READINGS IN
ANCIENT GREEK PHILOSOPHY

FROM THALES TO ARISTOTLE

Fourth Edition

Readings in

Ancient Greek Philosophy

from Thales to Aristotle

Fourth Edition

Edited by

S. MARC COHEN

PATRICIA CURD

C.D.C. REEVE

Hackett Publishing Company, Inc.
Indianapolis/Cambridge

Copyright © 2011 by Hackett Publishing Company, Inc.

14 13 12 11   1 2 3 4 5 6 7

For further information, please address:

Hackett Publishing Company, Inc.
P. O. Box 44937
Indianapolis, IN 46244-0937

www.hackettpublishing.com

Cover photograph copyright © 1985 by Peter Laytin

Interior design by Dan Kirklin
Composition by Agnew's, Inc.
Printed at Victor Graphics, Inc.

Library of Congress Cataloging-in-Publication Data

Readings in ancient Greek philosophy : from Thales to Aristotle / edited by S. Marc
Cohen, Patricia Curd, C.D.C. Reeve.—4th ed.
    p.   cm.
Includes bibliographical references.
ISBN 978-1-60384-462-8 (pbk.) — ISBN 978-1-60384-463-5 (cloth)
    1. Philosophy, Ancient. I. Cohen, S. Marc. II. Curd, Patricia, 1949–   III. Reeve,
C. D. C., 1948–
B171.R39   2011
180—dc22

                                                                    2010043404

CONTENTS

* Except where noted, translations of the Presocratics and the Sophists are by R. D. McKirahan.

Plato

Aristotle*

Appendixes

* Except as noted, Aristotle translations are reprinted from Aristotle, *Selections*, translated and edited by Terence Irwin and Gail Fine. Copyright © 1995 Terence Irwin and Gail Fine. Reprinted with permission. Glossary for Aristotle is adapted from the same work.

INTRODUCTION

This anthology is intended to introduce readers to a broad selection of the writings of some of the greatest of the ancient Greek philosophers—Heraclitus, Parmenides, Democritus, Protagoras, Plato, Aristotle, and many others. Together these thinkers brought about one of the most significant revolutions we know of, one that set the Western world on a path that—with minor and not so minor deviations—it has followed ever since. What they did, to put it boldly and oversimply, was to invent critical rationality and embody it in a tradition; for the theories they advanced, whether on the nature and origins of the cosmos or on ethics and politics, were not offered as gospels to be accepted on divine or human authority but as rational products to be accepted or rejected on the basis of evidence and argument: do not listen to me, Heraclitus says, but to my account. Every university and college, every intellectual discipline and scientific advance, every step toward freedom and away from ignorance, superstition, and enslavement to repressive dogma is eloquent testimony to the power of their invention. If they had not existed, our world would not exist.

Obviously, there is more to say about the achievements of Greek philosophy than this. But bold and oversimple as our claim is, and standing in need of modification and elaboration as it does, it points nonetheless to something central and vital, something that will surely be borne in upon any reader of the texts collected here: the world of Greek philosophy is an argumentative world.

As we weigh and consider the ideas and evaluate the arguments contained in the following pages, we will find ourselves thinking about the ultimate structure of reality, about the mind, about the nature of knowledge and scientific theorizing, about ethical values, and about the best kind of society for people to live in. Some of what we uncover we will no doubt find congenial; some we will want to criticize or reject. But as long as evidence and argument remain our touchstone, we will be joining in the enterprise that these philosophers both invented and did so much to develop. In the process, we will be to some degree becoming what some of them thought was the best thing to be—fully rational human beings.

This may sound attractive, but it may also seem one-sided, so it is perhaps important to add that the critical rationality vital to successful theorizing, while it is recommended as a very important ingredient in the best kind of life, is certainly not all that is recommended to us by these philosophers. For many of them, a successful life is one in which *all* the elements in our characters—needs, desires, emotions, and beliefs— are harmoniously integrated and in which we ourselves are harmoniously integrated with others into a flourishing society that is itself in harmony with the larger world of which it is a part. Moreover, many of the Greek philosophers—like their fellow poets and tragedians—recognized that there were profoundly nonrational elements in the world: the same Heraclitus who asks us to listen to his account also reminds us that "The Lord whose oracle is at Delphi neither speaks nor conceals, but gives a sign"; Socrates, the patron saint of rational self-scrutiny, is also a holy man, a servant of Apollo. Indeed, one of the most attractive features of Greek philosophy is its inclusivity, its manifest wish to see the world whole and see it right. Few contemporary philosophers offer us such all-encompassing visions of ourselves and our world as we find in Plato and Aristotle; few have the audacity to reach as far or as wide as the great Presocratics. That is not, surely, the only reason to make friends with these splendid thinkers, but it is, nonetheless, one major reason why they have never lost their power to challenge, inspire, and enlighten those who do befriend them.

We have divided the selection of readings into three sections, each with a separate introduction. Patricia Curd is primarily responsible for the section on the Presocratics and Sophists; David Reeve for the section on Plato; and Marc Cohen for the section on Aristotle. An excellent anthology of later Greek philosophical writers, which nicely complements this one, is B. Inwood and L. P. Gerson (eds.), *Hellenistic Philosophy: Introductory Readings,* second edition (Indianapolis: Hackett, 1997).

The fourth edition of *Readings in Ancient Greek Philosophy* features an extensive revision in the Presocratics unit, which had been untouched since the appearance of the first edition in 1995. Since then, Presocratic studies have grown rapidly. Exciting new material has been discovered: the Strasbourg Papyrus with its previously unknown lines of Empedocles, and the Derveni Papyrus, which shows how Presocratic philosophy was adopted into the wider intellectual world of ancient Greece. There have been new studies published, and numerous international conferences: scholars have asked novel questions, and offered fresh interpretations. For *Readings in Ancient Greek Philosophy,* the most important development has been Richard D. McKirahan's complete revision of his excellent volume, *Philosophy Before Socrates,* for its second edition. The translations prepared for that volume form the backbone of the Presocratics unit of this one.

In addition, all of the introductory material to this unit has been revised (in many cases to take advantage of recent interpretations), and much of the new material that has come to light (especially on Empedocles) has been included. The fragments in the Heraclitus and Empedocles chapters have been reordered, and the chapter on the Sophists has been changed in order to provide longer selections and a view of the Sophists more in keeping with contemporary scholarship. Finally, this edition includes the text of the intriguing Derveni Papyrus.

References to the Greek philosophers make use of certain standard editions of their words. Thus references to the Presocratics employ "Diels-Kranz numbers" because H. Diels and W. Kranz, *Die Fragmente der Vorsokratiker* (1903) was the first authoritative collection of Presocratic Texts. Testimonia about a philosopher written by someone else are identified by the letter "A," and fragments of the philosopher's own works by the letter "B." "22A2," for instance, refers to the second of the testimonia listed on Heraclitus, to whom the number 22 is assigned; 28B1 refers to the first fragment of Parmenides. References to Plato are to the edition of his works produced by Henri Estienne (known as Stephanus) in 1578, and are given by title and "Stephanus page number" (e.g., *Republic* 464d). References to Aristotle are to Immanuel Bekker's edition (1831) and are given by title and "Bekker page and line number" (e.g., *Politics* 1252a10).

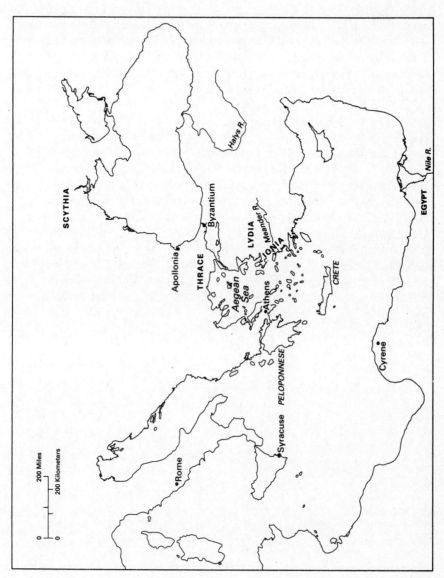

The Eastern
Mediterranean

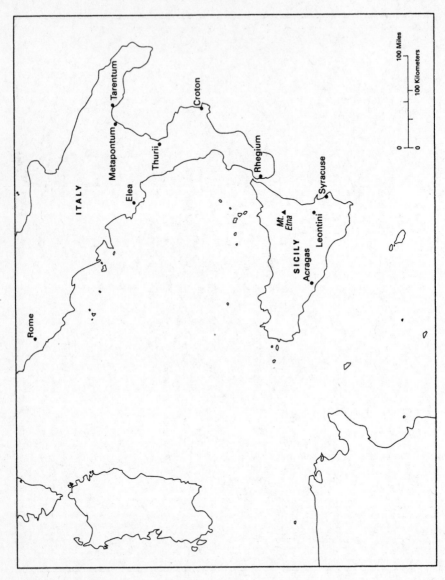

Sicily and
Southern Italy

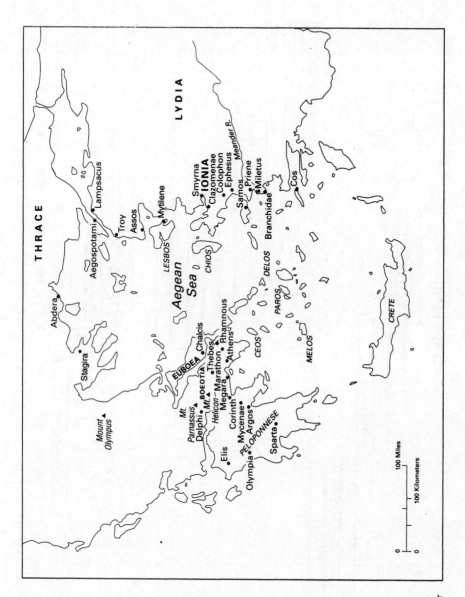

**Greece and
Western Asia Minor**

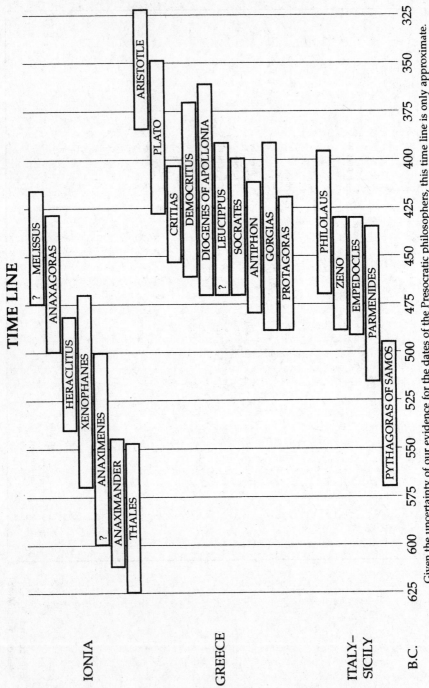

TIME LINE

IONIA

THALES
? ANAXIMANDER
ANAXIMENES
XENOPHANES
HERACLITUS
ANAXAGORAS
? MELISSUS

GREECE

PROTAGORAS
GORGIAS
ANTIPHON
SOCRATES
? LEUCIPPUS
DIOGENES OF APOLLONIA
DEMOCRITUS
CRITIAS
PLATO
ARISTOTLE

ITALY-SICILY

PYTHAGORAS OF SAMOS
PARMENIDES
EMPEDOCLES
ZENO
PHILOLAUS

B.C.

625 600 575 550 525 500 475 450 425 400 375 350 325

Given the uncertainty of our evidence for the dates of the Presocratic philosophers, this time line is only approximate.

ACKNOWLEDGMENTS

Excerpts from Richard D. McKirahan, *Philosophy Before Socrates: An Introduction with Texts and Commentary*, 2nd edition. Hackett Publishing Company, 2010. Copyright © 2010, Hackett Publishing Co. Reprinted by permission of the publisher.

Excerpts from Patricia Curd, *Anaxagoras of Clazomenae: Fragments and Testimonia. Texts and Translation with Notes and Essays* (The Phoenix Presocratics Series) University of Toronto Press, 2007. Copyright © 2007, University of Toronto Press. Reprinted by permission of the publisher.

Plato's *Euthyphro, Apology,* and *Crito,* translated by C.D.C. Reeve from *The Trials of Socrates,* edited by C.D.C. Reeve. Copyright © 2002 Hackett Publishing Co. Reprinted by permission of the publisher.

Excerpts from Plato's *Protagoras,* translated by Stanley Lombardo and Karen Bell. Copyright © 1992 Hackett Publishing Co. Reprinted by permission of the publisher.

Excerpts from Plato's *Gorgias,* translated by Donald Zeyl. Copyright © 1987 Hackett Publishing Co. Reprinted by permission of the publisher.

Plato's *Meno,* translated by G.M.A. Grube. Copyright © 1981 Hackett Publishing Co. Reprinted by permission of the publisher.

Plato's *Phaedo,* translated by G.M.A. Grube. Copyright © 1987 Hackett Publishing Co. Reprinted by permission of the publisher.

Plato's *Symposium,* translated by Alexander Nehamas and Paul Woodruff. Copyright © 1989 Hackett Publishing Co. Reprinted by permission of the publisher.

Plato's *Republic,* translated by G.M.A. Grube, revised by C.D.C. Reeve. Copyright © 1992 Hackett Publishing Co. Reprinted by permission of the publisher.

Plato's *Parmenides,* translated by Mary Louise Gill and Paul Ryan. Copyright © 1995 Hackett Publishing Co. Reprinted by permission of the translators and publisher.

Plato's *Timaeus,* translated by Donald Zeyl. Copyright © 1995 Hackett Publishing Co. Reprinted by permission of the translator and publisher.

Excerpts from Aristotle, *Nicomachean Ethics,* translated by Terence Irwin. Copyright © 1985 Hackett Publishing Co. Reprinted by permission of the translator and publisher.

Excerpts from Aristotle, *Selections,* translated by Terence Irwin and Gail Fine. Copyright © 1995 Hackett Publishing Co. Reprinted by permission of the translators and publisher.

Excerpts from Aristotle, *De Caelo,* translated by W.K.C. Guthrie (Cambridge, Mass.: Harvard University Press, 1939). Reprinted by permission of the publishers and the Loeb Classical Library.

Excerpt from Aristotle, *Meteorologica,* translated by S. Marc Cohen. Copyright © 1994 S. Marc Cohen. Reprinted by permission of the translator.

Excerpt from Aristotle, *Categories,* translated by S. Marc Cohen and Gareth B. Matthews. Copyright © 1995 S. Marc Cohen and Gareth B. Matthews. Reprinted by permission of the translators.

THE PRESOCRATICS
AND THE SOPHISTS

1. INTRODUCTION

Ancient tradition says that Thales of Miletus predicted an eclipse of the sun. Although we know none of the details of this supposed prediction, the event (an eclipse in 585 BCE) has traditionally marked the beginning of philosophy and science in Western thought. Aristotle, who was one of the earliest to think critically about the history of philosophy, speculated about why this kind of inquiry should have begun in Miletus, a Greek city on the Ionian coast of Asia minor (in what is now Turkey); like later scholars who have asked this question, Aristotle was unable to find an answer. So the circumstances surrounding the beginning of philosophy remain unclear; perhaps the question is unanswerable. Nevertheless, Thales, the titular first philosopher, stands at the beginning of a great tradition of rational inquiry and critical thought about the world and the place of human beings in it that continues to the present day.

Thales was the first of a succession of thinkers known as the Presocratics who lived in Greece in the sixth and fifth centuries BCE.[1] These thinkers do not belong to any unified school of thought, and they differed dramatically in their views. Yet they share intellectual attitudes and assumptions and they all display an enthusiasm for inquiry that justifies studying them as a group. It cannot be merely Thales' reported prediction of an eclipse that can justify our thinking of him as the first Western philosopher and scientist—after all, both the Babylonians and the Egyptians had complex astronomies. Nevertheless, for Aristotle and those

1. The name "Presocratics" comes from 19th-century classical scholars, who saw a fundamental break between the interests and methods of our group of thinkers and Socrates (470–399 BCE), and who regarded Socrates' interests in ethics as a radical advance in Western thought. Few would now agree with that evaluation, and it is worth pointing out that several of our Presocratics were actually contemporaries of or younger than Socrates. So, as a descriptive label, the name "Presocratics" is misleading, but as a designator for a recognized group of thinkers, it is quite useful, and I shall use it here in that sense. For more on this issue, see articles in Long.

1

who came after him, Thales, and his fellow-Milesians Anaximander and Anaximenes, shared an outlook that truly marks the beginning of philosophical inquiry. Part of this was a willingness to speculate and give reasons based on evidence and argument. Another aspect was a commitment to the view that the natural world (the entire universe) can be explained without needing to refer to anything beyond nature itself. For instance, Thales seems to have thought that everything is from water (although it is not clear whether he thought that water is the origin of all things, or that everything really is water in some form or another). This may strike us as a naïve and overly simplistic claim. Yet Aristotle saw in Thales' views something that suggested that Thales had reasons and arguments for them:

> [T]hey do not all agree about how many or what kinds of such principles there are, but Thales, the founder of this kind of philosophy, stated it to be water. (This is why he declared that the earth rests on water.) Perhaps he got this idea from seeing that the nourishment of all things is moist, and that even the hot itself comes to be from the moist and lives on it (the principle of all things is that from which they come to be)—getting this idea from this consideration and also because the seeds of all things have a moist nature; and water is the principle of the nature of moist things.
> (Aristotle, *Metaphysics* 1.3 983b18–27 = DK 11A12)

From Aristotle's comments, it is clear that he thought that Thales' claim was based on reasoning from observational evidence.

We may contrast Thales' account of the character of the natural world with the story Hesiod tells (probably in the century before Thales) about the origin of the cosmos:

> Tell me these things, Muses, who dwell on Olympus,
> From the beginning, and tell me, which of them was born first.
> First of all Chaos came into being. Next came
> broad-breasted Gaia [Earth], the secure dwelling place forever of
>   all
> the immortals who hold the peak of snowy Olympus.
> And murky Tartaros [Underworld] in a recess of the broad-roaded
>   Earth,
> and Eros [Love], who is the most beautiful among the immortal
>   gods, who
> loosens the limbs and overpowers the intentions and sensible
>   plans
> of all the gods and all humans too.
> From Chaos there came into being Erebos [Darkness] and black
>   Night.

From Night, Aithēr [bright upper air] and Hemera [Day] came
   into being,
which she conceived and bore after uniting in love with Erebos.
Gaia first brought forth starry Ouranos [Heaven]
equal to herself, to cover her all about
in order to be a secure dwelling place forever for the blessed gods.
She brought forth long mountains, beautiful shelters of divine
Nymphs who live in wooded mountains,
and also, without delightful love, gave birth to the barren sea,
Pontos, raging with its swelling waves. Then,
bedded by Ouranos, she gave birth to deep-swirling Ocean
and Koios and Kreios and Hyperion and Iapetos
and Theia and Rhea and Themis and Mnemosyne
and Phoebe with a golden wreath and lovely Tethys.
After them, last of all, was born crafty-minded Kronos,
the most terrible of the children, and he hated his mighty father.

(Hesiod, Theogony 114–38)

Hesiod requests the help of the Muses for the claims he will make. He then reports on the births of the gods with the Muses' authority as his source. In relying on the Muses, Hesiod does not infer his account of the cosmos from natural evidence. Nor does he think that appeals to evidence are necessary: the divine warrant offered by the Muses is sufficient for his purposes. Hesiod's account of the origins of the universe (his cosmogony) is in fact a story of the origins of the gods (a theogony). Each aspect of the cosmos is identified with the distinct characteristics and personality of a god, who controls that part of the universe. The change from the state of chaos to the presence of Gaia (Earth), Tartaros (the deepest underworld), Eros (desire), Erebos (the darkness under the earth), and Night is not explained in this passage.[2] Earth, Tartaros, and Eros simply came to be; there is no attempt to explain how this happened or justify why they came to be at exactly this moment rather than another. Once Eros is present, the model of generation is primarily sexual, although we are told that Gaia (Earth) gave birth to Pontos (sea) "without delightful love." These gods who, in some sense, are the different parts of the universe, behave like humans in their desires, emotions, and purposes. As in the Egyptian, Sumerian, and Hebrew creation myths, the Hesiodic story makes no clear distinction between a personality and a part of the cosmos: The natural and the supernatural coincide. Since Hesiod feels no compunction about asserting his claims without reasons to support them, he seems to think that the proper response to the story is acceptance. The hearer or reader should not subject it to critical scrutiny followed by rational agreement or disagreement.

2. Hesiod says that Chaos "came into being"; there is no explanation for this coming-to-be.

While the Presocratics rejected both the kind of account that Hesiod gave and his attitude toward uncritical belief, we must take care not to overstate the case: In the fragments of the Presocratics we shall find gaps in explanation, appeals to the Muses, apparent invocation of divine warrant, breaks in the connection between evidence and assertion. Despite all these apparent shortcomings, these early Greek thinkers took a bold leap in adopting a critical attitude. In the case of the Milesians, for instance, we find each proposing something different as the ultimate foundational reality of the cosmos. Anaximander, who followed Thales, apparently rejected the idea that water is the basic stuff; in its place he posited a single reality that he called the boundless (or the indefinite), something with no specific characteristics, out of which arise the other ingredients of the cosmos. Anaximander's follower Anaximenes, in turn rejects the boundless, apparently arguing that it was just too indefinite to do the job Anaximander required of it. Anaximenes claimed that air was the foundational stuff. Moreover, he seems to have seen that there was a gap in the earlier Milesian theories: Thales and Anaximander provided no mechanism to account for the transformations of their basic stuff. Anaximenes remedies this by proposing the processes of condensation and rarefaction: as air becomes more rarified or compacted, other stuffs are produced. Despite the disagreements among them, even this brief view shows that the Milesians worked within a shared framework of argument and justification.

Having adopted this critical attitude, the early Greek thinkers faced the question of what a human could justifiably claim to know. The Milesians might make claims about the basic stuff of the cosmos, and might give arguments for these claims, but how could they claim to have knowledge about an original or basic state of the universe, which they had never experienced? Hesiod would have an answer to this question: He could say that his information came from the Muses, and he could call on them to authenticate the truth of his claims about the coming-to-be of the gods. In the same way, we find Homer calling on the Muses when he wants to offer a catalogue of the leaders of the expedition to Troy. Because the Muses are divine they are immortal; since they were present for the gathering of the ships, they are appropriate as witnesses and can provide assurance that the story Homer tells is true:

Tell me now Muses, who have dwellings in Olympus
for you are goddesses and present and know everything,
while we hear only rumor and we know nothing;
Who were the Greek commanders and leaders?
The throngs I could never tell nor name,
Not even if ten tongues, ten mouths belonged to me,
a voice unbroken, and a bronze heart within me,

Unless the Olympian Muses, daughters of aegis-holding
Zeus, put into my mind those who came below Ilion.
(Homer, *Iliad* 2.484–92; tpc)

Although the contexts differ, Homer and Hesiod use the same invocation
of the Muses to guarantee their claims: historical for Homer, religious and
cosmogonical for Hesiod. Xenophanes of Colophon specifically rejects this
justification. "By no means," he says (21B18), "did the gods intimate all
things to mortals from the beginning, but in time, by inquiring, they discover better" (tpc). In rejecting divine authority for their claims, the Presocratics invite inquiry into the sources of human knowledge. A tantalizing mention of this problem appears in a fragment from Alcmaeon, who
echoes Homer's claims that the gods know all things, but apparently
offers a more pessimistic outlook for humans: "Concerning the unseen, the
gods have clarity, but it is for men to conjecture from signs . . ." (DK24B1;
tpc). We do not have the end of the fragment, but it is clear that Alcmaeon
is contrasting the limited epistemic status of humans with the exalted
certainty that the gods enjoy.

We find the Presocratics considering what separates sure and certain
knowledge from opinion or belief, and the roles of sense perception and
thought in acquiring knowledge, and, indeed, worrying about the very
possibility of such knowledge. Moreover, as competing theories about the
cosmos appear, the problem of theory justification comes to the fore.
Sometimes, as with the three Milesians, justification might be a question of
which theory appears to fit the evidence best; but there is another aspect to
theory justification, and that is the metatheoretical question about what
constitutes a genuine theory, regardless of the particular content. This
problem is raised most strikingly by Parmenides of Elea, and his powerful
arguments about what can be genuinely thought and said haunt the Greek
thinkers who come after him, including Plato and Aristotle.

Although we call these early Greek thinkers "philosophers," they would
probably not have called themselves by that name.[3] They were active in
many fields, and would not have thought that astronomy, physics, practical engineering, mathematics, and what we call philosophy were separate
disciplines, and most would not have thought that engaging in study of
any of these areas would preclude them from being active in politics. In a
society that was still more oral than literary, in which books (as scrolls, not
codices) were just beginning to be written and distributed, the Presocratics
thought and wrote about an astounding number of things. In the ancient
testimonies about the Presocratics, we find reports of writings on physics,
ethics, astronomy, epistemology, the gods and human worship of them,

3. The first use of the term may be in Heraclitus; it is Plato who tries to restrict the
name to a certain group of thinkers.

mathematics, metaphysics, meteorology, geometry, politics, the mechanism of sense perception, history (including the history of their own field),
and even painting and travel. They wrote in poetry and they wrote in
prose. They were as interested in the question of how a human being
ought to live as in the question of the basic stuffs of the cosmos. Struggling
to make philosophical notions clear in a language that did not yet have
technical philosophical terms, they used elegant images and awkward
analogies, straightforward arguments and intricate paradoxes. Much of
their work has not survived, and we know of most of it only through the
reports and quotations given by later philosophers and historians.[4] These
later scholars preserved or referred to those parts of Presocratic thought
that were most relevant for their own work; therefore most of what has
come down to us are fragments of and testimonia about their views on
natural philosophy, metaphysics, epistemology, and ethics, and so the
bulk of material included in this volume is on those topics.

In the latter part of the fifth century BCE, there was great interest in
social, political, and moral questions, and a number of thinkers explored
these topics almost exclusively. They were called Sophists, and they were
independent and often itinerant teachers of wisdom and practical political
skills. Many of them were accomplished and flamboyant rhetoricians.
They investigated questions about the nature of moral virtue and the best
way for a city to be governed, taking on paying pupils to whom they
taught their rhetorical skills and their social and political views. Most of
them were contemporaries of Socrates and some of Plato (who despised
them). Aristophanes, the great comic poet, represents Socrates himself as a
sophist in *Clouds* (423 BCE, revised 418–416). In the play, the character
Socrates has the traditional Presocratic interests in cosmological and meteorological subjects (although in Plato's dialogue *Phaedo,* Socrates stresses
that he gave up studying these questions). Moreover, at the same time as
philosophy was developing, so was medicine. Ancient medical practitioners were also interested in theory, and in the medical literature (collected in what is called the Hippocratic corpus) there are overlaps with
questions and problems that the Presocratics explored. All this suggests
that absolute distinctions among Sophists, Medical Practitioners, and Philosophers are too extreme.

In studying the Presocratics, the earliest Greek philosophers, we find
ourselves at the beginning of a great intellectual adventure. The metaphysical, epistemological, logical, and ethical problems and puzzles that

4. In the 1990s, fragments of a papyrus scroll in Strasbourg were pieced together
and discovered to contain text from Empedocles of Acragas. The Strasbourg Papyrus has both known and previously unknown lines, and may well be the only
direct transmission of a Presocratic text that we know (although scholars disagree
about this). Translations of the new material are included in Chapter 8, Empedocles
of Acragas.

engaged them became part of the philosophical project that Plato and Aristotle inherited and then passed on to other, later thinkers, including ourselves. We may find some of their assumptions and views to be strange, even a bit bizarre, and we may find some of their arguments difficult to comprehend. But these early Greek philosophers understood the importance of sustained rational inquiry and the critical evaluation of arguments and evidence. As we join them in this adventure, we, too, become part of that intellectual tradition that goes back to Miletus.

Sources

No Presocratic book has survived intact, and so what we know of the early Greek philosophers is gathered from other works. The Presocratics were quoted or referred to in many ancient works, ranging from philosophical treatises (e.g., Aristotle and the ancient commentators on Aristotle, or Sextus Empiricus) to works on grammar or entertaining treatises (e.g., Plutarch's "Table-Talk"). Our evidence is of two sorts, direct quotations (often simply called "the fragments") and summaries of Presocratic views, or references to the thinkers and their views (called "testimonia"). One must take care in using the fragments, as the extent of a quotation is often unclear; moreover there can be disagreements about the proper text when more than one source provides a passage. We must also be aware that the sources who quote or refer to our thinkers have their own reasons for doing so: very few are disinterested historians, and so the context may mislead us about the actual view of the philosopher quoted. Because of the fragmentary nature of the evidence, it is important to keep in mind that interpretations are tentative, and based on the best reconstruction of a view that one can offer, using as much evidence as one can. Fuller discussions of these problems may be found in the chapters by Mansfeld and by Runia in the anthologies edited by Long and by Curd and Graham cited in the bibliography on page 961.

Below is a short list of our most important sources for the Presocratic fragments and testimonia.

Both Plato and Aristotle referred to Presocratic thinkers and occasionally quoted them, but care must be used when dealing with evidence from these sources. Plato and Aristotle used views that they attributed to the earlier philosophers for polemical purposes, and both often gave short summaries of Presocratic positions, which are sometimes inaccurate.

Theophrastus, Eudemus, and Meno were students and associates of Aristotle, and they wrote treatises on the views of earlier thinkers (a project organized by Aristotle). Theophrastus wrote on their theories of perception in his book *On Sensation,* parts of which survive, and on their natural philosophy in a book called *Tenets in Natural Philosophy.* Eudemus concentrated on astronomy, mathematics, and theology, and Meno on medicine. Sadly, except for parts of *On Sensation,* these works are lost and survive only in fragments quoted by later scholars; but where they are available, they can provide important evidence for Presocratic thought.

The Roman orator Cicero (first century BCE) quotes from and refers to the early Greek thinkers in his accounts of philosophy, of which he was a serious student.

Clement of Alexandria (second half of the second century CE) was the author of a work called *Miscellanies,* comparing Greek and Christian thought. In the course of this, he often quotes Presocratic philosophers.

Sextus Empiricus, the skeptical philosopher of the second century CE, quotes many Presocratic views on sense perception and knowledge.

Plutarch, writing in the second century CE, quotes from many of our early Greek philosophers in his numerous essays, collected under the title *Moralia.*

The *Placita* (*Opinions*), a work from the second century CE, also gives information about the Presocratics. Though formerly attributed to Plutarch, it was in fact written by someone else. That person, about whom nothing else is known, is conventionally referred to as pseudo-Plutarch. The *Placita* is based on an earlier lost work, as is *Selections on Natural Philosophy* (*Eclogae Physicae*) by John Stobaeus (fifth century CE). The lost work, by Aëtius (c.100 CE), was itself based on earlier collections, and probably goes back to Theophrastus.

In the late second or early third century CE, Hippolytus, Bishop of Rome, wrote a book called *Refutation of All Heresies,* in which he argued that Christian heresies can be linked to Greek philosophical thought. In this ambitious work, he gives summaries of Presocratic views and quotes extensively from several of the early Greek philosophers.

Diogenes Laertius (third century CE) produced an entertaining and wide-ranging (but not entirely reliable) work called *Lives of the Philosophers,* drawing on many sources that are now lost. It contains biographical reports, lists of book titles, and summaries of views. Although it was influential in its time, it must be used with caution, as it contains much hearsay and invention.

The Neoplatonist philosopher Simplicius (sixth century CE) wrote detailed commentaries on Aristotle, and his commentary on Book I of Aristotle's *Physics* (in which Aristotle surveyed the views of his predecessors) is a valuable source for Presocratic scholars. In his commentaries, Simplicius provides quotations from a number of important Presocratics, especially Parmenides, Anaxagoras, and Empedocles (in all three cases, Simplicius is the only source for some passages). In the case of Parmenides, Simplicius tells us that he is quoting more of the material than is strictly necessary for his commentary, because copies of Parmenides' work have become rare and ought to be preserved. Alexander of Aphrodisias (c.200 CE) is another such commentator and source, as is Simplicius' contemporary John Philoponus.

On Abbreviations and Notes

The standard text collection for the Presocratics is H. Diels and W. Kranz, *Die Fragmente der Vorsokratiker* (6th edition, Berlin, 1951, and later printings), commonly referred to as *DK*. This collection has defined the scholarly conventions for referring to Presocratic texts, whether in Greek, Latin, or a modern translation. For each Presocratic philosopher DK assigns an identifying number: for example, Heraclitus is 22 and Anaxagoras is 59. DK uses the letter *A* to indicate testimony from ancient sources about that person, and the letter *B* to refer to what are taken to be direct quotations from that figure's work. These quotations are also referred to as the *fragments*, since all we have are small sections from longer works. Furthermore, DK identifies the testimonia and fragments by unique numbers. Thus text identified as 22A2 refers to Heraclitus (22) testimony (A) number two (2); and text identified as 59B12 refers to Anaxagoras (59) fragment (B) number twelve (12).

In this volume, DK numbers (where available) accompany every quotation; when all the passages in a chapter come from the same section of DK, the particular Presocratic's identifying number (22 or 59 in the examples just given) is listed only for the first passage. Hence fragment 1 from Anaxagoras will be identified as "(59B1)" and fragment 12 as "(B12)." Where texts come from more than one section, complete identifying DK numbers will be used as appropriate. In all cases, the source of the testimony or fragment from which DK drew the text appears at the end of the passage. For those texts that are not included in DK, the standard textual identification for the source is given along with the indication "not in DK." Where proper names follow textual references, the reference is to the editor of the standard edition of the relevant text. For example, in the Heraclitus chapter, the entry "Proclus, *Commentary on Plato's Alcibiades I* 117, Westerink" following selection 8 (B104) indicates that the fragment comes from Proclus' *Commentary on Plato's Alcibiades I*, and can be found on p. 117 of L. G. Westerink's 1954 edition of the text. References to two major papyrus collections use the standard abbreviations "P.Herc." and "P.Oxy."[5]

Unless otherwise indicated, translations are by Richard D. McKirahan. In the few places where I have modified his translations, "tmpc" appears in the source identification line; where I have translated the entire passage, "tpc" appears. All of the translations in Chapter 9 (Anaxagoras) are mine.

Notes on the texts are scattered throughout this collection. Notes from the translator (McKirahan) are marked as such; all other notes are mine.

Finally, in the translations of quoted passages from ancient authors, I use a system of brackets:

(. . .)   Parenthetical comment in the ancient text
< . . . >   Supplements to the text (either proposed by scholars, or added by the translator for the sake of clarity)
[. . .]   Alternative possible translations, explanatory remarks, or context for the quoted passage

2. THE MILESIANS

Thales, Anaximander, and Anaximenes were all from the city of Miletus in Ionia (now the western coast of Turkey) and make up what is referred to as the Milesian "school" of philosophy. Tradition reports that Thales was the teacher of Anaximander, who in turn taught Anaximenes. Aristotle begins his account of the history of philosophy as the search for causes and principles (in Metaphysics I) *with these three.*

2.1. Thales

Thales appears on lists of the seven sages of Greece, a traditional catalog of wise men. The chronicler Apollodorus suggests that he was born around 625 BCE. We should accept this date only with caution, as Apollodorus usually calculated birthdates by assuming that a man was forty years old at the time of his "acme," or greatest achievement. Thus, Apollodorus arrives at the date by assuming that Thales indeed predicted an eclipse in 585 BCE, and was forty at

5. P.Herc. is the Herculaneum Papyri, followed by the classification number of the papyrus. (More information can be found at http://163.1.169.40/cgi-bin/library?site=localhost&a=p&p=about&c=PHerc&ct+0&1=en&w=utf-8.) P.Oxy. is the Oxyrhynchus Papyri, followed by the classification number of the papyrus. (More information can be found at http://www.papyrology.ox.ac.uk/POxy/.)

the time. Plato and Aristotle tell stories about Thales that show that even in
ancient times philosophers had a mixed reputation for practicality.

1. (11A9) They say that once when Thales was gazing upwards while doing astronomy, he fell into a well, and that a witty and charming Thracian serving-girl made fun of him for being eager to know the things in the heavens but failing to notice what was just behind him and right by his feet.   (Plato, *Theaetetus* 174a)

2. (11A10) The story goes that when they were reproaching him for his poverty, supposing that philosophy is useless, he learned from his astronomy that the olive crop would be large. Then, while it was still winter, he obtained a little money and made deposits on all the olive presses both in Miletus and in Chios, and since no one bid against him, he rented them cheaply. When the time came, suddenly many requested the presses all at once, and he rented them out on whatever terms he wished, and so he made a great deal of money. In this way he proved that philosophers can easily be wealthy if they wish, but this is not what they are interested in.   (Aristotle, *Politics* 1.11 1259a9–18)

Thales reportedly studied astronomy (there is evidence for his interest in
eclipses, whether or not he had anything to say about the eclipse of 585 BCE),
geometry (he was said to have introduced the subject into Greece from Egypt),
and engineering (Herodotus reports that he changed the course of the Halys
river in order to aid the Lydian army). In his account of the cosmos, Thales
reportedly said that the basic stuff was water: This could mean that everything
comes from water as the originating source, or that everything really is water
in one form or another. Aristotle, the source of the reports, seems unsure about
which of these propositions Thales adopted. This shows that even by Aristotle's
time, Thales was probably not known by any direct written evidence but only
indirectly. According to the tradition that Aristotle follows, Thales also said
that the earth rests or floats on water. Aristotle also reports that Thales
thought that soul produces motion and that a magnetic lodestone has soul
because it causes iron to move.

3. Thales said that the sun suffers eclipse when the moon comes to be in front of it, the day in which the moon produces the eclipse being marked by its concealment.   (*P.Oxy.* 53.3710, col. 2, 37–40; not in DK)

4. Causes are spoken of in four ways, of which . . . one is matter. . . . Let us take as associates in our task our predecessors who considered the things that are and philosophized about the truth, for it is clear that they too speak of certain principles and causes, and so it will be useful to our present inquiry to survey them: either we will find some other

kind of cause or we will be more confident about the ones now being discussed.   (Aristotle, *Metaphysics* 1.3 983a26–b6; not in DK)

5. (11A12) Of those who first pursued philosophy, the majority believed that the only principles of all things are principles in the form of matter. For that of which all existing things are composed and that from which they originally come to be and that into which they finally perish—the substance persisting but changing in its attributes—this they state is the element and principle of the things that are. . . . For there must be one or more natures from which the rest come to be, while it is preserved. However, they do not all agree about how many or what kinds of such principles there are, but Thales, the founder of this kind of philosophy, stated it to be water. (This is why he declared that the earth rests on water.) He may have gotten this idea from seeing that the nourishment of all things is moist, and that even the hot itself comes to be from this and lives on this (the principle of all things is that from which they come to be)—getting this idea from this consideration and also because the seeds of all things have a moist nature; and water is the principle of the nature of moist things.
(Aristotle, *Metaphysics* 1.3 983b6–27)

6. (11A14) Some say [the earth] rests on water. This is the oldest account that we have inherited, and they say that Thales of Miletus said this. It rests because it floats like wood or some other such thing (for nothing is by nature such as to rest on air, but on water). He says this just as though the same argument did not apply to the water supporting the earth as to the earth itself!
(Aristotle, *On the Heavens* 2.13 294a28–34; tpc)

7. (11A22) Some say the soul is mixed in with the whole universe, and perhaps this is why Thales supposed that all things are full of gods.
(Aristotle, *On the Soul* 1.5 411a7–8; tpc)

8. (11A22) From what is related about him, it seems that Thales too held that the soul is something productive of motion, if indeed he said that the lodestone has soul, because it moves iron.
(Aristotle, *On the Soul* 1.2 405a19–21; tpc)

2.2. Anaximander

Diogenes Laertius says that Anaximander was sixty-four years old in 547/6BCE, and this dating agrees with the ancient reports that say that Anaximander was a pupil or follower of Thales. He was said to have been the first person to construct a map of the world, to have set up a gnomon at

*Sparta, and to have predicted an earthquake. Anaximander makes the
originating stuff of the cosmos something indefinite or boundless (apeiron in
Greek; later the word can also mean "infinite"). This indefinite stuff is moving,
directive of other things, and eternal; thus it qualifies as divine. The apeiron
gives rise to something productive of hot and cold, but Anaximander does not
say what this "something productive of hot and cold" is. The hot takes the
form of fire, the origin of the sun and the other heavenly bodies; while the cold
is a dark mist that can be transformed into air and earth. Both air and earth
are originally moist, but become drier because of the fire. In the first changes
from the originating apeiron, Anaximander postulates substantial opposites
(the hot, the cold) that act on one another and that are in turn the generating
stuffs for the sensible world. The reciprocal action of the opposites is the subject
of B1, the only direct quotation we have from Anaximander (and the extent of
the quotation is disputed by scholars). Here he stresses that changes in the
world are not capricious, but are ordered; with the mention of justice and
retribution he affirms that there are lawlike forces guaranteeing the orderly
processes of change between opposites. Anaximander also had theories about
the natures of the heavenly bodies and why the earth remains fixed where it is.
He made claims about meteorological phenomena, and about the origins of
living things, including human beings.*

9. (12A9 + 12B1) Of those who declared that the *arkhē*[6] is one, moving
   and *apeiron*, Anaximander . . . said that the *apeiron* was the *arkhē* and
   element of things that are, and he was the first to introduce this name
   for the *arkhē* [that is, he was the first to call the *arkhē apeiron*]. (In
   addition he said that motion is eternal, in which it occurs that the
   heavens come to be.) He says that the *arkhē* is neither water nor any of
   the other things called elements, but some other nature which is *apeiron*, out of which come to be all the heavens and the worlds in them.
   The things that are perish into the things from which they come to be,
   according to necessity, for they pay penalty and retribution to each
   other for their injustice in accordance with the ordering of time, as he
   says in rather poetical language.
   (Simplicius, *Commentary on Aristotle's Physics* 24.13–21)

10. (12A11) He says that the *arkhē* is neither water nor any of the other
    things called elements, but some nature which is *apeiron*, out of which
    come to be all the heavens and the worlds in them. This is eternal and
    ageless and surrounds all the worlds. . . . In addition he said that
    motion is eternal, in which it occurs that the heavens come to be.
    (Hippolytus, *Refutation of All Heresies* 1.6.1–2)

6. The word *arkhē* is left untranslated here. It means "originating point" or "first
principle."

11. (12A15) This [the infinite, *apeiron*] does not have an *arkhē*, but this seems to be the *arkhē* of the rest, and to contain all things and steer all things, as all declare who do not fashion other causes aside from the infinite [the *apeiron*] . . . and this is the divine. For it is deathless and indestructible, as Anaximander and most of the natural philosophers say.   (Aristotle, *Physics* 3.4 203b10–15)

12. (12A10) He declares that what arose from the eternal and is productive of [or, "capable of giving birth to"] hot and cold was separated off at the coming to be of this *kosmos*, and a kind of sphere of flame from this grew around the dark mist about the earth like bark about a tree. When it was broken off and enclosed in certain circles, the sun, moon, and stars came to be.   (Pseudo-Plutarch, *Miscellanies* 2)

13. (12A21) Anaximander says that the sun is equal to the earth, and the circle where it has its vent and on which it is carried is twenty-seven times <the size> of the earth.   (Aëtius 2.21.1)

14. (12A18) Anaximander says that the stars are borne by the circles and spheres on which each one is mounted.   (Aëtius 2.16.5)

15. (12A11) The earth is aloft and is not supported by anything. It stays at rest because its distance from all things is equal. The earth's shape is curved, round, like a stone column. We walk on one of the surfaces and the other one is set opposite. The stars come to be as a circle of fire separated off from the fire in the *kosmos* and enclosed by dark mist. There are vents, certain tube-like passages at which the stars appear. For this reason, eclipses occur when the vents are blocked. The moon appears sometimes waxing, sometimes waning as the passages are blocked or opened. The circle of the sun is twenty-seven times <that of the earth and> that of the moon <eighteen times>, and the sun is highest, and the circles of the fixed stars are lowest. Winds occur when the finest vapors of dark mist are separated off and collect together and then are set in motion. Rain results from the vapor arising from the earth under the influence of the sun. Lightning occurs whenever wind escapes and splits the clouds apart.

(Hippolytus, *Refutation of All Heresies* 1.6.3–7)

16. (12A23) Anaximander says that these [thunder, lightning, thunderbolts, waterspouts, and hurricanes] all result from wind. For whenever it [wind] is enclosed in a thick cloud and forcibly escapes because it is so fine and light, then the bursting [of the cloud] creates the noise and the splitting creates the flash against the blackness of the cloud.

(Aëtius 3.3.1)

17. (12A26) Some, like Anaximander . . . declare that the earth stays at rest because of equality. For it is no more fitting for what is situated at the center and is equally far from the extremes to move up rather than down or sideways. And it is impossible for it to move in opposite directions at the same time. Therefore, it stays at rest of necessity.

(Aristotle, *On the Heavens* 2.13 295b11–16)

18. (12A30) Anaximander says that the first animals were produced in moisture, enclosed in thorny barks. When their age advanced they came out onto the drier part, their bark broke off, and they lived a different mode of life for a short time.   (Aëtius 5.19.4)

19. (12A10) He also declares that in the beginning humans were born from animals of a different kind, since other animals quickly manage on their own, and humans alone require lengthy nursing. For this reason they would not have survived if they had been like this at the beginning.   (Pseudo-Plutarch, *Opinions* 2)

20. (12A30) Anaximander . . . believed that there arose from heated water and earth either fish or animals very like fish. In these, humans grew and were kept inside as embryos up to puberty. Then finally they burst, and men and women came forth already able to nourish themselves.   (Censorinus, *On the Day of Birth* 4.7)

2.3. Anaximenes

Ancient sources say that Anaximenes was a younger associate or pupil of Anaximander. Like Anaximander he agrees with Thales that there is a single originative stuff, but he disagrees with both Thales and Anaximander about what it is. He calls this basic stuff aēr *(usually translated "air," although* aēr *is more like a dense mist than what we think of as air, which is ideally transparent).* Aēr *is indefinite enough to give rise to the other things in the cosmos, but it is not as vague as Anaximander's* apeiron *(or indefinite). Anaximander seems to have left it unclear just what it is that comes from the* apeiron *and then produces the hot and the cold, and Anaximenes could well have argued that the* apeiron *was simply too indefinite to do the cosmic job Anaximander intended for it. In a major step away from Thales and Anaximander, Anaximenes explicitly includes condensation and rarefaction as the processes that transform* aēr *and the other stuffs of the cosmos. Like the other Presocratics, Anaximenes gave explanations of all sorts of meteorological and other natural phenomena.*

21. (13A5) Anaximenes . . . like Anaximander, declares that the underlying nature is one and unlimited [*apeiron*] but not indeterminate, as Anaximander held, but definite, saying that it is air. It differs in rarity and density according to the substances <it becomes>. Becoming finer, it comes to be fire; being condensed, it comes to be wind, then cloud; and when still further condensed, it becomes water, then earth, then stones, and the rest come to be from these. He too makes motion eternal and says that change also comes to be through it.

(Theophrastus, quoted by Simplicius, *Commentary on Aristotle's Physics* 24.26–25.1)

22. (13B2) Just as our soul, being air, holds us together and controls us, so do breath and air surround the whole *kosmos*.

(Pseudo-Plutarch, *Opinions* 876AB)

23. (13A10) Anaximenes determined that air is a god and that it comes to be and is without measure, infinite, and always in motion.

(Cicero, *On the Nature of the Gods* 1.10.26)

24. (13A7) Anaximenes . . . declared that the principle is unlimited [*apeiron*] air, from which come to be things that are coming to be, things that have come to be, and things that will be, and gods and divine things. The rest come to be out of the products of this. The form of air is the following: when it is most even, it is invisible, but it is revealed by the cold and the hot and the wet, and by its motion. It is always moving, for all the things that undergo change would not change if it were not moving. For when it becomes condensed or finer, it appears different. For when it is dissolved into a finer condition it becomes fire, and on the other hand air being condensed becomes winds. Cloud comes from air through felting,[7] and water comes to be when this happens to a greater degree. When condensed still more it becomes earth, and when it reaches the absolutely densest stage it becomes stones. (Hippolytus, *Refutation of All Heresies* 1.7.1–3)

25. (13B1) Or as Anaximenes of old believed, let us leave neither the cold nor the hot in the category of substance, but <hold them to be> common attributes of matter, which come as the results of its changes. For he declares that the contracted state of matter and the condensed state is cold, whereas what is fine and "loose" (calling it this way with this very word) is hot. As a result he claimed that it is not said unreasonably that a person releases both hot and cold from his mouth. For the breath becomes cold when compressed and condensed by the lips, and when the mouth is relaxed, the escaping breath becomes warm because of rareness. (Plutarch, *The Principle of Cold* 7 947F)

7. Translator's note: "Felting" is the production of nonwoven fabric by the application of heat, moisture, and pressure, as felt is produced from wool. The term here is extended to describe any other process in which the product is denser than and so has different properties from the ingredients.

26. (13A6) When the air was being felted the earth was the first thing to come into being, and it is very flat. This is why it rides upon the air, as is reasonable. (Pseudo-Plutarch, *Miscellanies* 3)

27. (13A20) Anaximenes, Anaxagoras, and Democritus say that its flatness is the cause of its staying at rest. For it does not cut the air below but covers it like a lid, as bodies with flatness apparently do; they are difficult for winds to move because of their resistance. They say that the earth does this same thing with respect to the air beneath because of its flatness. And the air, lacking sufficient room to move aside, stays at rest in a mass because of the air beneath. (Aristotle, *On the Heavens* 2.13 294b13–20)

28. (13A7) Likewise the sun and moon and all the other heavenly bodies, which are fiery, ride upon the air on account of their flatness. The stars came into being from the earth because moisture rises up out of it. When the moisture becomes fine, fire comes to be and the stars are formed of fire rising aloft. There are also earthen bodies in the region of the stars carried around together with them. He says that the stars do not move under the earth as others have supposed, but around it, as a felt cap turns around our head. The sun is hidden not because it is under the earth but because it is covered by the higher parts of the earth and on account of the greater distance it comes to be from us. Because of their distance the stars do not give heat. (Hippolytus, *Refutation of All Heresies* 1.7.4-6)

29. (13A17) Anaximenes stated that clouds occur when the air is further thickened. When it is condensed still more, rain is squeezed out. Hail occurs when the falling water freezes, and snow when some wind is caught up in the moisture. (Aëtius 3.4.1)

30. (13A21) Anaximenes declares that when the earth is being drenched and dried out it bursts, and earthquakes result from these hills breaking off and collapsing. This is why earthquakes occur in droughts and also in heavy rains. For in the droughts, as was said, the earth is broken while being dried out, and when it becomes excessively wet from the waters, it falls apart. (Aristotle, *Meteorology* 2.7 365b6–12)

3. PYTHAGORAS AND EARLY PYTHAGOREANISM

Pythagoras was born on the island of Samos in the eastern Aegean some time around 570 BCE; according to tradition his father was a gem-cutter or engraver. He reportedly traveled in Egypt and Babylonia, leaving Samos around 530 to escape the rule of the tyrant Polycrates. Eventually, Pythagoras settled in Croton, in southern Italy. There he was well-respected and gained political influence. He founded a community for himself and his followers that was philosophical, political, and religious. The exclusivity of the group angered some, and in about 500 there was an uprising in Croton (and elsewhere in Italy) against the Pythagoreans. The Pythagoreans were temporarily driven out of Croton, and many were killed. Pythagoras himself took refuge in Metapontum and died not long afterwards (some say he starved himself to death in a temple). Despite these and other setbacks—some Pythagoreans departed for the Greek mainland—there continued to be groups of Pythagoreans in southern Italy until about 400. Even then Archytas of Tarentum remained. He was a great mathematician and a friend of Plato.

Little is known of the views of Pythagoras himself, except that he had a reputation for great learning—a reputation that would later be mocked by Heraclitus—and that he was most likely the originator of the important and influential Pythagorean doctrine of the transmigration of souls, a view that Xenophanes ridiculed. This difficulty is noted by those in the ancient world who wrote about Pythagoras (see selection number 8 below). Sometime during his life or after his death, Pythagoras' followers split into two groups, which mirrored the two aspects of Pythagorean teaching. These groups were the mathēmatikoi *and the* akousmatikoi.[8] *The* akousmatikoi *were disciples who venerated Pythagoras' teachings on religion and the proper way to live, but had little interest in the philosophical aspects of Pythagoreanism. The* mathēmatikoi *had a great reputation in the ancient world for philosophical, mathematical, musical, and astronomical knowledge, while still following a Pythagorean way of life. All these different branches of study were connected in Pythagorean thought, for the Pythagoreans believed that number was the key to understanding the cosmos. Their original insight seemed to be that the apparent chaos of sound can be brought into rational, hence knowable, order by the imposition of number. They reasoned that the entire universe is a harmonious arrangement (*kosmos *in Greek), ordered by and so knowable*

---

8. The word *akousmatikoi* comes from *akousmata*, "things heard." The word *mathē-matikoi* comes from *mathēmata*, "things studied" or "learned." The later Pythago-reans Philolaus and Archytas (active in the first half of the fourth century) were members of the *mathēmatikoi*. Some scholars think the division belongs to later stages of Pythagoreanism.

through, number. The Pythagoreans apparently rejected the Ionian methods of inquiry, and turned from searching out the basic stuff of the universe to a study of the form that makes it a kosmos.

Note on the texts: The evidence about Pythagoras and Pythagoreanism is to be found in several chapters in DK. In the texts given here, the first number in parentheses is the DK number for the chapter in which the passage occurs.

1. (21B7) Once he passed by as a puppy was being beaten,
   the story goes, and in pity said these words:
   "Stop, do not beat him, since it is the soul of a man, a friend of mine,
   which I recognized when I heard it crying."
   (Diogenes Laertius, *Lives of the Philosophers* 8.36)

2. (22B40) Much learning ["polymathy"] does not teach insight. Otherwise it would have taught Hesiod and Pythagoras and moreover Xenophanes and Hecataeus.
   (Diogenes Laertius, *Lives of the Philosophers* 9.1)

3. (22B129) Pythagoras the son of Mnesarchus practiced inquiry [*historiē*] more than all other men, and making a selection of these writings constructed his own wisdom, polymathy, evil trickery.
   (Diogenes Laertius, *Lives of the Philosophers* 8.6)

4. (36B4) Thus he [Pherecydes] excelled in both manhood and
        reverence
   and even in death has a delightful life for his soul,
   if indeed Pythagoras was truly wise about all things,
   he who truly knew and had learned thoroughly the opinions of
        men.   (Diogenes Laertius, *Lives of the Philosophers* 1.120)

5. (31B129) There was a certain man among them who knew very holy
        matters,
   who possessed the greatest wealth of mind,
   mastering all sorts of wise deeds.
   For when he reached out with all his mind,
   easily he would survey every one of the things that are,
   yea, within ten and even twenty generations of humans.[9]
   (Porphyry, *Life of Pythagoras* 30)

9. This passage is from Empedocles, who does not mention Pythagoras by name here, and there is doubt (both ancient and modern) whether he meant to praise Pythagoras here or someone else. (Diogenes Laertius suggested that the verse was meant to honor Parmenides.)

6. (14,10)[10] Is Homer said to have been during his life a guide in education for people who delighted in associating with him and passed down to their followers a Homeric way of life? Pythagoras himself was greatly admired for this, and his followers even nowadays name a way of life Pythagorean and are conspicuous among others.

(Plato, *Republic* 10 600a–b)

7. (14,1) The Egyptians were the first to declare this doctrine, too, that the human soul is immortal, and each time the body perishes it enters into another animal as it is born. When it has made a circuit of all terrestrial, marine, and winged animals, it once again enters a human body as it is born. Its circuit takes three thousand years. Some Greeks have adopted this doctrine, some earlier and some later, as if it were peculiar to them. I know their names, but do not write them.

(Herodotus, *Histories* 2.123)

8. (14.8a) What he said to his associates, no one is able to say with any certainty, for they kept no ordinary silence among themselves. But it was especially well-known by all that first he declares that the soul is immortal; then that it changes into other kinds of animals; in addition that things that happen recur at certain intervals, that nothing is absolutely new, and that all things that come to be alive must be thought akin. Pythagoras seems to have been the first to introduce these opinions into Greece.   (Porphyry, *Life of Pythagoras* 19)

9. (58B40) Some of them [the Pythagoreans] declared that the soul is the motes in the air, and others that it is what makes the motes move.

(Aristotle, *On the Soul* 1.2 404a17)

10. (14.8) Heraclides of Pontus says that Pythagoras said the following about himself. Once he had been born Aethalides and was believed to be the son of Hermes. When Hermes told him to choose whatever he wanted except immortality, he asked to retain both alive and dead the memory of what happened to him. . . . Afterwards he entered into Euphorbus and was wounded by Menelaus. Euphorbus said that once he had been born as Aethalides and received the gift from Hermes, and told of the migration of his soul and what plants and animals it had belonged to and all it had experienced in Hades. When Euphorbus died his soul entered Hermotimus, who, wishing to provide evidence, went to Branchidae, entered the sanctuary of Apollo, and

---

10. The Pythagoras chapter of DK (14) is not divided into subsections, as are most of the rest of the chapters; thus there is no indication of "A" or "B" in references to texts collected there.

showed the shield Menelaus had dedicated. (He said that when Menelaus was sailing away from Troy he dedicated the shield to Apollo.)
The shield had already rotted away and only the ivory facing was
preserved. When Hermotimus died, it [the soul] became Pyrrhus the
Delian fisherman and again remembered everything. . . . When Pyrrhus died it became Pythagoras and remembered all that had been
said.   (Diogenes Laertius, *Lives of the Philosophers* 8.4–5)

11. (14,2, 58C4) There are two kinds of the Italian philosophy called
Pythagorean, since two types of people practiced it—the *akousmatikoi*
and the *mathēmatikoi*. Of these, the *akousmatikoi* were admitted to be
Pythagoreans by the others, but they, in turn, did not recognize the
mathēmatikoi but claimed that their pursuits were not those of Pythagoras, but of Hippasus. . . . The philosophy of the *akousmatikoi* consists
of unproved and unargued *akousmata* to the effect that one must act in
appropriate ways, and they also try to preserve all the other sayings of
Pythagoras as divine dogma. These people claim to say nothing of
their own invention and say that to make innovations would be
wrong. But they suppose that the wisest of their number are those who
have got the most *akousmata*.
                    (Iamblichus, *Life of Pythagoras* 81, 82; from Aristotle?)

12. (58C4) All the *akousmata* referred to in this way fall under three head-
ings: (a) Some indicate what something is; (b) others indicate what is
something in the greatest degree; and (c) others what must or must not
be done. (a) The following indicate what something is. What are the
Isles of the Blest? Sun and Moon. What is the oracle at Delphi? The
tetractys, which is the harmony in which the Sirens sing. (b) Others
indicate what is something in the greatest degree. What is most just?
To sacrifice. What is the wisest? Number, and second wisest is the
person who assigned names to things. What is the wisest thing in our
power? Medicine. What is most beautiful? Harmony.
                    (Iamblichus, *Life of Pythagoras* 82; from Aristotle?)

13. (58C3) <Pythagoras ordered his followers> not to pick up <food>
which had fallen, to accustom them not to eat self-indulgently or
because it fell on the occasion of someone's death . . . not to touch a
white rooster, because it is sacred to the Month and is a suppliant; it is
a good thing, and is sacred to the Month because it indicates the hours,
and white is of the nature of good, while black is of the nature of evil
. . . not to break bread, because friends long ago used to meet over a
single loaf just as foreigners still do, and not to divide what brings
them together. Others <explain this practice> with reference to the

judgment in Hades, others say that it brings cowardice in war, and still others that the whole universe begins from this.

(Aristotle, fr. 195 [Rose], quoted in Diogenes Laertius, *Lives of the Philosophers* 8.34ff.)

14. (58C6) Do not stir the fire with a knife.
Rub out the mark of a pot in the ashes.
Do not wear a ring.
Do not have swallows in the house.
Spit on your nail parings and hair trimmings.
Roll up your bedclothes on rising and smooth out the imprint of the body.
Do not urinate facing the sun.

(Selections from Iamblichus, *Protrepticus* 21; from Aristotle?)

15. (14.1) The Egyptians agree in this with those called Orphics . . . and with the Pythagoreans; for it is likewise unholy for anyone who takes part in these rites to be buried in woolen garments.

(Herodotus, *Histories* 2.81)

16. The tetractys is a certain number, which being composed of the four first numbers produces the most perfect number, 10. For 1 and 2 and 3 and 4 come to be 10. This number is the first tetractys and is called the source of ever-flowing nature, since according to them the entire *kosmos* is organized according to *harmonia*, and *harmonia* is a system of three concords, the fourth, the fifth, and the octave, and the proportions of these three concords are found in the aforementioned four numbers.

(Sextus Empiricus, *Against the Mathematicians* 7.94–95; not in DK)

17. (58B4) At the same time as these [Leucippus and Democritus] and, before them, those called Pythagoreans took hold of mathematics and were the first to advance that study; and being brought up in it, they believed that its principles are the principles of all things that are. Since numbers are naturally first among these, and in numbers they thought they observed many resemblances to things that are and that come to be . . . and since they saw the attributes and ratios of musical scales in numbers, and other things seemed to be made in the likeness of numbers in their entire nature, and numbers seemed to be primary in all nature, they supposed the elements of numbers to be the elements of all things that are.   (Aristotle, *Metaphysics* 1.5 985b23–28; 33–986a2)

18. (58B5)[11] The elements of number are the even and the odd, and of these the latter is limited and the former unlimited. The one is com-

11. This material may be based on Aristotle's study of Philolaus, and so it may refer to the later form of Pythagoreanism developed by Philolaus.

posed of both of these (for it is both even and odd), and number springs from the one; and numbers, as I have said, constitute the whole universe.   (Aristotle, *Metaphysics* 1.5 986a17–21)

19. (58B28) They say that the unlimited is the even. For when this is surrounded and limited by the odd it provides things with the quality of unlimitedness. Evidence of this is what happens with numbers. For when gnomons are placed around the one, and apart, in the one case the shape is always different, and in the other it is always one.
                    (Aristotle, *Physics* 3.4 203a10–15)

20. (58B5) Others of this same school declare that there are ten principles arranged in parallel columns:

limit	unlimited
odd	even
one	plurality
right	left
male	female
at rest	moving
straight	bent
light	darkness
good	evil
square	oblong

This is how Alcmaeon of Croton too seems to have understood things, and either he took this theory from them or they from him. . . . He says that most human matters are pairs, identifying as the oppositions not definite ones like the Pythagoreans . . . but the Pythagoreans described how many and what the oppositions are. (Aristotle, *Metaphysics* 1.5 986a22–b2)

4. XENOPHANES OF COLOPHON

Born in Colophon, a city on the west coast of what is now Turkey, near Miletus (home to Thales, Anaximander, and Anaximenes) and Ephesus (the city of Heraclitus), Xenophanes was an itinerant poet and philosopher. On his own evidence, he lived to a great age, and although the subjects discussed in the surviving fragments and testimonia give evidence of the scope of his travels, the details of his life are hazy. He was born c.570 BCE and seems to have left Colophon after it fell to the Medes in 546/5. He refers to Pythagoras and the doctrine of transmigration of souls in one fragment, and some in the ancient tradition say that he was a teacher of Parmenides (this is most unlikely).

Xenophanes wrote in verse, and while some of the surviving fragments deal with typical poetic topics, he also addressed what would now be called theological and philosophical questions. He rejected the traditional views of the Olympian gods, such as are found in Homer and Hesiod, and claimed that there was a supreme non-anthropomorphic god, who controls the cosmos by thought. Whether or not Xenophanes claimed that there was a single god or only that the supreme god was the greatest of an unnamed number of gods is debated by scholars. He rejected divination and the view that natural phenomena, such as rainbows, have divine significance and claimed that there is no divine communication to human beings. Humans must find out for themselves by inquiry; moreover, Xenophanes raises questions about the possibility of sure and certain knowledge, and suggests that humans must be satisfied with belief or opinion, although he probably thought that this must be backed with evidence. He had a keen interest in the natural world, which is not surprising, given his commitment to inquiry. He noted fossils of sea creatures in the mountains and developed a complicated "cloud astrophysics" to explain the phenomena of the heavens. He argued that the earth is indefinitely broad and extends downwards indefinitely, thus rejecting the view that the sun travels under the earth. Even in "traditional" areas for poets he seems to have held strong views: he gives instructions for a symposium (a drinking party) and laments the over-glorification of athletes. Recent scholarship has come to appreciate Xenophanes as a crucial figure in early Greek thought, whose views on knowledge and the divine were important for later thinkers.

1. (B1) For now the floor is clean, and the hands of all,
   and the cups. One is putting on the woven wreaths,
   another is offering fragrant myrrh in a bowl,
   a mixing bowl stands full of joy,
   another wine, gentle and scented of flowers, is at hand in
      wine-jars   5
   and boasts that it will never betray us.
   In the middle, frankincense is sending forth its holy scent.
   There is cold water sweet and pure.
   Golden loaves of bread are served and a magnificent table
   is laden with cheese and rich honey.   10
   In the center an altar is completely covered in flowers
   and the rooms are full of song and good cheer.
   Cheerful men should first sing a hymn to the god
   with well-omened words and pure speech.
   When they have poured an offering and prayed to be able
      to do acts of justice   15
   (for indeed these are the first things to pray for),
   it is not going too far (hubris) if you drink only as much as
      permits you to reach

home without assistance (unless you are very aged).
Praise the man who after drinking behaves nobly
in that he possesses memory and aims for excellence (*aretē*)   20
and relates neither battles of Titans nor Giants
nor Centaurs—the fictions of our fathers—
nor violent conflicts; there is no use in these,
but it is good always to have high regard for the gods.
                    (Athenaeus, *Scholars at Dinner* 11.462c; tmpc)

2. (B2) If anyone were to achieve a victory
at Zeus's sanctuary at Olympia by the streams of Pisa
in a foot race or the pentathlon or in wrestling
or the painful art of boxing
or the frightful contest they call the pankration,[12]   5
he would be more glorious in the eyes of the citizens.
They would grant him a seat of honor at the games,
he would enjoy meals at public expense
and a gift from the city for his children to inherit.
Even if he were to be victorious with horses he would
    obtain these things.   10
Though he is not as worthy of them as I. For superior to the
    strength
of men or horses is my wisdom.
But these ways are misguided and it is not right
to put strength ahead of wisdom, which is good.
If an excellent boxer were among the people   15
or someone excellent at the pentathlon or in wrestling
or in the foot race (which is the most highly honored
display of strength of all men's deeds in the contests);
that would not make a city be any more in a state of *eunomia*.[13]
A city will find little joy in a person   20
who wins in the contests by the banks of Pisa,
since this does not fatten the city's storerooms.
                    (Athenaeus, *Scholars at Dinner* 10.413f)

3. (B7) Once he passed by as a puppy was being beaten,
the story goes, and in pity said these words:
"Stop, do not beat him, since it is the soul of a man, a friend
    of mine,
which I recognized when I heard it crying."
                    (Diogenes Laertius, *Lives of the Philosophers* 8.36)

---

12. *Pankration*: A vicious sport combining boxing, wrestling, and kickboxing.
13. Translator's note: *Eunomia*: the condition in a city where the laws are good and people abide by them.

4. (B8) Already there are sixty-seven years
    tossing my speculation throughout the land of Greece,
    and from my birth there were twenty-five in addition to these,
    if indeed I know how to speak truly about these matters.
                  (Diogenes Laertius, *Lives of the Philosophers* 9.19)

5. (B10) Ever since the beginning all have learned according to Homer . . .
                  (Herodian, *On Doubtful Syllables* 296.6; tpc)

6. (B11) Both Homer and Hesiod have ascribed to the gods all deeds
    which among men are matters of reproach and blame:
    thieving, adultery, and deceiving one another.
                  (Sextus Empiricus, *Against the Mathematicians* 9.193)

7. (B12) . . . as they sang of many illicit acts of the gods
    thieving, adultery, and deceiving one another.
              (Sextus Empiricus, *Against the Mathematicians* 1.289; tpc)

8. (B14) But mortals suppose that the gods are born,
    have human clothing, and voice, and bodily form.
                  (Clement, *Miscellanies* 5.109)

9. (B15) If horses had hands, or oxen or lions,
    or if they could draw with their hands and produce works as men do,
    then horses would draw figures of gods like horses, and oxen like
      oxen,
    and each would render the bodies
    to be of the same frame that each of them have.
                  (Clement, *Miscellanies* 5.110; tpc)

10. (B16) Ethiopians say that their gods are snub-nosed and dark,
    Thracians, that theirs are grey-eyed and red-haired.
                  (Clement, *Miscellanies* 7.22; tpc)

11. (B17) . . . and bacchants [garlands] of pine set around the strong
    house.   (Scholium on Aristophanes, *Knights* 408; tpc)

12. (B18) By no means did the gods intimate all things to mortals from
    the beginning,
    but in time, inquiring, they discover better.
                  (Stobaeus, *Selections* 1.8.2; tpc)

13. (B23) One god, greatest among gods and men,
    not at all like mortals in form or thought.
                  (Clement, *Miscellanies*, 5.109; tpc)

14. (B24) . . . whole [he] sees, whole [he] thinks, and whole [he] hears.
> (Sextus Empiricus, *Against the Mathematicians* 9.144; tpc)

15. (B26) . . . always [he] remains in the same [state], changing not at all,
> nor is it fitting that [he] come and go to different places at different times.
> (Simplicius, *Commentary on Aristotle's Physics* 23.10; tpc)

16. (B25) . . . but completely without toil [he] agitates all things by the will of his mind.
> (Simplicius, *Commentary on Aristotle's Physics* 23.19; tpc)

17. (B27) For all things are from the earth and all return to the earth in the end.
> (Theodoretus, *Treatment of Greek Conditions* 4.5)

18. (B28) The earth's upper limit is seen here at our feet,
> touching the air. But the lower part goes down without limit.
> (Achilles Tatius, *Introduction to the Phaenomena of Aratus* 4.34.11)

19. (B29) All things that come into being and grow are earth and water.
> (John Philoponus, *Commentary on Aristotle's Physics* 1.5.125)

20. (B30) Sea is the source of water and the source of wind.
> For not without the wide sea would there come to be
> in clouds the force of wind blowing out from within,
> nor streams of rivers nor rain water from the sky,
> but the great wide sea is the sire of clouds and winds and rivers.
> (Geneva Scholium on *Iliad* 21.196)

21. (B31) . . . the sun passing high over the earth and warming it.
> (Heraclitus Homericus, *Homeric Allegories* 44.5; tpc)

22. (B32) She whom they call Iris, this too is by nature cloud:
> purple, and red, and greeny-yellow to behold.
> (Scholium BLT on *Iliad* 11.27; tpc)

23. (B33) We all come into being out of earth and water.
> (Sextus Empiricus, *Against the Mathematicians* 10.314)

24. (B34) . . . and of course the clear and certain truth no man has seen
> nor will there be anyone who knows about the gods and what I say
> about all things;

for even if, in the best case, someone happened to speak what has
been brought to pass,
nevertheless, he himself would not know, but opinion is ordained
for all.
(Sextus Empiricus, *Against the Mathematicians* 7.49.110; tpc)

25. (B35) Let these things be believed as resembling the truth.
(Plutarch, *Table Talk* 9.7.746b)

26. (B36) . . . however many they have made evident for mortals to behold.   (Herodian, *On Doubtful Syllables* 296.9)

27. (B38) If god had not fashioned yellow honey, they would say
that figs are far sweeter.   (Herodian, *On Peculiar Speech* 41.5)

28. (A12) Xenophanes used to say that those who say that the gods are
born are just as impious as those who say that they die, since either
way it follows that there is a time when the gods do not exist.
(Aristotle, *Rhetoric* 2.23 1399b6–9)

29. (A30) Some declared the universe to be a single substance . . . not
supposing, like some of the natural philosophers, that what-is is one,
and generating <the universe> out of the one as out of matter, but
speaking differently. For the others add change, since they generate
the universe, but these people say it is unchangeable. . . . Xenophanes,
who was the first of these to preach monism (Parmenides is said to
have been his student) made nothing clear . . . but looking off to the
whole heaven he declares that the one is god.
(Aristotle, *Metaphysics* 1.5 986b10–25)

30. (A32) He says that the sun is gathered together from many small
fires. . . . He declares that the earth is without limit and is not surrounded by air in every direction, that all things come into being from
the earth. And he says that sun and stars come into being from the
clouds.   (Pseudo-Plutarch, *Miscellanies* 4)

31. (A40) The sun <is constituted> out of incandescent clouds.[14]
(Stobaeus, *Opinions* 2.20.3)

32. (A38) <The stars> are constituted out of ignited clouds that die down
every day but become fiery again by night, just like coals.
(Aëtius 2.13.13)

---

14. Translator's note: The translation of this and the following two passages is
indebted to Mourelatos.

33. (A44) All things of this sort [comets, shooting stars, etc.] are aggregations of incandescent clouds.   (Aëtius 3.2.11)

34. (A33) [Xenophanes] says that the sun comes to be each day from the gathering together of many small fires, that the earth is unlimited and surrounded by neither the air nor the heavens. There are unlimited numbers of suns and moons, and everything is from the earth. He declared that the sea is salty because many mixtures flow together in it. . . . Xenophanes believes that earth is being mixed into the sea and over time it is dissolved by the moisture, saying that he has the following kinds of proofs: sea shells are found in the middle of earth and in mountains, and imprints of fish and seals have been found at Syracuse in the quarries, and the imprint of coral [or, "of a laurel leaf"] in the depth of the stone in Paros, and on Malta flat impressions of all forms of marine life. He says that these came about when all things were covered with mud long ago and the impressions were dried in the mud. All humans perish when the earth is carried down into the sea and becomes mud, and then there is another beginning of generation, and this change occurs in all the *kosmoi* [that is, in every such cycle].
(Hippolytus, *Refutation of All Heresies* 1.14.3–6)

35. (A39) <Concerning the stars that are called the *Dioscuri*>[15] Xenophanes says that the things like stars that appear on boats are small clouds that glimmer as a result of a certain kind of motion.
(Aëtius 2.18.1)

5. HERACLITUS OF EPHESUS

According to Diogenes Laertius, Heraclitus of Ephesus was born around 540 BCE. He was a member of one of the aristocratic families of that city, but turned his back on the sort of political life normally associated with persons of rank, ceding his hereditary ruling position to his brother. In the ancient world, he had a reputation for both misanthropy and obscurity—among his traditional nicknames were "the Obscure," and "the Riddler." The reputation is no doubt based on his rude comments about other philosophers, historians, and people in general, the nicknames on the enigmatic paradoxes he uses to present his views. He is said to have written a single book, of which fragment 1 was likely the beginning (or very near the beginning).

Although Heraclitus has cosmological views, many of which seem to have been influenced by Xenophanes, he is as interested in exploring questions

15. Translator's note: Literally, "sons of Zeus"; the term was used to refer to Castor and Polydeuces (Pollux). The phenomenon referred to is St. Elmo's Fire.

about knowledge, the soul, and the human condition as in making claims about the physical world. He asserted that a single divine law controls and steers the cosmos. He calls this the logos. *The word* logos *means, among other things, "account," or "thing said," or even "word." As with the English word "account," to give a* logos *is to say something, but also to give an explanation. Heraclitus is well aware of the ambiguities and complications possible in the words he uses, and he takes full advantage of the flexibility of the Greek language to make multiple points. Although the* logos *is an objective and independent truth available to all, Heraclitus is convinced that most people do not exercise the capacities required to come to understand it, and instead act like dreamers asleep in their own private worlds. Treating the* logos *as the divine law of the cosmos, the content of which is a truth to be grasped by humans who can (with difficulty) come to understand the cosmos, Heraclitus attempts to bridge the gap between divine and human knowledge pointed out by Homer, Hesiod, and Alcmaeon. The soul that understands the* logos *can, apparently, have the sure and certain knowledge that Xenophanes claimed "no man has seen." The path to this understanding is not, Heraclitus thinks, just the inquiry recommended by Xenophanes: Heraclitus ridicules those who have much learning but little understanding. The accumulation of facts without insight into the divine law-like workings of the cosmos is useless. Understanding how all things form a unity is a fundamental part of the necessary insight. Heraclitus offers signs of this unity in his paradoxical claims about the identity of opposites, insisting that despite unceasing change in the cosmos, there is an unchanging principle—the* logos*—that both governs and explains these changes. The physical sign of the* logos *is fire: always changing yet always the same.*

Note on the order of the fragments: Sextus Empiricus, our source for the first two fragments, says that they occurred at or near the beginning of Heraclitus' book, but we do not have similar information for the rest of the fragments. Their ordering is a controversial issue, as a particular order can impose an interpretation. In DK the fragments are ordered alphabetically by the name of the source. Here, the fragments are grouped more or less thematically, beginning with B1 and B2, and then going on to some general comments about the inadequacies of other thinkers and ordinary people. There are then observations on the difficulty of learning about the *logos*, but also encouraging remarks suggesting that proper thinking can lead people to the truth contained in the *logos*. There follow claims about the content of the *logos*, opposition and the unity of opposites, and the cosmos. Finally, there are fragments on soul, the human condition, and some remarks on religion. The reader should keep in mind that most Heraclitean sentences address several philosophical problems, and can be relevant for making a number of philosophical points. Fragments whose authenticity is disputed are marked with an asterisk (*).

1. (22B1) Although this *logos* holds always humans prove unable to understand it both before hearing it and when they have first heard it. For although all things come to be [or, "happen"] in accordance with this *logos,* humans are like the inexperienced when they experience such words and deeds as I set out, distinguishing each thing in accordance with its nature (*physis*) and saying how it is. But other people fail to notice what they do when awake, just as they forget what they do while asleep.

   (Sextus Empiricus, *Against the Mathematicians* 7.132)

2. (B2) For this reason it is necessary to follow what is common. But although the *logos* is common, most people live as if they had their own private understanding.

   (Sextus Empiricus, *Against the Mathematicians* 7.133)

3. (B40) Much learning ["polymathy"] does not teach insight. Otherwise it would have taught Hesiod and Pythagoras and moreover Xenophanes and Hecataeus. (Diogenes Laertius, *Lives of the Philosophers* 9.1)

4. (B129) Pythagoras the son of Mnesarchus practiced inquiry [*historiē*] more than all other men, and making a selection of these writings constructed his own wisdom, polymathy, evil trickery.

   (Diogenes Laertius, *Lives of the Philosophers* 8.6)

5. (B42) Heraclitus said that Homer deserved to be expelled from the contests and flogged, and Archilochus likewise.

   (Diogenes Laertius, *Lives of the Philosophers* 9.1)

6. (B39) In Priene was born Bias, son of Teutames, whose worth (*logos*) is greater than the others'.

   (Diogenes Laertius, *Lives of the Philosophers* 1.88)

7. (B57) Most men's teacher is Hesiod. They are sure he knew most things—a man who could not recognize day and night; for they are one. (Hippolytus, *Refutation of All Heresies* 9.10.2)

8. (B104) What understanding (*noos*) or intelligence (*phrēn*) have they? They put their trust in popular bards and take the mob for their teacher, unaware that most people are bad, and few are good.

   (Proclus, *Commentary on Plato's Alcibiades I* 117, Westerink)

9. (B86) Divine things for the most part escape recognition because of unbelief. (Plutarch, *Life of Coriolanus* 38 = Clement, *Miscellanies* 5.88.4)

10. (B108) Of all those whose accounts (*logoi*) I have heard, no one reaches the point of recognizing that what is wise is set apart from all.

(Stobaeus, *Selections* 3.1.174)

11. (B50) Listening not to me, but to the *logos*, it is wise to agree that all things are one.   (Hippolytus, *Refutation of All Heresies* 9.9.1)

12. (B123) Nature (*physis*) loves to hide.   (Themistius, *Orations* 5.69)

13. (B107) Eyes and ears are bad witnesses to people if they have barbarian[16] souls.   (Sextus Empiricus, *Against the Mathematicians* 7.126)

14.* (B46) [He said that] conceit is a holy disease[17] [and that] sight tells falsehoods.   (Diogenes Laertius, *Lives of the Philosophers* 9.7)

15. (B34) Uncomprehending when having heard, they are like the deaf. The saying describes them: being present they are absent.

(Clement, *Miscellanies* 5.115.3; tpc)

16. (B93) The Lord whose oracle is at Delphi neither speaks nor conceals but gives a sign.   (Plutarch, *On the Pythian Oracle* 404D)

17. (B113) Thinking (*phronein*) is common to all.

(Stobaeus, *Selections* 3.1.179)

18. (B112) Right thinking (*sōphronein*) is the greatest excellence, and wisdom (*sophia*) is to speak the truth and act in accordance with nature (*physis*) while paying attention to it.   (Stobaeus, *Selections* 3.1.178)

19.* (B73) One ought not to act and speak like people asleep.

(Marcus Aurelius, *Meditations* 4.43)

20. (B89) For the waking there is one common world, but when asleep each person turns away to a private one.

(Pseudo-Plutarch, *On Superstition* 166c)

21. (B26) A man in the night kindles a light for himself when his sight is extinguished; living he touches[18] the dead when asleep, when awake he touches the sleeper.   (Clement, *Miscellanies* 4.141.2)

16. Translator's note: A *barbaros* was originally anyone who did not speak Greek. Heraclitus uses the word here of people who do not understand the *logos*.
17. Translator's note: A reference to epilepsy, which was called the holy disease.
18. Translator's note: The Greek word for "kindles" and "touches" is the same.

22. (B21) What we see when awake is death, what we see asleep is sleep.
(Clement, *Miscellanies* 3.21.1)

23. (B114) Those who speak with understanding (*noos*) must rely firmly on what is common to all as a city must rely on [its?] law, and much more firmly. For all human laws are nourished by one law, the divine law; for it has as much power as it wishes and is sufficient for all and is still left over.   (Stobaeus, *Selections* 3.1.179)

24. (B18) Unless he hopes for the unhoped for, he will not find it, since it is not to be hunted out and is impassable.   (Clement, *Miscellanies* 2.17.4)

25. (B22) Those who seek gold dig up much earth but find little.
(Clement, *Miscellanies* 4.4.2)

26. (B17) For many, in fact all that come upon them, do not understand such things, nor when they have noticed them do they know them, but they seem to themselves <to do so>.   (Clement, *Miscellanies* 2.8.1)

27.* (B72) They are at odds with the *logos,* with which above all they are in continuous contact, and the things they meet every day appear strange to them.   (Marcus Aurelius, *Meditations* 4.46)

28.* (B70) [Heraclitus judged human opinions to be] children's play-things.   (Stobaeus, *Selections* 2.1.16)

29. (B19) [Rebuking some for their unbelief, Heraclitus says,] Knowing neither how to hear nor how to speak. (Clement, *Miscellanies,* 2.24.5)

30. (B28) The knowledge of the most famous persons, which they guard, is but opinion. . . . Justice will convict those who fabricate falsehoods and bear witness to them.   (Clement, *Miscellanies* 5.9.3)

31. (B87) A fool is excited by every word (*logos*).
(Plutarch, *On Listening to Lectures* 40f–41a)

32. (B97) Dogs bark at everyone they do not know.
(Plutarch, *Should Old Men Take Part in Politics?* 787c)

33. (B56) People are deceived about the knowledge of obvious things, like Homer, who was wiser than all the Greeks. For children who were killing lice deceived him by saying, "All we saw and caught we have left behind, but all we neither saw nor caught we bring with us."
(Hippolytus, *Refutation of All Heresies* 9.9.5)

34. (B47) Let us not make random conjectures about the greatest matters.
(Diogenes Laertius, *Lives of the Philosophers* 9.73)

35. (B116) It belongs to all people to know themselves and to think rightly
(*sōphronein*).   (Stobaeus, *Selections* 3.5.6)

36. (B35) Men who are lovers of wisdom must be inquirers into many
things indeed.   (Clement, *Miscellanies* 5.140.5)

37. (B101) I searched [*or:* inquired into] myself.
(Plutarch, *Against Colotes* 1118C)

38. (B54) An unapparent connection (*harmonia*) is stronger than an ap-
aparent one.   (Hippolytus, *Refutation of All Heresies* 9.9.5)

39. (B12) Upon those who step into the same rivers, different and again
different waters flow.   (Arius Didymus, fr. 39.2 = *Dox. Gr.* 471.4–5)

40. (B91) [It is not possible to step twice into the same river]. . . . It scatters
and again comes together, and approaches and recedes.
(Plutarch, *On the E at Delphi* 392b)

41.* (B49a) We step into and we do not step into the same rivers. We are
and we are not.   (Heraclitus Homericus, *Homeric Questions* 24)

42. (B78) Human nature has no insight, but divine nature has it.
(Origen, *Against Celsus* 6.12)

43. (B45) You would not discover the limits of the soul although you
traveled every road: so deep a *logos* does it have.
(Diogenes Laertius, *Lives of the Philosophers* 9.7)

44.* (B115) The soul has a self-increasing *logos*.
(Stobaeus, *Selections* 3.1.180)

45. (B30) This *kosmos*, the same for all, none of gods nor humans made, but
it was always and is and shall be: an ever-living fire, kindled in measures and extinguished in measures.
(Clement, *Miscellanies* 5.103.3; tpc)

46. (B41) The wise is one (*to sophon*), to know the intelligent plan (*gnōmē*)
by which all things are steered through all.
(Diogenes Laertius, *Lives of the Philosophers* 9.1; tpc)

47. (B32) The wise (*to sophon*) is one alone, both unwilling and willing to
be called by the name of Zeus.   (Clement, *Miscellanies* 5.115.1; tpc)

48. (B64) Thunderbolt steers all things.

> (Hippolytus, *Refutation of All Heresies* 9.10.7)

49. (B90) All things are an exchange for fire and fire for all things, as goods for gold and gold for goods.   (Plutarch, *On the E at Delphi* 338d–e)

50. (B65) Fire is want and satiety.

> (Hippolytus, *Refutation of All Heresies* 9.10.7)

51.* (B76) Fire lives the death of earth and *aēr* lives the death of fire, water lives the death of *aēr*, earth that of water.   (Maximus of Tyre, 41.4)

52. (B36) For souls to become water is to die; for water to become earth is to die; but from earth, water comes to be; from water, soul.

> (Clement, *Miscellanies* 6.17.2; tpc)

53. (B118) Gleam of light: the dry soul, wisest (*sophōtate*) and best.

> (Stobaeus, *Selections* 3.5.8)

54. (B117) A man when drunk is led by a boy, stumbling and not knowing where he goes, since his soul is moist.   (Stobaeus, *Selections* 3.5.7)

55. (B84a) Changing it rests.

> (Plotinus, *Enneads* 4.8.1)

56. (B125) Even the *Kykeōn* [posset][19] falls apart if it is not stirred.

> (Theophrastus, *On Vertigo* 9; tpc)

57. (B80) It is necessary to know that war is common and justice is strife and that all things happen in accordance with strife and necessity.

> (Origen, *Against Celsus* 6.42)

58. (B53) War is the father of all and king of all, and some he shows as gods, others as humans; some he makes slaves, others free.

> (Hippolytus, *Refutation of All Heresies* 9.9.4)

59. (B8) What is opposed brings together; the finest harmony [*harmonia*] is composed of things at variance, and everything comes to be [or, "occurs"] in accordance with strife.

> (Aristotle, *Nicomachean Ethics* 8.2 1155b4)

60. (B10) Things taken together are whole and not whole, <something that is> being brought together and brought apart, in tune and out of tune; out of all things there comes a unity and out of a unity all things.

> ([Aristotle], *On the World* 5 396b20)

---

19. The *Kykeōn* is a potion made of ground barley, grated cheese, and wine (sometimes with honey).

61. (B51) They do not understand how, though at variance with itself, it agrees with itself.[20] It is a backwards-turning[21] attunement like that of the bow and lyre.   (Hippolytus, *Refutation of All Heresies* 9.9.2)

62. (B55) All that can be seen, heard, experienced—these are what I prefer.
          (Hippolytus, *Refutation of All Heresies* 9.9.5)

63. (B101a) Eyes are more accurate witnesses than the ears.
          (Polybius, *Histories* 12.27.1)

64. (B7) If all things were smoke, nostrils would distinguish them.
          (Aristotle, *On the Senses and Their Objects* 5 443a23)

65. (B98) Souls [have use of the sense of] smell in Hades.
          (Plutarch, *On the Face in the Moon* 943E)

66. (B48) The name of the bow is life, but its work is death.[22]
          (*Etymologium Magnum* sv *bios*)

67. (B59) The track of writing [or, "the path of the carding wheels"][23] is straight and crooked.   (Hippolytus, *Refutation of All Heresies* 9.10.4)

68. (B60) The road up and the road down are one and the same.
          (Hippolytus, *Refutation of All Heresies* 9.10.4)

69. (B61) The sea is the purest and most polluted water: to fishes drinkable and bringing safety, to humans undrinkable and destructive.
          (Hippolytus, *Refutation of All Heresies* 9.10.5)

70.* (B82) The most beautiful of apes is ugly in comparison with the human race.   (Plato, *Hippias Major* 289a3–4)

71. (B13) Pigs rejoice in mud more than in pure water.
          (Clement, *Miscellanies* 1.2.2)

20. Translator's note: Or, "how by being at variance with itself it agrees with itself"; more literally, "how (by) being brought apart it is brought together."
21. Reading *palintropos* here. Translator's note: The sources disagree; some give *palintonos*, "backwards-stretching." There is no scholarly consensus on which word Heraclitus used.
22. Translator's note: The fragment exploits the identical spelling of the Greek words for bow (*biós*) and life (*bíos*); they differed in the accented syllables, but in Heraclitus' time accents were not yet written. Also, the fragment does not contain the word *biós* (bow), but uses the more common word *toxon*, thus requiring Heraclitus' readers (or hearers) to make the essential association themselves.
23. Translator's note: The manuscript reading *gnapheiōn* ("carding wheels") is emended by some editors to *grapheiōn* ("writing").

72. (B9) Asses would choose rubbish rather than gold.
(Aristotle, Nicomachean Ethics 10.5 1176a7)

73. (B4) We would call oxen happy when they find bitter vetch to eat.
(Albertus Magnus, On Vegetables 6.401)

74. (B37) Pigs wash themselves in mud, birds in dust or ash.
(Columella, On Agriculture 8.4.4)

75. (B11) Every beast is driven to pasture by blows.
([Aristotle], On the World 6 401a10)

76. (B83) The wisest of humans will appear as an ape in comparison with a god in respect to wisdom, beauty, and all other things.
(Plato, Hippias Major 289b4–5)

77. (B102) To god all things are beautiful and good and just, but humans have supposed some unjust and others just.
(Porphyry, Notes on Homer, on Iliad 4.4)

78. (B124) The most beautiful *kosmos* is a pile of things poured out at random.
(Theophrastus, Metaphysics 15)

79. (B103) The beginning and the end are common on the circumference of a circle.
(Porphyry, Notes on Homer, on Iliad 24.200)

80. (B126) Cold things grow hot, a hot thing cold, a moist thing withers, a parched thing is moistened.
(John Tzetzes, Notes on the Iliad, p. 126 Hermann)

81. (B67) God is day and night, winter and summer, war and peace, satiety and hunger, but changes the way <fire,(?)> when mingled with perfumes, is named according to the scent of each.
(Hippolytus, Refutation of All Heresies 9.10.8)

82. (B88) The same thing is both living and dead, and the waking and the sleeping, and young and old; for these things transformed are those, and those transformed back again are these.
(Pseudo-Plutarch, Consolation to Apollonius 106E)

83. (B23) They would not have known the name of justice if these things [unjust things] did not exist.
(Clement, Miscellanies 4.9.7)

84. (B111) Disease makes health pleasant and good, hunger satiety, weariness rest.
(Stobaeus, Selections 3.1.178)

85. (B58) Physicians who cut and burn complain that they receive no worthy pay, although they do these things.

(Hippolytus, *Refutation of All Heresies* 9.10.3)

86. (B62) Immortal mortals, mortal immortals, living the death of the others and dying their life.

(Hippolytus, *Refutation of All Heresies* 9.10.6)

87. (B31) The turnings of fire: first, sea; and of sea, half is earth and half fiery waterspout. . . . Earth is poured out as sea, and is measured according to the same ratio (*logos*) it was before it became earth.

(Clement, *Miscellanies* 5.104 3,5)

88. (B3 + B94) The sun by its nature is the width of a human foot, not exceeding in size the limits of its width . . . Otherwise, the Erinyes, ministers of Justice, will find him out.   (Derveni Papyrus, col. IV)

89. (B6) The sun is new each day.   (Aristotle, *Meteorology* 2.2 355a13)

90. (B99) If there were no sun, as far as concerns all the other stars it would be night.   (Plutarch, *Is Water or Fire the More Useful?* 957A)

91. (B120) Limits of dawn and evening are the Bear and opposite the Bear,[24] the limit of bright Zeus.   (Strabo, *Geography* 1.6)

92. (B136) Souls slain in war are purer than those that perish of diseases.

(Bodleian Scholium on Epictetus, lxxi Schenkel)

93. (B24) Gods and humans honor those slain in war.

(Clement, *Miscellanies* 4.16.1)

94. (B25) Greater deaths win greater destinies.

(Clement, *Miscellanies* 4.49.2)

95. (B27) Things unexpected and unthought of await humans when they die.   (Clement, *Miscellanies* 4.22.144)

96. (B63) They arise and become vigilant guardians of the living and the dead.   (Hippolytus, *Refutation of All Heresies* 9.10.6)

97. (B20) When they are born, they are willing to live and to have their destinies, and they leave children behind to become their destinies.

(Clement, *Miscellanies* 3.14.1)

24. Translator's note: The Bear is the constellation Ursa Major (the Big Dipper), and "opposite the Bear" refers to the star Arcturus, which was used as an indicator of the seasons.

98. (B16) How could one fail to be seen by that which does not set?
(Clement, *Pedagogue* 2.99.5)

99. (B96) Corpses are more fit to be thrown out than dung.
(Plutarch, *Table Talk* 669A)

100. (B121) Every grown man of the Ephesians should hang himself and leave the city to the boys; for they banished Hermodorus, the best man among them, saying "let no one of us excel, or if he does, be it elsewhere and among others."   (Strabo, *Geography* 14.25)

101. (B125a) May wealth never leave you, Ephesians, lest your wickedness be revealed.
(John Tzetzes, Scholium on Aristophanes' *Wealth* 88)

102. (B49) One person is ten thousand to me if he is best.
(Theodorus Prodromus, *Letters* 1)

103. (B52) A lifetime is a child playing, playing checkers; the kingdom belongs to a child.   (Hippolytus, *Refutation of All Heresies* 9.94)

104. (B44) The people must fight for the law as for the city wall.
(Diogenes Laertius, *Lives of the Philosophers* 9.2)

105. (B43) Willful violence [*hubris*] must be quenched more than a fire.
(Diogenes Laertius, *Lives of the Philosophers* 9.3)

106. (B119) A person's character is his divinity [or, "guardian spirit," *daimōn*].   (Stobaeus, *Selections* 4.40.23)

107. (B110) It is not better for humans to get all they want.
(Stobaeus, *Selections* 3.1.176)

108. (B95) It is better to conceal ignorance.   (Plutarch, *Table Talk* 644F)

109. (B85) It is difficult to fight against anger, for whatever it wants it buys at the price of the soul.   (Plutarch, *Life of Coriolanus* 22.2)

110. (B5) They vainly purify themselves with blood when defiled with it, as if a man who had stepped into mud were to wash it off with mud. He would be thought mad if anyone noticed him acting thus.
(Aristocritus, *Theosophia* 68; Origen, *Against Celsus* 7.62)

111. (B15) If it were not for Dionysus that they hold processions and sing hymns to the shameful parts [*phalli*], it would be a most shameless act; but Hades and Dionysus are the same, in whose honor they go mad and celebrate the Bacchic rites.   (Clement, *Protreptic* 34.5)

112. (B14) Nightwalkers, Magi, Bacchoi, Lenai, and the initiated. [These people Heraclitus threatens with what happens after death. . . .] For the secret rites practiced among humans are celebrated in an unholy manner.   (Clement, *Protreptic* 22)

113. (B92) The Sibyl with raving mouth uttering mirthless [and unadorned and unperfumed phrases, reaches a thousand years in her voice on account of the god]. (Plutarch, *On the Oracles at Delphi* 397A)

6. PARMENIDES OF ELEA

The most reliable reports on the life of Parmenides of Elea (an Italian town today called Velia near what is now Naples) imply that he was born around 515 BCE. Diogenes Laertius says that he was a pupil of Xenophanes, "but did not follow him" (i.e., he did not adopt Xenophanes' views). Diogenes Laertius also says that Parmenides was, at some time in his life associated with the Pythagoreans. There is no way of knowing whether or not these reports are true, but it seems clear that Parmenides is concerned with answering questions about knowledge that are generated by Xenophanes' views. (It is less clear that, as sometimes claimed, Xenophanes' account of his greatest god [see Chapter 4 fragment 13] influenced Parmenides' account of what-is.) It would not be surprising that Parmenides should know about Pythagoreanism, as Elea is in the southern part of Italy, which was home to the Pythagorean movement.

Like Xenophanes, Parmenides wrote in verse: His poem is in Homeric hexameters, and there are many Homeric images, especially from the Odyssey. *In the poem Parmenides presents a young man (kouros, in Greek), who is taken in a chariot to meet a goddess. He is told by her that he will learn "all things"; moreover, while the goddess says that what the kouros is told is true, she stresses that he himself must test and assess the arguments she gives. Parmenides is one of the most important and most controversial figures among the early Greek thinkers, and there is much disagreement among scholars about the details of his views. The poem begins with a long introduction (The Proem, B1); this is followed by a section traditionally called Truth (B2– B8.50). This is followed by the so-called Doxa section ("beliefs" or "opinions")—a cosmology that, the goddess warns, is in some way deceptive. In Truth, Parmenides argues that genuine thought and knowledge can only be about what genuinely is (what-is), for what-is-not is literally unsayable and unthinkable. Parmenides warns against what he calls the "beliefs of mortals," based entirely on sense-experience; in these, the goddess says, "there is no true trust." Rather, one must judge by understanding (the capacity to reason) what follows from the basic claim that what-is must be, and what-is-not cannot be. The poem proceeds (in the crucial fragment B8) to explore the features of genuine being: What-is must be whole, complete, unchanging, and one. It can neither come to be nor pass away, nor undergo any qualitative change. Only what is in this way can be grasped by thought and genuinely known.*

Given these arguments, the accounts of the way things are given by Parmenides' predecessors cannot be acceptable. The earlier views required fundamental changes in their theoretically basic entities, or relied on the reality of opposites and their unity; Parmenides argues that all these presuppose the reality of what-is-not, and so cannot succeed. For modern scholars, one particularly intriguing aspect of Parmenides' thought is that, having apparently rejected the world of sensory experience as unreal, the goddess then goes on, in the Doxa, to give a cosmological account of her own. Is this meant to be a parody of other views? Is it the best that can be said for the world that appears to human senses? Is it a lesson for the hearer, to test whether any cosmology could ever be acceptable on Parmenidean grounds? There is little agreement among Parmenides' readers on this. While Parmenides clearly shares with Xenophanes and Heraclitus interests in metaphysical and epistemological questions, Parmenides is the first to see the importance of metatheoretical questions about philosophical theories themselves, and to provide comprehensive arguments for his claims. These arguments are powerful, and Parmenides' views about knowledge, being, and change were a serious theoretical challenge, not only to later Presocratic thinkers, but also to Plato and Aristotle.

1. (28B1) The mares which carry me as far as my spirit ever
   aspired
   were escorting me, when they brought me and proceeded
   along the renowned route
   of the goddess, which brings a knowing mortal to all cities
   one by one.
   On this route I was being brought, on it wise mares were
   bringing me,
   straining the chariot, and maidens were guiding the way.   5
   The axle in the center of the wheel was shrilling forth the
   bright sound of a musical pipe,
   ablaze, for it was being driven forward by two rounded
   wheels at either end, as the daughters of the Sun
   were hastening to escort <me> after leaving the house of
   Night
   for the light, having pushed back the veils from their heads
   with their hands.   10
   There are the gates of the roads of Night and Day,
   and a lintel and a stone threshold contain them.
   High in the sky they are filled by huge doors
   of which avenging Justice holds the keys that fit them.

The maidens beguiled her with soft words   15
and skillfully persuaded her to push back the bar for them
quickly from the gates. They made
a gaping gap of the doors when they opened them,
swinging in turn in their sockets the bronze posts
fastened with bolts and rivets. There, straight through them
    then,   20
the maidens held the chariot and horses on the broad road.
And the goddess received me kindly, took my
right hand in hers, and addressed me with these words:
Young man, accompanied by immortal charioteers,
who reach my house by the horses which bring you,   25
welcome—since it was not an evil destiny that sent you
    forth to travel
this route (for indeed it is far from the beaten path of
    humans),
but Right and Justice. It is right that you learn all things—
both the unshaken heart of well-persuasive Truth
and the beliefs of mortals, in which there is no true trust.   30
But nevertheless you will learn these too—how it were
    right that the things that seem
be reliably, being indeed, the whole of things.
      (lines 1–30: Sextus Empiricus, *Against the Mathematicians*
          7.111–14; lines 28–32: Simplicius, *Commentary on*
              Aristotle's On the Heavens, 557.25–558.2; tmpc)

2. (B2) But come now, I will tell you—and you, when you
      have heard the story, bring it safely away—
which are the only routes of inquiry that are for thinking:
the one, that is and that it is not possible for it not to be,
is the path of Persuasion (for it attends upon Truth),
the other, that it is not and that it is right that it not be,   5
this indeed I declare to you to be a path entirely unable to
      be investigated:
For neither can you know what is not (for it is not to be
      accomplished)
nor can you declare it.
      (Proclus, *Commentary on Plato's Timaeus* 1.345.18; lines 3–8:
      Simplicius, *Commentary on Aristotle's Physics* 116.28; tmpc)

3. (B3) . . . for the same thing is for thinking and for being.[25]
         (Clement, *Miscellanies* 6.23; Plotinus, *Enneads* 5.1.8)

25. Translator's note: Alternative translations: "for the same thing both can be thought of and can be"; "for thinking and being are the same."

4. (B4) But gaze upon things which although absent are
     securely present to the mind.
   For you will not cut off what-is from clinging to what-is,
   neither being scattered everywhere in every way in order
   nor being brought together.   (Clement, *Miscellanies* 5.15)

5. (B5) . . . For me, it is indifferent
   from where I am to begin: for that is where I will arrive ~complete
     back again.
              (Proclus, *Commentary on Plato's Parmenides* 1.708)

6. (B6) It is right both to say and to think that it is what-is: for
     it can be,
   but nothing is not: these things I bid you to ponder.
   For I < 26 > you from this first route of inquiry,
   and then from that, on which mortals, knowing nothing,
   wander, two-headed: for helplessness in their   5
   breasts steers their wandering mind. They are borne along
   deaf and blind alike, dazed, hordes without judgment
   for whom to be and not to be are thought to be the same
   and not the same, and the path of all is backward-turning.
                  (Simplicius, *Commentary on Aristotle's Physics*
                              86.27–28; 117.4–13; tmpc)

7. (B7) For in no way may this prevail, that things that are not
     are;
   but you, hold your thought back from this route of inquiry
   and do not let habit, rich in experience, compel you along
     this route
   to direct an aimless eye and an echoing ear
   and tongue, but judge by reasoning (*logos*) the much-
     contested   5
   examination spoken by me.
         (lines 1–2: Plato, *Sophist* 242a; lines 2–6: Sextus Empiricus,
                         Against the Mathematicians 7.114; tmpc)

8. (B8) . . . Just one story of a route
   is still left: that it is. On this [route] there are signs
   very many, that what-is is ungenerated and imperishable,
                       ↳ what exists

26. There is a lacuna (gap) in all the manuscripts at this point. Diels supplied *eirgō*,
so the line would be translated "I hold you back." (This would imply that there are
three routes.) Two recent suggestions from scholars supply forms of the verb
archein, "to begin," so the goddess says either "I begin for you," or "You will
begin." (This implies two routes.)

a whole of a single kind, unshaken, and complete.
Nor was it ever, nor will it be, since it is now, all together   5
one, holding together: For what birth will you seek out for it?
How and from what did it grow? From what-is-not I will allow
you neither to say nor to think: For it is not to be said or
    thought
that it is not. What need would have roused it,
later or earlier, having begun from nothing, to grow?   10
In this way it is right either fully to be or not.
Nor will the force of true conviction ever permit anything to
    come to be
beside it from what-is-not. For this reason neither coming to
    be
nor perishing did Justice allow, loosening her shackles,
but she [Justice] holds it fast. And the decision about these
    things is in this: 15
is or is not; and it has been decided, as is necessary,
to leave the one [route] unthought of and unnamed (for it is
    not a true
route), so that the other [route] is and is genuine.
But how can what-is be hereafter? How can it come to be?
For if it came to be, it is not, not even if it is sometime going to
    be.   20
Thus coming-to-be has been extinguished and perishing
    cannot be investigated.
Nor is it divisible, since it is all alike,
and not at all more in any way, which would keep it from
    holding together,)
or at all less, but it is all full of what-is.
(Therefore it is all holding together; for what-is draws near to
    what-is.)   25
But unchanging in the limits of great bonds
it is without starting or ceasing, since coming-to-be and
    perishing
have wandered very far away; and true trust drove them away.
Remaining the same and in the same and by itself it lies
and so remains there fixed; for mighty Necessity   30
holds it in bonds of a limit which holds it in on all sides.
For this reason it is right for what-is to be not incomplete;
for it is not lacking; otherwise, what-is would be in want of
    everything.
What is for thinking is the same as that on account of which
    there is thought.

For not without what-is, on which it depends, having been
    solemnly pronounced,   35
will you find thinking; for nothing else either is or will be
except what-is, since precisely this is what Fate shackled
to be whole and changeless. Therefore it has been named all
    things
that mortals, persuaded that they are true, have posited
both to come to be and to perish, to be and not,   40
and to change place and alter bright color.
But since the limit is ultimate, it [namely, what-is] is complete
from all directions like the bulk of a ball well-rounded from all
    sides
equally matched in every way from the middle; for it is right
for it to be not in any way greater or lesser than in another.   45
For neither is there what-is-not—which would stop it from
    reaching
the same—nor is there any way in which what-is would be
    more than what-is in one way
and in another way less, since it is all inviolable;
for equal to itself from all directions, it meets uniformly with
    its limits.
At this point, I end for you my reliable account and thought   50
about truth. From here on, learn mortal opinions,
listening to the deceitful order of my words.
For they established two forms to name in their judgments,[27]
of which it is not right to name one—in this they have gone
    astray—
and they distinguished things opposite in body, and
    established signs   55
apart from one another—for one, the aetherial fire of flame,
mild, very light, the same as itself in every direction,
but not the same as the other; but that other one, in itself
is opposite—dark night, a dense and heavy body.
I declare to you all the ordering as it appears,   60
so that no mortal judgment may ever overtake you.
    (Simplicius, *Commentary on Aristotle's Physics* 145.1–146.25
            [lines 1–52]; 39.1–9 [lines 50–61]; tmpc)

9. (B9) But since all things have been named light and night
    and the things which accord with their powers have been
        assigned to these things and those,

27. Translator's note: Other manuscripts give a different form of the word rendered
"judgment" that requires another translation: "established judgments" (i.e., decided).

all is full of light and obscure night together,
of both equally, since neither has any share of nothing.
      (Simplicius, *Commentary on Aristotle's Physics* 180.9–12)

10. (B10) You shall know the nature of the Aithēr and all the
      signs in the Aithēr
and the destructive deeds of the shining sun's pure
torch and whence they came to be,
and you shall learn the wandering deeds of the round-faced
      moon
and its nature, and you shall know also the surrounding
      heaven,   5
from what it grew and how Necessity led and shackled it
to hold the limits of the stars.
                  (Clement, *Miscellanies* 5.14; 138.1)

11. (B11) . . . how earth and sun and moon
and the Aithēr that is common to all and the Milky Way
      and
furthest Olympus and the hot force of the stars surged forth
to come to be.
      (Simplicius, *Commentary on Aristotle's On the Heavens*
                            559.22–25)

12. (B12) For the narrower <wreaths> were filled with unmixed
      fire,
the ones next to them with night, but a due amount of fire
      is inserted among it,
and in the middle of these is the goddess who governs all
      things.
For she rules over hateful birth and union of all things,
sending the female to unite with male and in opposite fashion,   5
male to female.
           (Simplicius, *Commentary on Aristotle's Physics*
        39.14–16 [lines 1–3], 31.13–17 [lines 2–6])

13. (B13) First of all gods she contrived Love.
      (Simplicius, *Commentary on Aristotle's Physics* 39.18)

14. (B14) Night-shining foreign light wandering around earth.
              (Plutarch, *Against Colotes* 1116A)

15. (B15) Always looking toward the rays of the sun.
            (Plutarch, *On the Face in the Moon* 929A)

16. (B16) As on each occasion there is a mixture of the much-
     wandering limbs,
   so is mind present to humans; for the same thing
   is what the nature of the limbs thinks in men,
   both in all and in each; for the more is thought.
                         (Theophrastus, *On the Senses* 3; tpc)

17. (B17) [That the male is conceived in the right part of the
     uterus has been said by others of the ancients. For
     Parmenides says:]
   <The goddess brought> boys <into being> on the right
   <side of the uterus>, girls on the left.
                         (Galen, *Commentary on Book VI of
                         Hippocrates' Epidemics II* 46)

18. (B18) As soon as woman and man mingle the seeds of love
   <that come from> their veins, a formative power fashions
     well-constructed bodies
   from their two differing bloods, if it maintains a balance.
   For if when the seed is mingled the powers clash
   and do not create a single <power> in the body resulting
     from the mixture,
   with double seed they will dreadfully disturb the nascent
   sex <of the child>.
                         (Caelius Aurelianus, *On Chronic Diseases* VI.9)

19. (B19) In this way, according to opinion (*doxa*), these things
     have grown and now are
   and afterwards after growing up will come to an end.
   And upon them humans have established a name to mark
     each one.
   (Simplicius, *Commentary on Aristotle's On the Heavens* 558.9–11)

7. ZENO OF ELEA

*Almost everything we think we know about the life of Zeno of Elea comes from
Plato's dialogue* Parmenides. *According to Plato, Zeno was about twenty-five
years younger than Parmenides and was reported to have been his lover as well
as his philosophical associate. If Plato's claims are accepted, Zeno was born
around 490 BCE, and he and Parmenides visited Athens in about 450 when
Socrates was a young man. (It is quite unlikely that the conversation Plato
reports took place, but the chronological information from Plato may be based*

on fact.) The only other biographical claims about Zeno come from Diogenes Laertius' not entirely reliable Lives of the Philosophers *(9.25–9); according to Diogenes Laertius, Zeno bravely resisted a political tyranny and, despite being tortured, did not betray his comrades. Zeno explores the consequences of Parmenides' claims about what-is: in his ingenious arguments he purports to show that neither plurality nor motion is compatible with Parmenides' requirements for reality. Zeno challenges the seemingly incontrovertible evidence of our senses, and his arguments have worried and fascinated philosophers from ancient times to the present.*

1. (29A11, A12) Once Parmenides and Zeno came to Athens for the Great Panathenaic festival. Parmenides was quite an elderly man, very gray, but fine and noble in appearance, just about sixty-five years old. Zeno was then almost forty, of a good height and handsome to see. The story goes that he had been Parmenides' young lover. . . . Socrates and many others <were> eager to listen to Zeno's treatise, for he had then brought it to Athens for the first time. Socrates was then very young. Zeno himself read it to them. . . . When Socrates had heard it, he asked Zeno to read again the first hypothesis of the first argument. When he had read it, he said, "How do you mean this, Zeno? If things that are are many, they must therefore be both like and unlike, but this is impossible. For unlike things cannot be like, nor can like things be unlike. Isn't that what you are saying?"

   —*Zeno:* Yes.

   —*Socrates:* Now if it is impossible for unlike things to be like and for like things to be unlike, is it also impossible for things to be many? For if they were many they would have impossible attributes. Is this the point of your arguments—to contend, against all that is said, that things are not many? And do you think that each of your arguments proves this?

   —*Zeno:* You have well understood the purpose of the whole work.

   —*Socrates:* I understand, Parmenides, that Zeno here wants to be identified with you by his treatise as well as his friendship, for he has written somewhat in the same style as you, but by changing it he is trying to make us think he is saying something else. For in your poem you declare that the all is one and you do a good job of proving this, while he declares that it is not many, and furnishes many impressive proofs. Now when one of you says it is one and the other that it is not many, and each speaks so as to seem not to have said any of the same things, though you are saying practically the same things, what you have said appears beyond the rest of us.

   —*Zeno:* Yes, Socrates, but you have not completely understood the truth of the treatise. . . . It is actually a defense of Parmenides' argument against those who try to make fun of it, saying that if what-is is one, the argument has many ridiculous consequences which contradict it. Now my treatise opposes the advocates of plurality and pays them back the same and more, aiming to prove that their hypothesis, "if there are many things," suffers still more ridiculous consequences than the hypothesis that there is one, if anyone follows it through sufficiently. I wrote it in this spirit of competitiveness when I was young, and then someone stole it, so I did not even have the chance to consider whether it should be made public.

(Plato, *Parmenides* 127b–128d)

2. (A16) Zeno stated that if anyone could make clear to him what the one is, he would be able to speak of the things that are.

(Eudemus, *Physics* fr. 7, quoted in Simplicius,
Commentary on Aristotle's Physics 97.12–13)

3. (B2) For if it should be added to something else that exists, it would not make it any larger. For if it were of no size and were added, nothing it is added to could increase in size. And so it follows immediately that what is added is nothing. But if the other thing is no smaller when it is subtracted and it is not increased when it is added, clearly the thing added or subtracted is nothing.

(Simplicius, *Commentary on Aristotle's Physics* 139.11–15)

4. (B1) If it is, each thing must have some size and thickness, and part of it must be apart from the rest. And the same reasoning holds concerning the part that is in front. For that too will have size, and part of it will be in front. Now to say this once is the same thing as to keep saying it forever. For no such part of it will be the last or unrelated to another. Therefore if there are many things, they must be both small and large; so small as not to have size, but so large as to be infinite.

(Simplicius, *Commentary on Aristotle's Physics* 141.2–8)

5. (B3) If there are many, they must be just as many as they are, neither more nor less. But if they are as many as they are, they must be limited. If there are many things, the things that are are unlimited, since between things that are there are always others, and still others between those. Therefore the things that are are unlimited.

(Simplicius, *Commentary on Aristotle's Physics* 140.29–33)

6. (A25) There are four of Zeno's arguments about motion that present difficulties for those who try to solve them. First is the argument that says that there is no motion because that which is moving must reach the midpoint before the end. . . . It is always necessary to traverse half the distance, but these are infinite, and it is impossible to get through things that are infinite. . . .

(Aristotle, *Physics* 6.9 239b9–13; *Physics* 8.8 263a5–6)

7. (A26) The second <argument> is the one called the Achilles. This is to
the effect that the slowest as it runs will never be caught by the quickest. For the pursuer must first reach the point from which the pursued
departed, so that the slower must always be some distance in front.
This is the same argument as the Dichotomy,[28] but it differs in not
dividing the given magnitude in half.

(Aristotle, *Physics* 6.9 239b14–20)

8. (A25) For this reason Zeno's argument falsely assumes that it is impossible to traverse or come into contact with an infinite number of things
individually in a finite time. For both length and time and generally
everything that is continuous are called infinite in two ways: infinite in
division and infinite with respect to their extremities. Now it is impossible to come into contact with things infinite in quantity in a finite
time, but it is possible to do so with things that are infinite in division.
For time itself too is infinite in this way. And so, it follows that it
traverses the infinite in an infinite and not a finite time, and comes into
contact with infinite things in infinite, not finite times.

(Aristotle, *Physics* 6.2 233a21–31)

9. This solution is sufficient to use against the person who raised the
question (for he asked whether it is possible to traverse or count
infinite things in a finite time), but insufficient for the facts of the
matter and the truth.   (Aristotle, *Physics* 8.8 263a15–18; not in DK)

10. (A27) Zeno makes a mistake in reasoning. For if, he says, everything is
always at rest when it occupies a space equal to itself, and what is
moving is always "at a now," the moving arrow is motionless.

(Aristotle, *Physics* 6.9 239b5–7)

The third argument is the one just stated, that the arrow is stopped
while it is moving. This follows from assuming that time is composed
of "nows." If this is not conceded, the deduction will not go through.

(Aristotle, *Physics* 6.9 239b30–33)

11. (A28) The fourth argument is about equal bodies moving in a stadium
alongside equal bodies in the opposite direction, the one group moving from the end of the stadium, the other from the middle, at equal
speed. He claims in this argument that it follows that half the time is
equal to the double. The mistake is in thinking that an equal magnitude moving with equal speed takes an equal time in passing something moving as it does in passing something at rest. But this is false.
Let *A*'s represent the equal stationary bodies, *B*'s the bodies beginning

28. The Dichotomy is Aristotle's name for Zeno's first argument (A25, no. 6
above).

from the middle, equal in number and size to the *A*'s, and *C*'s the bodies beginning from the end, equal in number and size to these and having the same speed as the *B*'s. It follows that the first *B* is at the end at the same time as the first *C*, as the *B*'s and *C*'s move alongside one another, and the first *C* has completed the process of coming alongside all the *B*'s, but the first *B* has completed the process of coming alongside half the *A*'s. And so the time is half. For each of them is alongside each thing for an equal time. It follows simultaneously that the first *B* has moved alongside all the *C*'s, for the first *C* and the first *B* will be at the opposite ends simultaneously, because both have been alongside the *A*'s for an equal amount of time.

(Aristotle, *Physics* 6.9 239b33–240a17)

12.[29] (A24) If place exists, where is it? For everything that exists is in a place. Therefore if place exists, then place is in a place. This goes on to infinity. Therefore, place does not exist.

(Simplicius, *Commentary on Aristotle's Physics* 562.3–6; Aristotle, *Physics* 4.3 210b22–23, 4.1 209a23–25; Eudemus, *Physics* fr. 42, quoted by Simplicius, *Commentary on Aristotle's Physics* 563.25–28)

13. (A29)—*Zeno:* Tell me, Protagoras, does a single millet seed make a noise when it falls, or one ten-thousandth of a millet seed?

—*Protagoras:* No.

—*Zeno:* Does a bushel of millet seeds make a noise when it falls, or doesn't it?

—*Protagoras:* It does.

—*Zeno:* But isn't there a ratio between the bushel of millet seeds and one millet seed, or one ten-thousandth of a millet seed?

—*Protagoras:* Yes there is.

—*Zeno:* So won't there be the same ratios of their sounds to one another? For as the things that make the noise <are to one another>, so are the noises <to one another>. But since this is so, if the bushel of millet seeds makes a noise, so will a single millet seed and one ten-thousandth of a millet seed.

(Simplicius, *Commentary on Aristotle's Physics* 1108.18–25)

13a. (Response from Aristotle) It does not follow that if a given motive power causes a certain amount of motion, half that power will cause motion either of any particular amount or in any length of time: otherwise, one man might move a ship, if the power of the ship-haulers is divided into their number and the distance that all of them move it.

(Aristotle, *Physics* 7.5 250a16–19; not in DK)

29. Translator's note: This argument is reported variously; what follows is the gist of the argument.

8. EMPEDOCLES OF ACRAGAS

Born in Acragas, in Sicily, around 492 BCE, Empedocles belongs to the generation of Presocratics who come after Parmenides. He is known to have visited the southern Italian mainland, and while his work shows his familiarity with Parmenides, there are also signs of the influence of Pythagoreanism, the other great southern Italian philosophical movement. At home in Acragas, he seems to have been an active politician, supporting democracy against oligarchy, even though his own aristocratic family connections might have made that support unexpected. Empedocles was a philosopher, a medical man, and a truly flamboyant figure. According to ancient reports, he dressed ostentatiously (there are stories of rich purple robes, a golden diadem, and bronze sandals), he claimed remarkable powers for himself, and in fragment B112 (no. 1 below) he says of himself, "I go about among you, an immortal god, no longer mortal, / honored among all, as it seems, / wreathed with headbands and blooming garlands." There are many stories of his fantastic activities: reportedly a woman with no pulse who had stopped breathing was kept alive by him for a month; he diverted two streams in the city of Selinus (on the south coast of Sicily) in order to rid the city of a plague (and was said to have been honored as a god as a result). Empedocles was exiled from his home and was said to have died in the Peloponnese, although, given his character, it is not surprising that more exciting tales were told about his death. Diogenes Laertius reports that Empedocles, desiring to demonstrate that he was indeed a god, leapt into the crater of Mount Aetna.

Although these stories suggest a flashy and eccentric figure, we should not lose sight of the fact that Empedocles constructed a serious and complicated theory of the cosmos and the place of human beings in it. Like Parmenides, he wrote in verse; his subjects included both natural philosophy (physics and the development of the cosmos) and inquiry into how human beings ought to live (ethical and religious topics). For a long time scholars debated how, if at all, these two main areas of interest were related. New study, and the discovery of some new texts, now show without a doubt that Empedocles regarded these questions as connected, and that the material from the two was thoroughly integrated. There remains the question of how many different works Empedocles composed; traditionally there have been thought to be at least two separate poems, usually called Physics *and* Purifications. *Although we now know that the physical and purificatory material were not viewed by Empedocles as entirely distinct, the question of how many poems Empedocles wrote remains open.*

Empedocles claimed that the numerous basic realities of the cosmos are entities with the features of basic reality for which Parmenides had argued. Although these basic entities are eternally real and unchanging in their natures, their mixture and separation cause the world of the senses.

Empedocles says that there are six such basic things in the cosmos, each a genuine being in the Parmenidean sense: the roots (as Empedocles refers to them) Earth, Water, Air, and Fire (later called "elements" by Aristotle), and two forces, Love and Strife. The roots are mixed and separated (by Love and Strife) to produce the world that we sense and are a part of; this mixture and separation take the place of coming-to-be and passing-away, since the ingredients remain all through the changes. In selections 87 (B96) and 88 (B98) Empedocles provides "recipes" for such phenomenal things as bone and blood. At the same time, under the waxing and waning of the comparative strengths of the forces of Love and Strife the cosmos undergoes cycles from complete mixture of the roots to their complete separation: how many cycles there are, and the events within those cycles are subjects of controversy among commentators. Within the cycles, living things come to be and pass away; Empedocles' system includes daimones *(singular,* daimōn*) which are divinities of some sort. These* daimones *undergo many lives, apparently because of some transgression. Although they, like the gods, are called "long-lived" by Empedocles, they are not immortal, for they, like the roots of which they are made, are all absorbed into the complete mixture of the roots at the height of Love's power. Only the roots and Love and Strife are genuinely immortal, subject neither to coming-to-be or passing-away. The destiny of the* daimones *is connected with the sorts of lives they lead, and it is in the nature, behavior, and fates of the* daimones *that Empedocles' natural and religious views come together.*

Note on the text and the order of the fragments: In the 1990s scholars discovered that previously unexamined papyrus fragments contained some seventy-four lines of poetry (in varying states of completeness). Because the papyrus contained previously known lines as well as new, previously unknown material, the editors were able to identify the author as Empedocles. The Strasbourg Papyrus (so named because it has been in the collections of the Strasbourg library since the early part of the twentieth century), reconstructed and translated, provided important new material for Empedocles studies, and that material is included here. The ordering of the fragments of Empedocles is controversial; scholars have strong views and serious disagreements about the proper order. Here, the order is that of the translator, Richard McKirahan.[30]

1. (31B112) Friends who dwell in the great city on the yellow
   Acragas
   on the heights of the citadel, you whose care is good deeds,
   respectful havens for strangers, untouched by evil,

30. There are a few exceptions and omissions in the texts given here. For a discussion of McKirahan's ordering principles, see his *Philosophy Before Socrates*, 2nd edition, p. 230 n. 1.

hail! I go about among you, an immortal god, no longer
   mortal,
honored among all, as it seems,   5
wreathed with headbands and blooming garlands.
Wherever I go to their flourishing cities,
I am revered by all—men and women. And they follow
   together
in tens of thousands, inquiring where lies the path to profit,
some in need of prophecy, while others,   10
pierced for a long time with harsh pains,
asked to hear the voice of healing for all diseases.
               (Diogenes Laertius, *Lives of the Philosophers* 8.61–2
               [lines 1–10]; Clement, *Miscellanies* 6.30 [lines 9–11])

2. (B114) Friends, I know that truth is in the words
   I will speak. But very difficult
   for men and spiteful is the invasion of conviction into their
      minds.   (Clement, *Miscellanies* 5.9)

3. (B113) But why do I insist on these matters as if I were
      accomplishing something great,
   if I am superior to mortal humans who perish many times?
         (Sextus Empiricus, *Against the Mathematicians* 1.302)

4. (B128) Nor was there any god Ares among them nor
      Kudoimos ["battle-din"]
   nor King Zeus, nor Kronos nor Poseidon,
   but there was Queen Cypris. . . .
   Her they propitiated with reverent statues
   and painted figures and unguents with varied odors,   5
   and with offerings of unmixed myrrh and fragrant
      frankincense,
   pouring on the ground libations of yellow honey.
   No altar was drenched with the unspeakable slaughter of bulls,
   but this was the greatest abomination among humans,   10
   to tear out life and devour the noble limbs.
      (Porphyry, *On Abstinence* 2.20 [lines 1–8]; 2.27 [lines 8–11])

5. (B130) All were tame and kindly toward humans—
   both animals and birds—and friendliness burned brightly.
   (Scholium in Nicander, *Antidotes against Poisonous Bites* 453)

6. (B78) [Empedocles declares that evergreens and continuously
   fruiting trees flourish] with bounties of fruits in the air each
   year.   (Theophrastus, *On Plants: The Explanations* 1.13.2)

7. (B132) Blessed is he who possesses wealth of divine intelligence
   but wretched he is whose concern is a dim opinion about the
       gods.   (Clement, *Miscellanies* 5.140)

8. (B115) There is an oracle of Necessity, an ancient decree of
       the gods,
   eternal and sealed with broad oaths,
   that whenever anyone pollutes his own dear limbs with the
       sin of bloodshed,
   . . . [31] commits offense and swears a false oath
   —divinities (*daimones*) who possess immensely long life   5
   he wanders away from the blessed ones for thrice ten
       thousand seasons,
   through time growing to be all different kinds of mortals,
   taking the difficult paths of life one after another.
   For the force of Aithēr pursues them to the sea
   and the sea spits them out onto the surface of the earth, and the   10
       earth into the rays
   of the shining sun, and he [the sun] casts them into the
       vortices of Aithēr.
   One receives them after another, but all hate them.
   Of these I am now one, a fugitive from the gods and a wanderer,
   putting my reliance on raving Strife.
                 (Hippolytus, *Refutation of All Heresies* 7.29.14–23
       [lines 1–2, 4–14]; Plutarch, *On Exile* 607C [lines 1, 3, 5–13])

9. (B142) Neither, then, the roofed halls of aegis-bearing Zeus
   nor the house of Hades <? receives> him.
                       (Voll. Herc. N 1012 col 18)

10. (B125) For from living forms it [? Strife] was making dead
    ones, changing them.   (Clement, *Miscellanies* 3.14.2)

11. (B126) Wrapping <it> in an alien garb of flesh.
                    (Plutarch, *On Eating Flesh* 998c)

12. (B117) For I have already been born as a boy and a girl
    and a bush and a bird and a <mute> fish <from the sea>.
            (Diogenes Laertius, *Lives of the Philosophers* 8.77)

13. (B119) From such honor and how great an amount of bliss . . .
                 (Plutarch, *On Exile* 17 607D)

---

31. The first part of the line is missing, so lines 4 and 5 are unclear. They probably, as McKirahan says, "elaborate 'anyone' in line 3."

14. (B118) I wept and wailed upon seeing the unfamiliar place.
(Clement, *Miscellanies* 3.14)

15. (B121) . . . Joyless place,
where bloodshed, anger, and tribes of other spirits of death
and squalid diseases, rotting, and works of dissolution
wander in darkness through the meadow of disaster (*atē*).
(Hierocles, *Commentary on the Golden Verses* 54.2–3;
Proclus, *Commentary on Plato's Cratylus* 97.23)

16. (B124) Alas! Wretched race of mortals! Unfortunate!
Out of such quarreling and groaning were you born.
(Clement, *Miscellanies* 3.14)

17. (B136) Will you not cease from harsh-sounding bloodshed?
Do you not see
that you are devouring each other in the carelessness of
your thought?
(Sextus Empiricus, *Against the Mathematicians* 9.119)

18. (B138) Having drawn off life [*psychē*] with bronze.
(Aristotle, *Poetics* 1457b13)

19. (B137) A father lifts up his own dear son who has changed
form,
and, praying, slaughters him, committing a great folly. And
they are at a loss,
sacrificing him as he entreats them. But he, refusing to hear
the cries,
slaughters him and attends an evil feast in his halls.
Likewise a son seizes his father and children their mother,   5
and tearing out their life, devour the dear flesh.
(Sextus Empiricus, *Against the Mathematicians* 9.129)

20. (B145) Therefore, distraught with harsh evils,
you will never relieve your spirit from wretched distress.
(Clement, *Protrepticus* 2.27.3)

21. (B135) But what is lawful for all extends far through the
wide-ruling
Aithēr and through the immense glare.
(Aristotle, *Rhetoric* 1.13 1373b6–17)

22. (B144) Fast from evil. (Plutarch, *The Control of Anger* 464B)

23. (B140) Keep completely away from laurel leaves!

(Plutarch, *Table Talk* 646d)

24. (B141) Wretched, wholly wretched! Keep your hands off beans!

(Aulus Gellius, *Athenian Nights* 4.11.1–2 and 4.11.9–10)

25. (B127) Among beasts they come into being as lions whose lairs are in the mountains
and their beds on the ground, and as laurels among shaggy trees.

(Aelian, *Natural History* 12.7)

26. (B146) In the end they are prophets and bards and physicians
and chiefs among men on earth,
and from there they arise as gods mightiest in honors.

(Clement, *Miscellanies* 4.150)

27. (B147) Sharing the same hearth and table with other immortals
relieved of manly distress, unwearied.

(Clement, *Miscellanies* 5.122)

28. (B133) It is not possible to reach and approach <the divine> with our eyes
or grasp it with our hands, by which the most powerful
highway of persuasion strikes the minds of men.

(Clement, *Miscellanies* 5.81)

29. (B131) For if, immortal Muse, for the sake of any ephemeral creature
it pleased you that our concerns should come to your thoughts,
be present once again to me, Kalliopeia, now as I pray,
as I reveal a good account about the blessed gods.

(Hippolytus, *Refutation of All Heresies* 7.31.3)

30. (B1) But you listen, Pausanias, son of wise-minded Anchites.

(Diogenes Laertius, *Lives of the Philosophers* 8.60)

31. (B111) You will learn all the drugs there are as a safeguard against evils and old age,

since for you alone shall I bring to pass all these things.
You will stop the force of the tireless winds that rush
over the earth and devastate the plowed fields with their
    blasts.
And, if you wish, you will arouse their breath again.   5
You will change black rain into seasonable dryness
for people, and summer drought you will change
into tree-nourishing waters that dwell in the sky.
And you will bring back from Hades the strength of a dead
    man.   (Diogenes Laertius, *Lives of the Philosophers* 8.59)

32. (B5) [Empedocles advised Pausanias] to cover up [his
    teachings] within a voiceless heart (*phrēn*).
                              (Plutarch, *Table Talk* 728E)

33. (B4) It is highly typical of evil people to mistrust what
    prevails;
  but learn how the trustworthy reports from our Muse
    command,
  by splitting apart the account (*logos*) in your entrails.
                         (Clement, *Miscellanies* 5.18.4)

34. (B2) Narrow are the means of apprehension spread
    throughout the limbs.
  Many wretched things burst in which blunt the thoughts.
  People see a tiny part of life during their time
  and swift-fated they are taken away and fly like smoke,
  persuaded only of whatever each of them has chanced to
    meet   5
  as they were driven everywhere; but everyone boasts that
    he discovered the whole.
  These things are not in this way to be seen or heard by men
  or grasped with the mind. But you, since you have turned
    aside to this place,
  will learn; mortal cunning has reached no further.
            (Sextus Empiricus, *Against the Mathematicians* 7.123)

35. (B3b) Nor will it compel you to take away the blossoms of
    fair-famed honor from mortals
  on the condition that you say in rashness more than is
    holy—
  and <only> then sit upon the summits of wisdom.
  But come, look with every means of apprehension, in
    whatever way each thing is clear,

not holding any sight more in trust than <what comes>
    through hearing,   5
or loud-sounding hearing above the things made clear by
    the tongue,
and do not at all hold back trust in any of the other limbs,
wherever there is a channel for understanding, but
understand each thing in whatever way it is clear.
              (Sextus Empiricus, *Against the Mathematicians* 7.125)

36. (B3a) But, gods, avert their madness from my tongue,
and lead a pure stream from holy mouths.
And you, much-remembering maiden Muse with white
    arms,
I entreat—bring the things it is right for creatures of a day
to hear, driving your easily-steered chariot from the halls of
    reverence.
              (Sextus Empiricus, *Against the Mathematicians* 7.123)

37. (B6) Hear first the four roots of all things:
shining Zeus and life-bringing Hera and Aidoneus
and Nestis, who with her tears gives moisture to the source
   of mortals.   (Aëtius 1.3.20)

38. (B7) Ungenerated.
       (Hesychius, *Lexicon* s.v. *agennēta* [Empedocles used this
                          word to describe the elements])

39. (B8) I will tell you another thing. There is coming-to-be of
    not a single one of all
mortal things, nor is there any end of destructive death,
but only mixture, and separation of what is mixed,
and nature (*phusis*) is the name given to them by humans.
                 (Plutarch, *Against Colotes* 1111F–12A)

40. (B11) Fools. For their thoughts are not far-reaching—
those who expect that there comes to be what previously
    was not,
or that anything perishes and is completely destroyed.
                  (Plutarch, *Against Colotes* 1113C)

41. (B9) Whenever they arrive in the Aithēr mixed so as to
    form a man
or one of the wild beasts or bushes
or birds, that is when <people> speak of coming into being;

and whenever they are separated, that <is what they call>
the ill-starred fate of death.
They do not call it as is right, but I myself too assent to
their convention.   5
(Plutarch, Against Colotes 1113D)

42. (B15) A man who is wise in his thoughts (*phrēn*) would not
divine such things as this—
that as long as they live what they in fact call life
they are, and have things wretched and good,
but before they took on the fixed form of mortals and after
they have
dissolved, they are then nothing.
(Plutarch, Against Colotes 1113D)

43. (B12) For it is impossible to come to be from what in no
way is,
and it is not to be accomplished and is unheard of that
what is perishes absolutely.
For it will always be where a person thrusts it each time.
([Aristotle], Melissus, Xenophanes, Gorgias 2 975b1–4)

44. (B13) None of the whole is either empty or overfull.
(Aëtius 1.18.2)

45. (B14) Of the whole, nothing is empty; from where, then,
could anything come to be added to it?
([Aristotle], Melissus, Xenophanes, Gorgias 2 976b23)

46. (B16) For they are as they were previously and will be, and
never, I think,
will endless time be empty of both of these.
(Hippolytus, Refutation of All Heresies 7.29.9)

47. (B17 + Strasbourg Papyrus, *ensemble* a) I will tell a double
story. For
at one time they grew to be only one   (232)[32]
out of many, but at another they grew apart to be many out
of one.
Double is the generation of mortal things, and double their
decline.

32. Translator's note: The line numbers in parentheses are given as Empedocles'
text is reconstructed by Primavesi (2008). This numbering is based on the identification of the three hundredth line in the poem by a mark in the margin of the last
line in *ensemble a* of the Strasbourg Papyrus.

For the coming together of all things gives birth to one
    [namely,
generation and decline] and destroys it, (235)
and the other is nurtured and flies away when they grow
    apart again. 5
And these never cease continually interchanging,
at one time all coming together into one by Love
and at another each being borne apart by the hatred of Strife.
Thus in that they have learned to grow to be one out of
    many (240)
and in that they again spring apart as many when the one
    grows apart, 10
in that way they come to be, and their life is not lasting,
but in that they never cease interchanging continually,
in this way they are always unchanging in a cycle.
But come, listen to my words, for learning increases wisdom. (245)
For as I previously said, while declaring the bounds of my
    words, 15
I will tell a double story. For at one time they grew to be
    only one
out of many, but at another they grew apart to be many out
    of one:
fire and water and earth and the immense height of air,
and deadly Strife apart from them, equal in all directions (250)
and Love among them, equal in length and breadth. 20
Behold her with your mind, and do not sit with your eyes
    staring in amazement.
She is also recognized as innate in mortal limbs.
Through her they have kindly thoughts and do peaceful deeds,
calling her by the appellation Joy and also Aphrodite. (255)
No mortal man has seen her spinning 25
among them. But listen to the undeceitful course of my
    account.
For these [the four elements] are all equal and of the same
    age,
but each rules in its own province and possesses its own
    individual character,
but they dominate in their turn as time revolves. (260)
And nothing is added to them or subtracted, 30
for if they were perishing continuously, they would no
    longer be.
But what could increase this totality? And where would it
    come from?
And how could it perish, since nothing is empty of these?

But there are just these very things, and running through
    one another   (265)
at different times they come to be different things and yet
    are always and continuously the same.   35
{But under Love}[33] we come together into one *kosmos*,
{whereas under Strife it [that is, the ordered whole] grew
    apart, so as} to be many from one,
from which [that is, many things] all things that were and
    are and will be in the future
have sprouted: trees and men and women,   (270)
and beasts and birds and fishes nurtured in water,   40
and long-lived gods highest in honors.
{Under her [that is, Strife]} they never cease, continually
    darting in dense whirls . . .
without pausing, and never . . .   (275)
but {many} lifetimes before . . .   45
before passing from them . . .
{and never cease} continually darting {in all directions}
for neither the sun . . .
{the onrush full of this} . . .   (280)
nor any of the others . . .   50
but interchanging in a circle {they dart in all directions}
for at that time the impassable earth runs, and the sun as well
{and the sphere [that is, the celestial sphere]} as large as
    even now {it is judged} by men {to be}
in the same way all these things {were running} through
    one another   (285)
{and having been driven away, each of them reached}
    different {and peculiar} places   55
{self-willed}; and we were coming together in the mid-most
    places to be only one.

33. Translator's note: At this point begins the section for which the papyrus is our only evidence. There are numerous gaps in the preserved text, some of which can be restored with a good degree of confidence from other Empedoclean verses. For the rest, the choice is either to stay close to what the papyrus contains or to fill in the gaps by conjecture informed by one's knowledge of the author's vocabulary, style, and views. The translation provided is based on two versions of the Greek text and the accompanying translations: the original publication by Martin and Primavesi (1999), and the text printed in Inwood (2001). Inwood is more conservative, staying closer to the papyrus text, while Martin and Primavesi are more willing to propose ways to restore missing material. The words enclosed in curly brackets translate supplements of Martin and Primavesi that Inwood does not include. The purpose has been to offer a readable translation while marking places where there is a good chance that the text translated is not what Empedocles wrote.

But when indeed Strife passed through {and reached} the
    depths
{of the swirl,} and Love {comes to be} in the midst of the
    vortex,
{then} indeed all these things come together to be only one.   *(290)*
{Strive eagerly} so that {my account may arrive} not only
    through ears,   60
{and behold} the unerring truths that are around while you
    listen to me.
I shall show you also through your eyes {where they [that
    is, the elements] find} a larger body:
first, the coming together and development {of the offspring}
    . . . and all that now still remain of this {generation}   *(295)*
both among the {wild species} of mountain-roaming beasts   65
and among the twofold offspring of men, {and also among}
the offspring of root-bearing {fields} and vine-mounting
    {clusters of grapes}.
From these stories bring back to your mind undeceiving
    evidence,
for you will see the coming together and development of
    the offspring.   *(300)*
        (Simplicius, *Commentary on Aristotle's Physics* 158.1–159.4
        [lines 1–35] + Strasbourg Papyrus *ensemble* a [lines 26–69])

48. (B20 + Strasbourg Papyrus, *ensemble* c) {Where Love and
    Strife have} their guiding {counsels}   *(301)*
This is very clear in the mass of mortal limbs:
sometimes we come together through Love into one, all the
limbs that have obtained a body, at the peak of flourishing
    life,
while at other times, split apart through evil quarrels   *(305)* 5
they wander each kind separately on the furthest shore of
    life.
And it happens the same way for bushes and water-homed
    fishes
and mountain-dwelling beasts and wing-propelled birds.
        (Simplicius, *Commentary on Aristotle's Physics*
        1124.7–18 + Strasbourg Papyrus *ensemble* c)

49. (B21) But come, behold this witness of my previous discourse,   *(309)*
if anything in the foregoing was feeble in form:
the sun, brilliant to see and hot everywhere,
all the immortal things that are drenched in the heat and
    shining light,

and rain, in all things dark and cold,   5
and from earth stream forth things rooted and solid.
In Anger they are all apart and have separate forms,   (315)
but they come together in Love and yearn for one another.
From these all things that were and are and will be in the
    future
have sprouted: trees and men and women,   10
and beasts and birds and fishes nurtured in water,
and long-lived gods highest in honors.   (320)
For there are just these things, and running through one
    another
they come to have different appearances, for mixture
    changes them.
      (Simplicius, *Commentary on Aristotle's Physics* 159.13–26)

50. (B76 + Strasbourg Papyrus, *ensemble* b)
This [i.e., fire] is found in the case of heavy-backed shells of
    sea-dwelling creatures.   (324)
. . .   (325)
There you will see earth {dwelling} in the uppermost parts
    of the flesh . . .   (327)
and indeed truly [in the flesh] of stony-skinned tritons and
    turtles
. . . of horned stags
. . . saying   (330)
      (Plutarch, *The Face in the Moon* 14 927F–928A and *Table Talk*
              1.2.5 618B + Strasbourg Papyrus, *ensemble* b)

51. (B23) As when painters decorate votive offerings—
men through cunning well taught in their skill—
who when they take the many-colored pigments in their
    hands,
mixing in harmony more of these and less of those,
out of them they produce shapes similar to all things,   5
creating trees and men and women
and beasts and birds and fishes nurtured in water
and long-lived gods highest in honors.
So let not deception compel your mind (*phrēn*) to believe
    that there is from anywhere else
a source of mortal things, all the endless numbers of   10
things that have come to be manifest,
but know these things distinctly, having heard the story
    from a god.
      (Simplicius, *Commentary on Aristotle's Physics* 160.1–11)

52. (B26) They dominate in turn as the cycle evolves,
and they decrease into one another and grow in their turn,
    as destined.
For there are just these things, and running through one
    another
they come to be both humans and the tribes of other beasts,
at one time coming together into a single *kosmos* by Love   5
and at another each being borne apart again by the hatred
    of Strife,
until they grow together into one, the whole, and become
    subordinate.
Thus in that they have learned to grow to be one out of
    many
and in that they again spring apart as many when the one
    grows apart,
in that way they come to be and their life is not lasting,   10
but in that these never cease interchanging continually,
in this way they are always unchanging in a cycle.
        (Simplicius, *Commentary on Aristotle's Physics* 33.19–34.3)

53. (B139 + Strasbourg Papyrus, *ensemble* d)
    . . . to fall apart from one another and encounter their fate
    very much against their will, rotting through mournful
        necessity;
    But for those who now have Love . . .
    the Harpies will be present with the tokens {in the lottery}
        of death.
    Alas that the pitiless day did not destroy me   5
    before I devised with my claws wicked deeds for the sake
        of eating flesh.
    {But now} in vain in this {storm} I wet my cheeks
    {for we are approaching} a very deep {whirl,} I think,
    {and} although they do not wish it, {tens of thousands of}
        pains will be present in their mind
    {to humans,} but we will again mount {you} on {that} account: 10
    {when} an untiring flame happened to meet
    . . . bringing on a woeful mixture
    . . . things that could produce offspring were born
    . . . I entered the final place
    . . . with a scream and a cry   15
    . . . having obtained {the meadow of Disaster}
    . . . around . . . earth.
                    (Strasbourg Papyrus *ensemble* d + Porphyry
                        On Abstinence 2.31 [lines 5–6])

54. (B25) For indeed it is a fine thing to tell twice what one must.
(Scholium in Plato's *Gorgias* 498e)

55. (B22) For all these things—shining sun and earth and
heaven
and sea—are united with their own parts,
all that are split off and have come to be in mortal things.
In the same way, all that are more fitted for mixture
are made alike by Aphrodite and have come to love one
another.   5
But greatest enemies are those furthest separated from one
another
in birth and mixture and molded forms,
in every way unaccustomed to be together and very mournful
through their birth in Strife, because their births were in
anger.
(Simplicius, *Commentary on Aristotle's Physics* 160.26)

56. (B91) <Water> has a greater affinity with wine, but with olive
oil
it is unwilling <to mix>.
(Philoponus, *Commentary on Aristotle's
Generation of Animals* 123.19–20)

57. (B33) As when sap from a fig tree curdles and binds white
milk.   (Plutarch, *On Having Many Friends* 95A–B)

58. (B34) Having glued barley groats with water.
(Aristotle, *Meteorology* 381b31)

59. (B92) . . . like copper mixed with tin.
(Aristotle, *Generation of Animals* 2.8 747a34–b7)[34]

60. (B93) The brightness of gleaming saffron is mixed with linen.
(Plutarch, *On the Obsolescence of Oracles* 433b)

61. (B81) Wine is water from grape skin fermented in wood.
(Plutarch, *Natural Phenomena* 912b–c)

62. (B27) There neither the swift limbs of the sun are discerned,
nor the shaggy force of earth nor the sea.

34. Aristotle's comment: "On the question why mules are sterile, Empedocles
explains that the mixture of seeds becomes thick, although the seed of both the
horse and the ass is soft. For the hollow parts of each fit together with the thick
parts of the other, and as a result a hard substance comes from soft ones."

Thus by the dense concealment of Harmonia is held fast
a rounded sphere, exulting in its joyous solitude.
>   (Plutarch, *On the Face in the Moon* 926E; Simplicius,
>   *Commentary on Aristotle's Physics* 1183.24)

63. (B27a) No dissent or unseemly battle in its limbs.
>   (Plutarch, *Philosophers and Princes* 777c)

64. (B28) But equal to itself on all sides, and wholly without limit,
a rounded sphere, exulting in its joyous solitude.
>   (Stobaeus, *Selections* 1.15.2)

65. (B29) For two branches do not spring from its back
nor do feet or swift knees or organs of generation,
but it was a sphere and equal to itself on all sides.
>   (Hippolytus, *Refutation of All Heresies* 7.19.13)

66. (B134) For he is not furnished in his limbs with a human
     head.
Two branches do not spring from his back.
He has no feet, no swift knees, no hairy genitals,
but is only mind (*phrēn*), holy and indescribable,
darting through the entire *kosmos* with his swift thoughts.
(Ammonius, *Commentary on Aristotle's On Interpretation* 249.1)

5

67. (B30) But when great Strife had been nourished in its limbs
and leapt up to its prerogatives as the time was being
     fulfilled,
that is established for them in turn by a broad oath . . .
>   (Simplicius, *Commentary on Aristotle's Physics* 1184.12–13)

68. (B31) All the limbs of the god trembled, each in turn.
>   (Simplicius, *Commentary on Aristotle's Physics* 1184.3)

69. (B90) Thus sweet caught hold of sweet, bitter rushed
     toward bitter,
sour went to sour, and hot coupled with hot.
>   (Plutarch, *Table Talk* 4.1.3 663A;
>   Macrobius, *Saturnalia* 7.5.17–18)

70. (B38) But come, I shall first tell you the beginning . . .
from which all that we now look upon came to be clear—
earth and the sea with many waves and moist air
and the Titan Aithēr, squeezing all things round about in a
     circle.   (Clement, *Miscellanies* 5.48.3)

71. (B53, B54) For it sometimes happened to run this way, but
    often otherwise. . . .
Aithēr sank beneath the deep-rooted earth.
        (Aristotle, *On Generation and Corruption* 2.6 334a1–5)

72. (B44) \<The sun\> shines back toward Olympus with fearless
    face.   (Plutarch, *On the Oracles at Delphi* 400B)

73. (B42) \<The moon\> keeps off the sunlight
    when it goes above and darkens a portion of the earth
    the size of the breadth of the gray-eyed moon.
            (Plutarch, *On the Face in the Moon* 929CD)

74. (B47) For \<the moon\> gazes straight at the pure circle of her
    lord [i.e., the sun].
        (Anonymous, *Useful Expressions, Anecdota Graeca* 1.337.13)

75. (B43) Thus the sunlight, having struck the broad circle of the
    moon . . .   (Plutarch, *On the Face in the Moon* 929E)

76. (B45) A round alien light spins around the earth.
            (Achilles, *Introduction to Aratus* p.16 43.2–6)

77. (B46) It spins \<around the earth\> like the track of a chariot,
    and around the extremity it . . .
            (Plutarch, *On the Face in the Moon* 925B)

78. (B48) Earth makes night by obstructing \<the sun's\> rays.
            (Plutarch, *Platonic Questions* 1006e)

79. (B94) In the depths of a river, a dark color arises from the
    shadow,
    and is observed as well in deep caves.
                (Plutarch, *Natural Phenomena* 39)

80. (B55) The sea is the earth's sweat.
                (Aristotle, *Meteorology* 357a24)

81. (B56) Salt is solidified when blasted by the force of the sun.
            (Hephaiston, *Handbook* 1.3, p. 2.13)

82. (B71) If your faith in these matters were at all faint—
    \<about\> how when water, earth, Aithēr, and sun
    are mixed, as many shapes and colors of mortals came to be
    as now have come to be, fitted together by Aphrodite . . .
    (Simplicius, *Commentary on Aristotle's On the Heavens* 529.28)

83. (B151) Life-giving Aphrodite.   (Plutarch, *On Love* 756e)

84. (B73) As then Cypris, busily working on shapes moistened
     earth in rain,
and gave it to swift fire to strengthen . . .
     (Simplicius, *Commentary on Aristotle's On the Heavens* 530.6–7)

85. (B85) Mildly-shining flame chanced upon a little earth.
          (Simplicius, *Commentary on Aristotle's Physics* 331.3)

86. (B86) From which [the roots] divine Aphrodite fashioned
     tireless eyes.
(Simplicius, *Commentary on Aristotle's On the Heavens* 529.21)

87. (B96) Pleasant earth in her well-made crucibles
obtained two parts of bright Nestis out of the eight,
and four of Hephaestus, and white bones came into being,
fitted together by the divine glues of Harmonia.
          (Simplicius, *Commentary on Aristotle's Physics* 300.21–24)

88. (B98) Earth came together by chance in about equal
          quantity to these,
Hephaestus and rain and all-shining Aithēr,
anchored in the perfect harbors of Cypris,
either a bit more or a bit less of it among more of them.
From them blood came into being and other forms of flesh.   5
          (Simplicius, *Commentary on Aristotle's Physics* 32.6–10)

89. (B82) The same things become hairs and leaves and dense
     feathers of birds,
and scales on stout limbs.   (Aristotle, *Meteorology* 397b4)

90. (Empedocles fr. 152 in Wright's edition)
For all of them that exist with closely-packed roots below,
flourishing with more widely spaced shoots.
               (Herodian, *Universal Prosody*; not in DK)

91. (B75) . . . all of them that are dense within, while their
     exterior parts
are formed in a loose texture,
because they met with such moisture through the devices of
     Cypris.
                    (Simplicius, *Commentary on Aristotle's
                    On the Heavens* 530.9–10)

92. (B83) . . . but in hedgehogs
    sharp-pointed hairs bristle on their backs.
                                            (Plutarch, *On Chance* 98D)

93. (B79) In this way tall trees first lay eggs in the form of olives.
                        (Aristotle, *Generation of Animals* 731a4)

94. (B80) Therefore pomegranates and succulent apples are
        produced late
    in the season.   (Plutarch, *Table Talk* 683d)

95. (B62) Come now, hear how, as fire was being separated,
    it raised up the nocturnal shoots of men and women, full of
        wailing.
    For the story is not off the point or ignorant.
    First the whole-natured forms rose up out of the earth,
    having a portion of both water and heat.   5
    These the fire sent up, desiring to come to its like,
    and they did not yet show at all the lovely shape of limbs
    or a voice or the member native to men.
        (Simplicius, *Commentary on Aristotle's Physics* 381.29)

96. (B64) Indeed, longing for sexual intercourse comes upon
        him
    through sight.   (Plutarch, *Natural Phenomena* 917c)

97. (B66) Divided meadows of Aphrodite.[35]
            (Scholium on Euripides, *Phoenician Women* line 18)

98. (B65) They were poured in clean <places>. Some,
    encountering cold, become women.
                    (Aristotle, *Generation of Animals* 723a24)

99. (B67) That which has to do with males came to be in the
        warmer part of the earth,
    and this is why men are dark and have stronger limbs
    and more hair.
        (Galen, *Commentary on Hippocrates' Epidemics* 6, 2.46)

100. (B68) On the tenth day of the eighth month <the blood>
    becomes white pus.
                (Aristotle, *Generation of Animals* 4.8 777a7)

35. Translator's note: A "disgraceful" expression used of the female genitalia,
according to the source.

101. (B35) But I shall return to that path of songs
   that I recounted before, drawing off this account from
      another one.
   When Strife had reached the lowest depth
   of the vortex, and Love comes to be in the middle of the
      whirl,
   at this point all these things come together to be one single
      thing,   5
   not at once, but willingly combining, different ones from
      different places.
   As they were being mixed, myriads of tribes of mortal
      things poured forth,
   but many remained unmixed alternately with those that
      were being mingled—
   all that Strife still held back aloft. For it had not
   entirely completed its blameless retreat from them to the
      furthest limits of the circle,   10
   but some of its limbs remained, while others had departed.
   But however far it kept running out ahead, there followed
      in pursuit
   the gentle immortal onset of blameless Love.
   And immediately things grew to be mortal that formerly
      had learned to be immortal,
   and things previously unmixed <grew to be> mixed,
      interchanging their paths.   15
   And as they were mixed, myriads of tribes of mortal
      things poured forth,
   joined closely together with all kinds of forms, a wonder
      to behold.
      (Simplicius, *Commentary on Aristotle's On the Heavens*
      529.1–15 [lines 1–15]; *Commentary on Aristotle's Physics*
                        32.13–33.2 [lines 3–17])

102. (B36) And when they were coming together, Strife was
      retreating to the extremity.
                        (Stobaeus, *Selections* 1.10.11)

103. (B57) By her [Love] many neckless faces sprouted,
   and arms were wandering naked, bereft of shoulders,
   and eyes were roaming alone, in need of foreheads.
                        (Simplicius, *Commentary on Aristotle's
                        On the Heavens* 586.12; 587.1–2)

104. (B58) [In this situation, the limbs were still] single-limbed
   [as the result of the separation caused by Strife, and]

they wandered about [aiming at mixture with one
another.]
(Simplicius, Commentary on Aristotle's
On the Heavens 587.18–19)

105. (B60) Wobbly-footed with countless hands.
(Plutarch, Against Colotes 1123B)

106. (B61) Many grew with faces and chests on both sides,
man-faced ox-progeny, and some to the contrary rose up
as ox-headed things with the form of men, compounded
   partly from men
and partly from women, fitted with shadowy parts.
(Aelian, The Nature of Animals 16.29)

107. (B59) But when divinity was mixed to a greater extent
   with divinity,
these things began to fall together, however they chanced
   to meet,
and many others in addition arose continuously.
(Simplicius, Commentary on Aristotle's
On the Heavens 587.20, 23)

108. (B88) A single sight [visual impression] comes from both
[eyes].   (Aristotle, Poetics 1458a4–5)

109. (B84, B87)
As when someone planning for a journey prepares a lamp,
a flame of blazing fire in the wintry night,
attaching lantern-screens to protect it from all kinds of
   winds,
scattering the blast of the blowing winds,
but the light springs out, since it is finer,   5
and shines across the threshold with unwearying beams,
in the same way, after Aphrodite had enclosed the
   primeval fire
in membranes and equipped it with pegs of love,
she poured round-eyed Kore in fine-textured garments
that keep back the depth of water that flows around   10
but let the fire pass through since it is finer,
where they are pierced through with marvelous funnels.
(Aristotle, On the Senses and Their Objects 2 437b24–438a5;
Simplicius, Commentary on Aristotle's On the Heavens
529.21 [line 8])

110. (B99) Fleshy twig [what Empedocles called the ear].
(Theophrastus, On Sensation 9)

111. (B100) This is how all inhale and exhale: in all of them bloodless
tubes of flesh extend deep in the body.
At the mouths of the tubes, the furthest extremities of the
   nostrils
are pierced through with closely arranged holes, so that
   they retain the
blood, but a clear path for Aithēr is cut through.   5
Then whenever the delicate blood leaps back from there
the bubbling air leaps in with a raging swell,
and when it [the blood] springs up, the animal exhales
   again, as when a young girl
playing with a clepsydra of shining bronze
puts the passage of the pipe against her pretty hand   10
and dunks it into the delicate body of silvery water,
no liquid enters the vessel, but the bulk of air,
pressing from inside on the close-set holes, keeps it out
until she uncovers the compressed stream. But then
when the air is leaving, the water duly enters.   15
In the same way, when water occupies the vessel and the
   bronze
mouth and passage is blocked by mortal flesh,
the air striving eagerly to get in from without restrains the
   liquid,
commanding the approaches around the gates of the
   gurgling strainer,
until she removes her hand. At that point again, in reverse
   order,   20
as the air enters, the water duly runs out.
In the same way, when delicate blood in violent motion
   through the limbs
springs backward to the inmost recesses,
immediately a stream of air raging in a swell comes in,
and when the blood swells up, it exhales an equal amount
   back again.   25
                    (Aristotle, *On Respiration* 473a15)

112. (B101) Hunting with its nostrils the fragments of animals'
   limbs . . .
which they were leaving behind from their feet on the soft
   grass . . .
       (Plutarch, *On Being a Busybody* 520e; *Natural Phenomena*
                917e; Pseudo-Alexander, *Problems* 3.102)

113. (B102) So in this way all things have obtained both
   breathing and
the sense of smell.   (Theophrastus, *On Sensation* 22)

114. (B104) And to the extent that they happened to fall
together at great intervals . . . [or, "the finest things
happened to fall together"].
(Simplicius, *Commentary on Aristotle's Physics* 331.41)

115. (B109) For by earth we see earth, by water, water,
by Aithēr, divine Aithēr, and by fire, destructive fire,
yearning by yearning, and strife by mournful strife.
(Aristotle, *On the Soul* 1.2 404b11–15)

116. (B110) If you fix them in your strong intelligence
and gaze upon them propitiously with pure attention,
these things will all be very much present to you all your
life long,
and from them you will obtain many others. For these
very things
grow into each kind of character, depending on each
person's nature.   5
But if you reach out for other kinds of things, such as the
millions
of wretched things that are found among men that blunt
their thoughts,
indeed they will quickly leave you as time revolves,
longing to come to their own dear kind.
For know that all things possess thought and a portion of
intelligence.   10
(Hippolytus, *Refutation of All Heresies* 7.29.25)

117. (B106) Wisdom grows in humans in relation to what is present.   (Aristotle, *On the Soul* 3.4 427a21–23)

118. (B107) For from these [the roots] all things are joined and
compounded,
and by these they think and feel pleasure and pain.
(Theophrastus, *On Sensation* 10)

119. (B105) <The heart is> nurtured in the seas of rebounding
blood,
where most especially is what is called thought by humans,
for the blood around the heart in humans is thought.
(Porphyry, quoted by Stobaeus in *Selections* 1.49.53)

120. (B108) Insofar as they change and become different, so far
are different thoughts always present to them.
(Aristotle, *Metaphysics* 1009b19)

9. ANAXAGORAS OF CLAZOMENAE

*Although Presocratic thinkers after Parmenides had their own views and
theories about many of the traditional subjects, they were faced with the
problem of how to reconcile giving a successful rational account of the
changing world of sense experience with Parmenides' arguments against
coming-to-be and passing-away and his requirements for genuine being.
Anaxagoras of Clazomenae proposed one of the most intriguing of these
theories. Like the earlier Ionians he had an interest in explaining the cosmos,
but that interest was tempered by an awareness of the metaphysical
implications of the work of Parmenides. (As in Empedocles, some of the
passages in Anaxagoras are echoes of Parmenides.) Anaxagoras was born in
Clazomenae, in Ionia, probably around 500 BCE. He went to Athens, the first
of the early Greek philosophers to live there, and spent about thirty years in
the city, where he became an associate of Pericles, the politician. He was said
to have predicted the fall of a meteorite at Aegospotami in 467. This is no
doubt connected with his view that the sun and the other stars are fiery stones
that are snatched up from the surface of the earth by the force of the revolving
mass of ingredients and sometimes fall back to earth when shaken loose from
their orbits. His political associations combined with his nonconformist views
(he said that the heavenly bodies are stones and that none is a god) resulted in
his being prosecuted for impiety, a charge the Athenians would later make
against both Socrates and Aristotle. Convicted, Anaxagoras was exiled from
the city and went to Lampsacus, in northern Ionia. He was much revered in
that city, and died there in about 428. According to Aristotle, Anaxagoras was
older than Empedocles, but his work became known later than Empedocles'
did.*

*Anaxagoras envisions an original state of the cosmos in which, as he says,
"All things were together." All things except Mind (Nous), which is pure and
unmixed, and which knows and controls all things. At some point Nous sets
the original mixture of ingredients into motion: a rotation begins, and spreads
out through the unlimited mass of ingredients. As a result, ingredients begin
to be separated and recombined with one another, eventually producing the
world that we perceive. The details of Anaxagoras' theory are controversial,
but it is clear that he thinks that it is ingredients that are basic rather than
perceptible objects such as human beings, geological formations like mountains,
plants, and other animals, which are temporary emergences from the mixture
of ingredients.*

Note on the texts: The translations of the fragments and testimonia given
here are slightly revised versions of those by Patricia Curd in *Anaxagoras of
Clazomenae.*

1. (59B1) All things were together, unlimited both in amount and in smallness, for the small, too, was unlimited. And because all things were together, nothing was evident on account of smallness; for air and Aithēr dominated all things, both being unlimited, for these are the greatest among all things both in amount and in largeness.

    (Simplicius, *Commentary on Aristotle's Physics* 155.26–30)

2. (B2) . . . for both air and Aithēr are being separated off from the surrounding mass, and what is surrounding is unlimited in extent.

    (Simplicius, *Commentary on Aristotle's Physics* 155.31–156.1)

3. (B3) Nor of the small is there a smallest, but always a smaller (for what-is cannot not be)—but also of the large there is always a larger. And [the large] is equal to the small in extent (*plēthos*), but in relation to itself each thing is both large and small.

    (Simplicius, *Commentary on Aristotle's Physics* 155.26–30)

4. (B4) Since these things are so, it is right to think that there are many different things present in everything that is being combined, and seeds of all things, having all sorts of forms, colors, and flavors, and that humans and also the other animals were compounded, as many as have soul. Also that there are cities that have been constructed by humans and works made, just as with us, and that there are a sun and a moon and other heavenly bodies for them, just as with us, and the earth grows many different things for them, the most valuable of which they gather together into their household and use. I have said this about the separation off, because there would be separation off not only for us but also elsewhere. . . . Before there was separation off, because all things were together, there was not even any color evident; for the mixture of all things prevented it, of the wet and the dry and of the hot and the cold and of the bright and the dark, and there was much earth present and seeds unlimited in number, in no way similar to one another. For no one of the others is similar to another. Since these things are so, it is right to think that all things were present in the whole.

    (Simplicius, *Commentary on Aristotle's Physics* 34.29–35.9, 34.21–26)

5. (B5) Even though these things have been dissociated in this way, it is right to recognize that all things are in no way less or more (for it is impossible that they be more than all), but all things are always equal.

    (Simplicius, *Commentary on Aristotle's Physics* 156.10–12)

6. (B6) Since the shares of the large and the small are equal in number, in this way too, all things will be in everything; nor is it possible that [anything] be separate, but all things have a share of everything. Since

it is not possible that there is a least, it would not be possible that [anything] be separated, nor come to be by itself, but just as in the beginning, now too all things are together. In all things there are many things present, equal in number, both in the greater and in the lesser of the things being separated off.

> (Simplicius, *Commentary on Aristotle's Physics* 164.26–165.1)

7. (B7) . . . so as not to know the extent of the things being separated off, either in word or in deed.

> (Simplicius, *Commentary on Aristotle's On the Heavens* 608.26)

8. (B8) The things in the one *kosmos* have not been separated from one another, nor hacked apart with an axe—neither the hot from the cold nor the cold from the hot.

> (Simplicius, *Commentary on Aristotle's Physics* 175.12–14; 176.29)

9. (B9) . . . as these things are revolving in this way and being separated off by force and swiftness, the swiftness produces force; and their swiftness resembles the swiftness of nothing that is now present among humans, but is altogether many times as fast.

> (Simplicius, *Commentary on Aristotle's Physics* 35.14–18)

10. (B10) For how . . . can hair come from what is not hair, and flesh from what is not flesh?

> (Scholium on Gregory of Nazianzus, *Patrologia Graeca* 36.911)

11. (B11) In everything there is a share of everything except *Nous* (Mind), but there are some things in which *Nous*, too, is present.

> (Simplicius, *Commentary on Aristotle's Physics* 164.22)

12. (B12) The other things have a share of everything, but *Nous* is unlimited and self-ruling and has been mixed with no thing, but is alone itself by itself. For if it were not by itself, but had been mixed with anything else, then it would partake of all things, if it had been mixed with anything (for there is a share of everything in everything, just as I have said before); and the things mixed together with it would thwart it, so that it would control none of the things in the way that it in fact does, being alone by itself. For it is the finest of all things and the purest, and indeed it maintains all discernment (*gnōmē*) about everything and has the greatest strength. And *Nous* has control over all things that have soul, both the larger and the smaller. And *Nous* controlled the whole revolution, so that it started to revolve in the beginning. First it began to revolve from a small region, but it is revolving yet more, and it will revolve still more. And *Nous* knew (*egnō*) them all: the things that are

being mixed together, the things that are being separated off, and the things that are being dissociated. And whatever sorts of things were going to be, and whatever sorts were and now are not, and as many as are now and whatever sorts will be, all these *Nous* set in order. And *Nous* also ordered this revolution, in which the things being separated off now revolve, the stars and the sun and the moon and the air and the Aithēr. This revolution caused them to separate off. The dense is being separated off from the rare, and the warm from the cold, and the bright from the dark, and the dry from the moist. But there are many shares of many things; nothing is completely separated off or dissociated one from the other except *Nous*. All *Nous* is alike, both the greater and the smaller. Nothing else is like anything else, but each one is and was most manifestly those things of which there are the most in it.

(Simplicius, *Commentary on Aristotle's Physics* 164.24–25, 156.13–157.4)

13. (B13) When *Nous* began to move [things], there was separation off from the multitude that was being moved, and whatever *Nous* moved, all this was dissociated; and as things were being moved and dissociated, the revolution made them dissociate much more.

(Simplicius, *Commentary on Aristotle's Physics* 300.31–301.1)

14. (B14) *Nous*, which always is, most assuredly is even now where all the other things also are, in the surrounding multitude, and in the things that were joined together and in the things that have been separated off. (Simplicius, *Commentary on Aristotle's Physics* 157.7–9)

15. (B15) The dense and the wet and the cold and the dark came together here, where <the> earth is now; but the rare and the hot and the dry <and the bright> moved out to the far reaches of the Aithēr.

(Simplicius, *Commentary on Aristotle's Physics* 179.3–6)

16. (B16) From these, as they are being separated off, earth is compacted; for water is separated off from the clouds, and earth from the water, and from the earth stones are compacted by the cold, and these stones move farther out than the water.

(Simplicius, *Commentary on Aristotle's Physics* 179.8–10; 155.21–23)

17. (B17) The Greeks do not think correctly about coming-to-be and passing-away; for no thing comes to be or passes away, but is mixed together and dissociated from the things that are. And thus they would be correct to call coming-to-be mixing-together and passing-away dissociating.

(Simplicius, *Commentary on Aristotle's Physics* 163.20–24)

18. (B18) The sun places the light in the moon.

(Plutarch, *On the Face in the Moon* 929b)

19. (B19) We call the reflection of the sun in the clouds a rainbow.

(Scholium on *Iliad* 17.547)

20. (B21) Owing to their [the senses'] feebleness, we are not able to determine the truth.   (Sextus Empiricus, *Against the Mathematicians* 7.90)

21. (B21a) Appearances are a sight of the unseen . . .

(Sextus Empiricus, *Against the Mathematicians* 7.140)

22. (B22) . . . egg whites are bird's milk.

(Athenaeus, *Sophists at Dinner* 2.57B)

23. (A102) But in all these [physical skills that animals possess] we are more unfortunate than the beasts, but by experience and memory and wisdom and art according to Anaxagoras, we make use of their activity (?) and take their honey and milk them and herding them together, use them as we will. There is nothing of chance here, but all is wisdom and forethought.[36]   (Plutarch, *On Fortune* 3 98F)

24. (A52) Anaxagoras probably supposed [the principles] to be unlimited in this way because he accepted as true the common opinion of the physicists that nothing comes to be from what is not. That is why they say: "all things were together," and why Anaxagoras makes the generation of a thing of a certain sort into alteration.

(Aristotle, *Physics* 1.4 187a23–b6)

25. (A43) Anaxagoras says just the opposite of Empedocles about the elements. For [Empedocles] claims that fire and earth, and things of the same rank, are elements of bodies and that all things are compounded of them; but Anaxagoras says the opposite. For he claims that the homogeneous stuffs are elements—I mean, for instance, flesh and bone and each of the things of that sort—and that air and fire are mixtures of them and of all the other seeds; for each of them is a collection of all the invisible homogeneous stuffs.

(Aristotle *On the Heavens* 3.3 302a28)

26. (A46) [Anaxagoras] makes the homogeneous stuffs elements, for instance, bone and flesh and marrow and the others of which the part is called by the same name [as the whole].

(Aristotle, *On Coming to Be and Passing Away* I.1 314a18)

---

36. This phrase was given by DK as B21b. Following other scholars, I think it more likely that the passage is a testimonium. There are textual problems here; I read *sphōn ti* instead of *te*.

27. (A58) When someone said that *Nous* is present—in nature just as it is in animals—as the cause of the *kosmos* and of all its order, he appeared as a sober man among the random chatterers who preceded him. We know that Anaxagoras clearly held these views, but Hermotimus of Clazomenae gets the credit for holding them earlier.

(Aristotle, *Metaphysics* I.3.984b15)

28. (A117) Anaxagoras and Empedocles say that plants are moved by desire, and they also assert that they sense and can be made sad and happy. Anaxagoras said that they are animals and feel joy and sadness, taking the fall of their leaves as evidence. . . .

([Aristotle], *On Plants* I.1.815a15)

10. LEUCIPPUS AND DEMOCRITUS: FIFTH-CENTURY ATOMISM

Almost nothing is known of Leucippus, who was the founding theorist of atomism. Epicurus, a post-Aristotelian philosopher who adopted certain aspects of Presocratic atomism is even said to have denied that Leucippus existed. Leucippus' birthplace is variously given as Miletus, Abdera, and Elea (Miletus and Elea could represent the Milesian and Eleatic influences on his work, and Democritus, his pupil and associate was from Abdera). It is likely that Leucippus proposed the atomic system sometime around 440 to 430 BCE, thus he is contemporary with the other post-Eleatic thinkers Anaxagoras and Empedocles as well as Melissus. Two books are attributed to Leucippus: On Mind *and* The Great World System *(Makrokosmos).*

Democritus himself says that he was young when Anaxagoras was an old man; his birth date is usually placed at about 460; he lived well into the fourth century (tradition says he lived to be about 100 years old), and so was a contemporary of Socrates, Plato, and perhaps even the young Aristotle. Democritus was born in Abdera, in Thrace, a birthplace he shares with the sophist Protagoras, but he traveled widely throughout the ancient world (later sources say he went to India, but this is doubtful). Ancient sources list about seventy titles of books by Democritus on all sorts of subjects, both philosophical (on natural philosophy, ethics, mathematics, literature, and grammar) as well as on other perhaps more popular topics: He apparently wrote books on his travels; there are also reports of treatises on medicine, farming, military science, and painting. One of his books was called The Little World System *(Mikrokosmos), in obvious homage to his teacher and associate Leucippus.*

The selections included here concentrate on atomism, the scientific and metaphysical theory begun by Leucippus and continued by Democritus.

Unfortunately, very few passages from Leucippus and Democritus on atomism survive; most of the evidence we have about the view comes from Aristotle and the Aristotelian commentators.[37] We must keep in mind that these reports will also involve interpretation; atomism, which is a mechanistic theory, was the major competitor to the teleological systems of both Plato and Aristotle. The word atomos in Greek means "uncuttable," and so atoms are things that cannot be cut, split, or actually divided. The atomists claim that there is an indefinite number of these atoms, each of which is uniform, not subject to coming-to-be or passing-away, and unchangeable in any other way, except position, an external change that does not affect the inner core of atomic being. Atoms thus satisfy the Parmenidean requirements for reality. Individual atoms are imperceptible: most of them are very small, though Democritus may have said that there could be an atom as large as the cosmos. All atomic stuff is the same; atoms differ from one another only in shape and size (there is controversy about whether pre-Platonic atomists considered weight as a property of atoms).

The second player in the atomic system is "the empty" (void). Void is where the atoms are not, and atoms are able to move into the empty. The atomists explicitly call the void "the nothing" or the "what is not," whereas atoms are called "the something" or the "what is." Hence they explicitly challenge Parmenides' proscription against what-is-not; yet there is good evidence that they insisted that the void is real in its own right, and not simply the negation of what-is. Void separates atoms, which allows them to move and come close to one another without melding into each other. The mixing together and separating of the different types of atoms into different arrangements is responsible for all the aspects of the sensible world, and so what looks like coming-to-be and passing-away is merely rearrangement of the basic entities—atoms and void. All else is, as Democritus says, "by convention." Democritus offered complex accounts of the structure of physical objects (i.e., arrangements of atoms) and of perception, thought, and knowledge, as well as of many other aspects of human life. There are many fragments on ethical matters attributed to him, but the authenticity of these is unclear.

1. (67B2) No thing happens at random but all things as a result of a reason and by necessity.[38]   (Aëtius 1.25.4)

2. (67A1) Leucippus' opinion is this: All things are unlimited and they all turn around one another; the all [the universe] is both the empty [void] and the full. The worlds come to be when the atoms fall into the void and are entangled with one another. The nature of the stars

---

37. Aristotle wrote a multivolume work on Democritus; only fragments survive, thanks to Simplicius, who quotes some passages (see selection 5, below).
38. This is one of the few fragments that can be assigned to Leucippus with some confidence. Leucippus' DK number is 67, while Democritus' is 68.

comes to be from their motion, and from their increase [in entangle-ments]. The sun is carried around in a larger circle around the moon; and whirled around the center, the earth rides steady; its shape is drumlike. He was the first to make the atoms first principles.

(Diogenes Laertius, *Lives of the Philosophers* 9.30; tpc)

3. (67A6) Leucippus and his associate Democritus declare the full and the empty [void] to be the elements, calling the former "what-is" (*to on*) and the other "what-is-not" (*to mē on*). Of these, the one, "what-is," is full and solid, the other, "what-is-not," is empty [void] and rare. (This is why they say that what-is is no more than what-is-not, because the void is no less than body is.) These are the material causes of existing things. . . . They declare that the differences <among these> are the causes of the rest. Moreover, they say that the differences are three: shape, arrangement, and position. For they say that what-is differs only in "rhythm," "touching," and "turning"—and of these "rhythm" is shape, "touching" is arrangement, and "turning" is posi-tion. For *A* differs from *N* in shape, *AN* from *NA* in arrangement, and *Z* from *N* in position. Concerning the origin and manner of motion in existing things, these men too, like the rest, lazily neglected to give an account. (Aristotle, *Metaphysics* 1.4 985b4–20)

4. (67A9) After establishing the shapes, Democritus and Leucippus base their account of alteration and coming-to-be on them: coming-to-be and perishing by means of separation and combination, alteration by means of arrangement and position. Since they held that the truth is in the appearance, and appearances are opposite and infinite, they made the shapes infinite, so that by reason of changes of the composite, the same thing seems opposite to different people, and it shifts position when a small additional amount is mixed in, and it appears com-pletely different when a single thing shifts position. For tragedy and comedy come to be out of the same letters.

(Aristotle, *On Generation and Corruption* 1.1 315b6–15)

5. (68A37) Democritus believes that the nature of the eternal things is small substances (*ousiai*)[39] infinite in number. As a place for these he hypothesizes something else, infinite in size, and he calls their place by the names "the void," "not-hing" (*ouden*) and "the unlimited" [or, "infinite"] and he calls each of the substances "hing" (*den*) and "the compact" and "what-is." He holds that the substances are so small that they escape our senses. They have all kinds of forms and shapes and differences in size. Out of these as elements he generates and

39. Translator's note: *Ousia*, "substance," is a noun derived from the verb *einai*, "to be." There is a connection in language and meaning between *ousia* and *on*.

forms visible and perceptible bodies. <These substances> are at odds with one another and move in the void because of their dissimilarity and the other differences I have mentioned, and as they move they strike against one another and become entangled in a way that makes them be in contact and close to one another but does not make any thing out of them that is truly one, for it is quite foolish <to think> that two or more things could ever come to be one. The grounds he gives for why the substances stay together up to a point are that the bodies fit together and hold each other fast. For some of them are rough, some are hooked, others concave, and others convex, while yet others have innumerable other differences. So he thinks that they cling to each other and stay together until some stronger necessity comes along from the environment and shakes them and scatters them apart. He describes the generation and its contrary, separation, not only for animals but also for plants, *kosmoi*, and altogether for all perceptible bodies.

(Aristotle, *On Democritus*, quoted by Simplicius, *Commentary on Aristotle's On the Heavens* 295.1–22)

6. (67A8, 68A38) Leucippus . . . did not follow the same route as Parmenides and Xenophanes concerning things that are, but seemingly the opposite one. For while they made the universe one, immovable, ungenerated, and limited, and did not even permit the investigation of what-is-not, he posited the atoms as infinite and ever-moving elements, with an infinite number of shapes, on the grounds that they are no more like this than like that and because he observed that coming-to-be and change are unceasing among the things that are. Further, he posited that what-is is no more than what-is-not, and both are equally causes of things that come to be. For supposing the substance of the atoms to be compact and full, he said it is what-is and that it moves in the void, which he called "what-is-not" and which he declares is no less than what-is. His associate, Democritus of Abdera, likewise posited the full and the void as principles, of which he calls the former "what-is" and the latter "what-is-not." For positing the atoms as matter for the things that are, they generate the rest by means of their differences. These are three: rhythm, turning, and touching, that is, shape, position, and arrangement. For by nature like is moved by like, and things of the same kind move toward one another, and each of the shapes produces a different condition when arranged in a different combination. Thus, since the principles are infinite, they reasonably promised to account for all attributes and substances—how and through what cause anything comes to be. This is why they say that only those who make the elements infinite account for everything reasonably. They say that the number of the shapes among the atoms

is infinite on the grounds that they are no more like this than like that. For they themselves assign this as a cause of the infiniteness.

(Simplicius, *Commentary on Aristotle's Physics* 28.4–26)

7. (67A7) Leucippus and Democritus have accounted for all things very systematically and in a single theory, taking the natural starting point as their own. For some of the early philosophers held that what-is is necessarily one and immovable. For the void is not, and motion is impossible without a separate void, nor can there be many things without something to keep them apart. . . . But Leucippus thought he had arguments that assert what is generally granted to perception, not abolishing coming-to-be, perishing, motion, or plurality. Agreeing on these matters with the phenomena and agreeing with those who support the one [that is, the Eleatics] that there could be no motion without void, he asserts that void is what-is-not and that nothing of what-is is not, since what strictly is is completely full. But this kind of thing is not one thing but things that are infinite in number and invisible because of the minuteness of their size. These move in the void (for there is void), and they produce coming-to-be by combining and perishing by coming apart, and they act and are acted upon wherever they happen to come into contact (for in this way they are not one), and they generate <compounds> by becoming combined and entangled. A plurality could not come to be from what is in reality one, nor one from what is really many, but this is impossible.

(Aristotle, *On Generation and Corruption* 1.8 324b35–325a36)

8. (67A19) They declare that their [atoms'] nature is but one, as if each one were a separate piece of gold.

(Aristotle, *On the Heavens* 1.7 275b32–276a1)

9. (68A59) Plato and Democritus supposed that only the intelligible things are true (or, "real"); Democritus <held this view> because there is by nature no perceptible substrate, since the atoms, which combine to form all things, have a nature deprived of every perceptible quality.

(Sextus Empiricus, *Against the Mathematicians* 8.6)

10. (68A47) Democritus specified two <basic properties of atoms>: size and shape; and Epicurus added weight as a third.   (Aëtius 1.3.18)

11. (67A15) Since the bodies differ in shape, and the shapes are infinite, they declare the simple bodies to be infinite too. But they did not determine further what is the shape of each of the elements, beyond assigning a spherical shape to fire. They distinguished air and water and the others by largeness and smallness.

(Aristotle, *On the Heavens* 3.4 303a11–15)

12. (67A14) These men [Leucippus, Democritus, and Epicurus] said that the principles are infinite in multitude, and they believed them to be atoms and indivisible and incapable of being affected because they are compact and have no share of void. (For they claimed that division occurs where there is void in bodies.)

(Simplicius, *Commentary on Aristotle's On the Heavens* 242.18–21)

13. (67A13) Those who abandoned division to infinity on the grounds that we cannot divide to infinity and as a result cannot guarantee that the division cannot end, declared that bodies are composed of indivisible things and are divided into indivisibles. Except that Leucippus and Democritus hold that the cause of the primary bodies' indivisibility is not only their inability to be affected but also their minute size and lack of parts.

(Simplicius, *Commentary on Aristotle's Physics* 925.10–15)

14. (68A48b) Democritus would appear to have been persuaded by arguments that are appropriate to the science of nature. The point will be clear as we proceed. For there is a difficulty in supposing that there is a body, a magnitude, that is everywhere divisible and that this [the complete division] is possible. For what will there be that escapes the division? . . . Now since such a body is everywhere divisible, let it be divided. What, then, will be left? A magnitude? But that cannot be. For there will be something that has not been divided, whereas we supposed that it was everywhere divisible. But if there is no body or magnitude left and yet the division will take place, either <the original body> will consist of points and its components will be without magnitude, or it will be nothing at all so that even if it were to come to be out of nothing and be composed of nothing, the whole thing would then be nothing but an appearance. Likewise, if it is composed of points it will not be a quantity. For when they were in contact and there was a single magnitude and they coincided, they made the whole thing no larger. For when it is divided into two or more, the whole is no smaller or larger than before. And so even if all the points are put together they will not make any magnitude. . . . These problems result from supposing that any body whatever of any size is everywhere divisible. . . . And so, since magnitudes cannot be composed of contacts or points, it is necessary for there to be indivisible bodies and magnitudes.

(Aristotle, *On Generation and Corruption* 1.2 316a13–b16)

15. (67A7) When Democritus said that the atoms are in contact with each other, he did not mean contact, strictly speaking, which occurs when the surfaces of the things in contact fit perfectly with one another, but the condition in which the atoms are near one another and not far apart is what he called contact. For no matter what, they are separated by void.

> (Philoponus, *Commentary on Aristotle's On Generation and Corruption* 158.27–159.3)

16. (68B156) [When Democritus declares that] There is no more reason for the "hing" {Greek: *den*} to be than the nothing {Greek: *mēden*, nothing}, [he is calling thing body and nothing void, and declaring that this too (void) has some nature and existence of its own.]

> (Plutarch, *Against Colotes* 1108F; tpc)

17. (67A19) By "void" people mean an interval in which there is no perceptible body. Since they believe that everything that is is body, they say that void is that in which there is nothing at all. . . . So it is necessary to prove[40] . . . that there is no interval different from bodies . . . which breaks up the totality of body so that it is not continuous, as Democritus, Leucippus, and many other natural philosophers say, or that there is anything outside the totality of body, supposing that it is continuous. . . . They say that (1) there would be no change in place (that is, motion and growth), since it does not seem that there would be motion unless there were void, since what is full cannot admit anything else. . . . (2) Some things are seen to contract and be compressed; for example, they say that the jars hold the wine along with the wineskins, since the compressed body contracts into the empty places that are in it. Further, (3) all believe that growth takes place through void, since the nourishment is a body and two bodies cannot coincide. (4) They also use as evidence what happens with ash: it takes no less water to fill a jar that contains ashes than it does to fill the same jar when it is empty.   (Aristotle, *Physics* 4.6 213a27–b22)

18. (67A16) This is why Leucippus and Democritus, who say that the primary bodies are always moving in the void (that is, the infinite) must specify what motion they have and what is their natural motion.

> (Aristotle, *On the Heavens* 3.2 300b8–11)

19. (67A18) For they say that there is always motion. But why it is and what motion it is, they do not state, nor do they give the cause of its being of one sort rather than another.

> (Aristotle, *Metaphysics* 12.6 1071b33–35)

---

40. Translator's note: This passage forms part of Aristotle's treatment of void, in which he both presents the arguments offered in favor of the thesis that void exists and shows why they fail. Aristotle here says that he needs to refute the view that void exists.

20. (68A58) They say that motion occurs because of the void. For they, too, say that nature undergoes motion in respect of place.

(Aristotle, *Physics* 8.9 265b24–25)

21. (67A16) Leucippus and Democritus said that their primary bodies, the atoms, are always moving in the infinite void by compulsion.

(Simplicius, *Commentary on Aristotle's On the Heavens* 583.18–20)

22. (68A47) Democritus, saying that the atoms are by nature motionless, declares that they move "by a blow."

(Simplicius, *Commentary on Aristotle's Physics* 42.10–11)

23. (68A47) Democritus says that the primary bodies (these are the compact things) do not possess weight but move by striking against one another in the infinite, and there can be an atom the size of a *kosmos*.

(Aëtius 1.12.6)

24. (67A6) These men [Leucippus and Democritus] say that the atoms move by hitting and striking against each other, but they do not specify the source of their natural motion. For the motion of striking each other is compelled and not natural, and compelled motion is posterior to natural motion.

(Alexander, *Commentary on Aristotle's Metaphysics* 36.21–25)

25. (68A58) They said that moving by virtue of the weight in them, <the atoms> move with respect to place through the void, which yields and does not resist. For they said that they "are hurled all about." And they attribute this motion to the elements as not just their primary but in fact their only motion, whereas things composed of the elements have the other kinds of motion. For they grow and decrease, change, come to be, and perish through the combination and separation of the primary bodies.

(Simplicius, *Commentary on Aristotle's Physics* 1318.35–1319.5)

26. (68A47) Democritus holds that there is one kind of motion, that due to pulsation.

(Aëtius 1.23.3)

27. (68A60) Those <who call the primary bodies> solid can rather say that the larger ones are heavier. But since compounds do not appear to behave in this way, and we see many that are smaller in bulk but heavier, as bronze is heavier than wood, some think and say that the cause is different—that the void enclosed within makes the bodies light and sometimes makes larger things lighter, since they contain more void. . . . Those who make these distinctions must add not only that something contains more void if it is lighter but also that it contains less solid.   (Aristotle, *On the Heavens* 4.2 309a1–14)

28. (68A66) Democritus leaves aside purpose but refers all things which nature employs to necessity.
                              (Aristotle, *Generation of Animals* 5.8 789b2–4)

29. (68A66) <Concerning necessity> Democritus <says it is> the knocking against <each other> and the motion and "blow" of matter.
                                                      (Aëtius 1.26.2)

30. (68A68) <Democritus> seemed to employ chance in his cosmogony, but in his detailed discussions he declares that chance is the cause of nothing, and he refers to other causes.
             (Simplicius, *Commentary on Aristotle's Physics* 330.14–17)

31. (67A14) These atoms, which are separate from one another in the infinite void and differ in shape and size and position and arrangement, move in the void, and when they overtake one another they collide, and some rebound in whatever direction they may happen to, but others become entangled by virtue of the way their shapes, sizes, positions, and arrangements correspond, and they stay together, and this is how compounds are produced.
        (Simplicius, *Commentary on Aristotle's On the Heavens* 242.21–26)

32. (68A57) What does Democritus say? That atomic substances infinite in number, not different in kind, and moreover incapable of acting or being acted upon, are in motion, scattered in the void. When they approach one another or collide or become entangled, the compounds appear as water or fire or as a plant or a human, but all things are atoms, which he calls forms; there is nothing else. For there is no coming-to-be from what-is-not, and nothing could come to be from things that are, because on account of their hardness the atoms are not acted upon and do not change.
                              (Plutarch, *Against Colotes* 8 1110F–1111A)

33. (68B155) If a cone is cut by a plane parallel to the base, what should we think about the surfaces of the segments? Do they prove to be equal or unequal? If they are unequal they will make the cone uneven, with many step-like notches and rough spots, but if they are equal the segments will be equal, and the cone will appear to have the character of a cylinder, being composed of equal not unequal circles, which is most absurd.
                (Plutarch, *Against the Stoics on Common Conceptions* 1079E)

34. (67A14) Leucippus and Democritus, calling the smallest and primary bodies atoms, <say> that by virtue of differences in their shapes and position and order, some bodies come to be hot and fiery—those composed of rather sharp and minute primary bodies situated in a similar position, while others come to be cold and watery—those composed of the opposite kinds of bodies. And some come to be bright and shining, while others come to be dim and dark.

(Simplicius, *Commentary on Aristotle's Physics* 36.1–7)

35. (68A129) He makes sweet that which is round and good-sized; astringent that which is large, rough, polygonal, and not rounded; sharp-tasting, as its name indicates, sharp and angular in body, bent, fine, and not rounded; pungent, round, small, angular, and bent; salty, angular, good-sized, crooked, and equal-sided; bitter, round, smooth, crooked, and small-sized; oily, fine, round, and small.

(Theophrastus, *Causes of Plants* 6.1.6)

36. (68A135) Iron is harder and lead is heavier, since iron has its atoms arranged unevenly and has large quantities of void in many places . . . while lead has less void, but its atoms are arranged evenly throughout. This is why it is heavier but softer than iron.

(Theophrastus, *On Sensation* 62)

37. (67A1) <Leucippus> declares the universe to be infinite. . . . Of this, some is full and some is empty [void], and he declares these [full and void] to be elements. An infinite number of *kosmoi* arise out of these and perish into these. The *kosmoi* come into being in the following way. Many bodies of all sorts of shapes, being cut off from the infinite, move into a great void. They collect together and form a single vortex. In it they strike against one another and move around in all different ways, and they separate apart, like to like. When they are no longer able to rotate in equilibrium, the fine ones depart into the void outside as if sifted. The rest remain together, become entangled, move together in unison, and form a first spherical complex. This stands apart like a membrane, enclosing all kinds of bodies in it. As these whirl around by virtue of the resistance of the center, the surrounding membrane becomes thin, since the adjacent atoms join the motion when they come into contact with the vortex. And the earth came into being in this way when the atoms moving to the center remained together. And again the surrounding membrane-like thing itself grows because of the accretion of bodies from outside. As it moves in a vortex it acquires whatever it comes into contact with. Some of these become intertwined and form a complex that is at first damp and muddy, but when they have dried out and rotate with the vortex of the whole, they catch fire and form the nature of the stars.

(Diogenes Laertius, *Lives of the Philosophers* 9.31–32)

38. (68B164) Animals flock together with animals of the same kind—doves with doves, cranes with cranes, and likewise for the other irrational kinds. It is the same for inanimate things, as can be seen in the cases of seeds being sifted and pebbles on the shore. For through the swirling and separating motion of the sieve, lentils wind up together with lentils, wheat with wheat, and barley with barley, and through the motion of the waves, elongated pebbles are pushed to the same place as other elongated ones, and round ones to the same place as round ones, as if the similarity in these had some mutually attractive force for things.   (Sextus Empiricus, *Against the Mathematicians* 7.116)

39. (68A40) There are an infinite number of *kosmoi* of different sizes. In some there is no sun or moon. In some the sun and moon are larger than ours, and in others there are more. The distances between the *kosmoi* are unequal, and in one region there are more, in another fewer. Some are growing, some are at their peak, and some are declining, and here one is coming into being, there one is ceasing to be. They perish when they collide with one another. Some *kosmoi* have no animals, plants, or any moisture. In our own *kosmos* the earth came into being before the stars. The moon is lowest, then the sun, then the fixed stars. The planets too have unequal heights. A *kosmos* is at its peak until it is no longer able to take anything in from outside.
                    (Hippolytus, *Refutation of All Heresies* 1.13.2–4)

40. (67A1) The orbit of the sun is furthest out, that of the moon is nearest, and the others are in between. All the stars are on fire because of the speed of their motion; the sun too is on fire because of the stars, while the moon has only a small share of fire. The sun and moon suffer eclipses . . . [something is missing from the text—probably a reference to the ecliptic] because the earth is tilted toward the south. The regions to the north are always covered with snow and are very cold and frozen. The sun is eclipsed rarely, but the moon is eclipsed often because their orbits are unequal.
                    (Diogenes Laertius, *Lives of the Philosophers* 9.33)

41. (68A93) Democritus stated that thunder results from an uneven compound forcing the surrounding cloud to move downward. Lightning is the collision of clouds, as a result of which the atoms that generate fire are filtered through interstices containing much void (a process that involves friction) and collect in the same place. A thunderbolt occurs when there is a violent motion of fire-producing atoms that are very pure, fine, even, and "close-fitted" (the word Democritus himself uses). A waterspout occurs when compounds of fire containing much void are held back in regions with a lot of void and are wrapped in special membranes, and form bodies because of this rich mixture and make a rush toward the depth.   (Aëtius 3.3.11)

42. (68A104) Some say that the soul moves the body in which it is found in the same way as it is itself moved: Democritus, for example, who has a view like Philippos the comic poet, who says that Daedalus made the wooden statue of Aphrodite move by pouring quicksilver into it. Democritus speaks similarly, since he says that the indivisible spheres are in motion because their nature is never to stay still, and to draw the entire body along with them and move it. But we will ask if these same things also produce rest. How they will do so is difficult or impossible to state. In general, the soul does not appear to move the body in this way, but through choice of some kind and through thought.
                                       (Aristotle, *On the Soul* 1.3 406b16–25)

43. (68A135) The visual impression is not formed directly in the pupil, but the air between the eye and the object is contracted and stamped by the seen object and by the seeing thing. For there is a continual effluence from everything. Then this [air], which is solid and has a different color, forms an impression in the eyes, which are moist.
                                          (Theophrastus, *On Sensation* 50)

44. (68B9) Nonetheless [Democritus] is found condemning them [the senses]. For he says, "We in fact understand nothing exactly [or, "exact"], but what changes according to the disposition both of the body and of the things that enter it and offer resistance to it."
                             (Sextus Empiricus, *Against the Mathematicians* 7.136)

45. (68B11) There are two kinds of judgment, one legitimate and the other bastard. All the following belong to the bastard: sight, hearing, smell, taste, touch. The other is legitimate and is separate from this. When the bastard one is unable to see or hear or smell or taste or grasp by touch any further in the direction of smallness, but <we need to go still further> toward what is fine, <then the legitimate one enables us to carry on>.[41]   (Sextus Empiricus, *Against the Mathematicians* 7.138)

46. (68B9) By convention [or, "custom"], sweet; by convention, bitter; by convention, hot; by convention, cold; by convention, color; but in reality, atoms and void.
                             (Sextus Empiricus, *Against the Mathematicians* 7.135)

41. Translator's note: This fragment trails off into corruption, but there is general agreement about the sense of what is missing.

47. (68B6) A person must know by this rule [*kanōn*: measuring stick, standard] that he is separated from reality.
(Sextus Empiricus, *Against the Mathematicians* 7.136)

48. (68B8) In fact it will be clear that to know in reality what each thing is like is a matter of perplexity [or, "that people are at a loss to know in reality what each thing is like"].
(Sextus Empiricus, *Against the Mathematicians* 7.136)

49. (68B7) In reality we know nothing about anything, but for each person opinion is a reshaping [of the soul-atoms by the atoms entering from without].
(Sextus Empiricus, *Against the Mathematicians* 7.136)

50. (68A112) Either nothing is true, or at least to us it is unclear [or, "hidden"]. It is because these thinkers suppose intelligence to be sensation, and that, in turn, to be an alteration, that they say that what appears to our senses must be true (or, "real").
(Aristotle, *Metaphysics* 4.5 1009b11–15)

51. (68B117) In reality we know nothing, for truth is in the depths.
(Diogenes Laertius, *Lives of the Philosophers* 9.72)

52. (68B125) Wretched mind, do you take your evidence from us and then throw us down? Throwing us down is a fall for you!
(Galen, *On Medical Experience* 15.8)

53. (68B166) Democritus says that certain images of atoms approach humans, and of them some cause good and others evil, and as a result he prayed "to meet with propitious images." These are large and immense, and difficult to destroy though not indestructible. They indicate the future in advance to people when they are seen and emit voices. As a result people of ancient times, upon perceiving the appearances of these things, supposed that they are a god, though there is no other god aside from these having an indestructible nature.
(Sextus Empiricus, *Against the Mathematicians* 9.19)

54. (68B191) Cheerfulness arises in people through moderation of enjoyment and due proportion in life. Deficiencies and excesses tend to change suddenly and give rise to large movements in the soul. Souls that undergo motions involving large intervals are neither steady nor cheerful . . .
(Stobaeus, *Selections* 3.1.120)

55. (68A1) The goal of life is cheerfulness, which is not the same as pleasure . . . but the state in which the soul continues calmly and stably, disturbed by no fear or superstition or any other emotion. He also calls it "well-being" and many other names.

(Diogenes Laertius, *Lives of the Philosophers* 9.45)

56. (68B74) Accept nothing pleasant unless it is beneficial.

(Democrates, *Maxims*)

57. (68B69) To all humans the same thing is good and true, but different people find different things pleasant.   (Democrates, *Maxims*)

58. (68B214) Brave is not only he who masters the enemy but also he who masters pleasures. Some are lords of cities but slaves of women.

(Stobaeus, *Selections* 3.5.25)

59. (68B33) Nature and teaching are closely related. For teaching reshapes the person and by reshaping makes <his> nature.

(Clement, *Miscellanies* 4.151)

60. (68B189) Best for a person is to live his life being as cheerful and as little distressed as possible. This will occur if he does not make his pleasures in mortal things.   (Stobaeus, *Selections* 3.1.47)

61. (68B235) All those who make their pleasures from the belly, exceeding the right time for food, drink, or sex, have short-lived pleasures—only for as long as they eat or drink—but many pains.

(Stobaeus, *Selections* 3.18.35)

11. MELISSUS OF SAMOS

Melissus was an admiral as well as a philosopher. Although he lived on Samos (an island in the eastern Aegean that was the birthplace of Pythagoras), he adopted Parmenides' arguments. We do not know the year of his birth, but in 441 BCE he was the admiral of a fleet that defeated the Athenians under Pericles. Melissus' treatise was a sustained exploration of the consequences of Parmenides' views, and he even extends Parmenides' arguments. Melissus argues that only one thing can be, and that among other characteristics, the One (as he called it) must be changeless and full, not subject to changes in density and rarity, not subject to rearrangement, and not subject to pain or pleasure. These arguments seemingly take on the Milesians; Anaxagoras and

the Atomists, whose many ingredients change place and are rearranged (in
addition, the Atomists are committed to the reality of void); and Empedocles,
who has four ingredients that are rearranged, and whose divine sphere
"rejoices." Melissus was roundly abused by Aristotle, who said Melissus was
somewhat unrefined in his views, but Melissus sets out his arguments clearly
and uses Parmenides' claims about what-is to challenge the truth of the
evidence of the senses, and to call into question some basic assumptions of
post-Parmenidean theories.

1. (30B1) Whatever was, always was and always will be. For if it came to
   be, it is necessary that before it came to be it was nothing. Now if it was
   nothing, in no way could anything come to be out of nothing.
                    (Simplicius, *Commentary on Aristotle's Physics* 162.23–26)

2. (B2) Now since it did not come to be, it is and always was and always
   will be, and it does not have a beginning or an end, but it is unlimited.
   For if it had come to be it would have a beginning (for if it had come to
   be it would have begun at some time) and an end (for if it had come
   to be it would have ended at some time).[42] But since it neither began nor ended, and always was and always will be, it does not have
   a beginning or end. For whatever is not entire [or, "all"] cannot always be.
      (Simplicius, *Commentary on Aristotle's Physics* 29.22–26, 109.20–25)

3. (B3) [Just as he says that what came to be at some time is limited in its
   being, he also wrote clearly that what always is is unlimited in being,
   saying:] But just as it always is, so also it must always be unlimited in
   magnitude. [But by "magnitude" he does not mean what is extended
   in space.][43]   (Simplicius, *Commentary on Aristotle's Physics* 109.29–32)

4. (B4) Nothing that has both a beginning and an end is either eternal or
   unlimited.   (Simplicius, *Commentary on Aristotle's Physics* 110.2–4)

5. (B5) If it is not one, it will come to a limit in relation to something else.
                     (Simplicius, *Commentary on Aristotle's Physics* 110.5–6)

6. (B6) For if it is <unlimited>, it will be one. For if there were two, they
   could not be unlimited, but they would have limits in relation to each
   other.
         (Simplicius, *Commentary on Aristotle's On the Heavens* 557.14–17)

42. Translator's note: Although a better attested manuscript reading yields the
translations "it would have begun coming to be at some time," and "it would have
ended coming to be at some time," it is difficult to make sense of these claims.
43. Simplicius' comments are included in square brackets.

7. (B7) Thus it is eternal and unlimited and one and all alike.

And it cannot perish or become greater or be rearranged, nor does it feel pain or distress. For if it underwent any of these, it would no longer be one. For if it becomes different, it is necessary that what-is is not alike, but what previously was perishes, and what-is-not comes to be. Now if it were to become different by a single hair in ten thousand years, it would all perish in the whole of time.

But it is not possible for it to be rearranged either. For the arrangement that previously was is not destroyed, and an arrangement that is not does not come to be. But when nothing either comes to be in addition or is destroyed or becomes different, how could there be a rearrangement of things-that-are? For if it became at all different, it would thereby have in fact been rearranged.

Nor does it feel pain. For it could not be entire [or, "all"] if it were feeling pain. For a thing feeling pain could not always be. Nor does it have equal power to what is healthy. Nor would it be alike if it were feeling pain. For it would be feeling pain because something is either being taken away or added, and it would no longer be alike.

Nor could what is healthy feel pain. For what is healthy and what-is would perish and what-is-not would come to be.

And the same argument applies to feeling distress as to feeling pain.

Nor is any of it empty [or void]. For what is empty is nothing, and of course what is nothing cannot be. Nor does it move. For it cannot give way anywhere, but it is full. For if it were empty, it would give way into the empty part. But since it is not empty it has nowhere to give way.

It cannot be dense and rare. For it is impossible for the rare to be equally full as the dense, but the rare thereby proves to be emptier than the dense.

And we must make this the criterion of full and not full: If something yields or is penetrated, it is not full. But if it neither yields nor is penetrated, it is full.

Hence it is necessary that it is full if it is not empty. Hence if it is full it does not move.

(Simplicius, *Commentary on Aristotle's Physics* 111.18–112.15)

8. (B8) [After saying of what-is that it is one and ungenerated and motionless and interrupted by no void, but is a whole full of itself, he goes on:] Now this argument is the strongest indication that there is only one thing. But the following are indications too.

If there were many things, they must be such as I say the one is. For if there are earth and water and air and fire and iron and gold and the living and the dead and black and white and all the other things that people say are real—if these things really are and if we see and hear correctly, then each of them ought to be just as we thought at first, and it should not change or come to be different, but each thing always ought to be just as it is. But in fact we say that we see and hear and understand correctly.

We think that what is hot becomes cold and what is cold hot, that what is hard becomes soft and what is soft hard, and that the living dies and that it comes to be from the nonliving, and that all these things come to be different and that what was and what is now are not at all alike, but that iron, although hard, is worn away by contact with the finger, and also gold and stone and anything else that we think is enduring,[44] and that earth and stone come to be from water.

Hence these things do not agree with one another. For although we say that there are many eternal things that have definite forms and endurance, we think that all of them become different and change from what we see at any moment.

Hence it is clear that we do not see correctly and we are incorrect in thinking that those many things are. For they would not change if they were real, but each one would be just as we thought. For nothing can prevail over what is real.

But if it changes, what-is was destroyed, and what-is-not has come to be. Thus, if there are many things, they must be such as the one is.
(Simplicius, *Commentary on Aristotle's On the Heavens* 558.19–559.12)

9. (B9) [That he intends what-is to be bodiless he indicated, saying:] Now if it is, it must be one. But being one, it must not have body. But if it had thickness, it would have parts and no longer would be one.
(Simplicius, *Commentary on Aristotle's Physics* 109.34–110.2)

10. (B10) [For he himself proves that what-is is indivisible.]
For if what-is is divided, it moves. But if it moved, it would not be.
(Simplicius, *Commentary on Aristotle's Physics* 109.32–34)

11. (A5) Being one it is all alike. For if it were unlike, being more, it would no longer be one, but many.
(Pseudo-Aristotle, *On Melissus, Xenophanes, Gorgias* 1 974a12–14)

44. Translator's note: I follow Barnes (1979/1982) in omitting the words "so that it happens that we neither see nor know the things that are," which are found in this place in the manuscripts.

12. PHILOLAUS OF CROTON

Philolaus was born in Croton, the center of Pythagoreanism in southern Italy. The date of his birth is controversial, and is given from anywhere around 470 to about 430 BCE. He certainly never knew Pythagoras himself, who died before 490. He was probably the first of the Pythagoreans to write a book, which may have been one of Aristotle's chief sources for his accounts of Pythagoreanism. In Plato's Phaedo, *two associates of Socrates who are present at his death, Simmias and Cebes, are represented as Pythagoreans and said to have studied with Philolaus in Thebes when he visited mainland Greece. According to Philolaus, the cosmos is made up of what he calls limiters and unlimiteds, fitted together in what he calls a* harmonia *(literally a carpenter's joint; also a musical fitting together or harmony). A* harmonia *is expressible in a numerical ratio, and thus, according to Philolaus, can be known. On this view, the cosmos as a series of numerical relationships becomes intelligible to humans. In Philolaus, we see Pythagorean assumptions about the power of number at work, although it is possible that Aristotle's famous claim that the Pythagoreans said that everything* is *number is Aristotle's own interpretation rather than something any of the Pythagoreans actually said. It is not, for instance, present in any of the extant fragments of Philolaus.*

1. (44B1) Nature in the *kosmos* was joined from both unlimiteds and limiters, and the entire *kosmos* and all the things in it.
   (Diogenes Laertius, *Lives of the Philosophers* 8.85)

2. (B2) It is necessary that the things that are be all either limiters or unlimited or both limiters and unlimited; but not in all cases only unlimited. Now since it is evident that they are neither from things that are all limiters nor from things that are all unlimited, it is therefore clear that both the *kosmos* and the things in it were joined together from both limiters and unlimiteds. The behavior of these things in turn makes it clear. For those of them that are from limiters limit, those that are from both limiters and unlimiteds both limit and do not limit, and those that are from unlimiteds will evidently be unlimited.
   (Stobaeus, *Selections* 1.21.7a)

3. (B3) There will not be anything that is going to know at all, if all things are unlimited.
   (Iamblichus, *Commentary on Nicomachus' Introduction to Arithmetic* 7.8)

4. (B4) And in fact all the things that are known have number. For it is not possible for anything at all either to be comprehended or known without this.
   (Stobaeus, *Selections* 1.21.7b)

5. (B5) In fact, number has two proper kinds, odd and even and a third kind even-odd from both mixed together. Of each of the two kinds there are many forms, of which each thing itself gives signs.
(Stobaeus, *Selections* 1.21.7c)

6. (B6) Concerning nature and *harmonia* this is how it is:
the being of things, which is eternal—that is, in fact, their very nature—admits knowledge that is divine and not human, except that it was impossible for any of the things that are and are known by us to have come to be if there did not exist the being of the things from which the *kosmos* is constituted—both the limiters and the unlimiteds. But since the principles are not similar or of the same kind, it would be completely impossible for them to be brought into order [or, "for them to be kept in an orderly arrangement (*kosmos*)"] if *harmonia* had not come upon them in whatever way it did. Now things that are similar and of the same kind have no need of *harmonia*, but those that are dissimilar and not of the same kind or of the same speed must be connected together in *harmoniai* if they are going to be kept in an orderly arrangement (*kosmos*).   (Stobaeus, *Selections* 1.21.7d)

7. (B6a) The magnitude of the *harmonia* is the fourth plus the fifth. The fifth is greater than the fourth by a 9:8 ratio. For from the lowest string to the second string is a fourth, and from the second string to the highest string is a fifth, but from the highest string to the third string is a fourth, and from the third string to the lowest string is a fifth. What is between the third string and the second string is a 9:8 ratio; the fourth has a 4:3 ratio, the fifth a 3:2 ratio, and the octave a 2:1 ratio. Thus the *harmonia* is five 9:8 ratios plus two half tones, the fifth is three 9:8 ratios plus one half-tone, and the fourth two 9:8 ratios plus one half-tone.
(Stobaeus, *Selections* 1.21.7d)

8. (B7) The first thing that was joined [harmonized], the one in the middle of the sphere, is called the hearth.   (Stobaeus, *Selections* 1.21.8)

9. (B17) The *kosmos* is one. It began to come to be right up at the middle, and from the middle <it came to be> in an upward direction in the same way as it did in a downward direction, and the things above the middle are symmetrical with those below. For, in the lower <regions> the lowest part is like the highest part <in the upper regions>, and similarly for the rest. For both <the higher and the lower> have the same relationship to the middle, unless they have been moved to another location.
(Stobaeus, *Selections* 1.15.7; based on Huffman's translation)

10. (B16) Some *logoi* are stronger than we are.
(Aristotle, *Eudemian Ethics* 2.8 1225a30; Huffman's translation)

11. (B20) [Philolaus correctly called] the number 7 motherless. [For it alone is of a nature neither to generate nor to be generated.]
(John the Lydian, *On the Months* 2.12)

12. (B13) The head <is the location> of intellect, the heart of soul and sensation, the navel of the taking root and growth of the first <part>, the genital organs of the depositing of seed and of generation. The brain contains the principle of man, the heart <contains the principle> of animals, the navel that of plants, and the genital organs that of them all. For they all both flourish and grow from seed.
(Pseudo-Iamblichus, *Theological Arithmetic* 25.12)

13. (58B8) The Pythagoreans similarly posited two principles, but added something peculiar to themselves, not that the limited and the unlimited are distinct natures like fire or earth or something similar, but that the unlimited itself and the one itself are the substance of what they are predicated of. This is why they call number the substance of all things.   (Aristotle, *Metaphysics* 1.5 987a13–19)

14. (45, 3) Eurytus [late fifth century; pupil of Philolaus] assigned what was the number of what, for example, this is the number of a human, that is the number of a horse, like those who bring numbers into triangular and square figures, fashioning with pebbles the forms of plants.   (Aristotle, *Metaphysics* 14.5 1092b10–13)

15. (45, 3) For example, suppose the number 250 is the definition of human being. . . . After positing this, he [Eurytus] would take 250 pebbles, some green, some black, others red, and generally pebbles of all colors. Then he smeared a wall with lime and drew a human being in outline . . . and then fastened some of these pebbles in the drawn face, others in the hands, others elsewhere, and he completed the drawing of the human being there represented by means of pebbles equal to the units which he declared define human being. As a result of this procedure he would state that just as the particular sketched human being is composed of, say, 250 pebbles, so a real human being is defined by so many units.
(Alexander of Aphrodisias, *Commentary on Aristotle's Metaphysics* 827.9–19)

16. (58B4) In numbers they [Pythagoreans] thought they observed many resemblances to the things that are and that come to be . . . such and such an attribute of numbers being justice, another being soul and intellect, another being decisive moment, and similarly for virtually all other things . . . since all other things seemed to be made in the likeness of numbers in their entire nature.
(Aristotle, *Metaphysics* 1.5 985b28–33)

13. DIOGENES OF APOLLONIA

Theophrastus says that Diogenes of Apollonia was perhaps the last of the
physiologoi, the early Greek thinkers who concentrated on theories of the
natural world, the line of which began with Thales and the other Milesians. There
were several Apollonias in the ancient world, and it is most likely that Diogenes
came from the Apollonia on the Black Sea, which was a colony of Miletus;
Anaximander was connected with its founding. The best evidence suggests that
Diogenes was active after around 440 BCE; this makes him a contemporary of
Melissus and probably Anaxagoras, whose theories he seems to have known. He
lived at about the same time as Leucippus, although there is little evidence that he
was aware of Atomism. There are references to his work in the plays of the
Athenians Euripides and Aristophanes, and in Plato's Phaedo. *Nothing certain*
is known of his life, although his interest in the role of the brain in perception and
his studies of the veins suggest that he had an interest in medicine and was
perhaps a physician as well as a physicist. Simplicius in the sixth century CE had
seen a copy of Diogenes' book called On Nature, *and Simplicius suggests that*
Diogenes may have written at least three other books as well. Diogenes adopts
material monism: There is a single basic stuff, air, which undergoes alteration,
through the mechanism of condensation and rarefaction, to become all the other
elements of the cosmos; everything is a form of air. In fragment 2 (B2) he argues
for monism and against metaphysical pluralism. He also argues that air is
intelligent and divine. Thus, his cosmos is infused with intelligence and divinity;
the degree of intelligence anything has is determined by the comparative warmth
of its internal air. Diogenes wrote in prose, and his plain clear style (perhaps
influenced by Anaxagoras) makes his work more accessible to students of
philosophy and science than that of some of his Presocratic predecessors. Long
underestimated by scholars, Diogenes is now receiving more serious attention
than in the past.

1. (64B1) In my opinion, a person beginning any discourse must present
   a starting point that is indisputable and an explanation [or, "style"]
   that is simple and serious.

   (Diogenes Laertius, *Lives of the Philosophers* 9.57)[45]

2. (B2) [In *On Nature*, the only one of his works that has come into my
   hands, he proposes to give many proofs that in the principle he posits
   there is much intelligence. Immediately after the introduction he
   writes the following.][46] In my opinion, to sum it all up, all things that

45. Translator's note: Diogenes Laertius, who quotes this fragment, says that it
was the beginning of Diogenes' book.
46. B2–B5 are quoted by Simplicius in his *Commentary on Aristotle's Physics* 151.28–
153.17; some of Simplicius' comments are included in square brackets in the translations given here.

are are differentiated forms of the same thing and are the same thing. And this is manifest. For if the things that are now in this *kosmos*—earth, water, air, fire, and all the rest that are seen to exist in this *kosmos*—if any one of these were different from another, being different in its own nature, and if it were not the case that, being the same thing, it changed and was differentiated in many ways, they could not mix with each other in any way nor could help or harm come to one from another, nor could a plant grow from the earth nor an animal or anything else come to be, unless they were so constituted as to be the same thing. But all these things, being differentiated out of the same thing, come to be different things at different times and return into the same thing.

(Simplicius, *Commentary on Aristotle's Physics* 151.28–152.7)

3. (B3) [In what follows he shows that in this principle there is much intelligence.] For without intelligence it [the "same thing" in fragment 2] could not be distributed in such a way as to have the measures of all things—winter and summer, night and day, rains and winds and good weather. If anyone wants to think about the other things too, he would find that as they are arranged, they are as good as possible.

(Simplicius, *Commentary on Aristotle's Physics* 152.10–16)

4. (B4) [He continues as follows, saying that men and the other animals live and have soul and intelligence from this principle, which is air.] Moreover, in addition to the preceding indications, the following, too, are important. Humans and animals live by means of air through breathing. And this [air] is both soul and intelligence for them, as will be displayed manifestly in this book. And if this departs, they die and their intelligence fails.

(Simplicius, *Commentary on Aristotle's Physics* 152.15–21)

5. (B5) [Then, a little later he continues clearly.] And in my opinion, that which possesses intelligence is what people call air, and all humans are governed by it and it rules all things. For in my opinion this very thing is god, and it reaches everything and arranges all things and is in everything. And there is no single thing that does not share in this. But no single thing shares in it in the same way as anything else, but there are many forms both of air itself and of intelligence. For it is multiform—hotter and colder, drier and wetter, more stable and possessing a sharper movement, and unlimitedly many other alterations are in it, both of flavor and of color. And the soul of all animals is the same thing, air hotter than the air outside in which we are located, but much colder than the air near the sun. This heat is not identical in any two animals, since it is not identical even in any two humans, but it differs—not greatly, but so that they are similar. Moreover, it is impos-

sible for any of the things that are being differentiated to be exactly like one another without becoming the same thing. Now since the differentiation is multiform, also the animals are multiform and many and are like one another in neither shape nor way of life nor intelligence, on account of the large number of their differentiations. Nevertheless, all things live, see, and hear by means of the same thing, and all get the rest of their intelligence from the same thing.

(Simplicius, *Commentary on Aristotle's Physics* 152.21–153.13)

6. (B6) [And next he shows that the sperm of animals has the form of air, and thoughts come into being when air occupies the whole body through the veins, together with blood. In the course of this discussion he gives an accurate anatomy of the veins. In these words he is clearly seen to say that the principle is what people call air.]

This is an account of the blood vessels in humans. There are two very large ones. These run through the belly alongside the backbone, one on the right side and one on the left. Each goes toward the leg on the same side, and up toward the head alongside the collar bone through the throat. From these, blood vessels extend through the entire body, from the vessel on the right to the parts on the right, and from the vessel on the left to the parts on the left. The largest two go next to the backbone to the heart, and others, a little higher up, go through the chest under the armpit to the hand on the same side. One of them is called the splenetic vessel, the other the hepatic. Each of them is divided at the extremity, one part going to the thumb, the other to the palm, and from these, tiny vessels with many branches go to the rest of the hand and to the fingers. Other tinier vessels extend from the first vessels—from the one on the right side, to the liver, from the one on the left side, to the spleen and kidneys. The vessels that go to the legs branch at the junction of the legs and run through the entire length of the thigh and are visibly thick. Another one runs inside the thigh and is smaller and less thick than the other. Then they go next to the knee, to the shin and the foot in the same way as the ones that go to the hands, and they arrive at the sole of the foot, and from there they divide and go to the toes. Many tiny vessels branch off from them in the belly and ribs. Some go to the head through the throat and are visibly large in the neck. Many others branch off from the end of each of them and go to the head, some crossing from the right side to the left, and others from the left side to the right. They end at each ear. On each side there is another vessel in the neck next to the large vessel, a little smaller than it, to which most of the vessels that come from the head are connected. These too go through the throat on the inside, and from each of them others go under the shoulder blade to the hands, and they are visible next to the splenetic and hepatic vessels and other vessels that are a little smaller. These are the ones that [physicians] lance when there is pain under the skin. If there is pain in the region of the belly, they lance the hepatic and the splenetic vessels. Others begin from these and go to the breasts. There are others, tiny ones, that go from each of these through the spinal marrow to the testicles. Others go under the skin, through the flesh, to the kidneys and end at the testicles in men and in women at the uterus. The vessels from the belly are at first wider, and then they become narrower until they cross from right to left and from left to right. These are called the spermatic vessels. The thickest blood is absorbed by the fleshy parts of the body; the excess goes to these regions [the genital organs] and becomes thin, hot, and foamy.   (Aristotle, *History of Animals* 3.2 511b30–512b11)

7. (B7) And this very thing [air] is an eternal and immortal body, and by means of it some things come to be and others pass away.
   (Simplicius, *Commentary on Aristotle's Physics* 153.19–20)

8. (B8) But this seems clear to me, that it [air] is large and strong and eternal and immortal and knowing many things.
   (Simplicius, *Commentary on Aristotle's Physics* 153.20–21)

9. (A1) Air is the element. There are infinite *kosmoi* and infinite void. The air, by being condensed and rarefied, is generative of the *kosmoi*. Nothing comes to be from or perishes into what-is-not. The earth is round and is supported in the center [of the *kosmos*] and has undergone its process of formation through the rotation resulting from the hot and the solidification caused by the cold.
   (Diogenes Laertius, *Lives of the Philosophers* 9.57)

10. (A6) All things are in motion and there are infinite *kosmoi*. His account of cosmogony is the following: The whole is in motion and comes to be rare in one place, dense in another. Where the dense part chanced to come together it formed the earth by revolving, and the other things in the same way. The lightest things occupied the highest location and produced the sun.   (Pseudo-Plutarch, *Miscellanies* 12)

11. (A19) Diogenes attributes the senses, as well as life and thought, to air. . . . The sense of smell is due to the air around the brain. . . . Hearing occurs when the air in the ears is set in motion by the air outside and is passed on toward the brain. Sight occurs when things are reflected in the pupil, and the reflection, being mixed with the air inside, produces sensation. Evidence of this is the fact that if the veins [in the eyes] become inflamed, it [the reflection?] is not mixed with the air inside and we do not see, although the reflection is there just the

same. Taste occurs in the tongue because of its rare and soft nature. Concerning touch he declared nothing, neither its functioning nor its objects. . . . The interior air, which is a small part of god, is what perceives. Evidence of this is that often when we have our mind on other matters we neither see nor hear. Pleasure and pain arise in the following manner: pleasure whenever a large amount of air is mixed with the blood and makes it light, being in accordance with its nature and penetrating the whole body; and pain whenever the air is contrary to its nature and is not mixed, and the blood coagulates and becomes weaker and denser. Similarly also boldness and health and the opposites. . . . Thought, as was said, is due to air that is pure and dry. For moisture hinders the mind. For this reason thought is diminished when we are asleep, drunk, or full. . . . This is why children are foolish. . . . They are also prone to anger and in general easily roused and changeable because air, which is great in quantity, is separated by small intervals. This is also the cause of forgetfulness: When the air does not go through the entire body, people cannot comprehend.

(Theophrastus, *On Sensation* 39–45)

14. THE SOPHISTS

From the time of Homer onward Greek writers were concerned with questions about the best way of life for a human being and just what virtues or excellences a good person needed to cultivate. Herodotus and other early historians had also provided information about other cultures and their social and political systems and compared these with the Greeks. Yet it was primarily in the fifth century BCE that theories about moral, political, and social questions began to be developed. It was primarily the Sophists who raised and discussed these issues, although as we have seen, some of the Presocratic philosophers were also participants in these debates. Most of the Sophists were professional teachers and rhetoricians, but some active politicians in Athens came to be considered Sophists, and although they did not form a single school or group, there were enough similarities in their activities and viewpoints for them to be considered together. The word "sophist" has its roots in sophos *meaning "wise," and, in its earliest uses, someone who was a* sophistēs *was a master in his craft or an expert. In general, the Sophists can be considered as practitioners and teachers of wisdom. This obviously raises the question, "What is wisdom?" and the Sophists aimed to answer that question, as well as questions about the other excellences or virtues needed by a successful citizen of a Greek city-state, or* polis. *Travelling throughout Greece, teaching, giving rhetorical displays, and competing with one another for paying students and audiences, the Sophists were a major part of social and intellectual life, for the questions they raised were fundamental to life in a Greek* polis.

Our information about the Sophists comes mainly from Plato, who was not an impartial witness. Like Socrates, his intellectual hero, Plato was suspicious of sophistic teaching and claims to knowledge, and was scandalized by the fact that the Sophists charged for their teaching and would take on any pupil who could afford the price. Many of Plato's dialogues show Socrates demonstrating that one Sophist or another fails to understand his own views or the nature of the wisdom that the Sophist purports to teach. In his writings, Plato explicitly contrasts Socrates, the independent lover of wisdom (the philosophos) with the mere expert technician (the sophistēs) who pleases crowds rather than searching seriously for the truth. We should be wary of accepting Plato's views uncritically; and we should treat his evidence about the Sophists—in such dialogues as Protagoras, Gorgias, and the two named after Hippias—with great care.

The Sophists included here are representative of the movement and its methods; there are short claims illustrating views about knowledge and some longer speeches. The texts given here show that a sharp distinction between the philosophers and the Sophists may be untenable.

14.1. Protagoras

Protagoras was perhaps the most famous of the early Sophists. He was born in Abdera (home of Democritus as well) around 490 BCE and died about 420. He was often in Athens and part of the circle around Pericles (one wonders if he knew Anaxagoras), but he was also very well known in the western Greek cities of Sicily and Southern Italy. Plato's dialogue Protagoras presents an unforgettable (if perhaps not entirely trustworthy) picture of the excitement that Protagoras could generate.

1. (80A5) [Protagoras on what he teaches and the value of his teachings.] My boy, if you associate with me, the result will be that the very day you begin you will return home a better person, and the same will happen the next day too. Each day you will make constant progress toward being better. . . . [Protagoras teaches a young man] Good counsel concerning his personal affairs, so that he may best manage his own household, and also concerning the city's affairs, so that as far as the city's affairs go he may be most powerful in acting and in speaking.   (Plato, Protagoras 318a, 318e–319a)

2. (80B3) Teaching requires nature and training. . . . Learning must begin at an early age.   (Anecdota Parisiensia I 171, 31)

3. (80B10) Art (tekhnē) without practice and practice without art are nothing.   (Stobaeus, Selections 3.29.80)

4. (80B11) Education is not implanted in the soul unless one reaches a greater depth.   (Pseudo-Plutarch, On Training 178.25)

5. (80B4) Concerning the gods I am unable to know either that they are or that they are not or what their appearance is like. For many are the things that hinder knowledge: the obscurity of the matter and the shortness of human life.   (Eusebius, *Preparation of the Gospel* 14.3.7)

6. (80B7) [It is not true that geometry studies perceptible magnitudes . . .] For perceptible lines are not the kind of things the geometer talks about, since no perceptible thing is straight or curved in that way, nor is a circle tangent to a ruler at a point, but the way Protagoras used to say in refuting the geometers.   (Aristotle, *Metaphysics* 3.2 997b34–998a4)

7. Protagoras says of mathematics, the subject matter is unknowable and the terminology distasteful.
(Philodemus of Gadara, *On Poetry* P.Herc. 1676, col. 1.12–13; not in DK)

8. (80B1) A person is the measure of all things—of things that are, that they are, and of things that are not, that they are not.
(Sextus Empiricus, *Against the Mathematicians* 7.60)

9. (80A1) He was the first to use in dialectic the argument of Antisthenes that attempts to prove that contradiction is impossible.
(Diogenes Laertius, *Lives of the Philosophers* 9.53)

10. (80A1) Protagoras was the first to declare that there are two mutually opposed arguments on any subject.
(Diogenes Laertius, *Lives of the Philosophers* 9.51)

11. (80A21) Protagoras made the weaker and stronger argument and taught his students to blame and praise the same person.
(Stephanus of Byzantium, s.v. *Abdera*)

12. (80A21) [Aristotle on Protagoras' method.] This is making the weaker argument stronger. And people were rightly annoyed at Protagoras' promise.   (Aristotle, *Rhetoric* 2.24 1402a24–26)

What follows is an extract from the anonymous Dissoi Logoi *(Twofold* Arguments *or* Contrasting Arguments*), a sample collection of arguments for and against various claims, such as for and against Good and Bad, Truth and Falsity, Just and Unjust, and so on. It gives a sample of the sorts of arguments Protagoras or another Sophist might give.*

13. (90, 4) (1) Twofold arguments are also stated concerning the false and the true, of which one declares that true *logos* [speech, statement] and false *logos* are different from one another, and others that they are the

same. (2) And I say the following. First, that true and false *logos* are expressed in the same words. Second, when a *logos* is spoken, if events have occurred the way the *logos* is spoken, the *logos* is true, but if they have not occurred, the same *logos* is false. (3) Suppose it accuses someone of sacrilege. If the deed took place, the *logos* is true, but if it did not take place, it is false. And the *logos* of the defendant is the same. And the courts judge the same *logos* to be both false and true. (4) Next, if we are seated one next to the other, and we [each] say "I am an initiate of the mysteries," we will all say the same thing, but only I will be truthful, since in fact I am <the only> one <who is>. (5) Now it is obvious that the same *logos* is false whenever falsehood is present to it and true whenever truth is, in the same way a person is the same individual as a boy and as a youth and as an adult and as an old man. (6) It is also stated that false *logos* and true *logos* are different from one another, differing in name just as they differ in fact. For if anyone asks those who say that the same *logos* is both false and true which of the two [namely, false and true] the *logos* that they are stating is, then if it is false, clearly they [the true *logos* and the false *logos*] are two [and therefore not the same]. But if it is true, this same *logos* is also false. And if anyone has ever spoken or borne witness of things that are true, it follows that these same things are false. And if he knows any man to be true, also he knows the same man to be false. (7) As a result of the argument they say these things because if the thing occurred the *logos* is true, but if it did not then it is false. Therefore it is not their name that differs, but the fact of the matter. (8) Moreover, if anyone should ask the jurors what they are judging (since they are not present at the events), (9) these people too agree that the *logos* with which falsehood is mixed is false, and that with which truth is mixed is true. This is the entire difference.   (*Dissoi Logoi* 90.4)

14.2. Gorgias

Gorgias of Leontini in Sicily was a contemporary of Protagoras and was also born around 490 BCE; there are reports that he was well over 100 years old when he died. As well-known as Protagoras, Gorgias described himself as a teacher of rhetoric, and it appears that his formal and elaborate writing style was influential. He came to Athens on a diplomatic mission in 427 and was famous for his speeches, which he would give in public displays, some of which survive, and two of which are included below. One, a defense of Helen of Troy, explores the power of persuasion through rhetoric. The other, a fascinating response to (or parody of?) Eleatic metaphysics is called On Nature, or, On What Is Not. *This essay, written in the 440s and so contemporary with Melissus, influenced later philosophers, including Plato, and so it is given in full here.*

14. (82B11) *Praise of Helen* [in part]

(5) I will set forth the reasons for which it was likely that Helen's voyage to Troy took place. (6) She did what she did through the will of Fate and the designs of the gods and decrees of Necessity or because she was taken by force, persuaded by words (*logoi*), or conquered by Love. . . . (8) Not even if speech (*logos*) persuaded and deceived her soul, is it hard to make a defense against this charge and free her from blame, as follows. *Logos* is a powerful master, which by means of the smallest and most invisible body accomplishes most divine deeds. For it can put an end to fear, remove grief, instill joy, and increase pity. I will prove how this is so. (9) But it is to the opinion of my audience that I must prove it. I both consider and define all poetry to be speech (*logos*) with meter. Those who hear it are overcome with fearful shuddering, tearful pity, and mournful yearning, and over the good fortunes and ill-farings of other people and their affairs the soul experiences a feeling of its own, through the words (*logoi*). Come now, let me shift from one argument (*logos*) to another. (10) Inspired incantations bring on pleasure and bring away grief through words (*logoi*). For conversing with the soul's opinion the power of incantation charms, persuades, and changes it by witchcraft. Two arts of witchcraft and magic have been discovered—errors of the soul and deceptions of opinion. (11) All who have persuaded or who persuade anyone of anything do so by fashioning false *logos*. For if on all subjects everyone had memory of the past, <a conception> of the present, and foreknowledge of the future, *logos* would not be similarly similar as it is for people who, as things are, cannot easily remember the past, consider the present, or divine the future. Thus, on most matters, most people make opinion an adviser to their soul. But opinion is fallible and uncertain and involves those who make use of it in fallible and uncertain successes. (12) What, then, keeps us from supposing that Helen too, against her will, came under the influence of *logoi* just as if she had been taken by the force of mighty men? For it was possible to see how persuasion prevails, which lacks the appearance of necessity but has the same power.[47] For *logos*, which persuaded, compelled the soul, which it persuaded, both to believe what was said and to approve what was done. Therefore, the one who persuaded, since he compelled, is unjust, and the one who was persuaded, since she was compelled by *logos*, is wrongly blamed. (13) As to the fact that persuasion added to *logos* makes whatever impression it likes on the soul, one should attend first to the accounts (*logoi*) of the astronomers, who replace one opinion with another and so make things incredible and

47. Translator's note: The text of this sentence is corrupt. I follow Diels' suggestions (DK vol. 2, p. 291).

unclear seem apparent to the eyes of opinion; second, to compulsory competitions that use speeches (*logoi*) in which a single *logos* written with art (*tekhnē*) but not spoken with truth delights and persuades a large crowd; and third, to contests of philosophers' accounts (*logoi*), in which is revealed how easily the swiftness of thought makes our confidence in our opinion change. (14) The power of *logos* has the same relation (*logos*) to the order of the soul as the order of drugs has to the nature of bodies. For as different drugs expel different humors from the body, and some put an end to sickness and others to life, so some *logoi* cause grief, others joy, some fear, others render their hearers bold, and still others drug and bewitch the soul through an evil persuasion. (15) It has been stated that if she was persuaded by *logos* she did not do wrong but was unfortunate. . . . (21) By my account (*logos*) I have removed ill fame from a woman. I have stayed faithful to the rule (*nomos*) I stipulated at the beginning of my *logos*. I have attempted to put an end to the injustice of blame and the ignorance of opinion. I wanted to write the *logos* as a praise of Helen and an entertainment for myself.

15. (82B3)[48]*On What Is Not or On Nature*
(66) He concludes as follows that nothing is: if <something> is, either what-is is or what-is-not <is>, or both what-is and what-is-not <are>. But it is the case neither that what-is is, as he will show, nor that what-is-not is, as he will justify, nor that both what-is and what-is-not are, as he will teach this too. Therefore, it is not the case that anything is.

(67) And in fact, what-is-not is not. For if what-is-not is, it will be and not be at the same time. For in that it is considered as not being, it will not be, but in that it *is* not being, on the other hand, it will be. But it is completely absurd for something to be and not be at the same time. Therefore, it is not the case that what-is-not is.

And differently: if what-is-not is, what-is will not be, since they are opposites, and if being is an attribute of what-is-not, not-being will be an attribute of what-is. But it is certainly not the case that what what-is is not, and so neither will what-is-not be.

(68) Further, neither is it the case that what-is is. For if what-is is, it is either eternal or generated or eternal and generated at the same time. But it is neither eternal nor generated nor both, as we will show. Therefore it is not the case that what-is is. For if what-is is eternal (we must begin at this point), it does not have any beginning. (69) For everything that comes to be has some beginning, but what is eternal,

---

48. Translator's note: This is a translation of the version in Sextus Empiricus, *Against the Mathematicians* 7.65–86 = DK 82B3. The shorter summary in pseudo–Aristotle, *On Melissus, Xenophanes, and Gorgias,* Chs. 5–6 (not in DK), is preferable at some points.

being ungenerated did not have a beginning. But if it does not have a beginning it is unlimited, and if it is unlimited it is nowhere. For if it is anywhere, that in which it is is different from it, and so what-is will no longer be unlimited, since it is enclosed in something. For what encloses is larger than what is enclosed, but nothing is larger than what is unlimited, and so what is unlimited is not anywhere. (70) Further, it is not enclosed in itself, either. For "that in which" and "that in it" will be the same, and what-is will become two, place and body (for "that in which" is place, and "that in it" is body). But this is absurd, so what-is is not in itself, either. And so, if what-is is eternal it is unlimited, but if it is unlimited it is nowhere, and if it is nowhere it is not. So if what-is is eternal, it is not at all.

(71) Further, what-is cannot be generated either. For if it has come to be it did so either from a thing that is or from a thing that is not. But it has come to be neither from what-is (for if it is a thing that is, it has not come to be, but already is), nor from what-is-not (for what-is-not cannot generate anything, since what generates anything must of necessity share in existence). Therefore it is not the case that what-is is generated either. (72) In the same ways, it is not both eternal and generated at the same time. For these exclude one another, and if what-is is eternal it has not come to be, and if it has come to be it is not eternal. So if what-is is neither eternal nor generated nor both together, what-is would not be.

(73) And differently, if it is, it is either one or many. But it is neither one nor many, as will be shown. Therefore it is not the case that what-is is. For if it is one, it is either a quantity or continuous or a magnitude or a body. But whichever of these it is, it is not one, but being a quantity, it will be divided, and if it is continuous it will be cut. Similarly if conceived as a magnitude it will not be indivisible. And if it chances to be a body, it will be three-dimensional, for it will have length, width, and depth. But it is absurd to say that what-is is none of these. Therefore it is not the case that what-is is one. (74) Further, it is not many. For if it is not one it is not many either. For the many is a compound of individual ones, and so since <the thesis that what-is is> one is refuted, <the thesis that what-is is> many is refuted along with it. But it is altogether clear from this that neither what-is nor what-is-not is.

(75) It is easy to conclude that neither is it the case that both of them are, what-is and what-is-not. For if what-is-not is and what-is is, then what-is-not will be the same as what-is as regards being. And for this reason neither of them is. For it is agreed that what-is-not is not, and what-is has been shown to be the same as this. So it too will not be. (76) However, if what-is is the same as what-is-not, it is not possible for both to be. For if both <are>, then they are not the same, and if <they are> the same, then <it is> not <the case that> both <are>. It follows

that nothing is. For if neither what-is is nor what-is-not nor both, and nothing aside from these is conceived of, nothing is.

(77) Next in order is to teach that even if something is, it is unknowable and inconceivable by humans. For if things that are thought of, says Gorgias, are not things-that-are, what-is is not thought of. And reasonably so. For just as if things that are thought of have the attribute of being white, being thought of would be an attribute of white things, so if things that are thought of have the attribute of not being things-that-are, not to be thought of will necessarily be an attribute of things-that-are. (78) This is why the claim that if things that are thought of are not things-that-are, then what-is is not thought of is sound and preserves the sequence of argument. But things that are thought of (for we must assume this) are not things-that-are, as we will show. Therefore it is not the case that what-is is thought of. Further, it is completely clear that things that are thought of are not things-that-are. (79) For if things that are thought of are things-that-are, all things that are thought of are—indeed, however anyone thinks of them. But this is apparently false. For if someone thinks of a person flying or chariots racing in the sea, it is not the case that forthwith a person is flying or chariots racing in the sea. And so, it is not the case that things that are thought of are things-that-are. (80) In addition, if things that are thought of are things-that-are, things-that-are-not will not be thought of. For opposites have opposite attributes, and what-is-not is opposite to what-is. For this reason, if being thought of is an attribute of what-is, not being thought of will assuredly be an attribute of what-is-not. But this is absurd. For Scylla and Chimaera and many things-that-are-not are thought of. Therefore it is not the case that what-is is thought of. (81) And just as things that are seen are called visible because they are seen and things that are heard are called audible because they are heard, and we do not reject visible things because they are not heard or dismiss audible things because they are not seen (for each ought to be judged by its own sense, not by another), so also things that are thought of will be, even if they may not be seen by vision or heard by hearing, because they are grasped by their own criterion. (82) So if someone thinks that chariots race in the sea, even if he does not see them, he ought to believe that there are chariots racing in the sea. But this is absurd. Therefore it is not the case that what-is is thought of and comprehended.

(83) But even if it should be comprehended it cannot be expressed to another. For if things-that-are are visible and audible and generally perceptible and in fact are external objects, and of these the visible are comprehended by vision and the audible by hearing and not vice versa, how can these be communicated to another? (84) For that by which we communicate is *logos*, but *logos* is not the objects, the things-

that-are. Therefore it is not the case that we communicate things-that-are to our neighbors, but *logos*, which is different from the objects. So just as the visible could not become audible and vice versa, thus, since what-is is an external object, it could not become our *logos*. (85) But if it were not *logos*, it would not have been revealed to another. In fact, *logos*, he says, is composed from external things, that is, perceptible things, falling upon us. For from encountering flavor there arises in us the *logos* that is expressed with reference to this quality, and from the incidence on the senses of color arises the *logos* with reference to color. But if so, it is not the *logos* that makes manifest the external <object>, but the external <object> that comes to be communicative of the *logos*. (86) Further, it is not possible to say that *logos* is an object in the way visible and audible things are, so that objects that are can be communicated by it, which is an object that is. For, he says, even if *logos* is an object, it anyway differs from all other objects, and visible bodies differ most from *logos*. For the visible is grasped by one organ, *logos* by another. Therefore it is not the case that *logos* makes manifest the great number of objects, just as they do not reveal the nature of one another.

(Sextus Empiricus, *Against the Mathematicians* 7.65–86)

14.3. Prodicus

Prodicus was born on Ceos, an Aegean island near Attica, around 460 BCE, and probably lived into the fourth century. Growing wealthy from his teaching and speech-giving, he was well-traveled and was an acquaintance of Socrates (in some Platonic dialogues Socrates says that he had been a student of Prodicus; there is disagreement about how seriously to take this claim). Surviving fragments indicate that Prodicus was interested in rhetoric and logic, ethics and virtue, and the origins of religion: he was said to have denied the reality of the gods.

16. There is a reference to the paradoxical view of Prodicus that contradiction is impossible. What does this mean? It goes against everyone's judgment and opinion. For in both practical and intellectual matters we are constantly conversing with people who contradict us. He says dogmatically that contradiction is impossible, because if two people contradict one another they are both speaking, but they cannot both be speaking with reference to the same fact. He says that only the one who speaks the truth is reporting the fact as it is, while the person who contradicts him does not state the fact.

    (Didymus the Blind, *Commentary on Ecclesiastes;* not in DK)

17. (84B5) The ancients believed that the sun and moon, rivers and springs, and in general everything that benefits our life were gods because of the benefit deriving from them.

    (Sextus Empiricus, *Against the Mathematicians* 9.18)

18. He says that the gods worshipped by men neither exist nor have knowledge, but that the ancients exalted crops and everything else that is useful for life.   (P.Herc. 1428 col. 19.12–19; not in DK)

14.4. Hippias

Hippias was born in Elis, near Olympia in the Peloponnese; his birth date is unknown, but he was still living in the year of Socrates' death. He was another wealthy and successful Sophist. Plato makes fun of him as a polymath who can even make his own shoes, and presents him as rather dim-witted, but this is clearly a caricature. Hippias taught rhetoric, including mnemonics, and was interested in mathematics and geometry, where he made an important discovery, as well as in the arts. He was famous both for his rhetorical displays, many given at Olympia during the games, and for his "improvisational sophistry"—making speeches on any subject proposed by a member of his audience. He was also an early historian, compiling a list of Olympic victors, and most significantly, he collected texts of poets and philosophers, thus beginning the tradition of the history of philosophy.

19. (86B6) Some of these things may have been said by Orpheus, some by Musaeus—in short, in different places by different authors—some by Hesiod, Homer, or other poets, and some in prose works by Greeks or foreigners. From all of them I [Hippias] have collected the most important ones that are related, and I will compose out of them this original and multiform account.   (Clement of Alexandria, *Miscellanies* 6.2.15)

20. How can anyone suppose that laws are a serious matter or believe in them, since it often happens that the very people who make them repeal them and substitute and pass others in their place?[49]
(Xenophon, *Memorabilia* 4.4.14; not in DK)

14.5. Antiphon

The Sophist we know as Antiphon is probably Antiphon of Rhamnous. He was thus a native of Attica and a citizen of Athens and so was eligible to hold political office in Athens. Born around 480 BCE, he had wide philosophical and scientific interests, but it is for his views on justice that he is best known. Here he considers the relation between nature (phusis) and law or customs (nomos, pl. nomoi).

49. Translator's note: This passage occurs in conversation with Socrates in a work by Xenophon. How closely it reflects the actual views of Hippias is impossible to say.

21. (87A44a) (1) Justice is a matter of not transgressing what the *nomoi* prescribe in whatever city one is a citizen. A person would make most advantage of justice for himself if he treated the *nomoi* as important in the presence of witnesses and treated the decrees of *phusis* as important when alone and with no witnesses present. For the decrees of *nomoi* are extra additions, those of *phusis* are necessary; those of the *nomoi* are the products of agreement, not of natural growth, whereas those of *phusis* are the products of natural growth, not of agreement. (2) If those who made the agreement do not notice a person transgressing the prescriptions of *nomoi*, he is free from both disgrace and penalty, but not so if they do notice him. But if, contrary to possibility, anyone violates any of the things that are innate by *phusis*, the harm is no less if no one notices and no greater if all observe. For he does not suffer harm as a result of opinion but as a result of truth. . . .

This is the entire purpose of considering these matters—that most of the things that are just according to *nomos* are established in a way that is hostile to *phusis*. For *nomoi* have been established for the eyes as to what they must (3) see and what they must not, and for the ears as to what they must hear and what they must not, and for the tongue as to what it must say and what it must not, and for the hands as to what they must do and what they must not, and for the feet as to where they must go and where they must not, and for the mind as to what it must desire and what it must not. Now the things from which the *nomoi* deter humans are no more in accord with or suited to *phusis* than the things that they promote.

Living and dying are matters of *phusis*, and living results for them from what is advantageous, dying from what is not advantageous. (4) But the advantages that are established by the *nomoi* are bonds on *phusis*, and those established by *phusis* are free.

And so things that cause pain, at least when thought of correctly, do not help *phusis* more than things that give pleasure. Therefore it will not be painful things that are advantageous rather than pleasant things. For things that are truly advantageous must not cause harm but benefit. Now the things that are advantageous by *phusis* are among these. . . .

<But according to *nomos*, those are correct> who defend themselves after suffering (5) and are not first to do wrong, and those who do good to parents who are bad to them, and who permit others to accuse them on oath but do not themselves accuse on oath. You will find many of these cases hostile to *phusis*. They permit people to suffer more pain when less is possible and to have less pleasure when more is possible and to receive injury when it is not necessary.

Now if some assistance came from the *nomoi* for those who submitted to these conditions and some damage to those who do not submit but resist, (6) obedience to the *nomoi* would not be unhelpful. But as things are, it is obvious that the justice that stems from *nomos* is insufficient to aid those who submit. In the first place, it permits the one who suffers to suffer and the wrongdoer to do wrong, and it was not at the time of the wrongdoing able to prevent either the sufferer from suffering or the wrongdoer from doing wrong. And when the case is brought to trial for punishment, there is no special advantage for the one who has suffered over the wrongdoer. For he must persuade the jury that he suffered and that he is able to exact the penalty. And it is open to the wrongdoer to deny it. . . . (7) However convincing the accusation is on behalf of the accuser, the defense can be just as convincing. For victory comes through speech.[50]

(Oxyrhynchus Papyrus XI no. 1364, col. 1, line 6 to col. 7, line 15)

As the passage from Antiphon shows, the question of whether law and morality are grounded in nature or convention was a major subject of debate. Here are two texts that explore that question, the first from Critias, an aristocratic Athenian (related to Plato) and an associate of Socrates, who became one of the Thirty Tyrants after the defeat of Athens by Sparta in 404 BCE. Critias defends nomos *as the source of civilization. Finally, there is a late (for the Presocratic period) anonymous text called the* Anonymus Iamblichi *(usually dated to about 400), which argues that* nomos *is grounded in* phusis.

22. (88B25 lines 1–8) *Critias on nomos*
    There was a time when human life was without order,
    on the level of beasts, and subject to force;
    when there was no reward for the good
    or punishment for the bad.
    And then, I think, humans established
    nomoi as punishers, so that justice would be the mighty ruler
    of all equally and would have violence (*hubris*) as its slave,
    and anyone who did wrong would be punished.
                                (Sextus Empiricus, *Against the Mathematicians* 9.54)

23. (DK89.6 and 7) Selections from *The Anonymous Iamblichi*
    (6.1) No one should set out to maximize his own advantage or suppose that power used for one's advantage is *aretē* [virtue] and obedience to *nomoi* is cowardice. This is the most wicked thought, and it results in everything diametrically opposed to what is good: evil and harm. For if humans were by *phusis* unable to live singly but yielding to necessity came together to live with one another and discovered all their life and their contrivances for living, but it is impossible for them

---

50. Translator's note: The last part of the text is uncertain.

to live with one another and to conduct their lives in the absence of *nomoi* (since that way they would suffer more damage than they would by living alone)—on account of these necessities *nomos* and justice are kings among humans, and in no way can they depart. For they are firmly bound into our *phusis*.

(6.2) If, then, someone were born who had from the beginning the following sort of *phusis*: invulnerable in his flesh, not subject to disease, without feelings, superhuman, and hard as steel in body and soul—perhaps one might have thought that power used for personal advantage would be sufficient for such a person, since such a person could be scot-free even if he did not subject himself to the law (*nomos*). But this person does not think correctly. (6.3) Even if there were such a person, though there could not be, he would survive by being an ally of the laws (*nomoi*) and of justice, strengthening them and using his might for them and for what assists them, but otherwise he could not last. (6.4) For it would seem that all people would become enemies of a person with such a nature [*phunti*, related to *phusis*], and through their own observance of *nomos* and their numbers they would overcome him by craft or force and would prevail. (6.5) So it is obvious that power itself—real power—is preserved through *nomos* and justice.

(7)[51] It is worthwhile to learn these facts about *eunomia* and *anomia*—how big the difference is between them, and that *eunomia* is the best thing both for the community and for the individual, and *anomia* is the worst, for the greatest harm arises immediately from *anomia*. Let us begin by indicating first what results from *eunomia*. (7.1) In the first place, trust arises from *eunomia*, and this benefits all people greatly and is one of the great goods. For as a result of it, money becomes available, and so even if there is little it is sufficient, since it is in circulation, but without it not even a great deal of money would be enough. (7.2) Fortunes and misfortunes in money and life are managed most suitably for people as a result of *eunomia*. For those enjoying good fortune can use it in safety and without danger of plots, while those suffering ill fortune are aided by the fortunate through their mutual dealings and trust, which result from *eunomia*. (7.3) Through *eunomia*, moreover, the time people devote to *pragmata* [a word that can mean "government," "public business," or "troubles"] is idle, but that devoted to the activities of life is productive. (7.4) In *eunomia* people are free from the most unpleasant concern and engage in the most pleasant, since concern about *pragmata* is most unpleasant and

---

51. Translator's note: Here the *Anonymus Iamblichi* contrasts *eunomia* (a condition where the *nomoi* are good and people abide by them) and *anomia* (the opposite of *eunomia*), which the author seems to conceive as a condition in which each person pursues his or her own advantage in competition with others.

concern about one's activities is most pleasant. (7.5) Also when they go to sleep, which is a rest from troubles for people, they go to it without fear and unworried about painful matters, and when they rise from it they have other similar experiences and do not suddenly become fearful. Nor after this very pleasant change [that is, sleep] do they expect the day to bring poverty but they look forward to it without fear directing their concern without grief toward the activities of life, lightening their labors with trust and confident hopes that they will get good things as a result. For all these things *eunomia* is responsible.

(7.6) And war, which is the source of the greatest evils for people, leading as it does to destruction and slavery—this too comes more to those who practice *anomia*, less to those practicing *eunomia*. (7.7) There are many other goods found in *eunomia* that assist life, and also from it comes consolation for our difficulties. These are the evils that come from *anomia*. (7.8) In the first place, people do not have time for their activities and are engaged in the most unpleasant thing—*pragmata*, not activities—and because of mistrust and lack of mutual dealings they hoard money and do not make it available, so it becomes rare even if there is much. (7.9) Ill fortune and good fortune minister to the opposite results [from what occurs under *eunomia*]: good fortune is not safe in *anomia* but is plotted against, and bad fortune is not driven off but is strengthened through mistrust and the absence of mutual dealings. (7.10) War from outside is more frequently brought against a land, and domestic faction comes from the same cause, and if it did not occur earlier it happens then. Also it happens that people are always involved in *pragmata* because of plots that come from one another, which force them to live constantly on guard and to make counterplots against each other. (7.11) When they are awake their thoughts are not pleasant, and when they go to sleep their receptacle [that is, sleep] is not pleasant but full of fear, and their awakening is fearful and frightening and leads a person to sudden memories of his troubles. These and all the previously mentioned evils result from *anomia*.

(7.12) Also tyranny, so great and so foul an evil, arises from nothing else but *anomia*. Some people suppose—all who do not understand correctly—that a tyrant comes from some other source, and that people are deprived of their freedom without being themselves responsible but compelled by the tyrant when he has been established. But they do not consider this correctly. (7.13) For whoever thinks that a king or a tyrant arises from anything else than *anomia* and personal advantage is an idiot. For when everyone turns to evil, this is what happens. For it is impossible for humans to live without *nomoi* and justice. (7.14) So when these two things—*nomos* and justice—are missing from the mass of the people, that is exactly when the guardianship and protection of them passes to a single person. How else could solitary rule be transferred to a single person unless the *nomos* had been driven out that benefited the mass of the people? (7.15) For this man who is going to destroy justice and abolish *nomos*, which is common and advantageous to all, must be made of steel if he intends to strip these things from the mass of the people, he being one and they many. (7.16) But if he is made of flesh and is like the rest, he will not be able to accomplish this, but on the contrary if he reestablishes what is missing, he might rule alone. This is why some people fail to notice this occurring when it does.

(*Anonymus Iamblichi* fr. 6 and 7 = DK 89, 6; Vol. 2 402.21–404.32)

15. THE DERVENI PAPYRUS, COLUMNS IV–XXVI

The Derveni Papyrus was found in 1962, by workers constructing a highway in northern Greece, near the town of Derveni. It is a scroll, partially burnt and otherwise damaged (it was used in a funeral pyre in about 400 BCE), which contains parts of an Orphic poem with a commentary on the poem. Orpheus was a mythological musician and son of Apollo, who went to Hades and returned. Orphism is based on this myth, and the central texts of Orphism were based on material that supposedly went back to Orpheus himself. A fundamental belief was that the soul is immortal and undergoes transmigrations from one body to another. Following the Orphic way of life, after undergoing initiation, was supposed to bring eventual freedom from transmigration and release from punishment after death. The Derveni Papyrus combines an Orphic theogony similar to Hesiod's, along with a naturalizing explanation of the Orphic poem.[52] The author, who is familiar with Presocratic theories, interprets the theogony as an allegorical cosmology, and in doing so quotes Heraclitus and offers explanations that seem to indicate familiarity with Anaxagoras and perhaps Diogenes of Apollonia.

The papyrus contains twenty-six columns of text, all of which are more or less damaged; the first three columns contain practically no legible material, so our text begins with column IV.[53] The author weaves together quotations of parts of the Orphic poem with his commentary.

52. In the Orphic poem, there is first Night, who gives birth to Ouranos [the heavens]. Ouranos rules but is overthrown by Kronos, who is, in turn, overthrown by Zeus. It is Zeus who is responsible for the present state of the cosmos.
52. McKirahan describes it this way: "Imagine a rolled up newspaper partially burned in a fire, whose outer pages are destroyed, as are the top and bottom of the remaining pages, in which the fire, heat, and subsequent handling have created holes of varying sizes" (Philosophy Before Socrates, 2nd edition, p. 430).

Note on the text: McKirahan uses the conventions of three dots and square brackets to indicate gaps in the text. Three dots indicate a gap that he does not attempt to fill. Square brackets indicate supplements that seem likely. Question marks indicate supplements that are less certain. Angle brackets enclose material that is not in the Greek and is added for reasons of style. Parentheses are used for Greek words and English synonyms.

Column IV

. . . In the same way, Heraclitus [? using as evidence] things that are common, [overturns] things that are private, saying like an [? astronomer], "the sun . . . by its nature is the width of a human foot, not exceeding [? in size the limits of its width. Otherwise] the Erinyes, [the ministers of Justice] will find him out. . . .

Column V

. . . for them we enter the oracular shrine to [? inquire], for the sake of those who are seeking oracles, whether it is right. . . . Why do they disbelieve in the terrors of Hades? Since they do not understand dreams or any of the other things, what examples would be the grounds for their belief? [? For] overcome by error and pleasure as well they [neither] learn [nor] believe. Disbelief and failure to understand [? are the same thing. For if] they [neither] learn nor understand [it is not possible that they will believe] even when they see. . . .

Column VI

. . . prayers and sacrifices propitiate the [souls], and [the incantation] of the magi is able to remove the divinities that are in the way; divinities that are in the way [? are the enemies of souls]. For this reason the magi [perform] the sacrifice as if they are paying a penalty. On the offerings they pour water and milk, and from these they also make libations to the dead. They offer countless round knobby cakes because the souls too are countless. Initiates make a preliminary sacrifice to the Eumenides in the same way as the magi do, for the Eumenides are souls. On account of these things anyone who is going to sacrifice to the gods first [? must sacrifice] a bird. . . .

Column VII

. . . a hymn saying sound and lawful things. For [. . .] in the poem, and it is not possible to say [. . .] of words and the things that have been spoken. The poem is [alien] and enigmatic for people. [Orpheus] himself did not want to utter riddles that may be contested, but great matters in riddles. In fact he is narrating a holy discourse from the first word to the last, as [he shows] in the easily understood [verse]. For after bidding them to "put doors on their ears," he says that [he is not legislating for the] many . . . those [pure] in hearing . . .

Column VIII

. . . he shows [in this] verse:

who were born from Zeus, the [exceedingly mighty] king.
And how they begin he shows in this:
When Zeus from his father took the prophesied rule
and the strength in his hands, and the glorious divinity.

It is not noticed that these words are transposed. This is how they should be taken: "When Zeus took the strength from his father and the glorious divinity." When taken this way . . . not that Zeus hears [his father] but that he takes the strength [from him]. If taken [the other way he might seem to have taken the strength] contrary to the prophecies. . . .

Column IX

. . . So he made the [strength] belong to the most powerful just as a son belongs to his father. But those who do not understand what is said think that Zeus takes both the strength and the divinity from his own father. Now knowing that when fire is mixed up with the other things it agitates the things that are and prevents them from combining because of fomentation, he removed it far enough for it not, once it is removed, to prevent the things that are from being compounded. For whatever is kindled is dominated, and when dominated it is mixed with the other things. But regarding the words "he took in his hands," he was speaking in riddles as he was with the other things [? that previously appeared unclear, but which have been understood] with complete certainty. [Speaking in riddles,] then, he said that Zeus [took] by force [the strength and the] divinity just as if . . .

Column X

. . . and speaking; for it is [not] possible to speak without uttering. But he thought that speaking and uttering are the same. Also speaking and teaching mean the same thing. For it is impossible to teach without speaking whatever is taught through speech. Also, teaching is thought to take place through speaking. Therefore teaching was not considered separate from speaking, nor speaking from uttering, but uttering, speaking and teaching [mean] the same. Thus [nothing prevents] "all-uttering" and "teaching all things" from being the same thing. By calling her "nurse" he says in riddles that whatever the sun dissolves [by heating] the night [combines by cooling] . . . whatever the sun heated.

Column XI

. . . of Night. [He says] that she "proclaims oracles from the [innermost shrine (*aduton*)]," intending that the depth of the night is "never setting" (*aduton*). [For] it does not set as the light does, but the sunlight overtakes it as it remains in the same place. Further, "proclaim oracles" and "assist" mean the same thing. But it is important to consider what "assist" and "proclaim oracles" apply to. "Believing that this god proclaims oracles, they come to find out what they should do." [After this] he says:

> [And she] proclaimed all that it was [right] for him [to accomplish]

. . .

Column XII

. . . The next verse goes as follows:

> In order that he might [? rule] on the lovely dwelling place of snow-clad Olympus.

Olympus and time are the same thing. Those who think that Olympus and the heaven are the same are completely mistaken. They do not understand that the heaven cannot be longer rather than wider, but if someone were to call time long he would not be completely mistaken. Whenever he wanted to say "heaven" he added the epithet "wide," while whenever <he wanted to say> ["Olympus"] he never <added> "wide," [but "long"]. By saying that it is "snow-clad" he virtually [? likens time to what is] snowy; what is snowy [? is cold and] white . . .

Column XIII

When Zeus, having heard the prophecies from his father.
For he did not hear this, but it has been shown in what way he heard. Nor does Night give orders, but he makes it clear by saying as follows:

> He swallowed the genital organ, who was first to spring out of the Aithēr.

Because in all his poetry he is speaking in riddles about things, it is necessary to discuss each word individually. Seeing that people believe that generation depends on the [genital organs] and that without the genital organs there is [no] coming to be, he used this <word>, likening the sun to a genital organ, since without the sun it would be impossible for the things that are to come to be as they are. . . .

Column XIV

. . . spring out of the brightest and hottest, which had been separated from himself. So he says that this Kronos was born to Helios (Sun) and Gē (Earth), because it was through the sun that he <Kronos> was the cause of their <the things that are> striking against one another. This is why he says, "who did a great deed."
And the next verse,

Ouranos (Heaven), son of Evening, who was the first of all to reign.

Mind that strikes (*krouonta*) <the things that are> against one another he named Kronos and says that he did a great deed to Ouranos, since he deprived him of the kingship. He named him Kronos from his deed and <he named> the other things according to the [same] principle. For when all the things that are [? were not yet being struck, Mind,] as [? defining (*horizōn*)] nature, [? received the designation Ouranos. He says that he] was deprived [of his kingship] when the things that are [? were being struck].

Column XV

. . . [? in order to prevent the heat from] striking them <the things that are> against one another, and [in order to] make the things that are separate for the first time and stand apart from one another. For when the sun was being separated and confined in the middle, <Mind> coagulated them and it holds them fast, both those above the sun and those below. And the next verse:

After him in turn <reigned> Kronos, and then Zeus wise in counsel.

He means something like "from that time is the beginning from which the present rule reigns." It is related [that Mind,] by striking the things that are against one another and setting them apart toward their present reconfiguration, [did] not [make] them become different things, but things with different [qualities]. The words "and then [Zeus wise in counsel" make it clear] that it <Mind> is not different but the same. And he indicates this: "counsel . . . royal honor."

Column XVI

It has been shown [that] he called the sun a [genital organ]. He also says that the things that are now come to be from things that exist:

Of the genital organ of the first born king, on which all
the immortals grew, blessed gods and goddesses,
and rivers and lovely springs, and all other things
that had then been born, and he himself, therefore, came to be alone.
[He is now] king of all things [and will be] in the future.

In these verses he indicates that the things that are existed always and the things that are now come to be from things that exist. As for <the phrase>, "he himself, therefore, came to be alone," in saying this he shows that Mind, being alone, is worth everything [as] if the others were nothing. For without Mind it is not possible for the things that are now to be [? through them]. [Further in the next verse after this he said that Mind] is worth everything:

[? Clearly] Mind and [? the king of all things are the] same thing.

Column XVII

It existed before it was named. Then it was named. For air was a thing that is before the things that are now were formed, and it always will be. For it did not come to be, but it was. Why it was called air has been shown above. It was thought to have come to be because it had been named Zeus, as if it previously were not a thing that is. And he said that this will be "last" because it was named Zeus, and this will continue to be its name until the things that are now are formed into the same state in which they were previously floating as things that are. He [shows] that it is because of this <namely, air> that the things that are came to be such, and, having come to be, [? again] in this. . . . He indicates in the following words:

Zeus is the head, [Zeus the middle], and from Zeus all things [? are fashioned].

Head . . . he speaks in riddles . . . head . . . comes to be the beginning of formation . . . is formed . . .

Column XVIII

. . . and the things moving downward . . . saying . . . that this [earth] and all other things are in the air, being breath. Now Orpheus named this breath Moira [Fate]. Other people commonly say "Moira has spun for them" and "all that Moira has spun will be," speaking correctly but not knowing what either Moira or spinning is. For Orpheus called intelligence Moira, for this appeared to him the most suitable of the names that all people had given, since before it was called Zeus there existed Moira, the intelligence of the god, always and everywhere. But when it had been called Zeus, [it was thought] that he had come to be, even though he existed before without being named. [This is why he says] "Zeus came to be first." . . .

Column XIX

. . . the things that are are called each one after what dominates. According to the same principle all things were called Zeus. For air dominates all things as much as it wishes. In saying "Moira spun" they are saying that the intelligence of Zeus sanctioned the way in which the things that are, the things that come to be, and the things that will be should come to be and be and cease. He likens the air to a king—for among the names that are spoken this appeared to be appropriate to it—saying as follows:

Zeus the king, Zeus the ruler of all, he of the bright thunderbolt.

He says that he is [king] because one [of the authorities <namely, the royal authority>] has power over [? all the others] . . . and accomplishes all things. . . .

Column XX

. . . of people in cities, after performing the sacred rites, they saw. I wonder less that they do not understand. For it is impossible to hear what is being said and to learn it at the same time. But people who <have heard the rites> from a person who makes the holy rites his craft deserve to be wondered at and pitied: wondered at because before they performed the rites they think they will gain knowledge, but after performing them they go away before gaining knowledge, without even asking further questions, as if they had gained knowledge of the things they saw or heard or learned; and pitied because it was not enough that they spent their money in advance, but they go away deprived of their judgment as well. Before performing the rites they hoped that they would gain knowledge, but after performing them they go away deprived even of their hope. . . .

Column XXI

. . . nor the cold to the cold. By saying "jump" he shows that divided up into small pieces, they were moving and jumping in air, and as they were jumping the pieces of each kind were set together with one another. They continued to jump until each of them came to its like. Aphrodite Ourania (Heavenly Aphrodite) and Zeus, "aphrodizing" and jumping, *Peithō* (Persuasion) and *Harmonia* ("joining") are established as names of the same god. A man mingling with a woman is commonly said to aphrodize. Since the things that are now were mingled with one another, <the god> was named Aphrodite, and <he was named> *Peithō* because the things that are yielded to one another; yielding and persuading are the same thing. <He was named> *Harmonia* because he joined many of the things that are to each of them. For they existed previously [too], but were named as coming to be after they were separated apart. . . .

Column XXII

. . . [so] he named all things similarly, in the best way he could, knowing the nature of men, that they do not all have a like <nature> or want the same things. When they have power, each of them says whatever may come to his heart, whatever they may happen to want, never the same things, out of greed, and some things out of ignorance too. Gē (Earth), Mētēr (Mother), Rhea, and Hera are the same; she was called Gē by custom, Mētēr because all things come to be from her, Gē and Gaia according to each person's dialect. She was named Demeter as in Gē Mētēr—a single name from both, because they are the same. It is also said in the Hymns, "Demeter Rhea Gē Mētēr Hestia Dēiō." For she is called Dēiō because she was ravaged (edēiōthē) in the mingling. He will make it clear [. . .] in the verses that she [? is born]. <She is called> Rhea because many and . . . animals grew . . . from her.

Column XXIII

This verse is composed in a way that makes it misleading, and it is unclear to the many, although for those who understand correctly it is very clear that Oceanos is air and air is Zeus. Therefore it was not another Zeus that "contrived" Zeus, but Zeus himself contrived for himself "great strength." But those who do not understand suppose that Oceanos is a river because he added the epithet "wide-flowing." But he indicates his own meaning in customary words that are in current use. For people say that those who have great power "have flowed big." The next <verse>,

He inserted the sinews of silver-eddying Achelous.

[gives] the name Achelous to water. . . .

Column XXIV

. . . are equal measured from the middle, but those that are not circular cannot be equal-limbed. This makes it clear:

which shines for many mortals over the boundless earth.

Someone might suppose that this verse was said in a different sense, namely that if <the moon> is full, the things that are appear more than before it was full. But he does not mean that it is shining, for if this is what he meant he would have said not that it shines "for many" but "for all" at once—both those who work the land and those who sail when it is time for them that they should sail. For if there were no moon, people would not have discovered how to reckon the seasons or the winds . . . and everything else. . . .

Column XXV

. . . and brightness. But those of which the moon <is composed> are the whitest of all, divided according to the same principle, but they are not hot. There are others too now in air floating far from one another, but by day they are invisible because they are dominated by the sun, while at night it is evident that they are. They are dominated on account of their smallness. Each of them floats in necessity in order for them not to come together with one another. Otherwise all that have the same property as those from which the sun was formed would come together in a mass. If the god did not want the things that are now to exist, he would not have made the sun. But he made it the sort and size of thing as is related at the beginning of the account. The following <words> he composes as a blind, [not] wanting everyone to understand. He indicates in the following verse:

[but when the mind] of Zeus [contrived all] deeds.

Column XXVI

. . . "of mother" because Mind is the mother of the other things. "Good" because she is good. He makes it clear in the following verses as well that he means good.

Hermes, son of Maia, messenger, giver of good things.

He also makes it clear in the following:

At Zeus's threshold are placed two jars
of gifts such as they give—one of evils, one of goods.

Those who do not understand the word suppose it is "of his own mother." But if he wanted to show the god "wanting to mingle in love of his own mother," by altering the letters he could have said "of his mother," for in that way it would become "of his own," and he would be her [son].

PLATO

Plato is traditionally thought to have been born in 428 B.C. and to have died
in 347/8. His father, Ariston, was descended—or so legend has it—from
Codrus, the last king of Athens; his mother, Perictione, was related to
Solon, the first architect of the Athenian constitution. His family was
aristocratic and well off. He had two brothers, Glaucon and Adeimantus,
both of whom appear in the *Republic,* and a sister, Potone. While Plato was
still a boy, his father died and his mother married Pyrilampes, a friend of
the great Athenian statesman, Pericles. Thus Plato was no stranger to Athenian political life even from childhood. Because he was eighteen in 409,
when the Peloponnesian war with Sparta was still in progress, he almost
certainly served in the military in that period. He may have served again
around 395, when Athens was involved in the so-called Corinthian war.

Given his social class and family connections it would have been natural
for Plato to take a prominent role in Athenian political life. He did not do
so, however, and in his *Seventh Letter,* written when he was himself over
seventy, he explains why:

As a young man I went through the same experiences as many others.
I thought that as soon as I became my own master, I'd devote myself to
public affairs. Now, it happened that the course of political events gave
me the chance to do just that. The existing constitution came to be
reviled by many people, so that a revolution occurred . . . and thirty
rulers were set up with supreme powers. Some of these happened to be
relatives and friends of mine, and they immediately called on me to
join them, on the assumption that theirs was the sort of work appropriate for someone like me. It's no wonder, since I was a young man,
that my feeling was that they would govern the city by leading it from
an unjust way of life to a just one, and I was intensely interested to see
what would happen. But after a short time, I saw that these men made
the former constitution seem like a golden age by comparison. Among
other things, they sent my aged friend, Socrates, whom I wouldn't
hesitate to call the most just man of his time, along with some others
to fetch one of their fellow citizens by force, so that he could be
executed. Their purpose was to involve Socrates in their activities,

whether he wished it or not. He refused, however, and risked the most
extreme penalties rather than take part in their unholy deeds. When I
saw all this, and other similarly significant things, I withdrew in disgust from the evils then being practiced. Not long after that the Thirty
and their entire constitution were overthrown. Then, once more, but
this time more hesitantly, I was moved by the desire to take part in
public affairs and politics. To be sure, many offenses continued to take
place in those troublesome times as well, and it is hardly surprising
that during these revolutions some people took excessive revenge on
their enemies. But in general the restored democratic exiles exhibited
considerable decency. As it chanced, however, some of those in control
summoned our companion Socrates before the lawcourts and brought
a most unholy charge against him, one that he least of all deserved.
For they charged him with impiety, and the people condemned and put
to death the very man who, on the earlier occasion, when they themselves had the misfortune to be exiles, had refused to take part in the
arrest of one of their friends. . . . The result was that I, who had at
first been full of eagerness for public affairs, when I considered all this
and saw how things were shifting about every which way, at last
became dizzy. I didn't cease to consider ways of improving this particular situation, however, and, indeed, of reforming the whole constitution. But as far as action was concerned, I kept waiting for favorable
moments, and finally saw clearly that the constitutions of all actual
cities are bad, and that their laws are almost beyond redemption without extraordinary resources and luck as well. Hence I was compelled
to say in praise of the true philosophy that it enables us to discern
what is just for a city or an individual in every case, and that the
human race will have no respite from evils until those who are really
and truly philosophers acquire political power or until, through some
divine dispensation, those who rule and have political authority in
cities become real philosophers. (324b–326b)

At the heart of Plato's refusal to participate actively in politics, then, at the
heart of his turn from practical politics to political philosophy and education, we find the enigmatic figure of Socrates (470–399 B.C.).

Many of Socrates' contemporaries (for example, Aristophanes and
Xenophon) wrote about him, but it is exclusively Plato's portrait that we
meet in the following pages. In the *Euthyphro, Apology, Crito,* and *Republic*
Book I this portrait is probably a close approximation to the historical
Socrates. In the *Protagoras* and *Gorgias,* the approximation remains fairly
close, but the Socrates who appears in the *Meno, Phaedo, Symposium, Republic* II–X, *Parmenides,* and other later dialogues is a mouthpiece for Plato's
own doctrines. No doubt the true story is more complex than this—scholars
continue to disagree about how to tell it—but for present purposes the
simple version will suffice.

Philosophy for Socrates seems to have consisted almost entirely in examining people about justice, piety, courage, moderation, wisdom, friendship, and the other conventionally recognized virtues. He is always asking *Ti esti?* or What is it? about each of them. And he seems to presuppose that there are definite, unique answers to these questions, that justice, piety, courage, and the rest are each some definite characteristic—some definite *form*—whose nature can be captured in a unique definition or account (see *Euthyphro* 6d–e).

Socrates' method of examining is the so-called *elenchus*—we see it in operation in *Euthyphro, Crito, Protagoras, Gorgias,* and *Republic* I. The following example from the *Euthyphro* will help clarify its nature. Euthyphro defines piety as what is dear to the gods (7a). Socrates shows him that this is inconsistent with other things he firmly believes. The result is that Euthyphro modifies his original definition—piety is what is dear to *all* the gods (9e). Socrates shows him that this too is inconsistent with other beliefs he has. In the ideal situation, this process continues until a satisfactory definition emerges, one that is not inconsistent with other firmly held beliefs.

Most of the definitions Socrates encounters in the course of his elenctic examinations of others prove unsatisfactory, but a few doctrines do emerge more or less unscathed. Among them are the following four quintessentially Socratic doctrines. (1) The conventionally distinguished virtues—justice, piety, courage, and the rest—are all in fact identical to a single state of the soul, namely, wisdom or knowledge (*Meno* 87d–89a; cf. *Protagoras* selections). (2) Possession of this knowledge is necessary and sufficient for happiness (*Crito* 48b, *Gorgias* 470e, *Republic* 353e–354a). (3) No one ever does what he knows or believes to be other than the best, so that weakness of will, or acting against what one knows or believes to be best, is impossible (*Protagoras* selections). (4) It is better to suffer injustice than to do it (*Apology* 28b, *Gorgias* selection).

The goal of an elenchus is not simply to reach adequate definitions of the virtues or seemingly paradoxical doctrines about weakness of will and virtue, however; it also aims at moral reformation. For Socrates believes that regular elenctic philosophizing—leading the examined life—makes people happier and more virtuous than anything else (see *Apology* 30a, 36c–e, 38a, 41b–c). Perhaps he believes this because he believes that virtue is the very knowledge to which the elenchus leads. In any case, philosophizing is so important for human welfare, on Socrates' view, that he is willing to accept execution rather than give it up (29b–d).

I say "human" welfare advisedly, because one of the most striking facts about Socrates is his willingness to examine pretty well anyone—famous Sophists (Gorgias, Protagoras, Thrasymachus), illustrious generals, poets, politicians, ordinary Greek craftsmen, foreigners, women, even slaves. Everyone, it seems, has what it takes to lead the elenctically examined life and to benefit from leading it. Moreover, he believes that virtue is the same for all of them, Greek and foreigner, man and woman, slave and free. In these respects, he stands in marked contrast not only to the Sophists, who teach only those who can afford to pay, but also to Plato and Aristotle, both of whom have a far more elitist conception of philosophy and a far less egalitarian conception of virtue.

Going hand in hand with the use of the elenchus and the various philosophical doctrines that emerge from it are other Socratic claims and disclaimers that seem to stand in an uneasy and unstable relationship to them:

(1) Socrates presents himself in the *Apology* as someone who questions others about virtue and refutes them by means of an elenchus when they have answered inadequately. He also presents himself, however, as the servant of Apollo, as someone whose divinely inspired mission is not simply to refute people but to get them to care about virtue and their souls above everything else. How are we to reconcile the mission with the means of executing it? How are we to reconcile Socrates' commitment to the elenctic philosophy with his equally strong commitment to Apollonian religion?

(2) In addition to presenting himself as the servant of Apollo, Socrates often makes the disclaimer traditionally captured in the slogan "Socrates knows only that he knows nothing." But as we have seen, he makes a number of other specific claims which strongly suggest that this disclaimer is false or misleading. If he knows nothing, how does he know that virtue is knowledge, and so on? This problem is sharp enough, but it is further sharpened by the very content of these doctrines, for if Socrates' disclaimer of knowledge is sincere and if knowledge is indeed virtue, Socrates must lack not just knowledge but virtue too. Yet he seems to be virtuous and to present himself as such.

(3) Socrates is often characterized as a teacher—indeed, he has been called "the greatest teacher in European history." Yet he denies that he is a teacher, and he makes that denial part of his defense against the charge that he has corrupted the youth (*Apology* 33a–b). Is he lying to save his neck? Is he playing with us and with the jurors? Is he consciously and deliberately seeking martyrdom? Is he implicitly distinguishing elenctic philosophizing from teaching as traditionally conceived?

(4) Many have argued that if Socrates' disclaimers of knowledge and teaching are to be consistent with his possession of the knowledge he disclaims and with his elenctic activities, they must be *ironical*. The problem is to find a plausible role for irony in elenctic examination. That is difficult enough. But these Socratic disclaimers are not just restricted to the elenctic situation; they are also key components of his legal defense. If we resort to irony to solve the problems of Socratic ignorance and teaching, we must, therefore, find a plausible role for irony in that defense.

These four problems help to explain both why it is so difficult to command a clear view of Socrates and why he has fascinated so many different sorts of people for so long, achieving a place in popular thought that few philosophers of any age can equal.

It is obvious from the *Meno, Phaedo, Symposium,* and *Republic* that Plato shares Socrates' preoccupation with ethics, knowledge, and definitions, but it also seems obvious—especially perhaps from the *Republic*—that he soon abandons or significantly modifies Socrates' method of inquiry as well as some of his specific doctrines. After Book I, for example, the elenchus is conspicuous by its absence: "Socrates" stops merely asking questions and begins to give long and complex answers of his own. In Book VII, Plato suggests that the use of the elenchus on or by young people may result in their becoming immoral sensualists (538c ff.). That seems to be one reason why dialectic—which is a descendant of the Socratic elenchus—must be practiced only by mature people who have mastered the mathematical sciences (531d ff.). In Book IV, a subtle argument for the tripartition of the psyche or soul seems in part designed to allow for the possibility of some kinds of weakness of will (439e ff.). But despite these differences, Plato, like Socrates, is absolutely convinced that philosophy holds the key to human virtue and with it the key to human happiness and welfare (see 473c–e, 499a–c).

Socrates was no doubt the most important single influence on Plato, but there were others as well. Aristotle tells us, for example, that Plato was acquainted with the Heraclitean philosopher Cratylus "from his youth" (*Metaphysics* 987a32). Now, Cratylus, like his master Heraclitus, but perhaps carrying his doctrines to yet further extremes, believed that "everything flows," that everything is always changing, always in a state of flux. A similar doctrine is found in *Republic* V, where sensible things and characteristics—things and characteristics perceived by the senses—are described as "rolling around as intermediates between what is not and what purely is" (*Republic* 478a–479d; cf. *Timaeus* 52a). But whether or not this doctrine is a legacy of Cratylus' tutelage, it left Plato with a difficult problem. For if sensible things and characteristics are always in flux, how can justice and the other virtues be stable forms; how can there be fixed answers to Socrates' questions? And if there are no fixed answers to them, how can there be such a thing as ethical knowledge? More generally, if sensible things and characteristics are always in flux, always *becoming,* how can anything actually *be* something definite or determinate? If nothing actually is something definite or determinate, how can one know what anything is? It was reflection on these questions, Aristotle tells us, that led Plato to "separate" the forms from sensible things and characteristics (*Metaphysics* 987a29–b1). The allegories of the Sun, Line, and Cave, which divide reality into the intelligible and the visible (sensible), seem to embody this separation, as does the account of the creation of the universe in the *Timaeus* (especially 51b–e). Just what it amounts to is a matter of dispute; nonetheless, it is clear that Plato thought that it held the solution to the metaphysical and epistemological problems to which flux gives rise.

But, like many proposed solutions to philosophical problems, Plato's raises new problems of its own. If forms really are separate from the world of flux our senses reveal to us, how can we know them? If items in the world of flux really are separate from forms, how can they owe whatever determinate being they have to forms? In the *Meno* and *Phaedo* certainly, and perhaps also in the *Republic,* Plato answers the first of these questions with the so-called theory of recollection: We have knowledge of forms through prenatal direct contact with them; we forget this knowledge when our souls become embodied at birth; then we "recollect" it in this life when our memories are appropriately jogged (for example, when we undergo elenctic examination). In those same dialogues, he answers the second question by saying that items in the world of flux "participate" in forms by resembling them. The allegories of the Line and Cave in the *Republic* constitute his most detailed attempt to explain just how this resemblance is to be understood. But Plato will continue to reinvestigate and worry at these and other aspects of the theory of forms pretty much until the end of his life.

After the death of Socrates, Plato and some other Socratics seem to have taken refuge in Megara with the philosopher, Eucleides, a follower of Parmenides of Elea, whose doctrines are discussed in the Presocratics section of the present book. Eucleides seems to have tried to combine these puzzling doctrines with Socrates' ethical teaching, arguing that god, reason, the virtues, as well as the one unchanging being apparently defended by Parmenides are all identical to the good. The resulting metaphysical views find many echoes in Plato's writings: Things owe not just their knowability but their very being to the form of the good (*Republic* 509b), and forms in general seem to have most of the traits of Parmenidean being (see *Symposium* 211a–d, *Timaeus* 51b–52a).

When Plato was around forty, he may have made another journey away from Athens, this time to Italy and Sicily. It seems likely that he did so in order to visit the Pythagorean philosophers living there, especially the philosopher-statesman Archytas of Tarentum. (Some ancient sources actually list the Pythagorean Philolaus along with Cratylus as one of Plato's teachers.) But whether Plato went to Italy for this purpose or not, his dialogues clearly show the influence of Pythagorean doctrine, with its near-obsessive focus on number and ratio as the key to reality (see *Timaeus* selection). Archytas himself, for example, among many other significant achievements in mathematics and mechanics, discovered the ratios that underlie the relations between the successive notes in the enharmonic, harmonic, and chromatic scales. And one can easily imagine Plato seeing in such achievements the possibility of giving precise definitions in wholly mathematical terms of all characteristics, including such apparently vague and evaluative ones as harmony and disharmony, beauty and ugliness, justice and injustice, good and evil, and the other things of which Socrates sought definitions. Certainly, the *Republic* itself provides strong evidence that Plato thought that forms could not satisfactorily be defined in terms of sensible characteristics, but only in terms of numbers, ratios, and other precise mathematical notions (see 530d–533e).

The emergence to prominence of mathematics and science may seem like a major departure from the early dialogues in which ethics and politics are the near-exclusive focus. But it is also possible to see it as a deeper probing of the problems raised in those dialogues. Ethics and politics remain central, but Plato has become aware that they need to be treated as component parts of a much wider and deeper philosophical theory. The *Republic* offers us a brilliant attempt to articulate that theory, but it is characteristic of Plato's profoundly dialectical cast of mind—revealed in his unwillingness ever to appear as a speaker in his own dialogues—that no sooner has he laid his theory before us than he begins to criticize it. Indeed, some of the most apparently devastating criticisms of his own theory are developed in the *Parmenides*, a dialogue widely held to have been written soon after the *Republic* (see *Parmenides* selection). However, if the *Timaeus* is indeed one of Plato's latest works, as most scholars think it is, then Plato cannot have thought these criticisms to be fatal, since he there makes use of the theory of forms once again, adapting it to new explanatory purposes in cosmology.

From Italy Plato travelled to Sicily, where he made ardent friends with Dion, brother-in-law of the ruling tyrant Dionysius I. Dion became, in effect, Plato's pupil and under his influence came to prefer goodness to the pleasure and luxury with which he was surrounded. Exactly what subsequently transpired in Sicily is unclear, as is the precise length of Plato's stay. There is some reason to believe, however, that Plato was expelled by Dionysius and perhaps even sold into slavery by him, only to be rescued from the slave market by a benevolent stranger. But whatever exactly happened, Plato returned to Athens, bought some land in the precinct of the hero Academus, and there, around 385, founded his famous school, the Academy, which lasted until 529 A.D. With a few interruptions, Plato spent the remainder of his life as director of studies in the Academy (see *Republic* 528b–c).

It is not clear that Plato's school was the first European university—a prize that some would award to schools supposed to predate it on the Ionian coast of Asia Minor (the birthplace of Heraclitus and Herodotus, among others)—but it is the first of which we have any real knowledge, although that knowledge is far from extensive or detailed. Nonetheless, what evidence we do have makes it clear that the Academy was a center of research both in theoretical subjects and also in more practical ones. Metaphysics, epistemology, psychology, ethics, politics, and aesthetics all grew and developed there, as did mathematical science. Eudoxus (who gave a geometrical explanation of the revolutions of the sun, moon, and planets, and developed a general theory of proportion applicable to commensurable and incommensurable magnitudes) studied and taught in the Academy, as did Theaetetus (who developed solid geometry), and Heraclides Ponticus (who discovered the revolution of Venus and Mercury around the Sun)—Aristotle studied there for twenty years. But members of the Academy were also invited by a variety of cities—Arcadia, Pyrrha, Cidus, and Stagira are all mentioned—to help them develop new political constitutions. Thus it would be quite wrong to think that Plato and the other Academicians perpetually had their heads in the clouds. If this were so, they would hardly have been much use to politicians confronting practical constitutional problems.

The mixture of theory and practice—of abstract speculation and more practical application—was, no doubt, part of philosophy from its very founding. (Even for us, indeed, the word "wisdom" continues to connote both the esoteric and the down-to-earth.) But Plato does more, perhaps, than any of his predecessors to convince us that we may have to cast our net very wide and dig very deep—that we may have to understand how *things* in the broadest sense of the term *hang together* in the broadest sense of the term—if we are to obey the Socratic commandment to know ourselves or discover how best to live.

EUTHYPHRO APOLOGY CRITO

In 399 B.C., at the age of seventy, Socrates was brought to trial by Meletus on a writ of impiety. In the Euthyphro, *he is on his way to a preliminary hearing at which he will hear Meletus' formal charges for the first time and at which the official in charge of impiety cases—the King Archon—will determine whether or not there is a case to answer. Appropriately enough, the topic of the dialogue is the nature of piety. The* Apology *is (or purports to be) the speech of defense given at the trial itself. Under examination by Socrates, Meletus identifies his charges as these: Socrates is an atheist, who believes in strange daimonic activities, in the visitations of a* daimonion *or divine voice; he corrupts the youth by teaching these beliefs to them. A majority of the jurors found Socrates guilty of these charges. Athenian law allowed him to propose a counterpenalty to the death penalty demanded by Meletus and required the jury to choose which of them to impose. A yet larger majority of them voted for the death penalty. In the* Crito, *Socrates is in prison awaiting death by hemlock poisoning. Crito wants him to escape; Socrates explains why he cannot. The topic is legal or political obligation.*

EUTHYPHRO

EUTHYPHRO:[1] What's new, Socrates, to make you leave the Lyceum,[2] where you usually spend your time, to spend it here today at the court of

2

Translated by C.D.C. Reeve.

1. Euthyphro was a *mantis,* or prophet (3b9–c5, 3e3), a self-proclaimed authority on Greek religion (4e4–5a2), who takes very literally the stories embodied in its myths (5e3–6b6). If he is the Euthyphro mentioned in Plato's *Cratylus,* he was also interested in language and etymology (396d2–397a2).
2. The Lyceum was one of three great gymnasia outside the city walls of Athens (the others were the Cynosarges and the Academy). Plato's other dialogues also identify it as Socrates' favorite place to hold conversations (*Euthydemus* 271a1; *Symposium* 223d8–12). The Academy was later the site of Plato's own school; the Lyceum was that of Aristotle's.

the King Archon?[3] Surely, *you* don't have some sort of lawsuit before the King, as I do.

SOCRATES: *Athenians* don't call it a lawsuit, Euthyphro, but an indictment.

b   EUTHYPHRO: What? Someone has indicted you, apparently, for I'm not going to accuse *you* of indicting someone else!

SOCRATES: No, I certainly haven't.

EUTHYPHRO: But someone else has indicted you?

SOCRATES: Exactly.

EUTHYPHRO: Who is he?

SOCRATES: I hardly know the man myself, Euthyphro. He's young and unknown, it seems. But I believe his name's Meletus. He belongs to the Pitthean deme—if you recall a Meletus from that deme, with straight hair, not much of a beard, and a slightly hooked nose?

EUTHYPHRO: No, I don't recall him, Socrates. But tell me, what indictment has he brought against you?

c   SOCRATES: What indictment? Not a trivial one, it seems to me. I mean, it's no small thing for a young man to have come to know such an important matter. You see, according to him, he knows how the young men are being corrupted, and who's corrupting them. He's probably a wise man, who's seen that my own ignorance is corrupting his contemporaries, and is coming to accuse me to their mother the city, so to speak. In fact, he seems to me to be the only one who's starting up in politics correctly. For it

d   is correct to take care of the young first, to make them the best possible, just as it's reasonable for a good farmer to take care of the young plants first and all the others afterward. And so Meletus, too, is presumably first

3   weeding out those of us who corrupt the young shoots, as he claims. Then, after that, he'll clearly take care of the older people and bring about the greatest goods, both in number and in quality, for the city. That, at any rate, is the likely outcome of such a start.

EUTHYPHRO: I hope it happens, Socrates, but I'm terribly afraid the opposite may result. You see, by attempting to do an injustice to you, it seems to me he's simply starting out by wronging the city at its very hearth.[4] Tell me, what on earth does he say you're doing that corrupts the young?

b   SOCRATES: Strange things, my excellent friend, at any rate on first

---

3. The nine archons, chosen annually, were the chief public officials in Athens: one was civilian head of state, one was head of the army (*polemarchos*), and six had judicial roles (*thesmothetai*). The King Archon dealt with important religious matters (such as the indictment against Socrates for impiety) and also with homicide (the subject of Euthyphro's indictment). The King's court, or porch (*stoa*), was in the marketplace (*agora*).

4. The reference is to the communal hearth in the Prytaneum (*Apology* 36d7 note), which was the symbolic center of Athens.

hearing: he says I'm an inventor of gods. And because I invent new gods, and don't acknowledge the old ones, he's indicted me for the latter's sake, so he says.

EUTHYPHRO: I understand, Socrates. That's no doubt because you say your daimonic sign comes to you on each occasion. So he has written this indictment against you for making innovations in religious matters and comes before the court to slander you, knowing that such things are easy to misrepresent to the majority of people.[5] Why, they even mock *me* as if I were crazy, when I speak in the Assembly on religious matters and predict the future for them! And yet not one of my predictions has failed to come true. But all the same, they envy anyone like ourselves.[6] We mustn't give them a thought, though. Just meet them head on.

SOCRATES: Yes, my dear Euthyphro, but being mocked is presumably nothing to worry about. Athenians, it seems to me, aren't much concerned if they think someone's clever, so long as he doesn't teach his own wisdom. But if they think he's making other people wise like himself, they get angry, whether out of envy, as you say, or for some other reason.

EUTHYPHRO: As to that, I certainly have no desire to test their attitude toward *me*.

SOCRATES: Don't worry. They probably think you rarely put yourself at other people's disposal, and aren't willing to teach your own wisdom. But I'm afraid they think my love of people makes me tell whatever little I know unreservedly to any man,[7] not only without charging a fee,[8] but even glad to lose money, so long as someone cares to listen to me. So, as I was just saying, if they were going to mock me, as you say they do you, there'd be nothing unpleasant about their spending time in the law court playing around and laughing. But if they're going to be serious, the outcome's unclear, except to you prophets.

EUTHYPHRO: Well, it will probably come to nothing, Socrates, and you'll fight your case satisfactorily, as I think I'll fight mine.

SOCRATES: But now, Euthyphro, what *is* this case of yours? Are you defending or prosecuting?

EUTHYPHRO: Prosecuting.

SOCRATES: Whom?

EUTHYPHRO: Someone I'm again thought to be crazy for prosecuting.

SOCRATES: What's that? Is your prosecution a wild-goose chase?

c

d

e

4

---

5. Five hundred (or 501) of whom will serve on the jury that will eventually try Socrates.

6. That is, people who have the gift of prophecy. Socrates' sign is mantic or prophetic (*Apology* 40a4).

7. See *Apology* 30a3–5.

8. See *Apology* 19d8–20a2, 31a8–c3.

EUTHYPHRO: The goose is long past chasing: he's quite old.

SOCRATES: Who is he?

EUTHYPHRO: My father.

SOCRATES: My good man! Your own *father?*

EUTHYPHRO: Yes, indeed.

SOCRATES: But what's the charge? What's the lawsuit about?

EUTHYPHRO: Murder, Socrates.

SOCRATES: In the name of Heracles![9] Well, Euthyphro, I suppose most
b   people don't know how it can be correct to do this. I mean, I can't imagine
any ordinary person taking that action correctly, but only someone who's
already far advanced in wisdom.

EUTHYPHRO: Yes, by Zeus, Socrates, far advanced indeed.

SOCRATES: Is the man your father killed one of your relatives then? Of
course he must be, mustn't he? You'd hardly be prosecuting him for murder on behalf of a stranger.[10]

EUTHYPHRO: It's ridiculous, Socrates, for you to think it makes any
difference whether the dead man's a stranger or a relative. It's ridiculous
not to see that the sole consideration should be whether the killer killed
justly or not. If he did, let him go, if he didn't, prosecute—if, that is to say,
the killer shares your own hearth and table.[11] For the pollution's the same
c   if you knowingly associate with such a person and don't cleanse yourself
and him by bringing him to justice.

In point of fact, though, the victim was a day laborer[12] of mine, and
when we were farming on Naxos, he worked the land there for us. Well, he
got drunk, became enraged with one of our household slaves, and cut his
throat. So my father tied him hand and foot, threw him in a ditch, and sent
a man here to find out from the official interpreter what should be done. In
the meantime, he ignored and neglected his captive as a murderer, think-
d   ing it mattered nothing if he did die. And that's just what happened:
hunger, cold, and being tied up caused his death before the messenger got
back from the interpreter.

That's precisely why my father and my other relatives are angry with
me: because I'm prosecuting my father for murder on the murderer's

9. Heracles (Hercules) was a hero of legendary strength. His famous labors—
twelve extraordinarily difficult tasks—are alluded to at *Apology* 22a6–8.

10. Normally, the close relatives of the victim took responsibility for prosecuting
his murderer.

11. It is because Euthyphro shares hearth and table with his father—and so risks
being contaminated by the pollution (*miasma*) thought to adhere to murderers—
that he feels especially obliged to prosecute him.

12. A *pelatēs* or *thēs* (15d6) was a free man who worked for his daily hire. He was,
therefore, less a member of Euthyphro's household than even a slave would have
been.

behalf, when my father didn't even kill him, so they claim, and when, even if he definitely did kill him, it's wrong—since the dead man was a murderer—to concern yourself with the victim in that case. You see, it's impious, they say, for a son to prosecute his father for murder. Little *e* do they know, Socrates, about the gods' position on the pious and the impious!

SOCRATES: But, in the name of Zeus, Euthyphro, do you think *you* have such exact knowledge about the positions the gods take, and about the pious and the impious, that in the face of these events, you've no fear of acting impiously yourself in bringing your father to trial?

EUTHYPHRO: I'd be no use at all, Socrates, and Euthyphro would be no different from the majority of people, if I didn't have exact knowledge of 5 all such things.

SOCRATES: So, my excellent Euthyphro, the best thing, it seems, is for me to become your student, and to challenge Meletus on this very point before his case comes to trial, telling him that even in the past I always considered it of great importance to know about religious matters, and that now, when he says I've done wrong through improvising and innovating concerning the gods, I've become your student. Shouldn't I say to him, "Meletus, if *b* you agree that Euthyphro is wise about the gods, you should also regard me as correctly acknowledging them and drop the charge. But if you don't agree, prosecute this teacher of mine rather than me, for corrupting the old men—myself and his own father, me by his teaching, and his father by admonishment and punishment." If he isn't convinced by me, and doesn't drop the charge or prosecute you instead of me, shouldn't I say the same things in court as in my challenge to him?

EUTHYPHRO: Yes, by Zeus, Socrates, and if he tried bringing an indict-ment against *me,* I think I'd soon find his weak spots, and the question in *c* court would very quickly be about him rather than about me.

SOCRATES: I realize that as well as you do, my dear friend, and that's why I'm eager to become your student. I know that this Meletus, as well as others no doubt, pretends not to notice *you* at all, whereas he has seen *me* so sharply and so easily that he has indicted me for impiety.

Now then, in the name of Zeus, tell me what you were just claiming to know so clearly. What sort of thing would you say the holy and the unholy are, whether in cases of murder or of anything else? Or isn't the pious itself the same as itself in every action? And conversely, isn't the impious en-*d* tirely the opposite of the pious? And whatever's going to count as im-pious, isn't it itself similar to itself—doesn't it, as regards impiety, possess one single characteristic?

EUTHYPHRO: Absolutely, Socrates.

SOCRATES: Tell me, then, what do you say the pious and the impious are?

EUTHYPHRO: Very well, I say that what's pious is precisely what I'm doing now: prosecuting those who commit an injustice, such as murder or temple robbery, or those who've done some other such wrong, regardless
e of whether they're one's father or one's mother or anyone else whatever. Not prosecuting them, on the other hand, is what's impious.

Why, Socrates, look at the powerful evidence I have that the law requires this—evidence I've already offered to show other people that such actions are right, that one must not let an impious person go, no matter who he may happen to be. You see, those very people acknowledge Zeus
6 as the best and most just of the gods, and yet they agree that he put his own father in fetters because he unjustly swallowed down his children, and that *he*, in his turn, castrated *his* father because of other similar injustices.[13] Yet they're extremely angry with *me*, because I'm prosecuting *my* father for his injustice. And so they contradict themselves in what they say about the gods and about me.

SOCRATES: Could this be the reason, Euthyphro, I face indictment, that when people say such things about the gods, I find them somehow hard to accept? That, it seems, is why some people will say I'm a wrongdoer. But now if you, who know so much about such matters, share these views, it
b seems that the rest of us must assent to them too. I mean, what can we possibly say in reply, when we admit ourselves that we know nothing about them? But tell me, by the god of friendship, do you really believe those stories are true?

EUTHYPHRO: Yes, and still more amazing things, Socrates, that the majority of people don't know.

SOCRATES: And do you believe that there really is war among the gods? And terrible hostilities and battles, and other such things of the sort the poets relate, and that the good painters embroider on our sacred objects—
c I'm thinking particularly of the robe covered with embroideries of such scenes that's carried up to the Acropolis at the Great Panathenaean festival?[14] Are we to say that these are true, Euthyphro?

EUTHYPHRO: Not only those, Socrates, but as I mentioned just now, I will, if you like, tell you lots of other things about religious matters that I'm sure you'll be amazed to hear.

13. Cronus mutilated his father, Uranus (Sky), by cutting off his genitals when he was copulating with Gaea (Earth). He ate the children he had with his sister Rhea. Aided by her, however, their son Zeus escaped, overthrew Cronus, and fettered him. See Hesiod, *Theogony* 137–210, 456–508.
14. The Acropolis, set on the steep rocky hill that dominates Athens, was the central fortress and principal sanctuary of the goddess Athena. It was the site of the Parthenon, as well as of other temples. The Great Panathenaean festival took place every four years and was a more elaborate version of the yearly festival that marked Athena's birthday. At it, her statue in the Parthenon received a new robe embroidered with scenes from the mythical battle of the gods and the giants.

SOCRATES: I wouldn't be surprised. But tell me about them some other time, when we've the leisure. Now, however, try to answer more clearly the very question I asked before. You see, my friend, you didn't teach me *d* adequately earlier when I asked what the pious was, but you told me that what you're now doing is pious, prosecuting your father for murder.

EUTHYPHRO: Yes, and what I said was true, Socrates.

SOCRATES: Perhaps. But surely, Euthyphro, there are also many other things you call pious.

EUTHYPHRO: Yes, indeed.

SOCRATES: Do you remember, then, that what I urged you to do wasn't to teach me about one or two of the many pieties, but rather about the form itself, by virtue of which all the pieties are pious? You see, you said, I believe, that it was by virtue of one characteristic that the impieties are impious, and the pieties pious. Or don't you remember? *e*

EUTHYPHRO: I do indeed.

SOCRATES: Then teach me what that characteristic itself is, in order that by concentrating on it and using it as a model, I may call pious any action of yours or anyone else's that is such as it, and may deny to be pious whatever isn't such as it.

EUTHYPHRO: If that's what you want, Socrates, that's what I'll tell you.

SOCRATES: That *is* what I want.

EUTHYPHRO: In that case: what's loved by the gods is pious, and what's not loved by the gods is impious. *7*

SOCRATES: Excellent, Euthyphro! You've now given the sort of answer I was looking for. Whether it's true, however, that I don't know. But clearly you'll go on to demonstrate fully that what you say *is* true.

EUTHYPHRO: Yes, indeed.

SOCRATES: Come on, then, let's examine what it is we're saying. A god-loved thing or a god-loved person is pious, whereas a god-hated thing or a god-hated person is impious. And the pious isn't the same as the impious, but its exact opposite. Isn't that what we're saying?

EUTHYPHRO: It is indeed.

SOCRATES: And does it seem to be true?

EUTHYPHRO: It does seem so, Socrates. *b*

SOCRATES: And haven't we also said that the gods quarrel and differ with one another, and that there's mutual hostility among them?

EUTHYPHRO: Indeed, we did say that.

SOCRATES: But what are the issues, my good friend, on which differences produce hostility and anger? Let's examine it this way. If you and I differed about which of two groups was more numerous, would our differences on this issue make us hostile and angry toward one another? Or would we turn to calculation and quickly resolve our differences? *c*

EUTHYPHRO: Of course.

SOCRATES: Again, if we differed about which was larger or smaller, we'd turn to measurement and quickly put a stop to our difference.

EUTHYPHRO: That's right.

SOCRATES: And we'd turn to weighing, I imagine, to settle a dispute about which was heavier or lighter?

EUTHYPHRO: Certainly.

SOCRATES: Then what sorts of issues *would* make us angry and hostile toward one another if we disagreed about them and were unable to reach a settlement? Perhaps you can't say just offhand. But examine, while I'm speaking, whether they're issues about the just and unjust, fine and shameful, good and bad. Whenever we become enemies, aren't these the issues on which disagreement and an inability to reach a settlement make enemies of us—both you and I and all other human beings?

EUTHYPHRO: That is the difference, Socrates, and those are the things it has to do with.

SOCRATES: And what about the *gods,* Euthyphro? If indeed they differ, mustn't it be about those same things?

EUTHYPHRO: Absolutely.

SOCRATES: Then, according to your account, my noble Euthyphro, different sets of gods, too, consider different things to be just, or fine or shameful, or good or bad. For if they didn't differ about these, they wouldn't quarrel, would they?

EUTHYPHRO: That's right.

SOCRATES: Then are the very things that each group of them regards as fine, good, and just also the ones they love, and are the opposites of these the ones they hate?

EUTHYPHRO: Of course.

SOCRATES: But the very same things, so you say, that some gods consider to be just and others unjust are also the ones that lead them to quarrel and war with one another when they have disputes about them. Isn't that right?

EUTHYPHRO: It is.

SOCRATES: Then the same things, it seems, are both hated and loved by the gods, and so the same things would be both god-hated and god-loved.

EUTHYPHRO: It seems that way.

SOCRATES: So, on your account, Euthyphro, the same things would be both pious and impious.

EUTHYPHRO: Apparently.

SOCRATES: So, you haven't answered my question, my excellent friend. You see, I wasn't asking you what the selfsame thing is that's both pious and impious. But a thing that's god-loved is, it seems, also god-hated. It follows, Euthyphro, that it wouldn't be at all surprising if what you're now doing in prosecuting your father was something pleasing to Zeus but displeasing to Cronus and Uranus, or lovable to Hephaestus and displeasing to Hera,[15] and similarly for any other gods who may differ from one another on the matter.

EUTHYPHRO: But, Socrates, I think that on this point, at least, none of the gods do differ—that anyone who has unjustly killed another should be punished.

SOCRATES: Is that so? Well, what about men, Euthyphro? Have you never heard them arguing that someone who has killed unjustly or done anything else unjustly should *not* be punished?

EUTHYPHRO: Why yes, they never stop arguing like that, whether in the law courts or in other places. For people who've committed all sorts of injustices will do or say anything to escape punishment.

SOCRATES: But do they agree, Euthyphro, that they've committed injustice, and, in spite of agreeing, do they still say that they shouldn't be punished?

EUTHYPHRO: No, they certainly don't say that.

SOCRATES: So it isn't just anything that they'll do or say. You see, I don't think they'd dare to say or argue that if they act *unjustly*, they should not be punished. Instead, I think they deny acting unjustly, don't they?

EUTHYPHRO: That's true, they do.

SOCRATES: So they don't argue that someone who acts unjustly should not be punished, though they do, perhaps, argue about *who* acted unjustly, *what* his unjust action consisted of, and *when* he did it.

EUTHYPHRO: That's true.

SOCRATES: Then doesn't the very same thing happen to the gods as well—if indeed they do quarrel about just and unjust actions, as on your account they do, and if one lot says that others have done wrong, and another lot denies it? For surely no one, my excellent friend, whether god or human being, dares to say that one who acts unjustly should not be punished.

EUTHYPHRO: Yes, what you say is true, Socrates, at least the main point.

SOCRATES: I think that men and gods who argue, Euthyphro, if indeed gods really do argue, argue instead about *actions*. It's about some action that they differ, some of them saying that it was done justly, others unjustly. Isn't that so?

EUTHYPHRO: Of course.

SOCRATES: Come then, my dear Euthyphro, and teach me, too, that I may become wiser. A man committed murder while employed as a day laborer and died as a result of being tied up before the master who tied

15. Hephaestus, the god of fire and of blacksmithing, was armor maker to the gods. His mother, Hera, the wife and sister of Zeus, threw Hephaestus off Olympus because he was lame and deformed. This act pleased her, not him. In revenge, Hephaestus made her a throne that held her captive when she sat on it. This act pleased him, not her. Similarly, Cronus cannot have been pleased at being fettered by Zeus (see 6a4 note).

him up found out from the proper authorities what to do about him. What evidence do you have that all the gods consider this man to have been killed unjustly, and that it's right for a *son* to prosecute and denounce his

b   *father* for murder on behalf of such a man? Come, try to give me a clear proof that all gods undoubtedly consider this action to be right. If you can give me adequate proof of that, I'll never stop praising your wisdom.

EUTHYPHRO: But presumably that's no small task, Socrates, though I could of course prove it to you very clearly.

SOCRATES: I understand. You think I'm a slower learner than the jury, since it's clear that you'll prove to *them* that those actions of your father's were unjust and that the gods all hate them.

EUTHYPHRO: I'll prove it to them very clearly, Socrates, provided they'll listen to what I say.

c   SOCRATES: They'll listen all right, provided you seem to speak well. But a thought occurred to me while you were speaking, and I'm still examining it in my own mind: "Suppose Euthyphro so taught me that I became thoroughly convinced that all the gods do consider a death like that to be unjust. What more would I have learned from Euthyphro about what the pious and the impious are? *That action* would indeed be god-hated, so it seems. Yet it became evident just now that the pious and the impious aren't defined by that fact, since it became evident that what's god-hated is also god-loved. So I'll let you off on that point, Euthyphro. If you like, let's suppose that all the gods consider the action unjust, and that they all hate

d   it. Is that, then, the correction we're now making in the account, that what *all* the gods hate is impious while what they *all* love is pious, and that whatever some love and others hate is neither or both? Is that how you'd now like us to define the pious and the impious?

EUTHYPHRO: What's to prevent it, Socrates?

SOCRATES: Nothing on my part, Euthyphro. But you examine your own view, and whether by assuming it you'll most easily teach me what you promised.

e   EUTHYPHRO: All right, I'd say that the pious is what all the gods love, and its opposite, what all the gods hate, is the impious.

SOCRATES: Then aren't we going to examine that in turn, Euthyphro, to see whether what we said is true? Or are we going to let it alone and accept it from ourselves and from others just as it stands? And if someone merely asserts that something is so, are we going to concede that it's so? Or are we going to examine what the speaker says?

EUTHYPHRO: We're going to examine it. However, I for my part think that this time what we said *is* true.

10   SOCRATES: Soon, my good friend, we'll be better able to tell. Consider the following: is the pious loved by the gods because it's pious? Or is it pious because it's loved?

EUTHYPHRO: I don't know what you mean, Socrates.

SOCRATES: All right, I'll try to put it more clearly. We speak of a thing's being carried or carrying, and of its being led or leading, and of being seen or seeing. And you understand that these things are all different from one another and how they differ?

EUTHYPHRO: I think I understand, at any rate.

SOCRATES: Then is there also something that's loved, and is it different from something that's loving?

EUTHYPHRO: Certainly.

SOCRATES: Then tell me whether the carried thing is a carried thing   *b* because it's carried or because of something else.

EUTHYPHRO: No, it's because of that.

SOCRATES: Again, the led thing is so, then, because it's led and the seen thing because it's seen?

EUTHYPHRO: Of course.

SOCRATES: So it's not seen because it's a seen thing; on the contrary, it's a seen thing because it's seen; nor is it because it's a led thing that it's led, rather it's because it's led that it's a led thing; nor is something carried because it's a carried thing, rather it's a carried thing because it's carried. So is what I mean completely clear, Euthyphro? I mean this: if something's changed in some way or affected in some way, it's not changed because it's   *c* a changed thing; rather, it's a changed thing because it's changed. Nor is it affected because it's an affected thing; rather, it's an affected thing because it's affected. Or don't you agree with that?

EUTHYPHRO: I do.

SOCRATES: Then isn't a loved thing, too, either a thing changed or a thing affected by something?

EUTHYPHRO: Of course.

SOCRATES: And so the same holds of it as of our earlier examples: it's not because it's a loved thing that it's loved by those who love it; rather it's because it's loved that it's a loved thing?

EUTHYPHRO: Necessarily.

SOCRATES: Now what are we saying about the pious, Euthyphro? On   *d* your account, isn't it loved by all the gods?

EUTHYPHRO: Yes.

SOCRATES: So is that because it's pious or because of something else?

EUTHYPHRO: No, it's because it's pious.

SOCRATES: So it's loved because it's pious, not pious because it's loved?

EUTHYPHRO: Apparently.

SOCRATES: On the other hand, what's god-loved is loved—that is to say, god-loved—because the gods love it?

EUTHYPHRO: Certainly.

SOCRATES: Then the god-loved is not what's pious, Euthyphro, nor is the pious what's god-loved, as you claim, but one differs from the other.

EUTHYPHRO: How so, Socrates?   *e*

SOCRATES: Because we agreed that the pious is loved because it's pious, not pious because it's loved. Didn't we?

EUTHYPHRO: Yes.

SOCRATES: The god-loved, on the other hand, is so because it is loved by the gods; it's god-loved by the very fact of being loved. But it's not because it's god-loved that it's being loved.

EUTHYPHRO: That's true.

SOCRATES: But if the god-loved and the pious were really the same thing, my dear Euthyphro, then, if the pious were loved because it's pious, what's god-loved would in turn be loved because it's god-loved; and if *11* what's god-loved were god-loved because it was loved by the gods, the pious would in turn be pious because it was loved by them. But, as it is, you can see that the two are related in the opposite way, as things entirely different from one another. For one of them is lovable because it's loved, whereas the other is loved because it's lovable.

And so, Euthyphro, when you're asked what the pious is, it looks as though you don't want to reveal its being to me, but rather to tell me one of its affections—that this happens to the pious, that it's loved by all the gods. What explains it's being loved, however, you still haven't said. So *b* please don't keep it hidden from me, but rather say again from the beginning what it is that explains the pious's being loved by the gods or having some other affection—for we won't disagree about which ones it has. Summon up your enthusiasm, then, and tell me what the pious and the impious are.

EUTHYPHRO: But Socrates, *I* have no way of telling you what I have in mind. For whatever proposals we put forward keep somehow moving around and won't stay put.

SOCRATES: Your proposals, Euthyphro, seem to be the work of my an- *c* cestor, Daedalus! Indeed, if I were to state them and put them forward myself, you might perhaps make a joke of me, and say that it's because of my kinship with him that my works of art in words run away and won't stay put.[16] But, as it is, the proposals are your own. So you need a different joke, since it's for *you* that they won't stay put, as you can see yourself.

EUTHYPHRO: But it seems to me, Socrates, that pretty much the same joke does apply in the case of our definitions. You see, *I'm* not the one who makes them move around and not stay put. Rather, *you* seem to me to *d* be the Daedalus, since as far as I'm concerned they would have stayed put.

16. Daedalus was a legendary sculptor of great skill. His statues were so lifelike that they moved around by themselves just like living things. Socrates' father, Sophroniscus, is alleged to have been a sculptor or stone carver (Diogenes Laertius II.18), and some of the statues on the Acropolis may have been attributed to Socrates himself (Pausanias I.22).

SOCRATES: Then, my friend, it looks as though I've grown cleverer in my area of expertise than my venerated ancestor, in that he made only his own works not stay put, whereas I do this to my own, it seems, and also to other people's. And the most subtle thing about my area of expertise is that I'm wise in it without wanting to be. You see, I'd prefer to have accounts stay put and be immovably established for me than to acquire the wealth of Tantalus[17] and the wisdom of Daedalus combined. But enough of this. *e* Since you seem to me to be getting sated, I'll do my best to help you teach me about the pious—and don't you give up before you do. See whether you don't think that the pious as a whole must be just.

EUTHYPHRO: Yes, I do.

SOCRATES: Then is the just as a whole also pious? Or while the pious as a whole is just, is the just as a whole not pious, but part of it pious and part of *12* it something else?

EUTHYPHRO: I don't follow what you're saying, Socrates.

SOCRATES: And yet you're as much younger as wiser than I. But as I say, your wealth of wisdom has weakened you. Well, pull yourself together, my dear fellow. What I'm saying isn't hard to understand. You see, what I'm saying is just the opposite of what the poet said, who wrote:

With Zeus the maker, who caused all these things to come about,
You will not quarrel, since where there's dread there's shame too.[18]   *b*

I disagree with this poet. Shall I tell you where?

EUTHYPHRO: Of course.

SOCRATES: It doesn't seem to me that "where there's dread there's shame too." For many people seem to me to dread disease and poverty and many other things of that sort, but though they dread them, they feel no shame at what they dread. Or don't you agree?

EUTHYPHRO: Of course.

SOCRATES: But where there's shame, there is also dread. For if anyone feels shame at a certain action—if he's ashamed of it—doesn't he fear, doesn't he dread, a reputation for wickedness at the same time?   *c*

EUTHYPHRO: He certainly does dread it.

SOCRATES: Then it isn't right to say that "where there's dread, there's shame too." But where there's shame there's also dread, even though shame isn't found everywhere there's dread. You see, dread is broader

---

17. Tantalus, son of Zeus, was a legendary king proverbial for his wealth, who enjoyed the privilege of dining with the gods. He killed and cooked his son, Pelops, and mixed pieces of his flesh in with the gods' food to see whether they could detect it. He was punished in Hades by being "tantalized"—any food or water he reached for always eluded his grasp.

18. Author unknown.

than shame, I think. For shame is a part of fear, just as odd is of number. Hence where there's a number, there isn't something odd too, but where there's something odd there is also a number. Do you follow me now at least?

EUTHYPHRO: Of course.

SOCRATES: Well, that's the sort of thing I was asking just now: whenever there's something just, is there also something pious? Or is something just whenever it's pious, but not pious whenever it's just, because the pious is part of the just? Is that what we're to say, or do you disagree?

EUTHYPHRO: No, let's say that, since it seems to me you're right.

SOCRATES: Then consider the next point. If the pious is a part of what's just, we must, it seems, find out what part of the just the pious is. Now if you asked me about one of the things we just mentioned, for example, which part of number is the even—that is to say, what sort of number it is—I'd say that it's any number not indivisible by two, but divisible by it. Or don't you agree?

EUTHYPHRO: Yes, I do.

SOCRATES: Then you try to teach me in the same fashion what part of the just is pious. Then we can tell Meletus not to treat us unjustly any longer or indict us for impiety, since I've now been sufficiently instructed by you about what things are holy or pious and what aren't.

EUTHYPHRO: Well then, it seems to me, Socrates, that the part of the just that's holy or pious is the one concerned with tending to the gods, while the remaining part of the just is concerned with tending to human beings.

SOCRATES: You seem to me to have put that very well, Euthyphro. But I'm still lacking one small piece of information. You see, I don't yet understand this tending you're talking about. You surely don't mean that in just the way that there's tending to other things, there's tending to the gods too. We do speak this way, don't we? We say, for example, that not everyone knows how to tend to horses, but only horse trainers. Isn't that right?

EUTHYPHRO: Of course.

SOCRATES: Because horse training is expertise in tending to horses?

EUTHYPHRO: Yes.

SOCRATES: Nor does everyone know how to tend to dogs, but only dog trainers.

EUTHYPHRO: That's right.

SOCRATES: Because dog training is expertise in tending to dogs.

EUTHYPHRO: Yes.

SOCRATES: And cattle breeding is expertise in tending to cattle.

EUTHYPHRO: Of course.

SOCRATES: Well, but piety or holiness is tending to the gods, Euthyphro? That's what you're saying?

EUTHYPHRO: It is.

SOCRATES: But doesn't all tending accomplish the same end? I mean something like some good or benefit for what's being tended to—as you see that horses tended to by horse trainers are benefited and made better. Or don't you agree that they are?

EUTHYPHRO: Yes, I do.

SOCRATES: And so dogs, of course, are benefited by dog training and cattle by cattle breeding, and similarly for all the others. Or do you think   *c* that tending aims to harm what's being tended?

EUTHYPHRO: No, by Zeus, I don't.

SOCRATES: Rather, it aims to benefit it?

EUTHYPHRO: Certainly.

SOCRATES: Then if piety is tending to the gods, does it benefit the gods and make the gods better? Would you concede that whenever you do something pious, you're making some god better?

EUTHYPHRO: No, by Zeus, I wouldn't.

SOCRATES: No, I didn't think that that was what you meant, Euthyphro—far from it. But it is why I asked what you did mean by tending to the gods, because I didn't think you meant that sort of tending.   *d*

EUTHYPHRO: And you were right, Socrates, since that's not the sort I meant.

SOCRATES: All right. But then what sort of tending to the gods would the pious be?

EUTHYPHRO: The very sort of tending, Socrates, that slaves provide to their masters.

SOCRATES: I understand. Then it would seem to be some sort of service to the gods.

EUTHYPHRO: It is indeed.

SOCRATES: Now could you tell me about service to doctors? What result does that service—insofar as it is service—aim to produce? Don't you think it aims at health?

EUTHYPHRO: I do.

SOCRATES: What about service to shipbuilders? What result does the   *e* service aim to produce?

EUTHYPHRO: Clearly, Socrates, its aim is a ship.

SOCRATES: And in the case of service to builders, I suppose, the aim is a house?

EUTHYPHRO: Yes.

SOCRATES: Then tell me, my good friend, at what result does service to the gods aim? Clearly, you know, since you say you've a finer knowledge of religious matters than any other human being.

EUTHYPHRO: Yes, and what I say is true, Socrates.

SOCRATES: Then tell me, in the name of Zeus, what is that supremely fine result that the gods produce by using our services?

EUTHYPHRO: They produce many fine ones, Socrates.

14 SOCRATES: So too do generals, my friend. Nonetheless, you could easily tell me the main one, which is to produce victory in war, is it not?

EUTHYPHRO: Certainly.

SOCRATES: And farmers, too, I think, produce many fine results. Nonetheless, the main one is to produce food from the earth.

EUTHYPHRO: Of course.

SOCRATES: What, then, about the many fine results that the gods produce? Which is the main one they produce?

b EUTHYPHRO: I told you a moment ago, Socrates, that it's a pretty difficult task to learn the exact truth about all these matters. But to put it simply: if a person knows how to do and say the things that are pleasing to the gods in prayer and sacrifice—those are the ones that are pious. And actions like them preserve both the private welfare of households and the common welfare of the city, whereas those that are the opposite of pleasing are unholy, and they, of course, overturn and destroy everything.

SOCRATES: If you'd wanted to, Euthyphro, you could have put the main point I asked about much more briefly. But you're not eager to teach me—

c that's clear. You see, when you were just now on the point of answering you turned away. If you had given the answer, I'd already have been adequately instructed by you about piety. But as it is, the questioner must follow the one being questioned wherever he leads. Once again, then, what are you saying that the pious, or piety, is? Didn't you say that it was some sort of knowledge of sacrificing and praying?

EUTHYPHRO: Yes, I did.

SOCRATES: And sacrificing is giving to the gods, and praying is asking from them?

EUTHYPHRO: Yes, indeed, Socrates.

SOCRATES: So, on that account, piety would be knowing how to ask

d from the gods and how to give to them.

EUTHYPHRO: You've grasped my meaning perfectly, Socrates.

SOCRATES: Yes, my friend, that's because I really desire your wisdom and apply my mind to it, so that what you say won't fall on barren ground. But tell me, what is this service to the gods? You say it's asking for things from them and giving things to them?

EUTHYPHRO: I do.

SOCRATES: Well then, wouldn't asking in the right way consist of asking for the things we need from them?

EUTHYPHRO: What else could it be?

SOCRATES: And, conversely, giving in the right way would consist of

e giving them, in turn, the things they need from us? For surely giving someone what he didn't at all need isn't something that an expert in the art of giving would do.

EUTHYPHRO: That's true, Socrates.

SOCRATES: Then piety, Euthyphro, would be a sort of expertise in mutual trading between gods and men.

EUTHYPHRO: Yes, trading, if that's what you prefer to call it.

SOCRATES: I don't prefer anything, if it isn't true. But tell me, what benefit do the gods get from the gifts they receive from us? I mean, what they give is clear to everyone, since we possess nothing good that they don't give us. But how are they benefited by what they receive from us? Or do we get so much the better of them in the trade that we receive all our good things from them while they receive nothing from us?

EUTHYPHRO: But Socrates, do you really think gods are benefited by what they receive from us?

SOCRATES: If not, Euthyphro, what could those gifts of ours to gods possibly be?

EUTHYPHRO: What else do you think but honor and reverence and—as I said just now—what's pleasing to them.

SOCRATES: So is the pious pleasing to the gods, Euthyphro, but not beneficial to them or loved by them?

EUTHYPHRO: No, I think that it's in fact the most loved of all.

SOCRATES: So, once again, it seems, the pious is what's loved by the gods.

EUTHYPHRO: Absolutely.

SOCRATES: Well, if you say that, can you wonder that your accounts seem not to stay put but to move around? And will you accuse me of being the Daedalus who makes them move, when you yourself are far more expert than Daedalus in the art of making them move in a circle? Or don't you see that our account has circled back again to the same place? For surely you remember that earlier we discovered the pious and the god-loved are not the same, but different from one another. Or don't you remember that?

EUTHYPHRO: Yes, I do.

SOCRATES: Then don't you realize that you're now saying the pious is what the gods love? And that's the same, isn't it, as what's god-loved? Or is that not so?

EUTHYPHRO: Of course, it is.

SOCRATES: Then either we weren't right to agree before, or, if we were right, our present suggestion is wrong.

EUTHYPHRO: So it seems.

SOCRATES: So we must examine again from the beginning what the pious is, since I won't willingly give up until I learn this. Don't scorn me, but apply your mind to the matter in as many ways and as fully as you can, and then tell me the truth—for you must know it, if indeed any

15

b

c

d

human being does, and, like Proteus,[19] you mustn't be let go until you tell it. For if you didn't know with full clarity what the pious and the impious are, you'd never have ventured to prosecute your old father for murder on behalf of a day laborer. On the contrary, you wouldn't have risked acting wrongly because you'd have been afraid before the gods and ashamed before men. As things stand, however, I well know that you think you have fully clear knowledge of what's pious and what isn't. So tell me what you think it is, my excellent Euthyphro, and don't conceal it.

EUTHYPHRO: Some other time, Socrates. You see, I'm in a hurry to get somewhere, and it's time for me to be off.

SOCRATES: What a way to treat me, my friend! Going off like that and dashing the high hopes I had that I'd learn from you what things are pious and what aren't. Then I'd escape Meletus' indictment by showing him that Euthyphro had now made me wise in religious matters, and ignorance would no longer cause me to improvise and innovate about them. What's more, I'd live a better way for the rest of my life.

19. Proteus, the Old Man of the Sea, was a god who could change himself into any shape he wished. In this way, he avoided being captured, until his daughter, Eidothea, revealed this secret: keep tight hold of him, no matter what he changes into. See Homer, *Odyssey* iv.351–569.

APOLOGY

I don't know, men of Athens, how you were affected by my accusers. As for me, I was almost carried away by them, they spoke so persuasively. And yet almost nothing they said is true. Among their many falsehoods, however, one especially amazed me: that you must be careful not to be deceived by me, since I'm a dangerously clever speaker. That they aren't ashamed at being immediately refuted by the facts, once it becomes apparent that I'm not a clever speaker at all, that seems to me most shameless of them. Unless, of course, the one they call "clever" is the one who tells the truth. If that's what they mean, I'd agree that I'm an orator— although not one of their sort. No, indeed. Rather, just as I claimed, they have said little or nothing true, whereas from me you'll hear the whole truth. But not, by Zeus, men of Athens, expressed in elegant language like theirs, arranged in fine words and phrases. Instead, what you hear will be spoken extemporaneously in whatever words come to mind, and let none of you expect me to do otherwise—for I put my trust in the justice of what I say. After all, it wouldn't be appropriate at my age, gentlemen, to come before you speaking in polished, artificial language like a young man.

Indeed, men of Athens, this I positively entreat of you: if you hear me making my defense using the same sort of language that I'm accustomed to use both in the marketplace next to the bankers' tables—where many of you have heard me—and also in other places, please don't be surprised or create an uproar on that account. For the fact is that this is the first time I've appeared before a law court, although I'm seventy years old. So the language of this place is totally foreign to me. Now, if I were really a foreigner, you'd certainly forgive me if I spoke in the accents and manner in which I'd been raised. So now, too, I'm asking you, justly it seems to me, to overlook my manner of speaking (maybe it will be less good, maybe it will be better), but consider and apply your mind to this alone, whether I say what's just or not. For that's the virtue or excellence of a juror,[1] just as the orator's lies in telling the truth.

17

b

c

d

18

Translated by C.D.C. Reeve.
1. A member of an Athenian jury (a *dikastēs*) combined the responsibilities that are divided between judge and jury in our legal system. Hence *dikastēs* is sometimes translated as "judge" and sometimes (as in the present translation) as "juror."

The first thing justice demands, then, men of Athens, is that I defend myself from the first false accusations made against me and from my first accusers, and then from the later accusations and the later accusers. You see, many people have been accusing me in front of you for very many *b* years now—and nothing they say is true. And I fear them more than Anytus[2] and the rest, though the latter are dangerous as well. But the earlier ones, gentlemen, are more dangerous. They got hold of most of you from childhood and persuaded you with their accusations against me—accusations no more true than the current ones. They say there's a man called Socrates, a "wise" man, a thinker about things in the heavens, an investigator of all things below the earth, and someone who makes the *c* weaker argument the stronger. Those who've spread this rumor, men of Athens, are my dangerous accusers, since the people who hear them believe that those who investigate such things do not acknowledge the gods either. Moreover, those accusers are numerous and have been accusing me for a long time now. Besides, they also spoke to you at that age when you would most readily believe them, when some of you were children or young boys. Thus they simply won their case by default, as there was no defense. But what's most unreasonable in all this is that I can't discover even their names and tell them to you—unless one of them happens to be *d* a comic playwright. In any case, the ones who used malicious slander to persuade you—as well as those who persuaded others after having been persuaded themselves—all of these are impossible to deal with. One cannot bring any of them here to court or cross-examine them. One must literally fight with shadows to defend oneself and cross-examine with no one to respond.

So you too, then, should allow, as I claimed, that there are two groups of accusers: those who accused me just now and the older ones I've been discussing. Moreover, you should consider it proper for me to defend *e* myself against the latter first, since you've heard them accusing me earlier, and at much greater length, than these recent ones here.

All right. I must defend myself, then, men of Athens, and try to take *19* away in this brief time prejudices you acquired such a long time ago. Certainly, that's the outcome I'd wish for—if it's in any way better for you and for me—and I'd like to succeed in my defense. But I think it's a difficult task, and I am not at all unaware of its nature. Let it turn out, though,

2. Anytus was a democratic leader who helped restore democracy to Athens in 403 B.C. after the overthrow of the Thirty Tyrants (32c4 note), under whom he had lost most of his wealth. As a general in the Athenian army he faced indictment, but he allegedly "bribed the jury and was acquitted" (Aristotle, *Constitution of Athens* 27.5). There is evidence that he believed Socrates was responsible for the ruin of his son (Xenophon, *Socrates' Defense* 29–31) and that he was passionately opposed to the sophists (Plato, *Meno* 89e6–92c5).

in whatever way pleases the god. I have to obey the law and defend myself.

Let's examine, then, from the beginning, what the charge is from which the slander against me arose—the very one on which Meletus relied when   *b* he wrote the present indictment of me. Well, then, what exactly did the slanderers say to slander me? Just as if they were real accusers their affidavit must be read. It's something like this:

> Socrates commits injustice and is a busybody, in that he investigates the things beneath the earth and in the heavens, makes the weaker argument the stronger, and teaches these things to others.   *c*

Indeed, you saw these charges expressed yourselves in Aristophanes' comedy.[3] There, some fellow named Socrates swings around claiming he's walking on air and talking a lot of other nonsense on subjects that I know neither a lot nor a little but nothing at all about. Not that I mean to disparage this knowledge, if anyone's wise in such subjects—I don't want to have to defend myself against more of Meletus' lawsuits!—but I, men of Athens, take no part in them. I call on the majority of you as witnesses to this, and I appeal to you to make it perfectly plain to one another—those of   *d* you who've heard me conversing (as many of you have). Tell one another, then, whether any of you has ever heard me discussing such subjects, either briefly or at length, and from this you'll realize that the other things commonly said about me are of the same baseless character.

In any case, none of them is true. And if you've heard from anyone that I undertake to educate people and charge fees, that's not true either. Although, it also seems to me to be a fine thing if anyone's able to educate   *e* people in the way Gorgias of Leontini does, and Prodicus of Ceos, and Hippias of Elis.[4] For each of them, gentlemen, can enter any city and

---

3. The version of *Clouds* referred to here, which is earlier than the revised version we possess, was first staged in 423 B.C.

4. All three, like Evenus of Paros mentioned below, were sophists—itinerant professors who charged sometimes substantial fees for popular lectures and specialized instruction in a wide variety of fields, including natural science, rhetoric, grammar, ethics, and politics. Sophists did not constitute a single school or movement, however, and were neither doctrinally nor organizationally united. Gorgias of Leontini in Sicily (c. 480–376) was primarily a teacher of rhetoric, who was noted for his distinctive style. He is the author of the *Defense of Palamedes*, parts of which bear a striking resemblance to the *Apology* and may have either influenced or been influenced by it. Plato named a dialogue critical of rhetoric after him. Prodicus of Ceos, about whom little is known, was also a fifth-century teacher of rhetoric, with an interest in fine distinctions of meaning (*Protagoras* 337a1–c4) and the correctness of names (*Cratylus* 384a8–c2). Hippias of Elis, like Prodicus a contemporary of Socrates, claimed expertise in astronomy, physics, grammar, poetry, and other

persuade the young—who may associate with any of their own fellow citizens they want to free of charge—to abandon those associations, and as-
20   sociate with them instead, pay them a fee, and be grateful to them besides.

Since we're on that topic, I heard that there's another wise gentle-man here at present, from Paros. For I happened to run into a man who has spent more money on sophists than everyone else put together—Callias, the son of Hipponicus.[5] So I questioned him, since he has two sons himself.

"Callias," I said, "if your two sons had been born colts or calves, we could engage and pay a knowledgeable supervisor—one of those expert horse breeders or farmers—who could turn them into fine and good ex-
b   amples of their proper virtue or excellence. But now, seeing that they're human beings, whom do you have in mind to engage as a supervisor? Who is it that has the knowledge of *this* virtue, the virtue of human beings and of citizens? I assume you've investigated the matter, because you have two sons. Is there such a person," I asked, "or not?"

"Certainly," he replied.

"Who is he?" I said.

"His name's Evenus, Socrates," he replied, "from Paros. He charges five minas."[6]

I thought Evenus blessedly happy if he truly did possess that expertise
c   and taught it for so modest a fee. I, at any rate, would pride myself and give myself airs if I had knowledge of those things. But in fact, men of Athens, I don't know them.

Now perhaps one of you will interject: "But Socrates, what, then, is *your* occupation? What has given rise to these slanders against you? Surely if you weren't in fact occupied with something out of the ordinary, if you weren't doing something different from most people, all this rumor and talk wouldn't have arisen. Tell us, then, what it is, so that we don't judge
d   you hastily." These are fair questions, I think, for the speaker to ask, and I'll try to show you just what it is that has brought me this slanderous reputation. Listen, then. Perhaps, some of you will think I'm joking. But you may be sure that I'll be telling you the whole truth.

You see, men of Athens, I've acquired this reputation because of noth-ing other than a sort of wisdom. What sort of wisdom, you ask, is that? The very sort, perhaps, that is *human* wisdom. For it may just be that I

---

subjects. Two Platonic dialogues are named after him; he also appears in *Protagoras* (315b9–c7, 337c6–338b1).
5. Callias was one of the richest men in Greece and a patron of the sophists. Both Plato's *Protagoras* and Xenophon's *Symposium* are set in his house.
6. Evenus is described as a poet (*Phaedo* 60c8–e1) and as an orator (*Phaedrus* 267a1–5). A few fragments of his elegies survive. A drachma was a day's pay for someone engaged in public works; a mina was a hundred silver drachmas.

really do have that sort of wisdom, whereas the people I mentioned just now may, perhaps, be wise because they possess *superhuman* wisdom. I don't know what else to call it, since I myself certainly don't possess that knowledge, and whoever says I do is lying and speaking in order to slander me.

Please don't create an uproar, men of Athens, even if you think I'm somehow making grand claims. You see, I'm not the author of the story I'm about to tell, though I'll refer you to a reliable source. In fact, as a witness to the existence of my wisdom—if indeed it is a sort of wisdom—and to its nature, I'll present the god at Delphi to you.[7]

You remember Chaerephon, no doubt.[8] He was a friend of mine from youth and also a friend of your party, who shared your recent exile and restoration.[9] You remember, then, what sort of man Chaerephon was, how intense he was in whatever he set out to do.

Well, on one occasion in particular he went to Delphi and dared to ask the oracle[10]—as I said, please don't create an uproar, gentlemen—he asked, exactly as I'm telling you, whether anyone was wiser than myself.

e

21

---

7. Apollo, who was god of, among other things, healing, prophecy, purification, care for young citizens, music, and poetry.

8. A long-time companion of Socrates. He makes brief appearances in *Charmides* and *Gorgias,* and in *Clouds* 102–4, 144–47, 156 ff., 500–4, 831.

9. Members of the democratic party left Athens when the Thirty Tyrants came to power in 404 B.C. They returned to power when the tyrants were overthrown in 403.

10. The Delphic Oracle was one of the most famous in antiquity. There were two methods of consulting it. One method, involving the sacrifice of sheep and goats, was quite expensive but resulted in a written response. The other—the so-called method of the two beans—was substantially cheaper but resulted only in a response by lot. Since Chaerephon was notoriously poor, it seems probable that he consulted the oracle by the latter method (something also suggested by Socrates' characterization of the priestess as *drawing forth* the response at 21a6–7). The inscriptions on the walls of the temple well convey the spirit the oracle stood for: know thyself; do nothing in excess; observe the limit; hate hubris; bow before the divine; glory not in strength. There is no unambiguous record of the oracle's ever having praised anyone for what we would think of as his significant or noteworthy positive achievements or abilities. On the other hand, there are many stories of the following kind. Someone who is powerful, grand, famous for his wisdom, or in some other way noteworthy for his accomplishments, asks the oracle to say who is wisest, most pious, happiest, or what have you, expecting that he himself will be named. But the oracle names some unknown person living in humble and quiet obscurity. What we know about the oracle, then, makes it very unlikely that it was praising Socrates for his positive contributions to wisdom and very likely that it was using him—as he himself comes to believe that it was (23a5–b4)—as an example of someone who was wise because he made no hubristic claims to wisdom.

The Pythia drew forth the response that no one is wiser. His brother here will testify to you about it, since Chaerephon himself is dead.[11]

b   Please consider my purpose in telling you this, since I'm about to explain to you where the slander against me has come from. You see, when I heard these things, I thought to myself as follows: "What can the god be saying? What does his riddle mean? For I'm only too aware that I've no claim to being wise in anything either great or small. What can he mean, then, by saying that I'm wisest? Surely he can't be lying: that isn't lawful for him."

For a long time I was perplexed about what he meant. Then, very reluctantly, I proceeded to examine it in the following sort of way. I ap-proached one of the people thought to be wise, assuming that in his
c   company, if anywhere, I could refute the pronouncement and say to the oracle, "Here's someone wiser than I, yet you said I was wisest."

Then I examined this person—there's no need for me to mention him by name; he was one of our politicians. And when I examined him and talked with him, men of Athens, my experience was something like this: I thought this man seemed wise to many people, and especially to himself, but wasn't. Then I tried to show him that he thought himself wise, but
d   wasn't. As a result, he came to dislike me, and so did many of the people present. For my part, I thought to myself as I left, "I'm wiser than that person. For it's likely that neither of us knows anything fine and good, but he thinks he knows something he doesn't know, whereas I, since I don't in fact know, don't think that I do either. At any rate, it seems that I'm wiser than he in just this one small way: that what I don't know, I don't think I know." Next, I approached another man, one of those thought to be wiser than the first, and it seemed to me that the same thing occurred, and so I
e   came to be disliked by that man too, as well as by many others.

After that, then, I kept approaching one person after another. I realized, with distress and alarm, that I was arousing hostility. Nevertheless, I thought I must attach the greatest importance to what pertained to the god. So, in seeking what the oracle meant, I had to go to all those with any
22   reputation for knowledge. And, by the dog, men of Athens—for I'm obliged to tell the truth before you—I really did experience something like this: in my investigation in response to the god, I found that, where wis-dom is concerned, those who had the best reputations were practically the most deficient, whereas men who were thought to be their inferiors were much better off. Accordingly, I must present all my wanderings to you as if they were labors of some sort that I undertook in order to prove the oracle utterly irrefutable.

You see, after the politicians, I approached the poets—tragic, dithyram-
b   bic,[12] and the rest—thinking that in their company I'd catch myself in the

11. The brother is Chaerecrates (Xenophon, *Memorabilia* ii.3.1).
12. A dithyramb was a choral song in honor of the god Dionysus.

very act of being more ignorant than they. So I examined the poems with which they seemed to me to have taken the most trouble and questioned them about what they meant, in order that I might also learn something from them at the same time.

Well, I'm embarrassed to tell you the truth, gentlemen, but nevertheless it must be told. In a word, almost all the people present could have discussed these poems better than their authors themselves. And so, in the case of the poets as well, I soon realized it wasn't wisdom that enabled them to compose their poems, but some sort of natural inspiration, of just *c* the sort you find in seers and soothsayers. For these people, too, say many fine things, but know nothing of what they speak about. The poets also seemed to me to be in this sort of situation. At the same time, I realized that, because of their poetry, they thought themselves to be the wisest of people about the other things as well when they weren't. So I left their company, too, thinking that I had gotten the better of them in the very same way as of the politicians.

Finally, I approached the craftsmen. You see, I was conscious of knowing practically nothing myself, but I knew I'd discover that they, at least, *d* would know many fine things. And I wasn't wrong about this. On the contrary, they did know things that I didn't know, and in that respect they were wiser than I. But, men of Athens, the good craftsmen also seemed to me to have the very same flaw as the poets: because he performed his own craft well, each of them also thought himself to be wisest about the other things, the most important ones; and this error of theirs seemed to overshadow their wisdom. So I asked myself on behalf of the oracle whether *e* I'd prefer to be as I am, not in any way wise with their wisdom nor ignorant with their ignorance, or to have both qualities as they did. And the answer I gave to myself, and to the oracle, was that it profited me more to be just the way I was.

From this examination, men of Athens, much hostility has arisen against me of a sort that is harshest and most onerous. This has resulted in many *23* slanders, including that reputation I mentioned of being "wise." You see, the people present on each occasion think that I'm wise about the subjects on which I examine others. But in fact, gentlemen, it's pretty certainly the god who is really wise, and by his oracle he meant that human wisdom is worth little or nothing. And it seems that when he refers to the Socrates here before you and uses my name, he makes me an example, as if he were *b* to say, "That one among you is wisest, mortals, who, like Socrates, has recognized that he's truly worthless where wisdom's concerned."

So even now I continue to investigate these things and to examine, in response to the god, any person, citizen, or foreigner I believe to be wise. Whenever he seems not to be so to me, I come to the assistance of the god and show him that he's not wise. Because of this occupation, I've had no leisure worth talking about for either the city's affairs or my own domestic ones; rather, I live in extreme poverty because of my service to

c   the god.

In addition to these factors, the young people who follow me around of their own accord, those who have the most leisure, the sons of the very rich, enjoy listening to people being cross-examined. They often imitate me themselves and in turn attempt to cross-examine others. Next, I imagine they find an abundance of people who think they possess some knowledge, but in fact know little or nothing. The result is that those they question are angry not at themselves, but at me, and say that Socrates is a

d   thoroughly pestilential fellow who corrupts the young. Then, when they're asked what he's doing or teaching, they've nothing to say, as they don't know. Yet, so as not to appear at a loss, they utter the stock phrases used against all who philosophize: "things in the sky and beneath the earth," and "not acknowledging the gods," and "making the weaker argument the stronger." For they wouldn't be willing to tell the truth, I imagine: that it has become manifest they pretend to know, but know nothing. So, seeing that these people are, I imagine, ambitious, vehement, and nu-

e   merous, and have been speaking earnestly and persuasively about me, they've long been filling your ears with vehement slanders. On the basis of these slanders, Meletus has brought his charges against me, and Anytus and Lycon along with him: Meletus is aggrieved on behalf of the poets, Anytus on behalf of the artisans and politicians, and Lycon on behalf of the

24   orators. So, as I began by saying, I'd be amazed if I could rid your minds of this slander in the brief time available, when there's so much of it in them.

There, men of Athens, is the truth for you. I've spoken it without concealing or glossing over anything, whether great or small. And yet I pretty much know that I make enemies by doing these very things. And that's further evidence that I'm right—that this is the prejudice against me and

b   these its causes. Whether you investigate these matters now or later, you'll find it to be so.

Enough, then, for my defense before you against the charges brought by my first accusers. Next, I'll try to defend myself against Meletus—who is, he claims, both good and patriotic—and against my later accusers. Once again, then, just as if they were really a different set of accusers, their affidavit must be examined in turn. It goes something like this:

> Socrates is guilty of corrupting the young, and of not acknowledging the gods the city acknowledges, but new daimonic activities instead.

c   Such, then, is the charge. Let us examine each point in this charge.

Meletus says, then, that I commit injustice by corrupting the young. But I, men of Athens, reply that it's Meletus who is guilty of playing around with serious matters, of lightly bringing people to trial, and of professing

to be seriously concerned about things he has never cared about at all—
and I'll try to prove this.

Step forward, Meletus, and answer me. You regard it as most impor-
tant, do you not, that our young people be as good as possible?   *d*

I certainly do.

Come, then, and tell these jurors who improves them. Clearly you
know, since you care. For having discovered, as you assert, the one who
corrupts them—namely, myself—you bring him before these jurors and
accuse him. Come, then, speak up, tell the jurors who it is that improves
them. Do you see, Meletus, that you remain silent and have nothing to
say? Yet don't you think that's shameful and sufficient evidence of exactly
what I say, that you care nothing at all? Speak up, my good man. Who
improves them?

The laws.

But that's not what I'm asking, my most excellent fellow, but rather
which *person*, who knows the laws themselves in the first place, does this?   *e*

These gentlemen, Socrates, the jurors.

What are you saying, Meletus? Are they able to educate and improve
the young?

Most certainly.

All of them, or some but not others?

All of them.

That's good news, by Hera, and a great abundance of benefactors that
you speak of! What, then, about the audience present here? Do they improve the young or not?   25

Yes, they do so too.

And what about the members of the Council?[13]

Yes, the councilors too.

But, if that's so, Meletus, surely those in the Assembly, the assembly-
men, won't corrupt the young, will they? Won't they all improve them too?

Yes, they will too.

But then it seems that all the Athenians except for me make young
people fine and good, whereas I alone corrupt them. Is that what you're
saying?

Most emphatically, that's what I'm saying.

I find myself, if you're right, in a most unfortunate situation. Now
answer me this. Do you think that the same holds of horses? Do people
in general improve them, whereas one particular person corrupts them   *b*

---

13. The Council consisted of 500 male citizens over the age of 30, elected annually
by lot, 50 from each of the 10 tribes of Athens (32b3 note). The Council met daily
(except for some holidays and the like) as a steering committee for the Assembly.
Its responsibilities included state finance, public buildings, and the equipment of
navy and cavalry.

or makes them worse? Or isn't it wholly the opposite: one particular person—or the very few who are horse trainers—is able to improve them, whereas the majority of people, if they have to do with horses and make use of them, make them worse? Isn't that true, Meletus, both of horses and of all other animals? Of course it is, whether you and Anytus say so or not. Indeed, our young people are surely in a very happy situation if only one person corrupts them, whereas all the rest benefit them.

c   Well then, Meletus, it has been adequately established that you've never given any thought to young people—you've plainly revealed your indifference—and that you care nothing about the issues on which you bring me to trial.

Next, Meletus, tell us, in the name of Zeus, whether it's better to live among good citizens or bad ones. Answer me, sir. Surely, I'm not asking you anything difficult. Don't bad people do something bad to whoever's closest to them at the given moment, whereas good people do something good?

Certainly.

d   Now is there anyone who wishes to be harmed rather than benefited by those around him? Keep answering, my good fellow. For the law requires you to answer. Is there anyone who wishes to be harmed?

Of course not.

Well, then, when you summon me here for corrupting the young and making them worse, do you mean that I do so intentionally or unintentionally?

Intentionally, *I* say.

What's that, Meletus? Are you so much wiser at your age than I at mine, that you know bad people do something bad to whoever's closest to them at the given moment, and good people something good? Am I, by contrast,

e   so very ignorant that I don't know even this: that if I do something bad to an associate, I risk getting back something bad from him in return? And is the result, as you claim, that I do so very bad a thing intentionally?

I'm not convinced by you of that, Meletus, and neither, I think, is anyone else. No, either I'm not corrupting the young or, if I am corrupting

26   them, it's *un*intentionally, so that in either case what you say is false. But if I'm corrupting them unintentionally, the law doesn't require that I be brought to court for such mistakes—that is, unintentional ones—but that I be taken aside for private instruction and admonishment. For it's clear that if I'm instructed, I'll stop doing what I do unintentionally. You, however, avoided associating with me and were unwilling to instruct me. Instead, you bring me here, where the law requires you to bring those in need of punishment, not instruction.

Well, men of Athens, what I said before is absolutely clear by this point,

b   namely, that Meletus has never cared about these matters to any extent, great or small. Nevertheless, please tell us now, Meletus, how is it you say I corrupt the young? Or is it absolutely clear, from the indictment you wrote, that it's by teaching them not to acknowledge the gods the city acknowledges, but new daimonic activities instead? Isn't that what you say I corrupt them by teaching?

I most emphatically do say that.

Then, in the name of those very gods we're now discussing, Meletus, speak yet more clearly, both for my sake and for that of these gentlemen.   c
You see, I'm unable to tell what you mean. Is it that I teach people to acknowledge that some gods exist—so that I, then, acknowledge their existence myself and am not an out-and-out atheist and am not guilty of that—yet not, of course, the very ones acknowledged by the city, but different ones? Is that what you're charging me with, that they're different ones? Or are you saying that I myself don't acknowledge any gods at all, and that that's what I teach to others?

That's what I mean, that you don't acknowledge any gods at all.

You're a strange fellow, Meletus! What makes you say that? Do I not   d
even acknowledge that the sun and the moon are gods, then, as other men do?

No, by Zeus, gentlemen of the jury, he doesn't, since he says that the sun's a stone and the moon earth.

My dear Meletus, do you think it's Anaxagoras you're accusing?

Are you that contemptuous of the jury? Do you think they're so illiterate that they don't know that the books of Anaxagoras of Clazomenae are full of such arguments? And, in particular, do young people learn these views from me, views they can occasionally acquire in the Orchestra[14] for a drachma at most and that they'd ridicule Socrates for pretending were   e
his own—especially as they're so strange? In the name of Zeus, is that really how I seem to you? Do I acknowledge the existence of no god at all?

No indeed, by Zeus, none at all.

You aren't at all convincing, Meletus, not even, it seems to me, to yourself. You see, men of Athens, this fellow seems very arrogant and intemperate to me and to have written this indictment simply out of some sort of arrogance, intemperance, and youthful rashness. Indeed, he seems to have composed a sort of riddle in order to test me: "Will the so-called wise   27
Socrates recognize that I'm playing around and contradicting myself? Or will I fool him along with the other listeners?" You see, he seems to me to be contradicting himself in his indictment, as if he were to say, "Socrates is guilty of not acknowledging gods, but of acknowledging gods." And that's just childish playing around, isn't it?

Please examine with me, gentlemen, why it seems to me that this is what he's saying. And you, Meletus, answer us. But you, gentlemen,

14. The Orchestra was part of the marketplace (*agora*) in Athens.

b please remember what I asked of you at the beginning: don't create an uproar if I make my arguments in my accustomed manner.

Is there anyone, Meletus, who acknowledges that human activities exist but doesn't acknowledge human beings? Make him answer, gentlemen, and don't let him make one protest after another. Is there anyone who doesn't acknowledge horses but does acknowledge equine activities? Or who doesn't acknowledge that musicians exist but does acknowledge musical activities? There's no one, best of men—if you don't want to answer, I must answer for you and for the others here. But at least answer my next question. Is there anyone who acknowledges the existence of *c* daimonic activities but doesn't acknowledge daimons?

No, there isn't.

How good of you to answer, if reluctantly and when compelled to by these gentlemen. Well then, you say that I acknowledge daimonic activities, whether new or familiar, and teach about them. But then, on your account, I do at any rate acknowledge daimonic activities, and to this you've sworn in your indictment against me. However, if I acknowledge daimonic activities, surely it's absolutely necessary that I acknowledge daimons. Isn't that so? Yes, it is—I assume you agree, since you don't answer. But don't we believe that daimons are either gods or, at any rate, *d* children of gods? Yes or no?

Of course.

Then, if indeed I do believe in daimons, as you're saying, and if daimons are gods of some sort, that's precisely what I meant when I said that you're presenting us with a riddle and playing around: you're saying that I don't believe in gods and, on the contrary, that I do believe in gods, since in fact I do at least believe in daimons. But if, on the other hand, daimons are children of gods, some sort of bastard offspring of a nymph, or of whomever else tradition says each one is the child, what man could possibly believe that children of gods exist, but not gods? That would be just as *e* unreasonable as believing in the children of horses and asses—namely, mules—while not believing in the existence of horses and asses.

Well then, Meletus, you must have written these things to test us or because you were at a loss about what genuine injustice to charge me with. There's no conceivable way you could persuade any man with even the slightest intelligence that the same person believes in both daimonic activities and gods, and, on the contrary, that this same person believes *28* neither in daimons, nor in gods, nor in heroes.[15]

In fact, then, men of Athens, it doesn't seem to me to require a long defense to show that I'm not guilty of the charges in Meletus' indictment, but what I've said is sufficient. But what I was also saying earlier, that

15. Heroes are demigods (28c2), children of gods and mortals, whose existence therefore entails the existence of gods.

much hostility has arisen against me and among many people—you may be sure that's true. And *it's* what will convict me, if I am convicted: not Meletus or Anytus, but the slander and malice of many people. It has certainly convicted many other good men as well, and I imagine it will do so again. There's no danger it will stop with me.

But perhaps someone may say, "Aren't you ashamed, Socrates, to have engaged in the sort of occupation that has now put you at risk of death?" I, however, would be right to reply to him, "You're not thinking straight, sir, if you think that a man who's any use at all should give any opposing weight to the risk of living or dying, instead of looking to this alone whenever he does anything: whether his actions are just or unjust, the deeds of a good or bad man. You see, on your account, all those demigods who died on the plain of Troy were inferior people, especially the son of Thetis, who was so contemptuous of danger when the alternative was something shameful. When he was eager to kill Hector, his mother, since she was a goddess, spoke to him, I think, in some such words as these: 'My child, if you avenge the death of your friend Patroclus and slay Hector, you will die yourself immediately,' so the poem goes, 'as your death is fated to follow next after Hector's.' But though he heard that, he was contemptuous of death and danger, for he was far more afraid of living as a bad man and of failing to avenge his friends: 'Let me die immediately, then,' it continues, 'once I've given the wrongdoer his just deserts, so that I do not remain here by the curved ships, a laughingstock and a burden upon the earth.' Do you really suppose he gave a thought to death or danger?"

You see, men of Athens, this is the truth of the matter: Wherever someone has stationed himself because he thinks it best, or wherever he's been stationed by his commander, there, it seems to me, he should remain, steadfast in danger, taking no account at all of death or of anything else, in comparison to what's shameful. I'd therefore have been acting scandalously, men of Athens, if, when I'd been stationed in Potidea, Amphipolis, or Delium[16] by the leaders you had elected to lead me, I had, like many another, remained where they'd stationed me and run the risk of death. But if, when the god stationed me here, as I became thoroughly convinced he did, to live practicing philosophy, examining myself and others, I had—for fear of death or anything else—abandoned my station.

That would have been scandalous, and someone might have rightly and justly brought me to court for not acknowledging that gods exist, by disobeying the oracle, fearing death, and thinking I was wise when I wasn't. You see, fearing death, gentlemen, is nothing other than thinking one is wise when one isn't, since it's thinking one knows what one doesn't

16. Three battles in the Peloponnesian War between Athens and its allies and Sparta and its allies.

b   know. I mean, no one knows whether death may not be the greatest of all goods for people, but they fear it as if they knew for certain that it's the worst thing of all. Yet surely this is the most blameworthy ignorance of thinking one knows what one doesn't know. But I, gentlemen, may perhaps differ from most people by just this much in this matter too. And if I really were to claim to be wiser than anyone in any way, it would be in this: that as I don't have adequate knowledge about things in Hades, so too I don't think that I have knowledge. To act unjustly, on the other hand, to disobey someone better than oneself, whether god or man, that I do know to be bad and shameful. In any case, I'll never fear or avoid things that may for all I know be good more than things I know are bad.

c   Suppose, then, you're prepared to let me go now and to disobey Anytus, who said I shouldn't have been brought to court at all, but that since I had been brought to court, you had no alternative but to put me to death because, as he stated before you, if I were acquitted, soon your sons would all be entirely corrupted by following Socrates' teachings. Suppose, confronted with that claim, you were to say to me, "Socrates, we will not obey Anytus this time. Instead, we are prepared to let you go. But on the following condition: that you spend no more time on this investigation and

d   don't practice philosophy, and if you're caught doing so, you'll die." Well, as I just said, if you were to let me go on these terms, I'd reply to you, "I've the utmost respect and affection for you, men of Athens, but I'll obey the god rather than you, and as long as I draw breath and am able, I won't give up practicing philosophy, exhorting you and also showing the way to any of you I ever happen to meet, saying just the sorts of things I'm accustomed to say:

> My excellent man, you're an Athenian, you belong to the greatest city, renowned for its wisdom and strength; are you not ashamed that you take care to acquire as much wealth as possible—and repu-
e   tation and honor—but that about wisdom and truth, about how your soul may be in the best possible condition, you take neither care nor thought?

Then, if one of you disagrees and says that he *does* care, I won't let him go away immediately, but I'll question, examine, and test him. And if he doesn't seem to me to possess virtue, though he claims he does, I'll reproach him, saying that he treats the most important things as having the
30   least value, and inferior ones as having more. This I will do for anyone I meet, young or old, alien or fellow citizen—but especially for you, my fellow citizens, since you're closer kin to me. This, you may be sure, is what the god orders me to do. And I believe that no greater good for you has ever come about in the city than my service to the god. You see, I do nothing else except go around trying to persuade you, both young and old

alike, not to care about your bodies or your money as intensely as about   *b*
how your soul may be in the best possible condition. I say,

> It's not from wealth that virtue comes, but from virtue comes
> money, and all the other things that are good for human beings, both
> in private and in public life.

Now if by saying this, I'm corrupting the young, *this* is what you'd have to
think to be harmful. But if anyone claims I say something other than this,
he's talking nonsense."

"It's in that light," I want to say, "men of Athens, that you should obey
Anytus or not, and let me go or not—knowing that I wouldn't act in any
other way, not even if I were to die many times over."   *c*

Don't create an uproar, men of Athens. Instead, please abide by my
request not to create an uproar at what I say, but to listen. For I think it will
profit you to listen. You see, I'm certainly going to say some further things
to you at which you may perhaps exclaim—but by no means do so.

You may be sure that if you put me to death—a man of the sort I said I
was just now—you won't harm me more than you harm yourselves. Certainly, Meletus or Anytus couldn't harm me in any way: that's not possible. For I don't think it's lawful for a better man to be harmed by a worse.   *d*
He may, of course, kill me, or perhaps banish or disenfranchise me. And
these *he* believes to be very bad things, and others no doubt agree. But *I*
don't believe this. Rather, I believe that doing what he's doing now—
attempting to kill a man unjustly—is far worse.

So, men of Athens, I'm far from pleading in my own defense now, as
might be supposed. Instead, I'm pleading in yours, so that you don't
commit a great wrong against the god's gift to you by condemning me. If   *e*
you put me to death, you won't easily find another like me. For, even if it
seems ridiculous to say so, I've literally been attached to the city, as if to a
large thoroughbred horse that was somewhat sluggish because of its size
and needed to be awakened by some sort of gadfly. It's as just such a
gadfly, it seems to me, that the god has attached me to the city—one that
awakens, cajoles, and reproaches each and every one of you and never
stops alighting everywhere on you the whole day. You won't easily find   *31*
another like that, gentlemen. So if you obey me, you'll spare my life. But
perhaps you'll be resentful, like people awakened from a doze, and slap at
me. If you obey Anytus, you might easily kill me. Then you might spend
the rest of your lives asleep, unless the god, in his compassion for you,
were to send you someone else.

That I am indeed the sort of person to be given as a gift to the city by
the god, you may recognize from this: it doesn't seem a merely human   *b*
matter—does it?—for me to have neglected all my own affairs and to have
put up with this neglect of my domestic life for so many years now, but

always to have minded your business, by visiting each of you in private, like a father or elder brother, to persuade you to care about virtue. Of course, if I were getting anything out of it or if I were being paid for giving this advice, my conduct would be intelligible. But, as it is, you can plainly see for yourselves that my accusers, who so shamelessly accused me of

c   everything else, couldn't bring themselves to be so utterly shameless as to call a witness to say that I ever once accepted or asked for payment. In fact, it's *I* who can call what I think is a sufficient witness that I'm telling the truth—my poverty.

But perhaps it may seem strange that I, of all people, give this advice by going around and minding other people's business in private, yet do not venture to go before your Assembly and give advice to the city in public. The reason for that, however, is one you've heard me give many times and in many places: A divine and daimonic thing comes to me—the very thing

d   Meletus made mocking allusion to in the indictment he wrote. It's something that began happening to me in childhood: a sort of voice comes, which, whenever it does come, always holds me back from what I'm about to do but never urges me forward. *It* is what opposes my engaging in politics—and to me, at least, its opposition seems entirely right. For you may be sure, men of Athens, that if I'd tried to engage in politics I'd have perished long ago and have benefited neither you nor myself.

e   Please don't resent me if I tell you the truth. The fact is that no man will be spared by you or by any other multitude of people if he genuinely opposes a lot of unjust and unlawful actions and tries to prevent them

32   from happening in the city. On the contrary, anyone who really fights for what's just, if indeed he's going to survive for even a short time, must act privately not publicly.

I'll present substantial evidence of that—not words, but what you value, deeds. Listen, then, to what happened to me, so you may see that fear of death wouldn't lead me to submit to a single person contrary to what's just, not even if I were to perish at once for not submitting. The things I'll tell you are of a vulgar sort commonly heard in the law courts, but they're true nonetheless.

b   You see, men of Athens, I never held any other public office in the city, but I've served on the Council. And it happened that my own tribe, Antiochis, was presiding[17] when you wanted to try the ten generals—the ones

17. A *phulē* is not a tribe in our sense, but an administrative division of the citizen body, most probably of military origin. The presiding committee of the Council (25a5 note) consisted of the fifty members of one of the ten tribes, selected by lot to serve for one-tenth of the year. It arranged meetings of the Council and Assembly, received envoys and letters to the state, and conducted other routine business.

who failed to rescue the survivors of the naval battle—as a group.[18] That was unlawful, as you all came to recognize at a later time. On that occasion, I was the only presiding member opposed to your doing something illegal, and I voted against you. And though the orators were ready to lay information against me and have me summarily arrested,[19] and you were shouting and urging them on, I thought that I should face danger on the side of law and justice, rather than go along with you for fear of imprisonment or death when your proposals were unjust.

_c_

This happened when the city was still under democratic rule. But later, when the oligarchy had come to power, it happened once more. The Thirty[20] summoned me and four others to the Tholus[21] and ordered us to arrest Leon of Salamis[22] and bring him from Salamis to die. They gave many such orders to many other people too, of course, since they wanted to implicate as many as possible in their crimes. On _that_ occasion, however, I showed once again not by words but by deeds that I couldn't care less about death—if that isn't putting it too bluntly—but that all I care about is not doing anything unjust or impious. You see, that government, powerful though it was, didn't frighten me into unjust action: when we came out of the Tholus, the other four went to Salamis and arrested Leon, whereas I left and went home. I might have died for that if the government hadn't fallen shortly afterward.

_d_

There are many witnesses who will testify before you about these events.

_e_

Do you imagine, then, that I'd have survived all these years if I'd been regularly active in public affairs, and had come to the aid of justice like a good man, and regarded that as most important, as one should? Far from

---

18. After the naval battle at Arginusae on the Ionian coast of Asia Minor (406 B.C.), ten Athenian generals were indicted for failing to rescue survivors and to pick up the bodies of the dead. Both Council and Assembly voted to try them as a group, which was against Athenian law. See Xenophon, _Hellenica_ i.7.

19. _Endeiknunai . . . kai apagein: Endeixis_ (lay information against) and _apagoge_ (have summarily arrested) were formal legal actions of a specific sort.

20. After Athens was defeated by Sparta in 404 B.C., its democratic government was replaced by a brutal oligarchy, the so-called Thirty Tyrants, which survived barely eight months. During that time it allegedly executed some fifteen hundred people, and many more went into exile to escape. Two members of the Thirty— Critias and Charmides—were relatives of Plato and appear as Socratic interlocutors in the dialogues named after them. Socrates' association with them is often thought to have been one of the things that led to his indictment.

21. The Tholus was a dome-shaped building, also called the Skias ("parasol"). The presiding committee of the Council (32b3 note) took its meals there.

22. Leon is otherwise unknown. The episode, however, is widely reported (_Seventh Letter_ 324d8–325c5; Xenophon, _Hellenica_ ii.3.39, _Memorabilia_ iv.4.3).

it, men of Athens, and neither would any other man. But throughout my
33   entire life, in any public activities I may have engaged in, it was evident I
was the sort of person—and in private life I was the same—who never
agreed to anything with anyone contrary to justice, whether with others or
with those who my slanderers say are my students. In fact, I've never been
anyone's teacher at any time. But if anyone, whether young or old, wanted
to listen to me while I was talking and performing my own task, I never
begrudged that to him. Neither do I engage in conversation only when I
b   receive a fee and not when I don't. Rather, I offer myself for questioning to
rich and poor alike, or, if someone prefers, he may listen to me and answer
my questions. And if any one of these turned out well, or did not do so, I
can't justly be held responsible, since I never at any time promised any of
them that they'd learn anything from me or that I'd teach them. And if
anyone says that he learned something from me or heard something in
private that all the others didn't also hear, you may be sure he isn't telling
c   the truth.

Why, then, you may ask, do some people enjoy spending so much time
with me? You've heard the answer, men of Athens. I told you the whole
truth: it's because they enjoy listening to people being examined who
think they're wise but aren't. For it's not unpleasant. In my case, however,
it's something, you may take it from me, I've been ordered to do by the
god, in both oracles and dreams, and in every other way that divine
providence ever ordered any man to do anything at all.

All these things, men of Athens, are both true and easily tested. I mean,
d   if I really do corrupt the young or have corrupted them in the past, surely
if any of them had recognized when they became older that I'd given them
bad advice at some point in their youth, they'd now have come forward
themselves to accuse me and seek redress. Or else, if they weren't willing
to come themselves, some of their family members—fathers, brothers, or
other relatives—if indeed their kinsmen had suffered any harm from
me—would remember it now and seek redress.

In any case, I see many of these people present here: first of all, there's
e   Crito, my contemporary and fellow demesman, the father of Critobulus
here;[23] then there's Lysanius of Sphettus, father of Aeschines here;[24] next,
there's Epigenes' father, Antiphon of Cephisia here.[25] Then there are
others whose brothers have spent time in this way: Nicostratus, son of

23. Crito was a well-off farm owner (*Euthydemus* 291e8), able and willing to help
his friends financially (38b7, *Crito* 44b6–c5; Diogenes Laertius ii.20–21, 31, 105,
121).
24. Aeschines of Sphettus (fourth century B.C.) was a devoted follower of Socrates,
present at his death (*Phaedo* 59b8). He taught oratory and wrote speeches for the
law courts. He also wrote Socratic dialogues, only fragments of which are extant.
25. Epigenes was present at Socrates' death (*Phaedo* 59b8) and was a member of his
circle (Xenophon, *Memorabilia* iii.12).

Theozotides,[26] brother of Theodotus—by the way, Theodotus is dead, so that Nicostratus is at any rate not being held back by him; and Paralius here, son of Demodocus, whose brother was Theages;[27] and there's Adeimantus, the son of Ariston, whose brother is Plato here, and Aeantodorus, whose brother here is Apollodorus.[28] And there are many others I could mention, some of whom Meletus most certainly ought to have called as witnesses in the course of his own speech. If he forgot to do so, let him call them now—I yield time to him. Let him tell us if he has any such witness. No, it's entirely the opposite, gentlemen. You'll find that they're all prepared to come to my aid, their corruptor, the one who, Meletus and Anytus claim, is doing harm to their families. Of course, the corrupted ones themselves might indeed have reason to come to my aid. But the *un*corrupted ones, their relatives, who are older men now, what reason could they possibly have to support me, other than the right and just one: that they know perfectly well that Meletus is lying, whereas I am telling the truth?

Well then, gentlemen, those, and perhaps other similar things, are pretty much all I have to say in my defense. But perhaps one of you might be resentful when he recalls his own behavior. Perhaps when he was contesting even a lesser charge than this charge, he positively entreated the jurors with copious tears, bringing forward his children and many other relatives and friends as well, in order to arouse as much pity as possible. And then he finds that I'll do none of these things, not even when I'm facing what might be considered the ultimate danger. Perhaps someone with these thoughts might feel more willful where I'm concerned and, made angry by these very same thoughts, cast his vote in anger. Well, if there's someone like that among you—of course, I don't expect there to be, but *if* there is—I think it appropriate for me to answer him as follows: "I do indeed have relatives, my excellent man. As Homer puts it,[29] I too 'wasn't born from oak or from rock' but from human parents. And so I do have relatives, sons too, men of Athens, three of them, one already a young man while two are still children. Nonetheless, I won't bring any of them forward here and then entreat you to vote for my acquittal."

Why, you may ask, will I do none of these things? Not because I'm willful, men of Athens, or want to dishonor you—whether I'm boldly facing death or not is a separate story. The point has to do with reputation—yours and mine and that of the entire city: it doesn't seem noble to me to do these

34

b

c

d

e

26. Theozotides introduced two important democratic reforms after the fall of the Thirty Tyrants (32c4 note).
27. Otherwise largely unknown.
28. Apollodorus, an enthusiastic follower of Socrates, given to emotion (*Phaedo* 59a8–b1, 117c3–d6), is the narrator in the *Symposium*.
29. *Odyssey* xix.163.

things, especially at my age and with my reputation—for whether truly or falsely, it's firmly believed in any case that Socrates is superior to the
35   majority of people in some way. Therefore, if those of *you* who are believed to be superior—in either wisdom or courage or any other virtue whatever—behave like that, it would be shameful.

I've often seen people of this sort when they're on trial: they're thought to be someone, yet they do astonishing things—as if they imagined they'd suffer something terrible if they died and would be immortal if only you didn't kill them. People like that seem to me to bring such shame to the city that any foreigner might well suppose that those among the Athen-
b   ians who are superior in virtue—the ones they select from among themselves for political office and other positions of honor—are no better than women. I say this, men of Athens, because none of us who are in any way whatever thought to be someone should behave like that, nor, if we attempt to do so, should you allow it. On the contrary, you should make it clear you're far more likely to convict someone who makes the city despicable by staging these pathetic scenes than someone who minds his behavior.

Reputation aside, gentlemen, it doesn't seem just to me to entreat the
c   jury—nor to be acquitted by entreating it—but rather to inform it and persuade it. After all, a juror doesn't sit in order to grant justice as a favor, but to decide where justice lies. And he has sworn on oath not that he'll favor whomever he pleases, but that he'll judge according to law. We shouldn't accustom you to breaking your oath, then, nor should you become accustomed to doing so—neither of us would be doing something holy if we did. Hence don't expect me, men of Athens, to act toward you in
d   ways I consider to be neither noble, nor just, nor pious—most especially, by Zeus, when I'm being prosecuted for *impiety* by Meletus here. You see, if I tried to persuade and to force you by entreaties, after you've sworn an oath, I clearly would be teaching you not to believe in the existence of gods, and my defense would literally convict me of not acknowledging gods. But that's far from being the case: I do acknowledge them, men of Athens, as none of my accusers does. I turn it over to you and to the god to judge me in whatever way will be best for me and for yourselves.

•   •   •

e   There are many reasons, men of Athens, why I'm not resentful at this outcome—that you voted to convict me—and this outcome wasn't unex-
36   pected by me. I'm much more surprised at the number of votes cast on each side: I didn't think that the decision would be by so few votes but by a great many. Yet now, it seems, that if a mere thirty votes had been cast differently, I'd have been acquitted. Or rather, it seems to me that where

Meletus is concerned, I've been acquitted even as things stand. And not merely acquitted. On the contrary, one thing at least is clear to everyone: if Anytus had not come forward with Lycon to accuse me, Meletus would have been fined a thousand drachmas, since he wouldn't have received a fifth of the votes.

b

But be that as it may, the man demands the death penalty for me. Well then, what counterpenalty should I now propose to you, men of Athens? Or is it clear that it's whatever I deserve? What then should it be? What do I deserve to suffer or pay just because I didn't mind my own business throughout my life? Because I didn't care about the things most people care about—making money, managing an estate, or being a general, a popular leader, or holding some other political office, or joining the cabals and factions that come to exist in a city—but thought myself too honest, in truth, to engage in these things and survive? Because I didn't engage in things, if engaging in them was going to benefit neither you nor myself, but instead went to each of you privately and tried to perform what I claim is the greatest benefaction? That was what I did. I tried to persuade each of you to care first not about any of his possessions, but about himself and how he'll become best and wisest; and not primarily about the city's possessions, but about the city itself; and to care about all other things in the same way.

c

What, then, do I deserve to suffer for being such a man? Something good, men of Athens, if I'm indeed to propose a penalty that I truly deserve. Yes, and the sort of good thing, too, that would be appropriate for me. What, then, is appropriate for a poor man who is a public benefactor and needs to have the leisure to exhort you? Nothing could be more appropriate, men of Athens, than for such a man to be given free meals in the Prytaneum—much more so for him, at any rate, than for any one of you who has won a victory at Olympia, whether with a single horse or with a pair or a team of four.[30] You see, he makes you think you're happy, whereas I make you actually happy. Besides, he doesn't need to be sustained in that way, but I do need it. So if, as justice demands, I must propose a penalty I deserve, that's the penalty I propose: free meals in the Prytaneum.

d

e

37

Now perhaps when I say this, you may think I'm speaking in a quite willful manner—just as when I talked about appeals to pity and supplications. That's not so, men of Athens, rather it's something like this: I'm convinced that I never intentionally do injustice to any man—but I can't get you to share my conviction, because we've talked together a short time. I say this, because if you had a law, as other men in fact do, not to try

---

30. The Prytaneum, a building on the northeast slope of the Acropolis, was the symbolic center of Athens, where the communal hearth was housed.

b a capital charge in a single day, but over several, I think you'd be convinced. But as things stand, it isn't easy to clear myself of huge slanders in a short time.

Since *I'm* convinced that I've done injustice to no one, however, I'm certainly not likely to do myself injustice, to announce that I deserve something bad and to propose a penalty of that sort for myself. Why should I do that? In order not to suffer what Meletus proposes as a penalty for me, when I say that I don't know whether it's a good or a bad thing? As an alternative to that, am I then to choose one of the things I know very well to be bad and propose it? Imprisonment, for example? And why
c should I live in prison, enslaved to the regularly appointed officers, the Eleven?[31] All right, a fine with imprisonment until I pay? But in my case the effect would be precisely the one I just now described, since I haven't the means to pay.

Well then, should I propose exile? Perhaps that's what *you*'d propose for me. But I'd certainly have to have an excessive love of life, men of Athens, to be so irrational as to do that. I see that you, my fellow citizens, were unable to tolerate my discourses and discussions but came to find
d them so burdensome and odious that you're now seeking to get rid of them. Is it likely, then, that I'll infer that others will find them easy to bear? Far from it, men of Athens. It would be a fine life for me, indeed, a man of my age, to go into exile and spend his life exchanging one city for another, because he's always being expelled. You see, I well know that wherever I go, the young will come to hear me speaking, just as they do here. And if I drive them away, they will themselves persuade their elders to expel me; whereas if I don't drive them away, their fathers and relatives will expel
e me because of these same young people.

Now perhaps someone may say, "But by keeping quiet and minding your own business, Socrates, wouldn't it be possible for you to live in exile for us?" This is the very hardest point on which to convince some of you. You see, if I say that to do *that* would be to disobey the god, and that this is why I can't mind my own business, you won't believe me, since you'll
38 suppose I'm being ironical. But again, if I say it's the greatest good for a man to discuss virtue every day, and the other things you've heard me discussing and examining myself and others about, on the grounds that the unexamined life isn't worth living for a human being, you'll believe me even less when I say that. But in fact, things are just as I claim them to be, men of Athens, though it isn't easy to convince you of them. At the same time, I'm not accustomed to thinking that I deserve anything bad. If I had
b the means, I'd have proposed a fine of as much as I could afford to pay, since that would have done me no harm at all. But as things stand, I don't have them—unless you want me to propose as much as I'm in fact able to

31. Officials appointed by lot to be in charge of prisons and executions.

pay. Perhaps I could pay you about a mina of silver. So I propose a fine of that amount.

One moment, men of Athens. Plato here, and Crito, Critobulus, and Apollodorus as well, are urging me to propose thirty minas and saying that they themselves will guarantee it.[32] I propose a fine of that amount, therefore, and these men will be sufficient guarantors to you of the silver.

• • •

For the sake of a little time, men of Athens, you're going to earn from those who wish to denigrate our city both the reputation and the blame for having killed Socrates—that wise man. For those who wish to reproach you will, of course, claim that I'm wise, even if I'm not. In any case, if you'd waited a short time, this would have happened of its own accord. You, of course, see my age, you see that I'm already far along in life and close to death. I'm saying this not to all of you, but to those who voted for the death penalty. And to those same people I also say this: Perhaps you imagine, gentlemen, that I was convicted for lack of the sort of arguments I could have used to convince you, if I'd thought I should do or say anything to escape the penalty. Far from it. I *have* been convicted for a lack—not of arguments, however, but of bold-faced shamelessness and for being unwilling to say the sorts of things to you you'd have been most pleased to hear, with me weeping and wailing, and doing and saying many other things I claim are unworthy of me, but that are the very sorts of things you're used to hearing from everyone else. No, I didn't think then that I should do anything servile because of the danger I faced, and so I don't regret now that I defended myself as I did. I'd far rather die after such a defense than live like that.

You see, whether in a trial or in a war, neither I nor anyone else should contrive to escape death at all costs. In battle, too, it often becomes clear that one might escape death by throwing down one's weapons and turning to supplicate one's pursuers. And in each sort of danger there are many other ways one can contrive to escape death, if one is shameless enough to do or say anything. The difficult thing, gentlemen, isn't escaping death; escaping villainy is much more difficult, since it runs faster than death. And now I, slow and old as I am, have been overtaken by the slower runner while my accusers, clever and sharp-witted as they are, have been overtaken by the faster one—vice. And now I take my leave, convicted by you of a capital crime, whereas they stand forever convicted by the truth of wickedness and injustice. And just as I accept my penalty, so must they. Perhaps, things *had* to turn out this way, and I suppose it's good they have.

c

d

e

39

b

32. Thirty minas (three thousand silver drachmas) was almost ten years' salary for someone engaged in public works.

c   Next, I want to make a prophecy to those who convicted me. Indeed, I'm now at the point at which men prophesy most—when they're about to die. I say to you men who condemned me to death that as soon as I'm dead vengeance will come upon you, and it will be much harsher, by Zeus, than the vengeance you take in killing me. You did this now in the belief that you'll escape giving an account of your lives. But I say that quite the opposite will happen to you. There will be more people to test you, whom
d   I now restrain, though you didn't notice my doing so. And they'll be all the harsher on you, since they're younger, and you'll resent it all the more. You see, if you imagine that by killing people you'll prevent anyone from reproaching you for not living in the right way, you're not thinking straight. In fact, to escape is neither possible nor noble. On the contrary, what's best and easiest isn't to put down other people, but to prepare oneself to be the best one can. With that prophecy to those of you who voted to convict me, I take my leave.

e   However, I'd gladly discuss this result with those who voted for my acquittal while the officers of the court are busy and I'm not yet on my way to the place where I must die. Please stay with me, gentlemen, just for that short time. After all, there's nothing to prevent us from having a talk with one another while it's still in our power. To you whom I regard as friends
40   I'm willing to show the meaning of what has just now happened to me. You see, gentlemen of the jury—for in calling *you* "jurors" I no doubt use the term correctly—an amazing thing has happened to me. In previous times, the usual prophecies of my daimonic sign were always very frequent, opposing me even on trivial matters, if I was about do something that wasn't right. Now, however, something has happened to me, as you can see for yourselves, that one might think to be, and that's generally regarded as being, the worst of all bad things. Yet the god's sign didn't
b   oppose me when I left home this morning, or when I came up here to the law court, or anywhere in my speech when I was about to say something, even though in other discussions it has often stopped me in the middle of what I was saying. Now, however, where this affair is concerned, it has opposed me in nothing I either said or did.

    What, then, do I suppose is the explanation for that? I'll tell you. You see, it's likely that what has happened to me is a good thing and that those of you who suppose death to be bad make an incorrect supposition. I've
c   strong evidence of this, since there's no way my usual sign would have failed to oppose me, if I weren't about to achieve something good.

    But let's bear in mind that the following is also a strong reason to hope that death may be something good. Being dead is one of two things: either the dead are nothing, as it were, and have no awareness whatsoever of anything at all; or else, as we're told, it's some sort of change, a migration of the soul from here to another place. Now, if there's in fact no awareness, but it's like sleep—the kind in which the sleeper has no dream whatso- *d* ever—then death would be an amazing advantage. For I imagine that if someone had to pick a night in which he slept so soundly that he didn't even dream and had to compare all the other nights and days of his life with that one, and then, having considered the matter, had to say how many days or nights of his life he had spent better or more pleasantly than that night—I imagine that not just some private individual, but even the great king,[33] would find them easy to count compared to the other days *e* and nights. Well, if death's like that, *I* say it's an advantage, since, in that case, the whole of time would seem no longer than a single night.

On the other hand, if death's a sort of journey from here to another place, and if what we're told is true, and all who've died are indeed there, what could be a greater good than that, gentlemen of the jury? If on arriving in Hades and leaving behind the people who claim to be jurors *41* here, one's going to find those who are truly jurors or judges, the very ones who are said to sit in judgment there too—Minos,[34] Rhadamanthys, Aeachus, Triptolemus, and all the other demigods who were just in their own lifetimes—would the journey be a wretched one?

Or again, what would any one of you not give to talk to Orpheus and Museus, Hesiod and Homer?[35] I'd be willing to die many times over, if that were true. You see, for myself, at any rate, spending time there would *b* be amazing: when I met Palamedes or Ajax, the son of Telemon, or anyone else of old who died because of an unjust verdict, I could compare my own experience with theirs—as I suppose it wouldn't be unpleasing to do. And in particular, the most important thing: I could spend time examining and searching people there, just as I do here, to find out who among them is wise, and who thinks he is, but isn't.

What wouldn't one give, gentlemen of the jury, to be able to examine the leader of the great expedition against Troy, or Odysseus, or Sisyphus,[36] *c* or countless other men and women one could mention? To talk to them there, to associate with them and examine them, wouldn't that be inconceivable happiness? In any case, the people there certainly don't kill one for doing it. For if what we're told is true, the people there are both happier in all other respects than the people here and also deathless for the remainder of time.

But you too, gentlemen of the jury, should be of good hope in the face of death, and bear in mind this single truth: nothing bad can happen to a

33. The king of Persia, whose wealth and power made him a popular exemplar of human success and happiness.
34. Minos was a legendary king of Crete.
35. Orpheus was a legendary bard and founder of the mystical religion of Orphism. Museus, usually associated with Orpheus, was also a legendary bard.
36. Sisyphus is a legendary king and founder of Corinth.

d   good man, whether in life or in death, nor are the gods unconcerned about his troubles. What has happened to me hasn't happened by chance; rather, it's clear to me that to die now and escape my troubles was a better thing for me. It was for this very reason that my sign never opposed me. And so, for my part, I'm not at all angry with those who voted to condemn me or with my accusers. And yet this wasn't what they had in mind when they were condemning and accusing me. No, they thought to harm me—and for that they deserve to be blamed.

e   This small favor, however, I ask of them. When my sons come of age, gentlemen, punish them by harassing them in the very same way that I harassed you, if they seem to you to take care of wealth or anything before virtue, if they think they're someone when they're no one. Reproach them, just as I reproached you: tell them that they don't care for the things they should and think they're someone when they're worth nothing. If you will

42   do that, I'll have received my own just deserts from you, as will my sons.

    But now it's time to leave, I to die and you to live. Which of us goes to the better thing, however, is unclear to everyone except the god.

CRITO

SOCRATES: Why have you come at this hour, Crito? Isn't it still early?   43

CRITO: It is indeed.

SOCRATES: About what time?

CRITO: Just before dawn.

SOCRATES: I'm surprised the prison warden was willing to let you in.

CRITO: He knows me by now, Socrates, I come here so often. And besides I've done him a good turn.

SOCRATES: Have you just arrived or have you been here for a while?

CRITO: For quite a while.

SOCRATES: Then why didn't you wake me right away, instead of sitting   b
there in silence?

CRITO: In the name of Zeus, Socrates, I wouldn't do that! I only wish I weren't so sleepless and distressed myself. I've been amazed all this time to see how peacefully you were sleeping, and I deliberately kept from waking you, so that you could pass the time as pleasantly as possible. In the past—indeed, throughout my entire life—I've often counted you happy in your disposition, but never more so than in this present misfortune. You bear it so easily and calmly.

SOCRATES: Well, Crito, it would be an error for someone of my age to complain when the time has come when he must die.

CRITO: Other people get overtaken by such misfortunes too, Socrates,   c
but their age doesn't prevent them in the least from complaining about their fate.

SOCRATES: That's right. But tell me, why *have* you come so early?

CRITO: I bring bad news, Socrates. Not bad in your view, it seems to me, but bad and hard in mine and that of all your friends—and hardest of all, I think, for me to bear.

SOCRATES: What news is that? Or has the ship returned from Delos, at   d
whose return I must die?[1]

Translated by C.D.C. Reeve.
1. Legend had it that Athens was once obliged to send King Minos of Crete an annual tribute of seven young men and seven maidens to be given to the Minotaur—a monster, half man and half bull, that he kept in a labyrinth. With the help of a thread given to him by Minos' daughter Ariadne, Theseus, a legendary king of Athens, made his way through the labyrinth, killed the Minotaur, and escaped,

CRITO: No, it hasn't returned *yet*, but I think it will arrive today, judging from the reports of people who've come from Sunium,[2] where they left it. It's clear from these reports that it will arrive today. And so tomorrow, Socrates, you must end your life.

SOCRATES: I pray that it may be for the best, Crito. If it pleases the gods, let it be so. All the same, I don't think it will arrive today.

44   CRITO: What evidence have you for that?

SOCRATES: I'll tell you. I must die on the day after the ship arrives.

CRITO: That's what the authorities say, at least.

SOCRATES: Then I don't think it will arrive today, but tomorrow. My evidence for this comes from a dream I had in the night a short while ago. So it looks as though you chose the right time not to wake me.

CRITO: What was your dream?

SOCRATES: I thought a beautiful, graceful woman came to me, robed in
b   white. She called me and said, "Socrates, you will arrive 'in fertile Phthia' on the third day."[3]

CRITO: What a strange dream, Socrates.

SOCRATES: Yet its meaning is quite clear, Crito—at least, it seems so to me.

CRITO: All too clear, apparently. But look here, Socrates, it's still not too late to take my advice and save yourself. You see, if you die, I won't just suffer a single misfortune. On the contrary, not only will I lose a friend the like of whom I'll never find again, but, in addition, many people, who don't know you or me well, will think that I didn't care about you, since I
c   could have saved you if I'd been willing to spend the money. And indeed what reputation could be more shameful than being thought to value money more than friends? For the majority of people won't believe that it was you yourself who refused to leave this place, though we were urging you to do so.

SOCRATES: But my dear Crito, why should we care so much about what the majority think? After all, the most decent ones, who are worthier of consideration, will believe that matters were handled in just the way they were in fact handled.

d   CRITO: But you can surely see, Socrates, that one should care about majority opinion too. Your present situation itself shows clearly that the majority can do not just minor harms but the very worst things to someone who's been slandered in front of them.

---

thus ending the tribute. Each year, Athens commemorated these events by sending a mission of thanks to the sanctuary of Apollo on the sacred island of Delos. No executions could take place in Athens until the mission returned from its voyage. See *Phaedo* 58a3–c5.

2. A headland on the southeast coast of Attica, about 30 miles from Athens.

3. *Iliad* ix.363.

SOCRATES: I only wish, Crito, that the majority *could* do the very worst things, then they might also be able to do the very best ones—and everything would be fine. But as it is, they can do neither, since they can't make someone either wise or unwise—the effects *they* produce are really the result of chance.

CRITO: Well, if you say so. But tell me this, Socrates. You're not worried *e* about me and your other friends, are you—fearing that if you escaped, the informers[4] would give us trouble, and that we might be forced to give up all our property, pay heavy fines, or even suffer some further penalty? If you're afraid of anything like that, dismiss it from your mind. After all, *45* we're surely justified in running this risk to save you or an even greater one if need be. Now take my advice, and don't refuse me.

SOCRATES: Yes, those things do worry me, Crito, among many others.

CRITO: Then don't fear them: the sum of money that certain people I know will accept in order to save you and get you out of here isn't that large. Next, don't you see how cheap these informers are and how little money is needed to deal with them? My own wealth's available to you, and it, I think, should be enough. Next, even if your concern for me makes *b* you unwilling to spend my money, there are foreign visitors here who are willing to spend theirs. One of them, Simmias of Thebes, has even brought enough money for this very purpose; and Cebes, too, and a good many others are also willing to contribute. So, as I say, don't let these fears make you hesitate to save yourself. And don't let it trouble you, as you were saying in court, that if you went into exile you wouldn't know what to do with yourself. You see, wherever else you may go, there'll be people to *c* welcome you. If you want to go to Thessaly, I have friends there who'll make much of you and protect you, so that no one in Thessaly will give you any trouble.[5]

Besides, Socrates, I think that what you're doing isn't just: throwing away your life, when you could save it, and hastening the very sort of fate for yourself that your enemies would hasten—and indeed have hastened—in their wish to destroy you. What's more I think you're also betraying those sons of yours by going away and deserting them when you could bring them up and educate them. So far as you're concerned, *d* they must take their chances in life; and the chance they'll get, in all likelihood, is just the one that orphans usually get when they lose their parents. No. Either one shouldn't have children at all, or one ought to see their upbringing and education through to the end. But you seem to me to

4. The *sukophantai* were individuals who prosecuted others in order to get the reward offered in Athenian law to successful prosecutors as public benefactors, or as a way of blackmailing someone who would pay to avoid prosecution, or for personal or political gain of some other sort.
5. Thessaly is a region in the north of Greece.

be choosing the easiest way out, whereas one should choose whatever a good and brave man would choose—particularly when one claims to have cared about virtue throughout one's life.

e   I feel ashamed on your behalf and on behalf of myself and your friends. I fear that it's going to seem that this whole business of yours has been handled with a certain cowardice on our part. The case was brought to court when it needn't have been brought. Then there was the actual conduct of the trial. And now, to crown it all, this absurd finale to the affair. It's going to seem that we let the opportunity slip because of some vice, such

46   as cowardice, on our part, since we didn't save you nor did you save yourself, although it was quite possible had we been of even the slightest use.

See to it, then, Socrates, that all this doesn't turn out badly and a shameful thing both for you and for us. Come, deliberate—or rather, at this hour it's not a matter of deliberating but of having deliberated already—and only one decision remains. You see, everything must be done this coming night; and if we delay, it will no longer be possible. For all these reasons, Socrates, please take my advice and don't refuse me.

b   SOCRATES: My dear Crito, your enthusiasm's most valuable, provided it's of the right sort. But if it isn't, the greater it is, the more difficult it will be to deal with. We must therefore examine whether we should do what you advise or not. You see, I'm not the sort of person who's just now for the first time persuaded by nothing within me except the argument that on rational reflection seems best to me; I've *always* been like that. I can't now reject the arguments I stated before just because this misfortune has befallen me. On the contrary, they seem pretty much the same to me, and I

c   respect and value the same ones as I did before. So if we have no better ones to offer in the present situation, you can be sure I won't agree with you—not even if the power of the majority to threaten us, as if we were children, with the bogeymen of imprisonment, execution, and confiscation of property were far greater than it is now.

What, then, is the most reasonable way to examine these matters? Suppose we first take up the argument you stated about people's opinions. Is it

d   true or not that one should pay attention to some opinions but not to others? Or was it true before I had to die, whereas it's now clear that it was stated idly, for the sake of argument, and is really just childish nonsense? For my part, I'm eager to join you, Crito, in a joint examination of whether this argument will appear any differently to me, now that I'm here, or the same, and of whether we should dismiss it from our minds or be persuaded by it.

It used to be said, I think, by people who thought they were talking sense, that, as I said a moment ago, one should take some people's opinions seriously but not others. By the gods, Crito, don't you think that was true? You see, in all human probability, *you* are not going to die tomorrow, and so the present situation won't distort your judgment. Consider, then, don't you think it's a sound argument that one shouldn't value all the opinions people have, but some and not others, and not those of everyone, but those of some people and not of others? What do you say? Isn't that true?

CRITO: It is.

SOCRATES: And we should value good opinions, but not bad ones?

CRITO: Yes.

SOCRATES: And the good ones are those of wise people and the bad ones those of unwise people?

CRITO: Of course.

SOCRATES: Come then, what of such questions as this? When a man's primarily engaged in physical training, does he pay attention to the praise or blame or opinion of every man or only to those of the one man who's a doctor or a trainer?

CRITO: Only to those of the one man.

SOCRATES: Then he should fear the blame and welcome the praise of that one man, but not those of the majority of people.

CRITO: Clearly.

SOCRATES: So his actions and exercises, his eating and drinking, should be guided by the opinion of the one man, the knowledgeable and understanding supervisor, rather than on that of all the rest?

CRITO: That's right.

SOCRATES: Well, then, if he disobeys that one man and sets no value on his opinion or his praises but values those of the majority of people who have no understanding, won't something bad happen to him?

CRITO: Of course.

SOCRATES: And what is this bad effect? Where does it occur? In what part of the one who disobeys?

CRITO: Clearly, it's in his body, since that's what it destroys.

SOCRATES: That's right. And isn't the same true in other cases, Crito? No need to go through them all, but, in particular, in cases of just and unjust things, shameful and fine ones, good and bad ones—in cases of what we're now deliberating about—is it the opinion of the majority we should follow and fear? Or is it the opinion of the one man—if there is one who understands these things—we should respect and fear above all others? On the grounds that, if we don't follow it, we shall seriously damage and maim that part of us which, as we used to say, is made better by what's just but is destroyed by what's unjust. Or is there no truth in that?

CRITO: I certainly think there is, Socrates.

SOCRATES: Come then, suppose we destroy the part of us that is made better by what's healthy but is seriously damaged by what causes disease when we don't follow the opinion of people who have understanding. Would our lives be worth living once it has been seriously damaged? And that part, of course, is the body, isn't it?

CRITO: Yes.

SOCRATES: Then are our lives worth living with a wretched, seriously damaged body?

CRITO: Certainly not.

SOCRATES: But our lives *are* worth living when the part of us that's maimed by what's unjust and benefited by what's just is seriously damaged? Or do we consider it—whichever part of us it is to which justice and injustice pertain—to be inferior to the body?

CRITO: Certainly not.

SOCRATES: On the contrary, it's more valuable?

CRITO: Far more.

SOCRATES: Then, my very good friend, we should not give so much thought to what the majority of people will say about us, but think instead of what the person who understands just and unjust things will say—the one man and the truth itself. So your first claim—that we should give thought to the opinion of the majority about what's just, fine, good, and their opposites—isn't right.

"But," someone might say, "the majority can put us to death."

CRITO: That's certainly clear too. It would indeed be said, Socrates.

SOCRATES: That's right. And yet, my dear friend, the argument we've gone through still seems the same to me, at any rate, as it did before. And now examine this further one to see whether we think it still stands or not: the most important thing isn't living, but living well.

CRITO: Yes, it still stands.

SOCRATES: And the argument that living well, living a fine life, and living justly are the same—does it still stand or not?

CRITO: It still stands.

SOCRATES: Then in the light of these agreements, we should examine whether or not it would be just for me to try to get out of here when the Athenians haven't acquitted me. And if it does seem just, we should make the attempt, and if it doesn't, we should abandon the effort.

As for those other considerations you raise about loss of money and people's opinions and bringing up children—they, in truth, Crito, are appropriate considerations for people who readily put one to death and would as readily bring one back to life again if they could, without thinking; I mean, the majority of people. For us, however, the argument has made the decision. There's nothing else to be examined besides the very thing we just mentioned: whether we—both the ones who are rescued and also the rescuers themselves—will be acting justly if we pay money to those who would get me out of here and do them favors, or whether we will in truth be acting unjustly if we do those things. And if it appears that we will be acting unjustly in doing them, we have no need at all to give any opposing weight to our having to die—or suffer in some other way—if we stay here and mind our behavior when the alternative is doing injustice.

CRITO: What you *say* seems true to me, Socrates. But I wish you'd consider what we're to *do*.

SOCRATES: Let's examine that question together, my dear friend, and if you can oppose anything I say, oppose it, and I'll be persuaded by you. But if you can't, be a good fellow and stop telling me the same thing over and over, that I should leave here against the will of the Athenians. You see, I think it very important that I act in this matter having persuaded you, rather than against your will. Consider, then, the starting point of our inquiry, to see if you find it adequately formulated, and try to answer my questions as you really think best.

CRITO: I'll certainly try.

SOCRATES: Do we say that one should never do injustice intentionally? Or may injustice be done in some circumstances but not in others? Is doing injustice never good or fine, as we have often agreed in the past? Or have all these former agreements been discarded during these last few days? Can you and I at our age, Crito, have spent so long in serious discussion with one another without realizing that we ourselves were no better than a pair of children? Or is what we used to say true above all else: that whether the majority of people agree or not, and whether we must suffer still worse things than at present or ones that are easier to bear, it's true, all the same, that doing injustice in any circumstances is bad and shameful for the one who does it? Is that what we say or not?

CRITO: It is what we say.

SOCRATES: So one should never do injustice.

CRITO: Certainly not.

SOCRATES: So one shouldn't do injustice in return for injustice, as the majority of people think—seeing that one should *never* do injustice.

CRITO: Apparently not.

SOCRATES: Well then, should one do wrong or not?

CRITO: Certainly not, Socrates.

SOCRATES: Well, what about when someone does wrong in return for having suffered wrongdoing? Is that just, as the majority of people think, or not just?

CRITO: It's not just at all.

SOCRATES: No, for there's no difference, I take it, between doing wrong and doing injustice?

CRITO: That's right.

SOCRATES: So one must neither do injustice in return nor wrong any man, no matter what one has suffered at his hands. And, Crito, in agreeing to this, watch out that you're not agreeing to anything contrary to what you believe. You see, I know that only a few people do believe or will believe it. And between those who believe it and those who don't, there's no common basis for deliberation, but each necessarily regards the other with contempt when they see their deliberations. You too, then, should consider very carefully whether you share that belief with me and whether the following is the starting point of our deliberations: that it's never right to do injustice, or to do injustice in return, or to retaliate with bad treatment when one has been treated badly. Or do you disagree and not share this starting point? You see, I've believed this for a long time myself and still believe it now. But if you've come to some other opinion, say so. Instruct me. If you stand by the former one, however, then listen to my next point.

CRITO: Yes, I do stand by it and share it with you, so go on.

SOCRATES: Then I'll state the next point—or rather, ask a question: should one do the things one has agreed with someone to do, provided they are just, or should one cheat?

CRITO: One should do them.

SOCRATES: Then consider what follows. If we leave this place without having persuaded the city, are we treating some people badly—and those whom we should least of all treat in that way—or not? Are we standing by agreements that are just or not?

CRITO: I can't answer your question, Socrates, since I don't understand it.

SOCRATES: Well, look at it this way. Suppose we were about to run away from here—or whatever what we'd be doing should be called. And suppose the Laws and the city community came and confronted us, and said,

"Tell us, Socrates, what do you intend to do? Do you intend anything else by this act you're attempting than to destroy us Laws, and the city as a whole, to the extent that you can? Or do you think that a city can continue to exist and not be overthrown if the legal judgments rendered in it have no force, but are deprived of authority and undermined by the actions of private individuals?"

What shall we say in response to that question, Crito, and to others like it? For there's a lot that one might say—particularly, if one were an orator—on behalf of this law we're destroying, the one requiring that legal judgments, once rendered, have authority. Or shall we say to them, "Yes, that's what we intend, for the city treated us unjustly and didn't judge our lawsuit correctly." Is that what we're to say—or what?

CRITO: Yes, by Zeus, that's what we're to say, Socrates.

SOCRATES: Then what if the Laws replied, "Was that also part of the agreement between you and us, Socrates? Or did you agree to stand by whatever judgments the city rendered?" Then, if we were surprised at the words, perhaps they might say, "Don't be surprised at what we're saying,

Socrates, but answer us—since you're so accustomed to using question and answer. Come now, what charge have you to bring against the city and ourselves that you should try to destroy us? In the first place, wasn't it *d* we who gave you birth—wasn't it through us that your father married your mother and produced you? Tell us, do you have some complaint about the correctness of those of us Laws concerned with marriage?"

"No, I have no complaint," I'd reply.

"Well then, what about the Laws dealing with the bringing up and educating of children, under which you were educated yourself? Didn't those of us Laws who regulate that area prescribe correctly when we ordered your father to educate you in the arts and physical training?"

"They prescribed correctly," I'd reply.

"Good. Then since you were born, brought up, and educated, can you *e* deny, first, that you're our offspring and slave, both yourself and your ancestors? And if that's so, do you think that what's just is based on an equality between you and us, that whatever we try to do to you it's just for you to do to us in return? As regards you and your father (or you and your master, if you happened to have one), what's just isn't based on equality, and so you don't return whatever treatment you receive—answering back when you're criticized or striking back when you're struck, or doing many *51* other such things. As regards you and your fatherland and its Laws, then, are these things permitted? If we try to destroy you, believing it to be just, will you try to destroy us Laws and your fatherland, to the extent that you can? And will you claim that you're acting justly in doing so—you the man who really cares about virtue? Or are you so wise that it has escaped your notice that your fatherland is more worthy of honor than your mother and father and all your other ancestors; that it is more to be revered and more sacred and is held in greater esteem both among the gods and *b* among those human beings who have any sense; that you must treat your fatherland with piety, submitting to it and placating it more than you would your own father when it is angry; that you must either persuade it or else do whatever it commands; that you must mind your behavior and undergo whatever treatment it prescribes for you, whether a beating or imprisonment; that if it leads you to war to be wounded or killed, that's what you must do, and that's what is just—not to give way or retreat or leave where you were stationed, but, on the contrary, in war and law courts, and everywhere else, to do whatever your city or fatherland com- mands or else persuade it as to what is really just; and that while it is *c* impious to violate the will of your mother or father, it is yet less so than to violate that of your fatherland."

What are we to say to that, Crito? Are the Laws telling the truth or not?

CRITO: Yes, I think they are.

SOCRATES: "Consider, then, Socrates," the Laws might perhaps continue, "whether we're also telling the truth in saying this: that you aren't treating us justly in what you're now trying to do. You see, we gave you birth, upbringing, and education, and have provided you, as well as every
d   other citizen, with a share of all the fine things we could. Nonetheless, if any Athenian—who has been admitted to adult status and has observed both how affairs are handled in the city and ourselves, the Laws—is dissatisfied with us and wishes to leave, we grant him permission to take his property and go wherever he pleases. Not one of us Laws stands in his way or forbids it. If any one of you is dissatisfied with us and the city and wishes to go to a colony or to live as an alien elsewhere, he may go
e   wherever he wishes and hold on to what's his.

"*But* if any of you stays here, after he has observed the way we judge lawsuits and the other ways in which we manage the city, then we say that he has agreed with us by his action to do whatever we command. And we say that whoever does not obey commits a threefold injustice: he disobeys us as his parents; he disobeys us as those who brought him up; and, after having agreed to obey us, he neither obeys nor persuades us, if we're doing something that isn't right. Yet we offer him a choice and do not harshly command him to do what he's told. On the contrary, we offer two
52   alternatives: he must either persuade us or do what we say. And he does neither. These, then, are the charges, Socrates, to which we say you too will become liable, if you do what you have in mind—and you won't be among the least liable of the Athenians, but among the most."

Then, if I were to say, "Why is that?" perhaps they might justifiably reproach me by saying that I am among the Athenians who have made that agreement with them in the strongest terms.

b   "Socrates," they would say, "we have the strongest evidence that you were satisfied with us and with the city. After all, you'd never have stayed at home here so much more consistently than all the rest of the Athenians if you weren't also much more consistently satisfied. You never left the city for a festival, except once to go to the Isthmus.[6] You never went anywhere else, except for military service. You never went abroad as other people do. You had no desire to acquaint yourself with other cities or other laws. On
c   the contrary, we and our city sufficed for you. So emphatically did you choose us and agree to live as a citizen under us, that you even produced children here. *That's* how satisfied you were with the city.

"Moreover, even at your very trial, you could have proposed exile as a counterpenalty if you'd wished, and what you're now trying to do against the city's will, you could then have done with its consent. On that

---

6. The Isthmus is the narrow strip of land connecting the Peloponnese to the rest of Greece, where the Isthmian Games were held.

occasion, you prided yourself on not feeling resentful that you had to die. You'd choose death before exile—so you said. Now, however, you feel no shame at those words and show no regard for us Laws as you try to destroy us. You're acting exactly the way the most wretched slave would   *d* act by trying to run away, contrary to your commitments and your agreements to live as a citizen under us.

"First, then, answer us on this very point: are we telling the truth when we say that you agreed, by deeds not words, to live as a citizen under us? Or is that untrue?"

What are we to reply to that, Crito? Mustn't we agree?

CRITO: We must, Socrates.

SOCRATES: "Well then," they might say, "surely you're breaking the commitments and agreements you made with us. You weren't coerced or   *e* tricked into agreeing or forced to decide in a hurry. On the contrary, you had seventy years in which you could have left if you weren't satisfied with us or if you thought those agreements unjust. You, however, preferred neither Sparta nor Crete—places you often say have good law and order—nor any other Greek or foreign city. On the contrary, you went   *53* abroad less often than the lame, the blind, or other handicapped people. Hence it's clear that you, more than any other Athenian, have been consistently satisfied with your city and with us Laws—for who would be satisfied by a city but not by its laws? Won't you, then, stand by your agreements now? Yes, you will, if you're persuaded by us, Socrates, and at least you won't make yourself a laughingstock by leaving the city.

"For consider now: if you break those agreements, if you commit any of these wrongs, what good will you do yourself or your friends? You see, it's pretty clear that your friends will risk being exiled themselves as well as   *b* being disenfranchised and having their property confiscated. As for you, if you go to one of the nearest cities, Thebes or Megara—for they both have good laws—you will be arriving there, Socrates, as an enemy of their political systems, and those who care about their own cities will look on you with suspicion, regarding you as one who undermines laws. You will also confirm your jurors in their opinion, so that they will think they judged your lawsuit correctly. For anyone who undermines laws might   *c* very well be considered a corruptor of young and ignorant people.

"Will you, then, avoid cities with good law and order, and men of the most respectable kind? And if so, will your life be worth living? Or will you associate with these people and be shameless enough to converse with them? And what will you say, Socrates? The very things that you said here, about how virtue and justice are man's most valuable possessions, along with law and lawful conduct. Don't you think Socrates and everything about him will look unseemly? Surely, you must.

d   "Or will you keep away from those places and go to Crito's friends in
Thessaly? After all, there's complete disorder and laxity there, so perhaps
they'd enjoy hearing about your absurd escape from prison when you
dressed up in disguise, wore a peasant's leather jerkin or some other such
escapee's outfit, and altered your appearance. And will no one remark on
the fact that you, an old man, with probably only a short time left to live,
e   were so greedy for life that you dared to violate the most important laws?
Perhaps not, provided you don't annoy anyone. Otherwise, you'll hear
many disparaging things said about you. Will you live by currying favor
with every man and acting the slave—and do nothing in Thessaly besides
eat, as if you'd gone to live in Thessaly for a good dinner? As for those
54   arguments about justice and the rest of virtue, where, tell us, will they be?
          "Is it that you want to live for your children's sake, then, to bring them
up and educate them? Really? Will you bring them up and educate them
by taking them to Thessaly and making foreigners of them, so they can
enjoy that privilege too? If not, will they be better brought up and educated here without you, provided that you're still alive? 'Of course,' you
may say, because your friends will take care of them. Then will they take
care of them if you go to Thessaly, but not take care of them if you go to
Hades? If those who call themselves your friends are worth anything at all,
b   you surely can't believe that.
          "No, Socrates, be persuaded by us who reared you. Don't put a higher
value on children, on life, or on anything else than on what's just, so that
when you reach Hades you may have all this to offer as your defense
before the authorities there. For if you do do that, it doesn't seem that it
will be better for you *here,* or for any of your friends, or that it will be more
just or more pious. And it won't be better for you when you arrive *there*
either. As it is, you'll leave here—if you do leave—as one who has been
c   treated unjustly not by us Laws, but by men. But suppose you leave,
suppose you return injustice for injustice and bad treatment for bad treatment in that shameful way, breaking your agreements and commitments
with us and doing bad things to those whom you should least of all treat in
that way—yourself, your friends, your fatherland, and ourselves. Then
we'll be angry with you while you're still alive, and our brothers, the Laws
of Hades, won't receive you kindly there, knowing that you tried to
destroy us to the extent you could. Come, then, don't let Crito persuade
d   you to follow his advice rather than ours."
          That, Crito, my dear friend, is what I seem to hear them saying, you
may be sure. And, just like those Corybantes who think they are still
hearing the flutes,[7] the echo of their arguments reverberates in me and
makes me incapable of hearing anything else. No, as far as my present
thoughts go, at least, you may be sure that if you argue against them, you

---

7. See *Symposium* 215e4 note.

will speak in vain. All the same, if you think you can do any more, please tell me.

CRITO: No, Socrates, I've nothing to say.

SOCRATES: Then, let it be, Crito, and let's act in that way, since that's the   *e*
way the god is leading us.

PROTAGORAS

(317e–334c, 348c–362a)

*In the following selections, the great Sophist Protagoras (some fragments of
whose actual writings are included in this anthology) is made to explain his view
of virtue. When he finishes, Socrates beings to examine him on a series of related
topics that are central to his view: the unity of the virtues, the possibility of weakness of will, the identity of virtue and knowledge, and their bearing on the teach-
ability of virtue. The discussion ends in apparent aporia or puzzlement, because
the positions adopted and defended on these topics seem inconsistent.*

When we had all taken our seats, Protagoras said, "Now, then, Socrates,
since these gentlemen also are present, would you please say what it was
you brought up to me a little while ago on the young man's behalf."

318   "Well, Protagoras," I said, "as to why we have come, I'll begin as I did
before. Hippocrates here has gotten to the point where he wants to be your
student, and, quite naturally, he would like to know what he will get out of
it if he does study with you. That's really all we have to say."

Protagoras took it from there and said, "Young man, this is what you will
get if you study with me: The very day you start, you will go home a better

b   man, and the same thing will happen the day after. Every day, day after
day, you will get better and better."

When I heard this I said, "What you're saying, Protagoras, isn't very
surprising, but quite likely. Why, even you, though you are so old and wise,
would get better if someone taught you something you didn't happen to
know already. But what if the situation were a little different, and Hippocrates here all of a sudden changed his mind and set his heart on studying

c   with this young fellow who has just come into town, Zeuxippus of Her-
aclea,[1] and came to him, as he now comes to you, and heard from him the
very same thing as from you—that each day he spent with him he would
become better and make progress. If Hippocrates asked him in what way
he would become better, and toward what he would be making progress,
Zeuxippus would say at painting. And if he were studying with Orthagoras

Translated by Stanley Lombardo and Karen Bell.

1. Zeuxippus (more commonly spelled Zeuxis), a painter who flourished in the late
fifth century.

of Thebes[2] and he heard from him the same thing as he hears from you and asked him in what he would be getting better every day he studied with him, Orthagoras would say at flute-playing. It is in this way that you must tell me and the young man on whose behalf I am asking the answer to this *d* question: If Hippocrates studies with Protagoras, exactly how will he go away a better man and in what will he make progress each and every day he spends with you?"

Protagoras heard me out and then said, "You put your question well, Socrates, and I am only too glad to answer those who pose questions well. If Hippocrates comes to me he will not experience what he would if he studied with some other sophist. The others abuse young men, steering *e* them back again, against their will, into subjects the likes of which they have escaped from at school, teaching them arithmetic, astronomy, geometry, music, and poetry"—at this point he gave Hippias a significant look—"but if he comes to me he will learn only what he has come for. What I teach is sound deliberation, both in domestic matters—how best to manage *319* one's household, and in public affairs—how to realize one's maximum potential for success in political debate and action."

"Am I following what you are saying?" I asked. "You appear to be talking about the art of citizenship, and to be promising to make men good citizens."

"This is exactly what I claim, Socrates."

"Well, this is truly an admirable technique you have developed, if indeed you have. There is no point in my saying to you anything other than exactly what I think. The truth is, Protagoras, I have never thought that *b* this could be taught, but when you say it can be, I can't very well doubt it. It's only right that I explain where I got the idea that this is not teachable, not something that can be imparted from one human being to another. I maintain, along with the rest of the Greek world, that the Athenians are wise. And I observe that when we convene in the Assembly and the city has to take some action on a building project, we send for builders to advise us; if it has to do with the construction of ships, we send for shipwrights; and so forth for everything that is considered learnable and *c* teachable. But if anyone else, a person not regarded as a craftsman, tries to advise them, no matter how handsome and rich and well-born he might be, they just don't accept him. They laugh at him and shout him down until he either gives up trying to speak and steps down himself, or the archer-police remove him forcibly by order of the board. This is how they proceed in matters which they consider technical. But when it is a matter of deliberat- *d* ing on city management, anyone can stand up and advise them, carpenter, blacksmith, shoemaker, merchant, ship-captain, rich man, poor man, well-born, low-born—it doesn't matter—and nobody blasts him for presuming

2. Orthagoras, renowned for his excellent playing on the flute (*aulos*).

to give counsel without any prior training under a teacher. The reason for
e   this is clear: They do not think that this can be taught. Public life aside, the
same principle holds also in private life, where the wisest and best of our
citizens are unable to transmit to others the virtues that they possess. Look
at Pericles,[3] the father of these young men here. He gave them a superb
320   education in everything that teachers can teach, but as for what he himself
is really wise in, he neither teaches them that himself nor has anyone else
teach them either, and his sons have to browse like stray sacred cattle and
pick up virtue on their own wherever they might find it. Take a good look
at Cleinias, the younger brother of Alcibiades here. When Pericles became
his guardian he was afraid that he would be corrupted, no less, by Alcibiades. So he separated them and placed Cleinias in Ariphron's house and
tried to educate him there. Six months later he gave him back to Alcibiades
b   because he couldn't do anything with him. I could mention a great many
more, men who are good themselves but have never succeeded in making
anyone else better, whether family members or total strangers. Looking at
these things, Protagoras, I just don't think that virtue can be taught. But
when I hear what you have to say, I waver; I think there must be something
in what you are talking about. I consider you to be a person of enormous
experience who has learned much from others and thought through a great
many things for himself. So if you can clarify for us how virtue is teachable, please don't begrudge us your explanation."

c   "I wouldn't think of begrudging you an explanation, Socrates," he replied. "But would you rather that I explain by telling you a story, as an
older man to a younger audience, or by developing an argument?"

The consensus was that he should proceed in whichever way he wished.
"I think it would be more pleasant," he said, "if I told you a story.

"There once was a time when the gods existed but mortal races did not.
d   When the time came for their appointed genesis, the gods molded them
inside the earth, blending together earth and fire and various compounds
of earth and fire. When they were ready to bring them to light the gods put
Prometheus and Epimetheus in charge of assigning to each its appropriate
powers and abilities.

"Epimetheus begged Prometheus for the privilege of assigning the abil-
e   ities himself. 'When I've completed the distribution,' he said, 'you can inspect it.' Prometheus agreed, and Epimetheus started distributing abilities.

"To some he assigned strength without quickness; the weaker ones he
made quick. Some he armed; others he left unarmed but devised for them
321   some other means for preserving themselves. He compensated for small
size by issuing wings for flight or an underground habitat. Size was itself a
safeguard for those he made large. And so on down the line, balancing his

3. Pericles (c. 495–429 B.C.), the greatest fifth-century Athenian statesman and
general.

distribution, making adjustments, and taking precautions against the possible extinction of any of the races.

"After supplying them with defenses against mutual destruction, he devised for them protection against the weather. He clothed them with thick *b* pelts and tough hides capable of warding off winter storms, effective against heat, and serving also as built-in, natural bedding when they went to sleep. He also shod them, some with hooves, others with thick pads of bloodless skin. Then he provided them with various forms of nourishment, plants for some, fruit from trees for others, roots for still others. And there were some to whom he gave the consumption of other animals as their sustenance. To some he gave the capacity for few births; to others, ravaged by the former, he gave the capacity for multiple births, and so ensured the survival of their kind.

"But Epimetheus was not very wise, and he absentmindedly used up all *c* the powers and abilities on the nonreasoning animals; he was left with the human race, completely unequipped. While he was floundering about, at a loss, Prometheus arrived to inspect the distribution and saw that while the other animals were well provided with everything, the human race was naked, unshod, unbedded, and unarmed, and it was already the day on which all of them, human beings included, were destined to emerge from the earth into the light. It was then that Prometheus, desperate to find some *d* means of survival for the human race, stole from Hephaestus and Athena wisdom in the practical arts together with fire (without which this kind of wisdom is effectively useless) and gave them outright to the human race. The wisdom it acquired was for staying alive; wisdom for living together in society, political wisdom, it did not acquire, because that was in the keeping of Zeus. Prometheus no longer had free access to the high citadel that is the house of Zeus, and besides this, the guards there were terrifying. But he did sneak into the building that Athena and Hephaestus shared to *e* practice their arts, and he stole from Hephaestus the art of fire and from Athena her arts, and he gave them to the human race. And it is from this *322* origin that the resources human beings needed to stay alive came into being. Later, the story goes, Prometheus was charged with theft, all on account of Epimetheus.

"It is because humans had a share of the divine dispensation that they alone among animals worshipped the gods, with whom they had a kind of kinship, and erected altars and sacred images. It wasn't long before they were articulating speech and words and had invented houses, clothes, shoes, and blankets, and were nourished by food from the earth. Thus *b* equipped, human beings at first lived in scattered isolation; there were no cities. They were being destroyed by wild beasts because they were weaker in every way, and although their technology was adequate to obtain food, it was deficient when it came to fighting wild animals. This was because they did not yet possess the art of politics, of which the art of war is a part.

They did indeed try to band together and survive by founding cities. The outcome when they did so was that they wronged each other, because they did not possess the art of politics, and so they would scatter and again be destroyed. Zeus was afraid that our whole race might be wiped out, so he sent Hermes to bring justice and a sense of shame to humans, so that there would be order within cities and bonds of friendship to unite them. Hermes asked Zeus how he should distribute shame and justice to humans. 'Should I distribute them as the other arts were? This is how the others were distributed: one person practicing the art of medicine suffices for many ordinary people; and so forth with the other practitioners. Should I establish justice and shame among humans in this way, or distribute it to all?' 'To all,' said Zeus, 'and let all have a share. For cities would never come to be if only a few possessed these, as is the case with the other arts. And establish this law as coming from me: Death to him who cannot partake of shame and justice, for he is a pestilence to the city.'

"And so it is, Socrates, that when the Athenians (and others as well) are debating architectural excellence, or the virtue proper to any other professional specialty, they think that only a few individuals have the right to advise them, and they do not accept advice from anyone outside these select few. You've made this point yourself, and with good reason, I might add. But when the debate involves political excellence, which must proceed entirely from justice and temperance, they accept advice from anyone, and with good reason, for they think that this particular virtue, political or civic virtue, is shared by all, or there wouldn't be any cities. This must be the explanation for it, Socrates.

"And so you won't think you've been deceived, consider this as further evidence for the universal belief that all humans have a share of justice and the rest of civic virtue. In the other arts, as you have said, if someone claims to be a good flute-player or whatever, but is not, people laugh at him or get angry with him, and his family comes round and remonstrates with him as if he were mad. But when it comes to justice or any other social virtue, even if they know someone is unjust, if that person publicly confesses the truth about himself, they will call this truthfulness madness, whereas in the previous case they would have called it a sense of decency. They will say that everyone ought to claim to be just, whether they are or not, and that it is madness not to pretend to justice, since one must have some trace of it or not be human.

"This, then, is my first point: It is reasonable to admit everyone as an adviser on this virtue, on the grounds that everyone has some share of it. Next I will attempt to show that people do *not* regard this virtue as natural or self-generated, but as something taught and carefully developed in those in whom it is developed.

"In the case of evils that men universally regard as afflictions due to nature or bad luck, no one ever gets angry with anyone so afflicted or

reproves, admonishes, punishes, or tries to correct them. We simply pity them. No one in his right mind would try to do anything like this to someone who is ugly, for example, or scrawny or weak. The reason is, I assume, that they know that these things happen to people as a natural process or by chance, both these ills and their opposites. But in the case of the good things that accrue to men through practice and training and teaching, if someone does not possess these goods but rather their corre-   *e*
sponding evils, he finds himself the object of anger, punishment, and reproof. Among these evils are injustice, impiety, and in general everything   *324*
that is opposed to civic virtue. Offenses in this area are always met with anger and reproof, and the reason is clearly that this virtue is regarded as something acquired through practice and teaching. The key, Socrates, to the true significance of punishment lies in the fact that human beings consider virtue to be something acquired through training. For no one   *b*
punishes a wrong-doer in consideration of the simple fact that he has done wrong, unless one is exercising the mindless vindictiveness of a beast. Reasonable punishment is not vengeance for a past wrong—for one cannot undo what has been done—but is undertaken with a view to the future, to deter both the wrong-doer and whoever sees him being punished from repeating the crime. This attitude towards punishment as deterrence im-   *c*
plies that virtue is learned, and this is the attitude of all those who seek requital in public or in private. All human beings seek requital from and punish those who they think have wronged them, and the Athenians, your fellow citizens, especially do so. Therefore, by my argument, the Athenians are among those who think that virtue is acquired and taught. So it is with good reason that your fellow citizens accept a blacksmith's or a cobbler's advice in political affairs. And they do think that virtue is acquired and   *d*
taught. It appears to me that both these propositions have been sufficiently proved, Socrates.

"Now, on to your remaining difficulty, the problem you raise about good men teaching their sons everything that can be taught and making them wise in these subjects, but not making them better than anyone else in the particular virtue in which they themselves excel. On this subject, Socrates, I will abandon story for argument. Consider this: Does there or does there   *e*
not exist one thing which all citizens must have for there to be a city? Here and nowhere else lies the solution to your problem. For if such a thing exists, and this one thing is not the art of the carpenter, the blacksmith, or the potter, but justice, and temperance, and piety—what I may collect-   *325*
ively term the virtue of a man, and if this is the thing which everyone should share in and with which every man should act whenever he wants to learn anything or do anything, but should not act without it, and if we should instruct and punish those who do not share in it, man, woman, and   *b*
child, until their punishment makes them better, and should exile from our cities or execute whoever doesn't respond to punishment and instruction; if

this is the case, if such is the nature of this thing, and good men give their sons an education in everything but this, then we have to be amazed at how strangely our good men behave. For we have shown that they regard this thing as teachable both in private and public life. Since it is something that can be taught and nurtured, is it possible that they have their sons taught everything in which there is no death penalty for not understanding it, but when their children are faced with the death penalty or exile if they fail to

c   learn virtue and be nurtured in it—and not only death but confiscation of property and, practically speaking, complete familial catastrophe—do you think they do not have them taught this or give them all the attention possible? We must think that they do, Socrates.

"Starting when they are little children and continuing as long as they live, they teach them and correct them. As soon as a child understands what is said to him, the nurse, mother, tutor, and the father himself fight

d   for him to be as good as he possibly can, seizing on every action and word to teach him and show him that this is just, that is unjust, this is noble, that is ugly, this is pious, that is impious, he should do this, he should not do that. If he obeys willingly, fine; if not, they straighten him out with threats and blows as if he were a twisted, bent piece of wood. After this they send him to school and tell his teachers to pay more attention to his good con-

e   duct than to his grammar or music lessons. The teachers pay attention to these things, and when the children have learned their letters and are getting to understand writing as well as the spoken language, they are given the works of good poets to read at their desks and have to learn them

326   by heart, works that contain numerous exhortations, many passages describing in glowing terms good men of old, so that the child is inspired to imitate them and become like them. In a similar vein, the music teachers too foster in their young pupils a sense of moral decency and restraint, and when they learn to play the lyre they are taught the works of still more

b   good poets, the lyric and choral poets. The teachers arrange the scores and drill the rhythms and scales into the children's souls, so that they become gentler, and their speech and movements become more rhythmical and harmonious. For all of human life requires a high degree of rhythm and harmony. On top of all this, they send their children to an athletic trainer so that they may have sound bodies in the service of their now fit minds

c   and will not be forced to cowardice in war or other activities through physical deficiencies.

"This is what the most able, i.e., the richest, do. Their sons start going to school at the earliest age and quit at the latest age. And when they quit

d   school, the city in turn compels them to learn the laws and to model their lives on them. They are not to act as they please. An analogy might be drawn from the practice of writing-teachers, who sketch the letters faintly with a pen in workbooks for their beginning students and have them write the letters over the patterns they have drawn. In the same way the city has drawn up laws invented by the great lawgivers in the past and compels them to govern and be governed by them. She punishes anyone who goes beyond these laws, and the term for this punishment in your city and others is, because it is a corrective legal action, 'correction.'   *e*

"When so much care and attention is paid to virtue, Socrates, both in public and private, are you still puzzled about virtue being teachable? The wonder would be if it were not teachable.

"Why, then, do many sons of good fathers never amount to anything? I want you to understand this too, and in fact it's no great wonder, if what I've just been saying is true about virtue being something in which no one   *327* can be a layman if there is to be a city. For if what I am saying is true—and nothing could be more true: Pick any other pursuit or study and reflect upon it. Suppose, for instance, there could be no city unless we were all flute-players, each to the best of his ability, and everybody were teaching everybody else this art in public and private and reprimanding the poor players and doing all this unstintingly, just as now no one begrudges or   *b* conceals his expertise in what is just and lawful as he does his other professional expertise. For it is to our collective advantage that we each possess justice and virtue, and so we all gladly tell and teach each other what is just and lawful. Well, if we all had the same eagerness and generosity in teaching each other flute-playing, do you think, Socrates, that the sons of good flute-players would be more likely to be good flute-players than the sons of poor flute-players? I don't think so at all. When a son happened to be naturally disposed toward flute-playing, he would progress   *c* and become famous; otherwise, he would remain obscure. In many cases the son of a good player would turn out to be a poor one, and the son of a poor player would turn out to be good. But as flute-players, they would all turn out to be capable when compared with ordinary people who had never studied the flute. Likewise you must regard the most unjust person ever reared in a human society under law as a paragon of justice compared with   *d* people lacking education and lawcourts and the pervasive pressure to cultivate virtue, savages such as the playwright Pherecrates[4] brought on stage at last year's Lenaion. There's no doubt that if you found yourself among such people, as did the misanthropes in that play's chorus, you would be delighted to meet up with the likes of Eurybatus and Phrynondas[5] and would   *e* sorely miss the immorality of the people here. As it is, Socrates, you affect delicate sensibilities, because everyone here is a teacher of virtue, to the best of his ability, and you can't see a single one. You might as well look for a teacher of Greek; you wouldn't find a single one of those either. Nor   *328*

4. Pherecrates, an Athenian writer of comic plays and prize-winner at the Lenaion dramatic competition in the late fifth century.

5. Eurybatus and Phrynondas, historical individuals, whose names had in literature become synonymous with viciousness.

would you be any more successful if you asked who could teach the sons of our craftsmen the very arts which they of course learned from their fathers, to the extent that their fathers were competent, and their friends in the trade. It would be difficult to produce someone who could continue their education, whereas it would be easy to find a teacher for the totally unskilled. It is the same with virtue and everything else. If there is someone who is the least bit more advanced in virtue than ourselves, he is to be cherished.

b   "I consider myself to be such a person, uniquely qualified to assist others in becoming noble and good, and worth the fee that I charge and even more, so much so that even my students agree. This is why I charge accord-
c ing to the following system: a student pays the full price only if he wishes to; otherwise, he goes into a temple, states under oath how much he thinks my lessons are worth, and pays that amount.

"There you have it, Socrates, my mythic story and my argument that virtue is teachable and that the Athenians consider it to be so, and that it is no wonder that worthless sons are born of good fathers and good sons of worthless fathers, since even the sons of Polycleitus, of the same age as
d Paralus and Xanthippus here, are nothing compared to their father, and the same is true for the sons of other artisans. But it is not fair to accuse these two yet; there is still hope for them, for they are young."

Protagoras ended his virtuoso performance here and stopped speaking. I was entranced and just looked at him for a long time as if he were going to say more. I was still eager to listen, but when I perceived that he had really stopped I pulled myself together and, looking at Hippocrates, barely man-
e aged to say: "Son of Apollodorus, how grateful I am to you for suggesting that I come here. It is marvelous to have heard from Protagoras what I have just heard. Formerly I used to think there was no human practice by which the good become good, but now I am persuaded that there is, except for one small obstacle which Protagoras will explain away, I am sure, since he has
329 explained away so much already. Now, you could hear a speech similar to this from Pericles or some other competent orator if you happened to be present when one of them was speaking on this subject. But try asking one of them something, and they will be as unable to answer your question or to ask one of their own as a book would be. Question the least little thing in their speeches and they will go on like bronze bowls that keep ringing for a long time after they have been struck and prolong the sound indefinitely unless you dampen them. That's how these orators are: Ask them one
b little question and they're off on another long-distance speech. But Protagoras here, while perfectly capable of delivering a beautiful long speech, as we have just seen, is also able to reply briefly when questioned, and to put a question and then wait for and accept the answer—rare accomplishments these.

"Now, then, Protagoras, I need one little thing, and then I'll have it all, if

you'll just answer me this. You say that virtue is teachable, and if there's
any human being who could persuade me of this, it's you. But there is one
thing you said that troubles me, and maybe you can satisfy my soul. You   c
said that Zeus sent justice and a sense of shame to the human race. You
also said, at many points in your speech, that justice and temperance and
piety and all these things were somehow collectively one thing: virtue.
Could you go through this again and be more precise? Is virtue a single
thing, with justice and temperance and piety its parts, or are the things I   d
have just listed all names for a single entity? This is what still intrigues me."

   "This is an easy question to answer, Socrates," he replied. "Virtue is a
single entity, and the things you are asking about are its parts."

   "Parts as in the parts of a face: mouth, nose, eyes, and ears? Or parts as
in the parts of gold, where there is no difference, except for size, between
parts or between the parts and the whole?"

   "In the former sense, I would think, Socrates: as the parts of the face are   e
to the whole face."

   "Then tell me this. Do some people have one part and some another, or
do you necessarily have all the parts if you have any one of them?"

   "By no means, since many are courageous but unjust, and many again
are just but not wise."

   "Then these also are parts of virtue—wisdom and courage?"

   "Absolutely, and wisdom is the greatest part."   330

   "Is each of them different from the others?"

   "Yes."

   "And does each also have its own unique power or function? In the
analogy to the parts of the face, the eye is not like the ear, nor is its power
or function the same, and this applies to the other parts as well: They are
not like each other in power or function or in any other way. Is this how it
is with the parts of virtue? Are they unlike each other, both in themselves   b
and in their powers or functions? Is it not clear that this must be the case, if
our analogy is valid?"

   "Yes, it must be the case, Socrates."

   "Then, none of the other parts of virtue is like knowledge, or like justice,
or like courage, or like temperance, or like piety?"

   "Agreed."

   "Come on, then, and let's consider together what kind of thing each of
these is. Here's a good first question: Is justice a thing or is it not a thing? I   c
think it is. What about you?"

   "I think so too."

   "The next step, then: Suppose someone asked us, 'Protagoras and Socrates, tell me about this thing you just named, justice. Is it itself just or
unjust?' My answer would be that it is just. What would your verdict be?
The same as mine or different?"

   "The same."

"Then justice is the sort of thing that is just. That's how I would reply to the questioner. Would you also?"

"Yes."

d   "Suppose he questioned us further: 'Do you also say there is a thing called piety?' We would say we do, right?"

"Right."

"'Do you say this too is a thing?' We would say we do, wouldn't we?"

"That too."

e   "'Do you say that this thing is by nature impious or pious?' Myself, I would be irritated with this question and would say, 'Quiet, man! How could anything else be pious if piety itself is not?' What about you? Wouldn't you answer in the same way?"

"Absolutely."

"Suppose he asked us next: 'Then what about what you said a little while ago? Maybe I didn't hear you right. I thought you two said that the parts of virtue are related to each other in such a way that no part resembles any

331   other.' I would answer, 'There's nothing wrong with your hearing, except that I didn't say that. Protagoras here said that in answer to my question.' If he were to say then, 'Is he telling the truth, Protagoras? Are you the one who says that one part of virtue is not like another? Is this dictum yours?' how would you answer him?"

"I would have to admit it, Socrates."

"Well, if we accept that, Protagoras, what are we going to say if he asks next, 'Isn't piety the sort of thing that is just, and isn't justice the sort of thing that is pious? Or is it the sort of thing which is not pious? Is piety the

b   sort of thing to be not just, and therefore unjust, which is to say impious?' What are we going to say to him? Personally, I would answer both that justice is pious and piety is just, and I would give the same answer on your behalf (if you would let me), that justice is the same thing as piety, or very similar, and, most emphatically, that justice is the same kind of thing as piety, and piety as justice. What do you think? Will you veto this answer, or are you in agreement with it?"

c   "It's not so absolutely clear a case to me, Socrates, as to make me grant that justice is pious, and piety just. It seems a distinction is in order here. But what's the difference? If you want, we'll let justice be pious and piety just."

"Don't do that to me! It's not this 'if you want' or 'if you agree' business I want to test. It's you and me I want to put on the line, and I think the argument will be tested best if we take the 'if' out."

d   "Well, all right. Justice does have some resemblance to piety. Anything at all resembles any other thing in some way. There is a certain way in which white resembles black, and hard soft, and so on for all the usual polar opposites. And the things we were just talking about as having different

e   powers or functions and not being the same kinds of things—the parts of the face—these resemble each other in a certain way, and they are like each other. So by this method you could prove, if you wanted to, that these things too are all like each other. But it's not right to call things similar because they resemble each other in some way, however slight, or to call them dissimilar because there is some slight point of dissimilarity."

I was taken aback, and said to him, "Do you consider the relationship between justice and piety really only one of some slight similarity?"

"Not exactly, but not what you seem to think it is either."   332

"Well, then, since you seem to me to be annoyed about this, let's drop it and consider another point that you raised. Do you acknowledge that there is such a thing as folly?"

"Yes."

"And diametrically opposed to it is wisdom?"

"It seems so to me."

"And when people act correctly and beneficially, do they seem to you to be acting temperately or the opposite?"

"Temperately."

"Then it is by virtue of temperance that they are temperate?"

"It has to be."   b

"And those who do not act correctly act foolishly, and those who act this way are not temperate?"

"I agree."

"And the opposite of acting foolishly is acting temperately?"

"Yes."

"And foolish behavior comes from folly, just as temperate behavior comes from temperance?"

"Yes."

"And if something is done with strength, it is done strongly; if done with weakness, it is done weakly?"

"I agree."

"If it is done with quickness, it is done quickly, and if with slowness, slowly?"

"Yes."

"So whatever is done in a certain way is done through the agency of a   c
certain quality, and whatever is done in the opposite way is done through the agency of its opposite?"

"I agree."

"Then let's go on. Is there such a thing as beauty?"

"Yes."

"Is there any opposite to it except ugliness?"

"There is not."

"Is there such a thing as goodness?"

"There is."

"Is there any opposite to it except badness?"

"There is not."

"Is there such a thing as a shrill tone?"

"There is."

"Is there any opposite to it except a deep tone?"

"No, there is not."

d   "So for each thing that can have an opposite, there is only one opposite, not many?"

"I agree."

"Suppose we now count up our points of agreement. Have we agreed that there is one opposite for one thing, and no more?"

"Yes, we have."

"And that what is done in an opposite way is done through the agency of opposites?"

"Yes."

"And have we agreed that what is done foolishly is done in a way opposite to what is done temperately?"

"We have."

"And that what is done temperately is done through temperance, and what is done foolishly is done through folly?"

"Agreed."

e   "And it's true that if it's done in an opposite way, it is done through the agency of an opposite?"

"Yes."

"And one is done through temperance, the other through folly?"

"Yes."

"In an opposite way?"

"Yes."

"Through opposing agencies?"

"Yes."

"Then folly is the opposite of temperance?"

"It seems so."

"Well, then, do you recall our previous agreement that folly is the opposite of wisdom?"

"Yes, I do."

"And that one thing has only one opposite?"

"Of course."

333   "Then which of these propositions should we abandon, Protagoras? The proposition that for one thing there is only one opposite, or the one stating that wisdom is different from temperance and that each is a part of virtue, and that in addition to being distinct they are dissimilar, both in themselves and in their powers or functions, just like the parts of a face? Which should we abandon? The two statements are dissonant; they are not in harmony with one another. How could they be, if there is one and only one

b   opposite for each single thing, while folly, which is a single thing, evidently has two opposites, wisdom and temperance? Isn't this how it stands, Protagoras?"

He assented, although very grudgingly, and I continued: "Wouldn't that make wisdom and temperance one thing? And a little while ago it looked like justice and piety were nearly the same thing. Come on, Protagoras, we can't quit now, not before we've tied up these loose ends. So, does someone who acts unjustly seem temperate to you in that he acts unjustly?"

"I would be ashamed to say that is so, Socrates, although many people do   *c*
say it."

"Then shall I address myself to them or to you?"

"If you like, why don't you debate the majority position first?"

"It makes no difference to me, provided you give the answers, whether it is your own opinion or not. I am primarily interested in testing the argument, although it may happen both that the questioner, myself, and my respondent wind up being tested."

At first Protagoras played it coy, claiming the argument was too hard for   *d*
him to handle, but after a while he consented to answer.

"Let's start all over, then," I said, "with this question. Do you think some people are being sensible when they act unjustly?"

"Let us grant it," he said.

"And by 'sensible' you mean having good sense?"

"Yes."

"And having good sense means having good judgment in acting unjustly?"

"Granted."

"Whether or not they get good results by acting unjustly?"

"Only if they get good results."

"Are you saying, then, that there are things that are good?"

"I am."

"These good things constitute what is advantageous to people?"

"Good God, yes! And even if they are not advantageous to people, I can   *e*
still call them good."

I could see that Protagoras was really worked up and struggling by now and that he was dead set against answering any more. Accordingly, I carefully modified the tone of my questions.

"Do you mean things that are advantageous to no human being, Pro-   *334*
tagoras, or things that are of no advantage whatsoever? Do you call things like that good?"

"Of course not," he said. "But I know of many things that are disadvantageous to humans, foods and drinks and drugs and many other things, and some that are advantageous; some that are neither to humans but one or the other to horses; some that are advantageous only to cattle; some only to dogs; some that are advantageous to none of these but are so to trees; some that are good for the roots of a tree, but bad for its shoots, such   *b* as manure, which is good spread on the roots of any plant but absolutely ruinous if applied to the new stems and branches. Or take olive oil, which is extremely bad for all plants and is the worst enemy of the hair of all animals except humans, for whose hair it is beneficial, as it is for the rest of their bodies. But the good is such a multifaceted and variable thing that, in the case of oil, it is good for the external parts of the human body but very bad for the internal parts, which is why doctors universally forbid their sick patients to use oil in their diets except for the least bit, just enough to

c dispel a prepared meal's unappetizing aroma."

348c "Protagoras," I said, "I don't want you to think that my motive in talking with you is anything else than to take a good hard look at things that continually perplex me. I think that Homer said it all in the line,

d *Going in tandem, one perceives before the other.*[6]

Human beings are simply more resourceful this way in action, speech, and thought. If someone has a private perception, he immediately starts going around and looking until he finds somebody he can show it to and have it corroborated. And there is a particular reason why I would rather talk with you than anyone else: I think you are the best qualified to investigate the

e sort of things that decent and respectable individuals ought to examine, and virtue especially. Who else but you? Not only do you consider yourself to be noble and good but, unlike others who are themselves decent and respectable individuals yet unable to make others so, you are not only good yourself but able to make others good as well, and you have so much self-confidence that instead of concealing this skill, as others do, you advertise

349 it openly to the whole Greek world, calling yourself a sophist, highlighting yourself as a teacher of virtue, the first ever to have deemed it appropriate to charge a fee for this. How could I not solicit your help in a joint investigation of these questions? There is no way I could not.

"So right now I want you to remind me of some of the questions I first asked, starting from the beginning. Then I want to proceed together to take

b a good hard look at some other questions. I believe the first question was this: Wisdom, temperance, courage, justice, and piety—are these five names for the same thing, or is there underlying each of these names a unique thing, a thing with its own power or function, each one unlike any of the others? You said that they are not names for the same thing, that

c each of these names refers to a unique thing, and that all these are parts of virtue, not like the parts of gold, which are similar to each other and to the whole of which they are parts, but like the parts of a face, dissimilar to the whole of which they are parts and to each other, and each one having its

6. Homer, *Iliad* 10.224.

own unique power or function. If this is still your view, say so; if it's changed in any way, make your new position clear, for I am certainly not going to hold you accountable for what you said before if you want to say something at all different now. In fact, I wouldn't be surprised if you were just trying out something on me before."

d

"What I am saying to you, Socrates, is that all these are parts of virtue, and that while four of them are reasonably close to each other, courage is completely different from all the rest. The proof that what I am saying is true is that you will find many people who are extremely unjust, impious, intemperate, and ignorant, and yet exceptionally courageous."

"Hold it right there," I said. "This is worth looking into. Would you say courageous men are confident, or something else?"

e

"Confident, yes, and ready for action where most men would be afraid."

"Well, then, do you agree that virtue is something fine, and that you offer yourself as a teacher of it because it is fine?"

"The finest thing of all, unless I am quite out of my mind."

"Then is part of it worthless and part of it fine, or all of it fine?"

"Surely it is all as fine as can be."

"Do you know who dives confidently into wells?"

350

"Of course, divers."

"Is this because they know what they are doing, or for some other reason?"

"Because they know what they are doing."

"Who are confident in fighting from horseback? Riders or nonriders?"

"Riders."

"And in fighting with shields? Shieldmen or nonshieldmen?"

"Shieldmen, and so on down the line, if that's what you're getting at. Those with the right kind of knowledge are always more confident than those without it, and a given individual is more confident after he acquires it than he was before."

"But haven't you ever seen men lacking knowledge of all of these occupations yet confident in each of them?"

b

"I have, all too confident."

"Is their confidence courage?"

"No, because courage would then be contemptible. These men are out of their minds."

"Then what do you mean by courageous men? Aren't they those who are confident?"

"I still hold by that."

c

"Then these men who are so confident turn out to be not courageous but mad? And, on the other side, the wisest are the most confident and the most confident are the most courageous? And the logical conclusion would be that wisdom is courage?"

"You are doing a poor job of remembering what I said when I answered

your questions, Socrates. When I was asked if the courageous are confident, I agreed. I was not asked if the confident are courageous. If you had
d   asked me that, I would have said, 'Not all of them.' You have nowhere
shown that my assent to the proposition that the courageous are confident
was in error. What you did show next was that knowledge increases one's
confidence and makes one more confident than those without knowledge.
In consequence of this you conclude that courage and wisdom are the same
thing. But by following this line of reasoning you could conclude that
strength and wisdom are the same thing. First you would ask me if the
e   strong are powerful, and I would say yes. Then, if those who know how to
wrestle are more powerful than those who do not, and if individual
wrestlers became more powerful after they learn than they were before.
Again I would say yes. After I had agreed to these things, it would be open
to you to use precisely these points of agreement to prove that wisdom is
strength. But nowhere in this process do I agree that the powerful are
351   strong, only that the strong are powerful. Strength and power are not the
same thing. Power derives from knowledge and also from passionate emotion. Strength comes from nature and proper nurture of the body. So also
confidence and courage are not the same thing, with the consequence that
the courageous are confident, but not all those who are confident are courageous. For confidence, like power, comes from skill (and from passionate
emotion as well); courage, from nature and the proper nurture of the soul."
b   "Would you say, Protagoras, that some people live well and others live
badly?"
       "Yes."
       "But does it seem to you that a person lives well, if he lives distressed
and in pain?"
       "No, indeed."
       "Now, if he completed his life, having lived pleasantly, does he not seem
to you to have lived well?"
       "It seems that way to me."
c   "So, then, to live pleasantly is good, and unpleasantly, bad?"
       "Yes, so long as he lived having taken pleasure in honorable things."
       "What, Protagoras? Surely you don't, like most people, call some pleas-
ant things bad and some painful things good? I mean, isn't a pleasant thing
good just insofar as it is pleasant, that is, if it results in nothing other than
pleasure; and, on the other hand, aren't painful things bad in the same way,
just insofar as they are painful?"
       "I don't know, Socrates, if I should answer as simply as you put the
d   question—that everything pleasant is good and everything painful is bad. It
seems to me to be safer to respond not merely with my present answer in
mind but from the point of view of my life overall, that on the one hand,
there are pleasurable things which are not good, and on the other hand,

there are painful things which are not bad but some which are, and a third class which is neutral—neither bad nor good."

"You call pleasant things those which partake of pleasure or produce *e* pleasure?"

"Certainly."

"So my question is this: Just insofar as things are pleasurable are they good? I am asking whether pleasure itself is not a good."

"Just as you always say, Socrates, let us inquire into this matter, and if your claim seems reasonable and it is established that pleasure and the good are the same, then we will come to agreement; otherwise we will disagree."

"Do you wish to lead this inquiry, or shall I?"

"It is fitting for you to lead, for it is you who brought up the idea."

"All right, will this help to make it clear? When someone evaluates a *352* man's health or other functions of the body through his appearance, he looks at the face and extremities, and might say: 'Show me your chest and back too, so that I can make a better examination.' That's the kind of investigation I want to make. Having seen how you stand on the good and the pleasant, I need to say something like this to you: Come now, Pro- *b* tagoras, and reveal this about your mind: What do you think about knowl- edge? Do you go along with the majority or not? Most people think this way about it, that it is not a powerful thing, neither a leader nor a ruler. They do not think of it in that way at all; but rather in this way: while knowledge is often present in a man, what rules him is not knowledge but rather anything else—sometimes desire, sometimes pleasure, sometimes pain, at other times love, often fear; they think of his knowledge as being utterly dragged around by all these other things as if it were a slave. Now, *c* does the matter seem like that to you, or does it seem to you that knowl- edge is a fine thing capable of ruling a person, and if someone were to know what is good and bad, then he would not be forced by anything to act otherwise than knowledge dictates, and intelligence would be sufficient to save a person?"

"Not only does it seem just as you say, Socrates, but further, it would be shameful indeed for me above all people to say that wisdom and knowledge *d* are anything but the most powerful forces in human activity."

"Right you are. You realize that most people aren't going to be convinced by us. They are going to say that most people are unwilling to do what is best, even though they know what it is and are able to do it. And when I have asked them the reason for this, they say that those who act that way do so because they are overcome by pleasure or pain or are being ruled by *e* one of the things I referred to just now."

"I think people say a lot of other things erroneously too, Socrates."

"Come with me, then, and let's try to persuade people and to teach them

353   what is this experience which they call being overcome by pleasure, because of which they fail to do the best thing when they know what it is. For
perhaps if we told them that what they were saying isn't true, but is demon-
strably false, they would ask us: 'Protagoras and Socrates, if this is not the
experience of being overcome by pleasure, but something other than that,
what do you two say it is? Tell us.'"

       "Socrates, why is it necessary for us to investigate the opinion of ordi-
nary people, who will say whatever occurs to them?"

b   "I think this will help us find out about courage, how it is related to the
other parts of virtue. If you are willing to go along with what we agreed
just now, that I will lead us toward what I think will turn out to be the best
way to make things clear, then fine; if you are not willing, I will give it up."

       "No, you are right; proceed as you have begun."

c   "Going back, then; if they should ask us: 'We have been talking about
being overcome by pleasure. What do you say this is?' I would reply to
them this way: 'Listen. Protagoras and I will try to explain it to you. Have
you noticed, gentlemen, that this sort of thing happens to you, that you are
often overcome by pleasant things like food or drink or sex, and that you
do those things all the while knowing they are ruinous?' They would say
yes. Then you and I would ask them again: 'In what sense do you call these

d   things ruinous? Is it that each of these things is pleasant in itself and
produces immediate pleasure, or is it that later they bring about diseases
and poverty and many other things of that sort? Or even if it doesn't bring
about these things later, but gives only enjoyment, would it still be a bad
thing, just because it gives enjoyment in whatever way?' Can we suppose
then, Protagoras, that they would make any other answer than that bad
things are bad not because they bring about immediate pleasure, but rather
because of what happens later, disease and things like that?"

e   "I think that is how most people would answer."

       "'And in bringing about diseases and poverty, do they bring about pain?'
I think they would agree."

       "Yes."

       "'Does it not seem to you, my good people, as Protagoras and I maintain,
that these things are bad on account of nothing other than the fact that

354   they result in pain and deprive us of other pleasures?' Would they agree?"

       Protagoras concurred.

       "Then again, suppose we were to ask them the opposite question: 'You
who say that some painful things are good, do you not say that such things
as athletics and military training and treatments by doctors such as cautery, surgery, medicines, and starvation diet are good things even though
painful?' Would they say so?"

       "Yes."

b   "'Would you call these same things good for any other reason than that they bring about intense pain and suffering, or because they ultimately bring about health and good condition of bodies and preservation of cities and power over others and wealth?' Would they agree?"

"Yes."

"These things are good because of the fact that they result in pleasure and in the relief and avoidance of pain? 'Or do you have some other criterion in view, other than pleasure and pain, on the basis of which you would call these things good?' They would say no, I think."

"And I would agree with them."

"'So then you pursue pleasure as being good; avoid pain as bad?'"

"Yes."

"'So, this you regard as bad—pain, and this as good—pleasure, since you call the very enjoying of something bad whenever it deprives us of greater pleasures than it itself provides, or brings about greater pains than the very pleasures inherent in it? But if you call the very enjoying of something bad, then you are using some other criterion than the one I have suggested, and if so, then you could tell us what it is; but you won't be able to.'"

"I don't think they'll be able to either."

"'And likewise concerning the actual state of being in pain? Do you call the actual condition of being in pain good, whenever it relieves pains greater than the ones it contains or brings about greater pleasures than pains? Now, if you are using some other criterion than the one I have suggested, when you call the very condition of being pained good, you can tell us what it is; but you won't be able to do so.'"

"Truly spoken."

"Now, again, gentlemen, if you asked me: 'Why are you going on so much about this and in so much detail?' I would reply, forgive me. First of all, it is not easy to show what it is that you call 'being overcome by pleasure,' and then, it is upon this very point that all the arguments rest. But even now it is still possible to withdraw, if you are able to say that the good is anything other than pleasure or that the bad is anything other than pain, or is it enough for you to live life pleasantly without pain? If it is enough, and you are not able to say anything else than that the good and the bad are that which result in pleasure and pain, listen to this. For I say to you that if this is so, your position will become absurd, when you say that frequently a man, knowing the bad to be bad, nevertheless does that very thing, when he is able not to do it, having been driven and overwhelmed by pleasure; and again when you say that a man knowing the good is not willing to do it, on account of immediate pleasure, having been overcome by it. Just how absurd this is will become very clear, if we do not use so many names at the same time, 'pleasant' and 'painful,' 'good' and 'bad'; but since these appear to be only two things, let us instead agree on two names, first, 'good' and 'bad,' then later, 'pleasant' and 'painful.' On

c

d

e

355

b

c

that basis, then, let us say that a man knowing the bad, that it is bad, does it all the same. If then someone asks us: 'Why?' 'Having been overcome,' we shall reply. 'By what?' he will ask us. We are no longer able to say 'by pleasure,'—for it is taken on its other name, 'the good' instead of 'pleasure'—to him we will say and reply that 'he is overcome'—'By what?' he will ask. 'By the good,' we will say, 'for heaven's sake.' If by chance the

d   questioner is rude to us, he might burst out laughing and ask: 'What you're saying is ridiculous—someone does what is bad, knowing that it is bad, it not being necessary to do it, having been overcome by the good. So,' he will say, 'within yourself, does the good outweigh the bad or not?' We will clearly say in reply that it does not; for if it did, the person whom we say to be overcome by pleasure simply would not make any mistakes. 'In what respect,' he might say, 'does the good *outweigh* the bad or the bad the good?

e   In no other respect but that one is greater and one is smaller, or some are more and some are fewer.' We could not help but agree. 'So clearly then,' he will say, 'by "being overcome" you mean getting more bad things for the sake of getting fewer good things. That settles that, then.

"So let's now go back and apply the names 'the pleasant' and 'the painful' to these very same things, and now let us say that a man does what we

356   used to call 'the bad' and now shall call 'the painful,' and that he knows it is painful, but is overcome by the pleasant, although it is clear that the pleasant does not outweigh it. But how else does pleasure outweigh pain, except in relative excess or deficiency? Isn't it a matter (to use other terms) of larger and smaller, more or fewer, greater or lesser degree?

"For if someone were to say: 'But Socrates, the immediate pleasure is very much different from the pleasant and the painful at a later time,' I

b   would reply, 'They are not different in any other way than by pleasure and pain, for there is no other way that they could differ. Weighing is a good analogy; you put the pleasures together and the pains together, both the near and the remote, on the balance scale, and then say which of the two is more. For if you weigh pleasant things against pleasant, the greater and the more must always be taken; if painful things against painful, the fewer and the smaller. And if you weigh pleasant things against painful, and if the painful is exceeded by the pleasant—whether the near by the remote or the remote by the near—you have to perform that action in which the pleasant

c   prevails; on the other hand, if the pleasant is exceeded by the painful, you have to refrain from doing that. Does it seem any different to you, my friends?' I know that they would not say otherwise."

Protagoras assented.

"Since this is so, I will say to them: 'Answer me this: Do things of the same size appear to you larger when seen near at hand and smaller when seen from a distance, or not?' They would say they do. 'And similarly for thicknesses and pluralities? And equal sounds seem louder when near at

hand, softer when farther away?' They would agree. 'If then our well-being   *d*
depends upon this, doing and choosing large things, avoiding and not
doing the small ones, what would seem to be our salvation in life? Would it
be the art of measurement or the power of appearance? While the power
of appearance often makes us wander all over the place confused and
regretting our actions and choices with respect to thing large and small, the
art of measurment, in contrast, would make the appearances lose their power   *e*
by showing us the truth, would give us peace of mind firmly rooted in the
truth and would save our life.' Therefore, would men agree, with this in
mind, that the art of measurement would save us, or some other art?"

"I agree, the art of measurement would."

"What if our salvation in life depended on our choices of odd and even,
when the greater and the lesser had to be counted correctly, either the same
kind against itself or one kind against the other, whether it be near or   *357*
remote? What then would save our life? Surely nothing other than knowledge, specifically some kind of measurement, since that is the art of the
greater and the lesser? In fact, nothing other than arithmetic, since it's a
question of the odd and even? Would most people agree with us or not?"

Protagoras thought they would agree.

"Well, then, my good people: Since it has turned out that our salvation
in life depends on the right choice of pleasures and pains, be they more or
fewer, lesser or greater, farther or nearer, then doesn't our salvation seem   *b*
first of all, to be measurement, which is the study of relative excess and
deficiency and equality?"

"It must be."

"Since it is measurement, it must definitely be an art, and knowledge."

"They will agree."

"What exactly this art, this knowledge is, we shall inquire into later; that
it is knowledge of some sort is a good start for the demonstration which it
was necessary for Protagoras and me to give in order to answer the question which you asked us. You asked it, if you remember, when we were   *c*
agreeing that nothing was stronger or better than knowledge, which always
prevails, whenever it is present, over pleasure and everything else. At that
point you said that pleasure often rules even the man who knows; since we
disagreed, you went on to ask us this: 'Protagoras and Socrates, if this
experience is not being overcome by pleasure, what is it then; what do you   *d*
say it is? Tell us.' 'If immediately we had said to you "ignorance," you might
have laughed at us, but if you laugh at us now, you will be laughing at
yourselves. For you agreed with us that those who make mistakes with
regard to the choice of pleasure and pain, in other words, with regard to
good and bad, do so because of a lack of knowledge, and that it was not
merely a lack of knowledge but a lack of that knowledge you agreed was
measurement. And the mistaken act done without knowledge you must   *e*

know is one done from ignorance. So this is what "being overcome by pleasure" is—ignorance in the highest degree, and it is this which Protagoras and Prodicus and Hippias claim to cure. But you, thinking it to be something other than ignorance, do not yourselves go to sophists, nor do you send your children to them for instruction, believing as you do that we are dealing with something unteachable. By worrying about your money and not giving it to them, you all do badly in both private and public life.'

358   "This is how we would have answered the many. Now, I ask you, Hippias and Prodicus, as well as Protagoras—this is your conversation also—to say whether you think what I say is true or false." They all thought that what I said was marvelously true.

"So you agree, that the pleasant is good, the painful bad. I beg indulgence of Prodicus who distinguishes among words; for whether you call it
b   'pleasant' or 'delightful' or 'enjoyable,' or whatever way or manner you please to name this sort of thing, my excellent Prodicus, please respond to the intent of my question." Prodicus, laughing, agreed, as did the others.

"Well, then, men, what about this? Are not all actions leading toward living painlessly and pleasantly honorable and beneficial? And isn't honorable activity good and beneficial?"

They agreed.

"Then if the pleasant is the good, no one who knows or believes there is
c   something else better than what he is doing, something possible, will go on doing what he had been doing when he could be doing what is better. To give in to oneself is nothing other than ignorance, and to control oneself is nothing other than wisdom."

They all agreed.

"Well, then, do you say that ignorance is to have a false belief and to be deceived about matters of importance?"

They all agreed on this.

"Now, no one goes willingly toward the bad or what he believes to be
d   bad; neither is it in human nature, so it seems, to want to go toward what one believes to be bad instead of to the good. And when he is forced to choose between one of two bad things, no one will choose the greater if he is able to choose the lesser."

They agreed with all of that too.

"Well, then, is there something you call dread or fear? And I address this to you, Prodicus. I say that whether you call it fear or dread, it is an expectation of something bad."

Protagoras and Hippias thought that this was true of both dread and
e   fear, but Prodicus thought it applied to dread, but not to fear.

"Well, it does not really matter, Prodicus. This is the point. If what I have said up to now is true, then would anyone be willing to go toward what he dreads, when he can go toward what he does not? Or is this impossible from what we have agreed? For it was agreed that what one

fears one holds to be bad; no one goes toward those things which he holds
to be bad, or chooses those things willingly."

They all agreed.   *359*

"Well, Prodicus and Hippias, with this established, let Protagoras defend
for us the truth of his first answer. I don't mean his very first answer, for
then he said that while there are five parts of virtue, none is like any other,
but each one has its own unique power or function. I'm not talking about
this now, but about what he said later. For later he said that four of them   *b*
are very similar to each other, but that one differs very much from the
others, that one being courage. And he said that I would know this by the
following evidence: 'You will find, Socrates, many people who are extremely impious, unjust, intemperate, and ignorant, and yet exceptionally
courageous; by this you will recognize that courage differs very much from
all the other parts of virtue.' I was very surprised at his answer then, and
even more so now that I have gone over these things with you. I asked him
then if he said that the courageous were confident. And he said, 'Yes, and   *c*
ready for action too.' Do you remember giving this answer?"

He said he did.

"Well, then, tell us, for what actions are the courageous ready? The same
actions as the cowardly?"

"No."

"Different actions?"

"Yes."

"Do the cowardly go forward to things which are easily ventured, and
the courageous toward things to be feared?"

"So it is said by most people."

"Right, but I am not asking that. Rather, what do *you* say the courageous   *d*
go toward with daring: toward things to be feared, believing them to be
fearsome, or toward things not to be feared?"

"By what you have just said, the former is impossible."

"Right again; so, if our demonstration has been correct, then no one goes
toward those things he considers to be fearsome, since not to be in control
of oneself was found to be ignorance."

He agreed.

"But all people, both the courageous and the cowardly, go toward that
about which they are confident; both the cowardly and the courageous go   *e*
toward the same things."

"But, Socrates, what the cowardly go toward is completely opposite to
what the courageous go toward. For example, the courageous are willing to
go to war, but the cowardly are not."

"Is going to war honorable or is it disgraceful?"

"Honorable."

"Then, if it is honorable, we have agreed before, it is also good, for we
agreed that all honorable actions were good."

"Very true, and I always believed this."

360   "And rightly; but who would you say are not willing to go to war, war being honorable and good?"

"The cowardly."

"If a thing is noble and good, is it also pleasant?"

"That was definitely agreed upon."

"So, the cowardly, with full knowledge, are not willing to go toward the more honorable, the better, and more pleasant?"

"If we agree to that, we will undermine what we agreed on earlier."

"What about the courageous man: Does he go toward the more honorable, the better, and more pleasant?"

"We must agree to that."

"So, generally, when the courageous fear, their fear is not disgraceful; nor when they are confident is their confidence disgraceful."

b   "True."

"If not disgraceful, is it honorable?"

He agreed.

"If honorable, then also good?"

"Yes."

"Whereas the fear and confidence of the cowardly, the foolhardy, and madmen are disgraceful?"

He agreed.

"Is their confidence disgraceful and bad for any reason other than ignorance and stupidity?"

c   "No, it isn't."

"Now then; that through which cowardly people are cowardly, do you call it cowardice or courage?"

"Cowardice."

"And aren't cowards shown to be so through their ignorance of what is to be feared?"

"Absolutely."

"So they are cowards because of that ignorance?"

He agreed.

"You agreed that it is through cowardice that they are cowards?"

He said he did.

"So, can we conclude that cowardice is ignorance of what is and is not to be feared?"

He nodded.

d   "Now, courage is the opposite of cowardice."

He said yes.

"So then, wisdom about what is and is not to be feared is the opposite of this ignorance?"

He nodded again.

"And this ignorance is cowardice?"

He nodded again, very reluctantly.

"So the wisdom about what is and is not to be feared is courage and is the opposite of this ignorance?"

He would not even nod at this; he remained silent.

And I said, "What's this, Protagoras? Will you not say yes or no to my question?"

"Answer it yourself."

"I have only one more question to ask you. Do you still believe, as you *e* did at first, that some men are extremely ignorant and yet still very courageous?"

"I think that you just want to win the argument, Socrates, and that is why you are forcing me to answer. So I will gratify you and say that, on the basis of what we have agreed upon, it seems to me to be impossible."

"I have no other reason for asking these things than my desire to answer these questions about virtue, especially what virtue is in itself. For I know *361* that if we could get clear on that, then we would be able to settle the question about which we both have had much to say, I—that virtue cannot be taught, you—that it can.

"It seems to me that our discussion has turned on us, and if it had a voice of its own, it would say, mockingly, 'Socrates and Protagoras, how ridiculous you are, both of you. Socrates, you said earlier that virtue *b* cannot be taught, but now you are arguing the very opposite and have attempted to show that everything is knowledge—justice, temperance, courage—in which case, virtue would appear to be eminently teachable. On the other hand, if virtue is anything other than knowledge, as Protagoras has been trying to say, then it would clearly be unteachable. But, if it turns out to be wholly knowledge, as you now urge, Socrates, it would be very surprising indeed if virtue could not be taught. Now, Protagoras maintained at first that it could be taught, but now he thinks the opposite, *c* urging that hardly any of the virtues turn out to be knowledge. On that view, virtue could hardly be taught at all.'

"Now, Protagoras, seeing that we have gotten this topsy-turvy and terribly confused, I am most eager to clear it all up, and I would like us, having come this far, to continue until we come through to what virtue is in itself, *d* and then to return to inquire about whether it can or cannot be taught, so that Epimetheus might not frustrate us a second time in this inquiry, as he neglected us in the distribution of powers and abilities in your story. I liked the Prometheus character in your story better than Epimetheus. Since I take promethean forethought over my life as a whole, I pay attention to these things, and if you are willing, as I said at the beginning, I would be pleased to investigate them along with you."

"Socrates, I commend your enthusiasm and the way you find your way

e   through an argument. I really don't think I am a bad man, certainly the last
man to harbor ill will. Indeed, I have told many people that I admire you
more than anyone I have met, certainly more than anyone in your generation. And I say that I would not be surprised if you gain among men high
repute for wisdom. We will examine these things later, whenever you wish;
now it is time to turn our attention elsewhere."

362   "That is what we should do, if it seems right to you. It is long since time
for me to keep that appointment I mentioned. I stayed only as a favor to
our noble colleague Callias."

Our conversation was over, and so we left.

GORGIAS

(462a–481b)

In the following selection, Socrates examines Polus, a younger follower of Gorgias, the famous teacher of rhetoric (some fragments of whose writings are included in this anthology). The initial topic is the nature of rhetoric and its relation to politics. Very quickly, this is subsumed under a larger question about the goals of life (467a–468e). The discussion then focuses on the contribution of virtue to achieving those goals, with Socrates arguing, and Polus forced—kicking and screaming—to agree, that it is better to suffer injustice than to do it.

SOCRATES: You say, I take it, that you're an expert in the same craft as Gor- 462
gias is? Or don't you?

POLUS: Yes, I do.

SOCRATES: And don't you also invite people to ask you each time whatever they like, because you believe you give expert answers?

POLUS: Certainly.

SOCRATES: So now please do whichever of these you like: either ask ques- b
tions or answer them.

POLUS: Very well, I shall. Tell me, Socrates, since you think Gorgias is confused about oratory, what do *you* say it is?

SOCRATES: Are you asking me what *craft* I say it is?

POLUS: Yes, I am.

SOCRATES: To tell you the truth, Polus, I don't think it's a craft at all.

POLUS: Well then, what do you think oratory is?

SOCRATES: In the treatise that I read recently, it's the thing that you say c
has produced craft.

POLUS: What do you mean?

SOCRATES: I mean a knack.

POLUS: So you think oratory's a knack?

SOCRATES: Yes, I do, unless you say it's something else.

POLUS: A knack for what?

SOCRATES: For producing a certain gratification and pleasure.

POLUS: Don't you think that oratory's an admirable thing, then, to be able to give gratification to people?

Translated by D. J. Zeyl.

219

SOCRATES: Really, Polus! Have you already discovered from me what I
d   say it is, so that you go on to ask me next whether I don't think it's admirable?

POLUS: Haven't I discovered that you say it's a knack?

SOCRATES: Since you value gratification, would you like to gratify me on
a small matter?

POLUS: Certainly.

SOCRATES: Ask me now what craft I think pastry baking is.

POLUS: All right, I will. What craft is pastry baking?

SOCRATES: It isn't one at all, Polus. Now say, "What is it then?"

POLUS: All right.

SOCRATES: It's a knack. Say, "A knack for what?"

POLUS: All right.

e   SOCRATES: For producing gratification and pleasure, Polus.

POLUS: So oratory is the same thing as pastry baking?

SOCRATES: Oh no, not at all, although it *is* a part of the same practice.

POLUS: What practice do you mean?

SOCRATES: I'm afraid it may be rather crude to speak the truth. I hesitate
to do so for Gorgias's sake, for fear that he may think I'm satirizing what he
463 practices. I don't know whether this is the kind of oratory that Gorgias
practices—in fact in our discussion a while ago we didn't get at all clear on
just what he thinks it is. But what *I* call oratory is a part of some business
that isn't admirable at all.

GORGIAS: Which one's that, Socrates? Say it, and don't spare my feelings.

SOCRATES: Well then, Gorgias, I think there's a practice that's not craft-
like, but one that a mind given to making hunches takes to, a mind that's
b   bold and naturally clever at dealing with people. I call it flattery, basically. I
think that this practice has many other parts as well, and pastry baking,
too, is one of them. This part *seems* to be a craft, but in my account of it it
isn't a craft but a knack and a routine. I call oratory a part of this, too,
along with cosmetics and sophistry. These are four parts, and they're di-
c   rected to four objects. So if Polus wants to discover them, let him do so. He
hasn't discovered yet what sort of part of flattery I say oratory is. Instead,
it's escaped him that I haven't answered that question yet, and so he goes on
to ask whether I don't consider it to be admirable. And I won't answer him
whether I think it's admirable or shameful until I first tell what it is. That
wouldn't be right, Polus. If, however, you do want to discover this, ask me
what sort of part of flattery I say oratory is.

POLUS: I shall. Tell me what sort of part it is.

d   SOCRATES: Would you understand my answer? By my reasoning, oratory
is an image of a part of politics.

POLUS: Well? Are you saying that it's something admirable or shameful?

SOCRATES: I'm saying that it's a shameful thing—I call bad things shameful—since I must answer you as though you already know what I mean.

GORGIAS: By Zeus, Socrates, I myself don't understand what you mean, either!

SOCRATES: Reasonably enough, Gorgias. I'm not saying anything clear yet. This colt here is youthful and impulsive.   *e*

GORGIAS: Never mind him. Please tell me what you mean by saying that oratory is an image of a part of politics.

SOCRATES: All right, I'll try to describe my view of oratory. If this isn't what it actually is, Polus here will refute me. There is, I take it, something you call *body* and something you call *soul*?   464

GORGIAS: Yes, of course.

SOCRATES: And do you also think that there's a state of fitness for each of these?

GORGIAS: Yes, I do.

SOCRATES: All right. Is there also an apparent state of fitness, one that isn't real? The sort of thing I mean is this. There are many people who *appear* to be physically fit, and unless one is a doctor or one of the fitness experts, one wouldn't readily notice that they're not fit.

GORGIAS: That's true.

SOCRATES: I'm saying that this sort of thing exists in the case of both the body and the soul, a thing that makes the body and the soul *seem* fit when in fact they aren't any the more so.   *b*

GORGIAS: That's so.

SOCRATES: Come then, and I'll show you more clearly what I'm saying, if I can. I'm saying that of this pair of subjects there are two crafts. The one for the soul I call politics; the one for the body, though it is one, I can't give you a name for offhand, but while the care of the body is a single craft, I'm saying it has two parts: gymnastics and medicine. And in politics, the counterpart of gymnastics is legislation, and the part that corresponds to medicine is justice. Each member of these pairs has features in common   *c* with the other, medicine with gymnastics and justice with legislation, because they're concerned with the same thing. They do, however, differ in some way from each other. These, then, are the four parts, and they always provide care, in the one case for the body, in the other for the soul, with a view to what's best. Now flattery takes notice of them, and—I won't say by *knowing*, but only by *guessing*—divides itself into four, masks itself with each of the parts, and then pretends to be the characters of the masks. It   *d* takes no thought at all of whatever is best; with the lure of what's most pleasant at the moment, it sniffs out folly and hoodwinks it, so that it gives the impression of being most deserving. Pastry baking has put on the mask of medicine, and pretends to know the foods that are best for the body, so that if a pastry baker and a doctor had to compete in front of children, or in front of men just as foolish as children, to determine which of the two, the doctor or the pastry baker, had expert knowledge of good food and

bad, the doctor would die of starvation. I call this flattery, and I say that
465 such a thing is shameful, Polus—it's you I'm saying this to—because it
guesses at what's pleasant with no consideration for what's best. And I say
that it isn't a craft, but a knack, because it has no account of the nature of
whatever things it applies by which it applies them, so that it's unable to
state the cause of each thing. And I refuse to call anything that lacks such
an account a craft. If you have any quarrel with these claims, I'm willing to
submit them for discussion.

b   So pastry baking, as I say, is the flattery that wears the mask of medicine. Cosmetics is the one that wears that of gymnastics in the same way; a
mischievous, deceptive, disgraceful and illiberal thing, one that perpetrates
deception by means of shaping and coloring, smoothing out and dressing
up, so as to make people assume an alien beauty and neglect their own,
which comes through gymnastics. So that I won't make a long-style speech,
c I'm willing to put it to you the way the geometers do—for perhaps you
follow me now—that what cosmetics is to gymnastics, pastry baking is to
medicine; or rather, like this: what cosmetics is to gymnastics, sophistry is
to legislation, and what pastry baking is to medicine, oratory is to justice.
However, as I was saying, although these activities are naturally distinct in
this way, yet because they are so close, sophists and orators tend to be
mixed together as people who work in the same area and concern themselves with the same things. They don't know what to do with themselves,
and other people don't know what to do with them. In fact, if the soul
d didn't govern the body but the body governed itself, and if pastry baking
and medicine weren't kept under observation and distinguished by the soul,
but the body itself made judgments about them, making its estimates by
reference to the gratification it receives, then the world according to Anaxagoras would prevail, Polus my friend—you're familiar with these views—
all things would be mixed together in the same place, and there would be
no distinction between matters of medicine and health, and matters of
pastry baking.

You've now heard what I say oratory is. It's the counterpart in the soul to
e pastry baking, its counterpart in the body. Perhaps I've done an absurd
thing: I wouldn't let you make long speeches, and here I've just composed a
lengthy one myself. I deserve to be forgiven, though, for when I made my
statements short you didn't understand and didn't know how to deal with
the answers I gave you, but you needed a narration. So if I don't know how
466 to deal with your answers either, you must spin out a speech, too. But if I
do, just let me deal with them. That's only fair. And if you now know how
to deal with my answer, please deal with it.

POLUS: What is it you're saying, then? You think oratory is flattery?

SOCRATES: I said that it was a *part* of flattery. Don't you remember, Polus,
young as you are? What's to become of you?

POLUS: So you think that good orators are held in low regard in their cities, as flatterers?

SOCRATES: Is this a question you're asking, or some speech you're beginning?   *b*

POLUS: I'm asking a question.

SOCRATES: I don't think they're held in any regard at all.

POLUS: What do you mean, they're not held in any regard? Don't they have the greatest power in their cities?

SOCRATES: No, if by "having power" you mean something that's good for the one who has the power.

POLUS: That's just what I do mean.

SOCRATES: In that case I think that orators have the least power of any in the city.

POLUS: Really? Don't they, like tyrants, put to death anyone they want, and confiscate the property and banish from their cities anyone they see fit?   *c*

SOCRATES: By the Dog, Polus! I can't make out one way or the other with each thing you're saying whether you're saying these things for yourself and revealing your own view, or whether you're questioning me.

POLUS: I'm questioning you.

SOCRATES: Very well, my friend. In that case, are you asking me two questions at once?

POLUS: What do you mean, two?

SOCRATES: Weren't you just now saying something like "Don't orators, like tyrants, put to death anyone they want, don't they confiscate the property of anyone they see fit, and don't they banish them from their cities?"   *d*

POLUS: Yes, I was.

SOCRATES: In that case I say that these are two questions, and I'll answer you both of them. I say, Polus, that both orators and tyrants have the least power in their cities, as I was saying just now. For they do just about nothing they want to, though they certainly do whatever they see most fit to do.   *e*

POLUS: Well, isn't this having great power?

SOCRATES: No; at least Polus says it isn't.

POLUS: I say it isn't? I certainly say it is!

SOCRATES: You certainly don't, by . . . !, since you say that having great power is good for the one who has it.

POLUS: Yes, I do say that.

SOCRATES: Do you think it's good, then, if a person does whatever he sees most fit to do when he lacks intelligence? Do you call this "having great power" too?

POLUS: No, I do not.

SOCRATES: Will you refute me, then, and prove that orators do have intelligence, and that oratory is a craft, and not flattery? If you leave me   *467* unrefuted, then the orators who do what they see fit in their cities, and the tyrants, too, won't have gained any good by this. Power is a good thing, you say, but you agree with me that doing what one sees fit without intelligence is bad. Or don't you?

POLUS: Yes, I do.

SOCRATES: How then could it be that orators or tyrants have great power in their cities, so long as Socrates is not refuted by Polus to show that they do what they want?

b   POLUS: This fellow—

SOCRATES: —denies that they do what they want. Go ahead and refute me.

POLUS: Didn't you just now agree that they do what they see fit?

SOCRATES: Yes, and I still do.

POLUS: Don't they do what they want, then?

SOCRATES: I say they don't.

POLUS: Even though they do what they see fit?

SOCRATES: That's what I say.

POLUS: What an outrageous thing to say, Socrates! Perfectly monstrous!

SOCRATES: Don't attack me, my peerless Polus, to address you in your
c   own style. Instead, question me if you can, and prove that I'm wrong. Otherwise you must answer me.

POLUS: All right, I'm willing to answer, to get some idea of what you're saying.

SOCRATES: Do you think that when people do something, they want the thing they're doing at the time, or the thing for the sake of which they do what they're doing? Do you think that people who take medicines prescribed by their doctors, for instance, want what they're doing, the act of taking the medicine, with all its discomfort, or do they want to be healthy, the thing for the sake of which they're taking it?

POLUS: Obviously they want their being healthy.

d   SOCRATES: With seafarers, too, and those who make money in other ways, the thing they're doing at the time is not the thing they want—for who wants to make dangerous and troublesome sea voyages? What they want is their being wealthy, the thing for the sake of which, I suppose, they make their voyages. It's for the sake of wealth that they make them.

POLUS: Yes, that's right.

SOCRATES: Isn't it just the same in all cases, in fact? If a person does anything for the sake of something, he doesn't want this thing that he's
e   doing, but the thing for the sake of which he's doing it?

POLUS: Yes.

SOCRATES: Now is there any thing that isn't either *good*, or *bad*, or, what is between these, *neither good nor bad*?

POLUS: There can't be, Socrates.

SOCRATES: Do you say that wisdom, health, wealth and the like are *good*, and their opposites *bad*?

Polus: Yes, I do.

Socrates: And by things which are *neither good nor bad* you mean things which sometimes partake of what's good, sometimes of what's bad, and sometimes of neither, such as sitting or walking, running or making sea voyages, or stones and sticks and the like? Aren't these the ones you mean? Or are there any others that you call *things neither good nor bad?* 468

Polus: No, these are the ones.

Socrates: Now whenever people do things, do they do these intermediate things for the sake of good ones, or the good things for the sake of the intermediate ones?

Polus: The intermediate things for the sake of the good ones, surely. b

Socrates: So it's because we pursue what's good that we walk whenever we walk; we suppose that it's better to walk. And conversely, whenever we stand still, we stand still for the sake of the same thing, what's good. Isn't that so?

Polus: Yes.

Socrates: And don't we also put a person to death, if we do, or banish him and confiscate his property because we suppose that doing that is better for us than not doing it?

Polus: That's right.

Socrates: Hence, it's for the sake of what's good that those who do all these things do them.

Polus: I agree.

Socrates: Now didn't we agree that we want, not those things that we do for the sake of something, but that thing for the sake of which we do them? c

Polus: Yes, very much so.

Socrates: Hence, we don't simply want to slaughter people, or exile them from their cities and confiscate their property as such; we want to do these things if they are beneficial, but if they're harmful we don't. For we want the things that are good, as you agree, and we don't want those that are neither good nor bad, nor those that are bad. Right? Do you think that what I'm saying is true, Polus, or don't you? Why don't you answer?

Polus: I think it's true.

Socrates: Since we're in agreement about that then, if a person who's a d tyrant or an orator puts somebody to death or exiles him or confiscates his property because he supposes that doing so is better for himself when actually it's worse, this person, I take it, is doing what he sees fit, isn't he?

Polus: Yes.

Socrates: And is he also doing what he wants, if these things are actually bad? Why don't you answer?

Polus: All right, I don't think he's doing what he wants.

Socrates: Can such a man possibly have great power in that city, if in e fact having great power is, as you agree, something good?

POLUS: He cannot.

SOCRATES: So, what I was saying is true, when I said that it is possible for a man who does in his city what he sees fit not to have great power, nor to be doing what he wants.

POLUS: Really, Socrates! As if you wouldn't welcome being in a position to do what you see fit in the city, rather than not! As if you wouldn't be envious whenever you'd see anyone putting to death some person he saw fit, or confiscating his property or tying him up!

SOCRATES: Justly, you mean, or unjustly?

469   POLUS: Whichever way he does it, isn't he to be envied either way?

SOCRATES: Hush, Polus.

POLUS: What for?

SOCRATES: Because you're not supposed to envy the unenviable or the miserable. You're supposed to pity them.

POLUS: Really? Is this how you think it is with the people I'm talking about?

SOCRATES: Of course.

POLUS: So, you think that a person who puts to death anyone he sees fit, and does so justly, is miserable and to be pitied?

SOCRATES: No, I don't, but I don't think he's to be envied either.

POLUS: Weren't you just now saying that he's miserable?

b   SOCRATES: Yes, the one who puts someone to death unjustly is, my friend, and he's to be pitied besides. But the one who does so justly isn't to be envied.

POLUS: Surely the one who's put to death unjustly is the one who's both to be pitied and miserable.

SOCRATES: Less so than the one putting him to death, Polus, and less than the one who's justly put to death.

POLUS: How can that be, Socrates?

SOCRATES: It's because doing what's unjust is actually the greatest of evils.

POLUS: Really? Is *that* the greatest? Isn't suffering what's unjust a greater one?

SOCRATES: No, not in the least.

POLUS: So you'd want to suffer what's unjust rather than do it?

c   SOCRATES: I certainly wouldn't want either, but if it had to be one or the other, I would choose suffering over doing what's unjust.

POLUS: You wouldn't welcome being a tyrant, then?

SOCRATES: No, if by being a tyrant you mean what I do.

POLUS: I mean just what I said a while ago, to be in a position to do whatever you see fit in the city, whether it's putting people to death or exiling them, or doing any and everything just as you see fit.

SOCRATES: Well, my wonderful fellow! I'll put you a case, and you crit-
d   icize it. Imagine me in a crowded marketplace, with a dagger up my sleeve,

saying to you, "Polus, I've just got myself some marvelous tyrannical power. So, if I see fit to have any one of these people you see here put to death right on the spot, to death he'll be put. And if I see fit to have one of them have his head bashed in, bashed in it will be, right away. If I see fit to have his coat ripped apart, ripped it will be. That's how great my power in this city is!" Suppose you didn't believe me and I showed you the dagger.   e
On seeing it, you'd be likely to say, "But Socrates, *everybody* could have great power that way. For this way any house you see fit might be burned down, and so might the dockyards and triremes of the Athenians, and all their ships, both public and private." But then *that's* not what having great power is, doing what one sees fit. Or do you think it is?

POLUS: No, at least not like that.

SOCRATES: Can you then tell me what your reason is for objecting to this   470
sort of power?

POLUS: Yes, I can.

SOCRATES: What is it? Tell me.

POLUS: It's that the person who acts this way is necessarily punished.

SOCRATES: And isn't being punished a bad thing?

POLUS: Yes, it really is.

SOCRATES: Well then, my surprising fellow, here again you take the view that as long as acting as one sees fit coincides with acting beneficially, it is good, and this, evidently, is having great power. Otherwise it is a bad   b
thing, and is having little power. Let's consider this point, too. Do we agree that sometimes it's better to do those things we were just now talking about, putting people to death and banishing them and confiscating their property, and at other times it isn't?

POLUS: Yes, we do.

SOCRATES: This point is evidently agreed upon by you and me both?

POLUS: Yes.

SOCRATES: When do you say that it's better to do these things then? Tell me where you draw the line.

POLUS: Why don't you answer that question yourself, Socrates.

SOCRATES: Well then, Polus, if you find it more pleasing to listen to me, I   c
say that when one does these things justly, it's better, but when one does them unjustly, it's worse.

POLUS: How hard it is to refute you, Socrates! Why, even a child could refute you and show that what you're saying isn't true!

SOCRATES: In that case, I'll be very grateful to the child, and just as grateful to you if you refute me and rid me of this nonsense. Please don't falter now in doing a friend a good turn. Refute me.

POLUS: Surely, Socrates, we don't need to refer to ancient history to refute you. Why, current events quite suffice to do that, and to prove that many   d
people who behave unjustly are happy.

SOCRATES: What sorts of events are these?

POLUS: You can picture this man Archelaus, the son of Perdiccas, ruling Macedonia, I take it?

SOCRATES: Well, if I can't picture him, I do hear things about him.

POLUS: Do you think he's happy or miserable?

SOCRATES: I don't know, Polus. I haven't met the man yet.

e   POLUS: Really? You'd know this if you had met him, but without that you don't know straight off that he's happy?

SOCRATES: No, I certainly don't, by Zeus!

POLUS: It's obvious, Socrates, that you won't even claim to know that the Great King is happy![1]

SOCRATES: Yes, and that would be true, for I don't know how he stands in regard to education and justice.

POLUS: Really? Is happiness determined entirely by that?

SOCRATES: Yes, Polus, so I say anyway. I say that the admirable and good person, man or woman, is happy, but that the one who's unjust and wicked is miserable.

471   POLUS: So on your reasoning this man Archelaus is miserable?

SOCRATES: Yes, my friend, if he is in fact unjust.

POLUS: Why of course he's unjust! The sovereignty which he now holds doesn't belong to him at all, given the fact that his mother was a slave of Alcetas, Perdiccas's brother. By rights he was a slave of Alcetas, and if he wanted to do what's just, he'd still be a slave to Alcetas, and on your reasoning would be happy. As it is, how marvelously "miserable" he's turned out to be, now that he's committed the most heinous crimes. First he

b   sends for this man, his very own master and uncle, on the pretext of restoring to him the sovereignty that Perdiccas had taken from him. He entertains him, gets him drunk, both him and his son Alexander, his own cousin and a boy about his own age. He then throws them into a wagon, drives it away at night, and slaughters and disposes of them both. And although he's committed these crimes, he remains unaware of how "miserable" he's become, and feels no remorse either. He refuses to become "happy" by justly bringing up his brother and conferring the sovereignty

c   upon him, the legitimate son of Perdiccas, a boy of about seven to whom the sovereignty was by rights due to come. Instead, not long afterward, he throws him into a well and drowns him, telling the boy's mother Cleopatra that he fell into the well chasing a goose and lost his life. For this very reason now, because he's committed the most terrible of crimes of any in Macedonia, he's the most "miserable" of all Macedonians instead of the happiest, and no doubt there are some in Athens, beginning with yourself,

d   who'd prefer being any other Macedonian at all to being Archelaus.

SOCRATES: Already at the start of our discussions, Polus, I praised you

1. A title referring to the King of Persia, who embodied the popular idea of supreme happiness.

because I thought you were well educated in oratory. But I also thought that you had neglected the practice of discussion. And now is *this* all there is to the argument by which even a child could refute me, and do you suppose that when I say that a person who acts unjustly is not happy, I now stand refuted by you by means of *this* argument? Where did you get that idea, my good man? As a matter of fact, I disagree with every single thing you say!

POLUS: You're just unwilling to admit it. You really do think it's the way I   *e*
say it is.

SOCRATES: My wonderful man, you're trying to refute me in oratorical style, the way people in law courts do when they think they're refuting some claim. There, too, one side thinks it's refuting the other when it produces many reputable witnesses on behalf of the arguments it presents, while the person who asserts the opposite produces only one witness, or none at all. This "refutation" is worthless, as far as truth is concerned, for it might happen sometimes that an individual is brought down by the false   472
testimony of many reputable people. Now too, nearly every Athenian and alien will take your side on the things you're saying, if it's witnesses you want to produce against me to show that what I say isn't true. Nikias the son of Niceratus will testify for you, if you like, and his brothers along with him, the ones whose tripods are standing in a row in the precinct of Dionysus. Aristocrates the son of Scellius will too, if you like, the one to   *b*
whom that handsome votive offering in the precinct of Pythian Apollo belongs. And so will the whole house of Pericles, if you like, or any other local family you care to choose. Nevertheless, though I'm only one person, I don't agree with you. You don't compel me; instead you produce many false witnesses against me and try to banish me from my property, the truth. For my part, if I don't produce you as a single witness to agree with what I'm saying, then I suppose I've achieved nothing worth mentioning concerning the things we've been discussing. And I suppose you haven't either, if I don't   *c*
testify on your side, though I'm just one person, and you disregard all these other people.

There is, then, this style of refutation, the one you and many others accept. There's also another, one that I accept. Let's compare the one with the other and see if they'll differ in any way. It's true, after all, that the matters in dispute between us are not at all insignificant ones, but pretty nearly those it's most admirable to have knowledge about, and most shameful not to. For the heart of the matter is that of recognizing or failing to recognize who is happy and who is not. To take first the immediate ques-   *d*
tion our present discussion's about: you believe that it's possible for a man who behaves unjustly and who is unjust to be happy, since you believe Archelaus to be both unjust and happy. Are we to understand that this is precisely your view?

POLUS: That's right.

SOCRATES: And I say that that's impossible. This is one point in dispute between us. Fair enough. Although he acts unjustly, he'll be happy—that is, if he gets his due punishment?

POLUS: Oh no, certainly not! That's how he'd be the most miserable!

e   SOCRATES: But if a man who acts unjustly doesn't get his due, then, on your reasoning, he'll be happy?

POLUS: That's what I say.

SOCRATES: On my view of it, Polus, a man who acts unjustly, a man who is unjust, is thoroughly miserable, the more so if he doesn't get his due punishment for the wrongdoing he commits, the less so if he pays and receives what is due at the hands of both gods and men.

473   POLUS: What an absurd position you're trying to maintain, Socrates!

SOCRATES: Yes, and I'll try to get you to take the same position too, my good man, for I consider you a friend. For now, these are the points we differ on. Please look at them with me. I said earlier, didn't I, that doing what's unjust is worse than suffering it?

POLUS: Yes, you did.

SOCRATES: And you said that suffering it is worse.

POLUS: Yes.

SOCRATES: And I said that those who do what's unjust are miserable, and was "refuted" by you.

POLUS: You certainly were, by Zeus!

b   SOCRATES: So you think, Polus.

POLUS: So I *truly* think.

SOCRATES: Perhaps. And again, you think that those who do what's unjust are happy, so long as they don't pay what is due.

POLUS: I certainly do.

SOCRATES: Whereas I say that they're the most miserable, while those who pay their due are less so. Would you like to refute this too?

POLUS: Why, that's even more "difficult" to refute than the other claim, Socrates!

SOCRATES: Not difficult, surely, Polus. It's impossible. What's true is never refuted.

POLUS: What do you mean? Take a man who's caught doing something *c*   unjust, say, plotting to set himself up as tyrant. Suppose that he's caught, put on the rack, castrated, and has his eyes burned out. Suppose that he's subjected to a host of other abuses of all sorts, and then made to witness his wife and children undergo the same. In the end he's impaled or tarred. Will he be happier than if he hadn't got caught, had set himself up as tyrant, and lived out his life ruling in his city and doing whatever he liked, *d*   a person envied and counted happy by fellow citizens and aliens alike? Is *this* what you say is impossible to refute?

SOCRATES: This time you're spooking me, Polus, instead of refuting me. Just before, you were arguing by testimony. Still, refresh my memory on a small point: if the man plots to set himself up as tyrant *unjustly*, you said?

POLUS: Yes, I did.

SOCRATES: In that case neither of them will ever be the happier one, neither the one who gains tyrannical power unjustly, nor the one who pays what is due, for of two miserable people one could not be happier than the other. But the one who avoids getting caught and becomes a tyrant is the more miserable one. What's this, Polus? You're laughing? Is this now some further style of refutation, to laugh when somebody makes a point, instead of refuting him?   *e*

POLUS: Don't you think you've been refuted already, Socrates, when you're saying things the likes of which no human being would maintain? Just ask any one of these people.

SOCRATES: Polus, I'm not one of the politicians. Last year I was elected to the Council by lot, and when our tribe was presiding and I had to call for a vote, I came in for a laugh. I didn't know how to do it. So please don't tell   *474* me to call for a vote from the people present here. If you have no better "refutations" than these to offer, do as I suggested just now: let me have my turn, and you try the kind of refutation I think is called for. For I do know how to produce one witness to whatever I'm saying, and that's the man I'm having a discussion with. The majority I disregard. And I do know how to call for a vote from one man, but I don't even discuss things with the majority. See if you'll be willing to give me a refutation, then, by answering   *b* the questions you're asked. For I do believe that you and I and everybody else consider doing what's unjust worse than suffering it, and not paying what is due worse than paying it.

POLUS: And I do believe that I don't, and that no other person does, either. So you'd take suffering what's unjust over doing it, would you?

SOCRATES: Yes, and so would you and everyone else.

POLUS: Far from it! I wouldn't, you wouldn't, and nobody else would, either.

SOCRATES: Won't you answer, then?   *c*

POLUS: I certainly will. I'm eager to know what you'll say, in fact.

SOCRATES: So that you'll know, answer me as though this were my first question to you. Which do you think is worse, Polus, doing what's unjust or suffering it?

POLUS: I think suffering it is.

SOCRATES: You do? Which do you think is more shameful, doing what's unjust or suffering it? Tell me.

POLUS: Doing it.

SOCRATES: Now if doing it is in fact more shameful, isn't it also worse?

POLUS: No, not in the least.

SOCRATES: I see. Evidently you don't believe that *admirable* and *good* are   *d* the same, or that *bad* and *shameful* are.

POLUS: No, I certainly don't.

SOCRATES: Well, what about this? When you call all admirable things admirable, bodies, for example, or colors, shapes and sounds, or practices, is it with nothing in view that you do so each time? Take admirable bodies first. Don't you call them admirable either in virtue of their usefulness, relative to whatever it is that each is useful for, or else in virtue of some pleasure, if it makes the people who look at them get enjoyment from looking at them? In the case of the admirability of a body, can you mention anything other than these?

e   POLUS: No, I can't.

SOCRATES: Doesn't the same hold for all the other things? Don't you call shapes and colors admirable on account of either some pleasure or benefit or both?

POLUS: Yes, I do.

SOCRATES: Doesn't this also hold for sounds and all things musical?

POLUS: Yes.

SOCRATES: And certainly things that pertain to laws and practices—the admirable ones, that is—don't fall outside the limits of being either pleasant or beneficial, or both, I take it.

475   POLUS: No, I don't think they do.

SOCRATES: Doesn't the same hold for the admirability of the fields of learning, too?

POLUS: Yes indeed. Yes, Socrates, your present definition of the admirable in terms of pleasure and good is an admirable one.

SOCRATES: And so is my definition of the shameful in terms of the opposite, pain and evil, isn't it?

POLUS: Necessarily so.

SOCRATES: Therefore, whenever one of two admirable things is more admirable than the other, it is so because it surpasses the other either in one of these, pleasure or benefit, or in both.

POLUS: Yes, that's right.

SOCRATES: And whenever one of two shameful things is more shameful
b   than the other, it will be so because it surpasses the other either in pain or in evil. Isn't that necessarily so?

POLUS: Yes.

SOCRATES: Well now, what were we saying a moment ago about doing what's unjust and suffering it? Weren't you saying that suffering it is more evil, but doing it more shameful?

POLUS: I was.

SOCRATES: Now if doing what's unjust is in fact more shameful than suffering it, wouldn't it be so either because it is more painful and surpasses the other in pain, or because it surpasses it in evil, or both? Isn't that necessarily so, too?

POLUS: Of course it is.

SOCRATES: Let's look at this first: does doing what's unjust surpass suffer-   *c*
ing it in pain, and do people who do it hurt more than people who suffer it?

POLUS: No, Socrates, that's not the case at all!

SOCRATES: So it doesn't surpass it in pain, anyhow.

POLUS: Certainly not.

SOCRATES: So, if it doesn't surpass it in pain, it couldn't at this point
surpass it in both.

POLUS: Apparently not.

SOCRATES: This leaves it surpassing it only in the other thing.

POLUS: Yes.

SOCRATES: In evil.

POLUS: Evidently.

SOCRATES: So, because it surpasses it in evil, doing what's unjust would
be more evil than suffering it.

POLUS: That's clear.

SOCRATES: Now didn't the majority of mankind, and you earlier, agree   *d*
with us that doing what's unjust is more shameful than suffering it?

POLUS: Yes.

SOCRATES: And now, at least, it's turned out to be more evil.

POLUS: Evidently.

SOCRATES: Would you then welcome what's more evil and what's more
shameful over what is less so? Don't shrink back from answering, Polus.
You won't get hurt in any way. Submit yourself nobly to the argument, as
you would to a doctor, and answer me. Say yes or no to what I ask you.

POLUS: No, I wouldn't, Socrates.   *e*

SOCRATES: And would any other person?

POLUS: No, I don't think so, not on this reasoning, anyhow.

SOCRATES: I was right, then, when I said that neither you nor I nor any
other person would take doing what's unjust over suffering it, for it really is
more evil.

POLUS: So it appears.

SOCRATES: So you see, Polus, that when the one refutation is compared
with the other, there is no resemblance at all. Whereas everyone but me
agrees with you, you are all I need, although you're just a party of one, for   476
your agreement and testimony. It's you alone whom I call on for a vote; the
others I disregard. Let this be our verdict on this matter, then. Let's next
consider the second point in dispute between us, that is whether a wrongdoer's paying what is due is the greatest of evils, as you were supposing, or
whether his not paying it is a greater one, as I was.

Let's look at it this way. Do you call paying what is due and being justly
disciplined for wrongdoing the same?

POLUS: Yes, I do.

SOCRATES: Can you say, then, that all just things aren't admirable, insofar *b* as they are just? Think carefully and tell me.

POLUS: Yes, I think they are.

SOCRATES: Consider this point, too. If somebody acts upon something, there's necessarily also something that has something done to it by the one acting upon it?

POLUS: Yes, I think so.

SOCRATES: And that it has done to it what the thing acting upon it does, and in the sort of way the thing acting upon it does it? I mean, for example, that if somebody hits, there's necessarily something that is being hit?

POLUS: Necessarily.

c SOCRATES: And if the hitter hits hard or quickly, the thing being hit is hit that way, too?

POLUS: Yes.

SOCRATES: So the thing being hit gets acted upon in whatever way the hitting thing acts upon it?

POLUS: Yes, that's right.

SOCRATES: So, too, if somebody performs surgical burning, then necessarily something is being burned?

POLUS: Of course.

SOCRATES: And if he burns severely or painfully, the thing that's being burned is burned in whatever way the burning thing burns it?

POLUS: That's right.

SOCRATES: Doesn't the same account also hold if a person makes a surgical cut? For something is being cut.

POLUS: Yes.

SOCRATES: And if the cut is large or deep or painful, the thing being cut *d* is cut in whatever way the cutting thing cuts it?

POLUS: So it appears.

SOCRATES: Summing it up, see if you agree with what I was saying just now, that in all cases, in whatever way the thing acting upon something acts upon it, the thing acted upon is acted upon in just that way.

POLUS: Yes, I do agree.

SOCRATES: Taking this as agreed, is paying what is due a case of being acted upon or of acting upon something?

POLUS: It's necessarily a case of being acted upon, Socrates.

SOCRATES: By someone who acts?

POLUS: Of course. By the one administering discipline.

e SOCRATES: Now one who disciplines correctly disciplines justly?

POLUS: Yes.

SOCRATES: Thereby acting justly, or not?

POLUS: Yes, justly.

SOCRATES: So the one being disciplined is being acted upon justly when he pays what is due?

POLUS: Apparently.

SOCRATES: And it was agreed, I take it, that just things are admirable?

POLUS: That's right.

SOCRATES: So one of these men does admirable things, and the other, the one being disciplined, has admirable things done to him.

POLUS: Yes.

SOCRATES: If they're admirable, then, aren't they good? For they're either   477
pleasant or beneficial.

POLUS: Necessarily so.

SOCRATES: Hence, the one paying what is due has good things being done to him?

POLUS: Evidently.

SOCRATES: Hence, he's being benefited?

POLUS: Yes.

SOCRATES: Is his benefit the one I take it to be? Does his soul undergo improvement if he's justly disciplined?

POLUS: Yes, that's likely.

SOCRATES: Hence, one who pays what is due gets rid of evil in his soul?

POLUS: Yes.

SOCRATES: Now, is the evil he gets rid of the most serious one? Consider it this way: in the matter of a person's financial condition, do you detect   b
any evil other than poverty?

POLUS: No, just poverty.

SOCRATES: What about that of a person's physical condition? Would you say that evil here consists of weakness, disease, ugliness, and the like?

POLUS: Yes, I would.

SOCRATES: Do you believe that there's also some corrupt condition of the soul?

POLUS: Of course.

SOCRATES: And don't you call this condition injustice, ignorance, coward-ice, and the like?

POLUS: Yes, certainly.

SOCRATES: Of these three things, one's finances, one's body, and one's soul, you said there are three states of corruption, namely poverty, disease,   c
and injustice?

POLUS: Yes.

SOCRATES: Which of these states of corruption is the most shameful? Isn't it injustice, and corruption of one's soul in general?

POLUS: Very much so.

SOCRATES: And if it's the most shameful, it's also the most evil?

POLUS: What do you mean, Socrates?

SOCRATES: I mean this: What we agreed on earlier implies that what's most shameful is so always because it's the source either of the greatest pain, or of harm, or of both.

POLUS: Very much so.

SOCRATES: And now we've agreed that injustice, and corruption of soul
d   as a whole, is the most shameful thing.

POLUS: So we have.

SOCRATES: So either it's most painful and is most shameful because it
surpasses the others in pain, or else in harm, or in both?

POLUS: Necessarily so.

SOCRATES: Now is being unjust, undisciplined, cowardly, and ignorant
more painful than being poor or sick?

POLUS: No, I don't think so, Socrates, given what we've said, anyhow.

SOCRATES: So the reason that corruption of one's soul is the most shameful of them all is that it surpasses the others by same monstrously great
e   harm and astounding evil, since it doesn't surpass them in pain, according
to your reasoning.

POLUS: So it appears.

SOCRATES: But what is surpassing in greatest harm would, I take it,
certainly be the greatest evil there is.

POLUS: Yes.

SOCRATES: Injustice, then, lack of discipline and all other forms of corruption of soul are the greatest evil there is.

POLUS: Apparently so.

SOCRATES: Now, what is the craft that gets rid of poverty? Isn't it that of
financial management?

POLUS: Yes.

SOCRATES: What's the one that gets rid of disease? Isn't it that of medicine?

478   POLUS: Necessarily.

SOCRATES: What's the one that gets rid of corruption and injustice? If
you're stuck, look at it this way: where and to whom do we take people
who are physically sick?

POLUS: To doctors, Socrates.

SOCRATES: Where do we take people who behave unjustly and without
discipline?

POLUS: To judges, you mean?

SOCRATES: Isn't it so they'll pay what's due?

POLUS: Yes, I agree.

SOCRATES: Now don't those who administer discipline correctly employ a
kind of justice in doing so?

POLUS: That's clear.

SOCRATES: It's financial management, then, that gets rid of poverty, medi-
b   cine that gets rid of disease, and justice that gets rid of injustice and indis-
cipline.

POLUS: Apparently.

SOCRATES: Which of these, now, is the most admirable?

POLUS: Of which, do you mean?

SOCRATES: Of financial management, medicine, and justice.

POLUS: Justice is by far, Socrates.

SOCRATES: Doesn't it in that case provide either the most pleasure, or benefit, or both, if it really is the most admirable?

POLUS: Yes.

SOCRATES: Now, is getting medical treatment something pleasant? Do people who get it enjoy getting it?

POLUS: No, I don't think so.

SOCRATES: But it *is* beneficial, isn't it?

POLUS: Yes.

SOCRATES: Because they're getting rid of a great evil, so that it's worth   c
their while to endure the pain and so get well.

POLUS: Of course.

SOCRATES: Now, would a man be happiest, as far as his body goes, if he's under treatment, or if he weren't even sick to begin with?

POLUS: If he weren't even sick, obviously.

SOCRATES: Because happiness evidently isn't a matter of getting rid of evil; it's rather a matter of not even contracting it to begin with.

POLUS: That's so.

SOCRATES: Very well. Of two people, each of whom has an evil in either   d
body or soul, which is the more miserable one, the one who is treated and gets rid of the evil, or the one who doesn't but keeps it?

POLUS: The one who isn't treated, it seems to me.

SOCRATES: Now, wasn't paying what's due getting rid of the greatest evil, corruption?

POLUS: It was.

SOCRATES: Yes, because such justice makes people temperate, I take it, and more just. It proves to be a treatment against corruption.

POLUS: Yes.

SOCRATES: The happiest man, then, is the one who doesn't have evil in his soul, now that this has been shown to be the most serious kind of evil.

POLUS: That's clear.

SOCRATES: And second, I suppose, is the man who gets rid of it.   e

POLUS: Evidently.

SOCRATES: This is the man who gets lectured and lashed, the one who pays what is due.

POLUS: Yes.

SOCRATES: The man who keeps it, then, and who doesn't get rid of it, is the one whose life is the worst.

POLUS: Apparently.

SOCRATES: Isn't this actually the man who, although he commits the most

479 serious crimes and uses methods that are most unjust, succeeds in avoiding being lectured and disciplined and paying his due, as Archelaus according to you, and the other tyrants, orators, and potentates have put themselves in a position to do?

POLUS: Evidently.

SOCRATES: Yes, my good man, I take it that these people have managed to accomplish pretty much the same thing as a person who has contracted very serious illnesses, but, by avoiding treatment manages to avoid paying what's due to the doctors for his bodily faults, fearing, as would a child,

b cauterization or surgery because they're painful. Don't you think so, too?

POLUS: Yes, I do.

SOCRATES: It's because he evidently doesn't know what health and bodily excellence are like. For on the basis of what we're now agreed on, it looks as though those who avoid paying what is due also do the same sort of thing, Polus. They focus on its painfulness, but are blind to its benefit and are ignorant of how much more miserable it is to live with an unhealthy soul than with an unhealthy body, a soul that's rotten with injustice and impiety.

c This is also the reason they go to any length to avoid paying what is due and getting rid of the greatest evil. They find themselves funds and friends, and ways to speak as persuasively as possible. Now if what we're agreed on is true, Polus, are you aware of what things follow from our argument? Or would you like us to set them out?

POLUS: Yes, if you think we should anyhow.

SOCRATES: Does it follow that injustice, and doing what is unjust, is the greatest evil?

d POLUS: Yes, apparently.

SOCRATES: And it has indeed been shown that paying what is due is what gets rid of this evil?

POLUS: So it seems.

SOCRATES: And that if it isn't paid, the evil is retained?

POLUS: Yes.

SOCRATES: So, doing what's unjust is the second most serious evil. Not paying what's due when one has done what's unjust is by its nature the most serious and foremost of evil of all.

POLUS: Evidently.

SOCRATES: Now wasn't this the point in dispute between us, my friend?

e You consider Archelaus happy, a man who committed the gravest crimes without paying what was due, whereas I took the opposite view, that whoever avoids paying his due for his wrongdoing, whether he's Archelaus or any other man, deserves to be miserable beyond all other men, and that one who does what's unjust is always more miserable than the one who suffers it, and the one who avoids paying what's due always more miserable than the one who does pay it. Weren't these the things I said?

POLUS: Yes.

SOCRATES: Hasn't it been proved that what was said is true?

POLUS: Apparently.

SOCRATES: Fair enough. If these things are true then, Polus, what is the   *480*
great use of oratory? For on the basis of what we're agreed on now, what a
man should guard himself against most of all is doing what's unjust, knowing that he will have trouble enough if he does. Isn't that so?

POLUS: Yes, that's right.

SOCRATES: And if he or anyone else he cares about acts unjustly, he
should voluntarily go to the place where he'll pay his due as soon as
possible; he should go to the judge as though he were going to a doctor,   *b*
anxious that the disease of injustice shouldn't be protracted and cause his
soul to fester incurably. What else can we say, Polus, if our previous agreements really stand? Aren't these statements necessarily consistent with our
earlier ones in only this way?

POLUS: Well yes, Socrates. What else are we to say?

SOCRATES: So, if oratory is used to defend injustice, Polus, one's own or
that of one's relatives, companions, or children, or that of one's country
when it acts unjustly, it is of no use to us at all, unless one takes it to be   *c*
useful for the opposite purpose: that he should accuse himself first and
foremost, and then too his family and anyone else dear to him who happens to behave unjustly at any time; and that he should not keep his
wrongdoing hidden but bring it out into the open, so that he may pay his
due and get well; and compel himself and the others not to play the
coward, but to grit his teeth and present himself with grace and courage as
to a doctor for cauterization and surgery, pursuing what's good and admirable without taking any account of the pain. And if his unjust behavior
merits flogging, he should present himself to be whipped; if it merits   *d*
imprisonment, to be imprisoned; if a fine, to pay it; if exile, to be exiled;
and if execution, to be executed. He should be his own chief accuser, and
the accuser of other members of his family, and use his oratory for the
purpose of getting rid of the greatest evil, injustice, as the unjust acts are
being exposed. Are we to affirm or deny this, Polus?

POLUS: I think these statements are absurd, Socrates, though no doubt   *e*
you think they agree with those expressed earlier.

SOCRATES: Then either we should abandon those, or else these necessarily follow?

POLUS: Yes, that's how it is.

SOCRATES: And, on the other hand, to reverse the case, suppose a man
had to harm someone, an enemy or anybody at all, provided that he didn't
suffer anything unjust from this enemy himself—for this is something to be
on guard against—if the enemy did something unjust against another person, then our man should see to it in every way, both in what he does and
what he says, that his enemy does not go to the judge and pay his due. And   *481*
if he does go, he should scheme to get his enemy off without paying what's

due. If he's stolen a lot of gold, he should scheme to get him not to return it but to keep it and spend it in an unjust and godless way both on himself and his people. And if his crimes merit the death penalty, he should scheme to keep him from being executed, preferably never to die at all but to live forever in corruption, but failing that, to have him live as long as possible in that condition. Yes, this is the sort of thing I think oratory is useful for, Polus, since for the person who has no intention of behaving unjustly it doesn't seem to me to have much use—if in fact it has any use at all—since its usefulness hasn't in any way become apparent so far.

MENO PHAEDO SYMPOSIUM

These three dialogues are linked by the emergence and development in them of Plato's famous theory of forms. The Meno *begins with the question, also raised in the* Protagoras, *of whether virtue can be taught. This leads to an inquiry into virtue: what is the one form shared in common by all the virtues that makes each of them a virtue (72c–d)? Various answers are proposed and rejected. Then Meno introduces a general problem for the inquiry: if neither he nor Socrates knows what virtue is, how will they recognize it if they find it (80d)? Socrates answers with the theory of recollection, which he attempts to underwrite by the examination of the slave boy (81a–86c). The dialogue ends with a return to the original topic of whether or not virtue can be taught. The theory of recollection presupposes that the soul is immortal. In the* Phaedo, *explicit arguments are given in favor of this presupposition, the theory of recollection is modified and enriched, and we learn more about the nature of forms and about their role not just in ethics but in science and cosmology. The* Phaedo, *which—like the* Crito—*is set in the prison where Socrates spends his last days, ends with an account of his death. In the* Symposium, *Plato gives one of his most vivid accounts of the ascent of the soul from visible, tangible particulars to intelligible, abstract forms, and we learn that it is love (erōs) that leads us to make that ascent.*

MENO

Can you tell me, Socrates, can virtue be taught? Or is it not teachable but   70
the result of practice, or is it neither of these, but men possess it by nature
or in some other way?

Before now, Meno, Thessalians had a high reputation among the Greeks
and were admired for their horsemanship and their wealth, but now, it   b
seems to me, they are also admired for their wisdom, not least the fellow
citizens of your friend Aristippus of Larissa. The responsibility for this
reputation of yours lies with Gorgias, for when he came to your city he
found that the leading Aleuadae, your lover Aristippus among them, loved
him for his wisdom, and so did the leading Thessalians. He accustomed
you to give a bold and grand answer to any question you may be asked, as
experts are likely to do, as he himself was ready to answer any Greek who   c
wished to question him, and every question was answered. But here in

Translated by G.M.A. Grube.

241

Athens, my dear Meno, the opposite is the case, as if there were a dearth of
71   wisdom, and wisdom seems to have departed hence to go to you. If then
you want to ask one of us that sort of question, everyone will laugh and
say: "Good stranger, you must think me happy indeed if you think I know
whether virtue can be taught or how it comes to be; I am so far from
knowing whether virtue can be taught or not that I do not even have any
b   knowledge of what virtue itself is." I myself, Meno, am as poor as my
fellow citizens in this matter, and I blame myself for my complete ignorance about virtue. If I do not know what something is, how could I know
what qualities it possesses? Or do you think that someone who does not
know at all who Meno is could know whether he is good-looking or rich or
well-born, or the opposite of these? Do you think that is possible?

I do not; but, Socrates, do you really not know what virtue is? Are we to
c   report this to the folk back home about you?

Not only that, my friend, but also that, as I believe, I have never yet met
anyone else who did know.

How so? Did you not meet Gorgias when he was here?—I did.

Did you then not think that he knew?

I do not altogether remember, Meno, so that I cannot tell you now what I
thought then. Perhaps he does know; you know what he used to say, so you
d   remind me of what he said. You tell me yourself, if you are willing, for
surely you share his views.—I do.

Let us leave Gorgias out of it, since he is not here. But Meno, by the gods,
what do you yourself say that virtue is? Speak and do not begrudge us, so
that most fortunately I spoke an untruth when I said that I had never met
anyone who knew, if you and Gorgias are shown to know.

e   It is not hard to tell you, Socrates. First, if you want the virtue of a man,
it is easy to say that a man's virtue consists of being able to manage public
affairs and in so doing to benefit his friends and harm his enemies and to
be careful that no harm comes to himself; if you want the virtue of a
woman, it is not difficult to describe: she must manage the home well,
preserve its possessions, and be submissive to her husband; the virtue of a
child, whether male or female, is different again, and so is that of an
elderly man, if you want that, or if you want that of a free man or a slave.
72   And there are very many other virtues, so that one is not at a loss to say
what virtue is. There is virtue for every action and every age, for every task
of ours and every one of us—and Socrates, the same is true for wickedness.

I seem to be in great luck, Meno; while I am looking for one virtue, I
have found you to have a whole swarm of them. But, Meno, to follow
b   up the image of swarms, if I were asking you what is the nature of bees,
and you said that they are of all kinds, what would you answer if I asked
you: "Do you mean that they are many and varied and different from
one another in so far as they are bees? Or are they no different in that

regard, but in some other respect, in their beauty, for example, or their size or in some other such way?" Tell me, what would you answer if thus questioned?

I would say that they do not differ from one another in being bees.

If I went on to say: "Tell me, what is this very thing, Meno, in which *c* they are all the same and do not differ from one another?" Would you be able to tell me?—I would.

The same is true in the case of the virtues. Even if they are many and various, all of them have one and the same form which makes them virtues, and it is right to look to this when one is asked to make clear what virtue is. Or do you not understand what I mean? *d*

I think I understand, but I certainly do not grasp the meaning of the question as fully as I want to.

I am asking whether you think it is only in the case of virtue that there is one for man, another for woman and so on, or is the same true in the case of health and size and strength? Do you think that there is one for man and another for woman? Or, if it is health, does it have the same form everywhere, whether in man or in anything else whatever? *e*

The health of a man seems to me the same as that of a woman.

And so with size and strength? If a woman is strong, that strength will be the same and have the same form, for by "the same" I mean that strength is no different as far as being strength, whether in a man or a woman. Or do you think there is a difference?—I do not think so.

And will there be any difference in the case of virtue, as far as being virtue is concerned, whether it be in a child or an old man, in a woman or *73* in a man?

I think, Socrates, that somehow this is no longer like those other cases.

How so? Did you not say that the virtue of a man consists of managing the city well, and that of a woman of managing the household?— I did.

Is it possible to manage a city well, or a household, or anything else, while not managing it moderately and justly?—Certainly not.

Then if they manage justly and moderately, they must do so with justice *b* and moderation?—Necessarily.

So both the man and the woman, if they are to be good, need the same things, justice and moderation?—So it seems.

What about a child and an old man? Can they possibly be good if they are intemperate and unjust?—Certainly not.

But if they are moderate and just?—Yes.

So all men are good in the same way, for they become good by acquiring *c* the same qualities.—It seems so.

And they would not be good in the same way if they did not have the same virtue?—They certainly would not be.

Since then the virtue of all is the same, try to tell me and to remember what Gorgias, and you with him, said that that same thing is.

d   What else but to be able to rule over people, if you are seeking one description to fit them all.

That is indeed what I am seeking, but Meno, is the virtue of a child the same as that of a slave, namely, for them to be able to rule over a master, and do you think that he who rules is still a slave?—I do not think so at all, Socrates.

It is not likely, my good man. Consider this further point: you say that virtue is to be able to rule; shall we not add to this the word justly, not unjustly?

I think so, Socrates, for justice is virtue.

e   Is it virtue, Meno, or a virtue?—What do you mean?

As with anything else. For example, if you wish, take roundness about which I would say that it is a shape, but not simply that it is shape. I would not so speak of it because there are other shapes.

You are quite right. So I too say that not only justice is a virtue but there are many other virtues.

74   What are they? Tell me, as I could mention other shapes to you if you bade me do so, so do you mention other virtues.

I think courage is a virtue, and moderation, wisdom, and munificence, and very many others.

We are having the same trouble again, Meno, though in another way; we have found many virtues while looking for one, but we cannot find the one which covers all the others.

b   I cannot yet find, Socrates, what you are looking for, one virtue for them all, as in the other cases.

That is likely, but I am eager, if I can, that we should make progress, for you understand that the same applies to everything. If someone asked you what I mentioned just now: "What is shape, Meno?" and you told him that it was roundness, and if then he said to you what I did: "Is roundness shape or a shape?" you would surely tell him that it is a shape?—I certainly would.

c   That would be because there are other shapes?—Yes.

And if he asked you further what they were, you would tell him?—I would.

So too, if he asked you what colour is, and you said it is white, and your questioner interrupted you "Is white colour or a colour?" you would say that it is a colour, because there are also other colours?—I would.

And if he bade you mention other colours, you would mention others
d   that are no less colours than white is?—Yes.

Then if he pursued the argument as I did and said: "We always arrive at the many; do not talk to me in that way, but since you address all these many by one name, and say that no one of them is not a shape even though

they are opposites, tell me what this is which applies as much to the round
as to the straight and which you call shape, as you say the round is as much   *e*
a shape as the straight." Do you not say that?—I do.

When you speak like that, do you assert that the round is no more round
than it is straight, and that the straight is no more straight than it is
round?—Certainly not, Socrates.

Yet you say that the round is no more a shape than the straight is, nor the
one more than the other?—That is true.

What then is this to which the name shape applies? Try to tell me. If then
you answered the man who was questioning about shape or colour: "I do
not understand what you want, my man, nor what you mean," he would   75
probably wonder and say: "You do not understand that I am seeking that
which is the same in all these cases?" Would you still have nothing to say,
Meno, if one asked you: "What is this which applies to the round and the
straight and the other things which you call shapes and which is the same
in them all?" Try to say, that you may practise for your answer about
virtue.—No, Socrates, but you tell me.   *b*

Do you want me to do you this favour?—I certainly do.

And you will then be willing to tell me about virtue?—I will.

We must certainly press on. The subject is worth it.—It surely is.

Come then, let us try to tell you what shape is. See whether you
will accept that it is this: Let us say that shape is that which alone of
existing things always follows colour. Is that satisfactory to you, or do you
look for it in some other way? I should be satisfied if you defined virtue in   *c*
this way.

But that is foolish, Socrates.

How do you mean?

That shape, you say, always follows colour. Well then, if someone says
that he does not know what colour is, but that he has the same difficulty
as he had about shape, what would you think of the answer you have
given him?

That it is the truth, and if my questioner was one of those clever
and disputatious debaters, I would say to him: "I have given my answer;
if it is wrong, it is your job to refute it." Then, if they are friends as you   *d*
and I are, and want to discuss with each other, they must answer in a
manner more gentle and more proper to discussion. By this I mean that the
answers must not only be true, but in terms admittedly known to the questioner. I too will try to speak in these terms. Do you call some-   *e*
thing the end? I mean such a thing as a limit or boundary, for all those are,
I say, the same thing. Prodicus[1] might disagree with us, but you say a thing
is finished or completed—that is what I want to express, nothing elaborate.

I do, and I think I understand what you mean.

1. A well-known Sophist.

76   Further, you call something a plane, and something else a solid, as in geometry?—I do.

From this you may understand what I mean by shape, for I say this of every shape, that a shape is that which limits a solid; in a word, a shape is the limit of a solid.

And what do you say colour is, Socrates?

You are outrageous, Meno. You bother an old man to answer questions,
b but you yourself are not willing to recall and to tell me what Gorgias says that virtue is.

After you have answered this, Socrates, I will tell you.

Even someone who was blindfolded would know from your conversation that you are handsome and still have lovers.—Why so?

Because you are forever giving orders in a discussion, as spoiled people do, who behave like tyrants as long as they are young. And perhaps
c you have recognized that I am at a disadvantage with handsome people, so I will do you the favour of an answer.—By all means do me that favour.

Do you want me to answer after the manner of Gorgias, which you would most easily follow?—Of course I want that.

Do you both say there are effluvia of things, as Empedocles[2] does?— Certainly.

And that there are channels through which the effluvia make their way?—Definitely.

d   And some effluvia fit some of the channels, while others are too small or too big?—That is so.

And there is something which you call sight?—There is.

From this, "comprehend what I state," as Pindar said, for colour is an effluvium from a shape which fits the sight and is perceived.

That seems to me to be an excellent answer, Socrates.

Perhaps it was given in the manner to which you are accustomed. At the same time I think that you can deduce from this answer what sound is, and
e smell, and many such things.—Quite so.

It is a theatrical answer so it pleases you, Meno, more than that about shape.—It does.

It is not better, son of Alexidemus, but I am convinced that the other is, and I think you would agree, if you did not have to go away before the mysteries as you told me yesterday, but could remain and be initiated.

77   I would stay, Socrates, if you could tell me many things like these.

I shall certainly not be lacking in eagerness to tell you such things, both for your sake and my own, but I may not be able to tell you many. Come now, you too try to fulfill your promise to me and tell me the nature of virtue as a whole and stop making many out of one, as jokers say whenever

2. See Presocratics section pp. 52–74.

someone breaks something, but allow virtue to remain whole and sound, and tell me what it is, for I have given you examples.   *b*

I think, Socrates, that virtue is, as the poet says, "to find joy in beautiful things and have power." So I say that virtue is to desire beautiful things and have the power to acquire them.

Do you mean that the man who desires beautiful things desires good things?—Most certainly.

Do you assume that there are people who desire bad things, and others who desire good things? Do you not think, my good man, that all men   *c* desire good things?—I do not.

But some desire bad things?—Yes.

Do you mean that they believe the bad things to be good, or that they know they are bad and nevertheless desire them?—I think there are both kinds.

Do you think, Meno, that anyone, knowing that bad things are bad, nevertheless desires them?—I certainly do.

What do you mean by desiring? Is it to secure for oneself?—What else?

Does he think that the bad things benefit him who possesses them, or   *d* does he know they harm him?

There are some who believe that the bad things benefit them, others who know that the bad things harm them.

And do you think that those who believe that bad things benefit them know that they are bad?

No, that I cannot altogether believe.

It is clear then that those who do not know things to be bad do not desire what is bad, but they desire those things that they believe to be good but   *e* that are in fact bad. It follows that those who have knowledge of these things and believe them to be good clearly desire good things. Is that not so?—It is likely.

Well then, those whom you say desire bad things, believing that bad things harm their possessor, know that they will be harmed by them?— Necessarily.

And do they not think that those who are harmed are miserable to the   78 extent that they are harmed?—That too is inevitable.

And that those who are miserable are unhappy?—I think so.

Does anyone wish to be miserable and unhappy?—I do not think so, Socrates.

No one then wants what is bad, Meno, unless he wants to be such. For what else is being miserable but to desire bad things and secure them?

You are probably right, Socrates, and no one wants what is bad.   *b*

You said just now that virtue is to desire good things and have the power to secure them.—Yes, I did.

The desiring part of this statement is common to everybody, and one man is no better than another in this?—So it appears.

Clearly then, if one man is better than another, he must be better at securing them.—Quite so.

c This then is virtue according to your argument, the power of securing good things.

I think, Socrates, that the case is altogether as you now understand it.

Let us see then whether what you say is true, for you may well be right. You say that the capacity to acquire good things is virtue?—I do.

And by good things you mean, for example, health and wealth?

Yes, and also to acquire gold and silver, also honours and offices in the city.

By good things you do not mean other goods than these?

No, but I mean all things of this kind.

d Very well. According to Meno, the hereditary guest friend of the Great King, virtue is the acquisition of gold and silver. Do you add to this acquiring, Meno, the words justly and piously, or does it make no difference to you but even if one secures these things unjustly, you call it virtue none the less?—Certainly not, Socrates.

You would then call it wickedness?—Indeed I would.

It seems then that the acquisition must be accompanied by justice or e moderation or piety or some other part of virtue; if it is not, it will not be virtue, even though it provides good things.

How could there be virtue without these?

Then failing to secure gold and silver, whenever it would not be just to do so, either for oneself or another, is not this failure to secure them also virtue?—So it seems.

Then to provide these goods would not be virtue any more than not to 79 provide them, but whatever is done with justice will be virtue, and what is done without anything of the kind is wickedness?

I think it must necessarily be as you say.

We said a little while ago that each of these things was a part of virtue, namely justice and moderation and all such things?—Yes.

Then you are playing with me, Meno.—How so, Socrates?

Because I begged you just now not to break up or fragment virtue, and I gave examples of how you should answer. You paid no attention, but you b tell me that virtue is to be able to secure good things with justice, and this, you say, is a part of virtue.—I do.

It follows then from what you agree to, that to act in whatever you do with a part of virtue is virtue, for you say that justice is a part of virtue, as are all such qualities. Why do I say this? Because when I begged you to tell me about virtue as a whole, you are far from telling me what it is. Rather, you say that every action is virtue if it is performed with

a part of virtue, as if you had told me what virtue as a whole is, and I   *c*
would already know that, even if you fragment it into parts. I think you
must have the same question from the beginning, my dear Meno, namely,
what is virtue, if every action performed with justice is virtue? Do you
not think you should have the same question again, or do you think one
knows what a part of virtue is if one does not know virtue itself?—I do not
think so.

If you remember, when I was answering you about shape, we rejected   *d*
the kind of answer that tried to answer in terms still being the subject of
inquiry and not yet agreed upon.—And we were right to reject them.

Then surely, my good sir, you must not think, while the nature of virtue
as a whole is still under inquiry, that by answering in terms of the parts of
virtue you can make its nature clear to anyone or make anything else clear
by speaking in this way, but only that the same question must be put to you
again—what do you take the nature of virtue to be when you say what you   *e*
say? Or do you think there is no point in what I am saying?—I think what
you say is right.

Answer me again then from the beginning: What do you and your friend
say that virtue is?

Socrates, before I even met you I used to hear that you are always in a
state of perplexity and that you bring others to the same state, and now I   *80*
think you are bewitching and beguiling me, simply putting me under a
spell, so that I am quite perplexed. Indeed, if a joke is in order, you seem,
in appearance and in every other way, to be like the broad torpedo fish, for
it too makes anyone who comes close and touches it feel numb, and you
seem to have had that kind of effect on me, for both my mind and my   *b*
tongue are numb, and I have no answer to give you. Yet I have made many
speeches about virtue before large audiences on a thousand occasions, very
good speeches as I thought, but now I cannot even say what it is. I think
you are wise not to sail away from Athens to go and stay elsewhere, for if
you were to behave like this as a stranger in another city, you would be
driven away for practising sorcery.

You are a rascal, Meno, and you nearly deceived me.

Why so particularly, Socrates?

I know why you drew this image of me.   *c*

Why do you think I did?

So that I should draw an image of you in return. I know that all handsome men rejoice in images of themselves; it is to their advantage, for I
think that the images of beautiful people are also beautiful, but I will draw
no image of you in turn. Now if the torpedo fish is itself numb and so
makes others numb, then I resemble it, but not otherwise, for I myself do
not have the answer when I perplex others, but I am more perplexed than
anyone when I cause perplexity in others. So now I do not know what virtue

d   is; perhaps you knew before you contacted me, but now you are certainly
like one who does not know. Nevertheless, I want to examine and seek
together with you what it may be.

How will you look for it, Socrates, when you do not know at all what it
is? How will you aim to search for something you do not know at all? If
you should meet with it, how will you know that this is the thing that you
did not know?

e   I know what you want to say, Meno. Do you realize what a debater's
argument you are bringing up, that a man cannot search either for what he
knows or for what he does not know? He cannot search for what he
knows—since he knows it, there is no need to search—nor for what he does
not know, for he does not know what to look for.

Does that argument not seem sound to you, Socrates?

81   Not to me.

Can you tell my why?

I can. I have heard wise men and women talk about divine matters . . .

What did they say?

What was, I thought, both true and beautiful.

What was it, and who were they?

The speakers were among the priests and priestesses whose care it is to
b   be able to give an account of their practices. Pindar too says it, and many
others of the divine among our poets. What they say is this; see whether
you think they speak the truth: They say that the human soul is immortal;
at times it comes to an end, which they call dying, at times it is reborn, but
it is never destroyed, and one must therefore live one's life as piously as
possible:

Persephone will return to the sun above in the ninth year the souls of
those from whom she will exact punishment for old miseries, and from
c   these come noble kings, mighty in strength and greatest in wisdom,
and for the rest of time men will call them sacred heroes.

As the soul is immortal, has been born often and has seen all things here
and in the underworld, there is nothing which it has not learned; so it is in
no way surprising that it can recollect the things it knew before, both about
d   virtue and other things. As the whole of nature is akin, and the soul has
learned everything, nothing prevents a man, after recalling one thing
only—a process men call learning—discovering everything else for himself,
if he is brave and does not tire of the search, for searching and learning
are, as a whole, recollection. We must, therefore, not believe that debater's
argument, for it would make us idle, and fainthearted men like to hear it,
e   whereas my argument makes them energetic and keen on the search. I trust
that this is true, and I want to inquire along with you into the nature of
virtue.

Yes, Socrates, but how do you mean that we do not learn, but that what we call learning is recollection? Can you teach me that this is so?

As I said just now, Meno, you are a rascal. You now ask me if I can teach you, when I say there is no teaching but recollection, in order to show me up at once as contradicting myself.   82

No, by Zeus, Socrates, that was not my intention when I spoke, but just a habit. If you can somehow show me that things are as you say, please do so.

It is not easy, but I am nevertheless willing to do my best for your sake. Call one of these many attendants of yours, whichever you like, that I may prove it to you in his case.   b

Certainly. You there, come forward.

Is he a Greek? Does he speak Greek?

Very much so. He was born in my household.

Pay attention then whether you think he is recollecting or learning from me. —I will pay attention.

Tell me now, boy, you know that a square figure is like this?— I do.

A square then is a figure in which all these four sides are equal?   c —Yes indeed.

And it also has these lines through the middle equal?—Yes.

And such a figure could be larger or smaller?—Certainly.

If then this side were two feet, and this other side two feet, how many feet would the whole be? Consider it this way: if it were two feet this way, and only one foot that way, the figure would be once two feet? —Yes.

But if it is two feet also that way, it would surely be twice two feet?   d —Yes.

How many feet is twice two feet? Work it out and tell me.—Four, Socrates.

Now we could have another figure twice the size of this one, with the four sides equal like this one.—Yes.

How many feet will that be?—Eight.

Come now, try to tell me how long each side of this will be. The side of this is two feet. What about each side of the one which is its double?   e —Obviously, Socrates, it will be twice the length.

You see, Meno, that I am not teaching the boy anything, but all I do is question him. And now he thinks he knows the length of the line on which an eight-foot figure is based. Do you agree?—I do.

And does he know?—Certainly not.

He thinks it is a line twice the length?—Yes.

Watch him now recollecting things in order, as one must recollect. Tell me, boy, do you say that a figure double the size is based on a line double the length? Now I mean such a figure as this, not long on one side and   83 short on the other, but equal in every direction like this one, and double the size, that is, eight feet. See whether you still believe that it will be based on a line double the length. —I do.

Now the line becomes double its length if we add another of the same length here? —Yes indeed.

And the eight-foot square will be based on it, if there are four lines of that length? —Yes.

b   Well, let us draw from it four equal lines, and surely that is what you say is the eight-foot square? —Certainly.

And within this figure are four squares, each of which is equal to the four-foot square? —Yes.

How big is it then? Is it not four times as big? —Of course.

Is this square then, which is four times as big, its double? —No, by Zeus.

How many times bigger is it? —Four times.

c   Then, my boy, the figure based on a line twice the length is not double but four times as big? —You are right.

And four times four is sixteen, is it not? —Yes.

On how long a line then should the eight-foot square be based? On *this* line we have a square that is four times bigger, do we not? Now this four-foot square is based on this line here, half the length? —Yes.

Very well. Is the eight-foot square not double this one and half that one? —Yes.

Will it not be based on a line longer than this one and shorter than that
d   one? Is that not so? —I think so.

Good, you answer what you think. And tell me, was this one not two feet long, and that one four feet? —Yes.

The line on which the eight-foot square is based must then be longer than this one of two feet, and shorter than that one of four feet? —It must be.

e   Try to tell me then how long a line you say it is. —Three feet.

Then if it is three feet, let us add the half of this one, and it will be three feet? For these are two feet, and the other is one. And here, similarly, these are two feet and that one is one foot, and so the figure you mention comes to be? —Yes.

Now if it is three feet this way and three feet that way, will the whole figure be three times three feet? —So it seems.

How much is three times three feet? —Nine feet.

And the double square was to be how many feet? —Eight.

So the eight-foot figure cannot be based on the three-foot line? —Clearly not.

84   But on how long a line? Try to tell us exactly, and if you do not want to work it out, show me from what line. —By Zeus, Socrates, I do not know.

You realize, Meno, what point he has reached in his recollection. At first he did not know what the basic line of the eight-foot square was; even now he does not yet know, but then he thought he knew, and answered confidently as if he did know, and he did not think himself at a loss, but now he does think himself at a loss, and as he does not know, neither does he *b* think he knows.—That is true.

So he is now in a better position with regard to the matter he does not know.—I agree with that too.

Have we done him any harm by making him perplexed and numb as the torpedo fish does?—I do not think so.

Indeed, we have probably achieved something relevant to finding out how matters stand, for now, as he does not know, he would be glad to find out, whereas before he thought he could easily make many fine speeches to large audiences about the square of double size and said that it must have a *c* base twice as long.—So it seems.

Do you think that before he would have tried to find out that which he thought he knew though he did not, before he fell into perplexity and realized he did not know and longed to know?—I do not think so, Socrates.

Has he then benefitted from being numbed?—I think so.

Look then how he will come out of his perplexity while searching along with me. I shall do nothing more than ask questions and not teach him. Watch whether you find me teaching and explaining things to him instead *d* of asking for his opinion.

You tell me, is this not a four-foot figure? You understand?—I do.

We add to it this figure which is equal to it?—Yes.

And we add this third figure equal to each of them?—Yes.

Could we then fill in the space in the corner?—Certainly.

So we have these four equal figures?—Yes.

Well then, how many times is the whole figure larger than this one? *e* —Four times.

But we should have had one that was twice as large, or do you not remember?—I certainly do.

Does not this line from one corner to the other cut each of these figures 85 in two?—Yes.

So these are four equal lines which enclose this figure?—They are.

Consider now: how large is the figure?—I do not understand.

Within these four figures, each of these lines cuts off half of each, does it not?—Yes.

How many of this size are there in this figure?—Four.

How many in this?—Two.

What is the relation of four to two?—Double. *b*

How many feet in this?—Eight.

Based on what line?—This one.

That is, on the line that stretches from corner to corner of the four-foot figure?—Yes.

Clever men call this the diagonal, so that if diagonal is its name, you say

that the double figure would be that based on the diagonal?—Most certainly, Socrates.

What do you think, Meno? Has he, in his answers, expressed any opin-
c   ion that was not his own?

No, they were all his own.

And yet, as we said a short time ago, he did not know?—That is true.

So these opinions were in him, were they not?—Yes.

So the man who does not know has within himself true opinions about
the things that he does not know?—So it appears.

These opinions have now just been stirred up like a dream, but if he
were repeatedly asked these same questions in various ways, you know that
d   in the end his knowledge about these things would be as accurate as
anyone's.—It is likely.

And he will know it without having been taught but only questioned,
and find the knowledge within himself?—Yes.

And is not finding knowledge within oneself recollection?—Certainly.

Must he not either have at some time acquired the knowledge he now
possesses, or else have always possessed it?—Yes.

If he always had it, he would always have known. If he acquired it, he
e   cannot have done so in his present life. Or has someone taught him geometry? For he will perform in the same way about all geometry, and all other
knowledge. Has someone taught him everything? You should know, especially as he has been born and brought up in your house.

But I know that no one has taught him.

Yet he has these opinions, or doesn't he?

That seems indisputable, Socrates.

86   If he has not acquired them in his present life, is it not clear that he had
them and had learned them at some other time?—It seems so.

Then that was the time when he was not a human being?—Yes.

If then, during the time he exists and is not a human being he will have
true opinions which, when stirred by questioning, become knowledge, will
not his soul have learned during all time? For it is clear that during all time
he exists, either as a man or not.—So it seems.

b   Then if the truth about reality is always in our soul, the soul would be
immortal so that you should always confidently try to seek out and recollect what you do not know at present—that is, what you do not recollect?

Somehow, Socrates, I think that what you say is right.

I think so too, Meno. I do not insist that my argument is right in all other
respects, but I would contend at all costs both in word and deed as far as I
could that we will be better men, braver and less idle, if we believe that one
c   must search for the things one does not know, rather than if we believe that
it is not possible to find out what we do not know and that we must not
look for it.

In this too I think you are right, Socrates.

Since we are of one mind that one should seek to find out what one does not know, shall we try to find out together what virtue is?

Certainly. But Socrates, I should be most pleased to investigate and hear your answer to my original question, whether we should attack virtue as something teachable, or as a natural gift, or in whatever way it comes   *d* to men.

If I were directing you, Meno, and not only myself, we would not have investigated whether virtue is teachable or not before we had investigated what virtue itself is. But because you do not even attempt to rule yourself, in order that you may be free, but you try to rule me and do so, I will agree with you—for what can I do? So we must, it appears, inquire into the qualities of something the nature of which we do not yet know.   *e* However, please relax your rule a little bit for me and agree to investigate whether it is teachable or not by means of a hypothesis. I mean the way geometers often carry on their investigations. For example, if they are asked whether a specific area can be inscribed in the form of a triangle within a given circle, one of them might say: "I do not yet know whether   *87* that area has that property, but I think I have, as it were, a hypothesis that is of use for the problem, namely this: If that area is such that when one has applied it as a rectangle to the given straight line in the circle it is deficient by a figure similar to the very figure which is applied, then I think one alternative results, whereas another results if it is impossible for   *b* this to happen. So, by using this hypothesis, I am willing to tell you what results with regard to inscribing it in the circle—that is, whether it is impossible or not." So we can say about virtue also, since we do not know either what it is or what qualities it possesses, let us investigate whether it is teachable by means of a hypothesis, and say this: If among the things existing in the soul virtue has a certain quality, would it be teachable or not? Or, as we were saying just now, can it be recollected? First then, if it is other than knowledge—for let it make no difference to us whichever term   *c* we use—but can it be taught? Or is it plain to anyone that men cannot be taught anything but knowledge?

I think so.

But, if virtue is a kind of knowledge, it can clearly be taught?—Of course.

We have dealt with that question quickly, that if it is of one kind it can be taught, if it is of a different kind, it cannot.—We have indeed.

The next point to consider seems to be whether virtue is knowledge or something else.—That does seem to be the next point to consider.   *d*

Well now, do we say that virtue is itself something good, and will this hypothesis stand firm for us, that it is something good?—Of course.

If then there is anything else good that is different and separate from knowledge, virtue might well not be a kind of knowledge, but if there is

nothing good that knowledge does not encompass, we would be right to
suspect that it is a kind of knowledge?—That is so.

e   Surely virtue makes us good?—Yes.

And if we are good, we are beneficent, for all that is good is beneficial. Is
that not so?—Yes.

So virtue is something beneficial?

That necessarily follows from what has been agreed.

Let us then examine what kinds of things benefit us, taking them up one
by one: health, we say, and strength, and beauty, and also wealth. We say
that these things, and others of the same kind, benefit us, do we not?
—We do.

Yet we say that these same things also sometimes harm one. Do you
88   agree or not?—I do.

Look then, what directing factor determines in each case whether these
things benefit or harm us? Is it not the right use of them that benefits us,
and the wrong use that harms us?—Certainly.

Let us now look at the good of the soul. There is something you call
moderation, and justice, courage, intelligence, memory, munificence, and
all such things?—There is.

b   Consider whichever of these you believe not to be knowledge but different from it; do they not at times harm us, at other times benefit us?
Courage, for example, when it is not wisdom but like a kind of reckless-
ness: when a man is reckless without understanding, he is harmed, when
with understanding, he is benefitted.—Yes.

The same is true of moderation and mental quickness; when they are
learned and disciplined with understanding they are beneficial, but without
understanding they are harmful?—Very much so.

c   Therefore, in a word, all that the soul undertakes and endures, if directed by wisdom, ends in happiness, but if directed by ignorance, it ends
in the opposite.—That is likely.

If then virtue is something in the soul and it must be beneficial, it must
be knowledge, since all the qualities of the soul are in themselves neither
d   beneficial nor harmful, but accompanied by wisdom or folly they become
harmful or beneficial. This argument shows that virtue, being beneficial,
must be a kind of wisdom.—I agree.

Furthermore, those other things we were mentioning just now,
wealth and the like, are at times good and at times harmful. Just as for the
rest of the soul the direction of wisdom makes things beneficial, but harm-
e   ful if directed by folly, so in these cases, if the soul uses and directs them
right it makes them beneficial, but bad use makes them harmful?
—Quite so.

The wise soul directs them right, the foolish soul wrongly?—That is so.

So one may say that about everything: all other human activities depend

on the soul, and those of the soul itself depend on wisdom if they are to be
good. According to this argument the beneficial would be wisdom, and we   *89*
say that virtue is beneficial?—Certainly.

Wisdom then, as a whole or in part, is virtue?

What you say, Socrates, seems to me quite right.

Then, if that is so, the good are not so by nature?—I do not think
they are.

For if they were, this would follow: if the good were so by nature, we   *b*
would have people who knew which among the young were by nature
good; we would take those whom they had pointed out and guard them in
the Acropolis, sealing them up there much more carefully than gold so that
no one could corrupt them, and when they reached maturity they would be
useful to their cities.—Reasonable enough, Socrates.

Since the good are not good by nature, does learning make them so?   *c*

Necessarily, as I now think, Socrates, and clearly, on our hypothesis, if
knowledge is virtue, it can be taught.

Perhaps, by Zeus, but may it be that we were not right to agree to this?

Yet it seemed to be right at the time.

We should not only think it right at the time, but also now and in the
future if it is to be at all sound?

What is the difficulty? What do you have in mind that you do not like   *d*
about it and doubt that virtue is knowledge?

I will tell you, Meno. I am not saying that it is wrong to say that virtue is
teachable if it is knowledge, but look whether it is reasonable of me, to
doubt whether it is knowledge. Tell me this: if not only virtue but anything
whatever can be taught, should there not be of necessity people who teach
it and people who learn it?—I think so.

Then again, if on the contrary there are no teachers or learners of   *e*
something, we should be right to assume that the subject cannot be taught?

Quite so, but do you think that there are no teachers of virtue?

I have often tried to find out whether there were any teachers of it, but in
spite of all my efforts I cannot find any. I have searched for them with the
help of many people, especially those whom I believed to be most experienced in this matter. And now, Meno, Anytus[3] here has opportunely come
to sit down by us. Let us share our search with him. It would be reasonable
for us to do so, for Anytus, in the first place, is the son of Anthemion, a
man of wealth and wisdom, who did not become rich automatically or as   *90*
the result of a gift like Ismenias the Theban, who recently acquired the
possessions of Polycrates, but through his own wisdom and efforts. Further, he was not an arrogant or puffed up or offensive citizen in other ways,
but he was a well-mannered and well-behaved man. Also he gave our

---

3. A democratic leader and one of the instigators of the charges against Socrates.

b friend here a good upbringing and education, as the majority of Athenians believe, for they elected him to the highest offices. It is right then to look for the teachers of virtue with the help of men such as he, whether there are any and if so who they are. Do you therefore, Anytus, join me and your guest friend Meno here, in our inquiry as to who are the teachers of virtue? Look at it in this way: if we wanted Meno to become a good physician,

c to what teachers would we send him? Would we not send him to the physicians?

Certainly.

And if we wanted him to be a good shoemaker, to shoemakers?—Yes.

And so with other pursuits?—Certainly.

Tell me again on this same topic, like this: we say that we would be right to send him to the physicians if we want him to become a physician;

d whenever we say that, we mean that it would be reasonable to send him to those who practise the craft rather than to those who do not, and to those who exact fees for this very practice and have shown themselves to be teachers of anyone who wishes to come to them and learn. It is not with this in mind that we would be right to send him?

Yes.

And the same is true about flute-playing and the other crafts? It would

e be very foolish for those who want to make someone a flute-player to refuse to send him to those who profess to teach the craft and make money at it, but to send him to make trouble for others by seeking to learn from those who do not claim to be teachers or have a single pupil in that subject which we want the one we send to learn from them? Do you not think it very unreasonable to do so?

By Zeus I do, and also very ignorant.

Quite right. However, you can now deliberate with me about our guest

91 friend Meno here. He has been telling me for some time, Anytus, that he longs to acquire that wisdom and virtue which enables men to manage their households and their cities well, to take care of their parents, to know how to welcome and to send away both citizens and strangers as a good

b man should. Consider to whom we should be right to send him to learn this virtue. Or is it obvious in view of what was said just now that we should send him to those who profess to be teachers of virtue and have shown themselves to be available to any Greek who wishes to learn, and for this fix a fee and exact it?

And who do you say these are, Socrates?

You surely know yourself that they are those whom men call sophists.

c By Heracles, hush, Socrates. May no one of my household or friends, whether citizen or stranger, be mad enough to go to these people and be harmed by them, for they clearly cause the ruin and corruption of their followers.

How do you mean, Anytus? Are these people, alone of those who claim the knowledge to benefit one, so different from the others that they not only do not benefit what one entrusts to them but on the contrary corrupt it, even though they obviously expect to make money from *d* the process? I find I cannot believe you, for I know that one man, Protagoras, made more money from this knowledge of his than Phidias who made such notably fine works, and ten other sculptors. Surely what you say is extraordinary, if those who mend old sandals and restore clothes would be found out within the month if they returned the clothes and *e* sandals in a worse state than they received them; if they did this they would soon die of starvation, but the whole of Greece has not noticed for forty years that Protagoras corrupts those who frequent him and sends them away in a worse moral condition than he received them. I believe that he was nearly seventy when he died and had practised his craft for forty years. During all that time to this very day his reputation has stood high; and not only Protagoras but a great many others, some born before him and some still alive today. Are we to say that you maintain that they *92* deceive and harm the young knowingly, or that they themselves are not aware of it? Are we to deem those whom some people consider the wisest of men to be so mad as that?

They are far from being mad, Socrates. It is much rather those among the young who pay their fees who are mad, and even more the relatives who entrust their young to them and most of all the cities who allow them to *b* come in and do not drive out any citizen or stranger who attempts to behave in this manner.

Has some sophist wronged you, Anytus, or why are you so hard on them?

No, by Zeus, I have never met one of them, nor would I allow any one of my people to do so.

Are you then altogether without any experience of these men?

And may I remain so.

How then, my good sir, can you know whether there is any good in their *c* instruction or not, if you are altogether without experience of it?

Easily, for I know who they are, whether I have experience of them or not.

Perhaps you are a wizard, Anytus, for I wonder, from what you yourself say, how else you know about these things. However, let us not try to find out who the men are whose company would make Meno wicked—let them *d* be the sophists if you like—but tell us, and benefit your family friend here by telling him, to whom he should go in so large a city to acquire, to any worthwhile degree, the virtue I was just now describing.

Why did you not tell him yourself?

I did mention those whom I thought to be teachers of it, but you say I am *e*   wrong, and perhaps you are right. You tell him in your turn to whom among the Athenians he should go. Tell him the name of anyone you want.

Why give him the name of one individual? Any Athenian gentleman he may meet, if he is willing to be persuaded, will make him a better man than the sophists would.

And have these gentlemen become virtuous automatically, without learn-

93   ing from anyone, and are they able to teach others what they themselves never learned?

I believe that these men have learned from those who were gentlemen before them; or do you not think that there are many good men in this city?

I believe, Anytus, that there are many men here who are good at public affairs, and that there have been as many in the past, but have they been good teachers of their own virtue? That is the point we are discussing, not whether there are good men here or not, or whether there have been in the

b   past, but we have been investigating for some time whether virtue can be taught. And in the course of that investigation we are inquiring whether the good men of today and of the past knew how to pass on to another the virtue they themselves possessed, or whether a man cannot pass it on or receive it from another. This is what Meno and I have been investigating for some time. Look at it this way, from what you yourself have said. Would

c   you not say that Themistocles was a good man?

Yes. Even the best of men.

And therefore a good teacher of his own virtue if anyone was?

I think so, if he wanted to be.

But do you think he did not want some other people to be worthy men, and especially his own son? Or do you think he begrudged him this, and

d   deliberately did not pass on to him his own virtue? Have you not heard that Themistocles taught his son Cleophantus to be a good horseman? He could remain standing upright on horseback and shoot javelins from that position and do many other remarkable things which his father had him taught and made skillful at, all of which required good teachers. Have you not heard this from your elders?

I have.

So one could not blame the poor natural talents of the son for his failure in virtue?

e   Perhaps not.

But have you ever heard anyone, young or old, say that Cleophantus, the son of Themistocles, was a good and wise man at the same pursuits as his father?

Never.

Are we to believe that he wanted to educate his son in those other things but not to do better than his neighbors in that skill which he himself possessed, if indeed virtue can be taught?

Perhaps not, by Zeus.

And yet he was, as you yourself agree, among the best teachers of virtue in the past. Let us consider another man, Aristides, the son of Lysimachus. Do you not agree that he was good?

I very definitely do.

He too gave his own son Lysimachus the best Athenian education in matters which are the business of teachers, and do you think he made him a better man than anyone else? For you have been in his company and seen the kind of man he is. Or take Pericles, a man of such magnificent wisdom. You know that he brought up two sons, Paralus and Xanthippus?

I know.

You also know that he taught them to be as good horsemen as any Athenian, that he educated them in the arts, in gymnastics, and in all else that was a matter of skill not to be inferior to anyone, but did he not want to make them good men? I think he did, but this could not be taught. And lest you think that only a few most inferior Athenians are incapable in this respect, reflect that Thucydides[4] too brought up two sons, Melesias and Stephanus, that he educated them well in all other things. They were the best wrestlers in Athens—he entrusted the one to Xanthias and the other to Eudoxus, who were thought to be the best wrestlers of the day, or do you not remember?

I remember I have heard that said.

It is surely clear that he would not teach his boys what it costs money to teach, whereas it costs no money to make them good men, but he did not teach them this, if it could be taught. Or was Thucydides perhaps an inferior person who had not many friends among the Athenians and the allies? He belonged to a great house; he had great influence in the city and among the other Greeks, so that if virtue could be taught he would have found the man who could make his sons good men, be it a citizen or a stranger, if he himself did not have the time because of his public concerns. But, friend Anytus, virtue can certainly not be taught.

I think, Socrates, that you easily speak ill of people. I would advise you if you will listen to me to be careful. Perhaps also in another city, and certainly here, it is easier to injure people than to benefit them. I think you know that yourself.

I think, Meno, that Anytus is angry, and I am not at all surprised. He thinks, to begin with, that I am slandering those men, and then he believes himself to be one of them. If he ever realizes what slander is, he will cease from anger, but he does not know it now. You tell me, are there not worthy men among your people?—Certainly.

94

b

c

d

e

95

---

4. An Athenian statesman who was an opponent of Pericles and who was ostracized in 440 B.C.

b   Well now, are they willing to offer themselves to the young as teachers? Do they agree they are teachers, and that virtue can be taught?

No, by Zeus, Socrates, but sometimes you would hear them say that it can be taught, at other times, that it cannot.

Should we say that they are teachers of this subject, when they do not even agree on this point?—I do not think so, Socrates.

Further, do you think that these sophists, who alone profess to be so, are teachers of virtue?

c   I admire this most in Gorgias, Socrates, that you would never hear him promising this. Indeed, he ridicules the others when he hears them making this claim. He thinks one should make people clever speakers.

You do not think then that the sophists are teachers?

I cannot tell, Socrates; like most people, at times I think they are, at other times I think that they are not.

Do you know that not only you and the other public men at times think

d   that it can be taught, at other times that it cannot, but that the poet Theognis[5] says the same thing?—Where?

In his elegiacs: "Eat and drink with these men, and keep their company. Please those whose power is great, for you will learn goodness from the

e   good. If you mingle with bad men you will lose even what wit you possess." You see that here he speaks as if virtue can be taught?—So it appears.

Elsewhere, he changes somewhat: "If this could be done," he says, "and intelligence could be instilled," somehow those who could do this "would collect large and numerous fees," and further: "Never would a bad son be born of a good father, for he would be persuaded by wise words, but you

96   will never make a bad man good by teaching." You realize that the poet is contradicting himself on the same subject?—He seems to be.

Can you mention any other subject of which those who claim to be teachers are not, such as the teachers of other subjects, recognized as such, but not to have knowledge of it themselves, and are thought to be poor in

b   the very matter which they profess to teach, or any other subject of which those who are recognized as worthy men at one time say it can be taught and at other times that it cannot? Would you say that people who are so confused about a subject can be effective teachers of it?—No, by Zeus, I would not.

If then neither the sophists nor the worthy people themselves are teachers of this subject, clearly there would be no others?—I do not think there are.

c   If there are no teachers, neither are there pupils?—As you say.

And we agreed that a subject that has neither teachers nor pupils is not teachable?—We have so agreed.

---

5. Theognis was a poet of mid-sixth century B.C.

Now there seem to be no teachers of virtue anywhere?—That is so.

If there are no teachers, there are no learners?—That seems so.

Then virtue cannot be taught?

Apparently not, if we have investigated this correctly. I certainly wonder, *d*
Socrates, whether there are no good men either, or in what way good men
come to be.

We are probably poor specimens, you and I, Meno. Gorgias has not
adequately educated you, nor Prodicus me. We must then at all costs turn
our attention to ourselves and find someone who will in some way make us
better. I say this in view of our recent investigation, for it is ridiculous that *e*
we failed to see that it is not only under the guidance of knowledge that
men succeed in their affairs, and that is perhaps why the knowledge of how
good men come to be escapes us.

How do you mean, Socrates?

I mean this: we were right to agree that good men must be beneficent,
and that this could not be otherwise. Is that not so?—Yes.

And that they will be beneficent and useful if they give us correct guidance in our affairs. To this too we were right to agree? *97*
—Yes.

But that one cannot guide correctly if one does not have knowledge, to
this our agreement is likely to be incorrect.—How do you mean?

I will tell you. A man who knew the way to Larissa, or anywhere else
you like, and went there and guided others would surely lead them well
and correctly?—Certainly.

What if someone had had a correct opinion as to which was the way but *b*
had not gone there nor indeed had knowledge of it, would he not also lead
correctly?—Certainly.

And as long as he has the right opinion about that of which the other
has knowledge, he will not be a worse guide than the one who knows, as he
has a true opinion, though not knowledge?—In no way worse.

So true opinion is in no way a worse guide to correct action than knowledge? It is this that we omitted in our investigation of the nature of virtue,
when we said that only knowledge can lead to correct action, for true *c*
opinion can do so also?—So it seems.

So correct opinion is no less useful than knowledge?

Yes, to this extent, Socrates. But the man who has knowledge will always
succeed, whereas he who has true opinion will only succeed at times.

How do you mean? Will he who has the right opinion not always succeed, as long as his opinion is right?

That appears to be so of necessity, and it makes me wonder, Socrates,
this being the case, why knowledge is prized far more highly than right *d*
opinion, and why they are different.

Do you know why you wonder, or shall I tell you?—By all means tell me.

It is because you have paid no attention to the statues of Daedalus, but perhaps there are none in Thessaly.

What do you have in mind when you say this?

That they too run away and escape if one does not tie them down but
e   remain in place if tied down.—So what?

To acquire an untied work of Daedalus is not worth much, like acquiring a runaway slave, for it does not remain, but it is worth much if tied down, for his works are very beautiful. What am I thinking of when I say this? True beliefs. For true beliefs, as long as they remain, are a fine thing and all
98 they do is good, but they are not willing to remain long, and they escape from a man's mind, so that they are not worth much until one ties them down by (giving) an account of the reason why. And that, Meno my friend, is recollection, as we previously agreed. After they are tied down, in the first place they become knowledge, and then they remain in place. That is why knowledge is prized higher than correct opinion, and knowledge differs from correct opinion in being tied down.

Yes, by Zeus, Socrates, it seems to be something like that.

b   Indeed, I too speak as one who does not have knowledge but is guessing. However, I certainly do not think I am guessing that right opinion is a different thing than knowledge. If I claim to know anything else—and I would make that claim about few things—I would put this down as one of the things I know.—Rightly so, Socrates.

Well then, is it not correct that when true opinion guides the course of every action, it does no worse than knowledge?—I think you are right in this too.

c   Correct opinion is then neither inferior to knowledge nor less useful in directing actions, nor is the man who has it less so than he who has knowledge.—That is so.

And we agreed that the good man is useful?—Yes.

Since then it is not only through knowledge but also through right opinion that men are good, and beneficial to their cities when they are, and
d   neither knowledge nor true opinion come to men by nature but are acquired—or do you think either of these comes by nature?—I do not think so.

Then if they do not come by nature, men are not so by nature either.—Surely not.

As goodness does not come by nature, we inquired next whether it could be taught?—Yes.

We thought it could be taught, if it was knowledge?—Yes.

And that it was knowledge if it could be taught?—Quite so.

e   And that if there were teachers of it, it could be taught, but if there were not, it was not teachable?—That is so.

And then we agreed that there were no teachers of it?—We did.

So we agreed that it was neither teachable nor knowledge?—Quite so.

But we certainly agree that virtue is a good thing?—Yes.

And that which guides correctly is both useful and good?—Certainly.

And that only these two things, true belief and knowledge, guide cor-   99
rectly, and that if a man possesses these he gives correct guidance? The
things that turn out right by some chance are not due to human guidance,
but where there is correct human guidance it is due to two things, true
belief or knowledge?—I think that is so.

Now because it cannot be taught, virtue no longer seems to be
knowledge?—It seems not.

So one of the two good and useful things has been excluded, and knowl-   b
edge is not the guide in public affairs?—I do not think so.

So it is not by some kind of wisdom, or by being wise, that such men
lead their cities, those such as Themistocles and those mentioned by
Anytus just now? That is the reason why they cannot make others be like
themselves, because it is not knowledge which makes them what they are?

It is likely to be as you say, Socrates.

Therefore, if it is not through knowledge, the only alternative is that it is
through right opinion that statesmen follow the right course for their cities.   c
As regards knowledge, they are no different from soothsayers and
prophets. They too say many true things when inspired, but they have no
knowledge of what they are saying.—That is probably so.

And so, Meno, is it right to call divine these men who, without any
understanding, are right in much that is of importance in what they say
and do?—Certainly.

We should be right to call divine also those soothsayers and prophets
whom we just mentioned, and all the poets, and we should call no less   d
divine and inspired those public men who are no less under the gods'
influence and possession, as their speeches lead to success in many important matters, though they have no knowledge of what they are saying?—
Quite so.

Women too, Meno, call good men divine, and the Spartans, when they
eulogize someone, say, "This man is divine."

And they appear to be right, Socrates, though perhaps Anytus here will   e
be annoyed with you for saying so.

I do not mind that; we shall talk to him again, but if we were right in the
way in which we spoke and investigated in this whole discussion, virtue
would be neither an inborn quality nor taught, but come to those who
possess it as a gift from the gods which is not accompanied by understanding, unless there is someone among our statesmen who can make another   100
into a statesman. If there were one, he could be said to be among the living
as Homer said Teiresias was among the dead, namely, that he alone retained his wits while the others flitted about like shadows. In the same

manner such a man would, as far as virtue is concerned, here also be the only true reality compared, as it were, with shadows.

b   I think that is an excellent way to put it, Socrates.

It follows from this reasoning, Meno, that virtue appears to be present in those of us who may possess it as a gift from the gods. We shall have clear knowledge of this when, before we investigate how it comes to be present in men, we first try to find out what virtue in itself is. But now the time has come for me to go. You convince your guest friend Anytus here of these very things of which you have yourself been convinced, in order that he may be more amenable. If you succeed, you will also confer a benefit upon the Athenians.

PHAEDO

ECHECRATES: Were you with Socrates yourself, Phaedo, on the day when he drank the poison in prison, or did someone else tell you about it?

PHAEDO: I was there myself, Echecrates.

ECHECRATES: What are the things he said before he died? And how did he die? I should be glad to hear this. Hardly anyone from Phlius visits Athens nowadays, nor has any stranger come from Athens for some time *b* who could give us a clear account of what happened, except that he drank the poison and died, but nothing more.

PHAEDO: Did you not even hear how the trial went? 58

ECHECRATES: Yes, someone did tell us about that, and we wondered that he seems to have died a long time after the trial took place. Why was that, Phaedo?

PHAEDO: That was by chance, Echecrates. The day before the trial, as it happened, the prow of the ship that the Athenians send to Delos had been crowned with garlands.

ECHECRATES: What ship is that?

PHAEDO: It is the ship in which, the Athenians say, Theseus once sailed to Crete, taking with him the two lots of seven victims.[1] He saved them and was himself saved. The Athenians vowed then to Apollo, so the story *b* goes, that if they were saved they would send a mission to Delos every year. And from that time to this they send such an annual mission to the god. They have a law to keep the city pure while it lasts, and no execution may take place once the mission has begun until the ship has made its journey to Delos and returned to Athens, and this can sometimes take a long time if the winds delay it. The mission begins when the priest of *c* Apollo crowns the prow of the ship, and this happened, as I say, the day before Socrates' trial. That is why Socrates was in prison a long time between his trial and his execution.

ECHECRATES: What about his actual death, Phaedo? What did he say? What did he do? Who of his friends were with him? Or did the authorities not allow them to be present and he died with no friends present?

Translated by G.M.A. Grube.

1. Legend says that Minos, king of Crete, compelled the Athenians to send seven youths and seven maidens every year to be sacrificed to the Minotaur until Theseus saved them and killed the monster.

d   PHAEDO: By no means. Some were present, in fact, a good many.

ECHECRATES: Please be good enough to tell us all that occurred as fully as possible, unless you have some pressing business.

PHAEDO: I have the time and I will try to tell you the whole story, for nothing gives me more pleasure than to call Socrates to mind, whether talking about him myself, or listening to someone else do so.

ECHECRATES: Your hearers will surely be like you in this, Phaedo. So do try to tell us every detail as exactly as you can.

PHAEDO: I certainly found being there an astonishing experience. Al-
e   though I was witnessing the death of one who was my friend, I had no feeling of pity, for the man appeared happy in both manner and words as he died nobly and without fear, Echecrates, so that it struck me that even in
59   going down to the underworld he was going with the gods' blessing and that he would fare well when he got there, if anyone ever does. That is why I had no feeling of pity, such as would seem natural in my sorrow, nor indeed of pleasure, as we engaged in philosophical discussion as we were accustomed to do—for our arguments were of that sort—but I had a strange feeling, an unaccustomed mixture of pleasure and pain at the same time as I reflected that he was just about to die. All of us present were affected in much the same way, sometimes laughing, then weeping; espe-cially one of us, Apollodorus—you know the man and his ways.

b   ECHECRATES: Of course I do.

PHAEDO: He was quite overcome; but I was myself disturbed, and so were the others.

ECHECRATES: Who, Phaedo, were those present?

PHAEDO: Among the local people there was Apollodorus, whom I men-tioned, Critobulus and his father,[2] also Hermogenes, Epigenes, Aeschines, and Antisthenes. Ctesippus of Paeania was there, Menexenus and some others. Plato, I believe, was ill.

ECHECRATES: Were there some foreigners present?

c   PHAEDO: Yes, Simmias from Thebes with Cebes and Phaedondes, and from Megara, Euclides and Terpsion.

ECHECRATES: What about Aristippus and Cleombrotus? Were they there?

PHAEDO: No. They were said to be in Aegina.

2. The father of Critobulus is Crito, after whom the dialogue *Crito* is named. Several of the other friends of Socrates mentioned here also appear in other dia-logues. Hermogenes is one of the speakers in *Cratylus*. Epigenes is mentioned in *Apology* 33e, as is Aeschines, who was a writer of Socratic dialogues. Menexenus has a part in *Lysis* and has a dialogue named after him; Ctesippus appears in both *Lysis* and *Euthydemus*. Euclides and Terpsion are speakers in the introductory conversation of *Theaetetus,* and Euclides too wrote Socratic dialogues. Simmias and Cebes are mentioned in *Crito* 45b as having come to Athens with enough money to secure Socrates' escape.

ECHECRATES: Was there anyone else?

PHAEDO: I think these were about all.

ECHECRATES: Well then, what do you say the conversation was about?

PHAEDO: I will try to tell you everything from the beginning. On the previous days also both the others and I used to visit Socrates. We forgathered at daybreak at the court where the trial took place, for it was close to the prison, and each day we used to wait around talking until the prison should open, for it did not open early. When it opened we used to go in to Socrates and spend most of the day with him. On this day we gathered rather early, because when we left the prison on the previous evening we were informed that the ship from Delos had arrived, and so we told each other to come to the usual place as early as possible. When we arrived the gatekeeper who used to answer our knock came out and told us to wait and not go in until he told us to. "The Eleven,"[3] he said, "are freeing Socrates from his bonds and telling him how his death will take place today." After a short time he came and told us to go in. We found Socrates recently released from his chains, and Xanthippe—you know her—sitting by him, holding their baby. When she saw us, she cried out and said the sort of thing that women usually say: "Socrates, this is the last time your friends will talk to you and you to them." Socrates looked at Crito. "Crito," he said, "let someone take her home." And some of Crito's people led her away lamenting and beating her breast.

Socrates sat up on the bed, bent his leg, and rubbed it with his hand, and as he rubbed he said: "What a strange thing that which men call pleasure seems to be, and how astonishing the relation it has with what is thought to be its opposite, namely pain! A man cannot have both at the same time. Yet if he pursues and catches the one, he is almost always bound to catch the other also, like two creatures with one head. I think that if Aesop had noted this he would have composed a fable that a god wished to reconcile their opposition but could not do so, so he joined their two heads together, and therefore when a man has the one, the other follows later. This seems to be happening to me. My bonds caused pain in my leg, and now pleasure seems to be following."

Cebes intervened and said: "By Zeus, yes, Socrates, you did well to remind me. Evenus[4] asked me the day before yesterday, as others had done before, what induced you to write poetry after you came to prison, you who had never composed any poetry before, putting the fables of Aesop into verse and composing the hymn to Apollo. If it is of any concern to you that I should have an answer to give to Evenus when he repeats his question, as I know he will, tell me what to say to him."

3. The Eleven were the police commissioners of Athens.

4. Socrates refers to Evenus as a Sophist and teacher of the young in *Apology* 20a, c.

Tell him the truth, Cebes, he said, that I did not do this with the idea of rivaling him or his poems, for I knew that would not be easy, but I tried to
e find out the meaning of certain dreams and to satisfy my conscience in case it was this kind of art they were frequently bidding me to practice. The dreams were something like this: the same dream often came to me in the past, now in one shape now in another, but saying the same thing: "Socrates," it said, "practice and cultivate the arts." In the past I imagined that it was instructing and advising me to do what I was doing, such as
61 those who encourage runners in a race, that the dream was thus bidding me do the very thing I was doing, namely, to practice the art of philosophy, this being the highest kind of art, and I was doing that.

But now, after my trial took place, and the festival of the god was preventing my execution, I thought that, in case my dream was bidding me to practice this popular art, I should not disobey it but compose poetry.
b I thought it safer not to leave here until I had satisfied my conscience by writing poems in obedience to the dream. So I first wrote in honor of the god of the present festival. After that I realized that a poet, if he is to be a poet, must compose fables, not arguments. Being no teller of fables myself, I took the stories I knew and had at hand, the fables of Aesop, and I versified the first ones I came across. Tell this to Evenus, Cebes, wish him well and bid him farewell, and tell him, if he is wise, to follow me as soon
c as possible. I am leaving today, it seems, as the Athenians so order it.

Said Simmias: "What kind of advice is this you are giving to Evenus, Socrates? I have met him many times, and from my observation he is not at all likely to follow it willingly."

How so, said he, is Evenus not a philosopher?

I think so, Simmias said.

Then Evenus will be willing, like every man who partakes worthily of philosophy. Yet perhaps he will not take his own life, for that, they say, is
d not right. As he said this, Socrates put his feet on the ground and remained in this position during the rest of the conversation.

Then Cebes asked: "How do you mean Socrates, that it is not right to do oneself violence, and yet that the philosopher will be willing to follow one who is dying?"

Come now, Cebes, have you and Simmias, who keep company with Philolaus,[5] not heard about such things?

Nothing definite, Socrates.

Indeed, I too speak about this from hearsay, but I do not mind telling you what I have heard, for it is perhaps most appropriate for one who is
e about to depart yonder to tell and examine tales about what we believe that journey to be like. What else could one do in the time we have until sunset?

5. See pp. 97–99.

But whatever is the reason, Socrates, for people to say that it is not right to kill oneself? As to your question just now, I have heard Philolaus say this when staying in Thebes, and I have also heard it from others, but I have never heard anyone give a clear account of the matter.

Well, he said, we must do our best, and you may yet hear one. And it **62** may well astonish you if this subject, alone of all things, is simple, and it is never, as with everything else, better at certain times and for certain people to die than to live. And if this is so, you may well find it astonishing that those for whom it is better to die are wrong to help themselves, and that they must wait for someone else to benefit them.

And Cebes, lapsing into his own dialect, laughed quietly and said: "Zeus knows it is."

Indeed, said Socrates, it does seem unreasonable when put like that, but **b** perhaps there is reason to it. There is the explanation that is put in the language of the mysteries, that we men are in a kind of prison, and that one must not free oneself or run away. That seems to me an impressive doctrine and one not easy to understand fully. However, Cebes, this seems to me well expressed, that the gods are our guardians and that men are one of their possessions. Or do you not think so?

I do, said Cebes.

And would you not be angry if one of your possessions killed itself when you had not given any sign that you wished it to die, and if you had **c** any punishment you could inflict, you would inflict it?

Certainly, he said.

Perhaps then, put in this way, it is not unreasonable that one should not kill oneself before a god had indicated some necessity to do so, like the necessity now put upon us.

That seems likely, said Cebes. As for what you were saying, that phi- **d** losophers should be willing and ready to die, that seems strange, Socrates, if what we said just now is reasonable, namely, that a god is our protector and that we are his possessions. It is not logical that the wisest of men should not resent leaving this service in which they are governed by the best of masters, the gods, for a wise man cannot believe that he will look after himself better when he is free. A foolish man might easily think so, that he must escape from his master; he would not reflect that one must **e** not escape from a good master but stay with him as long as possible, because it would be foolish to escape. But the sensible man would want always to remain with one better than himself. So, Socrates, the opposite of what was said before is likely to be true; the wise would resent dying, whereas the foolish would rejoice at it.

I thought that when Socrates heard this he was pleased by Cebes' argumentation. Glancing at us, he said: "Cebes is always on the track of **63** some arguments; he is certainly not willing to be at once convinced by what one says."

Said Simmias: "But actually, Socrates, I think myself that Cebes has a point now. Why should truly wise men want to avoid the service of masters better than themselves, and leave them easily? And I think Cebes is aiming his argument at you, because you are bearing leaving us so lightly, and leaving those good masters, as you say yourself, the gods."

b You are both justified in what you say, and I think you mean that I must make a defense against this, as if I were in court.

You certainly must, said Simmias.

Come then, he said, let me try to make my defense to you more convincing than it was to the jury. For, Simmias and Cebes, I should be wrong not to resent dying if I did not believe that I should go first to other wise and good gods, and then to men who have died and are better than men are

c here. Be assured that, as it is, I expect to join the company of good men. This last I would not altogether insist on, but if I insist on anything at all in these matters, it is that I shall come to gods who are very good masters. That is why I am not so resentful, because I have good hope that some future awaits men after death, as we have been told for years, a much better future for the good than for the wicked.

Well now, Socrates, said Simmias, do you intend to keep this belief to

d yourself as you leave us, or would you share it with us? I certainly think it would be a blessing for us too, and at the same time it would be your defense if you convince us of what you say.

I will try, he said, but first let us see what it is that Crito here has, I think, been wanting to say for quite a while.

What else, Socrates, said Crito, but what the man who is to give you the poison has been telling me for some time, that I should warn you to talk as little as possible. People get heated when they talk, he says, and one

e should not be heated when taking the poison, as those who do must sometimes drink it two or three times.

Socrates replied: "Take no notice of him; only let him be prepared to administer it twice or, if necessary, three times."

I was rather sure you would say that, Crito said, but he has been bothering me for some time.

Let him be, he said. I want to make my argument before you, my judges, as to why I think that a man who has truly spent his life in philosophy is probably right to be of good cheer in the face of death and to be very

64 hopeful that after death he will attain the greatest blessings yonder. I will try to tell you, Simmias and Cebes, how this may be so. I am afraid that other people do not realize that the one aim of those who practice philosophy in the proper manner is to practice for dying and death. Now if this is true, it would be strange indeed if they were eager for this all their lives and then resent it when what they have wanted and practiced for a long time comes upon them.

Simmias laughed and said: "By Zeus, Socrates, you made me laugh, though I was in no laughing mood just now. I think that the majority, on   *b* hearing this, will think that it describes the philosophers very well, and our people in Thebes would thoroughly agree that philosophers are nearly dead and that the majority of men is well aware that they deserve to be.

And they would be telling the truth, Simmias, except for their being aware. They are not aware of the way true philosophers are nearly dead, nor of the way they deserve to be, nor of the sort of death they deserve.   *c*

But never mind them, he said, let us talk among ourselves. Do we believe that there is such a thing as death?

Certainly, said Simmias.

Is it anything else than the separation of the soul from the body? Do we believe that death is this, namely, that the body comes to be separated by itself apart from the soul, and the soul comes to be separated by itself apart from the body? Is death anything else than that?

No, that is what it is, he said.

Consider then, my good sir, whether you share my opinion, for this will lead us to a better knowledge of what we are investigating. Do you think it   *d* is the part of a philosopher to be concerned with such so-called pleasures as those of food and drink?

By no means.

What about the pleasures of sex?

Not at all.

What of the other pleasures concerned with the service of the body? Do you think such a man prizes them greatly, the acquisition of distinguished clothes and shoes and the other bodily ornaments? Do you think he values these or despises them, except insofar as one cannot do without them?   *e*

I think the true philosopher despises them.

Do you not think, he said, that in general such a man's concern is not with the body but that, as far as he can, he turns away from the body toward the soul?

I do.

So in the first place, such things show clearly that the philosopher more   65 than other men frees the soul from association with the body as much as possible?

Apparently.

A man who finds no pleasure in such things and has no part in them is thought by the majority not to deserve to live and to be close to death; the man, that is, who does not care for the pleasures of the body.

What you say is certainly true.

Then what about the actual acquiring of knowledge? Is the body an obstacle when one associates with it in the search for knowledge? I mean, for example, do men find any truth in sight or hearing, or are not even the   *b* poets forever telling us that we do not see or hear anything accurately, and surely if those two physical senses are not clear or precise, our other senses can hardly be accurate, as they are all inferior to these. Do you not think so?

I certainly do, he said.

When then, he asked, does the soul grasp the truth? For whenever it attempts to examine anything with the body, it is clearly deceived by it.

c   True.

Is it not in reasoning if anywhere that any reality becomes clear to the soul?

Yes.

And indeed the soul reasons best when none of these senses troubles it, neither hearing nor sight, nor pain nor pleasure, but when it is most by itself, taking leave of the body and as far as possible having no contact or association with it in its search for reality.

That is so.

d   And it is then that the soul of the philosopher most disdains the body, flees from it, and seeks to be by itself?

It appears so.

What about the following, Simmias? Do we say that there is such a thing as the Just itself, or not?

We do say so, by Zeus.

And the Beautiful, and the Good?

Of course.

And have you ever seen any of these things with your eyes?

In no way, he said.

Or have you ever grasped them with any of your bodily senses? I am speaking of all things such as Bigness, Health, Strength and, in a word, the

e   reality of all other things, that which each of them essentially is. Is what is most true in them contemplated through the body, or is this the position: whoever of us prepares himself best and most accurately to grasp that thing itself which he is investigating will come closest to the knowledge of it?

Obviously.

Then he will do this most perfectly who approaches the object with

66   thought alone, without associating any sight with his thought, or dragging in any sense perception with his reasoning, but who, using pure thought alone, tries to track down each reality pure and by itself, freeing himself as far as possible from eyes and ears, and in a word, from the whole body, because the body confuses the soul and does not allow it to acquire truth and wisdom whenever it is associated with it. Will not that man reach reality, Simmias, if anyone does?

What you say, said Simmias, is indeed true.

All these things will necessarily make the true philosophers believe and   b
say to each other something like this: "There is likely to be something such
as a path to guide us out of our confusion, because as long as we have a
body and our soul is fused with such an evil we shall never adequately
attain what we desire, which we affirm to be the truth. The body keeps us
busy in a thousand ways because of its need for nurture. Moreover, if
certain diseases befall it, they impede our search for the truth. It fills us   c
with wants, desires, fears, all sorts of illusions, and much nonsense, so
that, as it is said, in truth and in fact no thought of any kind ever comes to
us from the body. Only the body and its desires cause war, civil discord,
and battles, for all wars are due to the desire to acquire wealth, and it is the
body and the care of it, to which we are enslaved, which compel us to   d
acquire wealth, and all this makes us too busy to practice philosophy.

Worst of all, if we do get some respite from it and turn to some investigation, everywhere in our investigations the body is present and makes
for confusion and fear, so that it prevents us from seeing the truth.

"It really has been shown to us that, if we are ever to have pure knowledge, we must escape from the body and observe things in themselves with   e
the soul by itself. It seems likely that we shall, only then, when we are dead,
attain that which we desire and of which we claim to be lovers, namely,
wisdom, as our argument shows, not while we live; for if it is impossible to
attain any pure knowledge with the body, then one of two things is true:
either we can never attain knowledge or we can do so after death. Then and
not before, the soul is by itself apart from the body. While we live, we shall   67
be closest to knowledge if we refrain as much as possible from association
with the body and do not join with it more than we must, if we are not
infected with its nature but purify ourselves from it until the god himself
frees us. In this way we shall escape the contamination of the body's folly;
we shall be likely to be in the company of people of the same kind, and by
our own efforts we shall know all that is pure, which is presumably the
truth, for it is not permitted to the impure to attain the pure."   b

Such are the things, Simmias, that all those who love learning in the
proper manner must say to one another and believe. Or do you not think
so?

I certainly do, Socrates.

And if this is true, my friend, said Socrates, there is good hope that on
arriving where I am going, if anywhere, I shall acquire what has been our
chief preoccupation in our past life, so that the journey that is now ordered   c
for me is full of good hope, as it is also for any other man who believes that
his mind has been prepared and, as it were, purified.

It certainly is, said Simmias.

And does purification not turn out to be what we mentioned in our
argument some time ago, namely, to separate the soul as far as possible

from the body and accustom it to gather itself and collect itself out of every
d part of the body and to dwell by itself as far as it can both now and in the
future, freed, as it were, from the bonds of the body?

Certainly, he said.

And that freedom and separation of the soul from the body is called
death?

That is altogether so.

It is only those who practice philosophy in the right way, we say, who
always most want to free the soul; and this release and separation of the
soul from the body is the preoccupation of the philosophers?

So it appears.

Therefore, as I said at the beginning, it would be ridiculous for a man to
train himself in life to live in a state as close to death as possible, and then
e to resent it when it comes?

Ridiculous, of course.

In fact, Simmias, he said, those who practice philosophy in the right way
are in training for dying, and they fear death least of all men. Consider it
from this point of view: if they are altogether estranged from the body and
desire to have their soul by itself, would it not be quite absurd for them to
be afraid and resentful when this happens? If they did not gladly set out for
a place, where, on arrival, they may hope to attain that for which they had
68 yearned during their lifetime, that is, wisdom, and where they would be
rid of the presence of that from which they are estranged?

Many men, at the death of their lovers, wives, or sons, were willing to
go to the underworld, driven by the hope of seeing there those for whose
company they longed, and being with them. Will then a true lover of
wisdom, who has a similar hope and knows that he will never find it to
any extent except in Hades, be resentful of dying and not gladly undertake
the journey thither? One must surely think so, my friend, if he is a true
b philosopher, for he is firmly convinced that he will not find pure knowledge anywhere except there. And if this is so, then, as I said just now,
would it not be highly unreasonable for such a man to fear death?

It certainly would, by Zeus, he said.

Then you have sufficient indication, he said, that any man whom you
c see resenting death was not a lover of wisdom but a lover of the body, and
also a lover of wealth or of honors, either or both.

It is certainly as you say.

And, Simmias, he said, does not what is called courage belong especially to men of this disposition?

Most certainly.

And the quality of moderation which even the majority call by that
name, that is, not to get swept off one's feet by one's passions, but to treat
d them with disdain and orderliness, is this not suited only to those who
most of all despise the body and live the life of philosophy?

Necessarily so, he said.

If you are willing to reflect on the courage and moderation of other people, you will find them strange.

In what way, Socrates?

You know that they all consider death a great evil?

Definitely, he said.

And the brave among them face death, when they do, for fear of greater evils?

That is so.

Therefore, it is fear and terror that make all men brave, except the philosophers. Yet it is illogical to be brave through fear and cowardice.

It certainly is.   *e*

What of the moderate among them? Is their experience not similar? Is it license of a kind that makes them moderate? We say this is impossible, yet their experience of this unsophisticated moderation turns out to be similar: they fear to be deprived of other pleasures which they desire, so they keep away from some pleasures because they are overcome by others. Now to be mastered by pleasure is what they call license, but what happens to them is that they master certain pleasures because they are mastered by   *69* others. This is like what we mentioned just now, that in some way it is a kind of license that has made them moderate.

That seems likely.

My good Simmias, I fear this is not the right exchange to attain virtue, to exchange pleasures for pleasures, pains for pains, and fears for fears, the greater for the less like coins, but that the only valid currency for which   *b* all these things should be exchanged is wisdom. With this we have real courage and moderation and justice and, in a word, true virtue, with wisdom, whether pleasures and fears and all such things be present or absent. When these things are exchanged for one another in separation from wisdom, such virtue is only an illusory appearance of virtue; it is in fact fit for slaves, without soundness or truth, whereas, in truth, moderation and courage and justice are a purging away of all such things, and wisdom itself is a kind of cleansing or purification. It is likely that those   *c* who established the mystic rites for us were not inferior persons but were speaking in riddles long ago when they said that whoever arrives in the underworld uninitiated and unsanctified will wallow in the mire, whereas he who arrives there purified and initiated will dwell with the gods. There are indeed, as those concerned with the mysteries say, many who carry the thyrsus, but the Bacchants are few.[6] These latter are, in my opinion,   *d* no other than those who have practiced philosophy in the right way. I have in my life left nothing undone in order to be counted among these as far as

6. That is, the true worshippers of Dionysus, as opposed to those who only carry the external symbols of his worship.

possible, as I have been eager to be in every way. Whether my eagerness
was right and we accomplished anything, we shall, I think, know for
certain in a short time, god willing, on arriving yonder.

e   This is my defense, Simmias and Cebes, that I am likely to be right to
leave you and my masters here without resentment or complaint, believing that there, as here, I shall find good masters and good friends. If my
defense is more convincing to you than to the Athenian jury, it will be well.

When Socrates finished, Cebes intervened: Socrates, he said, everything
70   else you said is excellent, I think, but men find it very hard to believe what
you said about the soul. They think that after it has left the body it no
longer exists anywhere, but that it is destroyed and dissolved on the day
the man dies, as soon as it leaves the body; and that, on leaving it, it is
dispersed like breath or smoke, has flown away and gone, and is no longer
anything anywhere. If indeed it gathered itself together and existed by
itself and escaped those evils you were recently enumerating, there would
b   then be much good hope, Socrates, that what you say is true; but to believe
this requires a good deal of faith and persuasive argument, to believe that
the soul still exists after a man has died and that it still possesses some
capability and intelligence.

What you say is true, Cebes, Socrates said, but what shall we do? Do
you want to discuss whether this is likely to be true or not?

Personally, said Cebes, I should like to hear your opinion on the subject.

I do not think, said Socrates, that anyone who heard me now, not even a
c   comic poet, could say that I am babbling and discussing things that do not
concern me, so we must examine the question thoroughly, if you think we
should do so. Let us examine it in some such a manner as this: whether the
souls of men who have died exist in the underworld or not. We recall an
ancient theory that souls arriving there come from here, and then again
that they arrive here and are born here from the dead. If that is true, that
the living come back from the dead, then surely our souls must exist there,
d   for they could not come back if they did not exist, and this is a sufficient
proof that these things are so if it truly appears that the living never come
from any other source than from the dead. If this is not the case we should
need another argument.

Quite so, said Cebes.

Do not, he said, confine yourself to humanity if you want to understand
this more readily, but take all animals and all plants into account, and, in
e   short, for all things which come to be, let us see whether they come to be in
this way, that is, from their opposites if they have such, as the beautiful is
the opposite of the ugly and the just of the unjust, and a thousand other
things of the kind. Let us examine whether those that have an opposite
must necessarily come to be from their opposite and from nowhere else, as
for example when something comes to be larger it must necessarily become larger from having been smaller before.

Yes.

Then if something smaller comes to be, it will come from something larger before, which became smaller?   71

That is so, he said.

And the weaker comes to be from the stronger, and the swifter from the slower?

Certainly.

Further, if something worse comes to be, does it not come from the better, and the juster from the more unjust?

Of course.

So we have sufficiently established that all things come to be in this way, opposites from opposites?

Certainly.

There is a further point, something such as this, about these opposites: between each of those pairs of opposites there are two processes: from the   b
one to the other and then again from the other to the first; between the larger and the smaller there is increase and decrease, and we call the one increasing and the other decreasing?

Yes, he said.

And so too there is separation and combination, cooling and heating, and all such things, even if sometimes we do not have a name for the process, but in fact it must be everywhere that they come to be from one another, and that there is a process of becoming from each into the other?

Assuredly, he said.

Well then, is there an opposite to living, as sleeping is the opposite of   c
being awake?

Quite so, he said.

What is it?

Being dead, he said.

Therefore, if these are opposites, they come to be from one another, and there are two processes of generation between the two?

Of course.

I will tell you, said Socrates, one of the two pairs I was just talking about, the pair itself and the two processes, and you will tell me the other. I mean, to sleep and to be awake; to be awake comes from sleeping, and to   d
sleep comes from being awake. Of the two processes, one is going to sleep, the other is waking up. Do you accept that, or not?

Certainly.

You tell me in the same way about life and death. Do you not say that to be dead is the opposite of being alive?

I do.

And they come to be from one another?

Yes.

What comes to be from being alive?

Being dead.

And what comes to be from being dead?

One must agree that it is being alive.

Then, Cebes, living creatures and things come to be from the dead?

e So it appears, he said.

Then our souls exist in the underworld.

That seems likely.

Then in this case one of the two processes of becoming is clear, for dying is clear enough, is it not?

It certainly is.

What shall we do then? Shall we not supply the opposite process of becoming? Is nature to be lame in this case? Or must we provide a process of becoming opposite to dying?

We surely must.

And what is that?

Coming to life again.

72 Therefore, he said, if there is such a thing as coming to life again, it would be a process of coming from the dead to the living?

Quite so.

It is agreed between us then that the living come from the dead in this way no less than the dead from the living and, if that is so, it seems to be a sufficient proof that the souls of the dead must be somewhere whence they can come back again.

I think, Socrates, he said, that this follows from what we have agreed on.

Consider in this way, Cebes, he said, that, as I think, we were not wrong

b to agree. If the two processes of becoming did not always balance each other as if they were going round in a circle, but generation proceeded from one point to its opposite in a straight line and it did not turn back again to the other opposite or take any turning, do you realize that all things would ultimately be in the same state, be affected in the same way, and cease to become?

How do you mean? he said.

It is not hard to understand what I mean. If, for example, there was such a process as going to sleep, but no corresponding process of waking up, you realize that in the end everything would show the story of Endymion[7]

c to have no meaning. There would be no point to it because everything would have the same experience as he had and be asleep. And if everything were combined and nothing separated, the saying of Anaxagoras[8]

7. Endymion was granted eternal sleep by Zeus.

8. Anaxagoras of Clazomenae was born at the beginning of the fifth century B.C. He came to Athens as a young man and spent most of his life there in the study of

would soon be true," that all things were mixed together." In the same way, my dear Cebes, if everything that partakes of life were to die and remain in that state and not come to life again, would not everything ultimately have to be dead and nothing alive? Even if the living came from some other source, and all that lived died, how could all things avoid being absorbed in death?   *d*

It could not be, Socrates, said Cebes, and I think what you say is altogether true.

I think, Cebes, said he, that this is very definitely the case and that we were not deceived when we agreed on this: coming to life again in truth exists, the living come to be from the dead, and the souls of the dead exist.   *e*

Furthermore, Socrates, Cebes rejoined, such is also the case if that theory is true that you are accustomed to mention frequently, that for us learning is no other than recollection. According to this, we must at some previous time have learned what we now recollect. This is possible only if   73 our soul existed somewhere before it took on this human shape. So according to this theory too, the soul is likely to be something immortal.

Cebes, Simmias interrupted, what are the proofs of this? Remind me, for I do not quite recall them at the moment.

There is one excellent argument, said Cebes, namely that when men are interrogated in the right manner, they always give the right answer of their own accord, and they could not do this if they did not possess the knowledge and the right explanation inside them. Then if one shows them a   *b* diagram or something else of that kind, this will show most clearly that such is the case.[9]

If this does not convince you, Simmias, said Socrates, see whether you agree if we examine it in some such way as this, for do you doubt that what we call learning is recollection?

It is not that I doubt, said Simmias, but I want to experience the very thing we are discussing, recollection, and from what Cebes undertook to say, I am now remembering and am pretty nearly convinced. Nevertheless, I should like to hear now the way you were intending to explain it.

This way, he said. We surely agree that if anyone recollects anything, he   *c* must have known it before.

Quite so, he said.

Do we not also agree that when knowledge comes to mind in this way, it is recollection? What way do I mean? Like this: when a man sees or hears or in some other way perceives one thing and not only knows that thing

---

natural philosophy. He is quoted later in the dialogue (97c ff.) as claiming that the universe is directed by Mind (*Nous*). The reference here is to his statement that in the original state of the world, all its elements were thoroughly commingled.
9. Cf. *Meno* 81e ff., where Socrates does precisely that.

but also thinks of another thing of which the knowledge is not the same but different, are we not right to say that he recollects the second thing that comes into his mind?

d   How do you mean?

Things such as this: to know a man is surely a different knowledge from knowing a lyre.

Of course.

Well, you know what happens to lovers: whenever they see a lyre, a garment, or anything else that their beloved is accustomed to use, they know the lyre, and the image of the boy to whom it belongs comes into their mind. This is recollection, just as someone, on seeing Simmias, often recollects Cebes, and there are thousands of other such occurrences.

Thousands indeed, said Simmias.

Is this kind of thing not recollection of a kind? he said, especially so
e   when one experiences it about things that one had forgotten, because one had not seen them for some time?—Quite so.

Further, he said, can a man seeing the picture of a horse or a lyre recollect a man, or seeing a picture of Simmias recollect Cebes?—Certainly.

Or seeing a picture of Simmias, recollect Simmias himself?—He certainly can.

74   In all these cases the recollection can be occasioned by things that are similar, but it can also be occasioned by things that are dissimilar?—It can.

When the recollection is caused by similar things, must one not of necessity also experience this: to consider whether the similarity to that which one recollects is deficient in any respect or complete?—One must.

Consider, he said, whether this is the case: we say that there is something that is equal. I do not mean a stick equal to a stick or a stone to a stone, or anything of that kind, but something else beyond all these, the Equal itself. Shall we say that this exists or not?

b   Indeed we shall, by Zeus, said Simmias, most definitely.

And do we know what this is?—Certainly.

Whence have we acquired the knowledge of it? Is it not from the things we mentioned just now, from seeing sticks or stones or some other things that are equal we come to think of that other which is different from them? Or doesn't it seem to you to be different? Look at it also this way: do not equal stones and sticks sometimes, while remaining the same, appear to one to be equal and to another to be unequal?—Certainly they do.

c   But what of the equals themselves? Have they ever appeared unequal to you, or Equality to be Inequality?

Never, Socrates.

These equal things and the Equal itself are therefore not the same?

I do not think they are the same at all, Socrates.

But it is definitely from the equal things, though they are different from that Equal, that you have derived and grasped the knowledge of equality?

Very true, Socrates.

Whether it be like them or unlike them?

Certainly.

It makes no difference. As long as the sight of one thing makes you think of another, whether it be similar or dissimilar, this must of necessity be recollection?   *d*

Quite so.

Well then, he said, do we experience something like this in the case of equal sticks and the other equal objects we just mentioned? Do they seem to us to be equal in the same sense as what is Equal itself? Is there some deficiency in their being such as the Equal, or is there not?

A considerable deficiency, he said.

Whenever someone, on seeing something, realizes that that which he now sees wants to be like some other reality but falls short and cannot be   *e* like that other since it is inferior, do we agree that the one who thinks this must have prior knowledge of that to which he says it is like, but deficiently so?

Necessarily.

Well, do we also experience this about the equal objects and the Equal itself, or do we not?

Very definitely.

We must then possess knowledge of the Equal before that time when we first saw the equal objects and realized that all these objects strive to be   75 like the Equal but are deficient in this.

That is so.

Then surely we also agree that this conception of ours derives from seeing or touching or some other sense perception, and cannot come into our mind in any other way, for all these senses, I say, are the same.

They are the same, Socrates, at any rate in respect to that which our argument wishes to make plain.

Our sense perceptions must surely make us realize that all that we   *b* perceive through them is striving to reach that which is Equal but falls short of it; or how do we express it?

Like that.

Then before we began to see or hear or otherwise perceive, we must have possessed knowledge of the Equal itself if we were about to refer our sense perceptions of equal objects to it, and realized that all of them were eager to be like it, but were inferior.

That follows from what has been said, Socrates.

But we began to see and hear and otherwise perceive right after birth?

Certainly.

We must then have acquired the knowledge of the Equal before this.   *c*

Yes.

It seems then that we must have possessed it before birth.

It seems so.

Therefore, if we had this knowledge, we knew before birth and immediately after not only the Equal, but the Greater and the Smaller and all such things, for our present argument is no more about the Equal than

d   about the Beautiful itself, the Good itself, the Just, the Pious and, as I say, about all those things which we mark with the seal of "what it is," both when we are putting questions and answering them. So we must have acquired knowledge of them all before we were born.

That is so.

If, having acquired this knowledge in each case, we have not forgotten it, we remain knowing and have knowledge throughout our life, for to know is to acquire knowledge, keep it, and not lose it. Do we not call the losing of knowledge forgetting?

e   Most certainly, Socrates, he said.

But, I think, if we acquired this knowledge before birth, then lost it at birth, and then later by the use of our senses in connection with those objects we mentioned, we recovered the knowledge we had before, would not what we call learning be the recovery of our own knowledge, and we are right to call this recollection?

Certainly.

76   It was seen to be possible for someone to see or hear or otherwise perceive something, and by this to be put in mind of something else which he had forgotten and which is related to it by similarity or difference. One of two things follows, as I say: either we were born with the knowledge of it, and all of us know it throughout life, or those who later, we say, are learning, are only recollecting, and learning would be recollection.

That is certainly the case, Socrates.

Which alternative do you choose, Simmias? That we are born with this

b   knowledge or that we recollect later the things of which we had knowledge previously?

I have no means of choosing at the moment, Socrates.

Well, can you make this choice? What is your opinion about it? A man who has knowledge would be able to give an account of what he knows, or would he not?

He must certainly be able to do so, Socrates, he said.

And do you think everybody can give an account of the things we were mentioning just now?

I wish they could, said Simmias, but I'm afraid it is much more likely that by this time tomorrow there will be no one left who can do so adequately.

c   So you do not think that everybody has knowledge of those things?

No indeed.

So they recollect what they once learned?

They must.

When did our souls acquire the knowledge of them? Certainly not since we were born as men.

Indeed no.

Before that then?

Yes.

So then, Simmias, our souls also existed apart from the body before they took on human form, and they had intelligence.

Unless we acquire the knowledge at the moment of birth, Socrates, for that time is still left to us.

Quite so, my friend, but at what other time do we lose it? We just now *d* agreed that we are not born with that knowledge. Do we then lose it at the very time we acquire it, or can you mention any other time?

I cannot, Socrates. I did not realize that I was talking nonsense.

So this is our position, Simmias? he said. If those realities we are always talking about exist, the Beautiful and the Good and all that kind of reality, and we refer all the things we perceive to that reality, discovering that it existed before and is ours, and we compare these things with it, then, just *e* as they exist, so our soul must exist before we are born. If these realities do not exist, then this argument is altogether futile. Is this the position, that there is an equal necessity for those realities to exist, and for our souls to exist before we were born? If the former do not exist, neither do the latter?

I do not think, Socrates, said Simmias, that there is any possible doubt that it is equally necessary for both to exist, and it is opportune that our argument comes to the conclusion that our soul exists before we are born, *77* and equally so that reality of which you are now speaking. Nothing is so evident to me personally as that all such things must certainly exist, the Beautiful, the Good, and all those you mentioned just now. I also think that sufficient proof of this has been given.

Then what about Cebes? said Socrates, for we must persuade Cebes also.

He is sufficiently convinced I think, said Simmias, though he is the most difficult of men to persuade by argument, but I believe him to be fully convinced that our soul existed before we were born. I do not think myself, *b* however, that it has been proved that the soul continues to exist after death; the opinion of the majority which Cebes mentioned still stands, that when a man dies his soul is dispersed and this is the end of its existence. What is to prevent the soul coming to be and being constituted from some other source, existing before it enters a human body and then, having done so and departed from it, itself dying and being destroyed?

You are right, Simmias, said Cebes. Half of what needed proof has been *c* proved, namely, that our soul existed before we were born, but further proof is needed that it exists no less after we have died, if the proof is to be complete.

It has been proved even now, Simmias and Cebes, said Socrates, if you
are ready to combine this argument with the one we agreed on before, that
every living thing must come from the dead. If the soul exists before, it

d   must, as it comes to life and birth, come from nowhere else than death and
being dead, so how could it avoid existing after death since it must be born
again? What you speak of has, then, even now been proved. However, I
think you and Simmias would like to discuss the argument more fully. You
seem to have this childish fear that the wind would really dissolve and

e   scatter the soul, as it leaves the body, especially if one happens to die in a
high wind and not in calm weather.

Cebes laughed and said: Assuming that we were afraid, Socrates, try to
change our minds, or rather do not assume that we are afraid, but perhaps
there is a child in us who has these fears; try to persuade him not to fear
death like a bogey.

You should, said Socrates, sing a charm over him every day until you
have charmed away his fears.

78   Where shall we find a good charmer for these fears, Socrates, he said,
now that you are leaving us?

Greece is a large country, Cebes, he said, and there are good men in it;
the tribes of foreigners are also numerous. You should search for such a
charmer among them all, sparing neither trouble nor expense, for there is
nothing on which you could spend your money to greater advantage. You
must also search among yourselves, for you might not easily find people
who could do this better than yourselves.

b   That shall be done, said Cebes, but let us, if it pleases you, go back to the
argument where we left it.

Of course it pleases me.

Splendid, he said.

We must then ask ourselves something like this: what kind of thing is
likely to be scattered? On behalf of what kind of thing should one fear this,
and for what kind of thing should one not fear it? We should then examine
to which class the soul belongs, and as a result either fear for the soul or be
of good cheer.

What you say is true.

c   Is not anything that is composite and a compound by nature liable to be
split up into its component parts, and only that which is noncomposite, if
anything, is not likely to be split up?

I think that is the case, said Cebes.

Are not the things that always remain the same and in the same state
most likely not to be composite, whereas those that vary from one time to
another and are never the same are composite?

I think that is so.

Let us then return to those same things with which we were dealing

earlier, to that reality of whose existence we are giving an account in our   *d*
questions and answers; are they ever the same and in the same state, or do
they vary from one time to another; can the Equal itself, the Beautiful itself,
each thing in itself, the real, ever be affected by any change whatever? Or
does each of them that really is, being uniform by itself, remain the same
and never in any way tolerate any change whatever?

It must remain the same, said Cebes, and in the same state, Socrates.

What of the many beautiful particulars, be they men, horses, clothes, or   *e*
other such things, or the many equal particulars, and all those which bear
the same name as those others? Do they remain the same or, in total
contrast to those other realities, one might say, never in any way remain
the same as themselves or in relation to each other?

The latter is the case, they are never in the same state.

These latter you could touch and see and perceive with the other senses,   *79*
but those that always remain the same can be grasped only by the reasoning power of the mind? They are not seen but are invisible?

That is altogether true, he said.

Do you then want us to assume two kinds of existences, the visible and
the invisible?

Let us assume this.

And the invisible always remains the same, whereas the visible never
does?

Let us assume that too.

Now one part of ourselves is the body, another part is the soul?   *b*
Quite so.

To which class of existence do we say the body is more alike and akin?
To the visible, as anyone can see.

What about the soul? Is it visible or invisible?
It is not visible to men, Socrates, he said.

Well, we meant visible and invisible to human eyes; or to any others, do
you think?

To human eyes.

Then what do we say about the soul? Is it visible or not visible?
Not visible.

So it is invisible?—Yes.

So the soul is more like the invisible than the body, and the body more   *c*
like the visible?—Without any doubt, Socrates.

Haven't we also said some time ago that when the soul makes use of the
body to investigate something, be it through hearing or seeing or some
other sense—for to investigate something through the body is to do it
through the senses—it is dragged by the body to the things that are never
the same, and the soul itself strays and is confused and dizzy, as if it were
drunk, insofar as it is in contact with that kind of thing?

Certainly.

d But when the soul investigates by itself it passes into the realm of what is pure, ever existing, immortal, and unchanging, and being akin to this, it always stays with it whenever it is by itself and can do so; it ceases to stray and remains in the same state as it is in touch with things of the same kind, and its experience then is what is called wisdom?

Altogether well said and very true, Socrates, he said.

e Judging from what we have said before and what we are saying now, to which of these two kinds do you think that the soul is more alike and more akin?

I think, Socrates, he said, that on this line of argument any man, even the dullest, would agree that the soul is altogether more like that which always exists in the same state rather than like that which does not.

What of the body?

That is like the other.

80 Look at it also this way: when the soul and the body are together, nature orders the one to be subject and to be ruled, and the other to rule and be master. Then again, which do you think is like the divine and which like the mortal? Do you not think that the nature of the divine is to rule and to lead, whereas it is that of the mortal to be ruled and be subject?

I do.

Which does the soul resemble?

Obviously, Socrates, the soul resembles the divine, and the body resembles the mortal.

Consider then, Cebes, whether it follows from all that has been said that
b the soul is most like the divine, deathless, intelligible, uniform, indissoluble, always the same as itself, whereas the body is most like that which is human, mortal, multiform, unintelligible, soluble, and never consistently the same. Have we anything else to say to show, my dear Cebes, that this is not the case?

We have not.

Well then, that being so, is it not natural for the body to dissolve easily, and for the soul to be altogether indissoluble, or nearly so?

c Of course.

You realize, he said, that when a man dies, the visible part, the body, which exists in the visible world and which we call the corpse, whose natural lot it would be to dissolve, fall apart, and be blown away, does not immediately suffer any of these things but remains for a fair time, in fact, quite a long time if the man dies with his body in a suitable condition and at a favorable season? If the body is emaciated or embalmed, as in Egypt, it remains almost whole for a remarkable length of time, and even if the
d body decays, some parts of it, namely bones and sinews and the like, are nevertheless, one might say, deathless. Is that not so?—Yes.

Will the soul, the invisible part which makes its way to a region of the same kind, noble and pure and invisible, to Hades in fact, to the good and wise god whither, god willing, my soul must soon be going—will the soul, being of this kind and nature, be scattered and destroyed on leaving the body, as the majority of men say? Far from it, my dear Cebes and Simmias, *e* but what happens is much more like this: if it is pure when it leaves the body and drags nothing bodily with it, as it had no willing association with the body in life, but avoided it and gathered itself together by itself and always practiced this, which is no other than practicing philosophy in *81* the right way, in fact, training to die easily. Or is this not training for death?

It surely is.

A soul in this state makes its way to the invisible, which is like itself, the divine and immortal and wise, and arriving there it can be happy, having rid itself of confusion, ignorance, fear, violent desires, and the other human ills and, as is said of the initiates, truly spend the rest of time with the gods. Shall we say this, Cebes, or something different?

This, by Zeus, said Cebes.

But I think that if the soul is polluted and impure when it leaves the *b* body, having always been associated with it and served it, bewitched by physical desires and pleasures to the point at which nothing seems to exist for it but the physical, which one can touch and see or eat and drink or make use of for sexual enjoyment, and if that soul is accustomed to hate and fear and avoid that which is dim and invisible to the eyes but intelligible and to be grasped by philosophy—do you think such a soul will escape pure and by itself?

Impossible, he said. *c*

It is no doubt permeated by the physical, which constant intercourse and association with the body, as well as considerable practice, has caused to become ingrained in it?

Quite so.

We must believe, my friend, that this bodily element is heavy, ponderous, earthy, and visible. Through it, such a soul has become heavy and is dragged back to the visible region in fear of the unseen and of Hades. It wanders, as we are told, around graves and monuments, where shadowy *d* phantoms, images that such souls produce, have been seen, souls that have not been freed and purified but share in the visible, and are therefore seen.

That is likely, Socrates.

It is indeed, Cebes. Moreover, these are not the souls of good but of inferior men, which are forced to wander there, paying the penalty for their previous bad upbringing. They wander until their longing for that *e* which accompanies them, the physical, again imprisons them in a body, and they are then, as is likely, bound to such characters as they have practiced in their life.

What kind of characters do you say these are, Socrates?

Those, for example, who have carelessly practiced gluttony, violence, and drunkenness are likely to join a company of donkeys or of similar animals. Do you not think so?

Very likely.

Those who have esteemed injustice highly, and tyranny and plunder, will join the tribes of wolves and hawks and kites, or where else shall we say that they go?

Certainly to those, said Cebes.

And clearly, the destination of the others will conform to the way in which they have behaved?

Clearly, of course.

The happiest of these, who will also have the best destination, are those who have practiced popular and social virtue, which they call moderation and justice and which was developed by habit and practice, without philosophy or understanding?

How are they the happiest?

Because it is likely that they will again join a social and gentle group, either of bees or wasps or ants, and then again the same kind of human group, and so be moderate men.

That is likely.

No one may join the company of the gods who has not practiced philosophy and is not completely pure when he departs from life, no one but the lover of learning. It is for this reason, my friends Simmias and Cebes, that those who practice philosophy in the right way keep away from all bodily passions, master them, and do not surrender themselves to them; it is not at all for fear of wasting their substance and of poverty, which the majority and the money-lovers fear, nor for fear of dishonor and ill repute, like the ambitious and lovers of honors, that they keep away from them.

That would not be natural for them, Socrates, said Cebes.

By Zeus, no, he said. Those who care for their own soul and do not live for the service of their body dismiss all these things. They do not travel the same road as those who do not know where they are going but, believing that nothing should be done contrary to philosophy and their deliverance and purification, they turn to this and follow wherever philosophy leads.

How so, Socrates?

I will tell you, he said. The lovers of learning know that when philosophy gets hold of their soul, it is imprisoned in and clinging to the body, and that it is forced to examine other things through it as through a cage and not by itself, and that it wallows in every kind of ignorance. Philosophy sees that the worst feature of this imprisonment is that it is due to desires, so that the prisoner himself is contributing to his own incarceration most

of all. As I say, the lovers of learning know that philosophy gets hold of   *83*
their soul when it is in that state, then gently encourages it and tries to free
it by showing them that investigation through the eyes is full of deceit, as
is that through the ears and the other senses. Philosophy then persuades
the soul to withdraw from the senses insofar as it is not compelled to use
them and bids the soul to gather itself together by itself, to trust only itself
and whatever reality, existing by itself, the soul by itself understands, and   *b*
not to consider as true whatever it examines by other means, for this is
different in different circumstances and is sensible and visible, whereas
what the soul itself sees is intelligible and invisible. The soul of the true
philosopher thinks that this deliverance must not be opposed and so keeps
away from pleasures and desires and pains as far as he can; he reflects that
violent pleasure or pain or passion does not cause merely such evils as one
might expect, such as one suffers when one has been sick or extravagant   *c*
through desire, but the greatest and most extreme evil, though one does
not reflect on this.

What is that, Socrates? asked Cebes.

That the soul of every man, when it feels violent pleasure or pain in
connection with some object, inevitably believes at the same time that
what causes such feelings must be very clear and very true, which it is not.
Such objects are mostly visible, are they not?

Certainly.

And doesn't such an experience tie the soul to the body most completely?   *d*
How so?

Because every pleasure or pain provides, as it were, another nail to rivet
the soul to the body and to weld them together. It makes the soul corporeal, so that it believes that truth is what the body says it is. As it shares
the beliefs and delights of the body, I think it inevitably comes to share its
ways and manner of life and is unable ever to reach Hades in a pure state;
it is always full of body when it departs, so that it soon falls back into
another body and grows with it as if it had been sewn into it. Because of   *e*
this, it can have no part in the company of the divine, the pure and
uniform.

What you say is very true, Socrates, said Cebes.

This is why genuine lovers of learning are moderate and brave, or do
you think it is for the reasons the majority says they are?

I certainly do not.   *84*

Indeed no. This is how the soul of a philosopher would reason: it would
not think that while philosophy must free it, it should while being freed
surrender itself to pleasures and pains and imprison itself again, thus
laboring in vain like Penelope at her web. The soul of the philosopher
achieves a calm from such emotions; it follows reason and ever stays with
it contemplating the true, the divine, which is not the object of opinion.
Nurtured by this, it believes that one should live in this manner as long as   *b*

one is alive and, after death, arrive at what is akin and of the same kind, and escape from human evils. After such nurture there is no danger, Simmias and Cebes, that one should fear that, on parting from the body, the soul would be scattered and dissipated by the winds and no longer be anything anywhere.

c   When Socrates finished speaking there was a long silence. He appeared to be concentrating on what had been said, and so were most of us. But Cebes and Simmias were whispering to each other. Socrates observed them and questioned them. Come, he said, do you think there is something lacking in my argument? There are still many doubtful points and many objections for anyone who wants a thorough discussion of these matters. If you are discussing some other subject, I have nothing to say, but if you have some difficulty about this one, do not hesitate to speak for yourselves and expound it if you think the argument could be im-
d   proved, and if you think you will do better, take me along with you in the discussion.

I will tell you the truth, Socrates, said Simmias. Both of us have been in difficulty for some time, and each of us has been urging the other to question you because we wanted to hear what you would say, but we hesitated to bother you, lest it be displeasing to you in your present misfortune.

When Socrates heard this he laughed quietly and said: "Really, Sim-
e   mias, it would be hard for me to persuade other people that I do not consider my present fate a misfortune if I cannot persuade even you, and you are afraid that it is more difficult to deal with me than before. You seem to think me inferior to the swans in prophecy. They sing before too, but when they realize that they must die they sing most and most beau-
85   tifully, as they rejoice that they are about to depart to join the god whose servants they are. But men, because of their own fear of death, tell lies about the swans and say that they lament their death and sing in sorrow. They do not reflect that no bird sings when it is hungry or cold or suffers in any other way, neither the nightingale nor the swallow nor the hoopoe, though they do say that these sing laments when in pain. Nor do the
b   swans, but I believe that as they belong to Apollo, they are prophetic, have knowledge of the future, and sing of the blessings of the underworld, sing and rejoice on that day beyond what they did before. As I believe myself to be a fellow servant with the swans and dedicated to the same god, and have received from my master a gift of prophecy not inferior to theirs, I am no more despondent than they on leaving life. Therefore, you must speak and ask whatever you want as long as the authorities allow it."

Well spoken, said Simmias. I will tell you my difficulty, and then Cebes
c   will say why he does not accept what was said. I believe, as perhaps you do, that precise knowledge on that subject is impossible or extremely

difficult in our present life, but that it surely shows a very poor spirit not to examine thoroughly what is said about it, and to desist before one is exhausted by an all-around investigation. One should achieve one of these things: learn the truth about these things or find it for oneself, or, if that is impossible, adopt the best and most irrefutable of men's theories, and, borne upon this, sail through the dangers of life as upon a raft, unless someone should make that journey safer and less risky upon a firmer vessel of some divine doctrine. So even now, since you have said what you did, I will feel no shame at asking questions, and I will not blame myself in the future because I did not say what I think. As I examine what we said, both by myself and with Cebes, it does not seem to be adequate.

d

Said Socrates: "You may well be right, my friend, but tell me how it is inadequate."

e

In this way, as it seems to me, he said: "One might make the same argument about harmony, lyre, and strings, that a harmony is something invisible, without body, beautiful and divine in the attuned lyre, whereas the lyre itself and its strings are physical, bodily, composite, earthy, and akin to what is mortal. Then if someone breaks the lyre, cuts or breaks the strings, and then insists, using the same argument as you, that the harmony must still exist and is not destroyed because it would be impossible for the lyre and the strings, which are mortal, still to exist when the strings are broken, and for the harmony, which is akin and of the same nature as the divine and immortal, to be destroyed before that which is mortal; he would say that the harmony itself still must exist and that the wood and the strings must rot before the harmony can suffer. And indeed Socrates, I think you must have this in mind, that we really do suppose the soul to be something of this kind; as the body is stretched and held together by the hot and the cold, the dry and the moist, and other such things, and our soul is a mixture and harmony of those things when they are mixed with each other rightly and in due measure. If then the soul is a kind of harmony or attunement, clearly, when our body is relaxed or stretched without due measure by diseases and other evils, the soul must immediately be destroyed, even if it be most divine, as are the other harmonies found in music and all the works of artists, and the remains of each body last for a long time until they rot or are burned. Consider what we shall say in answer to one who deems the soul to be a mixture of bodily elements and to be the first to perish in the process we call death."

86

b

c

d

Socrates looked at us keenly, as was his habit, smiled, and said: "What Simmias says is quite fair. If one of you is more resourceful than I am, why did he not answer him, for he seems to have handled the argument competently. However, I think that before we answer him, we should hear Cebes' objection, in order that we may have time to deliberate on an answer. When we have heard him we should either agree with them, if we think

e

them in tune with us or, if not, defend our own argument. Come then, Cebes. What is troubling you?"

87   I tell you, said Cebes, the argument seems to me to be at the same point as before and open to the same objection. I do not deny that it has been very elegantly and, if it is not offensive to say so, sufficiently proved that our soul existed before it took on this present form, but I do not believe the same applies to its existing somewhere after our death. Not that I agree with Simmias' objection that the soul is not stronger and much more lasting than the body, for I think it is superior in all these respects. "Why then," the argument might say, "are you still unconvinced? Since you see that when the man dies, the weaker part continues to exist, do you not

b   think that the more lasting part must be preserved during that time?" On this point consider whether what I say makes sense.

Like Simmias, I too need an image, for I think this argument is much as if one said at the death of an old weaver that the man had not perished but was safe and sound somewhere, and offered as proof the fact that the cloak

c   the old man had woven himself and was wearing was still sound and had not perished. If one was not convinced, he would be asked whether a man lasts longer than a cloak which is in use and being worn, and if the answer was that a man lasts much longer, this would be taken as proof that the man was definitely safe and sound, since the more temporary thing had not perished. But Simmias, I do not think that is so, for consider what I say. Anybody could see that the man who said this was talking nonsense. That weaver had woven and worn out many such cloaks. He perished after

d   many of them, but before the last. That does not mean that a man is inferior and weaker than a cloak. The image illustrates, I think, the relationship of the soul to the body, and anyone who says the same thing about them would appear to me to be talking sense, that the soul lasts a long time while the body is weaker and more short-lived. He might say that each soul wears out many bodies, especially if it lives many years.

If the body were in a state of flux and perished while the man was still

e   alive, and the soul wove afresh the body that is worn out, yet it would be inevitable that whenever the soul perished it would be wearing the last body it wove and perish only before this last. Then when the soul perished, the body would show the weakness of its nature by soon decaying and disappearing. So we cannot trust this argument and be confident that

88   our soul continues to exist somewhere after our death. For, if one were to concede, even more than you do, to a man using that argument, if one were to grant him not only that the soul exists in the time before we are born, but that there is no reason why the soul of some should not exist and continue to exist after our death, and thus frequently be born and die in turn; if one were to grant him that the soul's nature is so strong that it can survive many bodies, but if, having granted all this, one does not further agree that the soul is not damaged by its many births and is not, in the end,

altogether destroyed in one of those deaths, he might say that no one knows which death and dissolution of the body brings about the destruc-   *b* tion of the soul, since not one of us can be aware of this. And in that case, any man who faces death with confidence is foolish, unless he can prove that the soul is altogether immortal. If he cannot, a man about to die must of necessity always fear for his soul, lest the present separation of the soul from the body bring about the complete destruction of the soul.

When we heard what they said we were all depressed, as we told each   *c* other afterward. We had been quite convinced by the previous argument, and they seemed to confuse us again, and to drive us to doubt not only what had already been said but also what was going to be said, lest we be worthless as critics or the subject itself admitted of no certainty.

ECHECRATES: By the gods, Phaedo, you have my sympathy, for as I listen to you now I find myself saying to myself: "What argument shall we   *d* trust, now that that of Socrates, which was extremely convincing, has fallen into discredit?" The statement that the soul is some kind of harmony has a remarkable hold on me, now and always, and when it was mentioned, it reminded me that I had myself previously thought so. And now I am again quite in need, as if from the beginning, of some other argument to convince me that the soul does not die along with the man. Tell me then, by Zeus, how Socrates tackled the argument. Was he obviously distressed, as you say you people were, or was he not, but quietly came to the rescue of   *e* his argument, and did he do so satisfactorily or inadequately? Tell us everything as precisely as you can.

PHAEDO: I have certainly often admired Socrates, Echecrates, but never more than on this occasion. That he had a reply was perhaps not strange.   *89* What I wondered at most in him was the pleasant, kind, and admiring way he received the young men's argument, and how sharply he was aware of the effect the discussion had on us, and then how well he healed our distress and, as it were, recalled us from our flight and defeat and turned us around to join him in the examination of their argument.

ECHECRATES: How did he do this?

PHAEDO: I will tell you. I happened to be sitting on his right by the couch on a low stool, so that he was sitting well above me. He stroked my   *b* head and pressed the hair on the back of my neck, for he was in the habit of playing with my hair at times. "Tomorrow, Phaedo," he said, "you will probably cut this beautiful hair."

Likely enough, Socrates, I said.

Not if you take my advice, he said.

Why not? said I.

It is today, he said, that I shall cut my hair and you yours, if our argument dies on us, and we cannot revive it. If I were you, and the argument escaped   *c* me, I would take an oath, as the Argives did, not to let my hair grow before I fought again and defeated the argument of Simmias and Cebes.

But, I said, they say that not even Heracles could fight two people.

Then call on me as your Iolaus, as long as the daylight lasts.

I shall call on you, but in this case as Iolaus calling on Heracles.

It makes no difference, he said, but first there is a certain experience we must be careful to avoid.

What is that? I asked.

d   That we should not become misologues, as people become misanthropes.

There is no greater evil one can suffer than to hate reasonable discourse.

Misology and misanthropy arise in the same way. Misanthropy comes when a man without knowledge or skill has placed great trust in someone and believes him to be altogether truthful, sound, and trustworthy; then, a short time afterward he finds him to be wicked and unreliable, and then this happens in another case; when one has frequently had that experience, especially with those whom one believed to be one's closest friends, then, in the end, after many such blows, one comes to hate all men and to believe that no one is sound in any way at all. Have you not seen this happen?

e

I surely have, I said.

This is a shameful state of affairs, he said, and obviously due to an attempt to have human relations without any skill in human affairs, for such skill would lead one to believe, what is in fact true, that the very good and the very wicked are both quite rare, and that most men are between those extremes.

90

How do you mean? said I.

The same as with the very tall and the very short, he said. Do you think anything is rarer than to find an extremely tall man or an extremely short one? Or a dog or anything else whatever? Or again, one extremely swift or extremely slow, ugly or beautiful, white or black? Are you not aware that in all those cases the most extreme at either end are rare and few, but those in between are many and plentiful?

Certainly, I said.

b   Therefore, he said, if a contest of wickedness were established, there too the winners, you think, would be very few?

That is likely, said I.

Likely indeed, he said, but arguments are not like men in this particular. I was merely following your lead just now. The similarity lies rather in this: it is as when one who lacks skill in arguments puts his trust in an argument as being true, then shortly afterward believes it to be false—as sometimes it is and sometimes it is not—and so with another argument and then another. You know how those in particular who spend their time studying contradiction in the end believe themselves to have become very wise and that they alone have understood that there is no soundness or reliability in any object or in any argument, but that all that exists simply

c

fluctuates up and down as if it were in the Euripus[10] and does not remain in the same place for any time at all.

What you say, I said, is certainly true.

It would be pitiable, Phaedo, he said, when there is a true and reliable argument and one that can be understood, if a man who has dealt with such arguments as appear at one time true, at another time untrue, should *d* not blame himself or his own lack of skill but, because of his distress, in the end gladly shift the blame away from himself to the arguments, and spend the rest of his life hating and reviling reasonable discussion and so be deprived of truth and knowledge of reality.

Yes, by Zeus, I said, that would be pitiable indeed.

This then is the first thing we should guard against, he said. We should *e* not allow into our minds the conviction that argumentation has nothing sound about it; much rather we should believe that it is we who are not yet sound and that we must take courage and be eager to attain soundness, you and the others for the sake of your whole life still to come, and I for *91* the sake of death itself. I am in danger at this moment of not having a philosophical attitude about this, but like those who are quite uneducated, I am eager to get the better of you in argument, for the uneducated, when they engage in argument about anything, give no thought to the truth about the subject of discussion but are only eager that those present will accept the position they have set forth. I differ from them only to this extent: I shall not be eager to get the agreement of those present that what I say is true, except incidentally, but I shall be very eager that I should myself be thoroughly convinced that things are so. For I am thinking—see in how contentious a spirit—that if what I say is true, it is a fine thing to be convinced; if, on the other hand, nothing exists after death, at least for this *b* time before I die I shall distress those present less with lamentations and my folly will not continue to exist along with me—that would be a bad thing—but will come to an end in a short time. Thus prepared, Simmias and Cebes, he said, I come to deal with your argument. If you will take my advice, you will give but little thought to Socrates but much more to the *c* truth. If you think that what I say is true, agree with me; if not, oppose it with every argument and take care that in my eagerness I do not deceive myself and you and, like a bee, leave my sting in you when I go.

We must proceed, he said, and first remind me of what you said if I do not appear to remember it. Simmias, as I believe, is in doubt and fear that the soul, though it is more divine and beautiful than the body, yet pre- *d* deceases it, being a kind of harmony. Cebes, I thought, agrees with me that the soul lasts much longer than the body, but that no one knows whether

10. The Euripus is the straits between the island of Euboea and Boeotia on the Greek mainland; its currents were both violent and variable.

the soul often wears out many bodies and then, on leaving its last body, is now itself destroyed. This then is death, the destruction of the soul, since the body is always being destroyed. Are these the questions, Simmias and Cebes, which we must investigate?

e   They both agreed that they were.

Do you then, he asked, reject all our previous statements, or some but not others?

Some, they both said, but not others.

What, he said, about the statements we made that learning is recollec-
92 tion and that, if this was so, our soul must of necessity exist elsewhere before us, before it was imprisoned in the body?

For myself, said Cebes, I was wonderfully convinced by it at the time, and I stand by it now also, more than by any other statement.

That, said Simmias, is also my position, and I should be very surprised if I ever changed my opinion about this.

But you must change your opinion, my Theban friend, said Socrates, if you still believe that a harmony is a composite thing and that the soul is a kind of harmony of the elements of the body in a state of tension, for surely
b   you will not allow yourself to maintain that a composite harmony existed before those elements from which it had to be composed, or would you?

Never, Socrates, he said.

Do you realize, he said, that this is what you are in fact saying when you state that the soul exists before it takes on the form and body of a man and that it is composed of elements which do not yet exist? A harmony is not like that to which you compare it; the lyre and the strings and the notes,
c   though still unharmonized, exist; the harmony is composed last of all, and is the first to be destroyed. How will you harmonize this statement with your former one?

In no way, said Simmias.

And surely, he said, a statement about harmony should do so more than any other.

It should, said Simmias.

So your statement is inconsistent? Consider which of your statements you prefer, that learning is recollection or that the soul is a harmony.

d   I much prefer the former, Socrates. I adopted the latter without proof, because of a certain probability and plausibility, which is why it appeals to most men. I know that arguments of which the proof is based on probability are pretentious and, if one does not guard against them, they certainly deceive one, in geometry and everything else. The theory of recollection and learning, however, was based on an assumption worthy of acceptance, for our soul was said to exist also before it came into the body, just as the reality does that is of the kind that we qualify by the
e   words "what it is," and I convinced myself that I was quite correct to

accept it. Therefore, I cannot accept the theory that the soul is a harmony either from myself or anyone else.

What of this, Simmias? Do you think it natural for a harmony, or any other composite, to be in a different state from that of the elements of which it is composed?

Not at all, said Simmias.

Nor, as I think, can it act or be acted upon in a different way than its elements?

He agreed.

One must therefore suppose that a harmony does not direct its components, but is directed by them.

He accepted this.

A harmony is therefore far from making a movement, or uttering a sound, or doing anything else, in a manner contrary to that of its parts.

Far from it indeed, he said.

Does not the nature of each harmony depend on the way it has been harmonized?

I do not understand, he said.

Will it not, if it is more and more fully harmonized, be more and more fully a harmony, and if it is less and less fully harmonized, it will be less and less fully a harmony?

Certainly.

Can this be true about the soul, that one soul is more and more fully a soul than another, or is less and less fully a soul, even to the smallest extent?

Not in any way.

Come now, by Zeus, he said. One soul is said to have intelligence and virtue and to be good, another to have folly and wickedness and to be bad. Are those things truly said?

They certainly are.

What will someone who holds the theory that the soul is a harmony say that those things are which reside in the soul, that is, virtue and wickedness? Are these some other harmony and disharmony? That the good soul is harmonized and, being a harmony, has within itself another harmony, whereas the evil soul is both itself a lack of harmony and has no other within itself?

I don't know what to say, said Simmias, but one who holds that assumption must obviously say something of that kind.

We have previously agreed, he said, that one soul is not more and not less a soul than another, and this means that one harmony is not more and more fully, or less and less fully, a harmony than another. Is that not so?

Certainly.

93

b

c

d

Now that which is no more and no less a harmony is not more or less harmonized. Is that so?

It is.

Can that which is neither more nor less harmonized partake more or less of harmony, or does it do so equally?

Equally.

e Then if a soul is neither more nor less a soul than another, it has been harmonized to the same extent?

This is so.

If that is so, it would have no greater share of disharmony or of harmony?

It would not.

That being the case, could one soul have more wickedness or virtue than another, if wickedness is disharmony and virtue harmony?

It could not.

94 But rather, Simmias, according to correct reasoning, no soul, if it is a harmony, will have any share of wickedness, for harmony is surely altogether this very thing, harmony, and would never share in disharmony.

It certainly would not.

Nor would a soul, being altogether this very thing, a soul, share in wickedness?

How could it, in view of what has been said?

So it follows from this argument that all the souls of all living creatures will be equally good, if souls are by nature equally this very thing, souls.

I think so, Socrates.

b Does our argument seem right, he said, and does it seem that it should have come to this, if the hypothesis that the soul is a harmony was correct?

Not in any way, he said.

Further, of all the parts of a man, can you mention any other part that rules him than his soul, especially if it is a wise soul?

I cannot.

Does it do so by following the affections of the body or by opposing them? I mean, for example, that when the body is hot and thirsty the soul draws him to the opposite, to not drinking; when the body is hungry, to

c not eating, and we see a thousand other examples of the soul opposing the affections of the body. Is that not so?

It certainly is.

On the other hand, we previously agreed that if the soul were a harmony, it would never be out of tune with the stress and relaxation and the striking of the strings or anything else done to its composing elements, but that it would follow and never direct them?

We did so agree, of course.

Well, does it now appear to do quite the opposite, ruling over all the

d elements of which one says it is composed, opposing nearly all of them

throughout life, directing all their ways, inflicting harsh and painful punishment on them, at times in physical culture and medicine, at other times
more gently by threats and exhortations, holding converse with desires
and passions and fears as if it were one thing talking to a different one, as
Homer wrote somewhere in the *Odyssey* where he says that Odysseus
"struck his breast and rebuked his heart saying, 'Endure, my heart, you
have endured worse than this.'"[11]

Do you think that when he composed this the poet thought that his soul   *e*
was a harmony, a thing to be directed by the affections of the body? Did he
not rather regard it as ruling over them and mastering them, itself a much
more divine thing than a harmony?

Yes, by Zeus, I think so, Socrates.

Therefore, my good friend, it is quite wrong for us to say that the soul is   95
a harmony, and in saying so we would disagree both with the divine poet
Homer and with ourselves.

That is so, he said.

Very well, said Socrates. Harmonia of Thebes seems somehow reasonably propitious to us. How and by what argument, my dear Cebes, can we
propitiate Cadmus?[12]

I think, Cebes said, that you will find a way. You dealt with the argument
about harmony in a manner that was quite astonishing to me. When
Simmias was speaking of his difficulties I was very much wondering   *b*
whether anyone would be able to deal with his argument, and I was quite
dumbfounded when right away he could not resist your argument's first
onslaught. I should not wonder therefore if that of Cadmus suffered the
same fate.

My good sir, said Socrates, do not boast, lest some malign influence
upset the argument we are about to make. However, we leave that to the
care of the god, but let us come to grips with it in the Homeric fashion, to
see if there is anything in what you say. The sum of your problem is this:
you consider that the soul must be proved to be immortal and indestruct-   *c*
ible before a philosopher on the point of death, who is confident that he will
fare much better in the underworld than if he had led any other kind of life,
can avoid being foolish and simpleminded in this confidence. To prove that
the soul is strong, that it is divine, that it existed before we were born as
men, all this, you say, does not show the soul to be immortal but only long-
lasting. That it existed for a very long time before, that it knew much and
acted much, makes it no more immortal because of that; indeed, its very   *d*
entering into a human body was the beginning of its destruction, like a

11. *Odyssey* xx.17–18.
12. Harmonia was in legend the wife of Cadmus, the founder of Thebes. Socrates'
punning joke is simply that, having dealt with Harmonia (harmony), we must now
deal with Cadmus (i.e., Cebes, the other Theban).

disease; it would live that life in distress and would in the end be destroyed in what we call death. You say it makes no difference whether it enters a body once or many times as far as the fear of each of us is concerned, for it is natural for a man who is no fool to be afraid, if he does not know and cannot prove that the soul is immortal. This, I think, is what you maintain, Cebes; I deliberately repeat it often, in order that no point may escape us, *e* and that you may add or subtract something if you wish.

And Cebes said: "There is nothing that I want to add or subtract at the moment. That is what I say."

Socrates paused for a long time, deep in thought. He then said: "This is *96* no unimportant problem that you raise, Cebes, for it requires a thorough investigation of the cause of generation and destruction. I will, if you wish, give you an account of my experience in these matters. Then if something I say seems useful to you, make use of it to persuade us of your position."

I surely do wish that, said Cebes.

Listen then, and I will, Cebes, he said. When I was a young man I was wonderfully keen on that wisdom which they call natural science, for I thought it splendid to know the causes of everything, why it comes to be, *b* why it perishes, and why it exists. I was often changing my mind in the investigation, in the first instance, of questions such as these: Are living creatures nurtured when heat and cold produce a kind of putrefaction, as some say? Do we think with our blood, or air, or fire, or none of these, and does the brain provide our senses of hearing and sight and smell, from which come memory and opinion, and from memory and opinion which has become stable, comes knowledge? Then again, as I investigated how these things perish and what happens to things in the sky and on the earth, *c* finally I became convinced that I have no natural aptitude at all for that kind of investigation, and of this I will give you sufficient proof. This investigation made me quite blind even to those things which I and others thought that I clearly knew before, so that I unlearned what I thought I knew before, about many other things and specifically about how men grew. I thought before that it was obvious to anybody that men grew *d* through eating and drinking, for food adds flesh to flesh and bones to bones, and in the same way appropriate parts were added to all other parts of the body, so that the man grew from an earlier small bulk to a large bulk later, and so a small man became big. That is what I thought then. Do you not think it was reasonable?

I do, said Cebes.

Then further consider this: I thought my opinion was satisfactory, that *e* when a large man stood by a small one he was taller by a head, and so a horse was taller than a horse. Even clearer than this, I thought that ten was more than eight because two had been added, and that a two-cubit length is larger than a cubit because it surpasses it by half its length.

And what do you think now about those things?

That I am far, by Zeus, from believing that I know the cause of any of those things. I will not even allow myself to say that where one is added to one, either the one to which it is added or the one that is added becomes two, or that the one added and the one to which it is added become two because of the addition of the one to the other. I wonder that, when each of them is separate from the other, each of them is one, nor are they then two, but that, when they come near to one another, this is the cause of their becoming two, the coming together and being placed closer to one another. Nor can I any longer be persuaded that when one thing is divided, this division is the cause of its becoming two, for just now the cause of becoming two was the opposite. At that time it was their coming close together and one was added to the other, but now it is because one is taken and separated from the other.

I do not any longer persuade myself that I know why a unit or anything else comes to be, or perishes or exists by the old method of investigation, and I do not accept it, but I have a confused method of my own. One day I heard someone reading, as he said, from a book of Anaxagoras, and saying that it is Mind that directs and is the cause of everything. I was delighted with this cause, and it seemed to me good, in a way, that Mind should be the cause of all. I thought that if this were so, the directing Mind would direct everything and arrange each thing in the way that was best. If then one wished to know the cause of each thing, why it comes to be or perishes or exists, one had to find what was the best way for it to be, or to be acted upon, or to act. On these premises, then, it befitted a man to investigate only, about this and other things, what is best. The same man must inevitably also know what is worse, for that is part of the same knowledge. As I reflected on this subject I was glad to think that I had found in Anaxagoras a teacher about the cause of things after my own heart, and that he would tell me, first, whether the earth is flat or round, and then would explain why it is so of necessity, saying which is better, and that it was better to be so. If he said it was in the middle of the universe, he would go on to show that it was better for it to be in the middle, and if he showed me those things I should be prepared never to desire any other kind of cause. I was ready to find out in the same way about the sun and the moon and the other heavenly bodies, about their relative speed, their turnings and whatever else happened to them, how it is best that each should act or be acted upon. I never thought that Anaxagoras, who said that those things were directed by Mind, would bring in any other cause for them than that it was best for them to be as they are. Once he had given the best for each as the cause for each and the general cause of all, I thought he would go on to explain the common good for all, and I would not have exchanged my hopes for a fortune. I eagerly acquired his books and read them as quickly as I could in order to know the best and the worst as soon as possible.

This wonderful hope was dashed as I went on reading and saw that the

man made no use of Mind, nor gave it any responsibility for the manage-
c   ment of things, but mentioned as causes air and ether and water and many
other strange things. That seemed to me much like saying that Socrates'
actions are all due to his mind, and then in trying to tell the causes of
everything I do, to say that the reason that I am sitting here is because my
body consists of bones and sinews, because the bones are hard and are
separated by joints, that the sinews are such as to contract and relax, that
d   they surround the bones along with flesh and skin which hold them together, then as the bones are hanging in their sockets, the relaxation and
contraction of the sinews enable me to bend my limbs, and that is the cause
of my sitting here with my limbs bent.

Again, he would mention other such causes for my talking to you:
sounds and air and hearing, and a thousand other such things, but he
would neglect to mention the true causes, that, after the Athenians decided
e   it was better to condemn me, for this reason it seemed best to me to sit here
and more right to remain and to endure whatever penalty they ordered.
For by the dog, I think these sinews and bones could long ago have been in
99   Megara or among the Boeotians, taken there by my belief as to the best
course, if I had not thought it more right and honorable to endure whatever
penalty the city ordered rather than escape and run away. To call those
things causes is too absurd. If someone said that without bones and sinews
and all such things, I should not be able to do what I decided, he would be
right, but surely to say that they are the cause of what I do, and not that I
have chosen the best course, even though I act with my mind, is to speak
b   very lazily and carelessly. Imagine not being able to distinguish the real
cause from that without which the cause would not be able to act as a cause.
It is what the majority appear to do, like people groping in the dark; they
call it a cause, thus giving it a name that does not belong to it. That is why
one man surrounds the earth with a vortex to make the heavens keep it in
c   place, another makes the air support it like a wide lid. As for their capacity
of being in the best place they could possibly be put, this they do not look
for, nor do they believe it to have any divine force, but they believe that
they will sometime discover a stronger and more immortal Atlas to hold
everything together more, and they do not believe that the truly good and
"binding" binds and holds them together. I would gladly become the
disciple of any man who taught the workings of that kind of cause. How-
d   ever, since I was deprived and could neither discover it myself nor learn it
from another, do you wish me to give you an explanation of how, as a
second-best, I busied myself with the search for the cause, Cebes?

I would wish it above all else, he said.

After this, he said, when I had wearied of investigating things, I thought
that I must be careful to avoid the experience of those who watch an eclipse
of the sun, for some of them ruin their eyes unless they watch its reflection
e   in water or some such material. A similar thought crossed my mind, and I

feared that my soul would be altogether blinded if I looked at things with my eyes and tried to grasp them with each of my senses.

So I thought I must take refuge in discussions and investigate the truth of things by means of words. However, perhaps this analogy is inadequate, for I certainly do not admit that one who investigates things by means of *100* words is dealing with images any more than one who looks at facts. However, I started in this manner: taking as my hypothesis in each case the theory that seemed to me the most compelling, I would consider as true, about cause and everything else, whatever agreed with this, and as untrue whatever did not so agree. But I want to put my meaning more clearly for I do not think that you understand me now.

No, by Zeus, said Cebes, not very well.

This, he said, is what I mean. It is nothing new, but what I have never *b* stopped talking about, both elsewhere and in the earlier part of our conversation. I am going to try to show you the kind of cause with which I have concerned myself. I turn back to those oft-mentioned things and proceed from them. I assume the existence of a Beautiful, itself by itself, of a Good and a Great and all the rest. If you grant me these and agree that they exist, I hope to show you the cause as a result, and to find the soul to be immortal.

Take it that I grant you this, said Cebes, and hasten to your conclusion. *c*

Consider then, he said, whether you share my opinion as to what follows, for I think that, if there is anything beautiful besides the Beautiful itself, it is beautiful for no other reason than that it shares in that Beautiful, and I say so with everything. Do you agree to this sort of cause?—I do.

I no longer understand or recognize those other sophisticated causes, *d* and if someone tells me that a thing is beautiful because it has a bright color or shape or any such thing, I ignore these other reasons—for all these confuse me—but I simply, naively, and perhaps foolishly cling to this, that nothing else makes it beautiful other than the presence of, or the sharing in, or however you may describe its relationship to that Beautiful we mentioned, for I will not insist on the precise nature of the relationship, but that all beautiful things are beautiful by the Beautiful. That, I think, is the safest answer I can give myself or anyone else. And if I stick to this I think I shall *e* never fall into error. This is the safe answer for me or anyone else to give, namely, that it is through Beauty that beautiful things are made beautiful. Or do you not think so too?—I do.

And that it is through Bigness that big things are big and the bigger are bigger, and that smaller things are made small by Smallness?—Yes.

And you would not accept the statement that one man is taller than another by a head and the shorter man shorter by the same, but you would *101* bear witness that you mean nothing else than that everything that is bigger is made bigger by nothing else than by Bigness, and that is the cause of its being bigger, and the smaller is made smaller only by Smallness and this is why it is smaller. I think you would be afraid that some opposite argument

would confront you if you said that someone is bigger or smaller by a head,
first, because the bigger is bigger and the smaller smaller by the same, then
b   because the bigger is bigger by a head which is small, and this would be
strange, namely, that someone is made bigger by something small. Would
you not be afraid of this?

I certainly would, said Cebes, laughing.

Then you would be afraid to say that ten is more than eight by two, and
that this is the cause of the excess, and not magnitude and because of
magnitude, or that two cubits is bigger than one cubit by half and not by
Bigness, for this is the same fear.—Certainly.

Then would you not avoid saying that when one is added to one it is the
c   addition and when it is divided it is the division that is the cause of two?
And you would loudly exclaim that you do not know how else each thing
can come to be except by sharing in the particular reality in which it shares,
and in these cases you do not know of any other cause of becoming two
except by sharing in Twoness, and that the things that are to be two must
share in this, as that which is to be one must share in Oneness, and you
would dismiss these additions and divisions and other such subtleties, and
leave them to those wiser than yourself to answer. But you, afraid, as they
d   say, of your own shadow and your inexperience, would cling to the safety
of your own hypothesis and give that answer. If someone then attacked
your hypothesis itself, you would ignore him and would not answer until
you had examined whether the consequences that follow from it agree with
one another or contradict one another.[13] And when you must give an
account of your hypothesis itself you will proceed in the same way: you
will assume another hypothesis, the one which seems to you best of the
e   higher ones until you come to something acceptable, but you will not
jumble the two as the debaters do by discussing the hypothesis and its
consequences at the same time, if you wish to discover any truth. This they
do not discuss at all nor give any thought to, but their wisdom enables
102   them to mix everything up and yet to be pleased with themselves, but if
you are a philosopher I think you will do as I say.

What you say is very true, said Simmias and Cebes together.

ECHECRATES: Yes, by Zeus, Phaedo, and they were right, I think he made
these things wonderfully clear to anyone of even small intelligence.

PHAEDO: Yes indeed, Echecrates, and all those present thought so too.

ECHECRATES: And so do we who were not present but hear of it now.
What was said after that?

PHAEDO: As I recall it, when the above had been accepted, and it was

13. Alternatively: "If someone should cling to your hypothesis itself, you would
dismiss him and would not answer until you had examined whether the consequences that follow from it agree with one another or contradict one another."

agreed that each of the Forms existed, and that other things acquired their   *b*
name by having a share in them, he followed this up by asking: if you say
these things are so, when you then say that Simmias is taller than Socrates
but shorter than Phaedo, do you not mean that there is in Simmias both
tallness and shortness?—I do.

But, he said, do you agree that the words of the statement "Simmias is
taller than Socrates" do not express the truth of the matter? It is not, surely,   *c*
the nature of Simmias to be taller than Socrates because he is Simmias but
because of the tallness he happens to have? Nor is he taller than Socrates
because Socrates is Socrates, but because Socrates has smallness compared
with the tallness of the other?—True.

Nor is he shorter than Phaedo because Phaedo is Phaedo, but because
Phaedo has tallness compared with the shortness of Simmias?—That is so.

So then Simmias is called both short and tall, being between the two,   *d*
presenting his shortness to be overcome by the tallness of one, and his
tallness to overcome the shortness of the other. He smilingly added, I seem
to be going to talk like a book, but it is as I say. The other agreed.

My purpose is that you may agree with me. Now it seems to me that not
only Tallness itself is never willing to be tall and short at the same time, but
also that the tallness in us will never admit the short or be overcome, but
one of two things happens: either it flees and retreats whenever its op-   *e*
posite, the short, approaches, or it is destroyed by its approach. It is not
willing to endure and admit shortness and be other than it was, whereas I
admit and endure shortness and still remain the same person and am this
short man. But Tallness, being tall, cannot venture to be small. In the same
way, the short in us is unwilling to become or to be tall ever, nor does any   *103*
other of the opposites become or be its opposite while still being what it
was; either it goes away or is destroyed when that happens.—I altogether
agree, said Cebes.

When he heard this, someone of those present—I have no clear memory
of who it was—said: "By the gods, did we not agree earlier in our discussion[14] to the very opposite of what is now being said, namely, that the
larger came from the smaller and the smaller from the larger, and that this
simply was how opposites came to be, from their opposites, but now I think
we are saying that this would never happen?"

On hearing this, Socrates inclined his head toward the speaker and said:
"You have bravely reminded us, but you do not understand the difference
between what is said now and what was said then, which was that an   *b*
opposite thing came from an opposite thing; now we say that the opposite
itself could never become opposite to itself, neither that in us nor that in
nature. Then, my friend, we were talking of things that have opposite

14. The reference is to 70d–71a above.

qualities and naming these after them, but now we say that these opposites themselves, from the presence of which in them things get their name,

c never can tolerate the coming to be from one another." At the same time he looked to Cebes and said: "Does anything of what this man says also disturb you?"

Not at the moment, said Cebes, but I do not deny that many things do disturb me.

We are altogether agreed then, he said, that an opposite will never be opposite to itself.—Entirely agreed.

Consider then whether you will agree to this further point. There is something you call hot and something you call cold.—There is.

d Are they the same as what you call snow and fire?—By Zeus, no.

So the hot is something other than fire, and the cold is something other than snow?—Yes.

You think, I believe, that being snow it will not admit the hot, as we said before, and remain what it was and be both snow and hot, but when the hot approaches it will either retreat before it or be destroyed.—Quite so.

So fire, as the cold approaches, will either go away or be destroyed; it will never venture to admit coldness and remain what it was, fire and

e cold.—What you say is true.

It is true then about some of these things that not only the Form itself deserves its own name for all time, but there is something else that is not the Form but has its character whenever it exists. Perhaps I can make my meaning clearer: the Odd must always be given this name we now mention. Is that not so?—Certainly.

104 Is it the only one of existing things to be called odd?—this is my question—or is there something else than the Odd which one must nevertheless also always call odd, as well as by its own name, because it is such by nature as never to be separated from the Odd? I mean, for example, the number three and many others. Consider three: do you not think that it must always be called both by its own name and by that of the Odd, which is not the same as three? That is the nature of three, and of five, and of half of

b all the numbers; each of them is odd, but it is not the Odd. Then again, two and four and the whole other column of numbers; each of them, while not being the same as the Even, is always even. Do you not agree?—Of course.

Look now. What I want to make clear is this: not only do those opposites not admit each other, but this is also true of those things which, while not being opposite to each other yet always contain the opposites, and it seems that these do not admit that Form which is opposite to that which is in

c them; when it approaches them, they either perish or give way. Shall we not say that three will perish or undergo anything before, while remaining three, becoming even?—Certainly, said Cebes.

Yet surely two is not the opposite of three?—Indeed it is not.

It is then not only opposite Forms that do not admit each other's approach, but also some other things that do not admit the onset of opposites.—Very true.

Do you then want us, if we can, to define what these are?—I surely do.

Would they be the things that compel whatever they occupy not only *d* to contain their form but also always that of some opposite?—How do you mean?

As we were saying just now, you surely know that what the Form of three occupies must be not only three but also odd.—Certainly.

And we say that the opposite Form to the Form that achieves this result could never come to it.—It could not.

Now it is Oddness that has done this?—Yes.

And opposite to this is the Form of the Even?—Yes.

So then the Form of the Even will never come to three?—Never. *e*

Then three has no share in the Even?—Never.

So three is uneven?—Yes.

As for what I said we must define, that is, what kind of things, while not being opposites to something, yet do not admit the opposite, as for example the triad, though it is not the opposite of the Even, yet does not admit it because it always brings along the opposite of the Even, and so the dyad in *105* relation to the Odd, fire to the Cold, and very many other things, see whether you would define it thus: not only does the opposite not admit its opposite, but that which brings along some opposite into that which it occupies, that which brings this along will not admit the opposite to that which it brings along. Refresh your memory, it is no worse for being heard often. Five does not admit the form of the Even, nor will ten, its double, admit the form of the Odd. The double itself is an opposite of something else, yet it will not admit the form of the Odd. Nor do one-and-a-half and other such fractions admit the form of the Whole, nor will one-third, and *b* so on, if you follow me and agree to this.

I certainly agree, he said, and I follow you.

Tell me again from the beginning, he said, and do not answer in the words of the question, but do as I do. I say that beyond that safe answer, which I spoke of first, I see another safe answer. If you should ask me what, coming into a body, makes it hot, my reply would not be that safe *c* and ignorant one, that it is heat, but our present argument provides a more sophisticated answer, namely, fire, and if you ask me what, on coming into a body, makes it sick, I will not say sickness but fever. Nor, if asked the presence of what in a number makes it odd, I will not say oddness but oneness, and so with other things. See if you now sufficiently understand what I want.—Quite sufficiently.

Answer me then, he said, what is it that, present in a body, makes it living?—A soul.

d   And is that always so?—Of course.

Whatever the soul occupies, it always brings life to it?—It does.

Is there, or is there not, an opposite to life?—There is.

What is it?—Death.

So the soul will never admit the opposite of that which it brings along, as we agree from what has been said?

Most certainly, said Cebes.

Well, and what do we call that which does not admit the form of the even?—The uneven.

What do we call that which will not admit the just and that which will not admit the musical?

e   The unmusical, and the other the unjust.

Very well, what do we call that which does not admit death?

The deathless, he said.

Now the soul does not admit death?—No.

So the soul is deathless?—It is.

Very well, he said. Shall we say that this has been proved, do you think?

Quite adequately proved, Socrates.

Well now, Cebes, he said, if the uneven were of necessity indestructible,

106   surely three would be indestructible?—Of course.

And if the nonhot were of necessity indestructible, then whenever anyone brought heat to snow, the snow would retreat safe and unthawed, for it could not be destroyed, nor again could it stand its ground and admit the heat?—What you say is true.

In the same way, if the noncold were indestructible, then when some cold attacked the fire, it would neither be quenched nor be destroyed, but retreat safely.—Necessarily.

b   Must then the same not be said of the deathless? If the deathless is also indestructible, it is impossible for the soul to be destroyed when death comes upon it. For it follows from what has been said that it will not admit death or be dead, just as three, we said, will not be even nor will the odd; nor will fire be cold, nor the heat that is in the fire. But, someone might say,

c   what prevents the odd, while not becoming even as has been agreed, from being destroyed, and the even to come to be instead? We could not maintain against the man who said this that it is not destroyed, for the uneven is not indestructible. If we had agreed that it was indestructible we could easily have maintained that at the coming of the even, the odd and the three have gone away and the same would hold for fire and the hot and the other things.—Surely.

d   And so now, if we are agreed that the deathless is indestructible, the soul, besides being deathless, is indestructible. If not, we need another argument.

—There is no need for one as far as that goes, for hardly anything could resist destruction if the deathless, which lasts forever, would admit destruction.

All would agree, said Socrates, that the god, and the Form of life itself, and anything that is deathless, are never destroyed.—All men would agree, by Zeus, to that, and the gods, I imagine, even more so.

If the deathless is indestructible, then the soul, if it is deathless, would   *e* also be indestructible?—Necessarily.

Then when death comes to man, the mortal part of him dies, it seems, but his deathless part goes away safe and indestructible, yielding the place to death.—So it appears.

Therefore the soul, Cebes, he said, is most certainly deathless and inde-   *107* structible and our souls will really dwell in the underworld.

I have nothing more to say against that, Socrates, said Cebes, nor can I doubt your arguments. If Simmias here or someone else has something to say, he should not remain silent, for I do not know to what further occasion other than the present he could put it off if he wants to say or to hear anything on these subjects.

Certainly, said Simmias, I myself have no remaining grounds for doubt after what has been said; nevertheless, in view of the importance of our subject and my low opinion of human weakness, I am bound still to have   *b* some private misgivings about what we have said.

You are not only right to say this, Simmias, Socrates said, but our first hypotheses require clearer examination, even though we find them convincing. And if you analyze them adequately, you will, I think, follow the argument as far as a man can, and if the conclusion is clear, you will look no further.—That is true.

It is right to think then, gentlemen, that if the soul is immortal, it re-   *c* quires our care not only for the time we call our life, but for the sake of all time, and that one is in terrible danger if one does not give it that care. If death were escape from everything, it would be a great boon to the wicked to get rid of the body and of their wickedness together with their soul. But now that the soul appears to be immortal, there is no escape from evil or   *d* salvation for it except by becoming as good and wise as possible, for the soul goes to the underworld possessing nothing but its education and upbringing, which are said to bring the greatest benefit or harm to the dead right at the beginning of the journey yonder.

We are told that when each person dies, the guardian spirit who was allotted to him in life proceeds to lead him to a certain place, whence those who have been gathered together there must, after being judged, proceed   *e* to the underworld with the guide who has been appointed to lead them thither from here. Having there undergone what they must and stayed there the appointed time, they are led back here by another guide after

108 long periods of time. The journey is not as Aeschylus' Telephus[15] describes it. He says that only one single path leads to Hades, but I think it is neither one nor simple, for then there would be no need of guides; one could not make any mistake if there were but one path. As it is, it is likely to have many forks and crossroads; and I base this judgment on the sacred rites and customs here.

The well-ordered and wise soul follows the guide and is not without familiarity with its surroundings, but the soul that is passionately attached

b to the body, as I said before, hovers around it and the visible world for a long time, struggling and suffering much until it is led away by force and with difficulty by its appointed spirit. When the impure soul which has performed some impure deed joins the others after being involved in unjust killings, or committed other crimes which are akin to these and are actions of souls of this kind, everybody shuns it and turns away, unwilling

c to be its fellow traveler or its guide; such a soul wanders alone completely at a loss until a certain time arrives and it is forcibly led to its proper dwelling place. On the other hand, the soul that has led a pure and moderate life finds fellow travelers and gods to guide it, and each of them dwells in a place suited to it.

There are many strange places upon the earth, and the earth itself is not such as those who are used to discourse upon it believe it to be in nature or size, as someone has convinced me.

d Simmias said: "What do you mean, Socrates? I have myself heard many things said about the earth, but certainly not the things that convince you. I should be glad to hear them."

Indeed, Simmias, I do not think it requires the skill of Glaucus[16] to tell you what they are, but to prove them true requires more than that skill, and I should perhaps not be able to do so. Also, even if I had the knowl-

e edge, my remaining time would not be long enough to tell the tale. However, nothing prevents my telling you what I am convinced is the shape of the earth and what its regions are.

Even that is sufficient, said Simmias.

109 Well then, he said, the first thing of which I am convinced is that if the earth is a sphere in the middle of the heavens, it has no need of air or any other force to prevent it from falling. The homogeneous nature of the heavens on all sides and the earth's own equipoise are sufficient to hold it, for an object balanced in the middle of something homogeneous will have no tendency to incline more in any direction than any other but will remain unmoved. This, he said, is the first point of which I am persuaded.

And rightly so, said Simmias.

15. The *Telephus* of Aeschylus is not extant.
16. This is a proverbial expression whose origin is obscure.

Further, the earth is very large, and we live around the sea in a small portion of it between Phasis and the pillars of Heracles, like ants or frogs *b* around a swamp; many other peoples live in many such parts of it. Everywhere about the earth there are numerous hollows of many kinds and shapes and sizes into which the water and the mist and the air have gathered. The earth itself is pure and lies in the pure sky where the stars are situated, which the majority of those who discourse on these subjects *c* call the ether. The water and mist and air are the sediment of the ether, and they always flow into the hollows of the earth. We, who dwell in the hollows of it, are unaware of this, and we think that we live above, on the surface of the earth. It is as if someone who lived deep down in the middle of the ocean thought he was living on its surface. Seeing the sun and the other heavenly bodies through the water, he would think the sea to be the *d* sky; because he is slow and weak, he has never reached the surface of the sea or risen with his head above the water or come out of the sea to our region here, nor seen how much purer and more beautiful it is than his own region, nor has he ever heard of it from anyone who has seen it.

Our experience is the same: living in a certain hollow of the earth, we believe that we live upon its surface; the air we call the heavens, as if the stars made their way through it; this too is the same: because of our weakness and slowness we are not able to make our way to the upper limit *e* of the air; if anyone got to this upper limit, if anyone came to it or reached it on wings and his head rose above it, then just as fish on rising from the sea see things in our region, he would see things there and, if his nature could endure to contemplate them, he would know that there is the true heaven, the true light, and the true earth, for the earth here, these stones and the *110* whole region, are spoiled and eaten away, just as things in the sea are by the salt water.

Nothing worth mentioning grows in the sea, nothing, one might say, is fully developed; there are caves and sand and endless slime and mud wherever there is earth—not comparable in any way with the beauties of our region. So those things above are in their turn far superior to the things we know. Indeed, if this is the moment to tell a tale, Simmias, it is worth *b* hearing about the nature of things on the surface of the earth under the heavens.

At any rate, Socrates, said Simmias, we should be glad to hear this story.

Well then, my friend, in the first place it is said that the earth, looked at from above, looks like those spherical balls made up of twelve pieces of leather; it is multicolored, and of these colors those used by our painters give us an indication; up there the whole earth has these colors, but much *c* brighter and purer than these; one part is sea-green and of marvelous beauty, another is golden, another is white, whiter than chalk or snow; the earth is composed also of the other colors, more numerous and beautiful than any we have seen. The very hollows of the earth, full of water and air, *d*   gleaming among the variety of other colors, present a color of their own so that the whole is seen as a continuum of variegated colors. On the surface of the earth the plants grow with corresponding beauty, the trees and the flowers and the fruits, and so with the hills and the stones, more beautiful in their smoothness and transparency and color. Our precious stones here

e   are but fragments, our cornelians, jaspers, emeralds, and the rest. All stones there are of that kind, and even more beautiful. The reason is that there they are pure, not eaten away or spoiled by decay and brine, or corroded by the water and air which have flowed into the hollows here and bring ugliness and disease upon earth, stones, the other animals, and

111 plants. The earth itself is adorned with all these things, and also with gold and silver and other metals. These stand out, being numerous and massive and occurring everywhere, so that the earth is a sight for the blessed. There are many other living creatures upon the earth, and also men, some living inland, others at the edge of the air, as we live on the edge of the sea, others again live on islands surrounded by air close to the mainland. In a word,

b   what water and the sea are to us, the air is to them, and the ether is to them what the air is to us. The climate is such that they are without disease, and they live much longer than people do here; their eyesight, hearing, and intelligence and all such are as superior to ours as air is superior to water and ether to air in purity; they have groves and temples dedicated to the gods, in which the gods really dwell, and they communicate with them by

c   speech and prophecy and by the sight of them; they see the sun and moon and stars as they are, and in other ways their happiness is in accord with this.

This then is the nature of the earth as a whole and of its surroundings; around the whole of it there are many regions in the hollows; some are deeper and more open than that in which we live; others are deeper and

d   have a narrower opening than ours, and there are some that have less depth and more width. All these are connected with each other below the surface of the earth in many places by narrow and broader channels, and thus have outlets through which much water flows from one to another as into mixing bowls; huge rivers of both hot and cold water thus flow beneath the earth eternally, much fire and large rivers of fire, and many of

e   wet mud, both more pure and more muddy, such as those flowing in advance of the lava and the stream of lava itself in Sicily. These streams then fill up every and all regions as the flow reaches each, and all these places move up and down with the oscillating movement of the earth. The natural cause of the oscillation is as follows: one of the hollows of the earth,

112 which is also the biggest, pierces through the whole earth; it is that which Homer mentioned when he said: "Far down where is the deepest pit below the earth . . . ,"[17] and which he elsewhere, and many other poets,

17. *Iliad* viii.14; cf. viii.481.

call Tartarus; into this chasm all the rivers flow together, and again flow
out of it, and each river is affected by the nature of the land through which   *b*
it flows. The reason for their flowing into and out of Tartarus is that this
water has no bottom or solid base, but it oscillates up and down in waves,
and the air and wind about it do the same, for they follow it when it flows
to this or that part of the earth. Just as when people breathe, the flow of air
goes in and out, so here the air oscillates with the water and creates terrible
winds as it goes in and out. Whenever the water retreats to what we call   *c*
the lower part of the earth, it flows into those parts and fills them up as if
the water were pumped in; when it leaves that part for this, it fills these
parts again, and the parts filled flow through the channels and through the
earth and in each case arrive at the places to which the channels lead and
create seas and marshes and rivers and springs. From there the waters
flow under the earth again, some flowing around larger and more nu-   *d*
merous regions, some around smaller and shallower ones, then flow back
into Tartarus, some at a point much lower than where they issued forth,
others only a little way, but all of them at a lower point, some of them at the
opposite side of the chasm, some on the same side; some flow in a wide
circle around the earth once or many times like snakes, then go as far
down as possible, then go back into the chasm of Tartarus. From each side
it is possible to flow down as far as the center, but not beyond, for this part   *e*
that faces the river flow from either side is steep.

There are many other large rivers of all kinds, and among these there
are four of note; the biggest which flows on the outside (of the earth) in a
circle is called Oceanus; opposite it and flowing in the opposite direction is
the Acheron; it flows through many other deserted regions and further   *113*
underground makes its way to the Acherusian lake to which the souls of
the majority come after death and, after remaining there for a certain
appointed time, longer for some, shorter for others, they are sent back to
birth as living creatures. The third river issues between the first two, and
close to its source it falls into a region burning with much fire and makes a
lake larger than our sea, boiling with water and mud. From there it goes in   *b*
a circle, foul and muddy, and winding on its way it comes, among other
places, to the edge of the Acherusian lake but does not mingle with its
waters; then, coiling many times underground it flows lower down into
Tartarus; this is called the Pyriphlegethon, and its lava streams throw off
fragments of it in various parts of the earth. Opposite this the fourth river   *c*
issues forth, which is called Stygion, and it is said to flow first into a
terrible and wild region, all of it blue-gray in color, and the lake that
this river forms by flowing into it is called the Styx. As its waters fall
into the lake they acquire dread powers; then diving below and winding around it flows in the opposite direction from the Pyriphlegethon
and into the opposite side of the Acherusian lake; its waters do not
mingle with any other; it too flows in a circle and into Tartarus opposite

the Pyriphlegethon. The name of that fourth river, the poets tell us, is Cocytus.[18]

d   Such is the nature of these things. When the dead arrive at the place to which each has been led by his guardian spirit, they are first judged as to whether they have led a good and pious life. Those who have lived an average life make their way to the Acheron and embark upon such vessels as there are for them and proceed to the lake. There they dwell and are

e   purified by penalties for any wrongdoing they may have committed; they are also suitably rewarded for their good deeds as each deserves. Those who are deemed incurable because of the enormity of their crimes, having committed many great sacrileges or wicked and unlawful murders and other such wrongs—their fitting fate is to be hurled into Tartarus never to emerge from it. Those who are deemed to have committed great but curable crimes, such as doing violence to their father or mother in a fit of

114 temper, but who have felt remorse for the rest of their lives, or who have killed someone in a similar manner, these must of necessity be thrown into Tartarus, but a year later the current throws them out, those who are guilty of murder by way of Cocytus, and those who have done violence to their parents by way of the Pyriphlegethon. After they have been carried along to the Acherusian lake, they cry out and shout, some for those they have

b   killed, others for those they have maltreated, and calling them they then pray to them and beg them to allow them to step out into the lake and to receive them. If they persuade them, they do step out and their punishment comes to an end; if they do not, they are taken back into Tartarus and from there into the rivers, and this does not stop until they have persuaded those they have wronged, for this is the punishment which the judges imposed on them.

c   Those who are deemed to have lived an extremely pious life are freed and released from the regions of the earth as from a prison; they make their way up to a pure dwelling place and live on the surface of the earth. Those who have purified themselves sufficiently by philosophy live in the future altogether without a body; they make their way to even more beautiful dwelling places which it is hard to describe clearly, nor do we now have the time to do so. Because of the things we have enunciated, Simmias, one must make every effort to share in virtue and wisdom in one's life, for the reward is beautiful and the hope is great.

d   No sensible man would insist that these things are as I have described them, but I think it is fitting for a man to risk the belief—for the risk is a noble one—that this, or something like this, is true about our souls and their dwelling places, since the soul is evidently immortal, and a man should repeat this to himself as if it were an incantation, which is why I

18. For these features of the underworld, see *Odyssey* x.511 ff., xi.157.

have been prolonging my tale. That is the reason why a man should be of good cheer about his own soul, if during life he has ignored the pleasures *e* of the body and its ornamentation as of no concern to him and doing him more harm than good, but has seriously concerned himself with the pleasures of learning, and adorned his soul not with alien but with its own ornaments, namely, moderation, righteousness, courage, freedom, and *115* truth, and in that state awaits his journey to the underworld.

Now you, Simmias, Cebes, and the rest of you, Socrates continued, will each take that journey at some other time, but my fated day calls me now, as a tragic character might say, and it is about time for me to have my bath, for I think it better to have it before I drink the poison and save the women the trouble of washing the corpse.

When Socrates had said this Crito spoke. Very well, Socrates, what are *b* your instructions to me and the others about your children or anything else? What can we do that would please you most?—Nothing new, Crito, said Socrates, but what I am always saying, that you will please me and mine and yourselves by taking good care of your own selves in whatever you do, even if you do not agree with me now, but if you neglect your own selves, and are unwilling to live following the tracks, as it were, of what we *c* have said now and on previous occasions, you will achieve nothing even if you strongly agree with me at this moment.

We shall be eager to follow your advice, said Crito, but how shall we bury you?

In any way you like, said Socrates, if you can catch me and I do not escape you. And laughing quietly, looking at us, he said: I do not convince Crito that I am this Socrates talking to you here and ordering all I say, but he *d* thinks that I am the thing which he will soon be looking at as a corpse, and so he asks how he shall bury me. I have been saying for some time and at some length that after I have drunk the poison I shall no longer be with you but will leave you to go and enjoy some good fortunes of the blessed, but it seems that I have said all this to him in vain in an attempt to reassure you and myself too. Give a pledge to Crito on my behalf, he said, the opposite pledge to that he gave the jury. He pledged that I would stay; you must *e* pledge that I will not stay after I die, but that I shall go away, so that Crito will bear it more easily when he sees my body being burned or buried and will not be angry on my behalf, as if I were suffering terribly, and so that he should not say at the funeral that he is laying out, or carrying out, or burying Socrates. For know you well, my dear Crito, that to express oneself badly is not only faulty as far as the language goes, but does some harm to the soul. You must be of good cheer, and say you are burying my body, and *116* bury it in any way you like and think most customary.

After saying this he got up and went to another room to take his bath, and Crito followed him and he told us to wait for him. So we stayed,

talking among ourselves, questioning what had been said, and then again
b   talking of the great misfortune that had befallen us. We all felt as if we had
lost a father and would be orphaned for the rest of our lives. When
he had washed, his children were brought to him—two of his sons
were small and one was older—and the women of his household came to
him.

He spoke to them before Crito and gave them what instructions he
wanted.

Then he sent the women and children away, and he himself joined us. It
was now close to sunset, for he had stayed inside for some time. He came
and sat down after his bath and conversed for a short while, when the
c   officer of the Eleven came and stood by him and said: "I shall not reproach
you as I do the others, Socrates. They are angry with me and curse me
when, obeying the orders of my superiors, I tell them to drink the poison.

"During the time you have been here I have come to know you in other
ways as the noblest, the gentlest, and the best man who has ever come
here. So now too I know that you will not make trouble for me; you know
who is responsible, and you will direct your anger against them. You
know what message I bring. Fare you well, and try to endure what you
d   must as easily as possible." The officer was weeping as he turned away
and went out. Socrates looked up at him and said: "Fare you well also; we
shall do as you bid us." And turning to us he said: "How pleasant the man
is! During the whole time I have been here he has come in and conversed
with me from time to time, a most agreeable man. And how genuinely he
now weeps for me. Come, Crito, let us obey him. Let someone bring the
poison if it is ready; if not, let the man prepare it."

e   But Socrates, said Crito, I think the sun still shines upon the hills and
has not yet set. I know that others drink the poison quite a long time after
they have received the order, eating and drinking quite a bit, and some of
them enjoy intimacy with their loved ones. Do not hurry; there is still some
time.

It is natural, Crito, for them to do so, said Socrates, for they think they
117   derive some benefit from doing this, but it is not fitting for me. I do not
expect any benefit from drinking the poison a little later, except to become
ridiculous in my own eyes for clinging to life, and be sparing of it when
there is none left. So do as I ask and do not refuse me.

Hearing this, Crito nodded to the slave who was standing near him; the
slave went out and after a time came back with the man who was to
administer the poison, carrying it made ready in a cup. When Socrates saw
him he said: "Well, my good man, you are an expert in this; what must one
b   do?"—"Just drink it and walk around until your legs feel heavy, and then
lie down and it will act of itself." And he offered the cup to Socrates, who
took it quite cheerfully, Echecrates, without a tremor or any change of

feature or color, but looking at the man from under his eyebrows as was his wont, asked: "What do you say about pouring a libation from this drink? It is allowed?"—"We only mix as much as we believe will suffice," said the man.

I understand, Socrates said, but one is allowed, indeed one must, utter a   c prayer to the gods that the journey from here to yonder may be fortunate. This is my prayer and may it be so.

And while he was saying this, he was holding the cup, and then drained it calmly and easily. Most of us had been able to hold back our tears reasonably well up until then, but when we saw him drinking it and after he drank it, we could hold them back no longer; my own tears came in floods against my will. So I covered my face. I was weeping for myself, not for him—for my misfortune in being deprived of such a comrade. Even   d before me, Crito was unable to restrain his tears and got up. Apollodorus had not ceased from weeping before, and at this moment his noisy tears and anger made everybody present break down, except Socrates. "What is this," he said, "you strange fellows. It is mainly for this reason that I sent the women away, to avoid such unseemliness, for I am told one should die   e in good-omened silence. So keep quiet and control yourselves."

His words made us ashamed, and we checked our tears. He walked around, and when he said his legs were heavy he lay on his back as he had been told to do, and the man who had given him the poison touched his body, and after a while tested his feet and legs, pressed hard upon his foot and asked him if he felt this, and Socrates said no. Then he pressed his   118 calves, and made his way up his body and showed us that it was cold and stiff. He felt it himself and said that when the cold reached his heart he would be gone. As his belly was getting cold Socrates uncovered his head—he had covered it—and said—these were his last words—"Crito, we owe a cock to Asclepius;[19] make this offering to him and do not forget."—"It shall be done," said Crito, "tell us if there is anything else." But there was no answer. Shortly afterward Socrates made a movement; the man uncovered him, and his eyes were fixed. Seeing this Crito closed his mouth and his eyes.

Such was the end of our comrade, Echecrates, a man who, we would say, was of all those we have known the best, and also the wisest and the most upright.

---

19. A cock was sacrificed to Asclepius by the sick people who slept in his temples, hoping for a cure. Socrates apparently means that death is a cure for the ills of life.

SYMPOSIUM

172   APOLLODORUS: In fact, your question does not find me unprepared. Just the other day, as it happens, I was walking to the city from my home in Phaleron when a man I know, who was making his way behind me, saw me and called from a distance:

"The gentleman from Phaleron!" he yelled, trying to be funny. "Hey, Apollodorus, wait!"

So I stopped and waited.

b   "Apollodorus, I've been looking for you!" he said. "You know there once was a gathering at Agathon's when Socrates, Alcibiades, and their friends had dinner together; I wanted to ask you about the speeches they made on Love. What were they? I heard a version from a man who had it from Phoenix, Philip's son, but it was badly garbled, and he said you were the one to ask. So please, will you tell me all about it? After all, Socrates is your friend—who has a better right than you to report his conversation? But before you begin," he added, "tell me this: were you there yourself?"

c   "Your friend must have really garbled his story," I replied, "if you think this affair was so recent that I could have been there."

"I did think that," he said.

173   "Glaucon, how could you? You know very well Agathon hasn't lived in Athens for many years, while it's been less than three that I've been Socrates' companion and made it my job to know exactly what he says and does each day. Before that, I simply drifted aimlessly. Of course, I used to think that what I was doing was important, but in fact I was the most worthless man on earth—as bad as you are this very moment: I used to think philosophy was the last thing a man should do."

"Stop joking, Apollodorus," he replied. "Just tell me when the party took place."

"When we were still children, when Agathon won the prize with his first tragedy. It was the day after he and his troupe held their victory celebration."

"So it really was a long time ago," he said. "Then who told you about it? Was it Socrates himself?"

b   "Oh, for god's sake, of course not!" I replied. "It was the very same man who told Phoenix, a fellow called Aristodemus, from Cydatheneum, a real

Translated by Alexander Nehamas and Paul Woodruff.

320

runt of a man, who always went barefoot. He went to the party because, I think, he was obsessed with Socrates—one of the worst cases at that time. Naturally, I checked part of his story with Socrates, and Socrates agreed with his account."

"Please tell me, then," he said. "You speak and I'll listen, as we walk to the city. This is the perfect opportunity."

So this is what we talked about on our way; and that's why, as I said *c* before, I'm not unprepared. Well, if I'm to tell *you* about it too—I'll be glad to. After all, my greatest pleasure comes from philosophical conversation, even if I'm only a listener, whether or not I think it will be to my advantage. All other talk, especially the talk of rich businessmen like you, bores me to tears, and I'm sorry for you and your friends because you think your affairs are important when really they're totally trivial. Perhaps, in your *d* turn, you think I'm a failure, and, believe me, I think that what you think is true. But as for all of you, I don't just *think* you are failures—I know it for a fact.

FRIEND: You'll never change, Apollodorus! Always nagging, even at yourself! I do believe you think everybody—yourself first of all—is totally worthless, except, of course, Socrates. I don't know exactly how you came to be called "the maniac," but you certainly talk like one, always furious with everyone, including yourself—but not with Socrates!

APOLLODORUS: Of course, my dear friend, it's perfectly obvious why I *e* have these views about us all: it's simply because I'm a maniac, and I'm raving!

FRIEND: It's not worth arguing about this now, Apollodorus. Please do as I asked: tell me the speeches.

APOLLODORUS: All right . . . Well, the speeches went something like this—but I'd better tell you the whole story from the very beginning, as *174* Aristodemus told it to me.

He said, then, that one day he ran into Socrates, who had just bathed and put on his fancy sandals—both very unusual events. So he asked him where he was going, and why he was looking so good.

Socrates replied, "I'm going to Agathon's for dinner. I managed to avoid yesterday's victory party—I really don't like crowds—but I promised to be there today. So, naturally, I took great pains with my appearance: I'm going to the house of a good-looking man; I had to look my best. But let me ask you this," he added. "I know you haven't been invited to the dinner; how would you like to come anyway?" *b*

And Aristodemus answered, "I'll do whatever you say."

"Come with me, then," Socrates said, "and we shall prove the proverb wrong; the truth is, 'Good men go uninvited to Goodman's feast.'[1] Even

---

1. Agathon's name could be translated "Goodman." The proverb is "Good men go uninvited to an inferior man's feast" (Eupolis frg. 289 Kock).

Homer himself, when you think about it, did not much like this proverb;
c   he not only disregarded it, he violated it. Agamemnon, of course, is one of
his great warriors, while he describes Menelaus as a 'limp spearman.' And
yet, when Agamemnon offers a sacrifice and gives a feast, Homer has the
weak Menelaus arrive uninvited at his superior's table."[2]

Aristodemus replied to this, "Socrates, I am afraid Homer's description
is bound to fit me better than yours. Mine is a case of an obvious inferior
arriving uninvited at the table of a man of letters. I think you'd better
figure out a good excuse for bringing me along, because, you know, I
d   won't admit I've come without an invitation. I'll say I'm your guest."

"Let's go," he said. "We'll think about what to say 'as we proceed the
two of us along the way.' "[3]

With these words, they set out. But as they were walking, Socrates began
to think about something, lost himself in thought, and kept lagging behind.
Whenever Aristodemus stopped to wait for him, Socrates would urge him
e   to go on ahead. When he arrived at Agathon's he found the gate wide open,
and that, Aristodemus said, caused him to find himself in a very embar-
rassing situation: a household slave saw him the moment he arrived and
took him immediately to the dining room, where the guests were already
lying down on their couches, and dinner was about to be served.

As soon as Agathon saw him, he called: "Welcome, Aristodemus! What
perfect timing! You're just in time for dinner! I hope you're not here for any
other reason—if you are, forget it. I looked all over for you yesterday, so I
could invite you, but I couldn't find you anywhere. But where is Socrates?
How come you didn't bring him along?"

So I turned around (Aristodemus said), and Socrates was nowhere to be
seen. And I said that it was actually Socrates who had brought *me* along as
his guest.
175   "I'm delighted he did," Agathon replied. "But where is he?"

"He was directly behind me, but I have no idea where he is now."

"Go look for Socrates," Agathon ordered a slave, "and bring him in.
Aristodemus," he added, "you can share Eryximachus' couch."

A slave brought water, and Aristodemus washed himself before he lay
down. Then another slave entered and said: "Socrates is here, but he's
gone off to the neighbor's porch. He's standing there and won't come in
even though I called him several times."

"How strange," Agathon replied. "Go back and bring him in. Don't
leave him there."

---

2. Menelaus calls on Agamemnon at *Iliad* ii.408. Menelaus is called a limp spearman at xvii.587–88.
3. An allusion to *Iliad* x.224, "When two go together, one has an idea before the
other."

But Aristodemus stopped him. "No, no," he said. "Leave him alone. It's   *b*
one of his habits: every now and then he just goes off like that and stands
motionless, wherever he happens to be. I'm sure he'll come in very soon,
so don't disturb him; let him be."

"Well, all right, if you really think so," Agathon said, and turned to the
slaves: "Go ahead and serve the rest of us. What you serve is completely
up to you; pretend nobody's supervising you—as if I ever did! Imagine
that we are all your own guests, myself included. Give us good reason to   *c*
praise your service."

So they went ahead and started eating, but there was still no sign of
Socrates. Agathon wanted to send for him many times, but Aristodemus
wouldn't let him. And, in fact, Socrates came in shortly afterward, as he
always did—they were hardly halfway through their meal. Agathon,
who, as it happened, was all alone on the farthest couch, immediately
called: "Socrates, come lie down next to me. Who knows, if I touch you, I   *d*
may catch a bit of the wisdom that came to you under my neighbor's
porch. It's clear *you've* seen the light. If you hadn't, you'd still be standing
there."

Socrates sat down next to him and said, "How wonderful it would be,
dear Agathon, if the foolish were filled with wisdom simply by touching
the wise. If only wisdom were like water, which always flows from a full
cup into an empty one when we connect them with a piece of yarn—well,   *e*
then I would consider it the greatest prize to have the chance to lie down
next to you. I would soon be overflowing with your wonderful wisdom.
My own wisdom is of no account—a shadow in a dream—while yours
is bright and radiant and has a splendid future. Why, young as you
are, you're so brilliant I could call more than thirty thousand Greeks as
witnesses."

"Now you've gone *too* far, Socrates," Agathon replied. "Well, eat your
dinner. Dionysus will soon enough be the judge of our claims to wisdom!"[4]   *176*

Socrates took his seat after that and had his meal, according to Aristodemus. When dinner was over, they poured a libation to the god, sang a
hymn, and—in short—followed the whole ritual. Then they turned their
attention to drinking. At that point Pausanias addressed the group:

"Well, gentlemen, how can we arrange to drink less tonight? To be
honest, I still have a terrible hangover from yesterday, and I could really
use a break. I daresay most of you could, too, since you were also part of
the celebration. So let's try not to overdo it."   *b*

Aristophanes replied: "Good idea, Pausanias. We've got to make a plan
for going easy on the drink tonight. I was over my head last night myself,
like the others."

---

4. Dionysus was the god of wine and drunkenness.

After that, up spoke Eryximachus, son of Acumenus: "Well said, both of you. But I still have one question: How do *you* feel, Agathon? Are you strong enough for serious drinking?"

"Absolutely not," replied Agathon. "I've no strength left for anything."

c "What a lucky stroke for us," Eryximachus said, "for me, for Aristodemus, for Phaedrus, and the rest—that you large-capacity drinkers are already exhausted. Imagine how weak drinkers like ourselves feel after last night! Of course I don't include Socrates in my claims: he can drink or not, and will be satisfied whatever we do. But since none of us seems particularly eager to overindulge, perhaps it would not be amiss for me to pro-

d vide you with some accurate information as to the nature of intoxication.

If I have learned anything from medicine, it is the following point: inebriation is harmful to everyone. Personally, therefore, I always refrain from heavy drinking; and I advise others against it—especially people who are suffering the effects of a previous night's excesses."

"Well," Phaedrus interrupted him, "I always follow your advice, especially when you speak as a doctor. In this case, if the others know what's good for them, they too will do just as you say."

e At that point they all agreed not to get drunk that evening; they decided to drink only as much as pleased them.

"It's settled, then," said Eryximachus. "We are resolved to force no one to drink more than he wants. I would like now to make a further motion: let us dispense with the flute-girl who just made her entrance; let her play for herself or, if she prefers, for the women in the house. Let us instead spend our evening in conversation. If you are so minded, I would like to

177 propose a subject."

They all said they were quite willing, and urged him to make his proposal. So Eryximachus said:

"Let me begin by citing Euripides' *Melanippe:* 'Not mine the tale.' What I am about to tell belongs to Phaedrus here, who is deeply indignant on this issue, and often complains to me about it:

"'Eryximachus,' he says, 'isn't it an awful thing! Our poets have composed hymns in honor of just about any god you can think of; but has a

b single one of them given one moment's thought to the god of love, ancient and powerful as he is? As for our fancy intellectuals, they have written volumes praising Heracles and other heroes (as did the distinguished Prodicus). Well, perhaps *that's* not surprising, but I've actually read a book

c by an accomplished author who saw fit to extol the usefulness of salt! How *could* people pay attention to such trifles and never, not even once, write a proper hymn to Love? How could anyone ignore so great a god?'

"Now, Phaedrus, in my judgment, is quite right. I would like, therefore, to take up a contribution, as it were, on his behalf, and gratify his wish.

d Besides, I think this a splendid time for all of us here to honor the god. If you agree, we can spend the whole evening in discussion, because I propose that each of us give as good a speech in praise of Love as he is capable of giving, in proper order from left to right. And let us begin with Phaedrus, who is at the head of the table and is, in addition, the father of our subject."

"No one will vote against that, Eryximachus," said Socrates. "How could *I* vote 'No,' when the only thing I say I understand is the art of   *e* love? Could Agathon and Pausanias? Could Aristophanes, who thinks of nothing but Dionysus and Aphrodite? No one I can see here now could vote against your proposal.

"And though it's not quite fair to those of us who have to speak last, if the first speeches turn out to be good enough and to exhaust our subject, I promise we won't complain. So let Phaedrus begin, with the blessing of Fortune; let's hear his praise of Love."

They all agreed with Socrates, and pressed Phaedrus to start. Of course,   *178* Aristodemus couldn't remember exactly what everyone said, and I myself don't remember everything he told me. But I'll tell you what he remembered best, and what I consider the most important points.

As I say, he said Phaedrus spoke first, beginning more or less like this:

Love is a great god, wonderful in many ways to gods and men, and most marvelous of all is the way he came into being. We honor him as one of the most ancient gods, and the proof of his great age is this: the parents of Love   *b* have no place in poetry or legend. According to Hesiod, the first to be born was Chaos,

> . . . but then came
> Earth, broad-chested, a seat for all, forever safe,
> And Love.[5]

And Acusilaus agrees with Hesiod: after Chaos came Earth and Love, these two.[6] And Parmenides tells of this beginning:

> The very first god [she] designed was Love.[7]

All sides agree, then, that Love is one of the most ancient gods. As such,   *c* he gives to us the greatest goods. I cannot say what greater good there is for a young boy than a gentle lover, or for a lover than a boy to love. There is a certain guidance each person needs for his whole life, if he is to live well; and nothing imparts this guidance—not high kinship, not public honor, not wealth—nothing imparts this guidance as well as Love. What   *d*

5. *Theogony* 116–20, 118 omitted.
6. Acusilaus was an early-fifth-century writer of genealogies.
7. Parmenides, B 13 Diels-Kranz.

guidance do I mean? I mean a sense of shame at acting shamefully, and a sense of pride in acting well. Without these, nothing fine or great can be accomplished, in public or in private.

What I say is this: if a man in love is found doing something shameful, or accepting shameful treatment because he is a coward and makes no defense, then nothing would give him more pain than being seen by the

e   boy he loves—not even being seen by his father or his comrades. We see the same thing also in the boy he loves, that he is especially ashamed before his lover when he is caught in something shameful. If only there were a way to start a city or an army made up of lovers and the boys they love! Theirs would be the best possible system of society, for they would

179   hold back from all that is shameful, and seek honor in each other's eyes. Even a few of them, in battle side by side, would conquer all the world, I'd say. For a man in love would never allow his loved one, of all people, to see him leaving ranks or dropping weapons. He'd rather die a thousand deaths! And as for leaving the boy behind, or not coming to his aid in danger—why, no one is so base that true Love could not inspire him with

b   courage, and make him as brave as if he'd been born a hero. When Homer says a god 'breathes might' into some of the heroes, this is really Love's gift to every lover.[8]

Besides, no one will die for you but a lover, and a lover will do this even if she's a woman. Alcestis is proof to everyone in Greece that what I say is

c   true.[9] Only she was willing to die in place of her husband, although his father and mother were still alive. Because of her love, she went so far beyond his parents in family feeling that she made them look like outsiders, as if they belonged to their son in name only. And when she did this her deed struck everyone, even the gods, as nobly done. The gods were so delighted, in fact, that they gave her the prize they reserve for a handful

d   chosen from the throngs of noble heroes—they sent her soul back from the dead. As you can see, the eager courage of love wins highest honors from the gods.

Orpheus, however, they sent unsatisfied from Hades, after showing him only an image of the woman he came for. They did not give him the woman herself, because they thought he was soft (he was, after all, a cithara-player) and did not dare to die like Alcestis for Love's sake, but contrived to enter living into Hades. So they punished him for that, and

e   made him die at the hands of women.[10]

---

8. Cf. *Iliad* x.482, xv.262; *Odyssey* ix.381.

9. Alcestis was the self-sacrificing wife of Admetus, whom Apollo gave a chance to live if anyone would go to Hades in his place.

10. Orpheus was a musician of legendary powers, who charmed his way into the underworld in search of his dead wife, Eurydice.

The honor they gave to Achilles is another matter. They sent him to the Isles of the Blest because he dared to stand by his lover Patroclus and avenge him, even after he had learned from his mother that he would die if *180* he killed Hector, but that if he chose otherwise he'd go home and end his life as an old man. Instead he chose to die for Patroclus, and more than that, he did it for a man whose life was already over. The gods were highly delighted at this, of course, and gave him special honor, because he made so much of his lover. Aeschylus talks nonsense when he claims Achilles was the lover;[11] he was more beautiful than Patroclus, more beautiful than all the heroes, and still beardless. Besides he was much younger, as Homer says.

In truth, the gods honor virtue most highly when it belongs to Love. *b*

They are more impressed and delighted, however, and are more generous with a loved one who cherishes his lover, than with a lover who cherishes the boy he loves. A lover is more godlike than his boy, you see, since he is inspired by a god. That's why they gave a higher honor to Achilles than to Alcestis, and sent him to the Isles of the Blest.

Therefore I say Love is the most ancient of the gods, the most honored, and the most powerful in helping men gain virtue and blessedness, whether they are alive or have passed away.

That was more or less what Phaedrus said according to Aristodemus. *c* There followed several other speeches which he couldn't remember very well. So he skipped them and went directly to the speech of Pausanias.

Phaedrus (Pausanias began), I'm not quite sure our subject has been well defined. Our charge has been simple—to speak in praise of Love. This would have been fine if Love himself were simple, too, but as a matter of fact, there are two kinds of Love. In view of this, it might be better to begin by making clear which kind of Love we are to praise. Let me therefore try *d* to put our discussion back on the right track and explain which kind of Love ought to be praised. Then I shall give him the praise he deserves, as the god he is.

It is a well-known fact that Love and Aphrodite are inseparable. If, therefore, Aphrodite were a single goddess, there could also be a single Love; but, since there are actually two goddesses of that name, there also are two kinds of Love. I don't expect you'll disagree with me about the two goddesses, will you? One is an older deity, the motherless daughter of Uranus, the god of heaven: she is known as Urania, or Heavenly Aphrodite. The other goddess is younger, the daughter of Zeus and Dione: her name is Pandemos, or Common Aphrodite. It follows, therefore, that there *e*

11. In his play, *The Myrmidons*. In Homer there is no hint of sexual attachment between Achilles and Patroclus.

is a Common as well as a Heavenly Love, depending on which goddess is Love's partner. And although, of course, all the gods must be praised, we must still make an effort to keep these two gods apart.

181   The reason for this applies in the same way to every type of action: considered in itself, no action is either good or bad, honorable or shameful. Take, for example, our own case. We had a choice between drinking, singing, or having a conversation. Now, in itself none of these is better than any other: how it comes out depends entirely on how it is performed. If it is done honorably and properly, it turns out to be honorable; if it is done improperly, it is disgraceful. And my point is that exactly this principle applies to being in love: Love is not in himself noble and worthy of praise; that depends on whether the sentiments he produces in us are themselves noble.

b   Now the Common Aphrodite's Love is himself truly common. As such, he strikes wherever he gets a chance. This, of course, is the love felt by the vulgar, who are attached to women no less than to boys, to the body more than to the soul, and to the least intelligent partners, since all they care about is completing the sexual act. Whether they do it honorably or not is of no concern. That is why they do whatever comes their way, sometimes good, sometimes bad; and which one it is is incidental to their purpose. For the Love who moves them belongs to a much younger goddess, who,
c through her parentage, partakes of the nature both of the female and the male.

    Contrast this with the Love of Heavenly Aphrodite. This goddess, whose descent is purely male (hence this love is for boys), is considerably older and therefore free from the lewdness of youth. That's why those who are inspired by her Love are attracted to the male: they find pleasure in what is by nature stronger and more intelligent. But, even within the
d group that is attracted to handsome boys, some are not moved purely by this Heavenly Love; those who are do not fall in love with little boys; they prefer older ones whose cheeks are showing the first traces of a beard—a sign that they have begun to form minds of their own. I am convinced that a man who falls in love with a young man of this age is generally prepared to share everything with the one he loves—he is eager, in fact, to spend the rest of his own life with him. He certainly does not aim to deceive him—to take advantage of him while he is still young and inexperienced and then,
e after exposing him to ridicule, to move quickly on to someone else.

    As a matter of fact, there should be a law forbidding affairs with young boys. If nothing else, all this time and effort would not be wasted on such an uncertain pursuit—and what is more uncertain than whether a particular boy will eventually make something of himself, physically or mentally? Good men, of course, are willing to make a law like this for themselves, but those other lovers, the vulgar ones, need external restraint. For just this
182 reason we have placed every possible legal obstacle to their seducing our

own wives and daughters. These vulgar lovers are the people who have given love such a bad reputation that some have gone so far as to claim that taking *any* man as a lover is in itself disgraceful. Would anyone make this claim if he weren't thinking of how hasty vulgar lovers are, and therefore how unfair to their loved ones? For nothing done properly and in accordance with our customs would ever have provoked such righteous disapproval.

I should point out, however, that, although the customs regarding Love in most cities are simple and easy to understand, here in Athens (and in Sparta as well) they are remarkably complex. In places where the people are inarticulate, like Elis or Boeotia, tradition straightforwardly approves taking a lover in every case. No one there, young or old, would ever consider it shameful. The reason, I suspect, is that, being poor speakers, they want to save themselves the trouble of having to offer reasons and arguments in support of their suits.

By contrast, in places like Ionia and almost every other part of the Persian empire, taking a lover is always considered disgraceful. The Persian empire is absolute; that is why it condemns love as well as philosophy and sport. It is no good for rulers if the people they rule cherish ambitions for themselves or form strong bonds of friendship with one another. That these are precisely the effects of philosophy, sport, and especially of Love is a lesson the tyrants of Athens learned directly from their own experience: Didn't their reign come to a dismal end because of the bonds uniting Harmodius and Aristogiton in love and affection?[12]

So you can see that plain condemnation of Love reveals lust for power in the rulers and cowardice in the ruled, while indiscriminate approval testifies to general dullness and stupidity.

Our own customs, which, as I have already said, are much more difficult to understand, are also far superior. Recall, for example, that we consider it more honorable to declare your love rather than to keep it a secret, especially if you are in love with a youth of good family and accomplishment, even if he isn't all that beautiful. Recall also that a lover is encouraged in every possible way; this means that what he does is not considered shameful. On the contrary, conquest is deemed noble, and failure shameful. And as for *attempts* at conquest, our custom is to praise lovers for totally extraordinary acts—so extraordinary, in fact, that if they performed them for any other purpose whatever, they would reap the most profound contempt. Suppose, for example, that in order to secure money, or a public post, or any other practical benefit from another person, a man were willing to do what lovers do for the ones they love. Imagine

---

12. Harmodius and Aristogiton attempted to overthrow the tyrant Hippias in 514 B.C. Although their attempt failed, the tyranny fell three years later, and the lovers were celebrated as tyrannicides.

that in pressing his suit he went to his knees in public view and begged in the most humiliating way, that he swore all sorts of vows, that he spent the night at the other man's doorstep, that he were anxious to provide services even a slave would have refused—well, you can be sure that everyone, his
b enemies no less than his friends, would stand in his way. His enemies would jeer at his fawning servility, while his friends, ashamed on his behalf, would try everything to bring him back to his senses. But let a lover act in any of these ways, and everyone will immediately say what a charming man he is! No blame attaches to his behavior: custom treats it as noble through and through. And what is even more remarkable is that, at least according to popular wisdom, the gods will forgive a lover even for break-
c ing his vows—a lover's vow, our people say, is no vow at all. The freedom given to the lover by both gods and men according to our custom is immense.

In view of all this, you might well conclude that in our city we consider the lover's desire and the willingness to satisfy it as the noblest things in the world. When, on the other hand, you recall that fathers hire attendants for their sons as soon as they're old enough to be attractive, and that an attendant's main task is to prevent any contact between his charge and his suitors; when you recall how mercilessly a boy's own friends tease him if they catch him at it, and how strongly their elders approve and even
d encourage such mocking—when you take all this into account, you're bound to come to the conclusion that we Athenians consider such behavior the most shameful thing in the world.

In my opinion, however, the fact of the matter is this. As I said earlier, love is, like everything else, complex: considered simply in itself, it is neither honorable nor a disgrace—its character depends entirely on the behavior it gives rise to. To give oneself to a vile man in a vile way is truly disgraceful behavior; by contrast, it is perfectly honorable to give oneself honorably to the right man. Now you may want to know who counts as
e vile in this context. I'll tell you: it is the common, vulgar lover, who loves the body rather than the soul, the man whose love is bound to be inconstant, since what he loves is itself mutable and unstable. The moment the body is no longer in bloom, "he flies off and away,"[13] his promises and vows in tatters behind him. How different from this is a man who loves the right sort of character, and who remains its lover for life, attached as he is
184 to something that is permanent.

We can now see the point of our customs: they are designed to separate the wheat from the chaff, the proper love from the vile. That's why we do everything we can to make it as easy as possible for lovers to press their suits and as difficult as possible for young men to comply; it is like a competition, a kind of test to determine to which sort each belongs. This

13. *Iliad* ii.71.

explains two further facts: First, why we consider it shameful to yield too quickly: the passage of time in itself provides a good test in these matters. Second, why we also consider it shameful for a man to be seduced by *b* money or political power, either because he cringes at ill-treatment and will not endure it or because, once he has tasted the benefits of wealth and power, he will not rise above them. None of these benefits is stable or permanent, apart from the fact that no genuine affection can possibly be based upon them.

Our customs, then, provide for only one honorable way of taking a man as a lover. In addition to recognizing that the lover's total and willing *c* subjugation to his beloved's wishes is neither servile nor reprehensible, we allow that there is one—and only one—further reason for willingly subjecting oneself to another which is equally above reproach: that is subjection for the sake of virtue. If someone decides to put himself at another's disposal because he thinks that this will make him better in wisdom or in any other part of virtue, we approve of his voluntary subjection: we consider it neither shameful nor servile. Both these principles—that is, both the principle governing the proper attitude toward the lover of young men and the principle governing the love of wisdom and of virtue in general— *d* must be combined if a young man is to accept a lover in an honorable way. When an older lover and a young man come together and each obeys the principle appropriate to him—when the lover realizes that he is justified in doing anything for a loved one who grants him favors, and when the young man understands that he is justified in performing any service for a lover who can make him wise and virtuous—and when the lover *is* able *e* to help the young man become wiser and better, and the young man *is* eager to be taught and improved by his lover—then, and only then, when these two principles coincide absolutely, is it ever honorable for a young man to accept a lover.

Only in this case, we should notice, is it never shameful to be deceived; in every other case it is shameful, both for the deceiver and the person he *185* deceives. Suppose, for example, that someone thinks his lover is rich and accepts him for his money; his action won't be any less shameful if it turns out that he was deceived and his lover was a poor man after all. For the young man has already shown himself to be the sort of person who will do anything for money—and that is far from honorable. By the same token, suppose that someone takes a lover in the mistaken belief that this lover is a good man and likely to make him better himself, while in reality the man is horrible, totally lacking in virtue; even so, it is noble for him to have been *b* deceived. For he too has demonstrated something about himself: that he is the sort of person who will do anything for the sake of virtue—and what could be more honorable than that? It follows, therefore, that giving in to your lover for virtue's sake is honorable, whatever the outcome. And this, of course, is the Heavenly Love of the heavenly goddess. Love's value to *c*   the city as a whole and to the citizens is immeasurable, for he compels the lover and his loved one alike to make virtue their central concern. All other forms of love belong to the vulgar goddess.

Phaedrus, I'm afraid this hasty improvisation will have to do as my contribution on the subject of Love.

When Pausanias finally came to a pause (I've learned this sort of fine figure from our clever rhetoricians), it was Aristophanes' turn, according to Aristodemus. But he had such a bad case of the hiccups—he'd probably stuffed himself again, though, of course, it could have been anything—that making a speech was totally out of the question. So he turned to the
d   doctor, Eryximachus, who was next in line, and said to him:

"Eryximachus, it's up to you—as well it should be. Cure me or take my turn."

"As a matter of fact," Eryximachus replied, "I shall do both. I shall take your turn—you can speak in my place as soon as you feel better—and I shall also cure you. While I am giving my speech, you should hold your
e   breath for as long as you possibly can. This may well eliminate your hiccups. If it fails, the best remedy is a thorough gargle. And if even this has no effect, then tickle your nose with a feather. A sneeze or two will cure even the most persistent case."

"The sooner you start speaking, the better," Aristophanes said. "I'll follow your instructions to the letter."

This, then, was the speech of Eryximachus:

Pausanias introduced a crucial consideration in his speech, though in my opinion he did not develop it sufficiently. Let me therefore try to carry his
186   argument to its logical conclusion. His distinction between the two species of Love seems to me very useful indeed. But if I have learned a single lesson from my own field, the science of medicine, it is that Love does not occur only in the human soul; it is not simply the attraction we feel toward human beauty: it is a significantly broader phenomenon. It certainly oc-
b   curs within the animal kingdom, and even in the world of plants. In fact, it occurs everywhere in the universe. Love is a deity of the greatest importance: he directs everything that occurs, not only in the human domain, but also in that of the gods.

Let me begin with some remarks concerning medicine—I hope you will forgive my giving pride of place to my own profession. The point is that our very bodies manifest the two species of Love. Consider for a moment the marked difference, the radical dissimilarity, between healthy and diseased constitutions and the fact that dissimilar subjects desire and love objects that are themselves dissimilar. Therefore, the love manifested in health is fundamentally distinct from the love manifested in disease. And
c   now recall that, as Pausanias claimed, it is as honorable to yield to a good man as it is shameful to consort with the debauched. Well, my point is that

the case of the human body is strictly parallel. Everything sound and healthy in the body must be encouraged and gratified; that is precisely the object of medicine. Conversely, whatever is unhealthy and unsound must be frustrated and rebuffed: that's what it is to be an expert in medicine.

In short, medicine is simply the science of the effects of Love on reple- *d* tion and depletion of the body, and the hallmark of the accomplished physician is his ability to distinguish the Love that is noble from the Love that is ugly and disgraceful. A good practitioner knows how to affect the body and how to transform its desires; he can implant the proper species of Love when it is absent and eliminate the other sort whenever it occurs.

The physician's task is to effect a reconciliation and establish mutual love between the most basic bodily elements. Which are those elements? They are, of course, those that are most opposed to one another, as hot is to cold, bitter to sweet, wet to dry, cases like those. In fact, our ancestor *e* Asclepius first established medicine as a profession when he learned how to produce concord and love between such opposites—that is what those poet fellows say, and—this time—I concur with them.

Medicine, therefore, is guided everywhere by the god of Love, and so *187* are physical education and farming as well. Further, a moment's reflection suffices to show that the case of poetry and music, too, is precisely the same. Indeed, this may have been just what Heraclitus had in mind, though his mode of expression certainly leaves much to be desired. The one, he says, "being at variance with itself is in agreement with itself" "like the attunement of a bow or a lyre."[14] Naturally, it is patently absurd to claim that an attunement or a harmony is in itself discordant or that its elements are still in discord with one another. Heraclitus probably meant that an expert musician creates a harmony by resolving the prior discord *b* between high and low notes. For surely there can be no harmony so long as high and low are still discordant; harmony, after all, is consonance, and consonance is a species of agreement. Discordant elements, as long as they are still in discord, cannot come to an agreement, and they therefore cannot produce a harmony. Rhythm, for example, is produced only when fast *c* and slow, though earlier discordant, are brought into agreement with each other. Music, like medicine, creates agreement by producing concord and love between these various opposites. Music is therefore simply the science of the effects of Love on rhythm and harmony.

These effects are easily discernible if you consider the constitution of rhythm and harmony in themselves; Love does not occur in both his forms in this domain. But the moment you consider, in their turn, the effects of rhythm and harmony on their audience—either through composition, *d*

14. Heraclitus of Ephesus, a philosopher of the early fifth century, was known for his enigmatic sayings. This one is quoted elsewhere in a slightly different form, frg. B 51 Diels-Kranz.

which creates new verses and melodies, or through musical education, which teaches the correct performance of existing compositions—complications arise directly, and they require the treatment of a good practitioner. Ultimately, the identical argument applies once again: the love felt by good people or by those whom such love might improve in this regard must be encouraged and protected. This is the honorable, heavenly species of *e* Love, produced by the melodies of Urania, the Heavenly Muse. The other, produced by Polyhymnia, the muse of many songs, is common and vulgar. Extreme caution is indicated here: we must be careful to enjoy his pleasures without slipping into debauchery—this case, I might add, is strictly parallel to a serious issue in my own field, namely, the problem of regulating the appetite so as to be able to enjoy a fine meal without unhealthy aftereffects.

In music, therefore, as well as in medicine and in all the other domains, in matters divine as well as in human affairs, we must attend with the *188* greatest possible care to these two species of Love, which are, indeed, to be found everywhere. Even the seasons of the year exhibit their influence. When the elements to which I have already referred—hot and cold, wet and dry—are animated by the proper species of Love, they are in harmony with one another: their mixture is temperate, and so is the climate. Harvests are plentiful; men and all other living things are in good health; no harm can come to them. But when the sort of Love that is crude and *b* impulsive controls the seasons, he brings death and destruction. He spreads the plague and many other diseases among plants and animals; he causes frost and hail and blights. All these are the effects of the immodest and disordered species of Love on the movements of the stars and the seasons of the year, that is, on the objects studied by the science called astronomy.

c Consider further the rites of sacrifice and the whole area with which the art of divination is concerned, that is, the interaction between men and gods. Here, too, Love is the central concern: our object is to try to maintain the proper kind of Love and to attempt to cure the kind that is diseased. For what is the origin of all impiety? Our refusal to gratify the orderly kind of Love, and our deference to the other sort, when we should have been guided by the former sort of Love in every action in connection with our parents, living or dead, and with the gods. The task of divination is to keep watch over these two species of Love and to doctor them as necessary. *d* Divination, therefore, is the practice that produces loving affection between gods and men; it is simply the science of the effects of Love on justice and piety.

Such is the power of Love—so varied and great that in all cases it might be called absolute. Yet even so it is far greater when Love is directed, in temperance and justice, toward the good, whether in heaven or on earth:

happiness and good fortune, the bonds of human society, concord with the gods above—all these are among his gifts.

Perhaps I, too, have omitted a great deal in this discourse on Love. If so, *e* I assure you, it was quite inadvertent. And if in fact I have overlooked certain points, it is now your task, Aristophanes, to complete the argument—unless, of course, you are planning on a different approach. In any case, proceed; your hiccups seem cured. *189*

Then Aristophanes took over (so Aristodemus said): "The hiccups have stopped all right—but not before I applied the Sneeze Treatment to them. Makes me wonder whether the 'orderly sort of Love' in the body calls for the sounds and itchings that constitute a sneeze, because the hiccups stopped immediately when I applied the Sneeze Treatment."

"You're good, Aristophanes," Eryximachus answered. "But watch what you're doing. You are making jokes before your speech, and you're forcing me to prepare for you to say something funny, and to put up my guard *b* against you, when otherwise you might speak at peace."

Then Aristophanes laughed. "Good point, Eryximachus. So let me 'unsay what I have said.' But don't put up your guard. I'm not worried about saying something funny in my coming oration. That would be pure profit, and it comes with the territory of my Muse. What I'm worried about is that I might say something ridiculous."

"Aristophanes, do you really think you can take a shot at me, and then escape? Use your head! Remember, as you speak, that you will be called upon to give an account. Though perhaps, if I decide to, I'll let you off." *c*

"Eryximachus," Aristophanes said, "indeed I do have in mind a different approach to speaking than the one the two of you used, you and Pausanias. You see, I think people have entirely missed the power of Love, because, if they had grasped it, they'd have built the greatest temples and altars to him and made the greatest sacrifices. But as it is, none of this is done for him, though it should be, more than anything else! For he loves *d* the human race more than any other god, he stands by us in our troubles, and he cures those ills we humans are most happy to have mended. I shall, therefore, try to explain his power to you; and you, please pass my teaching on to everyone else."

First you must learn what Human Nature was in the beginning and what has happened to it since, because long ago our nature was not what it is now, but very different. There were three kinds of human beings, that's my first point—not two as there are now, male and female. In addition to *e* these, there was a third, a combination of those two; its name survives, though the kind itself has vanished. At that time, you see, the word "androgynous" really meant something: a form made up of male and female elements, though now there's nothing but the word, and that's used as an insult. My second point is that the shape of each human being was completely round, with back and sides in a circle; they had four hands each, as *190* many legs as hands, and two faces, exactly alike, on a rounded neck. Between the two faces, which were on opposite sides, was one head with four ears. There were two sets of sexual organs, and everything else was the way you'd imagine it from what I've told you. They walked upright, as we do now, whatever direction they wanted. And whenever they set out to run fast, they thrust out all their eight limbs, the ones they had then, and spun rapidly, the way gymnasts do cartwheels, by bringing their legs around straight.

b   Now here is why there were three kinds, and why they were as I described them: The male kind was originally an offspring of the sun, the female of the earth, and the one that combined both genders was an offspring of the moon, because the moon shares in both. They were spherical, and so was their motion, because they were like their parents in the sky.

In strength and power, therefore, they were terrible, and they had great ambitions. They made an attempt on the gods, and Homer's story about Ephialtes and Otus was originally about them: how they tried to make an *c* ascent to heaven so as to attack the gods.[15] Then Zeus and the other gods met in council to discuss what to do, and they were sore perplexed. They couldn't wipe out the human race with thunderbolts and kill them all off, as they had the giants, because that would wipe out the worship they receive, along with the sacrifices we humans give them. On the other hand, they couldn't let them run riot. At last, after great effort, Zeus had an idea.

"I think I have a plan," he said, "that would allow human beings to exist *d* and stop their misbehaving: they will give up being wicked when they lose their strength. So I shall now cut each of them in two. At one stroke they will lose their strength and also become more profitable to us, owing to the increase in their number. They shall walk upright on two legs. But if I find they still run riot and do not keep the peace," he said, "I will cut them in two again, and they'll have to make their way on one leg, hopping."

e   So saying, he cut those human beings in two, the way people cut sorb-apples before they dry them or the way they cut eggs with hairs. As he cut each one, he commanded Apollo to turn its face and half its neck toward the wound, so that each person would see that he'd been cut and keep better order. Then Zeus commanded Apollo to heal the rest of the wound, and Apollo did turn the face around, and he drew skin from all sides over what is now called the stomach, and there he made one mouth, as in a

---

15. *Iliad* v.385; *Odyssey* xi.305 ff.

pouch with a drawstring, and fastened it at the center of the stomach. This
is now called the navel. Then he smoothed out the other wrinkles, of   *191*
which there were many, and he shaped the breasts, using some such tool
as shoemakers have for smoothing wrinkles out of leather on the form. But
he left a few wrinkles around the stomach and the navel, to be a reminder
of what happened long ago.

Now, since their natural form had been cut in two, each one longed for
its own other half, and so they would throw their arms about each other,
weaving themselves together, wanting to grow together. In that condition
they would die from hunger and general idleness, because they would not   *b*
do anything apart from each other. Whenever one of the halves died and
one was left, the one that was left still sought another and wove itself
together with that. Sometimes the half he met came from a woman, as we'd
call her now, sometimes it came from a man; either way, they kept on dying.

Then, however, Zeus took pity on them, and came up with another
plan: he moved their genitals around to the front! Before then, you see,
they used to have their genitals outside, like their faces, and they cast seed   *c*
and made children, not in one another, but in the ground, like cicadas. So
Zeus brought about this relocation of genitals, and in doing so he invented
interior reproduction, *by* the man *in* the woman. The purpose of this was
so that, when a man embraced a woman, he would cast his seed and they
would have children; but when male embraced male, they would at least
have the satisfaction of intercourse, after which they could stop embrac-
ing, return to their jobs, and look after their other needs in life. This, then,   *d*
is the source of our desire to love each other. Love is born into every
human being; it calls back the halves of our original nature together; it tries
to make one out of two and heal the wound of human nature.

Each of us, then, is a "matching half" of a human whole, because each
was sliced like a flatfish, two out of one, and each of us is always seeking
the half that matches him. That's why a man who is split from the double
sort (which used to be called "androgynous") runs after women. Many
lecherous men have come from this class, and so do the lecherous women   *e*
who run after men. Women who are split from a woman, however, pay no
attention at all to men; they are oriented more toward women, and les-
bians come from this class. People who are split from a male are male-
oriented. While they are boys, because they are chips off the male block,
they love men and enjoy lying with men and being embraced by men;   *192*
those are the best of boys and lads, because they are the most manly in
their nature. Of course, some say such boys are shameless, but they're
lying. It's not because they have no shame that such boys do this, you see,
but because they are bold and brave and masculine, and they tend to
cherish what is like themselves. Do you want me to prove it? Look, these
are the only kind of boys who grow up to be real men in politics. When   *b*
they're grown men, they are lovers of young men, and they naturally pay

no attention to marriage or to making babies, except insofar as they are required by local custom. They, however, are quite satisfied to live their lives with one another unmarried. In every way, then, this sort of man grows up as a lover of young men and a lover of Love, always rejoicing in his own kind.

And so, when a person meets the half that is his very own, whatever his orientation, whether it's to young men or not, then something wonderful happens: the two are struck from their senses by love, by a sense of belonging to one another, and by desire, and they don't want to be separated from one another, not even for a moment.

These are the people who finish out their lives together and still cannot say what it is they want from one another. No one would think it is the intimacy of sex—that mere sex is the reason each lover takes so great and deep a joy in being with the other. It's obvious that the soul of every lover longs for something else; his soul cannot say what it is, but like an oracle it has a sense of what it wants, and like an oracle it hides behind a riddle. Suppose two lovers are lying together and Hephaestus[16] stands over them with his mending tools, asking, "What is it you human beings really want from each other?" And suppose they're perplexed, and he asks them again: "Is this your heart's desire, then—for the two of you to become parts of the same whole, as near as can be, and never to separate, day or night? Because if that's your desire, I'd like to weld you together and join you into something that is naturally whole, so that the two of you are made into one. Then the two of you would share one life, as long as you lived, because you would be one being, and by the same token, when you died, you would be one and not two in Hades, having died a single death. Look at your love, and see if this is what you desire: wouldn't this be all the good fortune you could want?"

Surely you can see that no one who received such an offer would turn it down; no one would find anything else that he wanted. Instead, everyone would think he'd found out at last what he had always wanted: to come together and melt together with the one he loves, so that one person emerged from two. Why should this be so? It's because, as I said, we used to be complete wholes in our original nature, and now "Love" is the name for our pursuit of wholeness, for our desire to be complete.

Long ago we were united, as I said; but now the god has divided us as punishment for the wrong we did him, just as the Spartans divided the Arcadians.[17] So there's a danger that if we don't keep order before the

---

16. Cf. *Odyssey* viii.266 ff.

17. Arcadia included the city of Mantinea, which opposed Sparta and was rewarded by having its population divided and dispersed in 385 B.C. Aristophanes seems to be referring anachronistically to those events; such anachronisms are not uncommon in Plato.

gods, we'll be split in two again, and then we'll be walking around in the condition of people carved on gravestones in bas-relief, sawn apart between the nostrils, like half dice. We should encourage all men, therefore, to treat the gods with all due reverence, so that we may escape this fate *b* and find wholeness instead. And we will, if Love is our guide and our commander. Let no one work against him. Whoever opposes Love is hateful to the gods, but if we become friends of the god and cease to quarrel with him, then we shall find the young men that are meant for us and win their love, as very few men do nowadays.

Now don't get ideas, Eryximachus, and turn this speech into a comedy. *c*

Don't think I'm pointing this at Pausanias and Agathon. Probably, they both do belong to the group that are entirely masculine in nature. But I am speaking about everyone, men and women alike, and I say there's just one way for the human race to flourish: we must bring love to its perfect conclusion, and each of us must win the favors of his very own young man, so that he can recover his original nature. If that is the ideal, then, of course, the nearest approach to it is best in present circumstances, and that is to win the favor of young men who are naturally sympathetic to us.

If we are to give due praise to the god who can give us this blessing, *d* then, we must praise Love. Love does the best that can be done for the time being: he draws us toward what belongs to us. But for the future, Love promises the greatest hope of all: if we treat the gods with due reverence, he will restore to us our original nature, and by healing us, he will make us blessed and happy.

"That," he said, "is my speech about Love, Eryximachus. It is rather different from yours. As I begged you earlier, don't make a comedy of it. I'd prefer to hear what all the others will say—or, rather, what each of *e* them will say, since Agathon and Socrates are the only ones left."

"I found your speech delightful," said Eryximachus, "so I'll do as you say. Really, we've had such a rich feast of speeches on Love, that if I couldn't vouch for the fact that Socrates and Agathon are masters of the art of love, I'd be afraid that they'd have nothing left to say. But as it is, I have no fears on this score."

Then Socrates said, "That's because *you* did beautifully in the contest, *194* Eryximachus. But if you ever get in my position, or rather the position I'll be in after Agathon's spoken so well, then you'll really be afraid. You'll be at your wit's end, as I am now."

"You're trying to bewitch me, Socrates," said Agathon, "by making me think the audience expects great things of my speech, so I'll get flustered." *b*

"Agathon!" said Socrates, "How forgetful do you think I am? I saw how brave and dignified you were when you walked right up to the theater platform along with the actors and looked straight out at that enormous audience. You were about to put your own writing on display, and you weren't the least bit panicked. After seeing that, how could I expect you to be flustered by us, when we are so few?"

"Why, Socrates," said Agathon. "You must think I have nothing but theater audiences on my mind! So you suppose I don't realize that, if you're intelligent, you find a few sensible men much more frightening than a senseless crowd?"

c   "No," he said. "It wouldn't be very handsome of me to think you crude in any way, Agathon. I'm sure that if you ever run into people you consider wise, you'll pay more attention to them than to ordinary people. But you can't suppose we're in that class; we were at the theater too, you know, part of the ordinary crowd. Still, if you did run into any wise men, other than yourself, you'd certainly be ashamed at the thought of doing anything ugly in front of them. Is that what you mean?"

d   "That's true," he said. "On the other hand, you wouldn't be ashamed to do something ugly in front of ordinary people. Is that it?"

At that point Phaedrus interrupted: "Agathon, my friend, if you answer Socrates, he'll no longer care whether we get anywhere with what we're doing here, so long as he has a partner for discussion. Especially if he's handsome. Now, like you, I enjoy listening to Socrates in discussion, but it is my duty to see to the praising of Love and to exact a speech from every one of this group. When each of you two has made his offering to the god,

e   then you can have your discussion."

"You're doing a beautiful job, Phaedrus," said Agathon. "There's nothing to keep me from giving my speech. Socrates will have many opportunities for discussion later."

I wish first to speak of how I ought to speak, and only then to speak. In my opinion, you see, all those who have spoken before me did not so much celebrate the god as congratulate human beings on the good things that come to them from the god. But who it is who gave these gifts, what he is

195   like—no one has spoken about that. Now, only one method is correct for every praise, no matter whose: you must explain what qualities in the subject of your speech enable him to give the benefits for which we praise him. So now, in the case of Love, it is right for us to praise him first for what he is and afterward for his gifts.

I maintain, then, that while all the gods are happy, Love—if I may say so without giving offense—is the happiest of them all, for he is the most beautiful and the best. His great beauty lies in this: First, Phaedrus, he is

b   the youngest of the gods. He proves my point himself by fleeing old age in headlong flight, fast-moving though it is (that's obvious—it comes after us faster than it should). Love was born to hate old age and will come nowhere near it. Love always lives with young people and is one of them: the old story holds good that like is always drawn to like. And though on many other points I agree with Phaedrus, I do not agree with this: that

Love is more ancient than Cronus and Iapetus. No, I say that he is the   *c*
youngest of the gods and stays young forever.

Those old stories Hesiod and Parmenides tell about the gods—those
things happened under Necessity, not Love, if what they say is true. For
not one of all those violent deeds would have been done—no castrations,
no imprisonments—if Love had been present among them. There would
have been peace and brotherhood instead, as there has been now as long
as Love has been king of the gods.

So he is young. And besides being young, he is delicate. It takes a poet   *d*
as good as Homer to show how delicate the god is. For Homer says that
Mischief is a god and that she is delicate—well, that her feet are delicate,
anyway! He says:

> . . . hers are delicate feet: not on the ground
> Does she draw nigh; she walks instead upon the heads of men.[18]

A lovely proof, I think, to show how delicate she is: she doesn't walk on   *e*
anything hard; she walks only on what is soft. We shall use the same proof
about Love, then, to show that he is delicate. For he walks not on earth, not
even on people's skulls, which are not really soft at all, but in the softest of
all the things that are, there he walks, there he has his home. For he makes
his home in the characters, in the souls, of gods and men—and not even in
every soul that comes along: when he encounters a soul with a harsh
character, he turns away; but when he finds a soft and gentle character, he
settles down in it. Always, then, he is touching with his feet and with the
whole of himself what is softest in the softest places. He must therefore be   *196*
most delicate.

He is youngest, then, and most delicate; in addition he has a fluid,
supple shape. For if he were hard, he would not be able to enfold a soul
completely or escape notice when he first entered it or withdrew. Besides,
his graceful good looks prove that he is balanced and fluid in his nature.
Everyone knows that Love has extraordinary good looks, and between
ugliness and Love there is unceasing war.

And the exquisite coloring of his skin! The way the god consorts with
flowers shows that. For he never settles in anything, be it a body or a soul,   *b*
that cannot flower or has lost its bloom. His place is wherever it is flowery
and fragrant; there he settles, there he stays.

Enough for now about the beauty of the god, though much remains still
to be said. After this, we should speak of Love's moral character.[19] The
main point is that Love is neither the cause nor the victim of any injustice;
he does no wrong to gods or men, nor they to him. If anything has an effect

---

18. *Iliad* xix.92–93. "Mischief" translates *Atē*.
19. "Moral character": *aretē*, i.e., virtue.

c on him, it is never by violence, for violence never touches Love. And the effects he has on others are not forced, for every service we give to love we give willingly. And whatever one person agrees on with another, when both are willing, that is right and just; so say "the laws that are kings of society."[20]

And besides justice, he has the biggest share of moderation.[21] For moderation, by common agreement, is power over pleasures and passions, and no pleasure is more powerful than Love! But if they are weaker, they are under the power of Love, and *he* has the power; and because he has power over pleasures and passions, Love is exceptionally moderate.

d And as for manly bravery, "Not even Ares can stand up to" Love![22] For Ares has no hold on Love, but Love does on Ares—love of Aphrodite, so runs the tale.[23] But he who has hold is more powerful than he who is held; and so, because Love has power over the bravest of the others, he is bravest of them all.

Now I have spoken about the god's justice, moderation, and bravery; his wisdom remains.[24] I must try not to leave out anything that can be said
e on this. In the first place—to honor *our* profession as Eryximachus did his—the god is so skilled a poet that he can make others into poets: once Love touches him, *anyone* becomes a poet,

. . . howe'er uncultured he had been before.[25]

This, we may fittingly observe, testifies that Love is a good poet, good, in sum, at every kind of artistic production. For you can't give to another
197 what you don't have yourself, and you can't teach what you don't know.

And as to the production of animals—who will deny that they are all born and begotten through Love's skill?

20. This is a proverbial expression attributed by Aristotle (*Rhetoric* 1406a17–23) to the fourth-century liberal thinker and rhetorician Alcidamas.
21. *Sōphrosunē.* The word can be translated also as "temperance" and, most literally, "sound-mindedness." (Plato and Aristotle generally contrast *sōphrosunē* as a virtue with self-control: the person with *sōphrosunē* is naturally well-tempered in every way and so does not need to control himself or to hold himself back.)
22. From Sophocles, frg. 234b Dindorf: "Even Ares cannot withstand Necessity." Ares is the god of war.
23. See *Odyssey* viii.266–366. Aphrodite's husband Hephaestus made a snare that caught Ares in bed with Aphrodite.
24. "Wisdom" translates *sophia,* which Agathon treats as roughly equivalent to *technē* (professional skill); he refers mainly to the ability to produce things. Accordingly, "wisdom" translates *sophia* in the first instance; afterward in this passage it is "skill" or "art."
25. Euripides, *Stheneboea* (frg. 666 Nauck).

And as for artisans and professionals—don't we know that whoever has this god for a teacher ends up in the light of fame, while a man untouched by Love ends in obscurity? Apollo, for one, invented archery, medicine, and prophecy when desire and love showed the way. Even he, therefore, would be a pupil of Love, and so would the Muses in music, Hephaestus in bronze work, Athena in weaving, and Zeus in "the governance of gods and men."

b

That too is how the gods' quarrels were settled, once Love came to be among them—love of beauty, obviously, because love is not drawn to ugliness. Before that, as I said in the beginning, and as the poets say, many dreadful things happened among the gods, because Necessity was king. But once this god was born, all goods came to gods and men alike through love of beauty.

c

This is how I think of Love, Phaedrus: first, he is himself the most beautiful and the best; after that, if anyone else is at all like that, Love is responsible. I am suddenly struck by a need to say something in poetic meter,[26] that it is he who—

> Gives peace to men and stillness to the sea,
> Lays winds to rest, and careworn men to sleep.

d

Love fills us with togetherness and drains all of our divisiveness away.

Love calls gatherings like these together. In feasts, in dances, and in ceremonies, he gives the lead. Love moves us to mildness, removes from us wildness. He is giver of kindness, never of meanness. Gracious, kindly— let wise men see and gods admire! Treasure to lovers, envy to others, father of elegance, luxury, delicacy, grace, yearning, desire. Love cares well for good men, cares not for bad ones. In pain, in fear, in desire, or speech, Love is our best guide and guard; he is our comrade and our savior. Ornament of all gods and men, most beautiful leader and the best! Every man should follow Love, sing beautifully his hymns, and join with him in the song he sings that charms the mind of god or man.

e

This, Phaedrus, is the speech I have to offer. Let it be dedicated to the god, part of it in fun, part of it moderately serious, as best I could manage.

198

When Agathon finished, Aristodemus said, everyone there burst into applause, so becoming to himself and to the god did they think the young man's speech.

Then Socrates glanced at Eryximachus and said, "Now do you think I was foolish to feel the fear I felt before? Didn't I speak like a prophet a

---

26. After these two lines of poetry, Agathon continues with an extremely poetical prose peroration.

while ago when I said that Agathon would give an amazing speech and I would be tongue-tied?"

b "You were prophetic about one thing, I think," said Eryximachus, "that Agathon would speak well. But you, tongue-tied? No, I don't believe that."

"Bless you," said Socrates. "How am I not going to be tongue-tied, I or anyone else, after a speech delivered with such beauty and variety? The other parts may not have been so wonderful, but that at the end! Who would not be struck dumb on hearing the beauty of the words and phrases? Anyway, I was worried that I'd not be able to say anything that

c came close to them in beauty, and so I would almost have run away and escaped, if there had been a place to go. And, you see, the speech reminded me of Gorgias, so that I actually experienced what Homer describes: I was afraid that Agathon would end by sending the Gorgian head,[27] awesome at speaking in a speech, against my speech, and this would turn me to stone by striking me dumb. Then I realized how ridicu-

d lous I'd been to agree to join with you in praising Love and to say that I was a master of the art of love, when I knew nothing whatever of this business, of how anything whatever ought to be praised. In my foolishness, I thought you should tell the truth about whatever you praise, that this should be your basis, and that from this a speaker should select the most beautiful truths and arrange them most suitably. I was quite vain, thinking that I would talk well and that I knew the truth about praising anything whatever. But now it appears that this is not what it is to praise

e anything whatever; rather, it is to apply to the object the grandest and the most beautiful qualities, whether he actually has them or not. And if they are false, that is no objection; for the proposal, apparently, was that everyone here make the rest of us think he is praising Love—and not that he actually praise him. I think that is why you stir up every word and apply it

199 to Love; your description of him and his gifts is designed to make him look better and more beautiful than anything else—to ignorant listeners, plainly, for of course he wouldn't look that way to those who knew. And your praise did seem beautiful and respectful. But I didn't even know the method for giving praise; and it was in ignorance that I agreed to take part in this. So "the tongue" promised, and "the mind" did not.[28] Goodbye to that! I'm not giving another eulogy using that method, not at all—I

b wouldn't be able to do it!—but, if you wish, I'd like to tell the truth my way. I want to avoid any comparison with your speeches, so as not to give you a reason to laugh at me. So look, Phaedrus, would a speech like this

27. "Gorgian head" is a pun on "Gorgon's head." In his peroration Agathon had spoken in the style of Gorgias, and this style was considered to be irresistibly powerful. The sight of a Gorgon's head would turn a man to stone.
28. The allusion is to Euripides, *Hippolytus* 612.

satisfy your requirement? You will hear the truth about Love, and the words and phrasing will take care of themselves."

Then Aristodemus said that Phaedrus and the others urged him to speak in the way he thought was required, whatever it was.

"Well then, Phaedrus," said Socrates, "allow me to ask Agathon a few little questions, so that, once I have his agreement, I may speak on that basis."   c

"You have my permission," said Phaedrus. "Ask away." After that, said Aristodemus, Socrates began: "Indeed, Agathon, my friend, I thought you led the way beautifully into your speech when you said that one should first show the qualities of Love himself, and only then those of his deeds. I must admire that beginning. Come, then, since you have beautifully and magnificently expounded his qualities in other ways, tell me this, too,   d
about Love. Is Love such as to be a love of something or of nothing? I'm not asking if he is born *of* some mother or father (for the question whether Love is love of mother or of father would really be ridiculous), but it's as if I'm asking this about a father—whether a father is the father *of* something or not. You'd tell me, of course, if you wanted to give me a good answer, that it's *of* a son or a daughter that a father is the father. Wouldn't you?"

"Certainly," said Agathon.

"Then does the same go for the mother?" He agreed to that also.   e

"Well, then," said Socrates, "answer a little more fully, and you will understand better what I want. If I should ask, 'What about this: a brother, just insofar as he *is* a brother, is he the brother of something or not?'"

He said that he was. "And he's of a brother or a sister, isn't he?"

He agreed.

"Now try to tell me about love," he said. "Is Love the love of nothing or of something?"

"Of something, surely!"   200

"Then keep this object of love in mind, and remember what it is. But tell me this much: does Love desire that of which it is the love, or not?"

"Certainly," he said.

"At the time he desires and loves something, does he actually have what he desires and loves at that time, or doesn't he?"

"He doesn't. At least, that wouldn't be likely," he said.

"Instead of what's *likely*," said Socrates, "ask yourself whether it's *neces-*
sary that this be so: a thing that desires desires something of which it is in   b
need; otherwise, if it were not in need, it would not desire it. I can't tell you, Agathon, how strongly it strikes me that this is necessary. But how about you?"

"I think so too."

"Good. Now then, would someone who is tall, want to be tall? Or someone who is strong want to be strong?"

"Impossible, on the basis of what we've agreed."

"Presumably because no one is in need of those things he already has."

"True."

"But maybe a strong man could want to be strong," said Socrates, "or a
c   fast one fast, or a healthy one healthy: in cases like these, you might think
people really do want to be things they already are and do want to have
qualities they already have—I bring them up so they won't deceive us. But
in these cases, Agathon, if you stop to think about them, you will see that
these people are what they are at the present time, whether they want to be
or not, by a logical necessity. And who, may I ask, would ever bother to
desire what's necessary in any event? But when someone says 'I am
healthy, but that's just what I want to be,' or 'I am rich, but that's just what I
d   want to be,' or 'I desire the very things that I have,' let us say to him: 'You
already have riches and health and strength in your possession, my man,
what you want is to possess these things in time to come, since in the
present, whether you want to or not, you have them. Whenever you say, *I
desire what I already have,* ask yourself whether you don't mean this: *I want
the things I have now to be mine in the future as well.*' Wouldn't he agree?"

According to Aristodemus, Agathon said that he would.

So Socrates said, "Then this is what it is to love something which is not
at hand, which the lover does not have: it is to desire the preservation of
e   what he now has in time to come, so that he will have it then."

"Quite so," he said.

"So such a man or anyone else who has a desire desires what is not at
hand and not present, what he does not have, and what he is not, and that
of which he is in need; for such are the objects of desire and love."

"Certainly," he said.

"Come, then," said Socrates. "Let us review the points on which we've
agreed. Aren't they, first, that Love is the love of something, and, second,
201   that he loves things of which he has a present need?"

"Yes," he said.

"Now, remember, in addition to these points, what you said in your
speech about what it is that Love loves. If you like, I'll remind you. I think
you said something like this: that the gods' quarrels were settled by love of
beautiful things, for there is no love of ugly ones. Didn't you say something like that?"

"I did," said Agathon.

"And that's a suitable thing to say, my friend," said Socrates. "But if this
is so, wouldn't Love have to be a desire for beauty, and never for ugliness?"
b   He agreed.

"And we also agreed that he loves just what he needs and does not
have."

"Yes," he said.

"So Love needs beauty, then, and does not have it."

"Necessarily," he said.

"So! If something needs beauty and has got no beauty at all, would you still say that it is beautiful?"

"Certainly not."

"Then do you still agree that Love is beautiful, if those things are so?"

Then Agathon said, "It turns out, Socrates, I didn't know what I was talking about in that speech."

"It was a beautiful speech, anyway, Agathon," said Socrates. "Now take it a little further. Don't you think that good things are always beautiful as well?"

"I do."

"Then if Love needs beautiful things, and if all good things are beautiful, he will need good things too."

"As for me, Socrates," he said, "I am unable to contradict you. Let it be as you say."

"Then it's the truth, my beloved Agathon, that you are unable to contradict," he said. "It is not hard at all to contradict Socrates."

Now I'll let you go. I shall try to go through for you the speech about Love I once heard from a woman of Mantinea, Diotima—a woman who was wise about many things besides this: once she even put off the plague for ten years by telling the Athenians what sacrifices to make. She is the one who taught me the art of love, and I shall go through her speech as best I can on my own, using what Agathon and I have agreed to as a basis.

Following your lead, Agathon, one should first describe who Love is and what he is like, and afterward describe his works—I think it will be easiest for me to proceed the way Diotima did and tell you how she questioned me.

You see, I had told her almost the same things Agathon told me just now: that Love is a great god and that he belongs to beautiful things.[29] And she used the very same arguments against me that I used against Agathon; she showed how, according to my very own speech, Love is neither beautiful nor good.

So I said, "What do you mean, Diotima? Is Love ugly, then, and bad?"

But she said, "Watch your tongue! Do you really think that, if a thing is not beautiful, it has to be ugly?"

"I certainly do."

"And if a thing's not wise, it's ignorant? Or haven't you found out yet that there's something in between wisdom and ignorance?"

"What's that?"

29. The Greek is ambiguous between "Love loves beautiful things" and "Love is one of the beautiful things." Agathon had asserted the former (197b5, 201a5), and this will be a premise in Diotima's argument, but Agathon asserted the latter as well (195a7), and this is what Diotima proceeds to refute.

"It's judging things correctly without being able to give a reason. Surely you see that this is not the same as knowing—for how could knowledge be unreasoning? And it's not ignorance either—for how could what hits the truth be ignorance? Correct judgment, of course, has this character: it is *in between* understanding and ignorance."

b   "True," said I, "as you say."

"Then don't force whatever is not beautiful to be ugly, or whatever is not good to be bad. It's the same with Love: when you agree he is neither good nor beautiful, you need not think he is ugly and bad; he could be something in between," she said.

"Yet everyone agrees he's a great god," I said.

"Only those who don't know?" she said. "Is that how you mean 'everyone'? Or do you include those who do know?"

"Oh, everyone together."

c   And she laughed. "Socrates, how could those who say that he's not a god at all agree that he's a great god?"

"Who says that?" I asked.

"You, for one," she said, "and I for another."

"How can you say this!" I exclaimed.

"That's easy," said she. "Tell me, wouldn't you say that all gods are beautiful and happy? Surely you'd never say a god is not beautiful or happy?"

"Zeus! Not I," I said.

"Well, by calling anyone 'happy,' don't you mean they possess good and beautiful things?"

d   "Certainly."

"What about Love? You agreed he needs good and beautiful things, and that's why he desires them—because he needs them."

"I certainly did."

"Then how could he be a god if he has no share in good and beautiful things?"

"There's no way he could, apparently."

"Now do you see? You don't believe Love is a god either!"

"Then, what could Love be?" I asked. "A mortal?"

"Certainly not."

"Then, what is he?"

"He's like what we mentioned before," she said. "He is in between mortal and immortal."

"What do you mean, Diotima?"

e   "He's a great spirit, Socrates. Everything spiritual, you see, is in between god and mortal."

"What is their function?" I asked.

"They are messengers who shuttle back and forth between the two, conveying prayer and sacrifice from men to gods, while to men they bring commands from the gods and gifts in return for sacrifices. Being in the middle of the two, they round out the whole and bind fast the all to all. Through them all divination passes, through them the art of priests in sacrifice and ritual, in enchantment, prophecy, and sorcery. Gods do not mix with men; they mingle and converse with us through spirits instead, whether we are awake or asleep. He who is wise in any of these ways is a man of the spirit, but he who is wise in any other way, in a profession or any manual work, is merely a mechanic. These spirits are many and various, then, and one of them is Love."

203

"Who are his father and mother?" I asked.

b

"That's rather a long story," she said. "I'll tell it to you, all the same."

"When Aphrodite was born, the gods held a celebration. Poros, the son of Metis, was there among them.[30] When they had feasted, Penia came begging, as poverty does when there's a party, and stayed by the gates. Now Poros got drunk on nectar (there was no wine yet, you see) and, feeling drowsy, went into the garden of Zeus, where he fell asleep. Then Penia schemed up a plan to relieve her lack of resources: she would get a child from Poros. So she lay beside him and got pregnant with Love. That is why Love was born to follow Aphrodite and serve her: because he was conceived on the day of her birth. And that's why he is also by nature a lover of beauty, because Aphrodite herself is especially beautiful.

c

"As the son of Poros and Penia, his lot in life is set to be like theirs. In the first place, he is always poor, and he's far from being delicate and beautiful (as ordinary people think he is); instead, he is tough and shriveled and shoeless and homeless, always lying on the dirt without a bed, sleeping at people's doorsteps and in roadsides under the sky, having his mother's nature, always living with Need. But on his father's side he is a schemer after the beautiful and the good; he is brave, impetuous, and intense, an awesome hunter, always weaving snares, resourceful in his pursuit of intelligence, a lover of wisdom[31] through all his life, a genius with enchantments, potions, and clever pleadings.

d

"He is by nature neither immortal nor mortal. But now he springs to life when he gets his way; now he dies—all in the very same day. Because he is his father's son, however, he keeps coming back to life, but then anything he finds his way to always slips away, and for this reason Love is never completely without resources, nor is he ever rich.

e

"He is in between wisdom and ignorance as well. In fact, you see, none of the gods loves wisdom or wants to become wise—for they are wise— and no one else who is wise already loves wisdom; on the other hand, no one who is ignorant will love wisdom either or want to become wise. For

204

30. *Poros* means "way" or "resource." His mother's name, *Mētis*, means "cunning." *Penia* means "poverty."
31. I.e., a philosopher.

what's especially difficult about being ignorant is that you are content with yourself, even though you're neither beautiful and good nor intelligent. If you don't think you need anything, of course you won't want what you don't think you need."

b　　"In that case, Diotima, who *are* the people who love wisdom, if they are neither wise nor ignorant?"

"That's obvious," she said. "A child could tell you. Those who love wisdom fall in between those two extremes. And Love is one of them, because he is in love with what is beautiful, and wisdom is extremely beautiful. It follows that Love *must* be a lover of wisdom and, as such, is in between being wise and being ignorant. This, too, comes to him from his parentage, from a father who is wise and resourceful and a mother who is not wise and lacks resource.

c　　"My dear Socrates, that, then, is the nature of the Spirit called Love. Considering what you thought about Love, it's no surprise that you were led into thinking of Love as you did. On the basis of what you say, I conclude that you thought Love was *being loved,* rather than *being a lover.* I think that's why Love struck you as beautiful in every way: because it is what is really beautiful and graceful that deserves to be loved, and this is perfect and highly blessed; but being a lover takes a different form, which I have just described."

So I said, "All right then, my friend. What you say about Love is beauti-
d ful, but if you're right, what use is Love to human beings?"

"I'll try to teach you that, Socrates, after I finish this. So far I've been explaining the character and the parentage of Love. Now, according to you, he is love for beautiful things. But suppose someone asks us, 'Socrates and Diotima, what is the point of loving beautiful things?'

"It's clearer this way: 'The lover of beautiful things has a desire; what does he desire?' "

"That they become his own," I said.

"But that answer calls for still another question, that is, 'What will this man have, when the beautiful things he wants have become his own?' "
e　　I said there was no way I could give a ready answer to that question.

Then she said, "Suppose someone changes the question, putting 'good' in place of 'beautiful,' and asks you this: 'Tell me, Socrates, a lover of good things has a desire; what does he desire?' "

"That they become his own," I said.

"And what will he have, when the good things he wants have become his own?"

205　　"This time it's easier to come up with the answer," I said. "He'll have happiness."[32]

---

32. *Eudaimonia:* no English word catches the full range of this term, which is used for the whole of well-being and the good, flourishing life.

"That's what makes happy people happy, isn't it—possessing good things. There's no need to ask further, 'What's the point of wanting happiness?' The answer you gave seems to be final."

"True," I said.

"Now this desire for happiness, this kind of love—do you think it is common to all human beings and that everyone wants to have good things forever and ever? What would you say?"

"Just that," I said. "It is common to all."

"Then, Socrates, why don't we say that everyone is in love," she asked, *b* "since everyone always loves the same things? Instead, we say some people are in love and others not; why is that?"

"I wonder about that myself," I said.

"It's nothing to wonder about," she said. "It's because we divide out a special kind of love, and we refer to it by the word that means the whole— 'love'; and for the other kinds of love we use other words."

"What do you mean?" I asked.

"Well, you know, for example, that 'poetry' has a very wide range.[33] After all, everything that is responsible for creating something out of nothing is a kind of poetry; and so all the creations of every craft and *c* profession are themselves a kind of poetry, and everyone who practices a craft is a poet."

"True."

"Nevertheless," she said, "as you also know, these craftsmen are not called poets. We have other words for them, and out of the whole of poetry we have marked off one part, the part the Muses give us with melody and rhythm, and we refer to this by the word that means the whole. For this alone is called 'poetry,' and those who practice this part of poetry are called poets."

"True." *d*

"That's also how it is with love. The main point is this: every desire for good things or for happiness is 'the supreme and treacherous love' in everyone. But those who pursue this along any of its many other ways— through making money, or through the love of sports, or through philosophy—we don't say that *these* people are in love, and we don't call them lovers. It's only when people are devoted exclusively to one special kind of love that we use these words that really belong to the whole of it: 'love' and 'in love' and 'lovers.'"

"I am beginning to see your point," I said.

"Now there is a certain story," she said, "according to which lovers are *e* those people who seek their other halves. But according to my story, a

33. "Poetry" translates *poiēsis*, lit. "making," which can be used for any kind of production or creation. However, the word *poiētēs*, lit. "maker," was used mainly for poets—writers of metrical verses that were actually set to music.

lover does not seek the half or the whole, unless, my friend, it turns out to be good as well. I say this because people are even willing to cut off their own arms and legs if they think they are diseased. I don't think an individual takes joy in what belongs to him personally unless by 'belonging to me' he means 'good' and by 'belonging to another' he means 'bad.' That's

206 because what everyone loves is really nothing other than the good. Do you disagree?"

"Zeus! Not I," I said.

"Now, then," she said. "Can we simply say that people love the good?"

"Yes," I said.

"But shouldn't we add that, in loving it, they want the good to be theirs?"

"We should."

"And not only that," she said. "They want the good to be theirs forever, don't they?"

"We should add that too."

"In a word, then, love is wanting to possess the good forever."

b   "That's very true," I said.

"This, then, is the object of love," she said. "Now, how do lovers pursue it? We'd rightly say that when they are in love they do something with eagerness and zeal. But what is it precisely that they do? Can you say?"

"If I could," I said, "I wouldn't be your student, filled with admiration for your wisdom, and trying to learn these very things."

"Well, I'll tell you," she said. "It is giving birth in beauty,[34] whether in body or in soul."

c   "It would take divination to figure out what you mean. I can't."

"Well, I'll tell you more clearly," she said. "All of us are pregnant, Socrates, both in body and in soul, and, as soon as we come to a certain age, we naturally desire to give birth. Now no one can possibly give birth in anything ugly; only in something beautiful. That's because when a man and a woman come together in order to give birth, this is a godly affair. Pregnancy, reproduction—this is an immortal thing for a mortal animal to

d   do, and it cannot occur in anything that is out of harmony, but ugliness is out of harmony with all that is godly. Beauty, however, is in harmony with the divine. Therefore the goddess who presides at childbirth—she's called Moira or Eilithuia—is really Beauty.[35] That's why, whenever pregnant animals or persons draw near to beauty, they become gentle and joyfully

34. The preposition is ambiguous between "within" and "in the presence of." Diotima may mean that the lover causes the newborn (which may be an idea) to come to be within a beautiful person; or she may mean that he is stimulated to give birth to it in the presence of a beautiful person.

35. Moira is known mainly as a Fate, but she was also a birth goddess (*Iliad* xxiv.209) and was identified with the birth goddess Eilithuia (Pindar, *Olympian Odes* vi.42, *Nemean Odes* vii.1).

disposed and give birth and reproduce; but near ugliness they are foul-faced and draw back in pain; they turn away and shrink back and do not reproduce, and because they hold on to what they carry inside them, the labor is painful. This is the source of the great excitement about beauty that comes to anyone who is pregnant and already teeming with life: beauty *e* releases them from their great pain. You see, Socrates," she said, "what Love wants is not beauty, as you think it is."

"Well, what is it, then?"

"Reproduction and birth in beauty."

"Maybe," I said.

"Certainly," she said. "Now, why reproduction? It's because reproduc- tion goes on forever; it is what mortals have in place of immortality. A *207* lover must desire immortality along with the good, if what we agreed earlier was right, that Love wants to possess the good forever. It follows from our argument that Love must desire immortality."

All this she taught me, on those occasions when she spoke on the art of love. And once she asked, "What do you think causes love and desire, Socrates? Don't you see what an awful state a wild animal is in when it wants to reproduce? Footed and winged animals alike, all are plagued by *b* the disease of Love. First they are sick for intercourse with each other, then for nurturing their young—for their sake the weakest animals stand ready to do battle against the strongest and even to die for them, and they may be racked with famine in order to feed their young. They would do any- thing for their sake. Human beings, you'd think, would do this because they understand the reason for it; but what causes wild animals to be in *c* such a state of love? Can you say?"

And I said again that I didn't know.

So she said, "How do you think you'll ever master the art of love, if you don't know that?"

"But that's why I came to you, Diotima, as I just said. I knew I needed a teacher. So tell me what causes this, and everything else that belongs to the art of love."

"If you really believe that Love by its nature aims at what we have often agreed it does, then don't be surprised at the answer," she said. "For *d* among animals the principle is the same as with us, and mortal nature seeks so far as possible to live forever and be immortal. And this is possi- ble in one way only: by reproduction, because it always leaves behind a new young one in place of the old. Even while each living thing is said to be alive and to be the same—as a person is said to be the same from childhood until he turns into an old man—even then he never consists of the same things, though he is called the same, but he is always being renewed and in other respects passing away, in his hair and flesh and bones *e* and blood and his entire body. And it's not just in his body, but in his soul, too, for none of his manners, customs, opinions, desires, pleasures, pains,

or fears ever remains the same, but some are coming to be in him while others are passing away. And what is still far stranger than that is that not
208   only does one branch of knowledge come to be in us while another passes away and that we are never the same even in respect of our knowledge, but that each single piece of knowledge has the same fate. For what we call *studying* exists because knowledge is leaving us, because forgetting is the departure of knowledge, while studying puts back a fresh memory in place of what went away, thereby preserving a piece of knowledge, so that it seems to be the same. And in that way everything mortal is preserved,
b   not, like the divine, by always being the same in every way, but because what is departing and aging leaves behind something new, something such as it had been. By this device, Socrates," she said, "what is mortal shares in immortality, whether it is a body or anything else, while the immortal has another way. So don't be surprised if everything naturally values its own offspring, because it is for the sake of immortality that everything shows this zeal, which is Love."

c   Yet when I heard her speech I was amazed, and spoke: "Well," said I, "Most wise Diotima, is this really the way it is?"

         And in the manner of a perfect sophist she said, "Be sure of it, Socrates. Look, if you will, at how human beings seek honor. You'd be amazed at their irrationality, if you didn't have in mind what I spoke about and if you hadn't pondered the awful state of love they're in, wanting to become famous and 'to lay up glory immortal forever,' and how they're ready to brave any danger for the sake of this, much more than they are for their children; and they are prepared to spend money, suffer through all sorts of
d   ordeals, and even die for the sake of glory. Do you really think that Alcestis would have died for Admetus," she asked, "or that Achilles would have died after Patroclus, or that your Codrus would have died so as to preserve the throne for his sons,[36] if they hadn't expected the memory of their virtue—which we still hold in honor—to be immortal? Far from it," she said. "I believe that anyone will do anything for the sake of immortal
e   virtue and the glorious fame that follows; and the better the people, the more they will do, for they are all in love with immortality.

         "Now, some people are pregnant in body, and for this reason turn more to women and pursue love in that way, providing themselves through childbirth with immortality and remembrance and happiness, as they
209   think, for all time to come; while others are pregnant in soul—because there surely *are* those who are even more pregnant in their souls than in their bodies, and these are pregnant with what is fitting for a soul to bear and bring to birth. And what is fitting? Wisdom and the rest of virtue,

36. Codrus was the legendary last king of Athens. He gave his life to satisfy a prophecy that promised victory to Athens and salvation from the invading Dorians if their king was killed by the enemy.

which all poets beget, as well as all the craftsmen who are said to be creative. But by far the greatest and most beautiful part of wisdom deals with the proper ordering of cities and households, and that is called moderation and justice. When someone has been pregnant with these in his soul from early youth, while he is still a virgin, and, having arrived at the proper age, desires to beget and give birth, he too will certainly go about seeking the beauty in which he would beget; for he will never beget in anything ugly. Since he is pregnant, then, he is much more drawn to bodies that are beautiful than to those that are ugly; and if he also has the luck to find a soul that is beautiful and noble and well-formed, he is even more drawn to this combination; such a man makes him instantly teem with ideas and arguments about virtue—the qualities a virtuous man should have and the customary activities in which he should engage; and so he tries to educate him. In my view, you see, when he makes contact with someone beautiful and keeps company with him, he conceives and gives birth to what he has been carrying inside him for ages. And whether they are together or apart, he remembers that beauty. And in common with him he nurtures the newborn; such people, therefore, have much more to share than do the parents of human children, and have a firmer bond of friendship, because the children in whom they have a share are more beautiful and more immortal. Everyone would rather have such children than human ones, and would look up to Homer, Hesiod, and the other good poets with envy and admiration for the offspring they have left behind—offspring, which, because they are immortal themselves, provide their parents with immortal glory and remembrance. For example," she said, "those are the sort of children Lycurgus[37] left behind in Sparta as the saviors of Sparta and virtually all of Greece. Among you the honor goes to Solon for his creation of your laws. Other men in other places everywhere, Greek or barbarian, have brought a host of beautiful deeds into the light and begotten every kind of virtue. Already many shrines have sprung up to honor them for their immortal children, which hasn't happened yet to anyone for human offspring.

"Even you, Socrates, could probably come to be initiated into these rites of love. But as for the purpose of these rites when they are done correctly—that is the final and highest mystery, and I don't know if you are capable of it. I myself will tell you," she said, "and I won't stint any effort. And you must try to follow if you can.

"A lover who goes about this matter correctly must begin in his youth to devote himself to beautiful bodies. First, if the leader[38] leads aright, he should love one body and beget beautiful ideas there; then he should

37. Lycurgus was supposed to have been the founder of the oligarchic laws and stern customs of Sparta.
38. I.e., Love.

b   realize that the beauty of any one body is brother to the beauty of any other and that if he is to pursue beauty of form he'd be very foolish not to think that the beauty of all bodies is one and the same. When he grasps this, he must become a lover of all beautiful bodies, and he must think that this wild gaping after just one body is a small thing and despise it.

    "After this he must think that the beauty of people's souls is more valuable than the beauty of their bodies, so that if someone is decent in his
c   soul, even though he is scarcely blooming in his body, our lover must be content to love and care for him and to seek to give birth to such ideas as will make young men better. The result is that our lover will be forced to gaze at the beauty of activities and laws and to see that all this is akin to itself, with the result that he will think that the beauty of bodies is a thing of no importance. After customs he must move on to various kinds of
d   knowledge. The result is that he will see the beauty of knowledge and be looking mainly not at beauty in a single example—as a servant would who favored the beauty of a little boy or a man or a single custom (being a slave, of course, he's low and small-minded)—but the lover is turned to the great sea of beauty, and, gazing upon this, he gives birth to many gloriously beautiful ideas and theories, in unstinting love of wisdom,[39] until, having
e   grown and been strengthened there, he catches sight of such knowledge, and it is the knowledge of such beauty . . .

    "Try to pay attention to me," she said, "as best you can. You see, the man who has been thus far guided in matters of Love, who has beheld beautiful things in the right order and correctly, is coming now to the goal of Loving: all of a sudden he will catch sight of something wonderfully
211   beautiful in its nature; that, Socrates, is the reason for all his earlier labors:

    "First, it always *is* and neither comes to be nor passes away, neither waxes nor wanes. Second, it is not beautiful this way and ugly that way, nor beautiful at one time and ugly at another, nor beautiful in relation to one thing and ugly in relation to another; nor is it beautiful here but ugly there, as it would be if it were beautiful for some people and ugly for others. Nor will the beautiful appear to him in the guise of a face or hands or anything else that belongs to the body. It will not appear to him as one
b   idea or one kind of knowledge. It is not anywhere in another thing, as in an animal, or in earth, or in heaven, or in anything else, but itself by itself with itself, it is always one in form; and all the other beautiful things share in that, in such a way that when those others come to be or pass away, this does not become the least bit smaller or greater nor suffer any change. So when someone rises by these stages, through loving boys correctly, and
c   begins to see this beauty, he has almost grasped his goal. This is what it is to go aright, or be led by another, into the mystery of Love: one goes always upward for the sake of this Beauty, starting out from beautiful

    39. I.e., philosophy.

things and using them like rising stairs: from one body to two and from two to all beautiful bodies, then from beautiful bodies to beautiful customs, and from customs to learning beautiful things, and from these lessons he arrives in the end at this lesson, which is learning of this very Beauty, so that in the end he comes to know just what it is to be   *d* beautiful.

"And there in life, Socrates, my friend," said the woman from Mantinea, "there if anywhere should a person live his life, beholding that Beauty. If you once see that, it won't occur to you to measure beauty by gold or clothing or beautiful boys and youths—who, if you see them now, strike you out of your senses, and make you, you and many others, eager to be with the boys you love and look at them forever, if there were any way to do that, forgetting food and drink, everything but looking at them and being with them. But how would it be, in our view," she said, "if   *e* someone got to see the Beautiful itself, absolute, pure, unmixed, not polluted by human flesh or colors or any other great nonsense of mortality, but if he could see the divine Beauty itself in its one form? Do you think it   *212* would be a poor life for a human being to look there and to behold it by that which he ought, and to be with it? Or haven't you remembered," she said, "that in that life alone, when he looks at Beauty in the only way that Beauty can be seen—only then will it become possible for him to give birth not to images of virtue (because he's in touch with no images), but to true virtue (because he is in touch with the true Beauty). The love of the gods belongs to anyone who has given birth to true virtue and nourished it, and if any human being could become immortal, it would be he."   *b*

This, Phaedrus and the rest of you, was what Diotima told me. I was persuaded. And once persuaded, I try to persuade others too that human nature can find no better workmate for acquiring this than Love. That's why I say that every man must honor Love, why I honor the rites of Love myself and practice them with special diligence, and why I commend them to others. Now and always I praise the power and courage of Love so far as I am able. Consider this speech, then, Phaedrus, if you wish, a   *c* speech in praise of Love. Or if not, call it whatever and however you please to call it.

Socrates' speech finished to loud applause. Meanwhile, Aristophanes was trying to make himself heard over their cheers in order to make a response to something Socrates had said about his own speech. Then, all of a sudden, there was even more noise. A large drunken party had arrived at the courtyard door and they were rattling it loudly, accompanied by the shrieks of some flute-girl they had brought along. Agathon at that point called to his slaves:

"Go see who it is. If it's people we know, invite them in. If not, tell them   *d* the party's over, and we're about to turn in."

A moment later they heard Alcibiades shouting in the courtyard, very drunk and very loud. He wanted to know where Agathon was, he demanded to see Agathon at once. Actually, he was half-carried into the house by the flute-girl and by some other companions of his, but, at the door, he managed to stand by himself, crowned with a beautiful wreath of violets and ivy and ribbons in his hair.

"Good evening, gentlemen. I'm plastered," he announced. "May I join your party? Or should I crown Agathon with this wreath—which is all I came to do, anyway—and make myself scarce? I really couldn't make it yesterday," he continued, "but nothing could stop me tonight! See, I'm wearing the garland myself. I want this crown to come directly from my head to the head that belongs, I don't mind saying, to the cleverest and best-looking man in town. Ah, you laugh; you think I'm drunk! Fine, go ahead—I know I'm right anyway. Well, what do you say? May I join you on these terms? Will you have a drink with me or not?"

Naturally they all made a big fuss. They implored him to join them, they begged him to take a seat, and Agathon called him to his side. So Alcibiades, again with the help of his friends, approached Agathon. At the same time, he kept trying to take his ribbons off so that he could crown Agathon with them, but all he succeeded in doing was to push them further down his head until they finally slipped over his eyes. What with the ivy and all, he didn't see Socrates, who had made room for him on the couch as soon as he saw him. So Alcibiades sat down between Socrates and Agathon and, as soon as he did so, he put his arms around Agathon, kissed him, and placed the ribbons on his head.

Agathon asked his slaves to take Alcibiades' sandals off. "We can all three fit on my couch," he said.

"What a good idea!" Alcibiades replied. "But wait a moment! Who's the third?"

As he said this, he turned around, and it was only then that he saw Socrates. No sooner had he seen him than he leaped up and cried:

"Good lord, what's going on here? It's Socrates! You've trapped me again! You always do this to me—all of a sudden you'll turn up out of nowhere where I least expect you! Well, what do you want now? Why did you choose this particular couch? Why aren't you with Aristophanes or anyone else we could tease you about? But no, you figured out a way to find a place next to the most handsome man in the room!"

"I beg you, Agathon," Socrates said, "protect me from this man! You can't imagine what it's like to be in love with him: from the very first moment he realized how I felt about him, he hasn't allowed me to say two words to anybody else—what am I saying, I can't so much as look at an attractive man but he flies into a fit of jealous rage. He yells; he threatens; he can hardly keep from slapping me around! Please, try to keep him under control. Could you perhaps make him forgive me? And if you can't, if he gets violent, will you defend me? The fierceness of his passion terrifies me!"

"I shall never forgive you!" Alcibiades cried. "I promise you, you'll pay   *e*
for this! But for the moment," he said, turning to Agathon, "give me some of these ribbons. I'd better make a wreath for him as well—look at that magnificent head! Otherwise, I know, he'll make a scene. He'll be grumbling that, though I crowned you for your first victory, I didn't honor him even though he has never lost an argument in his life."

So Alcibiades took the ribbons, arranged them on Socrates' head, and lay back on the couch. Immediately, however, he started up again:

"Friends, you look sober to me; we can't have that! Let's have a drink! Remember our agreement? We need a master of ceremonies; who should it be? . . . Well, at least until you are all too drunk to care, I elect . . . myself! Who else? Agathon, I want the largest cup around . . . No! Wait! You! Bring me that cooling jar over there!"   214

He'd seen the cooling jar, and he realized it could hold more than two quarts of wine. He had the slaves fill it to the brim, drained it, and ordered them to fill it up again for Socrates.

"Not that the trick will have any effect on *him*," he told the group. "Socrates will drink whatever you put in front of him, but no one yet has seen him drunk."

The slave filled the jar and, while Socrates was drinking, Eryximachus said to Alcibiades:

"This is certainly most improper. We cannot simply pour the wine   *b*
down our throats in silence: we must have some conversation, or at least a song. What we are doing now is hardly civilized."

What Alcibiades said to him was this: "O Eryximachus, best possible son to the best possible, the most temperate father: Hi!"

"Greetings to you, too," Eryximachus replied. "Now what do you suggest we do?"

"Whatever you say. Ours to obey you, 'For a medical mind is worth a million others.'[40] Please prescribe what you think fit."

"Listen to me," Eryximachus said. "Earlier this evening we decided to   *c*
use this occasion to offer a series of encomia of Love. We all took our turn—in good order, from left to right—and gave our speeches, each according to his ability. You are the only one not to have spoken yet, though, if I may say so, you have certainly drunk your share. It's only proper, therefore, that you take your turn now. After you have spoken, you can decide on a topic for Socrates on your right; he can then do the same for the man to his right, and we can go around the table once again."

"Well said, O Eryximachus," Alcibiades replied. "But do you really think it's fair to put my drunken ramblings next to your sober orations?

40. *Iliad* xi.514.

d And anyway, my dear fellow, I hope you didn't believe a single word Socrates said: the truth is just the opposite! He's the one who will most surely beat me up if I dare praise anyone else in his presence—even a god!"

"Hold your tongue!" Socrates said.

"By god, don't you dare deny it!" Alcibiades shouted. "I would never—*never*—praise anyone else with you around."

e "Well, why not just do that, if you want?" Eryximachus suggested. "Why don't you offer an encomium to Socrates?"

"What do you mean?" asked Alcibiades. "Do you really think so, Eryximachus? Should I unleash myself upon him? Should I give him his punishment in front of all of you?"

"Now, wait a minute," Socrates said. "What do you have in mind? Are you going to praise me only in order to mock me? Is that it?"

"I'll only tell the truth—please, let me!"

"I would certainly like to hear the truth from you. By all means, go ahead," Socrates replied.

"Nothing can stop me now," said Alcibiades. "But here's what you can do: if I say anything that's not true, you can just interrupt, if you want, and
215 correct me; at worst, there'll be mistakes in my speech, not lies. But you can't hold it against me if I don't get everything in the right order—I'll say things as they come to mind. It is no easy task for one in my condition to give a smooth and orderly account of your bizarreness!"

I'll try to praise Socrates, my friends, but I'll have to use an image. And though he may think I'm trying to make fun of him, I assure you my image
b is no joke: it aims at the truth. Look at him! Isn't he just like a statue of Silenus? You know the kind of statue I mean; you'll find them in any shop in town. It's a Silenus sitting, his flute[41] or his pipes in his hands, and it's hollow. It's split right down the middle, and inside it's full of tiny statues of the gods. Now look at him again! Isn't he also just like the satyr Marsyas?[42]

Nobody, not even you, Socrates, can deny that you *look* like them. But the resemblance goes beyond appearance, as you're about to hear.

You are impudent, contemptuous, and vile! No? If you won't admit it, I'll bring witnesses. And you're quite a flute player, aren't you? In fact,

41. This is the conventional translation of the word, but the *aulos* was in fact a reed instrument and not a flute. It was held by the ancients to be the instrument that most strongly arouses the emotions.
42. Satyrs had the sexual appetites and manners of wild beasts and were usually portrayed with large erections. Sometimes they had horses' tails or ears, sometimes the traits of goats. Marsyas, in myth, dared to compete in music with Apollo and was skinned alive for his impudence.

you're much more marvelous than Marsyas, who needed instruments to c
cast his spells on people. And so does anyone who plays his tunes today—
for even the tunes Olympus[43] played are Marsyas' work, since Olympus
learned everything from him. Whether they are played by the greatest
flautist or the meanest flute-girl, his melodies have in themselves the
power to possess and so reveal those people who are ready for the god and
his mysteries. That's because his melodies are themselves divine. The only
difference between you and Marsyas is that you need no instruments; you d
do exactly what he does, but with words alone. You know, people hardly
ever take a speaker seriously, even if he's the greatest orator; but let
anyone—man, woman, or child—listen to you or even to a poor account
of what you say—and we are all transported, completely possessed.

If I were to describe for you what an extraordinary effect his words have
always had on me (I can feel it this moment even as I'm speaking), you e
might actually suspect that I'm drunk! Still, I swear to you, the moment he
starts to speak, I am beside myself: my heart starts leaping in my chest, the
tears come streaming down my face, even the frenzied Corybantes[44] seem
sane compared to me—and, let me tell you, I am not alone. I have heard
Pericles and many other great orators, and I have admired their speeches.
But nothing like this ever happened to me: they never upset me so deeply
that my very own soul started protesting that my life—*my* life!—was no
better than the most miserable slave's. And yet that is exactly how this
Marsyas here at my side makes me feel all the time: he makes it seem that 216
my life isn't worth living! You can't say that isn't true, Socrates. I know
very well that you could make me feel that way this very moment if I gave
you half a chance. He always traps me, you see, and he makes me admit
that my political career is a waste of time, while all that matters is just what
I most neglect: my personal shortcomings, which cry out for the closest
attention. So I refuse to listen to him; I stop my ears and tear myself away
from him, for, like the Sirens, he could make me stay by his side until I die. b

Socrates is the only man in the world who has made me feel shame—
ah, you didn't think I had it in me, did you? Yes, he makes me feel
ashamed: I know perfectly well that I can't prove he's wrong when he tells
me what I should do; yet, the moment I leave his side, I go back to my old
ways: I cave in to my desire to please the crowd. My whole life has become
one constant effort to escape from him and keep away, but when I see him,
I feel deeply ashamed, because I'm doing nothing about my way of life, c
though I have already agreed with him that I should. Sometimes, believe

---

43. Olympus was a legendary musician who was said to be loved by Marsyas
(*Minos* 318b5) and to have made music that moved its listeners out of their senses.
44. The Corybantes were legendary worshippers of Cybele, who brought about
their own derangement through music and dance.

me, I think I would be happier if he were dead. And yet I know that if he dies, I'll be even more miserable. I can't live with him, and I can't live without him! What *can* I do about him?

That's the effect of this satyr's music—on me and many others. But that's the least of it. He's like these creatures in all sorts of other ways; his powers are really extraordinary. Let me tell you about them, because, you

d   can be sure of it, none of you really understands him. But, now I've started, I'm going to show you what he really is.

To begin with, he's crazy about beautiful boys; he constantly follows them around in a perpetual daze. Also, he likes to say he's ignorant and knows nothing. Isn't this just like Silenus? Of course it is! And all this is just on the surface, like the outsides of those statues of Silenus. I wonder, my fellow drinkers, if you have any idea what a sober and temperate man he proves to be once you have looked inside. Believe me, it couldn't matter less to him whether a boy is beautiful. You can't imagine how little he cares

e   whether a person is beautiful, or rich, or famous in any other way that most people admire. He considers all these possessions beneath contempt, and that's exactly how he considers all of us as well. In public, I tell you, his whole life is one big game—a game of irony. I don't know if any of you have seen him when he's really serious. But I once caught him when he was open like Silenus' statues, and I had a glimpse of the figures he keeps

217   hidden within: they were so godlike—so bright and beautiful, so utterly amazing—that I no longer had a choice—I just had to do whatever he told me.

What I thought at the time was that what he really wanted was *me*, and that seemed to me the luckiest coincidence: all I had to do was to let him have his way with me, and he would teach me everything he knew— believe me, I had a lot of confidence in my looks. Naturally, up to that time we'd never been alone together; one of my attendants had always been

b   present. But with this in mind, I sent the attendant away, and met Socrates alone. (You see, in this company I must tell the whole truth: so pay attention. And, Socrates, if I say anything untrue, I want you to correct me.)

So there I was, my friends, alone with him at last. My idea, naturally, was that he'd take advantage of the opportunity to tell me whatever it is that lovers say when they find themselves alone; I relished the moment. But no such luck! Nothing of the sort occurred. Socrates had his usual sort

c   of conversation with me, and at the end of the day he went off.

My next idea was to invite him to the gymnasium with me. We took exercise together, and I was sure that this would lead to something. He took exercise and wrestled with me many times when no one else was present. What can I tell you? I got nowhere. When I realized that my ploy had failed, I decided on a frontal attack. I refused to retreat from a battle I myself had begun, and I needed to know just where matters stood. So what I did was to invite him to dinner, as if *I* were his lover and he my

young prey! To tell the truth, it took him quite a while to accept my   *d*
invitation, but one day he finally arrived. That first time he left right after
dinner: I was too shy to try to stop him. But on my next attempt, I started
some discussion just as we were finishing our meal and kept him talking
late into the night. When he said he should be going, I used the lateness of
the hour as an excuse and managed to persuade him to spend the night at
my house. He had had his meal on the couch next to mine, so he just made
himself comfortable and lay down on it. No one else was there.   *e*

Now you must admit that my story so far has been perfectly decent; I
could have told it in any company. But you'd never have heard me tell the
rest of it, as you're about to do, if it weren't that, as the saying goes,
"there's truth in wine when the slaves have left"—and when they're present, too. Also, would it be fair to Socrates for me to praise him and yet to
fail to reveal one of his proudest accomplishments? And, furthermore, you
know what people say about snakebite—that you'll only talk about it with
your fellow victims: only they will understand the pain and forgive you   *218*
for all the things it made you do. Well, something much more painful than
a snake has bitten me in my most sensitive part—I mean my heart, or my
soul, or whatever you want to call it, which has been struck and bitten by
philosophy, whose grip on young and eager souls is much more vicious
than a viper's and makes them do the most amazing things. Now, all you
people here, Phaedrus, Agathon, Eryximachus, Pausanias, Aristodemus,   *b*
Aristophanes—I need not mention Socrates himself—and all the rest,
have all shared in the madness, the Bacchic frenzy of philosophy. And
that's why you will hear the rest of my story; you will understand and
forgive both what I did then and what I say now. As for the house slaves
and for anyone else who is not an initiate, my story's not for you: block
your ears!

To get back to the story. The lights were out; the slaves had left; the time   *c*
was right, I thought, to come to the point and tell him freely what I had in
mind. So I shook him and whispered:

"Socrates, are you asleep?"

"No, no, not at all," he replied.

"You know what I've been thinking?"

"Well, no, not really."

"I think," I said, "you're the only worthy lover I have ever had—and
yet, look how shy you are with me! Well, here's how I look at it. It would be
really stupid not to give you anything you want: you can have me, my   *d*
belongings, anything my friends might have. Nothing is more important
to me than becoming the best man I can be, and no one can help me more
than you to reach that aim. With a man like you, in fact, I'd be much more
ashamed of what wise people would say if I did *not* take you as my lover,
than I would of what all the others, in their foolishness, would say if
I did."

He heard me out, and then he said in that absolutely inimitable ironic manner of his:

e   "Dear Alcibiades, if you are right in what you say about me, you are already more accomplished than you think. If I really have in me the power to make you a better man, then you can see in me a beauty that is really beyond description and makes your own remarkable good looks pale in comparison. But, then, is this a fair exchange that you propose? You seem to me to want more than your proper share: you offer me the merest appearance of beauty, and in return you want the thing itself, 'gold in 219   exchange for bronze.'[45]

"Still, my dear boy, you should think twice, because you could be wrong, and I may be of no use to you. The mind's sight becomes sharp only when the body's eyes go past their prime—and you are still a good long time away from that."

When I heard this I replied: "I really have nothing more to say. I've told you exactly what I think. Now it's your turn to consider what you think best for you and me."

b   "You're right about that," he answered. "In the future, let's consider things together. We'll always do what seems the best to the two of us."

His words made me think that my own had finally hit their mark, that he was smitten by my arrows. I didn't give him a chance to say another word. I stood up immediately and placed my mantle over the light cloak which, though it was the middle of winter, was his only clothing. I slipped *c*   underneath the cloak and put my arms around this man—this utterly unnatural, this truly extraordinary man—and spent the whole night next to him. Socrates, you can't deny a word of it. But in spite of all my efforts, this hopelessly arrogant, this unbelievably insolent man—he turned me down! He spurned my beauty, of which I was so proud, members of the jury—for this is really what you are: you're here to sit in judgment of Socrates' amazing arrogance and pride. Be sure of it, I swear to you by all *d*   the gods and goddesses together, my night with Socrates went no further than if I had spent it with my own father or older brother!

How do you think I felt after that? Of course, I was deeply humiliated, but also I couldn't help admiring his natural character, his moderation, his fortitude—here was a man whose strength and wisdom went beyond my wildest dreams! How could I bring myself to hate him? I couldn't bear to *e*   lose his friendship. But how could I possibly win him over? I knew very well that money meant much less to him than enemy weapons ever meant to Ajax,[46] and the only trap by means of which I had thought I might

---

45. *Iliad* vi.232–36 tells the famous story of the exchange by Glaucus of golden armor for bronze.

46. Ajax, a hero of the Greek army at Troy, carried an enormous shield and so was virtually invulnerable to enemy weapons.

capture him had already proved a dismal failure. I had no idea what to do, no purpose in life; ah, no one else has ever known the real meaning of slavery!

All this had already occurred when Athens invaded Potidaea,[47] where we served together and shared the same mess. Now, first, he took the hardships of the campaign much better than I ever did—much better, in fact, than anyone in the whole army. When we were cut off from our supplies, as often happens in the field, no one else stood up to hunger as   *220* well as he did. And yet he was the one man who could really enjoy a feast; and though he didn't much want to drink, when he had to, he could drink the best of us under the table. Still, and most amazingly, no one ever saw him drunk (as we'll straightaway put to the test).

Add to this his amazing resistance to the cold—and, let me tell you, the   *b* winter there is something awful. Once, I remember, it was frightfully cold; no one so much as stuck his nose outside. If we absolutely had to leave our tent, we wrapped ourselves in anything we could lay our hands on and tied extra pieces of felt or sheepskin over our boots. Well, Socrates went out in that weather wearing nothing but this same old light cloak, and even in bare feet he made better progress on the ice than the other soldiers did in their boots. You should have seen the looks they gave him; they   *c* thought he was only doing it to spite them!

So much for that! But you should hear what else he did during that same campaign,

> The exploit our strong-hearted hero dared to do.[48]

One day, at dawn, he started thinking about some problem or other; he just stood outside, trying to figure it out. He couldn't resolve it, but he wouldn't give up. He simply stood there, glued to the same spot. By midday, many soldiers had seen him, and, quite mystified, they told everyone that Socrates had been standing there all day, thinking about something. He was still there when evening came, and after dinner some Ionians moved their bedding outside, where it was cooler and more comfortable (all this took   *d* place in the summer), but mainly in order to watch if Socrates was going to stay out there all night. And so he did; he stood on the very same spot until dawn! He only left next morning, when the sun came out, and he made his prayers to the new day.

And if you would like to know what he was like in battle—this is a tribute he really deserves. You know that I was decorated for bravery

---

47. Potidaea, a city in Thrace allied to Athens, was induced by Corinth to revolt in 432 B.C. The city was besieged by the Athenians and was eventually defeated in a bloody local war, 432–430 B.C.
48. *Odyssey* iv.242, 271.

e during that campaign: well, during that very battle, Socrates single-handedly saved my life! He absolutely did! He just refused to leave me behind when I was wounded, and he rescued not only me but my armor as well. For my part, Socrates, I told them right then that the decoration really belonged to you, and you can blame me neither for doing so then nor for saying so now. But the generals, who seemed much more concerned with my social position, insisted on giving the decoration to me, and, I must say, you were more eager than the generals themselves for me to have it.

221 You should also have seen him at our horrible retreat from Delium.[49] I was there with the cavalry, while Socrates was a foot soldier. The army had already dispersed in all directions, and Socrates was retreating together with Laches. I happened to see them just by chance, and the moment I did I started shouting encouragements to them, telling them I was never going to leave their side, and so on. That day I had a better opportunity to watch *b* Socrates than I ever had at Potidaea, for, being on horseback, I wasn't in very great danger. Well, it was easy to see that he was remarkably more collected than Laches. But when I looked again, I couldn't get your words, Aristophanes, out of my mind: in the midst of battle he was making his way exactly as he does around town,

. . . with swagg'ring gait and roving eye.[50]

He was observing everything quite calmly, looking out for friendly troops and keeping an eye on the enemy. Even from a great distance it was obvious that this was a very brave man, who would put up a terrific fight if anyone approached him. This is what saved both of them. For, as a rule, you try to put as much distance as you can between yourself and such men *c* in battle; you go after the others, those who run away helter-skelter.

You could say many other marvelous things in praise of Socrates. Perhaps he shares some of his specific accomplishments with others. But, as a whole, he is unique; he is like no one else in the past and no one in the present—this is by far the most amazing thing about him. For we might be able to form an idea of what Achilles was like by comparing him to Brasidas or some other great warrior, or we might compare Pericles with *d* Nestor or Antenor or one of the other great orators.[51] There is a parallel for everyone—everyone else, that is. But this man here is so bizarre, his ways

49. At Delium, a town on the Boeotian coastline just north of Attica, a major Athenian expeditionary force was routed by a Boeotian army in 424 B.C. For another description of Socrates' action during the retreat, see *Laches* 181b.
50. Cf. Aristophanes, *Clouds* 362.
51. Brasidas, among the most effective Spartan generals during the Peloponnesian War, was mortally wounded while defeating the Athenians at Amphipolis in 422 B.C. Antenor (for the Trojans) and Nestor (for the Greeks) were legendary wise counselors during the Trojan War.

and his ideas are so unusual, that, search as you might, you'll never find anyone else, alive or dead, who's even remotely like him. The best you can do is not to compare him to anything human, but to liken him, as I do, to Silenus and the satyrs, and the same goes for his ideas and arguments.

Come to think of it, I should have mentioned this much earlier: even his ideas and arguments are just like those hollow statues of Silenus. If you *e* were to listen to his arguments, at first they'd strike you as totally ridiculous; they're clothed in words as coarse as the hides worn by the most vulgar satyrs. He's always going on about pack asses, or blacksmiths, or cobblers, or tanners; he's always making the same tired old points in the same tired old words. If you are foolish, or simply unfamiliar with him, you'd find it impossible not to laugh at his arguments. But if you see them 222 when they open up like the statues, if you go behind their surface, you'll realize that no other arguments make any sense. They're truly worthy of a god, bursting with figures of virtue inside. They're of great—no, of the greatest—importance for anyone who wants to become a truly good man.

Well, this is my praise of Socrates, though I haven't spared him my *b* reproach, either; I told you how horribly he treated me—and not only me but also Charmides, Euthydemus, and many others. He has deceived us all: he presents himself as your lover, and, before you know it, you're in love with him yourself! I warn you, Agathon, don't let him fool you! Remember our torments; be on your guard: don't wait, like the fool in the proverb, to learn your lesson from your own misfortune.[52] *c*

Alcibiades' frankness provoked a lot of laughter, especially since it was obvious that he was still in love with Socrates, who immediately said to him:

"You're perfectly sober after all, Alcibiades. Otherwise you could never have concealed your motive so gracefully: how casually you let it drop, almost like an afterthought, at the very end of your speech! As if the real point of all this has not been simply to make trouble between Agathon and *d* me! You think that I should be in love with you and no one else, while you, and no one else, should be in love with Agathon—well, we were *not* deceived; we've seen through your little satyr play. Agathon, my friend, don't let him get away with it: let no one come between us!"

Agathon said to Socrates: "I'm beginning to think you're right; isn't it *e* proof of that that he literally came between us here on the couch? Why would he do this if he weren't set on separating us? But he won't get away with it; I'm coming right over to lie down next to you."

"Wonderful," Socrates said. "Come here, on my other side."

"My god!" cried Alcibiades. "How I suffer in his hands! He kicks me when I'm down; he never lets me go. Come, don't be selfish, Socrates; at least, let's compromise: let Agathon lie down between us."

52. Cf. *Iliad* xvii.32.

"Why, that's impossible," Socrates said. "You have already delivered your praise of me, and now it's my turn to praise whoever's on my right. But if Agathon were next to you, he'd have to praise me all over again instead of having me speak in his honor, as I very much want to do in any case. Don't be jealous; let me praise the boy."

"Oh, marvelous," Agathon cried. "Alcibiades, nothing can make me stay next to you now. I'm moving no matter what. I simply *must* hear what Socrates has to say about me."

"There we go again," said Alcibiades. "It's the same old story: when Socrates is around, nobody else can get close to a good-looking man. Look how smoothly and plausibly he found a reason for Agathon to lie down next to him!"

And then, all of a sudden, while Agathon was changing places, a large drunken group, finding the gates open because someone was just leaving, walked into the room and joined the party. There was noise everywhere, and everyone was made to start drinking again in no particular order.

At that point, Aristodemus said, Eryximachus, Phaedrus, and some others among the original guests made their excuses and left. He himself fell asleep and slept for a long time (it was winter, and the nights were quite long). He woke up just as dawn was about to break; the roosters were crowing already. He saw that the others had either left or were asleep on their couches and that only Agathon, Aristophanes, and Socrates were still awake, drinking out of a large cup which they were passing around from left to right. Socrates was talking to them. Aristodemus couldn't remember exactly what they were saying—he'd missed the first part of their discussion, and he was half-asleep anyway—but the main point was that Socrates was trying to prove to them that authors should be able to write both comedy and tragedy: the skillful tragic dramatist should also be a comic poet. He was about to clinch his argument, though, to tell the truth, sleepy as they were, they were hardly able to follow his reasoning. In fact, Aristophanes fell asleep in the middle of the discussion, and very soon thereafter, as day was breaking, Agathon also drifted off.

But after getting them off to sleep, Socrates got up and left, and Aristodemus followed him, as always. He said that Socrates went directly to the Lyceum, washed up, spent the rest of the day just as he always did, and only then, as evening was falling, went home to rest.

REPUBLIC I

*On his way back from the Piraeus, where he has been attending a religious
festival, Socrates meets Polemarchus and goes with him to the house of his
father Cephalus (327a–328b). A discussion of what justice is ensues, which
begins with a lengthy examination of Polemarchus in which he is forced to
abandon a number of views about justice he has adopted along the way (331c–
336b). Thrasymachus is irritated by the examination of Polemarchus and
demands that Socrates give his own positive account of justice, instead of
simply refuting other people's. Socrates claims that he cannot give such an
account because he does not know what justice is, and persuades
Thrasymachus to give an account in his place (336b–338a). Thrasymachus
seems to be refuted but since Glaucon, Adeimantus, and even Socrates himself
(354b) are all dissatisfied with the outcome of Book I (358b, 367b), we must
wonder how successful Plato himself thought Socrates' refutations of
Thrasymachus actually were.*

I went down to the Piraeus yesterday with Glaucon, the son of Ariston. I   327
wanted to say a prayer to the goddess,[1] and I was also curious to see how
they would manage the festival, since they were holding it for the first
time. I thought the procession of the local residents was a fine one and that
the one conducted by the Thracians was no less outstanding. After we had
said our prayer and seen the procession, we started back towards Athens.
Polemarchus saw us from a distance as we were setting off for home and   b
told his slave to run and ask us to wait for him. The slave caught hold of
my cloak from behind: Polemarchus wants you to wait, he said. I turned
around and asked where Polemarchus was. He's coming up behind you,
he said, please wait for him. And Glaucon replied: All right, we will.

Just then Polemarchus caught up with us. Adeimantus, Glaucon's   c
brother, was with him and so were Niceratus, the son of Nicias, and some
others, all of whom were apparently on their way from the procession.

Polemarchus said: It looks to me, Socrates, as if you two are starting off
for Athens.

Translated by G.M.A. Grube, revised by C.D.C. Reeve.
1. The Thracian goddess Bendis, whose cult had recently been introduced in the
Piraeus, the harbor town of Athens.

It looks the way it is, then, I said.

Do you see how many we are? he said.

I do.

Well, you must either prove stronger than we are, or you will have to stay here.

Isn't there another alternative, namely, that we persuade you to let us go?

But could you persuade us, if we won't listen?

Certainly not, Glaucon said.

Well, we won't listen; you'd better make up your mind to that.

328   Don't you know, Adeimantus said, that there is to be a torch race on horseback for the goddess tonight?

On horseback? I said. That's something new. Are they going to race on horseback and hand the torches on in relays, or what?

In relays, Polemarchus said, and there will be an all-night festival that will be well worth seeing. After dinner, we'll go out to look at it. We'll be joined there by many of the young men, and we'll talk. So don't go; stay.

b   It seems, Glaucon said, that we'll have to stay.

If you think so, I said, then we must.

So we went to Polemarchus' house, and there we found Lysias and Euthydemus, the brothers of Polemarchus, Thrasymachus of Chalcedon, Charmantides of Paeania, and Clitophon the son of Aristonymus. Polemarchus' father, Cephalus, was also there, and I thought he looked quite

c   old, as I hadn't seen him for some time. He was sitting on a sort of cushioned chair with a wreath on his head, as he had been offering a sacrifice in the courtyard. There was a circle of chairs, and we sat down by him.

As soon as he saw me, Cephalus welcomed me and said: Socrates, you don't come down to the Piraeus to see us as often as you should. If it were still easy for me to walk to town, you wouldn't have to come here; we'd

d   come to you. But, as it is, you ought to come here more often, for you should know that as the physical pleasures wither away, my desire for conversation and its pleasures grows. So do as I say: Stay with these young men now, but come regularly to see us, just as you would to friends or relatives.

Indeed, Cephalus, I replied, I enjoy talking with the very old, for we should ask them, as we might ask those who have travelled a road that we

e   too will probably have to follow, what kind of road it is, whether rough and difficult or smooth and easy. And I'd gladly find out from you what you think about this, as you have reached the point in life the poets call "the threshold of old age."[2] Is it a difficult time? What is your report about it?

2. *Iliad* xxii.60, xxiv.487; *Odyssey* xv.246, 348, xxiii.212.

[Socrates/Polemarchus/Glaucon/Cephalus]

By god, Socrates, I'll tell you exactly what I think. A number of us, who   *329*
are more or less the same age, often get together in accordance with the old
saying.³ When we meet, the majority complain about the lost pleasures
they remember from their youth, those of sex, drinking parties, feasts, and
the other things that go along with them, and they get angry as if they had
been deprived of important things and had lived well then but are now
hardly living at all. Some others moan about the abuse heaped on old
people by their relatives, and because of this they repeat over and over   *b*
that old age is the cause of many evils. But I don't think they blame the real
cause, Socrates, for if old age were really the cause, I should have suffered
in the same way and so should everyone else of my age. But as it is, I've
met some who don't feel like that in the least. Indeed, I was once present
when someone asked the poet Sophocles: "How are you as far as sex goes,
Sophocles? Can you still make love with a woman?" "Quiet, man," the   *c*
poet replied, "I am very glad to have escaped from all that, like a slave
who has escaped from a savage and tyrannical master." I thought at the
time that he was right, and I still do, for old age brings peace and freedom
from all such things. When the appetites relax and cease to importune us,
everything Sophocles said comes to pass, and we escape from many mad
masters. In these matters and in those concerning relatives, the real cause *d*
isn't old age, Socrates, but the way people live. If they are moderate and
contented, old age, too, is only moderately onerous; if they aren't, both old
age and youth are hard to bear.

I admired him for saying that and I wanted him to tell me more, so I
urged him on: When you say things like that, Cephalus, I suppose that the   *e*
majority of people don't agree, they think that you bear old age more
easily not because of the way you live but because you're wealthy, for the
wealthy, they say, have many consolations.

That's true; they don't agree. And there is something in what they say,
though not as much as they think. Themistocles' retort is relevant here.
When someone from Seriphus insulted him by saying that his high reputation was due to his city and not to himself, he replied that, had he been a   *330*
Seriphian, he wouldn't be famous, but neither would the other even if he
had been an Athenian. The same applies to those who aren't rich and find
old age hard to bear: A good person wouldn't easily bear old age if he
were poor, but a bad one wouldn't be at peace with himself even if he were
wealthy.

Did you inherit most of your wealth, Cephalus, I asked, or did you make
it for yourself?

What did I make for myself, Socrates, you ask. As a money-maker I'm in
a sort of mean between my grandfather and my father. My grandfather   *b*
and namesake inherited about the same amount of wealth as I possess but

---

3. "God ever draws together like to like" (*Odyssey* xvii.218).

[Cephalus/Socrates]

multiplied it many times. My father, Lysanias, however, diminished that amount to even less than I have now. As for me, I'm satisfied to leave my sons here not less but a little more than I inherited.

The reason I asked is that you don't seem to love money too much. And those who haven't made their own money are usually like you. But those *c* who have made it for themselves are twice as fond of it as those who haven't. Just as poets love their poems and fathers love their children, so those who have made their own money don't just care about it because it's useful, as other people do, but because it's something they've made themselves. This makes them poor company, for they haven't a good word to say about anything except money.

That's true.

d It certainly is. But tell me something else. What's the greatest good you've received from being very wealthy?

What I have to say probably wouldn't persuade most people. But you know, Socrates, that when someone thinks his end is near, he becomes frightened and concerned about things he didn't fear before. It's then that the stories we're told about Hades, about how people who've been unjust here must pay the penalty there—stories he used to make fun of—twist *e* his soul this way and that for fear they're true. And whether because of the weakness of old age or because he is now closer to what happens in Hades and has a clearer view of it, or whatever it is, he is filled with foreboding and fear, and he examines himself to see whether he has been unjust to anyone. If he finds many injustices in his life, he awakes from sleep in terror, as children do, and lives in anticipation of bad things to come. But *331* someone who knows that he hasn't been unjust has sweet good hope as his constant companion—a nurse to his old age, as Pindar[4] says, for he puts it charmingly, Socrates, when he says that when someone lives a just and pious life

> Sweet hope is in his heart,
> Nurse and companion to his age.
> Hope, captain of the ever-twisting
> Minds of mortal men.

How wonderfully well he puts that. It's in this connection that wealth is most valuable, I'd say, not for every man but for a decent and orderly one. *b* Wealth can do a lot to save us from having to cheat or deceive someone against our will and from having to depart for that other place in fear because we owe sacrifice to a god or money to a person. It has many other uses, but, benefit for benefit, I'd say that this is how it is most useful to a man of any understanding.

4. Frg. 214 (Snell).

[Cephalus/Socrates]

A fine sentiment, Cephalus, but, speaking of this very thing itself, namely, justice, are we to say unconditionally that it is speaking the truth and paying whatever debts one has incurred? Or is doing these things sometimes just, sometimes unjust? I mean this sort of thing, for example: Everyone would surely agree that if a sane man lends weapons to a friend and then asks for them back when he is out of his mind, the friend shouldn't return them, and wouldn't be acting justly if he did. Nor should anyone be willing to tell the whole truth to someone who is out of his mind.

That's true.

Then the definition of justice isn't speaking the truth and repaying what one has borrowed.

It certainly is, Socrates, said Polemarchus, interrupting, if indeed we're to trust Simonides at all.[5]

Well, then, Cephalus said, I'll hand over the argument to you, as I have to look after the sacrifice.

So, Polemarchus said, am I then to be your heir in everything?

You certainly are, Cephalus said, laughing, and off he went to the sacrifice.

Then tell us, heir to the argument, I said, just what Simonides stated about justice that you consider correct.

He stated that it is just to give to each what is owed to him. And it's a fine saying, in my view.

Well, now, it isn't easy to doubt Simonides, for he's a wise and godlike man. But what exactly does he mean? Perhaps you know, Polemarchus, but I don't understand him. Clearly, he doesn't mean what we said a moment ago, that it is just to give back whatever a person has lent to you, even if he's out of his mind when he asks for it. And yet what he has lent to you is surely something that's owed to him, isn't it?

Yes.

But it is absolutely not to be given to him when he's out of his mind?

That's true.

Then it seems that Simonides must have meant something different when he says that to return what is owed is just.

Something different indeed, by god. He means that friends owe it to their friends to do good for them, never harm.

I follow you. Someone doesn't give a lender back what he's owed by giving him gold, if doing so would be harmful, and both he and the lender are friends. Isn't that what you think Simonides meant?

It is.

c

d

e

332

b

---

5. Simonides (c. 548–468 B.C.), a lyric and elegiac poet, was born in the Aegean island of Ceos.

[Socrates/Cephalus/Polemarchus]

But what about this? Should one also give one's enemies whatever is owed to them?

By all means, one should give them what is owed to them. And in my view what enemies owe to each other is appropriately and precisely—something bad.

It seems then that Simonides was speaking in riddles—just like a poet!—when he said what justice is, for he thought it just to give to each *c* what is appropriate to him, and this is what he called giving him what is owed to him.

What else did you think he meant?

Then what do you think he'd answer if someone asked him: "Simonides, which of the things that are owed or that are appropriate for someone or something to have does the craft[6] we call medicine give, and to whom or what does it give them?"

It's clear that it gives medicines, food, and drink to bodies.

And what owed or appropriate things does the craft we call cooking give, and to whom or what does it give them?

d   It gives seasonings to food.

Good. Now, what does the craft we call justice give, and to whom or what does it give it?

If we are to follow the previous answers, Socrates, it gives benefits to friends and does harm to enemies.

Simonides means, then, that to treat friends well and enemies badly is justice?

I believe so.

And who is most capable of treating friends well and enemies badly in matters of disease and health?

A doctor.

e   And who can do so best in a storm at sea?

A ship's captain.

What about the just person? In what actions and what work is he most capable of benefiting friends and harming enemies?

In wars and alliances, I suppose.

All right. Now, when people aren't sick, Polemarchus, a doctor is useless to them?

True.

And so is a ship's captain to those who aren't sailing?

Yes.

And to people who aren't at war, a just man is useless?

---

6. Here and in what follows "craft" translates *technē*. As Socrates conceives it a *technē* is a disciplined body of knowledge founded on a grasp of the truth about what is good and bad, right and wrong, in the matters of concern to it.

[Socrates/Polemarchus]

No, I don't think that at all.
Justice is also useful in peacetime, then?
It is.   333
And so is farming, isn't it?
Yes.
For getting produce?
Yes.
And shoemaking as well?
Yes.
For getting shoes, I think you'd say?
Certainly.
Well, then, what is justice useful for getting and using in peacetime?
Contracts, Socrates.
And by contracts do you mean partnerships, or what?
I mean partnerships.
Is someone a good and useful partner in a game of checkers because he's
just or because he's a checkers player?   b
Because he's a checkers player.
And in laying bricks and stones, is a just person a better and more useful
partner than a builder?
Not at all.
In what kind of partnership, then, is a just person a better partner than a
builder or a lyre-player, in the way that a lyre-player is better than a just
person at hitting the right notes?
In money matters, I think.
Except perhaps, Polemarchus, in using money, for whenever one needs
to buy a horse jointly, I think a horse breeder is a more useful partner, isn't
he?   c
Apparently.
And when one needs to buy a boat, it's a boatbuilder or a ship's captain?
Probably.
In what joint use of silver or gold, then, is a just person a more useful
partner than the others?
When it must be deposited for safekeeping, Socrates.
You mean whenever there is no need to use them but only to keep them?
That's right.
Then it is when money isn't being used that justice is useful for it?
I'm afraid so.   d
And whenever one needs to keep a pruning knife safe, but not to use it,
justice is useful both in partnerships and for the individual. When you
need to use it, however, it is skill at vine pruning that's useful?
Apparently.
You'll agree, then, that when one needs to keep a shield or a lyre safe

[Polemarchus/Socrates]

and not to use them, justice is a useful thing, but when you need to use them, it is soldiery or musicianship that's useful?

Necessarily.

And so, too, with everything else, justice is useless when they are in use but useful when they aren't?

It looks that way.

e   In that case, justice isn't worth much, since it is only useful for useless things. But let's look into the following point. Isn't the person most able to land a blow, whether in boxing or any other kind of fight, also most able to guard against it?

Certainly.

And the one who is most able to guard against disease is also most able to produce it unnoticed?

So it seems to me, anyway.

And the one who is the best guardian of an army is the very one who can
334   steal the enemy's plans and dispositions?

Certainly.

Whenever someone is a clever guardian, then, he is also a clever thief.

Probably so.

If a just person is clever at guarding money, therefore, he must also be clever at stealing it.

According to our argument, at any rate.

A just person has turned out then, it seems, to be a kind of thief. Maybe you learned this from Homer, for he's fond of Autolycus, the maternal
b   grandfather of Odysseus, whom he describes as better than everyone at lying and stealing.[7] According to you, Homer, and Simonides, then, justice seems to be some sort of craft of stealing, one that benefits friends and harms enemies. Isn't that what you meant?

No, by god, it isn't. I don't know any more what I did mean, but I still believe that to benefit one's friends and harm one's enemies is justice.

Speaking of friends, do you mean those a person believes to be good
c   and useful to him or those who actually are good and useful, even if he doesn't think they are, and similarly with enemies?

Probably, one loves those one considers good and useful and hates those one considers bad and harmful.

But surely people often make mistakes about this, believing many people to be good and useful when they aren't, and making the opposite mistake about enemies?

They do indeed.

And then good people are their enemies and bad ones their friends?

That's right.

d   And so it's just to benefit bad people and harm good ones?

---

7. *Odyssey* xix.392–98.

Apparently.

But good people are just and able to do no wrong?

True.

Then, according to your account, it's just to do bad things to those who do no injustice.

No, that's not just at all, Socrates; my account must be a bad one.

It's just, then, is it, to harm unjust people and benefit just ones?

That's obviously a more attractive view than the other one, anyway.

Then, it follows, Polemarchus, that it is just for the many, who are mistaken in their judgment, to harm their friends, who are bad, and benefit their enemies, who are good. And so we arrive at a conclusion opposite to *e* what we said Simonides meant.

That certainly follows. But let's change our definition, for it seems that we didn't define friends and enemies correctly.

How did we define them, Polemarchus?

We said that a friend is someone who is believed to be useful.

And how are we to change that now?

Someone who is both believed to be useful and is useful is a friend; someone who is believed to be useful but isn't, is believed to be a friend but isn't. And the same for the enemy. *335*

According to this account, then, a good person will be a friend and a bad one an enemy.

Yes.

So you want us to add something to what we said before about justice, when we said that it is just to treat friends well and enemies badly. You want us to add to this that it is just to treat well a friend who is good and to harm an enemy who is bad?

Right. That seems fine to me. *b*

Is it, then, the role of a just man to harm anyone?

Certainly, he must harm those who are both bad and enemies.

Do horses become better or worse when they are harmed?

Worse.

With respect to the virtue[8] that makes dogs good or the one that makes horses good?

The one that makes horses good.

And when dogs are harmed, they become worse in the virtue that makes dogs good, not horses?

8. I.e., *aretē*. *Aretē* is broader than our notion of virtue, which tends to be applied only to human beings, and restricted to good sexual behavior or helpfulness on their part to others. *Aretē* could equally be translated "excellence" or "goodness." Thus if something is a knife (say) its *aretē* or "virtue" as a knife is that state or property of it that makes it a good knife—having a sharp blade, and so on. So with the virtue of a man: this might include being intelligent, well-born, or courageous, as well as being just and sexually well-behaved.

Necessarily.

Then won't we say the same about human beings, too, that when they
c   are harmed they become worse in human virtue?

Indeed.

But isn't justice human virtue?

Yes, certainly.

Then people who are harmed must become more unjust?

So it seems.

Can musicians make people unmusical through music?

They cannot.

Or horsemen make people unhorsemanlike through horsemanship?
No.

Well, then, can those who are just make people unjust through justice? In
d   a word, can those who are good make people bad through virtue?

They cannot.

It isn't the function of heat to cool things but of its opposite?

Yes.

Nor the function of dryness to make things wet but of its opposite?

Indeed.

Nor the function of goodness to harm but of its opposite?

Apparently.

And a just person is good?

Indeed.

Then, Polemarchus, it isn't the function of a just person to harm a friend
or anyone else, rather it is the function of his opposite, an unjust person?

In my view that's completely true, Socrates.

e   If anyone tells us, then, that it is just to give to each what he's owed and
understands by this that a just man should harm his enemies and benefit
his friends, he isn't wise to say it, since what he says isn't true, for it has
become clear to us that it is never just to harm anyone?

I agree.

You and I shall fight as partners, then, against anyone who tells us that
Simonides, Bias, Pittacus, or any of our other wise and blessedly happy
men said this.

I, at any rate, am willing to be your partner in the battle.

336   Do you know to whom I think the saying belongs that it is just to benefit
friends and harm enemies?

Who?

I think it belongs to Periander, or Perdiccas, or Xerxes, or Ismenias of
Corinth, or some other wealthy man who believed himself to have great
power.[9]

9. The first three named are notorious tyrants or kings, the fourth a man famous
for his extraordinary wealth.

That's absolutely true.

All right, since it has become apparent that justice and the just aren't what such people say they are, what else could they be?

While we were speaking, Thrasymachus had tried many times to take over the discussion but was restrained by those sitting near him, who *b* wanted to hear our argument to the end. When we paused after what I'd just said, however, he couldn't keep quiet any longer. He coiled himself up like a wild beast about to spring, and he hurled himself at us as if to tear us to pieces.

Polemarchus and I were frightened and flustered as he roared into our midst: What nonsense have you two been talking, Socrates? Why do you act like idiots by giving way to one another? If you truly want to know *c* what justice is, don't just ask questions and then refute the answers simply to satisfy your competitiveness or love of honor. You know very well that it is easier to ask questions than answer them. Give an answer yourself, and tell us what you say the just is. And don't tell me that it's the right, the beneficial, the profitable, the gainful, or the advantageous, but tell me *d* clearly and exactly what you mean; for I won't accept such nonsense from you.

His words startled me, and, looking at him, I was afraid. And I think that if I hadn't seen him before he stared at me, I'd have been dumbstruck. But as it was, I happened to look at him just as our discussion began to exasperate him, so I was able to answer, and, trembling a little, I said: *e* Don't be too hard on us, Thrasymachus, for if Polemarchus and I made an error in our investigation, you should know that we did so unwillingly. If we were searching for gold, we'd never willingly give way to each other, if by doing so we'd destroy our chance of finding it. So don't think that in searching for justice, a thing more valuable than even a large quantity of gold, we'd mindlessly give way to one another or be less than completely serious about finding it. You surely mustn't think that, but rather—as I do—that we're incapable of finding it. Hence it's surely far more appropriate for us to be pitied by you clever people than to be given rough *337* treatment.

When he heard that, he gave a loud, sarcastic laugh. By Heracles, he said, that's just Socrates' usual irony. I knew, and I said so to these people earlier, that you'd be unwilling to answer and that, if someone questioned *you*, you'd be ironical and do anything rather than give an answer.

That's because you're a clever fellow, Thrasymachus. You knew very well that if you ask someone how much twelve is, and, as you ask, you warn him by saying "Don't tell me, man, that twelve is twice six, or three *b* times four, or six times two, or four times three, for I won't accept such nonsense," then you'll see clearly, I think, that no one could answer a question framed like that. And if he said to you: "What are you saying, Thrasymachus, am I not to give any of the answers you mention, not even

[Polemarchus/Socrates/Thrasymachus]

if twelve happens to be one of those things? I'm amazed. Do you want me to say something other than the truth? Or do you mean something else?" What answer would you give him?

Well, so you think the two cases are alike?

Why shouldn't they be alike? But even if they aren't alike, yet seem so to the person you asked, do you think him any less likely to give the answer that seems right to him, whether we forbid him to or not?

Is that what you're going to do, give one of the forbidden answers?

I wouldn't be surprised—provided that it's the one that seems right to me after I've investigated the matter.

What if I show you a different answer about justice than all these—and a better one? What would you deserve then?

What else than the appropriate penalty for one who doesn't know, namely, to learn from the one who does know? Therefore, that's what I deserve.

You amuse me, but in addition to learning, you must pay a fine.

I will as soon as I have some money.

He has some already, said Glaucon. If it's a matter of money, speak, Thrasymachus, for we'll all contribute for Socrates.

I know, he said, so that Socrates can carry on as usual. He gives no answer himself, and then, when someone else does give one, he takes up the argument and refutes it.

How can someone give an answer, I said, when he doesn't know it and doesn't claim to know it, and when an eminent man forbids him to express the opinion he has? It's much more appropriate for you to answer, since you say you know and can tell us. So do it as a favor to me, and don't begrudge your teaching to Glaucon and the others.

While I was saying this, Glaucon and the others begged him to speak. It was obvious that Thrasymachus thought he had a fine answer and that he wanted to earn their admiration by giving it, but he pretended that he wanted to indulge his love of victory by forcing me to answer. However, he agreed in the end, and then said: There you have Socrates' wisdom; he himself isn't willing to teach, but he goes around learning from others and isn't even grateful to them.

When you say that I learn from others you are right, Thrasymachus, but when you say that I'm not grateful, that isn't true. I show what gratitude I can, but since I have no money, I can give only praise. But just how enthusiastically I give it when someone seems to me to speak well, you'll know as soon as you've answered, for I think that you will speak well.

Listen, then. I say that justice is nothing other than the advantage of the stronger. Well, why don't you praise me? But then you'd do anything to avoid having to do that.

I must first understand you, for I don't yet know what you mean. The advantage of the stronger, you say, is just. What do you mean,

[Socrates/Thrasymachus]

Thrasymachus? Surely you don't mean something like this: Polydamus, the pancratist,[10] is stronger than we are; it is to his advantage to eat beef to build up his physical strength; therefore, this food is also advantageous and just for us who are weaker than he is?   *d*

You disgust me, Socrates. Your trick is to take hold of the argument at the point where you can do it the most harm.

Not at all, but tell us more clearly what you mean.

Don't you know that some cities are ruled by a tyranny, some by a democracy, and some by an aristocracy?

Of course.

And in each city this element is stronger, namely, the ruler?

Certainly.

And each makes laws to its own advantage. Democracy makes democratic laws, tyranny makes tyrannical laws, and so on with the others.   *e*
And they declare what they have made—what is to their own advantage—to be just for their subjects, and they punish anyone who goes against this as lawless and unjust. This, then, is what I say justice is, the same in all cities, the advantage of the established rule. Since the established rule is surely stronger, anyone who reasons correctly will conclude that the just *339* is the same everywhere, namely, the advantage of the stronger.

Now I see what you mean. Whether it's true or not, I'll try to find out. But you yourself have answered that the just is the advantageous, Thrasymachus, whereas you forbade that answer to me. True, you've added "of the stronger" to it.

And I suppose you think that's an insignificant addition.   *.b*

It isn't clear yet whether it's significant. But it is clear that we must investigate to see whether or not it's true. I agree that the just is some kind of advantage. But you add that it's *of the stronger*. I don't know about that. We'll have to look into it.

Go ahead and look.

We will. Tell me, don't you also say that it is just to obey the rulers? I do.

And are the rulers in all cities infallible, or are they liable to error?   *c*

No doubt they are liable to error.

When they undertake to make laws, therefore, they make some correctly, others incorrectly?

I suppose so.

And a law is correct if it prescribes what is to the rulers' own advantage and incorrect if it prescribes what is to their disadvantage? Is that what you mean?

It is.

10. The *pancration* was a mixture of boxing and wrestling combined with kicking and strangling. Biting and gouging were forbidden, but pretty well everything else, including breaking and dislocating limbs, was permitted.

[Socrates/Thrasymachus]

And whatever laws they make must be obeyed by their subjects, and this is justice?

Of course.

d   Then, according to your account, it is just to do not only what is to the advantage of the stronger, but also the opposite, what is not to their advantage.

What are you saying?

The same as you. But let's examine it more fully. Haven't we agreed that, in giving orders to their subjects, the rulers are sometimes in error as to what is best for themselves, and yet that it is just for their subjects to do whatever their rulers order? Haven't we agreed to that much?

I think so.

e   Then you must also think that you have agreed that it is just to do what is disadvantageous to the rulers and those who are stronger, whenever they unintentionally order what is bad for themselves. But you also say that it is just for the others to obey the orders they give. You're terribly clever, Thrasymachus, but doesn't it necessarily follow that it is just to do the opposite of what you said, since the weaker are then ordered to do what is disadvantageous to the stronger?

340   By god, Socrates, said Polemarchus, that's quite clear.

If you are to be his witness anyway, said Cleitophon, interrupting.

Who needs a witness? Polemarchus replied. Thrasymachus himself agrees that the rulers sometimes order what is bad for themselves and that it is just for the others to do it.

That, Polemarchus, is because Thrasymachus maintained that it is just to obey the orders of the rulers.

b   He also maintained, Cleitophon, that the advantage of the stronger is just. And having maintained both principles he went on to agree that the stronger sometimes gives orders to those who are weaker than he is—in other words, to his subjects—that are disadvantageous to the stronger himself. From these agreements it follows that what is to the advantage of the stronger is no more just than what is not to his advantage.

But, Cleitophon responded, he said that the advantage of the stronger is what the stronger believes to be his advantage. This is what the weaker must do, and this is what he maintained the just to be.

That isn't what he said, Polemarchus replied.

It makes no difference, Polemarchus, I said. If Thrasymachus wants to *c*   put it that way now, let's accept it. Tell me, Thrasymachus, is this what you wanted to say the just is, namely, what the stronger believes to be to his advantage, whether it is in fact to his advantage or not? Is that what we are to say you mean?

Not at all. Do you think I'd call someone who is in error stronger at the very moment he errs?

[Socrates/Thrasymachus/Polemarchus/Cleitophon]

I did think that was what you meant when you agreed that the rulers aren't infallible but are liable to error.

That's because you are a false witness in arguments, Socrates. When *d* someone makes an error in the treatment of patients, do you call him a doctor in regard to that very error? Or when someone makes an error in accounting, do you call him an accountant in regard to that very error in calculation? I think that we express ourselves in words that, taken literally, do say that a doctor is in error, or an accountant, or a grammarian. But each of these, insofar as he is what we call him, never errs, so that, according to *e* the precise account (and you are a stickler for precise accounts), no crafts- man ever errs. It's when his knowledge fails him that he makes an error, and in regard to that error he is no craftsman. No craftsman, expert, or ruler makes an error at the moment when he is ruling, even though every- one will say that a physician or a ruler makes errors. It's in this loose way that you must also take the answer I gave earlier. But the most precise answer is this. A ruler, insofar as he is a ruler, never makes errors and *341* unerringly decrees what is best for himself, and this his subject must do. Thus, as I said from the first, it is just to do what is to the advantage of the stronger.

All right, Thrasymachus, so you think I'm a false witness?

You certainly are.

And you think that I asked the questions I did in order to harm you in the argument?

I know it very well, but it won't do you any good. You'll never be able to *b* trick me, so you can't harm me that way, and without trickery you'll never be able to overpower me in argument.

I wouldn't so much as try, Thrasymachus. But in order to prevent this sort of thing from happening again, define clearly whether it is the ruler and stronger in the ordinary sense or in the precise sense whose advantage you said it is just for the weaker to promote as the advantage of the stronger.

I mean the ruler in the most precise sense. Now practice your harm- doing and false witnessing on that if you can—I ask no concessions from you—but you certainly won't be able to.

Do you think that I'm crazy enough to try to shave a lion or to bear false *c* witness against Thrasymachus?

You certainly tried just now, though you were a loser at that too.

Enough of this. Tell me: Is a doctor in the precise sense, whom you mentioned before, a money-maker or someone who treats the sick? Tell me about the one who is really a doctor.

He's the one who treats the sick.

What about a ship's captain? Is a captain in the precise sense a ruler of sailors or a sailor?

A ruler of sailors.

We shouldn't, I think, take into account the fact that he sails in a ship,
d and he shouldn't be called a sailor for that reason, for it isn't because of his
sailing that he is called a ship's captain, but because of his craft and his rule
over sailors?

That's true.

And is there something advantageous to each of these, that is, to bodies
and to sailors?

Certainly.

And aren't the respective crafts by nature set over them to seek and
provide what is to their advantage?

They are.

And is there any advantage for each of the crafts themselves except to be
as complete or perfect as possible?

e What are you asking?

This: If you asked me whether our bodies are sufficient in themselves, or
whether they need something else, I'd answer: "They certainly have
needs. And because of this, because our bodies are deficient rather than
self-sufficient, the craft of medicine has now been discovered. The craft of
medicine was developed to provide what is advantageous for a body." Do
you think that I'm right in saying this or not?

You are right.

342 Now, is medicine deficient? Does a craft need some further virtue, as the
eyes are in need of sight, and the ears of hearing, so that another craft is
needed to seek and provide what is advantageous to them? Does a craft
itself have some similar deficiency, so that each craft needs another, to seek
out what is to its advantage? And does the craft that does the seeking need
still another, and so on without end? Or does each seek out what is to its
b own advantage by itself? Or does it need neither itself nor another craft to
seek out what is advantageous to it, because of its own deficiencies? Or is it
that there is no deficiency or error in any craft? That it isn't appropriate for
any craft to seek what is to the advantage of anything except that of which
it is the craft? And that, since it is itself correct, it is without either fault or
impurity, as long as it is wholly and precisely the craft that it is? Consider
this with the preciseness of language you mentioned. Is it so or not?

It appears to be so.

Apparently so.

c Medicine doesn't seek its own advantage, then, but that of the body?

Yes.

And horse-breeding doesn't seek its own advantage, but that of horses?
Indeed, no other craft seeks its own advantage—for it has no further
needs—but the advantage of that of which it is the craft?

Apparently so.

Now, surely, Thrasymachus, the crafts rule over and are stronger than
the things of which they are the crafts?

Very reluctantly, he conceded this as well.

No kind of knowledge seeks or orders what is advantageous to itself, then, but what is advantageous to the weaker, which is subject to it.   *d*

He tried to fight this conclusion, but he conceded it in the end. And after he had, I said: Surely, then, no doctor, insofar as he is a doctor, seeks or orders what is advantageous to himself, but what is advantageous to his patient? We agreed that a doctor in the precise sense is a ruler of bodies, not a money-maker. Wasn't that agreed?

Yes.

So a ship's captain in the precise sense is a ruler of sailors, not a sailor?

That's what we agreed.   *e*

Doesn't it follow that a ship's captain or ruler won't seek and order what is advantageous to himself, but what is advantageous to a sailor?

He reluctantly agreed.

So, then, Thrasymachus, no one in any position of rule, insofar as he is a ruler, seeks or orders what is advantageous to himself, but what is advantageous to his subjects; the ones of whom he is himself the craftsman. It is to his subjects and what is advantageous and proper to them that he looks, and everything he says and does he says and does for them.

When we reached this point in the argument, and it was clear to all that his account of justice had turned into its opposite, instead of answering,   343 Thrasymachus said: Tell me, Socrates, do you still have a wet nurse?

What's this? Hadn't you better answer *my* questions rather than asking *me* such things?

Because she's letting you run around with a snotty nose, and doesn't wipe it when she needs to! Why, for all she cares, you don't even know about sheep and shepherds.

Just what is it I don't know?

You think that shepherds and cowherds seek the good of their sheep   *b* and cattle, and fatten them and take care of them, looking to something other than their master's good and their own. Moreover, you believe that rulers in cities—true rulers, that is—think about their subjects differently than one does about sheep, and that night and day they think of something besides their own advantage. You are so far from understanding   *c* about justice and what's just, about injustice and what's unjust, that you don't realize that justice is really the good of another, the advantage of the stronger and the ruler, and harmful to the one who obeys and serves. Injustice is the opposite, it rules the truly simple and just, and those it rules do what is to the advantage of the other and stronger, and they make the one they serve happy, but themselves not at all. You must look at it as follows, my most simple Socrates: A just man always gets less than an   *d* unjust one. First, in their contracts with one another, you'll never find, when the partnership ends, that a just partner has got more than an unjust one, but less. Second, in matters relating to the city, when taxes are to be

[Socrates/Thrasymachus]

paid, a just man pays more on the same property, an unjust one less, but when the city is giving out refunds, a just man gets nothing, while an

e unjust one makes a large profit. Finally, when each of them holds a ruling position in some public office, a just person, even if he isn't penalized in other ways, finds that his private affairs deteriorate because he has to neglect them, that he gains no advantage from the public purse because of his justice, and that he's hated by his relatives and acquaintances when he's unwilling to do them an unjust favor. The opposite is true of an unjust man in every respect. Therefore, I repeat what I said before: A person of

344 great power outdoes everyone else.[11] Consider him if you want to figure out how much more advantageous it is for the individual to be just rather than unjust. You'll understand this most easily if you turn your thoughts to the most complete injustice, the one that makes the doer of injustice happiest and the sufferers of it, who are unwilling to do injustice, most wretched. This is tyranny, which through stealth or force appropriates the property of others, whether sacred or profane, public or private, not little by little, but all at once. If someone commits only one part of injustice and

b is caught, he's punished and greatly reproached—such partly unjust people are called temple-robbers,[12] kidnappers, housebreakers, robbers, and thieves when they commit these crimes. But when someone, in addition to appropriating their possessions, kidnaps and enslaves the citizens as well, instead of these shameful names he is called happy and blessed, not only

c by the citizens themselves, but by all who learn that he has done the whole of injustice. Those who reproach injustice do so because they are afraid not of doing it but of suffering it. So, Socrates, injustice, if it is on a large enough scale, is stronger, freer, and more masterly than justice. And, as I said from the first, justice is what is advantageous to the stronger, while injustice is to one's own profit and advantage.

d   Having emptied this great flood of words into our ears all at once like a bath attendant, Thrasymachus intended to leave. But those present didn't let him and made him stay to give an account of what he had said. I too begged him to stay, and I said to him: After hurling such a speech at us, Thrasymachus, do you intend to leave before adequately instructing us or

e finding out whether you are right or not? Or do you think it a small matter

---

11. Outdoing *(pleonektein)* is an important notion in the remainder of the *Republic*. It is connected to *pleonexia*, which is what one succumbs to when one always wants to outdo everyone else by getting and having more and more. *Pleonexia* is, or is the cause of, injustice (359c), since always wanting to outdo others leads one to try to get what belongs to them, what isn't *one's own*. It is contrasted with *doing or having one's own*, which is, or is the cause of, justice (434a, 441e).

12. The temples acted as public treasuries, so that a temple robber is the equivalent of a present-day bank robber.

to determine which whole way of life would make living most worthwhile for each of us?

Is *that* what I seem to you to think? Thrasymachus said.

Either that, or else you care nothing for us and aren't worried about whether we'll live better or worse lives because of our ignorance of what you say you know. So show some willingness to teach it to us. It wouldn't be a bad investment for you to be the benefactor of a group as large as ours. For my own part, I'll tell you that I am not persuaded. I don't believe   345
that injustice is more profitable than justice, not even if you give it full scope and put no obstacles in its way. Suppose that there *is* an unjust person, and suppose he *does* have the power to do injustice, whether by trickery or open warfare; nonetheless, he doesn't persuade me that injustice is more profitable than justice. Perhaps someone here, besides myself, feels the same as I do. So come now, and persuade us that we are   *b*
wrong to esteem justice more highly than injustice in planning our lives.

And how am I to persuade you, if you aren't persuaded by what I said just now? What more can I do? Am I to take my argument and pour it into your very soul?

God forbid! Don't do that! But, first, stick to what you've said, and then, if you change your position, do it openly and don't deceive us. You see, Thrasymachus, that having defined the true doctor—to continue examining the things you said before—you didn't consider it necessary later to   *c*
keep a precise guard on the true shepherd. You think that, insofar as he's a shepherd, he fattens sheep, not looking to what is best for the sheep but to a banquet, like a guest about to be entertained at a feast, or to a future sale, like a money-maker rather than a shepherd. Shepherding is concerned only to provide what is best for the things it is set over, and it is itself   *d*
adequately provided with all it needs to be at its best when it doesn't fall short in any way of being the craft of shepherding. That's why I thought it necessary for us to agree before that every kind of rule, insofar as it rules, doesn't seek anything other than what is best for the things it rules and cares for, and this is true both of public and private kinds of rule. But do you think that those who rule cities, the true rulers, rule willingly?   *e*

I don't think it, by god, I know it.

But, Thrasymachus, don't you realize that in other kinds of rule no one wants to rule for its own sake, but they ask for pay, thinking that their ruling will benefit not themselves but their subjects? Tell me, doesn't every craft differ from every other in having a different function? Please don't   346
answer contrary to what you believe, so that we can come to some definite conclusion.

Yes, that's what differentiates them.

And each craft benefits us in its own peculiar way, different from the others. For example, medicine gives us health, navigation gives us safety while sailing, and so on with the others?

[Socrates/Thrasymachus]

Certainly.

And wage-earning gives us wages, for this is its function? Or would you
b call medicine the same as navigation? Indeed, if you want to define matters precisely, as you proposed, even if someone who is a ship's captain
becomes healthy because sailing is advantageous to his health, you
wouldn't for that reason call his craft medicine?

Certainly not.

Nor would you call wage-earning medicine, even if someone becomes
healthy while earning wages?

Certainly not.

Nor would you call medicine wage-earning, even if someone earns pay
while healing?

c   No.

We are agreed, then, that each craft brings its own peculiar benefit?

It does.

Then whatever benefit all craftsmen receive in common must clearly
result from their joint practice of some additional craft that benefits each of
them?

So it seems.

And we say that the additional craft in question, which benefits the
craftsmen by earning them wages, is the craft of wage-earning?

He reluctantly agreed.

Then this benefit, receiving wages, doesn't result from their own craft,
d but rather, if we're to examine this precisely, medicine provides health,
and wage-earning provides wages; house-building provides a house, and
wage-earning, which accompanies it, provides a wage; and so on with the
other crafts. Each of them does its own work and benefits the things it is set
over. So, if wages aren't added, is there any benefit that the craftsman gets
from his craft?

Apparently none.

e   But he still provides a benefit when he works for nothing?

Yes, I think he does.

Then, it is clear now, Thrasymachus, that no craft or rule provides for its
own advantage, but, as we've been saying for some time, it provides and
orders for its subject and aims at its advantage, that of the weaker, not of
the stronger. That's why I said just now, Thrasymachus, that no one willingly chooses to rule and to take other people's troubles in hand and
347 straighten them out, but each asks for wages; for anyone who intends to
practice his craft well never does or orders what is best for himself—at
least not when he orders as his craft prescribes—but what is best for his
subject. It is because of this, it seems, that wages must be provided to a
person if he's to be willing to rule, whether in the form of money or honor
or a penalty if he refuses.

[Socrates / Thrasymachus]

What do you mean, Socrates? said Glaucon. I know the first two kinds of
wages, but I don't understand what penalty you mean or how you can call
it a wage.

Then you don't understand the best people's kind of wages, the kind
that moves the most decent to rule, when they are willing to rule at all.
Don't you know that the love of honor and the love of money are despised,   *b*
and rightly so?

I do.

Therefore good people won't be willing to rule for the sake of either
money or honor. They don't want to be paid wages openly for ruling and
get called hired hands, nor to take them in secret from their rule and be
called thieves. And they won't rule for the sake of honor, because they
aren't ambitious honor-lovers. So, if they're to be willing to rule, some   *c*
compulsion or punishment must be brought to bear on them—perhaps
that's why it is thought shameful to seek to rule before one is compelled to.
Now, the greatest punishment, if one isn't willing to rule, is to be ruled by
someone worse than oneself. And I think that it's fear of this that makes
decent people rule when they do. They approach ruling not as something
good or something to be enjoyed, but as something necessary, since it can't
be entrusted to anyone better than—or even as good as—themselves. In a   *d*
city of good men, if it came into being, the citizens would fight in order *not*
to rule, just as they do now in order to rule. There it would be quite clear
that anyone who is really a true ruler doesn't by nature seek his own
advantage but that of his subjects. And everyone, knowing this, would
rather be benefited by others than take the trouble to benefit them. So I
can't at all agree with Thrasymachus that justice is the advantage of the
stronger—but we'll look further into that another time. What Thrasym-   *e*
achus is now saying—that the life of an unjust person is better than that of
a just one—seems to be of far greater importance. Which life would you
choose, Glaucon? And which of our views do you consider truer?

I certainly think that the life of a just person is more profitable.

Did you hear all of the good things Thrasymachus listed a moment ago   *348*
for the unjust life?

I heard, but I wasn't persuaded.

Then, do you want us to persuade him, if we're able to find a way, that
what he says isn't true?

Of course I do.

If we oppose him with a parallel speech about the blessings of the just
life, and then he replies, and then we do, we'd have to count and measure
the good things mentioned on each side, and we'd need a jury to decide
the case. But if, on the other hand, we investigate the question, as we've   *b*
been doing, by seeking agreement with each other, we ourselves can be
both jury and advocates at once.

[Glaucon/Socrates]

Certainly.

Which approach do you prefer? I asked.

The second.

Come, then, Thrasymachus, I said, answer us from the beginning. You say that complete injustice is more profitable than complete justice?

c   I certainly do say that, and I've told you why.

Well, then, what do you say about this? Do you call one of the two a virtue and the other a vice?

Of course.

That is to say, you call justice a virtue and injustice a vice?

That's hardly likely, since I say that injustice is profitable and justice isn't.

Then, what exactly do you say?

The opposite.

That justice is a vice?

No, just very high-minded simplicity.

d   Then do you call being unjust being low-minded?

No, I call it good judgment.

You consider unjust people, then, Thrasymachus, to be clever and good?

Yes, those who are completely unjust, who can bring cities and whole communities under their power. Perhaps, you think I meant pickpockets? Not that such crimes aren't also profitable, if they're not found out, but they aren't worth mentioning by comparison to what I'm talking about.

e   I'm not unaware of what you want to say. But I wonder about this: Do you really include injustice with virtue and wisdom, and justice with their opposites?

I certainly do.

That's harder, and it isn't easy now to know what to say. If you had declared that injustice is more profitable, but agreed that it is a vice or shameful, as some others do, we could have discussed the matter on the basis of conventional beliefs. But now, obviously, you'll say that injustice is fine and strong and apply to it all the attributes we used to apply to justice,

349   since you dare to include it with virtue and wisdom.

You've divined my views exactly.

Nonetheless, we mustn't shrink from pursuing the argument and looking into this, just as long as I take you to be saying what you really think. And I believe that you aren't joking now, Thrasymachus, but are saying what you believe to be the truth.

What difference does it make to you, whether *I* believe it or not? It's *my account* you're supposed to be refuting.

It makes no difference. But try to answer this further question: Do you

b   think that a just person wants to outdo someone else who's just?

Not at all, for he wouldn't then be as polite and innocent as he is.

Or to outdo someone who does a just action?

[Glaucon/Socrates/Thrasymachus]

No, he doesn't even want to do that.

And does he claim that he deserves to outdo an unjust person and believe that it is just for him to do so, or doesn't he believe that?

He'd want to outdo him, and he'd claim to deserve to do so, but he wouldn't be able.

That's not what I asked, but whether a just person wants to outdo an unjust person but not a just one, thinking that this is what he deserves?   *c*

He does.

What about an unjust person? Does he claim that he deserves to outdo a just person or someone who does a just action?

Of course he does; he thinks he deserves to outdo everyone.

Then will an unjust person also outdo an *unjust* person or someone who does an *unjust* action, and will he strive to get the most he can for himself from everyone?

He will.

Then, let's put it this way: A just person doesn't outdo someone like himself but someone unlike himself, whereas an unjust person outdoes both like and unlike.   *d*

Very well put.

An unjust person is clever and good, and a just one is neither?

That's well put, too.

It follows, then, that an unjust person is like clever and good people, while the other isn't?

Of course that's so. How could he fail to be like them when he has their qualities, while the other isn't like them?

Fine. Then each of them has the qualities of the people he's like?

Of course.

All right, Thrasymachus. Do you call one person musical and another   *e* nonmusical?

I do.

Which of them is clever in music, and which isn't?

The musical one is clever, of course, and the other isn't.

And the things he's clever in, he's good in, and the things he isn't clever in, he's bad in?

Yes.

Isn't the same true of a doctor?

It is.

Do you think that a musician, in tuning his lyre and in tightening and loosening the strings, wants to outdo another musician, claiming that this is what he deserves?

I do not.

But he does want to outdo a nonmusician?

Necessarily.

What about a doctor? Does he, when prescribing food and drink, want

350   to outdo another doctor or someone who does the action that medicine
prescribes?

Certainly not.

But he does want to outdo a nondoctor?

Yes.

In any branch of knowledge or ignorance, do you think that a knowledgeable person would intentionally try to outdo other knowledgeable
people or say something better or different than they do, rather than doing
or saying the very same thing as those like him?

Well, perhaps it must be as you say.

And what about an ignorant person? Doesn't he want to outdo both a
b   knowledgeable person and an ignorant one?

Probably.

A knowledgeable person is clever?

I agree.

And a clever one is good?

I agree.

Therefore, a good and clever person doesn't want to outdo those like
himself but those who are unlike him and his opposite.

So it seems.

But a bad and ignorant person wants to outdo both his like and his
opposite.

Apparently.

Now, Thrasymachus, we found that an unjust person tries to outdo
those like him and those unlike him? Didn't you say that?

I did.

c   And that a just person won't outdo his like but his unlike?

Yes.

Then, a just person is like a clever and good one, and an unjust is like an
ignorant and bad one.

It looks that way.

Moreover, we agreed that each has the qualities of the one he resembles.

Yes, we did.

Then, a just person has turned out to be good and clever, and an unjust
one ignorant and bad.

Thrasymachus agreed to all this, not easily as I'm telling it, but reluc-
d   tantly, with toil, trouble, and—since it was summer—a quantity of sweat
that was a wonder to behold. And then I saw something I'd never seen
before—Thrasymachus blushing. But, in any case, after we'd agreed that
justice is virtue and wisdom and that injustice is vice and ignorance, I said:
All right, let's take that as established. But we also said that injustice is
powerful, or don't you remember that, Thrasymachus?

I remember, but I'm not satisfied with what you're now saying. I could make a speech about it, but, if I did, I know that you'd accuse me of engaging in oratory. So either allow me to speak, or, if you want to ask   *e* questions, go ahead, and I'll say, "All right," and nod yes and no, as one does to old wives' tales.

Don't do that, contrary to your own opinion.

I'll answer so as to please you, since you won't let me make a speech. What else do you want?

Nothing, by god. But if that's what you're going to do, go ahead and do it. I'll ask my questions.

Ask ahead.

I'll ask what I asked before, so that we may proceed with our argument   *351* about justice and injustice in an orderly fashion, for surely it was claimed that injustice is stronger and more powerful than justice. But, now, if justice is indeed wisdom and virtue, it will easily be shown to be stronger than injustice, since injustice is ignorance (no one could now be ignorant of that). However, I don't want to state the matter so unconditionally, Thrasymachus, but to look into it in some such way as this. Would you say   *b* that it is unjust for a city to try to enslave other cities unjustly and to hold them in subjection when it has enslaved many of them?

Of course, that's what the best city will especially do, the one that is most completely unjust.

I understand that's your position, but the point I want to examine is this: Will the city that becomes stronger than another achieve this power without justice, or will it need the help of justice?

If what you said a moment ago stands, and justice is cleverness or wisdom, it will need the help of justice, but if things are as I stated, it will   *c* need the help of injustice.

I'm impressed, Thrasymachus, that you don't merely nod yes or no but give very fine answers.

That's because I'm trying to please you.

You're doing well at it, too. So please me some more by answering this question: Do you think that a city, an army, a band of robbers or thieves, or any other tribe with a common unjust purpose would be able to achieve it if they were unjust to each other?

No, indeed.   *d*

What if they weren't unjust to one another? Would they achieve more?

Certainly.

Injustice, Thrasymachus, causes civil war, hatred, and fighting among themselves, while justice brings friendship and a sense of common purpose. Isn't that so?

Let it be so, in order not to disagree with you.

You're still doing well on that front. So tell me this: If the effect of injustice is to produce hatred wherever it occurs, then, whenever it arises,

whether among free men or slaves, won't it cause them to hate one another, engage in civil war, and prevent them from achieving any common

e   purpose?

Certainly.

What if it arises between two people? Won't they be at odds, hate each
other, and be enemies to one another and to just people?

They will.

Does injustice lose its power to cause dissension when it arises within a
single individual, or will it preserve it intact?

Let it preserve it intact.

Apparently, then, injustice has the power, first, to make whatever it
arises in—whether it is a city, a family, an army, or anything else—

352   incapable of achieving anything as a unit, because of the civil wars and
differences it creates, and, second, it makes that unit an enemy to itself and
to what is in every way its opposite, namely, justice. Isn't that so?

Certainly.

And even in a single individual, it has by its nature the very same effect.
First, it makes him incapable of achieving anything, because he is in a state
of civil war and not of one mind; second, it makes him his own enemy, as
well as the enemy of just people. Hasn't it that effect?

Yes.

And the gods too are just?

Let it be so.

b   So an unjust person is also an enemy of the gods, Thrasymachus, while a
just person is their friend?

Enjoy your banquet of words! Have no fear, I won't oppose you. That
would make these people hate me.

Come, then, complete the banquet for me by continuing to answer as
you've been doing. We have shown that just people are cleverer and more
capable of doing things, while unjust ones aren't even able to act together,

c   for when we speak of a powerful achievement by unjust men acting together, what we say isn't altogether true. They would never have been able
to keep their hands off each other if they were completely unjust. But
clearly there must have been some sort of justice in them that at least
prevented them from doing injustice among themselves at the same time
as they were doing it to others. And it was this that enabled them to
achieve what they did. When they started doing unjust things, they were
only halfway corrupted by their injustice (for those who are all bad and
completely unjust are completely incapable of accomplishing anything).
These are the things I understand to hold, not the ones you first main-

d   tained. We must now examine, as we proposed before, whether just people
also live better and are happier than unjust ones. I think it's clear already
that this is so, but we must look into it further, since the argument concerns
no ordinary topic but the way we ought to live.

[Socrates/Thrasymachus]

Go ahead and look.

I will. Tell me, do you think there is such a thing as the function of a horse?

I do.   *e*

And would you define the function of a horse or of anything else as that which one can do only with it or best with it?

I don't understand.

Let me put it this way: Is it possible to see with anything other than eyes?

Certainly not.

Or to hear with anything other than ears?

No.

Then, we are right to say that seeing and hearing are the functions of eyes and ears?

Of course.

What about this? Could you use a dagger or a carving knife or lots of other things in pruning a vine?   353

Of course.

But wouldn't you do a finer job with a pruning knife designed for the purpose than with anything else?

You would.

Then shall we take pruning to be its function?

Yes.

Now, I think you'll understand what I was asking earlier when I asked whether the function of each thing is what it alone can do or what it does better than anything else.

I understand, and I think that this is the function of each.   *b*

All right. Does each thing to which a particular function is assigned also have a virtue? Let's go over the same ground again. We say that eyes have some function?

They do.

So there is also a virtue of eyes?

There is.

And ears have a function?

Yes.

So there is also a virtue of ears?

There is.

And all other things are the same, aren't they?

They are.

And could eyes perform their function well if they lacked their peculiar   *c*
virtue and had the vice instead?

How could they, for don't you mean if they had blindness instead of sight?

Whatever their virtue is, for I'm not now asking about that but about

[Thrasymachus/Socrates]

whether anything that has a function performs it well by means of its own peculiar virtue and badly by means of its vice?

That's true, it does.

So ears, too, deprived of their own virtue, perform their function badly?

That's right.

d   And the same could be said about everything else?

So it seems.

Come, then, and let's consider this: Is there some function of a soul that you couldn't perform with anything else, for example, taking care of things, ruling, deliberating, and the like? Is there anything other than a soul to which you could rightly assign these, and say that they are its peculiar function?

No, none of them.

What of living? Isn't that a function of a soul?

It certainly is.

And don't we also say that there is a virtue of a soul?

We do.

e   Then, will a soul ever perform its function well, Thrasymachus, if it is deprived of its own peculiar virtue, or is that impossible?

It's impossible.

Doesn't it follow, then, that a bad soul rules and takes care of things badly and that a good soul does all these things well?

It does.

Now, we agreed that justice is a soul's virtue, and injustice its vice?

We did.

Then, it follows that a just soul and a just man will live well, and an unjust one badly.

Apparently so, according to your argument.

And surely anyone who lives well is blessed and happy, and anyone

354   who doesn't is the opposite.

Of course.

Therefore, a just person is happy, and an unjust one wretched.

So be it.

It profits no one to be wretched but to be happy.

Of course.

And so, Thrasymachus, injustice is never more profitable than justice.

Let that be your banquet, Socrates, at the feast of Bendis.

Given by you, Thrasymachus, after you became gentle and ceased to give me rough treatment. Yet I haven't had a fine banquet. But that's my

b   fault not yours. I seem to have behaved like a glutton, snatching at every dish that passes and tasting it before properly savoring its predecessor. Before finding the answer to our first inquiry about what justice is, I let that go and turned to investigate whether it is a kind of vice and ignorance or a kind of wisdom and virtue. Then an argument came up about injustice

[Socrates/Thrasymachus]

being more profitable than justice, and I couldn't refrain from abandoning the previous one and following up on that. Hence the result of the discussion, as far as I'm concerned, is that I know nothing, for when I don't know   c what justice is, I'll hardly know whether it is a kind of virtue or not, or whether a person who has it is happy or unhappy.

[Socrates]

REPUBLIC II

Glaucon introduces a sophisticated division of goods into three classes and asks Socrates to which class justice belongs. Socrates places it in the highest class, consisting of things valued both because of themselves and because of their consequences (357a–358a). This conflicts with the general view that justice belongs in the lowest class, consisting of things harsh in themselves and valued only for their consequences. It is this view that Glaucon, with the help of Adeimantus, challenges Socrates to defeat. He does not complete his response until the end of Book IX.

His first step is to shift the debate from individual justice to political justice. He will construct an ideal or completely good city in theory, one in which everyone is as happy as possible. He knows on the basis of the argument that concludes Book I that such a city would have to be completely virtuous and so completely just (352d–354a). Having located justice in that city, he will then look for it in the soul.

The construction of the ideal city proceeds in stages. Socrates first introduces a city of people—the so-called first city—whose souls are ruled by their necessary appetites. But this city is not, given human psychology, a real possibility. For unnecessary appetites exist in all of us by nature (571b). The second stage in the construction of the ideal city—the so-called luxurious city—seems to be introduced to make this point (see 373a, b, d).

The result of the introduction of unnecessary appetites is war both civil and intercity (373d–e). To prevent this from destroying the city, soldier-police are needed to constrain both internal and external enemies (414b). These are the guardians. And like all the citizens of the ideal city, they must specialize in their job (see 370a–b, 374a–c, 394e, 423c–d, 433a, 443b, 453b).

The natural assets that a good guardian needs and the education he must have to develop them in the best possible way are, therefore, the next topic. The appropriate basic education for future guardians, Socrates claims, is the traditional one consisting of music and poetry, on the one hand, and physical training, on the other. His discussion of it continues into Book III.

357 When I said this, I thought I had done with the discussion, but it turned out to have been only a prelude. Glaucon showed his characteristic courage on this occasion too and refused to accept Thrasymachus' abandonment of

[Socrates]

the argument. Socrates, he said, do you want to seem to have persuaded us that it is better in every way to be just than unjust, or do you want truly to convince us of this?   *b*

I want truly to convince you, I said, if I can.

Well, then, you certainly aren't doing what you want. Tell me, do you think there is a kind of good we welcome, not because we desire what comes from it, but because we welcome it for its own sake—joy, for example, and all the harmless pleasures that have no results beyond the joy of having them?

Certainly, I think there are such things.

And is there a kind of good we like for its own sake and also for the sake of what comes from it—knowing, for example, and seeing and being   *c* healthy? We welcome such things, I suppose, on both counts.

Yes.

And do you also see a third kind of good, such as physical training, medical treatment when sick, medicine itself, and the other ways of making money? We'd say that these are onerous but beneficial to us, and we wouldn't choose them for their own sakes, but for the sake of the rewards and other things that come from them.   *d*

There is also this third kind. But what of it?

Where do you put justice?

I myself put it among the finest goods, as something to be valued by anyone who is going to be blessed with happiness, both because of itself   *358* and because of what comes from it.

That isn't most people's opinion. They'd say that justice belongs to the onerous kind, and is to be practiced for the sake of the rewards and popularity that come from a reputation for justice, but is to be avoided because of itself as something burdensome.

I know that's the general opinion. Thrasymachus faulted justice on these grounds a moment ago and praised injustice, but it seems that I'm a slow learner.

Come, then, and listen to me as well, and see whether you still have that   *b* problem, for I think that Thrasymachus gave up before he had to, charmed by you as if he were a snake. But I'm not yet satisfied by the argument on either side. I want to know what justice and injustice are and what power each itself has when it's by itself in the soul. I want to leave out of account their rewards and what comes from each of them. So, if you agree, I'll renew the argument of Thrasymachus. First, I'll state what kind of thing people consider justice to be and what its origins are. Second, I'll argue that   *c* all who practice it do so unwillingly, as something necessary, not as something good. Third, I'll argue that they have good reason to act as they do, for the life of an unjust person is, they say, much better than that of a just one.

It isn't, Socrates, that I believe any of that myself. I'm perplexed, indeed,

and my ears are deafened listening to Thrasymachus and countless others. But I've yet to hear anyone defend justice in the way I want, proving that it
d   is better than injustice. I want to hear it praised *by itself,* and I think that I'm most likely to hear this from you. Therefore, I'm going to speak at length in praise of the unjust life, and in doing so I'll show you the way I want to hear you praising justice and denouncing injustice. But see whether you want me to do that or not.

I want that most of all. Indeed, what subject could someone with any understanding enjoy discussing more often?

e   Excellent. Then let's discuss the first subject I mentioned—what justice is and what its origins are.

They say that to do injustice is naturally good and to suffer injustice bad, but that the badness of suffering it so far exceeds the goodness of doing it that those who have done and suffered injustice and tasted both, but who lack the power to do it and avoid suffering it, decide that it is profitable to
359   come to an agreement with each other neither to do injustice nor to suffer it. As a result, they begin to make laws and covenants, and what the law commands they call lawful and just. This, they say, is the origin and essence of justice. It is intermediate between the best and the worst. The best is to do injustice without paying the penalty; the worst is to suffer it without being able to take revenge. Justice is a mean between these two extremes. People value it not as a good but because they are too weak to do injustice with impunity. Someone who has the power to do this, however,
b   and is a true man wouldn't make an agreement with anyone not to do injustice in order not to suffer it. For him that would be madness. This is the nature of justice, according to the argument, Socrates, and these are its natural origins.

We can see most clearly that those who practice justice do it unwillingly
c   and because they lack the power to do injustice, if in our thoughts we grant to a just and an unjust person the freedom to do whatever they like. We can then follow both of them and see where their desires would lead. And we'll catch the just person red-handed travelling the same road as the unjust. The reason for this is the desire to outdo others and get more and more. This is what anyone's nature naturally pursues as good, but nature is forced by law into the perversion of treating fairness with respect.

The freedom I mentioned would be most easily realized if both people had the power they say the ancestor of Gyges of Lydia possessed. The
d   story goes that he was a shepherd in the service of the ruler of Lydia. There was a violent thunderstorm, and an earthquake broke open the ground and created a chasm at the place where he was tending his sheep. Seeing this, he was filled with amazement and went down into it. And there, in addition to many other wonders of which we're told, he saw a hollow bronze horse. There were windowlike openings in it, and, peeping in, he saw a corpse, which seemed to be of more than human size, wearing nothing but a gold

ring on its finger. He took the ring and came out of the chasm. He wore the   *e*
ring at the usual monthly meeting that reported to the king on the state of
the flocks. And as he was sitting among the others, he happened to turn the
setting of the ring towards himself to the inside of his hand. When he did
this, he became invisible to those sitting near him, and they went on talking
as if he had gone. He wondered at this, and, fingering the ring, he turned   *360*
the setting outwards again and became visible. So he experimented with
the ring to test whether it indeed had this power—and it did. If he turned
the setting inward, he became invisible; if he turned it outward, he became
visible again. When he realized this, he at once arranged to become one of
the messengers sent to report to the king. And when he arrived there, he
seduced the king's wife, attacked the king with her help, killed him, and   *b*
took over the kingdom.

Let's suppose, then, that there were two such rings, one worn by a just
and the other by an unjust person. Now, no one, it seems, would be so
incorruptible that he would stay on the path of justice or stay away from
other people's property, when he could take whatever he wanted from the
marketplace with impunity, go into people's houses and have sex with anyone he wished, kill or release from prison anyone he wished, and do all the   *c*
other things that would make him like a god among humans. Rather his
actions would be in no way different from those of an unjust person, and
both would follow the same path. This, some would say, is a great proof
that one is never just willingly but only when compelled to be. No one
believes justice to be a good when it is kept private, since, wherever either
person thinks he can do injustice with impunity, he does it. Indeed, every
man believes that injustice is far more profitable to himself than justice.
And any exponent of this argument will say he's right, for someone who   *d*
didn't want to do injustice, given this sort of opportunity, and who didn't
touch other people's property would be thought wretched and stupid by
everyone aware of the situation, though, of course, they'd praise him in
public, deceiving each other for fear of suffering injustice. So much for my
second topic.

As for the choice between the lives we're discussing, we'll be able to make
a correct judgment about that only if we separate the most just and the   *e*
most unjust. Otherwise we won't be able to do it. Here's the separation I
have in mind. We'll subtract nothing from the injustice of an unjust person
and nothing from the justice of a just one, but we'll take each to be complete in his own way of life. First, therefore, we must suppose that an unjust
person will act as clever craftsmen do: A first-rate captain or doctor, for
example, knows the difference between what his craft can and can't do. He   *361*
attempts the first but lets the second go by, and if he happens to slip, he can
put things right. In the same way, an unjust person's successful attempts at
injustice must remain undetected, if he is to be fully unjust. Anyone who is
caught should be thought inept, for the extreme of injustice is to be

[Glaucon]

believed to be just without being just. And our completely unjust person must be given complete injustice; nothing may be subtracted from it. We must allow that, while doing the greatest injustice, he has nonetheless provided himself with the greatest reputation for justice. If he happens to
b   make a slip, he must be able to put it right. If any of his unjust activities should be discovered, he must be able to speak persuasively or to use force. And if force is needed, he must have the help of courage and strength and of the substantial wealth and friends with which he has provided himself.

Having hypothesized such a person, let's now in our argument put beside him a just man, who is simple and noble and who, as Aeschylus says, doesn't want to be believed to be good but to be so. We must take away his
c   reputation, for a reputation for justice would bring him honor and rewards, so that it wouldn't be clear whether he is just for the sake of justice itself or for the sake of those honors and rewards. We must strip him of everything except justice and make his situation the opposite of an unjust person's. Though he does no injustice, he must have the greatest reputation for it, so that his justice may be tested full-strength and not diluted by wrong-doing and what comes from it. Let him stay like that unchanged until he dies—
d   just, but all his life believed to be unjust. In this way, both will reach the extremes, the one of justice and the other of injustice, and we'll be able to judge which of them is happier.

Whew! Glaucon, I said, how vigorously you've scoured each of the men for our competition, just as you would a pair of statues for an art competition.

I do the best I can, he replied. Since the two are as I've described, in any case, it shouldn't be difficult to complete the account of the kind of life that awaits each of them, but it must be done. And if what I say sounds crude,
e   Socrates, remember that it isn't I who speak but those who praise injustice at the expense of justice. They'll say that a just person in such circumstances will be whipped, stretched on a rack, chained, blinded with fire, and, at the end, when he has suffered every kind of evil, he'll be impaled, and will realize then that one shouldn't want to be just but to be believed to
362 be just. Indeed, Aeschylus' words are far more correctly applied to unjust people than to just ones, for the supporters of injustice will say that a really unjust person, having a way of life based on the truth about things and not living in accordance with opinion, doesn't want simply to be believed to be unjust but actually to be so—

b
> Harvesting a deep furrow in his mind,
> Where wise counsels propagate.[1]

He rules his city because of his reputation for justice; he marries into any family he wishes; he gives his children in marriage to anyone he wishes; he

1. *Seven Against Thebes*, 592–94.

[Glaucon/Socrates]

has contracts and partnerships with anyone he wants; and besides benefiting himself in all these ways, he profits because he has no scruples about doing injustice. In any contest, public or private, he's the winner and outdoes his enemies. And by outdoing them, he becomes wealthy, benefiting his friends and harming his enemies. He makes adequate sacrifices to the gods and sets up magnificent offerings to them. He takes better care of the gods, therefore (and, indeed, of the human beings he's fond of), than a just person does. Hence it's likely that the gods, in turn, will take better care of him than of a just person. That's what they say, Socrates, that gods and humans provide a better life for unjust people than for just ones.

When Glaucon had said this, I had it in mind to respond, but his brother Adeimantus intervened: You surely don't think that the position has been adequately stated?

Why not? I said.

The most important thing to say hasn't been said yet.

Well, then, I replied, a man's brother must stand by him, as the saying goes.[2] If Glaucon has omitted something, you must help him. Yet what he has said is enough to throw me to the canvas and make me unable to come to the aid of justice.

Nonsense, he said. Hear what more I have to say, for we should also fully explore the arguments that are opposed to the ones Glaucon gave, the ones that praise justice and find fault with injustice, so that what I take to be his intention may be clearer.

When fathers speak to their sons, they say that one must be just, as do all the others who have charge of anyone. But they don't praise justice itself, only the high reputations it leads to and the consequences of being thought to be just, such as the public offices, marriages, and other things Glaucon listed. But they elaborate even further on the consequences of reputation. By bringing in the esteem of the gods, they are able to talk about the abundant good things that they themselves and the noble Hesiod and Homer say that the gods give to the pious, for Hesiod says that the gods make the oak trees

> Bear acorns at the top and bees in the middle
> And make fleecy sheep heavy laden with wool

for the just, and tells of many other good things akin to these. And Homer is similar:

> When a good king, in his piety,
> Upholds justice, the black earth bears
> Wheat and barley for him, and his trees are heavy with fruit.

2. See *Odyssey* xvi.97–98.

[Glaucon/Socrates/Adeimantus]

His sheep bear lambs unfailingly, and the sea yields up its fish.[3]

Musaeus and his son make the gods give the just more headstrong goods than these.[4] In their stories, they lead the just to Hades, seat them on couches, provide them with a symposium of pious people, crown them with wreaths, and make them spend all their time drinking—as if they

d   thought drunkenness was the finest wage of virtue. Others stretch even further the wages that virtue receives from the gods, for they say that someone who is pious and keeps his promises leaves his children's children and a whole race behind him. In these and other similar ways, they praise justice. They bury the impious and unjust in mud in Hades; force them to carry water in a sieve; bring them into bad repute while they're still alive, and all those penalties that Glaucon gave to the just person they

e   give to the unjust. But they have nothing else to say. This, then, is the way people praise justice and find fault with injustice.

Besides this, Socrates, consider another form of argument about justice and injustice employed both by private individuals and by poets. All go on repeating with one voice that justice and moderation are fine things, but

364   hard and onerous, while licentiousness and injustice are sweet and easy to acquire and are shameful only in opinion and law. They add that unjust deeds are for the most part more profitable than just ones, and, whether in public or private, they willingly honor vicious people who have wealth and other types of power and declare them to be happy. But they dishonor and disregard the weak and the poor, even though they agree that they are

b   better than the others.

But the most wonderful of all these arguments concerns what they have to say about the gods and virtue. They say that the gods, too, assign misfortune and a bad life to many good people, and the opposite fate to their opposites. Begging priests and prophets frequent the doors of the rich and persuade them that they possess a god-given power founded on

c   sacrifices and incantations. If the rich person or any of his ancestors has committed an injustice, they can fix it with pleasant rituals. Moreover, if he wishes to injure some enemy, then, at little expense, he'll be able to harm just and unjust alike, for by means of spells and enchantments they can persuade the gods to serve them. And the poets are brought forward as witnesses to all these accounts. Some harp on the ease of vice, as follows:

Vice in abundance is easy to get;
d   The road is smooth and begins beside you,
But the gods have put sweat between us and virtue,

---

3. The two last quotations are from *Works and Days* 232 ff. and *Odyssey* xix.109–13, omitting 110, respectively.

4. Musaeus was a legendary poet closely associated with the mystery religion of Orphism.

[Adeimantus/Socrates]

and a road that is long, rough, and steep.[5] Others quote Homer to bear witness that the gods can be influenced by humans, since he said:

> The gods themselves can be swayed by prayer,
> And with sacrifices and soothing promises,
> Incense and libations, human beings turn them from their purpose   *e*
> When someone has transgressed and sinned.[6]

And they present a noisy throng of books by Musaeus and Orpheus, offspring as they say of Selene and the Muses, in accordance with which they perform their rituals.[7] And they persuade not only individuals but whole cities that the unjust deeds of the living or the dead can be absolved or purified through ritual sacrifices and pleasant games. These initiations,   *365* as they call them, free people from punishment hereafter, while a terrible fate awaits those who have not performed the rituals.

When all such sayings about the attitudes of gods and humans to virtue and vice are so often repeated, Socrates, what effect do you suppose they have on the souls of young people? I mean those who are clever and are able to flit from one of these sayings to another, so to speak, and gather from them an impression of what sort of person he should be and of how best to travel the road of life. He would surely ask himself Pindar's ques-   *b* tion, "Should I by justice or by crooked deceit scale this high wall and live my life guarded and secure?" And he'll answer: "The various sayings suggest that there is no advantage in my being just if I'm not also thought just, while the troubles and penalties of being just are apparent. But they tell me that an unjust person, who has secured for himself a reputation for justice, lives the life of a god. Since, then, 'opinion forcibly overcomes truth' and 'controls happiness,' as the wise men say, I must surely turn   *c* entirely to it.[8] I should create a façade of illusory virtue around me to deceive those who come near, but keep behind it the greedy and crafty fox of the wise Archilochus."[9]

"But surely," someone will object, "it isn't easy for vice to remain always hidden." We'll reply that nothing great is easy. And, in any case, if we're to be happy, we must follow the path indicated in these accounts. To remain   *d* undiscovered we'll form secret societies and political clubs. And there are teachers of persuasion to make us clever in dealing with assemblies and

5. *Works and Days* 287–89, with minor alterations.

6. *Iliad* ix.497–501, with minor alterations.

7. It is not clear whether Orpheus was a real person or a mythical figure. His fame in Greek myth rests on the poems in which the doctrines of the Orphic religion are set forth.

8. The quotation is attributed to Simonides, whom Polemarchus cites in Book I.

9. Archilochus of Paros (c. 756–716 B.C.) was an iambic and elegiac poet who composed a famous fable about the fox and the hedgehog.

[Adeimantus/Socrates]

law courts. Therefore, using persuasion in one place and force in another, we'll outdo others without paying a penalty.

"What about the gods? Surely, we can't hide from them or use violent force against them!" Well, if the gods don't exist or don't concern themselves with human affairs, why should we worry at all about hiding from

e them? If they do exist and do concern themselves with us, we've learned all we know about them from the laws and the poets who give their genealogies—nowhere else. But these are the very people who tell us that the gods can be persuaded and influenced by sacrifices, gentle prayers, and offerings. Hence, we should believe them on both matters or neither. If we believe them, we should be unjust and offer sacrifices from the fruits of

366 our injustice. If we are just, our only gain is not to be punished by the gods, since we lose the profits of injustice. But if we are unjust, we get the profits of our crimes and transgressions and afterwards persuade the gods by prayer and escape without punishment.

"But in Hades won't we pay the penalty for crimes committed here, either ourselves or our children's children?" "My friend," the young man will say as he does his calculation, "mystery rites have great power and the gods have great power of absolution. The greatest cities tell us this, as do

b those children of the gods who have become poets and prophets."

Why, then, should we still choose justice over the greatest injustice? Many eminent authorities agree that, if we practice such injustice with a false façade, we'll do well at the hands of gods and humans, living and dying as we've a mind to. So, given all that has been said, Socrates, how is

c it possible for anyone of any power—whether of mind, wealth, body, or birth—to be willing to honor justice and not laugh aloud when he hears it praised? Indeed, if anyone can show that what we've said is false and has adequate knowledge that justice is best, he'll surely be full not of anger but of forgiveness for the unjust. He knows that, apart from someone of godlike character who is disgusted by injustice or one who has gained knowl

d edge and avoids injustice for that reason, no one is just willingly. Through cowardice or old age or some other weakness, people do indeed object to injustice. But it's obvious that they do so only because they lack the power to do injustice, for the first of them to acquire it is the first to do as much injustice as he can.

And all of this has no other cause than the one that led Glaucon and me to say to you: "Socrates, of all of you who claim to praise justice, from the original heroes of old whose words survive, to the men of the present day,

e not one has ever blamed injustice or praised justice except by mentioning the reputations, honors, and rewards that are their consequences. No one has ever adequately described what each itself does of its own power by its presence in the soul of the person who possesses it, even if it remains hidden from gods and humans. No one, whether in poetry or in private conversations, has adequately argued that injustice is the worst thing a

[Adeimantus/Socrates]

soul can have in it and that justice is the greatest good. If you had treated
the subject in this way and persuaded us from youth, we wouldn't now be   *367*
guarding against one another's injustices, but each would be his own best
guardian, afraid that by doing injustice he'd be living with the worst thing
possible."

Thrasymachus or anyone else might say what we've said, Socrates, or
maybe even more, in discussing justice and injustice—crudely inverting
their powers, in my opinion. And, frankly, it's because I want to hear the
opposite from you that I speak with all the force I can muster. So don't   *b*
merely give us a theoretical argument that justice is stronger than injustice,
but tell us what each itself does, because of its own powers, to someone
who possesses it, that makes injustice bad and justice good. Follow Glaucon's advice, and don't take reputations into account, for if you don't
deprive justice and injustice of their true reputations and attach false ones
to them, we'll say that you are not praising them but their reputations and
that you're encouraging us to be unjust in secret. In that case, we'll say that   *c*
you agree with Thrasymachus that justice is the good of another, the
advantage of the stronger, while injustice is one's own advantage and
profit, though not the advantage of the weaker.

You agree that justice is one of the greatest goods, the ones that are
worth getting for the sake of what comes from them, but much more so for
their own sake, such as seeing, hearing, knowing, being healthy, and all   *d*
other goods that are fruitful by their own nature and not simply because of
reputation. Therefore, praise justice as a good of that kind, explaining
how—because of its very self—it benefits its possessors and how injustice
harms them. Leave wages and reputations for others to praise.

Others would satisfy me if they praised justice and blamed injustice in
that way, extolling the wages of one and denigrating those of the other. But
you, unless you order me to be satisfied, wouldn't, for you've spent your
whole life investigating this and nothing else. Don't, then, give us only a   *e*
theoretical argument that justice is stronger than injustice, but show what
effect each has because of itself on the person who has it—the one for good
and the other for bad—whether it remains hidden from gods and human
beings or not.

While I'd always admired the natures of Glaucon and Adeimantus, I
was especially pleased on this occasion, and I said: You are the sons of a   *368*
great man, and Glaucon's lover began his elegy well when he wrote,
celebrating your achievements at the battle of Megara,

Sons of Ariston, godlike offspring of a famous man.

That's well said in my opinion, for you must indeed be affected by the
divine if you're not convinced that injustice is better than justice and yet
can speak on its behalf as you have done. And I believe that you really are

[Adeimantus/Socrates]

b unconvinced by your own words. I infer this from the way you live, for if I had only your words to go on, I wouldn't trust you. The more I trust you, however, the more I'm at a loss as to what to do. I don't see how I can be of help. Indeed, I believe I'm incapable of it. And here's my evidence. I thought what I said to Thrasymachus showed that justice is better than injustice, but you won't accept it from me. On the other hand, I don't see how I can refuse my help, for I fear that it may even be impious to have breath in one's body and the ability to speak and yet to stand idly by and

c not defend justice when it is being prosecuted. So the best course is to give justice any assistance I can.

Glaucon and the others begged me not to abandon the argument but to help in every way to track down what justice and injustice are and what the truth about their benefits is. So I told them what I had in mind: The investigation we're undertaking is not an easy one but requires keen eye-

d sight. Therefore, since we aren't clever people, we should adopt the method of investigation that we'd use if, lacking keen eyesight, we were told to read small letters from a distance and then noticed that the same letters existed elsewhere in a larger size and on a larger surface. We'd consider it a godsend, I think, to be allowed to read the larger ones first and then to examine the smaller ones, to see whether they really are the same.

That's certainly true, said Adeimantus, but how is this case similar to

e our investigation of justice?

I'll tell you. We say, don't we, that there is the justice of a single man and also the justice of a whole city?

Certainly.

And a city is larger than a single man?

It is larger.

Perhaps, then, there is more justice in the larger thing, and it will be easier to learn what it is. So, if you're willing, let's first find out what sort of

369 thing justice is in a city and afterwards look for it in the individual, observing the ways in which the smaller is similar to the larger.

That seems fine to me.

If we could watch a city coming to be in theory, wouldn't we also see its justice coming to be, and its injustice as well?

Probably so.

And when that process is completed, we can hope to find what we are looking for more easily?

b Of course.

Do you think we should try to carry it out, then? It's no small task, in my view. So think it over.

We have already, said Adeimantus. Don't even consider doing anything else.

I think a city comes to be because none of us is self-sufficient, but we all need many things. Do you think that a city is founded on any other principle?

No.

And because people need many things, and because one person calls on a second out of one need and on a third out of a different need, many   *c* people gather in a single place to live together as partners and helpers. And such a settlement is called a city. Isn't that so?

It is.

And if they share things with one another, giving and taking, they do so because each believes that this is better for himself?

That's right.

Come, then, let's create a city in theory from its beginnings. And it's our needs, it seems, that will create it.

It is, indeed.

Surely our first and greatest need is to provide food to sustain life.   *d*

Certainly.

Our second is for shelter, and our third for clothes and such.

That's right.

How, then, will a city be able to provide all this? Won't one person have to be a farmer, another a builder, and another a weaver? And shouldn't we add a cobbler and someone else to provide medical care?

All right.

So the essential minimum for a city is four or five men?

Apparently.   *e*

And what about this? Must each of them contribute his own work for the common use of all? For example, will a farmer provide food for everyone, spending quadruple the time and labor to provide food to be shared by them all? Or will he not bother about that, producing one quarter the food in one quarter the time, and spending the other three quarters, one in   *370* building a house, one in the production of clothes, and one in making shoes, not troubling to associate with the others, but minding his own business on his own?

Perhaps, Socrates, Adeimantus replied, the way you suggested first would be easier than the other.

That certainly wouldn't be surprising, for, even as you were speaking it occurred to me that, in the first place, we aren't all born alike, but each of us differs somewhat in nature from the others, one being suited to one task, another to another. Or don't you think so?   *b*

I do.

Second, does one person do a better job if he practices many crafts or— since he's one person himself—if he practices one?

If he practices one.

It's clear, at any rate, I think, that if one misses the right moment in anything, the work is spoiled.

[Socrates/Adeimantus]

It is.

That's because the thing to be done won't wait on the leisure of the doer, but the doer must of necessity pay close attention to his work rather than treating it as a secondary occupation.

c

Yes, he must.

The result, then, is that more plentiful and better-quality goods are more easily produced if each person does one thing for which he is naturally suited, does it at the right time, and is released from having to do any of the others.

Absolutely.

Then, Adeimantus, we're going to need more than four citizens to provide the things we've mentioned, for a farmer won't make his own plough, not if it's to be a good one, nor his hoe, nor any of his other farming tools. Neither will a builder—and he, too, needs lots of things. And the same is true of a weaver and a cobbler, isn't it?

d

It is.

Hence, carpenters, metal workers, and many other craftsmen of that sort will share our little city and make it bigger.

That's right.

Yet it won't be a huge settlement even if we add cowherds, shepherds, and other herdsmen in order that the farmers have cows to do their ploughing, the builders have oxen to share with the farmers in hauling their materials, and the weavers and cobblers have hides and fleeces to use.

e

It won't be a small one either, if it has to hold all those.

Moreover, it's almost impossible to establish a city in a place where nothing has to be imported.

Indeed it is.

So we'll need yet further people to import from other cities whatever is needed.

Yes.

And if an importer goes empty-handed to another city, without a cargo of the things needed by the city from which he's to bring back what his own city needs, he'll come away empty-handed, won't he?

371

So it seems.

Therefore our citizens must not only produce enough for themselves at home but also goods of the right quality and quantity to satisfy the requirements of others.

They must.

So we'll need more farmers and other craftsmen in our city.

Yes.

And others to take care of imports and exports. And they're called merchants, aren't they?

Yes.

[Adeimantus/Socrates]

So we'll need merchants, too.

Certainly.

And if the trade is by sea, we'll need a good many others who know   *b*
how to sail.

A good many, indeed.

And how will those in the city itself share the things that each produces?
It was for the sake of this that we made their partnership and founded
their city.

Clearly, they must do it by buying and selling.

Then we'll need a marketplace and a currency for such exchange.

Certainly.

If a farmer or any other craftsman brings some of his products to mar-   *c*
ket, and he doesn't arrive at the same time as those who want to exchange
things with him, is he to sit idly in the marketplace, away from his own
work?

Not at all. There'll be people who'll notice this and provide the requisite
service—in well-organized cities they'll usually be those whose bodies are
weakest and who aren't fit to do any other work. They'll stay around the
market exchanging money for the goods of those who have something to   *d*
sell and then exchanging those goods for the money of those who want
them.

Then, to fill this need there will have to be retailers in our city, for aren't
those who establish themselves in the marketplace to provide this service
of buying and selling called retailers, while those who travel between
cities are called merchants?

That's right.

There are other servants, I think, whose minds alone wouldn't qualify
them for membership in our society but whose bodies are strong enough   *e*
for labor. These sell the use of their strength for a price called a wage and
hence are themselves called wage-earners. Isn't that so?

Certainly.

So wage-earners complete our city?

I think so.

Well, Adeimantus, has our city grown to completeness, then?

Perhaps it has.

Then where are justice and injustice to be found in it? With which of the
things we examined did they come in?

I've no idea, Socrates, unless it was somewhere in some need that these   372
people have of one another.

You may be right, but we must look into it and not grow weary. First,
then, let's see what sort of life our citizens will lead when they've been
provided for in the way we have been describing. They'll produce bread,
wine, clothes, and shoes, won't they? They'll build houses, work naked
and barefoot in the summer, and wear adequate clothing and shoes in the   *b*

[Socrates/Adeimantus]

winter. For food, they'll knead and cook the flour and meal they've made from wheat and barley. They'll put their honest cakes and loaves on reeds or clean leaves, and, reclining on beds strewn with yew and myrtle, they'll feast with their children, drink their wine, and, crowned with wreaths, hymn the gods. They'll enjoy sex with one another but bear no more children than their resources allow, lest they fall into either poverty or war.

It seems that you make your people feast without any delicacies, Glaucon interrupted.

True enough, I said, I was forgetting that they'll obviously need salt, olives, cheese, boiled roots, and vegetables of the sort they cook in the country. We'll give them desserts, too, of course, consisting of figs, chickpeas, and beans, and they'll roast myrtle and acorns before the fire, drinking moderately. And so they'll live in peace and good health, and when they die at a ripe old age, they'll bequeath a similar life to their children.

If you were founding a city for pigs, Socrates, he replied, wouldn't you fatten *them* on the same diet?

Then how should I feed these people, Glaucon? I asked.

In the conventional way. If they aren't to suffer hardship, they should recline on proper couches, dine at a table, and have the delicacies and desserts that people have nowadays.

All right, I understand. It isn't merely the origin of a city that we're considering, it seems, but the origin of a *luxurious* city. And that may not be a bad idea, for by examining it, we might very well see how justice and injustice grow up in cities. Yet the true city, in my opinion, is the one we've described, the healthy one, as it were. But let's study a city with a fever, if that's what you want. There's nothing to stop us. The things I mentioned earlier and the way of life I described won't satisfy some people, it seems, but couches, tables, and other furniture will have to be added, and, of course, all sorts of delicacies, perfumed oils, incense, prostitutes, and pastries. We mustn't provide them only with the necessities we mentioned at first, such as houses, clothes, and shoes, but painting and embroidery must be begun, and gold, ivory, and the like acquired. Isn't that so?

Yes.

Then we must enlarge our city, for the healthy one is no longer adequate. We must increase it in size and fill it with a multitude of things that go beyond what is necessary for a city—hunters, for example, and artists or imitators, many of whom work with shapes and colors, many with music. And there'll be poets and their assistants, actors, choral dancers, contractors, and makers of all kinds of devices, including, among other things, those needed for the adornment of women. And so we'll need more servants, too. Or don't you think that we'll need tutors, wet nurses, nannies, beauticians, barbers, chefs, cooks, and swineherds? We didn't need any of these in our earlier city, but we'll need them in this one. And

[Socrates/Glaucon]

we'll also need many more cattle, won't we, if the people are going to eat meat?

Of course.

And if we live like that, we'll have a far greater need for doctors than we did before?

Much greater.

And the land, I suppose, that used to be adequate to feed the population we had then, will cease to be adequate and become too small. What do you think?

The same.

Then we'll have to seize some of our neighbors' land if we're to have enough pasture and ploughland. And won't our neighbors want to seize part of ours as well, if they too have surrendered themselves to the endless acquisition of money and have overstepped the limit of their necessities?

That's completely inevitable, Socrates.

Then our next step will be war, Glaucon, won't it?

It will.

We won't say yet whether the effects of war are good or bad but only that we've now found the origins of war. It comes from those same desires that are most of all responsible for the bad things that happen to cities and the individuals in them.

That's right.

Then the city must be further enlarged, and not just by a small number, either, but by a whole army, which will do battle with the invaders in defense of the city's substantial wealth and all the other things we mentioned.

Why aren't the citizens themselves adequate for that purpose?

They won't be, if the agreement you and the rest of us made when we were founding the city was a good one, for surely we agreed, if you remember, that it's impossible for a single person to practice many crafts or professions well.

That's true.

Well, then, don't you think that warfare is a profession?

Of course.

Then should we be more concerned about cobbling than about warfare?

Not at all.

But we prevented a cobbler from trying to be a farmer, weaver, or builder at the same time and said that he must remain a cobbler in order to produce fine work. And each of the others, too, was to work all his life at a single trade for which he had a natural aptitude and keep away from all the others, so as not to miss the right moment to practice his own work well. Now, isn't it of the greatest importance that warfare be practiced well? And is fighting a war so easy that a farmer or a cobbler or any other craftsman can be a soldier at the same time? Though no one can become so

[Socrates/Glaucon]

d

much as a good player of checkers or dice if he considers it only as a sideline and doesn't practice it from childhood. Or can someone pick up a shield or any other weapon or tool of war and immediately perform adequately in an infantry battle or any other kind? No other tool makes anyone who picks it up a craftsman or champion unless he has acquired the requisite knowledge and has had sufficient practice.

If tools could make anyone who picked them up an expert, they'd be valuable indeed.

e

Then to the degree that the work of the guardians is most important, it requires most freedom from other things and the greatest skill and devotion.

I should think so.

And doesn't it also require a person whose nature is suited to that way of life?

Certainly.

Then our job, it seems, is to select, if we can, the kind of nature suited to guard the city.

It is.

By god, it's no trivial task that we've taken on. But insofar as we are able, we mustn't shrink from it.

375

No, we mustn't.

Do you think that, when it comes to guarding, there is any difference between the nature of a pedigree young dog and that of a well-born youth?

What do you mean?

Well, each needs keen senses, speed to catch what it sees, and strength in case it has to fight it out with what it captures.

They both need all these things.

And each must be courageous if indeed he's to fight well.

Of course.

And will a horse, a dog, or any other animal be courageous, if he isn't spirited? Or haven't you noticed just how invincible and unbeatable spirit

b

is, so that its presence makes the whole soul fearless and unconquerable?

I have noticed that.

The physical qualities of the guardians are clear, then.

Yes.

And as far as their souls are concerned, they must be spirited.

That too.

But if they have natures like that, Glaucon, won't they be savage to each other and to the rest of the citizens?

By god, it will be hard for them to be anything else.

Yet surely they must be gentle to their own people and harsh to the

c

enemy. If they aren't, they won't wait around for others to destroy the city but will do it themselves first.

[Socrates/Glaucon]

That's true.

What are we to do, then? Where are we to find a character that is both gentle and high-spirited at the same time? After all, a gentle nature is the opposite of a spirited one.

Apparently.

If someone lacks either gentleness or spirit, he can't be a good guardian. Yet it seems impossible to combine them. It follows that a good guardian cannot exist.   *d*

It looks like it.

I couldn't see a way out, but on reexamining what had gone before, I said: We deserve to be stuck, for we've lost sight of the analogy we put forward.

How do you mean?

We overlooked the fact that there *are* natures of the sort we thought impossible, natures in which these opposites are indeed combined.

Where?

You can see them in other animals, too, but especially in the one to which we compared the guardian, for you know, of course, that a pedigree dog naturally has a character of this sort—he is gentle as can be to those   *e* he's used to and knows, but the opposite to those he doesn't know.

I do know that.

So the combination we want is possible after all, and our search for the good guardian is not contrary to nature.

Apparently not.

Then do you think that our future guardian, besides being spirited, must also be by nature philosophical?

How do you mean? I don't understand.   376

It's something else you see in dogs, and it makes you wonder at the animal.

What?

When a dog sees someone it doesn't know, it gets angry before anything bad happens to it. But when it knows someone, it welcomes him, even if it has never received anything good from him. Haven't you ever wondered at that?

I've never paid any attention to it, but obviously that is the way a dog behaves.

Surely this is a refined quality in its nature and one that is truly   *b* philosophical.

In what way philosophical?

Because it judges anything it sees to be either a friend or an enemy, on no other basis than that it knows the one and doesn't know the other. And how could it be anything besides a lover of learning, if it defines what is its own and what is alien to it in terms of knowledge and ignorance?

It couldn't.

[Glaucon/Socrates]

But surely the love of learning is the same thing as philosophy or the love of wisdom?

It is.

Then, may we confidently assume in the case of a human being, too, that if he is to be gentle toward his own and those he knows, he must be a lover
c of learning and wisdom?

We may.

Philosophy, spirit, speed, and strength must all, then, be combined in the nature of anyone who is to be a fine and good guardian of our city.

Absolutely.

Then those are the traits a potential guardian would need at the outset. But how are we to bring him up and educate him? Will inquiry into that topic bring us any closer to the goal of our inquiry, which is to discover the
d origins of justice and injustice in a city? We want our account to be adequate, but we don't want it to be any longer than necessary.

I certainly expect, Glaucon's brother said, that such inquiry will further our goal.

Then, by god, Adeimantus, I said, we mustn't leave it out, even if it turns out to be a somewhat lengthy affair.

No, we mustn't.

Come, then, and just as if we had the leisure to make up stories, let's describe in theory how to educate our men.
e All right.

What will their education be? Or is it hard to find anything better than that which has developed over a long period—physical training for bodies and music and poetry for the soul?

Yes, it would be hard.

Now, we start education in music and poetry before physical training, don't we?

Of course.

Do you include stories under music and poetry?

I do.

Aren't there two kinds of story, one true and the other false?

Yes.

377 And mustn't our men be educated in both, but first in false ones?

I don't understand what you mean.

Don't you understand that we first tell stories to children? These are false, on the whole, though they have some truth in them. And we tell them to small children before physical training begins.

That's true.

And that's what I meant by saying that we must deal with music and poetry before physical training.

All right.

You know, don't you, that the beginning of any process is most important, especially for anything young and tender? It's at that time that it is most malleable and takes on any pattern one wishes to impress on it.   *b*

Exactly.

Then shall we carelessly allow the children to hear any old stories, told by just anyone, and to take beliefs into their souls that are for the most part opposite to the ones we think they should hold when they are grown up?

We certainly won't.

Then we must first of all, it seems, supervise the storytellers. We'll select their stories whenever they are fine or beautiful and reject them when they aren't. And we'll persuade nurses and mothers to tell their children the   *c*
ones we have selected, since they will shape their children's souls with stories much more than they shape their bodies by handling them. Many of the stories they tell now, however, must be thrown out.

Which ones do you mean?

We'll first look at the major stories, and by seeing how to deal with them, we'll see how to deal with the minor ones as well, for they exhibit the same pattern and have the same effects whether they're famous or not. Don't you think so?   *d*

I do, but I don't know which ones you're calling major.

Those that Homer, Hesiod, and other poets tell us, for surely they composed false stories, told them to people, and are still telling them.

Which stories do you mean, and what fault do you find in them?

The fault one ought to find first and foremost, especially if the falsehood isn't well told.

For example?

When a story gives a bad image of what the gods and heroes are like, the way a painter does whose picture is not at all like the things he's trying to   *e*
paint.

You're right to object to that. But what sort of thing in particular do you have in mind?

First, telling the greatest falsehood about the most important things doesn't make a fine story—I mean Hesiod telling us about how Uranus behaved, how Cronus punished him for it, and how he was in turn punished by his own son.[10] But even if it were true, it should be passed over in   *378*
silence, not told to foolish young people. And if, for some reason, it has to be told, only a very few people—pledged to secrecy and after sacrificing not just a pig but something great and scarce—should hear it, so that their number is kept as small as possible.

Yes, such stories are hard to deal with.

And they shouldn't be told in our city, Adeimantus. Nor should a young   *b*

10. See Hesiod, *Theogony* 154–210, 453–506.

[Socrates/Adeimantus]

person hear it said that in committing the worst crimes he's doing nothing out of the ordinary, or that if he inflicts every kind of punishment on an unjust father, he's only doing the same as the first and greatest of the gods.

No, by god, I don't think myself that these stories are fit to be told.

Indeed, if we want the guardians of our city to think that it's shameful to be easily provoked into hating one another, we mustn't allow *any* stories
c   about gods warring, fighting, or plotting against one another, for they aren't true. The battles of gods and giants, and all the various stories of the gods hating their families or friends, should neither be told nor even woven in embroideries. If we're to persuade our people that no citizen has ever hated another and that it's impious to do so, then *that's* what should be told to children from the beginning by old men and women; and as these children grow older, poets should be compelled to tell them the same
d   sort of thing. We won't admit stories into our city—whether allegorical or not—about Hera being chained by her son, nor about Hephaestus being hurled from heaven by his father when he tried to help his mother, who was being beaten, nor about the battle of the gods in Homer. The young can't distinguish what is allegorical from what isn't, and the opinions they absorb at that age are hard to erase and apt to become unalterable. For these reasons, then, we should probably take the utmost care to insure that
e   the first stories they hear about virtue are the best ones for them to hear.

That's reasonable. But if someone asked us what stories these are, what should we say?

You and I, Adeimantus, aren't poets, but we *are* founding a city. And it's
379   appropriate for the founders to know the patterns on which poets must base their stories and from which they mustn't deviate. But we aren't actually going to compose their poems for them.

All right. But what precisely are the patterns for theology or stories about the gods?

Something like this: Whether in epic, lyric, or tragedy, a god must always be represented as he is.

Indeed, he must.
b   Now, a god is really good, isn't he, and must be described as such?
What else?
And surely nothing good is harmful, is it?
I suppose not.
And can what isn't harmful do harm?
Never.
Or can what does no harm do anything bad?
No.
And can what does nothing bad be the cause of anything bad?
How could it?
Moreover, the good is beneficial?

[Socrates/Adeimantus]

Yes.

It is the cause of doing well?

Yes.

The good isn't the cause of all things, then, but only of good ones; it isn't the cause of bad ones.

I agree entirely.   c

Therefore, since a god is good, he is not—as most people claim—the cause of everything that happens to human beings but of only a few things, for good things are fewer than bad ones in our lives. He alone is responsible for the good things, but we must find some other cause for the bad ones, not a god.

That's very true, and I believe it.

Then we won't accept from anyone the foolish mistake Homer makes about the gods when he says: d

> There are two urns at the threshold of Zeus,
> One filled with good fates, the other with bad ones. . . .

and the person to whom he gives a mixture of these

> Sometimes meets with a bad fate, sometimes with good,

but the one who receives his fate entirely from the second urn,

> Evil famine drives him over the divine earth.

We won't grant either that Zeus is for us   e

> The distributor of both good and bad.

And as to the breaking of the promised truce by Pandarus, if anyone tells us that it was brought about by Athena and Zeus or that Themis and Zeus were responsible for strife and contention among the gods, we will not praise him. Nor will we allow the young to hear the words of Aeschylus: 380

> A god makes mortals guilty
> When he wants utterly to destroy a house.[11]

And if anyone composes a poem about the sufferings of Niobe, such as the one in which these lines occur, or about the house of Pelops, or the tale of Troy, or anything else of that kind, we must require him to say that these

---

11. The first three quotations are from *Iliad* xxiv.527–32. The sources for the fourth and for the quotation from Aeschylus are unknown. The story of Athena urging Pandarus to break the truce is told in *Iliad* iv.73–126.

[Adeimantus/Socrates]

things are not the work of a god. Or, if they are, then poets must look for
the kind of account of them that we are now seeking, and say that the
b   actions of the gods are good and just, and that those they punish are
benefited thereby. We won't allow poets to say that the punished are made
wretched and that it was a god who made them so. But we will allow them
to say that bad people are wretched because they are in need of punishment and that, in paying the penalty, they are benefited by the gods. And,
as for saying that a god, who is himself good, is the cause of bad things,
we'll fight that in every way, and we won't allow anyone to say it in his
own city, if it's to be well governed, or anyone to hear it either—whether
c   young or old, whether in verse or prose. These stories are not pious, not
advantageous to us, and not consistent with one another.

I like your law, and I'll vote for it.

This, then, is one of the laws or patterns concerning the gods to which
speakers and poets must conform, namely, that a god isn't the cause of all
things but only of good ones.

And it's a fully satisfactory law.

What about this second law? Do you think that a god is a sorcerer, able
d   to appear in different forms at different times, sometimes changing himself from his own form into many shapes, sometimes deceiving us by
making us think that he has done it? Or do you think he's simple and least
of all likely to step out of his own form?

I can't say offhand.

Well, what about this? If he steps out of his own form, mustn't he either
e   change himself or be changed by something else?

He must.

But the best things are least liable to alteration or change, aren't they?
For example, isn't the healthiest and strongest body least changed by food,
drink, and labor, or the healthiest and strongest plant by sun, wind, and
the like?

381   Of course.

And the most courageous and most rational soul is least disturbed or
altered by any outside affection?

Yes.

And the same account is true of all artifacts, furniture, houses, and
clothes. The ones that are good and well made are least altered by time or
anything else that happens to them.

That's right.

b   Whatever is in good condition, then, whether by nature or craft or both,
admits least of being changed by anything else.

So it seems.

Now, surely a god and what belongs to him are in every way in the best
condition.

How could they fail to be?

[Socates/Adeimantus]

Then a god would be least likely to have many shapes.

Indeed.

Then does he change or alter himself?

Clearly he does, if indeed he is altered at all.

Would he change himself into something better and more beautiful than himself or something worse and uglier?

It would have to be into something worse, if he's changed at all, for   c
surely we won't say that a god is deficient in either beauty or virtue.

Absolutely right. And do you think, Adeimantus, that anyone, whether god or human, would deliberately make himself worse in any way?

No, that's impossible.

Is it impossible, then, for gods to want to alter themselves? Since they are the most beautiful and best possible, it seems that each always and unconditionally retains his own shape.

That seems entirely necessary to me.

Then let no poet tell us about Proteus or Thetis, or say that   d

> The gods, in the likeness of strangers from foreign lands,
> Adopt every sort of shape and visit our cities.[12]

Nor must they present Hera, in their tragedies or other poems, as a priestess collecting alms for

> the life-giving sons of the Argive river Inachus,[13]

or tell us other stories of that sort. Nor must mothers, believing bad stories about the gods wandering at night in the shapes of strangers from foreign   e
lands, terrify their children with them. Such stories blaspheme the gods and, at the same time, make children more cowardly.

They mustn't be told.

But though the gods are unable to change, do they nonetheless make us believe that they appear in all sorts of ways, deceiving us through sorcery?

Perhaps.

What? Would a god be willing to be false, either in word or deed, by   382
presenting an illusion?

I don't know.

Don't you know that a *true* falsehood, if one may call it that, is hated by all gods and humans?

What do you mean?

I mean that no one is willing to tell falsehoods to the most important part

12. *Odyssey* xvii.485–86.
13. Inachus was the father of Io, who was persecuted by Hera because Zeus was in love with her. The source for the part of the story Plato quotes is unknown.

[Socrates/Adeimantus]

of himself about the most important things, but of all places he is most afraid to have falsehood there.

I still don't understand.

b   That's because you think I'm saying something deep. I simply mean that to be false to one's soul about the things that are, to be ignorant and to have and hold falsehood there, is what everyone would least of all accept, for everyone hates a falsehood in that place most of all.

That's right.

Surely, as I said just now, this would be most correctly called true falsehood—ignorance in the soul of someone who has been told a falsehood. Falsehood in words is a kind of imitation of this affection in the soul, an image of it that comes into being after it and is not a pure falsehood.

c   Isn't that so?

Certainly.

And the thing that is really a falsehood is hated not only by the gods but by human beings as well.

It seems so to me.

What about falsehood in words? When and to whom is it useful and so not deserving of hatred? Isn't it useful against one's enemies? And when any of our so-called friends are attempting, through madness or ignorance, to do something bad, isn't it a useful drug for preventing them? It is also useful in the case of those stories we were just talking about, the ones

d   we tell because we don't know the truth about those ancient events involving the gods. By making a falsehood as much like the truth as we can, don't we also make it useful?

We certainly do.

Then in which of these ways could a falsehood be useful to a god? Would he make false likenesses of ancient events because of his ignorance of them?

It would be ridiculous to think that.

Then there is nothing of the false poet in a god?

Not in my view.

Would he be false, then, through fear of his enemies?

e   Far from it.

Because of the ignorance or madness of his family or friends, then?

No one who is ignorant or mad is a friend of the gods.

Then there's no reason for a god to speak falsely?

None.

Therefore the daemonic and the divine are in every way free from falsehood.

Completely.

A god, then, is simple and true in word and deed. He doesn't change himself or deceive others by images, words, or signs, whether in visions or in dreams.

[Socrates/Adeimantus]

That's what I thought as soon as I heard you say it.   *383*

You agree, then, that this is our second pattern for speaking or composing poems about the gods: They are not sorcerers who change themselves,
nor do they mislead us by falsehoods in words or deeds.

I agree.

So, even though we praise many things in Homer, we won't approve of
the dream Zeus sent to Agamemnon, nor of Aeschylus when he makes
Thetis say that Apollo sang in prophecy at her wedding: *b*

> About the good fortune my children would have,
> Free of disease throughout their long lives,
> And of all the blessings that the friendship of the gods would bring
>   me,
> I hoped that Phoebus' divine mouth would be free of falsehood,
> Endowed as it is with the craft of prophecy.
> But the very god who sang, the one at the feast,
> The one who said all this, he himself it is
> Who killed my son.[14]

Whenever anyone says such things about a god, we'll be angry with him,
refuse him a chorus,[15] and not allow his poetry to be used in the education   *c*
of the young, so that our guardians will be as god-fearing and godlike as
human beings can be.

I completely endorse these patterns, he said, and I would enact them as
laws.

14. In *Iliad* ii.1–34, Zeus sends a dream to Agamemnon to promise success if he
attacks Troy immediately. The promise is false. The source for the quotation from
Aeschylus is unknown.
15. I.e., deny him the funding necessary to produce his play.

[Adeimantus/Socrates]

REPUBLIC III

Having completed his discussion of the content of stories about gods and heroes that the guardians should hear as part of their early training in music and poetry (392a), Socrates turns to the content of stories about human beings, only to postpone his discussion of it until Book X. The next topic is the selection of rulers or "complete guardians" from among the class of guardians (412b–414b). The final topic is the housing and life-styles of the rulers, which includes the so-called Myth of the Metals (414c–417b).

The luxurious city (372e) has now been "purified" (399e). This purified city, complete with guardians and rulers, is the second stage in Plato's account of his ideal city. It contains money-loving producers and honor-loving guardians, but no full-blown Platonic philosophers. For the educational institutions needed to produce such philosophers have not yet been provided for in the city's constitution.

386   Such, then, I said, are the kinds of stories that I think future guardians should and should not hear about the gods from childhood on, if they are to honor the gods and their parents and not take their friendship with one another lightly.

I'm sure we're right about that, at any rate.

What if they are to be courageous as well? Shouldn't they be told stories that will make them least afraid of death? Or do you think that anyone

b   ever becomes courageous if he's possessed by this fear?

No, I certainly don't.

And can someone be unafraid of death, preferring it to defeat in battle or slavery, if he believes in a Hades full of terrors?

Not at all.

Then we must supervise such stories and those who tell them, and ask them not to disparage the life in Hades in this unconditional way, but rather to praise it, since what they now say is neither true nor beneficial to

c   future warriors.

We must.

Then we'll expunge all that sort of disparagement, beginning with the following lines:

[Socrates/Adeimantus]

> To a man who is landless, with little to live on,
> Than be king over all the dead.[1]

and also these:

> He feared that his home should appear to gods and men   *d*
> Dreadful, dank, and hated even by the gods.[2]

and

> Alas, there survives in the Halls of Hades
> A soul, a mere phantasm, with its wits completely gone.[3]

and this:

> And he alone could think; the others are flitting shadows.[4]

and

> The soul, leaving his limbs, made its way to Hades,
> Lamenting its fate, leaving manhood and youth behind.[5]

and these: *387*

> His soul went below the earth like smoke,
> Screeching as it went . . .[6]

and

> As when bats in an awful cave
> Fly around screeching if one of them falls
> From the cluster on the ceiling, all clinging to one another,
> So their souls went screeching . . .[7]

We'll ask Homer and the other poets not to be angry if we delete these
passages and all similar ones. It isn't that they aren't poetic and pleasing to   *b*

1. *Odyssey* xi.489–91. Odysseus is being addressed by the dead Achilles in Hades.
2. *Iliad* xx.64–65. The speaker is the god of the underworld—who is afraid that
the earth will split open and reveal that his home is dreadful, etc.
3. *Iliad* xxiii.103–4. Achilles speaks these lines as the soul of the dead Patroclus
leaves for Hades.
4. *Odyssey* x.495. Circe is speaking to Odysseus about the prophet Tiresias.
5. *Iliad* xvi.856–57. The words refer to Patroclus, who has just been mortally
wounded by Hector.
6. *Iliad* xxiii.100–101. The soul referred to is Patroclus'.
7. *Odyssey* xxiv.6–9. The souls are those of the suitors of Penelope, whom Odysseus has killed.

[Socrates/Adeimantus]

the majority of hearers but that, the more poetic they are, the less they should be heard by children or by men who are supposed to be free and to fear slavery more than death.

Most certainly.

And the frightening and dreadful names for the underworld must be struck out, for example, "Cocytus" and "Styx,"[8] and also the names for the

c dead, for example, "those below" and "the sapless ones," and all those names of things in the underworld that make everyone who hears them shudder. They may be all well and good for other purposes, but we are afraid that our guardians will be made softer and more malleable by such shudders.

And our fear is justified.

Then such passages are to be struck out?

Yes.

And poets must follow the opposite pattern in speaking and writing?

Clearly.

Must we also delete the lamentations and pitiful speeches of famous

d men?

We must, if indeed what we said before is compelling.

Consider though whether we are right to delete them or not. We surely say that a decent man doesn't think that death is a terrible thing for someone decent to suffer—even for someone who happens to be his friend.

We do say that.

Then he won't mourn for him as for someone who has suffered a terrible fate.

Certainly not.

We also say that a decent person is most self-sufficient in living well and,

e above all others, has the least need of anyone else.

That's true.

Then it's less dreadful for him than for anyone else to be deprived of his son, brother, possessions, or any other such things.

Much less.

Then he'll least give way to lamentations and bear misfortune most quietly when it strikes.

Certainly.

We'd be right, then, to delete the lamentations of famous men, leaving them to women (and not even to good women, either) and to cowardly

388 men, so that those we say we are training to guard our city will disdain to act like that.

That's right.

8. "Cocytus" means river of wailing or lamenting; "Styx" means river of hatred or gloom.

[Socrates/Adeimantus]

Again, then, we'll ask Homer and the other poets not to represent Achilles, the son of a goddess, as

> Lying now on his side, now on his back, now again
> On his belly; then standing up to wander distracted
> This way and that on the shore of the unharvested sea.

Nor to make him pick up ashes in both hands and pour them over his head, weeping and lamenting in the ways he does in Homer. Nor to represent Priam, a close descendant of the gods, as entreating his men and

b

> Rolling around in dung,
> Calling upon each man by name.[9]

And we'll ask them even more earnestly not to make the gods lament and say:

> Alas, unfortunate that I am, wretched mother of a great son.[10]

c

But, if they do make the gods do such things, at least they mustn't dare to represent the greatest of the gods as behaving in so unlikely a fashion as to say:

> Alas, with my own eyes I see a man who is most dear to me
> Chased around the city, and my heart laments

or

> Woe is me, that Sarpedon, who is most dear to me, should be
> Fated to be killed by Patroclus, the son of Menoetius . . .[11]

d

If our young people, Adeimantus, listen to these stories without ridiculing them as not worth hearing, it's hardly likely that they'll consider the things described in them to be unworthy of mere human beings like themselves or that they'll rebuke themselves for doing or saying similar things when misfortune strikes. Instead, they'll feel neither shame nor restraint but groan and lament at even insignificant misfortunes.

What you say is completely true.

e

9. The last three references and quotations are to *Iliad* xxiv.3–12, *Iliad* xviii.23–24, and *Iliad* xxii.414–15, respectively.
10. *Iliad* xviii.54. Thetis, the mother of Achilles, is mourning his fate among the Nereids.
11. *Iliad* xxii.168–69 (Zeus is watching Hector being pursued by Achilles), and *Iliad* xvi.433–34.

[Socrates / Adeimantus]

Then, as the argument has demonstrated—and we must remain persuaded by it until someone shows us a better one—they mustn't behave like that.

No, they mustn't.

Moreover, they mustn't be lovers of laughter either, for whenever anyone indulges in violent laughter, a violent change of mood is likely to follow.

So I believe.

Then, if someone represents worthwhile people as overcome by laughter, we won't approve, and we'll approve even less if they represent gods
389 that way.

Much less.

Then we won't approve of Homer saying things like this about the gods:

> And unquenchable laughter arose among the blessed gods
> As they saw Hephaestus limping through the hall.[12]

According to your argument, such things must be rejected.
b If you want to call it mine, but they must be rejected in any case.

Moreover, we have to be concerned about truth as well, for if what we said just now is correct, and falsehood, though of no use to the gods, is useful to people as a form of drug, clearly we must allow only doctors to use it, not private citizens.

Clearly.

Then if it is appropriate for anyone to use falsehoods for the good of the city, because of the actions of either enemies or citizens, it is the rulers. But everyone else must keep away from them, because for a private citizen to
c lie to a ruler is just as bad a mistake as for a sick person or athlete not to tell the truth to his doctor or trainer about his physical condition or for a sailor not to tell the captain the facts about his own condition or that of the ship and the rest of its crew—indeed it is a worse mistake than either of these.

That's completely true.
d And if the ruler catches someone else telling falsehoods in the city—

> Any one of the craftsmen,
> Whether a prophet, a doctor who heals the sick, or a maker of
>   spears[13]

—he'll punish him for introducing something as subversive and destructive to a city as it would be to a ship.

He will, if practice is to follow theory.

What about moderation? Won't our young people also need that?

12. *Iliad* i.599–600.
13. *Odyssey* xvii.383–84.

[Socrates/Adeimantus]

Of course.

And aren't these the most important aspects of moderation for the majority of people, namely, to obey the rulers and to rule the pleasures of drink, sex, and food for themselves?

That's my opinion at any rate.

Then we'll say that the words of Homer's Diomedes are well put:

> Sit down in silence, my friend, and be persuaded by me.

and so is what follows:

> The Achaeans, breathing eagerness for battle,
> Marched in silence, fearing their commanders.

and all other such things.

Those *are* well put.

But what about this?

> Wine–bibber, with the eyes of a dog and the heart of a deer[14]

and the rest, is it—or any other headstrong words spoken in prose or poetry by private citizens against their rulers—well put?

No, they aren't.

I don't think they are suitable for young people to hear—not, in any case, with a view to making them moderate. Though it isn't surprising that they are pleasing enough in other ways. What do you think?

The same as you.

What about making the cleverest man say that the finest thing of all is when

> The tables are well laden
> With bread and meat, and the winebearer
> Draws wine from the mixing bowl and pours it in the cups.

or

> Death by starvation is the most pitiful fate.[15]

Do you think that such things make for self-control in young people? Or what about having Zeus, when all the other gods are asleep and he alone is

14. The last three citations are, respectively, *Iliad* iv.412, where Diomedes rebukes his squire and quiets him; *Iliad* iii.8 and iv.431, not in fact (in our Homer text) adjacent to one another or the preceding; and *Iliad* i.225 (Achilles is insulting his commander, Agamemnon).

15. Odysseus in *Odyssey* ix.8–10; *Odyssey* xii.342 (Eurylochus urges the men to slay the cattle of Helios in Odysseus' absence).

[Socrates/Adeimantus]

c   awake, easily forget all his plans because of sexual desire and be so overcome by the sight of Hera that he doesn't even want to go inside but wants
to possess her there on the ground, saying that his desire for her is even
greater than it was when—without their parents' knowledge—they were
first lovers? Or what about the chaining together of Ares and Aphrodite by
Hephaestus[16]—also the result of sexual passion?

No, by god, none of that seems suitable to me.

But if, on the other hand, there are words or deeds of famous men, who
d   are exhibiting endurance in the face of everything, surely they must be
seen or heard. For example,

> He struck his chest and spoke to his heart:
> "Endure, my heart, you've suffered more shameful things than
>   this."[17]

They certainly must.

Now, we mustn't allow our men to be money-lovers or to be bribable
with gifts.

e   Certainly not.

Then the poets mustn't sing to them:

> Gifts persuade gods, and gifts persuade revered kings.[18]

Nor must Phoenix, the tutor of Achilles, be praised as speaking with
moderation when he advises him to take the gifts and defend the
Achaeans, but not to give up his anger without gifts.[19] Nor should we
think such things to be worthy of Achilles himself. Nor should we agree
that he was such a money-lover that he would accept the gifts of Agamem-
391 non or release the corpse of Hector for a ransom but not otherwise.

It certainly isn't right to praise such things.

It is only out of respect for Homer, indeed, that I hesitate to say that it is
positively impious to accuse Achilles of such things or to believe others
who say them. Or to make him address Apollo in these words:

> You've injured me, Farshooter, most deadly of the gods;
> And I'd punish you, if I had the power.[20]

Or to say that he disobeyed the river—a god—and was ready to fight it, or
b   that he consecrated hair to the dead Patroclus, which was already conse-

16. *Odyssey* viii.266 ff.
17. *Odyssey* xx.17–18. The speaker is Odysseus.
18. The source of the passage is unknown. Cf. Euripides, *Medea* 964.
19. *Iliad* ix.602–5.
20. *Iliad* xxii.15, 20.

[Socrates/Adeimantus]

crated to a different river, Spercheius. It isn't to be believed that he did any of these. Nor is it true that he dragged the dead Hector around the tomb of Patroclus or massacred the captives on his pyre.[21] So we'll deny that. Nor will we allow our people to believe that Achilles, who was the son of a goddess and of Peleus (the most moderate of men and the grandson of Zeus) and who was brought up by the most wise Chiron, was so full of inner turmoil as to have two diseases in his soul—slavishness accompanied by the love of money, on the one hand, and arrogance towards gods and humans, on the other.

That's right.

We certainly won't believe such things, nor will we allow it to be said that Theseus, the son of Posidon, and Pirithous, the son of Zeus, engaged in terrible kidnappings,[22] or that any other hero and son of a god dared to do any of the terrible and impious deeds that they are now falsely said to have done. We'll compel the poets either to deny that the heroes did such things or else to deny that they were children of the gods. They mustn't say both or attempt to persuade our young people that the gods bring about evil or that heroes are no better than humans. As we said earlier, these things are both impious and untrue, for we demonstrated that it is impossible for the gods to produce bad things.[23]

Of course.

Moreover, these stories are harmful to people who hear them, for everyone will be ready to excuse himself when he's bad, if he is persuaded that similar things both are being done now and have been done in the past by

> Close descendants of the gods,
> Those near to Zeus, to whom belongs
> The ancestral altar high up on Mount Ida,
> In whom the blood of daemons has not weakened.[24]

For that reason, we must put a stop to such stories, lest they produce in the youth a strong inclination to do bad things.

Absolutely.

Now, isn't there a kind of story whose content we haven't yet discussed? So far we've said how one should speak about gods, heroes, daemons, and things in Hades.

We have.

Then what's left is how to deal with stories about human beings, isn't it?

21. The last four references are to *Iliad* xxi.232 ff., *Iliad* xxiii.141–52, *Iliad* xxiv.14–18, and *Iliad* xxiii.175, respectively.
22. According to some legends, Theseus and Pirithous abducted Helen and tried to abduct Persephone from Hades.
23. See 380d ff.
24. Thought to be from Aeschylus' lost play *Niobe*.

[Socrates/Adeimantus].

Obviously.

But we can't settle that matter at present.

Why not?

Because I think we'll say that what poets and prose-writers tell us about the most important matters concerning human beings is bad. They say *b* that many unjust people are happy and many just ones wretched, that injustice is profitable if it escapes detection, and that justice is another's good but one's own loss. I think we'll prohibit these stories and order the poets to compose the opposite kind of poetry and tell the opposite kind of tales. Don't you think so?

I know so.

But if you agree that what I said is correct, couldn't I reply that you've agreed to the very point that is in question in our whole discussion?

And you'd be right to make that reply.

c   Then we'll agree about what stories should be told about human beings only when we've discovered what sort of thing justice is and how by nature it profits the one who has it, whether he is believed to be just or not.

That's very true.

This concludes our discussion of the content of stories. We should now, I think, investigate their style, for we'll then have fully investigated both what should be said and how it should be said.

I don't understand what you mean, Adeimantus responded.

But you must, I said. Maybe you'll understand it better if I put it this *d* way. Isn't everything said by poets and storytellers a narrative about past, present, or future events?

What else could it be?

And aren't these narratives either narrative alone, or narrative through imitation, or both?

I need a clearer understanding of that as well.

I seem to be a ridiculously unclear teacher. So, like those who are incompetent at speaking, I won't try to deal with the matter as a whole, but I'll take up a part and use it as an example to make plain what I want to say. *e* Tell me, do you know the beginning of the *Iliad*, where the poet tells us that Chryses begs Agamemnon to release his daughter, that Agamemnon harshly rejects him, and that, having failed, Chryses prays to the god *393* against the Achaeans?

I do.

You know, then, that up to the lines:

> And he begged all the Achaeans
> But especially the two sons of Atreus, the commanders of the
>   army,[25]

25. *Iliad* i.15–16.

the poet himself is speaking and doesn't attempt to get us to think that the speaker is someone other than himself. After this, however, he speaks as if he were Chryses and tries as far as possible to make us think that the speaker isn't Homer but the priest himself—an old man. And he com-   *b* poses pretty well all the rest of his narrative about events in Troy, Ithaca, and the whole *Odyssey* in this way.

That's right.

Now, the speeches he makes and the parts between them are both narrative?

Of course.

But when he makes a speech as if he were someone else, won't we say that he makes his own style as much like that of the indicated speaker as   *c* possible?

We certainly will.

Now, to make oneself like someone else in voice or appearance is to imitate the person one makes oneself like.

Certainly.

In these passages, then, it seems that he and the other poets effect their narrative through imitation.

That's right.

If the poet never hid himself, the whole of his poem would be narrative   *d* without imitation. In order to prevent you from saying again that you don't understand, I'll show you what this would be like. If Homer said that Chryses came with a ransom for his daughter to supplicate the Achaeans, especially the kings, and after that didn't speak as if he had become Chryses, but still as Homer, there would be no imitation but rather simple narrative. It would have gone something like this—I'll speak without meter since I'm no poet: "And the priest came and prayed that the gods would allow them to capture Troy and be safe afterwards, that they'd   *e* accept the ransom and free his daughter, and thus show reverence for the god. When he'd said this, the others showed their respect for the priest and consented. But Agamemnon was angry and ordered him to leave and never to return, lest his priestly wand and the wreaths of the god should fail to protect him. He said that, before freeing the daughter, he'd grow old in Argos by her side. He told Chryses to go away and not to make him angry, if he wanted to get home safely. When the old man heard this, he   394 was frightened and went off in silence. But when he'd left the camp he prayed at length to Apollo, calling him by his various titles and reminding him of his own services to him. If any of those services had been found pleasing, whether it was the building of temples or the sacrifice of victims, he asked in return that the arrows of the god should make the Achaeans pay for his tears." That is the way we get simple narrative without   *b* imitation.

I understand.

[Socrates/Adeimantus]

Then also understand that the opposite occurs when one omits the words between the speeches and leaves the speeches by themselves.

I understand that too. Tragedies are like that.

c   That's absolutely right. And now I think that I can make clear to you what I couldn't before. One kind of poetry and story-telling employs only imitation—tragedy and comedy, as you say. Another kind employs only narration by the poet himself—you find this most of all in dithyrambs. A third kind uses both—as in epic poetry and many other places, if you follow me.

Now I understand what you were trying to say.

Remember, too, that before all that we said that we had dealt with *what* must be said in stories, but that we had yet to investigate *how* it must be said.

Yes, I remember.

d   Well, this, more precisely, is what I meant: We need to come to an agreement about whether we'll allow poets to narrate through imitation, and, if so, whether they are to imitate some things but not others—and what things these are, or whether they are not to imitate at all.

I divine that you're looking into the question of whether or not we'll allow tragedy and comedy into our city.

Perhaps, and perhaps even more than that, for I myself really don't know yet, but whatever direction the argument blows us, that's where we must go.

Fine.

Then, consider, Adeimantus, whether our guardians should be imitators
e   or not. Or does this also follow from our earlier statement that each individual would do a fine job of one occupation, not of many, and that if he tried the latter and dabbled in many things, he'd surely fail to achieve distinction in any of them?

He would indeed.

Then, doesn't the same argument also hold for imitation—a single individual can't imitate many things as well as he can imitate one?

No, he can't.

Then, he'll hardly be able to pursue any worthwhile way of life while at
395   the same time imitating many things and being an imitator. Even in the case of two kinds of imitation that are thought to be closely akin, such as tragedy and comedy, the same people aren't able to do both of them well. Did you not just say that these were both imitations?

I did, and you're quite right that the same people can't do both.

Nor can they be both rhapsodes and actors.

True.

Indeed, not even the same actors are used for tragedy and comedy. Yet
b   all these are imitations, aren't they?

[Socrates/Adeimantus]

They are.

And human nature, Adeimantus, seems to me to be minted in even smaller coins than these, so that it can neither imitate many things well nor do the actions themselves, of which those imitations are likenesses.

That's absolutely true.

Then, if we're to preserve our first argument, that our guardians must be kept away from all other crafts so as to be the craftsmen of the city's freedom, and be exclusively that, and do nothing at all except what contributes to it, they must neither do nor imitate anything else. If they do imitate, they must imitate from childhood what is appropriate for them, namely, people who are courageous, self-controlled, pious, and free, and their actions. They mustn't be clever at doing or imitating slavish or shameful actions, lest from enjoying the imitation, they come to enjoy the reality. Or haven't you noticed that imitations practiced from youth become part of nature and settle into habits of gesture, voice, and thought?

I have indeed.

Then we won't allow those for whom we profess to care, and who must grow into good men, to imitate either a young woman or an older one, or one abusing her husband, quarreling with the gods, or bragging because she thinks herself happy, or one suffering misfortune and possessed by sorrows and lamentations, and even less one who is ill, in love, or in labor.

That's absolutely right.

Nor must they imitate either male or female slaves doing slavish things.

No, they mustn't.

Nor bad men, it seems, who are cowards and are doing the opposite of what we described earlier, namely, libelling and ridiculing each other, using shameful language while drunk or sober, or wronging themselves and others, whether in word or deed, in the various other ways that are typical of such people. They mustn't become accustomed to making themselves like madmen in either word or deed, for, though they must know about mad and vicious men and women, they must neither do nor imitate anything they do.

That's absolutely true.

Should they imitate metal workers or other craftsmen, or those who row in triremes, or their time-keepers, or anything else connected with ships?

How could they, since they aren't to concern themselves with any of those occupations?

And what about this? Will they imitate neighing horses, bellowing bulls, roaring rivers, the crashing sea, thunder, or anything of that sort?

They are forbidden to be mad or to imitate mad people.

If I understand what you mean, there is one kind of style and narrative that someone who is really a gentleman would use whenever he wanted to narrate something, and another kind, unlike this one, which his opposite *c*   by nature and education would favor, and in which he would narrate.

Which styles are those?

Well, I think that when a moderate man comes upon the words or actions of a good man in his narrative, he'll be willing to report them as if he were that man himself, and he won't be ashamed of that kind of imitation. He'll imitate this good man most when he's acting in a faultless and

d   intelligent manner, but he'll do so less, and with more reluctance, when the good man is upset by disease, sexual passion, drunkenness, or some other misfortune. When he comes upon a character unworthy of himself, however, he'll be unwilling to make himself seriously resemble that inferior character—except perhaps for a brief period in which he's doing something good. Rather he'll be ashamed to do something like that, both because he's unpracticed in the imitation of such people and because he can't stand to shape and mold himself according to a worse pattern. He despises

e   this in his mind, unless it's just done in play.

That seems likely.

He'll therefore use the kind of narrative we described in dealing with the Homeric epics a moment ago. His style will participate both in imitation and in the other kind of narrative, but there'll be only a little bit of imitation in a long story. Or is there nothing in what I say?

That's precisely how the pattern for such a speaker must be.

397   As for someone who is not of this sort, the more inferior he is, the more willing he'll be to narrate anything and to consider nothing unworthy of himself. As a result, he'll undertake to imitate seriously and before a large audience all the things we just mentioned—thunder, the sounds of wind, hail, axles, pulleys, trumpets, flutes, pipes, and all the other instruments, even the cries of dogs, sheep, and birds. And this man's style will consist

b   entirely of imitation in voice and gesture, or else include only a small bit of plain narrative.

That too is certain.

These, then, are the two kinds of style I was talking about.

There are these two.

The first of these styles involves little variation, so that if someone provides a musical mode and rhythm appropriate to it, won't the one who speaks correctly remain—with a few minor changes—pretty well within

c   that mode and rhythm throughout?

That's precisely what he'll do.

What about the other kind of style? Doesn't it require the opposite if it is to speak appropriately, namely, all kinds of musical modes and all kinds of rhythms, because it contains every type of variation?

That's exactly right.

Do all poets and speakers adopt one or other of these patterns of style or a mixture of both?

[Socrates/Adeimantus]

Necessarily.

What are we to do, then? Shall we admit all these into our city, only one *d*
of the pure kinds, or the mixed one?

If my opinion is to prevail, we'll admit only the pure imitator of a decent
person.

And yet, Adeimantus, the mixed style is pleasant. Indeed, it is by far the
most pleasing to children, their tutors, and the vast majority of people.

Yes, it is the most pleasing.

But perhaps you don't think that it harmonizes with our constitution,
because no one in our city is two or more people simultaneously, since
each does only one job.   *e*

Indeed, it doesn't harmonize.

And isn't it because of this that it's only in our city that we'll find a
cobbler who is a cobbler and not also a captain along with his cobbling,
and a farmer who is a farmer and not also a juror along with his farming,
and a soldier who is a soldier and not a money-maker in addition to his
soldiering, and so with them all?

That's true.

It seems, then, that if a man, who through clever training can become
anything and imitate anything, should arrive in our city, wanting to give a *398*
performance of his poems, we should bow down before him as someone
holy, wonderful, and pleasing, but we should tell him that there is no one
like him in our city and that it isn't lawful for there to be. We should pour
myrrh on his head, crown him with wreaths, and send him away to another city. But, for our own good, we ourselves should employ a more
austere and less pleasure-giving poet and storyteller, one who would imitate the speech of a decent person and who would tell his stories in accor- *b*
dance with the patterns we laid down when we first undertook the education of our soldiers.

That is certainly what we'd do if it were up to us.

It's likely, then, that we have now completed our discussion of the part
of music and poetry that concerns speech and stories, for we've spoken
both of what is to be said and of how it is to be said.

I agree.

Doesn't it remain, then, to discuss lyric odes and songs?   *c*

Clearly.

And couldn't anyone discover what we would say about them, given
that it has to be in tune with what we've already said?

Glaucon laughed and said: I'm afraid, Socrates, that I'm not to be included under "anyone," for I don't have a good enough idea at the moment of what we're to say. Of course, I have my suspicions.

Nonetheless, I said, you know that, in the first place, a song consists of
three elements—words, harmonic mode, and rhythm.   *d*

[Adeimantus/Socrates/Glaucon]

Yes, I do know that.

As far as words are concerned, they are no different in songs than they are when not set to music, so mustn't they conform in the same way to the patterns we established just now?

They must.

Further, the mode and rhythm must fit the words.

Of course.

And we said that we no longer needed dirges and lamentations among our words.

We did, indeed.

e   What are the lamenting modes, then? You tell me, since you're musical.

The mixo-Lydian, the syntono-Lydian, and some others of that sort.

Aren't they to be excluded, then? They're useless even to decent women, let alone to men.

Certainly.

Drunkenness, softness, and idleness are also most inappropriate for our guardians.

How could they not be?

What, then, are the soft modes suitable for drinking-parties?

The Ionian and those Lydian modes that are said to be relaxed.

399   Could you ever use these to make people warriors?

Never. And now all you have left is the Dorian and Phrygian modes.

I don't know all the musical modes. Just leave me the mode that would suitably imitate the tone and rhythm of a courageous person who is active in battle or doing other violent deeds, or who is failing and facing wounds,

b   death, or some other misfortune, and who, in all these circumstances, is fighting off his fate steadily and with self-control. Leave me also another mode, that of someone engaged in a peaceful, unforced, voluntary action, persuading someone or asking a favor of a god in prayer or of a human being through teaching and exhortation, or, on the other hand, of someone submitting to the supplications of another who is teaching him and trying to get him to change his mind, and who, in all these circumstances, is acting with moderation and self-control, not with arrogance but with un-

c   derstanding, and is content with the outcome. Leave me, then, these two modes, which will best imitate the violent or voluntary tones of voice of those who are moderate and courageous, whether in good fortune or in bad.

The modes you're asking for are the very ones I mentioned.

Well, then, we'll have no need for polyharmonic or multistringed instruments to accompany our odes and songs.

It doesn't seem so to me at least.

Then we won't need the craftsmen who make triangular lutes, harps,

d   and all other such multistringed and polyharmonic instruments.

[Glaucon/Socrates]

Apparently not.

What about flute-makers and flute-players? Will you allow them into the city? Or isn't the flute the most "many-stringed" of all? And aren't the panharmonic instruments all imitations of it?[26]

Clearly.

The lyre and the cithara are left, then, as useful in the city, while in the country, there'd be some sort of pipe for the shepherds to play.

That is what our argument shows, at least.

Well, we certainly aren't doing anything new in preferring Apollo and *e* his instruments to Marsyas and his.[27]

By god, it doesn't seem as though we are.

And, by the dog, without being aware of it, we've been purifying the city we recently said was luxurious.

That's because we're being moderate.

Then let's purify the rest. The next topic after musical modes is the regulation of meter. We shouldn't strive to have either subtlety or great variety in meter. Rather, we should try to discover what are the rhythms of someone who leads an ordered and courageous life and then adapt the meter and the tune to his words, not his words to them. What these *400* rhythms actually are is for you to say, just as in the case of the modes.

I really don't know what to say. I can tell you from observation that there are three basic kinds of metrical feet out of which the others are constructed, just as there are four in the case of modes. But I can't tell you which sort imitates which sort of life.

Then we'll consult with Damon as to which metrical feet are suited to *b* slavishness, insolence, madness, and the other vices and which are suited to their opposites. I think I've heard him talking about an enoplion, which is a composite metrical phrase (although I'm not clear on this), and also about dactylic or heroic meter, which he arranged, I don't know how, to be equal up and down in the interchange of long and short. I think he called one foot an iambus, another a trochee, assigning a long and a short to both *c* of them. In the case of some of these, I think he approved or disapproved of the tempo of the foot as much as of the rhythm itself, or of some combination of the two—I can't tell you which. But, as I said, we'll leave these things to Damon, since to mark off the different kinds would require a long argument. Or do you think we should try it?

26. The instrument here is the *aulos*, which was not really a flute but a reed instrument. It was especially good at conveying emotion.

27. After Athena had invented the *aulos*, she discarded it because it distorted her features to play it. It was picked up by the satyr Marsyas, who was foolish enough to challenge Apollo (inventor of the lyre) to a musical contest. He was defeated, and Apollo flayed him alive. Satyrs were bestial in their behavior and desires—especially their sexual desires.

[Glaucon/Socrates]

No, I certainly don't.

But you can discern, can't you, that grace and gracelessness follow good and bad rhythm respectively?

Of course.

d   Further, if, as we said just now, rhythm and mode must conform to the words and not vice versa, then good rhythm follows fine words and is similar to them, while bad rhythm follows the opposite kind of words, and the same for harmony and disharmony.

To be sure, these things must conform to the words.

What about the style and content of the words themselves? Don't they conform to the character of the speaker's soul?

Of course.

And the rest conform to the words?

Yes.

Then fine words, harmony, grace, and rhythm follow simplicity of

e   character—and I do not mean this in the sense in which we use "simplicity" as a euphemism for "simple-mindedness"—but I mean the sort of fine and good character that has developed in accordance with an intelligent plan.

That's absolutely certain.

And must not our young people everywhere aim at these, if they are to do their own work?

They must, indeed.

Now, surely painting is full of these qualities, as are all the crafts similar

401 to it; weaving is full of them, and so are embroidery, architecture, and the crafts that produce all the other furnishings. Our bodily nature is full of them, as are the natures of all growing things, for in all of these there is grace and gracelessness. And gracelessness, bad rhythm, and disharmony are akin to bad words and bad character, while their opposites are akin to and are imitations of the opposite, a moderate and good character.

Absolutely.

b   Is it, then, only poets we have to supervise, compelling them to make an image of a good character in their poems or else not to compose them among us? Or are we also to give orders to other craftsmen, forbidding them to represent—whether in pictures, buildings, or any other works—a character that is vicious, unrestrained, slavish, and graceless? Are we to allow someone who cannot follow these instructions to work among us, so

c   that our guardians will be brought up on images of evil, as if in a meadow of bad grass, where they crop and graze in many different places every day until, little by little, they unwittingly accumulate a large evil in their souls? Or must we rather seek out craftsmen who are by nature able to pursue what is fine and graceful in their work, so that our young people will live in a healthy place and be benefited on all sides, and so that something of those fine works will strike their eyes and ears like a breeze that brings health from a good place, leading them unwittingly, from childhood on, to resemblance, friendship, and harmony with the beauty of reason? *d*

The latter would be by far the best education for them.

Aren't these the reasons, Glaucon, that education in music and poetry is most important? First, because rhythm and harmony permeate the inner part of the soul more than anything else, affecting it most strongly and bringing it grace, so that if someone is properly educated in music and poetry, it makes him graceful, but if not, then the opposite. Second, because anyone who has been properly educated in music and poetry will sense it acutely when something has been omitted from a thing and when it hasn't been finely crafted or finely made by nature. And since he has the right distastes, he'll praise fine things, be pleased by them, receive them into his soul, and, being nurtured by them, become fine and good. He'll rightly object to what is shameful, hating it while he's still young and *402* unable to grasp the reason, but, having been educated in this way, he will welcome the reason when it comes and recognize it easily because of its kinship with himself. *e*

Yes, I agree that those are the reasons to provide education in music and poetry.

It's just the way it was with learning how to read. Our ability wasn't adequate until we realized that there are only a few letters that occur in all sorts of different combinations, and that—whether written large or small[28]—they were worthy of our attention, so that we picked them out eagerly wherever they occurred, knowing that we wouldn't be competent readers until we knew our letters. *b*

True.

And isn't it also true that if there are images of letters reflected in mirrors or water, we won't know them until we know the letters themselves, for both abilities are parts of the same craft and discipline?

Absolutely.

Then, by the gods, am I not right in saying that neither we, nor the guardians we are raising, will be educated in music and poetry until we know the different forms of moderation, courage, frankness, high-mindedness, and all their kindred, and their opposites too, which are moving around everywhere, and see them in the things in which they are, both themselves and their images, and do not disregard them, whether they are written on small things or large, but accept that the knowledge of both large and small letters is part of the same craft and discipline? *c*

That's absolutely essential.

Therefore, if someone's soul has a fine and beautiful character and his body matches it in beauty and is thus in harmony with it, so that both *d*

28. See 368c–d.

share in the same pattern, wouldn't that be the most beautiful sight for anyone who has eyes to see?

It certainly would.

And isn't what is most beautiful also most loveable?

Of course.

And a musical person would love such people most of all, but he wouldn't love anyone who lacked harmony?

No, he wouldn't, at least not if the defect was in the soul, but if it was only in the body, he'd put up with it and be willing to embrace the boy *e* who had it.

I gather that you love or have loved such a boy yourself, and I agree with you. Tell me this, however: Is excessive pleasure compatible with moderation?

How can it be, since it drives one mad just as much as pain does?

What about with the rest of virtue?

403   No.

Well, then, is it compatible with violence and licentiousness?

Very much so.

Can you think of a greater or keener pleasure than sexual pleasure?

I can't—or a madder one either.

But the right kind of love is by nature the love of order and beauty that has been moderated by education in music and poetry?

That's right.

Therefore, the right kind of love has nothing mad or licentious about it?

No, it hasn't.

Then sexual pleasure mustn't come into it, and the lover and the boy he *b* loves must have no share in it, if they are to love and be loved in the right way?

By god, no, Socrates, it mustn't come into it.

It seems, then, that you'll lay it down as a law in the city we're establishing that if a lover can persuade a boy to let him, then he may kiss him, be with him, and touch him, as a father would a son, for the sake of what is fine and beautiful, but—turning to the other things—his association with *c* the one he cares about must never seem to go any further than this, otherwise he will be reproached as untrained in music and poetry and lacking in appreciation for what is fine and beautiful.

That's right.

Does it seem to you that we've now completed our account of education in music and poetry? Anyway, it has ended where it ought to end, for it ought to end in the love of the fine and beautiful.

I agree.

After music and poetry, our young people must be given physical training.

Of course.

[Socrates/Glaucon]

In this, too, they must have careful education from childhood throughout life. The matter stands, I believe, something like this—but you, too,   *d*
should look into it. It seems to me that a fit body doesn't by its own virtue
make the soul good, but instead that the opposite is true—a good soul by
its own virtue makes the body as good as possible. How does it seem to
you?

The same.

Then, if we have devoted sufficient care to the mind, wouldn't we be
right, in order to avoid having to do too much talking, to entrust it with the
detailed supervision of the body, while we indicate only the general patterns to be followed?   *e*

Certainly.

We said that our prospective guardians must avoid drunkenness, for it
is less appropriate for a guardian to be drunk and not to know where on
earth he is than it is for anyone else.

It would be absurd for a guardian to need a guardian.

What about food? Aren't these men athletes in the greatest contest?

They are.

Then would the regimen currently prescribed for athletes in training be   *404*
suitable for them?

Perhaps it would.

Yet it seems to result in sluggishness and to be of doubtful value for
health. Or haven't you noticed that these athletes sleep their lives away
and that, if they deviate even a little from their orderly regimen, they
become seriously and violently ill?

I have noticed that.

Then our warrior athletes need a more sophisticated kind of training.
They must be like sleepless hounds, able to see and hear as keenly as
possible and to endure frequent changes of water and food, as well as
summer and winter weather on their campaigns, without faltering in   *b*
health.

That's how it seems to me, too.

Now, isn't the best physical training akin to the simple music and poetry
we were describing a moment ago?

How do you mean?

I mean a simple and decent physical training, particularly the kind
involved in training for war.

What would it be like?

You might learn about such things from Homer. You know that, when
his heroes are campaigning, he doesn't give them fish to banquet on, even
though they are by the sea in the Hellespont, nor boiled meat either.
Instead, he gives them only roasted meat, which is the kind most easily   *c*
available to soldiers, for it's easier nearly everywhere to use fire alone than
to carry pots and pans.

[Socrates/Glaucon]

That's right.

Nor, I believe, does Homer mention sweet desserts anywhere. Indeed, aren't even the other athletes aware that, if one's body is to be sound, one must keep away from all such things?

They're right to be aware of it, at any rate, and to avoid such things.

d   If you think that, then it seems that you don't approve of Syracusan cuisine or of Sicilian-style dishes.

I do not.

Then you also object to Corinthian girlfriends for men who are to be in good physical condition.

Absolutely.

What about the reputed delights of Attic pastries?

I certainly object to them, too.

I believe that we'd be right to compare this diet and this entire life-style to the kinds of lyric odes and songs that are composed in all sorts of modes

e   and rhythms.

Certainly.

Just as embellishment in the one gives rise to licentiousness, doesn't it give rise to illness in the other? But simplicity in music and poetry makes for moderation in the soul, and in physical training it makes for bodily health?

That's absolutely true.

And as licentiousness and disease breed in the city, aren't many law

405   courts and hospitals opened? And don't medicine and law give themselves solemn airs when even large numbers of free men take them very seriously?

How could it be otherwise?

Yet could you find a greater sign of bad and shameful education in a city than that the need for skilled doctors and lawyers is felt not only by inferior people and craftsmen but by those who claim to have been brought up in the manner of free men? Don't you think it's shameful and a

b   great sign of vulgarity to be forced to make use of a justice imposed by others, as masters and judges, because you are unable to deal with the situation yourself?

I think that's the most shameful thing of all.

Yet isn't it even more shameful when someone not only spends a good part of his life in court defending himself or prosecuting someone else but, through inexperience of what is fine, is persuaded to take pride in being

c   clever at doing injustice and then exploiting every loophole and trick to escape conviction—and all for the sake of little worthless things and because he's ignorant of how much better and finer it is to arrange one's own life so as to have no need of finding a sleepy or inattentive judge?

This case is even more shameful than the other.

And doesn't it seem shameful to you to need medical help, not for

[Glaucon/Socrates]

wounds or because of some seasonal illness, but because, through idleness and the life-style we've described, one is full of gas and phlegm like a stagnant swamp, so that sophisticated Asclepiad doctors are forced to come up with names like "flatulence" and "catarrh" to describe one's diseases? *d*

It does. And those certainly are strange new names for diseases.

Indeed, I don't suppose that they even existed in the time of Asclepius himself. I take it as a proof of this that his sons at Troy didn't criticize either the woman who treated Eurypylus when he was wounded, or Patroclus *e* who prescribed the treatment, which consisted of Pramnian wine with barley meal and grated cheese sprinkled on it, though such treatment is now thought to cause inflammation.[29] *406*

Yet it's a strange drink to give someone in that condition.

Not if you recall that they say that the kind of modern medicine that plays nursemaid to the disease wasn't used by the Asclepiads before Herodicus. He was a physical trainer who became ill, so he mixed physical training with medicine and wore out first himself and then many others as *b* well.

How did he do that?

By making his dying a lengthy process. Always tending his mortal illness, he was nonetheless, it seems, unable to cure it, so he lived out his life under medical treatment, with no leisure for anything else whatever. If he departed even a little from his accustomed regimen, he became completely worn out, but because his skill made dying difficult, he lived into old age.

That's a fine prize for his skill.

One that's appropriate for someone who didn't know that it wasn't *c* because he was ignorant or inexperienced that Asclepius failed to teach this type of medicine to his sons, but because he knew that everyone in a well-regulated city has his own work to do and that no one has the leisure to be ill and under treatment all his life. It's absurd that we recognize this to be true of craftsmen while failing to recognize that it's equally true of those who are wealthy and supposedly happy.

How is that?

When a carpenter is ill, he expects to receive an emetic or a purge from *d* his doctor or to get rid of his disease through surgery or cautery. If anyone prescribed a lengthy regimen to him, telling him that he should rest with his head bandaged and so on, he'd soon reply that he had no leisure to be ill and that life is no use to him if he has to neglect his work and always be concerned with his illness. After that he'd bid good-bye to his doctor, *e* resume his usual way of life, and either recover his health or, if his body couldn't withstand the illness, he'd die and escape his troubles.

29. See *Iliad* xi.580 ff., 828–36, and 624–50.

[Socrates/Glaucon]

It is believed to be appropriate for someone like that to use medicine in this way.

407   Is that because his life is of no profit to him if he doesn't do his work? Obviously.

But the rich person, we say, has no work that would make his life unlivable if he couldn't do it.

That's what people say, at least.

That's because you haven't heard the saying of Phocylides that, once you have the means of life, you must practice virtue.[30]

I think he must also practice virtue before that.

We won't quarrel with Phocylides about this. But let's try to find out whether the rich person must indeed practice virtue and whether his life is not worth living if he doesn't or whether tending an illness, while it is an obstacle to applying oneself to carpentry and the other crafts, is no obstacle whatever to taking Phocylides' advice.

b

But excessive care of the body, over and above physical training, is pretty well the biggest obstacle of all. It's troublesome in managing a household, in military service, and even in a sedentary public office.

Yet the most important of all, surely, is that it makes any kind of learning, thought, or private meditation difficult, for it's always imagining some headaches or dizziness and accusing philosophy of causing them. Hence, wherever this kind of virtue is practiced and examined, excessive care of the body hinders it, for it makes a person think he's ill and be all the time concerned about his body.

c

It probably does.

Therefore, won't we say that Asclepius knew this, and that he taught medicine for those whose bodies are healthy in their natures and habits but have some specific disease? His medicine is for these people with these habits. He cured them of their disease with drugs or surgery and then ordered them to live their usual life so as not to harm their city's affairs. But for those whose bodies were riddled with disease, he didn't attempt to prescribe a regimen, drawing off a little here and pouring in a little there, in order to make their life a prolonged misery and enable them to produce offspring in all probability like themselves. He didn't think that he should treat someone who couldn't live a normal life, since such a person would be of no profit either to himself or to the city.

d

e

The Asclepius you're talking about was quite a statesman.

Clearly. And don't you see that because he was a statesman his sons turned out to be good men at Troy, practicing medicine as I say they did? Don't you remember that they "sucked out the blood and applied gentle potions" to the wound Pandarus inflicted on Menelaus, but without pre-

408

30. Phocylides of Miletus was a mid-sixth-century elegiac and hexameter poet best known for his epigrams.

[Glaucon/Socrates]

scribing what he should eat or drink after that, any more than they did for Eurypylus?[31] They considered their drugs to be sufficient to cure men who were healthy and living an orderly life before being wounded, even if they happened to drink wine mixed with barley and cheese right after receiv-   *b* ing their wounds. But they didn't consider the lives of those who were by nature sick and licentious to be profitable either to themselves or to anyone else. Medicine isn't intended for such people and they shouldn't be treated, not even if they're richer than Midas.

The sons of Asclepius you're talking about were indeed very sophisticated.

Appropriately so. But Pindar and the tragedians don't agree with us.[32] They say that Asclepius was the son of Apollo, that he was bribed with gold to heal a rich man, who was already dying, and that he was killed by lightning for doing so. But, in view of what we said before, we won't believe this. We'll say that if Asclepius was the son of a god, he was not a   *c* money-grubber, and that if he was a money-grubber, he was not the son of a god.

That's right. But what do you say about the following, Socrates? Don't we need to have good doctors in our city? And the best will surely be those who have handled the greatest number of sick and of healthy people. In the same way, the best judges will be those who have associated with   *d* people whose natures are of every kind.

I agree that the doctors and judges must be good. But do you know the kind I consider to be so?

If you'll tell me.

I'll try. But you ask about things that aren't alike in the same question.

In what way?

The cleverest doctors are those who, in addition to learning their craft, have had contact with the greatest number of very sick bodies from child-hood on, have themselves experienced every illness, and aren't very healthy by nature, for they don't treat bodies with their bodies, I   *e* suppose—if they did, we wouldn't allow their bodies to be or become bad. Rather they treat the body with their souls, and it isn't possible for the soul to treat anything well, if it is or has been bad itself.

That's right.

As for the judge, he *does* rule other souls with his own soul. And it isn't   *409* possible for a soul to be nurtured among vicious souls from childhood, to associate with them, to indulge in every kind of injustice, and come through it able to judge other people's injustices from its own case, as it can diseases of the body. Rather, if it's to be fine and good, and a sound

31. *Iliad* iv.218–19.
32. Cf. Aeschylus *Agamemnon* 1022 ff., Euripides *Alcestis* 3, Pindar *Pythians* 3.55–58.

[Socrates/Glaucon]

judge of just things, it must itself remain pure and have no experience of bad character while it's young. That's the reason, indeed, that decent people appear simple and easily deceived by unjust ones when they are

b young. It's because they have no models in themselves of the evil experiences of the vicious to guide their judgments.

That's certainly so.

Therefore, a good judge must not be a young person but an old one, who has learned late in life what injustice is like and who has become aware of it not as something at home in his own soul, but as something alien and present in others, someone who, after a long time, has recognized that injustice is bad by nature, not from his own experience of it, but through

c knowledge.

Such a judge would be the most noble one of all.

And he'd be good, too, which was what you asked, for someone who has a good soul is good. The clever and suspicious person, on the other hand, who has committed many injustices himself and thinks himself a wise villain, appears clever in the company of those like himself, because he's on his guard and is guided by the models within himself. But when he meets with good older people, he's seen to be stupid, distrustful at the wrong time, and ignorant of what a sound character is, since he has no

d model of this within himself. But since he meets vicious people more often than good ones, he seems to be clever rather than unlearned, both to himself and to others.

That's completely true.

Then we mustn't look for the good judge among people like that but among the sort we described earlier. A vicious person would never know either himself or a virtuous one, whereas a naturally virtuous person, when educated, will in time acquire knowledge of both virtue and vice. And it is someone like that who becomes wise, in my view, and not the bad

e person.

I agree with you.

Then won't you legislate in our city for the kind of medicine we mentioned and for this kind of judging, so that together they'll look after those

410 who are naturally well endowed in body and soul? But as for the ones whose bodies are naturally unhealthy or whose souls are incurably evil, won't they let the former die of their own accord and put the latter to death?

That seems to be best both for the ones who suffer such treatment and for the city.

However, *our* young people, since they practice that simple sort of music and poetry that we said produces moderation, will plainly be wary of coming to need a judge.

That's right.

And won't a person who's educated in music and poetry pursue physi-

cal training in the same way, and choose to make no use of medicine except *b*
when unavoidable?

I believe so.

He'll work at physical exercises in order to arouse the spirited part of his
nature, rather than to acquire the physical strength for which other athletes diet and labor.

That's absolutely right.

Then, Glaucon, did those who established education in music and poetry and in physical training do so with the aim that people attribute to *c*
them, which is to take care of the body with the latter and the soul with the
former, or with some other aim?

What other aim do you mean?

It looks as though they established both chiefly for the sake of the soul.

How so?

Haven't you noticed the effect that lifelong physical training, unaccom-
panied by any training in music and poetry, has on the mind, or the effect
of the opposite, music and poetry without physical training?

What effects are you talking about?

Savagery and toughness in the one case and softness and overcultiva- *d*
tion in the other.

I get the point. You mean that those who devote themselves exclusively
to physical training turn out to be more savage than they should, while
those who devote themselves to music and poetry turn out to be softer
than is good for them?

Moreover, the source of the savageness is the spirited part of one's
nature. Rightly nurtured, it becomes courageous, but if it's overstrained,
it's likely to become hard and harsh.

So it seems.

And isn't it the philosophic part of one's nature that provides the
cultivation? If it is relaxed too far, it becomes softer than it should, but if *e*
properly nurtured, it is cultivated and orderly.

So it is.

Now, we say that our guardians must have both these natures.

They must indeed.

And mustn't the two be harmonized with each other?

Of course.

And if this harmony is achieved, the soul is both moderate and
courageous? 411

Certainly.

But if it is inharmonious, it is cowardly and savage?

Yes, indeed.

Therefore, when someone gives music an opportunity to charm his soul
with the flute and to pour those sweet, soft, and plaintive tunes we mentioned through his ear, as through a funnel, when he spends his whole life

[Socrates/Glaucon]

humming them and delighting in them, then, at first, whatever spirit he has is softened, just as iron is tempered, and from being hard and useless, it is made useful. But if he keeps at it unrelentingly and is beguiled by the

b music, after a time his spirit is melted and dissolved until it vanishes, and the very sinews of his soul are cut out and he becomes "a feeble warrior."[33]

That's right.

And if he had a spiritless nature from the first, this process is soon completed. But if he had a spirited nature, his spirit becomes weak and unstable, flaring up at trifles and extinguished as easily. The result is that such people become quick-tempered, prone to anger, and filled with dis-

c content, rather than spirited.

That's certainly true.

What about someone who works hard at physical training and eats well but never touches music or philosophy? Isn't he in good physical condition at first, full of resolution and spirit? And doesn't he become more courageous than he was before?

Certainly.

d But what happens if he does nothing else and never associates with the Muse? Doesn't whatever love of learning he might have had in his soul soon become enfeebled, deaf, and blind, because he never tastes any learning or investigation or partakes of any discussion or any of the rest of music and poetry, to nurture or arouse it?

It does seem to be that way.

I believe that someone like that becomes a hater of reason and of music. He no longer makes any use of persuasion but bulls his way through every situation by force and savagery like a wild animal, living in ignorance and

e stupidity without either rhythm or grace.

That's most certainly how he'll live.

It seems, then, that a god has given music and physical training to human beings not, except incidentally, for the body and the soul but for the spirited and wisdom-loving parts of the soul itself, in order that these might be in harmony with one another, each being stretched and relaxed

412 to the appropriate degree.

It seems so.

Then the person who achieves the finest blend of music and physical training and impresses it on his soul in the most measured way is the one we'd most correctly call completely harmonious and trained in music, much more so than the one who merely harmonizes the strings of his instrument.

That's certainly so, Socrates.

Then, won't we always need this sort of person as an overseer in our city, Glaucon, if indeed its constitution is to be preserved?

---

33. *Iliad* xvii.588.

[Socrates/Glaucon]

It seems that we'll need someone like that most of all.   *b*

These, then, are the patterns for education and upbringing. Should we enumerate the dances of these people, or their hunts, chases with hounds, athletic contests, and horse races? Surely, they're no longer hard to discover, since it's pretty clear that they must follow the patterns we've already established.

Perhaps so.

All right, then what's the next thing we have to determine? Isn't it which of these same people will rule and which be ruled?

Of course.   *c*

Now, isn't it obvious that the rulers must be older and the ruled younger?

Yes, it is.

And mustn't the rulers also be the best of them?

That, too.

And aren't the best farmers the ones who are best at farming?

Yes.

Then, as the rulers must be the best of the guardians, mustn't they be the ones who are best at guarding the city?

Yes.

Then, in the first place, mustn't they be knowledgeable and capable, and mustn't they care for the city?

That's right.   *d*

Now, one cares most for what one loves.

Necessarily.

And someone loves something most of all when he believes that the same things are advantageous to it as to himself and supposes that if it does well, he'll do well, and that if it does badly, then he'll do badly too.

That's right.

Then we must choose from among our guardians those men who, upon examination, seem most of all to believe throughout their lives that they must eagerly pursue what is advantageous to the city and be wholly   *e* unwilling to do the opposite.

Such people would be suitable for the job at any rate.

I think we must observe them at all ages to see whether they are guardians of this conviction and make sure that neither compulsion nor magic spells will get them to discard or forget their belief that they must do what is best for the city.

What do you mean by discarding?

I'll tell you. I think the discarding of a belief is either voluntary or involuntary—voluntary when one learns that the belief is false, involuntary in the case of all true beliefs.   413

I understand voluntary discarding but not involuntary.

What's that? Don't you know that people are voluntarily deprived of

[Glaucon/Socrates]

bad things, but involuntarily deprived of good ones? And isn't being deceived about the truth a bad thing, while possessing the truth is good? Or don't you think that to believe the things that are is to possess the truth?

That's right, and I do think that people are involuntarily deprived of true opinions.

b But can't they also be so deprived by theft, magic spells, and compulsion?

Now, I don't understand again.

I'm afraid I must be talking like a tragic poet! By "the victims of theft" I mean those who are persuaded to change their minds or those who forget, because time, in the latter case, and argument, in the former, takes away their opinions without their realizing it. Do you understand now?

Yes.

By "the compelled" I mean those whom pain or suffering causes to change their mind.

I understand that, and you're right.

The "victims of magic," I think you'd agree, are those who change their *c* mind because they are under the spell of pleasure or fear.

It seems to me that everything that deceives does so by casting a spell.

Then, as I said just now, we must find out who are the best guardians of their conviction that they must always do what they believe to be best for the city. We must keep them under observation from childhood and set them tasks that are most likely to make them forget such a conviction or be *d* deceived out of it, and we must select whoever keeps on remembering it and isn't easily deceived, and reject the others. Do you agree?

Yes.

And we must subject them to labors, pains, and contests in which we can watch for these traits.

That's right.

Then we must also set up a competition for the third way in which people are deprived of their convictions, namely, magic. Like those who lead colts into noise and tumult to see if they're afraid, we must expose our young people to fears and pleasures, testing them more thoroughly than *e* gold is tested by fire. If someone is hard to put under a spell, is apparently gracious in everything, is a good guardian of himself and the music and poetry he has learned, and if he always shows himself to be rhythmical and harmonious, then he is the best person both for himself and for the *414* city. Anyone who is tested in this way as a child, youth, and adult, and always comes out of it untainted, is to be made a ruler as well as a guardian; he is to be honored in life and to receive after his death the most prized tombs and memorials. But anyone who fails to prove himself in this way is to be rejected. It seems to me, Glaucon, that rulers and guardians must be selected and appointed in some such way as this, though we've provided only a general pattern and not the exact details.

It also seems to me that they must be selected in this sort of way.

Then, isn't it truly most correct to call these people complete guardians,   *b*
since they will guard against external enemies and internal friends, so that
the one will lack the power and the other the desire to harm the city? The
young people we've hitherto called guardians we'll now call *auxiliaries*
and supporters of the guardians' convictions.

I agree.

How, then, could we devise one of those useful falsehoods we were
talking about a while ago,[34] one noble falsehood that would, in the best
case, persuade even the rulers, but if that's not possible, then the others in   *c*
the city?

What sort of falsehood?

Nothing new, but a Phoenician story which describes something that
has happened in many places. At least, that's what the poets say, and
they've persuaded many people to believe it too. It hasn't happened
among us, and I don't even know if it could. It would certainly take a lot of
persuasion to get people to believe it.

You seem hesitant to tell the story.

When you hear it, you'll realize that I have every reason to hesitate.

Speak, and don't be afraid.

I'll tell it, then, though I don't know where I'll get the audacity or even   *d*
what words I'll use. I'll first try to persuade the rulers and the soldiers and
then the rest of the city that the upbringing and the education we gave
them, and the experiences that went with them, were a sort of dream, that
in fact they themselves, their weapons, and the other craftsmen's tools
were at that time really being fashioned and nurtured inside the earth, and   *e*
that when the work was completed, the earth, who is their mother,
delivered all of them up into the world. Therefore, if anyone attacks the
land in which they live, they must plan on its behalf and defend it as their
mother and nurse and think of the other citizens as their earthborn
brothers.

It isn't for nothing that you were so shy about telling your falsehood.

Appropriately so. Nevertheless, listen to the rest of the story. "All of you   *415*
in the city are brothers," we'll say to them in telling our story, "but the god
who made you mixed some gold into those who are adequately equipped
to rule, because they are most valuable. He put silver in those who are
auxiliaries and iron and bronze in the farmers and other craftsmen. For the
most part you will produce children like yourselves, but, because you are
all related, a silver child will occasionally be born from a golden parent,   *b*
and vice versa, and all the others from each other. So the first and most
important command from the god to the rulers is that there is nothing that
they must guard better or watch more carefully than the mixture of metals

---

34. See 382a ff.

in the souls of the next generation. If an offspring of theirs should be found to have a mixture of iron or bronze, they must not pity him in any way, but *c* give him the rank appropriate to his nature and drive him out to join the craftsmen and farmers. But if an offspring of these people is found to have a mixture of gold or silver, they will honor him and take him up to join the guardians or the auxiliaries, for there is an oracle which says that the city will be ruined if it ever has an iron or a bronze guardian." So, do you have any device that will make our citizens believe this story?

d   I can't see any way to make them believe it themselves, but perhaps there is one in the case of their sons and later generations and all the other people who come after them.

I understand pretty much what you mean, but even that would help to make them care more for the city and each other. However, let's leave this matter wherever tradition takes it. And let's now arm our earthborn and lead them forth with their rulers in charge. And as they march, let them look for the best place in the city to have their camp, a site from which they *e* can most easily control those within, if anyone is unwilling to obey the laws, or repel any outside enemy who comes like a wolf upon the flock. And when they have established their camp and made the requisite sacrifices, they must see to their sleeping quarters. What do you say?

I agree.

And won't these quarters protect them adequately both in winter and summer?

Of course, for it seems to me that you mean their housing.

Yes, but housing for soldiers, not for money-makers.

416   How do you mean to distinguish these from one another?

I'll try to tell you. The most terrible and most shameful thing of all is for a shepherd to rear dogs as auxiliaries to help him with his flocks in such a way that, through licentiousness, hunger, or some other bad trait of character, they do evil to the sheep and become like wolves instead of dogs.

That's certainly a terrible thing.

b   Isn't it necessary, therefore, to guard in every way against our auxiliaries doing anything like that to the citizens because they are stronger, thereby becoming savage masters instead of kindly allies?

It is necessary.

And wouldn't a really good education endow them with the greatest caution in this regard?

But surely they have had an education like that.

Perhaps we shouldn't assert this dogmatically, Glaucon. What we can assert is what we were saying just now, that they must have the right education, whatever it is, if they are to have what will most make them *c* gentle to each other and to those they are guarding.

That's right.

[Socrates/Glaucon]

Now, someone with some understanding might say that, besides this
education, they must also have the kind of housing and other property
that will neither prevent them from being the best guardians nor encourage them to do evil to the other citizens.   *d*

That's true.

Consider, then, whether or not they should live in some such way as
this, if they're to be the kind of men we described. First, none of them
should possess any private property beyond what is wholly necessary.
Second, none of them should have a house or storeroom that isn't open for
all to enter at will. Third, whatever sustenance moderate and courageous
warrior-athletes require in order to have neither shortfall nor surplus in a   *e*
given year they'll receive by taxation on the other citizens as a salary for
their guardianship. Fourth, they'll have common messes and live together
like soldiers in a camp. We'll tell them that they always have gold and
silver of a divine sort in their souls as a gift from the gods and so have no
further need of human gold. Indeed, we'll tell them that it's impious for
them to defile this divine possession by any admixture of such gold, because many impious deeds have been done that involve the currency used
by ordinary people, while their own is pure. Hence, for them alone among   417
the city's population, it is unlawful to touch or handle gold or silver. They
mustn't be under the same roof as it, wear it as jewelry, or drink from gold
or silver goblets. In this way they'd save both themselves and the city. But
if they acquire private land, houses, and currency themselves, they'll be
household managers and farmers instead of guardians—hostile masters
of the other citizens instead of their allies. They'll spend their whole lives   *b*
hating and being hated, plotting and being plotted against, more afraid of
internal than of external enemies, and they'll hasten both themselves and
the whole city to almost immediate ruin. For all these reasons, let's say that
the guardians must be provided with housing and the rest in this way, and
establish this as a law. Or don't you agree?

I certainly do, Glaucon said.

REPUBLIC IV

The goal of the ideal city, Socrates responds, is not to make any one group in ths city outstandingly happy at the expense of others, as Thrasymachus claimed, but to make everyone as happy as his nature allows. It will be achieved, he argues, if everyone practices the craft for which his natural aptitude is highest, whether it is producing, guarding, or ruling (434a–c). Hence the guardians must above all protect their system of elementary education. For this provides the training in civic virtue without which no system of laws, no constitution, can hope to achieve anything worthwhile (423c–427a). The ideal city is pronounced established (427d). Since it is completely good (427e), it must have all the virtues of a city (see 352d–354a), namely, wisdom, courage, moderation, and justice. Therefore the search for the justice in it is guaranteed not to be futile. By the time that search has concluded (434d), wisdom, courage, moderation, and justice have each been identified with distinct structural features of the ideal city, but those identifications will not be secure until the very same structural features are shown to be identical to those virtues in the individual soul (434d–435a). This leads to the argument for the division of the soul into three parts—appetitive, spirited, rational—corresponding to the three major classes in the ideal city— producers, guardians, rulers (435c–441c). Once this argument is complete, it remains to find the virtues in the soul and to show that they are the same structural features of it as of the ideal city (441c–444e).

The final question raised in Book IV is the central one of the Republic, *namely, whether it is more profitable to be just or unjust (445a). Glaucon is ready to answer it at this point (445a–b) but Socrates is not (445b), for, in his view the question cannot be clearly answered until much more work has been done on virtue and vice (445b–e).*

419   And Adeimantus interrupted: How would you defend yourself, Socrates, he said, if someone told you that you aren't making these men very happy and that it's their own fault? The city really belongs to them, yet they derive no good from it. Others own land, build fine big houses, acquire furnishings to go along with them, make their own private sacrifices to the gods, entertain guests, and also, of course, possess what you were talking about just now, gold and silver and all the things that are thought to belong to people who are blessedly happy. But one might well say that your

[Adeimantus/Socrates]

guardians are simply settled in the city like mercenaries and that all they
do is watch over it.   420

Yes, I said, and what's more, they work simply for their keep and get no
extra wages as the others do. Hence, if they want to take a private trip
away from the city, they won't be able to; they'll have nothing to give to
their mistresses, nothing to spend in whatever other ways they wish, as
people do who are considered happy. You've omitted these and a host of
other, similar facts from your charge.

Well, let them be added to the charge as well.

Then, are you asking how we should defend ourselves?   b

Yes.

I think we'll discover what to say if we follow the same path as before.
We'll say that it wouldn't be surprising if these people were happiest just
as they are, but that, in establishing our city, we aren't aiming to make any
one group outstandingly happy but to make the whole city so, as far as
possible. We thought that we'd find justice most easily in such a city and
injustice, by contrast, in the one that is governed worst and that, by observing both cities, we'd be able to judge the question we've been inquiring into for so long. We take ourselves, then, to be fashioning the happy   c
city, not picking out a few happy people and putting them in it, but
making the whole city happy. (We'll look at the opposite city soon.[1])

Suppose, then, that someone came up to us while we were painting a
statue and objected that, because we had painted the eyes (which are the
most beautiful part) black rather than purple, we had not applied the most
beautiful colors to the most beautiful parts of the statue. We'd think it
reasonable to offer the following defense: "You mustn't expect us to paint
the eyes so beautifully that they no longer appear to be eyes at all, and the   d
same with the other parts. Rather you must look to see whether by dealing
with each part appropriately, we are making the whole statue beautiful."
Similarly, you mustn't force us to give our guardians the kind of happiness
that would make them something other than guardians. We know how to
clothe the farmers in purple robes, festoon them with gold jewelry, and tell   e
them to work the land whenever they please. We know how to settle our
potters on couches by the fire, feasting and passing the wine around, with
their wheel beside them for whenever they want to make pots. And we
can make all the others happy in the same way, so that the whole city is
happy. Don't urge us to do this, however, for if we do, a farmer wouldn't
be a farmer, nor a potter a potter, and none of the others would keep to the   421
patterns of work that give rise to a city. Now, if cobblers become inferior
and corrupt and claim to be what they are not, that won't do much harm to
the city. Hence, as far as they and the others like them are concerned, our

---

1. This discussion is announced at 445c, but doesn't begin until Book VIII.

argument carries less weight. But if the guardians of our laws and city are merely believed to be guardians but are not, you surely see that they'll destroy the city utterly, just as they alone have the opportunity to govern it well and make it happy.

If we are making true guardians, then, who are least likely to do evil to the city, and if the one who brought the charge is talking about farmers and *b* banqueters who are happy as they would be at a festival rather than in a city, then he isn't talking about a city at all, but about something else. With this in mind, we should consider whether in setting up our guardians we are aiming to give them the greatest happiness, or whether—since our aim is to see that the city as a whole has the greatest happiness—we must compel and persuade the auxiliaries and guardians to follow our other *c* policy and be the best possible craftsmen at their own work, and the same with all the others. In this way, with the whole city developing and being governed well, we must leave it to nature to provide each group with its share of happiness.

I think you put that very well, he said.

Will you also think that I'm putting things well when I make the next point, which is closely akin to this one?

Which one exactly?

Consider whether or not the following things corrupt the other workers, *d* so that they become bad.

What things?

Wealth and poverty.

How do they corrupt the other workers?

Like this. Do you think that a potter who has become wealthy will still be willing to pay attention to his craft?

Not at all.

Won't he become more idle and careless than he was?

Much more.

Then won't he become a worse potter?

Far worse.

And surely if poverty prevents him from having tools or any of the other things he needs for his craft, he'll produce poorer work and will teach his *e* sons, or anyone else he teaches, to be worse craftsmen.

Of course.

So poverty and wealth make a craftsman and his products worse.

Apparently.

It seems, then, that we've found other things that our guardians must guard against in every way, to prevent them from slipping into the city unnoticed.

What are they?

422   Both wealth and poverty. The former makes for luxury, idleness, and revolution; the latter for slavishness, bad work, and revolution as well.

[Socrates/Adeimantus]

That's certainly true. But consider this, Socrates: If our city hasn't got any money, how will it be able to fight a war, especially if it has to fight against a great and wealthy city?

Obviously, it will be harder to fight one such city and easier to fight two.   *b*

How do you mean?

First of all, if our city has to fight a city of the sort you mention, won't it be a case of warrior-athletes fighting against rich men?

Yes, as far as that goes.

Well, then, Adeimantus, don't you think that one boxer who has had the best possible training could easily fight two rich and fat non-boxers?

Maybe not at the same time.

Not even by escaping from them and then turning and hitting the one who caught up with him first, and doing this repeatedly in stifling heat and sun? Wouldn't he, in his condition, be able to handle even more than   *c* two such people?

That certainly wouldn't be surprising.

And don't you think that the rich have more knowledge and experience of boxing than of how to fight a war?

I do.

Then in all likelihood our athletes will easily be able to fight twice or three times their own numbers in a war.

I agree, for I think what you say is right.

What if they sent envoys to another city and told them the following truth: "We have no use for gold or silver, and it isn't lawful for us to   *d* possess them, so join us in this war, and you can take the property of those who oppose us for yourselves." Do you think that anyone hearing this would choose to fight hard, lean dogs, rather than to join them in fighting fat and tender sheep?

No, I don't. But if the wealth of all the cities came to be gathered in a single one, watch out that it doesn't endanger your nonwealthy city.   *e*

You're happily innocent if you think that anything other than the kind of city we are founding deserves to be called *a city*.

What do you mean?

We'll have to find a greater title for the others because each of them is a great many cities, not *a* city, as they say in the game. At any rate, each of them consists of two cities at war with one another, that of the poor and that of the rich, and each of these contains a great many. If you approach   423 them as one city, you'll be making a big mistake. But if you approach them as many and offer to give to the one city the money, power, and indeed the very inhabitants of the other, you'll always find many allies and few enemies. And as long as your own city is moderately governed in the way that we've just arranged, it will, even if it has only a thousand men to fight for it, be the greatest. Not in reputation; I don't mean that, but the greatest in fact. Indeed, you won't find a city as great as this one among either *b*   Greeks or barbarians, although many that are many times its size may seem to be as great. Do you disagree?

No, I certainly don't.

Then this would also be the best limit for our guardians to put on the size of the city. And they should mark off enough land for a city that size and let the rest go.

What limit is that?

I suppose the following one. As long as it is willing to remain *one* city, it may continue to grow, but it cannot grow beyond that point.

c   That is a good limit.

Then, we'll give our guardians this further order, namely, to guard in every way against the city's being either small or great in reputation instead of being sufficient in size and one in number.

At any rate, that order will be fairly easy for them to follow.

And the one we mentioned earlier is even easier, when we said that, if an offspring of the guardians is inferior, he must be sent off to join the other citizens and that, if the others have an able offspring, he must join the

d   guardians. This was meant to make clear that each of the other citizens is to be directed to what he is naturally suited for, so that, doing the one work that is his own, he will become not many but one, and the whole city will itself be naturally one not many.

That *is* easier than the other.

These orders we give them, Adeimantus, are neither as numerous nor as important as one might think. Indeed, they are all insignificant, provided, as the saying goes, that they guard the one great thing, though I'd rather

e   call it sufficient than great.

What's that?

Their education and upbringing, for if by being well educated they become reasonable men, they will easily see these things for themselves, as well as all the other things we are omitting, for example, that marriage, the having of wives, and the procreation of children must be governed as far

424   as possible by the old proverb: Friends possess everything in common.

That would be best.

And surely, once our city gets a good start, it will go on growing in a cycle. Good education and upbringing, when they are preserved, produce good natures, and useful natures, who are in turn well educated, grow up even better than their predecessors, both in their offspring and in other

b   respects, just like other animals.

That's likely.

To put it briefly, those in charge must cling to education and see that it isn't corrupted without their noticing it, guarding it against everything. Above all, they must guard as carefully as they can against any innovation in music and poetry or in physical training that is counter to the established order. And they should dread to hear anyone say:

[Socrates/Adeimantus]

> People care most for the song
> That is newest from the singer's lips.[2]

Someone might praise such a saying, thinking that the poet meant not new songs but new ways of singing. Such a thing shouldn't be praised, and the poet shouldn't be taken to have meant it, for the guardians must beware of changing to a new form of music, since it threatens the whole system. As Damon says, and I am convinced, the musical modes are never changed without change in the most important of a city's laws.   c

You can count me among the convinced as well, Adeimantus said.

Then it seems, I said, that it is in music and poetry that our guardians must build their bulwark.   d

At any rate, lawlessness easily creeps in there unnoticed.

Yes, as if music and poetry were only play and did no harm at all.

It is harmless—except, of course, that when lawlessness has established itself there, it flows over little by little into characters and ways of life. Then, greatly increased, it steps out into private contracts, and from private contracts, Socrates, it makes its insolent way into the laws and government, until in the end it overthrows everything, public and private.   e

Well, is that the way it goes?

I think so.

Then, as we said at first, our children's games must from the very beginning be more law-abiding, for if their games become lawless, and the children follow suit, isn't it impossible for them to grow up into good and law-abiding men?   425

It certainly is.

But when children play the right games from the beginning and absorb lawfulness from music and poetry, it follows them in everything and fosters their growth, correcting anything in the city that may have gone wrong before—in other words, the very opposite of what happens where the games are lawless.

That's true.

These people will also discover the seemingly insignificant conventions their predecessors have destroyed.

Which ones?

Things like this: When it is proper for the young to be silent in front of their elders, when they should make way for them or stand up in their presence, the care of parents, hair styles, the clothes and shoes to wear, deportment, and everything else of that sort. Don't you agree?   b

I do.

I think it's foolish to legislate about such things. Verbal or written decrees will never make them come about or last.

How could they?

2. *Odyssey* i.351–52, slightly altered.

[Socrates/Adeimantus]

At any rate, Adeimantus, it looks as though the start of someone's
c   education determines what follows. Doesn't like always encourage like?
It does.

And the final outcome of education, I suppose we'd say, is a single
newly finished person, who is either good or the opposite.
Of course.

That's why I wouldn't go on to try to legislate about such things.
And with good reason.

Then, by the gods, what about market business, such as the private
contracts people make with one another in the marketplace, for example,
d   or contracts with manual laborers, cases of insult or injury, the bringing of
lawsuits, the establishing of juries, the payment and assessment of whatever dues are necessary in markets and harbors, the regulation of market,
city, harbor, and the rest—should we bring ourselves to legislate about any
of these?

It isn't appropriate to dictate to men who are fine and good. They'll
e   easily find out for themselves whatever needs to be legislated about such
things.

Yes, provided that a god grants that the laws we have already described
are preserved.

If not, they'll spend their lives enacting a lot of other laws and then
amending them, believing that in this way they'll attain the best.

You mean they'll live like those sick people who, through licentiousness,
aren't willing to abandon their harmful way of life?
That's right.

426   And such people carry on in an altogether amusing fashion, don't they?
Their medical treatment achieves nothing, except that their illness becomes worse and more complicated, and they're always hoping that
someone will recommend some new medicine to cure them.

That's exactly what happens to people like that.

And isn't it also amusing that they consider their worst enemy to be the
person who tells them the truth, namely, that until they give up drunkenness, overeating, lechery, and idleness, no medicine, cautery, or surgery, no
b   charms, amulets, or anything else of that kind will do them any good?

It isn't amusing at all, for it isn't amusing to treat someone harshly when
he's telling the truth.

You don't seem to approve of such men.
I certainly don't, by god.

Then, you won't approve either if a whole city behaves in that way, as
we said. Don't you think that cities that are badly governed behave exactly
like this when they warn their citizens not to disturb the city's whole
c   political establishment on pain of death? The person who is honored and
considered clever and wise in important matters by such badly governed

[Socrates/Adeimantus]

cities is the one who serves them most pleasantly, indulges them, flatters them, anticipates their wishes, and is clever at fulfillling them.

Cities certainly do seem to behave in that way, and I don't approve of it at all.

What about those who are willing and eager to serve such cities? Don't you admire their courage and readiness?   *d*

I do, except for those who are deceived by majority approval into believing that they are true statesmen.

What do you mean? Have you no sympathy for such men? Or do you think it's possible for someone who is ignorant of measurement not to believe it himself when many others who are similarly ignorant tell him that he is six feet tall?   *e*

No, I don't think that.

Then don't be too hard on them, for such people are surely the most amusing of all. They pass laws on the subjects we've just been enumerating and then amend them, and they always think they'll find a way to put a stop to cheating on contracts and the other things I mentioned, not realizing that they're really just cutting off a Hydra's head.³

Yet that's all they're doing.   427

I'd have thought, then, that the true lawgiver oughtn't to bother with that form of law or constitution, either in a badly governed city or in a well-governed one—in the former, because it's useless and accomplishes nothing; in the latter, because anyone could discover some of these things, while the others follow automatically from the ways of life we established.

What is now left for us to deal with under the heading of legislation?   *b*

For us nothing, but for the Delphic Apollo it remains to enact the greatest, finest, and first of laws.

What laws are those?

Those having to do with the establishing of temples, sacrifices, and other forms of service to gods, daemons, and heroes, the burial of the dead, and the services that ensure their favor. We have no knowledge of these things, and in establishing our city, if we have any understanding, we won't be persuaded to trust them to anyone other than the ancestral   *c* guide. And this god, sitting upon the rock at the center of the earth,⁴ is without a doubt the ancestral guide on these matters for all people.

Nicely put. And that's what we must do.

Well, son of Ariston, your city might now be said to be established. The   *d* next step is to get an adequate light somewhere and to call upon your

3. The Hydra was a mythical monster. When one of its heads was cut off, two or three new heads grew in its place. Heracles had to slay the Hydra as one of his labors.

4. I.e., on the rock in the sanctuary at Delphi, which was believed to be the navel or center of the earth.

[Socrates/Adeimantus]

brother as well as Polemarchus and the others, so as to look inside it and see where the justice and the injustice might be in it, what the difference between them is, and which of the two the person who is to be happy should possess, whether its possession is unnoticed by all the gods and human beings or not.

You're talking nonsense, Glaucon said. You promised to look for them yourself because you said it was impious for you not to come to the rescue of justice in every way you could.

e

That's true, and I must do what I promised, but you'll have to help. We will.

I hope to find it in this way. I think our city, if indeed it has been correctly founded, is completely good.

Necessarily so.

Clearly, then, it is wise, courageous, moderate, and just.

Clearly.

Then, if we find any of these in it, what's left over will be the ones we haven't found?

428

Of course.

Therefore, as with any other four things, if we were looking for any one of them in something and recognized it first, that would be enough for us, but if we recognized the other three first, this itself would be sufficient to enable us to recognize what we are looking for. Clearly it couldn't be anything other than what's left over.

That's right.

Therefore, since there are four virtues, mustn't we look for them in the same way?

Clearly.

Now, the first thing I think I can see clearly in the city is wisdom, and there seems to be something odd about it.

b

What's that?

I think that the city we described is really wise. And that's because it has good judgment, isn't it?

Yes.

Now, this very thing, good judgment, is clearly some kind of knowledge, for it's through knowledge, not ignorance, that people judge well.

Clearly.

But there are many kinds of knowledge in the city.

Of course.

Is it because of the knowledge possessed by its carpenters, then, that the city is to be called wise and sound in judgment?

c

Not at all. It's called skilled in carpentry because of that.

Then it isn't to be called wise because of the knowledge by which it arranges to have the best wooden implements.

[Socrates/Glaucon]

No, indeed.

What about the knowledge of bronze items or the like?

It isn't because of any knowledge of that sort.

Nor because of the knowledge of how to raise a harvest from the earth, for it's called skilled in farming because of that.

I should think so.

Then, is there some knowledge possessed by some of the citizens in the city we just founded that doesn't judge about any particular matter but about the city as a whole and the maintenance of good relations, both internally and with other cities?   d

There is indeed.

What is this knowledge, and who has it?

It is guardianship, and it is possessed by those rulers we just now called complete guardians.

Then, what does this knowledge entitle you to say about the city?

That it has good judgment and is really wise.

Who do you think that there will be more of in our city, metal-workers or these true guardians?   e

There will be far more metal-workers.

Indeed, of all those who are called by a certain name because they have some kind of knowledge, aren't the guardians the least numerous?

By far.

Then, a whole city established according to nature would be wise because of the smallest class and part in it, namely, the governing or ruling one. And to this class, which seems to be by nature the smallest, belongs a share of the knowledge that alone among all the other kinds of knowledge   429 is to be called wisdom.

That's completely true.

Then we've found one of the four virtues, as well as its place in the city, though I don't know how we found it.

Our way of finding it seems good enough to me.

And surely courage and the part of the city it's in, the part on account of which the city is called courageous, aren't difficult to see.

How is that?

Who, in calling the city cowardly or courageous, would look anywhere   b other than to the part of it that fights and does battle on its behalf?

No one would look anywhere else.

At any rate, I don't think that the courage or cowardice of its other citizens would cause the city itself to be called either courageous or cowardly.

No, it wouldn't.

The city is courageous, then, because of a part of itself that has the power to preserve through everything its belief about what things are to c be feared, namely, that they are the things and kinds of things that the lawgiver declared to be such in the course of educating it. Or don't you call that courage?

I don't completely understand what you mean. Please, say it again.

I mean that courage is a kind of preservation.

What sort of preservation?

That preservation of the belief that has been inculcated by the law through education about what things and sorts of things are to be feared. And by preserving this belief "through everything," I mean preserving it
d and not abandoning it because of pains, pleasures, desires, or fears. If you like, I'll compare it to something I think it resembles.

I'd like that.

You know that dyers, who want to dye wool purple, first pick out from the many colors of wool the one that is naturally white, then they carefully prepare this in various ways, so that it will absorb the color as well as possible, and only at that point do they apply the purple dye. When
e something is dyed in this way, the color is fast—no amount of washing, whether with soap or without it, can remove it. But you also know what happens to material if it hasn't been dyed in this way, but instead is dyed purple or some other color without careful preparation.

I know that it looks washed out and ridiculous.

Then, you should understand that, as far as we could, we were doing something similar when we selected our soldiers and educated them in
430 music and physical training. What we were contriving was nothing other than this: That because they had the proper nature and upbringing, they would absorb the laws in the finest possible way, just like a dye, so that their belief about what they should fear and all the rest would become so fast that even such extremely effective detergents as pleasure, pain, fear, and desire wouldn't wash it out—and pleasure is much more potent than
b any powder, washing soda, or soap. This power to preserve through everything the correct and law-inculcated belief about what is to be feared and what isn't is what I call courage, unless, of course, you say otherwise.

I have nothing different to say, for I assume that you don't consider the correct belief about these same things, which you find in animals and slaves, and which is not the result of education, to be inculcated by law, and that you don't call it courage but something else.
c That's absolutely true.

Then I accept your account of courage.

Accept it instead as my account of *civic* courage, and you will be right. We'll discuss courage more fully some other time, if you like. At present, our inquiry concerns not it but justice. And what we've said is sufficient for that purpose.

You're quite right.

[Socrates/Glaucon]

There are now two things left for us to find in the city, namely, moderation and—the goal of our entire inquiry—justice.   *d*

That's right.

Is there a way we could find justice so as not to have to bother with moderation any further?

I don't know any, and I wouldn't want justice to appear first if that means that we won't investigate moderation. So if you want to please me, look for the latter first.

I'm certainly willing. It would be wrong not to be.   *e*

Look, then.

We will. Seen from here, it is more like a kind of consonance and harmony than the previous ones.

In what way?

Moderation is surely a kind of order, the mastery of certain kinds of pleasures and desires. People indicate as much when they use the phrase "self-control" and other similar phrases. I don't know just what they mean by them, but they are, so to speak, like tracks or clues that moderation has left behind in language. Isn't that so?

Absolutely.

Yet isn't the expression "self-control" ridiculous? The stronger self that does the controlling is the same as the weaker self that gets controlled, so that only one person is referred to in all such expressions.   *431*

Of course.

Nonetheless, the expression is apparently trying to indicate that, in the soul of that very person, there is a better part and a worse one and that, whenever the naturally better part is in control of the worse, this is expressed by saying that the person is self-controlled or master of himself. At any rate, one praises someone by calling him self-controlled. But when, on the other hand, the smaller and better part is overpowered by the larger, because of bad upbringing or bad company, this is called being self-defeated or licentious and is a reproach.   *b*

Appropriately so.

Take a look at our new city, and you'll find one of these in it. You'll say that it is rightly called self-controlled, if indeed something in which the better rules the worse is properly called moderate and self-controlled.

I am looking, and what you say is true.

Now, one finds all kinds of diverse desires, pleasures, and pains, mostly in children, women, household slaves, and in those of the inferior majority   *c*
who are called free.

That's right.

But you meet with the desires that are simple, measured, and directed by calculation in accordance with understanding and correct belief only in the few people who are born with the best natures and receive the best education.

That's true.

Then, don't you see that in your city, too, the desires of the inferior many
d   are controlled by the wisdom and desires of the superior few?

I do.

Therefore, if any city is said to be in control of itself and of its pleasures
and desires, it is this one.

Absolutely.

And isn't it, therefore, also moderate because of all this?

It is.

And, further, if indeed the ruler and the ruled in any city share the same
e   belief about who should rule, it is in this one. Or don't you agree?

I agree entirely.

And when the citizens agree in this way, in which of them do you say
moderation is located? In the ruler or the ruled?

I suppose in both.

Then, you see how right we were to divine that moderation resembles a
kind of harmony?

How so?

Because, unlike courage and wisdom, each of which resides in one part,
making the city brave and wise respectively, moderation spreads through-
432   out the whole. It makes the weakest, the strongest, and those in between—
whether in regard to reason, physical strength, numbers, wealth, or anything else—all sing the same song together. And this unanimity, this
agreement between the naturally worse and the naturally better as to
which of the two is to rule both in the city and in each one, is rightly called
moderation.

b   I agree completely.

All right. We've now found, at least from the point of view of our
present beliefs, three out of the four virtues in our city. So what kind of
virtue is left, then, that makes the city share even further in virtue? Surely,
it's clear that it is justice.

That is clear.

Then, Glaucon, we must station ourselves like hunters surrounding a
wood and focus our understanding, so that justice doesn't escape us and
vanish into obscurity, for obviously it's around here somewhere. So look
c   and try eagerly to catch sight of it, and if you happen to see it before I do,
you can tell me about it.

I wish I could, but you'll make better use of me if you take me to be a
follower who can see things when you point them out to him.

Follow, then, and join me in a prayer.

I'll do that, just so long as you lead.

I certainly will, though the place seems to be impenetrable and full of
shadows. It is certainly dark and hard to search though. But all the same,
we must go on.

[Glaucon/Socrates]

Indeed we must.   *d*

And then I caught sight of something. Ah ha! Glaucon, it looks as though there's a track here, so it seems that our quarry won't altogether escape us.

That's good news.

Either that, or we've just been stupid.

In what way?

Because what we are looking for seems to have been rolling around at our feet from the very beginning, and we didn't see it, which was ridiculous of us. Just as people sometimes search for the very thing they are holding in their hands, so we didn't look in the right direction but gazed   *e* off into the distance, and that's probably why we didn't notice it.

What do you mean?

I mean that, though we've been talking and hearing about it for a long time, I think we didn't understand what we were saying or that, in a way, we were talking about justice.

That's a long prelude for someone who wants to hear the answer.

Then listen and see whether there's anything in what I say. Justice, I   433 think, is exactly what we said must be established throughout the city when we were founding it—either that or some form of it. We stated, and often repeated, if you remember, that everyone must practice one of the occupations in the city for which he is naturally best suited.

Yes, we did keep saying that.

Moreover, we've heard many people say and have often said ourselves that justice is doing one's own work and not meddling with what isn't one's own.   *b*

Yes, we have.

Then, it turns out that this doing one's own work—provided that it comes to be in a certain way—is justice. And do you know what I take as evidence of this?

No, tell me.

I think that this is what was left over in the city when moderation, courage, and wisdom have been found. It is the power that makes it possible for them to grow in the city and that preserves them when they've grown for as long as it remains there itself. And of course we said that   *c* justice would be what was left over when we had found the other three.

Yes, that must be so.

And surely, if we had to decide which of the four will make the city good by its presence, it would be a hard decision. Is it the agreement in belief between the rulers and the ruled? Or the preservation among the soldiers of the law-inspired belief about what is to be feared and what isn't? Or the wisdom and guardianship of the rulers? Or is it, above all, the fact that   *d* every child, woman, slave, freeman, craftsman, ruler, and ruled each does his own work and doesn't meddle with what is other people's?

[Glaucon/Socrates]

How could this fail to be a hard decision?

It seems, then, that the power that consists in everyone's doing his own work rivals wisdom, moderation, and courage in its contribution to the virtue of the city.

e

It certainly does.

And wouldn't you call this rival to the others in its contribution to the city's virtue justice?

Absolutely.

Look at it this way if you want to be convinced. Won't you order your rulers to act as judges in the city's courts?

Of course.

And won't their sole aim in delivering judgments be that no citizen should have what belongs to another or be deprived of what is his own?

They'll have no aim but that.

Because that is just?

Yes.

Therefore, from this point of view also, the having and doing of one's own would be accepted as justice.

434

That's right.

Consider, then, and see whether you agree with me about this. If a carpenter attempts to do the work of a cobbler, or a cobbler that of a carpenter, or they exchange their tools or honors with one another, or if the same person tries to do both jobs, and all other such exchanges are made, do you think that does any great harm to the city?

Not much.

But I suppose that when someone, who is by nature a craftsman or some other kind of money-maker, is puffed up by wealth, or by having a major-

b

ity of votes, or by his own strength, or by some other such thing, and attempts to enter the class of soldiers, or one of the unworthy soldiers tries to enter that of the judges and guardians, and these exchange their tools and honors, or when the same person tries to do all these things at once, then I think you'll agree that these exchanges and this sort of meddling bring the city to ruin.

Absolutely.

Meddling and exchange between these three classes, then, is the greatest harm that can happen to the city and would rightly be called the worst

c

thing someone could do to it.

Exactly.

And wouldn't you say that the worst thing that someone could do to his city is injustice?

Of course.

Then, that exchange and meddling is injustice. Or to put it the other way around: For the money-making, auxiliary, and guardian classes each to do its own work in the city, is the opposite. That's justice, isn't it, and makes the city just?

I agree. Justice is that and nothing else.   *d*

Let's not take that as secure just yet, but if we find that the same form, when it comes to be in each individual person, is accepted as justice there as well, we can assent to it. What else can we say? But if that isn't what we find, we must look for something else to be justice. For the moment, however, let's complete the present inquiry. We thought that, if we first tried to observe justice in some larger thing that possessed it, this would make it easier to observe in a single individual. We agreed that this larger thing is a city, and so we established the best city we could, knowing well that justice would be in one that was good. So, let's apply what has come to   *e* light in the city to an individual, and if it is accepted there, all will be well. But if something different is found in the individual, then we must go back and test that on the city. And if we do this, and compare them side by side, we might well make justice light up as if we were rubbing fire-sticks   435 together. And, when it has come to light, we can get a secure grip on it for ourselves.

You're following the road we set, and we must do as you say.

Well, then, are things called by the same name, whether they are bigger or smaller than one another, like or unlike with respect to that to which that name applies?

Alike.

Then a just man won't differ at all from a just city in respect to the form of justice; rather he'll be like the city.   *b*

He will.

But a city was thought to be just when each of the three natural classes within it did its own work, and it was thought to be moderate, courageous, and wise because of certain other conditions and states of theirs.

That's true.

Then, if an individual has these same three parts in his soul, we will expect him to be correctly called by the same names as the city if he has the same conditions in them.   *c*

Necessarily so.

Then once again we've come upon an easy question, namely, does the soul have these three parts in it or not?

It doesn't look easy to me. Perhaps, Socrates, there's some truth in the old saying that everything fine is difficult.

Apparently so. But you should know, Glaucon, that, in my opinion, we will never get a precise answer using our present methods of argument— although there is another longer and fuller road that does lead to such an   *d* answer. But perhaps we can get an answer that's up to the standard of our previous statements and inquiries.

[Socrates/Glaucon]

Isn't that satisfactory? It would be enough for me at present.

In that case, it will be fully enough for me too.

Then don't weary, but go on with the inquiry.

Well, then, we are surely compelled to agree that each of us has within himself the same parts and characteristics as the city? Where else would they come from? It would be ridiculous for anyone to think that spiritedness didn't come to be in cities from such individuals as the Thracians, Scythians, and others who live to the north of us who are held to possess spirit, or that the same isn't true of the love of learning, which is mostly associated with our part of the world, or of the love of money, which one might say is conspicuously displayed by the Phoenicians and Egyptians.

It would.

That's the way it is, anyway, and it isn't hard to understand.

Certainly not.

But this *is* hard. Do we do these things with the same part of ourselves, or do we do them with three different parts? Do we learn with one part, get angry with another, and with some third part desire the pleasures of food, drink, sex, and the others that are closely akin to them? Or, when we set out after something, do we act with the whole of our soul, in each case? This is what's hard to determine in a way that's up to the standards of our argument.

I think so too.

Well, then, let's try to determine in that way whether these parts are the same or different.

How?

It is obvious that the same thing will not be willing to do or undergo opposites in the same part of itself, in relation to the same thing, at the same time. So, if we ever find this happening in the soul, we'll know that we aren't dealing with one thing but many.

All right.

Then consider what I'm about to say.

Say on.

Is it possible for the same thing to stand still and move at the same time in the same part of itself?

Not at all.

Let's make our agreement more precise in order to avoid disputes later on. If someone said that a person who is standing still but moving his hands and head is moving and standing still at the same time, we wouldn't consider, I think, that he ought to put it like that. What he ought to say is that one part of the person is standing still and another part is moving. Isn't that so?

It is.

And if our interlocutor became even more amusing and was sophisticated enough to say that whole spinning tops stand still and move at the

same time when the peg is fixed in the same place and they revolve, and
that the same is true of anything else moving in a circular motion on the
same spot, we wouldn't agree, because it isn't with respect to the same
parts of themselves that such things both stand still and move. We'd say
that they have an axis and a circumference and that with respect to the axis   *e*
they stand still, since they don't wobble to either side, while with respect
to the circumference they move in a circle. But if they do wobble to the left
or right, front or back, while they are spinning, we'd say that they aren't
standing still in any way.

And we'd be right.

No such statement will disturb us, then, or make us believe that the
same thing can be, do, or undergo opposites, at the same time, in the same
respect, and in relation to the same thing.   437

They won't make me believe it, at least.

Nevertheless, in order to avoid going through all these objections one by
one and taking a long time to prove them all untrue, let's hypothesize that
this is corrrect and carry on. But we agree that if it should ever be shown to
be incorrect, all the consequences we've drawn from it will also be lost.

We should agree to that.

Then wouldn't you consider all the following, whether they are doings   *b*
or undergoings, as pairs of opposites: Assent and dissent, wanting to have
something and rejecting it, taking something and pushing it away?

Yes, they are opposites.

What about these? Wouldn't you include thirst, hunger, the appetites as
a whole, and wishing and willing somewhere in the class we mentioned?   *c*
Wouldn't you say that the soul of someone who has an appetite for a thing
wants what he has an appetite for and takes to himself what it is his will to
have, and that insofar as he wishes something to be given to him, his soul,
since it desires this to come about, nods assent to it as if in answer to a
question?

I would.

What about not willing, not wishing, and not having an appetite? Aren't
these among the very opposites—cases in which the soul pushes and
drives things away?

Of course.   *d*

Then won't we say that there is a class of things called appetites and that
the clearest examples are hunger and thirst?

We will.

One of these is for food and the other for drink?

Yes.

Now, insofar as it is thirst, is it an appetite in the soul for more than that
for which we say that it is the appetite? For example, is thirst thirst for hot
drink or cold, or much drink or little, or, in a word, for drink of a certain
sort? Or isn't it rather that, where heat is present as well as thirst, it causes

e   the appetite to be for something cold as well, and where cold for something hot, and where there is much thirst because of the presence of muchness, it will cause the desire to be for much, and where little for little? But thirst itself will never be for anything other than what it is in its nature to be for, namely, drink itself, and hunger for food.

That's the way it is, each appetite itself is only for its natural object, while the appetite for something of a certain sort depends on additions.

438   Therefore, let no one catch us unprepared or disturb us by claiming that no one has an appetite for drink but rather good drink, nor food but good food, on the grounds that everyone after all has appetite for good things, so that if thirst is an appetite, it will be an appetite for good drink or whatever, and similarly with the others.

All the same, the person who says that has a point.

But it seems to me that, in the case of all things that are related to something, those that are of a particular sort are related to a particular sort
b   of thing, while those that are merely themselves are related to a thing that is merely itself.

I don't understand.

Don't you understand that the greater is such as to be greater than something?

Of course.

Than the less?

Yes.

And the much greater than the much less, isn't that so?

Yes.

And the once greater to the once less? And the going-to-be greater than the going-to-be less?

Certainly.

And isn't the same true of the more and the fewer, the double and the
c   half, heavier and lighter, faster and slower, the hot and the cold, and all other such things?

Of course.

And what about the various kinds of knowledge? Doesn't the same apply? Knowledge itself is knowledge of what can be learned itself (or whatever it is that knowledge is of), while a particular sort of knowledge is of a particular sort of thing. For example, when knowledge of building
d   houses came to be, didn't it differ from the other kinds of knowledge, and so was called knowledge of building?

Of course.

And wasn't that because it was a different sort of knowledge from all the others?

Yes.

And wasn't it because it was of a particular sort of thing that it itself

[Socrates/Glaucon]

became a particular sort of knowledge? And isn't this true of all crafts and kinds of knowledge?

It is.

Well, then, this is what I was trying to say—if you understand it now— when I said that of all things that are related to something, those that are merely themselves are related to things that are merely themselves, while those that are of a particular sort are related to things of a particular sort. However, I don't mean that the sorts in question have to be the same for *e* them both. For example, knowledge of health or disease isn't healthy or diseased, and knowledge of good and bad doesn't itself become good or bad. I mean that, when knowledge became, not knowledge of the thing itself that knowledge is of, but knowledge of something of a particular sort, the result was that it itself became a particular sort of knowledge, and this caused it to be no longer called knowledge without qualification, but—with the addition of the relevant sort—medical knowledge or whatever.

I understand, and I think that that's the way it is.

Then as for thirst, wouldn't you include it among things that are related to something? Surely thirst is related to . . .   *439*

I know it's related to drink.

Therefore a particular sort of thirst is for a particular sort of drink. But thirst itself isn't for much or little, good or bad, or, in a word, for drink of a particular sort. Rather, thirst itself is in its nature only for drink itself.

Absolutely.

Hence the soul of the thirsty person, insofar as he's thirsty, doesn't wish anything else but to drink, and it wants this and is impelled towards it.   *b*

Clearly.

Therefore, if something draws it back when it is thirsting, wouldn't that be something different in it from whatever thirsts and drives it like a beast to drink? It can't be, we say, that the same thing, with the same part of itself, in relation to the same, at the same time, does opposite things.

No, it can't.

In the same way, I suppose, it's wrong to say of the archer that his hands at the same time push the bow away and draw it towards him. We ought to say that one hand pushes it away and the other draws it towards him.

Absolutely.   *c*

Now, would we assert that sometimes there are thirsty people who don't wish to drink?

Certainly, it happens often to many different people.

What, then, should one say about them? Isn't it that there is something in their soul, bidding them to drink, and something different, forbidding them to do so, that overrules the thing that bids?

I think so.

Doesn't that which forbids in such cases come into play—if it comes into play at all—as a result of rational calculation, while what drives and drags them to drink is a result of feelings and diseases?

Apparently.

Hence it isn't unreasonable for us to claim that they are two, and different from one another. We'll call the part of the soul with which it calculates the rational part and the part with which it lusts, hungers, thirsts, and gets excited by other appetites the irrational appetitive part, companion of certain indulgences and pleasures.

Yes. Indeed, that's a reasonable thing to think.

Then, let these two parts be distinguished in the soul. Now, is the spirited part by which we get angry a third part or is it of the same nature as either of the other two?

Perhaps it's like the appetitive part.

But I've heard something relevant to this, and I believe it. Leontius, the son of Aglaion, was going up from the Piraeus along the outside of the North Wall when he saw some corpses lying at the executioner's feet. He had an appetite to look at them but at the same time he was disgusted and turned away. For a time he struggled with himself and covered his face, but, finally, overpowered by the appetite, he pushed his eyes wide open and rushed towards the corpses, saying, "Look for yourselves, you evil wretches, take your fill of the beautiful sight!"[5]

I've heard that story myself.

It certainly proves that anger sometimes makes war against the appetites, as one thing against another.

Besides, don't we often notice in other cases that when appetite forces someone contrary to rational calculation, he reproaches himself and gets angry with that in him that's doing the forcing, so that of the two factions that are fighting a civil war, so to speak, spirit allies itself with reason? But I don't think you can say that you've ever seen spirit, either in yourself or anyone else, ally itself with an appetite to do what reason has decided must not be done.

No, by god, I haven't.

What happens when a person thinks that he has done something unjust? Isn't it true that the nobler he is, the less he resents it if he suffers hunger, cold, or the like at the hands of someone whom he believes to be inflicting this on him justly, and won't his spirit, as I say, refuse to be aroused?

That's true.

But what happens if, instead, he believes that someone has been unjust

5. Leontius' desire to look at the corpses is sexual in nature, for a fragment of contemporary comedy tells us that Leontius was known for his love of boys as pale as corpses.

[Socrates/Glaucon]

to him? Isn't the spirit within him boiling and angry, fighting for what he believes to be just? Won't it endure hunger, cold, and the like and keep on till it is victorious, not ceasing from noble actions until it either wins, dies,   *d* or calms down, called to heel by the reason within him, like a dog by a shepherd?

Spirit is certainly like that. And, of course, we made the auxiliaries in our city like dogs obedient to the rulers, who are themselves like shepherds of a city.

You well understand what I'm trying to say. But also reflect on this further point.

What?   *e*

The position of the spirited part seems to be the opposite of what we thought before. Then we thought of it as something appetitive, but now we say that it is far from being that, for in the civil war in the soul it aligns itself far more with the rational part.

Absolutely.

Then is it also different from the rational part, or is it some form of it, so that there are two parts in the soul—the rational and the appetitive—instead of three? Or rather, just as there were three classes in the city that held it together, the money-making, the auxiliary, and the deliberative, is   *441* the spirited part a third thing in the soul that is by nature the helper of the rational part, provided that it hasn't been corrupted by a bad upbringing?

It must be a third.

Yes, provided that we can show it is different from the rational part, as we saw earlier it was from the appetitive one.

It isn't difficult to show that it is different. Even in small children, one can see that they are full of spirit right from birth, while as far as rational calculation is concerned, some never seem to get a share of it, while the majority do so quite late.   *b*

That's really well put. And in animals too one can see that what you say is true. Besides, our earlier quotation from Homer bears it out, where he says,

He struck his chest and spoke to his heart.

For here Homer clearly represents the part that has calculated about better and worse as different from the part that is angry without calculation.   *c*

That's exactly right.

Well, then, we've now made our difficult way through a sea of argument. We are pretty much agreed that the same number and the same kinds of classes as are in the city are also in the soul of each individual.

That's true.

Therefore, it necessarily follows that the individual is wise in the same way and in the same part of himself as the city.

[Socrates/Glaucon]

That's right.

And isn't the individual courageous in the same way and in the same
part of himself as the city? And isn't everything else that has to do with
virtue the same in both?

Necessarily.

Moreover, Glaucon, I suppose we'll say that a man is just in the same
way as a city.

That too is entirely necessary.

And we surely haven't forgotten that the city was just because each of
the three classes in it was doing its own work.

I don't think we could forget that.

Then we must also remember that each one of us in whom each part is
doing its own work will himself be just and do his own.

Of course, we must.

Therefore, isn't it appropriate for the rational part to rule, since it is
really wise and exercises foresight on behalf of the whole soul, and for the
spirited part to obey it and be its ally?

It certainly is.

And isn't it, as we were saying, a mixture of music and poetry, on the
one hand, and physical training, on the other, that makes the two parts
harmonious, stretching and nurturing the rational part with fine words
and learning, relaxing the other part through soothing stories, and making
it gentle by means of harmony and rhythm?

That's precisely it.

And these two, having been nurtured in this way, and having truly
learned their own roles and been educated in them, will govern the appetitive part, which is the largest part in each person's soul and is by nature
most insatiable for money. They'll watch over it to see that it isn't filled
with the so-called pleasures of the body and that it doesn't become so big
and strong that it no longer does its own work but attempts to enslave and
rule over the classes it isn't fitted to rule, thereby overturning everyone's
whole life.

That's right.

Then, wouldn't these two parts also do the finest job of guarding the
whole soul and body against external enemies—reason by planning, spirit
by fighting, following its leader, and carrying out the leader's decisions
through its courage?

Yes, that's true.

And it is because of the spirited part, I suppose, that we call a single
individual courageous, namely, when it preserves through pains and pleasures the declarations of reason about what is to be feared and what isn't.

That's right.

And we'll call him wise because of that small part of himself that rules in
him and makes those declarations and has within it the knowledge of

[Glaucon/Socrates]

what is advantageous for each part and for the whole soul, which is the community of all three parts.

Absolutely.

And isn't he moderate because of the friendly and harmonious relations between these same parts, namely, when the ruler and the ruled believe in common that the rational part should rule and don't engage in civil war against it?   *d*

Moderation is surely nothing other than that, both in the city and in the individual.

And, of course, a person will be just because of what we've so often mentioned, and in that way.

Necessarily.

Well, then, is the justice in us at all indistinct? Does it seem to be something different from what we found in the city?

It doesn't seem so to me.

If there are still any doubts in our soul about this, we could dispel them altogether by appealing to ordinary cases.   *e*

Which ones?

For example, if we had to come to an agreement about whether someone similar in nature and training to our city had embezzled a deposit of gold or silver that he had accepted, who do you think would consider him to have done it rather than someone who isn't like him?   443

No one.

And would he have anything to do with temple robberies, thefts, betrayals of friends in private life or of cities in public life?

No, nothing.

And he'd be in no way untrustworthy in keeping an oath or other agreement.

How could he be?

And adultery, disrespect for parents, and neglect of the gods would be more in keeping with every other kind of character than his.

With every one.

And isn't the cause of all this that every part within him does its own work, whether it's ruling or being ruled?   *b*

Yes, that and nothing else.

Then, are you still looking for justice to be something other than this power, the one that produces men and cities of the sort we've described?

No, I certainly am not.

Then the dream we had has been completely fulfilled—our suspicion that, with the help of some god, we had hit upon the origin and pattern of justice right at the beginning in founding our city.   *c*

Absolutely.

Indeed, Glaucon, the principle that it is right for someone who is by nature a cobbler to practice cobblery and nothing else, for the carpenter to

[Socrates/Glaucon]

practice carpentry, and the same for the others is a sort of image of justice—that's why it's beneficial.

Apparently.

And in truth justice is, it seems, something of this sort. However, it isn't concerned with someone's doing his own externally, but with what is

d inside him, with what is truly himself and his own. One who is just does not allow any part of himself to do the work of another part or allow the various classes within him to meddle with each other. He regulates well what is really his own and rules himself. He puts himself in order, is his own friend, and harmonizes the three parts of himself like three limiting notes in a musical scale—high, low, and middle. He binds together those parts and any others there may be in between, and from having been

e many things he becomes entirely one, moderate and harmonious. Only then does he act. And when he does anything, whether acquiring wealth, taking care of his body, engaging in politics, or in private contracts—in all of these, he believes that the action is just and fine that preserves this inner harmony and helps achieve it, and calls it so, and regards as wisdom the knowledge that oversees such actions. And he believes that the action that

444 destroys this harmony is unjust, and calls it so, and regards the belief that oversees it as ignorance.

That's absolutely true, Socrates.

Well, then, if we claim to have found the just man, the just city, and what the justice is that is in them, I don't suppose that we'll seem to be telling a complete falsehood.

No, we certainly won't.

Shall we claim it, then?

We shall.

So be it. Now, I suppose we must look for injustice.

Clearly.

b Surely, it must be a kind of civil war between the three parts, a meddling and doing of another's work, a rebellion by some part against the whole soul in order to rule it inappropriately. The rebellious part is by nature suited to be a slave, while the other part is not a slave but belongs to the ruling class. We'll say something like that, I suppose, and that the turmoil and straying of these parts are injustice, licentiousness, cowardice, ignorance, and, in a word, the whole of vice.

That's what they are.

So, if justice and injustice are really clear enough to us, then acting justly,

c acting unjustly, and doing injustice are also clear.

How so?

Because just and unjust actions are no different for the soul than healthy and unhealthy things are for the body.

In what way?

Healthy things produce health, unhealthy ones disease.

[Socrates/Glaucon]

Yes.

And don't just actions produce justice in the soul and unjust ones   *d*
injustice?

Necessarily.

To produce health is to establish the components of the body in a natural
relation of control and being controlled, one by another, while to produce
disease is to establish a relation of ruling and being ruled contrary to
nature.

That's right.

Then, isn't to produce justice to establish the parts of the soul in a
natural relation of control, one by another, while to produce injustice is to
establish a relation of ruling and being ruled contrary to nature?

Precisely.

Virtue seems, then, to be a kind of health, fine condition, and well-being
of the soul, while vice is disease, shameful condition, and weakness.   *e*

That's true.

And don't fine ways of living lead one to the possession of virtue,
shameful ones to vice?

Necessarily.

So it now remains, it seems, to inquire whether it is more profitable to act
justly, live in a fine way, and be just, whether one is known to be so or not,   *445*
or to act unjustly and be unjust, provided that one doesn't pay the penalty
and become better as a result of punishment.

But, Socrates, this inquiry looks ridiculous to me now that justice and
injustice have been shown to be as we have described. Even if one has
every kind of food and drink, lots of money, and every sort of power to
rule, life is thought to be not worth living when the body's nature is
ruined. So even if someone can do whatever he wishes, except what will   *b*
free him from vice and injustice and make him acquire justice and virtue,
how can it be worth living when his soul—the very thing by which he
lives—is ruined and in turmoil?

Yes, it is ridiculous. Nevertheless, now that we've come far enough to be
able to see most clearly that this is so, we mustn't give up.

That's absolutely the last thing we must do.

Then come here, so that you can see how many forms of vice there are,   *c*
anyhow that I consider worthy of examination.

I'm following you, just tell me.

Well, from the vantage point we've reached in our argument, it seems to
me that there is one form of virtue and an unlimited number of forms of
vice, four of which are worth mentioning.

How do you mean?

It seems likely that there are as many types of soul as there are specific
types of political constitution.

How many is that?

[Glaucon/Socrates]

d   Five forms of constitution and five of souls.

What are they?

One is the constitution we've been describing. And it has two names. If one outstanding man emerges among the rulers, it's called a kingship; if more than one, it's called an aristocracy.

That's true.

Therefore, I say that this is one form of constitution. Whether one man emerges or many, none of the significant laws of the city would be
e   changed, if they followed the upbringing and education we described.

Probably not.

REPUBLIC V

Book V continues the discussion of virtue and vice in souls and cities that was begun at the end of Book IV. But the discussion is immediately interrupted by Polemarchus and the other interlocutors, all of whom want Socrates to explain the remark he made in passing at 423e–424a about the guardians possessing their wives and children in common. Socrates' lengthy response to their request occupies the majority of the book (451c–471c). In it he makes the revolutionary proposal that children should be brought up by the city rather than by their biological parents and that men and women with the same natural ability should receive the same education and training and do the same kind of work.

Glaucon agrees that a city of the sort Socrates has described would be the best one, but he wonders whether or not it could ever really come about (471c–e). After some important clarification of the nature of the task (472a–473c), Socrates undertakes to show that it could. The smallest change that would transform an already existing city into the ideal city is if its kings or rulers became philosophers or if philosophers became its kings or rulers (473c–e). This proposal, Socrates thinks, is likely to produce even more outrage than those about women and children (473c), but he thinks that outrage will subside when he explains what true philosophers are really like (474b–c).

The remainder of Book V is occupied by the beginning of Socrates' portrait of these philosophers, which consists of a complex argument intended to show that only they can have access to forms and that without such access knowledge is impossible (474c–480a).

This is the kind of city and constitution, then, that I call good and correct, and so too is this kind of man. And if indeed this is the correct kind, all the others—whether as city governments or as organizations of the individual soul—are bad and mistaken. Their badness is of four kinds.

What are they? he said.

I was going to enumerate them and explain how I thought they developed out of one another, but Polemarchus, who was sitting a little further away than Adeimantus, extended his hand and took hold of the latter's cloak by the shoulder from above. He drew Adeimantus towards him, while he himself leaned forward and said something to him. We overheard nothing of what he said except the words "Shall we let it go, or what?"

449

b

We certainly won't let it go, Adeimantus said, now speaking aloud.

And I asked: What is it that you won't let go?

You, he said.

c   For what reason in particular?

We think that you're slacking off and that you've cheated us out of a whole important section of the discussion in order to avoid having to deal with it. You thought we wouldn't notice when you said—as though it were something trivial—that, as regards wives and children, anyone could see that the possessions of friends should be held in common.

But isn't that right, Adeimantus?

Yes it is. But this "right," like the other things we've discussed, requires an explanation—in this case, an explanation of the manner in which they are to be held in common, for there may be many ways of doing this. So don't

d   omit telling us about the particular one you mean. We've been waiting for some time, indeed, for you to tell us about the production of children— how they'll be produced and, once born, how they'll be brought up—and about the whole subject of having wives and children in common. We think that this makes a considerable difference—indeed all the difference— to whether a constitution is correct or not. So now, since you are beginning to describe another constitution before having adequately discussed these things, we are resolved, as you overheard, not to let you off until you

450   explain all this as fully as the rest.

Include me, Glaucon said, as a partner in this resolution.

In fact, Socrates, Thrasymachus added, you can take this as the resolution of all of us.

What a thing you've done, I said, in stopping me! What an argument you've started up again from the very beginning, as it were, about the constitution! I was delighted to think that it had already been described and was content to have these things accepted as they were stated before. You don't realize what a swarm of arguments you've stirred up by calling

b   me to account now. I saw the swarm and passed the topic by in order to save us a lot of trouble.

Well, said Thrasymachus, are we here to search for gold[1] or to listen to an argument?

The latter, I said, but within reason.

It's within reason, Socrates, Glaucon said, for people with any understanding to listen to an argument of this kind their whole life long. So don't mind about us, and don't get tired yourself. Rather, tell us at length what your thoughts are on the topic we inquired about, namely, what the com-

c   mon possession of wives and children will amount to for the guardians and

---

1. Literally: to refine gold. A proverbial expression applied to those who neglect the task at hand for some more fascinating but less profitable pursuit. Thrasymachus seems to be reminding Socrates of his own words at 336e.

[Adeimantus/Socrates/Glaucon/Thrasymachus]

how the children will be brought up while they're still small, for the time between birth and the beginning of education seems to be the most difficult period of all. So try to tell us what the manner of this upbringing must be.

It isn't an easy subject to explain, for it raises even more incredulity than the topics we've discussed so far. People may not believe that what we say is possible or that, even if it could be brought about, it would be for the best. It's for this reason that I hesitated to bring it up, namely, that our argument might seem to be no more than wishful thinking. *d*

Then don't hesitate, for your audience isn't inconsiderate, incredulous, or hostile.

Are you trying to encourage me by saying that?

I am.

Well, you're doing the opposite. Your encouragement would be fine, if I could be sure I was speaking with knowledge, for one can feel both secure and confident when one knows the truth about the dearest and most important things and speaks about them among those who are themselves wise and dear friends. But to speak, as I'm doing, at a time when one is *e* unsure of oneself and searching for the truth, is a frightening and insecure thing to do. I'm not afraid of being laughed at—that would be childish *451* indeed. But I am afraid that, if I slip from the truth, just where it's most important not to, I'll not only fall myself but drag my friends down as well. So I bow to Adrasteia[2] for what I'm going to say, for I suspect that it's a lesser crime to kill someone involuntarily than to mislead people about fine, good, and just institutions. Since it's better to run this risk among enemies than among friends, you've well and truly encouraged me! *b*

Glaucon laughed and said: Well, Socrates, if we suffer from any false note you strike in the argument, we'll release you and absolve you of any guilt as in a homicide case: your hands are clean, and you have not deceived us. So take courage and speak.

I will, for the law says that someone who kills involuntarily is free of guilt when he's absolved by the injured party. So it's surely reasonable to think the same is true in my case as well.

With that as your defense, speak.

Then I'll have to go back to what should perhaps have been said in *c* sequence, although it may be that this way of doing things is in fact right and that after the completion of the male drama, so to speak, we should then go through the female one—especially as you insist on it so urgently.

For men born and educated as we've described there is, in my opinion, no right way to acquire and use women and children other than by following

2. Adrasteia was a kind of Nemesis, a punisher of pride and proud words. The "bow to Adrasteia" is therefore an apology for the kind of act or statement that might otherwise spur her to take action.

the road on which we started them. We attempted, in the argument, to set up the men as guardians of the herd.

Yes.

d   Then let's give them a birth and rearing consistent with that and see whether it suits us or not.

How?

As follows: Do we think that the wives of our guardian watchdogs should guard what the males guard, hunt with them, and do everything else in common with them? Or should we keep the women at home, as incapable of doing this, since they must bear and rear the puppies, while the males work and have the entire care of the flock?

e   Everything should be in common, except that the females are weaker and the males stronger.

And is it possible to use any animals for the same things if you don't give them the same upbringing and education?

No, it isn't.

Therefore, if we use the women for the same things as the men, they must also be taught the same things.

452   Yes.

Now, we gave the men music and poetry and physical training.

Yes.

Then we must give these two crafts, as well as those having to do with warfare, to the women also to use in the same way as the men use them.

That seems to follow from what you say.

But perhaps much of what we are saying, since it is contrary to custom, would incite ridicule if it were carried out in practice as we've described.

It certainly would.

What is the most ridiculous thing that you see in it? Isn't it obviously the women exercising naked in the palestras[3] with the men? And not just the young women, but the older ones too—like old men in gymnasiums who,

b   even though their bodies are wrinkled and not pleasant to look at, still love to do physical training.

Yes, that would look really ridiculous as things stand at present.

But surely, now that we've started to speak about this, we mustn't fear the various jokes that wits will make about this kind of change in music and

c   poetry, physical training, and—last but not least—in bearing arms and riding horses.

You're right.

And now that we've begun to speak about this, we must move on to the tougher part of the law, begging these people not to be silly (though that is their own work!) but to take the matter seriously. They should remember that it wasn't very long ago that the Greeks themselves thought it shameful

3. A palestra is a wrestling school and training ground.

[Socrates/Glaucon]

and ridiculous (as the majority of the barbarians still do) for even men to be seen naked and that when the Cretans and then the Lacedaemonians began the gymnasiums, the wits of those times could also have ridiculed it all. Or don't you think so?   *d*

I do.

But I think that, after it was found in practice to be better to strip than to cover up all those parts, then what was ridiculous to the eyes faded away in the face of what argument showed to be the best. This makes it clear that it's foolish to think that anything besides the bad is ridiculous or to try to raise a laugh at the sight of anything besides what's stupid or bad or (putting it the other way around) it's foolish to take seriously any standard   *e* of what is fine and beautiful other than the good.

That's absolutely certain.

However, mustn't we first agree about whether our proposals are possible or not? And mustn't we give to anyone who wishes the opportunity to question us—whether in jest or in earnest—about whether female human nature *can* share all the tasks of that of the male, or none of them, or some   453 but not others, and to ask in which class the waging of war belongs? Wouldn't this, as the best beginning, also be likely to result in the best conclusion?

Of course.

Shall we give the argument against ourselves, then, on behalf of those who share these reservations, so that their side of the question doesn't fall by default?

There's no reason not to.   *b*

Then let's say this on their behalf: "Socrates and Glaucon, there's no need for others to argue with you, for you yourselves, when you began to found your city, agreed that each must do his own work in accordance with his nature."

And I think we certainly did agree to that.

"Can you deny that a woman is by nature very different from a man?"

Of course not.

"And isn't it appropriate to assign different work to each in accordance with its nature?"

Certainly.   *c*

"How is it, then, that you aren't mistaken and contradicting yourselves when you say that men and women must do the same things, when their natures are so completely separate and distinct?"

Do you have any defense against that attack?

It isn't easy to think of one on the spur of the moment, so I'll ask you to explain the argument on our side as well, whatever it is.

This and many other such things, Glaucon, which I foresaw earlier, were what I was afraid of, so that I hesitated to tackle the law concerning the possession and upbringing of women and children.   *d*

By god, it doesn't seem to be an easy topic.

It isn't. But the fact is that whether someone falls into a small diving pool or into the middle of the biggest ocean, he must swim all the same.

He certainly must.

Then we must swim too, and try to save ourselves from the sea of argument, hoping that a dolphin will pick us up or that we'll be rescued by some other desperate means.

e   It seems so.

Come, then. Let's see if we can find a way out. We've agreed that different natures must follow different ways of life and that the natures of men and women are different. But now we say that those different natures must follow the same way of life. Isn't that the accusation brought against us?

That's it exactly.

454   Ah! Glaucon, great is the power of the craft of disputation.

Why is that?

Because many fall into it against their wills. They think they are having not a quarrel but a conversation, because they are unable to examine what has been said by dividing it up according to forms. Hence, they pursue mere verbal contradictions of what has been said and have a quarrel rather than a conversation.

That does happen to lots of people, but it isn't happening to us at the moment, is it?

b   It most certainly is, for it looks to me, at any rate, as though we are falling into disputation against our will.

How?

We're bravely, but in a quarrelsome and merely verbal fashion, pursuing the principle that natures that aren't the same must follow different ways of life. But when we assigned different ways of life to different natures and the same ones to the same, we didn't at all examine the form of natural difference and sameness we had in mind or in what regard we were distinguishing them.

No, we didn't look into that.

c   Therefore, we might just as well, it seems, ask ourselves whether the natures of bald and long-haired men are the same or opposite. And, when we agree that they are opposite, then, if the bald ones are cobblers, we ought to forbid the long-haired ones to be cobblers, and if the long-haired ones are cobblers, we ought to forbid this to the bald ones.

That would indeed be ridiculous.

And aren't we in this ridiculous position because at that time we did not introduce every form of difference and sameness in nature, but focused on the one form of sameness and difference that was relevant to the particular ways of life themselves? We meant, for example, that a male and female

d   doctor have souls of the same nature. Or don't you think so?

[Glaucon/Socrates]

I do.

But a doctor and a carpenter have different ones?

Completely different, surely.

Therefore, if the male sex is seen to be different from the female with regard to a particular craft or way of life, we'll say that the relevant one must be assigned to it. But if it's apparent that they differ only in this respect, that the females bear children while the males beget them, we'll say that there has been no kind of proof that women are different from men with respect to what we're talking about, and we'll continue to believe that   *e* our guardians and their wives must have the same way of life.

And rightly so.

Next, we'll tell anyone who holds the opposite view to instruct us in this: With regard to what craft or way of life involved in the constitution of the city are the natures of men and women not the same but different?   455

That's a fair question, at any rate.

And perhaps he'd say, just as you did a moment ago, that it isn't easy to give an immediate answer, but with enough consideration it should not be difficult.

Yes, he might say that.

Shall we ask the one who raises this objection to follow us and see whether we can show him that no way of life concerned with the management of the city is peculiar to women?   *b*

Of course.

"Come, now," we'll say to him, "give us an answer: Is this what you meant by one person being naturally well suited for something and another being naturally unsuited? That the one learned it easily, the other with difficulty; that the one, after only a brief period of instruction, was able to find out things for himself, while the other, after much instruction, couldn't even remember what he'd learned; that the body of the one adequately served his thought, while the body of the other opposed his. Are there any other things besides these by which you distinguished those who are natu-   *c* rally well suited for anything from those who are not?"

No one will claim that there are any others.

Do you know of anything practiced by human beings in which the male sex isn't superior to the female in all these ways? Or must we make a long story of it by mentioning weaving, baking cakes, and cooking vegetables, in which the female sex is believed to excel and in which it is most ridiculous of all for it to be inferior?   *d*

It's true that one sex is much superior to the other in pretty well everything, although many women are better than many men in many things. But on the whole it is as you say.

Then there is no way of life concerned with the management of the city that belongs to a woman because she's a woman or to a man because he's a man, but the various natures are distributed in the same way in both

[Glaucon/Socrates]

e   creatures. Women share by nature in every way of life just as men do, but in all of them women are weaker than men.

Certainly.

Then shall we assign all of them to men and none to women?

How can we?

We'll say, I suppose, that one woman is a doctor, another not, and that one is musical by nature, another not.

Of course.

And, therefore, won't one be athletic or warlike, while another is un-
456   warlike and no lover of physical training?

I suppose so.

Further, isn't one woman philosophical or a lover of wisdom, while another hates wisdom? And isn't one spirited and another spiritless?

That too.

So one woman may have a guardian nature and another not, for wasn't it qualities of this sort that we looked for in the natures of the men we selected as guardians?

Certainly.

Therefore, men and women are by nature the same with respect to guarding the city, except to the extent that one is weaker and the other stronger.

Apparently.

Then women of this sort must be chosen along with men of the same
b   sort to live with them and share their guardianship, seeing that they are adequate for the task and akin to the men in nature.

Certainly.

And mustn't we assign the same way of life to the same natures?

We must.

We've come round, then, to what we said before and have agreed that it isn't against nature to assign an education in music, poetry, and physical training to the wives of the guardians.

Absolutely.

c   Then we're not legislating impossibilities or indulging in mere wishful thinking, since the law we established is in accord with nature. It's rather the way things are at present that seems to be against nature.

So it seems.

Now, weren't we trying to determine whether our proposals were both possible and optimal?

Yes, we were.

And haven't we now agreed that they're possible?

Yes.

Then mustn't we next reach agreement about whether or not they're optimal?

Clearly.

[Socrates/Glaucon]

Should we have one kind of education to produce women guardians, then, and another to produce men, especially as they have the same natures to begin with?   *d*

No.

Then, what do you think about this?

What?

About one man being better and another worse. Or do you think they're all alike?

Certainly not.

In the city we're establishing, who do you think will prove to be better men, the guardians, who receive the education we've described, or the cobblers, who are educated in cobblery?

Your question is ridiculous.

I understand. Indeed, aren't the guardians the best of the citizens?   *e*

By far.

And what about the female guardians? Aren't they the best of the women?

They're by far the best.

Is there anything better for a city than having the best possible men and women as its citizens?

There isn't.

And isn't it music and poetry and physical training, lending their support in the way we described, that bring this about?   *457*

Of course.

Then the law we've established isn't only possible; it is also optimal for a city?

Yes.

Then the guardian women must strip for physical training, since they'll wear virtue or excellence instead of clothes. They must share in war and the other guardians' duties in the city and do nothing else. But the lighter parts must be assigned to them because of the weakness of their sex. And the man who laughs at naked women doing physical training for the sake of what is best is "plucking the unripe fruit" of laughter and doesn't know,   *b* it seems, what he's laughing at or what he's doing, for it is and always will be the finest saying that the beneficial is beautiful, while the harmful is ugly.

Absolutely.

Can we say, then, that we've escaped one wave of criticism in our discussion of the law about women, that we haven't been altogether swept away by laying it down that male and female guardians must share their entire way of life, and that our argument is consistent when it states that this is   *c* both possible and beneficial?

And it's certainly no small wave that you've escaped.

You won't think that it's so big when you get a look at the next one.

[Socrates/Glaucon]

Tell me about it, and I'll decide.

I suppose that the following law goes along with the last one and the others that preceded it.

Which one?

That all these women are to belong in common to all the men, that none are to live privately with any man, and that the children, too, are to be
d   possessed in common, so that no parent will know his own offspring or any child his parent.

This wave is far bigger than the other, for there's doubt both about its possibility and about whether or not it's beneficial.

I don't think that its being beneficial would be disputed or that it would be denied that the common possession of women and children would be the greatest good, if indeed it is possible. But I think that there would be a lot of disagreement about whether or not it is possible.

e   There could very well be dispute about both.

You mean that I'll have to face a coalition of arguments. I thought I'd escape one of them, if you believed that the proposal was beneficial, and that I'd have only the one about whether or not it's possible left to deal with.

But you didn't escape unobserved, so you have to give an argument for both.

Well, then, I'll have to accept my punishment. But do me this favor. Let me, as if on a holiday, do what lazy people do who feast on their own
458   thoughts when out for a solitary walk. Instead of finding out how something they desire might actually come about, these people pass that over, so as to avoid tiring deliberations about what's possible and what isn't. They assume that what they desire is available and proceed to arrange the rest, taking pleasure in thinking through everything they'll do when they
b   have what they want, thereby making their lazy souls even lazier. I'm getting soft myself at the moment, so I want to delay consideration of the feasibility of our proposal until later. With your permission, I'll assume that it's feasible and examine how the rulers will arrange these matters when they come to pass. And I'll try to show that nothing could be more beneficial to the city and its guardians than those arrangements. These are the things I'll examine with you first, and I'll deal with the other question later, but only if you'll permit me to do it this way.

You have my permission, so carry on with your examination.

I suppose that our rulers and auxiliaries—if indeed they're worthy of the
c   names—will be willing to command and to obey respectively. In some cases, the rulers will themselves be obeying our laws, and in others, namely, the ones we leave to their discretion, they'll give directions that are in the spirit of our laws.

Probably so.

Then you, as their lawgiver, will select women just as you did men, with natures as similar to theirs as possible, and hand them over to the men.

And since they have common dwellings and meals, rather than private
ones, and live together and mix together both in physical training and in *d*
the rest of their upbringing, they will, I suppose, be driven by innate
necessity to have sex with one another. Or don't you think we're talking
about necessities here?

The necessities aren't geometrical but erotic, and they're probably better
than the others at persuading and compelling the majority of people.

That's right. But the next point, Glaucon, is that promiscuity is impious
in a city of happy people, and the rulers won't allow it. *e*

No, for it isn't right.

Then it's clear that our next task must be to make marriage as sacred as
possible. And the sacred marriages will be those that are most beneficial.

Absolutely.

How, then, will they be most beneficial? Tell me this, Glaucon: I see that
you have hunting dogs and quite a flock of noble fighting birds at home. *459*
Have you noticed anything about their mating and breeding?

Like what?

In the first place, although they're all noble, aren't there some that are the
best and prove themselves to be so?

There are.

Do you breed them all alike, or do you try to breed from the best as
much as possible?

I try to breed from the best.

And do you breed from the youngest or the oldest or from those in their · *b*
prime?

From those in their prime.

And do you think that if they weren't bred in this way, your stock of
birds and dogs would get much worse?

I do.

What about horses and other animals? Are things any different with
them?

It would be strange if they were.

Dear me! If this also holds true of human beings, our need for excellent
rulers is indeed extreme.

It does hold of them. But what of it? *c*

Because our rulers will then have to use a lot of drugs. And while an
inferior doctor is adequate for people who are willing to follow a regimen
and don't need drugs, when drugs are needed, we know that a bolder
doctor is required.

That's true. But what exactly do you have in mind?

I mean that it looks as though our rulers will have to make considerable
use of falsehood and deception for the benefit of those they rule. And we
said that all such falsehoods are useful as a form of drug. *d*

And we were right.

[Socrates/Glaucon]

Well, it seems we were right, especially where marriages and the producing of children are concerned.

How so?

It follows from our previous agreements, first, that the best men must have sex with the best women as frequently as possible, while the opposite is true of the most inferior men and women, and, second, that if our herd is to be of the highest possible quality, the former's offspring must be *e* reared but not the latter's. And this must all be brought about without being noticed by anyone except the rulers, so that our herd of guardians remains as free from dissension as possible.

That's absolutely right.

Therefore certain festivals and sacrifices will be established by law at which we'll bring the brides and grooms together, and we'll direct our poets to compose appropriate hymns for the marriages that take place. We'll leave *460* the number of marriages for the rulers to decide, but their aim will be to keep the number of males as stable as they can, taking into account war, disease, and similar factors, so that the city will, as far as possible, become neither too big nor too small.

That's right.

Then there'll have to be some sophisticated lotteries introduced, so that at each marriage the inferior people we mentioned will blame luck rather than the rulers when they aren't chosen.

There will.

And among other prizes and rewards the young men who are good in *b* war or other things must be given permission to have sex with the women more often, since this will also be a good pretext for having them father as many of the children as possible.

That's right.

And then, as the children are born, they'll be taken over by the officials appointed for the purpose, who may be either men or women or both, since our offices are open to both sexes.

Yes.

I think they'll take the children of good parents to the nurses in charge *c* of the rearing pen situated in a separate part of the city, but the children of inferior parents, or any child of the others that is born defective, they'll hide in a secret and unknown place, as is appropriate.

It is, if indeed the guardian breed is to remain pure.

And won't the nurses also see to it that the mothers are brought to the rearing pen when their breasts have milk, taking every precaution to insure that no mother knows her own child and providing wet nurses if the *d* mother's milk is insufficient? And won't they take care that the mothers suckle the children for only a reasonable amount of time and that the care of sleepless children and all other such troublesome duties are taken over by the wet nurses and other attendants?

[Socrates/Glaucon]

You're making it very easy for the wives of the guardians to have children.

And that's only proper. So let's take up the next thing we proposed. We said that the children's parents should be in their prime.

True.

Do you share the view that a woman's prime lasts about twenty years and a man's about thirty?   *e*

Which years are those?

A woman is to bear children for the city from the age of twenty to the age of forty, a man from the time that he passes his peak as a runner until he reaches fifty-five.

At any rate, that's the physical and mental prime for both.   *461*

Then, if a man who is younger or older than that engages in reproduction for the community, we'll say that his offense is neither pious nor just, for the child he begets for the city, if it remains hidden, will be born in darkness, through a dangerous weakness of will, and without the benefit of the sacrifices and prayers offered at every marriage festival, in which the priests and priestesses, together with the entire city, ask that the children of good and beneficial parents may always prove themselves still better and more beneficial.   *b*

That's right.

The same law will apply if a man still of begetting years has a child with a woman of child-bearing age without the sanction of the rulers. We'll say that he brings to the city an illegitimate, unauthorized, and unhallowed child.

That's absolutely right.

However, I think that when women and men have passed the age of having children, we'll leave them free to have sex with whomever they wish, with these exceptions: For a man—his daughter, his mother, his daughter's children, and his mother's ancestors; for a woman—her son and   *c* his descendants, her father and his ancestors. Having received these instructions, they should be very careful not to let a single fetus see the light of day, but if one is conceived and forces its way to the light, they must deal with it in the knowledge that no nurture is available for it.

That's certainly sensible. But how will they recognize their fathers and daughters and the others you mentioned?   *d*

They have no way of knowing. But a man will call all the children born in the tenth or seventh month after he became a bridegroom his sons, if they're male, and his daughters, if they're female, and they'll call him father. He'll call their children his grandchildren, and they'll call the group to which he belongs grandfathers and grandmothers. And those who were born at the same time as their mothers and fathers were having children they'll call their brothers and sisters. Thus, as we were saying, the relevant   *e* groups will avoid sexual relations with each other. But the law will allow

[Glaucon/Socrates]

brothers and sisters to have sex with one another if the lottery works out that way and the Pythia⁴ approves.

That's absolutely right.

This, then, Glaucon, is how the guardians of your city have their wives and children in common. We must now confirm that this arrangement is both consistent with the rest of the constitution and by far the best. Or how else are we to proceed?

462 In just that way.

Then isn't the first step towards agreement to ask ourselves what we say is the greatest good in designing the city—the good at which the legislator aims in making the laws—and what is the greatest evil? And isn't the next step to examine whether the system we've just described fits into the tracks of the good and not into those of the bad?

Absolutely.

Is there any greater evil we can mention for a city than that which tears it apart and makes it many instead of one? Or any greater good than that
b which binds it together and makes it one?

There isn't.

And when, as far as possible, all the citizens rejoice and are pained by the same successes and failures, doesn't this sharing of pleasures and pains bind the city together?

It most certainly does.

But when some suffer greatly, while others rejoice greatly, at the same things happening to the city or its people, doesn't this privatization of
c pleasures and pains dissolve the city?

Of course.

And isn't that what happens whenever such words as "mine" and "not mine" aren't used in unison? And similarly with "someone else's"?

Precisely.

Then, is the best-governed city the one in which most people say "mine" and "not mine" about the same things in the same way?

It is indeed.

What about the city that is most like a single person? For example, when one of us hurts his finger, the entire organism that binds body and soul together into a single system under the ruling part within it is aware of this, and the whole feels the pain together with the part that suffers. That's
d why we say that the man has a pain in his finger. And the same can be said about any part of a man, with regard either to the pain it suffers or to the pleasure it experiences when it finds relief.

Certainly. And, as for your question, the city with the best government *is* most like such a person.

4. The priestess of Apollo at Delphi.

[Socrates/Glaucon]

Then, whenever anything good or bad happens to a single one of its citizens, such a city above all others will say that the affected part is its own and will share in the pleasure or pain as a whole.

If it has good laws, that must be so.

It's time now to return to our own city, to look there for the features we've agreed on, and to determine whether it or some other city possesses them to the greatest degree.

Then that's what we must do.

What about those other cities? Aren't there rulers and people in them, as well as in ours?

There are.

Besides fellow citizens, what do the people call the rulers in those other cities?

In many they call them despots, but in democracies they are called just this—rulers.

What about the people in our city? Besides fellow citizens, what do they call their rulers?

Preservers and auxiliaries.

And what do they in turn call the people?

Providers of upkeep and wages.

What do the rulers call the people in other cities?

Slaves.

And what do the rulers call each other?

Co-rulers.

And ours?

Co-guardians.

Can you tell me whether a ruler in those other cities could address some of his co-rulers as his kinsmen and others as outsiders?

Yes, many could.

And doesn't he consider his kinsman to be his own, and doesn't he address him as such, while he considers the outsider not to be his own?

He does.

What about your guardians? Could any of them consider a co-guardian as an outsider or address him as such?

There's no way he could, for when he meets any one of them, he'll hold that he's meeting a brother or sister, a father or mother, a son or daughter, or some ancestor or descendant of theirs.

You put that very well. But tell me this: Will your laws require them simply to use these kinship names or also to do all the things that go along with the names? Must they show to their "fathers" the respect, solicitude, and obedience we show to our parents by law? Won't they fare worse at the hands of gods and humans, as people whose actions are neither pious nor just, if they do otherwise? Will these be the oracular sayings they hear

[Socrates/Glaucon]

from all the citizens from their childhood on, or will they hear something else about their fathers—or the ones they're told are their fathers—and other relatives?

The former. It would be absurd if they only mouthed kinship names *e*   without doing the things that go along with them.

Therefore, in our city more than in any other, they'll speak in unison the words we mentioned a moment ago. When any one of them is doing well or badly, they'll say that "mine" is doing well or that "mine" is doing badly.

That's absolutely true.

464   Now, didn't we say that the having and expressing of this conviction is closely followed by the having of pleasures and pains in common?

Yes, and we were right.

Then won't our citizens, more than any others, have the same thing in common, the one they call "mine"? And, having that in common, won't they, more than any others, have common pleasures and pains?

Of course.

And, in addition to the other institutions, the cause of this is the having of wives and children in common by the guardians?

That more than anything else is the cause.

But we agreed that the having of pains and pleasures in common is the greatest good for a city, and we characterized a well-governed city in terms *b*   of the body's reaction to pain or pleasure in any one of its parts.

And we were right to agree.

Then, the cause of the greatest good for our city has been shown to be the having of wives and children in common by the auxiliaries.

It has.

And, of course, this is consistent with what we said before, for we said somewhere that, if they're going to be guardians, they mustn't have private houses, property, or possessions, but must receive their upkeep from the *c*   other citizens as a wage for their guardianship and enjoy it in common.

That's right.

Then isn't it true, just as I claimed, that what we are saying now, taken together with what we said before, makes even better guardians out of them and prevents them from tearing the city apart by not calling the same thing "mine"? If different people apply the term to different things, one would drag into his own house whatever he could separate from the others, and another would drag things into a different house to a different wife *d*   and children, and this would make for private pleasures and pains at private things. But our people, on the other hand, will think of the same things as their own, aim at the same goal, and, as far as possible, feel pleasure and pain in unison.

Precisely.

And what about lawsuits and mutual accusations? Won't they pretty well disappear from among them, because they have everything in common

[Socrates/Glaucon]

except their own bodies? Hence they'll be spared all the dissension that
arises between people because of the possession of money, children, and
families.   *e*

They'll necessarily be spared it.

Nor could any lawsuits for insult or injury justly occur among them, for
we'll declare that it's a fine and just thing for people to defend themselves
against others of the same age, since this will compel them to stay in good
physical shape.

That's right.

This law is also correct for another reason: If a spirited person vents his   *465*
anger in this way, it will be less likely to lead him into more serious
disputes.

Certainly.

But an older person will be authorized to rule and punish all the younger
ones.

Clearly.

And surely it's also obvious that a younger person won't strike or do any
sort of violence to an older one or fail to show him respect in other ways,
unless the rulers command it, for there are two guardians sufficient to
prevent him from doing such things—shame and fear. Shame will prevent
him from laying a hand on his parents, and so will the fear that the others
would come to the aid of the victim, some as his sons, some as his brothers,   *b*
and some as his fathers.

That's the effect they'll have.

Then, in all cases, won't the laws induce men to live at peace with one
another?

Very much so.

And if there's no discord among the guardians, there's no danger that the
rest of the city will break into civil war, either with them or among themselves.

Certainly not.

I hesitate to mention, since they're so unseemly, the pettiest of the evils
the guardians would therefore escape: The poor man's flattery of the rich,
the perplexities and sufferings involved in bringing up children and in   *c*
making the money necessary to feed the household, getting into debt,
paying it off, and in some way or other providing enough money to hand
over to their wives and household slaves to manage. All of the various
troubles men endure in these matters are obvious, ignoble, and not worth
discussing.

They're obvious even to the blind.   *d*

They'll be free of all these, and they'll live a life more blessedly happy
than that of the victors in the Olympian games.

How?

The Olympian victors are considered happy on account of only a small

[Socrates/Glaucon]

part of what is available to our guardians, for the guardians' victory is even greater, and their upkeep from public funds more complete. The victory they gain is the preservation of the whole city, and the crown of victory that they and their children receive is their upkeep and all the necessities of life. They receive rewards from their own city while they live, and at their *e* death they're given a worthy burial.

Those are very good things.

Do you remember that, earlier in our discussion, someone—I forget who—shocked us by saying that we hadn't made our guardians happy, that it was possible for them to have everything that belongs to the citizens, yet *466* they had nothing? We said, I think, that if this happened to come up at some point, we'd look into it then, but that our concern at the time was to make our guardians true guardians and the city the happiest we could, rather than looking to any one group within it and moulding it for happiness.

I remember.

Well, then, if the life of our auxiliaries is apparently much finer and *b* better than that of Olympian victors, is there any need to compare it to the lives of cobblers, farmers, or other craftsmen?

Not in my opinion.

Then it's surely right to repeat here what I said then: If a guardian seeks happiness in such a way that he's no longer a guardian and isn't satisfied with a life that's moderate, stable, and—as we say—best, but a silly, adolescent idea of happiness seizes him and incites him to use his power to take *c* everything in the city for himself, he'll come to know the true wisdom of Hesiod's saying that somehow "the half is worth more than the whole."[5]

If he takes my advice, he'll keep to his own life-style.

You agree, then, that the women and men should associate with one another in education, in things having to do with children, and in guarding the other citizens in the way we've described; that both when they remain in the city and when they go to war, they must guard together and hunt *d* together like dogs and share in everything as far as possible; and that by doing so they'll be doing what's best and not something contrary either to woman's nature as compared with man's or to the natural association of men and women with one another.

I agree.

Then doesn't it remain for us to determine whether it's possible to bring about this association among human beings, as it is among animals, and to say just how it might be done?

You took the words right out of my mouth.

e As far as war is concerned, I think it's clear how they will wage it.

How so?

Men and women will campaign together. They'll take the sturdy children

5. *Works and Days* 40.

with them, so that, like the children of other craftsmen, they can see what they'll have to do when they grow up. But in addition to observing, they can serve and assist in everything to do with the war and help their mothers and fathers. Haven't you noticed in the other crafts how the chil-   *467* dren of potters, for example, assist and observe for a long time before actually making any pots?

I have indeed.

And should these craftsmen take more care in training their children by appropriate experience and observation than the guardians?

Of course not; that would be completely ridiculous.

Besides, every animal fights better in the presence of its young.   *b*

That's so. But, Socrates, there's a considerable danger that in a defeat—and such things are likely to happen in a war—they'll lose their children's lives as well as their own, making it impossible for the rest of the city to recover.

What you say is true. But do you think that the first thing we should provide for is the avoidance of all danger?

Not at all.

Well, then, if people will probably have to face some danger, shouldn't it be the sort that will make them better if they come through it successfully?

Obviously.

And do you think that whether or not men who are going to be warriors observe warfare when they're still boys makes such a small difference that it isn't worth the danger of having them do it?   *c*

No, it does make a difference to what you're talking about.

On the assumption, then, that the children are to be observers of war, if we can contrive some way to keep them secure, everything will be fine, won't it?

Yes.

Well, then, in the first place, their fathers won't be ignorant, will they, about which campaigns are dangerous and which are not, but rather as knowledgeable about this as any human beings can be?   *d*

Probably so.

Then they'll take the children to some campaigns and not to others?

Correct.

And they'll put officers in charge of them whose age and experience qualifies them to be leaders and tutors?

Appropriately so.

But, as we say, the unexpected often occurs.

Indeed.

With this in mind, we must provide the children with wings when they're small, so that they can fly away and escape.

What do you mean?   *e*

We must mount them on horses as early as possible—not on spirited or aggressive horses, but on very fast and manageable ones—and when they've learned to ride, they must be taken to observe a war. In this way, they'll get the best look at their own work and, if the need arises, make the securest possible escape to safety, following their older guides.

I think you're right.

468   What about warfare itself? What attitude should your soldiers have to each other and to the enemy? Are my views about this right or not?

First, tell me what they are.

If one of them leaves his post or throws away his shield or does anything else of that sort through cowardice, shouldn't he be reduced to being a craftsman or farmer?

Certainly.

And shouldn't anyone who is captured alive be left to his captors as a gift to do with as they wish?

b   Absolutely.

But don't you think that anyone who distinguishes himself and earns high esteem should, while still on the campaign, first be crowned with wreaths by each of the adolescents and children who accompany the expedition?

I do.

And what about shaken by the right hand?

That too.

But I suppose that you wouldn't go this far?

Namely?

That he should kiss and be kissed by each of them.

That most of all. And I'd add this to the law: As long as the campaign lasts, no one he wants to kiss shall be allowed to refuse, for then, if one of

c   them happens to be in love with another, whether male or female, he'll be all the more eager to win the rewards of valor.

Excellent. And we've already stated that, since he's a good person, more marriages will be available to him, and he'll be selected for such things more frequently than the others, so that he'll beget as many children as possible.

Yes, we did say that.

Indeed, according to Homer too, it is just to honor in such ways those young people who are good, for he says that Ajax, when he distinguished

d   himself in battle, "was rewarded with the long cut off the backbone."[6] And that's an appropriate honor for a courageous young man, since it will both honor him and increase his strength.

That's absolutely right.

Then we'll follow Homer in these matters at least. And insofar as good people have shown themselves to be good, we'll honor them at sacrifices and all such occasions with hymns, "seats of honor, meats, and well-filled

6. *Iliad* 7.321.

[Socrates/Glaucon]

cups of wine,"[7] and in all the other ways we mentioned, so that, in addition to honoring good men and women, we'll continue to train them.   e

That's excellent.

All right. And as for those who died on the campaign, won't we say, first of all, that, if their deaths were distinguished, they belong to the golden race?

That above all.

And won't we believe with Hesiod that, whenever any of that race die, they become

> Sacred daimons living upon the earth,   469
> Noble spirits, protectors against evil, guardians of articulate mortals?[8]

We'll certainly believe that.

Then we'll inquire from the god what kind of distinguished funeral we should give to daimonic and godlike people, and we'll follow his instructions.

Of course.

And for the remainder of time, we'll care for their graves and worship at them as we would at those of daimons. And we'll follow the same rites for anyone whom we judge to have lived an outstandingly good life, whether   b
he died of old age or in some other way.

That is only just.

Now, what about enemies? How will our soldiers deal with them?

In what respect?

First, enslavement. Do you think it is just for Greeks to enslave Greek cities, or, as far as they can, should they not even allow other cities to do so, and make a habit of sparing the Greek race, as a precaution against being enslaved by the barbarians?   c

It's altogether and in every way best to spare the Greek race.

Then isn't it also best for the guardians not to acquire a Greek slave and to advise the other Greeks not to do so either?

Absolutely. In that way they'd be more likely to turn against the barbarians and keep their hands off one another.

What about despoiling the dead? Is it a good thing to strip the dead of anything besides their armor after a victory? Or don't cowards make this an excuse for not facing the enemy—as if they were doing something of   d
vital importance in bending over a corpse? And haven't many armies been lost because of such plundering?

Indeed, they have.

Don't you think it's slavish and money-loving to strip a corpse? Isn't it

---

7. *Iliad* 8.162.

8. *Works and Days* 122.

[Socrates/Glaucon]

small-minded and womanish to regard the body as your enemy, when the
enemy himself has flitted away, leaving behind only the instrument with
which he fought? Or do you think such behavior any different from that of
e dogs who get angry with the stone that hits them and leave the thrower
alone?

It's no different at all.

Then may our soldiers strip corpses or refuse the enemy permission to
pick up their dead?

No, by god, they certainly may not.

Moreover, we won't take enemy arms to the temples as offerings, and if
we care about the goodwill of other Greeks, we especially won't do this
470 with *their* arms. Rather we'd be afraid of polluting the temples if we
brought them such things from our own people, unless, of course, the god
tells us otherwise.

That's absolutely right.

What about ravaging the land of the Greeks and burning their houses?
Will your soldiers do things of this sort to their enemies?

I'd like to hear *your* opinion about that.

Well, I think they should do neither of these things but destroy the year's
b harvest only. Do you want me to tell you why?

Of course.

It seems to me that as we have two names, "war" and "civil war," so there
are two things and the names apply to two kinds of disagreements arising
in them. The two things I'm referring to are what is one's own and akin, on
the one hand, and what's foreign and strange, on the other. The name "civil
war" applies to hostilities with one's own, while "war" applies to hostilities
with strangers.

That's certainly to the point.

Then see whether this is also to the point: I say that the Greek race is its
c own and akin, but is strange and foreign to barbarians.

That's right.

Then when Greeks do battle with barbarians or barbarians with Greeks,
we'll say that they're natural enemies and that such hostilities are to be
called war. But when Greeks fight with Greeks, we'll say that they are
natural friends and that in such circumstances Greece is sick and divided
d into factions and that such hostilities are to be called civil war.

I, at any rate, agree to think of it that way.

Now, notice that, wherever something of the sort that's currently called
civil war occurs and a city is divided, if either party ravages the land of the
others and burns their houses, it's thought that this is abominable and that
neither party loves their city, since otherwise they'd never have ravaged
their very nurse and mother. However, it *is* thought appropriate for the
victors to carry off the harvest of the vanquished. Nonetheless, their atti-
e tude of mind should be that of people who'll one day be reconciled and
who won't always be at war.

[Socrates/Glaucon]

This way of thinking is far more civilized than the other.

What about the city you're founding? It is Greek, isn't it?

It has to be.

Then, won't your citizens be good and civilized?

Indeed they will.

Then, won't they love Greece? Won't they consider Greece as their own and share the religion of the other Greeks?

Yes, indeed.

Then won't they consider their differences with Greeks—people who are *471* their own—not as war but as civil war?

Of course.

And won't they quarrel like people who know that one day they'll be reconciled?

Certainly.

Then they'll moderate their foes in a friendly spirit, not punish them with enslavement and destruction, for they're moderators, not enemies.

That's right.

And being Greeks, they won't ravage Greece or burn her houses, nor will they agree that in any of her cities all the inhabitants—men, women, and children—are their enemies, but that whatever differences arise are caused by the few enemies that any city inevitably contains. Because of this, because the majority are friendly, they won't ravage the country or destroy the houses, and they'll continue their quarrel only to the point at which *b* those who caused it are forced to pay the penalty by those who were its innocent victims.

I agree that this is the way our citizens must treat their enemies, and they must treat barbarians the way Greeks currently treat each other.

Then shall we also impose this law on the guardians: Neither ravage the country nor burn the houses? *c*

Consider it imposed. And let's also assume that this law and its predecessors are all fine. But I think, Socrates, that if we let you go on speaking about this subject, you'll never remember the one you set aside in order to say all this, namely, whether it's possible for this constitution to come into being and in what way it could be brought about. I agree that, if it existed, all the things we've mentioned would be good for the city in which they occurred. And I'll add some that you've left out. The guardians would be excellent fighters against an enemy because they'd be least likely to desert each other, since they know each other as brothers, fathers, and sons, and call each other by those names. Moreover, if their women joined *d* their campaigns, either in the same ranks or positioned in the rear to frighten the enemy and in case their help should ever be needed, I know that this would make them quite unbeatable. And I also see all the good things that they'd have at home that you've omitted. Take it that I agree that all these things would happen, as well as innumerable others, if this kind *e* of constitution came into being, and say no more on that subject. But

[Socrates/Glaucon]

rather let's now try to convince ourselves that it is possible and how it is possible, and let the rest go.

472   This is a sudden attack that you've made on my argument, and you show no sympathy for my delay. Perhaps you don't realize that, just as I've barely escaped from the first two waves of objections, you're bringing the third—the biggest and most difficult one—down upon me. When you see and hear it, you'll surely be completely sympathetic, and recognize that it was, after all, appropriate for me to hesitate and be afraid to state and look into so paradoxical a view.

The more you speak like that, the less we'll let you off from telling us how it's possible for this constitution to come into being. So speak instead

b   of wasting time.

Well, then, we must first remember that we got to this point while trying to discover what justice and injustice are like.

We must. But what of it?

Nothing. But if we discover what justice is like, will we also maintain that the just man is in no way different from the just itself, so that he is like justice in every respect? Or will we be satisfied if he comes as close to it as

c   possible and participates in it far more than anyone else?

We'll be satisfied with that.

Then it was in order to have a model that we were trying to discover what justice itself is like and what the completely just man would be like, if he came into being, and what kind of man he'd be if he did, and likewise with regard to injustice and the most unjust man. We thought that, by looking at how their relationship to happiness and its opposite seemed to us, we'd also be compelled to agree about ourselves as well, that the one

d   who was most like them would have a portion of happiness most like theirs. But we weren't trying to discover these things in order to prove that it's possible for them to come into being.

That's true.

Do you think that someone is a worse painter if, having painted a model of what the finest and most beautiful human being would be like and having rendered every detail of his picture adequately, he could not prove that such a man could come into being?

No, by god, I don't.

Then what about our own case? Didn't we say that we were making a

e   theoretical model of a good city?

Certainly.

So do you think that our discussion will be any less reasonable if we can't prove that it's possible to found a city that's the same as the one in our theory?

Not at all.

Then that's the truth of the matter. But if, in order to please you, I must also be willing to show how and under what conditions it would most be possible to found such a city, then you should agree to make the same concessions to me, in turn, for the purposes of this demonstration.

Which ones?

Is it possible to do anything in practice the same as in theory? Or is it in the nature of practice to grasp truth less well than theory does, even if some people don't think so? Will you first agree to this or not?   *473*

I agree.

Then don't compel me to show that what we've described in theory can come into being exactly as we've described it. Rather, if we're able to discover how a city could come to be governed in a way that most closely approximates our description, let's say that we've shown what you ordered us to show, namely, that it's possible for our city to come to be. Or wouldn't you be satisfied with that? *I* would be satisfied with it.   *b*

So would I.

Then next, it seems, we should try to discover and point out what's now badly done in cities that keeps them from being governed in that way and what's the smallest change that would enable our city to reach our sort of constitution—one change, if possible, or if not one, two, and if not two, then the fewest in number and the least extensive.

That's absolutely right.   *c*

There is one change we could point to that, in my opinion, would accomplish this. It's certainly neither small nor easy, but it is possible.

What is it?

Well, I've now come to what we likened to the greatest wave. But I shall say what I have to say, even if the wave is a wave of laughter that will simply drown me in ridicule and contempt. So listen to what I'm going to say.

Say on.

Until philosophers rule as kings or those who are now called kings and leading men genuinely and adequately philosophize, that is, until political power and philosophy entirely coincide, while the many natures who at   *d* present pursue either one exclusively are forcibly prevented from doing so, cities will have no rest from evils, Glaucon, nor, I think, will the human race. And, until this happens, the constitution we've been describing in theory will never be born to the fullest extent possible or see the light of   *e* the sun. It's because I saw how very paradoxical this statement would be that I hesitated to make it for so long, for it's hard to face up to the fact that there can be no happiness, either public or private, in any other city.

Socrates, after hurling a speech and statement like that at us, you must expect that a great many people (and not undistinguished ones either) will cast off their cloaks and, stripped for action, snatch any available weapon, and make a determined rush at you, ready to do terrible things. So, unless   *474* you can hold them off by argument and escape, you really will pay the penalty of general derision.

[Socrates/Glaucon]

Well, you are the one that brought this on me.

And I was right to do it. However, I won't betray you, but rather defend you in any way I can—by goodwill, by urging you on, and perhaps by being able to give you more appropriate answers than someone else. So, with the promise of this assistance, try to show the unbelievers that things
b   are as you say they are.

I must try it, then, especially since you agree to be so great an ally. If we're to escape from the people you mention, I think we need to define for them who the philosophers are that we dare to say must rule. And once that's clear, we should be able to defend ourselves by showing that the people we mean are fitted by nature both to engage in philosophy and to
c   rule in a city, while the rest are naturally fitted to leave philosophy alone and follow their leader.

This would be a good time to give that definition.

Come, then, follow me, and we'll see whether or not there's some way to set it out adequately.

Lead on.

Do you need to be reminded or do you remember that, if it's rightly said that someone loves something, then he mustn't love one part of it and not another, but he must love all of it.
d   I think you'll have to remind me, for I don't understand it at all.

That would be an appropriate response, Glaucon, for somebody else to make. But it isn't appropriate for an erotically inclined man to forget that all boys in the bloom of youth pique the interest of a lover of boys and arouse him and that all seem worthy of his care and pleasure. Or isn't that the way you people behave to fine and beautiful boys? You praise a snub-nosed one as cute, a hook-nosed one you say is regal, one in between is well proportioned, dark ones look manly, and pale ones are children of the
e   gods. And as for a honey-colored boy, do you think that this very term is anything but the euphemistic coinage of a lover who found it easy to tolerate sallowness, provided it was accompanied by the bloom of youth?
475   In a word, you find all kinds of terms and excuses so as not to reject anyone whose flower is in bloom.

If you insist on taking me as your example of what erotically inclined men do, then, for the sake of the argument, I agree.

Further, don't you see wine-lovers behave in the same way? Don't they love every kind of wine and find any excuse to enjoy it?

Certainly.

And I think you see honor-lovers, if they can't be generals, be captains, and, if they can't be honored by people of importance and dignity, they put
b   up with being honored by insignificant and inferior ones, for they desire the whole of honor.

Exactly.

Then do you agree to this or not? When we say that someone desires

[Glaucon/Socrates]

something, do we mean that he desires everything of that kind or that he desires one part of it but not another?

We mean he desires everything.

Then won't we also say that the philosopher doesn't desire one part of wisdom rather than another, but desires the whole thing?

Yes, that's true.

And as for the one who's choosy about what he learns, especially if he's young and can't yet give an account of what is useful and what isn't, we won't say that he is a lover of learning or a philosopher, for we wouldn't say   c
that someone who's choosy about his food is hungry or has an appetite for food or is a lover of food—instead, we'd say that he is a bad eater.

And we'd be right to say it.

But the one who readily and willingly tries all kinds of learning, who turns gladly to learning and is insatiable for it, is rightly called a philosopher, isn't he?

Then many strange people will be philosophers, for the lovers of sights   d
seem to be included, since they take pleasure in learning things. And the lovers of sounds are very strange people to include as philosophers, for they would never willingly attend a serious discussion or spend their time that way, yet they run around to all the Dionysiac festivals, omitting none, whether in cities or villages, as if their ears were under contract to listen to every chorus. Are we to say that these people—and those who learn similar   e
things or petty crafts—are philosophers?

No, but they are *like* philosophers.

And who are the true philosophers?

Those who love the sight of truth.

That's right, but what exactly do you mean by it?

It would not be easy to explain to someone else, but I think that you will agree to this.

To what?

Since the beautiful is the opposite of the ugly, they are two.

Of course.   476

And since they are two, each is one?

I grant that also.

And the same account is true of the just and the unjust, the good and the bad, and all the forms. Each of them is itself one, but because they manifest themselves everywhere in association with actions, bodies, and one another, each of them appears to be many.

That's right.

So, I draw this distinction: On one side are those you just now called lovers of sights, lovers of crafts, and practical people; on the other side are those we are arguing about and whom one would alone call philosophers.   b

How do you mean?

The lovers of sights and sounds like beautiful sounds, colors, shapes, and

[Socrates/Glaucon]

everything fashioned out of them, but their thought is unable to see and embrace the nature of the beautiful itself.

That's for sure.

In fact, there are very few people who would be able to reach the beautiful itself and see it by itself. Isn't that so?

c   Certainly.

What about someone who believes in beautiful things,[9] but doesn't believe in the beautiful itself and isn't able to follow anyone who could lead him to the knowledge of it? Don't you think he is living in a dream rather than a wakened state? Isn't this dreaming: whether asleep or awake, to think that a likeness is not a likeness but rather the thing itself that it is like?

I certainly think that someone who does that is dreaming.

But someone who, to take the opposite case, believes in the beautiful itself, can see both it and the things that participate in it and doesn't believe

d   that the participants are it or that it itself is the participants—is he living in a dream or is he awake?

He's very much awake.

So we'd be right to call his thought knowledge, since he knows, but we should call the other person's thought opinion, since he opines?

Right.

What if the person who has opinion but not knowledge is angry with us and disputes the truth of what we are saying? Is there some way to console

e   him and persuade him gently, while hiding from him that he isn't in his right mind?

There must be.

Consider, then, what we'll say to him. Won't we question him like this? First, we'll tell him that nobody begrudges him any knowledge he may have and that we'd be delighted to discover that he knows something. Then we'll say: "Tell us, does the person who knows know something or nothing?" You answer for him.

He knows something.

Something that is or something that is not?[10]

477   Something that is, for how could something that is not be known?

Then we have an adequate grasp of this: No matter how many ways we

9. Socrates may be referring here either to particular things that are beautiful or to the various beauties in them, which are properties or universals. The same is true later when Socrates speaks of "the many just things," "the many doubles," and the rest.

10. Because of the ambiguity of the verb *einai* ("to be"), Socrates could be asking any or all of the following questions: (1) "Something that exists or something that does not exist?" (existential "is"); (2) "Something that is beautiful (say) or something that is not beautiful?" (predicative "is"); (3) "Something that is true or something that is not true?" (veridical "is").

examine it, what is completely is completely knowable and what is in no way is in every way unknowable?

A most adequate one.

Good. Now, if anything is such as to be and also not to be, won't it be intermediate between what purely is and what in no way is?

Yes, it's intermediate.

Then, as knowledge is set over what is, while ignorance is of necessity set over what is not, mustn't we find an intermediate between knowledge and ignorance to be set over what is intermediate between what is and what is not, if there is such a thing?   *b*

Certainly.

Do we say that opinion is something?

Of course.

A different power from knowledge or the same?

A different one.

Opinion, then, is set over one thing, and knowledge over another, according to the power of each.

Right.

Now, isn't knowledge by its nature set over what is, to know it as it is? But first maybe we'd better be a bit more explicit.

How so?

Powers are a class of the things that are that enable us—or anything else   *c* for that matter—to do whatever we are capable of doing. Sight, for example, and hearing are among the powers, if you understand the kind of thing I'm referring to.

I do.

Here's what I think about them. A power has neither color nor shape nor any feature of the sort that many other things have and that I use to distinguish those things from one another. In the case of a power, I use only what it is set over and what it does, and by reference to these I call   *d* each the power it is: what is set over the same things and does the same I call the same power; what is set over something different and does something different I call a different one. Do you agree?

I do.

Then let's back up. Is knowledge a power, or what class would you put it in?

It's a power, the strongest of them all.

And what about opinion, is it a power or some other kind of thing?   *e*

It's a power as well, for it is what enables us to opine.

A moment ago you agreed that knowledge and opinion aren't the same.

How could a person with any understanding think that a fallible power is the same as an infallible one?

Right. Then we agree that opinion is clearly different from knowledge.   478

It is different.

Hence each of them is by nature set over something different and does something different?

[Socrates/Glaucon]

Necessarily.

Knowledge is set over what is, to know it as it is?

Yes.

And opinion opines?

Yes.

Does it opine the very thing that knowledge knows, so that the knowable and the opinable are the same, or is this impossible?

It's impossible, given what we agreed, for if a different power is set over something different, and opinion and knowledge are different powers, then

b the knowable and the opinable cannot be the same.

Then, if what is is knowable, the opinable must be something other than what is?

It must.

Do we, then, opine what is not? Or is it impossible to opine what is not? Think about this. Doesn't someone who opines set his opinion over something? Or is it possible to opine, yet to opine nothing?

It's impossible.

But someone who opines opines some one thing?

Yes.

Surely the most accurate word for that which is not isn't 'one thing' but

c 'nothing'?

Certainly.

But we had to set ignorance over what is not and knowledge over what is?

That's right.

So someone opines neither what is nor what is not?

How could it be otherwise?

Then opinion is neither ignorance nor knowledge?

So it seems.

Then does it go beyond either of these? Is it clearer than knowledge or darker than ignorance?

No, neither.

Is opinion, then, darker than knowledge but clearer than ignorance?

It is.

d Then it lies between them?

Yes.

So opinion is intermediate between those two?

Absolutely.

Now, we said that, if something could be shown, as it were, to be and not to be at the same time, it would be intermediate between what purely is and what in every way is not, and that neither knowledge nor ignorance would be set over it, but something intermediate between ignorance and knowledge?

Correct.

And now the thing we call opinion has emerged as being intermediate between them?

[Glaucon/Socrates]

It has.

Apparently, then, it only remains for us to find what participates in both being and not being and cannot correctly be called purely one or the other, in order that, if there is such a thing, we can rightly call it the opinable, thereby setting the extremes over the extremes and the intermediate over the intermediate. Isn't that so?

It is.

Now that these points have been established, I want to address a question to our friend who doesn't believe in the beautiful itself or any form of the beautiful itself that remains always the same in all respects but who does believe in the many beautiful things—the lover of sights who wouldn't allow anyone to say that the beautiful itself is one or that the just is one or any of the rest: "My dear fellow," we'll say, "of all the many beautiful things, is there one that will not also appear ugly? Or is there one of those just things that will not also appear unjust? Or one of those pious things that will not also appear impious?"

There isn't one, for it is necessary that they appear to be beautiful in a way and also to be ugly in a way, and the same with the other things you asked about.

What about the many doubles? Do they appear any the less halves than doubles?

Not one.

So, with the many bigs and smalls and lights and heavies, is any one of them any more the thing someone says it is than its opposite?

No, each of them always participates in both opposites.

Is any one of the manys what someone says it is, then, any more than it is not what he says it is?

No, they are like the ambiguities one is entertained with at dinner parties or like the children's riddle about the eunuch who threw something at a bat—the one about what he threw at it and what it was in,[11] for they are ambiguous, and one cannot understand them as fixedly being or fixedly not being or as both or as neither.

Then do you know how to deal with them? Or can you find a more appropriate place to put them than intermediate between being and not being? Surely, they can't *be* more than what is or *not be* more than what is not, for apparently nothing is darker than what is not or clearer than what is.

e

479

b

c

d

11. The riddle seems to have been: A man who is not a man saw and did not see a bird that was not a bird in a tree (*xulon*) that was not a tree; he hit (*ballō*) and did not hit it with a stone that was not a stone. The answer is that a eunuch with bad eyesight saw a bat on a rafter, threw a pumice stone at it and missed. "He saw a bird" is ambiguous between "he saw what was actually a bird" and "he saw what he took to be a bird," *xulon* means both "tree" and "rafter" or "roof tree," and *ballō* means both "to throw" and "to hit." The rest is obvious.

Very true.

We've now discovered, it seems, that according to the many conventions of the majority of people about beauty and the others, they are rolling around as intermediates between what is not and what purely is.

We have.

And we agreed earlier that anything of that kind would have to be called the opinable, not the knowable—the wandering intermediate grasped by the intermediate power.

We did.

e   As for those who study the many beautiful things but do not see the beautiful itself and are incapable of following another who leads them to it, who see many just things but not the just itself, and so with everything— these people, we shall say, opine everything but have no knowledge of anything they opine.

Necessarily.

What about the ones who in each case study the things themselves that are always the same in every respect? Won't we say that they know and don't opine?

That's necessary too.

Shall we say, then, that these people love and embrace the things that

480   knowledge is set over, as the others do the things that opinion is set over? Remember we said that the latter saw and loved beautiful sounds and colors and the like but wouldn't allow the beautiful itself to be anything?

We remember, all right.

We won't be in error, then, if we call such people lovers of opinion rather than philosophers or lovers of wisdom and knowledge? Will they be angry with us if we call them that?

Not if they take my advice, for it isn't right to be angry with those who speak the truth.

As for those who in each case embrace the thing itself, we must call them philosophers, not lovers of opinion?

Most definitely.

REPUBLIC VI

Only the philosophers have knowledge, and that alone is sufficient to qualify them to be the rulers, provided that they are not inferior to the nonphilosophers in virtue (484d). So Socrates tries to show that they are in fact supremely virtuous (485a–487a). Adeimantus accepts his arguments, but points out that the majority of people will simply go on believing that philosophers are unsuited to rule because they know from experience that most philosophers are vicious while the few decent ones are useless (487a–d). Socrates surprisingly agrees with the majority about this. The people the majority take to be philosophers are either vicious or useless (487d–496e), but that is because the few decent ones, who possess a true philosophical nature, are not raised under the right sort of constitution (497a–b). If the majority ever saw a philosopher who had been raised in that way, they too would agree that he should rule their city (500e–501a).

The guardians in the most exact sense of the term must be philosophers (503b), then, and they must have all the traits already mentioned, but they must also be tested to see whether or not they can master the most important subjects (503e). These are the subjects that enable someone to come to know the good itself, i.e., the form of the good (504e–505b). Socrates cannot explain directly what the good itself is, but he describes "what is apparently an offspring of the good and most like it" (506b–e). This description is the famous Sun analogy (507a–509c). It is completed by the Line analogy, which occupies the remainder of the book (509d–511e).

And so, Glaucon, I said, after a somewhat lengthy and difficult discussion, both the philosophers and the nonphilosophers have revealed who they are.   484

It probably wouldn't have been easy, he said, to have them do it in a shorter one.

Apparently not. But for my part, I think that the matter would have been better illuminated if we had only it to discuss and not all the other things that remain to be treated in order to discover the difference between the just life and the unjust one.   b

What's our next topic?

What else but the one that's next in order? Since those who are able to grasp what is always the same in all respects are philosophers, while those who are not able to do so and who wander among the many things that vary in every sort of way are not philosophers, which of the two should be the leaders in a city?

What would be a sensible answer to that?

We should establish as guardians those who are clearly capable of guard-
c   ing the laws and the ways of life of the city.

That's right.

And isn't it clear that the guardian who is to keep watch over everything should be keen-sighted rather than blind?

Of course it's clear.

Do you think, then, that there's any difference between the blind and those who are really deprived of the knowledge of each thing that is? The latter have no clear model in their souls, and so they cannot—in the manner of painters—look to what is most true, make constant reference to it,
d   and study it as exactly as possible. Hence they cannot establish here on earth conventions about what is fine or just or good, when they need to be established, or guard and preserve them, once they have been established.

No, by god, there isn't much difference between them.

Should we, then, make these blind people our guardians or rather those who know each thing that is and who are not inferior to the others, either in experience or in any other part of virtue?

It would be absurd to choose anyone but philosophers, if indeed they're not inferior in these ways, for the respect in which they are superior is pretty well the most important one.

Then shouldn't we explain how it is possible for someone to have both
485   these sorts of qualities?

Certainly.

Then, as we said at the beginning of this discussion, it is necessary to understand the nature of philosophers first, for I think that, if we can reach adequate agreement about that, we'll also agree that the same people *can* have both qualities and that no one but they should be leaders in cities.

How so?

Let's agree that philosophic natures always love the sort of learning that makes clear to them some feature of the being that always is and does not
b   wander around between coming to be and decaying.

And further, let's agree that, like the honor-lovers and erotically inclined men we described before, they love all such learning and are not willing to give up any part of it, whether large or small, more valuable or less so.

That's right.
c   Consider next whether the people we're describing must also have this in their nature?

What?

They must be without falsehood—they must refuse to accept what is false, hate it, and have a love for the truth.

That's a reasonable addition, at any rate.

It's not only reasonable, it's entirely necessary, for it's necessary for a man who is erotically inclined by nature to love everything akin to or belonging to the boy he loves.

That's right.

And could you find anything that belongs more to wisdom than truth does?

Of course not.

Then is it possible for the same nature to be a philosopher—a lover of wisdom—and a lover of falsehood?   *d*

Not at all.

Then someone who loves learning must above all strive for every kind of truth from childhood on.

Absolutely.

Now, we surely know that, when someone's desires incline strongly for one thing, they are thereby weakened for others, just like a stream that has been partly diverted into another channel.

Of course.

Then, when someone's desires flow towards learning and everything of that sort, he'd be concerned, I suppose, with the pleasures of the soul itself by itself, and he'd abandon those pleasures that come through the body—if indeed he is a true philosopher and not merely a counterfeit one.

That's completely necessary.   *e*

Then surely such a person is moderate and not at all a money-lover. It's appropriate for others to take seriously the things for which money and large expenditures are needed, but not for him.

That's right.

And of course there's also this to consider when you are judging whether *486* a nature is philosophic or not.

What's that?

If it is at all slavish, you should not overlook that fact, for pettiness is altogether incompatible with a soul that is always reaching out to grasp everything both divine and human as a whole.

That's completely true.

And will a thinker high-minded enough to study all time and all being consider human life to be something important?

He couldn't possibly.

Then will he consider death to be a terrible thing?   *b*

He least of all.

Then it seems a cowardly and slavish nature will take no part in true philosophy.

Not in my opinion.

And is there any way that an orderly person, who isn't money-loving, slavish, a boaster, or a coward, could become unreliable or unjust?

There isn't.

[Socrates/Glaucon]

Moreover, when you are looking to see whether a soul is philosophic or not, you'll look to see whether it is just and gentle, from youth on, or savage and hard to associate with.

Certainly.

c   And here's something I think you won't leave out.

What?

Whether he's a slow learner or a fast one. Or do you ever expect anyone to love something when it pains him to do it and when much effort brings only small return?

No, it couldn't happen.

And what if he could retain nothing of what he learned, because he was full of forgetfulness? Could he fail to be empty of knowledge?

How could he?

Then don't you think that, if he's laboring in vain, he'd inevitably come to hate both himself and that activity in the end?

Of course.

Then let's never include a forgetful soul among those who are sufficiently
d   philosophical for our purposes, but look for one with a good memory.

Absolutely.

Now, we'd certainly say that the unmusical and graceless element in a person's nature draws him to lack of due measure.

Of course.

And do you think that truth is akin to what lacks due measure or to what is measured?

To what is measured.

Then, in addition to those other things, let's look for someone whose thought is by nature measured and charming and is easily led to the form of each thing that is.

Of course.

Well, then, don't you think the properties we've enumerated are compatible with one another and that each is necessary to a soul that is to have an
e   adequate and complete grasp of that which is?
487   They're all completely necessary.

Is there any objection you can find, then, to a way of life that no one can adequately follow unless he's by nature good at remembering, quick to learn, high-minded, graceful, and a friend and relative of truth, justice, courage, and moderation?

Not even Momus[1] could find one.

When such people have reached maturity in age and education, wouldn't you entrust the city to them and to them alone?

And Adeimantus replied: No one would be able to contradict the things you've said, Socrates, but on each occasion that you say them, your hearers
b   are affected in some such way as this. They think that, because they're

---

1. Momus is a personification of blame or censure.

[Socrates/Glaucon/Adeimantus]

inexperienced in asking and answering questions, they're led astray a little
bit by the argument at every question and that, when these little bits are
added together at the end of the discussion, great is their fall, as the opposite
of what they said at the outset comes to light. Just as inexperienced checkers
players are trapped by the experts in the end and can't make a move, so
they too are trapped in the end and have nothing to say in this different   c
kind of checkers, which is played not with disks but with words. Yet the
truth isn't affected by this outcome. I say this with a view to the present
case, for someone might well say now that he's unable to oppose you as you
ask each of your questions, yet he sees that of all those who take up
philosophy—not those who merely dabble in it while still young in order to
complete their upbringing and then drop it, but those who continue in it for
a longer time—the greatest number become cranks, not to say completely   d
vicious, while those who seem completely decent are rendered useless to
the city because of the studies you recommend.

When I'd heard him out, I said: Do you think that what these people say
is false?

I don't know, but I'd be glad to hear what you think.

You'd hear that they seem to me to speak the truth.

How, then, can it be true to say that there will be no end to evils in our   e
cities until philosophers—people we agree to be useless—rule in them?

The question you ask needs to be answered by means of an image or
simile.

And you, of course, aren't used to speaking in similes!

So! Are you making fun of me now that you've landed me with a claim
that's so hard to establish? In any case, listen to my simile, and you'll
appreciate all the more how greedy for images I am. What the most decent   488
people experience in relation to their city is so hard to bear that there's no
other single experience like it. Hence to find an image of it and a defense
for them, I must construct it from many sources, just as painters paint goat-
stags by combining the features of different things. Imagine, then, that
something like the following happens on a ship or on many ships. The
shipowner is bigger and stronger than everyone else on board, but he's hard
of hearing, a bit short-sighted, and his knowledge of seafaring is equally   b
deficient. The sailors are quarreling with one another about steering the
ship, each of them thinking that he should be the captain, even though he's
never learned the art of navigation, cannot point to anyone who taught it to
him, or to a time when he learned it. Indeed, they claim that it isn't
teachable and are ready to cut to pieces anyone who says that it is. They're
always crowding around the shipowner, begging him and doing everything
possible to get him to turn the rudder over to them. And sometimes, if they   c
don't succeed in persuading him, they execute the ones who do succeed or
throw them overboard, and then, having stupefied their noble shipowner
with drugs, wine, or in some other way, they rule the ship, using up what's
in it and sailing in the way that people like that are prone to do. Moreover,

[Adeimantus/Socrates]

they call the person who is clever at persuading or forcing the shipowner
d   to let them rule a "navigator," a "captain," and "one who knows ships,"
and dismiss anyone else as useless. They don't understand that a true
captain must pay attention to the seasons of the year, the sky, the stars,
the winds, and all that pertains to his craft, if he's really to be the ruler
of a ship. And they don't believe there is any craft that would enable
him to determine how he should steer the ship, whether the others want
e   him to or not, or any possibility of mastering this alleged craft or of
practicing it at the same time as the craft of navigation. Don't you think
that the true captain will be called a real stargazer, a babbler, and a good-
489   for-nothing by those who sail in ships governed in that way, in which
such things happen?

I certainly do.

I don't think that you need to examine the simile in detail to see that the
ships resemble cities and their attitude to the true philosophers, but you
already understand what I mean.

Indeed, I do.

Then first tell this simile to anyone who wonders why philosophers aren't
honored in the cities, and try to persuade him that there would be far more
b   cause for wonder if they were honored.

I will tell him.

Next tell him that what he says is true, that the best among the philosophers are useless to the majority. Tell him not to blame those decent people
for this but the ones who don't make use of them. It isn't natural for the
captain to beg the sailors to be ruled by him nor for the wise to knock at
the doors of the rich—the man who came up with that wisecrack made a
mistake. The natural thing is for the sick person, rich or poor, to knock at
c   the doctor's door, and for anyone who needs to be ruled to knock at the
door of the one who can rule him. It isn't for the ruler, if he's truly any use,
to beg the others to accept his rule. Tell him that he'll make no mistake in
likening those who rule in our cities at present to the sailors we mentioned
just now, and those who are called useless stargazers to the true captains.

That's absolutely right.

Therefore, it isn't easy for the best ways of life to be highly esteemed by
people who, as in these circumstances, follow the opposite ways. By far the
greatest and most serious slander on philosophy, however, results from
d   those who profess to follow the philosophic way of life. I mean those of
whom the prosecutor of philosophy declared that the greatest number are
completely vicious and the most decent useless. And I admitted that what
he said was true, didn't I?

Yes.

And haven't we explained why the decent ones are useless?

Yes, indeed.

Then, do you next want us to discuss why it's inevitable that the greater

[Socrates/Adeimantus]

number are vicious and to try to show, if we can, that philosophy isn't
responsible for this either?   *e*

Certainly.

Then, let's begin our dialogue by reminding ourselves of the point at
which we began to discuss the nature that someone must have if he is to
become a fine and good person. First of all, if you remember, he had to be
guided by the truth and always pursue it in every way, or else he'd really be   *490*
a boaster, with no share at all in true philosophy.

That's what was said.

And isn't this view completely contrary to the opinions currently held
about him?

It certainly is.

Then, won't it be reasonable for us to plead in his defense that it is the
nature of the real lover of learning to struggle toward what is, not to
remain with any of the many things that are believed to be, that, as he
moves on, he neither loses nor lessens his erotic love until he grasps the   *b*
being of each nature itself with the part of his soul that is fitted to grasp it,
because of its kinship with it, and that, once getting near what really is and
having intercourse with it and having begotten understanding and truth, he
knows, truly lives, is nourished, and—at that point, but not before—is
relieved from the pains of giving birth?

That is the most reasonable defense possible.

Well, then, will such a person have any part in the love of falsehood, or
will he entirely hate it?

He'll hate it.   *c*

And if truth led the way, we'd never say, I suppose, that a chorus of evils
could ever follow in its train.

How could it?

But rather a healthy and just character, with moderation following it.

That's right.

What need is there, then, to marshal all over again from the beginning
the members of the philosophic nature's chorus in their inevitable array?
Remember that courage, high-mindedness, ease in learning, and a good
memory all belong to it. Then you objected, saying that anyone would be
compelled to agree with what we said, but that, if he abandoned the   *d*
argument and looked at the very people the argument is about, he'd say
that some of them were useless, while the majority had every kind of vice.
So we examined the reason for this slander and have now arrived at the
point of explaining why the majority of them are bad. And it's for this
reason that we've again taken up the nature of the true philosophers and
defined what it necessarily has to be.

That's true.   *e*

We must now look at the ways in which this nature is corrupted, how it's
destroyed in many people, while a small number (the ones that are called

[Adeimantus/Socrates]

useless rather than bad) escape. After that, we must look in turn at the natures of the souls that imitate the philosophic nature and establish themselves in its way of life, so as to see what the people are like who thereby arrive at a way of life they are unworthy of and that is beyond them and who, because they often strike false notes, bring upon philosophy the reputation that you said it has with everyone everywhere.

In what ways are they corrupted?

I'll try to enumerate them for you if I can. I suppose that everyone would agree that only a few natures possess all the qualities that we just now said were essential to becoming a complete philosopher and that seldom occur naturally among human beings. Or don't you think so?

I certainly do.

Consider, then, the many important ways in which these few can be corrupted.

What are they?

What will surprise you most, when you hear it, is that each of the things we praised in that nature tends to corrupt the soul that has it and to drag it away from philosophy. I mean courage, moderation, and the other things we mentioned.

That does sound strange.

Furthermore, all the things that are said to be good also corrupt it and drag it away—beauty, wealth, physical strength, relatives who are powerful in the city, and all that goes with these. You understand what I have in mind?

I do, and I'd be glad to learn even more about it.

If you correctly grasp the general point I'm after, it will be clear to you, and what I've said before won't seem so strange.

What do you want me to do?

We know that the more vigorous any seed, developing plant, or animal is, the more it is deficient in the things that are appropriate for it to have when it is deprived of suitable food, season, or location. For the bad is more opposed to the good than is the merely not good.

Of course.

Then it's reasonable to say that the best nature fares worse, when unsuitably nurtured, than an ordinary one.

It is.

Then won't we say the same thing about souls too, Adeimantus, that those with the best natures become outstandingly bad when they receive a bad upbringing? Or do you think that great injustices and pure wickedness originate in an ordinary nature rather than in a vigorous one that has been corrupted by its upbringing? Or that a weak nature is ever the cause of either great good or great evil?

No, you're right.

Now, I think that the philosophic nature as we defined it will inevitably

[Socrates/Adeimantus]

grow to possess every virtue if it happens to receive appropriate instruc-   *492*
tion, but if it is sown, planted, and grown in an inappropriate environment,
it will develop in quite the opposite way, unless some god happens to come
to its rescue. Or do you agree with the general opinion that certain young
people are actually corrupted by sophists—that there are certain sophists
with significant influence on the young who corrupt them through private
teaching? Isn't it rather the very people who say this who are the greatest
sophists of all, since they educate most completely, turning young and old,
men and women, into precisely the kind of people they want them to be?   *b*
    When do they do that?
    When many of them are sitting together in assemblies, courts, theaters,
army camps, or in some other public gathering of the crowd, they object
very loudly and excessively to some of the things that are said or done and
approve others in the same way, shouting and clapping, so that the very
rocks and surroundings echo the din of their praise or blame and double it.   *c*
In circumstances like that, what is the effect, as they say, on a young
person's heart? What private training can hold out and not be swept away
by that kind of praise or blame and be carried by the flood wherever it
goes, so that he'll say that the same things are beautiful or ugly as the
crowd does, follow the same way of life as they do, and be the same sort of
person as they are.
    He will be under great compulsion to do so, Socrates.   *d*
    And yet we haven't mentioned the greatest compulsion of all.
    What's that?
    It's what these educators and sophists impose by their actions if their
words fail to persuade. Or don't you know that they punish anyone who
isn't persuaded, with disenfranchisement, fines, or death?
    They most certainly do.
    What other sophist, then, or what private conversations do you think
will prevail in opposition to these?
    I don't suppose that any will.   *e*
    No, indeed, it would be very foolish even to try to oppose them, for there
isn't now, hasn't been in the past, nor ever will be in the future anyone with
a character so unusual that he has been educated to virtue in spite of the
contrary education he received from the mob—I mean, a human character;
the divine, as the saying goes, is an exception to the rule. You should realize
that if anyone is saved and becomes what he ought to be under our present
constitutions, he has been saved—you might rightly say—by a divine dis-   *493*
pensation.
    I agree.
    Well, then, you should also agree to this.
    What?
    Not one of those paid private teachers, whom the people call sophists
and consider to be their rivals in craft, teaches anything other than the

[Adeimantus/Socrates]

convictions that the majority express when they are gathered together. Indeed, these are precisely what the sophists call wisdom. It's as if someone were learning the moods and appetites of a huge, strong beast that he's

b   rearing—how to approach and handle it, when it is most difficult to deal with or most gentle and what makes it so, what sounds it utters in either condition, and what sounds soothe or anger it. Having learned all this through tending the beast over a period of time, he calls this knack wisdom, gathers his information together as if it were a craft, and starts to teach it. In truth, he knows nothing about which of these convictions is fine or shameful, good or bad, just or unjust, but he applies all these names in

c   accordance with how the beast reacts—calling what it enjoys good and what angers it bad. He has no other account to give of these terms. And he calls what he is compelled to do just and fine, for he hasn't seen and cannot show anyone else how much compulsion and goodness really differ. Don't you think, by god, that someone like that is a strange educator?

I do indeed.

Then does this person seem any different from the one who believes that it is wisdom to understand the moods and pleasures of a majority gathered

d   from all quarters, whether they concern painting, music, or, for that matter, politics? If anyone approaches the majority to exhibit his poetry or some other piece of craftsmanship or his service to the city and gives them mastery over him to any degree beyond what's unavoidable, he'll be under Diomedean compulsion,[2] as it's called, to do the sort of thing of which they approve. But have you ever heard anyone presenting an argument that such things are truly good and beautiful that wasn't absolutely ridiculous?

e   No, and I don't expect ever to hear one.

Keeping all this in mind, recall the following question: Can the majority in any way tolerate or accept the reality of the beautiful itself, as opposed to the many beautiful things, or the reality of each thing itself, as opposed

494   to the corresponding many?

Not in any way.

Then the majority cannot be philosophic.

They cannot.

Hence they inevitably disapprove of those who practice philosophy?

Inevitably.

And so do all those private individuals who associate with the majority and try to please them.

Clearly.

---

2. The origin of the phrase is uncertain but a likely source is in the following story. Odysseus attempted to kill Diomedes when the two were returning from Troy to the Greek camp, but failed. Diomedes punished him by tying his arms together and driving him home with blows from the flat of his sword. But, whatever the source, the phrase refers to inescapable compulsion.

[Socrates/Adeimantus]

Then, because of all that, do you see any salvation for someone who is by nature a philosopher, to insure that he'll practice philosophy correctly to the end? Think about what we've said before. We agreed that ease in learning, a good memory, courage, and high-mindedness belong to the   *b* philosophic nature.

Yes.

And won't someone with a nature like that be first among the children in everything, especially if his body has a nature that matches that of his aoul?

How could he not be?

Then I suppose that, as he gets older, his family and fellow citizens will want to make use of him in connection with their own affairs.

Of course.

Therefore they'll pay court to him with their requests and honors, trying by their flattery to secure for themselves ahead of time the power that is   *c* going to be his.

That's what usually happens, at any rate.

What do you think someone like that will do in such circumstances, especially if he happens to be from a great city, in which he's rich, well-born, good-looking, and tall? Won't he be filled with impractical expectations and think himself capable of managing the affairs, not only of the Greeks, but of the barbarians as well? And as a result, won't he exalt himself to great heights and be brimming with pretension and pride that is empty and lacks understanding?   *d*

He certainly will.

And if someone approaches a young man in that condition and gently tells him the truth, namely, that that there's no understanding in him, that he needs it, and that it can't be acquired unless he works like a slave to attain it, do you think that it will be easy for him to listen when he's in the midst of so many evils?

Far from it.

And even if a young man of that sort somehow sees the point and is guided and drawn to philosophy because of his noble nature and his kinship with reason, what do you think those people will do, if they believe   *e* that they're losing their use of him and his companionship? Is there anything they won't do or say to him to prevent him from being persuaded? Or anything they won't do or say about his persuader—whether plotting against him in private or publicly bringing him into court—to prevent him from such persuasion?

There certainly isn't.   *495*

Then, is there any chance that such a person will practice philosophy?

None at all.

Do you see, then, that we weren't wrong to say that, when someone with a philosophic nature is badly brought up, the very components of his

[Socrates/Adeimantus]

nature—together with the other so-called goods, such as wealth and other similar advantages—are themselves in a way the cause of his falling away from the philosophic way of life?

I do, and what we said was right.

These, then, are the many ways in which the best nature—which is already rare enough, as we said—is destroyed and corrupted, so that it *b* cannot follow the best way of life. And it is among these men that we find the ones who do the greatest evils to cities and individuals and also—if they happen to be swept that way by the current—the greatest good, for a petty nature will never do anything great, either to an individual or a city.

That's very true.

When these men, for whom philosophy is most appropriate, fall away *c* from her, they leave her desolate and unwed, and they themselves lead lives that are inappropriate and untrue. Then others, who are unworthy of her, come to her as to an orphan deprived of the protection of kinsmen and disgrace her. These are the ones who are responsible for the reproaches that you say are cast upon philosophy by those who revile her, namely, that some of those who consort with her are useless, while the majority deserve to suffer many bad things.

Yes, that is indeed what is said.

And it's a reasonable thing to say, for other little men—the ones who are most sophisticated at their own little crafts—seeing that this position, which is full of fine names and adornments, is vacated, leap gladly from *d* those little crafts to philosophy, like prisoners escaping from jail who take refuge in a temple. Despite her present poor state, philosophy is still more high-minded than these other crafts, so that many people with defective natures desire to possess her, even though their souls are cramped and spoiled by the mechanical nature of their work, in just the way that their *e* bodies are mutilated by their crafts and labors. Isn't that inevitable?

It certainly is.

Don't you think that a man of this sort looks exactly like a little bald-headed tinker who has come into some money and, having been just released from jail, has taken a bath, put on a new cloak, got himself up as a bridegroom, and is about to marry the boss's daughter because she is poor and abandoned?

496   They're exactly the same.

And what kind of children will that marriage produce. Won't they be illegitimate and inferior.

They have to be.

What about when men who are unworthy of education approach philosophy and consort with her unworthily? What kinds of thoughts and opinions are we to say they beget? Won't they truly be what are properly called sophisms, things that have nothing genuine about them or worthy of being called true wisdom?

[Adeimantus/Socrates]

That's absolutely right.

Then there remains, Adeimantus, only a very small group who consort with philosophy in a way that's worthy of her: A noble and well brought-up character, for example, kept down by exile, who remains with philosophy according to his nature because there is no one to corrupt him,   *b* or a great soul living in a small city, who disdains the city's affairs and looks beyond them. A very few might be drawn to philosophy from other crafts that they rightly despise because they have good natures. And some might be held back by the bridle that restrains our friend Theages—for he's in every way qualified to be tempted away from philosophy, but his physical illness restrains him by keeping him out of politics. Finally, my own   *c* case is hardly worth mentioning—my daimonic sign—because it has happened to no one before me, or to only a very few. Now, the members of this small group have tasted how sweet and blessed a possession philosophy is, and at the same time they've also seen the madness of the majority and realized, in a word, that hardly anyone acts sanely in public affairs and that there is no ally with whom they might go to the aid of justice and survive, that instead they'd perish before they could profit either their city   *d* or their friends and be useless both to themselves and to others, just like a man who has fallen among wild animals and is neither willing to join them in doing injustice nor sufficiently strong to oppose the general savagery alone. Taking all this into account, they lead a quiet life and do their own work. Thus, like someone who takes refuge under a little wall from a storm of dust or hail driven by the wind, the philosopher—seeing others filled with lawlessness—is satisfied if he can somehow lead his present life free from injustice and impious acts and depart from it with good hope, blameless and content.   *e*

Well, that's no small thing for him to have accomplished before departing.   *497*

But it isn't the greatest either, since he didn't chance upon a constitution that suits him. Under a suitable one, his own growth will be fuller, and he'll save the community as well as himself. It seems to me that we've now sensibly discussed the reasons why philosophy is slandered and why the slanderer is unjust—unless, of course, you have something to add.

I have nothing to add on that point. But which of our present constitutions do you think is suitable for philosophers?

None of them. That's exactly my complaint: None of our present constitutions is worthy of the philosophic nature, and, as a result, this nature is   *b* perverted and altered, for, just as a foreign seed, sown in alien ground, is likely to be overcome by the native species and to fade away among them, so the philosophic nature fails to develop its full power and declines into a different character. But if it were to find the best constitution, as it is itself   *c* the best, it would be clear that it is really divine and that other natures and ways of life are merely human. Obviously you're going to ask next what the best constitution is.

[Socrates/Adeimantus]

You're wrong there; I wasn't going to ask that, but whether it was the constitution we described when we were founding our city or some other one.

In the other respects, it is that one. But we said even then that there must always be some people in the city who have a theory of the constitution, *d* the same one that guided you, the lawgiver, when you made the laws.

We did say that.

Yes, but we didn't emphasize it sufficiently, for fear of what your objections have made plain, namely, that its proof would be long and difficult. And indeed what remains is by no means easy to go through.

What's that?

How a city can engage in philosophy without being destroyed, for all great things are prone to fall, and, as the saying goes, fine things are really hard to achieve.

e Nevertheless, to complete our discussion, we'll have to get clear about this.

If anything prevents us from doing it, it won't be lack of willingness but lack of ability. At least you'll see how willing *I* am, for notice again how enthusiastically and recklessly I say that the manner in which a city ought to take up the philosophic way of life is the opposite of what it does at present.

How?

At present, those who study philosophy do so as young men who have just left childhood behind and have yet to take up household management *498* and money-making. But just when they reach the hardest part—I mean the part that has to do with giving a rational account—they abandon it and are regarded as fully trained in philosophy. In later life, they think they're doing well if they are willing to be in an invited audience when others are doing philosophy, for they think they should do this only as a sideline. And, with a few exceptions, by the time they reach old age, their eagerness for philosophy is quenched more thoroughly than the sun of Heraclitus, *b* which is never rekindled.

What should they do?

Entirely the opposite. As youths and children, they should put their minds to youthful education and philosophy and take care of their bodies at a time when they are growing into manhood, so as to acquire a helper for philosophy. As they grow older and their souls began to reach maturity, they should increase their mental exercises. Then, when their strength begins to fail and they have retired from politics and military service, they should graze freely in the pastures of philosophy and do nothing else—I *c* mean the ones who are to live happily and, in death, add a fitting destiny in that other place to the life they have lived.

You seem to be speaking with true enthusiasm, Socrates. But I'm sure that most of your hearers, beginning with Thrasymachus, will oppose you with even greater enthusiasm and not be at all convinced.

[Socrates/Adeimantus]

Don't slander Thrasymachus and me just as we've become friends—not
that we were enemies before. We won't relax our efforts until we either   *d*
convince him and the others or, at any rate, do something that may benefit
them in a later incarnation, when, reborn, they happen upon these arguments again.

That's a short time you're talking about!

It's nothing compared to the whole of time. All the same, it's no wonder
that the majority of people aren't convinced by our arguments, for they've
never seen a *man* that fits our *plan* (and the rhymes of this sort they have
heard are usually intended and not, like this one, the product of mere
chance). That is to say, they've never seen a man or a number of men who   *e*
themselves rhymed with virtue, were assimilated to it as far as possible,
and ruled in a city of the same type. Or do you think they have?   *499*

I don't think so at all.

Nor have they listened sufficiently to fine and free arguments that search
out the truth in every way for the sake of knowledge but that keep away
from the sophistications and eristic quibbles that, both in public trials and
in private gatherings, aim at nothing except reputation and disputation.

No, they haven't.

It was because of this, because we foresaw these difficulties, that we
were afraid. Nonetheless, we were compelled by the truth to say that no
city, constitution, or individual man will ever become perfect until either   *b*
some chance event compels those few philosophers who aren't vicious (the
ones who are now called useless) to take charge of a city, whether they
want to or not, and compels the city to obey them, or until a god inspires
the present rulers and kings or their offspring with a true erotic love for
true philosophy. Now, it cannot be reasonably maintained, in my view, that
either of these things is impossible, but if it could, we'd be justly ridiculed   *c*
for indulging in wishful thinking. Isn't that so?

It is.

Then, if in the limitless past, those who were foremost in philosophy
were forced to take charge of a city or if this is happening now in some
foreign place far beyond our ken or if it will happen in the future, we are
prepared to maintain our argument that, at whatever time the muse of   *d*
philosophy controls a city, the constitution we've described will also exist at
that time, whether it is past, present, or future. Since it is not impossible for
this to happen, we are not speaking of impossibilities. That it is *difficult* for
it to happen, however, we agree ourselves.

That's my opinion, anyway.

But the majority don't share your opinion—is that what you are going
to say?

They probably don't.

You should not make such wholesale charges against the majority, for
they'll no doubt come to a different opinion, if instead of indulging your

[Adeimantus/Socrates]

e   love of victory at their expense, you soothe them and try to remove their slanderous prejudice against the love of learning, by pointing out what you mean by a philosopher and by defining the philosophic nature and way of

500   life, as we did just now, so that they'll realize that you don't mean the same people as they do. And if they once see it your way, even you will say that they'll have a different opinion from the one you just attributed to them and will answer differently. Or do you think that anyone who is gentle and without malice is harsh with someone who is neither irritable nor malicious? I'll anticipate your answer and say that a few people may have such a harsh character, but not the majority.

And, of course, I agree.

b   Then don't you also agree that the harshness the majority exhibit towards philosophy is caused by those outsiders who don't belong and who've burst in like a band of revellers, always abusing one another, indulging their love of quarrels, and arguing about human beings in a way that is wholly inappropriate to philosophy?

I do indeed.

No one whose thoughts are truly directed towards the things that are, Adeimantus, has the leisure to look down at human affairs or to be filled with envy and hatred by competing with people. Instead, as he looks at and

c   studies things that are organized and always the same, that neither do injustice to one another nor suffer it, being all in a rational order, he imitates them and tries to become as like them as he can. Or do you think that someone can consort with things he admires without imitating them?

I do not. It's impossible.

Then the philosopher, by consorting with what is ordered and divine and despite all the slanders around that say otherwise, himself becomes as

d   divine and ordered as a human being can.

That's absolutely true.

And if he should come to be compelled to put what he sees there into people's characters, whether into a single person or into a populace, instead of shaping only his own, do you think that he will be a poor craftsman of moderation, justice, and the whole of popular virtue?

He least of all.

And when the majority realize that what we are saying about the philosopher is true, will they be harsh with him or mistrust us when we say

e   that the city will never find happiness until its outline is sketched by painters who use the divine model?

They won't be harsh, if indeed they realize this. But what sort of sketch

501   do you mean?

They'd take the city and the characters of human beings as their sketching slate, but first they'd wipe it clean—which isn't at all an easy thing to do. And you should know that this is the plain difference between them and others, namely, that they refuse to take either an individual or a city in

[Adeimantus/Socrates]

hand or to write laws, unless they receive a clean slate or are allowed to clean it themselves.

And they'd be right to refuse.

Then don't you think they'd next sketch the outline of the constitution? Of course.

And I suppose that, as they work, they'd look often in each direction,   *b* towards the natures of justice, beauty, moderation, and the like, on the one hand, and towards those they're trying to put into human beings, on the other. And in this way they'd mix and blend the various ways of life in the city until they produced a human image based on what Homer too called "the divine form and image" when it occurred among human beings.[3]

That's right.

They'd erase one thing, I suppose, and draw in another until they'd made characters for human beings that the gods would love as much as possible.   *c*

At any rate, that would certainly result in the finest sketch.

Then is this at all persuasive to those you said were straining to attack us—that the person we were praising is really a painter of constitutions? They were angry because we entrusted the city to him: Are they any calmer, now that they've heard what we had to say?

They'll be much calmer, if they have any moderation.

Indeed, how could they possibly dispute it? Will they deny that philoso-phers are lovers of what is or of the truth?   *d*

That would be absurd.

Or that their nature as we've described it is close to the best?

They can't deny that either.

Or that such a nature, if it follows its own way of life, isn't as completely good and philosophic as any other? Or that the people we excluded are more so?

Certainly not.   *e*

Then will they still be angry when we say that, until philosophers take control of a city, there'll be no respite from evil for either city or citizens, and the constitution we've been describing in theory will never be com-pleted in practice?

They'll probably be less angry.

Then if it's all right with you, let's not say that they'll simply be less angry but that they'll become altogether gentle and persuaded, so that they'll be shamed into agreeing with us, if nothing else.   *502*

It's all right with me.

Let's assume, therefore, that they've been convinced on this point. Will anyone dispute our view that the offspring of kings or rulers could be born with philosophic natures?

No one would do that.

---

3. See, for example, *Iliad* 1.131.

[Socrates/Adeimantus]

Could anyone claim that, if such offspring are born, they'll inevitably be corrupted? We agree ourselves that it's hard for them to be saved from corruption, but could anyone claim that in the whole of time not one of
b   them could be saved?

How could he?

But surely one such individual would be sufficient to bring to completion all the things that now seem so incredible, provided that his city obeys him.

One would be sufficient.

If a ruler established the laws and ways of life we've described, it is surely not impossible that the citizens would be willing to carry them out.

Not at all.

And would it be either astonishing or impossible that others should think as we do?

c   I don't suppose it would.

But I think our earlier discussion was sufficient to show that these arrangements are best, if only they are possible.

Indeed it was.

Then we can now conclude that this legislation is best, if only it is possible, and that, while it is hard for it to come about, it is not impossible.

We can.

Now that this difficulty has been disposed of, we must deal with what remains, namely, how the saviors of our constitution will come to be in the city, what subjects and ways of life will cause them to come into being, and
d   at what ages they'll take each of them up.

Indeed we must.

It wasn't very clever of me to omit from our earlier discussion the troublesome topics of acquiring wives, begetting children, and appointing rulers, just because I knew that the whole truth would provoke resentment and would be hard to bring about in practice, for as it turned out, I had to go through these matters anyway. The subject of women and children has
e   been adequately dealt with, but that of the rulers has to be taken up again from the beginning. We said, if you remember, that they must show themselves to be lovers of their city when tested by pleasure and pain and that
503   they must hold on to their resolve through labors, fears, and all other adversities. Anyone who was incapable of doing so was to be rejected, while anyone who came through unchanged—like gold tested in a fire— was to be made ruler and receive prizes both while he lived and after his death. These were the sorts of things we were saying while our argument, afraid of stirring up the very problems that now confront us, veiled its face
b   and slipped by.

That's very true; I do remember it.

We hesitated to say the things we've now dared to say anyway. So let's now also dare to say that those who are to be made our guardians in the most exact sense of the term must be philosophers.

Let's do it.

[Socrates/Adeimantus]

Then you should understand that there will probably be only a few of them, for they have to have the nature we described, and its parts mostly grow in separation and are rarely found in the same person.

What do you mean?   c

You know that ease of learning, good memory, quick wits, smartness, youthful passion, high-mindedness, and all the other things that go along with these are rarely willing to grow together in a mind that will choose an orderly life that is quiet and completely stable, for the people who possess the former traits are carried by their quick wits wherever chance leads them and have no stability at all.

That's true.

On the other hand, people with stable characters, who don't change easily, who aren't easily frightened in battle, and whom one would employ because of their greater reliability, exhibit similar traits when it comes to   d
learning: They are as hard to move and teach as people whose brains have become numb, and they are filled with sleep and yawning whenever they have to learn anything.

That's so.

Yet we say that someone must have a fine and goodly share of both characters, or he won't receive the truest education, honors, or rule.

That's right.

Then, don't you think that such people will be rare?

Of course.

Therefore they must be tested in the labors, fears, and pleasures we   e
mentioned previously. But they must also be exercised in many other subjects—which we didn't mention but are adding now—to see whether they can tolerate the most important subjects or will shrink from them like the cowards who shrink from other tests.   504

It's appropriate to examine them like that. But what do you mean by the most important subjects?

Do you remember when we distinguished three parts in the soul, in order to help bring out what justice, moderation, courage, and wisdom each is?

If I didn't remember that, it wouldn't be just for me to hear the rest.

What about what preceded it?

What was that?

We said, I believe, that, in order to get the finest possible view of these   b
matters, we would need to take a longer road that would make them plain to anyone who took it but that it was possible to give demonstrations of what they are that would be up to the standard of the previous argument. And you said that that would be satisfactory. So it seems to me that our discussion at that time fell short of exactness, but whether or not it satisfied you is for you to say.

I thought you gave us good measure and so, apparently, did the others.

Any measure of such things that falls short in any way of that which is is   c

[Adeimantus/Socrates]

not good measure, for nothing incomplete is the measure of anything, although people are sometimes of the opinion that an incomplete treatment is nonetheless adequate and makes further investigation unnecessary.

Indeed, laziness causes many people to think that.

It is a thought that a guardian of a city and its laws can well do without.

Probably so.

Well, then, he must take the longer road and put as much effort into learning as into physical training, for otherwise, as we were just saying, he *d* will never reach the goal of the most important subject and the most appropriate one for him to learn.

Aren't these virtues, then, the most important things? he asked. Is there anything even more important than justice and the other virtues we discussed?

There is something more important. However, even for the virtues themselves, it isn't enough to look at a mere sketch, as we did before, while neglecting the most complete account. It's ridiculous, isn't it, to strain every nerve to attain the utmost exactness and clarity about other things of little *e* value and not to consider the most important things worthy of the greatest exactness?

It certainly is. But do you think that anyone is going to let you off without asking you what this most important subject is and what it concerns?

No, indeed, and you can ask me too. You've certainly heard the answer often enough, but now either you aren't thinking or you intend to make trouble for me again by interrupting. And I suspect the latter, for you've *505* often heard it said that the form of the good is the most important thing to learn about and that it's by their relation to it that just things and the others become useful and beneficial. You know very well now that I am going to say this, and, besides, that we have no adequate knowledge of it. And you also know that, if we don't know it, even the fullest possible knowledge of other things is of no benefit to us, any more than if we acquire any possession without the good of it. Or do you think that it is any advantage to have *b* every kind of possession without the good of it? Or to know everything except the good, thereby knowing nothing fine or good?

No, by god, I don't.

Furthermore, you certainly know that the majority believe that pleasure is the good, while the most sophisticated believe that it is knowledge.

Indeed I do.

And you know that those who believe this can't tell us what sort of knowledge it is, however, but in the end are forced to say that it is knowledge of the good.

And that's ridiculous.

c Of course it is. They blame us for not knowing the good and then turn around and talk to us as if we did know it. They say that it is knowledge of the good—as if we understood what they're speaking about when they utter the word "good."

[Socrates/Adeimantus]

That's completely true.

What about those who define the good as pleasure? Are they any less full of confusion than the others? Aren't even they forced to admit that there are bad pleasures?

Most definitely.

So, I think, they have to agree that the same things are both good and bad. Isn't that true?

Of course.   *d*

It's clear, then, isn't it, why there are many large controversies about this?

How could it be otherwise?

And isn't this also clear? In the case of just and beautiful things, many people are content with what are believed to be so, even if they aren't really so, and they act, acquire, and form their own beliefs on that basis. Nobody is satisfied to acquire things that are merely believed to be good, however, but everyone wants the things that really *are* good and disdains mere belief here.

That's right.

Every soul pursues the good and does whatever it does for its sake. It   *e* divines that the good is something but it is perplexed and cannot ade-quately grasp what it is or acquire the sort of stable beliefs it has about other things, and so it misses the benefit, if any, that even those other things may give. Will we allow the best people in the city, to whom we entrust everything, to be so in the dark about something of this kind and   *506* of this importance?

That's the last thing we'd do.

I don't suppose, at least, that just and fine things will have acquired much of a guardian in someone who doesn't even know in what way they are good. And I divine that no one will have adequate knowledge of them until he knows this.

You've divined well.

But won't our constitution be perfectly ordered, if a guardian who knows these things is in charge of it?   *b*

Necessarily. But, Socrates, you must also tell us whether you consider the good to be knowledge or pleasure or something else altogether.

What a man! It's been clear for some time that other people's opinions about these matters wouldn't satisfy you.

Well, Socrates, it doesn't seem right to me for you to be willing to state other people's convictions but not your own, especially when you've spent so much time occupied with these matters.   *c*

What? Do you think it's right to talk about things one doesn't know as if one does know them?

Not as if one knows them, he said, but one ought to be willing to state one's opinions as such.

What? Haven't you noticed that opinions without knowledge are shameful and ugly things? The best of them are blind—or do you think that those who express a true opinion without understanding are any different from blind people who happen to travel the right road?

They're no different.

d   Do you want to look at shameful, blind, and crooked things, then, when you might hear illuminating and fine ones from other people?

By god, Socrates, Glaucon said, don't desert us with the end almost in sight. We'll be satisfied if you discuss the good as you discussed justice, moderation, and the rest.

That, my friend, I said, would satisfy me too, but I'm afraid that I won't be up to it and that I'll disgrace myself and look ridiculous by trying. So let's abandon the quest for what the good itself is for the time being, for

e   even to arrive at my own view about it is too big a topic for the discussion we are now started on. But I am willing to tell you about what is apparently an offspring of the good and most like it. Is that agreeable to you, or would you rather we let the whole matter drop?

It is. The story about the father remains a debt you'll pay another time.

507   I wish that I could pay the debt in full, and you receive it instead of just the interest. So here, then, is this child and offspring of the good. But be careful that I don't somehow deceive you unintentionally by giving you an illegitimate account of the child.[4]

We'll be as careful as possible, so speak on.

I will when we've come to an agreement and recalled some things that we've already said both here and many other times.

b   Which ones?

We say that there are many beautiful things and many good things, and so on for each kind, and in this way we distinguish them in words.

We do.

And beauty itself and good itself and all the things that we thereby set down as many, reversing ourselves, we set down according to a single form of each, believing that there is but one, and call it "the being" of each.[5]

That's true.

And we say that the many beautiful things and the rest are visible but not intelligible, while the forms are intelligible but not visible.

That's completely true.

c   With what part of ourselves do we see visible things?

With our sight.

And so audible things are heard by hearing, and with our other senses we perceive all the other perceptible things.

---

4. Throughout, Socrates is punning on the word *tokos*, which means either a child or the interest on capital.

5. The "being" of something is sometimes taken to refer to what we call its essence. Socrates would then be saying that the essence of the fineness present in many things is the form of the fine.

[Socrates/Adeimantus/Glaucon]

That's right.

Have you considered how lavish the maker of our senses was in making the power to see and be seen?

I can't say I have.

Well, consider it this way. Do hearing and sound need another kind of thing in order for the former to hear and the latter to be heard, a third thing in whose absence the one won't hear or the other be heard?   *d*

No, they need nothing else.

And if there are any others that need such a thing, there can't be many of them. Can you think of one?

I can't.

You don't realize that sight and the visible have such a need?

How so?

Sight may be present in the eyes, and the one who has it may try to use it, and colors may be present in things, but unless a third kind of thing is present, which is naturally adapted for this very purpose, you know that sight will see nothing, and the colors will remain unseen.   *e*

What kind of thing do you mean?

I mean what you call light.

You're right.

Then it isn't an insignificant kind of link that connects the sense of sight and the power to be seen—it is a more valuable link than any other linked   *508* things have got, if indeed light is something valuable.

And, of course, it's very valuable.

Which of the gods in heaven would you name as the cause and controller of this, the one whose light causes our sight to see in the best way and the visible things to be seen?

The same one you and others would name. Obviously, the answer to your question is the sun.

And isn't sight by nature related to that god in this way?

Which way?

Sight isn't the sun, neither sight itself nor that in which it comes to be, namely, the eye.   *b*

No, it certainly isn't.

But I think that it is the most sunlike of the senses.

Very much so.

And it receives from the sun the power it has, just like an influx from an overflowing treasury.

Certainly.

The sun is not sight, but isn't it the cause of sight itself and seen by it?

That's right.

Let's say, then, that this is what I called the offspring of the good, which the good begot as its analogue. What the good itself is in the intelligible realm, in relation to understanding and intelligible things, the sun is in the visible realm, in relation to sight and visible things.   *c*

[Socrates/Glaucon]

How? Explain a bit more.

You know that, when we turn our eyes to things whose colors are no longer in the light of day but in the gloom of night, the eyes are dimmed and seem nearly blind, as if clear vision were no longer in them.

Of course.

Yet whenever one turns them on things illuminated by the sun, they see
d   clearly, and vision appears in those very same eyes.

Indeed.

Well, understand the soul in the same way: When it focuses on something illuminated by truth and what is, it understands, knows, and apparently possesses understanding, but when it focuses on what is mixed with obscurity, on what comes to be and passes away, it opines and is dimmed, changes its opinions this way and that, and seems bereft of understanding.

It does seem that way.

So that what gives truth to the things known and the power to know to
e   the knower is the form of the good. And though it is the cause of knowledge and truth, it is also an object of knowledge. Both knowledge and truth are beautiful things, but the good is other and more beautiful than they. In the visible realm, light and sight are rightly considered sunlike, but it is
509   wrong to think that they are the sun, so here it is right to think of knowledge and truth as goodlike but wrong to think that either of them is the good—for the good is yet more prized.

This is an inconceivably beautiful thing you're talking about, if it provides both knowledge and truth and is superior to them in beauty. You surely don't think that a thing like that could be pleasure.

Hush! Let's examine its image in more detail as follows.
b   How?

You'll be willing to say, I think, that the sun not only provides visible things with the power to be seen but also with coming to be, growth, and nourishment, although it is not itself coming to be.

How could it be?

Therefore, you should also say that not only do the objects of knowledge owe their being known to the good, but their being is also due to it, although the good is not being, but superior to it in rank and power.
c   And Glaucon comically said: By Apollo, what a daimonic superiority!

It's your own fault; you forced me to tell you my opinion about it.

And I don't want you to stop either. So continue to explain its similarity to the sun, if you've omitted anything.

I'm certainly omitting a lot.

Well, don't, not even the smallest thing.

I think I'll have to omit a fair bit, but, as far as is possible at the moment, I won't omit anything voluntarily.

Don't.
d   Understand, then, that, as we said, there are these two things, one sovereign of the intelligible kind and place, the other of the visible (I don't say

[Socrates/Glaucon]

"of heaven" so as not to seem to you to be playing the sophist with the name). In any case, you have two kinds of thing, visible and intelligible.

Right.

It is like a line divided into two unequal sections.[6] Then divide each section—namely, that of the visible and that of the intelligible—in the same ratio as the line. In terms now of relative clarity and opacity, one subsection of the visible consists of images. And by images I mean, first, shadows, then reflections in water and in all close-packed, smooth, and shiny materials, and everything of that sort, if you understand.

    e

    510

I do.

In the other subsection of the visible, put the originals of these images, namely, the animals around us, all the plants, and the whole class of manufactured things.

Consider them put.

Would you be willing to say that, as regards truth and untruth, the division is in this proportion: As the opinable is to the knowable, so the likeness is to the thing that it is like?

Certainly.

    b

Consider now how the section of the intelligible is to be divided.

How?

As follows: In one subsection, the soul, using as images the things that were imitated before, is forced to investigate from hypotheses, proceeding not to a first principle but to a conclusion. In the other subsection, however, it makes its way to a first principle that is *not* a hypothesis, proceeding from a hypothesis but without the images used in the previous subsection, using forms themselves and making its investigation through them.

I don't yet fully understand what you mean.

Let's try again. You'll understand it more easily after the following preamble. I think you know that students of geometry, calculation, and the like

    c

6. The line is illustrated below:

Understanding (*noēsis*)

Thought (*dianoia*)

Belief (*pistis*)

Imagination (*eikasia*)

[Glaucon/Socrates]

hypothesize the odd and the even, the various figures, the three kinds of angles, and other things akin to these in each of their investigations, as if they knew them. They make these their hypotheses and don't think it necessary to give any account of them, either to themselves or to others, as if they were clear to everyone. And going from these first principles through the remaining steps, they arrive in full agreement about what they
d   set out to investigate.

I certainly know that much.

Then you also know that, although they use visible figures and make claims about them, their thought isn't directed to them but to those other things that they are like. They make their claims for the sake of the square itself and the diagonal itself, not the diagonal they draw, and similarly with
e   the others. These figures that they make and draw, of which shadows and reflections in water are images, they now in turn use as images, in seeking to see those others themselves that one cannot see except by means of
511   thought.

That's true.

This, then, is the kind of thing that, on the one hand, I said is intelligible, and, on the other, is such that the soul is forced to use hypotheses in the investigation of it, not travelling up to a first principle, since it cannot reach beyond its hypotheses, but using as images those very things of which images were made in the section below, and which, by comparison to their images, were thought to be clear and to be valued as such.
b   I understand that you mean what happens in geometry and related sciences.

Then also understand that, by the other subsection of the intelligible, I mean that which reason itself grasps by the power of dialectic. It does not consider these hypotheses as first principles but truly as hypotheses— stepping stones to take off from, enabling it to reach the unhypothetical first principle of everything. Having grasped this principle, it reverses itself and, keeping hold of what follows from it, comes down to a conclusion without
c   making use of anything visible at all, but only of forms themselves, moving on from forms to forms, and ending in forms.

I understand, if not yet adequately (for in my opinion you're speaking of an enormous task), that you want to distinguish the intelligible part of that which is, the part studied by the science of dialectic, as clearer than the part studied by the so-called sciences, for which their hypotheses are first principles. And although those who study the objects of these sciences are forced to do so by means of thought rather than sense perception, still,
d   because they do not go back to a genuine first principle, but proceed from hypotheses, you don't think that they understand them, even though, given such a principle, they are intelligible. And you seem to me to call the state of the geometers thought but not understanding, thought being intermediate between opinion and understanding.

[Socrates/Glaucon]

Your exposition is most adequate. Thus there are four such conditions in the soul, corresponding to the four subsections of our line: Understanding for the highest, thought for the second, belief for the third, and imaging for the last. Arrange them in a ratio, and consider that each shares in clarity to the degree that the subsection it is set over shares in truth.

I understand, agree, and arrange them as you say.

REPUBLIC VII

*Book VII begins with another unforgettable image, the allegory of the Cave,
which fits together with the Sun and Line (517b), and which illustrates the effects
of education on the soul (514a). It leads to a brief but important discussion of
education (518b–519b), in which Socrates makes it clear that the aim of education is to turn the soul around by changing its desires.*

*The next topic is the education of the philosopher-kings. (1) Their initial edu-
cation is in music and poetry, physical training, and elementary mathematics
(535a–537b). (2) This is followed by two or three years of compulsory physical
training, rather like the military service that some countries still have (537b–c).
(3) Those who are most successful in these studies next receive ten years of education in mathematical science (537c–d, 522c–531d). (4) Those who are again
most successful receive five years of training in dialectic (537d–540a, 531e–535a).
(5) Those who are still most successful receive fifteen years of practical political
training (539e–540a). Finally, (6) those who are also successful in practical politics are "compelled to lift up the radiant light of their souls" to the good itself
(540a) and are equipped to be philosopher-kings.*

*The third city, which contains philosopher-kings and the educational institu-
tions necessary to produce them, constitutes the final stage in Plato's construction
of his ideal city (535a–536d, 543c–544a).*

Next, I said, compare the effect of education and of the lack of it on our
514 nature to an experience like this: Imagine human beings living in an underground, cavelike dwelling, with an entrance a long way up, which is both
open to the light and as wide as the cave itself. They've been there since
childhood, fixed in the same place, with their necks and legs fettered, able
to see only in front of them, because their bonds prevent them from turning their heads around. Light is provided by a fire burning far above and
b behind them. Also behind them, but on higher ground, there is a path
stretching between them and the fire. Imagine that along this path a low
wall has been built, like the screen in front of puppeteers above which they
show their puppets.

I'm imagining it.

Then also imagine that there are people along the wall, carrying all
kinds of artifacts that project above it—statues of people and other ani-

[Socrates/Glaucon]

mals, made out of stone, wood, and every material. And, as you'd expect,   c
some of the carriers are talking, and some are silent.   515

It's a strange image you're describing, and strange prisoners.

They're like us. Do you suppose, first of all, that these prisoners see
anything of themselves and one another besides the shadows that the fire
casts on the wall in front of them?

How could they, if they have to keep their heads motionless throughout life?   b

What about the things being carried along the wall? Isn't the same true
of them?

Of course.

And if they could talk to one another, don't you think they'd suppose
that the names they used applied to the things they see passing before
them?

They'd have to.

And what if their prison also had an echo from the wall facing them?
Don't you think they'd believe that the shadows passing in front of
them were talking whenever one of the carriers passing along the wall was
doing so?

I certainly do.

Then the prisoners would in every way believe that the truth is nothing   c
other than the shadows of those artifacts.

They must surely believe that.

Consider, then, what being released from their bonds and cured of their
ignorance would naturally be like. When one of them was freed and suddenly compelled to stand up, turn his head, walk, and look up toward the
light, he'd be pained and dazzled and unable to see the things whose
shadows he'd seen before. What do you think he'd say, if we told him that   d
what he'd seen before was inconsequential, but that now—because he is a
bit closer to the things that are and is turned towards things that are
more—he sees more correctly? Or, to put it another way, if we pointed to
each of the things passing by, asked him what each of them is, and compelled him to answer, don't you think he'd be at a loss and that he'd believe
that the things he saw earlier were truer than the ones he was now being
shown?

Much truer.

And if someone compelled him to look at the light itself, wouldn't
his eyes hurt, and wouldn't he turn around and flee towards the things he's   e
able to see, believing that they're really clearer than the ones he's being
shown?

He would.

And if someone dragged him away from there by force, up the rough,
steep path, and didn't let him go until he had dragged him into the sunlight,
wouldn't he be pained and irritated at being treated that way? And when he

[Socrates/Glaucon]

516   came into the light, with the sun filling his eyes, wouldn't he be unable to
see a single one of the things now said to be true?

He would be unable to see them, at least at first.

I suppose, then, that he'd need time to get adjusted before he could see
things in the world above. At first, he'd see shadows most easily, then
images of men and other things in water, then the things themselves. Of
these, he'd be able to study the things in the sky and the sky itself more
easily at night, looking at the light of the stars and the moon, than during
b   the day, looking at the sun and the light of the sun.

Of course.

Finally, I suppose, he'd be able to see the sun, not images of it in water or
some alien place, but the sun itself, in its own place, and be able to study it.

Necessarily so.

And at this point he would infer and conclude that the sun provides the
seasons and the years, governs everything in the visible world, and is in
c   some way the cause of all the things that he used to see.

It's clear that would be his next step.

What about when he reminds himself of his first dwelling place, his
fellow prisoners, and what passed for wisdom there? Don't you think that
he'd count himself happy for the change and pity the others?

Certainly.

And if there had been any honors, praises, or prizes among them for the
one who was sharpest at identifying the shadows as they passed by and
who best remembered which usually came earlier, which later, and which
d   simultaneously, and who could thus best divine the future, do you think
that our man would desire these rewards or envy those among the prisoners who were honored and held power? Instead, wouldn't he feel, with
Homer, that he'd much prefer to "work the earth as a serf to another, one
without possessions,"[1] and go through any sufferings, rather than share
their opinions and live as they do?

e   I suppose he would rather suffer anything than live like that.

Consider this too. If this man went down into the cave again and sat
down in his same seat, wouldn't his eyes—coming suddenly out of the sun
like that—be filled with darkness?

They certainly would.

And before his eyes had recovered—and the adjustment would not be
quick—while his vision was still dim, if he had to compete again with the
517   perpetual prisoners in recognizing the shadows, wouldn't he invite ridicule?
Wouldn't it be said of him that he'd returned from his upward journey with
his eyesight ruined and that it isn't worthwhile even to try to travel upward? And, as for anyone who tried to free them and lead them upward, if
they could somehow get their hands on him, wouldn't they kill him?

1. *Odyssey* 11.489–90. The shade of the dead Achilles speaks these words to Odysseus, who is visiting Hades.

[Socrates/Glaucon]

They certainly would.

This whole image, Glaucon, must be fitted together with what we said   *b*
before. The visible realm should be likened to the prison dwelling, and the
light of the fire inside it to the power of the sun. And if you interpret the
upward journey and the study of things above as the upward journey of
the soul to the intelligible realm, you'll grasp what I hope to convey, since
that is what you wanted to hear about. Whether it's true or not, only the
god knows. But this is how I see it: In the knowable realm, the form of the
good is the last thing to be seen, and it is reached only with difficulty. Once
one has seen it, however, one must conclude that it is the cause of all that is
correct and beautiful in anything, that it produces both light and its source   *c*
in the visible realm, and that in the intelligible realm it controls and provides truth and understanding, so that anyone who is to act sensibly in
private or public must see it.

I have the same thought, at least as far as I'm able.

Come, then, share with me this thought also: It isn't surprising that the
ones who get to this point are unwilling to occupy themselves with human
affairs and that their souls are always pressing upwards, eager to spend
their time above, for, after all, this is surely what we'd expect, if indeed
things fit the image I described before.   *d*

It is.

What about what happens when someone turns from divine study to the
evils of human life? Do you think it's surprising, since his sight is still dim,
and he hasn't yet become accustomed to the darkness around him, that he
behaves awkwardly and appears completely ridiculous if he's compelled,
either in the courts or elsewhere, to contend about the shadows of justice or
the statues of which they are the shadows and to dispute about the way
these things are understood by people who have never seen justice itself?   *e*

That's not surprising at all.

No, it isn't. But anyone with any understanding would remember that the   518
eyes may be confused in two ways and from two causes, namely, when
they've come from the light into the darkness *and* when they've come from
the darkness into the light. Realizing that the same applies to the soul,
when someone sees a soul disturbed and unable to see something, he won't
laugh mindlessly, but he'll take into consideration whether it has come from
a brighter life and is dimmed through not having yet become accustomed
to the dark or whether it has come from greater ignorance into greater light
and is dazzled by the increased brilliance. Then he'll declare the first soul
happy in its experience and life, and he'll pity the latter—but even if he
chose to make fun of it, at least he'd be less ridiculous than if he laughed at   *b*
a soul that has come from the light above.

What you say is very reasonable.

If that's true, then here's what we must think about these matters: Education isn't what some people declare it to be, namely, putting knowledge into
souls that lack it, like putting sight into blind eyes.   *c*

[Glaucon/Socrates]

They do say that.

But our present discussion, on the other hand, shows that the power to learn is present in everyone's soul and that the instrument with which each learns is like an eye that cannot be turned around from darkness to light without turning the whole body. This instrument cannot be turned around from that which is coming into being without turning the whole soul until

d   it is able to study that which is and the brightest thing that is, namely, the one we call the good. Isn't that right?

Yes.

Then education is the craft concerned with doing this very thing, this turning around, and with how the soul can most easily and effectively be made to do it. It isn't the craft of putting sight into the soul. Education takes for granted that sight is there but that it isn't turned the right way or looking where it ought to look, and it tries to redirect it appropriately.

So it seems.

Now, it looks as though the other so-called virtues of the soul are akin to those of the body, for they really aren't there beforehand but are added

e   later by habit and practice. However, the virtue of reason seems to belong above all to something more divine, which never loses its power but is either useful and beneficial or useless and harmful, depending on the way

519 it is turned. Or have you never noticed this about people who are said to be vicious but clever, how keen the vision of their little souls is and how sharply it distinguishes the things it is turned towards? This shows that its sight isn't inferior but rather is forced to serve evil ends, so that the sharper it sees, the more evil it accomplishes.

Absolutely.

However, if a nature of this sort had been hammered at from childhood and freed from the bonds of kinship with becoming, which have been fastened to it by feasting, greed, and other such pleasures and which, like

b   leaden weights, pull its vision downwards—if, being rid of these, it turned to look at true things, then I say that the same soul of the same person would see these most sharply, just as it now does the things it is presently turned towards.

Probably so.

And what about the uneducated who have no experience of truth? Isn't it likely—indeed, doesn't it follow necessarily from what was said before— that they will never adequately govern a city? But neither would those who've been allowed to spend their whole lives being educated. The former

c   would fail because they don't have a single goal at which all their actions, public and private, inevitably aim; the latter would fail because they'd refuse to act, thinking that they had settled while still alive in the faraway Isles of the Blessed.[2]

2. A place where good people are said to live in eternal happiness, normally after death.

[Socrates/Glaucon]

That's true.

It is our task as founders, then, to compel the best natures to reach the study we said before is the most important, namely, to make the ascent and see the good. But when they've made it and looked sufficiently, we mustn't allow them to do what they're allowed to do today.   *d*

What's that?

To stay there and refuse to go down again to the prisoners in the cave and share their labors and honors, whether they are of less worth or of greater.

Then are we to do them an injustice by making them live a worse life when they could live a better one?

You are forgetting again that it isn't the law's concern to make any one class   *e* in the city outstandingly happy but to contrive to spread happiness throughout the city by bringing the citizens into harmony with each other through persuasion or compulsion and by making them share with each other the benefits that each class can confer on the community. The law produces such people in the city, not in order to allow them to turn in whatever   *520* direction they want, but to make use of them to bind the city together.

That's true, I had forgotten.

Observe, then, Glaucon, that we won't be doing an injustice to those who've become philosophers in our city and that what we'll say to them, when we compel them to guard and care for the others, will be just. We'll say: "When people like you come to be in other cities, they're justified in not sharing in their city's labors, for they've grown there spontaneously,   *b* against the will of the constitution. And what grows of its own accord and owes no debt for its upbringing has justice on its side when it isn't keen to pay anyone for that upbringing. But we've made you kings in our city and leaders of the swarm, as it were, both for yourselves and for the rest of the city. You're better and more completely educated than the others and are better able to share in both types of life. Therefore each of you in turn   *c* must go down to live in the common dwelling place of the others and grow accustomed to seeing in the dark. When you are used to it, you'll see vastly better than the people there. And because you've seen the truth about fine, just, and good things, you'll know each image for what it is and also that of which it is the image. Thus, for you and for us, the city will be governed, not like the majority of cities nowadays, by people who fight over shadows and struggle against one another in order to rule—as if that were a great good—but by people who are awake rather than dreaming, for the truth is surely this: A city whose prospective rulers are least eager to rule must of   *d* necessity be most free from civil war, whereas a city with the opposite kind of rulers is governed in the opposite way."

Absolutely.

Then do you think that those we've nurtured will disobey us and refuse to share the labors of the city, each in turn, while living the greater part of their time with one another in the pure realm?

[Socrates/Glaucon]

e   It isn't possible, for we'll be giving just orders to just people. Each of them will certainly go to rule as to something compulsory, however, which is exactly the opposite of what's done by those who now rule in each city.

   This is how it is. If you can find a way of life that's better than ruling for the prospective rulers, your well-governed city will become a possibility, *521*   for only in it will the truly rich rule—not those who are rich in gold but those who are rich in the wealth that the happy must have, namely, a good and rational life. But if beggars hungry for private goods go into public life, thinking that the good is there for the seizing, then the well-governed city is impossible, for then ruling is something fought over, and this civil and domestic war destroys these people and the rest of the city as well.

   That's very true.

b   Can you name any life that despises political rule besides that of the true philosopher?

   No, by god, I can't.

   But surely it is those who are not lovers of ruling who must rule, for if they don't, the lovers of it, who are rivals, will fight over it.

   Of course.

   Then who will you compel to become guardians of the city, if not those who have the best understanding of what matters for good government and who have other honors than political ones, and a better life as well?

   No one.

   Do you want us to consider now how such people will come to be in our *c*   city and how—just as some are said to have gone up from Hades to the gods—we'll lead them up to the light?

   Of course I do.

   This isn't, it seems, a matter of spinning a potsherd, but of turning a soul from a day that is a kind of night to the true day—the ascent to what is, which we say is true philosophy.

   Indeed.

   Then mustn't we try to discover the subjects that have the power to bring *d*   this about?

   Of course.

   So what subject is it, Glaucon, that draws the soul from the realm of becoming to the realm of what is? And it occurs to me as I'm speaking that we said, didn't we, that it is necessary for the prospective rulers to be athletes in war when they're young?

   Yes, we did.

   Then the subject we're looking for must also have this characteristic in addition to the former one.

   Which one?

   It mustn't be useless to warlike men.

   If it's at all possible, it mustn't.

   Now, prior to this, we educated them in music and poetry and physical *e*   training.

[Socrates/Glaucon]

We did.

And physical training is concerned with what comes into being and dies, for it oversees the growth and decay of the body.

Apparently.

So it couldn't be the subject we're looking for.

No, it couldn't.   522

Then, could it be the music and poetry we described before?

But that, if you remember, is just the counterpart of physical training. It educated the guardians through habits. Its harmonies gave them a certain harmoniousness, not knowledge; its rhythms gave them a certain rhythmical quality; and its stories, whether fictional or nearer the truth, cultivated other habits akin to these. But as for the subject you're looking for now, there's nothing like that in music and poetry.   b

Your reminder is exactly to the point; there's really nothing like that in music and poetry. But, Glaucon, what is there that does have this? The crafts all seem to be base or mechanical.

How could they be otherwise? But apart from music and poetry, physical training, and the crafts, what subject is left?

Well, if we can't find anything apart from these, let's consider one of the subjects that touches all of them.

What sort of thing?

For example, that common thing that every craft, every type of thought, and every science uses and that is among the first compulsory subjects for   c everyone.

What's that?

That inconsequential matter of distinguishing the one, the two, and the three. In short, I mean number and calculation, for isn't it true that every craft and science must have a share in that?

They certainly must.

Then so must warfare.

Absolutely.

In the tragedies, at any rate, Palamedes[3] is always showing up Agamemnon as a totally ridiculous general. Haven't you noticed? He says that, by inventing numbers, he established how many troops there were in the   d Trojan army and counted their ships and everything else—implying that they were uncounted before and that Agamemnon (if indeed he didn't know how to count) didn't even know how many feet he had? What kind of general do you think that made him?

A very strange one, if that's true.

Then won't we set down this subject as compulsory for a warrior, so that   e he is able to count and calculate?

More compulsory than anything. If, that is, he's to understand any-

---

3. Palamades is a proverbially clever warrior best known for his cunning while serving under Agamemnon.

[Glaucon/Socrates]

thing about setting his troops in order or if he's even to be properly human.

Then do you notice the same thing about this subject that I do?

What's that?

That this turns out to be one of the subjects we were looking for that naturally lead to understanding. But no one uses it correctly, namely, as 523 something that is really fitted in every way to draw one towards being.

What do you mean?

I'll try to make my view clear as follows: I'll distinguish for myself the things that do or don't lead in the direction we mentioned, and you must study them along with me and either agree or disagree, and that way we may come to know more clearly whether things are indeed as I divine.

Point them out.

I'll point out, then, if you can grasp it, that some sense perceptions *don't* summon the understanding to look into them, because the judgment of b   sense perception is itself adequate, while others encourage it in every way to look into them, because sense perception seems to produce no sound result.

You're obviously referring to things appearing in the distance and to *trompe l'oeil* paintings.

You're not quite getting my meaning.

Then what do you mean?

The ones that don't summon the understanding are all those that don't go off into opposite perceptions at the same time. But the ones that do go off c   in that way I call *summoners*—whenever sense perception doesn't declare one thing any more than its opposite, no matter whether the object striking the senses is near at hand or far away. You'll understand my meaning better if I put it this way: These, we say, are three fingers—the smallest, the second, and the middle finger.

That's right.

Assume that I'm talking about them as being seen from close by. Now, this is my question about them.

What?

It's apparent that each of them is equally a finger, and it makes no difference in this regard whether the finger is seen to be in the middle or at d   either end, whether it is dark or pale, thick or thin, or anything else of that sort, for in all these cases, an ordinary soul isn't compelled to ask the understanding what a finger is, since sight doesn't suggest to it that a finger is at the same time the opposite of a finger.

No, it doesn't.

Therefore, it isn't likely that anything of that sort would summon or e   awaken the understanding.

No, it isn't.

But what about the bigness and smallness of fingers? Does sight perceive

[Socrates/Glaucon]

them adequately? Does it make no difference to it whether the finger is in the middle or at the end? And is it the same with the sense of touch, as regards the thick and the thin, the hard and the soft? And do the other senses reveal such things clearly and adequately? Doesn't each of them rather do the following: The sense set over the hard is, in the first place, of *524* necessity also set over the soft, and it reports to the soul that the same thing is perceived by it to be both hard and soft?

That's right.

And isn't it necessary that in such cases the soul is puzzled as to what this sense means by the hard, if it indicates that the same thing is also soft, or what it means by the light and the heavy, if it indicates that the heavy is light, or the light, heavy?

Yes, indeed, these are strange reports for the soul to receive, and they do *b* demand to be looked into.

Then it's likely that in such cases the soul, summoning calculation and understanding, first tries to determine whether each of the things announced to it is one or two.

Of course.

If it's evidently two, won't each be evidently distinct and one?

Yes.

Then, if each is one, and both two, the soul will understand that the two are separate, for it wouldn't understand the inseparable to be two, but rather one.   *c*

That's right.

Sight, however, saw the big and small, not as separate, but as mixed up together. Isn't that so?

Yes.

And in order to get clear about all this, understanding was compelled to see the big and the small, not as mixed up together, but as separate—the opposite way from sight.

True.

And isn't it from these cases that it first occurs to us to ask what the big is and what the small is?

Absolutely.

And, because of this, we called the one the intelligible and the other the visible.

That's right.   *d*

This, then, is what I was trying to express before, when I said that some things summon thought, while others don't. Those that strike the relevant sense at the same time as their opposites I call summoners, those that don't do this do not awaken understanding.

Now I understand, and I think you're right.

Well, then, to which of them do number and the one belong?

I don't know.

[Socrates/Glaucon]

Reason it out from what was said before. If the one is adequately seen itself by itself or is so perceived by any of the other senses, then, as we were saying in the case of fingers, it wouldn't draw the soul towards being.

e But if something opposite to it is always seen at the same time, so that nothing is apparently any more one than the opposite of one, then something would be needed to judge the matter. The soul would then be puzzled, would look for an answer, would stir up its understanding, and would ask what the one itself is. And so this would be among the subjects

525 that lead the soul and turn it around towards the study of that which is.

But surely the sight of the one does possess this characteristic to a remarkable degree, for we see the same thing to be both one and an unlimited number at the same time.

Then, if this is true of the one, won't it also be true of all numbers?

Of course.

Now, calculation and arithmetic are wholly concerned with numbers.

That's right.

b Then evidently they lead us towards truth.

Supernaturally so.

Then they belong, it seems, to the subjects we're seeking. They are compulsory for warriors because of their orderly ranks and for philosophers because they have to learn to rise up out of becoming and grasp being, if they are ever to become rational.

That's right.

And our guardian must be both a warrior and a philosopher.

Certainly.

Then it would be appropriate, Glaucon, to legislate this subject for those who are going to share in the highest offices in the city and to persuade them to turn to calculation and take it up, not as laymen do, but staying

c with it until they reach the study of the natures of the numbers by means of understanding itself, nor like tradesmen and retailers, for the sake of buying and selling, but for the sake of war and for ease in turning the soul around, away from becoming and towards truth and being.

Well put.

Moreover, it strikes me, now that it has been mentioned, how sophisticated the subject of calculation is and in how many ways it is useful for our

d purposes, provided that one practices it for the sake of knowing rather than trading.

How is it useful?

In the very way we were talking about. It leads the soul forcibly upward and compels it to discuss the numbers themselves, never permitting anyone to propose for discussion numbers attached to visible or tangible bodies. You know what those who are clever in these matters are like: If, in the course of the argument, someone tries to divide the one itself, they laugh

e and won't permit it. If you divide it, they multiply it, taking care that one thing never be found to be many parts rather than one.

[Glaucon/Socrates]

That's very true.

Then what do you think would happen, Glaucon, if someone were to ask them: "What kind of numbers are you talking about, in which the one is as *526* you assume it to be, each one equal to every other, without the least difference and containing no internal parts?"

I think they'd answer that they are talking about those numbers that can be grasped only in thought and can't be dealt with in any other way.

Then do you see that it's likely that this subject really is compulsory for *b* us, since it apparently compels the soul to use understanding itself on the truth itself?

Indeed, it most certainly does do that.

And what about those who are naturally good at calculation or reasoning? Have you already noticed that they're naturally sharp, so to speak, in all subjects, and that those who are slow at it, if they're educated and exercised in it, even if they're benefited in no other way, nonetheless improve and become generally sharper than they were?

That's true.

Moreover, I don't think you'll easily find subjects that are harder to learn *c* or practice than this.

No, indeed.

Then, for all these reasons, this subject isn't to be neglected, and the best natures must be educated in it.

I agree.

Let that, then, be one of our subjects. Second, let's consider whether the subject that comes next is also appropriate for our purposes.

What subject is that? Do you mean geometry?

That's the very one I had in mind.

Insofar as it pertains to war, it's obviously appropriate, for when it comes *d* to setting up camp, occupying a region, concentrating troops, deploying them, or with regard to any of the other formations an army adopts in battle or on the march, it makes all the difference whether someone is a geometer or not.

But, for things like that, even a little geometry—or calculation for that matter—would suffice. What we need to consider is whether the greater and more advanced part of it tends to make it easier to see the form of the good. And we say that anything has that tendency if it compels the soul to *e* turn itself around towards the region in which lies the happiest of the things that are, the one the soul must see at any cost.

You're right.

Therefore, if geometry compels the soul to study being, it's appropriate, but if it compels it to study becoming, it's inappropriate.

So we've said, at any rate.

Now, no one with even a little experience of geometry will dispute that *527* this science is entirely the opposite of what is said about it in the accounts of its practitioners.

How do you mean?

They give ridiculous accounts of it, though they can't help it, for they speak like practical men, and all their accounts refer to doing things. They talk of "squaring," "applying," "adding," and the like, whereas the entire
b subject is pursued for the sake of knowledge.

Absolutely.

And mustn't we also agree on a further point?

What is that?

That their accounts are for the sake of knowing what always is, not what comes into being and passes away.

That's easy to agree to, for geometry *is* knowledge of what always is.

Then it draws the soul towards truth and produces philosophic thought by directing upwards what we now wrongly direct downwards.

As far as anything possibly can.
c Then as far as *we* possibly can, we must require those in your fine city not to neglect geometry in any way, for even its by-products are not insignificant.

What are they?

The ones concerned with war that you mentioned. But we also surely know that, when it comes to better understanding any subject, there is a world of difference between someone who has grasped geometry and someone who hasn't.

Yes, by god, a world of difference.

Then shall we set this down as a second subject for the young?

Let's do so, he said.

And what about astronomy? Shall we make it the third? Or do you
d disagree?

That's fine with me, for a better awareness of the seasons, months, and years is no less appropriate for a general than for a farmer or navigator.

You amuse me: You're like someone who's afraid that the majority will think he is prescribing useless subjects. It's no easy task—indeed it's very difficult—to realize that in every soul there is an instrument that is purified and rekindled by such subjects when it has been blinded and destroyed by
e other ways of life, an instrument that it is more important to preserve than ten thousand eyes, since only with it can the truth be seen. Those who share your belief that this is so will think you're speaking incredibly well, while those who've never been aware of it will probably think you're talking nonsense, since they see no benefit worth mentioning in these subjects. So decide right now which group you're addressing. Or are your arguments
528 for neither of them but mostly for your own sake—though you won't begrudge anyone else whatever benefit he's able to get from them?

The latter: I want to speak, question, and answer mostly for my own sake.

Then let's fall back to our earlier position, for we were wrong just now about the subject that comes after geometry.

[Socrates/Glaucon]

What was our error?

After plane surfaces, we went on to revolving solids before dealing with solids by themselves. But the right thing to do is to take up the third dimension right after the second. And this, I suppose, consists of cubes and   *b*
of whatever shares in depth.

You're right, Socrates, but this subject hasn't been developed yet.

There are two reasons for that: First, because no city values it, this difficult subject is little researched. Second, the researchers need a director, for, without one, they won't discover anything. To begin with, such a director is hard to find, and, then, even if he could be found, those who currently do research in this field would be too arrogant to follow him. If an   *c*
entire city helped him to supervise it, however, and took the lead in valuing it, then he would be followed. And, if the subject was consistently and vigorously pursued, it would soon be developed. Even now, when it isn't valued and is held in contempt by the majority and is pursued by researchers who are unable to give an account of its usefulness, nevertheless, in spite of all these handicaps, the force of its charm has caused it to develop somewhat, so that it wouldn't be surprising if it were further developed even as things stand.

The subject *has* outstanding charm. But explain more clearly what you   *d*
were saying just now. The subject that deals with plane surfaces you took to be geometry.

Yes.

And at first you put astronomy after it, but later you went back on that.

In my haste to go through them all, I've only progressed more slowly. The subject dealing with the dimension of depth was next. But because it is in a ridiculous state, I passed it by and spoke of astronomy (which deals with the motion of things having depth) after geometry.   *e*

That's right.

Let's then put astronomy as the fourth subject, on the assumption that solid geometry will be available if a city takes it up.

That seems reasonable. And since you reproached me before for praising astronomy in a vulgar manner, I'll now praise it your way, for I think it's clear to everyone that astronomy compels the soul to look upward and   *529*
leads it from things here to things there.

It may be obvious to everyone except me, but that's not my view about it.

Then what *is* your view?

As it's practiced today by those who teach philosophy, it makes the soul look very much downward.

How do you mean?

In my opinion, your conception of "higher studies" is a good deal too generous, for if someone were to study something by leaning his head back and studying ornaments on a ceiling, it looks as though you'd say he's studying not with his eyes but with his understanding. Perhaps you're right,   *b*
and I'm foolish, but I can't conceive of any subject making the soul look

[Socrates/Glaucon]

upward except one concerned with that which is, and that which is is invisible. If anyone attempts to learn something about sensible things, whether by gaping upward or squinting downward, I'd claim—since there's no knowledge of such things—that he never learns anything and that, even

c   if he studies lying on his back on the ground or floating on it in the sea, his soul is looking not up but down.

You're right to reproach me, and I've been justly punished, but what did you mean when you said that astronomy must be learned in a different way from the way in which it is learned at present if it is to be a useful subject for our purposes?

It's like this: We should consider the decorations in the sky to be the most beautiful and most exact of visible things, seeing that they're embroidered on a visible surface. But we should consider their motions to

d   fall far short of the true ones—motions that are really fast or slow as measured in true numbers, that trace out true geometrical figures, that are all in relation to one another, and that are the true motions of the things carried along in them. And these, of course, must be grasped by reason and thought, not by sight. Or do you think otherwise?

Not at all.

Therefore, we should use the embroidery in the sky as a model in the study of these other things. If someone experienced in geometry were to come upon plans very carefully drawn and worked out by Daedalus or

e   some other craftsman or artist, he'd consider them to be very finely executed, but he'd think it ridiculous to examine them seriously in order to

530   find the truth in them about the equal, the double, or any other ratio.

How could it be anything other than ridiculous?

Then don't you think that a real astronomer will feel the same when he looks at the motions of the stars? He'll believe that the craftsman of the heavens arranged them and all that's in them in the finest way possible for such things. But as for the ratio of night to day, of days to a month, of a month to a year, or of the motions of the stars to any of them or to each other, don't you think he'll consider it strange to believe that they're always

b   the same and never deviate anywhere at all or to try in any sort of way to grasp the truth about them, since they're connected to body and visible?

That's my opinion anyway, now that I hear it from you.

Then if, by really taking part in astronomy, we're to make the naturally intelligent part of the soul useful instead of useless, let's study astronomy by means of problems, as we do geometry, and leave the things in the

c   sky alone.

The task you're prescribing is a lot harder than anything now attempted in astronomy.

And I suppose that, if we are to be of any benefit as lawgivers, our prescriptions for the other subjects will be of the same kind. But have you any other appropriate subject to suggest?

[Glaucon/Socrates]

Not offhand.

Well, there isn't just one form of motion but several. Perhaps a wise person could list them all, but there are two that are evident even to us.   *d*

What are they?

Besides the one we've discussed, there is also its counterpart.

What's that?

It's likely that, as the eyes fasten on astronomical motions, so the ears fasten on harmonic ones, and that the sciences of astronomy and harmonics are closely akin. This is what the Pythagoreans[4] say, Glaucon, and we agree, don't we?

We do.

Therefore, since the subject is so huge, shouldn't we ask them what they   *e* have to say about harmonic motions and whether there is anything else besides them, all the while keeping our own goal squarely in view?

What's that?

That those whom we are rearing should never try to learn anything incomplete, anything that doesn't reach the end that everything should reach—the end we mentioned just now in the case of astronomy. Or don't you know that people do something similar in harmonics? Measuring aud-   *531* ible consonances and sounds against one another, they labor in vain, just like present-day astronomers.

Yes, by the gods, and pretty ridiculous they are too. They talk about something they call a "dense interval" or quartertone[5]—putting their ears to their instruments like someone trying to overhear what the neighbors are saying. And some say that they hear a tone in between and that *it* is the shortest interval by which they must measure, while others argue that this tone sounds the same as a quarter tone. Both put ears before understanding.   *b*

You mean those excellent fellows who torment their strings, torturing them, and stretching them on pegs. I won't draw out the analogy by speaking of blows with the plectrum or the accusations or denials and boastings on the part of the strings; instead I'll cut it short by saying that these aren't the people I'm talking about. The ones I mean are the ones we just said we were going to question about harmonics, for they do the same as the astronomers. They seek out the numbers that are to be found in these audible   *c* consonances, but they do not make the ascent to problems. They don't investigate, for example, which numbers are consonant and which aren't or what the explanation is of each.

But that would be a superhuman task.

Yet it's useful in the search for the beautiful and good. But pursued for any other purpose, it's useless.

4. See Presocratics Sections pp. 18–23 and 97–99.

5. A dense interval is evidently the smallest difference in pitch recognized in ancient music.

[Socrates/Glaucon]

Probably so.

Moreover, I take it that, if inquiry into all the subjects we've mentioned brings out their association and relationship with one another and draws
d   conclusions about their kinship, it does contribute something to our goal and isn't labor in vain, but that otherwise it is in vain.

I, too, divine that this is true. But you're still talking about a very big task, Socrates.

Do you mean the prelude, or what? Or don't you know that all these subjects are merely preludes to the song itself that must also be learned? Surely you don't think that people who are clever in these matters are
e   dialecticians.

No, by god, I don't. Although I have met a few exceptions.

But did it ever seem to you that those who can neither give nor follow an account know anything at all of the things we say they must know?

My answer to that is also no.

532   Then isn't this at last, Glaucon, the song that dialectic sings? It is intelligible, but it is imitated by the power of sight. We said that sight tries at last to look at the animals themselves, the stars themselves, and, in the end, at the sun itself. In the same way, whenever someone tries through argument and apart from all sense perceptions to find the being itself of each thing and doesn't give up until he grasps the good itself with understanding itself,
b   he reaches the end of the intelligible, just as the other reached the end of the visible.

Absolutely.

And what about this journey? Don't you call it dialectic?

I do.

Then the release from bonds and the turning around from shadows to statues and the light of the fire and, then, the way up out of the cave to the sunlight and, there, the continuing inability to look at the animals, the plants, and the light of the sun, but the newly acquired ability to look at
c   divine images in water and shadows of the things that are, rather than, as before, merely at shadows of statues thrown by another source of light that is itself a shadow in relation to the sun—all this business of the crafts we've mentioned has the power to awaken the best part of the soul and lead it upward to the study of the best among the things that are, just as, before,
d   the clearest thing in the body was led to the brightest thing in the bodily and visible realm.

I accept that this is so, even though it seems very hard to accept in one way and hard not to accept in another. All the same, since we'll have to return to these things often in the future, rather than having to hear them just once now, let's assume that what you've said is so and turn to the song itself, discussing it in the same way as we did the prelude. So tell us: what is the sort of power dialectic has, what forms is it divided into, and what
e   paths does it follow? For these lead at last, it seems, towards that place

[Socrates/Glaucon]

which is a rest from the road, so to speak, and an end of journeying for the one who reaches it.

You won't be able to follow me any longer, Glaucon, even though there is   533
no lack of eagerness on my part to lead you, for you would no longer be seeing an image of what we're describing, but the truth itself. At any rate, that's how it seems to me. That it is really so is not worth insisting on any further. But that there is some such thing to be seen, *that* is something we must insist on. Isn't that so?

Of course.

And mustn't we also insist that the power of dialectic could reveal it only to someone experienced in the subjects we've described and that it cannot reveal it in any other way?

That too is worth insisting on.

At any rate, no one will dispute it when we say that there is no other   b
inquiry that systematically attempts to grasp with respect to each thing itself what the being of it is, for all the other crafts are concerned with human opinions and desires, with growing or construction, or with the care of growing or constructed things. And as for the rest, I mean geometry and the subjects that follow it, we described them as to some extent grasping what is, for we saw that, while they do dream about what is, they are unable to command a waking view of it as long as they make use of hypotheses that they leave untouched and that they cannot give any ac-   c
count of. What mechanism could possibly turn any agreement into knowledge when it begins with something unknown and puts together the conclusion and the steps in between from what is unknown?

None.

Therefore, dialectic is the only inquiry that travels this road, doing away with hypotheses and proceeding to the first principle itself, so as to be   d
secure. And when the eye of the soul is really buried in a sort of barbaric bog, dialectic gently pulls it out and leads it upwards, using the crafts we described to help it and cooperate with it in turning the soul around. From force of habit, we've often called these crafts sciences or kinds of knowledge, but they need another name, clearer than opinion, darker than knowledge. We called them thought somewhere before. But I presume that we won't dispute about a name when we have so many more important   e
matters to investigate.

Of course not.

It will therefore be enough to call the first section knowledge, the second thought, the third belief, and the fourth imaging, just as we did before. The last two together we call opinion, the other two, intellect. Opinion is con-   534
cerned with becoming, intellect with being. And as being is to becoming, so intellect is to opinion, and as intellect is to opinion, so knowledge is to belief and thought to imaging. But as for the ratios between the things these are set over and the division of either the opinable or the intelligible

section into two, let's pass them by; Glaucon, lest they involve us in arguments many times longer than the ones we've already gone through.

I agree with you about the others in any case, insofar as I'm able to
b   follow.

Then, do you call someone who is able to give an account of the being of each thing dialectical? But insofar as he's unable to give an account of something, either to himself or to another, do you deny that he has any understanding of it?

How could I do anything else?

Then the same applies to the good. Unless someone can distinguish in an account the form of the good from everything else, can survive all refuta-
c   tion, as if in a battle, striving to judge things not in accordance with opinion but in accordance with being, and can come through all this with his account still intact, you'll say that he doesn't know the good itself or any other good. And if he gets hold of some image of it, you'll say that it's through opinion, not knowledge, for he is dreaming and asleep throughout his present life, and, before he wakes up here, he will arrive in Hades and
d   go to sleep forever.

Yes, by god, I'll certainly say all of that.

Then, as for those children of yours whom you're rearing and educating in theory, if you ever reared them in fact, I don't think that you'd allow them to rule in your city or be responsible for the most important things while they are as irrational as incommensurable lines.

Certainly not.

Then you'll legislate that they are to give most attention to the education that will enable them to ask and answer questions most knowledgeably?
e   I'll legislate it along with you.

Then do you think that we've placed dialectic at the top of the other subjects like a coping stone and that no other subject can rightly be placed above it, but that our account of the subjects that a future ruler must learn
535   has come to an end?

Probably so.

Then it remains for you to deal with the distribution of these subjects, with the question of to whom we'll assign them and in what way.

That's clearly next.

Do you remember what sort of people we chose in our earlier selection of rulers?

Of course I do.

In the other respects, the same natures have to be chosen: we have to select the most stable, the most courageous, and as far as possible the most graceful. In addition, we must look not only for people who have a noble
b   and tough character but for those who have the natural qualities conducive to this education of ours.

Which ones exactly?

[Socrates/Glaucon]

They must be keen on the subjects and learn them easily, for people's souls give up much more easily in hard study than in physical training, since the pain—being peculiar to them and not shared with their body—is more their own.

That's true.

We must also look for someone who has got a good memory, is per-   *c*
sistent, and is in every way a lover of hard work. How else do you think he'd be willing to carry out both the requisite bodily labors and also complete so much study and practice?

Nobody would, unless his nature was in every way a good one.

In any case, the present error, which as we said before explains why philosophy isn't valued, is that she's taken up by people who are unworthy of her, for illegitimate students shouldn't be allowed to take her up, but only legitimate ones.

How so?

In the first place, no student should be lame in his love of hard work,   *d*
really loving one half of it, and hating the other half. This happens when someone is a lover of physical training, hunting, or any kind of bodily labor and isn't a lover of learning, listening, or inquiry, but hates the work involved in them. And someone whose love of hard work tends in the opposite direction is also lame.

That's very true.

Similarly with regard to truth, won't we say that a soul is maimed if it hates a voluntary falsehood, cannot endure to have one in itself, and is greatly angered when it exists in others, but is nonetheless content to accept   *e*
an involuntary falsehood, isn't angry when it is caught being ignorant, and bears its lack of learning easily, wallowing in it like a pig?

Absolutely.   *536*

And with regard to moderation, courage, high-mindedness, and all the other parts of virtue, it is also important to distinguish the illegitimate from the legitimate, for when either a city or an individual doesn't know how to do this, it unwittingly employs the lame and illegitimate as friends or rulers for whatever services it wants done.

That's just how it is.

So we must be careful in all these matters, for if we bring people who are sound of limb and mind to so great a subject and training, and educate them in it, even justice itself won't blame us, and we'll save the city and its   *b*
constitution. But if we bring people of a different sort, we'll do the opposite, and let loose an even greater flood of ridicule upon philosophy.

And it would be shameful to do that.

It certainly would. But I seem to have done something a bit ridiculous myself just now.

What's that?

I forgot that we were only playing, and so I spoke too vehemently. But I

c   looked upon philosophy as I spoke, and seeing her undeservedly be-
smirched, I seem to have lost my temper and said what I had to say too
earnestly, as if I were angry with those responsible for it.

That certainly wasn't my impression as I listened to you.

But it was mine as I was speaking. In any case, let's not forget that in our
earlier selection we chose older people but that that isn't permitted in this
one, for we mustn't believe Solon when he says that as someone grows older

d   he's able to learn a lot. He can do that even less well than he can run races,
for all great and numerous labors belong to the young.

Necessarily.

Therefore, calculation, geometry, and all the preliminary education required for dialectic must be offered to the future rulers in childhood, and
not in the shape of compulsory learning either.

Why's that?

e   Because no free person should learn anything like a slave. Forced bodily
labor does no harm to the body, but nothing taught by force stays in
the soul.

That's true.

Then don't use force to train the children in these subjects; use play
instead. That way you'll also see better what each of them is naturally

537 fitted for.

That seems reasonable.

Do you remember that we stated that the children were to be led into
war on horseback as observers and that, wherever it is safe to do so, they
should be brought close and taste blood, like puppies?

I remember.

In all these things—in labors, studies, and fears—the ones who always
show the greatest aptitude are to be inscribed on a list.

b   At what age?

When they're released from compulsory physical training, for during
that period, whether it's two or three years, young people are incapable of
doing anything else, since weariness and sleep are enemies of learning.
At the same time, how they fare in this physical training is itself an important test.

Of course it is.

And after that, that is to say, from the age of twenty, those who are
chosen will also receive more honors than the others. Moreover, the subjects they learned in no particular order as children they must now bring

c   together to form a unified vision of their kinship both with one another
and with the nature of that which is.

At any rate, only learning of that sort holds firm in those who receive it.

It is also the greatest test of who is naturally dialectical and who isn't, for
anyone who can achieve a unified vision is dialectical, and anyone who
can't isn't.

[Socrates/Glaucon]

I agree.

Well, then, you'll have to look out for the ones who most of all have this ability in them and who also remain steadfast in their studies, in war, and in the other activities laid down by law. And after they have reached their thirtieth year, you'll select them in turn from among those chosen earlier and assign them yet greater honors. Then you'll have to test them by means of the power of dialectic, to discover which of them can relinquish his eyes and other senses, going on with the help of truth to that which by itself is. And this is a task that requires great care.

d

What's the main reason for that?

Don't you realize what a great evil comes from dialectic as it is currently practiced?

e

What evil is that?

Those who practice it are filled with lawlessness.

They certainly are.

Do you think it's surprising that this happens to them? Aren't you sympathetic?

Why isn't it surprising? And why should I be sympathetic?

Because it's like the case of a child brought up surrounded by much wealth and many flatterers in a great and numerous family, who finds out, when he has become a man, that he isn't the child of his professed parents and that he can't discover his real ones. Can you divine what the attitude of someone like that would be to the flatterers, on the one hand, and to his supposed parents, on the other, before he knew about his parentage, and what it would be when he found out? Or would you rather hear what I divine about it?

538

I'd rather hear your views.

Well, then, I divine that during the time that he didn't know the truth, he'd honor his father, mother, and the rest of his supposed family more than he would the flatterers, that he'd pay greater attention to their needs, be less likely to treat them lawlessly in word or deed, and be more likely to obey them than the flatterers in any matters of importance.

b

Probably so.

When he became aware of the truth, however, his honor and enthusiasm would lessen for his family and increase for the flatterers, he'd obey the latter far more than before, begin to live in the way that they did, and keep company with them openly, and, unless he was very decent by nature, he'd eventually care nothing for that father of his or any of the rest of his supposed family.

c

All this would probably happen as you say, but in what way is it an image of those who take up arguments?

As follows. We hold from childhood certain convictions about just and fine things; we're brought up with them as with our parents, we obey and honor them.

[Socrates/Glaucon]

Indeed, we do.

d   There are other ways of living, however, opposite to these and full of pleasures, that flatter the soul and attract it to themselves but which don't persuade sensible people, who continue to honor and obey the convictions of their fathers.

That's right.

And then a questioner comes along and asks someone of this sort, "What is the fine?" And, when he answers what he has heard from the traditional lawgiver, the argument refutes him, and by refuting him often and in many places shakes him from his convictions, and makes him believe that the fine is no more fine than shameful, and the same with the *e*   just, the good, and the things he honored most. What do you think his attitude will be then to honoring and obeying his earlier convictions?

Of necessity he won't honor or obey them in the same way.

Then, when he no longer honors and obeys those convictions and can't discover the true ones, will he be likely to adopt any other way of life than *539*   that which flatters him?

No, he won't.

And so, I suppose, from being law-abiding he becomes lawless.

Inevitably.

Then, as I asked before, isn't it only to be expected that this is what happens to those who take up arguments in this way, and don't they therefore deserve a lot of sympathy?

Yes, and they deserve pity too.

Then, if you don't want your thirty-year-olds to be objects of such pity, you'll have to be extremely careful about how you introduce them to arguments.

That's right.

And isn't it one lasting precaution not to let them taste arguments while they're young? I don't suppose that it has escaped your notice that, when *b*   young people get their first taste of arguments, they misuse it by treating it as a kind of game of contradiction. They imitate those who've refuted them by refuting others themselves, and, like puppies, they enjoy dragging and tearing those around them with their arguments.

They're excessively fond of it.

Then, when they've refuted many and been refuted by them in turn, they forcefully and quickly fall into disbelieving what they believed before. *c*   And, as a result, they themselves and the whole of philosophy are discredited in the eyes of others.

That's very true.

But an older person won't want to take part in such madness. He'll imitate someone who is willing to engage in discussion in order to look for the truth, rather than someone who plays at contradiction for sport. He'll *d*   be more sensible himself and will bring honor rather than discredit to the philosophical way of life.

[Socrates/Glaucon]

That's right.

And when we said before that those allowed to take part in arguments should be orderly and steady by nature, not as nowadays, when even the unfit are allowed to engage in them—wasn't all that also said as a precaution?

Of course.

Then if someone continuously, strenuously, and exclusively devotes himself to participation in arguments, exercising himself in them just as he did in the bodily physical training, which is their counterpart, would that be enough?

Do you mean six years or four?   e

It doesn't matter. Make it five. And after that, you must make them go down into the cave again, and compel them to take command in matters of war and occupy the other offices suitable for young people, so that they won't be inferior to the others in experience. But in these, too, they must be tested to see whether they'll remain steadfast when they're pulled this way and that or shift their ground.   540

How much time do you allow for that?

Fifteen years. Then, at the age of fifty, those who've survived the tests and been successful both in practical matters and in the sciences must be led to the goal and compelled to lift up the radiant light of their souls to what itself provides light for everything. And once they've seen the good itself, they must each in turn put the city, its citizens, and themselves in order, using it as their model. Each of them will spend most of his time   b
with philosophy, but, when his turn comes, he must labor in politics and rule for the city's sake, not as if he were doing something fine, but rather something that has to be done. Then, having educated others like himself to take his place as guardians of the city, he will depart for the Isles of the Blessed and dwell there. And, if the Pythia agrees, the city will publicly establish memorials and sacrifices to him as a daimon, but if not, then as a   c
happy and divine human being.

Like a sculptor, Socrates, you've produced ruling men that are completely fine.

And ruling women, too, Glaucon, for you mustn't think that what I've said applies any more to men than it does to women who are born with the appropriate natures.

That's right, if indeed they are to share everything equally with the men, as we said they should.

Then, do you agree that the things we've said about the city and its   d
constitution aren't altogether wishful thinking, that it's hard for them to come about, but not impossible? And do you also agree that they can come about only in the way we indicated, namely, when one or more true philosophers come to power in a city, who despise present honors, thinking them slavish and worthless, and who prize what is right and the honors that come from it above everything, and regard justice as the most impor-   e

tant and most essential thing, serving it and increasing it as they set their city in order?

How will they do that?

541   They'll send everyone in the city who is over ten years old into the country. Then they'll take possession of the children, who are now free from the ethos of their parents, and bring them up in their own customs and laws, which are the ones we've described. This is the quickest and easiest way for the city and constitution we've discussed to be established, become happy, and bring most benefit to the people among whom it's established.

b   That's by far the quickest and easiest way. And in my opinion, Socrates, you've described well how it would come into being, if it ever did.

Then, isn't that enough about this city and the man who is like it? Surely it is clear what sort of man we'll say he has to be.

It is clear, he said. And as for your question, I think that we have reached the end of this topic.

REPUBLIC VIII

*The description of the ideal city and of the man whose character resembles it—
the philosopher-king—is now complete, and Socrates returns to the argument
interrupted at the beginning of Book V. He describes four individual character
types and the four types of constitutions that result when people who possess
them rule in a city (544d–545d). He presents these as four stages in the
increasing corruption or decline of the ideal city, and he explains why the ideal
city will decline by appeal to a mathematical myth (546a–b). However,
embedded in the myth is the serious philosophical suggestion that the ideal city
will decline because the philosopher-kings have to rely on sense perception in
putting their eugenics policy into practice (546b–c).*

*The first of the bad cities Socrates describes is a timocracy. It is ruled by
people whose souls are themselves ruled by the spirited part of their soul, in
which the desire for honor, victories, and good reputation are located (550b). It
is the second-best city to the ideal. The third-best city is an oligarchy. It is
ruled by people whose souls are ruled by their necessary appetites (544a). The
fourth-best city is a democracy. It is ruled by people whose souls are ruled by
unnecessary appetites (561a–b). The worst city of all is a tyranny. It is ruled
by someone whose soul is ruled by its lawless unnecessary appetites (571a).*

Well, then, Glaucon, we've agreed to the following: If a city is to achieve   543
the height of good government, wives must be in common, children and
all their education must be in common, their way of life, whether in peace
or war, must be in common, and their kings must be those among them
who have proved to be best, both in philosophy and in warfare.

We have agreed to that, he said.

Moreover, we also agreed that, as soon as the rulers are established, they
will lead the soldiers and settle them in the kind of dwellings we de-   *b*
scribed, which are in no way private but common to all. And we also
agreed, if you remember, what kind of possessions they will have.

I remember that we thought that none of them should acquire any of the
things that the other rulers now do but that, as athletes of war and guardians, they should receive their yearly upkeep from the other citizens as a
wage for their guardianship and look after themselves and the rest of the   *c*
city.

That's right. But since we have completed this discussion, let's recall the point at which we began the digression that brought us here, so that we can continue on the same path from where we left off.

That isn't difficult, for, much the same as now, you were talking as if you had completed the description of the city. You said that you would class both the city you described and the man who is like it as good, even *d* though, as it seems, you had a still finer city and man to tell us about. But, *544* in any case, you said that, if this city was the right one, the others were faulty. You said, if I remember, that there were four types of constitution remaining that are worth discussing, each with faults that we should observe, and we should do the same for the people who are like them. Our aim was to observe them all, agree which man is best and which worst, and then determine whether the best is happiest and the worst most wretched or whether it's otherwise. I was asking you which four constitu- *b* tions you had in mind when Polemarchus and Adeimantus interrupted. And that's when you took up the discussion that led here.

That's absolutely right.

Well, then, like a wrestler, give me the same hold again, and when I ask the same question, try to give the answer you were about to give before.

If I can.

I'd at least like to hear what four constitutions you meant.

c That won't be difficult since they're the ones for which we have names. First, there's the constitution praised by most people, namely, the Cretan or Laconian.[1] The second, which is also second in the praise it receives, is called oligarchy and is filled with a host of evils. The next in order, and antagonistic to it, is democracy. And finally there is genuine tyranny, sur- passing all of them, the fourth and last of the diseased cities. Or can you think of another type of constitution—I mean another whose form is distinct from these? Dynasties and purchased kingships and other con- *d* stitutions of that sort, which one finds no less among the barbarians than among the Greeks, are somewhere intermediate between these four.

At any event, many strange ones are indeed talked about.

And do you realize that of necessity there are as many forms of human character as there are of constitutions? Or do you think that constitutions are born "from oak or rock"[2] and not from the characters of the people who live in the cities governed by them, which tip the scales, so to speak, *e* and drag the rest along with them?

No, I don't believe they come from anywhere else.

Then, if there are five forms of city, there must also be five forms of the individual soul.

Of course.

1. I.e., the Spartan constitution.
2. See e.g. *Odyssey* xix.163.

[Socrates/Glaucon]

Now, we've already described the one that's like aristocracy, which is rightly said to be good and just.

We have.   *545*

Then mustn't we next go through the inferior ones, namely, the victory-loving and honor-loving (which corresponds to the Laconian form of constitution), followed by the oligarchic, the democratic, and the tyrannical, so that, having discovered the most unjust of all, we can oppose him to the most just? In this way, we can complete our investigation into how pure justice and pure injustice stand, with regard to the happiness or wretchedness of those who possess them, and either be persuaded by Thrasymachus to practice injustice or by the argument that is now coming to light to practice justice.   *b*

That's absolutely what we have to do.

Then, just as we began by looking for the virtues of character in a constitution, before looking for them in the individual, thinking that they'd be clearer in the former, shouldn't we first examine the honor-loving constitution? I don't know what other name there is for it, but it should be called either timocracy or timarchy. Then shouldn't we examine an individual who is related to that constitution, and, after that, oligarchy and an oligarchic person, and democracy and a democratic person? And finally, having come to a city under a tyrant and having examined it,   *c* shouldn't we look into a tyrannical soul, trying in this way to become adequate judges of the topic we proposed to ourselves?

That would be a reasonable way for us to go about observing and judging, at any rate.

Well, then, let's try to explain how timocracy emerges from aristocracy. Or is it a simple principle that the cause of change in any constitution is civil war breaking out within the ruling group itself, but that if this group—however small it is—remains of one mind, the constitution can-   *d* not be changed?

Yes, that's right.

How, then, Glaucon, will our city be changed? How will civil war arise, either between the auxiliaries and the rulers or within either group? Or do you want us to be like Homer and pray to the Muses to tell us "how civil war first broke out?"[3] And shall we say that they speak to us in tragic   *e* tones, as if they were in earnest, playing and jesting with us as if we were children?

What will they say?

Something like this. "It is hard for a city composed in this way to change,   *546* but everything that comes into being must decay. Not even a constitution such as this will last forever. It, too, must face dissolution. And this is how it will be dissolved. All plants that grow in the earth, and also all animals

---

3. An adaptation of *Iliad* xvi.112–13.

[Socrates/Glaucon]

that grow upon it, have periods of fruitfulness and barrenness of both soul
and body as often as the revolutions complete the circumferences of their
circles. These circumferences are short for the short-lived, and the opposite for their opposites.[4] Now, the people you have educated to be
leaders in your city, even though they are wise, still won't, through

b   calculation together with sense perception, hit upon the fertility and barrenness of the human species, but it will escape them, and so they will at
some time beget children when they ought not to do so. For the birth of a
divine creature, there is a cycle comprehended by a perfect number. For a
human being, it is the first number in which are found root and square
increases, comprehending three lengths and four terms, of elements that
make things like and unlike, that cause them to increase and decrease, and
that render all things mutually agreeable and rational in their relations to

c   one another. Of these elements, four and three, married with five, give two
harmonies when thrice increased. One of them is a square, so many times a
hundred. The other is of equal length one way but oblong. One of its sides
is one hundred squares of the rational diameter of five diminished by one
each or one hundred squares of the irrational diameter diminished by two
each. The other side is a hundred cubes of three. This whole geometrical
number controls better and worse births.[5] And when your rulers, through
ignorance of these births, join brides and grooms at the wrong time, the

d   children will be neither good natured nor fortunate. The older generation
will choose the best of these children but they are unworthy nevertheless,
and when they acquire their fathers' powers, they will begin, as guardians,
to neglect us Muses. First, they will have less consideration for music and
poetry than they ought, then they will neglect physical training, so that
your young people will become less well educated in music and poetry.

e   Hence, rulers chosen from among them won't be able to guard well the
testing of the golden, silver, bronze, and iron races, which are Hesiod's and
your own.[6] The intermixing of iron with silver and bronze with gold that

4. The reference is to the fertility and gestation periods of different species of
plants and animals and their (supposedly related) life spans.

5. The human geometrical number is the product of 3, 4, and 5 "thrice increased,"
multiplied by itself three times, i.e., $(3 \cdot 4 \cdot 5)^4$ or 12,960,000. This can be represented
geometrically as a square whose sides are 3600 or as an oblong or rectangle whose
sides are 4800 and 2700. The first is "so many times a hundred," viz. 36 times. The
latter is obtained as follows. The "rational diameter" of 5 is the nearest rational
number to the real diagonal of a square whose sides are 5, i.e., to $\sqrt{50}$. This number
is 7. Since the square of 7 is 49, we get the longer side of the rectangle by diminish-
ing 49 by 1 and multiplying the result by 100. This gives 4800. The "irrational
diameter" of 5 is $\sqrt{50}$. When squared, diminished by 2, and multiplied by 100 this,
too, is 4800. The short side, "a hundred cubes of three," is 2700.

6. See *Works and Days* 109–202.

results will engender lack of likeness and unharmonious inequality, and   *547*
these always breed war and hostility wherever they arise. Civil war, we
declare, is always and everywhere 'of this lineage'."[7]

And we'll declare that what the Muses say is right.

It must be, since they're Muses.

What do the Muses say after that?   *b*

Once civil war breaks out, both the iron and bronze types pull the
constitution towards money-making and the acquisition of land, houses,
gold, and silver, while both the gold and silver types—not being poor, but
by nature rich or rich in their souls—lead the constitution towards virtue
and the old order. And thus striving and struggling with one another, they
compromise on a middle way: They distribute the land and houses as
private property, enslave and hold as serfs and servants those whom they
previously guarded as free friends and providers of upkeep, and occupy
themselves with war and with guarding against those whom they've   *c*
enslaved.

I think that is the way this transformation begins.

Then, isn't this constitution a sort of midpoint between aristocracy and
oligarchy?

Absolutely.

Then, if that's its place in the transformation, how will it be managed
after the change? Isn't it obvious that it will imitate the aristocratic constitution in some respects and oligarchy in others, since it's between them,   *d*
and that it will also have some features of its own?

That's right.

The rulers will be respected; the fighting class will be prevented from
taking part in farming, manual labor, or other ways of making money; it
will eat communally and devote itself to physical training and training for
war; and in all such ways, won't the constitution be like the aristocratic
one?

Yes.

On the other hand, it will be afraid to appoint wise people as rulers, on
the grounds that they are no longer simple and earnest but mixed, and will   *e*
incline towards spirited and simpler people, who are more naturally suited
for war than peace; it will value the tricks and stratagems of war and spend
all its time making war. Aren't most of these qualities peculiar to it?   *548*

Yes.

Such people will desire money just as those in oligarchies do, passionately adoring gold and silver in secret. They will possess private treasuries
and storehouses, where they can keep it hidden, and have houses to en-

7. See e.g. *Iliad* vi.211.

[Socrates/Glaucon]

b   close them, like private nests, where they can spend lavishly either on
      women or on anyone else they wish.

      That's absolutely true.

      They'll be mean with their own money, since they value it and are not
allowed to acquire it openly, but they'll love to spend other people's because of their appetites. They'll enjoy their pleasures in secret, running
away from the law like boys from their father, for since they've neglected
the true Muse—that of discussion and philosophy—and have valued
physical training more than music and poetry, they haven't been educated
c   by persuasion but by force.

      The constitution you're discussing is certainly a mixture of good and
bad.

      Yes, it is mixed, but because of the predominance of the spirited ele-
ment, one thing alone is most manifest in it, namely, the love of victory and
the love of honor.

      Very much so.

      This, then, is the way this constitution would come into being and what
it would be like, for, after all, we're only sketching the shape of the constitution in theory, not giving an exact account of it, since even from a
d   sketch we'll be able to discern the most just and the most unjust person.
And, besides, it would be an intolerably long task to describe every constitution and every character without omitting any detail.

      That's right.

      Then who is the man that corresponds to this constitution? How does he
come to be, and what sort of man is he?

      I think, said Adeimantus, that he'd be very like Glaucon here, as far as
the love of victory is concerned.

      In that respect, I said, he might be, but, in the following ones, I don't
think his nature would be similar.

e   Which ones?

      He'd be more obstinate and less well trained in music and poetry,
though he's a lover of it, and he'd love to listen to speeches and arguments,
though he's by no means a rhetorician. He'd be harsh to his slaves rather
than merely looking down on them as an adequately educated person
549   does. He'd be gentle to free people and very obedient to rulers, being
himself a lover of ruling and a lover of honor. However, he doesn't base his
claim to rule on his ability as a speaker or anything like that, but, as he's a
lover of physical training and a lover of hunting, on his abilities and
exploits in warfare and warlike activities.

      Yes, that's the character that corresponds to this constitution.

      Wouldn't such a person despise money when he's young but love it
more and more as he grows older, because he shares in the money-loving
b   nature and isn't pure in his attitude to virtue? And isn't that because he
lacks the best of guardians?

                                            [Glaucon/Adeimantus]

What guardian is that? Adeimantus said.

Reason, I said, mixed with music and poetry, for it alone dwells within the person who possesses it as the lifelong preserver of his virtue.

Well put.

That, then, is a timocratic youth; he resembles the corresponding city.

Absolutely.   c

And he comes into being in some such way as this. He's the son of a good father who lives in a city that isn't well governed, who avoids honors, office, lawsuits, and all such meddling in other people's affairs, and who is even willing to be put at a disadvantage in order to avoid trouble.

Then how does he come to be timocratic?

When he listens, first, to his mother complaining that her husband isn't one of the rulers and that she's at a disadvantage among the other women as a result. Then she sees that he's not very concerned about money and that he doesn't fight back when he's insulted, whether in private or in   d
public in the courts, but is indifferent to everything of that sort. She also sees him concentrating his mind on his own thoughts, neither honoring nor dishonoring her overmuch. Angered by all this, she tells her son that his father is unmanly, too easy-going, and all the other things that women repeat over and over again in such cases.   e

Yes, Adeimantus said, it's like them to have many such complaints.

You know, too, I said, that the servants of men like that—the ones who are thought to be well disposed to the family—also say similar things to the son in private. When they see the father failing to prosecute someone who owes him money or has wronged him in some other way, they urge the son to take revenge on all such people when he grows up and to be more of a man than his father. The boy hears and sees the same kind of   550
things when he goes out: Those in the city who do their own work are called fools and held to be of little account, while those who meddle in other people's affairs are honored and praised. The young man hears and sees all this, but he also listens to what his father says, observes what he does from close at hand, and compares his ways of living with those of the others. So he's pulled by both. His father nourishes the rational part of his   b
soul and makes it grow; the others nourish the spirited and appetitive parts. Because he isn't a bad man by nature but keeps bad company, when he's pulled in these two ways, he settles in the middle and surrenders the rule over himself to the middle part—the victory-loving and spirited part—and becomes a proud and honor-loving man.

I certainly think that you've given a full account of how this sort of man comes to be.

Then we now have the second constitution and the second man.   c

We have.

Then shall we next talk, as Aeschylus says, of "another man ordered like another city,"[8] or shall we follow our plan and talk about the city first?

We must follow our plan.

And I suppose that the one that comes after the present constitution is oligarchy.

And what kind of constitution would you call oligarchy?

The constitution based on a property assessment, in which the rich rule, *d* and the poor man has no share in ruling.

I understand.

So mustn't we first explain how timarchy is transformed into oligarchy?

Yes.

And surely the manner of this transformation is clear even to the blind.

What is it like?

The treasure house filled with gold, which each possesses, destroys the constitution. First, they find ways of spending money for themselves, then they stretch the laws relating to this, then they and their wives disobey the laws altogether.

They would do that.

And as one person sees another doing this and emulates him, they make *e* the majority of the others like themselves.

They do.

From there they proceed further into money-making, and the more they value it, the less they value virtue. Or aren't virtue and wealth so opposed that if they were set on a scales, they'd always incline in opposite directions?

That's right.

So, when wealth and the wealthy are valued or honored in a city, virtue *551* and good people are valued less.

Clearly.

And what is valued is always practiced, and what isn't valued is neglected.

That's right.

Then, in the end, victory-loving and honor-loving men become lovers of making money, or money-lovers. And they praise and admire wealthy people and appoint them as rulers, while they dishonor poor ones.

Certainly.

Then, don't they pass a law that is characteristic of an oligarchic constitution, one that establishes a wealth qualification—higher where the constitution is more oligarchic, less where it's less so—and proclaims that *b* those whose property doesn't reach the stated amount aren't qualified to rule? And they either put this through by force of arms, or else, before it comes to that, they terrorize the people and establish their constitution that way. Isn't that so?

8. Perhaps an adaptation of *Seven Against Thebes* 451.

[Socrates/Adeimantus]

Of course it is.

Generally speaking, then, that's the way this kind of constitution is established.

Yes, but what is its character? And what are the faults that we said it contained?   c

First of all, the very thing that defines it is one, for what would happen if someone were to choose the captains of ships by their wealth, refusing to entrust the ship to a poor person even if he was a better captain?

They would make a poor voyage of it.

And isn't the same true of the rule of anything else whatsoever?

I suppose so.

Except a city? Or does it also apply to a city?

To it most of all, since it's the most difficult and most important kind of rule.

That, then, is one major fault in oligarchy.   d

Apparently.

And what about this second fault? Is it any smaller than the other?

What fault?

That of necessity it isn't one city but two—one of the poor and one of the rich—living in the same place and always plotting against one another.

By god, that's just as big a fault as the first.

And the following is hardly a fine quality either, namely, that oligarchs probably aren't able to fight a war, for they'd be compelled either to arm and use the majority, and so have more to fear from them than the enemy, or not to use them and show up as true oligarchs—few in number—on the   e battlefield. At the same time, they'd be unwilling to pay mercenaries, because of their love of money.

That certainly isn't a fine quality either.

And what about the meddling in other people's affairs that we condemned before? Under this constitution, won't the same people be farmers, money-makers, and soldiers simultaneously? And do you think it's right for things to be that way?   552

Not at all.

Now, let's see whether this constitution is the first to admit the greatest of all evils.

Which one is that?

Allowing someone to sell all his possessions and someone else to buy them and then allowing the one who has sold them to go on living in the city, while belonging to none of its parts, for he's neither a money-maker, a craftsman, a member of the cavalry, or a hoplite, but a poor person without means.

It is the first to allow that.   b

At any rate, this sort of thing is not forbidden in oligarchies. If it were,

[Adeimantus/Socrates]

some of their citizens wouldn't be excessively rich, while others are totally impoverished.

That's right.

Now, think about this. When the person who sells all his possessions was rich and spending his money, was he of any greater use to the city in the ways we've just mentioned than when he'd spent it all? Or did he merely seem to be one of the rulers of the city, while in truth he was neither ruler nor subject there, but only a squanderer of his property?

That's right. He seemed to be part of the city, but he was nothing but a
c   squanderer.

Should we say, then, that, as a drone exists in a cell and is an affliction to the hive, so this person is a drone in the house and an affliction to the city?

That's certainly right, Socrates.

Hasn't the god made all the winged drones stingless, Adeimantus, as well as some wingless ones, while other wingless ones have dangerous stings? And don't the stingless ones continue as beggars into old age,
d   while those with stings become what we call evildoers?

That's absolutely true.

Clearly, then, in any city where you see beggars, there are thieves, pick-pockets, temple-robbers, and all such evildoers hidden.

That is clear.

What about oligarchic cities? Don't you see beggars in them?

Almost everyone except the rulers is a beggar there.
e   Then mustn't we suppose that they also include many evildoers with stings, whom the rulers carefully keep in check by force?

We certainly must.

And shall we say that the presence of such people is the result of lack of education, bad rearing, and a bad constitutional arrangement?

We shall.

This, then, or something like it, is the oligarchic city. It contains all these evils and probably others in addition.

That's pretty well what it's like.

Then, let's take it that we've disposed of the constitution called
553   oligarchy—I mean the one that gets its rulers on the basis of a property assessment—and let's examine the man who is like it, both how he comes to be and what sort of man he is.

All right.

Doesn't the transformation from the timocrat we described to an oligarch occur mostly in this way?

Which way?

The timocrat's son at first emulates his father and follows in his footsteps. Then he suddenly sees him crashing against the city like a ship
b   against a reef, spilling out all his possessions, even his life. He had held a

generalship or some other high office, was brought to court by false witnesses, and was either put to death or exiled or was disenfranchised and had all his property confiscated.

That's quite likely.

The son sees all this, suffers from it, loses his property, and, fearing for his life, immediately drives from the throne in his own soul the honor-loving and spirited part that ruled there. Humbled by poverty, he turns greedily to making money, and, little by little, saving and working, he *c* amasses property. Don't you think that this person would establish his appetitive and money-making part on the throne, setting it up as a great king within himself, adorning it with golden tiaras and collars and girding it with Persian swords?

I do.

He makes the rational and spirited parts sit on the ground beneath appetite, one on either side, reducing them to slaves. He won't allow the *d* first to reason about or examine anything except how a little money can be made into great wealth. And he won't allow the second to value or admire anything but wealth and wealthy people or to have any ambition other than the acquisition of wealth or whatever might contribute to getting it.

There is no other transformation of a young man who is an honor-lover into one who is a money-lover that's as swift and sure as this.

Then isn't this an oligarchic man? *e*

Surely, he developed out of a man who resembled the constitution from which oligarchy came.

Then let's consider whether he resembles the oligarchic constitution?

All right. *554*

Doesn't he resemble it, in the first place, by attaching the greatest importance to money?

Of course.

And, further, by being a thrifty worker, who satisfies only his necessary appetites, makes no other expenditures, and enslaves his other desires as vain.

That's right.

A somewhat squalid fellow, who makes a profit from everything and hoards it—the sort the majority admires. Isn't this the man who resembles such a constitution? *b*

That's my opinion, anyway. At any rate, money is valued above everything by both the city and the man.

I don't suppose that such a man pays any attention to education.

Not in my view, for, if he did, he wouldn't have chosen a blind leader for his chorus and honored him most.[9]

---

9. Plutus, the god of wealth, is represented as being blind.

[Socrates/Adeimantus]

Good. But consider this: Won't we say that, because of his lack of education, the dronish appetites—some beggarly and others evil—exist in him,
c   but that they're forcibly held in check by his carefulness?

Certainly.

Do you know where you should look to see the evildoings of such people?

Where?

To the guardianship of orphans or something like that, where they have ample opportunity to do injustice with impunity.

True.

And doesn't this make it clear that, in those other contractual obligations, where he has a good reputation and is thought to be just, he's forcibly holding his other evil appetites in check by means of some decent
d   part of himself? He holds them in check, not by persuading them that it's better not to act on them or taming them with arguments, but by compulsion and fear, trembling for his other possessions.

That's right.

And, by god, you'll find that most of them have appetites akin to those of the drone, once they have other people's money to spend.

You certainly will.

Then someone like that wouldn't be entirely free from internal civil war and wouldn't be one but in some way two, though generally his better
e   desires are in control of his worse.

That's right.

For this reason, he'd be more respectable than many, but the true virtue of a single-minded and harmonious soul far escapes him.

I suppose so.

Further, this thrifty man is a poor individual contestant for victory in a city or for any other fine and much-honored thing, for he's not willing to
555   spend money for the sake of a fine reputation or on contests for such things. He's afraid to arouse his appetites for spending or to call on them as allies to obtain victory, so he fights like an oligarch, with only a few of his resources. Hence he's mostly defeated but remains rich.

That's right.

Then have we any further doubt that a thrifty money-maker is like an
b   oligarchic city?

None at all.

It seems, then, that we must next consider democracy, how it comes into being, and what character it has when it does, so that, knowing in turn the character of a man who resembles it, we can present him for judgment.

That would be quite consistent with what we've been doing.

Well, isn't the city changed from an oligarchy to a democracy in some such way as this, because of its insatiable desire to attain what it has set before itself as the good, namely, the need to become as rich as possible?

[Socrates/Adeimantus]

In what way?

Since those who rule in the city do so because they own a lot, I suppose   *c*
they're unwilling to enact laws to prevent young people who've had no
discipline from spending and wasting their wealth, so that by making
loans to them, secured by the young people's property, and then calling
those loans in, they themselves become even richer and more honored.

That's their favorite thing to do.

So isn't it clear by now that it is impossible for a city to honor wealth and
at the same time for its citizens to acquire moderation, but one or the other
is inevitably neglected?   *d*

That's pretty clear.

Because of this neglect and because they encourage bad discipline,
oligarchies not infrequently reduce people of no common stamp to
poverty.

That's right.

And these people sit idle in the city, I suppose, with their stings and
weapons—some in debt, some disenfranchised, some both—hating those
who've acquired their property, plotting against them and others, and
longing for a revolution.   *e*

They do.

The money-makers, on the other hand, with their eyes on the ground,
pretend not to see these people, and by lending money they disable any of
the remainder who resist, exact as interest many times the principal sum,
and so create a considerable number of drones and beggars in the city.   *556*

A considerable number indeed.

In any case, they are unwilling to quench this kind of evil as it flares up
in the city, either in the way we mentioned, by preventing people from
doing whatever they like with their own property or by another law which
would also solve the problem.

What law?

The second-best one, which compels the citizens to care about virtue by
prescribing that the majority of voluntary contracts be entered into at the
lender's own risk, for lenders would be less shameless then in their pur-   *b*
suit of money in the city and fewer of those evils we were mentioning just
now would develop.

Far fewer.

But as it is, for all these reasons, the rulers in the city treat their subjects
in the way we described. But as for themselves and their children, don't
they make their young fond of luxury, incapable of effort either mental or
physical, too soft to stand up to pleasures or pains, and idle besides?   *c*

Of course.

And don't they themselves neglect everything except making money,
caring no more for virtue than the poor do?

Yes.

[Adeimantus/Socrates]

But when rulers and subjects in this condition meet on a journey or some other common undertaking—it might be a festival, an embassy, or a campaign, or they might be shipmates or fellow soldiers—and see one another in danger, in these circumstances are the poor in any way despised by the

d rich? Or rather isn't it often the case that a poor man, lean and suntanned, stands in battle next to a rich man, reared in the shade and carrying a lot of excess flesh, and sees him panting and at a loss? And don't you think that he'd consider that it's through the cowardice of the poor that such people are rich and that one poor man would say to another when they met in

e private: "These people are at our mercy; they're good for nothing"?

I know very well that's what they would do.

Then, as a sick body needs only a slight shock from outside to become ill and is sometimes at civil war with itself even without this, so a city in the same condition needs only a small pretext—such as one side bringing in allies from an oligarchy or the other from a democracy—to fall ill and to fight with itself and is sometimes in a state of civil war even without any external influence.

557 Absolutely.

And I suppose that democracy comes about when the poor are victorious, killing some of their opponents and expelling others, and giving the rest an equal share in ruling under the constitution, and for the most part assigning people to positions of rule by lot.

Yes, that's how democracy is established, whether by force of arms or because those on the opposing side are frightened into exile.

Then how do these people live? What sort of constitution do they have?

b It's clear that a man who is like it will be democratic.

That is clear.

First of all, then, aren't they free? And isn't the city full of freedom and freedom of speech? And doesn't everyone in it have the license to do what he wants?

That's what they say, at any rate.

And where people have this license, it's clear that each of them will arrange his own life in whatever manner pleases him.

It is.

Then I suppose that it's most of all under this constitution that one finds

c people of all varieties.

Of course.

Then it looks as though this is the finest or most beautiful of the constitutions, for, like a coat embroidered with every kind of ornament, this city, embroidered with every kind of character type, would seem to be the most beautiful. And many people would probably judge it to be so, as women and children do when they see something multicolored.

They certainly would.

[Socrates/Adeimantus]

It's also a convenient place to look for a constitution.   *d*

Why's that?

Because it contains all kinds of constitutions on account of the license it gives its citizens. So it looks as though anyone who wants to put a city in order, as we were doing, should probably go to a democracy, as to a supermarket of constitutions, pick out whatever pleases him, and establish that.

He probably wouldn't be at a loss for models, at any rate.   *e*

In this city, there is no requirement to rule, even if you're capable of it, or again to be ruled if you don't want to be, or to be at war when the others are, or at peace unless you happen to want it. And there is no requirement in the least that you not serve in public office as a juror, if you happen to want to serve, even if there is a law forbidding you to do so. Isn't that a divine and pleasant life, while it lasts?   *558*

It probably is—while it lasts.

And what about the calm of some of their condemned criminals? Isn't that a sign of sophistication? Or have you never seen people who've been condemned to death or exile under such a constitution stay on at the center of things, strolling around like the ghosts of dead heroes, without anyone staring at them or giving them a thought?

Yes, I've seen it a lot.

And what about the city's tolerance? Isn't it so completely lacking in   *b*
small-mindedness that it utterly despises the things we took so seriously when we were founding our city, namely, that unless someone had transcendent natural gifts, he'd never become good unless he played the right games and followed a fine way of life from early childhood? Isn't it magnificent the way it tramples all this underfoot, by giving no thought to what someone was doing before he entered public life and by honoring him if only he tells them that he wishes the majority well?   *c*

Yes, it's altogether splendid!

Then these and others like them are the characteristics of democracy. And it would seem to be a pleasant constitution, which lacks rulers but not variety and which distributes a sort of equality to both equals and unequals alike.

We certainly know what you mean.

Consider, then, what private individual resembles it. Or should we first inquire, as we did with the city, how he comes to be?

Yes, we should.

Well, doesn't it happen like this? Wouldn't the son of that thrifty oligarch be brought up in his father's ways?   *d*

Of course.

Then he too rules his spendthrift pleasures by force—the ones that aren't money-making and are called unnecessary.

[Socrates/Adeimantus]

Clearly.

But, so as not to discuss this in the dark, do you want us first to define which desires are necessary and which aren't?

I do.

Aren't those we can't desist from and those whose satisfaction benefits us rightly called necessary, for we are by nature compelled to satisfy them both? Isn't that so?

e

Of course.

559

So we'd be right to apply the term "necessary" to them?

We would.

What about those that someone could get rid of if he practiced from youth on, those whose presence leads to no good or even to the opposite? If we said that all of them were unnecessary, would we be right?

We would.

Let's pick an example of each, so that we can grasp the patterns they exhibit.

We should do that.

Aren't the following desires necessary: the desire to eat to the point of health and well-being and the desire for bread and delicacies?

b

I suppose so.

The desire for bread is necessary on both counts; it's beneficial, and unless it's satisfied, we die.

Yes.

The desire for delicacies is also necessary to the extent that it's beneficial to well-being.

Absolutely.

What about the desire that goes beyond these and seeks other sorts of foods, that most people can get rid of, if it's restrained and educated while they're young, and that's harmful both to the body and to the reason and moderation of the soul? Would it be rightly called unnecessary?

c

It would indeed.

Then wouldn't we also say that such desires are spendthrift, while the earlier ones are money-making, because they profit our various projects?

Certainly.

And won't we say the same about the desire for sex and about other desires?

Yes.

And didn't we say that the person we just now called a drone is full of such pleasures and desires, since he is ruled by the unnecessary ones, while a thrifty oligarch is ruled by his necessary desires?

d

We certainly did.

Let's go back, then, and explain how the democratic man develops out of the oligarchic one. It seems to me as though it mostly happens as follows.

[Adeimantus/Socrates]

How?

When a young man, who is reared in the miserly and uneducated manner we described, tastes the honey of the drones and associates with wild and dangerous creatures who can provide every variety of multicolored pleasure in every sort of way, this, as you might suppose, is the beginning of his transformation from having an oligarchic constitution within him to having a democratic one.   *e*

It's inevitable that this is how it starts.

And just as the city changed when one party received help from like-minded people outside, doesn't the young man change when one party of his desires receives help from external desires that are akin to them and of the same form?

Absolutely.

And I suppose that, if any contrary help comes to the oligarchic party within him, whether from his father or from the rest of his household, who exhort and reproach him, then there's civil war and counterrevolution within him, and he battles against himself.   560

That's right.

Sometimes the democratic party yields to the oligarchic, so that some of the young man's appetites are overcome, others are expelled, a kind of shame rises in his soul, and order is restored.

That does sometimes happen.

But I suppose that, as desires are expelled, others akin to them are being nurtured unawares, and because of his father's ignorance about how to bring him up, they grow numerous and strong.   *b*

That's what tends to happen.

These desires draw him back into the same bad company and in secret intercourse breed a multitude of others.

Certainly.

And, seeing the citadel of the young man's soul empty of knowledge, fine ways of living, and words of truth (which are the best watchmen and guardians of the thoughts of those men whom the gods love), they finally occupy that citadel themselves.

They certainly do.   *c*

And in the absence of these guardians, false and boastful words and beliefs rush up and occupy this part of him.

Indeed, they do.

Won't he then return to these lotus-eaters and live with them openly? And if some help comes to the thrifty part of his soul from his household, won't these boastful words close the gates of the royal wall within him to prevent these allies from entering and refuse even to receive the words of older private individuals as ambassadors? Doing battle and controlling things themselves, won't they call reverence foolishness and moderation   *d* cowardice, abusing them and casting them out beyond the frontiers like

[Adeimantus/Socrates]

disenfranchised exiles? And won't they persuade the young man that measured and orderly expenditure is boorish and mean, and, joining with many useless desires, won't they expel it across the border?

They certainly will.

Having thus emptied and purged these from the soul of the one they've possessed and initiated in splendid rites, they proceed to return insolence, anarchy, extravagance, and shamelessness from exile in a blaze of torchlight, wreathing them in garlands and accompanying them with a vast chorus of followers. They praise the returning exiles and give them fine names, calling insolence good breeding, anarchy freedom, extravagance magnificence, and shamelessness courage. Isn't it in some such way as this that someone who is young changes, after being brought up with necessary desires, to the liberation and release of useless and unnecessary pleasures?

Yes, that's clearly the way it happens.

And I suppose that after that he spends as much money, effort, and time on unnecessary pleasures as on necessary ones. If he's lucky, and his frenzy doesn't go too far, when he grows older, and the great tumult within him has spent itself, he welcomes back some of the exiles, ceases to surrender himself completely to the newcomers, and puts his pleasures on an equal footing. And so he lives, always surrendering rule over himself to whichever desire comes along, as if it were chosen by lot. And when that is satisfied, he surrenders the rule to another, not disdaining any but satisfying them all equally.

That's right.

And he doesn't admit any word of truth into the guardhouse, for if someone tells him that some pleasures belong to fine and good desires and others to evil ones and that he must pursue and value the former and restrain and enslave the latter, he denies all this and declares that all pleasures are equal and must be valued equally.

That's just what someone in that condition would do.

And so he lives on, yielding day by day to the desire at hand. Sometimes he drinks heavily while listening to the flute; at other times, he drinks only water and is on a diet; sometimes he goes in for physical training; at other times, he's idle and neglects everything; and sometimes he even occupies himself with what he takes to be philosophy. He often engages in politics, leaping up from his seat and saying and doing whatever comes into his mind. If he happens to admire soldiers, he's carried in that direction, if money-makers, in that one. There's neither order nor necessity in his life, but he calls it pleasant, free, and blessedly happy, and he follows it for as long as he lives.

You've perfectly described the life of a man who believes in legal equality.

I also suppose that he's a complex man, full of all sorts of characters, fine

[Socrates/Adeimantus]

and multicolored, just like the democratic city, and that many men and women might envy his life, since it contains the most models of constitutions and ways of living.

That's right.

Then shall we set this man beside democracy as one who is rightly called democratic?   562

Let's do so.

The finest constitution and the finest man remain for us to discuss, namely, tyranny and a tyrannical man.

They certainly do.

Come, then, how does tyranny come into being? It's fairly clear that it evolves from democracy.

It is.

And doesn't it evolve from democracy in much the same way that democracy does from oligarchy?   b

What way is that?

The good that oligarchy puts before itself and because of which it is established is wealth, isn't it?

Yes.

And its insatiable desire for wealth and its neglect of other things for the sake of money-making is what destroyed it, isn't it?

That's true.

And isn't democracy's insatiable desire for what it defines as the good also what destroys it?

What do you think it defines as the good?

Freedom: Surely you'd hear a democratic city say that this is the finest thing it has, so that as a result it is the only city worth living in for someone   c
who is by nature free.

Yes, you often hear that.

Then, as I was about to say, doesn't the insatiable desire for freedom and the neglect of other things change this constitution and put it in need of a dictatorship?

In what way?

I suppose that, when a democratic city, athirst for freedom, happens to get bad cupbearers for its leaders, so that it gets drunk by drinking more than it should of the unmixed wine of freedom, then, unless the rulers are   d
very pliable and provide plenty of that freedom, they are punished by the city and accused of being accursed oligarchs.

Yes, that is what it does.

It insults those who obey the rulers as willing slaves and good-for-nothings and praises and honors, both in public and in private, rulers who behave like subjects and subjects who behave like rulers. And isn't it inevitable that freedom should go to all lengths in such a city?   e

Of course.

[Socrates/Adeimantus]

It makes its way into private households and in the end breeds anarchy even among the animals.

What do you mean?

I mean that a father accustoms himself to behave like a child and fear his sons, while the son behaves like a father, feeling neither shame nor fear in front of his parents, in order to be free. A resident alien or a foreign visitor

563   is made equal to a citizen, and he is their equal.

Yes, that is what happens.

It does. And so do other little things of the same sort. A teacher in such a community is afraid of his students and flatters them, while the students despise their teachers or tutors. And, in general, the young imitate their elders and compete with them in word and deed, while the old stoop to the level of the young and are full of play and pleasantry, imitating the

b   young for fear of appearing disagreeable and authoritarian.

Absolutely.

The utmost freedom for the majority is reached in such a city when bought slaves, both male and female, are no less free than those who bought them. And I almost forgot to mention the extent of the legal equality of men and women and of the freedom in the relations between them.

What about the animals? Are we, with Aeschylus, going to "say what-

c   ever it was that came to our lips just now" about them?

Certainly. I put it this way: No one who hasn't experienced it would believe how much freer domestic animals are in a democratic city than anywhere else. As the proverb says, dogs become like their mistresses; horses and donkeys are accustomed to roam freely and proudly along the streets, bumping into anyone who doesn't get out of their way; and all the

d   rest are equally full of freedom.

You're telling me what I already know. I've often experienced that sort of thing while travelling in the country.

To sum up: Do you notice how all these things together make the citizens' souls so sensitive that, if anyone even puts upon *himself* the least degree of slavery, they become angry and cannot endure it. And in the end, as you know, they take no notice of the laws, whether written or

e   unwritten, in order to avoid having any master at all.

I certainly do.

This, then, is the fine and impetuous origin from which tyranny seems to me to evolve.

It is certainly impetuous. But what comes next?

The same disease that developed in oligarchy and destroyed it also develops here, but it is more widespread and virulent because of the general permissiveness, and it eventually enslaves democracy. In fact, excessive action in one direction usually sets up a reaction in the opposite

[Socrates/Adeimantus]

direction. This happens in seasons, in plants, in bodies, and, last but not least, in constitutions.   *564*

That's to be expected.

Extreme freedom can't be expected to lead to anything but a change to extreme slavery, whether for a private individual or for a city.

No, it can't.

Then I don't suppose that tyranny evolves from any constitution other than democracy—the most severe and cruel slavery from the utmost freedom.

Yes, that's reasonable.

But I don't think that was your question. You asked what was the disease that developed in oligarchy and also in democracy, enslaving it.   *b*

That's true.

And what I had in mind as an answer was that class of idle and extravagant men, whose bravest members are leaders and the more cowardly ones followers. We compared them to stinged and stingless drones, respectively.

That's right.

Now, these two groups cause problems in any constitution, just as phlegm and bile do in the body. And it's against them that the good doctor and lawgiver of a city must take advance precautions, first, to prevent their   *c* presence and, second, to cut them out of the hive as quickly as possible, cells and all, if they should happen to be present.

Yes, by god, he must cut them out altogether.

Then let's take up the question in the following way, so that we can see what we want more clearly.

In what way?

Let's divide a democratic city into three parts in theory, this being the way that it is in fact divided. One part is this class of idlers, that grows here no less than in an oligarchy, because of the general permissiveness.   *d*

So it does.

But it is far fiercer in democracy than in the other.

How so?

In an oligarchy it is fierce because it's disdained, but since it is prevented from having a share in ruling, it doesn't get any exercise and doesn't become vigorous. In a democracy, however, with a few exceptions, this class is the dominant one. Its fiercest members do all the talking and acting, while the rest settle near the speaker's platform and buzz and refuse to tolerate the opposition of another speaker, so that, under a democratic constitution, with the few exceptions I referred to before, this class manages everything.   *e*

That's right.

Then there's a second class that always distinguishes itself from the majority of people.

Which is that?

When everybody is trying to make money, those who are naturally most organized generally become the wealthiest.

Probably so.

Then they would provide the most honey for the drones and the honey that is most easily extractable by them.

Yes, for how could anyone extract it from those who have very little?

Then I suppose that these rich people are called drone-fodder.

Something like that.

565 The people—those who work with their own hands—are the third class. They take no part in politics and have few possessions, but, when they are assembled, they are the largest and most powerful class in a democracy.

They are. But they aren't willing to assemble often unless they get a share of the honey.

And they always do get a share, though the leaders, in taking the wealth of the rich and distributing it to the people, keep the greater part for themselves.

b   Yes, that is the way the people get their share.

And I suppose that those whose wealth is taken away are compelled to defend themselves by speaking before the people and doing whatever else they can.

Of course.

And they're accused by the drones of plotting against the people and of being oligarchs, even if they have no desire for revolution at all.

That's right.

So in the end, when they see the people trying to harm them, they truly
c   do become oligarchs and embrace oligarchy's evils, whether they want to or not. But neither group does these things willingly. Rather the people act as they do because they are ignorant and are deceived by the drones, and the rich act as they do because they are driven to it by the stinging of those same drones.

Absolutely.

And then there are impeachments, judgments, and trials on both sides.

That's right.

Now, aren't the people always in the habit of setting up one man as their special champion, nurturing him and making him great?

They are.

d   And it's clear that, when a tyrant arises, this special leadership is the sole root from which he sprouts.

It is.

What is the beginning of the transformation from leader of the people to tyrant? Isn't it clear that it happens when the leader begins to behave like the man in the story told about the temple of the Lycean Zeus[10] in Arcadia?

What story is that?

That anyone who tastes the one piece of human innards that's chopped up with those of other sacrificial victims must inevitably become a wolf. Haven't you heard that story?

I have.

Then doesn't the same happen with a leader of the people who dominates a docile mob and doesn't restrain himself from spilling kindred blood? He brings someone to trial on false charges and murders him (as tyrants so often do), and, by thus blotting out a human life, his impious tongue and lips taste kindred citizen blood. He banishes some, kills others, and drops hints to the people about the cancellation of debts and the redistribution of land. And because of these things, isn't a man like that inevitably fated either to be killed by his enemies or to be transformed from a man into a wolf by becoming a tyrant?

It's completely inevitable.

He's the one who stirs up civil wars against the rich.

He is.

And if he's exiled but manages, despite his enemies, to return, doesn't he come back as a full-fledged tyrant?

Clearly.

And if these enemies are unable to expel him or to put him to death by accusing him before the city, they plot secretly to kill him.

That's usually what happens at least.

And all who've reached this stage soon discover the famous request of the tyrant, namely, that the people give him a bodyguard to keep their defender safe for them.

That's right.

And the people give it to him, I suppose, because they *are* afraid for his safety but aren't worried at all about their own.

That's right.

And when a wealthy man sees this and is charged with being an enemy of the people because of his wealth, then, as the oracle to Croesus put it, he

Flees to the banks of the many-pebbled Hermus,
Neither staying put nor being ashamed of his cowardice.

He wouldn't get a second chance of being ashamed.

That's true, for if he was caught, he'd be executed.

He most certainly would.

10. Zeus the wolf-god.

[Adeimantus/Socrates]

But, as for the leader, he doesn't lie on the ground "mighty in his might,"[11] but, having brought down many others, he stands in the city's

d   chariot, a complete tyrant rather than a leader.

What else?

Then let's describe the happiness of this man and of the city in which a mortal like him comes to be.

Certainly, let's do so.

During the first days of his reign and for some time after, won't he smile in welcome at anyone he meets, saying that he's no tyrant, making all sorts of promises both in public and in private, freeing the people from debt,

e   redistributing the land to them and to his followers, and pretending to be gracious and gentle to all?

He'd have to.

But I suppose that, when he has dealt with his exiled enemies by making peace with some and destroying others, so that all is quiet on that front, the first thing he does is to stir up a war, so that the people will continue to feel the need of a leader.

Probably so.

But also so that they'll become poor through having to pay war taxes, for

567   that way they'll have to concern themselves with their daily needs and be less likely to plot against him.

Clearly.

Besides, if he suspects some people of having thoughts of freedom and of not favoring his rule, can't he find a pretext for putting them at the mercy of the enemy in order to destroy them? And for all these reasons, isn't it necessary for a tyrant to be always stirring up war?

It is.

b   And because of this, isn't he all the more readily hated by the citizens?

Of course.

Moreover, don't the bravest of those who helped to establish his tyranny and who hold positions of power within it speak freely to each other and to him, criticizing what's happening?

They probably do.

Then the tyrant will have to do away with all of them if he intends to rule, until he's left with neither friend nor enemy of any worth.

Clearly.

He must, therefore, keep a sharp lookout for anyone who is brave, large-minded, knowledgeable, or rich. And so happy is he that he must be the

c   enemy of them all, whether he wants to be or not, and plot against them until he has purged them from the city.

That's a fine sort of purge!

---

11. See *Iliad* xvi.776.

Yes, for it's the opposite of the one that doctors perform on the body. They draw off the worst and leave the best, but he does just the opposite.

Yet I expect he'll have to do this, if he's really going to rule.

It's a blessedly happy necessity he's bound by, since it requires him either to live with the inferior majority, even though they hate him, or not to live at all.   *d*

Yet that's exactly his condition.

And won't he need a larger and more loyal bodyguard, the more his actions make the citizens hate him?

Of course.

And who will these trustworthy people be? And where will he get them from?

They'll come swarming of their own accord, if he pays them.

Drones, by the dog! All manner of foreign drones! That's what I think you're talking about.   *e*

You're right.

But what about in the city itself? Wouldn't he be willing . . .

Willing to what?

To deprive citizens of their slaves by freeing them and enlisting them in his bodyguard?

He certainly would, since they'd be likely to prove most loyal to him.

What a blessedly happy sort of fellow you make the tyrant out to be, if these are the sort of people he employs as friends and loyal followers after he's done away with the earlier ones.   568

Nonetheless, they're the sort he employs.

And these companions and new citizens admire and associate with him, while the decent people hate and avoid him.

Of course.

It isn't for nothing, then, that tragedy in general has the reputation of being wise and that Euripides is thought to be outstandingly so.

Why's that?

Because among other shrewd things he said that "tyrants are wise who associate with the wise." And by "the wise" he clearly means the sort of people that we've seen to be the tyrant's associates.   *b*

Yes. And he and the other poets eulogize tyranny as godlike and say lots of other such things about it.

Then, surely, since the tragic poets are wise, they'll forgive us and those whose constitutions resemble ours, if we don't admit them into our city, since they praise tyranny.

I suppose that the more sophisticated among them will.   *c*

And so I suppose that they go around to other cities, draw crowds, hire people with fine, big, persuasive voices, and lead their constitutions to tyranny and democracy.

[Socrates/Adeimantus]

They do indeed.

And besides this, they receive wages and honors, especially—as one might expect—from the tyrants and, in second place, from the democracies, but the higher they go on the ascending scale of constitu-

d   tions, the more their honor falls off, as if unable to keep up with them for lack of breath.

Absolutely.

But we digress. So let's return to that fine, numerous, diverse, and ever-changing bodyguard of the tyrant and explain how he'll pay for it.

Clearly, if there are sacred treasuries in the city, he'll use them for as long as they last, as well as the property of the people he has destroyed, thus requiring smaller taxes from the people.

e   What about when these give out?

Clearly, both he and his fellow revellers—his companions, male or female—will have to feed off his father's estate.

I understand. You mean that the people, who fathered the tyrant, will have to feed him and his companions.

They'll be forced to do so.

And what would you have to say about this? What if the people get angry and say, first, that it isn't just for a grown-up son to be fed by his father but, on the contrary, for the father to be fed by his son; second, that they didn't father him and establish him in power so that, when

569   he'd become strong, they'd be enslaved to their own slave and have to feed both him and his slaves, along with other assorted rabble, but because they hoped that, with him as their leader, they'd be free from the rich and the so-called fine and good people in the city; third, that they therefore order him and his companions to leave the city, just as a father might drive a son and his troublesome fellow revellers from his house?

Then, by god, the people will come to know what kind of creature they have fathered, welcomed, and made strong and that they are the weaker

b   trying to drive out the stronger.

What do you mean? Will the tyrant dare to use violence against his father or to hit him if he doesn't obey?

Yes—once he's taken away his father's weapons.

You mean that the tyrant is a parricide and a harsh nurse of old age, that his rule has become an acknowledged tyranny at last, and that—as the saying goes—by trying to avoid the frying pan of enslavement to free men, the people have fallen into the fire of having slaves as their masters,

c   and that in the place of the great but inappropriate freedom they enjoyed under democracy, they have put upon themselves the harshest and most bitter slavery to slaves.

[Adeimantus/Socrates]

That's exactly what I mean.

Well, then, aren't we justified in saying that we have adequately described how tyranny evolves from democracy and what it's like when it has come into being?

We certainly are, he said.

REPUBLIC IX

Book VIII ends with the description of tyranny. Book IX begins with a long and brilliant description of the tyrannical person himself, notable for its psychological realism and insight. When it is complete, Socrates is ready to respond to the challenge Glaucon raised in Book II.

His response consists of three complex arguments. The first appeals to the foregoing description of the five cities and the five character types. It concludes that a philosopher-king is the happiest and most just of people, a timocrat is second in virtue and happiness, an oligarch third, a democrat fourth, and a tyrant is the most unjust and most wretched of all (580a–c).

The second argument (580d–583b) appeals to the tripartition of the soul. In it Socrates argues that a philosopher's assessment of the relative pleasantness of his life and those of money-lovers and honor-lovers is more reliable than their assessments of the relative pleasantness of his life and theirs.

The third argument (583b–588a), described by Socrates as "the greatest and most decisive of the overthrows," is also the most complex. It uses the metaphysical theory developed in Books V–VII, together with the psychological theory of Book IV, to develop a complex theory of pleasure. It concludes that a philosopher's pleasures are truer and purer than those of a money-lover or honor-lover.

The book ends with a powerful image of what the soul of an unjust person is like.

571   It remains, I said, to consider the tyrannical man himself, how he evolves from a democrat, what he is like when he has come into being, and whether he is wretched or blessedly happy.

Yes, he said, he is the one who is still missing.

And do you know what else I think is still missing?

What?

I don't think we have adequately distinguished the kinds and numbers of our desires, and, if that subject isn't adequately dealt with, our entire investigation will be less clear.

b   Well, isn't now as fine a time as any to discuss the matter?

It certainly is. Consider, then, what I want to know about our desires. It's this: Some of our unnecessary pleasures and desires seem to me to be lawless. They are probably present in everyone, but they are held in check

         [Socrates/Adeimantus]

by the laws and by the better desires in alliance with reason. In a few people, they have been eliminated entirely or only a few weak ones remain, while in others they are stronger and more numerous.   *c*

What desires do you mean?

Those that are awakened in sleep, when the rest of the soul—the rational, gentle, and ruling part—slumbers. Then the beastly and savage part, full of food and drink, casts off sleep and seeks to find a way to gratify itself. You know that there is nothing it won't dare to do at such a time, free of all control by shame or reason. It doesn't shrink from trying to have sex with a mother, as it supposes, or with anyone else at all, whether man, god,   *d* or beast. It will commit any foul murder, and there is no food it refuses to eat. In a word, it omits no act of folly or shamelessness.

That's completely true.

On the other hand, I suppose that someone who is healthy and moderate with himself goes to sleep only after having done the following: First, he rouses his rational part and feasts it on fine arguments and speculations; second, he neither starves nor feasts his appetites, so that they will slumber   *e* and not disturb his best part with either their pleasure or their pain, but they'll leave it alone, pure and by itself, to look for something—it knows   572 not what—and to try to perceive it, whether it is past, present, or future; third, he soothes his spirited part in the same way, for example, by not falling asleep with his spirit still aroused after an outburst of anger. And when he has quieted these two parts and aroused the third, in which reason resides, and so takes his rest, you know that it is then that he best grasps the truth and that the visions that appear in his dreams are least lawless.   *b*

Entirely so.

However, we've been carried away from what we wanted to establish, which is this: Our dreams make it clear that there is a dangerous, wild, and lawless form of desire in everyone, even in those of us who seem to be entirely moderate or measured. See whether you think I'm talking sense and whether or not you agree with me.

I do agree.

Recall, then, what we said a democratic man is like. He was produced by being brought up from youth by a thrifty father who valued only those desires that make money and who despised the unnecessary ones that aim   *c* at frivolity and display. Isn't that right?

Yes.

And by associating with more sophisticated men, who are full of the latter desires, he starts to indulge in every kind of insolence and to adopt their form of behavior, because of his hatred of his father's thrift. But, because he has a better nature than his corrupters, he is pulled in both directions and settles down in the middle between his father's way of life and theirs. And enjoying each in moderation, as he supposes, he leads a life

[Socrates/Adeimantus]

d   that is neither slavish nor lawless and from having been oligarchic he becomes democratic.

That was and is our opinion about this type of man.

Suppose now that this man has in turn become older and that *he* has a son who is brought up in *his* father's ethos.

All right.

And further suppose that the same things that happened to his father now happen to him. First, he is led to all the kinds of lawlessness that those *e*   who are leading him call freedom. Then his father and the rest of household come to the aid of the middle desires, while the others help the other ones. Then, when those clever enchanters and tyrant-makers have no hope of keeping hold of the young man in any other way, they contrive to plant in him a powerful erotic love, like a great winged drone, to be the leader of those idle desires that spent whatever is at hand. Or do you think that 573   erotic love is anything other than an enormous drone in such people?

I don't think that it could be anything else.

And when the other desires—filled with incense, myrrh, wreaths, wine, and the other pleasures found in their company—buzz around the drone, nurturing it and making it grow as large as possible, they plant the sting of longing in it. Then this leader of the soul adopts madness as its bodyguard *b*   and becomes frenzied. If it finds any beliefs or desires in the man that are thought to be good or that still have some shame, it destroys them and throws them out, until it's purged him of moderation and filled him with imported madness.

You've perfectly described the evolution of a tyrannical man.

Is this the reason that erotic love has long been called a tyrant?

It looks that way.

c   Then doesn't a drunken man have something of a tyrannical mind?

Yes, he has.

And a man who is mad and deranged attempts to rule not just human beings, but gods as well, and expects that he will be able to succeed.

He certainly does.

Then a man becomes tyrannical in the precise sense of the term when either his nature or his way of life or both of them together make him drunk, filled with erotic desire, and mad.

Absolutely.

This, then, it seems, is how a tyrannical man comes to be. But what way does he live?

d   No doubt *you're* going to tell *me*, just as posers of riddles usually do.

I am. I think that someone in whom the tyrant of erotic love dwells and in whom it directs everything next goes in for feasts, revelries, luxuries, girlfriends, and all that sort of thing.

Necessarily.

And don't many terrible desires grow up day and night beside the tyrannical one, needing many things to satisfy them?

[Socrates/Adeimantus]

Indeed they do.

Hence any income someone like that has is soon spent.

Of course.

Then borrowing follows, and expenditure of capital.   *e*

What else?

And when everything is gone, won't the violent crowd of desires that has nested within him inevitably shout in protest? And driven by the stings of the other desires and especially by erotic love itself (which leads all of them as its bodyguard), won't he become frenzied and look to see who possesses anything that he could take, by either deceit or force?   *574*

He certainly will.

Consequently, he must acquire wealth from every source or live in great pain and suffering.

He must.

And just as the pleasures that are latecomers outdo the older ones and steal away their satisfactions, won't the man himself think that he deserves to outdo his father and mother, even though he is younger than they are—to take and spend his father's wealth when he's spent his own share?

Of course.

And if they won't give it to him, won't he first try to steal it from them by   *b* deceitful means?

Certainly.

And if that doesn't work, wouldn't he seize it by force?

I suppose so.

And if the old man and woman put up a fight, would he be careful to refrain from acting like a tyrant?

I'm not very optimistic about their fate, if they do.

But, good god, Adeimantus, do you think he'd sacrifice his long-loved and irreplaceable mother for a recently acquired girlfriend whom he can do without? Or that for the sake of a newfound and replaceable boyfriend in the bloom of youth, he'd strike his aged and irreplaceable father, his oldest   *c* friend? Or that he'd make his parents the slaves of these others, if he brought them under the same roof?

Yes, indeed he would.

It seems to be a very great blessing to produce a tyrannical son!

It certainly does!

What about when the possessions of his father and mother give out? With that great swarm of pleasures inside him, won't he first try to break   *d* into someone's house or snatch someone's coat late at night? Then won't he try to loot a temple? And in all this, the old traditional opinions that he had held from childhood about what is fine or shameful—opinions that are accounted just—are overcome by the opinions, newly released from slavery, that are now the bodyguard of erotic love and hold sway along with it. When he himself was subject to the laws and his father and had a demo-   *e*

[Adeimantus/Socrates]

cratic constitution within him, these opinions used only to be freed in sleep. Now, however, under the tyranny of erotic love, he has permanently become while awake what he used to become occasionally while asleep, and he won't hold back from any terrible murder or from any kind of food or act. But, rather, erotic love lives like a tyrant within him, in complete

575   anarchy and lawlessness as his sole ruler, and drives him, as if he were a city, to dare anything that will provide sustenance for itself and the unruly mob around it (some of whose members have come in from the outside as a result of his keeping bad company, while others have come from within, freed and let loose by his own bad habits). Isn't this the life that a tyrannical man leads?

It is indeed.

Now, if there are only a few such men in a city, and the rest of the people are moderate, this mob will leave the city in order to act as a

b   bodyguard to some other tyrant or to serve as mercenaries if there happens to be a war going on somewhere. But if they chance to live in a time of peace and quiet, they'll remain in the city and bring about lots of little evils.

What sort of evils do you mean?

They steal, break into houses, snatch purses, steal clothes, rob temples, and sell people into slavery. Sometimes, if they are good speakers, they become sycophants and bear false witness and accept bribes.

These evils *are* small, provided that there happen to be only a few such

c   people.

Yes, for small things are small by comparison to big ones. And when it comes to producing wickedness and misery in a city, all these evils together don't, as the saying goes, come within a mile of the rule of a tyrant. But when such people become numerous and conscious of their numbers, it is they—aided by the foolishness of the people—who create a tyrant. And he,

d   more than any of them, has in his soul the greatest and strongest tyrant of all.

Naturally, for he'd be the most tyrannical.

That's if the city happens to yield willingly, but if it resists him, then, just as he once chastised his mother and father, he'll now chastise his fatherland, if he can, by bringing in new friends and making his fatherland and his dear old motherland (as the Cretans call it) their slaves and keeping them that way, for this is surely the end at which such a man's desires are directed.

e   It most certainly is.

Now, in private life, before a tyrannical man attains power, isn't he this sort of person—one who associates primarily with flatterers who are ready to obey him in everything? Or if he himself happens to need anything from other people, isn't he willing to fawn on them and make every gesture of friendship, as if he were dealing with his own family? But once he gets

576   what he wants, don't they become strangers again?

[Socrates/Adeimantus]

Yes, they certainly do.

So someone with a tyrannical nature lives his whole life without being friends with anyone, always a master to one man or a slave to another and never getting a taste of either freedom or true friendship.

That's right.

Wouldn't we be right to call someone like that untrustworthy?

Of course.

And isn't he as unjust as anyone can be? If indeed what we earlier agreed   b
about justice was right.

And it certainly was right.

Then, let's sum up the worst type of man: His waking life is like the nightmare we described earlier.

That's right.

And he evolves from someone by nature most tyrannical who achieves sole rule. And the longer he remains tyrant, the more like the nightmare he becomes.

That's inevitable, said Glaucon, taking over the argument.

Well, then, I said, isn't the man who is clearly most vicious also clearly most wretched? And isn't the one who for the longest time is most of all a tyrant, most wretched for the longest time? If, that is to say, truth rather   c
than majority opinion is to settle these questions.

That much is certain, at any rate.

And isn't a tyrannical man like a city ruled by a tyrant, a democratic man like a city ruled by a democracy, and similarly with the others?

Of course.

And won't the relations between the cities with respect to virtue and happiness be the same as those between the men?

Certainly.   d

Then how does the city ruled by a tyrant compare to the city ruled by kings that we described first?

They are total opposites: one is the best, and the other the worst.

I won't ask you which is which, since it's obvious. But is your judgment the same with regard to their happiness and wretchedness? And let's not be dazzled by looking at one man—a tyrant—or at the few who surround him, but since it is essential to go into the city and study the whole of it, let's not give our opinion, till we've gone down and looked into every corner.   e

That's right, for it's clear to everyone that there is no city more wretched than one ruled by a tyrant and none more happy than one ruled by kings.

Would I be right, then, to make the same challenge about the individuals, assuming, first, that the person who is fit to judge them is someone who in   577
thought can go down into a person's character and examine it thoroughly, someone who doesn't judge from outside, the way a child does, who is dazzled by the façade that tyrants adopt for the outside world to see, but is

[Socrates/Adeimantus/Glaucon]

able to see right through that sort of thing? And, second, that he's someone—since we'd all listen to him if he were—who is competent to judge, because he has lived in the same house with a tyrant and witnessed his behavior at home and his treatment of each member of his household when he is stripped of his theatrical façade, and has also seen how he

b behaves when in danger from people? Shouldn't we ask the person who has seen all that to tell us how the tyrant compares to the others in happiness and wretchedness?

That's also right.

Then do you want us to pretend that we are among those who can give such a judgment and that we have already met tyrannical people, so that we'll have someone to answer our questions?

I certainly do.

c Come, then, and look at it this way for me: Bearing in mind the resemblance between the city and the man, look at each in turn and describe its condition.

What kinds of things do you want me to describe?

First, speaking of the city, would you say that a tyrannical city is free or enslaved?

It is as enslaved as it is possible to be.

Yet you see in it people who are masters and free.

I do see a few like that, but the whole city, so to speak, and the most decent part of it are wretched, dishonored slaves.

d Then, if man and city are alike, mustn't the same structure be in him too? And mustn't his soul be full of slavery and unfreedom, with the most decent parts enslaved and with a small part, the maddest and most vicious, as their master?

It must.

What will you say about such a soul then? Is it free or slave?

Slave, of course.

And isn't the enslaved and tyrannical city least likely to do what it wants?

Certainly.

Then a tyrannical soul—I'm talking about the whole soul—will also be least likely to do what it wants and, forcibly driven by the stings of a

e dronish gadfly, will be full of disorder and regret.

How could it be anything else?

Is a tyrannically ruled city rich or poor?

Poor.

578 Then a tyrannical soul, too, must always be poor and unsatisfiable.

That right.

What about fear? Aren't a tyrannical city and man full of it?

Absolutely.

[Socrates/Glaucon]

And do you think that you'll find more wailing, groaning, lamenting, and grieving in any other city?

Certainly not.

Then, are such things more common in anyone besides a tyrannical man, who is maddened by his desires and erotic loves?

How could they be?

It is in view of all these things, I suppose, and others like them, that you judged this to be the most wretched of cities.   *b*

And wasn't I right?

Of course you were. But what do you say about a tyrannical man, when you look at these same things?

He's by far the most wretched of all of them.

There you're no longer right.

How is that?

I don't think that this man has yet reached the extreme of wretchedness.

Then who has?

Perhaps you'll agree that this next case is even more wretched.

Which one?

The one who is tyrannical but doesn't live a private life, because some   *c*
misfortune provides him with the opportunity to become an actual tyrant.

On the basis of what was said before, I assume that what you say is true.

Yes, but in matters of this sort, it isn't enough just to assume these things; one needs to investigate carefully the two men in question by means of argument, for the investigation concerns the most important thing, namely, the good life and the bad one.

That's absolutely right.

Then consider whether I'm talking sense or not, for I think our investigation will be helped by the following examples.   *d*

What are they?

We should look at all the wealthy private citizens in our cities who have many slaves, for, like a tyrant, they rule over many, although not over so many as he does.

That's right.

And you know that they're secure and do not fear their slaves.

What have they got to be afraid of?

Nothing. And do you know why?

Yes. It's because the whole city is ready to defend each of its individual citizens.

You're right. But what if some god were to lift one of these men, his fifty   *e*
or more slaves, and his wife and children out of the city and deposit him with his slaves and other property in a deserted place, where no free person could come to his assistance? How frightened would he be that he himself and his wife and children would be killed by the slaves?

[Glaucon/Socrates]

Very frightened indeed.

579
And wouldn't he be compelled to fawn on some of his own slaves, promise them lots of things, and free them, even though he didn't want to? And wouldn't he himself have become a panderer to slaves?

He'd have to or else be killed.

What if the god were to settle many other neighbors around him, who wouldn't tolerate anyone to claim that he was the master of another and who would inflict the worst punishments on anyone they caught doing it?

b
I suppose that he'd have even worse troubles, since he'd be surrounded by nothing but vigilant enemies.

And isn't this the kind of prison in which the tyrant is held—the one whose nature is such as we have described it, filled with fears and erotic loves of all kinds? Even though his soul is really greedy for it, he's the only

c
one in the whole city who can't travel abroad or see the sights that other free people want to see. Instead, he lives like a woman, mostly confined to his own house, and envying any other citizen who happens to travel abroad and see something worthwhile.

That's entirely so.

Then, isn't this harvest of evils a measure of the difference between a tyrannical man who is badly governed on the inside—whom you judged to be most wretched just now—and one who doesn't live a private life but is compelled by some chance to be a tyrant, who tries to rule others when he can't even control himself. He's just like an exhausted body without any self-control, which, instead of living privately, is compelled to compete and

d
fight with other bodies all its life.

That's exactly what he's like, Socrates, and what you say is absolutely true.

And so, Glaucon, isn't this a completely wretched condition to be in, and doesn't the reigning tyrant have an even harder life than the one you judged to be hardest?

He certainly does.

In truth, then, and whatever some people may think, a real tyrant is really a slave, compelled to engage in the worst kind of fawning, slavery, and pandering to the worst kind of people. He's so far from satisfying his

e
desires in any way that it is clear—if one happens to know that one must study his whole soul—that he's in the greatest need of most things and truly poor. And, if indeed his state is like that of the city he rules, then he's full of fear, convulsions, and pains throughout his life. And it is like it, isn't it?

Of course it is.

580
And we'll also attribute to the man what we mentioned before, namely, that he is inevitably envious, untrustworthy, unjust, friendless, impious, host and nurse to every kind of vice, and that his ruling makes him even

[Glaucon/Socrates]

more so. And because of all these, he is extremely unfortunate and goes on to make those near him like himself.

No one with any understanding could possibly contradict you.

Come, then, and like the judge who makes the final decision, tell me who among the five—the king, the timocrat, the oligarch, the democrat, and the tyrant—is first in happiness, who second, and so on in order.   *b*

That's easy. I rank them in virtue and vice, in happiness and its opposite, in the order of their appearance, as I might judge choruses.

Shall we, then, hire a herald, or shall I myself announce that the son of Ariston has given as his verdict that the best, the most just, and the most happy is the most kingly, who rules like a king over himself, and that the   *c* worst, the most unjust, and the most wretched is the most tyrannical, who most tyrannizes himself and the city he rules.

Let it be so announced.

And shall I add to the announcement that it holds, whether these things remain hidden from every god and human being or not?

Add it.

Good. Then that is one of our proofs. And there'd be a second, if you happen to think that there is anything in this.   *d*

In what?

In the fact that the soul of each individual is divided into three parts, in just the way that a city is, for that's the reason I think that there is another proof.

What is it?

This: it seems to me that there are three pleasures corresponding to the three parts of the soul, one peculiar to each part, and similarly with desires and kinds of rule.

What do you mean?

The first, we say, is the part with which a person learns, and the second the part with which he gets angry. As for the third, we had no one special name for it, since it's multiform, so we named it after the biggest and strongest thing in it. Hence we called it the appetitive part, because of the   *e* intensity of its appetites for food, drink, sex, and all the things associated with them, but we also called it the money-loving part, because such appetites are most easily satisfied by means of money.   581

And rightly so.

Then, if we said that its pleasure and love are for profit, wouldn't that best determine its central feature for the purposes of our argument and insure that we are clear about what we mean when we speak of this part of the soul, and wouldn't we be right to call it money-loving and profit-loving?

That's how it seems to me, at least.

What about the spirited part? Don't we say that it is wholly dedicated to the pursuit of control, victory, and high repute?

[Socrates/Glaucon]

b   Certainly.

Then wouldn't it be appropriate for us to call it victory-loving and honor-loving?

It would be most appropriate.

Now, it is clear to everyone that the part with which we learn is always wholly straining to know where the truth lies and that, of the three parts, it cares least for money and reputation.

By far the least.

Then wouldn't it be appropriate for us to call it learning-loving and philosophical?

Of course.

And doesn't this part rule in some people's souls, while one of the other
c   parts—whichever it happens to be—rules in other people's?

That's right.

And isn't that the reason we say that there are three primary kinds of people: philosophic, victory-loving, and profit-loving?

That's it precisely.

And also three forms of pleasure, one assigned to each of them?

Certainly.

And do you realize that, if you chose to ask three such people in turn to tell you which of their lives is most pleasant, each would give the highest praise to his own? Won't a money-maker say that the pleasure of being
d   honored and that of learning are worthless compared to that of making a profit, if he gets no money from them?

He will.

What about an honor-lover? Doesn't he think that the pleasure of making money is vulgar and that the pleasure of learning—except insofar as it brings him honor—is smoke and nonsense?

He does.

And as for a philosopher, what do you suppose he thinks the other pleasures are worth compared to that of knowing where the truth lies and
e   always being in some such pleasant condition while learning? Won't he think that they are far behind? And won't he call them really necessary, since he'd have no need for them if they weren't necessary for life.

He will: we can be sure of that.

Then, since there's a dispute between the different forms of pleasure and between the lives themselves, not about which way of living is finer or more shameful or better or worse, but about which is more pleasant and
582   less painful, how are we to know which of them is speaking most truly?

Don't ask me.

Look at it this way: How are we to judge things if we want to judge them well? Isn't it by experience, reason, and argument? Or could anyone have better criteria than these?

[Socrates/Glaucon]

How could he?

Consider, then: Which of the three men has most experience of the pleasures we mentioned? Does a profit-lover learn what the truth itself is like or acquire more experience of the pleasure of knowing it than a philosopher does of making a profit?   *b*

There's a big difference between them. A philosopher has of necessity tasted the other pleasures since childhood, but it isn't necessary for a profit-lover to taste or experience the pleasure of learning the nature of the things that are and how sweet it is. Indeed, even if he were eager to taste it, he couldn't easily do so.

Then a philosopher is far superior to a profit-lover in his experience of both their pleasures.

He certainly is.   *c*

What about an honor-lover? Has he more experience of the pleasure of knowing than a philosopher has of the pleasure of being honored?

No, for honor comes to each of them, provided that he accomplishes his aim. A rich man is honored by many people, so is a courageous one and a wise one, but the pleasure of studying the things that are cannot be tasted by anyone except a philosopher.

Then, as far as experience goes, he is the finest judge of the three.   *d*

By far.

And he alone has gained his experience in the company of reason.

Of course.

Moreover, the instrument one must use to judge isn't the instrument of a profit-lover or an honor-lover but a philosopher.

What instrument is that?

Arguments, for didn't we say that we must judge by means of them?

Yes.

And argument is a philosopher's instrument most of all.

Of course.

Now, if wealth and profit were the best means of judging things, the praise and blame of a profit-lover would necessarily be truest.   *e*

That's right.

And if honor, victory, and courage were the best means, wouldn't it be the praise and blame of an honor-lover?

Clearly.

But since the best means are experience, reason, and argument . . .

The praise of a wisdom-lover and argument-lover is necessarily truest.

Then, of the three pleasures, the most pleasant is that of the part of the soul with which we learn, and the one in whom that part rules has the most   *583* pleasant life.

How could it be otherwise? A person with knowledge at least speaks with authority when he praises his own life.

[Socrates/Glaucon]

To what life and to what pleasure does the judge give second place?

Clearly, he gives it to those of a warrior and honor-lover, since they're closer to his own than those of a money-maker.

Then the life and pleasure of a profit-lover come last, it seems.

Of course they do.

b   These, then, are two proofs in a row, and the just person has defeated the unjust one in both. The third is dedicated in Olympic fashion to Olympian Zeus the Savior.[1] Observe then that, apart from those of a knowledgeable person, the other pleasures are neither entirely true nor pure but are like a shadow-painting, as I think I've heard some wise person say. And yet, if this were true, it would be the greatest and most decisive of the overthrows.

It certainly would. But what exactly do you mean?

I'll find out, if I ask the questions, and you answer.

Ask, then.

Tell me, don't we say that pain is the opposite of pleasure?

Certainly.

And is there such a thing as feeling neither pleasure nor pain?

There is.

Isn't it intermediate between these two, a sort of calm of the soul by comparison to them? Or don't you think of it that way?

I do.

And do you recall what sick people say when they're ill?

Which saying of theirs do you have in mind?

That nothing gives more pleasure than being healthy, but that they hadn't

d   realized that it was most pleasant until they fell ill.

I do recall that.

And haven't you also heard those who are in great pain say that nothing is more pleasant than the cessation of their suffering?

I have.

And there are many similar circumstances, I suppose, in which you find people in pain praising, not enjoyment, but the absence of pain and relief from it as most pleasant.

That may be because at such times a state of calm becomes pleasant enough to content them.

e   And when someone ceases to feel pleasure, this calm will be painful to him.

Probably so.

Then the calm we described as being intermediate between pleasure and pain will sometimes be both.

---

1. The first toast at a banquet was to the Olympian Zeus, the third to Zeus the Savior. By combining the two aspects of Zeus in a single form of address, Plato seems to be emphasizing the importance of this final proof.

[Glaucon/Socrates]

So it seems.

Now, is it possible for that which is neither to become both?

Not in my view.

Moreover, the coming to be of either the pleasant or the painful in the soul is a sort of motion, isn't it?

Yes.

And didn't what is neither painful nor pleasant come to light just now as *584*
a calm state, intermediate between them?

Yes, it did.

Then, how can it be right to think that the absence of pain is pleasure or that the absence of pleasure is pain?

There's no way it can be.

Then it isn't right. But when the calm is next to the painful it appears pleasant, and when it is next to the pleasant it appears painful. However, there is nothing sound in these appearances as far as the truth about pleasure is concerned, only some kind of magic.

That's what the argument suggests, at any rate.

Take a look at the pleasures that don't come out of pains, so that you *b*
won't suppose in their case also that it is the nature of pleasure to be the cessation of pain or of pain to be the cessation of pleasure.

Where am I to look? What pleasures do you mean?

The pleasures of smell are especially good examples to take note of, for they suddenly become very intense without being preceded by pain, and when they cease they leave no pain behind. But there are plenty of other examples as well.

That's absolutely true.

Then let no one persuade us that pure pleasure is relief from pain or that *c*
pure pain is relief from pleasure.

No, let's not.

However, most of the so-called pleasures that reach the soul through the body, as well as the most intense ones are of this form—they are some kind of relief from pain.

Yes, they are.

And aren't the pleasures and pains of anticipation, which arise from the expectation of future pleasures or pains, also of this form?

They are.

Do you know what kind of thing they are and what they most re- *d*
semble?

No, what is it?

Do you believe that there is an up, a down, and a middle in nature?

I do.

And do you think that someone who was brought from down below to the middle would have any other belief than that he was moving upward? And if he stood in the middle and saw where he had come from, would he

[Socrates/Glaucon]

believe that he was anywhere other than the upper region, since he hasn't seen the one that is truly upper?

By god, I don't see how he could think anything else.

And if he was brought back, wouldn't he suppose that he was being
e brought down? And wouldn't he be right?

Of course.

Then wouldn't all this happen to him because he is inexperienced in what is really and truly up, down, and in the middle?

Clearly.

Is it any surprise, then, if those who are inexperienced in the truth have unsound opinions about lots of other things as well, or that they are so disposed to pleasure, pain, and the intermediate state that, when they descend to the painful, they believe truly and are really in pain, but that,
585 when they ascend from the painful to the intermediate state, they firmly believe that they have reached fulfillment and pleasure? They are inexperienced in pleasure and so are deceived when they compare pain to painlessness, just as they would be if they compared black to grey without having experienced white.

No, by god, I wouldn't be surprised. In fact, I'd be very surprised if it were any other way.

b Think of it this way: Aren't hunger, thirst, and the like some sort of empty states of the body?

They are.

And aren't ignorance and lack of sense empty states of the soul?

Of course.

And wouldn't someone who partakes of nourishment or strengthens his understanding be filled?

Certainly.

Does the truer filling up fill you with that which is less or that which is more?

Clearly, it's with that which is more.

And which kinds partake more of pure being? Kinds of filling up such as filling up with bread or drink or delicacies or food in general? Or the kind of filling up that is with true belief, knowledge, understanding, and, in sum, with all of virtue? Judge it this way: That which is related to what
c is always the same, immortal, and true, is itself of that kind, and comes to be in something of that kind—this is more, don't you think, than that which is related to what is never the same and mortal, is itself of that kind, and comes to be in something of that kind?

That which is related to what is always the same is far more.

And does the being of what is always the same participate more in being than in knowledge?

Not at all.

Or more than in truth?

Not that either.

And if less in truth, then less in being also?

Necessarily.

And isn't it generally true that the kinds of filling up that are concerned with the care of the body share less in truth and being than those con-   *d*
cerned with the care of the soul?

Yes, much less.

And don't you think that the same holds of the body in comparison to the soul?

Certainly.

And isn't that which is more, and is filled with things that are more, really more filled than that which is less, and is filled with things that are less?

Of course.

Therefore, if being filled with what is appropriate to our nature is pleasure, that which is more filled with things that are more enjoys more really and truly a more true pleasure, while that which partakes of things that are   *e*
less is less truly and surely filled and partakes of a less trustworthy and less true pleasure.

That's absolutely inevitable.

Therefore, those who have no experience of reason or virtue, but are always occupied with feasts and the like, are brought down and then back   *586*
up to the middle, as it seems, and wander in this way throughout their lives, never reaching beyond this to what is truly higher up, never looking up at it or being brought up to it, and so they aren't filled with that which really is and never taste any stable or pure pleasure. Instead, they always look down at the ground like cattle, and, with their heads bent over the dinner table, they feed, fatten, and fornicate. To outdo others in these things, they kick and butt them with iron horns and hooves, killing each   *b*
other, because their desires are insatiable. For the part that they're trying to fill is like a vessel full of holes, and neither it nor the things they are trying to fill it with are among the things that are.

Socrates, you've exactly described the life of the majority of people, just like an oracle.

Then isn't it necessary for these people to live with pleasures that are mixed with pains, mere images and shadow-paintings of true pleasures? And doesn't the juxtaposition of these pleasures and pains make them appear intense, so that they give rise to mad erotic passions in the foolish,   *c*
and are fought over in just the way that Stesichorus tells us the phantom of Helen was fought over at Troy by men ignorant of the truth?

Something like that must be what happens.

And what about the spirited part? Mustn't similar things happen to someone who satisfies it? Doesn't his love of honor make him envious and his love of victory make him violent, so that he pursues the satisfaction of *d*   his anger and of his desires for honors and victories without calculation or understanding?

Such things must happen to him as well.

Then can't we confidently assert that those desires of even the money-loving and honor-loving parts that follow knowledge and argument and pursue with their help those pleasures that reason approves will attain the truest pleasures possible for them, because they follow truth, and the ones

e   that are most their own, if indeed what is best for each thing is most its own?

And indeed it is best.

Therefore, when the entire soul follows the philosophic part, and there is no civil war in it, each part of it does its own work exclusively and is just,

587   and in particular it enjoys its own pleasures, the best and truest pleasures possible for it.

Absolutely.

But when one of the other parts gains control, it won't be able to secure its own pleasure and will compel the other parts to pursue an alien and untrue pleasure.

That's right.

And aren't the parts that are most distant from philosophy and reason the ones most likely to do this sort of compelling?

They're much more likely.

And isn't whatever is most distant from reason also most distant from law and order?

Clearly.

And didn't the erotic and tyrannical desires emerge as most distant from

b   these things?

By far.

And weren't the kingly and orderly ones least distant?

Yes.

Then I suppose that a tyrant will be most distant from a pleasure that is both true and his own and that a king will be least distant.

Necessarily.

So a tyrant will live most unpleasantly, and a king most pleasantly.

Necessarily.

Do you know how much more unpleasant a tyrant's life is than a king's?

I will if you tell me.

There are, it seems, three pleasures, one genuine and two illegitimate, and a tyrant is at the extreme end of the illegitimate ones, since he flees

c   both law and reason and lives with a bodyguard of certain slavish pleasures. But it isn't easy, all the same, to say just how inferior he is to a king, except perhaps as follows. A tyrant is somehow third from an oligarch, for a democrat was between them.

[Glaucon/Socrates]

Yes.

Then, if what we said before is true, doesn't he live with an image of pleasure that is third from an oligarch's with respect to truth?[2]

He does.

Now, an oligarch, in turn, is third from a king, if we identify a king and an aristocrat.   *d*

Yes, he's third.

So a tyrant is three times three times removed from true pleasure.

Apparently so.

It seems then, on the basis of the magnitude of its number, that the image of tyrannical pleasure is a plane figure.

Exactly.

But then it's clear that, by squaring and cubing it, we'll discover how far a tyrant's pleasure is from that of a king.

It is clear to a mathematician, at any rate.

Then, turning it the other way around, if someone wants to say how far a king's pleasure is from a tyrant's, he'll find, if he completes the calculation, that a king lives seven hundred and twenty-nine times more pleas-   *e* antly than a tyrant and that a tyrant is the same number of times more wretched.

That's an amazing calculation of the difference between the pleasure and pain of the two men, the just and the unjust.   *588*

Yet it's a true one, and one appropriate to human lives, if indeed days, nights, months, and years are appropriate to them.

And of course they are appropriate.

Then, if a good and just person's life is that much more pleasant than the life of a bad and unjust person, won't its grace, fineness, and virtue be incalculably greater?

By god, it certainly will.

All right, then. Since we've reached this point in the argument, let's   *b* return to the first things we said, since they are what led us here. I think someone said at some point that injustice profits a completely unjust person who is believed to be just. Isn't that so?

It certainly is.

Now, let's discuss this with him, since we've agreed on the respective powers that injustice and justice have.

How?

By fashioning an image of the soul in words, so that the person who says this sort of thing will know what he is saying.

What sort of image?   *c*

2. Third because the Greeks always counted the first as well as the last member of a series, e.g. the day after tomorrow was the third day.

One like those creatures that legends tell us used to come into being in ancient times, such as the Chimera, Scylla, Cerberus,[3] or any of the multitude of others in which many different kinds of things are said to have grown together naturally into one.

Yes, the legends do tell us of such things.

Well, then, fashion a single kind of multicolored beast with a ring of many heads that it can grow and change at will—some from gentle, some from savage animals.

d   That's work for a clever artist. However, since words are more malleable than wax and the like, consider it done.

Then fashion one other kind, that of a lion, and another of a human being. But make the first much the largest and the other second to it in size.

That's easier—the sculpting is done.

Now join the three of them into one, so that they somehow grow together naturally.

They're joined.

Then, fashion around them the image of one of them, that of a human being so that anyone who sees only the outer covering and not what's inside

e   will think it is a single creature, a human being.

It's done.

Then, if someone maintains that injustice profits this human being and that doing just things brings no advantage, let's tell him that he is simply saying that it is beneficial for him, first, to feed the multiform beast well and make it strong, and also the lion and all that pertains to him; second,

589   to starve and weaken the human being within, so that he is dragged along wherever either of the other two leads; and, third, to leave the parts to bite and kill one another rather than accustoming them to each other and making them friendly.

Yes, that's absolutely what someone who praises injustice is saying.

But, on the other hand, wouldn't someone who maintains that just things are profitable by saying, first, that all our words and deeds should insure that the human being within this human being has the most control; sec-

b   ond, that he should take care of the many-headed beast as a farmer does his animals, feeding and domesticating the gentle heads and preventing the savage ones from growing; and, third, that he should make the lion's nature his ally, care for the community of all his parts, and bring them up in such a way that they will be friends with each other and with himself?

Yes, that's exactly what someone who praises justice is saying.

From every point of view, then, anyone who praises justice speaks truly,

---

3. The Chimera was "lion in the front, serpent in the back, and she-goat in the middle" (*Iliad* 6.181). Scylla had six heads, each with three rows of teeth, and twelve feet (see *Odyssey* 12.85 ff., 245 ff.). Cerberus was a huge dog guarding the entrance to Hades; he had three heads and a serpent's tail.

[Glaucon/Socrates]

and anyone who praises injustice speaks falsely. Whether we look at the
matter from the point of view of pleasure, good reputation, or advantage, a
praiser of justice tells the truth, while one who condemns it has nothing   c
sound to say and condemns without knowing what he is condemning.

In my opinion, at least, he knows nothing about it.

Then let's persuade him gently—for he isn't wrong of his own will—by
asking him these questions. Should we say that this is the original basis for
the conventions about what is fine and what is shameful? Fine things are
those that subordinate the beastlike parts of our nature to the human—or
better, perhaps, to the divine; shameful ones are those that enslave the   d
gentle to the savage? Will he agree or what?

He will, if he takes my advice.

In light of this argument, can it profit anyone to acquire gold unjustly if,
by doing so, he enslaves the best part of himself to the most vicious? If he
got the gold by enslaving his son or daughter to savage and evil men, it
wouldn't profit him, no matter how much gold he got. How, then, could he   e
fail to be wretched if he pitilessly enslaves the most divine part of himself
to the most godless and polluted one and accepts golden gifts in return for a
more terrible destruction than Eriphyle's when she took the necklace in   590
return for her husband's soul?[4]

A much more terrible one, Glaucon said. I'll answer for him.

And don't you think that licentiousness has long been condemned for
just these reasons, namely, that because of it, that terrible, large, and multiform beast is let loose more than it should be?

Clearly.

And aren't stubbornness and irritability condemned because they inhar-
moniously increase and stretch the lionlike and snakelike part?   b

Certainly.

And aren't luxury and softness condemned because the slackening and
loosening of this same part produce cowardice in it?

Of course.

And aren't flattery and slavishness condemned because they subject the
spirited part to the moblike beast, accustoming it from youth on to being
insulted for the sake of the money needed to satisfy the beast's insatiable
appetites, so that it becomes an ape instead of a lion?

They certainly are.   c

Why do you think that the condition of a manual worker is despised? Or
is it for any other reason than that, when the best part is naturally weak in
someone, it can't rule the beasts within him but can only serve them and
learn to flatter them?

4. Eriphyle was bribed by Polynices to persuade her husband, Amphiaraus, to take
part in an attack on Thebes. He was killed, and she was murdered by her son in
revenge. See *Odyssey* 11.326–7; Pindar, *Nemean* 9.37 ff.

[Socrates/Glaucon]

Probably so.

Therefore, to insure that someone like that is ruled by something similar to what rules the best person, we say that he ought to be the slave of that best person who has a divine ruler within himself. It isn't to harm the slave *d* that we say he must be ruled, which is what Thrasymachus thought to be true of all subjects, but because it is better for everyone to be ruled by divine reason, preferably within himself and his own, otherwise imposed from without, so that as far as possible all will be alike and friends, governed by the same thing.

Yes, that's right.

This is clearly the aim of the law, which is the ally of everyone. But it's also our aim in ruling our children, we don't allow them to be free until we establish a constitution in them, just as in a city, and—by fostering their best part with our own—equip them with a guardian and ruler similar to *591* our own to take our place. Then, and only then, we set them free.

Clearly so.

Then how can we maintain or argue, Glaucon, that injustice, licentiousness, and doing shameful things are profitable to anyone, since, even though he may acquire more money or other sort of power from them, they make him more vicious?

There's no way we can.

Or that to do injustice without being discovered and having to pay the penalty is profitable? Doesn't the one who remains undiscovered become *b* even more vicious, while the bestial part of the one who is discovered is calmed and tamed and his gentle part freed, so that his entire soul settles into its best nature, acquires moderation, justice, and reason, and attains a more valuable state than that of having a fine, strong, healthy body, since the soul itself is more valuable than the body?

That's absolutely certain.

Then won't a person of understanding direct all his efforts to attaining *c* that state of his soul? First, he'll value the studies that produce it and despise the others.

Clearly so.

Second, he won't entrust the condition and nurture of his body to the irrational pleasure of the beast within or turn his life in that direction, but neither will he make health his aim or assign first place to being strong, healthy, and beautiful, unless he happens to acquire moderation as a result. *d* Rather, it's clear that he will always cultivate the harmony of his body for the sake of the consonance in his soul.

He certainly will, if indeed he's to be truly trained in music and poetry.

Will he also keep order and consonance in his acquisition of money, with that same end in view? Or, even though he isn't dazzled by the size of the majority into accepting their idea of blessed happiness, will he increase his wealth without limit and so have unlimited evils?

[Socrates/Glaucon]

Not in my view.

Rather, he'll look to the constitution within him and guard against dis-   *e*
turbing anything in it, either by too much money or too little. And, in this
way, he'll direct both the increase and expenditure of his wealth, as far as
he can.

That's exactly what he'll do.

And he'll look to the same thing where honors are concerned. He'll
willingly share in and taste those that he believes will make him better, but   *592*
he'll avoid any public or private honor that might overthrow the established
condition of his soul.

If that's his chief concern, he won't be willing to take part in politics.

Yes, by the dog, he certainly will, at least in his own kind of city. But he
may not be willing to do so in his fatherland, unless some divine good luck
chances to be his.

I understand. You mean that he'll be willing to take part in the politics of
the city we were founding and describing, the one that exists in theory, for
I don't think it exists anywhere on earth.   *b*

But perhaps, I said, there is a model of it in heaven, for anyone who
wants to look at it and to make himself its citizen on the strength of what
he sees. It makes no difference whether it is or ever will be somewhere, for
he would take part in the practical affairs of that city and no other.

Probably so, he said.

[Glaucon/Socrates]

REPUBLIC X

(595a–621d)

The main argument of the Republic is now complete. Hence Socrates is in a position to discuss the kind of poetry about human beings that is permitted in the ideal city, a discussion that had to be postponed in Book III (392a–c). Given the importance Socrates attributes to music and poetry and physical training (424b–425a) and the importance of Homer and Hesiod in Greek education, the return to this topic is hardly an anticlimax. It is rather the moment at which the new philosophy-based education confronts the traditional education based on poetry.

Socrates' critique of poetry is extremely subtle. The question on which it focuses is whether what one needs to know in order to be a good poet qualifies one as a teacher of virtue. Socrates argues that it does not.

Having completed his account of poetry, Socrates turns to the topic of the immortality of the soul and to the previously excluded consequences of justice and injustice (609b–612e). He argues that the good consequences of justice both in this life and the next far outweigh those of injustice. This completes his argument that justice belongs in the best of the three classes of goods that Glaucon distinguished at the beginning of Book II, since it is choiceworthy both for its own sake and for its consequences.

595   Indeed, I said, our city has many features that assure me that we were entirely right in founding it as we did, and, when I say this, I'm especially thinking of poetry.

What about in particular? Glaucon said.

That we didn't admit any that is imitative. Now that we have distinguished the separate parts of the soul, it is even clearer, I think, that
b   such poetry should be altogether excluded.

What do you mean?

Between ourselves—for *you* won't denounce me to the tragic poets or any of the other imitative ones—all such poetry is likely to distort the thought of anyone who hears it, unless he has the knowledge of what it is really like, as a drug to counteract it.

What exactly do you have in mind in saying this?

I'll tell you, even though the love and respect I've had for Homer since I was a child make me hesitate to speak, for he seems to have been the first

[Socrates/Glaucon]

teacher and leader of all these fine tragedians. All the same, no one is to be
honored or valued more than the truth. So, as I say, it must be told.   *c*

That's right.

Listen then, or, rather, answer.

Ask and I will.

Could you tell me what imitation in general is? I don't entirely understand what sort of thing imitations are trying to be.

Is it likely, then, that *I'll* understand?

That wouldn't be so strange, for people with bad eyesight often see things
before those whose eyesight is keener.   *596*

That's so, but even if something occurred to me, I wouldn't be eager to
talk about it in front of you. So I'd rather that you did the looking.

Do you want us to begin our examination, then, by adopting our usual
procedure? As you know, we customarily hypothesize a single form in
connection with each collection of many things to which we apply the
same name. Or don't you understand?

I do.

Then let's now take any of the manys you like. For example, there are
many beds and tables.   *b*

Of course.

But there are only two forms of such furniture, one of the bed and one
of the table.

Yes.

And don't we also customarily say that their makers look towards the
appropriate form in making the beds or tables we use, and similarly in the
other cases? Surely no craftsman makes the form itself. How could he?

There's no way he could.

Well, then, see what you'd call *this* craftsman?

Which one?   *c*

The one who makes all the things that all the other kinds of craftsmen
severally make.

That's a clever and wonderful fellow you're talking about.

Wait a minute, and you'll have even more reason to say that, for this
same craftsman is able to make, not only all kinds of furniture, but all
plants that grow from the earth, all animals (including himself), the earth
itself, the heavens, the gods, all the things in the heavens and in Hades
beneath the earth.

He'd be amazingly clever!   *d*

You don't believe me? Tell me, do you think that there's no way any
craftsman could make all these things, or that in one way he could and in
another he couldn't? Don't you see that there is a way in which you yourself
could make all of them?

What way is that?

It isn't hard: You could do it quickly and in lots of places, especially if you were willing to carry a mirror with you, for that's the quickest way of all. With it you can quickly make the sun, the things in the heavens, the earth, yourself, the other animals, manufactured items, plants, and everything else mentioned just now.

Yes, I could make them appear, but I couldn't make the things themselves as they truly are.

Well put! You've extracted the point that's crucial to the argument. I suppose that the painter too belongs to this class of makers, doesn't he?

Of course.

But I suppose you'll say that he doesn't truly make the things he makes. Yet, in a certain way, the painter does make a bed, doesn't he?

Yes, he makes the appearance of one.

What about the carpenter? Didn't you just say that he doesn't make the form—which is our term for the being of a bed—but only *a* bed?

Yes, I did say that.

Now, if he doesn't make the being of a bed, he isn't making that which is, but something which is like that which is, but is not it. So, if someone were to say that the work of a carpenter or any other craftsman is completely that which is, wouldn't he risk saying what isn't true?

That, at least, would be the opinion of those who busy themselves with arguments of this sort.

Then let's not be surprised if the carpenter's bed, too, turns out to be a somewhat dark affair in comparison to the true one.

All right.

Then, do you want us to try to discover what an imitator is by reference to these same examples?

I do, if you do.

We get, then, these three kinds of beds. The first is in nature a bed, and I suppose we'd say that a god makes it, or does someone else make it?

No one else, I suppose.

The second is the work of a carpenter.

Yes.

And the third is the one the painter makes. Isn't that so?

It is.

Then the painter, carpenter, and god correspond to three kinds of bed?

Yes, three.

Now, the god, either because he didn't want to or because it was necessary for him not to do so, didn't make more than one bed in nature, but only one, the very one that is the being of a bed. Two or more of these have not been made by the god and never will be.

Why is that?

Because, if he made only two, then again one would come to light whose form they in turn would both possess, and *that* would be the one that is the being of a bed and not the other two.

[Socrates/Glaucon]

That's right.

The god knew this, I think, and wishing to be the real maker of the truly real bed and not just *a* maker of *a* bed, he made it to be one in nature.   *d*

Probably so.

Do you want us to call him its natural maker or something like that?

It would be right to do so, at any rate, since he is by nature the maker of this and everything else.

What about a carpenter? Isn't he the maker of a bed?

Yes.

And is a painter also a craftsman and maker of such things?

Not at all.

Then what do you think he does do to a bed?

He imitates it. He is an imitator of what the others make. That, in my view, is the most reasonable thing to call him.   *e*

All right. Then wouldn't you call someone whose product is third from the natural one an imitator?

I most certainly would.

Then this will also be true of a tragedian, if indeed he is an imitator. He is by nature third from the king and the truth, as are all other imitators.

It looks that way.

We're agreed about imitators, then. Now, tell me this about a painter. Do you think he tries in each case to imitate the thing itself in nature of the   *598* works of craftsmen?

The works of craftsmen.

As they are or as they appear? You must be clear about that.

How do you mean?

Like this. If you look at a bed from the side or the front or from anywhere else is it a different bed each time? Or does it only appear different, without being at all different? And is that also the case with other things?

That's the way it is—it appears different without being so.

Then consider this very point: What does painting do in each case? Does it imitate that which is as it is, or does it imitate that which appears as it   *b* appears? Is it an imitation of appearances or of truth?

Of appearances.

Then imitation is far removed from the truth, for it touches only a small part of each thing and a part that is itself only an image. And that, it seems, is why it can produce everything. For example, we say that a painter can paint a cobbler, a carpenter, or any other craftsman, even though he knows nothing about these crafts. Nevertheless, if he is a good painter and   *c* displays his painting of a carpenter at a distance, he can deceive children and foolish people into thinking that it is truly a carpenter.

Of course.

Then this, I suppose, is what we must bear in mind in all these cases. Hence, whenever someone tells us that he has met a person who knows all the crafts as well as all the other things that anyone else knows and that his knowledge of any subject is more exact than any of theirs is, we must

d assume that we're talking to a simple-minded fellow who has apparently encountered some sort of magician or imitator and been deceived into thinking him omniscient and that the reason he has been deceived is that he himself can't distinguish between knowledge, ignorance, and imitation.

That's absolutely true.

Then, we must consider tragedy and its leader, Homer. The reason is this: We hear some people say that poets know all crafts, all human affairs

e concerned with virtue and vice, and all about the gods as well. They say that if a good poet produces fine poetry, he must have knowledge of the things he writes about, or else he wouldn't be able to produce it at all. Hence, we have to look to see whether those who tell us this have encountered these imitators and have been so deceived by them that they don't realize that their works are at the third remove from that which is and are

599 easily produced without knowledge of the truth (since they are only images, not things that are), or whether there is something in what these people say, and good poets really do have knowledge of the things most people think they write so well about.

We certainly must look into it.

Do you think that someone who could make both the thing imitated and

b its image would allow himself to be serious about making images and put this at the forefront of his life as the best thing to do?

No, I don't.

I suppose that, if he truly had knowledge of the things he imitates, he'd be much more serious about actions than about imitations of them, would try to leave behind many fine deeds as memorials to himself, and would be more eager to be the subject of a eulogy than the author of one.

I suppose so, for these things certainly aren't equally valuable or equally beneficial either.

Then let's not demand an account of any of these professions from Homer or the other poets. Let's not ask whether any of them is a doctor

c rather than an imitator of what doctors say, or whether any poet of the old or new school has made anyone healthy as Asclepius did, or whether he has left any students of medicine behind as Asclepius did his sons. And let's not ask them about the other crafts either. Let's pass over all that. But about the most important and most beautiful things of which Homer undertakes to speak—warfare, generalship, city government, and people's education—about these it *is* fair to question him, asking him this: "Homer,

d if you're not third from the truth about virtue, the sort of craftsman of images that we defined an imitator to be, but if you're even second and capable of knowing what ways of life make people better in private or in public, then tell us which cities are better governed because of you, as Sparta is because of Lycurgus, and as many others—big and small—are because of many other men? What city gives you credit for being a good lawgiver who benefited it, as Italy and Sicily do to Charondas,[1] and as we *e* do to Solon? Who gives such credit to you?" Will he be able to name one?

I suppose not, for not even the Homeridae[2] make that claim for him.

Well, then, is any war in Homer's time remembered that was won be- *600* cause of his generalship and advice?

None.

Or, as befits a wise man, are many inventions and useful devices in the crafts or sciences attributed to Homer, as they are to Thales of Miletus and Anacharsis the Scythian?[3]

There's nothing of that kind at all.

Then, if there's nothing of a public nature, are we told that, when Homer was alive, he was a leader in the education of certain people who took pleasure in associating with him in private and that he passed on a Homeric way of life to those who came after him, just as Pythagoras did? *b* Pythagoras is particularly loved for this, and even today his followers are conspicuous for what they call the Pythagorean way of life.

Again, we're told nothing of this kind about Homer. If the stories about him are true, Socrates, his companion, Creophylus,[4] seems to have been an even more ridiculous example of education than his name suggests, for they tell us that while Homer was alive, Creophylus completely neglected him. *c*

They do tell us that. But, Glaucon, if Homer had really been able to educate people and make them better, if he'd known about these things and not merely about how to imitate them, wouldn't he have had many companions and been loved and honored by them? Protagoras of Abdera, Prodicus of Ceos, and a great many others are able to convince anyone who associates with them in private that he wouldn't be able to manage his household or city unless they themselves supervise his education, and they are so intensely loved because of this wisdom of theirs that their disciples *d* do everything but carry them around on their shoulders. So do you suppose that, if Homer had been able to benefit people and make them more virtuous, his companions would have allowed either him or Hesiod to wander around as rhapsodes? Instead, wouldn't they have clung tighter to

1. Charondas probably lived in the sixth century B.C. and gave laws to Catane and other cities in Italy and Sicily.

2. The Homeridae were the rhapsodes and poets who recited and expounded Homer throughout the Greek world.

3. Ancharsis, who lived around 600 B.C. and is often included among the Seven Sages, is credited with beginning Greek geometry and with being able to calculate the distance of ships at sea. On Thales, see Presocratics Section pp. 8–10.

4. Creophylus is said to have been an epic poet from Chios. His name comes from two words, *kreas*, meaning "meat," and *phylon*, meaning "race" or "kind." A modern equivalent, with parallel comic overtones, would be "meathead."

[Socrates/Glaucon]

them than to gold and compelled them to live with them in their homes, or,
if they failed to persuade them to do so, wouldn't they have followed them
e   wherever they went until they received sufficient education?

It seems to me, Socrates, that what you say is entirely true.

Then shall we conclude that all poetic imitators, beginning with Homer,
imitate images of virtue and all the other things they write about and have
no grasp of the truth? As we were saying just now, a painter, though he
knows nothing about cobblery, can make what seems to be a cobbler to
601   those who know as little about it as he does and who judge things by their
colors and shapes.

That's right.

And in the same way, I suppose we'll say that a poetic imitator uses
words and phrases to paint colored pictures of each of the crafts. He
himself knows nothing about them, but he imitates them in such a way
that others, as ignorant as he, who judge by words, will think he speaks
extremely well about cobblery or generalship or anything else whatever,
provided—so great is the natural charm of these things—that he speaks
with meter, rhythm, and harmony, for if you strip a poet's works of their
b   musical colorings and take them by themselves, I think you know what
they look like. You've surely seen them.

I certainly have.

Don't they resemble the faces of young boys who are neither fine nor
beautiful after the bloom of youth has left them?

Absolutely.

Now, consider this. We say that a maker of an image—an imitator—
knows nothing about that which is but only about its appearance. Isn't
c   that so?

Yes.

Then let's not leave the discussion of this point halfway, but examine it
fully.

Go ahead.

Don't we say that a painter paints reins and a mouth-bit?

Yes.

And that a cobbler and a metal-worker makes them?

Of course.

Then, does a painter know how the reins and mouth-bit have to be? Or is
it the case that even a cobbler and metal-worker who make them don't
know this, but only someone who knows how to use them, namely, a
horseman?

That's absolutely true.

And won't we say that the same holds for everything?

What?

d   That for each thing there are these three crafts, one that uses it, one that
makes it, and one that imitates it?

Yes.

Then aren't the virtue or excellence, the beauty and correctness of each manufactured item, living creature, and action related to nothing but the use for which each is made or naturally adapted?

They are.

It's wholly necessary, therefore, that a user of each thing has most experience of it and that he tell a maker which of his products performs well or badly in actual use. A flute-player, for example, tells a flute-maker about the flutes that respond well in actual playing and prescribes what kind of flutes he is to make, while the maker follows his instructions.

e

Of course.

Then doesn't the one who knows give instructions about good and bad flutes, and doesn't the other rely on him in making them?

Yes.

Therefore, a maker—through associating with and having to listen to the one who knows—has right opinion about whether something he makes is fine or bad, but the one who knows is the user.

602

That's right.

Does an imitator have knowledge of whether the things he makes are fine or right through having made use of them, or does he have right opinion about them through having to consort with the one who knows and being told how he is to paint them?

Neither.

Therefore an imitator has neither knowledge nor right opinion about whether the things he makes are fine or bad.

Apparently not.

Then a poetic imitator is an accomplished fellow when it comes to wisdom about the subjects of his poetry!

Hardly.

Nonetheless, he'll go on imitating, even though he doesn't know the good or bad qualities of anything, but what he'll imitate, it seems, is what appears fine or beautiful to the majority of people who know nothing.

b

Of course.

It seems, then, that we're fairly well agreed that an imitator has no worthwhile knowledge of the things he imitates, that imitation is a kind of game and not something to be taken seriously, and that all the tragic poets, whether they write in iambics or hexameters, are as imitative as they could possibly be.

That's right.

Then is this kind of imitation concerned with something that is third from the truth, or what?

c

Yes, it is.

And on which of a person's parts does it exert its power?

What do you mean?

This: Something looked at from close at hand doesn't seem to be the same size as it does when it is looked at from a distance.

No, it doesn't.

And something looks crooked when seen in water and straight when seen out of it, while something else looks both concave and convex because our eyes are deceived by its colors, and every other similar sort of confusion is clearly present in our soul. And it is because they exploit this

d   weakness in our nature that *trompe l'oeil* painting, conjuring, and other forms of trickery have powers that are little short of magical.

That's true.

And don't measuring, counting, and weighing give us most welcome assistance in these cases, so that we aren't ruled by something's looking bigger, smaller, more numerous, or heavier, but by calculation, measurement, or weighing?

Of course.

And calculating, measuring, and weighing are the work of the rational

e   part of the soul.

They are.

But when this part has measured and has indicated that some things are larger or smaller or the same size as others, the opposite appears to it at the same time.

Yes.

And didn't we say that it is impossible for the same thing to believe opposites about the same thing at the same time?

We did, and we were right to say it.

Then the part of the soul that forms a belief contrary to the measure-

603   ments couldn't be the same as the part that believes in accord with them.

No, it couldn't.

Now, the part that puts its trust in measurement and calculation is the best part of the soul.

Of course.

Therefore, the part that opposes it is one of the inferior parts in us.

Necessarily.

This, then, is what I wanted to get agreement about when I said that painting and imitation as a whole produce work that is far from the truth, namely, that imitation really consorts with a part of us that is far from reason, and the result of their being friends and companions is neither

b   sound nor true.

That's absolutely right.

Then imitation is an inferior thing that consorts with another inferior thing to produce an inferior offspring.

So it seems.

Does this apply only to the imitations we see, or does it also apply to the ones we hear—the ones we call poetry?

[Glaucon/Socrates]

It probably applies to poetry as well.

However, we mustn't rely solely on a mere probability based on the analogy with painting; instead, we must go directly to the part of our thought with which poetic imitations consort and see whether it is inferior or something to be taken seriously.

Yes, we must.

Then let's set about it as follows. We say that imitative poetry imitates human beings acting voluntarily or under compulsion, who believe that, as a result of these actions, they are doing either well or badly and who experience either pleasure or pain in all this. Does it imitate anything apart from this?

Nothing.

Then is a person of one mind in all these circumstances? Or, just as he was at war with himself in matters of sight and held opposite beliefs about the same thing at the same time, does he also fight with himself and engage in civil war with himself in matters of action? But there is really no need for us to reach agreement on this question now, for I remember that we already came to an adequate conclusion about all these things in our earlier arguments, when we said that our soul is full of a myriad of such oppositions at the same time.

And rightly so.

It *was* right, but I think we omitted some things then that we must now discuss.

What are they?

We also mentioned somewhere before that, if a decent man happens to lose his son or some other prized possession, he'll bear it more easily than the other sorts of people.

Certainly.

But now let's consider this. Will he not grieve at all, or, if that's impossible, will he be somehow measured in his response to pain?

The latter is closer to the truth.

Now, tell me this about him: Will he fight his pain and put up more resistance to it when his equals can see him or when he's alone by himself in solitude?

He'll fight it far more when he's being seen.

But when he's alone I suppose he'll venture to say and do lots of things that he'd be ashamed to be heard saying or seen doing.

That's right.

And isn't it reason and law that tells him to resist his pain, while his experience of it tells him to give in?

True.

And when there are two opposite inclinations in a person in relation to the same thing at the same time, we say that he must also have two parts.

Of course.

[Glaucon/Socrates]

Isn't one part ready to obey the law wherever it leads him?

How so?

The law says, doesn't it, that it is best to keep as quiet as possible in misfortunes and not get excited about them? First, it isn't clear whether such things will turn out to be good or bad in the end; second, it doesn't make the future any better to take them hard; third, human affairs aren't
c   worth taking very seriously; and finally, grief prevents the very thing we most need in such circumstances from coming into play as quickly as possible.

What are you referring to?

Deliberation. We must accept what has happened as we would the fall of the dice, and then arrange our affairs in whatever way reason determines to be best. We mustn't hug the hurt part and spend our time weeping and wailing like children when they trip. Instead, we should always accustom our souls to turn as quickly as possible to healing the disease and putting
d   the disaster right, replacing lamentation with cure.

That would be the best way to deal with misfortune, at any rate.

Accordingly, we say that it is the best part of us that is willing to follow this rational calculation.

Clearly.

Then won't we also say that the part that leads us to dwell on our misfortunes and to lamentation, and that can never get enough of these things, is irrational, idle, and a friend of cowardice?

We certainly will.

Now, this excitable character admits of many multicolored imitations.
e   But a rational and quiet character, which always remains pretty well the same, is neither easy to imitate nor easy to understand when imitated, especially not by a crowd consisting of all sorts of people gathered together at a theater festival, for the experience being imitated is alien to them.
605   Absolutely.

Clearly, then, an imitative poet isn't by nature related to the part of the soul that rules in such a character, and, if he's to attain a good reputation with the majority of people, his cleverness isn't directed to pleasing it. Instead, he's related to the excitable and multicolored character, since it is easy to imitate.

Clearly.

Therefore, we'd be right to take him and put him beside a painter as his counterpart. Like a painter, he produces work that is inferior with respect to truth and that appeals to a part of the soul that is similarly inferior
b   rather than to the best part. So we were right not to admit him into a city that is to be well-governed, for he arouses, nourishes, and strengthens this part of the soul and so destroys the rational one, in just the way that someone destroys the better sort of citizens when he strengthens the vicious ones and surrenders the city to them. Similarly, we'll say that an

[Socrates/Glaucon]

imitative poet puts a bad constitution in the soul of each individual by making images that are far removed from the truth and by gratifying the irrational part, which cannot distinguish the large and the small but believes that the same things are large at one time and small at another.   c

That's right.

However, we haven't yet brought the most serious charge against imitation, namely, that with a few rare exceptions it is able to corrupt even decent people, for that's surely an altogether terrible thing.

It certainly is, if indeed it can do that.

Listen, then, and consider whether it can or not. When even the best of us hear Homer or some other tragedian imitating one of the heroes sorrowing and making a long lamenting speech or singing and beating his breast, you know that we enjoy it, give ourselves up to following it, sympathize   d
with the hero, take his sufferings seriously, and praise as a good poet the one who affects us most in this way.

Of course we do.

But when one of us suffers a private loss, you realize that the opposite happens. We pride ourselves if we are able to keep quiet and master our grief, for we think that this is the manly thing to do and that the behavior we praised before is womanish.   e

I do realize that.

Then are we right to praise it? Is it right to look at someone behaving in a way that we would consider unworthy and shameful and to enjoy and praise it rather than being disgusted by it?

No, by god, that doesn't seem reasonable.

No, at least not if you look at it in the following way.   606

How?

If you reflect, first, that the part of the soul that is forcibly controlled in our private misfortunes and that hungers for the satisfaction of weeping and wailing, because it desires these things by nature, is the very part that receives satisfaction and enjoyment from poets, and, second, that the part of ourselves that is best by nature, since it hasn't been adequately educated either by reason or habit, relaxes its guard over the lamenting part when it is watching the sufferings of somebody else. The reason it does so is this: It thinks that there is no shame involved for it in praising and pitying another   b
man who, in spite of his claim to goodness, grieves excessively. Indeed, it thinks that there is a definite gain involved in doing so, namely, pleasure. And it wouldn't want to be deprived of that by despising the whole poem. I suppose that only a few are able to figure out that enjoyment of other people's sufferings is necessarily transferred to our own and that the pitying part, if it is nourished and strengthened on the sufferings of others, won't be easily held in check when we ourselves suffer.

That's very true.   c

And doesn't the same argument apply to what provokes laughter? If there are any jokes that you yourself would be ashamed to tell but that you very much enjoy hearing and don't detest as something evil in comic plays or in private, aren't you doing the same thing as in the case of what provokes pity? The part of you that wanted to tell the jokes and that was held back by your reason, for fear of being thought a buffoon, you then release, not realizing that, by making it strong in this way, you will be led into becoming a figure of fun where your own affairs are concerned.

Yes, indeed.

d   And in the case of sex, anger, and all the desires, pleasures, and pains that we say accompany all our actions, poetic imitation has the very same effect on us. It nurtures and waters them and establishes them as rulers in us when they ought to wither and be ruled, for that way we'll become better and happier rather than worse and more wretched.

I can't disagree with you.

e   And so, Glaucon, when you happen to meet those who praise Homer and say that he's the poet who educated Greece, that it's worth taking up his works in order to learn how to manage and educate people, and that one should arrange one's whole life in accordance with his teachings, you should welcome these people and treat them as friends, since they're as *607*   good as they're capable of being, and you should agree that Homer is the most poetic of the tragedians and the first among them. But you should also know that hymns to the gods and eulogies to good people are the only poetry we can admit into our city. If you admit the pleasure-giving Muse, whether in lyric or epic poetry, pleasure and pain will be kings in your city instead of law or the thing that everyone has always believed to be best, namely, reason.

That's absolutely true.

Then let this be our defense—now that we've returned to the topic of *b*   poetry—that, in view of its nature, we had reason to banish it from the city earlier, for our argument compelled us to do so. But in case we are charged with a certain harshness and lack of sophistication, let's also tell poetry that there is an ancient quarrel between it and philosophy, which is evidenced by such expressions as "the dog yelping and shrieking at its master," "great in the empty eloquence of fools," "the mob of wise men that has *c*   mastered Zeus," and "the subtle thinkers, beggars all." Nonetheless, if the poetry that aims at pleasure and imitation has any argument to bring forward that proves it ought to have a place in a well-governed city, we at least would be glad to admit it, for we are well aware of the charm it exercises. But, be that as it may, to betray what one believes to be the truth is impious. What about you, Glaucon, don't you feel the charm of the *d*   pleasure-giving Muse, especially when you study her through the eyes of Homer?

Very much so.

Therefore, isn't it just that such poetry should return from exile when it has successfully defended itself, whether in lyric or any other meter?

[Socrates/Glaucon]

Certainly.

Then we'll allow its defenders, who aren't poets themselves but lovers of poetry, to speak in prose on its behalf and to show that it not only gives pleasure but is beneficial both to constitutions and to human life. Indeed, we'll listen to them graciously, for we'd certainly profit if poetry were shown to be not only pleasant but also beneficial.

e

How could we fail to profit?

However, if such a defense isn't made, we'll behave like people who have fallen in love with someone but who force themselves to stay away from him, because they realize that their passion isn't beneficial. In the same way, because the love of this sort of poetry has been implanted in us by the upbringing we have received under our fine constitutions, we are well disposed to any proof that it is the best and truest thing. But if it isn't able to produce such a defense, then, whenever we listen to it, we'll repeat the argument we have just now put forward like an incantation so as to preserve ourselves from slipping back into that childish passion for poetry which the majority of people have. And we'll go on chanting that such poetry is not to be taken seriously or treated as a serious undertaking with some kind of hold on the truth, but that anyone who is anxious about the constitution within him must be careful when he hears it and must continue to believe what we have said about it.

608

b

I completely agree.

Yes, for the struggle to be good rather than bad is important, Glaucon, much more important than people think. Therefore, we mustn't be tempted by honor, money, rule, or even poetry into neglecting justice and the rest of virtue.

After what we've said, I agree with you, and so, I think, would anyone else.

And yet we haven't discussed the greatest rewards and prizes that have been proposed for virtue.

c

They must be inconceivably great, if they're greater than those you've already mentioned.

Could anything really great come to pass in a short time? And isn't the time from childhood to old age short when compared to the whole of time?

It's a mere nothing.

Well, do you think that an immortal thing should be seriously concerned with that short period rather than with the whole of time?

d

I suppose not, but what exactly do you mean by this?

Haven't you realized that our soul is immortal and never destroyed?

He looked at me with wonder and said: No, by god, I haven't. Are you really in a position to assert that?

I'd be wrong not to, I said, and so would you, for it isn't difficult.

It is for me, so I'd be glad to hear from you what's not difficult about it.

Listen, then.

Just speak, and I will.

Do you talk about good and bad?

I do.

e   And do you think about them the same way I do?

What way is that?

The bad is what destroys and corrupts, and the good is what preserves and benefits.

I do.

And do you say that there is a good and a bad for everything? For example, ophthalmia for the eyes, sickness for the whole body, blight for
609 grain, rot for wood, rust for iron or bronze. In other words, is there, as I say, a natural badness and sickness for pretty well everything?

There is.

And when one of these attaches itself to something, doesn't it make the thing in question bad, and in the end, doesn't it disintegrate it and destroy it wholly?

Of course.

Therefore, the evil that is natural to each thing and the bad that is peculiar to it destroy it. However, if they don't destroy it, nothing else will, for the good would never destroy anything, nor would anything neither
b   good nor bad.

How could they?

Then, if we discover something that has an evil that makes it bad but isn't able to disintegrate and destroy it, can't we infer that it is naturally incapable of being destroyed?

Probably so.

Well, what about the soul? Isn't there something that makes it bad?

Certainly, all the things we were mentioning: Injustice, licentiousness,
c   cowardice, and lack of learning.

Does any of these disintegrate and destroy the soul? Keep your wits about you, and let's not be deceived into thinking that, when an unjust and foolish person is caught, he has been destroyed by injustice, which is evil in a soul. Let's think about it this way instead: Just as the body is worn out, destroyed, and brought to the point where it is a body no longer by disease, which is evil in a body, so all the things we mentioned just now reach the point at which they cease to be what they are through their own peculiar evil, which attaches itself to them and is present in them. Isn't that
d   so?

Yes.

Then look at the soul in the same way. Do injustice and the other vices that exist in a soul—by their very presence in it and by attaching themselves to it—corrupt it and make it waste away until, having brought it to the point of death, they separate it from the body?

That's not at all what they do.

[Glaucon/Socrates]

But surely it's unreasonable to suppose that a thing is destroyed by the badness proper to something else when it is not destroyed by its own?

That is unreasonable.

Keep in mind, Glaucon, that we don't think that a body is destroyed by the badness of food, whether it is staleness, rottenness, or anything else. *e* But if the badness of the food happens to implant in the body an evil proper to a body, we'll say that the body was destroyed by its own evil, namely, disease. But, since the body is one thing and food another, we'll never judge that the body is destroyed by the badness of food, unless it *610* implants in it the body's own natural and peculiar evil.

That's absolutely right.

By the same argument, if the body's evil doesn't cause an evil in the soul that is proper to the soul, we'll never judge that the soul, in the absence of its own peculiar evil, is destroyed by the evil of something else. We'd never accept that *anything* is destroyed by an evil proper to something else.

That's also reasonable.

Then let's either refute our argument and show that we were wrong, or, as long as it remains unrefuted, let's never say that the soul is destroyed by a fever or any other disease or by killing either, for that matter, not even if the body is cut up into tiny pieces. We mustn't say that the soul is even *b* close to being destroyed by these things until someone shows us that these conditions of the body make the soul more unjust and more impious. When something has the evil proper to something else in it, but its own peculiar evil is absent, we won't allow anyone to say that it is destroyed, no matter whether it is a soul or anything else whatever. *c*

And you may be sure that no one will ever prove that the souls of the dying are made more unjust by death.

But if anyone dares to come to grips with our argument, in order to avoid having to agree that our souls are immortal, and says that a dying man does become more vicious and unjust, we'll reply that, if what he says is true, then injustice must be as deadly to unjust people as a disease, and those who catch it must die of it because of its own deadly nature, with the *d* worst cases dying quickly and the less serious dying more slowly. As things now stand, however, it isn't like that at all. Unjust people do indeed die of injustice, but at the hands of others who inflict the death penalty on them.

By god, if injustice were actually fatal to those who contracted it, it wouldn't seem so terrible, for it would be an escape from their troubles. But I rather think that it's clearly the opposite, something that kills other people if it can, while, on top of making the unjust themselves lively, it *e* even brings them out at night. Hence it's very far from being deadly to its possessors.

You're right, for if the soul's own evil and badness isn't enough to kill and destroy it, an evil appointed for the destruction of something else will

[Socrates/Glaucon]

hardly kill it. Indeed, it won't kill anything at all except the very thing it is appointed to destroy.

"Hardly" is right, or so it seems.

Now, if the soul isn't destroyed by a single evil, whether its own or something else's, then clearly it must always be. And if it always is, it is 611 immortal.

Necessarily so.

So be it. And if it is so, then you realize that there would always be the same souls, for they couldn't be made fewer if none is destroyed, and they couldn't be made more numerous either. If anything immortal is increased, you know that the increase would have to come from the mortal, and then everything would end up being immortal.

That's true.

Then we mustn't think such a thing, for the argument doesn't allow it, nor must we think that the soul in its truest nature is full of multicolored b variety and unlikeness or that it differs with itself.

What do you mean?

It isn't easy for anything composed of many parts to be immortal if it isn't put together in the finest way, yet this is how the soul now appeared to us.

It probably isn't easy.

Yet our recent argument and others as well compel us to believe that the soul *is* immortal. But to see the soul as it is in truth, we must not study it as it is while it is maimed by its association with the body and other evils— c which is what we were doing earlier—but as it is in its pure state, that's how we should study the soul, thoroughly and by means of logical reasoning. We'll then find that it is a much finer thing than we thought and that we can see justice and injustice as well as all the other things we've discussed far more clearly. What we've said about the soul is true of it as it appears at present. But the condition in which we've studied it is like that of the sea god Glaucus, whose primary nature can't easily be made out by d those who catch glimpses of him. Some of the original parts have been broken off, others have been crushed, and his whole body has been maimed by the waves and by the shells, seaweeds, and stones that have attached themselves to him, so that he looks more like a wild animal than his natural self. The soul, too, is in a similar condition when we study it, beset by many evils. That, Glaucon, is why we have to look somewhere else in order to discover its true nature.

To where?

To its philosophy, or love of wisdom. We must realize what it grasps and e longs to have intercourse with, because it is akin to the divine and immortal and what always is, and we must realize what it would become if it followed this longing with its whole being, and if the resulting effort lifted 612 it out of the sea in which it now dwells, and if the many stones and shells (those which have grown all over it in a wild, earthy, and stony profusion because it feasts at those so-called happy feastings on earth) were hammered off it. Then we'd see what its true nature is and be able to determine whether it has many parts or just one and whether or in what manner it is put together. But we've already given a decent account, I think, of what its condition is and what parts it has when it is immersed in human life.

We certainly have.

And haven't we cleared away the various other objections to our argument without having to invoke the rewards and reputations of justice, as you said Homer and Hesiod did?[5] And haven't we found that justice itself   b
is the best thing for the soul itself, and that the soul—whether it has the ring of Gyges or even it together with the cap of Hades[6]—should do just things?

We have. That's absolutely true.

Then can there now be any objection, Glaucon, if in addition we return to justice and the rest of virtue both the kind and quantity of wages that they obtain for the soul from human beings and gods, whether in this life   c
or the next?

None whatever.

Then will you give me back what you borrowed from me during the discussion?

What are you referring to in particular?

I granted your request that a just person should seem unjust and an unjust one just, for you said that, even if it would be impossible for these things to remain hidden from both gods and humans, still, this had to be granted for the sake of argument, so that justice itself could be judged in relation to injustice itself. Don't you remember that?   d

It would be wrong of me not to.

Well, then, since they've now been judged, I ask that the reputation justice in fact has among gods and humans be returned to it and that we agree that it does indeed have such a reputation and is entitled to carry off the prizes it gains for someone by making him seem just. It is already clear that it gives good things to anyone who is just and that it doesn't deceive those who really possess it.

That's a fair request.   e

Then won't you first grant that it doesn't escape the notice of the gods at least as to which of the two is just and which isn't?

We will.

Then if neither of them escapes the gods' notice, one would be loved by the gods and the other hated, as we agreed at the beginning.

5. See 357–367e.
6. The ring of Gyges is discussed at 359d–360a. The cap of Hades also made its wearer invisible.

That's right.

And won't we also agree that everything that comes to someone who is loved by gods, insofar as it comes from the gods themselves, is the best

613 possible, unless it is the inevitable punishment for some mistake he made in a former life?

Certainly.

Then we must suppose that the same is true of a just person who falls into poverty or disease or some other apparent evil, namely, that this will end well for him, either during his lifetime or afterwards, for the gods never neglect anyone who eagerly wishes to become just and who makes himself as much like a god as a human can by adopting a virtuous way of

b   life.

It makes sense that such a person not be neglected by anyone who is like him.

And mustn't we suppose that the opposite is true of an unjust person?

Definitely.

Then these are some of the prizes that a just person, but not an unjust one, receives from the gods.

That's certainly my opinion.

What about from human beings? What does a just person get from them? Or, if we're to tell the truth, isn't this what happens? Aren't clever but unjust people like runners who run well for the first part of the course but not for the second? They leap away sharply at first, but they become ridiculous by the end and go off uncrowned, with their ears drooping on their shoulders like those of exhausted dogs, while true runners, on the

c   other hand, get to the end, collect the prizes, and are crowned. And isn't it also generally true of just people that, towards the end of each course of action, association, or life, they enjoy a good reputation and collect the prizes from other human beings?

Of course.

Then will you allow me to say all the things about them that you your-self said about unjust people? I'll say that it is just people who, when

d   they're old enough, rule in their own cities (if they happen to want ruling office) and that it is they who marry whomever they want and give their children in marriage to whomever they want. Indeed, all the things that you said about unjust people I now say about just ones. As for unjust people, the majority of them, even if they escape detection when they're young, are caught by the end of the race and are ridiculed. And by the time they get old, they've become wretched, for they are insulted by foreigners and citizens, beaten with whips, and made to suffer those punishments, such as racking and burning, which you rightly described as crude. Imag-

e   ine that I've said that they suffer all such things, and see whether you'll allow me to say it.

Of course I will. What you say is right.

[Glaucon/Socrates]

Then these are the prizes, wages, and gifts that a just person receives from gods and humans while he is alive and that are added to the good things that justice itself provides.   614

Yes, and they're very fine and secure ones too.

Yet they're nothing in either number or size compared to those that await just and unjust people after death. And these things must also be heard, if both are to receive in full what they are owed by the argument.

Then tell us about them, for there aren't many things that would be more pleasant to hear.   b

It isn't, however, a tale of Alcinous that I'll tell you but that of a brave Pamphylian man called Er, the son of Armenias, who once died in a war.[7] When the rest of the dead were picked up ten days later, they were already putrefying, but when he was picked up, his corpse was still quite fresh. He was taken home, and preparations were made for his funeral. But on the twelfth day, when he was already laid on the funeral pyre, he revived and, having done so, told what he had seen in the world beyond. He said that, after his soul had left him, it travelled together with many others until they came to a marvellous place, where there were two adjacent openings in the   c earth, and opposite and above them two others in the heavens, and between them judges sat. These, having rendered their judgment, ordered the just to go upwards into the heavens through the door on the right, with signs of the judgment attached to their chests, and the unjust to travel downward through the opening on the left, with signs of all their deeds on their backs. When Er himself came forward, they told him that he was to   d be a messenger to human beings about the things that were there, and that he was to listen to and look at everything in the place. He said that he saw souls departing after judgment through one of the openings in the heavens and one in the earth, while through the other two souls were arriving. From the door in the earth souls came up covered with dust and dirt and from the door in the heavens souls came down pure. And the souls who were arriving all the time seemed to have been on long journeys, so that   e they went gladly to the meadow, like a crowd going to a festival, and camped there. Those who knew each other exchanged greetings, and those who came up from the earth asked those who came down from the heavens about the things there and were in turn questioned by them about the things below. And so they told their stories to one another, the former weeping as they recalled all they had suffered and seen on their journey   615 below the earth, which lasted a thousand years, while the latter, who had come from heaven, told about how well they had fared and about the inconceivably fine and beautiful sights they had seen. There was much to tell, Glaucon, and it took a long time, but the main point was this: For each

7. Books ix–xi of the *Odyssey* were traditionally referred to as the tales of Alcinous.

[Socrates/Glaucon]

in turn of the unjust things they had done and for each in turn of the people they had wronged, they paid the penalty ten times over, once in every century of their journey. Since a century is roughly the length of a *b* human life, this means that they paid a tenfold penalty for each injustice. If, for example, some of them had caused many deaths by betraying cities or armies and reducing them to slavery or by participating in other wrong-doing, they had to suffer ten times the pain they had caused to each individual. But if they had done good deeds and had become just and pious, they were rewarded according to the same scale. He said some other things about the stillborn and those who had lived for only a short *c* time, but they're not worth recounting. And he also spoke of even greater rewards or penalties for piety or impiety towards gods or parents and for murder with one's own hands.

For example, he said he was there when someone asked another where the great Ardiaeus was. (This Ardiaeus was said to have been tyrant in some city in Pamphylia a thousand years before and to have killed his aged father and older brother and committed many other impious deeds *d* as well.) And he said that the one who was asked responded: "He hasn't arrived here yet and never will, for this too was one of the terrible sights we saw. When we came near the opening on our way out, after all our sufferings were over, we suddenly saw him together with some others, pretty well all of whom were tyrants (although there were also some private individuals among them who had committed great crimes). They *e* thought that they were ready to go up, but the opening wouldn't let them through, for it roared whenever one of these incurably wicked people or anyone else who hadn't paid a sufficient penalty tried to go up. And there were savage men, all fiery to look at, who were standing by, and when they heard the roar, they grabbed some of these criminals and led them away, but they bound the feet, hands, and head of Ardiaeus and the *616* others, threw them down, and flayed them. Then they dragged them out of the way, lacerating them on thorn bushes, and telling every passer-by that they were to be thrown into Tartarus, and explaining why they were being treated in this way." And he said that of their many fears the greatest each one of them had was that the roar would be heard as he came up and that everyone was immensely relieved when silence greeted him. Such, then, were the penalties and punishments and the rewards corresponding *b* to them.

Each group spent seven days in the meadow, and on the eighth they had to get up and go on a journey. On the fourth day of that journey, they came to a place where they could look down from above on a straight column of light that stretched over the whole of heaven and earth, more like a rain-bow than anything else, but brighter and more pure. After another day, they came to the light itself, and there, in the middle of the light, they saw the extremities of its bonds stretching from the heavens, for the light binds

[Socrates]

the heavens like the cables girding a trireme and holds its entire revolution   c
together. From the extremities hangs the spindle of Necessity, by means of
which all the revolutions are turned. Its stem and hook are of adamant,
whereas in its whorl[8] adamant is mixed with other kinds of material. The
nature of the whorl was this: Its shape was like that of an ordinary whorl,   d
but, from what Er said, we must understand its structure as follows. It was
as if one big whorl had been made hollow by being thoroughly scooped
out, with another smaller whorl closely fitted into it, like nested boxes, and
there was a third whorl inside the second, and so on, making eight whorls
altogether, lying inside one another, with their rims appearing as circles
from above, while from the back they formed one continuous whorl   e
around the spindle, which was driven through the center of the eighth.
The first or outside whorl had the widest circular rim; that of the sixth was
second in width; the fourth was third; the eighth was fourth; the seventh
was fifth; the fifth was sixth; the third was seventh; and the second was
eighth. The rim of the largest was spangled; that of the seventh was brightest; that of the eighth took its color from the seventh's shining on it; the
second and fifth were about equal in brightness, more yellow than the
others; the third was the whitest in color; the fourth was rather red; and the   617
sixth was second in whiteness. The whole spindle turned at the same
speed, but, as it turned, the inner spheres gently revolved in a direction
opposite to that of the whole. Of these inner spheres, the eighth was the
fastest; second came the seventh, sixth, and fifth, all at the same speed; it
seemed to them that the fourth was third in its speed of revolution; the   b
fourth, third; and the second, fifth. The spindle itself turned on the lap of
Necessity. And up above on each of the rims of the circles stood a Siren,
who accompanied its revolution, uttering a single sound, one single note.
And the concord of the eight notes produced a single harmony. And there
were three other beings sitting at equal distances from one another, each
on a throne. These were the Fates, the daughters of Necessity: Lachesis,
Clotho, and Atropos. They were dressed in white, with garlands on their   c
heads, and they sang to the music of the Sirens. Lachesis sang of the past,
Clotho of the present, and Atropos of the future. With her right hand,
Clotho touched the outer circumference of the spindle and helped it turn,
but left off doing so from time to time; Atropos did the same to the inner
ones; and Lachesis helped both motions in turn, one with one hand and
one with the other.   d
    When the souls arrived at the light, they had to go to Lachesis right
away. There a Speaker arranged them in order, took from the lap of Lachesis a number of lots and a number of models of lives, mounted a high
pulpit, and spoke to them: "Here is the message of Lachesis, the maiden
daughter of Necessity: 'Ephemeral souls, this is the beginning of another

    8. A whorl is the weight that twirls a spindle.

[Socrates]

e   cycle that will end in death. Your daemon or guardian spirit will not be
assigned to you by lot; you will choose him. The one who has the first lot
will be the first to choose a life to which he will then be bound by necessity.
Virtue knows no master; each will possess it to a greater or less degree,
depending on whether he values or disdains it. The responsibility lies with
the one who makes the choice; the god has none.'" When he had said this,
the Speaker threw the lots among all of them, and each—with the exception of Er, who wasn't allowed to choose—picked up the one that fell next
to him. And the lot made it clear to the one who picked it up where in the
order he would get to make his choice. After that, the models of lives were

618 placed on the ground before them. There were far more of them than there
were souls present, and they were of all kinds, for the lives of animals were
there, as well as all kinds of human lives. There were tyrannies among
them, some of which lasted throughout life, while others ended halfway
through in poverty, exile, and beggary. There were lives of famous men,
some of whom were famous for the beauty of their appearance, others for
their strength or athletic prowess, others still for their high birth and the
virtue or excellence of their ancestors. And there were also lives of men

b   who weren't famous for any of these things. And the same for lives of
women. But the arrangement of the soul was not included in the model
because the soul is inevitably altered by the different lives it chooses. But
all the other things were there, mixed with each other and with wealth,
poverty, sickness, health, and the states intermediate to them.

Now, it seems that it is here, Glaucon, that a human being faces the
greatest danger of all. And because of this, each of us must neglect all other

c   subjects and be most concerned to seek out and learn those that will enable
him to distinguish the good life from the bad and always to make the best
choice possible in every situation. He should think over all the things we
have mentioned and how they jointly and severally determine what the
virtuous life is like. That way he will know what the good and bad effects
of beauty are when it is mixed with wealth, poverty, and a particular state

d   of the soul. He will know the effects of high or low birth, private life or
ruling office, physical strength or weakness, ease or difficulty in learning,
and all the things that are either naturally part of the soul or are acquired,
and he will know what they achieve when mixed with one another. And
from all this he will be able, by considering the nature of the soul, to reason
out which life is better and which worse and to choose accordingly, calling
a life worse if it leads the soul to become more unjust, better if it leads the

e   soul to become more just, and ignoring everything else: We have seen that
this is the best way to choose, whether in life or death. Hence, we must go
down to Hades holding with adamantine determination to the belief that

619 this is so, lest we be dazzled there by wealth and other such evils, rush into
a tyranny or some other similar course of action, do irreparable evils, and

suffer even worse ones. And we must always know how to choose the mean in such lives and how to avoid either of the extremes, as far as possible, both in this life and in all those beyond it. This is the way that a human being becomes happiest.   *b*

Then our messenger from the other world reported that the Speaker spoke as follows: "There is a satisfactory life rather than a bad one available even for the one who comes last, provided that he chooses it rationally and lives it seriously. Therefore, let not the first be careless in his choice nor the last discouraged."

He said that when the Speaker had told them this, the one who came up first chose the greatest tyranny. In his folly and greed he chose it without adequate examination and didn't notice that, among other evils, he was fated to eat his own children as a part of it. When he examined at leisure,   *c* the life he had chosen, however, he beat his breast and bemoaned his choice. And, ignoring the warning of the Speaker, he blamed chance, daemons, or guardian spirits, and everything else for these evils but himself. He was one of those who had come down from heaven, having lived his previous life under an orderly constitution, where he had participated in virtue through habit and without philosophy. Broadly speaking, indeed, most of those who were caught out in this way were souls who had come   *d* down from heaven and who were untrained in suffering as a result. The majority of those who had come up from the earth, on the other hand, having suffered themselves and seen others suffer, were in no rush to make their choices. Because of this and because of the chance of the lottery, there was an interchange of goods and evils for most of the souls. However, if someone pursues philosophy in a sound manner when he comes to live here on earth and if the lottery doesn't make him one of the last to   *e* choose, then, given what Er has reported about the next world, it looks as though not only will he be happy here, but his journey from here to there and back again won't be along the rough underground path, but along the smooth heavenly one.

Er said that the way in which the souls chose their lives was a sight worth seeing, since it was pitiful, funny, and surprising to watch. For the   *620* most part, their choice depended upon the character of their former life. For example, he said that he saw the soul that had once belonged to Orpheus choosing a swan's life, because he hated the female sex because of his death at their hands, and so was unwilling to have a woman conceive and give birth to him. Er saw the soul of Thamyris[9] choosing the life of a nightingale, a swan choosing to change over to a human life, and other

---

9. Thamyris was a legendary poet and singer, who boasted that he could defeat the Muses in a song contest. For this they blinded him and took away his voice. He is mentioned at *Iliad* ii.596–600.

[Socrates]

musical animals doing the same thing. The twentieth soul chose the life of
b a lion. This was the soul of Ajax, son of Telamon.[10] He avoided human life
because he remembered the judgment about the armor. The next soul was
that of Agamemnon, whose sufferings also had made him hate the human
race, so he changed to the life of an eagle. Atalanta[11] had been assigned a
place near the middle, and when she saw great honors being given to a
male athlete, she chose his life, unable to pass them by. After her, he saw
the soul of Epeius, the son of Panopeus, taking on the nature of a craftswo-
c man.[12] And very close to last, he saw the soul of the ridiculous Thersites
clothing itself as a monkey.[13] Now, it chanced that the soul of Odysseus got
to make its choice last of all, and since memory of its former sufferings had
relieved its love of honor, it went around for a long time, looking for the
life of a private individual who did his own work, and with difficulty it
found one lying off somewhere neglected by the others. He chose it gladly
and said that he'd have made the same choice even if he'd been first. Still
d other souls changed from animals into human beings, or from one kind of
animal into another, with unjust people changing into wild animals, and
just people into tame ones, and all sorts of mixtures occurred.

After all the souls had chosen their lives, they went forward to Lachesis
in the same order in which they had made their choices, and she assigned
to each the daemon it had chosen as guardian of its life and fulfiller of its
e choice. This daemon first led the soul under the hand of Clotho as it turned
the revolving spindle to confirm the fate that the lottery and its own choice
had given it. After receiving her touch, he led the soul to the spinning of
Atropos, to make what had been spun irreversible. Then, without turning
around, they went from there under the throne of Necessity and, when all
of them had passed through, they travelled to the Plain of Forgetfulness in
621 burning, choking, terrible heat, for it was empty of trees and earthly vege-
tation. And there, beside the River of Unheeding, whose water no vessel
can hold, they camped, for night was coming on. All of them had to drink a
certain measure of this water, but those who weren't saved by reason
drank more than that, and as each of them drank, he forgot everything and
went to sleep. But around midnight there was a clap of thunder and an
b earthquake, and they were suddenly carried away from there, this way

10. Ajax is a great Homeric hero. He thought that he deserved to be awarded the
armor of the dead Achilles, but instead it went to Odysseus. Ajax was maddened
by this injustice and finally killed himself because of the terrible things he had done
while mad. See Sophocles, *Ajax*.
11. Atalanta was a mythical huntress, who would marry only a man who could
beat her at running. In most versions of the myth, losers were killed.
12. Epeius is mentioned at *Odyssey* viii.493 as the man who helped Athena make
the Trojan Horse.
13. Thersites is an ordinary soldier who criticizes Agamemnon at *Iliad* ii.211–77.
Odysseus beats him for his presumption and is widely approved for doing so.

[Socrates]

and that, up to their births, like shooting stars. Er himself was forbidden to drink from the water. All the same, he didn't know how he had come back to his body, except that waking up suddenly he saw himself lying on the pyre at dawn.

And so, Glaucon, his story wasn't lost but preserved, and it would save us, if we were persuaded by it, for we would then make a good crossing of the River of Forgetfulness, and our souls wouldn't be defiled. But if we are *c* persuaded by me, we'll believe that the soul is immortal and able to endure every evil and every good, and we'll always hold to the upward path, practicing justice with reason in every way. That way we'll be friends both to ourselves and to the gods while we remain here on earth and afterwards—like victors in the games who go around collecting their *d* prizes—we'll receive our rewards. Hence, both in this life and on the thousand-year journey we've described, we'll do well and be happy.

[Socrates]

PARMENIDES

(127b–135d)

*The following brief selection shows the young Socrates in the company of
Parmenides and Zeno, talking not about ethics but about profound and very
abstract metaphysical issues: Are things many or—as Plato takes Parmenides to
have argued in his poem—only one? Socrates introduces the theory of forms
(128e-130a) as a response to Zeno. Parmenides counters with a series of powerful criticisms of that theory. Since Plato wrote Parmenides' lines, this dialogue is
a good example of Plato's willingness to submit even his own cherished views to
critical scrutiny.*

127 Antiphon said that Pythodorus said that Zeno and Parmenides once
b came to the Great Panathenaia. Parmenides was already quite venerable,
very gray but of distinguished appearance, about sixty-five years old. Zeno
was at that time near forty, a tall, handsome man, who had been, as rumor
had it, the object of Parmenides' affections when he was a boy. Antiphon
c said that the two of them were staying with Pythodorus, outside the wall in
the Potters' Quarter, and that Socrates had come there, along with quite a
few others, because they were eager to hear Zeno read his book, which he
and Parmenides had just brought to Athens for the first time. Socrates was
then quite young.

Zeno himself was reading to them; Parmenides happened to be out. Very
d little remained to be read when Pythodorus, as he related it, came in, and
with him Parmenides and Aristotle (the one who later became one of the
Thirty). They listened to a little of the book at the very end. But
Pythodorus had himself heard Zeno read it before.

Then Socrates, after he had heard it, asked Zeno to read the first hypothesis of the first argument again; and when he had read it, asked, "Zeno,
e what do you mean by this: if things are many, they must then be both like
and unlike, but that is impossible, because unlike things can't be like or like
things unlike? That's what you say, isn't it?"

"It is," Zeno said.

"So if it's impossible for unlike things to be like and like things unlike, it
follows that it's also impossible for them to be many? Because, if they were

Translated by M. L. Gill and P. Ryan.

many, they would have incompatible properties. Is this the point of your arguments—simply to maintain, in opposition to everything that is commonly said, that things are not many? And so you suppose that each of your arguments is proof for this position, so that you think you give as many proofs that things are not many as your book has arguments? Is that what you're saying—or do I misunderstand?"   128

"No," Zeno replied. "On the contrary, you grasp the general point of the book splendidly."

"Parmenides," Socrates said, "I understand that Zeno wants to be on intimate terms with you not only in friendship but also in his book. He has, in a way, written the same thing as you, but by changing it round he tries to fool us into thinking he is saying something different. You say in your poem that the all is one, and you give splendid and excellent proofs for   b that; he, for his part, says that it is not many and gives a vast array of very grand proofs of his own. So, with one of you saying 'one,' and the other 'not many,' and with each of you speaking in a way that suggests that you've said not at all the same thing—although you mean practically the same thing—what you've said you appear to have said over the heads of the rest of us."

"Yes, Socrates," Zeno said. "Still, you haven't completely discerned the truth about my book, even though you chase down its arguments and follow their spoor as well as a young Spartan hound. First of all, you have   c missed this point: the book doesn't at all preen itself on having been written with the intent you described, while disguising it from people, as if that were some great accomplishment. You have mentioned something that happened accidentally. The truth is that the book comes to the defense of Parmenides' argument against those who try to make fun of it by claiming that, if it is one, many absurdities and self-contradictions result from his   d argument. Accordingly, this book argues against those who assert the many and pays them back in kind with something for good measure, since it aims to make clear that their hypothesis, if it is many, would, if someone examined the matter thoroughly, suffer consequences even more absurd than those suffered by the hypothesis of its being one. I wrote a book, then, in that competitive spirit when I was a young man. Someone made an unauthorized copy, so I didn't even have a chance to decide for myself whether or not it should see the light. So this eluded you, Socrates: you   e think it was written not out of a young man's competitiveness, but out of a mature man's vainglory. Still, as I said, your portrayal was not bad."

"I take your point," Socrates said, "and I believe it was as you say. But tell   129 me this: don't you acknowledge that there is a form, itself by itself, of likeness, and another form, opposite to this, which is just what it is to be unlike? Don't you and I and the other things we call 'many' get a share of those two entities? And don't things that get a share of likeness come to be like in that way and to the extent that they get a share, while things that get a share of unlikeness come to be unlike, and things that get a share of both come to be both? And even if all things get a share of both, though they are opposites, and, by partaking of them, are both like and unlike themselves, what's astonishing about that?

b   "If someone showed that the likes themselves come to be unlike or the unlikes like—that, I think, would be a marvel; but if he shows that things that partake of both of these have both properties, there seems to me nothing outlandish about that, Zeno—not even if someone shows that all things are one by partaking of oneness, and that these same things are also many by partaking of multitude.[1] But if he should demonstrate that this thing itself, just what it is to be one, is many or that, conversely, the many

c   are one—at this I'll be astonished.

"And it's the same with all the others: if he could show that the kinds and forms[2] themselves have in themselves these opposite properties, that would call for astonishment. But if someone should demonstrate that I am one thing and also many, what's astonishing about that? He will say, when he wants to show that I'm many, that my right side is different from my left, and my front from my back, and likewise with my upper and lower parts— since I take it I do partake of multitude. But when he wants to show that I'm one thing, he will say I'm one person among the seven of us, because I

d   also partake of oneness. Thus he shows that both are true.

"So if—in the case of stones and sticks and such things—someone tries to show that the same thing is many and one, we'll say that he is demonstrating that *something* is many and one, not that the one is many or the many one—and we'll say that he is saying nothing astonishing, but just what all of us would agree to. But if someone first distinguishes as separate the forms, themselves by themselves, of the things I was talking about a moment ago—for example, likeness and unlikeness, multitude and oneness,

e   rest and motion, and everything of that sort—and then shows that in themselves they can mix together and separate, I for my part," he said, "would be utterly amazed, Zeno. I think these issues have been handled resolutely indeed in your book; but I would, as I say, be much more impressed if someone were able to display this same difficulty, which you

---

1. Like *to hen* ("the one," "oneness"), the expression *plēthos* ("multitude") is also ambiguous. It can refer to a form, to any group of many things (whether concrete particulars or forms), or the character things have if they are many. Corresponding to the ambiguity in the meaning of "one," between "single" and "unified," there is an ambiguity in the meaning of "multitude." It can specify a plurality of definite individuals or some mass that lacks unity and definiteness.

2. In this dialogue Plato uses three different abstract expressions to specify forms, two of which occur here: *genos*, which we render as "kind" and *eidos*, which we render as "form." Later he will use a third term *idea*, which we render as "character."

and Parmenides went through in the case of visible things, also similarly
entwined in multifarious ways in the forms themselves—in things that are   *130*
grasped by reasoning."

Pythodorus said that, while Socrates was saying all this, he himself kept
from moment to moment expecting Parmenides and Zeno to get annoyed;
but they both paid close attention to Socrates and often glanced at each
other and smiled, as though they admired him. In fact what Parmenides
said when Socrates had finished confirmed this impression. "Socrates," he
said, "You are much to be admired for the impulse that drives you to   *b*
argument! Tell me. Have you yourself distinguished as separate, in the way
you mention, certain forms themselves, and also as separate the things that
partake of them? And do you think that likeness itself is something,
separate from a likeness we possess? And one and many and all the things
you heard Zeno reading about a while ago?"

"I do indeed," Socrates replied.

"And what about these?" asked Parmenides. "Is there a form, itself by
itself, of just, and beautiful, and good, and everything of that sort?"

"Yes," he said.

"What about a form of human being, separate from us and all those like   *c*
us? Is there a form itself of human being, or fire, or water?"

Socrates said, "Parmenides, I've often found myself in doubt whether one
should talk about those in the same way as the others or differently."

"And what about these, Socrates? Things that might seem absurd, like
hair and mud and dirt, or anything else totally undignified and worthless?
Are you doubtful whether or not one should say that there is a form
separate for each of these, too, which in turn is other than anything we   *d*
touch with our hands?"

"Not at all," Socrates answered. "On the contrary, these things are in fact
just what we see. Surely it's too outlandish to think there is a form for them.
Not that the thought that the same thing might hold in all cases hasn't
troubled me from time to time. Then, when I get bogged down in that, I
hurry away, afraid that I may fall into some pit of nonsense and come to
harm; but when I arrive back in the vicinity of the things we agreed a
moment ago have forms, I linger there and occupy myself with them."

"That's because you are still young, Socrates," said Parmenides, "and   *e*
philosophy has not yet gripped you as, in my opinion, it will in the future,
once you begin to consider none of the cases beneath your notice. Now,
though, you still care about what people think, because of your youth.

"But tell me this: is it your view that, as you say, there are certain forms,
whose names these other things have through getting a share of them—as,
for instance, they come to be like by getting a share of likeness, large   *131*
by getting a share of largeness, and just and beautiful by getting a share of
justice and beauty?"

"It certainly is," Socrates replied.

"So does each thing that gets a share get a share of the form as a whole or of a part of it? Or could there be some other means of getting a share apart from these two?"

"How could there be?" he said.

"Do you think, then, that the form as a whole—one thing—is in each of the many? Or what do you think?"

"What's to prevent its being one, Parmenides?" asked Socrates.

b   "So, being one and the same, it will be at the same time, as a whole, in things that are many and separate; and thus it would be separate from itself."

"No it wouldn't," Socrates said. "Not if it's like a day. One and the same day is in many places at the same time and is none the less not separate from itself. If that's what it's like, each of the forms might be, at the same time, one and the same in all."

"Socrates," he said, "how neatly you make one and the same thing be in many places at the same time! It's as if you were to cover many people with a sail, and then say that one thing as a whole is over many. Or isn't that the sort of thing you mean to say?"

c   "Perhaps," he replied.

"In that case would the sail be, as a whole, over each person, or would a part of it be over one person and another part over another?"

"A part."

"So the forms themselves are divisible, Socrates," he said, "and the things that partake of them would partake of a part; no longer would a whole form, but only a part of it, be in each thing."

"It does appear that way."

"Then are you willing to say, Socrates, that our one form is really divided? Will it still be one?"

"Not at all," he replied.

"Look," said Parmenides, "suppose you are going to divide largeness

d   itself. If each of the many large things is to be large by a part of largeness smaller than largeness itself, won't that appear unreasonable?"

"It certainly will," he replied.

"What about this? Will each thing that has received a small part of the equal have something by which to be equal to anything, when its portion is less than the equal itself?"

"That's impossible."

"Well, suppose one of us is going to have a part of the small. The small will be larger than that part of it, since the part is a part of it: so the small

e   itself will be larger! And that to which the part subtracted is added will be smaller, not larger, than it was before."

"That surely couldn't happen," he said.

"Socrates, in what way, then, will the other things get a share of your forms, if they can do so neither by getting parts nor by getting wholes?"

"By Zeus!" Socrates exclaimed, "I don't think it's at all easy to sort that out!"

"And what do you think about the following?"

"What's that?"

"I suppose you think each form is one on the following ground: when-   132
ever some many things seem to you to be large, perhaps there seems to be some one character—the same—as you look at them all, and from that you conclude that the large is one thing."

"That's true," he said.

"What about the large itself and the other large things? If you look at them all in the same way with the mind's eye, again won't some one thing appear large, by which all these appear large?"

"It seems so."

"So another form of largeness will make its appearance, which has emerged alongside largeness itself and the things that partake of it, and in   b
turn another over all these, by which all of them will be large. No longer will each of your forms be one, but unlimited in multitude."

"But, Parmenides, maybe each of the forms is a thought of the many," Socrates said, "and properly occurs only in minds. In this way each of them might be one and yet not face the difficulties mentioned just now."

"What do you mean?" he asked. "Is each of the thoughts one thing, but a thought of nothing?"

"On the contrary, that's impossible," he said.

"Of something, rather?"

"Yes."

"Of something that is, or of something that is not?"   c

"Of something that is."

"Isn't it of some *one* thing, which that thought thinks is over all the instances, being some one character?"

"Yes."

"Then won't this thing that is thought to be one, being always the same over all the instances, be a form?"

"That, too, appears to be necessary."

"And what about this?" said Parmenides. "Given your claim that other things partake of forms, won't you necessarily think either that each thing is composed of thoughts and all things think, or that, being thoughts, they are not thought?"

"That isn't reasonable either, Parmenides," he said. "No, what appears most likely to me is this: these forms are like patterns set in nature, and   d
other things resemble them and are likenesses; and this partaking of the forms is, for the other things, simply being likened to them."

"If something resembles the form," he said, "can that form not be like what has been likened to it, to the extent that the thing has been made like it? Or is there any way for something like to be like what is not like it?"

"There is not."

"And isn't there a compelling necessity for that which is like to partake of
the same one thing as what is like it?"

"There is."

"And if like things are like by partaking of something, won't that thing
be the form itself?"

"Absolutely."

"Therefore something cannot be like the form, nor can the form be like
something else. Otherwise, alongside the form another form will always
make its appearance, and if that form is like anything, yet another; and
if the form proves to be like what partakes of it, a fresh form will never
cease emerging."

"That's very true."

"So other things don't get a share of the forms by means of likeness; we
must seek some other means by which they get a share."

"So it seems."

"Then do you see, Socrates," he said, "how great the difficulty turns out
to be if one marks things off as forms, themselves by themselves?"

"Quite clearly."

"I assure you," he said, "that you do not yet, if I may put it so, have an
inkling of how great the difficulty is if you are going to posit one form in
each case every time you make a distinction among things."

"How so?" he asked.

"There are many other reasons," Parmenides said, "but the main one is
this: suppose someone were to say that if the forms are such as we claim
they must be, they cannot even be known? If anyone should raise that
objection, you wouldn't be able to show him that he is wrong, unless the
objector happened to be widely experienced and not ungifted, and consented to pay attention while in your effort to show him you dealt with
many distant considerations. Otherwise, the person who insists that they
are necessarily unknowable would remain unconvinced."

"Why is that, Parmenides?" Socrates asked.

"Because I think that you, Socrates, and anyone else who posits that
there is for each thing some being, itself by itself, would agree, to begin
with, that none of these beings is in us."

"Yes—how could it still be itself by itself?" Socrates replied.

"Very good," said Parmenides. "And so all the characters that are what
they are in relation to each other have their being in relation to themselves
but not in relation to things that belong to us. And whether one posits these
as likenesses or in some other way, it is by partaking of them that we come
to be called by their various names. These things that belong to us, although they have the same names as the forms, are in their turn what they
are in relation to themselves but not in relation to the forms; and all the
things named in this way are so named of themselves but not of the forms."

"What do you mean?" Socrates asked.

"Take an example," said Parmenides. "If one of us is somebody's master or somebody's slave, he is surely not a slave of master itself—of just what a master is—nor is the master a master of slave itself—of just what a slave is. On the contrary, being a human being, he is a master or slave of a human being. Mastery itself, on the other hand, is what it is of slavery itself; and, in the same way, slavery itself is slavery of mastery itself. Things in us do not have their power in relation to the forms, nor do they have theirs in relation to us; but, I repeat, the forms are what they are *of* themselves and in relation to themselves, and things that belong to us are, in the same way, what they are in relation to themselves. You do understand what I mean?" *134*

"Certainly," Socrates said, "I understand."

"So too," he said, "knowledge itself, just what knowledge is, would be knowledge of that truth itself, which is just what truth is?"

"Certainly."

"Furthermore, each particular knowledge, just what that knowledge is, would be knowledge of some particular thing, of just what that thing is. Isn't that so?"

"Yes."

"But wouldn't knowledge that belongs to us be of the truth here, where we are? And wouldn't it follow that each particular knowledge that belongs to us is in turn knowledge of some particular thing here?" *b*

"Necessarily."

"But, as you agree, we neither possess the forms themselves nor can they belong to us."

"Yes, you're quite right."

"And surely the form of knowledge knows the kinds themselves, just what each of them is?"

"Yes."

"But we don't possess it."

"No, we don't."

"So none of the forms is known by us, because we don't partake of knowledge itself."

"It seems not."

"Then the beautiful itself, just what it is, cannot be known by us, nor can the good nor, indeed, can any of the things we take to be characters themselves." *c*

"It looks that way."

"Look—here's something even more shocking than that."

"What's that?"

"Surely you would say that if in fact there is knowledge—a kind itself— it is much more precise than is knowledge that belongs to us. And the same applies to beauty and all the others."

"Yes."

"Well, if anything at all partakes of knowledge itself, wouldn't you say that a god more than anyone else possesses this most precise knowledge?"

"Necessarily."

d   "Tell me, will the god, possessing knowledge itself, then be able to know the things here, where we are?"

"Yes, why not?"

"Because we have agreed, Socrates," Parmenides said, "that those forms do not have their power in relation to things here, and things here do not have theirs in relation to the forms, but that things in each group have their power in relation to themselves."

"Yes, we did agree on that."

"Well then, if this most precise mastery and this most precise knowledge belong to the divine, the gods' mastery could never master us, nor could

e   their knowledge know us or anything that belongs to us. No, just as we do not govern them by our governance and know nothing of the divine by our knowledge, so they in their turn are, for the same reason, neither our masters nor, being gods, do they know human affairs."

"If god is to be stripped of knowing," he said, "our argument may be getting too bizarre."

"And yet, Socrates," said Parmenides, "the forms inevitably involve these

135   objections and a host of others besides—if there are those characters for things, and one is to mark off each form as 'something itself'. As a result, whoever hears about them is doubtful and objects that they do not exist, and that, even if they *do*, they must by strict necessity be unknowable to human nature; and in saying this he seems to have a point and, besides that, as we said, he is extraordinarily hard to win over. Only a very gifted man can come to know that for each thing there is some kind, a being itself

b   by itself; but only a prodigy more remarkable still will discover that and be able to teach someone else who has sifted all these difficulties thoroughly and critically for himself."

"I agree with you, Parmenides," Socrates said. "That's very much what I think too."

"Yet on the other hand, Socrates," said Parmenides, "if someone won't allow that there are forms for things, because he has an eye on all the difficulties we have just brought up and others of the same sort, and won't mark off a form for each one thing, he won't have a direction for his

c   thought, since he doesn't allow that for each thing there is a character that is always the same. In this way he will destroy the power of discourse entirely. But I think you are only too well aware of that."

"What you say is true," Socrates said.

"What then will you do about philosophy? Where will you turn, while these difficulties remain unresolved?"

"I don't think I have anything clearly in view, at least not at present."

"Socrates, that's because you are trying to mark off something beautiful,

and just, and good, and each one of the forms, too soon," he said, "before
you have been properly trained. I noticed that the other day too, as I   *d*
listened to you discoursing with Aristotle here. The impulse you bring to
argument is noble and divine, make no mistake about it. But while you are
still young, put your back into it and get more training through something
people think useless—what the crowd call idle talk. Otherwise, the truth
will escape you."

TIMAEUS

(27e–58c)

The following selection deals with the creation of the universe. It makes use of the theory of forms, not now in an ethical or metaphysical context, but to deal with the kind of cosmological and scientific issues familiar from the writings of the Presocratics.

TIMAEUS: As I see it, then, we must begin by making the following distinction: What is *that which always is* and has no becoming, and what is *that which becomes* but never is? The former is apprehended by understanding which involves a reasoned account. It is unchanging. The latter is grasped by opinion, which involves unreasoning sense perception. It becomes and passes away, but never really is. Now of necessity, everything that comes to be[1] must come to be by the agency of some cause, for it is impossible for anything to come to be without a cause. So whenever the craftsman looks at what is always changeless and, using a thing of that kind as his model, reproduces its form and character, then, of necessity, all that he so completes is beautiful. But were he to look at a thing that has come to be and use as his model something that has been begotten, his work will lack beauty.

Now as to the whole universe [*ouranos*], or world order [*cosmos*]—let's just call it by whatever name is most acceptable in a given context—there is a question we need to consider first. This is the sort of question one should begin with in inquiring into any subject. Has it always existed? Was there no origin [*archē*] from which it came to be? Or did it come to be and take its start from some origin? It has come to be. For it is both visible and tangible and it has a body—and all things of that kind are perceptible. And, as we have shown, perceptible things are grasped by opinion, which involves sense perception. As such, they are things that come to be, things that are begotten. Further, we maintain that, necessarily, that which comes to be must come to be by the agency of some cause. Now to find the maker and father of this universe [*to pan*] is hard enough, and even if I succeeded, to declare him to everyone is impossible. And so we must go back and raise

28

b

c

Translated by D. J. Zeyl

1. *Becoming* and *coming to be* here as elsewhere translate the same Greek word, *genesis*, and its cognates.

this question about the universe: Which of the two models did the maker use when he fashioned it? Was it the one that does not change and stays the same, or the one that has come to be? Well, if this world of ours is beautiful and its craftsman good, then clearly he looked at the eternal model. But if what it's blasphemous to even say is the case, then he looked at one that has come to be. Now surely it's clear to all that it was the eternal model he looked at, for, of all the things that have come to be, our universe is the most beautiful, and of causes the craftsman is the most excellent. This, then, is how it has come to be: It is a work of craft, modeled after that which is changeless and is grasped by a rational account, that is, by wisdom.

Since these things are so, it follows by unquestionable necessity that this world is an image of something. Now in every subject it is of utmost importance to begin at the natural beginning, and so, on the subject of an image and its model, we must make the following specification: the accounts we give of things have the same character as the subjects they set forth. So accounts of what is stable and fixed and transparent to understanding are themselves stable and unshifting. We must do our very best to make these accounts as irrefutable and invincible as any account may be. On the other hand, accounts we give of that which has been formed to be like that reality, since they are accounts of what is a likeness, are themselves likely, and stand in proportion to the previous accounts, i.e., what being is to becoming, truth is to conviction. Don't be surprised then, Socrates, if it turns out repeatedly that we won't be able to produce accounts on a great many subjects—on gods or the coming to be of the universe—that are completely and perfectly consistent and accurate. Instead, if we can come up with accounts no less likely than any, we ought to be content, keeping in mind that both I, the speaker, and you, the judges, are only human. So we should accept the likely tale on these matters. It behooves us not to look for anything beyond this.

SOCRATES: Bravo, Timaeus! By all means! We must accept it as you say we should. This overture of yours was marvellous. Go on now and let us have the work itself.

The Achievement of Intellect

TIMAEUS: Very well then. Now why did he who framed this whole universe of becoming frame it? Let us state the reason why: He was good, and one who is good can never become envious of anything. And so, being free of envy, he wanted everything to become as much like himself as was possible. In fact, men of wisdom will tell you (and you couldn't do better than to accept their claim) that this, more than anything else, was the most pre-eminent reason for the origin of the world's coming into being. The god wanted everything to be good and nothing to be bad so far as that was

29

b

c

d

e

30

possible, and so he took over all that was visible—not at rest but in discordant and disorderly motion—and brought it from a state of disorder to one of order, because he believed that order was in every way better than disorder. Now it wasn't permitted (nor is it now) that one who is supremely

b   good should do anything but what is best. Accordingly, the god reasoned and concluded that in the realm of things naturally visible no unintelligent thing could as a whole be better than anything which does possess intelligence as a whole, and he further concluded that it is impossible for anything to come to possess intelligence apart from soul. Guided by this reasoning, he put intelligence in soul, and soul in body, and so he constructed the universe. He wanted to produce a piece of work that would be as excellent and supreme as its nature would allow. This, then, in keeping with our likely account, is how we must say divine providence brought our

c   world into being as a truly living being, endowed with soul and intelligence.

This being so, we have to go on to speak about what comes next. When the maker made our world, what living being did he make it resemble? Let us not stoop to think that it was any of those that have the natural character of a part, for nothing that is a likeness of anything incomplete could ever turn out beautiful. Rather, let us lay it down that the universe resembles more closely than anything else that Living Being of which all other living beings are parts, both individually and by kinds. For that Living Being comprehends within itself all intelligible living beings, just as our

d   world is made up of us and all the other visible creatures. Since the god wanted nothing more than to make the world like the best of the intelligible beings, complete in every way, he made it a single visible living being,

31   which contains within itself all the living beings whose nature it is to share its kind.

Have we been correct in speaking of *one* universe, or would it have been more correct to say that there are many, in fact infinitely many universes? There is but one universe, if it is to have been crafted after its model. For that which contains all of the intelligible living beings couldn't ever be one of a pair, since that would require there to be yet another Living Being, the one that contained those two, of which they then would be parts, and then it would be more correct to speak of our universe as made in the likeness,

b   now not of those two, but of that other, the one that contains them. So, in order that this living being should be like the complete Living Being in respect of uniqueness, the Maker made neither two, nor yet an infinite number of worlds. On the contrary, our universe came into being as the one and only thing of its kind, is so now and will continue to be so in the future.

Now that which comes into being must have bodily form, and be both visible and tangible, but nothing could ever become visible apart from fire, nor tangible without something solid, nor solid without earth. That is why, as he began to put the body of the universe together, the god came to make it out of fire and earth. But it isn't possible to combine two things well all by themselves, without a third; there has to be some bond between the two c that unites them. Now the best bond is one that really and truly makes a unity of itself together with the things bonded by it, and this in the nature of things is best accomplished by proportion. For whenever of three numbers which are either solids or squares the middle term between any two 32 of them is such that what the first term is to it, it is to the last, and, conversely, what the last term is to the middle, it is to the first, then, since the middle term turns out to be both first and last, and the last and the first likewise both turn out to be middle terms, they will all of necessity turn out to have the same relationship to each other, and, given this, will all be unified.

So if the body of the universe were to have come into being as a two-dimensional plane, a single middle term would have sufficed to bind to- b gether its conjoining terms with itself. As it was, however, the universe was to be a solid, and solids are never joined together by just one middle term but always by two. Hence the god set water and air between fire and earth, and made them as proportionate to one another as was possible, so that what fire is to air, air is to water, and what air is to water, water is to earth. He then bound them together and thus he constructed the visible and tangible universe. This is the reason why these four particular constituents c were used to beget the body of the world, making it a symphony of proportion.[2] They bestowed friendship upon it, so that, having come to-gether into a unity with itself, it could not be undone by anyone but the one who had bound it together.

Now each one of the four constituents was entirely used up in the pro-cess of building the world. The builder built it from all the fire, water, air and earth there was, and left no part or power of any of them out. His intentions in so doing were these: First, that as a living being it should be as d whole and complete as possible and made up of complete parts. Second, 33 that it should be just one universe, in that nothing would be left over from which another one just like it could be made. Third, that it should not get old and diseased. He realized that when heat or cold or anything else that possesses strong powers surrounds a composite body from outside and attacks it, it destroys that body prematurely, brings disease and old age upon it and so causes it to waste away. That is why he concluded that he should fashion the world as a single whole, composed of all wholes, com-

---

2. A simple example of a proportionate progression that satisfies Plato's require-ments in 32a might be that of 2, 4, 8. So: 2:4::4:8 (the first term is to the middle what the middle is to the last, the last term is to the middle what the middle is to the first); 4:2::8:4 or 4:8::2:4 (the middle term turns out to be first and last and the first and last terms turn out to be middles). Since, however, the body of the world is three-dimensional, its components must be represented by "solid" numbers, i.e., numbers that are the products of three numbers. This will require two middle terms.

plete and free of old age and disease, and why he fashioned it that way.

b And he gave it a shape appropriate to the kind of thing it was. The appropriate shape for that living being that is to contain within itself all the living beings would be the one which embraces within itself all the shapes there are. Hence he gave it a round shape, the form of a sphere, with its center equidistant from its extremes in all directions. This of all shapes is the most complete and most like itself, which he gave to it because he believed that likeness is incalculably more excellent than unlikeness. And

c he gave it a smooth round finish all over on the outside, for many reasons. It needed no eyes, since there was nothing visible left outside it; nor did it need ears, since there was nothing audible there, either. There was no air enveloping it that it might need for breathing, nor did it need any organ by which to take in food or, again, expel it when it had been digested. For since there wasn't anything else, there would be nothing to leave it or come to it from anywhere. It supplied its own waste for its food. Anything that it

d did or experienced it was designed to do or experience within itself and by itself. For the builder thought that if it were self-sufficient, it would be a better thing than if it required other things.

And since it had no need to catch hold of or fend off anything, the god thought that it would be pointless to attach hands to it. Nor would it need

34 feet or any support to stand on. In fact, he awarded it the movement suited to its body—that one of the seven motions which is especially associated with understanding and intelligence. And so he set it turning continuously in the same place, spinning around upon itself. All the other six motions he took away, and made its movement free of their wanderings. And since it didn't need feet to follow this circular path, he begat it without legs or feet.

b Applying this entire train of reasoning to the god that was yet to be, the eternal god made it smooth and even all over, equal from the center, a whole and complete body itself, but also made up of complete bodies. In its center he set a soul, which he extended throughout the whole body, and with which he then covered the body outside. And he set it to turn in a circle, a single solitary universe, whose very excellence enables it to keep its own company without requiring anything else. For its knowledge of and friendship with itself is enough. All this, then, explains why this world which he begat for himself is a blessed god.

As for the world's soul, even though we are now embarking on an ac-

c count of it *after* we've already given an account of its body, it isn't the case that the god devised it to be younger than the body. For the god would not have united them and then allow the elder to be ruled by the younger. We have a tendency to be casual and random in our speech, reflecting, no doubt, the whole realm of the casual and random of which we are a part. The god, however, gave priority and seniority to the soul, both in its coming into being and in the degree of its excellence, to be the body's mistress and to rule over it as her subject.

35 The components from which he made the soul and the way in which he made it were as follows: In between the *Being* that is indivisible and always changeless, and the one that is divisible and comes into being in the corporeal realm, he mixed a third, intermediate form of being, derived from the other two. Similarly, he made a mixture of *the Same*, and then one of *the Different*, in between their indivisible and their corporeal, divisible counterparts. And he took the three mixtures and mixed them together to make a uniform mixture, forcing the Different, which was hard to mix, into conformity with the Same. Now when he had mixed these two together *b* with Being, and from the three had made a single mixture, he redivided the whole mixture into as many parts as his task required, each part remaining a mixture of the Same, the Different, and of Being. This is how he began the division: First he took one portion away from the whole, and then he took another, twice as large, followed by a third, one and a half times as large as the second and three times as large as the first. The fourth portion he took was twice as large as the second, the fifth three times as large as the third, the sixth eight times that of the first, and the seventh twenty-seven times that of the first.

After this he went on to fill the double and triple intervals by cutting off *36* still more portions from the mixture and placing these between them, in such a way that in each interval there were two middle terms, one exceeding the first extreme by the same fraction of the extremes by which it was exceeded by the second, and the other exceeding the first extreme by a number equal to that by which it was exceeded by the second. These connections produced intervals of 3/2, 4/3, and 9/8 within the previous intervals. He then proceeded to fill all the 4/3 intervals with the 9/8 inter- *b* val, leaving a small portion over every time. The terms of this interval of the portion left over made a numerical ratio of 256/243. And so it was that the mixture, from which he had cut off these portions, was eventually completely used up.[3]

3. The construction of the world's soul follows three stages:

(1) *The creation of the mixture:* Three preliminary mixtures are created. The first is a mixture of indivisible, changeless Being with divisible Being. The second and third are likewise mixtures of indivisible with divisible Sameness and Difference, respectively. These three preliminary mixtures are themselves mixed to create the final mixture.

(2) *The division of the mixture:* Seven "portions" of the mixture are now marked off, possessing the following numerical values:

First portion:	1	Fifth portion:	9
Second portion	2	Sixth portion:	8
Third portion:	3	Seventh portion:	27
Fourth portion:	4		

(3) *The filling of the intervals:* The values of the first, second, fourth and sixth portions form a series such that each successive portion is twice that of its pre-

Next, he sliced this entire compound in two along its length, joined the
two halves together center to center like an X, and bent them back in a
circle, attaching each half to itself end to end and to the ends of the other
half at the point opposite to the one where they had been joined together.
He then included them in that motion which revolves in the same place
without variation, and began to make the one the outer, and the other the
inner circle. And he decreed that the outer movement should be the movement of *the Same*, while the inner one should be that of *the Different*. He
made the movement of the Same revolve toward the right by way of the
side, and that of the Different toward the left by way of the diagonal, and
he made the revolution of the Same, i.e., the uniform, the dominant one in
that he left this one alone undivided, while he divided the inner one six
times, to make seven unequal circles. His divisions corresponded to the
several double and triple intervals, of which there were three each. He set
the circles to go in contrary directions: three to go at the same speed, and

---

decessor. The values of the first, third, fifth and seventh portions form a series such
that each successive portion is three times that of its predecessor. Thus intervals
between successive portions of the first series are called "double intervals," and
those between successive portions of the second series are called "triple intervals."
Within each interval there are two "middle terms." The first of these is such that its
value is that of the first extreme plus $1/x$ of the first extreme, which is equal to the
value of the second extreme minus $1/x$ of the second extreme. This is the "harmonic middle." The second middle term is such that its value is the median between
the extremes. This is the "arithmetical middle." Inserting the two middle terms
within the original intervals in the first series, we get:

$1 - 4/3 - 3/2 - 2 - 8/3 - 3 - 4 - 16/3 - 6 - 8$;

and doing the same with the second series produces:

$1 - 3/2 - 2 - 3 - 9/2 - 6 - 9 - 27/2 - 18 - 27$.

Combining the two series in ascending order and omitting duplication we get:

$1 - 4/3 - 3/2 - 2 - 8/3 - 3 - 4 - 9/2 - 16/3 - 6 - 8 - 9 - 27/2 - 18 - 27$.

In this series the value of each term but the first is either 4/3 or 3/2 or 9/8 the value
of its predecessor. Finally, the intervals of 4/3 (e.g., between 1 and 4/3, or between
3/2 and 2, or 3 and 4) are now themselves "filled" by intervals of 9/8. In the
interval between 1 and 4/3, for example, we can insert new intervals each
of which multiplies its predecessor by 9/8, but we can do so no more than twice
$(1 - 9/8 - 81/64 \ldots 4/3)$, since a third attempt (729/512) would exceed 4/3. The
interval between 81/64 can only be filled up with a "leftover," a number by which
81/64 can be multiplied to equal 4/3. This number turns out to be 256/243.

the other four to go at speeds different from both each other's and that of the other three. Their speeds, however, were all proportionate to each other.[4]

Once the whole soul had acquired a form that pleased him, he who formed it went on to fashion inside it all that is corporeal, and, joining center to center, he fitted the two together. The soul was woven together with the body from the center on out in every direction to the outermost limit of the universe, and covered it all around on the outside. And, revolving within itself, it initiated a divine beginning of unceasing, intelligent life for all time. Now while the body of the universe had come into being as a visible thing, the soul was invisible. But even so, because it shares in reason

e

4. By speaking of "circles" instead of spheres, Plato seems to have in mind the model of an armillary sphere, a skeleton structure which, by representing whole spheres as rings, enables a viewer to examine the axial positions of spheres within the outer sphere. The circle of *the Same* is a ring of one half of the just described soul compound which in its motion represents the entire sphere, from the center of the earth to the outer limit, the realm of the fixed stars. This sphere moves "toward the right," i.e., from east to west along its axis between the poles along the plane of the equator. The observation point is presumably that of an observer in a northern latitude looking toward the south. The circle of *the Different* is a ring of the remaining half of the soul compound, which is subsequently subdivided into seven smaller rings (spheres), the orbits of the moon, the sun, and the five planets. Their movements are "toward the left," i.e., in the opposite direction of the movement of the sphere that embraces them, that of *the Same*. The planes of these seven rings are parallel to "the diagonal," i.e., the plane of the ecliptic, and presumably all seven rings move within the limits of the Zodiac, that band of constellations which parallels, and is bisected along its length by, the ecliptic. The relation of the plane of the equator to that of the ecliptic, following Plato's suggestion that the latter is "diagonal" to the former, may be illustrated as follows:

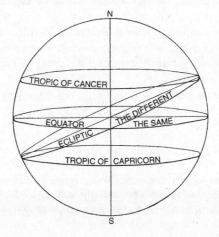

37   and harmony, the soul came into being as the most excellent of all the
       things begotten by him who is himself most excellent of all that is intelli-
       gible and eternal.

       Because the soul is a mixture of the Same, the Different and Being (the
       three components we've described), because it was divided up and bound
       together in various proportions, and because it circles round upon itself,
       then, whenever it comes into contact with something whose being is scat-
       terable or else with something whose being is indivisible, it is stirred
       throughout its whole self. It then declares what exactly that thing is the

b   same as, or what it is different from, and in what respect and in what
       manner, as well as when, it turns out that they are the same or different
       and are characterized as such.[5] This applies both to the things that come to
       be, and to those that are always changeless. And when this contact gives
       rise to an account that is equally true whether it is about what is different
       or about what is the same, and is borne along without utterance or sound
       within the self-moved thing, then, whenever the account concerns anything
       that is perceptible, the circle of the Different goes straight and proclaims it
       throughout its whole soul. This is how firm and true opinions and convic-

c   tions come about. Whenever, on the other hand, the account concerns any
       object of reasoning, and the circle of the Same runs well and reveals it, the
       necessary result is understanding and knowledge. And if anyone should
       ever call that in which these two arise, not soul but something else, what he
       says will be anything but true.

       Now when the Father who had begotten the universe observed it set in
       motion and alive, a thing that had come into being as a shrine for the
       everlasting gods, he was well pleased, and in his delight he thought of

d   making it more like its model still. So, as the model was itself an everlast-
       ing Living Being, he set himself to bringing this universe to completion in
       such a way that it, too, would have that character to the extent that was
       possible. Now the Living Being's nature was to be eternal, but it isn't possi-
       ble to bestow eternity fully upon anything that is begotten. And so he
       began to think of making a moving image of eternity: at the same time as
       he brought order to the universe, he would make an eternal image, moving
       according to number, of eternity remaining in unity. This image, of course,
       is what we now call "time."

e   For before the heavens came into being, there were no days or nights, no
       months or years. But now, at the same time as he framed the heavens, he

---

5. Plato relies on a principle, common to some fifth-century natural philosophers
(e.g., Empedocles), that "like is known by like": In order for a knowing subject to be
able to know a given object, the subject must possess some of the same or similar
characteristics as the object. Thus because the soul is itself composed of sameness
and difference it can recognize A as being the same as or different from B, and the
respects, manners and times when this is so.

devised their coming into being. These all are parts of time, and *was* and *will be* are forms of time that have come into being. Such notions we unthinkingly but incorrectly apply to everlasting being. For we say that it *was* and *is* and *will be*, but according to the true account only *is* is appropri- 38 ately said of it. *Was* and *will be* are properly said about the becoming that passes in time, for these two are motions. But that which is always change-less and motionless cannot become either older or younger in the course of time—it neither ever became so, nor is it now such that it has become so, nor will it ever be so in the future. And all in all, none of the characteristics that becoming has bestowed upon the things that are borne about in the realm of perception are appropriate to it. These, rather, are forms of time that have come into being—time that imitates eternity and circles accord-ing to number. And what is more, we also say things like these: that what   *b* has come to be *is* what has come to be, that what is coming to be *is* what is coming to be, and also that what will come to be *is* what will come to be, and that what is not *is* what is not. None of these expressions of ours is accurate. But I don't suppose this is a good time right now to be too meticulous about these matters.

Time, then, came into being together with the universe so that just as they were begotten together, they might also be undone together, should there ever be an undoing of them. And it came into being after the model of that which is sempiternal, so that it might be as much like its model as   *c* possible. For the model is something that has being *for all eternity*, while it, on the other hand, has been, is, and shall be *for all time*, forevermore. Such was the reason, then, such the god's design for the coming into being of time, that he brought into being the Sun, the Moon and five other stars, for the begetting of time. These are called "wanderers" [*planeta*], and they came into being to set limits to and stand guard over the numbers of time. When the god had finished making a body for each of them, he placed them into the orbits traced by the period of the Different—seven bodies in seven orbits. He set the Moon in the first circle, around the earth, and the   *d* Sun in the second, above it. The Dawnbearer [the Morning Star, or Venus] and the star said to be sacred to Hermes [Mercury] he set to run in circles that equal the Sun's in speed, though they received the power contrary to its power. As a result, the Sun, the star of Hermes and the Dawnbearer alike overtake and are overtaken by one another. As for the other bodies, if I were to spell out where he situated them, and all his reasons for doing so, my account, already a digression, would make more work than its purpose   *e* calls for. Perhaps later on we could at our leisure give this subject the ex-position it deserves.

Now when each of the bodies that were to cooperate in producing time had come into the movement prepared for carrying it and when, bound by bonds of soul, these bodies had been begotten with life and learned their assigned tasks, they began to revolve along the movement of the Different,

39 which is oblique and which goes through the movement of the Same, by which it is also dominated. Some bodies would move in a larger circle, others in a smaller one, the latter moving more quickly and the former more slowly. Indeed, because of the movement of the Same, the ones that go around most quickly appeared to be overtaken by those going more slowly, even though in fact they were overtaking them. For as it revolves, this movement gives to all these circles a spiral twist, because they are

b moving forward in two contrary directions at once. As a result, it makes that body which departs most slowly from it—and it is the fastest of the movements—appear closest to it.

And so that there might be a conspicuous measure of their relative slowness and quickness with which they move along in their eight revolutions, the god kindled a light in the orbit second from the earth, the light that we now call the Sun. Its chief work would be to shine upon the whole universe and to bestow upon all those living beings appropriately endowed and taught by the revolution of the Same and the uniform, a share in

c number. In this way and for these reasons night-and-day, the period of a single circling, the wisest one, came into being. A month has passed when the Moon has completed its own cycle and overtaken the Sun; a year when the Sun has completed its own cycle.

As for the periods of the other bodies, all but a scattered few have failed to take any note of them. Nobody has given them names or investigated their numerical measurements relative to each other. And so people are all

d but ignorant of the fact that time really is the wanderings of these bodies, bewilderingly numerous as they are and astonishingly variegated. It is none the less possible, however, to discern that the perfect number of time brings to completion the perfect year at that moment when the relative speeds of all eight periods have been completed together and, measured by the circle of the Same that moves uniformly, have achieved their consummation. This, then, is how as well as why those stars were begotten which, on their way through the universe, would have turnings. The purpose was

e to make this living being as like as possible to that perfect and intelligible Living Being, by way of imitating its sempiternity.

Prior to the coming into being of time, the universe had already been made to resemble in various respects the model in whose likeness the god was making it, but the resemblance still fell short in that it didn't yet contain all the living beings that were to have come into being within it. This remaining task he went on to perform, casting the world into the nature of its model. And so he determined that the living being he was making should possess the same kinds and numbers of living beings as those which, according to the discernment of Understanding, are contained within the real Living Being. Now there are four of these kinds: first, the

40 heavenly race of gods; next, the kind that has wings and travels through

the air; third, the kind that lives in water; and fourth, the kind that has feet and lives on land. The gods he made mostly out of fire, to be the brightest and fairest to the eye.[6] He made them well-rounded, to resemble the universe, and placed them in the wisdom of the dominant circle [i.e., of the Same], to follow the course of the universe. He spread the gods throughout the whole heaven to be a true adornment [cosmos] for it, an intricately wrought whole. And he bestowed two movements upon each of them. The first was rotation, an unvarying movement in the same place, by which the god would always think the same thoughts about the same things. The other was revolution, a forward motion under the dominance of the circular carrying movement of the Same and uniform. The gods are devoid of motion and stand still in respect of any of the other five motions, in order that each of them may come as close as possible to attaining perfection.

   This, then, was the reason why all those everlasting and unwandering stars—divine living beings which stay fixed by revolving without variation in the same place—came into being. Those that have turnings and thus wander in that sort of way came into being as previously described.

   The Earth he devised to be our nurturer, and, because it curls around the axis that stretches throughout the universe, also to be the maker and guardian of day and night. Of the gods that have come into being within the universe, Earth ranks as the foremost, the one with greatest seniority.

   To describe the dancing movements of these gods, their juxtapositions and the back-circlings and advances of their circular courses on themselves; to tell which of the gods come into line with one another at their conjunctions and how many of them are in opposition, and in what order and at which times they pass in front of or behind one another, so that some are occluded from our view to reappear once again, thereby bringing terrors and portents of things to come to those who cannot reason—to tell all this without the use of visible models would be labor spent in vain. We will make do with this account, and so let this be the conclusion of our discussion of the nature of the visible and generated gods.

   As for the other spiritual beings [daimones], it is beyond our task to know and speak of how they came into being. We should accept on faith the assertions of those figures of the past who claimed to be the offspring of gods. They must surely have been well informed about their own ancestors. So we cannot avoid believing the children of gods, even though their accounts lack plausible or compelling proofs. Rather, we should follow custom and believe them, on the ground that what they claim to be reporting are matters of their own concern. Accordingly, let us accept their account of how these gods came into being and state what it is.

6. These are the fixed stars, i.e., those other than the planets, which have already been created (cf. below, 40b).

Earth and Heaven gave birth to Ocean and Tethys, who in turn gave birth
41   to Phorkys, Cronus and Rhea and all the gods in that generation. Cronus
and Rhea gave birth to Zeus and Hera, as well as all those siblings who are
called by names we know. These in turn gave birth to yet another generation. In any case, when all the gods had come into being, both the ones
who make their rounds conspicuously and the ones who present themselves only to the extent that they are willing, the begetter of this universe
spoke to them. This is what he said:

"O gods, works divine whose maker and father I am, whatever has come
into being by my hands cannot be undone but by my consent. Now while it
b   is true that anything that is bound is liable to being undone, till, only one
who is evil would consent to the undoing of what has been well fitted
together and is in fine condition. This is the reason why you, as creatures
that have come into being, are neither completely immortal nor exempt
from being undone. Still, you will not be undone nor will death be your
portion, since you have received the guarantee of my will—a greater, more
sovereign bond than those with which you were bound when you came into
being. Learn now, therefore, what I declare to you. There remain still three
kinds of mortal beings that have not yet been begotten; and as long as they
have not come into being, the universe will be incomplete, for it will still
c   lack within it all the kinds of living beings it must have if it is to be
sufficiently complete. But if these creatures came into being and came to
share in life by my hand, they would rival the gods. It is you, then, who
must turn yourselves to the task of fashioning these living beings, as your
nature allows. This will assure their mortality, and this whole universe will
really be a completed whole. Imitate the power I used in bringing you into
being. And to the extent that it is fitting for them to possess something that
shares our name of 'immortal', something described as divine and ruling
within those of them who always consent to follow after justice and after
d   you, I shall begin by sowing that seed, and then hand it over to you. The
rest of the task is yours. Weave what is mortal to what is immortal, fashion
and beget living beings. Give them food, cause them to grow, and when
they perish, receive them back again."

When he had finished this speech, he turned again to the mixing bowl he
had used before, the one in which he had blended and mixed the soul of
the universe. He began to pour into it what remained of the previous
ingredients and to mix them in somewhat the same way, though these were
no longer invariably and constantly pure, but of a second and third grade
of purity. And when he had compounded it all, he divided the mixture into
e   a number of souls equal to the number of the stars and assigned each soul
to a star. He mounted each soul in a carriage, as it were, and showed it the
nature of the universe. He described to them the laws that had been fore-
ordained: They would all be assigned one and the same initial birth, so that

none would be less well treated by him than any other. Then he would sow
each of the souls into that instrument of time suitable to it, where they
were to acquire the nature of being the most god-fearing of living beings,   42
and, since humans have a twofold nature, the superior kind should be such
as would from then on be called "man". So, once the souls were of necessity implanted in bodies, and these bodies had things coming to them and
leaving them, mingled with pleasure and pain. And they would come to
have fear and spiritedness as well, plus whatever goes with having these   b
emotions, as well as all their natural opposites. And if they could master
these emotions, their lives would be just, whereas if they were mastered by
them, they would be unjust. And if a person lived a good life throughout
the due course of his time, he would at the end return to his dwelling place
in his companion star, to live a life of happiness that agreed with his
character. But if he failed in this, he would be born a second time, now as a   c
woman. And if even then he still could not refrain from wickedness, he
would be changed once again, this time into some wild animal that resembled the wicked character he had acquired. And he would have no rest
from these toilsome transformations until he had dragged that massive
accretion of fire-water-air-earth into conformity with the revolution of the
Same and uniform within him, and so subdued that turbulent, irrational   d
mass by means of reason. This would return him to his original condition
of excellence.

Having set out all these ordinances to them—which he did to exempt
himself from responsibility for any evil they might afterwards do—the god
proceeded to sow some of them into the Earth, some into the Moon, and
others into the various other instruments of time. After the sowing, he
handed over to the young gods the task of weaving mortal bodies. He had
them make whatever else remained that the human soul still needed to   e
have, plus whatever goes with those things. He gave them the task of ruling
over these mortal living beings and of giving them the finest, the best
possible guidance they could give, without being responsible for any evils
these creatures might bring upon themselves.

When he had finished assigning all these tasks, he proceeded to abide at
rest in his own customary nature. His children immediately began to attend
to and obey their father's assignment. Now that they had received the
immortal principle of the mortal living being, they began to imitate the
craftsman who had made them. They borrowed parts of fire, earth, water
and air from the world, intending to pay them back again, and bonded   43
together into a unity the parts they had taken, but not with those indissoluble bonds by which they themselves were held together. Instead, they
proceeded to fuse them together with copious rivets so small as to be
invisible, thereby making each body a unit made up of all the components.
And they went on to invest this body—into and out of which things were

to flow—with the orbits of the immortal soul. These orbits, now bound within a mighty river, neither mastered that river nor were mastered by it,
b   but tossed it violently and were violently tossed by it. Consequently the living being as a whole did indeed move, but it would proceed in a disorderly, random and irrational way that involved all six of the motions.[7] It would go forwards and backwards, then back and forth to the right and the left, and upwards and downwards, wandering every which way in these six directions. For mighty as the nourishment-bearing billow was in its ebb and flow, mightier still was the turbulence produced by the disturbances [*pathēmata*] caused by the things that struck against the living beings. Such
c   disturbances would occur when the body encountered and collided with external fire (i.e., fire other than the body's own) or for that matter with a hard lump of earth or with the flow of gliding waters, or when it was caught up by a surge of air-driven winds. The motions produced by all these encounters would then be conducted through the body to the soul, and strike against it. (That is no doubt why these motions as a group came afterwards to be called "sensations," as they are still called today.) It was just then, at that very instant, that they produced a very long and intense
d   commotion. They cooperated with the continually flowing channel to stir and violently shake the orbits of the soul. They completely bound that of the Same by flowing against it in the opposite direction, and held it fast just as it was beginning to go its way. And they further shook the orbit of the Different right through, with the result that they twisted every which way the three intervals of the double and the three of the triple, as well as the middle terms of the ratios of 3/2, 4/3 and 9/8 that connect them. [These agitations did not undo them, however,] because they cannot be completely undone except by the one who had bound them together. They mutilated
e   and disfigured the circles in every possible way so that the circles barely held together and though they remained in motion, they moved without rhyme or reason, sometimes in the opposite direction, sometimes sideways and sometimes upside down—like a man upside down, head propped against the ground and holding his feet up against something. In that position his right side will present itself both to him and to those looking at him as left, and his left side as right. It is this very thing—and others like
44 it—that had such a dramatic effect upon the revolutions of the soul. Whenever they encounter something outside of them characterizable as *same* or *different*, they will speak of it as "the same as" something, or as "different from" something else when the truth is just the opposite, so proving themselves to be misled and unintelligent. Also, at this stage souls do not have a ruling orbit taking the lead. And so when certain sensations come in from

---

7. Timaeus is here describing the uncontrolled movements of a newborn animal. He goes on to describe the confusion produced in its soul by its first sensations.

outside and attack them, they sweep the soul's entire vessel along with them. It is then that these revolutions, however much in control they seem to be, are actually under their control. All these disturbances are no doubt the reason why even today and not only at the beginning, whenever a soul is bound within a mortal body, it at first lacks intelligence. But as the *b* stream that brings growth and nourishment diminishes and the soul's orbits regain their composure, resume their proper courses and establish themselves more and more with the passage of time, their revolutions are set straight, to conform to the configuration each of the circles takes in its natural course. They then correctly identify what is the same and what is different, and render intelligent the person who possess them. And to be sure, if such a person also gets proper nurture to supplement his education, he'll turn out perfectly whole and healthy, and will have escaped the most *c* grievous of illnesses. But if he neglects this, he'll limp his way through life and return to Hades uninitiated and unintelligent.

But this doesn't happen until later. Our present subject, on the other hand, needs a more detailed treatment. We must move on to treat the prior questions—the ones that deal with how bodies came into being, part by part, as well as the soul. What were the gods' reasons, what was their plan when they brought these into being? In discussing these questions we shall *d* hold fast to what is most likely, and proceed accordingly.

Copying the revolving shape of the universe, the gods bound the two divine orbits into a ball-shaped body, the part that we now call our head. This is the most divine part of us, and master of all our other parts. They then assembled the rest of the body and handed the whole of it to the head, to be in its service. They intended it to share in all the motions there were to be. To keep the head from rolling around on the ground without *e* any way of getting up over its various high spots and out of the low, they gave it the body as a vehicle to make its way easy. This is the reason why the body came to have length and grow four limbs that could flex and extend themselves, divinely devised for the purpose of getting about. Holding on and supporting itself with these limbs, it would be capable of making its way through all regions, while carrying at the top the dwelling **45** place of that most divine, most sacred part of ourselves. This is how as well as why we have all grown arms and legs. And considering the front side to be more honorable and more commanding than the back, the gods gave us the ability to travel for the most part in this direction. Human beings no doubt ought to have the front sides of their bodies distinguishable from and dissimilar to their backs, and so the gods began by setting the face on that side of the the head, the soul's vessel. They bound organs inside it to provide completely for the soul, and they assigned this side, the *b* natural front, to be the part that takes the lead.

The eyes were the first of the organs to be fashioned by the gods, to conduct light. The reason why they fastened them within the head is this. They contrived that such fire as was not for burning but for providing a gentle light should become a body, proper to each day. Now the pure fire inside us, cousin to that fire, they made to flow through the eyes: so they made the eyes—the eye as a whole but its middle in particular—close-

c   textured, smooth and dense, to enable them to keep out all the other, coarser stuff, and let that kind of fire pass through pure by itself. Now whenever daylight surrounds the visual stream, like makes contact with like and coalesces with it to make up a single homogeneous body aligned with the direction of the eyes. This happens wherever the internal fire strikes and presses against an external object it has connected with. And because this body of fire has become uniform throughout and thus uni-

d   formly affected, it transmits the motions of whatever it comes in contact with as well as of whatever comes in contact with it, to and through the whole body until they reach the soul. This brings about the sensation we call "seeing." At night, however, the kindred fire has departed and so the visual stream is cut off. For now it exits only to encounter something unlike itself. No longer able to bond with the surrounding air, which now has lost its fire, it undergoes changes and dies out. So it not only stops seeing, but even begins to induce sleep. For when the eyelids—which the gods devised

e   to keep eyesight safe—are closed, they shut in the power of the internal fire, which then disperses and evens out the internal motions, and when these have been evened out, a state of quietness ensues. And if this quietness is deep, one falls into an all but dreamless sleep. But if some fairly

46   strong motions remain, they produce images similar in kind and in number to the kind of motions they are, and the kind of regions in which they remain—images which, though formed within, are recalled upon waking as external objects.

And so there is no longer any difficulty in understanding how images are produced in mirrors or in any other smooth reflecting surfaces. On such occasions the internal fire joins forces with the external fire, to form on the smooth surface a single fire which is reshaped in a multitude of ways. So

b   once the fire from the face comes to coalesce with the fire from sight on the smooth and bright surface, you have the inevitable appearance of all images of this sort. What is left will appear as right, because the parts of the fire from sight connect with the opposite parts of the fire from the face, contrary to the usual manner of encounter. But, on the other hand, what is right does appear as right, and what is left as left whenever light switches sides in the process of coalescing with the light with which it coalesces.

c   And this happens whenever the mirror's smooth surface is curled upwards on both sides, thereby bending the right part of the fire from sight towards the left, and the left part towards the right. And when this same smooth surface is turned along the length of the face [i.e., vertically], it makes the whole object appear upside down, because it bends the lower part of the ray toward the top, and the upper part toward the bottom.[8]

Now all of the above are among the auxiliary causes employed in the service of the god as he does his utmost to bring to completion the character of what is most excellent. But because they make things cold or hot,   *d* compact or disperse them, and produce all sorts of similar effects, most people regard them not as auxiliary causes, but as the actual causes of all things. Things like these, however, are totally incapable of possessing any reason or understanding about anything. We must pronounce the soul to be the only thing there is that properly possesses understanding. The soul is an invisible thing, whereas fire, water, earth and air have all come into being as visible bodies. So anyone who is a lover of understanding and knowledge must of necessity pursue as primary causes those that belong to intelligent nature, and as secondary all those that arise from other things—   *e* things which are subject to being moved by others and which set still others in motion by necessity. We too, surely, must do likewise: we must describe both types of causes, distinguishing those which possess understanding and thus fashion what is beautiful and good, from those which are devoid of intelligence and so produce only haphazard and disorderly effects every time.

Let us conclude, then, our discussion of the accompanying auxiliary causes that gave our eyes the power which they now possess. We must next speak of that supremely beneficial function for which the god gave them to   47 us. As my account has it, our sight has indeed proved to be a source of supreme benefit to us, in that none of our present statements about the universe could ever have been made if we had never seen any stars, sun or heaven. As it is, however, our ability to see the periods of day-and-night, of

8. According to 46b-c, direct vision of an object in daylight occurs when fire exiting from the eyes coalesces with fire (daylight) travelling from the object to make a uniform, linear column of fire. In the case of seeing an object reflected in a mirror, the left side of the object will appear as its right side would appear if the object were directly seen, and vice versa, as the following diagram illustrates:

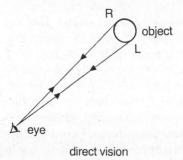

direct vision

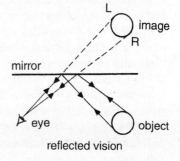

reflected vision

months and of years, of equinoxes and solstices, has led to the invention of number, and has given us the idea of time and opened the path to inquiry

b into the nature of the universe. These pursuits have given us philosophy, a gift from the gods to the mortal race whose value neither has been nor ever will be surpassed. I'm quite prepared to declare this to be the supreme good our eyesight offers us. Why then should we exalt all the lesser good things, which a non-philosopher struck blind would "lament and bewail in vain"? Let us rather declare that the cause and purpose of this supreme good is this: the god invented sight and gave it to us so that we might observe the orbits of intelligence in the universe and apply them to the revolutions of

c our own understanding. For there is a kinship between them, even though our revolutions are disturbed, whereas the universal orbits are undisturbed. So once we have come to know them and to share in the ability to make correct calculations according to nature, we should stabilize the straying revolutions within ourselves by imitating the completely unstraying revolutions of the god.

Likewise, the same account goes for sound and hearing—these too are the gods' gifts, given for the same purpose and intended to achieve the same result. Speech (*logos*) was designed for this very purpose—it plays the

d greatest part in its achievement. And all such composition (*mousikē*) as lends itself to making audible musical sound (*phōnē*) is given in order to express harmony, and so serves this purpose as well. And harmony, whose movements are akin to the orbits within our souls, is a gift of the Muses, if our dealings with them are guided by understanding, not for irrational pleasure, for which people nowadays seem to make use of it, but to serve as an ally in the fight to bring order to any orbit in our souls that has become unharmonized, and make it concordant with itself. Rhythm, too, has like-

e wise been given us by the Muses for the same purpose, to assist us. For with most of us our condition is such that we have lost all sense of measure, and are lacking in grace.

Now in all but a brief part of the discourse I have just completed I have presented what has been crafted by Intellect (*nous*). But I need to match this account by providing a comparable one concerning the things that

48 have come about by Necessity (*anankē*). For this ordered world is of mixed birth: it is the offspring of a union of Necessity and Intellect. Intellect prevailed over Necessity by persuading it to direct most of the things that come into being toward what is best, and the result of this subjugation of Necessity to wise persuasion was the initial formation of this universe. So if I'm to tell the story of how it really came into being in this way, I'd also have to introduce the character of the Straying Cause—how it is its nature

b to set things adrift. I shall have to retrace my steps, then, and, armed with a second starting point that also applies to these same things, I must go back once again to the beginning and start my present inquiry from there, just as I did with my earlier one.

The Contribution of Necessity

We shall of course have to study the intrinsic nature of fire, water, air and earth prior to the heaven's coming into being, as well as the characteristics (*pathē*) they had then. So far no one has as yet revealed how these four came into being. We tend to posit them as the elemental "letters" of the universe and tell people they are its "principles" (*archai*) on the assumption that they know what fire and the other three are. In fact, however, they shouldn't even be compared to syllables.[9] Only a very unenlightened person might be expected to make such a comparison. So let me now proceed with my treatment in the following way: for the present I cannot state "the principle" or "principles" of all things, or however else I think about them, for the simple reason that it is difficult to show clearly what my view is if I follow my present manner of exposition. Please do not expect me to do so then. I couldn't convince even myself that I could be right to commit myself to undertaking a task of such magnitude. I shall keep to what I stated at the beginning, the virtue of likely accounts, and so shall try right from the start to say about things, both individually and collectively, what is no less likely than any, more likely, in fact, than what I have said before. Let us therefore at the outset of this discourse call upon the god to be our savior this time, too, to give us safe passage through a strange and unusual exposition, and lead us to a view of what is likely. And so let me begin my speech again.

48c

d

e

    The new starting point in my account of the universe needs to be more complex than the earlier one. Then we distinguished two kinds, but now we must specify a third, one of a different sort. The earlier two sufficed for our previous account: one was proposed as a model, intelligible and always changeless, a second as an imitation of the model, something that possesses becoming and is visible. We did not distinguish a third kind at the time, because we thought that we could make do with the two of them. Now, however, it appears that our account compels us to attempt to illuminate in words a kind that is difficult and vague. What must we suppose it to do and to be? This above all: it is a *receptacle* of all becoming—its wetnurse, as it were.

49

    However true that statement may be, we must nevertheless describe it more clearly. This is a difficult task, particularly because it requires us to raise a preliminary problem about fire and the other three:

b

    It is difficult to say of each of them—in a way that employs a reliable

9. Plato is criticizing Empedocles and his followers, who made the familiar four elements the ultimate material constituents (the "roots") of things. As he argues later (53b–56c), the elements are composites made up of things that are themselve composite: They are composed of solid geometrical figures which are themselves composed of triangles. It is the solid figures and not the four elements themselves that rank as "syllables" to the triangles (the "letters").

and stable account—which one is the sort of thing one should really call *water* rather than *fire*, or which one one should call some one of these rather than just any and every one of them. What problem, then, do they present for us to work through in likely fashion? And then how and in what manner are we to go on to speak about this third kind?[10]

First, we see (or think we see) the thing that we have just now been calling *water* condensing and turning to stones and earth. Next, we see this same thing dissolving and dispersing, turning to wind and air, and air, when ignited, turning to fire. And then we see fire being condensed and extinguished and turning back to the form of air, and air coalescing and thickening and turning back into cloud and mist. When these are compressed still more we see them turning into flowing water, which we see turning to earth and stones once again. In this way, then, they transmit their coming into being one to the other in a cycle, or so it seems. Now then, since none of these appears ever to remain the same, which one of them can one categorically assert, without embarrassment, to be some particular thing, *this* one, and not something else? One can't. Rather, the safest course by far is to propose that we speak about these things in the following way: What we invariably observe becoming different at different times—fire for example—to characterize that, i.e., fire, not as "this", but each time as "what is such", and speak of water not as "this", as but always as "what is such". And never to speak of anything else as "this", as though it has some stability, of all the things at which we point and use the expressions "that" and "this" and so think we are designating something. For it gets away without abiding the charge of "that" and "this", or any other expression that indicts them of being stable. It is in fact safest not to refer to it by any of these expressions. Rather, "what is such"—coming around like what it was, again and again—*that's* the thing to call it in each and every case. So fire—and generally everything that has becoming—it is safest to call "what is altogether such." But that *in* which they each appear to keep coming in to being and *from* which they subsequently pass out of being, *that's* the only thing to refer to by means of the expressions "that" and "this". A thing that is some "such" or other, however—hot or white, say, or any one of the opposites, and all things constituted by these—should be called none of these things [i.e., "this" or "that"].

I must make one more effort to describe it, more clearly still. Suppose you were molding gold into every shape there is, going on non-stop remolding one shape into the next. If someone then were to point at one of them and ask you, "What *is* it?" your safest answer by far, with respect to truth, would be to say, "gold," but never "triangle" or any of the other shapes that

10. Lit. "this thing itself," a reference to the receptacle. The "preliminary problem" concerning fire and the others is raised in b7–d3 and a solution is proposed at d3–e7. The solution then provides the correct way of thinking and speaking of the receptacle (d7–50a6).

come to be in the gold, as though it *is* these, because they change even while you're making the statement. However, that answer, too, should be satisfactory, as long the shapes are willing to accept "what is such" as someone's designation. This has a degree of safety.

Now the same account, in fact, holds also for that nature which receives all the bodies. We must always refer to it by the same term, for it does not depart from its own character in any way. Not only does it always receive all things, it has never in any way whatever taken on any characteristic *c* similar to any of the things that enter it. Its nature is to be available for anything to make its impression upon, and it is modified, shaped and reshaped by the things that enter it. These are the things that make it appear different at different times. The things that enter and leave it are imitations of those things that always are, imprinted after their likeness in a marvellous way that is hard to describe. This is something we shall pursue at another time. For the moment, we need to keep in mind three types of things: (i) *that which comes to be*, (ii) *that in which it comes to be*, *d* and (iii) *that after which the thing coming to be is modeled, and which is its source*. It is in fact appropriate to compare (ii) the receiving thing to a mother, (iii) the source to a father, and (i) the nature between them to their offspring. We also must understand that if the imprints are to be varied, with all the varieties there to see, this thing upon which the imprints are to be formed could not be well prepared for that role if it were not itself devoid of any of those characters that it is to receive from elsewhere. For if *e* it resembled any of the things that enter it, it could not successfully copy their opposites or things of a totally different nature whenever it were to receive them. It would be showing its own face as well. This is why the thing that is to receive in itself all the [elemental] kinds must be totally devoid of any characteristics. Think of people who make fragrant ointments. They expend skill and ingenuity to come up with something just like this [i.e., a neutral base], to have on hand to start with. The liquids that are to receive the fragrances they make as odorless as possible. Or think of people who work at impressing shapes upon soft materials. They emphatically refuse to allow any such material to already have some definite shape. Instead, they'll even it out and make it as smooth as it can be. In the *51* same way, then, if the thing that is to receive repeatedly throughout its whole self the likenesses of the intelligible objects, the things which always are—if it is to do so successfully, then it ought to be devoid of any inherent characteristics of its own. This, of course, is the reason why we shouldn't call the mother or receptacle of what has come to be, of what is visible or perceivable in every other way, either earth or air, fire or water, or any of their compounds or their constituents. But if we speak of it as an invisible and characterless sort of thing, one that receives all things and shares in a *b* most perplexing way in what is intelligible, a thing extremely difficult to comprehend, we shall not be misled. And insofar as it is possible to arrive at its nature on the basis of what we've said so far, the most correct way to speak of it may well be this: the part of it that gets ignited appears on each occasion as fire, the dampened part as water, and parts as earth or air insofar as it receives the imitations of these.

But we must prefer to conduct our inquiry by means of rational argument. Hence we should make a distinction like the following: Is there such a thing as a Fire *by itself*? Do all these things of which we always say that each of them is something "by itself" really exist? Or are the things we see, and whatever else we perceive through the body, the only things that possess this kind of actuality, so that there is absolutely nothing else besides them at all? Is our perpetual claim that there exists an intelligible Form for each thing a vacuous gesture, in the end nothing but mere talk? Now we certainly will not do justice to the question before us if we dismiss it, leaving it undecided and unadjudicated, and just insist that such things exist, but neither must we append a further lengthy digression to a discourse already quite long. If, however, a significant distinction formulated in few words were to present itself, that would suit our present needs best of all. So here's how I cast my own vote: If understanding and true opinion are distinct, then these "by themselves" things definitely exist—these Forms, the objects not of our sense perception, but of our understanding only. But if—as some people think—true opinion does not differ in any way from understanding, then all the things we perceive through our bodily senses must be assumed to be the most stable things there are. But we do have to speak of understanding and true opinion as distinct, of course, because we can come to have one without the other, and the one is not like the other. It is through instruction that we come to have understanding, and through persuasion that we come to have true belief. Understanding always involves a true account while true belief lacks any account. And while understanding remains unmoved by persuasion, true belief gives in to persuasion. And of true belief, it must be said, all men have a share, but of understanding, only the gods and a small group of people do.

Since these things are so, we must agree that (i) that which keeps its own form unchangingly, which has not been brought into being and is not destroyed, which neither receives into itself anything else from anywhere else, nor itself enters into anything else anywhere, is one thing. It is invisible—it cannot be perceived by the senses at all—and it is the role of understanding to study it. (ii) The second thing is that which shares the other's name and resembles it. This thing can be perceived by the senses, and it has been begotten. It is constantly borne along, now coming into being in a certain place and then perishing out of it. It is apprehended by opinion, which involves sense perception. (iii) And the third type is space, which exists always and cannot be destroyed. It provides a location for all things that come into being. It is itself apprehended by a kind of bastard reasoning that does not involve sense perception, and it is hardly even an object of conviction [*pistis*]. We look at it as in a dream when we say that everything that exists must of necessity be somewhere, in some place and occupying some space, and that that which doesn't exist somewhere, whether on earth or in heaven, doesn't exist at all.

We prove unable to draw all these distinctions and others related to them—even in the case of that unsleeping, truly existing reality—because our dreaming state renders us incapable of waking up and stating the truth, which is this: Since that for which an image has come into being is not at all intrinsic to the image, which is invariably borne along to picture something else, it stands to reason that the image should therefore come into being *in* something else, somehow clinging to being, or else be nothing at all. But that which really is receives support from the accurate, true account, which is that as long as the one is distinct from the other, neither ever comes to be in the other in such a way that they at the same time become one and the same, and also two.[11]

Let this, then, be a summary of the account I would offer, as computed by my "vote." There are (a) being, (b) space and (c) becoming, three distinct things which existed even before the universe came into being.

Now as the wetnurse of becoming turns watery and fiery and receives the character of earth and air, and as it acquires all the properties that come with these characters, it takes on a variety of visible aspects, but because it is filled with powers that are neither similar nor evenly balanced, no part of it is in balance. It sways irregularly in every direction as it is shaken by those things, and being set in motion it in turn shakes them. And as they are moved, they drift continually, some in one direction and others in others, separating from one another. They are winnowed out, as it were, like grain that is sifted by winnowing sieves or other such implements. They are carried off and settle down, the dense and heavy ones in one direction, and the rare and light ones to another place.

That is how at that time the four kinds were being shaken by the receiver, which was itself agitating like a shaking machine, separating the kinds most unlike each other furthest apart and pushing those most like each other closest together into the same region. This, of course, explains how these different kinds came to occupy different regions of space, even

11. Plato's argument in this terse paragraph seems to be the following: A's being an image of B is a relation which supervenes upon A's intrinsic properties, and thus is not itself among A's intrinsic properties. Such a relation requires a subject with a certain set of intrinsic properties to sustain it. For example, if a certain lump of bronze formed in a particular way or a certain canvas covered with oil pigments in a particular configuration are *images* of JFK, they must be, respectively, an image "in bronze" or "on canvas". Images that aren't "in" or "on" anything are "nothing at all". The final sentence reasserts the absence of the "being in" relation (and perhaps by extension the "being of" relation) between the model (Forms) and the subject (receptacle): whereas the image is "in" the latter (and "of" the former), they neither are "of" nor "in" each other.

before their constitution rendered the universe orderly at its coming into being. Indeed, it is a fact that before this took place the four kinds all lacked proportion and measure, and at the time the ordering of the universe was undertaken, fire, water, earth and air initially possessed certain traces of what they are now. They were indeed in the condition one would expect thoroughly god-forsaken things to be in. So, finding them in this natural condition, the first thing the god then did was to give them their distinctive shapes, using forms and numbers.

Here is a proposition we shall always affirm above all else: *The god fashioned these four kinds to be as perfect and excellent as possible, when they were not so before.* It will now be my task to explain to you what structure each of them acquired, and how each came into being. My account will be an unusual one, but since you are well schooled in the fields of learning in terms of which I must of necessity proceed with my exposition, I'm sure you'll follow me.

First of all, everyone knows, I'm sure, that fire, earth, water and air are bodies. Now everything that has bodily form also has depth. Depth, moreover, is of necessity comprehended within surface, and any surface bounded by straight lines is composed of triangles. Every triangle, moreover, derives from two triangles, each of which has one right angle and two acute angles. Of these two triangles, one [the isosceles right-angled triangle] has at each of the other two vertices an equal part of a right angle, determined by its division by equal sides; while the other [the scalene right-angled triangle] has unequal parts of a right angle at its other two vertices, determined by the division of the right angle by unequal sides. This, then, we presume to be the originating principle [archē] of fire and of the other bodies, as we pursue our likely account in terms of Necessity. Principles yet more ultimate than these are known only to the god, and to any man he may hold dear.

We should now say which are the most excellent four bodies that can come into being. They are quite unlike each other, though some of them are capable of breaking up and turning into others and vice-versa. If our account is on the mark, we shall have the truth about how earth and fire and their proportionate intermediates [water and air] came into being. For we shall never concede to anyone that there are any visible bodies more excellent than these, each conforming to a single kind. So we must wholeheartedly proceed to fit together the four kinds of bodies of surpassing excellence, and to declare that we have come to grasp their natures well enough.

Of the two [right-angled] triangles, the isosceles has but one nature, while the scalene has infinitely many. Now we have to select the most excellent one from among the infinitely many, if we are to get a proper start. So if anyone can say that he has picked out one that is more excellent for the construction of these bodies [than the one we are going to pick out], his victory will be that of a friend, not an enemy. Of the many [scalene right-angled] triangles, then, we posit as the one most excellent, surpassing the others, that one from [a pair of] which the equilateral triangle is constructed as a third figure. Why this is so is too long a story to tell now. But *b* if anyone puts this claim to the test and discovers that it isn't so, his be the prize, with our congratulations. So much, then, for the selection of the two triangles out of which the bodies of fire and the other bodies are constructed—the [right-angled] isosceles, and [the right-angled] scalene whose longer side squared is always triple its shorter side squared [i.e., the half-equilateral].[12]

At this point we need to formulate more precisely something that was not stated clearly earlier. For then it appeared that all four kinds of bodies could turn into one another by successive stages. But the appearance is wrong. While there are indeed four kinds of bodies that come into being *c* from the [right-angled] triangles we have selected, three of them come from triangles that have unequal sides, whereas the fourth alone is fashioned out of isosceles triangles. Thus not all of them have the capacity of breaking up and turning into one another, with a large number of small bodies turning into a small number of large ones and vice versa. There are three that can do this. For all three are made up of a single type of triangle, so that when once the larger bodies are broken up, the same triangles can go to make up a large number of small bodies, assuming shapes appropriate to them. And likewise, when numerous small bodies are fragmented *d* into their triangles, these triangles may well combine to make up some single massive body belonging to another kind.

So much, then, for our account of how these bodies turn into one another. Let us next discuss the form that each of them has come to have, and the various numbers that have combined to make them up.

Leading the way will be the primary form, the tiniest structure,[13] whose elementary triangle is the one whose hypotenuse is twice the length of its shorter side. Now when a pair of such triangles are juxtaposed along the

12. Plato's argument in 53c–54b can be summarized and interpreted as follows:

1. All bodies are three-dimensional and hence bounded by surfaces.
2. All surfaces bounded by straight lines are divisible into triangles.
3. All triangles are or are divisible into right-angled triangles (by drawing from an appropriately selected angle a line that is perpendicular to the opposite side).
4. All right-angled triangles are either isosceles (with all angles of fixed size) or scalene (with two angles of varying size).
5. The most perfect of the scalene right-angled triangles is the half-equilateral, whose right angle is bounded by lines the lengths of which are in the ratio of n^2 to $3n^2$ (or, as Plato says later (54d6,7), whose hypotenuse is twice the length of its shorter side).

13. The pyramid.

e

55

diagonal [i.e., their hypotenuses] and this is done three times, and their
diagonals and short sides converge upon a single point as center, the result
is a single equilateral triangle, composed of six such triangles.[14] When four
of these equilateral triangles are combined, a single solid angle is produced
at the junction of three plane angles. This, it turns out, is the angle which
comes right after the most obtuse of the plane angles.[15] And once four such
solid angles have been completed, we get the primary solid form, which is
one that divides the entire circumference [sc. of the sphere in which it is
inscribed] into equal and similar parts.

The second solid form[16] is constructed out of the same [elementary]
triangles which, however, are now arranged in eight equilateral triangles
and produce a single solid angle out of four plane angles. And when six
such solid angles have been produced, the second body has reached its
completion.

b

Now the third body[17] is made up of a combination of one hundred and
twenty of the elementary triangles, and of twelve solid angles, each enclosed by five plane equilateral triangles. This body turns out to have
twenty equilateral triangular faces. And let us take our leave of this one of
the elementary triangles, the one that has begotten the above three kinds of
bodies and turn to the other one, the isosceles [right-angled] triangle,
which has begotten the fourth.[18] Arranged in sets of four whose right

14. Juxtaposing AOD and AOE along their common side AO, and similarly BOD
and BOF along BO, and COE and COF along CO, and then joining the resulting
trapezia at O.

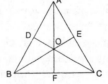

15. I.e., the conjunction of three 60° angles, totalling 180°. All obtuse angles are
<180°.

16. The octahedron, produced by joining four equilateral triangles to form a solid
angle, will require eight such triangles joined at six solid angles for its completion.

17. The icosahedron, produced by joining five equilateral triangles to form a solid
angle. It requires one hundred twenty elemental "perfect" scalene right-angled
triangles, arranged in twenty equilateral triangles, joined at twelve solid angles for
its completion.

18. The cube, made up of squares, produced by juxtaposing AOB, BOC, COD and
AOD at O.

angles come together at the center, the isosceles triangle produced a single equilateral quadrangle [i.e., a square]. And when six of these quadrangles were combined together, they produced eight solid angles, each of which was constituted by three plane right angles. The shape of the resulting body so constructed is a cube, and it has six quadrangular equilateral faces.

One other construction, a fifth, still remained, and this one the god used for the whole universe, embroidering figures on it.[19]

Anyone following this whole line of reasoning might very well be puzzled about whether we should say that there are infinitely many worlds or a finite number of them. If so, he would have to conclude that to answer, "infinitely many," is to take the view of one who is really "unfinished" in things he ought to be "finished" in. He would do better to stop with the question whether we should say that there's really just one world or five and be puzzled about that. Well, our "probable account" answer declares there to be but one world, a god—though someone else, taking other things into consideration, will come to a different opinion. We must set him aside, however.

Let us now assign to fire, earth, water and air the structures which have just been given their formations in our speech. To earth let us give the cube, because of the four kinds of bodies earth is the most immobile and the most pliable—which is what the solid whose faces are the most secure must of necessity turn out to be, more so than the others. Now of the [right-angled] triangles we originally postulated, the face belonging to those that have equal sides has a greater natural stability than that belonging to triangles that have unequal sides, and the surface that is composed of the two triangles, the equilateral quadrangle [the square], holds its position with greater stability than does the equilateral triangle, both in their parts and as wholes. Hence, if we assign this solid figure to earth, we are preserving our "likely account." And of the solid figures that are left, we shall next assign the least mobile of them to water, to fire the most mobile, and to air the one in between. This means that the tiniest body belongs to fire, the largest to water, and the intermediate one to air—and also that the body with the sharpest edges belongs to fire, the next sharpest to air, and the third sharpest to water. Now in all these cases the body that has the fewest faces is of necessity the most mobile, in that it, more than any other, has edges that are the sharpest and best fit for cutting in every direction. It is also the lightest, in that it is made up of the least number of identical parts. The second body ranks second in having these same properties, and the third ranks third. So let us follow our account, which is not only likely but also correct, and take the solid form of the pyramid that we saw constructed as the element or the seed of fire. And let us say that the

19. The dodecahedron, the remaining one of the regular solids. It has twelve faces, each of which is a regular pentagon. It cannot be constructed out of either of the two elemental right-angled triangles.

second form in order of generation is that of air, and the third that of water.

Now we must think of all these bodies as being so small that due to their
c   small size none of them, whatever their kind, is visible to us individually. When, however, a large number of them are clustered together, we do see them in bulk. And in particular, as to the proportions among their numbers, their motions and their other properties, we must think that when the god had brought them to complete and exact perfection (to the degree that Necessity was willing to comply obediently), he arranged them together proportionately.

Given all we have said so far about the kinds of elemental bodies, the
d   following account [of their transformations] is the most likely: When earth encounters fire and is broken up by fire's sharpness, it will drift about—whether the breaking up occurred within fire itself, or within a mass of air or water—until its parts meet again somewhere, refit themselves together and become earth again. The reason is that the parts of earth will never pass into another form. But when water is broken up into parts by fire or even by air, it could happen that the parts recombine to form one corpuscle
e   of fire and two of air. And the fragments of air could produce, from any single particle that is broken up, two fire corpuscles. And conversely, whenever a small amount of fire is enveloped by a large quantity of air or water or perhaps earth and is agitated inside them as they move, and in spite of its resistance is beaten and shattered to bits, then any two fire corpuscles may combine to constitute a single form of air. And when air is overpowered and broken down, then two and one half entire forms of air will be consolidated into a single, entire form of water.[20]

Let us recapitulate and formulate our account of these transformations as
57   follows: Whenever one of the other kinds is caught inside fire and gets cut up by the sharpness of fire's angles and edges, then if it is reconstituted as fire, it will stop getting cut. The reason is that a thing of any kind that is alike and uniform is incapable of effecting any change in, or being affected by, anything that is similar to it. But as long as something involved in a transformation has something stronger than it to contend with, the process of its dissolution will continue non-stop. And likewise, when a few of the
b   smaller corpuscles are surrounded by a greater number of bigger ones, they

---

20. A corpuscle (sōma) of water is an icosahedron, consisting of twenty equilateral triangles or one hundred twenty elementary triangles, sufficient to constitute one pyramid (four equilateral or twenty-four elementary triangles) and two octahedra (eight equilateral or forty-eight elementary triangles each). A corpuscle of air is an octahedron, and so sufficient to constitute two pyramids. Conversely, two fire corpuscles have the required constituent triangles to make up one of air, and two and a half air corpuscles can make up a water corpuscle (or perhaps better: five air corpuscles can make up two of water). Plato seems to use "corpuscle" and "form" (eidos) interchangeably in this passage.

will be shattered and quenched. The quenching will stop when these smaller bodies are willing to be reconstituted into the form of the kind that prevailed over them, and so from fire will come air, and from air, water. But if these smaller corpuscles are in process of turning into these and one of the other kinds encounters them and engages them in battle, their dissolution will go on non-stop until they are either completely squeezed and broken apart and escape to their own likes, or else are defeated, and, melding from many into one, they are assimilated to the kind that prevailed over them, and come to share its abode from then on. And, what is more, as they undergo these processes, they all exchange their territories: for as a result of the Receptacle's agitation the masses of each of the kinds are separated from one another, with each occupying its own region, but because some parts of a particular kind do from time to time become unlike their former selves and like the other kinds, they are carried by the shaking towards the region occupied by whatever masses they are becoming like to.

c

These, then, are the sorts of causes by which the unalloyed primary bodies have come into being. Now the fact that different varieties are found within their respective forms is to be attributed to the constructions of each of the elements [sc. the two elementary right-angled triangles]. Each of these two constructions did not originally yield a triangle that had just one size, but triangles that were both smaller and larger, numerically as many as there are varieties within a given form. That is why when they are mixed with themselves and with each other they display an infinite variety, which those who are to employ a likely account in their study of nature ought to take note of.

d

Now as for motion and rest, unless there is agreement on the manner and the conditions in which these two come into being, we will have many obstacles to face in our subsequent course of reasoning. Although we have already said something about them, we need to say this as well: *there will be no motion in a state of uniformity.* For it is difficult, or rather impossible, for something to be moved without something to set it in motion, or something to set a thing in motion without something to be moved by it. When either is absent, there is no motion, but [when they are present] it is quite impossible for them to be uniform. And so let us always presume that rest is found in a state of uniformity and to attribute motion to non-uniformity. The latter, moreover, is caused by inequality, the origin of which we have already discussed.[21]

e

58

21. The reference of the discussion of "the origin of inequality" is unclear. Perhaps Plato is thinking of the discussion of the "powers that are neither similar nor evenly balanced" (52e) in the primal chaos. Or perhaps, more specifically, he has in mind the origin of the differences among the elemental structures. These differences are due to the dissimilarity of the two primal triangles, their different sizes and the different possible combinations and recombinations of the scalene right-angled triangles.

We have not explained, however, how it is that the various corpuscles have not reached the point of being thoroughly separated from each other kind by kind, so that their transformations into each other and their movement [toward their own regions] would have come to a halt. So let us return to say this about it: Once the circumference of the universe has comprehended the [four] kinds, then, because it is round and has a natural tendency to gather in upon itself, it constricts them all and allows no empty

b   space to be left over. This is why fire, more than the other three, has come to infiltrate all of the others, with air in second place, since it is second in degree of subtlety, and so on for the rest. For the bodies that are generated from the largest parts will have the largest gaps left over in their construction, whereas the smallest bodies will have the tiniest. Now this gathering, contracting process squeezes the small parts into the gaps inside the big ones. So now, as the small parts are placed among the large ones and the smaller ones tend to break up the larger ones while the larger tend to cause the smaller to coalesce, they all shift, up and down, into their own

c   respective regions. For as each changes in quantity, it also changes the position of its region. This, then, is how and why the occurrence of non-uniformity is perpetually preserved, and so sets these bodies in perpetual motion, both now and in the future without interruption.

ARISTOTLE

Aristotle was born of a well-to-do family in the Macedonian town of Stagira in 384 B.C. His father, Nicomachus, was a physician who died when Aristotle was young. In 367, when Aristotle was seventeen, his uncle, Proxenus, sent him to Athens to study at Plato's Academy. There he remained, first as a pupil, later as an associate, for the next twenty years.

When Plato died in 347, the Academy came under the control of his nephew Speusippus, who favored mathematical aspects of Platonism that Aristotle, who was more interested in biology, found uncongenial. Perhaps for this reason—but more likely because of growing anti-Macedonian sentiment in Athens—Aristotle decided to leave. He accepted the invitation of Hermeias, his friend and a former fellow student in the Academy, to join his philosophical circle on the coast of Asia Minor in Assos, where Hermeias (a former slave) had become ruler. Aristotle remained there for three years. During this period he married Hermeias's niece, Pythias, with whom he had a daughter, also named Pythias.

In 345, Aristotle moved to Mytilene, on the nearby island of Lesbos, where he joined another former Academic, Theophrastus, who was a native of the island. Theophrastus, at first Aristotle's pupil and then his closest colleague, remained associated with him until Aristotle's death. While they were on Lesbos the biological research of Aristotle and Theophrastus flourished. In 343, Philip of Macedon invited Aristotle to his court to serve as tutor to his son Alexander, then thirteen years old. What instruction Aristotle gave to the young man who was to become Alexander the Great is not known, but it seems likely that Aristotle's own interest in politics increased during his stay at the Macedonian court. In 340 Alexander was appointed regent for his father, and his studies with Aristotle ended.

The events of the next five years are uncertain. Perhaps Aristotle stayed at the court; perhaps he went back to Stagira. But in 335, after the death of Philip, he returned to Athens for his second long sojourn. Just outside the city he rented some buildings and established his own school, the Lyceum, where he lectured, wrote, and discussed philosophy with his pupils and associates. Under his direction, they carried out research on biological and other philosophical and scientific topics. Theophrastus worked on botany, Aristoxenus on music; Eudemus wrote a history of mathematics and astronomy, Meno of medicine, and Theophrastus of physics, cosmology, and psychology. In addition, Aristotle and his group produced a monumental account of the constitutions of 158 Greek city-states—an account Aristotle draws on in his own *Politics.*

While he was in Athens, Aristotle's wife Pythias died. He subsequently began a union with a woman named Herpyllis, like Aristotle a native of Stagira. Although they apparently never married, they had a son, whom they named Nicomachus, after Aristotle's father.

Aristotle's work during his twelve or thirteen years at the Lyceum was prodigious. Most of his surviving works were probably written during this period. But when Alexander died in 323, Athens once again became a hostile environment for a Macedonian, and Aristotle was accused of impiety (the same charge that had been leveled against both Anaxagoras and Socrates). Leaving the Lyceum in the hands of Theophrastus, Aristotle fled northward to the Macedonian stronghold of Chalcis (his mother's birthplace); he is said to have remarked that he would "not allow the Athenians to sin twice against philosophy." Removed from the cultural center of Athens, he lamented his isolation and died in 322 at the age of sixty-two.

Of Aristotle's writings, only about one fifth to one quarter have survived. Still, the great variety of subjects that they cover provides a good indication of the range and depth of his interests. The notorious difficulty these writings pose for the contemporary reader is in part explained by the nature of the works themselves. Far from being polished pieces of prose intended for publication, they are for the most part working papers and lecture notes, terse and compressed often to the point of unintelligibility. (Ancient sources tell us that in his published works—now lost—Aristotle displayed an exemplary literary style, and there are occasional glimpses of it in the surviving works.)

Aristotle was above all driven by a desire for knowledge and understanding in every possible realm. His works are teeming with detailed observations about the natural world as well as abstract speculations of the most general sort. As both a scientist and a philosopher, Aristotle could easily make the transition from describing the feeding behavior of eels and limpets to theorizing about the divine intellect that is the uncaused cause of everything else in the universe. But his philosophical and scientific interests are rooted in the natural world—about one quarter of the surviving works deal with topics in biology. This he combined with an unshakeable confidence in the ability of the human mind, aided by the system of deductive logic he invented and by close and detailed observation of natural phenomena, to comprehend the fundamental nature of objective reality.

Aristotle did not suppose that he was the first person to attempt this task. He was a keen student of the writings of his scientific and philosophical predecessors. The influence of Plato's thought is apparent throughout Aristotle's works, even where he disagrees with his teacher most. He pays a great deal of attention to the Presocratics, seldom agreeing with them, but often crediting them with important (albeit usually partial) insights. His typical approach to a subject is to review its history and then, making what use he can of the received opinions, to set out his own account. Often his position is a kind of compromise that incorporates the best features while avoiding the excesses of rival schemes that are too extreme.

All of the sciences (*epistēmai,* literally "knowledges") can be divided into three branches: theoretical, practical, and productive. Whereas practical sciences, such as ethics and politics, are concerned with human action, and productive sciences with making things, theoretical sciences, such as theology, mathematics, and the natural sciences, aim at truth and are pursued for their own sake. Aristotle was unique in pursuing all three. His *Rhetoric* and *Poetics,* which provide the foundation for the study of speech and literary theory, are his contributions to the productive sciences. The *Ethics* and *Politics* are devoted to the practical sciences. In the remainder of his works, Aristotle directs his attention to the theoretical sciences.

A science, according to Aristotle, can be set out as an axiomatic system in which necessary first principles lead by inexorable deductive inferences to all of the truths about the subject matter of the science (*Posterior Analytics* I.6). Some of these first principles are peculiar to the science in question, as the definition of a straight line is to geometry. Some—such as the principle of noncontradiction—are so general that they are common to all the sciences (*Metaphysics* IV.3). Scientific knowledge is therefore demonstrative; what we know scientifically is what we can derive, directly or indirectly, from first principles that do not themselves require proof.

What, then, is the status of the first principles? They clearly cannot be known in the same way as the consequences derived from them, i.e., demonstratively, yet Aristotle is confident that they must be known—for how could knowledge be derived from what is not knowledge? They are, Aristotle tells us, grasped by the mind (Aristotle's term is *nous,* usually translated as *intuition* or *understanding*). This way of putting the matter makes it seem as if an Aristotelian science is an entirely *a priori* enterprise in which reason alone grasps first principles and logic takes over from there to arrive at all of the truths of science. And Aristotle does say that it is dialectic—a process of deductive reasoning—that provides a path to first principles (*Topics* I.2).

It is clear, however, that Aristotle does not think that this alone is the way a scientist goes about acquiring his knowledge, for in his own scientific treatises, he does not begin by announcing the first principles and deducing their consequences. Rather, he sets out the puzzles the science is trying to solve and the observations that have been made and the opinions that have been held about them. Perhaps he thinks of the axiomatic presentation as a kind of ideal that is possible only for a completed science and is appropriate for teaching it rather than for making discoveries in it. As for the acquisition of first principles, Aristotle appeals to what sounds somewhat like an inductive procedure. Beginning with the perception of particulars, which are "better known to us," and moving through memory and experience, we arrive at knowledge of universals, which are "better known in themselves" (*Posterior Analytics* II.19, *Metaphysics* I.1). Aristotle's approach thus seems to combine features of both rationalism and empiricism.

Each of the special sciences studies some particular realm of being, some part of what there is. But there is also, Aristotle maintains (*Metaphysics* IV.1), a more general study of what there is, a study of being *qua* being. ('*Qua*' translates a technical expression Aristotle uses to indicate an aspect under which something is to be considered). The study of being *qua* being concerns the most general class of things, viz., everything that exists. And it studies them under their most general aspect, namely, as things that exist. It thus raises the question of what it is for something to exist.

Now, on Aristotle's view what it is for a horse to exist is different in kind from what it is for whiteness or courage to exist. "Being," he tells us, "is said in many ways" (*Metaphysics* IV.2). So it might seem that there could not be a unified answer to the question of what it is for something in general to exist. But he also thinks that there is a connection among these modes of being (or senses of 'exist') which is deep enough to make a unified answer possible. The existence of whiteness is derivative; there is such a thing as whiteness because something, for example some horse, is white. Whiteness is not an independent entity, capable of existing on its own. Horses and other biological specimens, on the other hand, are independent entities. Such independently existing entities Aristotle called *substances*. (The Greek word traditionally translated as 'substance' may with equal plausibility be rendered 'basic reality'.) The existence of everything else is somehow dependent on its relation to substances. Hence Aristotle tells us that the ancient and perennial question "What is being?" really comes down to the question "What is substance?" (*Metaphysics* VII.1).

Substances, then, are the most fundamental realities. But not all of Aristotle's predecessors would have agreed with him about what the substances are. Empedocles would have said that the four *elements* are the only substances; Democritus would call the *atoms* substances; for Plato, the substances are his independently existing and immaterial *forms*. Much of Aristotle's *Metaphysics* is spent trying to steer a middle course between the materialism of these Presocratics, on the one hand, and Platonism, on the other. How successful he is in this effort—and indeed, even the precise details of his solution—are matters of dispute.

In his earliest ontological writings, Aristotle maintains that individual biological specimens—this man, or that tree—are the primary substances (*Categories* 5). The species to which they belong, *man* and *tree*, are substances in a secondary sense. But he subsequently (*Metaphysics* VII–VIII) begins to raise the question of what it is that makes this man or that tree a substance—what the substance *of* these things is, as he puts it. He intimates that the answer to this question will tell us what primary substance is. His convoluted and difficult investigation of this question leads him to the conclusion that it is *form* or *essence* that is primary substance. This suggests a tilt in the direction of Platonism, but Aristotle insists that his answer is different from Plato's, for on his view Platonic forms are separate from and independent of their material instantiations, whereas Aristotelian essences in some sense are not. Still, much remains unclear about Aristotle's answer. For example, there is no consensus among scholars about whether Aristotle thought of essences as being particular (so that each individual horse has its own unique essence) or specific (in which case the essence of all horses will be the same).

Aristotle's universe is finite, eternal, and geocentric: a stationary earth surrounded by concentric spheres that carry the sun, moon, planets, and stars in their circular orbits about the earth. Everything below the sphere of the moon is made of four fundamental elements—earth, water, air, and fire—that interact and are capable of transforming into one another. Each element is characterized by a pair of properties from among the contraries hot, cold, wet, and dry. Earth is cold and dry, water cold and wet, air hot and wet, fire hot and dry. The heavenly bodies are made of a different kind of matter altogether, a fifth element ("quintessence"). Each element has a natural place and a natural movement. The four sublunary elements tend to move in a straight line, earth downward toward the center of the universe, fire up toward the extreme reaches of the universe, and air and water toward intermediate places. Once in its natural place, each of these four remains at rest unless something else causes it to move. The natural movement of the fifth element in the heavens is circular and eternal. All of this movement and change is ultimately explained in terms of an "unmoved mover"—a cause of change that is itself uncaused and outside of the universe (*On the Heavens* I–III, *On Generation and Corruption* II.4, *Physics* VIII.6, *Metaphysics* XII.6–9).

It is the job of natural science to study things whose nature it is to undergo change. In the face of influential Parmenidean arguments against the possibility of change, Aristotle attempted to set out a framework that would make change intelligible. Every change involves three essential ingredients: a pair of opposed characteristics or states (from which and to which, respectively, the change occurs) and a subject which underlies the change and persists through it. Schematically, every change, every case of "coming to be," can be described in this way: Something, x, goes from being F to being not F, or vice versa. A musician comes to be because a man goes from being unmusical to being musical; a statue comes to be because some shapeless bronze takes on a definite form. Contrary to what Parmenides argued, coming to be does not involve getting *something from nothing*; it involves getting something which is F from something which is (among other things) not F (*Physics* I.7–9).

These are the necessary preconditions for change. But what is change?

Aristotle defines it in terms of his concepts of *actuality* and *potentiality*. Change, he tells us, is "the actuality of what is potentially, *qua* such" (*Physics* III.1). The process of building a house, for example, is the actuality of the buildable materials, *qua* buildable. The materials that are potentially a house are already actual even before the building begins—they are bricks and boards, etc. So the actuality with which Aristotle identifies change is that of the bricks and boards, not *qua* bricks and boards, but *qua* buildable. It is precisely when the house is in the process of being built that this potentiality of the materials actually (and not merely potentially) exists *qua* potentiality. Once the process is completed, that potentiality has been replaced by a corresponding actuality, that of the completed house. The precise meaning of Aristotle's definition of change is a subject of scholarly debate. For present purposes it is sufficient to note that, in undergoing change, a thing is actualizing a potentiality that it already has even before it changes. It is thus already part of its nature to be able to undergo change of that sort.

It is the job of a theoretical science to explain things, and that means that it must answer "Why?" questions. To answer such a question is to give a *cause*. (Aristotle's word is *aition*; 'explanation' is an equally appropriate translation.) But 'cause' is "said in many ways" (*Physics* II.3). In one sense, the cause of something is the material out of which it comes to be (material cause). In another sense, it is the form or essence stated in the definition of the thing (formal cause). In a third, it is the source of change or stability (efficient cause). In a fourth, it is the end (*telos*), what the thing is *for* (final cause). Note that it is not just events that have causes, in Aristotle's view; houses and tigers have causes just as much as eclipses and explosions do. Note also that there can be more than one cause of the same thing (e.g., bronze is the material cause of a statue, whereas a certain shape is its formal cause). Indeed, two things may be causes of each other, as exercise is the (efficient) cause of health, and health is the (final) cause of exercise.

A complete account of something will mention all of the causes that are appropriate to it. Artifacts clearly have causes in all four senses: A house is made of wood, by a builder, with a form and structure suitable to provide a shelter for human beings and their possessions. Mathematical objects, since they do not undergo change, have no efficient or final causes. Natural objects, such as plants and animals, clearly have the first three kinds of cause, for they come into being, are composed of matter (ultimately of the four elements), and have essential natures. But are there final causes in nature? Aristotle maintains, notoriously, that there are (*Physics* II.8, *Parts of Animals* I.1). His teleological account of nature is central to his entire philosophical system.

His position here may strike us as an aberration if we identify final causes with conscious intentions. The final causes of artifacts are found in the minds of the artisans who made them; they are in that sense external to the artifacts themselves. (It is for this reason that artifacts do not count for Aristotle as genuine substances. Lacking final causes that are internal to them, they do not engage in activity of their own, and hence they have no essence, strictly speaking.) But final causes in nature are not like this at all. Rather, Aristotle's idea is that the final causes of natural objects are internal to those objects. Consider the living creatures that populate the natural world. They behave in certain characteristic ways: They interact with their environment, nourish themselves, reproduce. Their being is defined by these functions and these characteristic activities. The parts of which they are composed enable them to fulfill these functions more or less successfully. It is not by accident that animals have teeth or eyes; these organs clearly have functions—they are *for* something. And what they are for is typically beneficial for the organism; they enable it to survive and to engage in the activities that define its being. It is function and activity, not purpose, that Aristotle claims to discern in nature.

This understanding of Aristotle's teleology helps to explain why he believes that final, formal, and efficient causes often coincide (*Physics* II.7). Just as the various parts and organs of an animal contribute toward its well-being and survival, the *telos* of the animal itself is to be a good (i.e., successful) specimen of its kind. So the final cause of a tiger is just to be a tiger, as specified in its formal cause (i.e., its definition). The coincidence of the efficient cause with the final and the formal can be seen most easily in the case of reproduction and development. The efficient cause of a tiger cub is a tiger (in Aristotle's view, its father). As the cub grows, its process of development tends almost invariably (in the normal case—occasionally things go awry) toward the same outcome: a mature individual that, like its parents, satisfies the definition of a tiger.

The being of a living thing is thus inextricably bound up in its being alive and living the life that a thing of its kind lives. What is it that differentiates the living from the nonliving? Aristotle's answer is: the presence of the soul (*psuchē*). We notice immediately an important difference between this and later conceptions of soul: *Psuchē* for Aristotle is linked with life in general, rather than with mind, thought, or personality in particular. All living things have souls. But there are different degrees or levels of soul, associated with different capacities or functions. At the most fundamental level is the nutritive soul, the kind of soul common to all living things, for all plants and animals have the capacity to take in nourishment. Higher levels of soul account for the appetitive, locomotive, and perceptive capacities of humans and other animals. At the highest level is the rational soul, peculiar to humans.

But what is the soul? Aristotle defines it to be the *form* of the body. More precisely, it is the "first actuality of a natural body that has life potentially" (*De Anima* II.1). The term 'first actuality' needs some explanation. As Aristotle uses the expression, a first actuality is not itself an activity or bit of behavior (a 'second actuality'), but a capacity or ability to act or to behave. It is thus a kind of potentiality (a 'second potentiality'), an organizing principle that enables a living thing to go about the business of living. To have a soul, then, is to have the capacity to engage in certain characteristic activities. In the most general case, it is the capacity to metabolize. For higher levels of soul, it is the capacity to move about, to have desires and to fulfill them, to perceive, to contemplate.

The soul is therefore neither a material part of an animal, nor some immaterial thing capable of existing in separation from the body. For the soul is a set of capacities that a living thing has, and these capacities are incapable of existing on their own—they are the capacities of a living thing. Aristotle thus resists both a materialistic conception of the soul as some kind of bodily part and a Platonic conception which holds the soul to be independent of and, indeed, impeded by the body.

Much of Aristotle's discussion of the soul concerns the topic of sense-perception (*De Anima* II.5–12). He discusses the physiology of each of the five senses in detail and defines perception in general as the reception in the soul of the perceptible form of an external object. His account of thought to some extent mirrors what he says about perception. In thinking, the mind takes on the intelligible form of its object and in so doing becomes, in a sense, identical to it. Aristotle thereby avoids the problem of having somehow to relate a mental representation to an object external to the mind. But thought differs from perception in an important respect: Whereas there are sense organs, there is, for Aristotle, no organ of thought (*De Anima* III.4). For this reason he holds that thought, unlike other psychic functions, is somehow separable from the body. It is not clear how well this aspect of Aristotle's theory can be made to harmonize with his otherwise hylomorphic conception of the soul.

Thus far we have looked at some of Aristotle's answers to the questions of the theoretical sciences. As we shall see, his approach to the practical sciences builds on those answers. The central question of ethics is how to live, i.e., what the good life is, and Aristotle's answer is basically naturalistic. He takes it to be uncontroversial that all of our actions are aimed at some good. So the good, he reasons, is "that at which all things aim" (*Nicomachean Ethics* I.1). And what is this good? It must be something that is chosen for its own sake, and not for the sake of something else. Aristotle's answer is that it is happiness (*eudaimonia*) in the sense of well-being or flourishing. (It would be a mistake to think of happiness here in the narrow sense of a kind of mental or emotional state.) The well-being of a thing consists in its fulfilling its basic functions and performing its characteristic activities. Human happiness or well-being, then, consists in fulfilling the functions and performing the activities that define life for human beings. All animals nourish themselves, and grow, and perceive. What is distinctively human is the rational faculty, and that is what determines our well-being. *Eudaimonia* is therefore an "activity of soul in accordance with virtue or excellence (*aretē*)" (*Nicomachean Ethics* I.7). We flourish, then, when we do well the things that are distinctively human.

The remainder of Aristotle's *Ethics* consists of an unpacking of this basic conception of *eudaimonia*. He distinguishes virtues of character from intellectual virtues, and discusses all of them in detail (*Nicomachean Ethics* II–VI). Intellectual virtues are excellences of the rational element in the soul. But the irrational element also has an aspect that is rational, in that it is capable of being persuaded by reason, and the excellences of this part of the soul are virtues of character, or moral virtues (*Nicomachean Ethics* I.13). Such a virtue is a disposition to choose actions that are intermediate between the extremes of excess and deficiency. (For example, courage is a mean between cowardice and rashness.) These choices must be made in accordance with reason, as would be determined by a person of practical wisdom. So possession of the moral virtues implies the possession of the intellectual virtues, as well, since practical wisdom is an intellectual virtue. Of the intellectual virtues, the highest is that of theoretical contemplation. This, finally, is the activity of the soul with which Aristotle identifies the highest form of *eudaimonia* (*Nicomachean Ethics* X.7).

In Aristotle's view, politics is continuous with ethics, for just as it is part of human nature to seek happiness, it is also part of human nature to live in communities. We are, Aristotle asserts, social animals (*Politics* I.2). The state is the highest form of community; it is a natural entity, and does not exist merely by convention. (The kind of state Aristotle has in mind is the relatively small city-state of fourth-century Greece.) Plato had argued that the structure of the soul was like that of the state, with different psychic functions corresponding to different classes of citizens. For Aristotle, the analogy works the other way around. The state has a proper function and a nature in the same way that an individual organism does. Hence, to say what a state is we must determine what its proper function is.

Aristotle believes that a state exists for the sake of the good or happy life, so that the best form of government will be one which promotes the well-being of all of its citizens, and he goes on, after considering a variety of alternatives, to describe such a state in considerable detail (*Politics* VII). In his emphasis on the rule of law and the role of a constitution in defining a state, Aristotle's ideas are still timely today. There are other aspects of his thought, however, such as his belief that there are natural rulers and natural slaves, that the contemporary reader will no doubt find repugnant.

Aristotle has had a profound influence on the history of philosophy. From late antiquity through the middle ages, it was standard procedure for philosophers to couch their own writings in the form of commentaries on his works. His logic was so thoroughly accepted that the subject remained virtually unchanged for the next two millennia. His concepts of subject and predicate, matter and form, essence and accident, species and genus, among others, have become a standard part of the philosophical vernacular. Although many of his ideas have been discredited or superseded, much of what he has to say remains relevant to issues of vital contemporary interest. In terms of the breadth of his intellectual curiosity and the vastness of his influence, Aristotle is without equal in the history of human thought.

About the Translations

We are grateful to Gail Fine and T. H. Irwin for making their new translations of Aristotle available for use in this volume. What we have included
here is part of a larger collection of translations that appear in their Hackett
anthology, Aristotle, *Selections*. Readers whose appetite for Aristotle has
been whetted by the current volume are encouraged to turn next to *Selections*, which also includes a much expanded set of explanatory notes and a
more complete and detailed glossary.

Words contained in angle brackets < > do not correspond directly to
anything in the Greek text, and have been supplied to complete the sense
and make the translation more intelligible. Terms occurring in SMALL CAP-
ITAL LETTERS in the footnotes refer the reader to a more detailed discussion
in the Glossary.

CATEGORIES

Translated by S. Marc Cohen and Gareth B. Matthews

In this brief but important work, Aristotle gives an account of predication, i.e., of the application of the terms of a language to things in the world. (The Greek word katēgoriai, *from which the English 'categories' is derived, comes from the verb meaning "to predicate.") On the basis of this account he develops a theory of classification of "the things that there are." In the excerpt presented here he introduces the notion of a substance (ousia), his term for an independently existing entity, a fundamental ingredient of reality. Everything else, he argues, depends for its existence on the existence of substances.*

1

1a Things are called *homonymous* when they have only a name in common but a different definition[1] corresponding to the name. For example, both a human and a drawing are animals.[2] But while the name of these two things is common to them both, the definition corresponding to the name is dif-

5 ferent. For if one gives an account of what it is for each of them to be an animal, one will give a distinctive definition for each.

Things are called *synonymous* when they have a name in common and also the same definition corresponding to the name. Thus, for example, both a human and an ox are animals. Each of them is called by the same

10 name, 'animal'; moreover, the definition of what they are is the same. For if one gives a definition of what it is for each of these to be what it is, an animal, one will give the same definition.

Things are called *paronymous* in case one gets its name from another with some difference in grammatical form. Thus, for example, the gram-

15 marian gets his name from grammar, the brave man from bravery.

1. 'Definition', here and elsewhere in this chapter, translates *logos tēs ousias*, literally, 'account of being'.

2. The Greek word *zōon* can mean either an animal or a figure in a picture; the latter need not be the figure of an animal.

2

Among things that are said, some are said in combination, some without combination. Examples of things said in combination are 'man runs', 'man wins'. Examples of things said without combination are 'man', 'ox', 'runs', 'wins'.

Among the things that there are: 20

(a) Some are said of a subject but are not in any subject. For example, man is said of a subject, the individual man, but is not in any subject.
(b) Some are in a subject but are not said of any subject. (I call 'in a subject' what is in something, not as a part, and cannot exist separately 25 from what it is in.) For example, this bit of grammar is in a subject, the soul, but it is not said of any subject; and this individual white is in a subject, the body, for all color is in body, but it is not said of any subject.
(c) Some are both said of a subject and in a subject. For example, knowl- 1b edge is in a subject, the soul, and is said of a subject, grammar.
(d) Some are neither in a subject nor said of a subject, for example the individual man or the individual horse. Nothing of this sort is either in 5 a subject or said of a subject.

Without exception, things that are individual and one in number are not said of any subject, but nothing prevents some of them from being in a subject. This bit of grammar is among the things in a subject.

3

Whenever one thing is predicated of another as of a subject, everything 10 said of what is predicated will also be said of the subject. For example, man is predicated of the individual man, and animal is predicated of man; therefore animal will also be predicated of the individual man. For the individual man is both a man and an animal. 15

Differentiae of genera that are different and not subordinate to one another are also different in kind—for example, differentiae of animal and of knowledge. For the differentiae of animal are *footed, winged, aquatic,* and *two-footed,* but none of these is a differentia of knowledge—one sort of knowledge does not differ from another by being two-footed. Yet if one 20 genus is subordinate to another, nothing prevents their differentiae from being the same. For the higher genera are predicated of those beneath them, so that all differentiae of what is predicated will be differentiae of the subject as well.

4

Each of the things said without any combination signifies either a substance, or how much [quantity], or of what sort [quality], or related to what [relative], or where, or when, or being arranged, or having on, or doing, or being affected. To give a general indication of what these things are, here are some examples:

Substance	man, horse
Quantity	two cubits, three cubits
Quality	white, grammatical
Relative	double, half, larger
Where	in the Lyceum, in the marketplace
When	yesterday, last year
Being arranged	lying, sitting
Having on	wearing shoes, being armed
Doing	cutting, burning
Being affected	being cut, being burned

Said by itself, each of the things mentioned above is no assertion, but, in combination with others of these, it becomes an assertion. For it seems that every assertion is either true or false; but none of the things said without combination—such as 'man', 'white', 'runs', 'wins'—is either true or false.

5

Substance in the most proper sense of the word, that which is *primarily* and most of all called substance, is neither said of any subject, nor is it in any subject—for example, the individual man and the individual horse. What are called *secondary* substances are both the species which the things primarily called substances fall under and the genera of these species. For example, the individual man falls under the species, man, and the genus of the species is animal. So these things, for example man and animal, are called secondary substances.

It is evident from what has been said that both the name and the definition of a thing *said of a subject* must be predicable of the subject. For example, man is said of a subject, the individual man, and so the name is predicated—for you will be predicating 'man' of the individual man; and also the definition of man will be predicated of the individual man—for the individual man is also a man. Thus, both the name and the definition will be predicated of the subject.

But, for the most part, neither the name nor the definition of what is *in a subject* is predicated of the subject. Sometimes, however, nothing prevents the name from being predicated of the subject, but the definition cannot be predicated. For example, white, which is in a subject (body) is predicated of the subject—for the body is called white—but the definition of white will never be predicated of body.

All other things are either said of primary substances as subjects or in them as subjects. This is evident from a consideration of cases. For example, animal is predicated of man, and therefore of the individual man (for if it were predicated of no individual man, it would not be predicated of man at all). Again, color is in body, and therefore in an individual body (for if it were not in any individual, it would not be in body at all). Thus, all other things are either said of primary substances as subjects or in them as subjects. Therefore, if there were no primary substances, there could not be anything else.

Among secondary substances, the species is more a substance than the genus; for it is closer to the primary substance. If one were to give an account of what some primary substance is, it would be more informative and more appropriate to give the species than to give the genus. For example, we would give a more informative account of an individual man if we give 'man' rather than 'animal'; for the former is more distinctive of an individual man, while the latter is more general. And in giving an account of an individual tree it is more informative to give 'tree' in our account than to give 'plant'. Further, primary substances are subjects for all other things, and all other things are predicated of them or are in them, and it is for this reason that they are called substances most of all. But as primary substances are to other things, so species is to genus—for a species is a subject for its genus. And while genera are predicated of their species, the converse does not hold—that is, species are not predicated of their genera. Thus for this reason, too, the species is more a substance than is the genus.

Among species that are not themselves genera, none is more a substance than another. For it is no more appropriate to give 'man' in an account of an individual man than it is to give 'horse' in an account of an individual horse. Similarly, among primary substances none is more a substance than another, for an individual man is no more a substance than is an individual ox.

It is reasonable that, after primary substances, species and genera alone among everything else should be called secondary substances. For they alone among things predicated reveal primary substance. If we were to give an account of what an individual man is we should properly give the species or the genus—and we should do this more informatively by giving 'man' than by giving 'animal'. But to give any of the other things will be out of place—for example, to give 'white' or 'runs' or anything whatsoever like that. So it is reasonable that only these among the other things are called substances.

Moreover, it is because they are subjects for everything else that primary substances are most properly called substances. But as primary substances

35

2b

5

10

15

20

25

30

35

3a

are to everything else, so species and genera of primary substances are to all the rest; for all the rest are predicated of these. Thus if you call an individual man grammatical you will be calling both a man and an animal grammatical—and likewise for the rest.

Not being in a subject is something common to all substances. For a primary substance is neither said of a subject nor is it in a subject. It is also quite clear that secondary substances are not in a subject either. For man is said of a subject, the individual man; but it is not in a subject, for man is not in the individual man. In similar fashion animal is also said of a subject, the individual man; but animal is not in the individual man. Moreover, although nothing prevents the name of a thing that is in a subject from sometimes being predicated of the subject, the definition of such a thing cannot be predicated of it. In the case of secondary substances, however, the definition as well as the name can be predicated of the subject. For you will predicate of the individual man both the definition of man and the definition of animal. Therefore no substance is among the things in a subject.

This, however, is not peculiar to substance; their differentiae are not in a subject either. For *footed* and *two-footed* are said of a subject, man, but they are not in a subject—neither *two-footed* nor *footed* is in man. Moreover, the definition of a differentia is predicated of that of which the differentia would be said. For example, if *footed* is said of man, the definition of *footed* will also be predicated of man, since man is footed.

We shouldn't be afraid that we might have to say that the parts of a substance are not themselves substances since they are in a subject, namely, the whole substance. For 'things in a subject' was not being used to mean things belonging to something as parts.

It is a characteristic of substances and differentiae that they are said synonymously of everything they are said of. For every such predicate is predicated either of individuals or of species. (While a primary substance yields no predicate—for a primary substance is not said of any subject—among secondary substances the species is predicated of the individual and the genus is predicated both of the species and of the individual. Similarly, differentiae are predicated both of species and of individuals.) Moreover, primary substances are given the definition of both their species and their genera, and a species is given that of its genus. (For whatever is said of the predicate is also said of the subject.) Similarly, both species and individuals are given the definition of their differentiae. But we saw that synonymous things are those that have both a name in common and the same definition. Therefore substances and differentiae are said synonymously of everything they are said of.

Each substance seems to signify a particular *this*. As far as primary substances are concerned, it is indisputably true that each signifies a particular *this*, for what is indicated is individual and one in number. As far as

secondary substances are concerned, it seems from the appearance of the
name when one says 'man' or 'animal' that they, too, signify a particular   15
this. But it is not really so. Rather, each signifies a particular sort.[3] For the
subject is not one, as is primary substance, but man and animal are said of
many things. Yet a secondary substance does not signify simply a particular sort, as white does. White signifies nothing but a sort, whereas species   20
and genus distinguish a sort with respect to substance; for each of them
signifies a particular sort of substance. (With a genus one encompasses
more than with a species. For saying 'animal' embraces more than saying
'man'.)

It is also a characteristic of substances not to have a contrary. For what   25
would be the contrary of a primary substance? For example, nothing is the
contrary of an individual man, nor is anything the contrary of man or of
animal. But this is not peculiar to substance—it holds also of many other
things, such as quantity. For nothing is the contrary of two cubits, or of   30
ten, or of any other such thing—although someone might say that many is
the contrary of few, or large the contrary of small. But nothing is the
contrary of any definite quantity.

It appears that substance does not admit of more or less. I do not mean
that one substance is not more a substance than another—indeed, I said   35
that it is—rather, I mean that no substance is said to be more or less just
what it is. For example, if this substance is a man, he will not be more or
less a man than himself or than another man. One man is not more a man
than another, as one white thing is whiter than another or one thing is   4a
more beautiful than another. And yet something may be said to be more or
less than itself, as when a white body is said to be whiter now than before,
and what is hot is said to be more or less hot. But no substance is spoken of   5
in this way. A man is not said to be more a man now than before, nor is any
other substance. Therefore, substance does not admit of more or less.

Most characteristic of substance seems to be the fact that something one   10
and the same in number can receive contraries. In no other case can one
cite something one in number that is able to receive contraries. For example,
a color that is one and the same in number will not be white and black; nor   15
will the same action, one in number, be both bad and good; and similarly
for other things that are not substance. But a substance, one and the same
in number, can receive contraries. An individual man, for example, being
one and the same, becomes now pale and now dark, now hot and now cold,   20
now bad and now good. This sort of thing is to be seen in no other case.

Someone might object by saying that statements and beliefs are things of
this sort, for the same statement seems to be both true and false. For
example, if the statement that someone is sitting is true, when the person   25
stands the same statement will be false. It is the same with beliefs, also. If

3. 'Sort' here translates *poion*, usually rendered 'quality'. See QUALITY.

one holds the true belief that someone is sitting, when the person stands—
if one holds the same belief about him—the belief will be false. But even if
we agree to this, there is still a difference in how this happens. In the case
30   of substances it is because *they* change that they are able to receive contraries. For what turns from hot to cold, or from dark to pale, or from good
to bad, has changed (because it has altered). Similarly in other cases, each
thing is able to receive contraries by itself admitting the change. Statements
35   and beliefs, however, remain themselves entirely unchanged; it is because
the facts change that the contrary comes to hold of a statement or belief.
4b   For the statement that someone is sitting remains the same, but it becomes
now true and now false because the facts change. It is the same with beliefs,
5   also. Thus even if one were to allow that statements and beliefs can receive
contraries, it would still be characteristic of a substance that it can receive
contraries in this way—by a change in *itself*.

Yet this is not true. For statements and beliefs are said to be able to
receive contraries not because they receive anything themselves, but because something else has been affected. It is because of what the facts are,
10   or are not, that a statement is said to be either true or false, not by its being
able to receive contraries. For no statement or belief is changed by anything
at all. So, since nothing comes about in them, they are not able to receive
contraries. But a substance itself receives contraries, and this is the reason it
15   is said to be able to receive contraries. For it receives illness and health, or
paleness and darkness, and it is said to be able to receive contraries because
it itself receives each thing of this sort. Thus it is distinctive of substance
that what is one and the same in number can receive contraries. Let this
much, then, be said about substance.

DE INTERPRETATIONE

The second in a series of works on logic, De Interpretatione *(literally, "On Interpretation") presents an analysis of the structure of statement-making sentences. It is thus one of the first attempts to answer the questions of what is today called philosophy of language. In chapter 9 Aristotle raises a famous puzzle about the present truth of statements concerning events in the future.*

1

We must first establish what names and verbs are, then what negations,   *16a*
affirmations, statements, and sentences are.

Spoken sounds are symbols of affections in the soul, and written marks
are symbols of spoken sounds; and just as written marks are not the same   *5*
for everyone, neither are spoken sounds. But the primary things that these
signify (the affections in the soul) are the same for everyone, and what
these affections are likenesses of (actual things) are also the same for
everyone. We have discussed these questions in *On the Soul*; they belong to
another inquiry.

Some thoughts in the soul are neither true nor false, while others must be   *10*
one or the other; the same is true of spoken sounds. For falsity and truth
involve combination and division. Names and verbs by themselves, when
nothing is added (for instance, 'man' and 'pale') are like thoughts without   *15*
combination and separation, since they are not yet either true or false. A
sign of this is the fact that 'goatstag' signifies something but is not yet true
or false unless 'is' or 'is not' is added, either without qualification or with
reference to time.

2

A name is a spoken sound that is significant by convention, without time,   *20*
of which no part is significant in separation. For in 'Grancourt', the 'court'
does not signify anything in itself, as it does in the phrase 'a grand court'.
But complex names are not the same as simple ones; for in simple names

701

25   the part is not at all significant, whereas in complex names the part has
some force but does not signify anything in separation—for instance, 'fact'
in 'artifact'. I say 'by convention' because nothing is a name by nature;
something is a name only if it becomes a symbol. For even inarticulate
noises—of beasts, for example—reveal something, but they are not names.
30   'Not-man' is not a name, nor is any established name rightly applied to it,
since neither is it a sentence or a negation. Let us call it an indefinite name.
16b   'Philo's', 'to-Philo', and the like are not names but inflections of names.
The same account applies to them as to names, except that a name with 'is'
or 'was' or 'will be' added is always true or false, whereas an inflection with
them added is neither true nor false. For example, in 'Philo's is' or 'Philo's is
5   not' nothing is yet either true or false.

3

A verb is <a spoken sound> of which no part signifies separately, and
which additionally signifies time; it is a sign of things said of something
else. By 'additionally signifies time', I mean that, for instance, 'recovery' is a
name but 'recovers' is a verb; for it additionally signifies something's hold-
10   ing now. And it is always a sign of something's holding, i.e. of something's
holding of a subject.
I do not call 'does not recover' and 'does not ail' verbs; for, although they
additionally signify time and always hold of something, there is a difference for which there is no established name. Let us call them indefinite
15   verbs, since they hold of anything whether it is or is not.[1]
Similarly, 'recovered' and 'will-recover' are not verbs, but inflections of
verbs. They differ from verbs because verbs additionally signify the present time, whereas inflections of verbs signify times outside the present.
20   A verb said just by itself is a name and signifies something, since the
speaker fixes his thought and the hearer pauses; but it does not yet signify
whether something is or is not. For 'being' or 'not being' is not a sign of an
object (not even if you say 'what is' without addition);[2] for by itself it is
nothing, but it additionally signifies some combination, which cannot be
25   thought of without the components.

1. **is or is not**: Perhaps 'exists or does not exist', or 'is the case or is not the case'. Cf.
APo 71a12.
2. **For being . . . without addition**: The text and interpretation are doubtful. (1)
Aristotle may be using the verb 'to be' to stand for any verb (cf. 21b6) and pointing
out that the verb 'run' (e.g.) uttered by itself does not say *what* runs or does not
run. (2) Alternatively, he may be taking the verb 'to be' as his example, because it
would be most tempting to suppose that this verb all by itself could say that
something is or is not.

4

A sentence[3] is a significant spoken sound, of which some part is significant in separation as an expression, not as an affirmation. I mean that 'animal', for instance, signifies something, but not that it is or is not (but if something is added, there will be an affirmation or negation), whereas the *30* single syllables of 'animal' signify nothing. Nor is the 'ice' in 'mice' significant; here it is only a spoken sound. In the case of double names, as was said, a part signifies, but not by itself.

Every sentence is significant, not because it is a <naturally suitable> *17a* instrument but, as we said, by convention. But not every sentence is a statement; only those sentences that are true or false are statements. Not every sentence is true or false; a prayer, for instance, is a sentence but it is neither true nor false. Let us set aside these other cases, since inquiry into them is more appropriate for rhetoric or poetics; our present study concerns affirmations. . . .

7

Some things are universals, others are particulars. By 'universal' I mean what is naturally predicated of more than one thing; by 'particular', what *40* is not. For example, man is a universal, and Callias is a particular. *17b*

Necessarily, then, when one says that something does or does not hold of something, one sometimes says this of a universal, sometimes of a particular. Now if one states universally of a universal that something does or does not hold, there will be contrary statements. (By 'stating universally of *5* a universal' I mean, for instance, 'Every man is pale', 'No man is pale'.) But when one states something of a universal, but not universally, the statements are not contrary, though contrary things may be revealed. (By 'stating of a universal but not universally', I mean, for instance, 'A man is *10* pale',[4] 'A man is not pale'. For although man is a universal, it is not used universally in the statement; for 'every' does not signify the universal, but rather signifies that it is used universally.)

In the case of what is predicated, it is not true to predicate a universal universally; for there will be no affirmation in which the universal is pred- *15* icated universally of what is predicated, as in, for instance, 'Every man is every animal'.

I call an affirmation and a negation contradictory opposites when what one signifies universally the other signifies not universally—for instance,

3. **sentence:** See REASON #2.

4. 'A man is pale': There is no indefinite article (or anything corresponding to it) in the Greek.

'Every man is pale' and 'Not every man is pale', or 'No man is pale' and 'Some man is pale'. But the universal affirmation and the universal negation—for instance, 'Every man is just' and 'No man is just'— are contrary opposites. That is why they cannot both be true at the same time, but their <contradictory> opposites may both be true about the same thing—for instance, 'Not every man is pale' and 'Some man 25 is pale'.

Of contradictory universal statements about a universal, one or the other must be true or false; similarly if they are about particulars—for instance, 'Socrates is pale' and 'Socrates is not pale'. But if they are about 30 universals, but are not universal <statements>, it is not always the case that one is true, the other false. For it is true to say at the same time that a man is pale and that a man is not pale, and that a man is handsome and that a man is not handsome; for if ugly, then not handsome. And if something is becoming F, it is also not F. This might seem strange at first 35 sight, since 'A man is not pale' might appear to signify at the same time that no man is pale; but it does not signify the same, nor does it necessarily hold at the same time.

It is clear that a single affirmation has a single negation. For the negation 40 must deny the same thing that the affirmation affirms, and deny it of the 18a same <subject>—either of a particular or of a universal, either universally or not universally, as, for instance, in 'Socrates is pale' and 'Socrates is not pale'. (But if something else is denied, or the same thing is denied of a different <subject>, that will not be the opposite statement but a different 5 one.) The opposite of 'Every man is pale' is 'Not every man is pale'; of 'Some man is pale', 'No man is pale'; of 'A man is pale', 'A man is not pale'.

We have explained, then, that a single affirmation has a single negation as its contradictory opposite, and which these are; that contrary statements are different, and which these are; and that not all contradictory pairs are true or false, and why and when they are true or false.

9[5]

In the case of what is and what has been, then, it is necessary that the 30 affirmation or negation be true or false. And in the case of universal statements about universals, it is always <necessary> for one to be true and the other false; and the same is true in the case of particulars, as we have said. But in the case of universals not spoken of universally, this is not

5. This chapter discusses an argument for fatalism—the view that since everything that happens happens necessarily, it is impossible for us to affect or control what happens. Aristotle rejects this view (see 19a1–11). The chapter has aroused much dispute; in the following notes we mention only a few of the interpretative options.

necessary; we have also discussed this.[6] But in the case of particulars that are going to be, it is not the same.[7]

For if every affirmation or negation is true or false, then it is also necessary that everything either is the case or is not the case. And so if[8] someone   35 says that something will be and another denies the same thing, clearly it is necessary for one of them to speak truly, if every affirmation is true or false. For both will not be the case at the same time in such cases.

For if it is true to say that something is pale or not pale, it is necessary   18b for it to be pale or not pale; and if it is pale or not pale, it was true to affirm or deny this. And if it is not the case, one speaks falsely; and if one speaks falsely, it is not the case. Hence it is necessary for the affirmation or the negation to be true or false.[9]

Therefore nothing either is or happens by chance or as chance has it; nor will it be nor not be <thus>. Rather, everything <happens> from necessity and not as chance has it, since either the affirmer or the denier speaks truly. For otherwise, it might equally well happen or not happen; for what happens as chance has it neither is nor will be any more this way than that.

Further, if something is pale now, it was true to say previously that it   10 would be pale, so that it was always true to say of any thing that has happened that it would be. But if it was always true to say that it was or would be, it could not not be, or not be going to be. But if something cannot not happen, it is impossible for it not to happen; and what cannot not happen necessarily happens. Everything, then, that will be will be   15 necessarily. Therefore, nothing will be as chance has it or by chance; for if it is by chance it is not from necessity.

But it is not possible to say that neither is true—that, for example, it neither will be nor will not be. For, first, <if this is possible, then> though

6. **we have also discussed this**: See 17b29.

7. **not the same**: lit. 'not likewise'. Aristotle might mean (i) that the previous claim ('one contradictory true, one false') is not true of future singular statements, or (ii) that it is true in a different way.

8. **And so if**: Read *hōste ei*. Some mss. read 'for if' (*ei gar*).

9. **Hence it is . . . to be true or false**: This paragraph might be taken in two ways: (1) Aristotle means that it is necessary that (if *p* is true, then the state of affairs described by *p* obtains); he does not mean that if *p* is true, then the state of affairs described by *p* is necessary. The necessity governs the conditional, not its consequent. In the next paragraph (which seems to argue fallaciously from the necessity of the conditional to the necessity of the consequent) Aristotle articulates the fatalist's argument, which he goes on to reject. (2) In this paragraph Aristotle himself argues that if *p* is true, then the state of affairs described by *p* is necessary; he ascribes necessity to the consequent, as well as to the whole conditional. In that case the next paragraph expresses his own view.

the affirmation is false, the negation is not true; and though the negation is
20   false, it turns out <on this view> that the affirmation is not true.

Moreover, if it is true to say that it is pale and dark,[10] both must be the
case; and if <both> will be the case tomorrow, <both> must be the case
tomorrow. But if it neither will nor will not be tomorrow, even so, the sea
battle, for instance, will not happen as chance has it; for in this case, the sea
battle would have to neither happen nor not happen.

These and others like them are the absurd consequences if in every
affirmation and negation (either about universals spoken of universally or
about particulars) it is necessary that one of the opposites be true and the
30   other false, and nothing happens as chance has it, but all things are and
happen from necessity. Hence there would be no need to deliberate or to
take trouble, thinking that if we do this, that will be, and if we do not, it
will not be; for it might well be that ten thousand years ago one person said
35   that this would be and another denied it, so that whichever it was true to
affirm at that time will be so from necessity.

Nor does it make a difference whether or not anyone made the contradictory statements; for clearly things are thus even if someone did not affirm
it and another deny it. For it is not because of the affirming or denying that
19a   it will be or will not be the case, nor is this any more so for ten thousand
years ago than for any other time.

Hence if in the whole of time things were such that one or the other
statement was true, it was necessary for this to happen, and each thing that
happened was always such as to happen from necessity. For if someone has
5   said truly that something will happen, it cannot not happen; and it was
always true to say of something that has happened that it would be.

But surely this is impossible. For we see that both deliberation and action
originate things that will be; and, in general, we see in things that are not
10   always in actuality that there is the possibility both of being and of not
being; in these cases both being and not being, and hence both happening
and not happening, are possible.

We find that this is clearly true of many things. It is possible, for instance, for this cloak to be cut up, though <in fact> it will not be cut up but
15   will wear out first instead. Similarly, its not being cut up is also possible;
for its wearing out first would not have been the case unless its not being
cut up were possible. Hence the same is true for other things that happen,
since this sort of possibility is ascribed to many of them.

Evidently, then, not everything is or happens from necessity. Rather,
20   some things happen as chance has it, and the affirmation is no more true

10. **pale and dark**: The fatalists insist that we cannot escape their argument by
denying the Principle of Non-Contradiction and saying that something is both pale
and dark. (Some mss. read 'pale and large'.)

than the negation.[11] In other cases, one alternative <happens> more than the other and happens usually, but it is still possible for the other to happen and for the first not to happen.

It is necessary for what is, whenever it is, to be, and for what is not, whenever it is not, not to be. But not everything that is necessarily is; and not everything that is not necessarily is not. For everything's being from necessity when it is is not the same as everything's being from necessity without qualification; and the same is true of what is not.[12]

The same argument also applies to contradictories. It is necessary for everything either to be or not to be, and indeed to be going to be or not be going to be. But one cannot divide <the contradictories> and say that one or the other is necessary.[13] I mean that, for instance, it is necessary for there to be or not to be a sea battle tomorrow, but it is not necessary for a sea battle to happen tomorrow, nor is it <necessary> for one not to happen. It is necessary, however, for it either to happen or not to happen.

And so, since the truth of statements corresponds to how things are, it is clear that, for however many things are as chance has it and are such as to admit contraries, it is necessary for the same to be true of the contradictories. This is just what happens with things that neither always are nor

11. **the affirmation . . . the negation**: Aristotle is probably thinking of a sentence type, irrespective of its tense (e.g. 'It will rain (or: it rained) this year on Independence Day') whose tokens are true on some occasions (i.e. when uttered before (or: after) 4 July in years in which it rains on 4 July) and false on others. If this is his point, he is not saying that a token sentence (uttered on a particular occasion) is neither true nor false.

12. **It is necessary . . . true of what is not**: This paragraph might be understood in two ways: (1) Aristotle uncovers the fatalist's fallacy, by distinguishing necessity without qualification from conditional necessity. It is true to say that necessarily (when x is, x is); but we cannot validly infer from this that when x is, x necessarily is. Certainly x is conditionally necessary, in that, necessarily (when x is, x is); but x is not necessary without qualification, i.e. necessary on its own. (2) Aristotle affirms that when x is (i.e. is present), then x necessarily is. He affirms the necessity of the present and past, in contrast to the non-necessity of the future.

These two interpretations correspond to the two interpretations of Aristotle's previous argument (see notes 9 and 11), and imply two different views of the next paragraph.

13. **But one . . . is necessary**: From necessarily (p or not-p), we cannot infer the disjunction (either necessarily p or necessarily not-p). On 'dividing' see *Met.* 1008a19. If the first interpretation of the previous paragraph is correct, the present paragraph illustrates the fatalists' modal fallacy in a different case. If the second interpretation is correct, Aristotle seeks to show that it is true that (either there will or will not be a sea battle tomorrow), but it is neither true that there will be a sea battle nor true that there will not be a sea battle.

always are not. For in these cases it is necessary for one of the contradictories to be true and the other false. It is not, however, <necessary> for this
or that one <more than the other one to be true or false>. Rather, <it is
true or false> as chance has it; or <in the case of things that happen
usually> one is more true than the other, but not thereby true or false
<without qualification>.[14]

19b   Clearly, then, it is not necessary that of every affirmation and negation
of opposites, one is true and one false. For what holds for things that are
<always> does not also hold for things that are not <always> but are
capable of being and of not being; in these cases it is as we have said.

14. **For in these cases . . .   . . . qualification>**: There are again two possible interpretations: (1) This is a third explanation of the fallacy. In the statement involving
contradictories (p or not-p), it is necessary that one of p and not-p be true, the
other false. But it does not follow that whichever of them is true is necessarily true,
or that whichever of them is false is necessarily false. This third case differs from
the second, in that it applies to statements whereas the second applies to states of
affairs. (2) Aristotle claims that from '(p or not-p) is true' we cannot infer 'either
(p is true) or (not-p is true)'. If this is our view, we will translate the last two sentences as follows: 'It is not, however, <necessary> for this or that one <to be true
or false>, but rather as chance has it; or one rather than the other is true, but is not
already true or false'.

TOPICS[1]

This early work is a manual of argumentation. In the brief excerpt presented here, Aristotle discusses the role of dialectic in obtaining first principles (chapters 1 and 2). He also defines some concepts central to his thought (chapter 5).

BOOK I

1

The purpose of our discussion is to discover a line of inquiry that will   *100a* allow us to reason deductively from common beliefs on any problem pro-   *20* posed to us, and to give an account ourselves without saying anything contradictory. First, then, we must say what a deduction is and what different types of it there are, so that we can grasp what dialectical deduction is—for this is what we are looking for in our proposed discussion.

A deduction, then, is an argument in which, if p and q are assumed, then   *25* something else r, different from p and q, follows necessarily through p and q.[2] It is a demonstration whenever the deduction proceeds from true and primary premises or our knowledge of the premises is originally derived from primary and true premises. A dialectical deduction is the one that   *30* proceeds from common beliefs.

The premises that are true and primary are those that produce convic-   *100b* tion not through other things, but through themselves. For in the principles of knowledge we must not search further for the reason why; rather, each   *20* of the principles must be credible itself in its own right.

The common beliefs are the things believed by everyone or by most people or by the wise (and among the wise by all or by most or by those most known and commonly recognized[3]). A contentious deduction is one

---

1. The *Topics* is about *topoi*, 'places' (hence 'commonplaces'). 'Places' probably refers to a technique for remembering a list of items by correlating them with a previously-learned grid or list of places. Hence the dialectical 'places' are common forms of argument to be remembered for use in dialectical discussions.

2. **if p and q . . . p and q**: Lit., 'when some things have been laid down, something other than the things laid down comes about by necessity, through the things laid down'.

3. **commonly recognized**: *endoxos*. 'Common beliefs' translates *endoxa*.

25   proceeding from apparent common beliefs that are not really common
      beliefs, or one apparently proceeding from real or apparent common be-
      liefs. <We speak of 'apparent' common beliefs,> because not everything
      that appears to be a common belief really is one; for none of the things
      called common beliefs has the appearance entirely on the surface. On this
      point they differ from what happens in the case of the principles of conten-
30   tious arguments. For in the latter case the nature of the falsity is especially
      clear straightaway to those with even a little ability to trace consequences.
101a The first kind of deduction that we have called contentious, then, should
      indeed count as a genuine deduction, whereas the other kind is a conten-
      tious deduction, but not a genuine deduction, since it appears to make a
      deduction, but does not actually do so.
(5)   Further, besides all the types of deduction just mentioned, there are
      fallacious arguments that start from premises that are proper to a given
      science, as happens in the case of geometry and cognate sciences. For this
      type of argument would seem to be different from the types of deduction
10   previously mentioned; for someone who draws the wrong diagram deduces
      a conclusion neither from true and primary premises nor from common
      beliefs. He does not fall into either class, since he does not accept what is
      believed by all, or by most people, or by the wise (either all or most or the
      most commonly recognized of these), but produces his deduction by ac-
15   cepting things that are proper to the science but are not true. For example,
      he produces his fallacious argument[4] either by describing the semicircles
      wrongly or by drawing lines wrongly.
          These, then, are, in outline, the types of deduction. In general, both in
20   all the cases we have discussed and in all those to be discussed later, this
      degree of determinateness is to be taken as adequate. For <in undertaking
      this discussion> the account we decide to give on any subject is not an
      exact account, but enough for us to describe it in outline. We assume that
      the ability to recognize these things in some way is entirely adequate for
      the proposed line of inquiry.

      2

      Our next task is to say what areas, and how many, there are in which our
      discussion is useful. It is useful, then, for three purposes—for training, for
      encounters, and for the philosophical sciences.
          Its usefulness for training is immediately evident; for if we have a line of
25   inquiry, we will more easily be able to take on a question proposed to us. It
      is useful for encounters, because once we have catalogued the beliefs of the
      many, our approach to them will begin from their own views, not from
      other people's, and we will redirect them whenever they appear to us to be

      4. **fallacious argument**: Aristotle is thinking of attempts to square the circle.

wrong. It is useful for the philosophical sciences, because the ability to   35
survey the puzzles on each side of a question makes it easier to notice what
is true and false. Moreover it is useful for finding the primary things in
each science. For from the principles proper to the science proposed for
discussion nothing can be derived about the principles themselves, since
the principles are primary among all <the truths contained in the science>;
instead they must be discussed through the common beliefs in a given area.   101b
This is distinctive of dialectic, or more proper to it than to anything else;
for since it cross-examines, it provides a way towards the principles of all
lines of inquiry.

5

We must say, then, what a definition, a distinctive property, a genus, and a
coincident are.

A definition is an account[5] that signifies the essence. One provides either   102a
an account to replace a name or an account to replace an account—for it is
also possible to define some of the things signified by an account. Those
who merely provide a name, whatever it is, clearly do not provide the
definition of the thing, since every definition is an account. Still, this sort   5
of thing—for example, 'the fine is the fitting'[6]—should also be counted as
definitory. In the same way one should also count as definitory a question
such as 'Are perception and knowledge the same or different?'; for most of
the discussion about definition is occupied with whether things are the
same or different. Speaking without qualification, we may count as definitory everything that falls under the same line of inquiry that includes   10
definition.

It is clear immediately that all the things just mentioned meet this condition. For if we are able to argue dialectically that things are the same and
that they are different, we will in the same way be well supplied to take on
definitions;[7] for once we have shown that two things are not the same, we   15
will have undermined the <attempted> definition. The converse of this
point, however, does not hold; for showing that two things are the same is
not enough to establish a definition, whereas showing that two things are
not the same is enough to destroy a definition.

A distinctive property is one that does not reveal what the subject is,
though it belongs only to that subject and is reciprocally predicated of it. It

5. **account**: *logos*; see REASON #4–5. This is not necessarily (see 101b22n) a linguis-
tic expression (though here the contrast with names suggests that this is what
Aristotle has in mind).

6. **'the fine is the fitting'**: Aristotle objects that this provides a single word ('fitting')
instead of a *logos* as a definition.

7. **take on**: especially for the purpose of attacking them.

20 is distinctive of man, for instance, to be receptive of grammatical knowledge; for if someone is a man, he is receptive of grammatical knowledge, and if someone is receptive of grammatical knowledge, he is a man. For no one counts as a distinctive property what admits of belonging to something else—for instance, no one counts being asleep as a distinctive property of a man, even if at some time it happens to belong only to him. If, then,

25 something of this sort were to be called a distinctive property, it would be called distinctive not without qualification, but at a time, or in relation to something; being on the right, for instance, is distinctive of something at a particular time, while being a biped is distinctive of one thing in relation to another—of man, for instance, in relation to horse and dog. It is clear that nothing that admits of belonging to something else is reciprocally predi-

30 cated of its subject; it is not necessary, for instance, that what is asleep is a man.

A genus is what is essentially predicated[8] of a plurality of things differing in species. Let us count as essentially predicated whatever it is appropriate to mention if we are asked what a given thing is; when we are asked

35 what man is, for instance, it is appropriate to say that it is an animal. It is also relevant to the genus to say whether two things are in the same genus, or each is in a different genus, since this also falls under the same line of inquiry as the genus. If, for instance, we argue dialectically that animal is the genus of man, and also of ox, we will have argued that they are in the

102b same genus; and if we prove that something is the genus of one thing but not of another, we will have argued that these two things are not in the same genus.

5 A coincident is what though it is none of these things—neither a definition nor a distinctive property nor a genus—belongs to the subject. Again, it is whatever admits both of belonging and of not belonging to one and the same subject. Being seated, for instance, admits both of belonging and of not belonging to one and the same subject, and so does being pale, since the same subject may easily be pale at one time and not pale at another.

10 The second of these two definitions of coincident is better. For if the first is stated, we will not understand it unless we first know what a definition, a distinctive property, and a genus are; the second, however, is sufficient in its own right for our knowing what is meant.

15 Let us also add to the <class of> coincidents the comparisons between things whose descriptions are derived in some way from the coincident. These include, for instance, the question whether the fine or the advantageous is more choiceworthy, or whether the life of virtue or the life of gratification is pleasanter, and any other questions similar to these. For in

20 all such cases the question proves to be about whether the thing predicated is more <properly> a coincident of the one subject or of the other.

8. **essentially predicated**: lit. 'predicated in the what-it-is'.

It is immediately clear that a coincident may easily be distinctive of a subject at a particular time and in relation to a particular thing. Whenever, for instance, someone is the only one seated, being seated, which is a coincident, is distinctive at that time; and when he is not the only one seated, being seated is distinctive of him in relation to those not seated. Hence a coincident may easily turn out to be distinctive in relation to a particular thing and at a particular time, but it is not a distinctive property without qualification.

25

POSTERIOR ANALYTICS

The Posterior Analytics *contains Aristotle's epistemology and philosophy of science. His approach is broadly speaking foundational. Some of what we know can be justified by being shown to follow logically from other things that we know, but some of what we know does not need to be justified in this way. Such items of foundational knowledge are the first principles of the various sciences. In the excerpts below, Aristotle sets out the axiomatic structure of a science and presents his theory of explanation. The final chapter provides a tantalizing but obscure presentation of his ideas on the acquisition of first principles.*

BOOK I

1

71a   All teaching and all intellectual learning result from previous cognition. This is clear if we examine all the cases; for this is how the mathematical
5   sciences and all crafts arise. This is also true of both deductive and inductive arguments, since they both succeed in teaching because they rely on previous cognition: deductive arguments begin with premises we are assumed to understand, and inductive arguments prove the universal by relying on the fact that the particular is already clear. Rhetorical arguments
10   also persuade in the same way, since they rely either on examples (and hence on induction) or on argumentations (and hence on deduction).

    Previous cognition is needed in two ways. In some cases we must presuppose that something is[1] (for example, that it is true that everything is either asserted or denied truly <of a given subject>). In other cases we must
15   comprehend what the thing spoken of is (for example, that a triangle signifies this); and in other cases we must do both (for example, we must both comprehend what a unit signifies and presuppose that there is such a thing). For something different is needed to make each of these things clear to us.

    We may also recognize that *q* by having previously recognized that *p* and

---

1. **that something is**: lit. 'that (subject unexpressed) is', *hoti estin*. We render this by 'that it is true' in 71a14 and by 'that there is such a thing' in 71a16. Cf. 93b33, *Phys.* 193a3, 217b31.

acquiring recognition of q at the same time <as we acquire recognition of r>. This is how, for instance, we acquire recognition of the cases that fall under the universal of which we have cognition; for we previously knew that, say, every triangle has angles equal to two right angles, but we recognize that 20 this figure in the semicircle is a triangle at the same time as we perform the induction <showing that this figure has two right angles>. For in some cases we learn in this way, (rather than recognizing the last term through the middle); this is true when we reach particulars, i.e. things not said of any subject.

Before we perform the induction or the deduction, we should presumably 25 be said to know in one way but not in another. For if we did not know without qualification whether <a given triangle> is, how could we know without qualification that it has two right angles? But clearly we know it insofar as we know it universally, but we do not know it without qualification. Otherwise we will face the puzzle in the *Meno*, since we will turn out 30 to learn either nothing or else nothing but what we <already> know.[2]

For we should not agree with some people's attempted solution to this puzzle. Do you or do you not know that every pair is even? When you say you do, they produce a pair that you did not think existed and hence did not think was even. They solve this puzzle by saying that one does not know that every pair is even, but rather one knows that what one knows to be a pair is even. In fact, however, <contrary to this solution>, one knows 71b that of which one has grasped and still possesses the demonstration, and the demonstration one has grasped is not about whatever one knows to be a triangle or a number, but about every number or triangle without qualification; for <in a demonstration> a premiss is not taken to say that what you know to be a triangle or rectangle is so and so, but, on the contrary, it is taken to apply to every case.

But, I think, it is quite possible for us to know in one way what we are learning, while being ignorant of it in another way. For what is absurd is not that we <already> know in some way the very thing we are learning; the absurdity arises only if we already know it to the precise extent and in the precise way in which we are learning it.

2. **Otherwise we . . . <already know>**: Plato presents the puzzle (*Meno* 80a–d) as follows: (1) For any item x, either one knows x or one does not know x. (2) If one knows x, one cannot inquire into x. (3) If one does not know x, one cannot inquire into x. (4) Therefore, whether one knows or does not know x, one cannot inquire into x. Aristotle solves the puzzle by rejecting (2) and distinguishing different sorts of knowledge: one can inquire into what one knows in some way, so long as one is inquiring in order to know it in another way, or in order to know some different fact about it. (The beginning of *APo* i 1 may allow that one can inquire in the absence of knowledge, so long as one has suitable beliefs, in which case Aristotle rejects not only (3) but also (2).)

2

10 We think we know a thing without qualification, and not in the sophistic, coincidental way, whenever we think we recognize the explanation[3] because of which the thing is <so>, and recognize both that it is the explanation of that thing and that it does not admit of being otherwise. Clearly, then, knowing is something of this sort; for both those who lack knowledge and those who have it think they are in this condition, but those who 15 have the knowledge are really in it. So whatever is known without qualification cannot be otherwise.

We shall say later whether there is also some other way of knowing; but we certainly say that we know through demonstration. By 'demonstration' I mean a deduction expressing knowledge; by 'expressing knowledge' I mean that having the deduction constitutes having knowledge.

20 If, then, knowing is the sort of thing we assumed it is, demonstrative knowledge must also be derived from things that are true, primary, immediate, better known[4] than, prior to, and explanatory of the conclusion; for this will also ensure that the principles are proper to what is being proved. For these conditions are not necessary for a deduction, but they are neces-25 sary for a demonstration, since without them a deduction will not produce knowledge.

<The conclusions> must be true, then, because we cannot know what is not <true> (for example, that the diagonal is commensurate). They must be derived from <premisses> that are primary and indemonstrable, because we will have no knowledge unless we have a demonstration of these <premisses>; for to have non-coincidental knowledge of something demonstrable is to have a demonstration of it.

30 They must be explanatory, better known, and prior. They must be explanatory, because we know something whenever we know its explanation. They must be prior if they are indeed explanatory. And they must be previously cognized not only in the sense that we comprehend them, but also in the sense that we know that they are <true>. Things are prior and better known in two ways; for what is prior by nature is not the same as 72a what is prior to us, nor is what is better known <by nature> the same as what is better known to us. By 'what is prior and better known to us' I mean what is closer to perception, and by 'what is prior and better known without qualification' I mean what is further from perception. What is most

3. **explanation**: or 'cause', *aitia*. Aristotle is thinking not only of an explanatory statement, but also of the event or state of affairs that the statement refers to.

4. **better known**: *gnōrimōterōn*. The term is cognate with the verb (*gnōrizein*) that we translate 'cognize' or 'recognize'. Aristotle applies it both to things that are 'more knowable' in themselves and to things that are 'more familiar' to us (see 72a1ff); hence we translate it uniformly as 'better known'.

universal is furthest from perception, and particulars are closest to it;   5
particular and universal are opposite to each other.

Derivation from primary things is derivation from proper principles. (I
mean the same by 'primary things' as I mean by 'principles'.) A principle of
demonstration is an immediate premiss, and a premiss is immediate if no
others are prior to it. A premiss is one or the other part of a contradiction,[5]
and it says one thing of one thing. It is dialectical if it takes either part   10
indifferently, demonstrative if it determinately takes one part because it is
true.[6] A contradiction is an opposition which, in itself, has nothing in the
middle. The part of the contradiction that asserts something of something
is an affirmation, and the part that denies something of something is a
denial.

By 'thesis' I mean an immediate principle of deduction that cannot be   15
proved, but is not needed if one is to learn anything at all. By 'axiom' I
mean a principle one needs in order to learn anything at all; for there are
some things of this sort, and it is especially these to which we usually
apply the name.

If a thesis asserts one or the other part of a contradiction—for example,   20
that something is or that something is not—it is an assumption; otherwise
it is a definition. For a definition is a thesis (since the arithmetician, for
example, lays it down that a unit is what is indivisible in quantity), but it is
not an assumption (since what it is to be a unit and that a unit is are not the
same).

Since our conviction and knowledge about a thing must be based on our   25
having the sort of deduction we call a demonstration, and since we have
this sort of deduction when its premisses obtain, not only must we have
previous cognition about all or some of the primary things, but we must
also know them better. For if x makes y F, x is more F than y; if, for   30
instance, we love y because of x, x is loved more than y. Hence if the
primary things produce knowledge and conviction, we must have more
knowledge and conviction about them, since they also produce it about
subordinate things.

Now if we know q, we cannot have greater conviction about p than
about q unless we either know p or are in some condition better than
knowledge about p.[7] This will result, however, unless previous knowledge   35

5. **contradiction**: reading *antiphaseōs*, and omitting *apophanseōs . . . morion*, b11–
12. 'Pleasure is good' and 'Pleasure is not good' (i.e. it is not the case that pleasure is
good) are the two parts of a contradiction.

6. **dialectical . . . demonstrative**: see *Top.* 100a25–b23.

7. **Now if we know . . . than knowledge about** p: More literally: 'We cannot have
greater conviction about things that we neither know nor are better disposed towards than if we knew, than <we have> about things we know.'

<of the principles> is the basis of conviction produced by demonstration; for we must have greater conviction about all or some of the principles than about the conclusion.

If we are to have knowledge through demonstration, then not only must we know the principles better and have greater conviction about them than 72b about what is proved, but we must also not find anything more convincing or better known that is opposed to the principles and allows us to deduce a mistaken conclusion contrary <to the correct one>. For no one who has knowledge without qualification can be persuaded out of it.

3

5   Some people think that because <knowledge through demonstration> requires knowledge of the primary things, there is no knowledge; others think that there is knowledge, and that everything <knowable> is demonstrable. Neither of these views is either true or necessary.

The first party—those who assume that there is no knowledge at all—claim that we face an infinite regress. They assume that we cannot know posterior things because of prior things, if there are no primary things. Their assumption is correct, since it is impossible to go through an infinite series. If, on the other hand, the regress stops, and there are principles, these are, in their view, unrecognizable, since these principles cannot be demonstrated, and, in these people's view, demonstration is the only way of knowing. But if we cannot know the primary things, then neither can we 15 know without qualification or fully the things derived from them; we can know them only conditionally, on the assumption that we can know the primary things.

The other party agree that knowledge results only from demonstration, but they claim that it is possible to demonstrate everything, since they take circular and reciprocal demonstration to be possible.

We reply that not all knowledge is demonstrative, and in fact knowledge 20 of the immediate premisses is indemonstrable. Indeed, it is evident that this must be so; for if we must know the prior things (i.e. those from which the demonstration is derived), and if eventually the regress stops, these immediate premisses must be indemonstrable. Besides this, we also say that there is not only knowledge but also some origin of knowledge, which gives us cognition of the definitions.

25   Unqualified demonstration clearly cannot be circular, if it must be derived from what is prior and better known. For the same things cannot be both prior and posterior to the same things at the same time, except in different ways (so that, for example, some things are prior relative to us, and others are prior without qualification—this is the way induction makes something known). If this is so, our definition of unqualified knowledge 30 will be faulty, and there will be two sorts of knowledge; or <rather>

perhaps the second sort of demonstration is not unqualified demonstration, since it is derived from what is <merely> better known to us.

Those who allow circular demonstration must concede not only the previous point, but also that they are simply saying that something is if it is. On these terms it is easy to prove anything. This is clear if we consider   35
three terms—for it does not matter whether we say the demonstration turns back through many or few terms, or through few or two. For suppose that if A is, necessarily B is, and that if B is, necessarily C is; it follows that if A is, C will be. Suppose, then, that if A is, then B necessarily is, and if B is, A   73a
is (since this is what circular argument is), and let A be C. In that case, to say that if B is, A is is to say that <if B is,> C is; this <is to say> that if A is, C is. But since C is the same as A, it follows that those who allow circular demonstration simply say that if A is, then A is. On these terms it   5
is easy to prove anything.

But not even this is possible, except for things that are reciprocally predicated, such as distinctive properties. If, then, one thing is laid down, we have proved that it is never necessary for anything else to be the case. (By 'one thing' I mean that neither one term nor one thesis is enough; two   10
theses are the fewest <needed for a demonstration>, since they are also the fewest needed for a deduction.) If, then, A follows from B and C, and these follow from each other and from A, then in this way it is possible to prove all the postulates from each other in the first figure, as we proved in the discussion of deduction. We also proved that in the other figures, the result   15
is either no deduction or none relevant to the things assumed. But it is not at all possible to give a circular proof of things that are not reciprocally predicated. And so, since there are few things that are reciprocally predicated in demonstrations, it is clearly empty and impossible to say that demonstration is reciprocal and that for this reason everything is demon-   20
strable.

4

Since what is known without qualification cannot be otherwise, what is known by demonstrative knowledge will be necessary. Demonstrative knowledge is what we have by having a demonstration; hence a demonstration is a deduction from things that are necessary. We must, then, find from   25
what and from what sorts of things demonstrations are derived. Let us first determine what we mean by '<belonging> in every case', 'in its own right', and 'universal'.

By '<belonging> in every case' I mean what belongs not <merely> in some cases, or at some times, as opposed to others. If, for example, animal   30
belongs to every man, it follows that if it is true to say that this is a man, it is also true to say that he is an animal, and that if he is a man now, he is also an animal now. The same applies if it is true to say that there is a point

in every line. A sign of this is the fact that when we are asked whether something belongs in every case, we advance objections by asking whether it fails to belong either in some cases or at some times.

A belongs to B in its own right in the following cases:

35   (a) A belongs to B in what B is, as, for example, line belongs to triangle, and point to line; for here the essence of B is composed of A, and A is present in the account that says what B is.

   (b) A belongs to B, and B itself is present in the account revealing what A is. In this way straight and curved, for instance, belong to line, while
40   odd and even, prime and compound, equilateral and oblong, belong in
73b   this way to number. In all these cases either line or number is present in the account saying what <straight or odd, for example,> is. Similarly in other cases, this is what I mean by saying that A belongs to B in its
5   own right. What belongs in neither of these ways I call coincidental— as, for instance, musical or pale belongs to animal.

   (c) A is not said of something else B that is the subject of A. A walker or a pale thing, for example, is a walker or a pale thing by being something else;[8] but a substance—i.e. whatever signifies a this—is not what it is by being something else. I say, then, that what is not said of a subject is
10   <a thing> in its own right, whereas what is said of a subject is a coincident.

   (d) Moreover, in another way, if A belongs to B because of B itself, then A belongs to B in its own right; if A belongs to B, but not because of B itself, then A is coincidental to B. If, for example, lightning flashed while you were walking, that was coincidental; for the lightning was not caused by your walking but, as we say, was a coincidence. If, however, A belongs to B because of B itself, then it belongs to B in its own right. If, for example, an animal was killed in being sacrificed, the
15   killing belongs to the sacrificing in its own right, since the animal was killed because it was sacrificed, and it was not a coincidence that the animal was killed in being sacrificed.

Hence in the case of unqualified objects of knowledge, whenever A is said to belong to B in its own right, either because B is present in A and A is predicated of B, or because A is present in B, then A belongs to B because of B itself and necessarily. <It belongs necessarily> either because it is impossible for A not to belong to B or because it is impossible for
20   neither A nor its opposite (for example, straight and crooked, or odd and even) to belong to B (for example, a line or a number). For a contrary is

8. **A walker or a pale thing**: lit. 'the walking', 'the pale' (neuter adjectives). **by being something else**: i.e. by being (e.g.) a man. Cf. *Met.* 1028a24–31.

either a privation or a contradiction in the same genus; even, for example, is what is not odd among numbers, insofar as this follows. Hence, if it is necessary either to affirm or to deny, then what belongs to a subject in its own right necessarily belongs to that subject.   25

Let this, then, be our definition of what belongs in every case and of what belongs to something in its own right.

By 'universal' I mean what belongs to its subject in every case and in its own right, and insofar as it is itself. It is evident, then, that what is universal belongs to things necessarily. What belongs to the subject in its own right is the same as what belongs to it insofar as it is itself. A point and straightness, for instance, belong to a line in its own right, since they   30 belong to a line insofar as it is a line. Similarly, two right angles belong to a triangle insofar as it is a triangle, since a triangle is equal in its own right to two right angles.

A universal belongs <to a species> whenever it is proved of an instance that is random and primary. Having two right angles, for instance, is not universal to figure; for though you may prove that some figure has two right angles, you cannot prove it of any random figure, nor do you use any random figure in proving it, since a quadrilateral is a figure but does not have angles equal to two right angles. Again, a random isosceles triangle has angles equal to two right angles, but it is not the primary case, since the triangle is prior. If, then, a random triangle is the primary case that is   40 proved to have two right angles, or whatever it is, then that property belongs universally to this case primarily, and the demonstration holds   74a universally of this case in its own right. It holds of the other cases in a way, but not in their own right; it does not even hold universally of the isosceles triangle, but more widely.

5

We must not fail to notice that we often turn out to be mistaken and that   5 what we are proving does not belong primarily and universally in the way we think we are proving it to belong. We are deceived in this way in these cases: (1) We cannot find any higher <kind> besides a particular <less general kind>. (2) We can find <such a kind>, but it is nameless, applying to things that differ in species. (3) The <kind> we are proving something about is in fact a partial whole; for the demonstration will apply to the   10 particular instances <of the partial whole>, but still it will not apply universally to this <kind> primarily. I say that a demonstration applies to a given <kind> primarily, insofar as it is this <kind>, whenever it applies universally to <this kind> primarily.

If, then, one were to prove that right angles do not meet, one might think that the demonstration applied to this case because it holds for all right   15 angles. This is not so, however, since this <conclusion> results not because they are equal in this <specific> way <by both being right angles>, but insofar as they are equal at all.

Again, if there were no triangles other than isosceles, then <what applies to triangles insofar as they are triangles> would seem to apply to isosceles triangles insofar as they are isosceles.

Again, <it might seem> that proportion alternates in numbers insofar as they are numbers. lines insofar as they are lines, solids insofar as they are solids, and times insofar as they are times; indeed it once used to be
20   proved separately <for each of these cases>. In fact it can be proved by a single demonstration; but because all of these (numbers, lengths, times, solids) do not constitute one <kind> with a name, but differ from each other in species, they used to be taken separately. Now it is proved universally; for it does not belong to them insofar as they are lines or numbers,
25   but insofar as they are this other thing that is assumed to belong universally.

That is why, even if for each <kind of> triangle you prove by one or by more than one demonstration that it has two right angles, taking equilateral, scalene, and isosceles triangles separately, you do not thereby know (except in the sophistical way) that the triangle has angles equal to two right angles—not even if there is no other <kind of> triangle besides these.
30   For you do not know that it belongs to a triangle insofar as it is a triangle, nor that it belongs to every triangle; you know it for every triangle taken numerically, but not for every triangle taken as a kind—even if there is no triangle for which you do not know it.

When, then, do you not know universally, and when do you know without qualification? Clearly, if being a triangle were the same as being equilateral (for each or for all), <then you would know without qualifica-
35   tion>. But if being a triangle is not the same as being equilateral, and if <having two right angles> belongs to a triangle insofar as it is a triangle, then you do not know.

Then does having two right angles belong to a triangle insofar as it is a triangle, or to an isosceles triangle insofar as it is isosceles? When does it belong to a triangle primarily in respect of its being a triangle? To what does the demonstration apply universally? It is clear that it applies universally to F whenever it applies to F primarily, after <other things> have been abstracted. For instance, two right angles belong to the bronze isosceles
74b   triangle, but they still belong when being bronze and and being isosceles have been abstracted. But they do not belong when figure or limit has been abstracted. Still, these are not the first <whose abstraction makes the property cease to belong>. Then what is the first <whose abstraction has this result>? If it is triangle, then it is in respect of being a triangle that having two right angles belongs to the other things too, and the demonstration applies to this universally.

6

We have found that demonstrative knowledge is derived from necessary   5
principles (since what is known cannot be otherwise) and that what belongs to things in their own right is necessary (for in the one case it belongs
in the essence, and in the other case it belongs in the essence of the things
predicated of it, and one or the other of the opposites necessarily belongs   10
to it). Evidently, then, demonstrative deduction will be derived from what
belongs to something in its own right; for whatever belongs to a subject
belongs to it either in its own right or coincidentally, and coincidents are
not necessary. We must either say this or else lay it down as a principle that
demonstration is of what is necessary and that what is demonstrated cannot be otherwise. It follows, then, that this deduction must be derived from   15
necessary premisses; for non-demonstrative deduction is possible from true
premisses, but not from necessary premisses, since deduction from necessary premisses is characteristic of demonstration.

The character of the objections that are raised against demonstrations is
evidence for our claim that demonstration is from necessary premisses; for   20
we object <to an alleged demonstration> by saying that <some part of it>
is not necessary, if we think that it is possible (either in general or for the
sake of argument) for it to be otherwise. This also shows how silly it is to
think that, if the premiss is commonly believed and true, we have the right
grasp of the principles (as the sophists think, since they assume that to
know is simply to have knowledge). For a principle is not something we
commonly believe, but what is primary in the genus relevant to our proofs;   25
moreover, not every truth is proper <to the relevant genus>.

A further argument shows that <demonstrative> deduction must be derived from necessary premisses. When a conclusion is demonstrable, we do
not know it if we have no account of the reason why it is true; but A might
belong to C necessarily, while B, the middle term through which this con-   30
clusion was <allegedly> demonstrated, <belongs to C, but> not necessarily. In that case we do not know the reason <why the conclusion is
true>; for the middle term is not the reason, since it is possible for the
middle term not to be, whereas the conclusion is necessary.

Further, if we do not now know, although we have the account and we
still exist, and the object still exists, and we have not forgotten, then we did
not know before either. But the middle term might cease to exist, if it is not
necessary; hence we might have the account, and we would still exist, and   35
the object would still exist, but we would not know, so that we did not
know previously either. If the middle term still exists, but its non-existence
is possible, the result we have described is possible and might arise; someone in that state cannot possibly know.

Whenever, then, the conclusion is necessary, the middle through which it   75a was proved may well not be necessary; for what is necessary can be deduced even from what is not necessary, just as a truth can be deduced from what is not true. But whenever the middle is necessary, the conclusion will also be necessary, just as truths always result in truth. (For let A be said of B necessarily, and B of C <necessarily>; it is also necessary, then, for A to belong to C <necessarily>.) But when the conclusion is not necessary, the middle cannot be necessary either. (For let A belong to C not necessarily, but to B necessarily; and let B belong to C necessarily; then A will also belong to C necessarily. But it was assumed not to.)

Since, then, what we know demonstratively must belong necessarily, it is clear that we must also demonstrate through a middle that is necessary. Otherwise we will not know either the reason why or that it is necessary for this to be; either we will think but not know (if we take what is not necessary to be necessary), or we will not even think it (whether we know the fact through the middle terms or know the reason and know it through immediate premisses).

There is no demonstrative knowledge of coincidents that do not belong to things in their own right (according to our determination of what belongs to things in their own right); for the conclusion cannot be proved necessarily, since it is possible for a coincident not to belong (this is the sort of coincident I mean). Still, one might be puzzled about the point of asking questions about these things, if the conclusion is not necessary; for it would make no difference if we asked any old random questions and then stated the conclusion. We are right to ask the questions, however, not because we assume that they make <the conclusion> necessary, but because someone who gives these answers must then necessarily affirm the conclusion and must affirm it truly, if the answers are true.

Since in each genus what belongs to something in its own right and insofar as it is a given <sort of thing> belongs necessarily, it is clear that demonstrations that express knowledge are about, and are derived from, things that belong to a subject in its own right. For since coincidents are not necessary, we do not necessarily know why a conclusion <derived from them> holds, even if it holds of the subject in every case, but not in its own right (for example, deduction through signs). For in that case you will know something that <in fact> belongs to something in its own right, but you will not know it <as belonging to something> in its own right, nor will you know the reason why it belongs. (And to know the reason why is to know through the explanation.) The middle, then, must belong to the third, and the first to the middle, because of itself.

10

By 'principles' in each genus I mean the things whose truth cannot be proved. What the primary things, and the things derived from them, signify is assumed, and the truth of the principles must also be assumed; but the truth of the rest must be proved. For instance, we must assume what a unit, or straight and a triangle, signify, and that there is such a thing as a 35 unit and a magnitude, but we must prove the other things.

Of the principles used in demonstrative science, some are distinctive of a given science and others are common. The common ones are common by analogy, since each is useful to the extent that it applies to the genus falling under the science. A distinctive principle is, for instance, that a line or the 40 straight is this sort of thing. A common principle is, for instance, that if equals are removed from equals, equals are left. Each of these is adequate to the extent that it applies to a given genus; for the effect will be the same if it is not assumed to hold of everything whatever, but only of magnitudes 76b <for the geometer>, and of numbers for the arithmetician.

BOOK II

8

We must consider over again what is right and what is wrong in what has 93ʋ been said, and what a definition is, and whether or not there is any sort of demonstration of what something is.

Now, we say that knowing what a thing is is the same as knowing the explanation[9] of whether it is. The argument for this is that there is some 5 explanation <of whether a thing is> and this is either the same <as what the thing is> or something else, and if it is something else, then it is either demonstrable or indemonstrable. If, then, it is something else and is demonstrable, the explanation must be a middle term, and must be proved in the first figure, since what is being proved is universal and affirmative.

One type of proof, then, would be the one examined just now—proving 10 what something is through something else. For in proofs of what a thing is it is necessary for the middle term to be what <the thing> is, and in proofs of distinctive properties it is necessary for the middle term to be a distinctive property. Hence in one case you will, and in another case you will not, prove the essence of the same object. Now this type of proof, as has been said before, is not a demonstration, but a logical deduction of what something is. 15

Let us say, then, starting again from the beginning, how a demonstration is possible. In some cases we seek the reason for something when we have already grasped the fact,[10] and in other cases they both become clear at the

9. **explanation**: See CAUSE #2. In this discussion 'cause' would sometimes be more suitable (since Aristotle is treating substances and events, rather than propositions, facts, or properties, as *aitiai*). We have retained 'explanation' for the sake of uniformity with Bk i.

10. **the reason . . . the fact**: lit. 'the why (*to dihoti*) . . . the that (*to hoti*)'. Cf. *EN* 1095b7, CAUSE #2.

same time; but it is never possible to recognize the reason before the fact. It is clear, then, that in the same way we cannot recognize the essence of a
20   thing without knowing that the thing is; for it is impossible to know what a thing is if we do not know whether the thing is.

Our grasp of whether a thing is is in some cases <merely> coincidental, while in other cases we grasp whether a thing is by grasping some aspect of the thing itself. We may grasp, for instance, whether thunder is, by grasping that it is some sort of noise in the clouds; whether an eclipse is, by grasping that it is some sort of deprivation of light; whether a man is, by grasping that he is some sort of animal; and whether a soul is, by grasping that it initiates its own motion.

25   In cases where we know <only> coincidentally that a thing is, we necessarily have no grasp of what the thing is, since we do not even know that the thing is; to inquire into what a thing is when we have not grasped that the thing is is to inquire into nothing. But in the cases where we do grasp some <aspect of the thing itself>, it is easier <to inquire into what the thing is>. And so we acquire knowledge of what the thing is to the extent that we know that the thing is.

As a case where we grasp some aspect of what a thing is, let us take first
30   of all the following: Let A be an eclipse, C the moon, and B blocking by the earth. Then to inquire into whether it is eclipsed or not is to inquire into whether B is or not. This question is just the same as the question whether there is an account of <A>; and if there is an account of <A>, we also say that <A> is. Or perhaps we ask which of two contradictories—for exam-
35   ple, the triangle's having or not having two right angles—satisfies the account.

When we find <the account>, we know both the fact and the reason at the same time, if <we reach the fact> through immediate <premisses>; if <the premisses are not immediate>, then we know the fact, but not the reason. For instance, let C be the moon, A an eclipse, and B the inability to cast a shadow at the full moon when there is nothing apparent between us
93b   and it. Suppose, then, that B (inability to cast a shadow when there is nothing between us and it) belongs to C, and that A (being eclipsed) belongs to B. In that case it is clear that the moon has been eclipsed, but it is not thereby clear why it has been eclipsed; we know that there is an eclipse, but we do not know what it is.

5   If it is clear that A belongs to C, then <to inquire into> why it belongs is to inquire into what B is—whether it is the blocking <by the earth> or the rotation of the moon or its extinguishing. And this is the account of one extreme term—in this case the account of A, since an eclipse is a blocking by the earth.

<Or take another example:> What is thunder? Extinguishing of fire in a cloud. Why does it thunder? Because the fire is extinguished in the cloud.
10   Let C be a cloud, A thunder, B extinguishing of fire. Then B belongs to C, a cloud (since the fire is extinguished in it), and A, the noise, belongs to B;

and in fact B is the account of A, the first extreme term. And if there is a further middle term <explaining> B, this will be found from the remaining accounts <of A>.   *15*

We have said, then, how one grasps the what-it-is, and how it comes to be recognized. And so it turns out that though the what-it-is is neither deduced nor demonstrated, still it is made clear through deduction and demonstration. Hence, in the case where the explanation of a thing is something other than the thing, a demonstration is required for recognition of what the thing is, even though there is no demonstration of what the thing is, as we also said in setting out the puzzles.[11]   *20*

9

Some things have something else as their explanation, while other things do not; and so it is clear that in some cases the what-it-is is immediate and a principle. In these cases we must assume (or make evident in some other way) both that it is and what it is—as the students of arithmetic do, since they assume both what the unit is and that it is. In the other cases—those   *25* that have a middle term, and where something else is the explanation of their essence—it is possible, as we said, to make clear what something is through demonstration, even though the what-it-is is not demonstrated.

10

Since a definition is said to be an account of the what-it-is, it is evident that   *30* one type will be an account of what a name or some other name-like account signifies[12]—for example, what triangle signifies. When we have grasped that <a thing> is <this>,[13] we inquire into why it is; but it is difficult to grasp in this way <why a thing is>, given that we do not know that the thing is.[14] The reason for this difficulty has been mentioned before: <if we know only what a thing's name signifies>, we do not even know whether or not the thing is, unless <we know this> coincidentally.[15] (An

11. **setting out the puzzles**: This was done in ii 3.

12. **an account of . . . account signifies**: This is often (though not by Aristotle) called a 'nominal definition'.

13. **When we . . . is <this>**: Or: 'when we have grasped that a thing exists' (lit. 'having which, that it is').

14. **but it is difficult . . . the thing is**: Or 'But it is difficult to have this sort of grasp <i.e. the sort we get through a nominal definition> about things whose existence we do not know'. This might be taken to mean (contrary to our supplements) that we cannot grasp a nominal definition of x without knowing that x exists.

15. **<if we know . . . know this> coincidentally**: According to our translation and supplements, knowledge of x's nominal definition does not supply knowledge of

account is unified in either of two ways—either by connection, like the Iliad, or by revealing one <property> of one <subject> non-coincidentally.)

This, then, is one definition of definition; another sort of definition is an account revealing why something is.[16] Hence the first type of definition signifies but does not prove, whereas the second type will clearly be a sort of demonstration of what something is, but differently arranged—for saying why it thunders is different from saying what thunder is. We will answer the first question by saying 'Because fire is extinguished in the clouds'. And what is thunder? A noise of fire being extinguished in the clouds. These are two different statements, then, of the same account; the first is a continuous demonstration, the second a definition. Moreover, a definition of thunder is noise in the clouds, which is the conclusion of a demonstration of what it is. In contrast to this, the definition of something immediate is an indemonstrable positing of what it is.

One sort of definition, then, is an indemonstrable account of the what-it-is; a second is a deduction of the what-it-is, differing in arrangement from a demonstration; and a third is the conclusion of a demonstration of the what-it-is.

What we have said, then, has made it evident, first, in what way the what-it-is is demonstrable and in what way it is not, and what things are demonstrable and what things are not; secondly, in how many ways a definition is spoken of, in what way it proves the what-is-it and in what way it does not, and what things have definitions and what things do not; and, thirdly, how definition is related to demonstration, and in what way there can be both definition and demonstration of the same thing and in what way there cannot.

19

99b It is evident, then, what deduction and demonstration are and how they come about; the same holds for demonstrative knowledge, since it is the same <as demonstration>. But how do we come to recognize principles, and what state recognizes them? This will be clear from the following argument, if we first state the puzzles.

20 We said before that we cannot know through demonstration without

---

whether x is (exists)—if we knew what triangle signifies and also happened to know that triangles exist, the second piece of knowledge would be coincidental to the first. Both knowledge of x's nominal definition and knowledge that x exists are needed for knowledge of why x is. A different conclusion emerges from other accounts of these two sentences (see previous two notes).

16. **another sort . . . something is:** This is often called (though not by Aristotle), a 'real', as opposed to a 'nominal', definition.

recognizing the first, immediate principles.[17] But one might be puzzled about whether cognition of the immediate principles is or is not the same <as knowledge of truths derived from them>; whether there is knowledge of each, or knowledge of one but something else of the other; and whether   25
the states are acquired rather than <innately> present in us without our noticing them.[18]

It would be absurd if we had the principles <innately>; for then we would possess cognition that is more exact than demonstration, but without noticing it. If, on the other hand, we acquire the principles and do not previously possess them, how could we recognize and learn them from no prior knowledge? That is impossible, as we also said in the case of demon-   30
stration. Evidently, then, we can neither possess the principles <innately> nor acquire them if we are ignorant and possess no state <of knowledge>. Hence we must have some <suitable> potentiality, but not one that is at a level of exactness superior to that of the knowledge we acquire.[19]

All animals evidently have <such a potentiality>, since they have the   35
innate discriminative potentiality called perception.[20] Some animals that have perception (though not all of them) also retain <in memory> what they perceive; those that do not retain it have no cognition outside percep-tion (either none at all or none about what is not retained), but those that do retain it keep what they have perceived in their souls even after they   100a
have perceived. When this has happened many times a <further> dif-ference arises: in some, but not all, cases, a rational account arises from the retention of perceptions.

From perception, then, as we say, memory arises, and from repeated memory of the same thing experience arises; for a number of memories   5
make up one experience. From experience, or <rather> from the whole universal that has settled in the soul—the one apart from the many, what-ever is present as one and the same in all of them—arises a principle of craft (if it is about what comes to be) or of science (if it is about what is).

Hence the relevant states are not <innate> in us in any determinate   10
character and do not arise from states that have a better grasp on cogni-tion; rather, they arise from perception. It is like what happens in a battle

17. **We said . . . principles**: see 72b18–25.

18. **and not <innately> . . . noticing them**: Aristotle probably has in mind Plato, *Meno* 81a–86c.

19. **but at . . . acquire**: lit. 'but not to have such a one as will be more honorable than these in respect of exactness.'

20. In what follows Aristotle may mean to explain (1) the acquisition of universal concepts (e.g., the concept of horse) from perception (e.g., of particular horses) or (2) the acquisition of knowledge of universal truths (e.g., that horses have four legs) from perception (e.g., that this horse has four legs, that horse ... etc.) or (3) both (1) and (2). On perception, memory and knowledge cf. *Met.* 980a21–981a12.

when there is a retreat: first one soldier makes a stand, then a second, then another, until they reach a starting point.[21] The soul's nature gives it a potentiality to be affected in this way.

15   Let us state again, then, what we stated, but not perspicuously, before. When one of the undifferentiated things[22] makes a stand, that is the first universal in the soul; for though one perceives the particular, perception is
100b of the universal—of man, for instance, not of Callias the man. Again, in these <universals something else> makes a stand, until what has no parts and is universal makes a stand—first, for example, a certain sort of animal makes a stand, until animal does, and in this <universal> something else makes a stand in the same way. Clearly, then, we must recognize the first
5   things[23] by induction; for that is also how perception produces the universal in us.

        Among our intellectual states that grasp the truth, some—knowledge and understanding[24]—are always true, whereas others—for example, belief and reasoning—admit of being false; and understanding is the only sort of state that is more exact than knowledge. Since the principles of demonstra-
10   tion are better known <than the conclusions derived from them>, and since all knowledge requires an account, it follows that we can have no knowledge of the principles. Since only understanding can be truer than knowledge, we must have understanding of the principles.

21. **It is like . . . starting point:** Aristotle exploits the different uses of 'archē'; see PRINCIPLE #3. When soldiers rally and gather to make a stand, they reach a starting point (archē), which provides a beginning (archē) for a new advance. Similarly, perceptions 'gather' until they produce a starting point (archē), which is a suitable principle (archē) for demonstrations explaining the facts initially grasped by perception.

22. **undifferentiated things:** Probably these are the lowest species (e.g., man), not further differentiated into species. It is less probable that Aristotle refers to particular perceptible things.

23. **first things:** These are the most determinate universals, e.g., man. Probably they are the same as the 'undifferentiated things' mentioned in 100a16.

24. **understanding:** *nous.* See UNDERSTANDING #3, *DA* 429a14n. Here *nous* is used in a specialized sense, not applying to every sort of thought, or even to every sort of intellectual knowledge (hence it has a narrower scope than in *DA* iii 3). It is restricted to the state that grasps ultimate first principles as such, without any further account, as being 'recognized through themselves' (cf. *Phys.* 193a4–7, *APr* 64b35–6). This is the sort of cognitive grasp that was demanded in i 3, to avoid a circle or infinite regress of justification.

        In this passage the distinction between cognition (*gnōsis*) and knowledge (*epistēmē*) is important. We have cognition of the first principles, and indeed they are better known (i.e., cognized) than the conclusions derived from them; but we have no knowledge of the principles, since knowledge requires DEMONSTRATION and the first principles are indemonstrable.

The same conclusion follows from the further point that since the principle of a demonstration is not a demonstration, the principle of knowledge
is not knowledge. If, then, the only sort of state besides knowledge that is   *15*
<always> true is understanding, understanding must be the principle of
knowledge. The principle, then, will grasp the principle, and, similarly, all
knowledge will grasp its object.

PHYSICS

The Greek title of this work, ta phusika, *comes from the word for nature*
*(*phusis*). It thus refers to the study of natural phenomena in general, and not just*
to physics in the narrow sense. In books I and III Aristotle defends and defines
the concept of change. In book II he presents his doctrine of the four causes, dis-
cusses the topics of chance and necessity, and argues for the existence of ends
(or "final causes") in nature. In parts of the book not included in this anthology,
he discusses place, time, the void, the infinite, continuity, and the eternity of
change. Finally, in book VIII he argues for the eternal existence of an "unmoved
mover"—an uncaused cause of change.

BOOK I

1

184a In every line of inquiry into something that has principles[1] or causes or
elements, we achieve knowledge—that is, scientific knowledge[2]—by cogniz-
ing them; for we think we cognize a thing when we know its primary
causes and primary principles, all the way to its elements. Clearly, then, it
15 is also true in the science of nature that our first task is to determine the
principles.

  The natural path is to start from what is better known and more perspicuous to us, and to advance to what is more perspicuous and better
known by nature; for what is better known to us is not the same as what is
better known without qualification. We must advance in this way, then,
20 from what is less perspicuous by nature but more perspicuous to us, to
what is more perspicuous and better known by nature.

  The things that, most of all, are initially clear and perspicuous to us are
inarticulate wholes; later, as we articulate them, the elements and principles come to be known from them. We must, then, advance from universals
25 to particulars;[3] for the whole is better known in perception, and the univer-

1. **principles**: 'Origins' would often be appropriate in Bk i (see PRINCIPLE); but to
display the connection of thought, we have kept 'principles' throughout.

2. **scientific knowledge**: just one word in Greek (*epistēmē*).

3. **from universals to particulars**: Aristotle is concerned with the process of clarify-
ing very general principles that we do not fully understand at the start. The passage

sal is a sort of whole, since it includes many things as parts. The same is   *184b*
true, in a way, of names in relation to their accounts. For a name—for
instance, 'circle'—signifies a sort of whole and signifies indefinitely,
whereas the definition <of a circle> articulates it by stating the particular
<properties>. Again, children begin by calling all men 'father' and all
women 'mother'; only later do they distinguish different men and different
women.

5[4]

We must first of all grasp the fact that nothing that exists is naturally such   *188a*
as to act or be affected in just any old way by the agency of just any old
thing; nor does something come to be just any old thing from just any old
thing, unless you consider coincidents. For how could <something> come   *35*
to be pale from being musical, unless musical were a coincident of the not-
pale or the dark thing?[5] Rather, something comes to be pale from being
not-pale—and not simply from being not-pale, but from being dark or   *188b*
something between dark and pale. Similarly, something becomes musical
from being not-musical, and not from just any way of being not-musical
but from being unmusical or from being something (if there is anything)
between musical and unmusical.

Nor, on the other hand, does anything perish primarily into just any old
thing. The pale thing, for instance, does not perish into the musical thing
(unless it does so coincidentally), but into the not-pale thing, and not into   *5*
just any old not-pale thing, but into the dark thing or into something
between pale and dark. In the same way the musical thing perishes into the
not-musical thing, and not into just any old not-musical thing, but into the
unmusical thing or into something between musical and unmusical.

The same is true in the other cases as well, since the same account
applies to things that are not simple but composite; but we do not notice   *10*
that this is so, because the opposite condition in each case has no name. For
whatever is ordered must necessarily come to be from something disordered, and what is disordered from something ordered, and whatever is

---

is not inconsistent (despite appearances) with *APo* 72a4, where Aristotle is concerned with a different process—the inductive progress from awareness of particular facts to universal generalizations.

4. In i 2–4 Aristotle discusses (1) arguments of the Eleatics against the reality of
COMING TO BE and (2) views of other Presocratics on the sorts of principles needed
to account for coming to be. He rejects (1) and now turns to offer his own account
of the principles considered in (2).

5. **the not-pale or the dark thing**: Aristotle uses just the neuter definite article and
adjective. The exact interpretation of these phrases is often difficult, since they
might refer either to the quality or to the subject that has it; cf. *Met.* 1031b22–8.

15 ordered must necessarily perish into disorder, and not into just any old
disorder, but into the one opposed to that order.

It makes no difference whether we speak of order or arrangement or
combination, since it is evident that the same account applies to them all.
Now, a house, a statue, and any other <artifact> comes to be in the same
way. For a house comes to be from these <bricks etc.> which were not
combined, but dispersed in this way; and a statue, or whatever is shaped,
20 comes to be from shapelessness; and each of these is a case of arrangement
or combination.

If, then, this is true, everything that comes to be or perishes does so from
one contrary into the other, or from or into the intermediate. And the
intermediates are from the contraries, as, for instance, colors are from pale
25 and dark. And so all the things that come to be naturally are either contraries or from contraries.[6]

6

189a . . . The following puzzle might arise if we do not assume some other
nature as subject for the contraries. For we see that contraries are not the
30 substance of anything that is, and a principle must not be said of any
subject; for if it were, then the <alleged> principle would itself have a
principle, since a subject seems to be a principle of, and prior to, what is
predicated of it. Further, we say that one substance is not contrary to
another. How, then, could a non-substance be prior to a substance?
35 That is why someone who takes both the previous argument and this one
189b to be correct must, if he is to retain them both, assume a third thing as
subject, as those theorists do who take the whole universe to be some one
nature—water, fire, or something intermediate. And in fact something intermediate seems more reasonable, since fire, earth, air, and water are
essentially[7] involved with contrarieties. . . .

7

30 Let us, then, give our own account of coming to be, in the following way.
And first let us deal with all of coming to be; for the natural procedure is
to speak first about what is common to every case, and then to study what
is special to each case.

When we say that something comes to be one thing from being another
and different thing, we are speaking about either simple or compound
35 things. What I mean is this: It is possible that a man comes to be musical,

6. Aristotle continues in i 5 by showing how the various Presocratic views confirm
his conclusion.

7. **essentially**: lit. 'already'.

that the not-musical thing comes to be musical, and that the not-musical   *190a*
man comes to be a musical man. By 'simple thing coming to be <*F*>' I mean
the man and the not-musical thing; and by 'simple thing that comes into
being'⁸ I mean the musical thing. By 'compound' I mean both the thing that
comes into being and what comes to be that thing, whenever we say that
the not-musical man comes to be a musical man.   5

In one type of case we say not only that something comes to be *F*, but
also that it comes to be *F from* being *G*;⁹ for instance, <the man not only
comes to be musical, but also comes to be> musical from being not-
musical. But we do not say this for all <properties>; for <the man> did not
come to be musical from being a man, but rather the man came to be
musical.

When something comes to be *F* (in the sense in which we say a simple
thing comes to be <something>), in some cases it remains when it comes   10
to be *F*, and in other cases it does not remain. The man, for instance, remains a man and is still a man when he comes to be musical, whereas the
not-musical or unmusical thing, either simple or compound, does not
remain.

Now that we have made these distinctions, here is something we can
grasp from every case of coming to be, if we look at them all in the way
described. In every case there must be some subject that comes to be   15
<something>; even if it is one in number, it is not one in form, since being
a man is not the same as being an unmusical thing. (By 'in form' I mean the
same as 'in account'.) One thing <that comes to be> remains, and one does
not remain. The thing that is not opposite remains, since the man remains;
but the not-musical thing, or the unmusical thing, does not remain. Nor   20
does the thing compounded from both (for instance, the unmusical man)
remain.

We say that something comes to be *F* from being *G*, but not that the *G*
comes to be *F*, more often in cases where *G* does not remain; for instance,
we say that <a man> comes to be musical from being unmusical, but not
that <the unmusical comes to be musical> from a man. Still, sometimes we
speak in the same way in cases where *G* remains; we say, for instance, that   25
a statue comes to be from bronze, but not that the bronze comes to be a

8. **thing that comes into being'**: This refers to the product of the coming to be—in
this case, to the musical thing that comes into being as a result of the man becoming musical.

9. **not only . . . being G**: Or: 'not only that it comes to be, but also that it comes to
be from *F*. The second rendering is less likely, since Aristotle seems to introduce '*F*
comes to be' (i.e. comes to be without qualification) for the first time at 190a31. We
have supplied the dummy letters ('*F*, etc.); Aristotle uses either nothing (leaving the
reference to be gathered from the context) or demonstrative pronouns ('this comes
to be this', etc.).

statue. If, however, something comes to be F from being G, where G is opposite to F and G does not remain, we speak in both ways, saying both that something comes to be F from being G and that the G comes to be F; for it is true both that the man comes to be musical from being unmusical and that the unmusical one comes to be musical. That is why we also say

30   the same about the compound: we say both that the musical man comes to be musical from being an unmusical man and that the unmusical man comes to be musical.

Things are said to come to be in many ways, and some things are said not to come to be, but to come to be something; only substances are said to come to be without qualification. In the other cases it is evident that there must be some subject that comes to be <something>; for in fact, when

35   <something> comes to be of some quantity or quality, or relative to another, or somewhere, something is the subject <underlying the change>, because a substance is the only thing that is never said of any other subject,

190b whereas everything else is said of a substance.[10]

However, substances—the things that are without qualification—also come to be from some subject. This will become evident if we examine it. For in every case there is something that is a subject from which the thing

5   that comes to be comes to be, as plants and animals come to be from seed.

Some of the things that come to be without qualification do so by change of figure (for instance, a statue); some by addition (for instance, growing things); some by subtraction (for instance, Hermes from the stone); some by composition (for instance, a house); some by alteration (for instance, things changing in accordance with their matter). It is evident that every-

10   thing that comes to be in this way comes to be from a subject.

And so it is clear from what has been said that in every case, what comes to be is composite: there is something that comes into being and something that comes to be this. And this latter thing is of two sorts: either the subject or the opposite. I mean, for instance, that the unmusical is opposite, and the man is subject; and that the lack of figure, shape, and order is the opposite,

15   and the bronze, stone, or gold is the subject.

Suppose, then, that there are indeed causes and principles of natural things, from which they primarily are and have come to be—not come to be coincidentally, but come to be what each thing is called in accordance

20   with its essence. It evidently follows that everything comes to be from the subject and the shape. For in a way the musical man is composed from man and musical, since you will analyze him into their accounts. It is clear, then, that whatever comes to be does so from these things.

10. **said of a substance**: Aristotle uses 'said of a subject' more broadly here than in *Catg*. 1a21. In the *Catg*. the phrase is confined to the predication of essential properties. Here (and elsewhere; cf. *Met*. 1028b26) it also includes non-essential properties (and so includes the cases where the *Catg*. speaks of being 'in a subject').

The subject is one in number but two in form. Man, gold, and matter in   *25*
general, is countable, since it is a this more <than the privation is>, and
what comes to be comes to be from it not coincidentally. The privation—
the contrariety—is a coincident. The form is one—for instance, structure,
musicality, or anything else predicated in this way.

Hence we should say that in one way there are two principles, and that
in another way there are three. In one way they are contraries—if, for   *30*
instance, one were to speak of the musical and the unmusical, or the hot
and the cold, or the ordered and the disordered. But in another way they
are not contraries, since contraries cannot be affected by each other. This
<puzzle about how becoming is possible> is also solved by the fact that the
subject is something different, since it is not a contrary.   *35*

Hence, in a way the principles are no more numerous than the contraries,
but, one might say, they are two in number. On the other hand, because
they differ in being, they are not two in every way, but three; for being   *191a*
man is different from being unmusical, and being shapeless is different
from being bronze.

We have said, then, how many principles are relevant to the coming to be
of natural things, and we have described the different ways they should be
counted. And it is clear that some subject must underlie the contraries, and *5*
that there must be two contraries. In another way, however, there need not
be two; for just one of the contraries is enough, by its absence or presence,
to produce the thing.

The nature that is subject is knowable by analogy. For as bronze is to a
statue, or wood is to a bed, or as the shapeless before it acquires a shape is *10*
to anything else that has a shape, so the nature that is subject is to a
substance, a this, and a being.

This, then, is one principle; it is not one or a being in the way a this is.
Another principle is the one specified by the account, and a third is the
contrary of this, the privation. The way in which these are two, and the
way in which they are more than two, has been stated above.   *15*

First, then, it was said that only the contraries were principles. Later we
added that something further is needed as subject and that there must be
three principles. And from what we have said now it is evident how the
contraries differ, how the principles are related to one another, and what
the subject is. It is not yet clear, however, whether the form or the subject is *20*
substance.[11] Still, it is clear that there are three principles, and in what way
there are three, and what sorts of things they are. This, then, should allow
us to observe how many principles there are, and what they are.

---

11. **whether . . . substance:** It is surprising that Aristotle considers only the matter
and the form, and omits the statue (which might seem to be a compound of matter
and form) as a candidate for being substance. See further *Met.* vii 3, 10–11,
1042a26–31, FORM.

8

This is also the only solution to the puzzle raised by the earlier philoso-
25 phers, as we shall now explain. Those who were the first to search for the
truth philosophically and for the nature of beings were diverted and, so to
speak, pushed off the track by inexperience. They say that nothing that is
either comes to be or perishes. For, they say, what comes to be must come
to be either from what is or from what is not, and coming to be is impossible in both cases; for what is cannot come to be (since it already is), while
nothing can come to be from what is not (since there must be some subject). And then, having reached this result, they make things worse by
going on to say that there is no plurality, but only being itself.

They accepted this belief for the reason mentioned. We reply as follows:
30 The claim that something comes to be from what is or from what is not, or
that what is or what is not acts on something or is acted on or comes to be
191b anything whatever, is in one way no different from the claim that, for instance, a doctor acts on something or is acted on, or is or comes to be
something from being a doctor. We say this about a doctor in two ways;
and so, clearly, we also speak in two ways when we say that something is or
comes to be something from what is, and that what is is acting on something or being acted on.

Now a doctor builds a house, not insofar as he is a doctor, but insofar as
5 he is a housebuilder; and he becomes pale, not insofar as he is a doctor, but
insofar as he is dark. But he practices medicine, or loses his medical knowledge, insofar as he is a doctor. We speak in the fullest sense of a doctor
acting on something or being acted on, or coming to be something, from
being a doctor, if it is insofar as he is a doctor that he is acted on in this
way or produces these things or comes to be these things. So it is also clear
that coming to be from what is not signifies this: coming to be from it
10 insofar as it is not.

The early philosophers failed to draw this distinction and gave up the
question. This ignorance led them into more serious ignorance—so serious
that they thought nothing else <besides what already is> either is or comes
to be, and so they did away with all coming to be.

We agree with them in saying that nothing comes to be without
qualification from what is not, but we say that things come to be in a
15 way—for instance, coincidentally—from what is not. For something comes
to be from the privation, which in itself is not and which does not belong to
the thing <when it has come to be>. But this causes surprise, and it seems
impossible that something should come to be in this way from what is not.

Similarly, there is no coming to be, except coincidentally, from what is,
or of what is. But coincidentally what is also comes to be, in the same way
20 as if animal came to be from animal and a certain animal from a certain
animal. Suppose, for instance, that a dog came to be from a horse. For the

dog would come to be not only from a certain animal, but also from animal, though not insofar as it is animal (for that is already present). But if a certain <sort of> animal is to come to be, not coincidentally, it will not be from animal; and if a certain thing that is <is to come to be>, it will not be from what is, nor from what is not. For we have said what 'from what is   25 not' signifies—i.e. insofar as it is not. Further, we are not doing away with <the principle that> everything is or is not.

This is one way <of solving this puzzle>. Another is <to note> that the same things can be spoken of in accordance with potentiality and actuality; this is discussed more exactly elsewhere.

And so, as we have said, we have solved the puzzles that compelled   30 people to do away with some of the things we have mentioned. For this is why earlier thinkers were also diverted from the road leading them to <an understanding of> coming to be, perishing, and change in general. For if they had seen this nature <of the subject>, that would have cured all their ignorance.

9

Admittedly other people touched on the nature of the subject, but did not   35 grasp it adequately. For first they agree that a thing comes to be without qualification from what is not and that to this extent Parmenides is right;   192a but then it appears to them that if a thing is one in number, it is also only one in potentiality—whereas in fact the two are very different.

For we say that matter and privation are different and that matter is coincidentally a not-being, whereas the privation is a not-being in its own   5 right. Moreover, we say that matter is close <to being substance> and in a way is substance, whereas the privation is not substance in any way. Previous thinkers, however, identify both the great and the small (taken both together or each separately) with what is not, so that their conception of the three things involved must be quite different from ours. For they got as far as seeing that there must be some nature that is the subject, but they   10 take this to be one—for even though someone takes it to be a pair (calling it the great and small), he still does the same thing <in taking it to be one>, since he overlooked the other nature.

For the nature that remains[12] is a joint cause, together with the form, of what comes to be, as a mother is; but the other part of the contrariety might often appear not to be at all, if one focuses on its evildoing aspect.   15 For we say that one principle is divine, good, and an object of striving, while a second is contrary to the first, and the third naturally strives for the first and tends towards it in accordance with its own nature. In their view, by contrast, the contrary tends towards its own destruction. In fact, how-

12. **nature that remains**: i.e. matter.

ever, the form cannot strive for itself, since it does not lack <itself>; nor does the contrary strive for it, since contraries destroy each other. Hence what strives for the form must be the matter. It is as though the female strove to be male, or the ugly to be beautiful—except that <the matter> is
25   not ugly or female in its own right, but coincidentally.

The <matter> perishes and comes to be in a way, and in a way it does not.[13] For as that in which <the privation is present> it perishes in its own right, since what perishes—the privation—is present in this; but as what is potentially <formed, the matter> does not come to be or perish in its own right, but must be without coming to be or perishing. For if it was coming to be, there has to be some primary subject from which it was coming to be and which is present in it; and this is the very nature of matter. And so <if
30   we assume that the matter comes to be,> it will already be before it has come to be—for by 'matter' I mean a thing's primary subject, from which the thing comes to be and which is present in the thing non-coincidentally. And on the other hand, if the matter perishes, it will come finally to <matter>, so that <if we assume that the matter perishes>, it will have perished before it has perished.

An exact determination of questions about the formal principle—whether it is one or many, and what it is in each case—is a task for first
192b   philosophy, and so we may put it off to that occasion.[14] Natural and perishable forms, however, will be discussed in the following exposition.

We have now determined, then, that there are principles, what they are, and how many they are. Let us now continue, after first making a fresh start.

BOOK II

1

Some existing things are natural, while others are due to other causes. Those that are natural are animals and their parts, plants, and the simple bodies, such as earth, fire, air and water; for we say that these things and things of this sort are natural. All these things evidently differ from those that are not naturally constituted, since each of them has within itself[15] a

13. **The <matter> . . . does not**: The following argument shows that in every case of coming to be there is some matter that, in that process, does not come to be (and correspondingly for perishing). It does not show that there is some matter that never comes to be or perishes.

14. **we may . . . occasion**: Such an inquiry is found in *Met.* vii–ix, xii.

15. **within itself**: This does not imply that they do not also have an external origin of their motions. Animals, for example, are moved not only by their internal principles but also by external forces and stimuli.

principle of motion[16] and stability in place, in growth and decay, or in   *15*
alteration.

In contrast to these, a bed, a cloak, or any other <artifact>—insofar as it
is described as such, <i.e. as a bed, a cloak, or whatever>, and to the extent
that it is a product of a craft—has no innate impulse to change; but insofar
as it is coincidentally made of stone or earth or a mixture of these, it has   *20*
an innate impulse to change, and just to that extent. This is because a
nature[17] is a type of principle and cause of motion and stability within
those things to which it primarily belongs in their own right and not
coincidentally. (By 'not coincidentally' I mean, for instance, the following:
Someone who is a doctor might cause himself to be healthy, but it is not   *25*
insofar as he is being healed that he has the medical science; on the contrary, it is coincidental that the same person is a doctor and is being healed,
and that is why the two characteristics are sometimes separated from each
other.)

The same is true of everything else that is produced, since no such thing
has within itself the principle of its own production. In some things (for   *30*
instance, a house or any other product of handicraft) the principle comes
from outside, and it is within other things. In other things (those that might
turn out to be coincidental causes for themselves) the principle is within
them, but not in their own right.

A nature, then, is what we have said; and the things that have a nature
are those that have this sort of principle. All these things are substances;
for <a substance> is a sort of subject, and a nature is invariably in a
subject. The things that are in accordance with nature include both these   *35*
and whatever belongs to them in their own right, as traveling upwards
belongs to fire—for this neither is nor has a nature, but is natural and in   *193a*
accordance with nature. We have said, then, what nature is, and what is
natural and in accordance with nature.

To attempt to prove that there is such a thing as nature would be
ridiculous; for it is evident that there are many things of the sort we have
described. To prove what is evident from what is not evident betrays an   *5*
inability to discriminate what is known because of itself from what is not.

16. **motion**: This renders *kinēsis*. **Change** renders *metabolē*. Aristotle does not seem
to intend any distinction between the two in this context, though elsewhere he does;
see MOTION.

17. **a nature**: or just 'nature'. Since Greek has no indefinite article, it is sometimes
difficult to know when it should be inserted in a translation. Moreover it is often
difficult to choose between 'the nature' (of a particular thing or kind of thing) and
'nature' (in general), since Greek uses a definite article in both cases. In this chapter, however, Aristotle's examples suggest that he is primarily concerned to say what
it is for something (a tree or a dog, for instance) to have a nature, rather than to
describe nature (the natural order) as a whole.

(It is clearly possible to suffer from this inability: someone blind from birth might still make deductions about colors.) And so such people are bound to argue about <mere> names and to understand nothing.

10   Some people think that the nature and substance of a natural thing is the primary constituent present in it, having no order in its own right, so that the nature of a bed, for instance, <would be> the wood, and the nature of a statue <would be> the bronze. A sign of this, according to Antiphon, is the fact that, if you were to bury a bed and the rotting residue were to become able to sprout, the result would be wood, not a bed. He thinks that

15   this is because the conventional arrangement, i.e. the craft <making the wood into a bed>, is a <mere> coincident of the wood, whereas the substance is what remains continuously while it is affected in these ways. And if each of these things is related to something else in the same way (bronze and gold, for instance, to water; bones and wood to earth; and so

20   on with anything else), that thing is their nature and substance.

This is why some people say that fire or earth or air or water is the nature of the things that exist; some say it is some of these, others say it is all of them. For whenever any of these people supposed one, or more than one, of these things to be <the primary constituent>, he takes this or these

25   to be all the substance there is, and he takes everything else to be attributes, states, and conditions of these things; and each of these is held to be everlasting, since they do not change from themselves, but the other things come to be and are destroyed an unlimited number of times.

This, then, is one way we speak of a nature: as the primary matter that is

30   a subject for each thing that has within itself a principle of motion and change.

In another way the nature is the shape, i.e. the form in accordance with the account. For just as we speak of craftsmanship in what is in accordance with craft and is crafted, so also we speak of nature in what is in accordance with nature and is natural. But if something were only potentially a

35   bed and still lacked the form of a bed, we would not yet speak of craftsmanship or of a product in accordance with craft; nor would we say the corresponding thing about anything that is constituted naturally. For what

193b   is only potentially flesh or bone does not have its nature, and is not naturally flesh or bone, until it acquires the form in accordance with the account by which we define flesh or bone and say what it is. In another way, then, the nature is the shape and form of things that have within themselves a principle of motion; this form is not separable except in account.

5   (What is composed of form and matter—for instance, a man—is not a nature, but is natural.)

Indeed, the form is the nature more than the matter is. For something is called <flesh, bone, and so on> when it is actually so, more than when it is only potentially so. Further, a man comes to be from a man, but not a bed from a bed. In fact that is why some say that the nature of the bed is not

the shape but the wood, because if it were to sprout the result would be   10
wood, not a bed. If this shows that the wood is the nature, then the shape is
also the nature, since a man comes to be from a man. Further, nature, as
applied to coming to be, is really a road towards nature; it is not like
medical treatment, which is a road not towards medical science, but towards health. For medical treatment necessarily proceeds *from* medical   15
science, not *towards* medical science. But nature <as coming to be> is not
related to nature in this way; rather, what is growing, insofar as it is
growing, proceeds from something towards something <else>. What is it,
then, that grows? Not what it is growing from, but what it is growing into.
Therefore, the shape is the nature.

Shape and nature are spoken of in two ways; for the privation is also
form in a way. We must consider later whether or not there is a privation   20
and a contrary in unqualified coming to be.

2

Since we have distinguished the different ways we speak of nature, we
should next consider how the mathematician differs from the student of
nature; for natural bodies certainly have surfaces, solids, lengths, and   25
points, which are what the mathematician studies. We should also consider
whether astronomy is different from or a part of the study of nature; for it
would be absurd if a student of nature ought to know what the sun or
moon is but need not know any of their coincidents in their own right—
especially since it is evident that students of nature also discuss the shape
of the sun and moon, and specifically whether or not the earth and heaven   30
are spherical.

These things are certainly the concern of both the mathematician and
the student of nature. But the mathematician is not concerned with them
insofar as each is the limit of a natural body, and he does not study the
coincidents of a natural body insofar as they belong to a natural body.
That is why he also separates these coincidents; for they are separable in
thought from motion, and his separating them makes no difference and   35
results in no falsehood.

Those who say there are Ideas do not notice that they do this too; for
they separate natural objects, though these are less separable than mathe-   194a
matical objects. This would be clear if one tried to state the formulae of
both natural and mathematical objects—of the things themselves and of
their coincidents. For odd and even, straight and curved, and also number,   5
line, and point do not involve motion, whereas flesh, bones, and man do—
we speak of them as we speak of the snub nose, not as we speak of the
curved.[18]

18. **we speak . . . the curved**: To speak of them as we speak of **the snub nose** is to
speak of them as involving matter.

This is also clear from the parts of mathematics that are more related to the study of nature—for instance, optics, harmonics, and astronomy. These are in a way the reverse of geometry; for geometry investigates natural lines, but not insofar as they are natural, whereas optics investigates mathematical lines, but insofar as they are natural, not insofar as they are mathematical.

Since we speak of nature in two ways—both as form and as matter—we should study it as though we were investigating what snubness is, and so we should study natural objects neither independently of their matter nor <simply> insofar as they have matter. For indeed, since there are these two types of nature, there might be a puzzle about which one the student of nature should study.[19] Perhaps the compound of the two? If so, then also each of them. Then is it the same or a different discipline that knows each one of them?

If we judge by the early thinkers, the student of nature would seem to study <only> matter, since Empedocles and Democritus touched only slightly on form and essence. Craft, however, imitates nature,[20] and the same science knows both the form and the matter up to a point. The doctor, for instance, knows health, and also the bile and phlegm in which health <is realized>; similarly, the housebuilder knows both the form of the house and that its matter is bricks and wood; and the same is true in the other cases. The science of nature, therefore, must also know both types of nature.

Moreover the same discipline studies both what something is for—i.e. the end—and whatever is for the end. Nature is an end and what something is for; for whenever a continuous motion has some end this sort of terminus is also what the motion is for. That is why it was ludicrous for the poet to say 'He has reached the end he was born for'; it was ludicrous because by 'end' we mean not every terminus but only the best one.

For crafts produce their matter (some by producing it without qualification, others by making it suitable for their work); and we use all <matter> as being for our sake,[21] since we are also an end in a way. (For what something is for is of two sorts,[22] as we said in On Philosophy.[23])

194b There are two crafts that control the matter and involve knowledge: the craft that uses <the matter> and the craft that directs this productive craft. Hence the using craft also directs in a way, but with the difference that the

19. **a puzzle . . . study**: For this puzzle cf. DA 403a27, PA 641a22.

20. **Craft . . . nature**: See 199a15.

21. **as being for our sake**: This might mean 'as we would if it were for our sake', or 'because we believe it is for our sake' or perhaps 'because it is for our sake'.

22. **two sorts**: cf. DA 415 62–63.

23. *On Philosophy*: A work of Aristotle's that survives only in fragments.

directing craft knows the form, whereas the productive craft knows the matter. For instance, the pilot knows what sort of form the rudder has, and   5
he prescribes <how to produce it>, whereas the boatbuilder knows what sort of wood and what sorts of motions are needed to make it. With products of a craft, then, we produce the matter for the sake of the product; with natural things, the matter is already present.

Further, matter is relative; for there is one <sort of> matter for one form, and another for another.

How much, then, must the student of nature know about form and what-   10
it-is? Perhaps as much as the doctor knows about sinews, or the smith about bronze—enough to know what something is for. And he must confine himself to things that are separable in form but are in matter—for a man is born from a man and the sun. But it is a task for first philosophy to   15
determine what is separable and what the separable is like.

3

Now that we have determined these points, we should consider how many and what sorts of causes there are. For our inquiry aims at knowledge; and we think we know something only when we find the reason why it is so, i.e. when we find its primary cause. Clearly, then, we must also find the reason   20
why in the case of coming to be, perishing, and every sort of natural change, so that when we know their principles we can try to refer whatever we are searching for to these principles.

In one way, then, that from which, as a <constituent> present in it, a thing comes to be is said to be that thing's cause—for instance, the bronze   25
and silver, and their genera, are causes of the statue and the bowl.

In another way, the form—i.e. the pattern—is a cause. The form is the account (and the genera of the account) of the essence (for instance, the cause of an octave is the ratio two to one, and in general number), and the parts that are in the account.

Further, the source of the primary principle of change or stability[24] is a   30
cause. For instance, the adviser is a cause <of the action>, and a father is a cause of his child; and in general the producer is a cause of the product, and the initiator of the change is a cause of what is changed.

Further, something's end—i.e. what it is for—is its cause, as health is of walking. For why does he walk? We say, 'To be healthy'; and in saying this we think we have provided the cause. The same is true of all the intermedi-   35
ate steps that are for the end, where something else has initiated the

24. **the source of the primary principle of change or stability**: lit. 'that from which the primary PRINCIPLE of change or stability <comes>'. Sometimes Aristotle refers to the moving (or 'efficient') cause more briefly, omitting 'that from which' from the formula.

motion, as, for example, slimming, purging, drugs, or instruments are for
195a health; all of these are for the end, though they differ in that some are
activities, while others are instruments.

We may take these, then, to be the ways we speak of causes.

5   Since causes are spoken of in many ways, there are many non-
coincidental causes of the same thing. Both the sculpting craft and the
bronze, for instance, are causes of the statue, not insofar as it is something
else, but insofar as it is a statue. But they are not causes in the same way:
the bronze is a cause as matter, the sculpting craft as the source of the
motion. Some things are causes of each other: hard work, for instance, is
10   the cause of fitness, and fitness of hard work. But they are not causes in the
same way: fitness is what the hard work is for, whereas hard work is the
principle of motion. Further, the same thing is the cause of contraries; for
sometimes if a thing's presence causes F, that thing is also, by its absence,
taken to cause the contrary of F, so that, for instance, if a pilot's presence
would have caused the safety of a ship, we take his absence to have caused
15   the shipwreck.

All the causes just mentioned are of four especially evident types: (1)
Letters are the cause of syllables, matter of artifacts, fire and such things of
bodies, parts of the whole, and the assumptions of the conclusion, as that
out of which. In each of these cases one thing—for instance, the parts—is
20   cause as subject, while (2) the other thing—the whole, the composition, and
the form—is cause as essence. (3) The seed, the doctor, the adviser and, in
general, the producer, are all sources of the principle of change or stability.
(4) In other cases, one thing is a cause of other things by being the end and
25   the good. For what the other things are for is taken to be[25] the best and
their end—it does not matter <for present purposes> whether we call it the
good or the apparent good.[26] These, then, are the number of kinds of
causes there are.

Although there are many types of causes, they are fewer when they are
arranged under heads. For causes are spoken of in many ways, and even
30   among causes of the same type, some are prior and others posterior. For
example, the cause of health is a doctor and <speaking more generally> a
craftsman, and the cause of an octave is the double and <speaking more
generally> number; in every case the inclusive causes are posterior to the
particular.

Further, some things and their genera are coincidental causes. Polycleitus
and the sculptor, for instance, are causes of the statue in different ways,
35   because being Polycleitus is coincidental to the sculptor. What includes the
coincident is also a cause—if, for example, the man or, quite generally, the
195b animal is a cause of the statue. Some coincidental causes are more remote

25. **is taken to be**: Or perhaps 'tends to be', *ethelei einai*.

26. **the good or the apparent good**: For the difference see *DA* 433a28, *EN* 1113a22–4.

or more proximate than others; if, for instance, the pale man or the musician were said to be the cause of the statue <it would be a more remote cause than Polycleitus is>.

We may speak of any <moving> cause, whether proper or coincidental, either as having a potentiality or as actualizing it; for instance, we may say   5
either that the housebuilder, or that the housebuilder actually building, is causing the house to be built.

Similar things may also be said about the things of which the causes are causes. For example, we may speak of the cause of this statue, or of a statue, or of an image in general; or of this bronze, or of bronze, or of matter in general. The same is true of coincidents. We may speak in this   10
same way of combinations—of Polycleitus the sculptor, for instance, instead of Polycleitus or a sculptor.

Still, all these ways amount to six, each spoken of in two ways. For there is (1) the particular and (2) the genus, and (3) the coincident and (4) the genus of the coincident; and these may be spoken of either (5) in combina-   15
tion or (6) simply. Each of these may be either active or potential. The difference is the following. Active and particular causes exist and cease to exist simultaneously with the things they cause, so that, for instance, this one practicing medicine exists simultaneously with this one being made healthy, and in the same way this one housebuilding exists simultaneously   20
with this thing being built into a house.[27] But this is not true of every cause that is potential; for the house and the housebuilder do not perish simultaneously.

Here as elsewhere, we must always seek the most precise[28] cause. A man, for example, is building because he is a builder, and he is a builder insofar as he has the building craft; his building craft, then, is the prior cause, and   25
the same is true in all cases. Further, we must seek genera as causes of genera, and particulars as causes of particulars; a sculptor, for instance, is the cause of a statue, but this sculptor of this statue. And we must seek a potentiality as the cause of a potential effect, and something actualizing a potentiality as the cause of an actual effect.

This, then, is an adequate determination of the number of causes, and of the ways in which they are causes.

4

Luck and chance are also said to be causes, and many things are said to be   30
and to come to be because of them. We must, then, investigate how luck

27. **Active and . . . a house**: Aristotle thinks of an active cause as a substance in a particular condition (e.g., the builder in the condition of building), not as an event (the building engaged in by the builder) or a fact (the fact that the builder is building).

28. **most precise**: Or perhaps 'highest' (lit. 'most extreme').

and chance are included in the causes we have mentioned, whether luck is
35   or is not the same as chance, and, in general, what they are.
196a   Some people even wonder whether luck and chance exist. For they say
that nothing results from luck; rather, everything that is said to result from
chance or luck has some definite cause. If, for instance, as a result of luck
someone comes to the marketplace and finds the person he wanted to meet
but did not expect, they say the cause is his wanting to go to market.
5   Similarly, for every other supposed result of luck, they say it is possible to
find some cause other than luck. For if there were such a thing as luck, it
would appear truly strange and puzzling that none of the early philoso-
10   phers who discussed the causes of coming to be and perishing ever determined anything about luck; in fact it would seem that they also thought
that nothing results from luck. But this too is surprising; for surely many
things come to be and exist as a result of luck and chance. Though people
know perfectly well that everything that comes to be can be referred to
15   some cause, as the old argument doing away with luck says, everyone
nonetheless says that some of these things result from luck and that others
do not.

That is why the early philosophers should have mentioned luck in
some way or other. But they certainly did not think luck was among the
causes they recognized—for instance, love or strife or mind or fire or anything else of that sort. In either case, then, it is strange, whether they
supposed there was no such thing as luck, or supposed there was such a
20   thing but omitted to discuss it. It is especially strange considering that they
sometimes appeal to luck. Empedocles, for example, appeals to luck when
he says that air is separated out on top, not always but as luck has it; at
least, he says in his cosmogony that 'it happened to run that way at that
time, but often otherwise'.[29] And he says that most of the parts of animals
result from luck.

25   Other people make chance the cause of our heaven and of all worlds. For
they say that the vortex, and the motion that dispersed and established
everything in its present order, resulted from chance. And this is certainly
30   quite amazing. For animals and plants, they say, neither are nor come to be
from luck, but rather nature or mind or something of that sort is the cause,
since it is not just any old thing that comes to be from a given type of seed,
but an olive-tree comes from one type, and a man from another; and yet
they say that the heaven and the most divine of visible things result from
35   chance and have no cause of the sort that animals and plants have.

If this is so, it deserves attention, and something might well have been
196b said about it. For in addition to the other strange aspects of what they say,
it is even stranger to say all this when they see that nothing in the heavens

29. 'it happened . . . otherwise': Empedocles DK 31B53.

results from chance, whereas many things happen as a result of luck to things whose existence is not itself a result of luck. Surely the contrary   5
would have been likely.

Other people suppose that luck is a cause, but they take it to be divine and superhuman, and therefore obscure to the human mind.

And so we must consider chance and luck, and determine what each is, and whether they are the same or different, and see how they fit into the causes we have distinguished.

5

First, then, we see that some things always, others usually, come about   10
in the same way. Evidently neither luck nor anything that results from luck is said to be the cause of either of these things—either of what is of necessity and always or of what is usually. But since besides these there is a third sort of event[30] which everyone says results from luck, it is evi-   15
dent that there is such a thing as luck and chance; for we know that this third sort of event results from luck and that the results of luck are of this sort.

Further, some events are for something and others are not. Among the former, some are in accordance with a decision while others are not, but both sorts are for something. And so it is clear that even among events that   20
are neither necessary nor usual there are some that admit of being for something. (Events that are for something include both the actions that result[31] from thought and also the results of nature.) This, then, is the sort of event that we regard as a result of luck, whenever an event of that sort comes about coincidentally. For just as some things are something in their own right, and others are something coincidentally, so also it is possible for   25
a cause to be of either sort. For example, the cause of a house is, in its own right, the housebuilder, but coincidentally the pale or musical thing. Hence the cause in its own right is determinate, but the coincidental cause is indeterminate, since one thing might have an unlimited number of coincidents.

As has been said, then, whenever this <coincidental causation> occurs   30
among events of the sort that are for something the events <that have these coincidental causes> are said to result from chance and luck. The difference between chance and luck will be determined later; we may take it as evident for the moment that both are found among events of the sort that are for something.

30. **event:** lit. 'thing coming to be'.

31. **that result:** Reading *an prachthē(i)*. Alternatively (reading *an prachtheiē*) 'that might result'.

For instance, A would have come when B was collecting subscriptions, in order to recover the debt from B, if A had known <B would be there>.[32] In fact, however, A did not come in order to do this; it was a coincidence that

35   A came <when B happened to be there>, and so met B in order to collect
197a   the debt[33]—given that A neither usually nor of necessity frequents the place <for that purpose>. The end—collecting the debt—is not a cause <of A's action> in A, but it is the sort of thing that one decides to do and that results from thought. And in this case A's coming is said to result from luck; but if A always or usually frequented the place because he had

5   decided to and for the purpose of collecting the debt, then <A's being there when B was there> would not result from luck.

Clearly, then, luck is a coincidental cause found among events of the sort that are for something, and specifically among those of the sort that are in accordance with a decision. Hence thought (since decision requires thought) and luck concern the same things.

Now the causes whose results might be matters of luck are bound to be indeterminate. That is why luck also seems to be something indeterminate

10   and obscure to human beings, and why, in one way, it might seem that nothing results from luck. For, as we might reasonably expect, all these claims are correct. For in one way things do result from luck, since they are coincidental results and luck is a coincidental cause. But luck is not the unqualified <and hence non-coincidental> cause of anything. The

15   <unqualified> cause of a house, for instance, is a housebuilder, and the coincidental cause a flute-player; and the man's coming and collecting the debt, without having come to collect it, has an indefinite number of coincidental causes—he might have come because he wished to see someone, or was going to court or to the theater.

It is also correct to say that luck is contrary to reason. For rational

20   judgment tells us what is always or usually the case, whereas luck is found in events that happen neither always nor usually. And so, since causes of this sort are indeterminate, luck is also indeterminate.

Still, in some cases one might be puzzled about whether just any old

32. **For instance . . . would be there>**: The example Aristotle has in mind seems to be this: A wants to collect a debt from B; one day A comes to the marketplace for some other reason (e.g., wanting to sell his olives) and meets B who happens to be there at the same time collecting subscriptions for a club of which B is the treasurer. Unfortunately Aristotle's use of 'collect' is sometimes ambiguous in this passage (between 'A's collecting the debt from B' and 'B's collecting subscriptions for his club').

33. **it was a coincidence . . . the debt**: Text and interpretation uncertain. Lit. 'it was a coincidence that he came and did this for the sake of collecting'. **In order to collect the debt** states not the cause of A's being in the marketplace at this time, but A's purpose once he had coincidentally found B in the marketplace.

thing might be a cause of a lucky outcome. Surely the wind or the sun's warmth, but not someone's haircut, might be the cause of his health; for some coincidental causes are closer than others to what they cause.

Luck is called good when something good results, bad when something   25
bad results; it is called good and bad fortune when the results are large. That is why someone who just misses great evil or good as well <as someone who has it is> fortunate or unfortunate; for we think of him as already having <the great evil or good>, since the near miss seems to us to   30
be no distance. Further, it is reasonable that good fortune is unstable; for luck is unstable, since no result of luck can be either always or usually the case.

As we have said, then, both luck and chance are coincidental causes, found in events of the sort that are neither without exception nor usual,   35
and specifically in events of this sort that might be for something.[34]

6

Chance is not the same as luck, since it extends more widely; for results of luck also result from chance, but not all results of chance result from luck.   197b
For luck and its results are found in things that are capable of being fortunate and in general capable of action, and that is why luck must concern what is achievable by action. A sign of this is the fact that good fortune seems to be the same or nearly the same as being happy, and being   5
happy is a sort of action, since it is doing well in action.[35] Hence what cannot act cannot do anything by luck either. Hence neither inanimate things nor beasts nor children do anything by luck, because they are incapable of decision. Nor do they have good or bad fortune, except by a <mere> similarity—as Protarchus[36] said that the stones from which altars   10
are made are fortunate, because they are honored, while their fellows are trodden underfoot. Still, even these things are affected by the results of luck in a way, whenever an agent affects them by some lucky action; but otherwise they are not.

Chance, on the other hand, applies both to animals other than man and to many inanimate things. We say, for instance, that the horse came by   15
chance, since it was saved because it came but did not come in order to be saved. And the tripod fell by chance, because it did not fall in order to be sat on, although it was left standing in order to be sat on.

34. events of the sort . . . for something: A simplified paraphrase. More literally: 'things that are capable of coming about not without exception nor usually, and among however many of these might come about for something'.

35. doing well in action: See EN 1139b3. On good luck and happiness see EN 1099b6–8.

36. Protarchus: An orator and pupil of Gorgias.

Hence it is evident that among types of events that are for something
(speaking without qualification), we say that a particular event of such a
type results from chance if it has an external cause and the actual result is
20   not what it is for; and we say that it results from luck if it results from
chance and is an event of the sort that is decided on by an agent who is
capable of decision. A sign of this is the fact that we say an event is
pointless[37] if it <is of the sort that> is for some result but <in this case>
that result is not what it is for. If, for instance, walking is for evacuating the
bowels, but when he walked on this occasion it was not <for that reason>,
25   then we say that he walked pointlessly and that his walking is pointless. We
assume that an event is pointless if it is naturally for something else, but
does not succeed in <being for> what it is naturally for. For if someone
said that his washing himself was pointless because the sun was not
eclipsed, he would be ridiculous, since washing is not for producing
eclipses. So also, then, an event happens by chance (as the name suggests)
30   whenever it is pointless.[38] For the stone did not fall in order to hit someone;
it fell by chance, because it might have fallen because someone threw it to
hit someone.

The separation of chance from luck is sharpest in natural events. For if
35   an event is contrary to nature, we regard it as a result of chance, not of
luck. But even this is different from <other cases of chance; the other
cases> have an external cause, but <events contrary to nature> have an
internal cause.

198a   We have said, then, what chance and luck are and how they differ.
Each of them falls under the sort of cause that is the source of the principle
of motion. For in every case they are either among natural causes or among
5   those resulting from thought, and the number of these is indeterminate.

Chance and luck are causes of events <of the sort> that mind or nature
might have caused, in cases where <particular> events <of this sort> have
some coincidental cause. Now nothing coincidental is prior to anything
that is in its own right; hence clearly no coincidental cause is prior to
10   something that is a cause in its own right. Chance and luck are therefore
posterior to mind and nature. And so however true it might be that chance

37. **pointless:** *matēn*. Alternatively 'in vain', i.e. unsuccessful. See NATURE #6. This
sense for *matēn* would require the following translation of Aristotle's example:
'. . . if the result that it was done for does not come about. If, for instance, walking
is for evacuating the bowels, but when he walked, he did not succeed in doing this,
we say that he walked in vain and that his walking was in vain. We assume that
something is done in vain if it is naturally for something else, but does not succeed
in achieving the result that it is naturally for'.

38. **by chance**, *automaton* . . . **pointless**, *matēn*. Aristotle appeals to (alleged) etymology.

is the cause of the heavens, still it is necessary for mind and nature to be prior causes of this universe and of many other things.

7

It is clear, then, that there are causes, and that there are as many different types as we say there are; for the reason why something is so includes all these different types <of causes>. For we refer the ultimate reason why (1) in the case of unmoved things, to the what-it-is (for instance, in mathematics; for there we refer ultimately to the definition of straight or commensurate or something else), or (2) to what first initiated the motion (for instance, why did they go to war?—because the other side raided them), or (3) to what it is for (for instance, in order to set themselves up as rulers), or (4) in the case of things that come to be, to the matter.

It is evident, then, that these are the causes and that this is their number. Since there are four of them, the student of nature ought to know them all; and in order to give the sort of reason that is appropriate for the study of nature, he must trace it back to all the causes—to the matter, the form, what initiated the motion, and what something is for. The last three often amount to one; for what something is and what it is for are one, and the first source of the motion is the same in species as these, since a man generates a man; and the same is true generally of things that initiate motion by being in motion.

Things that initiate motion without being in motion are outside the scope of the study of nature. For although they initiate motion, they do not do so by having motion or a principle of motion within themselves, but they are unmoved. Hence there are three inquiries: one about what is unmoved, one about what is in motion but imperishable, and one about what is perishable.

And so the reason why is given by referring to the matter, to the what-it-is, and to what first initiated the motion. For in cases of coming to be, this is the normal way of examining the causes—by asking what comes to be after what, and what first acted or was acted on, and so on in order in every case.

Two sorts of principles initiate motion naturally. One of these principles is not itself natural, since it has no principle of motion within itself; this is true of whatever initiates motion without itself being in motion—for instance, what is entirely without motion (i.e. the first of all beings) and also the what-it-is (i.e. the form), since this is the end and what something is for. And so, since natural processes are for something, this cause too must be known.

The reason why should be stated in all these ways. For instance, (1) this necessarily results from that (either without exception or usually); (2) if this is to be (as the conclusion from the premisses); (3) that this is the essence; and (4) because it is better thus—not unqualifiedly better, but better in relation to the essence of a given thing.

8

10   We must first say why nature is among the causes that are for something, and then how necessity applies to natural things. For everyone refers things to necessity, saying that since the hot, the cold, and each element have a certain nature, certain other things are and come to be of necessity. For if
15   they mention any cause other than necessity (as one thinker mentions love or strife, and another mentions mind), they just touch on it, then let it go.

A puzzle now arises: why not suppose that nature acts not for something or because it is better, but of necessity? Zeus's rain does not fall in order to make the grain grow, but of necessity. For it is necessary that what has
20   been drawn up is cooled, and that what has been cooled and become water comes down, and it is coincidental that this makes the grain grow. Similarly, if someone's grain is spoiled on the threshing-floor, it does not rain in order to spoil the grain, and the spoilage is coincidental.

Why not suppose, then, that the same is true of the parts of natural organisms? On this view, it is of necessity that, for example, the front teeth
25   grow sharp and well adapted for biting, and the back ones broad and useful for chewing food; this <useful> result was coincidental, not what they were for. The same will be true of all the other parts that seem to be for something. On this view, then, whenever all the parts came about
30   coincidentally as though they were for something, these animals survived, since their constitution, though coming about by chance, made them suitable <for survival>. Other animals, however, were differently constituted and so were destroyed; indeed they are still being destroyed, as Empedocles says of the man-headed calves.[39]

This argument, then, and others like it, might puzzle someone. In fact, however, it is impossible for things to be like this. For these <teeth and
35   other parts> and all natural things come to be as they do either always or usually, whereas no result of luck or chance comes to be either always or
199a   usually. (For we do not regard frequent winter rain or a summer heat wave, but only summer rain or a winter heat wave, as a result of luck or coincidence.) If, then, these seem either to be coincidental results or to be for
5   something, and they cannot be coincidental or chance results, they are for something. Now surely all such things are natural, as even those making these claims <about necessity> would agree. We find, then, among things that come to be and are by nature, things that are for something.

Further, whenever <some sequence of actions> has an end, the whole sequence of earlier and later actions is directed towards the end. Surely

---

39. **man-headed calves**: Empedocles DK 31B61.

what is true of action[40] is also true of nature, and what is true of nature is   *10*
true of each action, if nothing prevents it. Now actions are for something;
therefore, natural sequences are for something. For example, if a house
came to be naturally, it would come to be just as it actually does by craft,
and if natural things came to be not only naturally but also by craft, they   *15*
would come to be just as they do naturally; one thing, then, is what the
other is for. In general, craft either completes the work that nature is unable
to complete or imitates nature. If, then, the products of a craft are for
something, clearly the products of nature are also for something; for there
is the same relation of later stages to earlier in productions of a craft and in
productions of nature.

This is most evident in the case of animals other than man, since they   *20*
use neither craft nor inquiry nor deliberation in producing things—indeed
this is why some people are puzzled about whether spiders, ants, and other
such things operate by understanding or in some other way. If we advance
little by little along the same lines, it is evident that even in plants things
come to be that promote the end—leaves, for instance, grow for the protec-   *25*
tion of the fruit. If, then, a swallow makes its nest and a spider its web both
naturally and for some end, and if plants grow leaves for the sake of the
fruit, and send roots down rather than up for the sake of nourishment, it
evidently follows that this sort of cause is among things that come to be   *30*
and are by nature. And since nature is of two sorts, nature as matter and
nature as form, and the form is the end, and since everything else is for the
end, the form must be what things are for.

Errors occur even in productions of craft; grammarians, for instance,
have written incorrectly, and doctors have given the wrong medicine.   *35*
Clearly, then, errors are also possible in productions of nature.   *199b*

In some productions by crafts, the correct action is for something, and in
cases of error the attempt is for something but misses the mark. The same
will be true, then, of natural things; freaks will be errors, missing what
they are for. Hence in the original formations of things, a defective princi-   *5*
ple would also have brought the <man-headed> calves into being, if they
were unable to reach any definite term and end—just as, in the actual state
of things, <freaks> come to be when the seed is defective. Further, it is
necessary for the seed to come into being first, and not the animal straightaway; in fact the 'all-natured first'[41] was seed.

Further, in plants as well as in animals things happen for something,   *10*
though in a less articulate way. Then what about plants? Did olive-headed
vines keep coming into being, as he says <man-headed> calves did? Surely

40. **action**: Aristotle is not thinking of all sequences of movements, but only of
those rational human ACTIONS (including productions) that have an END (*telos*), i.e.
are goal-directed.

41. **'all-natured first'**: Empedocles DK 31B61–2.

not—that is absurd—but surely they would have to have come into being, if the animals did.

Further, <on Empedocles' view> coming to be would also have to be merely a matter of chance among seeds. But whoever says this does away
15   entirely with nature and natural things. For things are natural when they are moved continuously from some principle in themselves and so arrive at some end. From each principle comes, not the same thing in each case, but not just any old thing either; in every case it proceeds to the same <end>, if nothing prevents it.

Now certainly both the end that a process is for and the process that is
20   for this end might also result from luck. We say, for instance, that a friend in a foreign country came by luck and paid the ransom and then went away, when he did the action as though he had come in order to do it, though in fact that was not what he came to do. This end is achieved coincidentally, since (as we said before) luck is one of the coincidental
25   causes. But whenever the end results always or usually, it is neither coincidental nor a result of luck. And in natural things that is how it is in every case, unless something prevents it.

Besides, it is strange for people to think there is no end unless they see an agent initiating the motion by deliberation. Even crafts do not deliberate. Moreover, if the shipbuilding craft were in the wood, it would produce a
30   ship in the same way that nature would. And so if what something is for is present in craft, it is also present in nature. This is clearest when a doctor applies medical treatment to himself—that is what nature is like.

It is evident, then, that nature is a cause, and in fact the sort of cause that is for something.

9

35   Is the necessity present <in nature only> conditional, or is it also unqualified?
200a   The sort of necessity that is ascribed nowadays to things that come to be is the sort there would be if someone supposed that a wall came into being of necessity. On this view, heavy things naturally move downwards, and light things upwards, and that is why the stones and the foundations are below, while the earth is above because of its lightness, and the wooden
5   logs are on the very top because they are lightest of all.

Nonetheless, though the wall certainly requires these things, it did not come to be because of them (except insofar as they are its material cause), but in order to give shelter and protection.

The same is true in all other cases that are for something: although they require things that have a necessary nature, they do not come to be because
10   of these things (except insofar as they are the material cause), but for some

end. For instance, why does a saw have such and such features? In order to perform this function, and for this end. But this end cannot come to be unless the saw is made of iron; and so it is necessary for it to be made of iron if there is to be a saw performing its function. What is necessary, then, is conditional, but not <necessary> as an end; for necessity is in the matter, whereas the end is in the form.   15

Necessity is found both in mathematics and in things that come to be naturally, and to some extent the two cases are similar. For instance, since the straight is what it is, it is necessary for a triangle to have angles equal to two right angles. It is not because the triangle has angles equal to two right angles that the straight is what it is; but if the triangle does not have angles equal to two right angles, the straight will not be what it is either.

The reverse is true in the case of things that come to be for an end: if the   20
end is or will be, then the previous things are or will be too. Just as, in the mathematical case, if the conclusion <about the triangle> is false, the principle <about the straight> will not be true either, so also in nature if the <materials> do not exist, the end that the process is for will not come about either. For the end is also a principle; it is a principle not of the action, but of the reasoning. (In the mathematical case <also> the principle is the principle of the reasoning, since in this case there is no action.)

And so, if there is to be a house, it is necessary for these things to come   25
to be or to be present; and in general, the matter that is for something must exist (for example, bricks and stones if there is to be a house). The end, however, does not exist because of these things, except insofar as they are the material cause, nor will it come about because of them; still, in general, the end (the house or the saw) requires them (the stones or the iron). Similarly, in the mathematical case the principles require the triangle to   30
have two right angles.

Evidently, then, necessity in natural things belongs to the material cause and to the motions of matter. The student of nature should mention both causes, but more especially what something is for, since this is the cause of the matter, whereas the matter is not the cause of the end. The end is what something is for, and the principle comes from the definition and the form.   35

The same is true in productions of craft. For instance, since a house is   200b
this sort of thing, these things must come to be and be present of necessity; and since health is this, these things must come to be and be present of necessity. In the same way, if a man is this, these things must come to be and be present of necessity; and if these, then these.

But presumably necessity is present in the form as well <as in the matter>. Suppose, for instance, that we define the function of sawing as a   5
certain sort of cutting; this sort of cutting requires a saw with teeth of a certain sort, and these require a saw made of iron. For the form, as well as the matter, has parts in it as matter of the form.

BOOK III

1

200b Since nature is a principle of motion and change, and since our line of inquiry is about nature, we must find out what motion is; for if we do not
15 know what it is, neither can we know what nature is. Once we have determined what motion is, we should try the same approach to the things that come next in order.

Motion seems to be continuous, and the first thing discerned in the continuous is the infinite. That is why those who define the continuous
20 often turn out to be relying on the account of the infinite as well, since they assume that what is infinitely divisible is continuous. Moreover, it seems impossible for there to be motion without place, void, and time.

It is clear, then, both because of these <connections> and because these things are common to everything and universal, that we should undertake a discussion of each of them, since the study of special topics comes after
25 the study of common topics; and first, as we said, we should discuss motion.

Some things are only in actuality,⁴² and others are in potentiality and in actuality—thises, or quantities, or qualities, or one of the other predications of being. Among relatives, some are spoken of with reference to
30 excess and deficiency, and others with reference to acting and being affected, and in general with reference to initiating motion and to being moved—for what initiates motion initiates it in what is moved, and what is moved is moved by what initiates motion.

There is no motion apart from things <that are moved>. For what changes always does so either in substance or in quantity or in quality or in
35 place, and we claim that there is nothing that is common and applies to all
201a of these—i.e. is neither a this nor a quantity nor a quality nor any of the other things predicated. Hence there is no motion or change of anything apart from the things mentioned, since there is nothing apart from these things.

Each of these things belongs to everything in <one of> two ways. This is true, for instance, of the this, which in some cases is form and in other
5 cases privation; of quality, which in some cases is pale and in other cases dark; and of quantity, which in some cases is complete and in other cases incomplete. It is true in the same way of local motion, which in some cases is upward and in other cases is downward, or <in other words> where some things are light and others heavy. Hence there are as many kinds of motion and change as there are of being.

---

42. **actuality**: *entelecheia*. In this chapter both *energeia* and *entelecheia* are translated by 'actuality', since no difference seems to be intended. See ACTUALITY #1.

In each kind of thing we distinguish what is actually F from what is   *10*
potentially F.[43] Hence the actuality of what is F potentially, insofar as it is F
potentially, is motion. The actuality of the alterable, for instance, insofar as
it is alterable, is alteration; the actuality of what is capable of growing or
its opposite, decaying (since there is no name that covers both), is growing
or decaying; the actuality of what is capable of coming to be or perishing
is coming to be or perishing; the actuality of what is capable of local   *15*
movement is local movement. That this is what motion is is clear from the
following. Whenever the buildable, insofar as we say it is buildable, is in
actuality, it is being built, and this is building. The same applies to learning, curing, rolling, jumping, ripening, and aging.

In some cases, the same things are both in potentiality and in actuality,   *20*
though not at the same time or in the same way, but rather they are, for
instance, actually hot and potentially cold. It follows that many things will
both act on and be affected by each other, since everything of this sort will
be capable both of acting and of being affected. Hence what naturally
initiates motion is also movable; for everything of this sort initiates motion
by itself being moved. Hence some people even believe that whatever initi-   *25*
ates motion is itself moved. The truth about this, however, will be clear
from other considerations; for in fact there is something that initiates motion without being movable.[44] In any case, the actuality of what is potentially F, whenever, being in actuality, it is active[45]—not insofar as it is itself,
but insofar as it is movable—is motion.

By 'insofar as' I mean the following: Though bronze is potentially a   *30*
statue, it is not the actuality of bronze, insofar as it is bronze, that is
motion. For being bronze is not the same as being potentially something;
for if they were the same without qualification, i.e. in definition, the actuality of bronze insofar as it is bronze would be motion. but in fact, as we
have said, they are not the same. This point is clear in the case of con-   *35*
traries. For being potentially healthy is not the same as being potentially ill; *201b*
if they were the same, then being ill and being healthy would also be the
same. Rather, the subject (whether it is moisture or blood) that is healthy
and ill <at different times> is one and the same. The two potentialities,
therefore, <of F insofar as it is F, and of F insofar as it is movable> are not
the same, just as color and the visible are not the same; and so it is evident
that the actuality of what is potentially F, insofar as it is potentially F,   *5*
is motion.

It is clear, then, that this actuality is motion, and that something is in fact

43. **actually F . . . potentially F**: In the following discussion 'F is added to make
the form of Aristotle's definition clear, in conformity with his explanation below.

44. **without being movable**: or 'without being moved'. The ending represented by
'-able' is sometimes ambiguous between these two readings.

45. **active**: *energein*, cognate with *energeia*.

in motion just when the actuality is this one, and neither earlier nor later. For it is possible for something—for instance, the buildable—to be at one time actual and at another not, and the actuality of the buildable, insofar

10 as it is buildable, is building. For the actuality is either the <process of> building or the house; but when the house exists, it is no longer buildable,[46] whereas what is being built is something buildable; necessarily, then, the actuality is <the process of> building. Now, building is a type of motion; moreover, the same account will also fit the other cases of motion.

2

That this account is correct is clear both from what other people say about motion and from the fact that it is not easy to define it in any other way. For motion and change cannot be assigned to any other genus, as is clear if

20 we examine what some people assign them to. They assert that motion is difference, or inequality, or what is not; but none of these—different things or unequal things or things that are not—is necessarily in motion, and change is no more into these or from these than it is from their opposites.

25 The reason why they assign motion to these genera is that motion seems to be something indefinite, and the principles in the second column[47] are indefinite because they are privative; for none of them is a this, or of any quality, or any of the other predications. The reason why motion seems to be indefinite is that it cannot be assigned either to the potentiality or to the

30 actuality of beings. For neither what potentially has a given quantity nor what actually has it is necessarily in motion. Moreover, motion seems to be some sort of actuality, but an incomplete one; this is because the potential, of which motion is an actuality, is incomplete. This, then, is why it is difficult to grasp what motion is; for it has to be assigned either to priva-

35 tion or to potentiality or to unqualified actuality, but none of these appears possible.

202a The remaining option, then, is the way <of understanding motion> that we have described: to say that it is a sort of actuality, and, in fact, the sort we have mentioned,[48] which is difficult to notice but possible to be.

As we have said, everything that initiates motion is also moved, provided that it has a potentiality to be moved and that its lack of motion is rest (for,

5 in the case of things that undergo motion, lack of motion is rest). For to act on this sort of thing <i.e., something movable>, insofar as it is of this sort, is just what it is to move it. <The agent> does this by contact, so that it is

46. **it is no longer buildable**: Or 'the buildable no longer exists'.

47. **second column**: On the columns of opposites see *GC* 319a15n and *Met.* 1004b27n.

48. **mentioned**: See 201a27.

itself acted on at the same time. That is why motion is the actuality of the movable insofar as it is movable; this comes about by contact with the mover,[49] so that <the mover> is also acted on at the same time. In each case the mover will bring some form—either a this or of this quality or of this quantity—that will be the principle and cause of motion whenever the mover initiates motion; for instance, an actual man makes something else actually a man from being potentially a man.

10

3

It is also evident how to answer the puzzle, by saying that the motion is in the thing moved.[50] For it is the actuality of the thing moved, brought about by the agency of the mover. The actuality of the mover is not different from this; for there must be an actuality of both mover and thing moved, since the mover is an initiator of motion by its potentiality, and it initiates motion by its actuality, but it is the thing moved that it brings to actuality. And so both mover and moved have one actuality, in the way in which the same interval is the interval from one to two and the interval from two to one, and <the same road> is the uphill and the downhill <road>. For these things are one, but their account is not one; and the same applies to the mover and the thing moved.

15

20

This, however, raises a logical puzzle. For presumably there must be some actuality of the agent and of what is acted on. The former actuality is *acting on* something, and the latter actuality is *being acted on*; and the achievement[51] and end of the former is an action, and of the latter a way of being acted on. Both of these actualities, then, are motions; if, then, they are different, what are they in?

25

Either both are in the thing that is affected and moved, or else the acting is in the agent and the being acted on is in the thing acted on. (If this being acted on is <also> to be called acting, then acting will be homonymous.) But now, if this is so, then the motion will be in the mover, since the same account applies to the mover and to the thing moved <as applies to the agent and to the thing acted on>. And so either the mover will be moved or it will have motion and yet not be moved.

30

Suppose that, on the contrary, both the acting and the being acted on are in the thing that is moved and acted on, and that both teaching and learning, being two <motions>, are in the learner. In that case, first of all, the actuality of a given <subject> will not be in that <subject>. Secondly,

49. **mover**: i.e. what initiates motion. See MOTION #1.

50. **puzzle . . . moved**: Aristotle has not actually mentioned the puzzle he alludes to here, about whether motion is in the mover or in the thing moved.

51. **achievement**: or 'work', *ergon*. Here the *ergon* is the outcome. See FUNCTION.

it is absurd that <the thing acted on> should undergo two motions at the
35 same time. For what will be the two alterations of one <subject> into one
form? That is impossible.

Suppose, then, that the actuality <of the mover and the thing moved>
202b are one. But it is unreasonable for two things that are different in form to
have one and the same actuality. Moreover if <the processes of> teaching
and learning, or <the processes of> acting and being acted on, are the
same, then to teach will be the same as to learn, and to act will be the same
5 as to be acted on, so that it will be necessary for the one teaching to be
learning <everything that he is teaching>, and for the agent to be acted on
<by its own action>.

Perhaps, however, it is not absurd for the actuality of one thing to be in
another thing; for teaching is the actuality of what is capable of teaching,
but in some subject <acted on>. It is not cut off, but is the actuality of this
<agent> in this <thing acted on>. And perhaps it is not impossible for two
things to have one and the same actuality—not in such a way that the
10 actuality is one in being, but in the way in which the potential is related to
the actual.

Nor is it necessary for the one teaching to be learning, even if acting and
being acted on are the same, given that they are not the same in such a way
that one and the same account states the essence of both, as it does for cape
and cloak; rather, they are the same in the way in which the road from
Thebes to Athens is the same as the road from Athens to Thebes, as has
15 been said before.[52] For if things are <merely> the same in some way, it does
not follow that all the same things belong to them; this follows only if their
being is the same.

Moreover, even if <the process of> teaching is the same thing as learning, it does not follow that to teach is the same as to learn, just as, even if
there is one interval between the two things separated by it, it does not
follow that to be separated by the interval from here to there is one and the
same as to be separated by the interval from there to here. And, to speak
generally, <the process of teaching> is not the same thing in the full sense
20 as learning, nor is acting the same <in the full sense> as being acted on.
What is one is the motion to which both the properties <of being a teaching and being a learning> belong. For being the actuality of this <subject>
in that one is different in account from being the actuality of that <sub-
ject> by the agency of this one.

We have said, then, what motion is, both in general and in particular
25 cases. For it is clear how each species of it will be defined. Alteration, for
instance, will be the actuality of the alterable insofar as it is alterable. To
make it still better known: <Motion will be> the actuality of what has the
potentiality for acting and being acted on, insofar as it has that potentiality.

52. **said before:** See 202a18–20.

This is true without qualification, and again in particular cases—for instance in building or healing. The same account will be given of each of the other types of motion.

BOOK VIII

6

Since motion must be everlasting and must never fail, there must be some 258b everlasting first mover, one or more than one. The question whether each of the unmoved movers[53] is everlasting is irrelevant to this argument; but it will be clear in the following way that there must be something that is itself unmoved and outside all change, either unqualified or coincidental, but 15 initiates motion in something else.

Let us suppose, then, if you like, that in the case of some things it is possible for them to be at one time and not to be at another without any coming to be or perishing—for if something has no parts, but it is at one time and is not at another time, perhaps it is necessary for it to be at one 20 time and not to be at another without changing.[54] Let us also suppose that, among the principles that are unmoved but initiate motion, it is possible for some to be at one time and not to be at another time.

Still, this is not possible for every principle of that sort; for it is clear that there is something that causes the self-movers to be at one time and not to be at another time. For every self-mover necessarily has some magnitude, if 25 nothing that lacks parts is moved; but from what we have said it is not necessary for every mover to have magnitude. Hence the cause explaining why some things come to be and other things perish, and in a continuous sequence, cannot be any of the things that are unmoved but do not always exist; nor can some things be the cause of some <parts of the sequence> and other things the cause of other <parts>; for neither any one of them 30 nor all of them together is the cause explaining why the sequence is everlasting and continuous. For the sequence is everlasting and necessary, whereas all these movers are infinitely many and they do not all exist at the same time.

It is clear, then, that however many unmoved movers and self-movers 259a perish and are succeeded by others, so that one unmoved mover moves one thing and another moves another, still there is something that embraces them all and is apart from each of them, which is the cause explaining why some exist and some do not exist, and why the change is continuous. This is 5 the cause of motion in these <other movers>, and these are the cause of motion in the other things.

53. **unmoved movers**: i.e. souls.

54. **without changing**: i.e. without undergoing any process of change.

If, then, motion is everlasting, the first mover is also everlasting, if there is just one; and if there are many, there are many everlasting movers. But we must suppose there is one rather than many, and a finite rather than an infinite number. For in every case where the results <of either assumption> are the same, we should assume a finite number <of causes>; for among natural things what is finite and better must exist rather <than its opposite> if this is possible. And one mover is sufficient; it will be first and everlasting among the unmoved things, and the principle of motion for the other things.

ON GENERATION
AND CORRUPTION

In this work on the topic of coming into (and going out of) existence, Aristotle opposes the atomists' contention that these phenomena involve the association (and dissociation) of atoms. There are no atoms (i.e., indivisible bodies) in Aristotle's view. Rather, every body has the potential to be divided at any point, although no body can be actually divided into an infinite number of parts.

In the excerpts presented here, Aristotle distinguishes coming to be from alteration (Book I) and discusses the reciprocal transformation of the four elements (Book II).

BOOK I

1

We must distinguish the causes and accounts of coming to be and perishing   *314a* that are common to everything that comes to be and perishes naturally. We must also ask what growth and alteration are and whether alteration and coming to be should be taken to have the same nature, or separate natures   *5* that correspond to their distinct names.

Some of the early <philosophers> say that what is called unqualified coming to be is <really nothing but> alteration, while others say that alteration is different from coming to be. For those who say that the whole universe is some one thing and make everything come to be from one thing have to say that <so-called> coming to be is <really> alteration, and that   *10* what <allegedly> comes to be in the full sense is <really only> altered. But those who say that matter is more than one thing—for instance, Empedocles, Anaxagoras, Leucippus—have to say that coming to be and alteration are different.

And yet <among these pluralists> Anaxagoras misunderstood his own statements. At any rate, he says that coming to be and perishing are the   *15* same as alteration, even though, like others, he says that there are many elements. For Empedocles says that there are four bodily elements, but that the total number of elements, including the <two> sources of motion, is six, while Anaxagoras, Leucippus and Democritus say that the elements are unlimited <in number>. For the elements that Anaxagoras recognizes are uniform things—for instance, bone, flesh, marrow, and everything else   *20* whose parts are synonymous with the whole. Democritus and Leucippus, by contrast, say that everything else is composed of indivisible bodies that are infinite both in number and in shapes, and that <differences in> these components and <in> their position and arrangement make the compounds different from each other. For the views of Anaxagoras and his supporters are evidently contrary to those of Empedocles and his supporters. For Empedocles says that fire, water, air, and earth, rather than flesh, bone, and similar uniform things, are <the only> four elements and that only these are simple, whereas Anaxagoras and his supporters say that these <uniform things> are simple and elemental, while earth, fire, water, and air are compounds—for these four, they say, are a common seed-bed of the uniform things.

Those, then, who constitute everything out of some one thing must say that <so-called> coming to be and perishing are <nothing but> alteration. For in their view, in every <change> the subject remains one and the same; and that is the sort of thing that we say is altered. On the other hand, those who recognize more than one kind of thing must distinguish alteration from coming to be; for when things <of different kinds> are combined there is coming to be, and when they are dissolved there is perishing. That is why Empedocles also speaks in this way, when he says 'There is no birth of anything, but only mixture and the dissolution of things that have been mixed'.

It is clear, then, that this account fits their assumption, and that this is what they actually say. But they must also distinguish alteration from coming to be; yet their own statements make this impossible. It is easy to see that we are right about this. For just as we see a substance remaining stable while its size changes (this is called growth and decay), so also we see alteration; and yet the views of those who recognize more than one principle make alteration impossible. For the attributes that we take to be <gained or lost> when something is altered—i.e. hot and cold, pale and dark, dry and wet, soft and hard, etc.—are differentiae of the elements.[1] Empedocles also says this: 'The sun is pale to the eye and hot all over, but rain is dark and cold throughout' (and he distinguishes the other <elements> in the same way). If, then, water cannot come to be from fire, or earth from water, then neither will anything be dark from being pale, or hard from being soft; and the same argument applies to the other cases. But we agreed that this is what alteration is.

Hence it is also evident that in every case we must assume a single matter for the contraries <involved in change>, whether the change involves place, or growth and decay, or alteration. Moreover, the existence of this matter and of alteration are equally necessary; for if there is any alteration, it follows both that the subject is a single element and also that

---

1. **differentiae of the elements**: If they are DIFFERENTIAE, they must be essential properties of the elements. Since alteration involves only nonessential properties, these differentiae cannot enter into alteration.

all the <contraries> that allow change into each other have a single matter. And equally, if the subject is one, there is such a thing as alteration.

3

Now that we have determined these points, the next question is this: Does *317a32* anything come to be without qualification or perish, or does nothing come to be in the full sense, so that in each case a thing comes to be *F* from being *G*[2]—comes to be healthy, for instance, from being sick and sick from being *35* healthy, or comes to be small from being large and large from being small, and everything else in the same way? For if there is such a thing as *317b* unqualified coming to be, then something would come to be without qualification from what it is not, so that it will be true to say that not being belongs to some things. For a thing comes to be *F* from what is not *F* (for instance, not pale or not beautiful), and a thing comes to be without *5* qualification from what is-not without qualification.

Now, 'without qualification' signifies either what is primary in a given predication of being, or what is universal and includes everything. If, then, <'not-being without qualification' signifies not being> the primary thing, then substance will come to be from non-substance; but if a thing is not a substance and a this,[3] then clearly it has none of the other predications *10* either—for instance, quality, quantity, or location—for if it had, attributes would be separable from substance. Alternatively, if <'not-being without qualification' signifies> not being at all, it will be the universal negation of everything, so that what comes to be <without qualification> will have to come to be from nothing.[4]

The puzzles about this issue have been thoroughly examined, and the <necessary> distinctions drawn more fully, in other discussions;[5] but we *15* should also state the points concisely here. In one way, something comes to be <without qualification> from what is-not without qualification, but in another way it comes to be, in every case, from what is. For something that

2. *F* **from being** *G*: lit. 'something from something'.

3. **and a this**: Here and in 317b20 the 'and' may be equivalent to 'i.e.'.

4. **come to be from nothing**: Aristotle refers to the puzzle about coming to be that he mentions at *Phys.* 191a23–33. We may be willing to agree that qualified coming to be (i.e., alteration, etc.) is possible, because it does not involve coming to be from what is-not without qualification, but only the coming to be of what is *F* (the musical man) from what is not *F* (the unmusical man). But if some type of coming to be is different from qualified coming to be because it involves the coming to be of a new SUBSTANCE (cf. *Phys.* 190a31–b1), does it not involve coming to be from nothing (from what is-not without qualification)? This is the puzzle that Aristotle tries to resolve.

5. **other discussions**: See *Phys.* 191a33–b27.

is *F* potentially, but is not *F* actually, must precede <any coming to be of
F>, and this is spoken of in both ways <as being and as not being>.

But even when these distinctions have been drawn, a further question is
remarkably puzzling, and we must go back to it again: How can there be
20   unqualified coming to be, either from what potentially is or in any other
way? For it is a puzzling question whether there is any coming to be of a
substance and a this, rather than <merely> of a quality or quantity or
location (and the same applies to perishing). For if something[6] comes to be,
then clearly there will be some potential but not actual substance from
25   which <the substance> will come to be and into which the <substance>
will have to change when it perishes. Will this, then, actually have any of
the other things (quantity, quality, or location) if it is only potentially a this
and a being, and is neither a this nor a being without qualification? For if it
has none of these actually, but has all of them potentially, then it turns out
that what lacks all these sorts of being is separable, and moreover that
30   something comes to be from nothing preceding it—the very thing that
always most alarmed the earliest philosophers. If, on the other hand, it is
not a this or a substance but has one of the other <predications> we
mentioned, then, as we said, attributes will turn out to be separable from
substance.

We must, therefore, work on these questions as much as we can. We must
35   also ask what is the cause of there always being coming to be, both unqualified coming to be and coming to be in a particular respect.

318a   One sort of cause is the one we call the source of the principle of
motion, and one sort is matter. Here we ought to discuss the second sort
of cause; for we have discussed the first sort earlier, in the treatment of
motion,[7] where we said that one sort of <principle of motion> is unmoved
5   for all time, and the other sort is always in motion. A consideration of the
first sort of cause is a task for a different and prior <branch of> philosophy; and later we will discuss the <principle> that initiates motion in other
things by being in continuous motion itself, and say which particular thing
of this sort is the cause. But for now let us discuss the material cause,
10   explaining why perishing and coming to be never fail in nature. For, presumably, in making this clear we will also make clear both the answer to
the present puzzle and the right account of unqualified perishing and
coming to be.

It is puzzling enough to know what causes the continuity of coming to
15   be, if what perishes passes into what is not and what is not is nothing—
since what is not neither is something nor has any quality, quantity, or
location. If, then, at every time something that is is passing away, why has

6. **something**: Aristotle uses 'something' to refer to SUBSTANCE. Cf. 318a15, 319a25.
7. **the treatment of motion**: i.e. *Phys.* viii 6.

everything not been used up and vanished long ago, if it is indeed true that there was only a limited amount from which everything coming to be comes to be? For surely the reason that coming to be does not fail is not that there is an infinite source from which things come to be. That view is *20* impossible; for since nothing is infinite in actuality, and something can be infinite in potentiality only by division, it follows that division into ever smaller things is the only type of coming to be that never fails—and that is not what we see happen. Alternatively, then, does the fact that the perishing of F [8] is the coming to be of G, and the coming to be of F is the perishing of G, explain why change is necessarily ceaseless?

This, then, should be regarded as an adequate explanation for all cases, *25* of why coming to be and perishing belong to each being alike. If, however, we agree that the coming to be of F is the perishing of G, and the perishing *30* of F is the coming to be of G, we must reconsider why we say that some things come to be or perish without qualification, whereas others do so only with some qualification; for we need to give some account of this. For sometimes we say that a thing is now perishing without qualification, not that F is perishing, and that one event is an unqualified coming to be, and another an unqualified perishing. Moreover, sometimes the F comes to be G, but the F does not come to be without qualification;[9] for we say, for instance, that the learner comes to be expert, not that he comes to be *35* without qualification.

Now we often draw a distinction by saying that some things signify a *318b* this,[10] and others do not; and this is why our present question arises. For it all depends on what the subject is changing into; presumably, for instance, turning into fire is both an unqualified coming to be and the perishing of something (for instance, of earth), whereas the coming to be of earth is *5* both a sort of coming to be (not an unqualified coming to be) and an unqualified perishing (for instance, of fire). This is Parmenides' view when he mentions two things <that something can change into>, and asserts that what is is fire and that what is not is earth. (It does not matter whether we assume fire and earth or other such things, since we are inquiring about the type, not the subject, of the change.) Turning into what is-not without qualification, therefore, is <unqualified> perishing, and turning into what *10*

8. **perishing of** F: We have used 'F' and 'G' where Aristotle simply uses 'this'. He might be referring either to (e.g.) paleness or to the pale thing.

9. **the** F **comes . . . qualification**: In this sentence Aristotle uses 'this' where we have 'the F' and 'the G'. His example suggests that here at least the subject is (e.g.) the pale thing that comes to be dark.

10. **signify a this**: In this chapter 'this' is applied both (a) to the category of substance, and (b) to the positive property as opposed to the negative (e.g. to the form rather than the privation). Aristotle does not argue that (a) and (b) coincide.

is without qualification is unqualified coming to be. And so one of the two elements that mark the distinction (whether they are fire and earth, or other things) will be what is, and the other will be what is not.[11]

This, then, is one way to distinguish unqualified from qualified coming to be or perishing. Another way appeals to the character of the matter. For if the differentiae of a type of matter signify a this to a higher degree, what they signify is itself a substance to a higher degree; if they signify a privation, what they signify is not-being. If heat, for instance, is a <positive> predication and form, and cold a privation, and these differentiate earth and fire, <then fire will be being and earth not-being>.

Most people, however, are more inclined to believe that <coming to be and perishing> are distinguished by whether <the product> is perceptible or not: whenever there is a change into perceptible matter, they say it is a coming to be, and when it is into imperceptible matter, they say it is a perishing. For they distinguish being from not-being by whether something is perceived or not, just as what is known is what is and what is not known is what is not—for perception <in their view> counts as knowledge. Hence, just as they think they are alive and have their being by perceiving or being capable of it, so they think things have their being <by being perceived or by being perceptible>. In a way, then, they are on the track of the truth, though what they actually say is not true.

In reality, then, unqualified coming to be and perishing turn out to be different from what they are commonly believed to be. For from the point of view of perception, wind and air are beings to a lesser extent <than earth is>. Hence people say that what perishes without qualification perishes by changing into one of them, and that something comes to be <without qualification> when something changes into what is tangible (i.e. earth). In reality, however, each of them is more of a this and a form than earth is.

We have explained, then, why there is unqualified coming to be that is also something's perishing, and unqualified perishing that is also something's coming to be. The reason is that there are different types of matter, so that the matter out of which and that into which <the change occurs> may be either substance and non-substance, or substances to different degrees, or more and less perceptible.

But why are some things said to come to be without qualification, and others said merely to come to be *F*, in other cases besides those in which things come to be from each other in the way we have described? For so far we have only determined why we do not speak in the same way of coming to be and perishing in all cases of things that change into each other, even though every coming to be is the perishing of something else

11. **what is . . . what is not**: These are not the existent and the non-existent, but the positive and the negative.

and every perishing is the coming to be of something else. But our further question raises a different puzzle, about why the learner is said merely to come to be expert, not to come to be without qualification, whereas <a plant> growing <from a seed> is said to come to be <without qualification>. 10

These cases, then, are distinguished by reference to the predications; for some things signify a this, some quality,[12] some quantity. Whatever does not signify a substance, then, is said to come to be *F*, not to come to be without qualification. Still, in every case we speak of coming to be in <only the positive> one of the two columns;[13] for instance, we recognize a coming to be in the case of substance if fire rather than earth comes to be, and in the case of quality if someone comes to be expert rather than inexpert. 15

We have said, then, why some things do and others do not come to be without qualification, both in general and also in the case of substances themselves. We have also explained why the subject is the material cause of the continuity of coming to be—because it is capable of changing from one contrary to another, and in every case where substances are involved, the coming to be of one thing is the perishing of another, and the perishing of one thing is the coming to be of another. 20

Nor should we be puzzled about why there is coming to be even though things are always being destroyed. For just as people speak of unqualified perishing whenever a thing passes into something imperceptible and into what is not, so also they speak of coming to be from what is not, whenever a thing comes to be from something imperceptible. And so whether or not the subject is something, a thing comes to be from what is not, so that things come to be from what is not and likewise perish into what is not. It is not surprising, then, that coming to be never ceases; for coming to be is the perishing of what is not, and perishing is the coming to be of what is not. 25

30

But is what is-not without qualification also one of a pair of contraries? For instance, is earth (i.e. the heavy) a thing that is not, and is fire (i.e. the light) a thing that is, or is earth also a thing that is, and is the common matter of earth and air a thing that is not? And is the matter of each one different, or <must it be the same, since otherwise> they would not come to be from each other and from their contraries? For the contraries are present in these—in fire, earth, water, and air. Or is it in a way the same and in a way different? <Apparently so;> for the subject, whatever it may be <at a particular time> is the same <subject>, but what it is <at different times> is not the same. So much, then, for these questions. 319b

12. **quality**: lit. 'such'. See QUALITY.

13. **two columns**: These are columns listing the pairs of contrary (positive and negative) properties. See *Met.* 1004b27.

4

Let us now describe the difference between coming to be and alteration, since we say that these changes are different from each other.

A subject is different from an attribute that is by its nature said of the subject, and each of these may change. Alteration occurs whenever the subject, being perceptible, remains but changes in its attributes, these being either contraries or intermediates. A body, for instance, is at one time healthy and at another time sick, still remaining the same <body>; and the bronze is at one time round and at another time angular, still remaining the same <bronze>.

But whenever the whole <subject> changes and something perceptible does not remain as the same subject[14] (as, for instance, blood comes to be from the whole seed, or air from <the whole of the> water, or water from the whole of the air), then this is a case of the coming to be of one thing, <for instance, the blood>, and the perishing of the other, <for instance, the seed>. This is so especially if the change is from something imperceptible to something perceptible (perceptible by touch, or by all the senses)— whenever, for instance, water comes to be, or perishes into air (since air is fairly imperceptible).

In such cases <of unqualified coming to be>, sometimes the same attribute (which is one of a pair of contraries) that belongs to the thing that has perished remains in the thing that has come to be, when water, for instance, comes to be from air, if both are transparent or cold. But in these cases the thing resulting from the change must not itself be an attribute of this <attribute that remains>—if it were, the change would be an alteration. Suppose that a musical man, for instance, perished, and an unmusical man came to be, and the man remains as the same thing. If, then, musicality and unmusicality were not attributes of the man in their own right,[15] it would have been a coming to be of the unmusical and a perishing of the musical.[16] In fact, however, each of these is an attribute of the thing that remains; that is why they are attributes of the man, and it is <only> a coming to be or perishing of the musical or unmusical man. That is why such cases count as alterations.

14. **something perceptible . . . subject**: This might mean either (a) there is some perceptible thing that does not remain as subject, or (b) there is no perceptible subject that remains. While (a) leaves open the possibility that some perceptible subject remains (as long as some other perceptible subject does not remain), (b) rules out this possibility. Normally Aristotle's account of unqualified coming to be requires only (a).

15. **attributes in their own right**: This is the second sense of IN ITS OWN RIGHT distinguished at *APo* 73a34–b24.

16. **of the unmusical . . . of the musical**: lit. 'of the one . . . of the other'.

A change between contrary quantities, then, is growth or decay; between contrary places it is locomotion; and between contrary attributes and qualities it is alteration. But when nothing remains that has <the contrary resulting from the change> as its attribute or as any sort of coincident, the change is a coming to be, and <its contrary> is a perishing.

Matter is most of all and most fully the subject that admits the <unqualified> coming to be and perishing <of another thing>; but the subject for the other types of change is also matter in a way, since every subject admits <its proper> contraries.

Let this, then, be our account of whether or not there is coming to be and in what way there is, and of alteration.

BOOK II

1

Our view is that there is some matter of perceptible bodies, but that it is not separable but rather is always accompanied by one of a pair of contrary properties, from which[17] the so-called elements come to be. A more precise account of them[18] has been given elsewhere. Nevertheless, since it is in just this way that the primary bodies come to be from the matter, we must also give an account of these,[19] in which we take as a first principle the matter that is inseparable yet is subject for the contraries. For the hot is not matter for the cold, nor it for the hot, but what underlies is matter for both. Therefore the principle is, first, what is potentially a perceptible body, but secondly it is the pairs of contrary properties (I mean, e.g., heat and cold), and thirdly it is fire and water and the like. For the latter change into one another, and not in the way that Empedocles and others say (for there would be no alteration), but the contrary properties do not change. Nonetheless we must discuss how many and what kind <of contrary properties> are principles of body. For other people postulate and use them, and say nothing about why these or why this many. (*Translated S. M. Cohen*)

17. The reference of 'which' here is unclear. It might refer to the 'pair of contrary properties' that immediately precedes, but more likely to the 'matter' at the beginning of the sentence.

18. Again, the reference of 'them' is unclear. It might refer to (a) matter and contrary properties, but more likely to (b) the elements. On option (a), the reference would be to *Physics* I.6–9; on (b), to *De Caelo* III–IV.

19. 'These' clearly refers to something different from 'them' in the previous sentence (see previous note). On option (a), 'these' refers to the primary bodies, i.e., the elements; on the preferable option (b), it refers to the pairs of contrary properties, which are discussed in the next chapter.

2

329b7   Since we are seeking the principles of perceptible body, that is to say, of tangible body, and since what is tangible is what is perceived by the sense of touch, it is evident that not all contrary properties, but only contrary

10   tangible properties, constitute forms and principles of bodies; for <primary bodies> are distinguished not only by having contrary properties but specifically by having contrary tangible properties. That is why neither paleness and darkness nor sweetness and bitterness nor, equally, any of the other pairs of perceptible contraries constitute any element. Admittedly,

15   since sight is prior to touch, the <visible> subject is also prior; but it is not an attribute of tangible body in so far as it is tangible, but in so far as it is something else that may indeed be naturally prior.

     Among the tangible properties themselves, we must first distinguish the primary differentiae and pairs of contraries. The pairs of contraries corre-

20   sponding to touch are the these: hot and cold, dry and wet, heavy and light, hard and soft, sticky and brittle, rough and smooth, coarse and fine. Among these, heavy and light neither act nor are affected; for these are not called what they are called by acting on or by being affected by anything else, whereas the elements must be capable of mutual action and affection,

25   since they combine and change into each other.

     Hot and cold, dry and wet, however, are so called in so far as they either act or are affected. Hot is what holds together things of the same kind; for dispersal, which is said to be the action of fire, is really holding together things of the same kind, since the result of the dispersal is the removal of

30   the foreign things. Cold is what brings and holds together both things of the same kind and things of different kinds. Wet is what is not confined by any limit of its own, but is easily confined within <another> limit. Dry is what is easily confined within its own limit, but is hard to confine within <another> limit . . .

3

330b22   Fire, earth, and the other things we have mentioned[20] are not simple, but mixed. The simple bodies are similar to these, but they are not the same. If, for instance, there is a simple body that is similar to fire, it is fiery but not

25   fire, and the one similar to air is airy, and so on. Fire is a predominance of heat, just as ice is a predominance of cold; for freezing and boiling are types of predominance—of cold and heat, respectively. If, then, ice is the freezing of what is wet and cold, fire is the boiling of what is dry and hot— that is why nothing comes to be from ice or from fire. . . .

20. **Fire . . . mentioned:** i.e. the recognized 'four elements'.

4

We have previously determined that the simple bodies come to be from one another. Moreover, perception makes this evident; for if they did not, there would be no alteration, since alteration involves the attributes of tangible things. We must, then, describe the way they change into each other, and consider whether each of them can come to be from every other one, or only some can, and others cannot.

It is evident that all of them naturally change into each other; for coming to be begins from one contrary and ends in the other, and each element has some quality contrary to a quality of each of the others, since their differentiae are contraries. For some <elements>—fire and water—have both properties contrary <to each other> (since fire is dry and hot, and water is wet and cold), while others—air and water—have only one property contrary <to that of the other element>, (since air is wet and hot, and water is wet and cold).

In general, therefore, it is evident that each <element> naturally comes to be from each of the others. It is easy to see how this is so when we come to particular cases; for each will come from each, but the process will be quicker or slower, and harder or easier. For if bodies have corresponding qualities, change from one to the other is quick; otherwise it is slow, since one quality changes more easily than many. Air, for instance, will come from fire when just one quality changes; for fire is hot and dry, and air hot and wet, so that if the dry is overcome by the wet, air will result. Again, water will result from air if the hot is overcome by the old; for air is hot and wet, and water is cold and wet, so that if the hot changes, water will result. . . .

331a7
10

15

20

25

30

5

But let us also consider the following points about <the elements>. If fire, earth, and so on are, as some people think, the matter of natural bodies, there must be either one or two or more than two of them. Now they cannot all be one—for instance, they cannot all be air or all water or all fire or all earth—since change is into contraries. For if they are all air, then, since this will remain, there will be alteration, not coming to be; and besides, it does not seem to happen in such a way that water would at the same time be air or any other <element>. There will therefore be some contrariety and differentia of which <water will have one member> and some <element> will have the other member, as fire, for instance, has heat. Nor again is fire hot air; for in that case <the change from air to fire> would be an alteration, but this is not what it appears to be. Moreover, if air came from fire, it would come from hot changing into its contrary, so that this contrary would be present in air, and air would be something cold. Hence fire cannot be hot air, since that would make the same thing both hot and cold.

332a3
5

10

15

Both <air and fire>, then, must be some other thing that is the same for both, i.e. some other matter common to them.[21] The same argument applies to all the elements, showing that there is no one of them from which everything comes.

Nor again is there anything else besides these—something intermediate, for instance, between air and water (coarser than air, but finer than water) or between fire and air (coarser than fire but finer than air). For this intermediate element will be air and fire (respectively) when a contrariety is added to it; but since one of a pair of contraries is a privation, the intermediate element cannot exist alone at any time (as some people say the indefinite and all-inclusive does). It is therefore one or another of the elements, or nothing.

If, then, nothing (or nothing perceptible at least) is prior to these elements, they will be everything. They must, then, either always remain without changing into each other, or else change into each other; if they change, then either all of them do, or else some do and some do not, as Plato wrote in the *Timaeus*.[22] We have shown previously that they must change into each other, and that one does not come to be from another equally quickly in each case, because those that have a corresponding property come to be more quickly from each other, and those that have none come to be more slowly.

If, then, the elements change within just one pair of contraries, there must be two of them; for the matter, being imperceptible and inseparable, is intermediate between them. But since we see that there are more than two elements, there must also be at least two pairs of contraries; and if there are two <pairs of contraries>, there must be, as in fact there appear to be, four elements, not three. For that is the number of combinations <of qualities>; though there are six <describable combinations>, two of them cannot occur because they are contrary to one another. . . .

21. **matter common to them:** This is usually taken to be a reference to 'prime (i.e. first, most basic) matter'; see MATTER #3. This matter underlies the four elements and is the subject of the changes between them (since, for the reasons Aristotle gives here, none of the elements can be the appropriate sort of subject). This prime matter (on the usual interpretation) (a) has none of the qualities of the elements essentially, but (b) is capable of having all of them at different times, and (c) necessarily has the qualities of some element or other at any given time (i.e. it cannot exist without being hot or cold or . . . , but it is neither necessarily hot nor necessarily cold nor . . .).
22. **in the *Timaeus*:** see 54b–d.

ON THE HEAVENS

Translated by W. K. C. Guthrie

This work contains Aristotle's account of the physical universe—the earth, moon, sun, planets, and stars. In parts not included in this anthology, he argues that the universe is unique and eternal, that the earth is stationary at the center of the universe, and that the other heavenly bodies revolve around it in circular orbits. In the chapters excerpted here he discusses the elements of which everything on the earth is composed. He argues that they are four in number and that they cannot be reduced to a smaller number. They are not eternal but are capable of being generated out of one another.

Book I

2

The question of the nature of this Whole, whether it is of infinite magni- 268b11
tude or its total bulk is limited, must be left until later. We have now to
speak of its formally distinct parts, and we may start from this, that al-
lnatural bodies and magnitudes are capable of moving of themselves in   15
space; for nature we have defined as the principle of motion in them.[1] Now
all motion in space (locomotion) is either straight or circular or a compound of the two, for these are the only simple motions, the reason being
that the straight and circular lines are the only simple magnitudes. By
"circular motion" I mean motion around the center, by "straight," motion   20
up and down. "Up" means away from the center, "down" towards the
center. It follows that all simple locomotion is either away from the center
or towards the center or around the center. This appears to follow consis-   25
tently on what was said at the beginning: body was completed by the
number three, and so now is its motion.

   Of bodies some are simple, and some are compounds of the simple. By
"simple" I mean all bodies which contain a principle of natural motion, like

Excerpts from Aristotle, *De Caelo* translated by W.K.C. Guthrie (Cambridge, Mass.: Harvard University Press 1939). Reprinted by permission of the publishers and the Loeb Classical Library.

1. *Phys.* II.1.192b20.

fire and earth and their kinds, and the other bodies of the same order.
30   Hence motions also must be similarly divisible, some simple and others
269a compound in one way or another; simple bodies will have simple motions
and composite bodies composite motions, though the movement may be
according to the prevailing element in the compound.

If we take these premisses, (a) that there is such a thing as simple motion,
(b) that circular motion is simple, (c) that simple motion is the motion of a
5   simple body (for if a composite body moves with a simple motion, it is only
by virtue of a simple body prevailing and imparting its direction to the
whole), then it follows that there exists a simple body naturally so constituted as to move in a circle in virtue of its own nature. By force it can be
brought to move with the motion of another, different body, but not naturally, if it is true that each of the simple bodies has one natural motion
10   only. Moreover, granted that (a) unnatural motion is the contrary of natural, (b) a thing can have only one contrary, then circular motion, seeing it is
one of the simple motions, must, if it is not the motion natural to the
moved body, be contrary to its nature. Suppose now that the body which is
moving in a circle be fire or some other of the four elements, then its
natural motion must be contrary to the circular. But a thing can have only
15   one contrary, and the contrary of upward is downward, and *vice versa*.
Suppose on the other hand that this body which is moving in a circle
contrary to its own nature is something other than the elements, there must
be some other motion which is natural to it. But that is impossible: for if
the motion were upward, the body would be fire or air, if downward, water
or earth.

20   Furthermore, circular motion must be primary. That which is complete is
prior in nature to the incomplete, and the circle is a complete figure,
whereas no straight line can be so. An infinite straight line cannot, for to be
complete it would have to have an end or completion, nor yet a finite, for
all finite lines have something beyond them: any one of them is capable of
being extended. Now if (a) a motion which is prior to another is the motion
25   of a body prior in nature, (b) circular motion is prior to rectilinear, (c)
rectilinear motion is the motion of the simple bodies (as *e.g.* fire moves in a
straight line upwards and earthy bodies move downwards towards the
center), then circular motion also must of necessity be the motion of some
simple body. (We have already made the reservation that the motion of
composite bodies is determined by whatever simple body predominates in
30   the mixture.) From all these premisses therefore it clearly follows that there
exists some physical substance besides the four in our sublunary world, and
moreover that it is more divine than, and prior to, all these. The same can
also be proved on the further assumption that all motion is either natural
or unnatural, and that motion which is unnatural to one body is natural to
35   another, as the motions up and down are natural or unnatural to fire and
269b earth respectively; from these it follows that circular motion too, since it is
unnatural to these elements, is natural to some other. Moreover, if circular

motion is natural to anything, it will clearly be one of the simple and primary bodies of such a nature as to move naturally in a circle, as fire moves upward and earth downward. If on the other hand it be maintained that the revolutionary motion of the body which is carried round in a circle is unnatural, it is strange, in fact quite absurd, that being unnatural it should yet be the only continuous and eternal motion, seeing that in the rest of nature what is unnatural is the quickest to fall into decay. And so, if fire be the body carried round, as some say, this motion will be no less unnatural to it than motion downwards; for we see the natural motion of fire to be in a straight line away from the center.

Thus the reasoning from all our premisses goes to make us believe that there is some other body separate from those around us here, and of a higher nature in proportion as it is removed from the sublunary world.

Book III

3

It remains to decide what bodies are subject to generation, and why. Since, then, knowledge is always to be sought through what is primary, and the primary constituents of bodies are their elements, we must consider which of such bodies are elements, and why, and afterwards how many of them there are and what is their character. The answer will be plain once we have laid down what is the nature of an element. Let us then define the element in bodies as that into which other bodies may be analyzed, which is present in them either potentially or actually (which of the two, is a matter for future debate), and which cannot itself be analyzed into constituents differing in kind. Some such definition of an element is what all thinkers are aiming at throughout.

Now if this definition is correct, elemental bodies must exist. In flesh and wood, for instance, and all such substances, fire and earth are potentially present, for they may be separated out and become apparent. But flesh or wood are not present in fire, either potentially or actually; otherwise they could be separated out. Even if there only existed one single element, they would not be present in it. It may be flesh, bone etc. are to be produced from it, but that does not immediately involve saying that they are potentially present in it. One must also take into consideration the manner of their generation.

Anaxagoras is opposed to Empedocles on the subject of the elements. Empedocles' view is that fire and earth and the other substances of the same order are the elements of bodies, and everything is composed of them. According to Anaxagoras, on the other hand, the uniform bodies[2]

2. **uniform bodies:** *homoiomerē*, translated by Guthrie as "homoeomeries." Cf. *Met.*, 389b25n.

302b are elements (flesh, bone and other substances of that order), whereas air and fire are a mixture of these and all the other seeds, for each consists of an agglomeration of all the uniform bodies in invisible quantities. That is why everything is generated from these two. (He makes no distinction
5 between fire and *aither*.) But since (i) every natural body has its proper motion, (ii) some motions are simple and others composite, and (iii) simple motions are of simple bodies, composite of composite, it clearly follows that certain simple bodies must exist. For there are simple motions. Thus we see both that there are elements and why.

4

10 The next question that arises is whether they are finite or infinite in number, and if finite, how many. First then we must observe that they are not infinite, as some think, and we may begin with those who, like Anaxagoras, regard all uniform substances as elements. None of those who hold
15 this opinion have a proper conception of an element, for many composite bodies also can be seen to be divisible into uniform parts, *e.g.* flesh, bone, wood, stone. If, then, what is composite is not an element, an element is not any uniform body, but only, as we said before, one which cannot be ana-
20 lyzed into constituents differing in kind.

Moreover, even with their conception of an element, it was unnecessary to make them infinite in number, for should a finite number be assumed, it will give all the same results. The same result will be obtained if there are only two or three such bodies, as Empedocles tries to show. Even with an
25 infinite number, they do not succeed in forming everything out of uniform parts—they do not construct a face out of faces, nor any other finished products of nature similarly—so that it would clearly be much better to make the principles finite, and indeed as few as possible provided that all
30 the same effects can be demonstrated. Mathematicians are certainly of this opinion: they always take, as principles, data which are limited either in kind or in quantity.

Finally, if bodies are distinguished from one another by their proper differentiae, and bodily differentiae are finite in number (it is in their sensible qualities that they differ, and these are finite, though this is some-
303a thing which awaits demonstration), it is clear that the elements themselves must be finite.

There is another view, championed by Leucippus and Democritus of
5 Abdera, whose conclusions are no more acceptable to reason. According to this view the primary magnitudes are infinite in number and not divisible in magnitude. Generation is neither of many out of one, nor of one out of many, but consists entirely in the combination and entanglement of these bodies. In a way these thinkers too are saying that everything that exists is
10 numbers, or evolved from numbers; they may not show it clearly, but

nevertheless that is what they mean. Besides, if shape is the distinguishing feature of bodies, and there is an infinite number of shapes, they are asserting an infinite number of simple bodies. Yet they never went so far as to define or characterize the shape of each element, except to assign the sphere to fire. Air and water and the rest they distinguished by greatness and smallness, as if it were their nature to be a sort of "seed-mixture" of all the elements.

First of all, then, this school makes the same mistake of failing to grasp that the elements are finite in number, though they could have drawn all the same conclusions. Also, the limitation of bodily differentiae proves that the number of elements must be limited. Moreover by positing indivisible bodies they cannot help coming into conflict with mathematics, and undermining many accepted beliefs and facts of observation. These we have discussed already in the works on time and motion. At the same time they are even forced to contradict themselves, for if the elements are indivisible it is impossible for air and earth and water to be differentiated by greatness and smallness. If they are, they cannot be generated from one another, for the supply of large atoms will fail in the continual separating process by which, according to them, this mutual generation between water and air and earth takes place. Again, even their theory does not seem to demand an infinite number of elements. Bodies, they say, differ on account of differing shapes, but all shapes are constructed out of pyramids, rectilinear from rectilinear and the sphere from its eight parts. Shapes must have certain principles, and whether these are one or two or more, the simple bodies will be of the same number. Finally, every element has its proper motion, and the motion of a simple body is simple. But there is not an infinite number of simple motions, because the directions of movement are limited to two and the places also are limited. On this argument also there cannot be an infinite number of elements.

15

20

25

30

303b

5

5

Having established that the number of the elements must be limited, it remains for us to consider whether there are more than one. Some philosophers posit one alone, either water or air or fire or a substance rarer than water but denser than air, and this they say is infinite in extent and embraces all the worlds.

Now all those who posit as the single element water or air or the substance intermediate in density between the two, and generate everything else from this by a process of condensation and rarefaction, are unwittingly assuming the existence of a substance more fundamental than their element. Generation from the elements, they say, is a synthesis, and back into the elements an analysis. If so, then the substance with finer particles must be prior in nature. Since therefore they agree that fire is the finest of all

10

15

20

bodies, fire must be primary in the order of nature. Whether it is fire or not does not matter; in any case it must be one of the others that is primary and not the intermediate.

Secondly, to attribute generation to density or rarity is the same as
25   attributing it to coarseness and fineness, for fine is what they mean by rare, and coarse by dense. To attribute it to coarseness and fineness is, in its turn, to attribute it to greatness and smallness, for fine = composed of small parts, coarse = composed of large parts, seeing that fine means extended over a wide area, and that is the condition of a body composed of small parts. In fact, therefore, they are making greatness and smallness the dis-
30   tinguishing mark of bodies other than the primary. But on this criterion all the names which they give must be relative: it cannot be said simply of one thing that it is fire, of another water, and of another air, but the same body
304a will be fire relatively to this, and air relatively to something else. Those who posit a plurality of elements, but distinguish them by greatness and smallness, are in the same position. For since it is quantity that dis- tinguishes each one, their magnitudes must bear a certain ratio to one
5   another, and hence those which exhibit this ratio must be air, fire, earth and water with respect to each other, seeing that the same ratios may be found among the larger bodies as among the smaller.

As for those who make fire the element, they escape this difficulty, but
10   cannot avoid other absurd consequences. Some fit a shape to fire, e.g. those who make it a pyramid. Among them we find (a) the cruder argument that the pyramid is the sharpest of figures and fire the sharpest of bodies, and (b) the subtler reasoning put forward that all bodies are built up out of the
15   finest body, and solid figures out of pyramids, and that therefore, since fire is the finest of bodies, and the pyramid the finest and the primary among figures, the primary figure belongs to the primary body, therefore fire is pyramidal. Others leave aside the question of shape, and simply postulate
20   it as the finest body, from the agglomeration of which, as of filings blown together, the other bodies are generated.

Both views are open to the same objections. (a) If they make the first body indivisible, our former arguments recur to refute their hypothesis. In
25   any case, no one who wishes to look at the matter scientifically can speak as they do. For if all bodies are comparable in respect of size, and the magnitudes of uniform substances stand in the same ratio to one another as do their elements (for instance, as the magnitude of the whole mass of water is to that of the whole mass of air, so that of the element of water is
30   to that of the element of air, and so on), and if, further, air is more widely extended than water, and in general the finer body than the coarser, then clearly the element of water will be smaller than the element of air. If
304b therefore the smaller magnitude is contained in the greater, the element of air must be divisible. The same applies to the element of fire and of the finer bodies in general. (b) Suppose on the other hand they make it divis-

ible. Then those who assign a figure to fire will discover that a part of fire
is not fire, since a pyramid is not composed of pyramids; also that not   5
every body is either an element or composed of the elements, for a part of
fire will be neither fire nor any other element. Those on the other hand
who make size the differentia must admit that there is an element prior to
their element, and so on to infinity, once granted that every body is divisible and that the finest is the element. Moreover these too are in the   10
position of saying that the same body is fire in relation to this and air in
relation to that, and again water or earth.

The mistake common to all those who postulate a single element only is
that they allow for only one natural motion shared by everything. We
know that every natural body contains a principle of motion. If then all
bodies are one substance, they must all have the same motion, and they   15
will move the more swiftly with this motion, the more abundantly its
source is available, just as with fire, the more of it there is, the faster it
performs its proper motion upward. But in fact there are many things
which move faster *downward* the more there is of them. For this reason,
and taking into account our earlier decision that there are several natural   20
motions, it is clearly impossible that there should be one element only. The
elements, then, are neither infinite in number nor reducible to one, and
must therefore be (*a*) a plurality but (*b*) a limited number.

6

First however we must inquire whether they are eternal or come to be and
perish; for a demonstration of this will make clear their number and   25
character as well.

Eternal they cannot be, for both fire and water and indeed each of the
simple bodies are observed in process of dissolution. This process must
either be infinite or come to a stop. (*a*) If infinite, the time which it takes
will also be infinite, and also the time of the synthesis which follows; for
the dissolution and the synthesis of each part take place successively. Inev- 30
itably therefore there will be a second infinite time apart from the first, in
every case where the time of synthesis is infinite and the time of dissolution precedes it. Thus we have two infinites side by side, which is impos-   305a
sible. (*b*) If there is a term to the process of dissolution, the body left when
it stops must be either indissoluble or destined never to be dissolved; the
latter is what Empedocles seems to aim at describing. Our previous arguments forbid that it should be indissoluble: nor on the other hand can it be   5
capable of, but destined never to undergo, dissolution. A smaller body is
always more perishable than a larger: if therefore the larger body itself
submits to destruction by this process of being broken up into smaller
parts, it is likely that the smaller will submit to it even more readily. Now
fire may be observed to perish in two ways: it may be quenched, *i.e.*   10

destroyed by its opposite, or it may die out, destroyed by its own action. A smaller quantity is acted upon by a greater, and the smaller it is the quicker the effect. The elements of bodies, therefore, must be subject to destruction and generation.

15 Since they are generated, their generation must be either from the incorporeal or from the corporeal, and if from the corporeal, either from some extraneous body or from each other. The theory which generates them from the incorporeal involves a void separate from body; for everything which comes to be comes to be *in* something, and that in which its coming to be takes place must be either incorporeal or corporeal: if corporeal, 20 there will be two bodies in the same place at once, that which is in process of formation and that which was there before: if incorporeal, there must be a separate void. But the impossibility of this has been proved before. On the other hand there is no body from which the elements could be generated, for that would mean that some other body was prior to the elements. 25 If this body has weight or lightness, it will itself be one of the elements: if it has no impulse in any direction, it will be unmoved, *i.e.* a mathematical object. But in that case it will not occupy a place. If it rests in a place, it will be possible for it to move in that place, if by force, then unnaturally, or if not by force, then naturally. If then it occupies a place somewhere, it will 30 be one of the elements. If not, nothing can be generated from it, for that which comes to be and that from which it is generated must be together. Seeing therefore that the elements can neither be generated from the incorporeal nor from an extraneous body, it remains to suppose that they are generated from each other.

METEOROLOGICA

Translated by S. Marc Cohen

As its name implies, this work is devoted primarily to a study of meteorological phenomena, such as wind, rain, lightning, and thunder, along with certain astronomical phenomena, such as comets, that Aristotle mistakenly considers to be meteorological. Book IV discusses the way in which the four elements combine in composite bodies such as metals and tissues; in the final chapter, presented here, Aristotle brings out the role of function in the accounts of even the four elements.

Book IV

12

Now that we have made these distinctions, let us discuss in particular what *389b23* flesh is, and bone, and the rest of the uniform[1] parts. For it is through *25* understanding the generation of the uniform parts that we understand the elements of which they are naturally constituted, the genera under which they fall, and the particular genus of each one. Uniform parts are made up of the elements, and themselves serve as the matter for all the products of nature.

The aforementioned elements are the matter of which all these parts are composed, but their essence is in their form. That this is so is always clearer in the more developed products and in general in those things that *30* are like instruments and are *for* something. It is clearer, for example, that a corpse is a human being only homonymously. So, too, a hand of a dead person is called a hand only homonymously, in just the way that stone *390a* flutes might still be called flutes; for these also seem to be instruments of a kind. But that this is so is less clear in the case of flesh and bone, and less clear still in the case of fire and water. The reason is that being *for* some-

1. In Aristotle's terminology, flesh and bone are "uniform parts" (or "homoiomeries," *homoiomerē*, lit. "like-parted,") in the sense that flesh can be divided into parts that are themselves flesh. A face, on the other hand, is a non-uniform part, since no part of a face is itself a face.

5 thing is least clear where matter dominates. It's like this: if you take the extremes, matter is nothing other than matter, and essence nothing other than form, but each intermediate thing is proportional to the nearer extreme. Every one of these is *for* something, and is not water or fire or flesh
10 or viscera in every condition in which it may occur. This is even more so with a face or a hand. They are all defined by their function. The capacity to perform its function constitutes what each of them truly is. For example, an eye is an eye if it can see, but when it is incapable of doing this it is an eye only homonymously, like one that is dead or made of stone. Nor is a wooden saw really a saw any more than one in a picture. It is the same,
15 moreover, with flesh as well, but its function is less clear than that of the tongue. It is similar with fire, too, although its function is perhaps even less clear in nature than that of flesh. It is similar, too, with the parts of plants and with inanimate things, like bronze and silver. They are all what they are in virtue of some capacity to act or to be acted upon, just like flesh and
20 sinew. But their definitions cannot be given precisely, so that it is not easy to discern when they are present and when they are not unless their capacities are so thoroughly weakened that only their shapes remain. For example, the bodies of ancient corpses suddenly become ashes in their graves,
390b and extremely old fruit retains only its shape but not its perceptible qualities. So, too, with solids formed from milk.

Parts such as these—I mean such uniform parts as flesh, bone, hair, sinew, and the like—can be generated by heat and cold and the motions
5 they produce as the parts are solidified by the hot and the cold. They are all differentiated by the differentiae mentioned above—tension, attraction, pulverization, hardness, softness, and the rest—all of which are produced
10 by the hot and the cold and the combination of their motions. But no one would suppose this to be true of the non-uniform parts that are composed of these, like a head or a hand or a foot. In just the same way, although cold and heat and their motion cause the generation of bronze and silver, they do not cause the generation of a saw or a bowl or a box. In these cases the cause is a craft, while in the case of the non-uniform parts it is nature or some other cause.
15 Now that we understand which genus each of the uniform parts falls under, we must take on the question of what each of them is, for example, what blood is, or flesh or semen or any of the others. For we know what each thing is and why it is when we grasp either the matter or the form involved in its generation and destruction, but especially when we have
20 both, and also know what the source of its motion is. After the uniform parts have been clarified we must similarly study the non-uniform ones, and finally the compounds made up of the latter, such as humans, plants, and other such things.

PARTS OF ANIMALS[1]

*Explanations in biology, according to Aristotle, are fundamentally teleological in
character: Parts and systems are explained in terms of what they do and what
they are for. In this study of the physiology of animals, he provides a number of
such explanations. In the two chapters excerpted here, he defends both the study
of biology in general and the teleological approach in particular.*

Book I

1

In every sort of study and line of inquiry, more humble and more honor-   639a
able alike, there appear to be two sorts of competence. One of these is
rightly called scientific knowledge of the subject, and the other is a certain   5
type of education; for it is characteristic of an educated person to be able
to reach a judgment based on a sound estimate of when people expound
their conclusions in the right or wrong way. For this is in fact what we take
to be characteristic of a generally educated person, and this is the sort of
ability that we identify with being educated. We expect one and the same
individual with this general education to be able to judge in practically   10
all subjects; but if someone <is educated in some narrower area>, we
take him to have this ability <only> for some determinate area—for it is
possible for someone to have the ability of an educated person about a
restricted area.

Clearly, then, in inquiry into nature as elsewhere, there must be norms[2]
of this sort that we can refer to in deciding whether to accept the way in
which a conclusion is proved, apart from whether or not the conclusion   15
is true.

Should we, for instance, consider each single substance[3]—the nature of
man, for instance, or ox or any other <species>, taking them one at a
time—and determine what belongs to it in its own right? Or should we

1. The actual study of the parts of animals begins in Book ii. The chapters translated from Book i are a general discussion of the methods and value of biological
studies.

2. **norms**, *horoi* (lit. 'boundaries' or 'limits'). We usually render *horos* by 'formula'.

3. **substance**: This refers to the 'secondary SUBSTANCE' described in *Catg.* 2a14.

20   begin with the coincidents that belong to them all in so far as they have
some common property? For often the same properties—for instance, sleep,
breathing, growth, shrinkage, death, and all the other attributes and conditions of this sort—belong to many different kinds[4] of things.

For, as things are, the right way to discuss these questions is unclear and
indeterminate. Evidently, if we discuss them one species[5] at a time, we will
25   repeat ourselves on many topics. For in fact each of the properties mentioned actually belongs to horses, dogs, and men; and so, if we describe the
coincidents one species at a time, we will be compelled to describe the same
things many times over—in the case of each property that belongs to
specifically different animals but is not itself different in each species.
30   Presumably, though, there are also properties that have the same predicate
639b   but differ specifically in the different species. The mobility of animals, for
instance, is apparently not specifically one, since flying, swimming, walking, and creeping differ from one another.

Hence we should consider the right way to examine such questions:
5   Should we begin by studying a whole genus in common before going on to
study the special properties of the different species? Or should we study
the particular species one at a time? For, as things are, this has not been
determined.

Another question that has not been determined is this: Should the student of nature follow the procedure of the mathematician who proves
truths about astronomy? If he does, he will first study the appearances
10   about animals and about the parts of each type of animal, and then go on
to state the reason why and the causes. Or should he follow some other
procedure?

Further, we see that natural coming to be has more than one cause—for
instance, both the cause that is for something and the cause that is the
source of the principle of motion. We must, then, also determine which is
15   primary and which is secondary among these.

The primary cause is apparently the one that we say is for something.
For this is the form, and the form is the principle, both in the products of
craft and equally in naturally constituted things. For the doctor or the
builder begins by focussing, by thought or perception, on the definition of
health or a house, and goes on to supply the forms and the causes of each
20   thing he produces, explaining why it should be produced in this way. And,
moreover, what something is for—i.e. the fine result—is more fully present
in the products of nature than in the products of craft.

Further, what is of necessity is not present in the same way in everything
that is in accordance with nature. Practically all <students of nature>,

4. **kinds**: *genos*, usually rendered 'genus', but here applied to species.

5. **species**: We supply 'species' throughout this paragraph, since the next paragraph
implies that Aristotle has had species in mind.

however, try to refer their accounts back to what is of necessity, without having distinguished the different ways necessity is spoken of.

Unqualified necessity belongs to everlasting things, whereas conditional necessity belongs to everything that comes to be, just as it belongs to the products of crafts—to a house, for instance, and to anything else of that sort. In such cases it is necessary for the right sort of matter to be present if there is to be a house or some other end; first this must come to be and be moved, then this, and so on in order in the same way, until it reaches the end for which a thing comes to be and is.[6] And the same is true of what comes to be by nature.

The appropriate type of demonstration and necessity, however, is not the same in the study of nature as it is in the theoretical sciences; we have discussed this in another work. For in the latter case the principle we begin from is what something is, but in the former case it is what will be. For since F (for instance, health or a man) is of this sort, it is necessary for G to be or to come to be, whereas it is not true that since G is or has come to be, F is or will be of necessity. Nor can you combine the necessity of such demonstration for ever, so as to say that since one thing is, another thing is. In another work we have discussed both these questions, and also the sorts of things that are necessary, and in what cases necessities are reciprocal, and why.

We must also consider whether we should follow the procedure of our predecessors, by studying how a thing naturally comes to be rather than how it is. For it matters quite a bit which procedure we follow.

Now, it would seem that in the case of coming to be we should begin from how things are; for, just as we said before, we must begin with the appearances about a given kind of thing and then go on to state their causes. For in the case of building also, this comes about because the form of a house is of this sort, whereas it is not true that a house is of this sort because this is how it comes to be; for coming to be is for the sake of being,[7] but being is not for the sake of coming to be.

That is why Empedocles was wrong to say that many things belong to animals because they came about coincidentally in the course of the animals' coming to be. He says, for instance, that the backbone has vertebrae because of the coincidence that the fetus got twisted and the backbone was broken. He did not know, first, that the seed resulting in the animal must already have the right potentiality, and, secondly, that the producer is prior in time as well as in account—for a man generates a man, so that the character of the parent explains the way in which the offspring comes to be.

6. **In such cases . . . and is:** Cf. *Phys.* 200a5–15.

7. **being:** *ousia.* Aristotle uses this as the abstract noun corresponding to 'be' in contrast to 'become', *gignesthai.*

The same point applies to the <natural> things that seem to come to be by chance, as it also does in the case of things produced by craft. For some things—for instance, health—are the same when they come to be by chance
30   as when they come to be from craft. In those cases, then, where the producer comes first (in statue-making, for instance), the product does not come to be by chance. The craft is the account (without the matter) of the product; and the same is true for things resulting from luck, since how they come to be corresponds to the character of the craft.

35   Hence the best thing to say is that since being a man is this, this is why he has these parts, since it is impossible for him to be without these parts. If we cannot say this, we must come as close as we can, and say either that it
640b was quite impossible any other way or that it is done well this way. And these <means to the end> follow: since this is the character of the product, it is necessary for the coming to be to have this character and to happen in this way—that is why first this part comes to be, and then this part. And the same is true equally in the case of everything that is naturally con-
5   stituted.

The early philosophers, the first to study nature, investigated the material principle and cause, to see what it is and of what sort, how the whole universe comes to be from it, and what initiates the motion. <In their view>, strife, for instance, or love, or mind, or chance initiates the motion, and the matter that is the subject necessarily has a certain sort of nature;
10   fire, for instance, has a hot and light nature, earth a cold and heavy nature. This, indeed, is their account of how the world-order comes into being.

They give the same sort of account of how animals and plants come into being. On their account, for example, the flowing of water in the body results in the coming to be of the stomach and of every receptacle for food
15   and waste, and the flow of air results in the breaking open of the nostrils. Air and water are the matter of <living> bodies, since all <these philosophers> constitute nature from <elementary> bodies of this sort.

If, however, men and animals and their parts are natural, then we should
20   discuss flesh, bone, blood, and all the uniform parts, and equally all the non-uniform parts, for instance, face, hand, and foot; and we should ask what gives each of them its character, and what potentiality is involved.

For it is not enough to say what constituents each of these parts is made of—of fire or earth, for instance. If we were speaking of a bed or any other
25   <artifact>, we would try to distinguish its form rather than its matter (for instance, bronze or wood), or at any rate <the relevant matter> would be the matter of the compound. For a bed is this form in this matter, or this matter of this sort.[8] And so we ought to speak of the thing's figure and the sort of character it has as well <as of its matter>, since the nature corre-
30   sponding to the form is more important than the material nature.

If, then, an animal and its parts have their being by having their figure

8. **this form . . . sort**: Lit. 'this in this or this such'. Cf. *Met.* 1036b23–24, QUALITY.

and color, what Democritus says will turn out to be right, since this is what he seems to suppose. At any rate he says it is clear to everyone what the human form is, on the assumption that man is recognized by his <visible> figure and his color. <This is false>, however, <since> a dead man has the same <visible> shape and figure that the living man has, but still it is not a man. Further, it is impossible for something <with the right figure and color> to be a hand, if it is not in the right condition—if, for instance, it is a bronze or wooden hand; in that case it can be a hand only homonymously, just as the doctor <painted in a picture is a doctor only homonymously>. For it will lack the potentiality to perform the function of a hand, just as the painted doctor or stone flute lacks the potentiality to perform the function of a doctor or flute. Similarly, none of the parts of a dead man is any longer the relevant sort of part—an eye or a hand, for instance.

Hence Democritus' claim lacks the appropriate qualifications; it is no better than a carpenter claiming that a wooden hand is a hand. For such a claim is typical of the naturalists' account of the coming to be and the causes of something's figure. For suppose we ask, 'What potentialities produced this?'. Presumably the carpenter will mention an axe or an auger, whereas the naturalist will mention air and earth. The carpenter, however, gives the better answer.[9] For he will not suppose that it is enough to say that when his tool struck the wood, this part became hollow and this part plane. He will also mention the cause that explains why and for what end he struck this sort of blow—that is to say, in order to produce this or that sort of shape.

It is clear, then, that the natural philosophers are wrong, and that we must say that an animal has the <formal> character we have described. We must say, both about the animal itself and about each of its parts, what it is and what sort of thing it is, just as we also speak of the form of the bed.

Now, this form is either the soul or a part of the soul, or requires the soul. At any rate, when the soul has left, the animal no longer exists, and none of its parts remains the same, except in figure, like the things in stories that are turned to stone. If this is so, it is the task of the student of nature to discuss and to know about the soul—if not about all soul, then about the soul in so far as it makes the animal the sort of thing it is. He should know what the soul is, or what the relevant part of it is, and he should know about the coincidents that belong to it in so far as it has this sort of substance.

This is especially important because nature is, and is spoken of, in two ways, as matter and as substance. Now, substance is both the cause initiating motion and the end; and the soul, all or part of it, is both sorts of cause of the animal.[10] Hence, for this reason also, the student of nature should discuss the soul more than the matter, to the extent that the <animal's>

9. **better answer**: Cf. *Phys.* 199b34–200a7.

10. **the soul . . . cause of the animal**: On the soul as cause cf. *DA* ii 415b8–28.

matter is its nature because of the soul, rather than the other way round—
for the wood is a bed or a tripod because it is one potentially.

Reflection on what we have said might raise a puzzle about whether the
35   study of nature should consider all soul, or only some. If it considers all
soul, then there will be no branch of philosophy apart from the science of
641b   nature. For since understanding grasps the objects of understanding, the
study of nature will be knowledge of everything. For if two correlatives fall
under the same study, as perception and its object do, and if understanding
and its object are correlatives, then the same study will be concerned both
with understanding and with its object.

5   Perhaps, however, not all soul, and not every part of soul, is a principle
of motion. Rather, perhaps the principle of growth is the same part as in
plants, the principle of alteration is the perceiving part, and the principle of
local motion is some other part distinct from understanding, since local
motion is found in other animals as well as in men, but understanding is
not found in any of them. It is clear, then, that we should not discuss all
10   soul; for it is not all soul, but only one or more parts of it, that is nature.

Further, it is impossible for natural science to study any product of
abstraction, because nature produces everything for something. For it is
apparent that, just as craft is present in artifacts, so also in natural things
themselves there is another cause and principle of this sort, which we get,
15   as we get the hot and the cold, from the whole universe. Hence it is more
plausible to suppose that the heaven has come to be by such a cause (if
indeed it has come to be at all) and remains in being because of it, than to
suppose this about mortal animals. For what is ordered and determinate is
20   far more apparent in the heavens than in us, whereas variations from one
time to another and matters of chance are more apparent in mortal things.

Some other people, however, hold that whereas every animal comes to be
and remains in being by nature, the heaven was constituted as it is from
luck and chance. They say this even though nothing at all resulting from
luck and disorder is apparent in the heaven.[11]

25   Again, whenever some end is apparent towards which a motion pro-
gresses if nothing impedes, we say that the motion is for the end. Hence it
is evident that there is something of this sort, which we call nature. For not
just any old thing comes to be from a given type of seed, but this sort of
thing from this sort of seed; nor does any old body produce any old seed.
Hence the <body> that the seed comes from is the principle that produces
30   the seed that comes from it. For this happens naturally—at any rate, the
body grows naturally from the seed.

But prior still is what it is the seed of. For the seed is a case of becoming,
and the end is being. And what produces the seed is prior both to the seed
and to what comes from the seed. For it is a seed in two ways—as the seed

11. **They say . . . heaven:** Cf. *Phys.* 196a24–b5.

produced by something and as the seed of something.[12] For in fact it is the   *35*
seed of what produced it (for instance, a horse), and also the seed of what
comes to be from it (for instance, a mule), but it is not the seed of both in
the same way; it is the seed of each in the way just described. Moreover,
the seed is potentially <the organism>, and we know how potentiality is   *642a*
related to actuality.

There are, then, two causes—what something is for and what is of
necessity (since many things come to be because it is necessary <for them
to come to be>. And presumably a puzzle might arise about the sort of
necessity that is meant by those who speak of what is of necessity; for   *5*
neither of the two types defined in our treatises on philosophy[13] can apply
to this case.

There is a third type, however, in things that come to be. For we speak of
food as necessary in neither of these two ways, but because an organism
cannot exist without it. This, one might say, is conditional necessity. For   *10*
instance, since an axe is needed for splitting wood, it is necessary for it to
be hard; and in that case it is necessary for it to be made of iron.[14] In the
same way, the body is also an instrument, since each of its parts, and the
whole likewise, is for something; it is necessary, then, for it to be of this
sort and to be composed of things of this sort, if what it is for is to result.

It is clear, then, that there are two types of cause and that in what we say   *15*
we must either find both of them or, alternatively, try to make it clear, at
any rate, that we cannot find both.[15] It is also clear that people who do not
do this might be said to tell us nothing about nature; for nature is a
principle more than matter is.

Sometimes, indeed, Empedocles is led by the truth itself, and stumbles on
the right sort of cause, and is compelled to say that the form is a thing's   *20*
substance and nature. When, for instance, he expounds what bone is, he
does not say that it is one, two, three, or all of its elements, but that it is the
form of their mixture. It is clear, then, that flesh and every other part of
that sort have this character.

The reason our predecessors did not discover this character is that they   *25*
did not grasp the essence or the practice of defining substance. Democritus
was the first to make some contact with them, but that was all he did—and
not because he supposed it to be necessary for the study of nature, but
because the facts themselves carried him away <from his own views>. In
the time of Socrates, this <concern with essence and definition> grew, but
investigation into nature stopped, and philosophers turned away to study-   *30*
ing the virtue that is relevant to the conduct of life, and to political study.

---

12. **For it is . . . seed of something:** For these two ways cf. *Met.* 1072b30–1073a3.

13. **our treatises on philosophy:** It is not clear what work Aristotle refers to.

14. **since an axe . . . of iron:** Cf. *Phys.* 200a11–15.

15. **try to . . . both:** Read *dēlon ge peirasthai poiein, dēlon.*

Our proof should be on these lines—that respiration, for instance, is for this, but this comes about because of these things of necessity. Necessity sometimes signifies that if that end is to result, it is necessary for these
35   things to be; and sometimes that they are so by nature. <In the second case> it is necessary, for instance, for the hot to go out and to come back in
642b when it meets resistance, and for the air to flow in. This is all necessary; and when the hot that is inside resists as cooling goes on, the air outside enters or leaves.

This, then, is the procedure of our line of inquiry, and these are the sorts of things whose causes we must find.

5

644b22 Among the substances constituted by nature, some, we say, neither come to
25   be nor perish for all time, and others share in coming to be and perishing. It turns out that we have fewer ways of studying the first type of substances, honorable and divine though they are; for very few things indeed are apparent in perception to give us a basis for inquiry into what we would like to know about these things. We are better supplied, however,
30   with opportunities for knowledge about perishable plants and animals, since we live among them. For someone willing to undertake the appropriate labor can discover many of the facts about each kind of plant and animal.

Each of the two types of substance has some appeal. For even though we have little contact with the divine substances, still their honorable nature makes it pleasanter to know them than to know all the things around us—
35   just as a chance glimpse of some small part of someone we love is pleasan-
645a ter than an exact view of many other great things. On the other hand, since we can know better and know more about the substances around us, the knowledge of them has some superiority. Further, the fact that they are closer to us and more akin to our nature compensates to some degree for <the superior attraction of> philosophy about divine things.
5   We have finished our discussion of divine things,[16] saying what appears to us. The remaining task, then, is to speak of animal nature, whether more or less honorable, leaving nothing out, as far as we are able. For even though some of the animals we study are unattractive to perception, still
10   the nature that has produced them provides amazing pleasures for those who are capable of recognizing the causes and who are naturally philosophers. For in studying representations of them, we also delight in studying the painter's or sculptor's craft that has produced them; how absurd it would be, then, not to like studying those naturally constituted things
15   themselves, provided, of course, that we are able to notice the causes.

16. **divine things:** in *On the Heavens.*

That is why we must avoid childish complaints about examining the less
honorable animals; for in all natural things there is something admirable.   *20*
The story goes that when some strangers wanted to see Heraclitus, they
stopped on their way in, since they saw him warming himself at the oven;
but he kept urging them, 'Come in, and don't worry; for there are gods here
also.' In the same way, then, we must go forward without embarrassment
with our search into each type of animal, assuming that there is something
natural and fine in each of them.

For <processes> that are for something and are not a matter of luck are
most characteristic of the products of nature; and the end for which these   *25*
things are constituted or have come to be counts as something admirable.
And anyone who regards the study of other animals as dishonorable ought
to take the same view about himself; for one is bound to feel great distaste
at the constituents of the human species[17]—blood, flesh, bones, veins, and   *30*
parts of that sort.

Similarly, when someone is discussing some part or equipment, we
should not suppose that he is drawing attention <simply> to the matter, or
that he is concerned with it for its own sake; he is concerned with the form
as a whole. In the case of a house, for instance, <we are concerned with the
form>, not with the bricks, mud, and wood. So also, in studying nature we   *35*
are concerned with the composite structure and with the substance as a
whole, not with the things that are never found in separation from their
substance.

---

17. **species:** *genos,* usually translated 'genus'.

METAPHYSICS

Although everything in the Metaphysics *was written by Aristotle, it was probably not written as a single work but was put into its present form and probably
given its present title by a later editor (Andronicus of Rhodes, first century A.D.).
The meaning of the title is unclear. It may mean "Beyond natural things," indicating that this work goes beyond the study of nature. Or it may mean simply "After the* Physics," *referring to its place in the Aristotelian curriculum. Aristotle's
own term for its subject matter is "first philosophy." The* Metaphysics *is generally regarded to be the most difficult work in the Aristotelian corpus.*

*In the excerpts presented here, Aristotle discusses the history of the notion of
causes (Book I); the nature of the study of being* qua *being (Book IV); the question "What is substance?" and the ideas of matter, form, essence, and universals
(Books VII and VIII); and the unmoved mover (Book XII).*

BOOK I

1

980a21   All human beings by nature desire to know. A sign of this is our liking for
the senses; for even apart from their usefulness we like them for themselves
especially the sense of sight, since we choose seeing above practically all
the others, not only as an aid to action, but also when we have no intention
25   of acting. The reason is that sight, more than any of the other senses, gives
us knowledge of things and clarifies many differences between them.

Animals possess sense-perception by nature at birth. In some but not all
980b   of these, perception results in memory, making them more intelligent and
better at learning than those that cannot remember. Some animals that
cannot hear sounds (for instance, bees and similar kinds of animal) are
25   intelligent but do not learn; those that both perceive sounds and have
memory also learn.

Non-human animals live by appearances and memories but have little
share in experience, whereas human beings also live by craft[1] and reasoning. In human beings experience results from memory, since many memo-

1. **craft.** *Technē*, like *epistēmē*, applies both to the state of having knowledge and to
what someone in that state knows.

ries of the same thing result in the capacity for a single experience.[2] Experi-   *981a*
ence seems to be quite like science and craft, and indeed human beings
attain science and craft through experience; for, as Polus[3] correctly says,
experience has produced craft, but inexperience only luck.   *5*

A craft arises when many thoughts that arise from experience result in
one universal judgment about similar things. For the judgment that in this
illness this treatment benefited Callias, Socrates, and others, in many par-
ticular cases, is characteristic of experience, but the judgment that it bene-   *10*
fited everyone of a certain sort (marked out by a single kind) suffering
from a certain disease (for instance, phlegmatic or bilious people when
burning with fever) is characteristic of craft.

For practical purposes, experience seems no worse than craft; indeed we
even see that experienced people are actually more successful than those
who have a rational account but lack experience. The reason is that experi-   *15*
ence is cognition of particulars, whereas craft is cognition of universals.
Moreover, each action and event concerns a particular; in medical treatment, for instance, we do not heal man (except coincidentally) but Callias
or Socrates or some other individual who is coincidentally a man.[4] If, then,   *20*
someone has a rational account but lacks experience, and recognizes the
universal but not the particular falling under it, he will often give the
wrong treatment, since treatment is applied to the particular.

Nonetheless, we attribute knowing and comprehending to craft more   *25*
than to experience, and we judge that craftsmen are wiser than experienced
people, on the assumption that in every case knowledge, rather than experience, implies wisdom. This is because craftsmen know the cause, but
<merely> experienced people do not; for experienced people know the fact
that something is so but not the reason why it is so, whereas craftsmen
recognize the reason why, i.e. the cause.   *30*

That is why we believe that the master craftsmen in a given craft are
more honorable, know more, and are wiser than the manual craftsmen,   *981b*
because they know the causes of what is produced. The manual craftsmen,
we think, are like inanimate things that produce without knowing what
they produce, in the way that, for instance, fire burns; the latter produce
their products by a natural tendency, while the manual craftsmen produce
theirs because of habit. We assume, then, that some craftsmen are wiser   *5*
than others not because they are better in practice, but because they have a
rational account and recognize the causes.

And in general, a sign that distinguishes those who know from those

2. **experience:** See *APo* 100a3–6.

3. **Polus:** a rhetorical theorist of the mid–fifth century, a pupil of Gorgias. He is a
character in Plato's *Gorgias*.

4. **coincidentally a man:** i.e. coincidentally from the point of view of healing.
Aristotle does not mean that being a man is a COINCIDENTAL property of Socrates.

who do not is their ability to teach. Hence we think craft, rather than
experience, is knowledge, since craftsmen can teach, while merely experienced people cannot.

Further, we do not think any of the senses is wisdom, even though they
are the most authoritative ways of recognizing particulars. They do not tell
us why anything is so; for instance, they do not tell us why fire is hot, but
only that it is hot.

It is not surprising, then, that in the earliest times anyone who discovered any craft that went beyond the perceptions common to all was
admired not only because he discovered something useful, but also for
being a wise person, superior to others. Later on, as more crafts were
discovered—some related to necessities, others to <leisuretime> pursuits—
those who discovered these latter crafts were in every case judged to be
wiser than the others, because their sciences did not aim at practical utility.
Hence, finally, after all these crafts had been established, the sciences that
aim neither at pleasure nor at necessities were discovered, initially in the
places where people had leisure. This is why mathematical crafts arose first
in Egypt; for there the priestly class were allowed to be at leisure.

The difference between craft and science and other similar sorts of
things has been discussed in the Ethics.[5] The point of our present discussion is to show that in everyone's judgment any discipline deserving the
name of wisdom must describe the first causes, i.e. the principles. And so,
as we said earlier, the experienced person seems to be wiser than those who
have just any old perception; the craftsman seems to be wiser than those
with nothing more than experience; the master craftsman wiser than the
manual craftsman; and the purely theoretical sciences wiser than the productive sciences. It is clear, then, that wisdom is knowledge of certain sorts
of principles and causes.

2

Since this is the science we are looking for, we should consider what sorts
of causes and principles wisdom is the science of. Perhaps this will become
clearer if we consider our judgments about the wise person. First, we judge
that he has knowledge about all things as far as possible, without, however,
having it about each particular <kind of thing>. Next, the one who is
capable of knowing difficult things, i.e. things not easily known by human
beings, is the wise person; for sense-perception is common to everyone, and
that is why it is easy and not characteristic of wisdom. Further, someone is
wiser in a given science if he is more exact, and a better teacher of the
causes. Again, if one of two sciences is choiceworthy for itself—<purely>
for the sake of knowing it—and the other is choiceworthy <only> for the
sake of its results, the first has a better claim to be wisdom than the

5. *the Ethics*: See *EN* vi 2.

second. Moreover, the superior science has a better claim than the subordinate science; for the wise person must give orders, not take them, and those who are less wise must follow his orders, not he theirs. These, then, are our judgments about wisdom and wise people.

Of these features, we judge that knowledge about everything necessarily belongs to the one who has the best claim to universal science; for he in a way knows everything that is a subject for a science. These most universal things are also just about the most difficult for human beings to know, since they are furthest from perceptions.[6] Further, the most exact sciences are those that, more than the others, study the first things; for the sciences that are derived from fewer principles—for instance, arithmetic—are more exact than those—for instance, geometry—that require further principles. Moreover, the science that studies the causes is more of a teacher, since teachers are those who state something's causes. Besides, knowledge and science for their own sake are most characteristic of the science of the most appropriate object of knowledge. For one who chooses knowledge for its own sake will choose above all the science that is a science to the highest degree. This science is the science of the most appropriate objects of knowledge; these objects are the first things, i.e. the causes, since we know the subordinate things because of these and from these, not the other way round. Further, the most superior science—the one that is superior to any subordinate science—is the one that knows the end for which a given thing should be done; this end is something's good, and in general the end is what is best in every sort of nature.

From everything that has been said, then, we find that the name under discussion, <i.e., 'wisdom'>, applies to the same science; for we find that wisdom must study the first principles and causes, and the good, the end, is one of the causes.

The fact that this science is not productive is also clear from those who first engaged in philosophy. For human beings originally began philosophy, as they do now, because of wonder, at first because they wondered at the strange things in front of them, and later because, advancing little by little, they found greater things puzzling—what happens to the moon, the sun and the stars, how the universe comes to be. Someone who wonders and is puzzled thinks he is ignorant (this is why the myth-lover is also a philosopher in a way, since myth is composed of wonders); since, then, they engaged in philosophy to escape ignorance, they were evidently pursuing scientific knowledge <simply> for the sake of knowing, not for any further use.

What actually happened is evidence for this view. For it was only when practically everything required for necessities and for ease and <leisure-time> pursuits was supplied that they began to seek this sort of understanding; clearly, then, we do not seek it for some further use. Just as we

20

25

30

982b

5

10

15

20

25

6. **furthest from perceptions**: cf. *APo* 72a1–5.

describe a free person as one who exists for his own sake and not for someone else's, so we also describe this as the only free science, since it is the only one that exists for its own sake.

30   Hence the possession of this science might justifiably be thought to be beyond human capacity. For in many ways human nature is in slavery, so that, as Simonides says, 'the god alone would have this privilege', and it is unfitting for human beings to transgress their own level in their search for the science. If there actually is something in what the poets say, and the

983a   divine nature is spiteful, divine spite would be likely in this case, and all those who go too far would suffer misfortunes. The divine nature, however, cannot be spiteful: as the proverb says, 'Poets tell many lies'.

          Nor ought we to take any science to be more honorable than this one,
5   since the most divine science is also the most honorable, and this science that we are describing is the most divine. It alone is most divine in two ways: for the divine science <may be understood> as (i) the one that a god more than anyone else would be expected to have, or as (ii) the science of divine things. Only this science <of first causes> satisfies both conditions <for being divine>. For (i) the god seems to be among the causes of all things, and to be some sort of principle, and (ii) this is the sort of science
10   that the god, alone or more than anyone else, would be expected to have. Hence all the other sciences are more necessary than this one, but none is better.

          However, the possession of this science must in a way leave us in a condition contrary to the one we were in when we began our search. For, as we said, everyone begins from wonder that something is the way it is, as
15   they wonder at toys that move spontaneously, or the turnings of the sun, or the incommensurability of the diagonal (for people who have not yet studied the cause are filled with wonder that there is something that is not measured by the smallest length). But we must end up in the contrary and (according to the proverb) the better state, the one that people achieve by
20   learning <the cause> in these other cases as well—for nothing would be more amazing to a geometer than if the diagonal turned out to be commensurable.

          We have described, then, the nature of the science we are seeking, and the goal that our search and our whole line of inquiry must reach.

          3

          It is evident, then, that we must acquire knowledge of the original causes,
25   since we say we know a thing whenever we think we recognize its primary cause. Causes are spoken of in four ways. One of these, we say, is the being and essence; for the reason why is traced back ultimately to the account, and the primary reason why is the cause and principle. Another is the
30   matter and subject. A third is the source of the principle of motion. The

fourth is what something is for, i.e. the good—the opposite to the third cause, since it is the end of all coming to be and motion.

We have studied these causes adequately in our work on nature.[7] Still, let us also enlist those who previously took up the investigation of beings and pursued philosophical study about the truth; for it is clear that they also mention causes and principles of some sort. A discussion of their views, then, will advance our present line of inquiry; for either we shall find some other kind of cause or we shall be more convinced about those we have just mentioned.

Most of the first philosophers, then, thought that the only principles of all things were material. For, they say, there is some <subject> that all beings come from, the first thing they come to be from and the last thing they perish into, the substance remaining throughout but changing in respect of its attributes. This, they say, is the element and the principle of beings. And for this reason they think that nothing either comes to be or is destroyed, on the assumption that this nature <that is the subject> persists in every change, just as we say that Socrates does not come to be without qualification when he comes to be good or musical, and that he is not destroyed when he loses these states (because the subject, Socrates himself, remains)—so also they say that nothing else either comes to be or perishes without qualification (for there must be some nature, either one or more than one, that persists while everything else comes to be from it).

But they do not all agree about the number or type of this material principle. Thales, the originator of this sort of philosophy, says it is water (that is why he also declared that the earth rests on water). Presumably he reached this judgment from seeing that what nourishes all things is wet and that the hot itself comes from the wet and is kept alive by it (and what all things come to be from is their principle). He also reached this judgment because he thought that the seeds of all things have a wet nature (and water is the principle of the nature of wet things).

Some people think that even those who first gave accounts of the gods in very ancient times, long before the present, accepted this judgment about nature. For the ancients made Oceanus and Tethys the parents of coming to be and described the oath of the gods as water, which they called Styx; for what is oldest is most honored, and what is most honored is the oath. It is perhaps unclear whether this belief about nature is in fact old or even ancient, but at any rate this is what Thales is said to have declared about the first cause. (No one would think of including Hippon among these philosophers, given the triviality of his thought.)

Anaximenes and Diogenes take air to be both prior to water and also the primary principle of all the simple bodies, while Hippasus of Metapontium and Heraclitus of Ephesus say this about fire. Empedocles takes the four

983b

5

10

15

20

25

30

984a

5

---

7. **on nature:** See *Phys.* ii 3.

bodies to be principles, adding earth as a fourth to the ones mentioned.
These, he says, always remain, and do not come to be, except in so far as
they come to be more or fewer, being combined into one and dispersed
from one into many.

Anaxagoras of Clazomenae, who was older than Empedocles but wrote
later, says that the principles are unlimited; for he says that practically all
the uniform things[8] (for instance, water or fire) come to be and are destroyed only in the ways we have mentioned, by being combined and
dispersed; they do not come to be or get destroyed in any other way, but
always remain.

If one went by these views, one might judge that the material cause is the
only sort of cause. But as people thus advanced, reality itself showed them
the way and compelled them to search. For however true it might be that all
coming to be and perishing is from one (or more than one) thing, still, why
does this happen, and what is the cause? For certainly the subject does not
produce change in itself. I mean, for instance, neither the wood nor the
bronze causes itself to change, nor does the wood itself produce a bed, or
the bronze a statue, but something else causes the change. And to search for
this is (in our view) to search for the second principle—the source of the
principle of motion.

Those who were the very first to undertake this line of inquiry into
nature, who said that the subject is one, were quite satisfied with this. But
at least some of those who said that the subject is one, as though defeated
by this search <for an explanation of change>, said that the one, i.e. nature
as a whole, is immobile, not only as regards coming to be and perishing
(that was an old belief agreed on by all), but also as regards every other
sort of change. This view is distinctive of them.

Of those who said that the universe is one element, none managed to
notice this <second> cause, unless Parmenides did; he noticed it only in so
far as he posited not only one cause, but also in a way two causes. Indeed
those who recognize more than one element—for instance, hot and cold, or
fire and earth—make it easier to state <the cause that initiates motion>,
since they regard fire as having a nature that initiates motion, and water,
earth, and other such things as having natures contrary to this.

After these sorts of principles were proposed by these people, other
people found them inadequate to generate the nature of beings; once again,
as we said, it was as though the truth itself compelled them, and so they
began to search for the next sort of principle. For presumably it is unlikely
that fire or earth or anything else of that sort would cause some things to
be in a good and fine state and would cause other things to come to be in
that state, and unlikely that people would think so; still, it was unsatisfac-

8. **uniform things**: lit. 'things with parts similar to the wholes', *homoiomere*.

tory to entrust so great a result to chance and luck. And so when one of
them said that mind is present (in nature just as in animals) as the cause of
the world order and of all its arrangement, he seemed like a sober person,
and his predecessors seemed like babblers in comparison. We know that
Anaxagoras evidently made a start on giving such accounts, but an earlier
statement of them is ascribed to Hermotimus of Clazomenae. Those who
held this view posited a principle of beings that is at once both the cause of
things' turning out well and the sort of cause that is the source of motion
for beings.

4

One might suspect that the first to search for this sort of cause was Hesiod
and anyone else who counted desire or appetite among beings as a principle, as Parmenides, for instance, also did. For he too, in describing the
coming to be of the whole universe, says: 'Desire was the first of all the
gods she devised'. And Hesiod says: 'Before everything else that came to
be, there was chaos, and then the broad-fronted earth, and desire, preemi-
nent among all the immortals.'[9] He assumes that there must be some cause
among beings to initiate motion in things and to bring them together. Let us
leave it till later to determine which of these people was the first <to
discover this sort of cause>.

Moreover, the contraries of good things (i.e. disorder and ugliness no
less than order and beauty) were also apparent in nature, and bad things
were apparently more numerous than good things, and base things more
numerous than beautiful things. For this reason someone else introduced
love and strife so that each of them would be the cause of one of these two
sorts of things. For if we follow Empedocles' argument, and do not confine
ourselves to his mumbling way of expressing it, but attend to what he has
in mind, we will find that love is the cause of good things, and strife of
bad. And so, if one were to claim that in a way Empedocles said—indeed
was the first to say—that the good and the bad are principles, one would
perhaps be right, if the cause of all goods is the good itself.

These people, then, as we say, evidently made this much progress in
fastening on two of the four causes that we distinguished in our work on
nature—the matter and the principle of motion. But they did so dimly and
not at all perspicuously. They were like unskilled boxers in fights, who, in
the course of moving around, often land good punches, but are not guided
by knowledge; in the same way these thinkers would seem not to know
what they are saying, since they evidently make practically no use of these
causes, except to a slight degree.

9. 'Before . . . immortals': An inaccurate quotation (probably, like many of Aristotle's quotations, from memory) of Hesiod, *Theogony* 116–20.

Anaxagoras, for instance, uses mind[10] as an ad hoc device[11] for the production of the universe; it is when he is puzzled about the cause of something's being necessarily as it is that he drags in mind, but in other cases he
recognizes anything but mind as the cause of things that come to be.
Empedocles, admittedly, uses these causes more than Anaxagoras does, but
he too still makes insufficient use of them, and he does not succeed in
using them consistently. At any rate, he often makes love draw things apart,
and strife draw them together. For whenever strife scatters the universe into
its elements, all the fire is gathered into one, and so is each of the other
elements; and whenever love brings things back together again into one,
the parts from each element are necessarily scattered again.

Empedocles, then, went beyond his predecessors. He was the first to
distinguish this cause and to introduce it; he did not take the principle of
motion to be one, but assumed different and contrary principles. Moreover,
he was the first to say that there are four material elements. In fact, though,
he does not use all four, but treats them as two, treating fire in its own right
as one nature, and its opposites—earth, air, and water—as together con-
stituting another; this may be gathered from studying his poems. As we
say, then, this is how many principles he recognized, and this is what he
said about them.

Leucippus and his colleague Democritus, on the other hand, say that the
elements are the full and the empty, and that, of these, the full and solid is
what is, and the empty is what is not. That is why they also say that what is
is no more of a being than what is not, because body is no more of a being
than the empty is. They take these to be the material causes of beings.

Those who take the substance that is the subject to be one explain how
everything else comes to be by referring to the ways in which the subject is
affected, taking the rare and the dense to be the principle of the ways it is
affected. In the same way, Leucippus and Democritus take the differentiae[12]
to be the causes of the other things. They say, however, that there are three
of these differentiae—shape, order, and position. For they say that what is
is differentiated only by rhythm, touching, and turning.[13] Of these rhythm
is shape, touching is order, and turning is position; for A differs from N in

10. **mind**: *nous*.

11. **ad hoc device**: Literally 'machine'. Aristotle probably alludes to the theatrical
device of the 'god from the machine' (*deus ex machina*), brought out on a crane
above the stage at the end of the play to provide an artificially tidy ending. Cf. *Poet.*
1454a39–b3.

12. **differentiae**: i.e. of the atoms, the solid bodies referred to in general terms as
'the full'.

13. **rhythm, touching, and turning**: These are the Atomists' own terms, which
Aristotle explains; the illustration using letters (*stoicheia*, also translated 'elements';
cf. 1041b15) is probably theirs too.

shape, AN from NA in order, and Z from N in position. Like the other   *20*
people, however, they were too lazy to take up the question about motion
and to ask from what source and in what way it arises in beings.

This, then, would seem to be the extent, as we say, of the earlier thinkers'
search for these two causes.

6

Plato's work came after the philosophical views we have mentioned;[14] it   *987a29*
agreed with them in most ways, but it also had distinctive features setting it   *30*
apart from the philosophy of the Italians. For in his youth Plato first
became familiar with Cratylus and with the Heraclitean beliefs that all
perceptible things are always flowing and that there is no knowledge of
them; he held these views later too. Socrates, on the other hand, was   *987b*
concerned with ethics and not at all with nature as a whole; he was seeking
the universal in ethics and was the first to turn his thought to definitions.
Plato agreed with Socrates, but because of his Heraclitean views he took   *5*
these definitions to apply not to perceptible things but to other things; for,
he thought, the common formula could not be of any of the perceptible
things, since they are always changing. Beings of this sort <that definitions
are of>, then, he called Ideas, and he said that perceptible things are apart
from these, and are all called after them, since the things with the same
names as the Forms are what they are[15] by participation in them.   *10*

In speaking of 'participation' he changed only the name; for the
Pythagoreans say that things are what they are by imitating numbers, and
Plato (changing the name) said they are what they are by participating <in
Forms>. But they left it to others to investigate what it is to participate in or
to imitate Forms.

Further, he says that, apart from perceptible things and Forms, there are   *15*
also mathematical objects in between. These differ from perceptible things
in being everlasting and immobile; they differ from Forms in that there are
many of the same kind, whereas there is only one Form for each kind of
thing.[16]

Since the Forms are the causes of other things, he thought that their
elements are the elements of all beings. The great and the small, then, as   *20*
matter, and the one, as substance, are principles; for Forms come from
these, by participating in the one. And yet he said, agreeing with the
Pythagoreans, that the one is substance, and that it is not said to be one by

14. **views we have mentioned**: Aristotle has been discussing the Eleatics and
Pythagoreans, whom he calls the 'Italians'.

15. **are what they are**: Lit. just 'are', and hence perhaps 'exist' (and also in the rest
of the paragraph).

16. **there is only one Form for each kind of thing**: Lit. 'each Form itself is only one'.

being something else. He also agreed with them in saying that numbers are
25 the causes of the being of other things; but in positing a duality instead of
treating the indeterminate as one, and in taking the great and small to
constitute the indeterminate, he held a distinctive view of his own. Moreover, in his view numbers exist apart from perceptible things; whereas the
Pythagoreans take the objects themselves to be numbers, and do not place
mathematical objects between perceptible things and Forms.

30   His claim that the one and numbers exist apart from the other objects (in
contrast to the Pythagorean view) and his introduction of the Forms were
the result of his investigation of arguments; for none of his predecessors
engaged in dialectic. He made the other nature <besides the One> a duality because he thought that numbers (except the primes) could be neatly
988a produced from the duality, as though from something malleable.

What actually happens, though, is the contrary of this, and it is implaus-
ible to think it would happen in the way they <the Platonists> say. For in
their view many things are made out of the matter, but the Form generates
only once; in fact, however, only one table is apparently made out of one
<bit of> matter, whereas the agent who applies the form, though he is one,
5   makes many tables. Similarly, in the case of male and female, the female is
impregnated from one copulation, whereas the male impregnates many
females. And yet these things are imitations of those principles <that they
believe in>.

This, then, was what Plato determined about the questions we are investigating. It is evident from what has been said that he used only two causes,
10   the cause involving the what-it-is and the material cause; for the Forms are
causes of the what-it-is of other things, and the one is the cause of the
what-it-is of Forms. The nature of the matter that is the subject for the
Forms (in the case of perceptible things) and for the one (in the case of
Forms) is also evident: it is the duality, the great and the small. Further, he
15   has assigned the cause of good and bad to the elements, one to each, as we
say some earlier philosophers, such as Empedocles and Anaxagoras, also
sought to do.

9

990a34   . . . As for those who posited Ideas, the first objection is that in seeking to
990b   grasp the causes of the beings in this world, they introduced different
things, equal in number to them. It is as though someone wanted to count
things and thought he could not do it if there were fewer of them, but
5   could do it if he added more. For the Forms they resorted to in their search
for the causes of things in this world are practically equal in number to—or
at any rate are no fewer than—the things in this world. For take each <kind
of> thing that has a one over many, both substances and non-substances,
both things in this world and everlasting things; in each case there is some
<one over many> that has the same name <as the many>.

Further, none of the proofs we[17] offer to show that there are Forms
appears to succeed; for some of them are invalid, while some also yield   *10*
Forms of things that we think have no Forms. For the arguments from the
sciences yield Forms of all the things of which there are sciences; the one
over many yields Forms even of negations; and the argument from thinking about something that has perished yields Forms of things that perish,   *15*
since there is an appearance[18] of these. Further, among the more accurate
arguments, some produce Ideas of relatives, whereas we deny that these
are a kind of things that are in their own right; others introduce the
Third Man.

And in general the arguments for Forms undermine the existence of
things that matter more to us than the existence of the Ideas does. For they
imply that number, not duality, is first and that what is relative is prior to   *20*
what is in its own right, and they lead to all the other <unacceptable>
conclusions that some people have been led to believe by following the beliefs
about the Ideas, even though these beliefs conflict with their own principles.

Further, the reasoning that leads us to say that there are Ideas also yields
Forms of many other things as well as of substances. For a thought is one   *25*
not only in the case of substances but also in other cases; there are sciences
of other things as well as of substance; and thousands of other such
difficulties arise.

On the other hand, it is necessary, and follows from the beliefs about
Forms, that if things can participate in Forms, only substances can have
Ideas; for a thing does not participate in a Form coincidentally, but insofar   *30*
as it is not said of a subject. (If, for instance, something participates in the
Double itself, it also participates in the Everlasting, but coincidentally, since
it is coincidental that the Double is everlasting.) Hence the Forms will be
substances. But the same things signify substances among the Forms as in   *991a*
this world—otherwise what will the claim that there is something apart
from these things, the one over many, amount to? And if the Idea and the
things participating in it have the same form, they will have something in
common—for why should <what it is to be> two be one and the same thing
in all the perishable twos and in all the many everlasting twos, but not one   *5*
and the same thing in the Two itself and in some particular two? But if
they do not have the same form, they will be <merely> homonymous; it
will be like calling both Callias and a wooden <statue> a man, when one
has observed no common <nature> that they share.

One might be especially puzzled about what on earth Forms contribute
to perceptible things, either to those that are everlasting or to those that   *10*
come to be and perish; for they cause neither motion nor any change in

---

17. **we**: Aristotle thinks of himself as one of the Platonic school—though he does
not endorse their position. In the rest of this chapter 'we' and 'our' also refer to the
Platonists, not to Aristotle's independent views.

18. **appearance**: *phantasma*, usually rendered 'object of appearance'.

them. Nor do they contribute to knowledge of other things, since they are
not their substance—if they were, they would be in the other things. Nor
do they contribute to the being of other things, since Forms are not present
15   in the things that participate in them. For if they were present, they might
perhaps be thought to be causes, as white is if it is mixed in a white object.
This argument was first stated by Anaxagoras and then by Eudoxus and
certain others. It is easily upset, since it is easy to collect many impossible
consequences that challenge such a belief.

20   Nor can the other things be from Forms in any of the ways things are
normally said to be from something. And to say that Forms are patterns
and that other things participate in them is empty talk, mere poetic meta-
phors. For what is it that looks to the Ideas when it produces things? And it
is possible for one thing to be, or to come to be, like another without being
25   copied from it, so that whether or not Socrates exists someone like Socrates
might come to be; and clearly the same would be true even if Socrates were
everlasting. Further, there will be many patterns of the same thing, hence
many Forms; the Forms of man, for instance, will be Animal and Biped as
30   well as Man-itself. Further, the Forms will be patterns not only of perceptible things, but also of themselves—the genus, for instance, of its species—
991b so that the same thing will be both pattern and copy.

Further, it would seem impossible for a substance to be separate from
what it is the substance of. How, then, if the Ideas are the substances of
things, could they be separate from them?

According to the *Phaedo*,[19] the Forms are the causes both of being and of
5   coming to be. But what participates in the Forms does not come to be, even
if the Forms exist, unless something initiates the motion. And in addition to
these <natural things>, many things—for instance, a house or a ring—
which in our view have no Forms, come to be. Hence it is clearly also
possible for the <natural> things to be and to come to be because of causes
of the sort just mentioned.

10   Further, if the Forms are numbers, how can they be causes? Is it because
beings are other numbers, so that one number, for instance, is man, another
is Socrates, and another is Callias? If so, why are one lot of numbers
causes of the other lot? It makes no difference if the Forms are everlasting
and the other things are not. But if it is because things in this world—for
instance, a harmony—are ratios of numbers, it is clear that the things of
which they are ratios are some one <kind of> thing. But if there is this one
15   thing, i.e. the matter, then evidently the numbers themselves will also be
ratios of one thing to another. If, for instance, Callias is a numerical ratio
of fire, earth, water, and air, then his Idea will also be the number of
certain other subjects. And Man-itself, even if it is in some way numerical,
20   will nonetheless be a numerical ratio of certain things, not <properly> a
number. This argument, then, does not show that any Idea is a number.

19. *Phaedo*: See Plato, *Phaedo* 100a–105c.

. . . In general, it is impossible to find the elements of beings without   *992b18*
distinguishing the ways they are spoken of, since in fact beings are spoken
of in many ways. It is especially impossible to find them if we search in   *20*
this way for the sorts of elements that compose beings. For what elements
compose acting or being affected or the straight? Presumably these cannot
be found; at most the elements of substances can be found. Hence it is incorrect either to seek the elements of all beings or to think one has found them.

And how could one even learn the elements of all things? For clearly one   *25*
cannot begin with previous cognition. If, for instance, we are learning
geometry, we may have previous knowledge of other things <outside geom-
etry>, but we have no previous cognition about the subject matter of the
science we are to learn about; the same is true in other cases. Hence if there
is some science of all things, such as some say there is, we could not have   *30*
previous cognition of anything before we learn this science. And yet all
learning, either through demonstration or through definitions, relies on
previous cognition of either all or some things; for one must previously
know the elements of the definition, and they must be well known; the
same is true for learning through induction. Then is this science actually   *993a*
innate? If so, it is remarkable that we manage not to notice that we possess
the supreme science.

Further, how is one to acquire recognition of the elements, and how is
this knowledge to be made clear? For there is a puzzle here too, since our
answers might be disputed, as in the case of certain syllables; for some say   *5*
that ZA is from S, D, and A, while others say it is a different sound, and
none of the well-known ones.

Further, how could one recognize perceptible things without perception?
And yet one would have to, if the elements composing all things are indeed
the same, as complex sounds are <composed of> their proper elements.   *10*

Book IV

1

There is a science that studies being insofar as it is being,[20] and also the   *1003a21*
properties of being in its own right. It is not the same as any of the so-
called special sciences. For none of them considers being quite generally, in
so far as it is being; rather, each of them cuts off some part of being and   *25*
studies the relevant coincident of that part, as, for instance, the mathematical sciences do.

20. **insofar as**: or 'qua', *hē(i)*. For this way of focussing on a special set of properties of a given object see INSOFAR AS. Aristotle is not referring to some special kind
of being (as though something had the properties of being qua being, but not the
properties of any specific sort of being). He is thinking of ordinary beings studied
with reference to the properties that belong to them as beings. For this explanation
see 1004b10–17.

Since we are seeking the principles, i.e. the highest causes, clearly they must be the causes of the nature of some subject as it is in its own right. If, then, those who were seeking the elements of beings were also seeking these highest principles, the elements must also be the elements of being not coincidentally, but in so far as it is being. That is why we also ought to find the first causes of being in so far as it is being.

2

Being is spoken of in many ways, but always with reference to one thing—i.e. to some one nature—and not homonymously.[21] Everything healthy, for instance, is spoken of with reference to health—one thing because it preserves health, another because it produces health, another because it indicates health, another because it can receive health. Similarly, the medical is spoken of with reference to medical science; for one thing is called medical because it has the medical science, another because it is naturally suited to medical science, another because it is the function of medical science, and we shall find other things spoken of in ways similar to these.

Similarly, then, being is spoken of in many ways, but in all cases it is spoken of with reference to one principle. For some things are called beings because they are substances, others because they are attributes of substance, others because they are a road to substance, or because they are perishings or privations or qualities of substance, or productive or generative of substance or of things spoken of with reference to it, or because they are negations of one of these or of substance. This is why we also say that not being is—i.e. is not being.

A single science studies all healthy things, and the same applies in the other cases. For it is not only things that are spoken of in accordance with one <common property> that are studied by a single science; the same is true of things that are spoken of with reference to one nature, since these things are also, in a way, spoken of in accordance with one <common property>. Clearly, then, it is also the task of a single science to study beings in so far as they are beings.

In every case the dominant concern of a science is with its primary object, the one on which the others depend and because of which they are spoken of as they are. If, then, this primary object is substance, the philosopher must grasp the principles and causes of substances.[22]

There are as many parts of philosophy as there are <types of> sub-

---

21. **not homonymously:** This is a bit surprising, since the relation between beings that Aristotle describes here seems to fit his usual conditions for HOMONYMY. Probably then he means by 'not homonymously' what he elsewhere conveys by 'not *merely* homonymously'.

22. The following paragraph consists of 1004a2–9 transposed to an apparently more suitable place.

(marginal line numbers: 30, 35, 1003b, 5, 10, 15, 1004a2)

stances, and so there must be a first philosophy, and a second philosophy following it; for being is divided immediately into genera, which is why the sciences will also conform to these. For the philosopher is spoken of in the same way as the mathematician is; for mathematical science also has parts, and in mathematics there is a first and a second science and others succeeding in order.

For every single genus there is a single <sort of> perception and a single science; there is, for instance, a single grammatical science, and it studies all the <types of> sounds. Hence it is also the task of a science that is one in genus to study all the species of being in so far as it is being; it is the task of the species of that science to study the species <of being>.

Being and unity are the same and a single nature, since they imply each other, as principle and cause do, though they are not one and the same in the sense of being revealed by the same account (though indeed it does not matter if we take them to have the same account; that would be even more suitable for our purpose). For one man is the same as a man,[23] and moreover a man who is is the same as a man, and 'he is a man and a man who is'[24] reveals nothing different by the repetition in what is said, since clearly a man and a man who is are separated neither in coming to be nor in perishing. The same also applies to unity. It is evident, then, that in these cases the addition <of 'one'> reveals the same thing <as 'is' reveals>, and that unity is nothing different from being. Moreover, the substance of a thing is non-coincidentally one thing; and similarly it is essentially[25] some being.

It follows that there are as many species of being as of unity. Hence it is a task for a science that is the same in genus to study the what-it-is about these species—for instance, about same, similar and other such things. Practically all the contraries are referred to this principle; our study of these in the Selection of Contraries[26] will suffice.

It is the task of one science to study opposites, and plurality is the opposite of unity. It is also the task of one science to study negation and privation, since in both cases we study the one thing of which it is the negation or the privation. For either we say without qualification that something does not belong to the subject, or we say that it does not belong to some genus of the subject. In the latter case a differentia is added besides what is in the negation—for the negation is the absence of that property, but the privation also involves some nature that is the subject of which the privation is said.

And so it is also the task of the science we have mentioned to know

5

1003b19
20

25

30

35

1004a
10

15

23. **as a man**: Read *heis anthrōpos <kai anthrōpos>*.

24. **'he is a man and a man who is'**: Read *estin anthrōpos kai estin ōn anthrōpos*.

25. **essentially**: *hoper*. See ESSENCE #2(d).

26. **Selection of Contraries**: Perhaps this is a separate treatise, now lost.

about the contraries of the things we have mentioned—different, unlike, unequal, and everything else that is spoken of either with respect to these

20 or with respect to plurality and unity. Contrariety is also one of these; for it is a type of difference, and difference is a type of otherness. And so, since unity is spoken of in many ways, these will also be spoken of in many ways; but still it is the task of a single science to know them all. For the mere fact that things are spoken of in many ways does not imply that they cannot be studied by one and the same science; different sciences are required only if it is true both that the things have no one <common

25 property> and that their accounts are not referred to one thing.

Since in each case everything is referred to the primary thing (for instance, everything that is called one is referred to the primary unity), this is also what we ought to say about same, different, and contraries. And so we should first distinguish how many ways each thing is spoken of, and then show how each of the things we have distinguished is spoken of with

30 reference to the primary thing in each predication; for some things will be spoken of as they are because they have that primary thing, others because they produce it, others in other such ways.

Evidently, then, it is the task of a single science to take account both of these things and of substance (this was one of the questions that raised

1004b puzzles), and it is the philosopher's task to be able to study all <these> things. For if this is not his task, who will consider whether Socrates is the same as seated Socrates, or whether one thing has <just> one contrary, or what contrariety is, or how many ways it is spoken of? And the same is true for other questions of that sort.

5 We have found, then, that these are attributes of unity in so far as it is unity, and of being in so far as it is being; each is an attribute of unity and being in their own right, not in so far as they are numbers or lines or fire. Hence it is clearly the task of that science <of being> to know both what being and unity are, and also their coincidents. The mistake of those who currently consider these questions is not that they fail to practice philosophy but that, although substance is prior, they comprehend nothing about it.

10 There are attributes distinctive of number in so far as it is number (for instance, oddness and evenness, commensurability and inequality, being more and being less), and these belong to numbers both in their own right and in relation to one another. Likewise there are other attributes distinctive of the solid, both moved and unmoved, and <of the moved>, both

15 weightless and having weight. In the same way, then, there are also some attributes distinctive of being in so far as it is being, and it is the philosopher's task to investigate the truth about these.

Here is a sign <to show that it is his task>. Dialecticians and sophists assume the same guise as the philosopher. For sophistic has the appearance

20 of wisdom, though nothing more, and dialecticians practice dialectic about

all things; being is common to all things, and clearly they practice dialectic about all things because all things are proper to philosophy. For sophistic and dialectic treat the same genus as philosophy, but philosophy differs from dialectic in the type of power it has, and it differs from sophistic in its decision about how to live. Dialectic tests in the area where philosophy achieves knowledge, while sophistic has the appearance <of knowledge>, but not the reality.

Further, one column of contraries[27] is privation, and all contraries are referred to being and not being, and to unity and plurality—for instance, stability belongs to unity, motion to plurality. And practically everyone agrees that beings and substance are composed of contraries. At any rate, they all say that the principles are contrary; for some say that they are the odd and even, some that they are the hot and cold, some that they are the determinate and indeterminate, others that they are love and strife. All the other contraries are also evidently referred to unity and plurality (let us assume this referral), and the principles recognized by others fall completely under unity and plurality as their genera.

This also makes it evident, then, that it is the task of a single science to study being in so far as it is being; for all things are either contraries or composed of contraries, and unity and plurality are principles of the contraries. Unity and plurality belong to one science, whether or not they are spoken of as having one <common property> (and presumably in fact they are not). Even if unity is indeed spoken of in many ways, still the non-primary unities will be spoken of with reference to the primary unity; the same applies to the contraries. This is true even if being or unity is neither universal and the same over them all nor separable; and presumably it is neither of these, but rather some <beings and unities> are spoken of with reference to one thing, and others in succession. That is why it is not the geometer's task to study what a contrary is or what completeness is, or to study unity, or being, or same, or different, but only to study them on the basis of an assumption.

Clearly, then, it is the task of a single science to study both being in so far as it is being and also the things that belong to it in so far as it is being. And clearly the same science studies not only substances but also their attributes—both those we have mentioned and also prior and posterior, genus and species, whole and part, and the other things of this sort.

3

We ought to say whether it is the task of one and the same science or of different sciences to study both the axioms (as they are called in mathematics) and substance. Evidently it is also the task of one and the same

25

30

1005a

5

10

15

20

27. **column of contraries:** Cf. *GC* 319a15n.

science—the philosopher's—to examine these, since these belong to all beings and are not distinctive of one genus in separation from the others.

Every scientist uses the axioms because they belong to being insofar as it is being, and each genus is a being. But each uses them to the extent he needs them, and that is however far the genus about which he presents his demonstrations extends. Clearly, then, the axioms belong to all things in so far as they are beings (for this is what all things have in common); and so it is also the task of the one who knows being in so far as it is being to study the axioms.

This is why none of those who investigate a special area—for instance, a geometer or an arithmetician—undertakes to say anything about whether or not the axioms are true. The ones who did so were some of the students of nature; and it is not surprising that they did this, since they were the only ones who thought they were examining the whole of nature and examining being. In fact, however, there is someone still higher than the student of nature, since nature is only one kind of being; and so investigating these axioms will also be a task of this universal scientist, the one who studies primary substance. The study of nature is also a type of wisdom, but not the primary type.

Now, some of those who argue about when a conclusion should properly be accepted as true object that one should not accept <principles that have not been demonstrated>. They do this because they lack education in analytics;[28] for someone who comes <to the science of being> must already know about analytics and not ask about it when he studies <the science of being>.

Clearly, then, study of the principles of deductions is also a task for the philosopher—i.e. for the one who studies the nature of all substance. Whoever has the best claim to knowledge of a given genus ought to be able to state the firmest principles of his subject matter; hence whoever has the best claim to knowledge of beings in so far as they are beings should be able to state the firmest principles of all things—and this person is the philosopher.

The firmest principle of all is one about which it is impossible to be mistaken. For this sort of principle must be known best (for what we make mistakes about is invariably what we do not know), and it cannot be an assumption. For a principle that we must already possess in order to understand anything at all about beings is not an assumption; and what we must know in order to know anything at all is a principle we must already possess. Clearly, then, this sort of principle is the firmest of all.

Let us next say what this principle is: that it is impossible for the same thing both to belong and not to belong at the same time to the same thing and in the same respect (and let us assume we have drawn all the further

---

28. Now some . . . in analytics: The translation includes supplementation derived from 1006a5-8, to make the point clearer. Lit. 'As for as many things as those people undertake who speak about the truth, in what way it should be accepted, they do this because of lack of education . . .'.

distinctions that might be drawn to meet logical complaints). This, then, is the firmest principle of all, since it has the distinguishing feature previously mentioned.

For it is impossible for anyone to suppose that the same thing is and is not, though some people take Heraclitus to say this; for what one says need not be what one supposes to be true. For it is impossible for contraries to belong at the same time to the same thing (and let us assume that the customary further distinctions are added to this statement). But what is contrary to a belief is the belief in its contradictory. Hence evidently it is impossible for the same person at the same time to suppose that the same thing is and is not, since someone who makes this mistake would have contrary beliefs at the same time. This is why all those who demonstrate refer back to this belief as ultimate; for this is by nature the principle of all the other axioms as well.

BOOK VII

1

Being is spoken of in many ways, which we distinguished previously in the work on how many ways things are spoken of. For one <type of being> signifies what-it-is and a this; another signifies quality, or quantity, or any of the other things predicated in this way. But while being is spoken of in this number of ways, it is evident that among these the primary being is the what-it-is, which signifies substance. For whenever we say what quality this has, we call it good or bad, not three cubits long or a man, whereas whenever we say what it is, we call it man or god, not pale or hot or three cubits long; and the other things are called beings by belonging to this type of being—some as quantities, some as qualities, some as affections, some in some other such way.

That is why someone might actually be puzzled about whether walking, flourishing, or sitting signifies a being;[29] for none of these either is in its own right or is capable of being separated from substance, but it is more true that the walking or sitting or flourishing thing is a being—if indeed it is a being. This latter type of thing is apparently more of a being because it has some definite subject—the substance and the particular—which is discerned in such a predication; for this subject is implied in speaking of the good or sitting thing. Clearly, then, it is because of substance that each of those other things is also a being,[30] so that what is in the primary way, what is not something,[31] but is without qualification a being, is substance.

Now the primary is so spoken of in many ways, but still, substance is

29. **signifies a being**: Read *on sēmainei*.

30. **is also a being**: Lit. just 'is'.

31. **what is not something**: i.e. what is not something *else*, as the sitting thing is something else, e.g., a man. (Or 'what is not a certain sort of being'.)

primary in every way: in nature, in account, and in knowledge.[32] For none
of the other things predicated is separable, but only substance. Substance is

35 also primary in account, since its account is necessarily present in the
account of each thing. Moreover, we think we know a thing most of all
whenever we know what, for instance, man or fire is, rather than when we

1028b1 know its quality or quantity or place; for indeed we know each of these
only when we know *what* the quantity or the quality *is*.

Indeed, the old question—always pursued from long ago till now, and
always raising puzzles—'What is being?' is just the question 'What is sub-

5 stance?'. For it is substance that some say is one and others say is more than
one, some saying that it is limited in number, others that it is unlimited.
And so we too must make it our main, our primary, indeed practically our
only, task to study what it is that is in this way.

2

The most evident examples of substances seem to be bodies. That is why

10 we say that animals and plants and their parts are substances, and also
natural bodies, such as fire, water, earth, and all such things, and whatever
is either a part of these or composed of all or some of them—for instance,
the universe and its parts, the stars, moon, and sun. But we ought to

15 consider: Are these the only substances there are, or are there also others?
Or are only some of these things substances, or some of these and also
some other things? Or are none of these things substances, but only some
other things?

Some people think that the limits of a body—for instance, surface, line,
point, and unit—are substances, and are so to a higher degree than a body
and a solid. Further, some think there are no substances apart from perceptible things, while to others it seems that there are also everlasting substances, which are more numerous and are beings to a higher degree. Plato,

20 for example, thinks that Forms and mathematicals are two types of substances, and that the substance of perceptible bodies is a third type.
Speusippus posits even more substances, beginning with the one, and posits
a principle for each type of substance—one for numbers, another for magnitudes, and then another for soul; and in this way he multiplies the sub-

25 stances. Some say that Forms and numbers have the same nature, and that
everything else comes after them—lines, planes, and everything else, extending to the substance of the universe and to perceptible things.

We must consider, then, which of these views are correct or incorrect;
what substances there are; whether or not there are any substances besides

30 perceptible substances, and in what way these perceptible substances are

---

32. **in nature . . . knowledge**: Read *kai phusei kai logō(i) kai gnōsei*. OCT: 'in account, in knowledge, and in time'. The next three sentences explain how substance
is prior in each of the three ways just distinguished.

<substances>; and whether or not there is any separable substance besides perceptible ones, and, if there is, why there is, and in what way it is <substance>. But before doing this, we must first sketch what substance is.

3

Substance is spoken of, if not in several ways, at any rate in four main cases. For the essence, the universal and the genus seem to be the substance of a given thing, and the fourth of these cases is the subject.

Now, the subject is that of which the other things are said, but which is not itself in turn said of any other thing; hence we must first determine what it is, since the primary subject seems to be substance most of all.

What is spoken of in this way <as the primary subject> is in one way the matter, in another way the form, and in a third way the thing composed of these. (By the matter I mean, for example, the bronze, by the form I mean the arrangement of the figure, and by the thing composed of them I mean the statue, i.e., the compound.) And so if the form is prior to the matter, and more[33] of a being, it will also, by the same argument, be prior to the thing composed of both.

We have now said in outline, then, what substance is: it is what is not said of a subject but has the other things said of it.

However, we must not confine ourselves to this answer. For it is inadequate: for, first, it is itself unclear; and further, the matter turns out to be substance. For if the matter is not substance, it is hard to see what other substance there is; for when all the other things are removed, nothing <but the matter> evidently remains.[34] For the other things are affections, products, and potentialities of bodies; and length, breadth, and depth[35] are kinds of quantities but not substances (for quantity is not substance), but the primary <subject> to which these belong is more of a substance than they are. But when length, breadth, and depth are abstracted, we see that nothing is left, except whatever is determined by these. And so, if we examine it in this way, the matter necessarily appears as the only substance.

By matter I mean what is spoken of in its own right neither as being something, nor as having some quantity, nor as having any of the other things by which being is determined. For there is something of which each of these is predicated, something whose being is different from that of each of the things predicated; for the other things are predicated of the substance, and the substance is predicated of the matter. And so the last thing

35

1029a

5

10

15

20

33. **more**: The translation of *mallon* (see MORE) makes a considerable difference to the interpretation of Aristotle's claims about matter in this chapter.

34. **nothing . . . evidently remains**: This is ambiguous between (a) 'It is not evident that anything remains' and (b) 'It is evident that nothing remains'. The weaker claim (a) is all that is needed for the argument.

35. **length, breadth, and depth**: These are the essential properties of bodies.

25   is in its own right neither something nor of some quantity nor any other
     <of the things mentioned>; nor is it <in its own right> the negations of
     these, since what we have said implies that the negations as well <as the
     positive properties> belong to it <only> coincidentally.

     And so, if we study it from this point of view, the result is that the
     matter is substance; but that is impossible. For being separable and being a
     this seem to belong to substance most of all; that is why the form and the
     <compound> of both <matter and form> would seem to be substance
30   more than the matter is.

     And so the substance composed of both—I mean composed of the mat-
     ter and the form—should be set aside, since it is posterior to the other two,
     and clear. The matter is also evident in a way. We must, then, consider the
     third type of substance, since it is the most puzzling.
1029b   Since some of the perceptible substances are agreed to be substances, we
     should begin our search with these.

4

     Since we began by distinguishing the things by which we define substance
     and since essence seems to be one of these, we ought to study it. For it is
     useful to advance towards what is better known, since this is how anyone
5   succeeds in learning, by advancing through what is less well known by nature
     to what is better known. In questions about action, our task is to advance
     from what is good to ourselves, and so to make what is good without reserva-
     tion[36] good to ourselves; in the same way, then, we should advance from what
     is better known to ourselves, and so make what is well known by nature well
     known to ourselves. Admittedly, what is well known and known first to any
10   given type of person is only slightly known and has little or no hold on being;
     still, we must begin from what is poorly known but known by us and try to
     come to know what is known without reservation, by advancing, as has been
     said, through the very things that are known to us.

     First let us make some logical remarks about it. The essence of a thing is
15   what the thing is said to be in its own right. For being you[37] is not the same
     as being a musician, since you are not a musician in your own right; hence
     your essence is what you are in your own right.

     Nor indeed is your essence all of what you are in your own right. For a
     thing's essence is not what belongs to it in its own right in the way that pale

36. **without reservation:** *holōs*, usually rendered by 'in general'. Here its force is
similar to that of 'WITHOUT QUALIFICATION'.

37. **being you:** In this chapter 'being *x*' translates phrases of the form *to x einai*,
which in vii 6 are translated by 'the essence of *x*'. Aristotle uses 'being *x*' equivalently with 'the essence of *x*' (*to ti ēn einai x*), except that he seems to regard the
first phrase as easier to understand, and therefore useful for explaining what the
second phrase means.

belongs in its own right to a surface; for being a surface[38] is not the same as being pale. But neither is a thing's essence the same as the combination of the thing and what belongs in its own right to it—for instance, being a pale surface, since here surface is added. It follows that the account of a thing's essence is the account that describes but does not mention the thing; and so if being a pale surface is the same as being a smooth surface, being pale and being smooth are one and the same.

There are composites <not only among substances but> also in the other predications, since each of these (for instance, quality, quantity, when, where, and motion) has a subject; hence we should ask whether there is an account of the essence of each of these composites, and whether an essence belongs to them—to a pale man, for instance—as well as to substances. Let us, then, call this composite 'cloak'. What is being a cloak?

One might object, however, that a cloak is not spoken of in its own right either. <We reply:> There are two ways in which we speak of what is not in its own right; one way is from addition, the other is not. In the first case, something is said <not to be in its own right> because the thing to be defined is added to something else—if, for instance, one gave the account of pale man as a definition of pale. In the second case, something is said not to be in its own right because something else is added to it—if, for instance, 'cloak' signified a pale man, but one were to define cloak as pale. A pale man, then, is pale, but is not what being pale is.

But is being a cloak an essence at all? Perhaps not, for this reason: An essence is what something essentially is,[39] but whenever one thing is said of another, the composite of the two is not essentially a this; the pale man, for instance, is not essentially a this, since only a substance is a this. Hence the things that have an essence are those whose account is a definition. But the mere fact that a name and an account signify the same thing does not imply that the account is a definition; if it did, then all accounts would be formulae (since for every account, we can find a name that signifies the same), so that even the *Iliad* would be a definition. Rather, an account is a definition <only> if it is of some primary thing; primary things are those that are spoken of in a way that does not consist in one thing's being said of another. Hence essence will belong only to species of a genus and to nothing else,[40] since <only> these seem to be spoken of in a way that does

---

38. **being a surface**: The indefinite article makes more natural English, but corresponds to nothing in the Greek. The Greek leaves open the question whether Aristotle has in mind the essences of particulars or of universals.

39. **what something essentially is**: Read *hoper ti*. (OCT: 'what a this essentially is'.) On *hoper* see ESSENCE #2 (d).

40. **Hence essence . . . to nothing else**: Two possible interpretations: (1) Essences are found only within species and genera (of substances), i.e. only members of these substantial species and genera have essences. (2) Species and genera (as opposed to individual members of them) are the only things that have essences.

not consist in one thing's participating in another, or in one thing's being an
attribute or coincident of another. Admittedly, everything else <besides
members of a species>, if it has a name, will also have an account saying
what it signifies (i.e. that this belongs to this) or, instead of an unqualified
account, a more exact one; but nothing else will have a definition or essence.

Perhaps, however, definitions, like what-it-is, are spoken of in several
ways. For in fact what-it-is in one way signifies substance and a this, and in
another way signifies each of the things predicated—quantity, quality, and
all the rest. For just as being belongs to them all—not in the same way, but
to substance primarily and to the other things derivatively—so also the
what-it-is belongs without qualification to substance and derivatively to the
other things. For we might ask what a quality is, so that quality is also a
what-it-is, though not without qualification; just as some people say, speaking logically, that not-being is (not that it is without qualification, but that
it is not-being), so also we say what a quality is.

We must certainly consider what ought to be said about a particular
question, but we must consider no less how things really are. That is why,
in this case, since what is said is evident <we must consider how things
are>; we find that essence, like what-it-is, belongs primarily and without
qualification to substance and belongs derivatively to the other things also,
where it will be the essence of quality or quantity, not the essence without
qualification. For we must say that these <non-substances> are beings
either homonymously or by addition and subtraction, as we say that what
is not known is known <not to be known>. The right answer is that they
are beings neither homonymously nor in the same way. What is medical,
for instance, is spoken of with reference to one and the same thing, not by
being one and the same thing, but not homonymously either—for a body, a
procedure, and an instrument are called medical neither homonymously
nor by having one <nature>, but with reference to one thing. The same
applies to beings.

It does not matter which alternative we accept: in either case substances
evidently have a definition and essence of the primary type, i.e., a definition and essence without qualification. Certainly other beings also have
definitions and essences, but not primarily. For if we accept this view of
definition, not every name that signifies the same as an account will necessarily have a definition corresponding to it; rather, in order to be a definition, the account must be of the right type, namely an account of something that is one—and something that is one not merely by continuity (like
the *Iliad*, or like things that are tied together) but that is one in one of the
ways in which one is spoken of. Now, one is spoken of in the same ways as
being, and one type of being signifies a this, another quantity, another
quality. That is why there will also be an account and a definition of the
pale man, but not in the way that there is of pale and of the substance.

6

We should investigate whether a given thing is the same as or different   *15*
from its essence. For this is useful for our investigation of substance; for a
given thing seems to be nothing other than its own substance, and something's substance is said to be its essence.

In the case of things spoken of coincidentally, a thing might seem to be   *20*
different from its essence; a pale man, for instance, is different from being a
pale man. For if it is the same, then being a man is the same as being a pale
man; for, they say, a man is the same as a pale man, so that being a pale
man is the same as being a man.

Perhaps, however, it is not necessary for things to be the same if one is a   *25*
coincident of the other, since the extreme terms are not the same in the
same way. But presumably it might seem to follow that the extremes, the
coincidental things, turn out to be the same—for instance, being pale and
being musical. In fact, however, it seems not to follow.

But is it necessary for a thing spoken of in its own right to be the same as
its essence? For instance, what about a substance of the sort some say an
Idea is, one that has no other substance or nature prior to it? Suppose that   *30*
the good itself <the Idea> is different from the essence of good, and the
animal itself from the essence of animal, and the being itself from the
essence of being. In that case, there will be further substances, natures, and   *1031b*
Ideas apart from those mentioned, and these will be prior substances and
substances to a higher degree, if essence is substance.

If, then, <the Ideas and the essences> are severed from each other, it
follows that <the Ideas> will not be known and that <the essences> will
not be beings. (By 'severed' I mean that the essence of good does not   *5*
belong to the good itself, and being good does not belong to the essence of
good.) For we know a thing whenever we recognize its essence. Further,
what applies to good applies equally to the other essences; if the essence of
good is not good, then neither will the essence of being be, nor the essence
of one be one. But since all essences alike either are or are not, it follows   *10*
that, if not even the essence of being is a being, none of the other essences
is a being either. Moreover, if the essence of good does not belong to a
given thing, that thing is not good.

The good, then, is necessarily one with the essence of good, and the fine
with the essence of fine. The same applies to all the primary things, those
spoken of in their own right and not insofar as they belong to something
else.[41] For if this is true <i.e. that something is a primary being>, it already
implies <that the primary being is identical to its essence>, even if it is not
a Form—though presumably <the conclusion> is all the more <necessary>   *15*
if the thing is a Form.

41. **insofar . . . something else:** Lit. 'in accordance with something else'.

Further, if the Ideas are what some people say they are, then clearly the subject will not be substance. For Ideas must be substances, but not by <being said> of a subject, since <if they were said of a subject>, they would exist <only> by being participated in.

20 From these arguments, then, we find that a thing itself and its essence are non-coincidentally one and the same, and that knowing a thing is knowing its essence; and so even isolating the Forms shows that a thing and its essence must be some one thing.

But because what is spoken of coincidentally—for instance, the musical or the pale—signifies two <different> things, it is not true to say that it is
25 the same as its essence. For the pale signifies both the subject of which pale is a coincident and the coincident <itself>;[42] and so in a way it is the same as its essence, and in a way it is not the same—for <the pale> is not the same as man or as pale man, but it is the same as the attribute.

We can also see that it is absurd <for something not to be the same as its essence>, if we give a name to each essence; for apart from that essence there will be another essence as well—for instance, another essence will be
30 the essence of the essence of horse. But why not let some things be essences at once, going no further, since essence is substance? Moreover, not
1032a only is <a thing> one <with its essence>, but their account is also the same; for one and being one are non-coincidentally one. Moreover, if there is another essence, the essences will go on to infinity; for one thing will be the essence of the one, and another will be the one, so that the same
5 argument will also apply in their case.

Clearly, then, in the case of the primary things, those spoken of in their own right, a thing and its essence are one and the same. And it is evident that the sophistical refutations aimed against this position are all resolved in the same way as is the puzzle of whether Socrates and being Socrates are the same; for there is no difference in the premisses from which one would
10 ask the questions or in the premisses from which one would find a solution.

We have said, then, in what way something's essence is the same as the thing, and in what way it is not.

10

1034b A definition is an account, and every account has parts; and a part of the account corresponds to a part of the thing defined in the way the whole account corresponds to the whole thing. Hence a puzzle arises about whether or not the account of the parts must be present in the account of

---

42. **the pale . . . itself>:** We can use 'the pale' (neuter article + adjective) to refer (i) to the man who is pale (i.e. to the pale thing) or (ii) to his quality (i.e. his paleness). On this double use of the neuter adjective see *Phys.* 188a36n, 189b35, *Met.* 1028a24.

the whole. For in some cases the accounts of the parts evidently are present and in some cases they evidently are not; the account of a circle, for instance, does not include that of the segments, but the account of a syllable includes that of the letters, even though the circle is divided into its segments just as the syllable is divided into its letters.

Moreover, if a part is prior to a whole, and an acute angle is part of a right angle, and a finger of an animal, then an acute angle would be prior to a right angle, and a finger to a man. In fact, however, the whole seems to be prior, since the account of the part refers to the whole, and the whole is prior by being independent.

Alternatively, perhaps a part is spoken of in many ways, and a quantitative measure is only one type of part; leaving this type aside, we should examine the parts that compose substance.

If, then, there is matter, form, and the compound of these, and matter, form, and the compound of them are all substance, then it follows that in one way matter is also called a part of something, but in another way it is not, and in this second way only the components of the account[43] of the form are parts. For example, flesh is not a part of concavity (since it is the matter in which concavity comes to be), but it is a part of snubness. Again, bronze is a part of the compound statue, but not a part of the statue spoken of as form. For it is the form of the statue—i.e., the statue insofar as it has form—and never the material aspect in its own right, that should be spoken of as the statue.[44]

This is why the account of a circle does not include that of the segments, whereas the account of a syllable does include that of the letters; for the letters are not matter, but parts of the account of the form, while the segments are parts as matter in which the form comes to be. Still, the segments are nearer to the form than bronze is to the circle in the cases where circularity comes to be in bronze.

In a way, however, not every sort of letters—for instance, those in wax or those in air—will be included in the account of the syllable; for these also <like the bronze in the circle> are a part of the syllable as its perceptible matter. For if a line is divided and perishes into halves, or a man into bones, sinews, and bits of flesh, it does not follow that these compose the whole as parts of the substance, but only that they compose it as its matter. They are parts of the compound, but when we come to the form, which is what the account is of, they are not parts of it; that is why they are not included in accounts either.

43. **account**: *logos*. Sometimes Aristotle seems to use *logos* to refer (as we would say) to what the definition is a definition of, rather than to the definition itself.

44. **For it is the form . . . the statue**: Lit. 'For the form and insofar as it has form should be called a given thing, but the material should never in its own right be called'.

Hence the account of some things will include that of these material parts, but the account of other things, if it is not of something combined with matter, must not[45] include it. For this reason, the principles composing a given thing are, in some but not all cases, the material parts into which it perishes.

25

If, then, something—for instance, the snub or the bronze circle—is form and matter combined, then it perishes into these <material parts>, and matter is a part of it. But if something is without matter, not combined with it, so that its account is only of the form, then it does not perish—

30   either not at all, or at least not in this way. Hence these <material parts> are parts and principles of things combined with matter, but neither parts nor principles of the form.

That is why the clay statue perishes into clay, the ball into bronze, and Callias into flesh and bones. Moreover, the circle perishes into its segments,

1035b   because one type of circle is combined with matter; for the circle spoken of without qualification and the particular circle are called circles homonymously, because the particular[46] has no distinctive name.

We have now given the true answer, but let us take up the question again,

5   and state the answer more perspicuously. Parts of the account—i.e., the things into which the account is divided—are, either all or some of them, prior to the whole. The account of the right angle, by contrast, does not include that of the acute angle, but, on the contrary, that of the acute angle includes that of the right angle; for we use the right angle in defining the acute, which is <defined as> less than a right angle. This is also the relation

10   of the circle to a semicircle, since the semicircle is defined by the circle. Similarly, a finger is defined by reference to the whole, since this sort of part of a man is a finger.

And so all the material parts—i.e., those into which the whole is divided as its matter—are posterior to it, but the parts that are parts of the account and of the substance corresponding to the account are, either all or some of them, prior to the whole.

15   Now, an animal's soul—the substance of what is ensouled—is the substance corresponding to the account; it is the form and essence of the right sort of body. At any rate, a proper definition of each part[47] requires reference to its function, and this function requires perception. Hence the parts of the soul, either all or some of them, are prior to the compound animal, and the same is true in the case of the particular.

45. **must not**: Or 'need not'.

46. **the particular**: This is the material particular ring (which is 'combined with matter'). The Greek 'kuklos' is used both for 'circle' and for 'ring'; hence Aristotle remarks that it is homonymous ('ring' is the distinctive name in English that Greek lacks).

47. **each part**: Retain *to meros*, deleted in OCT.

The body and its parts are posterior to this substance <i.e., the soul>,   *20*
and its parts are the matter into which the compound, but not this substance, is divided. In a way they are prior to the compound, but in a way
they are not, since they cannot exist when they are separated; for a finger is
not an animal's finger in all conditions—on the contrary, a dead finger is   *25*
only homonymously a finger. Some of them are simultaneous, if they are
the controlling parts, those on which the account and the substance primarily depend—the heart or the brain, for instance (for it does not matter
which of the two it is).

Now, man or horse or anything else that applies in this way to particulars, but universally, is not a substance, but a sort of compound of this
account and this matter as universal. When we come to particulars, Soc-   *30*
rates is composed of ultimate matter, and the same is true in the other
cases.

A part may be either of the form (by 'form' I mean the essence), or of
the compound of the form and the matter, or of the matter itself. But only
parts of the form are parts of the account, and the account is of the
universal; for being circle is the same as circle, and being soul is the same   *1036a*
as soul. But a compound such as this particular circle, either a perceptible
(for instance, bronze or wooden) compound or an intelligible (for instance,
mathematical) compound, has no definition, but we know it with the help   *5*
of thought or perception. When it has departed from actual thought or
perception, it is unclear whether or not it exists; but still, we always speak
of it and know it by means of the universal account, whereas the matter is
unknowable in its own right.

One sort of matter is perceptible, another intelligible. Examples of per-   *10*
ceptible matter are, for instance, bronze and wood, and all matter that is
capable of motion; intelligible matter is the matter present in perceptible
things (as, for instance, mathematical objects are present in them), but not
insofar as they are perceptible.

We have now stated the facts about whole and part and about prior and
posterior. If someone asks whether the right angle, or circle, or animal is   *15*
prior to the parts composing it, i.e., the parts into which it is divided, or
whether, alternatively, the parts are prior to the whole, we must answer
that neither is true without qualification.

For suppose first that the soul is the animal, or rather the ensouled thing,
or that a thing's soul is the thing itself, that being circle is the circle, and
that being right angle, i.e., the essence of the right angle, is the right angle.
In that case, we should say that <the particular compound>—both the
bronze right angle including <perceptible> matter and the right angle in
particular lines—is posterior to the things in the account and to one sort of   *20*
right angle, and that the right angle without matter is posterior to the
things in its account, but prior to the parts in the particular. We should
<add these conditions and> not give an unqualified answer. Suppose, alter-

natively, that the soul is not the animal but different from it. In this case
25   too we should say that some things are <prior> and some are not, as we
have said.

11

Not surprisingly, a further puzzle arises: What sorts of parts are parts of
the form, and what sorts are parts of the combined thing, not of the form?
If this is not clear, we cannot define anything; for definition is of the
universal and of the form. If, then, it is not evident which sorts of parts
30   count as matter and which do not, it will not be evident what an account is
either.

In cases where something evidently occurs in different kinds of things,
as a circle, for instance, is found in bronze, stone, and wood, it seems clear
that the bronze or stone (for instance) is not part of the substance of a
35   circle, because a circle is <also found> separated from it. Even if it is not
1036b   seen to be separated, the case may still be similar to those just mentioned.
This would be true if, for example, all the circles that were seen were
bronze; for it would still be true that the bronze is not part of the form <of
circle>, even though it is hard to remove the bronze in thought. Now the
form of man, for instance, always appears in flesh and bones, and in parts
5   of this sort. Does it follow that these are also parts of the form and the
account? Perhaps not; perhaps they are only matter, and we are incapable
of separating them from the form because it does not also occur in other
<sorts of material parts>.

Since this sort of thing seems to be possible, but it is unclear when <it is
possible>, some people are puzzled even when they come to a circle or a
triangle. They suppose that it is not suitably defined by lines and by the
10   continuous, and that we speak of these in the same way as we were speaking of the flesh and bones of a man, or the bronze or stone of a statue.
Hence they reduce everything to numbers, and say that the account of the
line is the account of the two.

Those talk about the Ideas are also affected by this puzzle. Some of them
15   say that the dyad is line-itself; others say that it is the form of line since,
they say, in some cases—for instance, dyad and the form of dyad—the
form is the same as the thing whose form it is, but in the case of the line it
is not. The result is that there is one form for many things whose form
appears different (this was also the result of the Pythagorean view); and
20   then it is possible to make this form the one form of all things, and to make
nothing else a form. On this argument, however, all things will be one.

We have said, then, that questions about definitions raise a puzzle, and
why they raise it. That is why this reduction of everything <to numbers
and Forms> and the abstracting of matter goes too far; for presumably
some things are <essentially> this form in this matter, or these material

parts with this form.[48] And Socrates the Younger was wrong in his habitual 25
comparison of an animal <and its parts with circle and bronze>. For his
comparison leads us away from the truth; it makes us suppose that a man
can exist without his parts, as a circle can exist without bronze. But in fact
the two cases are not similar; for an animal is a perceiver,[49] and cannot be
defined without reference to motion, and therefore to parts in the right 30
condition. For a hand is not a part of man in just any condition, but only
when it is capable of fulfilling its function, and hence only when it is
ensouled—when it is not ensouled, it is not a part <of a man>.

But in the case of mathematical objects, why are accounts <of parts>, of
semicircles, for instance, not parts of accounts <of wholes>, of circles, for
instance? For these are not perceptible. Perhaps, however, this makes no 35
difference; for some non-perceptible things have matter too, and in fact 1037a
everything that is not an essence and form itself in its own right, but a this,
has some sort of matter. Hence these semicircles will not be parts of the
universal circle, but they will be parts of particular circles, as we said
before; for one sort of matter is perceptible, one sort intelligible. 5

It is also clear that the soul is the primary substance, the body is matter,
and man or animal is composed of the two as universal. As for Socrates or
Coriscus, if <Socrates'> soul[50] is also Socrates, he is spoken of in two
ways; for some speak of him as soul, some as the compound. But if he is
without qualification this soul and this body, then what was said about the 10
universal also applies to the particular.

We must postpone an investigation of whether there is another sort of
matter apart from the matter of these <perceptible> substances, and
whether we must search for some other sort of substance—for instance,
numbers or something of the sort. For we also have this in view in trying to
determine <the answers to questions> about perceptible substances as well
<as non-perceptible substances>, since in a way the study of nature, i.e., 15
second philosophy, has the task of studying perceptible substances. For the
student of nature must know not only about matter but also, and even
more, about the substance corresponding to the account.

We must also postpone an investigation of the way in which the things in
the account are parts of the definition, and of why the definition is one
account. For it is clear that the thing defined is one. But what makes it one, 20
given that it has parts?

We have said generally, then, about all cases, what the essence is; in what
way it is itself in its own right; why in some cases the account of the

48. **this form . . . this form**: Lit. 'this in this or these in this condition'. Cf. *PA* 640b27.

49. **perceiver**: Read *aisthētikon*. (OCT: 'perceptible'.)

50. **<Socrates'> soul**: Lit. 'the soul'. Probably (not certainly) Aristotle is thinking of a particular soul (and therefore of a particular form); see FORM #9.

essence includes the parts of the thing defined and in some cases it does
not; and that in the account of substance the parts that are matter will not
be present, because they are parts of the compound substance, not of the
substance corresponding to the account.

The compound substance has an account in one way, but in another way
it has no account. Taken together with matter, it has no account, since that
is indefinable; but it has an account corresponding to the primary substance, so that the account of man, for instance, is the account of soul. For
<the primary> substance is the form present in the thing, and the com-
pound substance is spoken of as composed of the form and the matter.
Concavity, for instance, <is a form of this sort>; for snub nose and snubness are composed of concavity and nose (for nose will be present twice in
these). And the compound substance (for instance snub nose or Callias)
will also have matter in it.

We have also said that in some cases, as in the case of primary substances, a thing and its essence are the same; curvature, for instance, is the
same as being curvature, if curvature is primary.[51] (By 'primary substance'
I mean the substance that is so called not because x is in y and y is the
subject of x by being the matter of x.) But if a thing is <a substance> by
being matter or by being combined with matter, it is not the same as its
essence. Nor, however, are they[52] one <only> coincidentally, as Socrates
and the musical are; for these are the same <only> coincidentally.[53]

13

Since we are investigating substance, let us return to it again. Just as the
subject and the essence[54] are said to be substance, so too is the universal.
We have discussed the first two of these, namely essence and subject; we
have seen that something is a subject in one of two ways, either by being a
this (as an animal is the subject for its attributes) or as matter is the subject
for the actuality. But some also think that the universal is a cause and
principle more than anything else is; that is why we should discuss the
universal as well. For it would seem impossible for anything spoken of
universally to be substance.

For, first, the substance of a thing is the substance that is distinctive of it,
which does not belong to anything else, whereas the universal is common—
for what is called universal is what naturally belongs to more than one
thing. Then which thing's substance will the universal be? For it must be

51. **curvature, for instance . . . is primary**: Deleted in OCT.

52. **Nor . . . are they**: Read *oude*. (OCT: 'not even if they are . . .'.)

53. **as Socrates . . . coincidentally**: See vii 6, esp. 1031a21.

54. **the subject and the essence**: OCT adds: 'and the thing composed of these'.
Aristotle returns to the criteria for substance that he mentioned at 1028b33.

the substance either of all or of none of them. It cannot be the substance of all; if it is the substance of one of them, then the others will be this one too, since things that have one substance also have one essence and are themselves one.[55]

Further, what is called substance is what is not said of a subject, whereas every universal is said of a subject.

Now, suppose someone says: 'Admittedly, a universal cannot belong to something as its essence. Still, it is present in the essence, as animal is present in man and horse.' Surely it is clear that it will be some account of <the essence it is present in>. It does not matter even if it is not an account of everything in the substance; for this <universal> will still be the substance of something, as man is of the man in which it is present. And so the result will be the same once again; for <the universal>—for instance, animal—will be the substance of whatever it is present in by being its distinctive property.[56]

Further, it is both impossible and absurd for a this and substance, if it is composite, to be composed not from substances and not from a this, but from a sort of thing;[57] for it will follow that a non-substance, a sort of thing, will be prior to substance, to a this. But that is impossible; for attributes cannot be prior to substance, either in account or in time or in knowledge[58]—for if they were, they would also be separable.

Moreover, a substance will be present in <the substance> Socrates, so that <the universal> will be the substance of two things.

In general, if a man[59] and things spoken of in this way are substances, it follows that nothing in their account is the substance of any of them or exists separately from them or in anything else. I mean, for instance, that there is no animal, or anything else mentioned in the accounts, apart from the particular animals.[60]

If we study them in this way, then, it is evident that nothing that belongs universally is a substance and that what is predicated in common signifies

15

20

25

30

35

1039a1

55. **since things . . . are themselves one**: If, then, the universal is the substance of all its instances, all its instances will be one (given the principle conceded in 1038b10–12). Hence the universal must be the substance of none of its instances. Alternative rendering: 'since things that have one substance and [or 'i.e.'] one essence are themselves one'.

56. **for <the . . . property**: And so all animals will be one, by the first argument against universal substances. Read *hoion to zō(i)on, en hō(i) hōs idion huparchei.* (OCT: 'for it will be the substance of that species in which it is present . . .'.)

57. **sort of thing**: *poion*. Or 'such'. See 1039a2n, QUALITY.

58. **in knowledge**: Read *gnōsei*. (OCT: 'in coming to be'.)

59. **a man**: i.e. a particular man. Alternatively, 'man', i.e. the species.

60. **apart from the particular animals**: Or 'apart from the various species of animals'.

this sort of thing, not a this. If it is a this, then many <difficulties> result, including the Third Man.

Further, our conclusion can also be made clear from the following points. Substance cannot be composed of substances that are actually present in it; for things that are actually two in this way are never actually one, but if they are potentially two they are <actually> one. A double line, for instance, is composed of halves that are <only> potentially two things; for the actuality separates them. And so if substance is one, it will not be composed of substances that are actually present in it. Democritus is right about actuality, when he says that one cannot come to be from two, or two from one; he says this because he regards the indivisible magnitudes as the substances. Clearly, then, the same will apply in the case of number if, as some say, number is a combination of units; for either the pair is not one or else a unit is not actually in it.

This conclusion, however, raises a puzzle. For if no substance can be composed of universals (because a universal signifies this sort of thing, not a this) and if no substance can be composed of substances actually present in it, then it follows that every substance will be incomposite, so that none will have any account. And yet, it seems to everyone, and we have said much earlier,[61] that substances alone, or most of all, have formulae, whereas now they too turn out not to have them. And so either nothing will have a definition or else in a way things will have definitions, and in a way they will not. What this means will be clearer from what follows.

15

We have found that the compound and the form are different sorts of substance; I mean that the first sort of substance is substance by being the form combined with matter, and the second sort is the form without qualification.

Now, all the substances spoken of as compounds perish, since all of them also come to be; but the form does not perish in such a way that it is ever <in the process of> perishing, since neither is it ever <in the process of> coming to be. For it is the essence of this house, not the essence of house, that is <in the process of> coming to be, whereas forms are and are not without <any process of> coming to be and perishing, since we have shown that no one generates or produces them.

For this reason there is neither definition nor demonstration about particular perceptible substances, because they have matter whose nature admits of both being and not being; that is why all perceptible particulars are perishable.

61. **much earlier:** Cf. 1030a2–27.

Now, demonstrations and definitions that express knowledge are of necessary things.[62] And just as knowledge cannot be knowledge at one time and ignorance at another, but what admits of such variation is belief, so also neither demonstration nor definition admits of such variation; belief is what is concerned with what admits of being otherwise. It clearly follows that there will be neither definition nor demonstration of these <particular perceptible things>. For whenever perishing things pass from perception, they are unclear to those with knowledge, and though the accounts still remain in the souls of those with knowledge, there will be neither definition nor demonstration <about perceptible things>. That is why, whenever anyone who looks for a formula is defining a particular, he ought to realize that the definition can in every case be undermined, since particulars cannot be defined.

Nor, indeed, can Ideas be defined. For Ideas are particulars, they say, and separable. But accounts must be composed of names, and the definer will not make a <new> name (since it would be unknown); yet each of the established names is common to all <the particulars of a given kind>, and so they must also belong to something else <as well as to a given particular>. If, for instance, someone defines you, he will say you are a thin or pale animal, or something else that belongs to something else as well as to you.

Someone might say: 'Even though each name <in the definition> belongs separately to many things, still it is possible that all together belong only to this.' We should answer, first, that biped animal, for instance, belongs both to animal and to biped—indeed, this must be so with everlasting things, since they are prior to and parts of the composite thing. Moreover, they are also separable if man is separable; for either none of the three is separable or both animal and biped are. And so if none of them is separable, the genus will not exist apart from the species; but if the genus is separable, so is the differentia. Moreover, <animal and biped> are prior in being <to biped animal>, and therefore they are not destroyed when it is.

Further, if Ideas are composed of Ideas (for the things they are composed of are less composite), then the components of the Idea—for instance, animal and biped—will also have to be predicated of many things. If they are not, how will they be known? For there will be an Idea which cannot be predicated of more than one thing. But that does not seem to be so; on the contrary, every Idea can, it seems, be participated in.

As has been said, then, we fail to notice that everlasting things <that are particulars> are indefinable. This is especially true in the case of those that are unique—for instance, the sun and the moon. For sometimes people not

1040a

5

10

15

20

25

30

62. Now . . . necessary things: Or (assuming a different text): 'Now, demonstrations are of necessary things, and definitions express knowledge'.

only go wrong by adding the sorts of things (for instance, going around the earth, or being hidden at night) that can be removed from the sun without its ceasing to be the sun. (For <this sort of definition implies that> if it stops going around or shows at night, it will no longer be the sun; but that is absurd, since the sun signifies a certain substance.) They also <sometimes go wrong by mentioning only the features> that can be found in something else as well. If, for instance, something else of this sort comes to be, then clearly, <according to the alleged definition>, it will also have to be the sun, and in that case the account will be common <to the two>. But in fact the sun is a particular, as Cleon and Socrates are.

<These objections show why Ideas are indefinable.> For why does none of those <who believe in Ideas> present a formula of any Idea? If they tried to do so, the truth of what we have just said would become clear.

1040b

17

1041a But let us make a sort of new beginning, and say over again what, and what sort of thing, substance should be said to be; for presumably our answer will also make things clear about the substance that is separated from perceptible substances. Since, then, substance is some sort of princi-
10 ple and cause, we should proceed from here.

In every case, we search for the reason why by asking why one thing belongs to another. For if we ask why a musical man is a musical man, either we are searching for what we have mentioned—for instance, why the man is musical—or else we are searching for something else. Now, to ask
15 why something is itself is to search for nothing. For that <it is so> and its being so—I mean, for instance, that the moon is eclipsed—must be clear already; and the answer 'because it is itself' is one account and one cause applying to every case, to why a man is a man or a musician a musician. Perhaps, however, someone might answer 'because each thing is indivisible
20 from itself, since this is what it is to be one'. But this is a short answer common to all cases.

However, we might ask why a man is this sort of animal. Here, then, we are clearly not asking why something that is a man is a man. We are asking, then, why one thing belongs to another; that it does belong must already be clear, since otherwise we are searching for nothing. For in-
25 stance, when we ask why it thunders, we are asking why there is a noise in the clouds; here we ask why one thing belongs to another. Similarly, we ask why these things—for instance, bricks and stones—are a house.

Evidently, then, we are searching for the cause; and this is the essence, to speak from a logical point of view. In some cases—for instance, presum-
30 ably, a house or a bed—the cause is what something is for; sometimes it is what first initiated the motion, since this is also a cause. We search for

the latter type of cause in the case of coming to be and perishing; in the case of being as well <as in the case of coming to be> we search for the former type of cause.

What we are searching for is most easily overlooked when one thing is not said of another (as when we ask, for instance, what a man is), because *1041b* we speak without qualification and do not specify that we are asking why these things are this thing. Instead of speaking without qualification, we must articulate our question before we search, since otherwise we will not have distinguished a genuine search from a search for nothing. Since we must take it as given that the subject exists, clearly we search for why the *5* matter is something. We ask, for instance, 'Why are these things a house?'. Because the essence of house belongs to them. Similarly, a man is this, or rather is this body having this. Hence we search for the cause on account of which the matter is something, i.e., for the form;[63] and this cause is the substance.

Evidently, then, there is neither searching nor teaching about incom- *10* posite things; the approach to them is different from searching.

Now, a composite is composed of something in such a way that the whole thing is one, not as a heap is, but as a syllable is. A syllable is not the same as its letters—for instance, B and A are not the same thing as BA, nor is flesh fire and earth. For when the components are dispersed, the flesh or *15* syllable no longer exists, though the letters or the fire and earth still do. Hence the syllable is something, and not only the vowel and the consonant but some further thing; and similarly, flesh is not only fire and earth, or the hot and cold, but some further thing.

Now suppose that this further thing must be either an element or com- *20* posed of elements. If it is an element, there will be the same argument over again; for flesh will be composed of this <new element>, plus fire and earth, plus some further thing, so that it will go on without limit. If the further thing is composed of an element, it is clearly not composed of just one (otherwise it would itself be this one), but of more than one; and then we will repeat the same argument about it as about flesh or a syllable. *25*

It would seem, however, that this further thing is something, and not an element, and that it is the cause of one thing's being flesh and another thing's being a syllable, and similarly in the other cases.

Now this is the substance of a given thing; for this is the primary cause of the thing's being <what it is>. Some things are not substances, but the things that are substances are naturally constituted; hence this nature—the *30* one that is not an element but a principle—will apparently be substance. An element is what is present in something as the matter into which the thing is divided—for instance, the A and the B in the syllable.

---

63. **i.e., for the form**: Deleted by OCT.

BOOK VIII

1

1042a3   We must, then, draw the conclusions from what has been said, gather
together the main points, and so complete the discussion. Here, then, is
5   what we have said:[64]

(1) We are searching for the causes, principles, and elements of substances.

(2) Some substances are agreed by everyone to be substances, while some
people have held distinctive views of their own about some other things
<that they count as substances>. The agreed substances are the natural
ones—for instance, fire, earth, water, air, and the other simple bodies, then
10   plants and their parts, animals and their parts, and, finally, the heaven and
its parts. In some people's distinctive views, Forms and mathematical objects are substances.

(3) Some arguments imply that the essence is substance, others that the
subject is substance. Other arguments imply that the genus is substance
more than the species are, and that the universal is substance more than the
15   particulars are. The Ideas are closely related to the universal and the genus,
since the same argument makes all of them seem to be substances.

(4) Since the essence is substance and a definition is an account of the
essence, we have discussed definition and what is in its own right.

20   (5) Since a definition is an account and an account has parts, we also had
to consider what a part is, to see what sorts of parts are parts of the
substance, and what sorts are not, and whether the same parts <that are
parts of the substance> are also parts of the definition.

(6) Further, neither the universal nor the genus is substance.

(7) We should examine Ideas and mathematical objects later, since some
say that these are substances apart from perceptible substances.

25   For now, let us proceed with a discussion of the agreed substances; these
are the perceptible ones, and all perceptible substances have matter.

The subject is substance. In one way, matter <is a subject>.[65] (By 'matter'
I mean what is potentially but not actually a this.) In another way, the
account and the form, which, being a this, is separable in account, <is a
30   subject>. The third <sort of subject> is the composite of these two. Only it
comes to be and perishes, and it is separable without qualification; for
among substances that correspond to the account some are <separable
without qualification> and some are not.

64. **what we have said**: The numbered points that follow summarize the argument
of Bk VII.

65. **<is a subject>**: Less probably, '<is a substance>'. The same question arises in
the rest of the paragraph.

Now, clearly matter as well <as form and compound> is substance; for
in all changes between opposites there is some subject for the change.
Changes in place, for instance, have a subject that is here at one time,
elsewhere at another time; those involving growth have one that is this size   35
at one time, smaller or bigger at another time; changes involving alteration
have one that is, <for instance,> healthy at one time, sick at another time.   1042b
Similarly, changes involving substance have a subject that is at one time in
<process of> coming to be, at another time in <process of> perishing, and
at one time is the sort of subject that is a this and at another time is the sort
of subject that corresponds to a privation.

Coming to be and perishing imply all the other sorts of change, but one   5
or two of the other sorts do not imply this sort. For if something has
matter for change in place, it need not also have matter for coming to be
and perishing. The difference between unqualified and qualified coming to
be has been described in the works on nature.[66]

2

The substance that is subject and matter is agreed; this is the substance that   10
is something potentially. It remains, then, to describe the substance of
perceptible things that is actuality.

Democritus would seem to think that there are three differentiae; in his
view, the body that is the subject—the matter—is one and the same, but
<perceptible things> differ either by 'balance', i.e. figure, or by 'turning',
i.e. position, or by 'contact', i.e. arrangement.[67] It is evident, however, that   15
there are many differentiae. For things are differentiated by the way their
matter is combined (blended together, for instance, as honey-water is); or
tied together (for instance, a bundle); or glued (for instance, a book); or
nailed (for instance, a box); or by more than one of these; or by having a
specific position (a threshold or a lintel, for instance, since their differentia
is being in a certain position); or by a specific time (for instance, dinner   20
and breakfast); or by a specific place (for instance, the winds); or by having
different perceptible attributes (for instance, hardness or softness, thickness
or thinness, dryness or wetness), either some or all of them, and, in general, by excess or deficiency <of them>.   25

Clearly, then, 'is' is also said in just as many ways. Something is a
threshold, for instance, because it has this position, and its being a threshold signifies its having this position; and similarly, being ice signifies
<water's> having solidified in this way. The being of some things will be
defined by all of these things—by some things being mixed, some blended,   30

66. **works on nature:** See *Phys.* i 7, COMING TO BE.

67. **'balance'** . . . **arrangement:** Aristotle seems to quote Democritus' actual terms
(marked here by quotation marks), which he then explains.

some bound together, some solidified, and some (a hand or foot, for instance) having the other differentiae.

We must grasp, then, what kinds of differentiae there are, since they will be the principles of <a thing's> being <what it is>. For instance, things differentiated by more and less, or thick and thin, or by other such things, are all differentiated by excess and deficiency; things differentiated by shape, or by roughness and smoothness, are all differentiated by straight and bent; and the being of other things will be being mixed,[68] and their not being will be the opposite.

It is evident from what we have said, then, that if substance is the cause of a thing's being, we should seek the cause of the being of each of these things in these <differentiae>. Although none of them is substance even when combined <with matter>, still it is in each case analogous to substance; and just as in substances what is predicated of the matter is the actuality itself, so also in other definitions what is predicated is what is closest to being the actuality.[69] If, for instance, we have to define a threshold, we will say it is wood or stone in this position; we will define a house as bricks and timber in this position (or in some cases we mention the end as well). If we have to define ice, we will say it is water frozen or solidified in this way; we will say harmony is this sort of blending of high and low; and the same is true in the other cases.

It is evident from this that each different sort of matter has a different actuality and account. For in some cases the actuality is the composition, in some it is the mixture, and in others one of the other things we have mentioned.

That is why some people who offer definitions say what a house is by saying it is stones, bricks, and timber; in saying this, they speak of what is potentially a house, since these things are matter. Others say that a house is a container sheltering possessions and <living> bodies (or add something else of that sort); in saying this, they speak of the actuality. Others combine the matter and the actuality; in doing this, they speak of the third sort of substance, which is composed of the first two. For the account giving the differentiae would seem to be the account of the form and the actuality, and the one giving the constituents present in the house would seem to be more an account of the matter. The same is true of the sorts of formulae that Archytas used to accept; for these are accounts of the composite. What, for instance, is calm weather? Quiet in a large expanse of air; for air is the matter, and quiet is the actuality of the substance. What is calm? Smoothness of sea; the material subject is the sea, and the actuality and form is the smoothness.

It is evident from what we have said, then, both what perceptible sub-

---

68. **being mixed**: Read *to memichthai*. OCT: 'by being mixed'.

69. **is what . . . actuality**: lit. 'is most of all the actuality'.

stance is and what sort of being it has; for one sort is substance as matter, another is substance as form and actuality, and the third is the substance that is composed of these.

6

Let us now return to the puzzle we mentioned about definitions and about 1045a7
numbers, namely about the cause of their being one. If something has
several parts, but all together it is not a sort of heap, but, on the contrary, 10
the whole is something apart from the parts, then there is a cause of its
being one, since, even among bodies, in some cases the cause of being one
is contact, and in others it is viscosity or some other such attribute.

A definition is an account that is one, not by being tied together (like the
Iliad),[70] but by being of one thing. What, then, is it that makes man one?
Why is he one, and not more than one—animal and two-footed, for 15
instance—especially if, as some say, there is some animal itself and two-
footed itself?[71] For why is man not these things themselves? If so, men
will exist by participating, not in one thing (man), but in two (animal and
two-footed); and in general, man would be more than one (animal and two- 20
footed) and not one.

Now, it is evident that it is impossible to explain and solve the puzzle if
one continues to define and to speak as they normally do. But if, as we say,
one thing is matter and another is form, and the one is <something>
potentially, the other actually, then what we are searching for no longer 25
seems to be a puzzle. For this puzzle is the same as the question whether the
round bronze is the formula of cloak. <If it is,> then this name <'cloak'> is
a sign of the account, and so what we are searching for is what causes the
round and the bronze to be one. There no longer appears to be a puzzle,
then, because one of them is the matter, and the other is the form.

What, then, causes something that is potentially to be actually? That is 30
to say, what is the cause apart from the agent that produced it (in the case
of things that come to be)? There is no cause other than <the fact that> the
potential sphere is an actual sphere;[72] this is the essence of both <the
potential and the actual sphere>.

Some matter is intelligible, some perceptible; and in every account one
part is the matter, one the actuality. 35

If something has neither intelligible nor perceptible matter, it is thereby 1045b
essentially one thing, just as it is also essentially a being—a this, a quality,
a quantity; this is why neither being nor one is present in definitions.

70. *Iliad*: Cf. 1030a9.

71. **animal itself and two-footed itself**: i.e. the Platonic FORMS.

72. **There is . . . actual sphere**: Or: 'Nothing else is the cause of <the fact that> the
potential sphere is an actual sphere.'

Moreover, the essence of these things is thereby one thing, just as it is also a being. Hence none of these things has any other cause than being one or being a being; for each is some being and some one <thing> immediately <by its own nature>, not by being in the genus of being or of one, and not in such a way that <being and one> are separable apart from particulars.

This puzzle leads some to speak of participating and to be puzzled about its cause and about what it is. Others speak of communion: Lycophron, for instance, says that knowledge is a communion of knowing and the soul. Others say that life is a compounding or tying together of the soul with the body. But the same thing can be said about all these attempts. For according to them being healthy, for instance, will also be a communion or tying together or compounding of soul and health; and the bronze's being a triangle will be a compounding of bronze and triangle; and something's being pale will be a compounding of surface and paleness. The reason they say these things is that they are searching for an account that makes potentiality and actuality one, and <in doing so> they are searching for the differentia.

In fact, however, as we have said, the ultimate matter and the form are one and the same; the matter <is something> potentially, and the form <is that thing> actually. Hence <to search for what causes them to be one> is like searching for the cause of one and of being one. For each thing <that has matter and form> is some one thing; and what is potentially and what is actually are in a way one. And so nothing else causes <them to be one>, unless something has initiated the motion from potentiality to actuality. Anything that lacks matter is without qualification some one thing essentially.

BOOK XII

6

1071b3 Since we have found that there are three types of substance, two of them natural and one unmoved, we must discuss the third kind, to show that there must be an everlasting unmoved substance. For substances are the primary beings, and if all substances are perishable, then everything is perishable. But motion cannot come to be or perish (since it has always been), nor can time (since there cannot be a before and an after if there is no time). Motion is also continuous, then, in the same way that time is, since time is either the same as motion or an attribute of it. But the only continuous motion is local motion—specifically, circular motion.

Now if there is something that is capable of initiating motion or of acting, but it does not actually do so, there will be no motion; for what has a potentiality need not actualize it. It will be no use, then, to assume

everlasting substances, as believers in Forms do, unless these include some   *15*
principle capable of initiating change. And even this, or some other type of
substance besides the Forms, is not sufficient; for if it does not actualize its
potentiality, there will be no motion. Nor yet is it sufficient if it actualizes
its potentiality, but its essence is potentiality; for there will be no everlasting motion, since what has a potentiality need not actualize it. There must,
then, be a principle of the sort whose essence is actuality. Further, these   *20*
substances must be without matter; for they must be everlasting if anything
else is to be everlasting, and hence they must be actuality.

Now a puzzle arises. For it seems that whatever actualizes a potentiality
must have it, but not everything that has a potentiality also actualizes it;
and so potentiality is prior. But now, if this is so, nothing that exists will   *25*
exist, since things can have the potentiality to exist without actualizing it.
And yet, if those who have written about the gods are right to generate
everything from night,[73] or if the natural philosophers are right to say that
'all things were together',[74] the same impossibility results. For how will
things be moved if there is no cause <initiating motion> in actuality? For
surely matter will not initiate motion in itself, but carpentry, <for instance,   *30*
must initiate the motion>; nor will the menstrual fluid or the earth initiate
motion in themselves, but the semen and the seeds <must initiate the
motion>.

Hence some people—Leucippus and Plato, for instance—believe in everlasting actuality; for they say that there is always motion. But they do not
say why there is this motion, or what kind of motion it is, and neither do
they state the cause of something's being moved in this way or that. For
nothing is moved at random, but in every case there must be some   *35*
<cause>—as in fact things are moved in one way by nature and in another
by force or by the agency of mind[75] or something else. Further, what sort of
motion is primary? For that makes an enormous difference. Nor can Plato   *1072a*
say that the principle is of the sort that he sometimes thinks it is—what
initiates its own motion. For he also says that the soul is later <than
motion> and comes into being at the same time as the universe.[76]

The view that potentiality is prior to actuality is in a way correct and in
a way incorrect—we have explained how this is so. The priority of actu-   *5*
ality is attested by Anaxagoras (since mind is actuality), and by Empedocles (who makes love and strife prior), and by those who say that there is
always motion, as Leucippus does. And so chaos or night did not exist for

73. **from night**: Hesiod.

74. **all things were together**: Anaxagoras.

75. **mind**: *nous*, usually 'UNDERSTANDING'.

76. **Nor can Plato . . . universe**: Aristotle is probably thinking of *Timaeus* 34b.
Plato identifies what moves itself with soul, but he describes soul as coming into
existence when some sort of motion already exists.

an infinite time, but the same things have always existed (either in a cycle or in some other way), if actuality is prior to potentiality.

10   If, then, the same things always exist in a cycle, something must always remain actually operating in the same way. And if there is to be coming to be and perishing, then there must be something else that always actually operates, in one way at one time and in another way at another time. This <second mover>, then, must actually operate in one way because of itself and in another way because of something else, and hence either because of some third mover or because of the first mover. Hence it must be because
15   of the first mover; for <otherwise> the first mover will cause the motion of both the second and the third. Then surely it is better if the first mover is the cause. For we have seen that it is the cause of what is always the same, and a second mover is the cause of what is different at different times. Clearly both together cause this everlasting succession. Then surely this is also how the motions occur. Why, then, do we need to search for any other principles?

7

Since it is possible for things to be as we have said they are, and since the
20   only alternative is for everything to come to be from night and from all things being together and from what is not, this may be taken as the solution of the puzzles. There is something, then, that is always being moved in a ceaseless motion, and this motion is circular (this is clear not only from argument but also from what actually happens); and so the first heaven is everlasting. Hence there is also something that initiates motion. And since whatever both is moved and initiates motion is an intermediary,
25   there is something[77] that initiates motion without being moved, something that is everlasting and a substance and actuality.

This is how an object of understanding or desire initiates motion; it initiates motion without being moved. The primary objects of desire and of understanding are the same. For what appears fine is the object of appetite, and what is fine[78] is the primary object of wish; and we desire something because it seems <fine>, rather than its seeming <fine> because
30   we desire it—for understanding is the principle.[79]

Understanding is moved by its object, and the first column <of opposites> is what is understood in its own right. In this column substance is primary; and the primary substance is the substance that is simple and actually operating. (Being one and being simple are not the same; for being

77. intermediary, there is something . . .: Text uncertain. Read *kinoun meson, esti toinun*.

78. what appears fine . . . what is fine: Cf. *DA* 433a26–30, *EN* 1113a15–22.

79. understanding is the principle: Cf. *DA* 433a21, *EN* 1139a31–36.

one signifies a measure, while being simple signifies that something is itself in a particular condition.) Further, what is fine and what is choiceworthy for itself are in the same column; and what is primary is in every case either the best or what is analogous to the best.

Division shows that what something is for is among the things that are unmoved. For it is either the end for some <beneficiary> or the end <aimed at> in some <process>; the first of these is moved, and the second is unmoved. The <end> initiates motion by being an object of love, and it initiates motion in the other things by <something else's> being moved.

If, then, something is moved, it can be otherwise. And so, if something's actuality is the primary type of local motion,[80] it follows that in so far as it is in motion, in this respect it admits of being otherwise, in place if not in substance. But since there is something that initiates motion without itself being moved, and this is actually operating, it cannot be otherwise in any respect at all. For local motion is the primary type of motion, and the primary type of local motion is circular motion; and this is the sort of motion that the primary mover initiates. Hence the primary mover exists necessarily; and in so far as it exists necessarily, its being is fine, and in so far as its being is fine, it is a principle. For what is necessary is spoken of in a number of ways—as what is forced because it is contrary to the subject's impulse, as that without which the good cannot be, and as what cannot be otherwise but is necessary without qualification.

This, then, is the sort of principle on which the heaven[81] and nature depend. Its way of life has the same character as our own way of life at its best has for a short time. For the primary mover is always in this state <of complete actuality>, whereas we cannot always be in it; for its actuality is also pleasure (that is why being awake, perceiving, and thinking are pleasantest, while expectations and memories are pleasant because of these).

Understanding in its own right is of what is best in its own right, and the highest degree of understanding is of what is best to the highest degree in its own right. And understanding understands itself by sharing the character of the object of understanding; for it becomes an object of understanding by being in contact with and by understanding its object, so that understanding and its object are the same.[82] For understanding is what is capable of receiving the object of understanding and the essence, and it is actually understanding when it possesses its object; and so it is this <actual understanding and possession> rather than <the potentiality to receive the object> that seems to be the divine aspect of understanding, and its actual attention to the object of understanding is pleasantest and best.

80. **if something's . . . motion:** Read *ei phora prōtē hē energeia estin*.

81. **the heaven:** Aristotle uses 'heaven', *ouranos*, both for the upper universe in contrast to the earth and for the universe including the earth (as in 1074a31).

82. **understanding and its object are the same:** Cf. *DA* 430a3.

35
1072b

5

10

15

20

25 If, then, the god is always in the good state that we are in sometimes, that deserves wonder; if he is in a better state, that deserves still more wonder. And that is indeed the state he is in. Further, life belongs to the god. For the actuality of understanding is life, and the god is that actuality; and his actuality in its own right is the best and everlasting life. We say, then, that the god is the best and everlasting living being,[83] so that contin-

30 uous and everlasting life and duration belong to the god; for that is what the god is.

Some, however, suppose, as the Pythagoreans and Speusippus do, that what is finest and best is not present in the principle, claiming that the principles of plants and animals are their causes, whereas what is fine and

35 complete is found in what results from these. Their view is mistaken. For the seed comes from other <principles> that are prior and complete; and

1073a what is primary is not the seed, but the complete <organism>; for instance,[84] one would say that the man is prior to the seed (not the man who comes into being from the seed, but another one, from whom the seed comes).

It is evident from what has been said, then, that there is an everlasting,

5 unmoved substance that is separated from perceptible things. It has also been proved that this substance cannot have any magnitude, but must be without parts and indivisible; for it initiates motion for an infinite time, but nothing finite has infinite potentiality. And since every magnitude is either

10 infinite or finite, <the primary mover> cannot have a finite magnitude, and it cannot have an infinite magnitude, because there is no infinite magnitude at all. Besides, it has also been proved that this substance is not affected or altered, since all other motions depend on local motion. It is clear, then, why these things are so.

8

We must also consider, however, whether we should take there to be one

15 such substance, or more than one, and, if more than one, how many; and we must remember that, on the question about how many there are, other people's views have contributed nothing that can be perspicuously stated. The views about the Ideas, for instance, include no special discussion of the question. For those who speak of Ideas say that the Ideas are numbers, but

20 when they speak of numbers, they sometimes speak as though numbers were infinite, sometimes as though they were finite and went only as far as the number ten; and they make no serious effort to demonstrate the reason why there should be just this many numbers. Let us, however, take what has been laid down and determined as a basis for discussion.

83. **living being:** *zōon*, usually rendered 'animal'.
84. **for instance . . .:** Read *hoion proteron*.

The principle and primary being is unmoved both in its own right and coincidentally, and it initiates the everlasting and single primary motion. *25* Now, what is moved must be moved by something, but the primary mover is unmoved in its own right. Further, an everlasting motion is initiated by an everlasting mover, and a single motion is initiated by a single mover; but we see that besides the simple local motion of the whole, which we say is *30* initiated by the primary and unmoved substance, there are also the everlasting local motions of the planets (for a body that moves in a circle has an everlasting and unceasing motion, as was shown in our work on nature). Hence it necessarily follows that each of these motions is also initiated by the agency of some substance that is unmoved in its own right and everlasting. For the nature of the stars is everlasting and is a type of substance; and *35* what initiates motion is everlasting and prior to what is moved; and what is prior to a substance must be a substance. It is evident, then, that there must be this number of substances that are everlasting in their nature and unmoved in their own right, and (for the reason given above) without magni- *1073b* tude.

It is evident, then, that there are substances, and that one of them is first and another second, in an order corresponding to the motions of the stars. But when we come to the number of these motions, we must examine it on the basis of the mathematical science that is closest[85] to philosophy, i.e. as- *5* tronomy. For astronomy studies a kind of substance that is perceptible, but still everlasting, whereas the other mathematical sciences—those concerned with numbers and with geometry, for instance—do not study any substance at all.

Now it is evident, even on moderate acquaintance, that there are more motions than there are bodies moved, since each of the planets has more *10* than one motion. On the question of how many motions there are, we now state what some of the mathematicians say, in order to form some conception <of an answer>, so that we can suppose some definite number in our thinking. Beyond this <provisional answer> we must on some points inquire ourselves and on other points find out from other people's inquiries. If something different from what is now said appears correct to later *15* students, we must be friends to both sides, but must follow the more exact investigators.

Eudoxus thought that the motion of the sun and the moon in each case involves three spheres. The first is the sphere of the fixed stars; the second moves in the circle along the middle of the zodiac; the third moves in the *20* circle inclined across the breadth of the zodiac; and the moon's circle is inclined at a greater angle than the sun's circle. The motion of each planet involves four spheres. The first and second of these are the same as for the *25*

85. **closest**: or 'most proper', 'most akin', *oikeion*.

sun and the moon; for the sphere of the fixed stars is the one that moves all the spheres, and the sphere placed under this, moving in the circle along the middle of the zodiac, is also common to all the spheres. But the third sphere of each of the planets has its poles in the circle along the middle of

30 the zodiac; and the fourth moves along the circle inclined at an angle to the equator of the third sphere. And the poles of the third sphere are different for each of the planets, except that for Venus and Mercury they are the same.

Callippus agreed with Eudoxus about the position of the spheres. On

35 their number, he agreed with Eudoxus for Jupiter and Saturn, but for the sun and the moon he thought two further spheres must be added in order to yield the appearances, and that one must be added for each of the other planets.

1074a In fact, however, it is necessary, if all the combined spheres together are to yield the appearances, to admit further spheres (one fewer <than those mentioned>) that counteract <the previous spheres>, and in each case restore to the same position the first sphere of the star that is placed

5 beneath the given star. For only in that way is it possible for all the combined spheres to produce the motions of the planets.

And so the spheres in which the planets themselves move are eight and twenty-five; and only the spheres in which the lowest-placed planet moves need no counteracting spheres. Hence the spheres counteracting the spheres

10 of the first two planets will be six, and those counteracting the spheres of the next four will be sixteen. Hence the total number of the <forward-> moving and counteracting spheres will be fifty-five. If we do not add to the moon and sun the motions we mentioned, then the total number of the spheres will be forty-seven.

15 Let this, then, be the number of the spheres. In that case the supposition that this is also the number of unmoved substances and principles is reasonable—we can leave talk of necessity to stronger people.

And if every local motion <in the heaven> must contribute to the motion of a star, and if every nature and every substance that is unaffected

20 and that in its own right has achieved the best must be regarded as an end, it follows that there can be no other natures besides these, and that this must be the number of substances. For if there were other substances, they would have to initiate motions by being the end of local motion; but there cannot be any other local motion besides those mentioned above. It is

25 reasonable to infer this from the bodies that are moved. For if everything that initiates local motion is for the sake of what is moved, and if every motion is the motion of something that is moved, then no motion is for its own sake or for the sake of some other motion, but every motion is for the sake of the stars. For if every motion were for the sake of some further motion, then that further motion would have to be for the sake of something else; and so, since it cannot go on to infinity, one of the divine bodies that is moved in the heaven must be the end of every motion. 30

It is evident that there is only one heaven.[86] For if there were a number of heavens, as there are a number of men, then the principle—one for each heaven—would be specifically one but numerically many. Now, things that are numerically many all have matter; for many <particulars> have one and the same account—that of man, for instance—but Socrates is one 35 <particular>. But the primary essence has no matter, since it is actuality. Hence the primary and unmoved mover is one in number and account; so also, then, is what is always and continuously moved; and so there is only one heaven.

There is a tradition handed down from the distant past to later genera- 1074b tions, that these stars are gods and that the whole of nature is divine. The rest of the tradition is a mythical accretion, added to persuade the many 5 and to use in upholding what is lawful and advantageous; for those who handed it down say that the gods have human form or are similar to other animals, and they add other features following from these and similar to them. But if we separate the first point—that they thought the primary substances were gods—from these accretions, and consider it alone, we will 10 regard it as a divine insight, on the assumption that every craft and philo- sophical discipline has probably often been discovered, as far as people could manage it, and has often been forgotten, and that this belief has survived like remains from earlier generations until the present. And so <the truth of> the ancestral beliefs coming from the earliest times is evi- dent to us only to this extent.

9

The nature of <divine> understanding[87] raises a number of puzzles. For 15 understanding seems to be the most divine of the things we observe, but many difficulties arise about what state it must be in if it is to be so divine. For if it understands nothing, what is so impressive about it? It would be like someone asleep. If, on the other hand, it does understand, but some- thing else controls whether it understands (since its essence is not actual 20 understanding, but the potentiality for it), it is not the best substance; for what makes it valuable comes from <actual> understanding.

And in any case, whether its essence is potential or actual understand- ing, what does it understand? It must understand either itself or something else; if something else, then either always the same thing or else different

86. **heaven**: See 1072b14n.

87. **understanding**: *nous*. 'Thought' might also be defended in this chapter. Cf. in general *DA* iii 4.

things at different times. Then does it make any difference whether the
25   object of its understanding is fine or is just any old thing? Surely there are
some things that it would be absurd for it to think about. Clearly, then, it
understands what is most divine and most valuable, and it does not
change; for the change would be to something worse, and it would thereby
also be a motion.

First, then, if it is potential, not actual, understanding, it is reasonable to
expect that the continuous <exercise of> understanding would be tiring for
30   it. Moreover, clearly something other than understanding—namely the object of understanding—would be more valuable. For indeed both the potentiality and the activity of understanding[88] will belong even to someone
who understands the worst thing; and if this is to be avoided (since there
are also some things it is better not to see than to see), then the activity of
understanding is not the best thing.

<The divine understanding,> then, must understand itself, so that its
35   understanding is an understanding of understanding. In every case, however, knowledge, perception, belief, and thought have something other than
themselves as their object; each has itself as its object as a by-product.
Further, if to understand and to be understood are different, which is
responsible for the presence of the good? For to be an act of understanding
is not the same as to be understood.

1075a   Well, perhaps in some cases the knowledge is the object. In the productive <sciences, the knowledge is> the substance and essence <of the prod-
uct> without the matter, and in the theoretical sciences, the account is both
the object and the understanding. In these cases, then, where the object of
understanding does not differ from understanding—i.e., in cases where the
object has no matter—the object and the understanding will be the same,
5   and the activity of understanding will be one with its object.

One puzzle still remains: Is the object of understanding composite? If it
were composite, understanding would change in <understanding dif-
ferent> parts of the whole. Perhaps we should say that whatever has no
matter is indivisible. <On this view, the condition of actual understanding
is> the condition that human understanding (or rather, the understanding
of any composite beings) reaches over a certain length of time; for it does
not possess the good at this or that time, but achieves the best, which
10   is something other than it, in some whole <period of time>. And this is
the condition the understanding that understands itself is in throughout
all time.

88. **both the . . . of understanding:** Or 'both thinking (*noein*) and the act of thinking (*noēsis*)'.

DE ANIMA

The subject matter of this work is psychology, the study of the soul. (The title means "On the Soul.") For Aristotle this study is a part of biology; he identifies the soul with the form of a living thing. In the excerpts presented here, he sets out the problems he wishes to solve and indicates why the subject is so difficult (I.1), proposes his own definition of the soul (II.1–2), and describes a hierarchy of souls (II.3). The remainder of book II contains his theory of perception; book III considers the characteristic activity of the highest level of soul: thinking.

BOOK I

1

We suppose that knowing is fine and honorable, and that one type of   402a
knowing is finer and more honorable than another either because it is more
exact or because it is concerned with better and more wonderful things. On
both grounds, we might reasonably place inquiry into the soul in the first
rank. Moreover, knowledge of it seems to make an important contribution   5
to <knowledge of> the truth as a whole, and especially to the <knowledge
of> nature, since the soul is a sort of principle of animals. We seek to
study and know the nature and essence of the soul, and then all of its
coincidental properties; some of these seem to be distinctive attributes of
the soul, while others also seem to belong to animals because they have   10
souls.

And yet it is altogether in every way a most difficult task to reach any
conviction about the soul. For, as in many other areas of study, we are
seeking the essence and the what-it-is; and so someone might perhaps
think some single line of inquiry is appropriate for every case where we
want to know the substance—just as demonstration suits all coincidental   15
properties that are distinctive of a given subject. On this view, then, we
should seek this single line of inquiry. If, however, no single line of inquiry
is suitable for the what-it-is, our task turns out to be still more difficult,
since in that case we must discover how to study each area. But even if it is
evident whether demonstration or division or some further line of inquiry   20
is the right one, the question of where to begin our investigation causes
many puzzles and confusions; for different things—for instance, numbers
and surfaces—have different principles.

First of all, presumably, we must determine the soul's genus and what it is. Is it, in other words, a this and a substance, or a quality, or a quantity, or something in one of the other predications that we have distinguished? Further, is it something potential or is it more of an actuality? That makes quite a bit of difference. We should also examine whether it is divisible into parts or has no parts. Do all souls belong to the same species or not? If not, do they differ in species, or in genus? As things are, those who discuss and inquire into the soul would seem to examine only the human soul. Nor should we forget to ask whether there is just one account of the soul, as there is of animal, or a different account for each type of soul—for instance, of horse, dog, man, god—so that the universal animal either is nothing or else is posterior to these. The same will apply to any other common thing predicated.

Further, if there are not many types of soul, but <one type of soul with many> parts, must we begin by inquiring into the whole soul, or by inquiring into the parts? It is also difficult to determine which parts differ in nature from each other and whether we should begin by inquiring into the parts or for their functions. Should we, for instance, begin with understanding, perceiving, and so on, or with the part that understands and the part that perceives? And if we should begin with the functions, we might be puzzled anew about whether we should investigate the corresponding objects before the functions—the object of perception, for instance, before perceiving, and the object of understanding before understanding.

It would indeed seem useful to know the what-it-is, in order to study the causes of the coincidental properties of substances. In mathematics, for instance, it is useful to know what straight and curved are or what a line and a surface are, in order to notice how many right angles the angles of a triangle are equal to. Conversely, however, the <knowledge of the> coincidental properties also is also very important for knowing the what-it-is. For we can state the essence best once we can describe how all or most of the coincidental properties appear to be;[1] for since the what-it-is is the principle of all demonstration, a definition will clearly be dialectical and empty unless it results in knowledge, or at least in ready conjecture, about the coincidental properties.

A further puzzle arises about whether all the affections[2] of the soul also belong to what has the soul or there is also some affection that is distinctive of the soul itself. We must find the answer, but it is not easy.

---

1. **appear to be:** Lit. 'according to the appearance'. Aristotle is setting out the APPEARANCES or COMMON BELIEFS (endoxa).

2. **affections:** pathē. Pathos is often most appropriately rendered by 'ATTRIBUTE'. But in this section the connection with being affected (paschein) is especially close; hence 'affection' has been preferred.

In most cases (for instance, being angry or confident, having an appetite, or perceiving in general), it appears that without the body the soul neither is affected nor acts. Understanding, more than the other affections, would seem to be distinctive <of the soul>; but if it is also some sort of appearance[3] or requires appearance, then understanding also requires a body. 10 And so if some function or affection of the soul is distinctive of it, then the soul would be separable; but if not, then it would not be separable. Similarly, the straight, insofar as it is straight, has many coincidental properties—for instance, that it touches a bronze sphere at a point—but if it is separated, it will not touch the sphere in this way; for it is inseparable, 15 given that in every case it requires some body.

In fact, all the affections of the soul—emotion, gentleness, fear, pity, confidence, and, further, joy, loving, and hating—would seem to require a body, since whenever we have them the body is affected in some way. An indication of this is the fact that sometimes, though something severe and obvious affects us, we are not provoked or frightened; and sometimes we 20 are moved by something small and faint, if the body is swelling and in the condition that accompanies anger. It is still more evident that sometimes, though nothing frightening is happening, people are affected just as a frightened person is.

If this is so, then clearly affections are forms that involve matter. Hence 25 the formulae will be, for instance:[4] 'Being angry is a certain motion of this sort of body or part or capacity by this agency for this end'. Hence study of the soul—either every sort or this sort—turns out to be a task for the student of nature.

The student of nature and the dialectician would give different definitions of each of these affections—of anger, for instance. The dialectician 30 would define it as a desire to inflict pain in return for pain, or something of that sort, whereas the student of nature would define it as a boiling of the blood and of the hot <element> around the heart. The student of nature 403b describes the matter, whereas the dialectician describes the form and the account: for desire, for instance, is the form of the thing, but its existence requires this sort of matter. Similarly, the account of a house is of this sort—that it is a shelter preventing destruction by wind, rain, or heat; 5 someone else[5] will say that it is stones, bricks, and timber; and someone else will say that it is the form in these <stones, for instance,> for the sake of this end. Who, then, is the <real> student of nature—the one who is

3. **some sort of appearance**: i.e. a state of being appeared to (in which it is true that *x* appears *F* to me). See APPEARANCE.

4. **will be, for instance**: Or perhaps 'will be such (sc. involving matter). For instance . . .'.

5. **someone else**: Or perhaps 'another account'.

concerned with the matter but is ignorant of the account, or the one who is concerned only with the account? Or is the <real> student of nature more properly the one who mentions both form and matter? If so, then what is each of the first two?

10   Perhaps in fact there is no one who is concerned with the inseparable affections of matter but not concerned with them insofar as they are separable. Rather, the student of nature is concerned with all the actions and affections of this sort of body and this sort of matter; what is not of this sort concerns someone else, perhaps a craftsman (for instance, a carpenter 15   or a doctor). Inseparable affections, insofar as they are not affections of this sort of body but <are considered> by abstraction, concern the mathematician; insofar as they are separated, they concern first philosophy.

    We should return to where our discussion began. We were saying, then, that the affections of the soul (for instance, emotion and fear) are, insofar as they are affections of the soul, inseparable[6] (unlike surface and line) from the natural matter of animals.

4

408b   We say that the soul feels pain or enjoyment, and confidence or fear, and also that it is angry or perceives or thinks; and all of these seem to be 5   motions. Hence one might infer that the soul is in motion; but this does not necessarily follow.

    For let us by all means grant that feeling pain, feeling enjoyment, and thinking are motions, and that to be in these conditions is to be moved, and that the soul initiates the motion—so that to be angry or afraid, for instance, is for the heart to undergo this motion, while thinking is presumably a motion of this part or of something else, and this comes about in 10   some cases by the local motion of some things, in other cases by alteration (to say which things and what sort of motion requires another discussion). Still, to say that the soul is angry is like saying that the soul weaves or builds houses. For presumably it is better to say, not that the soul feels pity or learns or thinks, but that the human being does so by 15   the soul. And this is true not because the motion is in the soul, but because sometimes it reaches as far as the soul, and sometimes it begins from the soul. Perception, for instance, begins from these <external> things <and reaches as far as the soul>, while recollection begins from the soul and extends to the motions or to the traces remaining in the sense-organs. . . .

6. **inseparable**: They cannot exist without matter, though they are SEPARABLE in account and definition. See further *Met.* vii 10–11.

BOOK II

1

So much for the views on the soul that our predecessors have handed   412a3
down. Let us now return and make a new start, trying to determine what   5
the soul is and what account of it best applies to all souls in common.

We say, then, that one kind of being is substance. One sort of substance
is matter, which is not a this in its own right; another sort is shape or form,
which makes <matter> a this; and the third sort is the compound of matter
and form. Matter is potentiality, and form is actuality; actuality is either,   10
for instance, <the state of> knowing or <the activity of> attending <to
what one knows>.

What seem to be substances most of all are bodies, and especially natural bodies, since these are the sources[7] of the others. Some natural bodies
are alive and some are not—by 'life' I mean self-nourishment, growth, and   15
decay.[8]

It follows that every living natural body is a substance and, <more
precisely,> substance as compound. But since every such body is also this
sort of body—i.e. the sort that is alive—the soul cannot be a body, since
the body <is substance> as subject and matter and is not said of a subject.
The soul, then, must be substance as the form of a natural body that is   20
potentially alive. Now, substance is actuality; hence the soul will be the
actuality of this specific sort of body.

Actuality is spoken of in two ways—one corresponding to <the state of>
knowing and the other to attending to <what one knows>. Evidently, then,
the soul is the same sort of actuality that knowing is. For both being asleep
and being awake require the presence of the soul; being awake corresponds   25
to attending and being asleep to the state of inactive knowing. Moreover,
in the same subject the state of knowing precedes the activity. Hence the
soul is the first actuality[9] of a natural body that is potentially alive.

The sort of natural body that is potentially alive is an organic one. The   412b
parts of plants are also organs, though altogether simple ones; the leaf, for
instance, is a shelter for the shell, and the shell for the fruit, and similarly
the roots correspond to a mouth, since both draw in food. And so, if we
must give an account common to every sort of soul, we will say that the   5
soul is the first actuality of a natural organic body.

---

7. **sources:** *archai.* See PRINCIPLE #2. Aristotle means that artifacts are made from
natural bodies; cf. *Phys.* 192b19.

8. **self-** . . . **decay.** 'Self-' governs 'growth' and 'decay' as well as 'nourishment',
since in living creatures these all have an internal *archē*.

9. **first actuality:** Aristotle applies this term to the state exemplified by having
knowledge, contrasted with attending to what one knows.

Hence we need not ask whether the soul and body are one, any more than we need to ask this about the wax and the seal[10] or, in general, about the matter and the thing of which it is the matter. For while one and being are spoken of in several ways, the actuality <and what it actualizes> are fully one.[11]

10 We have said in general, then, that the soul is substance that corresponds to the account; and this <sort of substance> is the essence of this sort of body. Suppose some instrument—an axe, for instance—were a natural body; then being an axe would be its substance, and its soul would also be this <i.e. being an axe>; and if this substance were separated from it, it 15 would no longer be an axe, except homonymously. In fact, however, it is an axe; for the soul is not the essence and form of this sort of body but of the specific sort of natural body that has in itself a principle of motion and rest.

We must also study this point by applying it to the parts <of living things>. If the eye, for instance, were an animal, sight would be its soul. 20 For sight is the eye's substance that corresponds to the account, while the eye is the matter of sight; if an eye loses its sight, it is no longer an eye, except homonymously, as a stone eye or a painted eye is. We must apply this point about the part to the whole living body; for what holds for the relation of part <of the faculty of perception> to part <of the body> holds 25 equally for the relation of the whole <faculty of> perception to the whole perceptive body, insofar as it is perceptive. The sort of body that is potentially alive is not the one that has lost its soul but the one that has it; and the seed or the fruit is potentially this sort of body.

Being awake, then, is <a second> actuality, corresponding to cutting or 413a seeing. The soul is <a first> actuality, corresponding to <the faculty of> sight and to the potentiality of the instrument <to cut>; and the body is potentially this. And as an eye is the pupil plus sight, so an animal is soul plus body.

It is clear, then, that the soul is not separable from the body. At least, 5 some parts of it are not, if it is divisible into parts; for the actuality of some <parts of the soul> is <the actuality> of the parts <of the body> themselves. Still, some <parts of the soul> might well not be actualities of any body and might therefore be separable. Moreover, it is still unclear whether the soul is the actuality of the body in the way a sailor is of a ship. 10 Let this, then, be our outline definition and sketch of the soul.

10. **seal**: Or perhaps 'shape'.

11. **the actuality . . . one**: Or perhaps: 'The strict sense <of 'one'> is that of actuality'.

2

Since what is perspicuous and better known from the point of view of reason emerges from what is less perspicuous but more evident, we must start again and apply this approach to the soul. For the defining account must not confine itself, as most definitions do, to showing the fact; it must 15 also contain and indicate its cause. The accounts that are customarily stated in formulae are like conclusions, so that if we ask, for instance, what squaring is, we are told that it is making an equilateral rectangle equal to an oblong rectangle. This sort of formula is an account of the conclusion, whereas the one that defines squaring as the finding of the mean states the 20 cause of the fact.

To begin our inquiry, then, we say that living is what distinguishes things with souls from things without souls. Living is spoken of in several ways— for instance, understanding, perception, locomotion and rest, and also the motion involved in nourishment, and decay and growth. And so whatever 25 has even one of these is said to be alive.

This is why all plants as well <as animals> seem to be alive, since they evidently have an internal potentiality and principle through which they both grow and decay in contrary directions. For they grow up and down and in all directions alike, not just up rather than down; they are con- tinually nourished, and they stay alive as long as they can absorb nourish- 30 ment. This <sort of life> can be separated from the others, but in mortal things the others cannot be separated from it. This is evident in the case of plants, since they have no other potentiality of the soul.

This principle, then, is what makes something alive. What makes some- 413b thing an animal is primarily perception; for whatever has perception, even without motion or locomotion, is said to be an animal, not simply to be alive. Touch is the primary type of perception belonging to all animals, and 5 it can be separated from the other senses, just as the nutritive <potenti- ality> can be separated from touch and the other senses.

The part of the soul that belongs to plants as well as to animals is called nutritive; and all animals evidently have the sense of touch. Later we will 10 state the explanation of each of these facts.[12] For now let us confine our- selves to saying that the soul is the principle of the <potentialities> we have mentioned—for nutrition, perception, understanding, and motion— and is defined by them.

Is each of these a soul or a part of a soul? And if a part, is it the sort that is separable only in account, or is it also separable in place? In some cases 15 the answer is easily seen, but some parts raise a puzzle. For some plants are evidently still alive when they are cut <from one plant> and are separated

---

12. **explanation . . . facts**: A teleological explanation is given in iii 12 (not re- printed in this volume).

20   from each other; for, we assume, the soul in each plant is actually one but potentially more than one. And we see that the same is also true of other differentiae of the soul. <This is clear> in the case of insects that are cut in two. For each part has both perception and locomotion; if it has perception, then it also has appearance and desire. For if it has perception, then it has pain and pleasure, and if it has these, then it necessarily also has appetite.

25   So far, however, nothing is evident about understanding and the potentiality for theoretical study. It would seem to be a different kind of soul,[13] and the only part that can be separated,[14] in the way in which the everlasting can be separated from the perishable.

30   It evidently follows, however, that the other parts of the soul are not separable, as some say they are. But they evidently differ in account; for perceiving is different from believing, and hence being the perceptive part is different from being the believing part, and so on for each of the other parts mentioned.

414a   Further, animals are differentiated by the fact that some of them have all of these parts, some have some of them, and some have only one; we should investigate the reason for this later. Practically the same is true of the senses; some animals have all of them, some have some of them, and some have only the most necessary one, touch.

5   When we say we live and perceive by something, we speak in two ways, just as we do when we say we know by something. For we say we know either by knowledge or by the soul, since we say we know by each of these; and similarly, we are healthy in one way by health, in another way by some part or the whole of the body. In these cases, knowledge or health is a sort

10   of shape and form, i.e. an account and a sort of actuality of what is receptive of knowledge or health; for the actuality of the agent seems to occur in the thing that is acted on and suitably disposed.

    Now the soul is that by which we primarily live, perceive, and think, and

15   so it will be an account and a form, not matter and subject. For substance, as we said, is spoken of in three ways, as form, matter, and the compound of both; of these, matter is potentiality, form actuality. Since, therefore, the compound of body and soul is ensouled, body is not the actuality of soul, but the soul is the actuality of some sort of body.

20   This vindicates the view of those who think that the soul is not a body but requires a body; for it is not a body, but it belongs to a body, and for that reason it is present in a body, and in this sort of body. Our pre-

13. **different kind of soul**: Or perhaps 'different kind (*genos*) of thing from soul'.

14. **and the . . . separated**: Read *endechesthai*, 413b26. OCT: 'and it is the only part that can be separated'.

decessors were wrong, then, in trying to fit the soul into a body without further determining the proper sort of body, even though it appears that not just any old thing receives any old thing. Our view, however, is quite reasonable, since a thing's actuality naturally comes to be in what has the potentiality for it, i.e. in the proper matter.

It is evident from this, then, that the soul is a certain sort of actuality and form of what has the potentiality to be of this sort.

3

As we said, some things have all the potentialities of the soul that were previously mentioned, while other things have some of these potentialities, and others have only one. The potentialities we mentioned were those for nutrition, perception, desire, locomotion, and understanding. Now, plants have only the nutritive part. Other things have the nutritive part and also the perceptive part, and if they have the perceptive part, they also have the desiring part. For desire includes appetite, emotion, and wish; but all animals have at least the sense of touch, and whatever has any perception has pleasure and pain and finds things pleasant or painful. Whatever finds things pleasant and painful also has appetite, since appetite is desire for what is pleasant.

Further, animals have the perception of nourishment; for touch is perception of nourishment, since all living things are nourished by things that are dry and wet and hot and cold, and touch is the perception of these. Animals are nourished by other objects of perception[15] only coincidentally, since neither sound nor color nor smell contributes anything to nourishment, and flavor is an object of touch. Now, hunger and thirst are appetites for the dry and hot, and the wet and cold, respectively, while flavor is a sort of pleasant relish belonging to these.

We must make these points clear later on. For now let us confine ourselves to saying that living things that have touch also have desire. Whether they all have appearance is not clear, and must be considered later.

Besides these parts, some things have the locomotive part. Others— human beings, for instance, and any thinking being that is different from, or superior to, a human being[16]—also have the thinking part and intellect.

Clearly, then, soul will have one single account in the same way that figure has; for just as figure is nothing besides the triangle and the figures that follow in order, so equally the soul is nothing besides those <potenti-

25

30

414b

5

10

15

20

---

15. **other objects of perception**: Read *tois d'allois tōn aisthētōn*.

16. **any thinking . . . human being**: Or: 'anything else that is similar or superior to a human being'.

alities> we have mentioned. Still, in the case of figures we can find a
common account that fits all of them and is distinctive of none; the same is
25   true for the souls we have mentioned. It is ridiculous, then, in these and
other such cases, to seek a common account that is not distinctive of any
being and does not fit the proper and indivisible species, if we neglect this
32   <distinctive> account. Hence[17] we must ask what the soul of each particu-
33   lar <kind of thing>—for instance, a plant, a human being, or a beast—is.
28   What is true of the soul is similar to what is true of figure; for in both
cases the earlier is invariably present potentially in its successor—for in-
415a   stance, the triangle in the square, and the nutritive in the perceptive. We
must consider why they are in this order. For the perceptive part requires
the nutritive, but in plants the nutritive is separated from the perceptive.
Again, each of the other senses requires touch, whereas touch is found
5   without the other senses, since many animals lack sight, hearing, and
smell. Among things that perceive, some but not all have the locomotive
part. Finally and most rarely, some have reasoning and understanding. For
perishable things that have reasoning also have all the other parts of the
10   soul; but not all of those that have each of the other parts also have
reasoning—on the contrary, some animals lack appearance, while some live
by appearance alone. Theoretical intellect requires a different account.
     Clearly, then, the account of each of these parts of the soul is also the
most proper account of <each type of> soul.

     4

15   If we are to investigate these <parts of the soul> we must find what each of
them is and then inquire into the next questions and those that follow. And
if we ought to say what, for instance, the understanding or the perceptive
or the nutritive part is, we should first say what it is to understand or
20   perceive, since actualities and actions are prior in account to potentialities.
If this is so, and if in addition the objects corresponding to the actualities
are prior to them and so must[18] be studied first, then we must, for the same
reason, begin by determining the objects corresponding to nutrition, sense,
and understanding. And so we should first discuss nourishment and generation; for the nutritive soul belongs to other living things as well as <to
25   plants>, and it is the first and most widely shared potentiality of the soul,
the one that makes all living things alive.
     Its functions are generation and the use of nourishment. For the most
natural of all functions for a living thing, if it is complete and not defective
and does not come to be by chance, is to produce another thing of the same

17. **Hence . . . beast is:** 414b32–33 have been transposed to 414b28.

18. **and so must . . .:** Read *kai dei*.

sort as itself (an animal, if it is an animal, and a plant, if it is a plant), in
order to share as far as it can in the everlasting and divine. For this is the   *415b*
end they all strive for, and for its sake they do every action that accords
with nature. (What something is for is of two types—the goal and the
beneficiary.) These living things cannot share in the everlasting and divine
by continuously existing, since no perishable thing can remain numerically
one and the same; hence they share in it as far as they can, to different   *5*
degrees, and what remains is not the <parent> itself, but something else of
the same sort as <the parent>—something that is specifically, not numerically, one with <the parent>.

The soul is the cause and principle of the living body. Now, causes are
spoken of in many ways, and the soul is a cause in three of the ways   *10*
distinguished—as the source of motion, as what something is for, and as
the substance of ensouled bodies.

It is clearly the cause as substance; for a thing's substance is the cause of
its being, and the being of living things is their living, the cause and
principle of which is soul. Moreover, the actuality is the form of what is
potentially.

The soul is evidently also a cause by being what something is for. For just   *15*
as productive thought aims at something, so does nature, and what it aims
at is its end. In living things[19] the natural end is the soul; for all natural
bodies, of plants no less than of animals, are organs of the soul, since they   *20*
are for the sake of the soul. (The end for the sake of which is of two types,
either the goal or the beneficiary.)

Moreover, the soul is also the source of locomotion, though not all living
things have this potentiality. Alteration and growth also depend on the
soul; for perception seems to be some kind of alteration, and nothing that   *25*
lacks a soul perceives. The same applies to growth and decay; for nothing
either decays or grows naturally without being nourished, and nothing that
has no share of life is nourished.

Empedocles is wrong when he adds that plants grow by putting down
roots because earth naturally moves downwards, and that plants grow by   *416a*
extending upwards because fire naturally moves upwards. His conception
of up and down is wrong. For up and down are not the same for each
particular <sort of> thing as they are for the universe as a whole; in fact, if   *5*
we ought to call organs the same or different in accordance with their
functions, a plant's roots correspond to an animal's head. Besides, what is it
that holds the fire and earth together when they are moving in contrary
directions? For they will be torn apart unless something prevents it; whatever prevents it will be the soul, the cause of growing and being nourished.

Some think the nature of fire is the unqualified cause of nourishment   *10*

19. **living things**: Read *zōsin*.

and growth, since it is the only body that is evidently nourished and grows, and hence one might suppose that it also performs this function in both plants and animals. In fact, however, fire is a sort of joint cause, but not the unqualified cause; it is the soul, rather than fire, that is the unqualified cause. For while fire grows without limit, as long as there is fuel, the size and growth of everything naturally constituted has a limit and form, which are characteristic of soul, not of fire—i.e., of the form rather than of the matter.

Since one and the same potentiality of the soul is both nutritive and generative, we must first determine the facts about nutrition; for this is the function that distinguishes the nutritive potentiality from others.

Contrary seems to nourish contrary, not in every case, but only when they not only come to be but also grow from each other; for many things come to be from each other (healthy from sick, for instance) without gaining any quantity. And not even those contraries that grow seem to nourish each other in the same way; water, for instance, nourishes fire, but fire does not nourish water. It seems to be true, then, of the simple bodies more than of other things, that one thing nourishes and the other is nourished.

A puzzle arises: while some say that like nourishes like, just as (they say) like grows by like, others, as we have said, hold the opposite view, that contrary nourishes contrary; for, they say, like is unaffected by like, but nourishment changes and is digested, and everything changes into its opposite or into the intermediate. Moreover, nourishment is affected by the thing nourished, whereas the thing nourished is unaffected by the nourishment—just as the matter is affected by the carpenter, who is unaffected by it and merely changes from inactivity to activity.[20]

It matters for this question whether nourishment is the first or last thing added. Perhaps it is both, if undigested nourishment is added first, and digested nourishment last. If so, then it would be possible to speak of nourishment in both ways; for insofar as nourishment is undigested, contrary nourishes contrary, and insofar as it has been digested, like nourishes like. Evidently, then, each view is in a way both correct and incorrect.

Since nothing is nourished except what has a share of life, the ensouled body, insofar as it is ensouled, is what is nourished. Nourishment, therefore, is also relative, not coincidentally, to an ensouled thing. However, nourishing something is not the same as making it grow; for an ensouled thing is caused to grow insofar as it has some quantity, but it is nourished insofar as it is a this and a substance. For it preserves its substance and exists as long as it is nourished; and what it generates is not itself, but something else of the same sort—for its own substance already exists, and a thing does not generate, but preserves, itself.

Hence this sort of principle in the soul is a potentiality of the sort that

---

20. **activity**: *energeia*, usually rendered 'actuality'.

preserves the ensouled thing, insofar as it is ensouled, and nourishment
equips it for its actuality; and so if it has been deprived of nourishment it   20
cannot exist. Further,[21] since a thing's end rightly determines what we   23
should call it, and in this case the end is the generation of another thing of
the same sort, this first soul will be the generative soul, generating another   25
thing of the same sort.

We must distinguish three things—what is nourished, what it is nour-   20
ished by, and what nourishes. What nourishes is this first soul, what is
nourished is the ensouled body, and what it is nourished by is the nourishment. What the soul nourishes by is of two types—just as what we steer by
is both the hand and the rudder: The first both initiates motion and undergoes it, and the second simply undergoes it. Since all nourishment must be
digestible and the hot element produces digestion, every ensouled thing
contains heat.

This, then, is an outline of what nutrition is; we should describe it more   30
clearly later in the discussions proper to it.

5

Now that we have determined this, let us discuss perception in general.
Perception occurs in being moved and affected, as we have said, since it
seems to be a type of alteration. Some also say that like is affected by like;   35
we have said in our general discussion of acting and being affected how   417a
this is or is not possible.

A puzzle arises about why we do not perceive the senses themselves, and
about why they do not produce perception without external objects, despite
the presence of fire, earth, and the other elements, whose intrinsic or   5
coincidental properties are the things that are perceived. Clearly, then, the
perceptive part is <what it is> by merely potential, not actual, <perceiving>,
and so it does not perceive <without an external object>—just as what is
combustible is not burnt all by itself without something to burn it, since
otherwise it would burn itself with no need of actual fire.

We speak of perceiving in two ways; for we say that something sees or   10
hears both in the case of something that has the potentiality for seeing or
hearing, even though it is asleep at the time, and in the case of something
that is actually seeing or hearing at the time. It follows that perception is
also spoken of in two ways, as potential and as actual, and in the same way
both what is potentially perceived and what is actually perceived are called
objects of perception.

First, then, let us speak as though the actuality were the same as being   15
affected and moved—for motion is in fact a sort of actuality, though an

---

21. **Further, since . . . same sort:** 416b23–25 are transposed to 416b20.

incomplete one, as we have said elsewhere.[22] Now, everything is affected
and moved by an agent that has the relevant property in actuality, so that

20   in a way like is affected by like, and in a way unlike by unlike—for what
is being affected is unlike the agent, but when it has been affected it is like
the agent.

We must also distinguish types of potentiality and actuality, since just
now we were speaking of them without qualification. One way in which
someone might know is the way we have in mind in saying that a man
knows because man is a kind of thing that knows and has knowledge;

25   another way is the way we have in mind in saying that someone who has
grammatical knowledge knows. These knowers have different sorts of
potentiality—the first has a potentiality because he has the right sort of
genus and matter, whereas the second has a potentiality because he has the
potentiality to attend to something when he wishes, if nothing external
prevents it. A third sort <of knower> is someone who is attending to
something at the time, actualizing his knowledge and fully knowing (for

30   instance) this A. In the first and second case we pass from potentially to
actually knowing; but in the first case we do so by being altered through
learning, and by frequent changes from the contrary state, while in the sec-

417b ond case—where we pass from having arithmetical or grammatical knowledge without actualizing it, to actualizing it—we do so in another way.

Further, there is not just one way of being affected. On the contrary, one
way of being affected is a destruction of contrary by contrary, while the
other way is more properly preservation, not destruction, of a potential F

5   by an actual F, when the potential F is <not contrary, but> like the actual F,
in the way that a potentiality is like its actuality. For the second case—
where the possessor of knowledge comes to attend to what he knows—
either is not a case of alteration at all (since the addition leads to <the
knowledge> itself and to the actuality) or is a different kind of alteration.
That is why we should not say that the intelligent subject is altered in
exercising his intelligence, just as we should not say that the builder is
altered in <actually> building.

10   First, then, when an understanding and intelligent subject is led from
potentiality to actuality, we should not call this teaching but give it some
other name. Again, if a subject with potential knowledge learns and acquires knowledge from a teacher with actual knowledge, then we should
say either, as we said, that this is not a case of being affected, or that there

15   are two ways of being altered, one of which is a change into a condition of
deprivation, and the other of which is a change into possession of a state
and into <the fulfillment of the subject's> nature.

In the perceiver, the first change is produced by its parent; and at birth it
possesses perception corresponding to <the second type of> knowledge.

22. **said elsewhere**: See *Phys.* iii 1.

We speak of actual perceiving in a way that corresponds to attending,
except that the visible, audible, and other perceptible objects that produce   *20*
the actuality are external. This is because actual perception is of particulars, while knowledge is of universals, which are, in a way, in the soul
itself; hence it is up to us to think whenever we want to, but it is not up to   *25*
us to perceive whenever we want to, since perception requires the presence
of its object. The same is true for the types of knowledge that are about
perceptible things, and for the same reason—namely that perceptible things
are particulars and external.

There may be an opportunity to explain these points more perspicuously   *30*
another time, but for the moment let us be content with the distinctions we
have made. There are different types of potentiality: One is what is meant
in saying that a child is potentially a general. A second is what is meant in
attributing the potentiality to someone of the right age, and <this second
type> applies to the perceptive part. Since the difference between these   *418a*
cases has no name, though our distinctions have shown that they are different, and in what ways, we have to use 'being affected' and 'being altered'
as though they were the strictly correct names.

The perceiver is potentially what the perceptible object actually is already, as we have said. When it is being affected, then, it is unlike the   *5*
object; but when it has been affected it has been made like the object and
has acquired its quality.

6

We should first discuss the objects of perception, taking each sense in turn.
An object of perception is spoken of in three ways: Two types are perceived intrinsically, and one coincidentally. One type of intrinsic object is   *10*
proper to each sense, and the other type of intrinsic object is common to
all the senses.

By 'proper object' I mean the one that cannot be perceived by another
sense and about which we cannot be deceived. Sight, for instance, is of
color; hearing of sound; taste of flavor; and touch has a number of different objects. At any rate, each sense discriminates among its proper   *15*
objects, and a sense is not deceived about whether, for instance, something
is a color or a sound, but can be deceived about whether or where the
colored or sounding thing is. These objects, then, are said to be proper to
each sense.

Motion, rest, number, shape, and size are the common objects, since they
are not proper to any one sense, but are common to them all—a certain
sort of motion, for instance, is perceptible by both touch and sight.   *20*

Something is said to be coincidentally perceptible if, for instance, the
pale <thing> is the son of Diares. For we perceive the son of Diares
coincidentally, since he coincides with the pale thing we perceive, and

hence we are not affected at all by the perceptible object insofar as it is
<the son of Diares>.

25   Among the intrinsic objects of perception, the proper objects are most
properly perceptible, and the essence of each sense is by nature relative to
these. . . .

11

423b27   . . . The objects of touch are the differentiae of body insofar as it is body,
i.e. those that distinguish the elements—hot, cold, dry, and wet; we have
30   discussed these earlier in what we said about the elements. Their tactile
sense-organ, the primary seat of the sense called touch, is the part that has
424a   these qualities potentially. For perceiving is a way of being affected; hence
the agent causes the thing that is affected, which potentially has the quality
that the agent has, to have that quality actually.

Hence we do not perceive anything that is as dry or wet, or hard or soft,
<as the organ>, but only the excesses in either direction, because the sense
5   is a sort of intermediate condition between the contraries in objects of
perception. And that is why a sense discriminates among its objects; for
what is intermediate discriminates, since in relation to each extreme it
becomes the other extreme. And just as what is going to perceive both pale
and dark must be actually neither pale nor dark but potentially both, and
10   similarly in the other cases, so also in the case of touch, <what is going to
perceive the contraries> must be neither hot nor cold.

Further, just as we found that sight in a way perceives both the visible
and the invisible, and similarly the other senses perceive the opposites, so
also touch perceives the tangible and the intangible. What is intangible is
either something that either has altogether very few of the differentiating
properties of tangibles—air, for instance—or has an excess of tangible
15   qualities—for instance, things that destroy <the sense>.

We have spoken in outline, then, of the senses, one by one.

12

A general point to be grasped is that each sense receives the perceptible
forms without the matter. Wax, for instance, receives the design on a
20   signet-ring without the iron or gold; it acquires the design in the gold or
bronze, but not insofar as the design is gold or bronze. Similarly, each sense
is affected by the thing that has color or flavor or sound, but not insofar as
it is said to be that thing <for instance, a horse>, but insofar as it has a
given quality <for instance, color> and in accordance with the form <of
the sense>.

25   The primary sense-organ is the seat of this sort of potentiality. Hence
the organ and the capacity are one, but their being is different. For though

<the sense-organ> that perceives is of some magnitude, being perceptive is not, and <so> the sense is not something with magnitude but is a <specific sort of> form and potentiality of the organ.

It is also evident from this why excesses in objects of perception destroy the sense-organs. For if the motion is too strong for the sense-organ, then the form, i.e. the sense, is destroyed, just as the harmony and tension are destroyed if the strings of an instrument are struck heavily. 30

This also makes it evident why plants do not perceive, even though they have one part of soul, and are affected in some ways by objects of touch, since they are chilled and heated. The reason is that they lack a <suitable> intermediate condition and a principle suitable for receiving the form of perceptible things; instead, they are affected <by the form> with the matter. 424b

A puzzle arises about whether something that cannot smell can be at all affected by odor, or something that cannot see can be affected by color, and so on for the other cases. If the object of smell is odor, then anything produced by odor must be <the act of> smelling; hence nothing that is incapable of smelling anything can be affected by odor (the same applies to the other cases), and any such thing must be affected insofar as it is a perceiver. A further argument makes the same conclusion clear. For a body is affected neither by light and darkness nor by sound nor by odor, but only by their subject, as, for instance, the air that comes with the thunder splits the log. 5

10

On the other hand, tangible <qualities> and flavors affect bodies; otherwise, what would affect and alter soulless things? Then will the other objects of perception also affect bodies? Perhaps not every body is liable to be affected by odor and sound, and those that are affected are indefinite and impermanent—air, for instance, since it acquires an odor as though affected in some way. 15

Then what is there to smelling, besides being affected? Perhaps smelling is <not only being affected, but> also perceiving, while air that is affected <by odor>, by contrast, soon becomes an object of perception <not a perceiver>.

BOOK III

3

. . . If appearance[23] is that in virtue of which some object appears to us,[24] in contrast to what is so called metaphorically, then is it one of those 428a1

---

23. **appearance**: This might also be translated 'imagination' in this chapter.

24. **object appears to us**: Lit. 'some object-of-appearance (*phantasma*) arises for us'.

5 potentialities or states in virtue of which we discriminate and attain truth or falsity? These are perception, belief, knowledge, and understanding.

It is clear as follows that appearance is not the same as perception. For perception is either a potentiality, such as sight, or an actuality, such as seeing; but we have appearances when we have neither of these—in dreams, for instance. Moreover, perception is present in every <animal>, but appearance is not. If they were the same in actuality, then it would be 10 possible for all beasts to have appearance, whereas in fact it does not seem possible <for all>; ants or bees, for instance, and grubs <do not have it>.[25] Further, perceptions are always true, whereas most appearances are false. Again, whenever we are actually perceiving accurately, we do not say that this appears to us <to be> a man; we are more inclined to say <that 15 something appears to be so> in cases where we do not see clearly whether something is true or false. Further, as we were saying before, sights appear to us even when we have our eyes closed.

The remaining question is whether appearance is belief; for belief may 20 also be either true or false. Belief, however, implies conviction—since one cannot believe things if one does not find them convincing—whereas no beasts have conviction, though many have appearance. Further, belief implies conviction, conviction implies being persuaded, and persuasion implies reason, whereas no beasts have reason, though some have appearance.

25 It is evident, then, that appearance is neither belief that involves perception, nor belief that is produced through perception, nor a combination of belief and perception. This is so both for the reasons given and also because <on this view> belief will not be about anything other than the thing, if there is one, that is the object of perception.

I mean, for instance, that the combination of a belief about the pale and 30 a perception of the pale will turn out to be appearance; for surely it will not be the combination of a belief about the good and a perception of the 428b pale—for appearance will be having a belief non-coincidentally about the very thing one perceives. In fact, however, we sometimes have false appearances about the same things at the same time as we have a true supposition about them, as when, for instance, the sun appears a foot across, even though we are convinced that it is bigger than the inhabited world.

5 It turns out, then, <on the view being considered> that either we have lost the true belief we had, even though the thing still exists and we have neither forgotten our belief nor been persuaded to change it, or else, if we still have the true belief, the same belief must at the same time be both true and false. But in fact it could have become false only if the thing changed without our noticing it. It follows, then, that appearance cannot be any of these things, nor a product of them.

25. **ants or . . . have it**: Text uncertain. A plausible emendation: 'ants or bees, for instance, <have it>, but grubs do not'.

It is possible, however, when one thing has been set in motion, for a   10
second thing to be set in motion by the first. Moreover, appearance seems
to be a sort of motion, to involve perception, to be present in things that
have perception, and to be about the objects of perception. Now, it is also
possible for motion to result from actual perception, and this motion must
be similar to the perception.

Hence this motion cannot occur without perception or in things that do   15
not have perception. Things that have appearance act and are affected in
many ways in accordance with it, and it can be either true or false. . . .

4

Now we must consider the part by which the soul has knowledge and   429a10
intelligence, and ask whether it is separable, or it is not separable in magnitude but only in account; and what its differentia is, and how understanding comes about.

Now, if understanding[26] is like perceiving, it consists either in being
affected by the object of intellect or in something else of the same sort.   15
Hence the intellect must be unaffected, but receptive of the form; it must
have the quality <of the object> potentially, not actually; and it must be
related to its object as the perceiving part is related to the objects of
perception.

Hence the intellect, since it understands all things, must be unmixed, in
order, as Anaxagoras says, to 'master' them (i.e. to know them); for the   20
intrusion of any foreign thing would hinder and obstruct it. And so it has
no nature except this—that it is potential. Hence the part of the soul called
intellect (by which I mean that by which the soul thinks and supposes) is
not actually, before it understands, any of the things there are. It is also   25
unreasonable, then, for intellect to be mixed with the body, since it would
then acquire some quality (for instance, hot or cold) or even, like the
perceiving part, have some organ, whereas in fact it has none.

And so those who say that the soul is a place of forms are right, except
that it is the intellectual soul, not the whole soul, which is—potentially, not
actually—the forms.

The condition of the sense-organ and of the faculty of perception makes   30
it evident that the perceiving part and the intellectual part are unaffected in
different ways. For after a sense perceives something very perceptible, it   429b
cannot perceive; after hearing very loud sounds, for instance, it cannot
hear sound, and after seeing vivid colors or smelling strong odors, it can-

---

26. **understanding**: In this chapter *noein* is rendered 'understand', and the term for
the relevant faculty, *nous*, by 'intellect'. Probably Aristotle (in this chapter) is primarily treating *noein* as a form of knowledge, not simply as thinking about things;
but it is not always clear which he has in mind. See UNDERSTANDING #2. 'Thought'
and 'thinking' are reserved for *dianoia* and *dianoeisthai*. See *APo* 100b8n.

not see or smell. But whenever intellect understands something that is very
intelligible, it understands more, not less, about inferior objects; for intellect is separable, whereas the perceiving part requires a body.

When the intellect becomes each thing <that it understands>, as it does
when someone is said to have actual knowledge (this comes about whenever someone is able to actualize his knowledge through himself), even
then it is still potential in a way, though not in the same way as before it
learnt or discovered; and then it is capable of understanding itself.[27]

Magnitude is different from being magnitude and water from being water; and the same applies in many other cases too, though not in all, since
in some cases the thing is the same as its being.[28] It follows that to discriminate being flesh we use something different, or something in a different
state, from what we use in discriminating flesh; for flesh requires matter,
and, like the snub, it is this <form> in this <matter>. Hence to discriminate the hot and the cold and the things of which flesh is some sort of
form, we use the perceptive part; but to discriminate being flesh, we use
something else that is either separable <from body> or related to it as a
formerly bent line is related to the straight line it has become.

Further, if we turn to things whose being depends on abstraction, the
straight is similar to the snub, since it requires something continuous. But if
being straight is different from the straight, then so is the essence of
straight (duality, let us say) different from the straight, and therefore to
discriminate it we use something different, or something in a different
state. In general, then, the <separability> of intellect corresponds to the
way in which objects are separable from matter.

A puzzle arises. If intellect is simple and unaffected, having, as Anaxagoras says, nothing in common with anything, then how can it understand, if understanding consists in being affected? For it seems that two
things must have something in common if one is to affect the other. Again,
is intellect itself an object of intellect? For if nothing other <than itself>
makes it an object of intellect, and if all objects of intellect are one in
species, then the other objects of intellect will also be intellect; alternatively, it will need something mixed into it, to make it an object of
intellect in the same way as the other objects of intellect are.

On the other hand, our previous discussion of ways of being affected
because of something in common has shown that the intellect is in a way
potentially the objects of intellect, but before it understands them, it is
none of them actually. Its potentiality is that of a writing tablet with
nothing actually written on it—which is also true of intellect.

Further, intellect itself is an object of intellect in the same way as its
objects are. For in the case of things without matter, the understanding

27. **understanding itself**: Reading *de hauton*. OCT: 'it is capable of understanding
through itself'.

28. **the thing is the same as its being**: See *Met.* 1036a1.

part and its object are one,[29] since actual knowledge and its object are the   5
same. (We should investigate why it is not <engaged in the activity of>
understanding all the time.) In things that have matter, each object of
intellect is potentially present; hence intellect will not be in them (since it is
a potentiality for being such things without their matter), but it will be an
object of intellect.

5[30]

In the whole of nature each kind of thing has something as its matter,   10
which is potentially all the things in the kind, and something else as the
cause and producer, which produces them all—for instance, the craft in
relation to its matter. These differences, then, must also be found in the
soul. One sort of intellect corresponds to matter, since it becomes all   15
things. Another sort corresponds to the producer by producing all things in
the way that a state, such as light, produces things—for in a way light
makes potential colors into actual colors. This second sort of intellect is
separable, unaffected, and unmixed, since its essence is actuality.

For in every case the producer is more valuable than the thing affected,
and the principle is more valuable than the matter. Actual knowledge is the   20
same as its object; potential knowledge is temporally prior in an individual
<knower>, but in general it is not even temporally prior. But <productive
intellect> does not understand at one time and not at another.

Only when it has been separated is it precisely what it is, all by itself.
And this alone is immortal and everlasting. But <when it is separated>[31] we
do not remember, because this <productive intellect> is unaffected,
whereas the intellect that is affected is perishable. And without this   25
<productive intellect>[32] nothing understands. . . .

10

There are apparently two parts that move us—both intellect and desire, if   433a9
we take appearance to be a kind of understanding. For many people follow   10
their appearances against their knowledge, and the other animals have
appearance but lack understanding and reasoning. Both intellect and de-

29. **the understanding . . . are one**: Cf. *Met.* 1072b18–21.

30. The text, translation, and interpretation of this chapter are all extremely doubtful. There are disputes about whether the productive intellect is a part of an
individual soul or something common to all souls, about its role in thought, and
about its dependence on or independence of the senses and the body.

31. <**when it is separated**>: Or perhaps <when it is embodied>. The Greek at this
point is very elliptical and ambiguous.

32. **without this** <**productive intellect**>: Or perhaps 'without this <passive intel-
lect>'.

sire, then, move us from place to place. This is the intellect that reasons for
some goal and is concerned with action; its <concern with an> end distinguishes it from theoretical intellect. All desire also aims at some goal; for
the object of desire is the starting point[33] of intellect concerned with action, and the last stage <of our reasoning> is the starting point of action.

Hence it is reasonable to regard these two things—desire, and thought
concerned with action—as the movers. For the object of desire moves us,
and thought moves us because its starting point is the object of desire.
Moreover, whenever appearance moves us, it requires desire.

And so there is one mover, the desiring part. For if there were two—
intellect and desire—they would move us insofar as they had a common
form. In fact, however, intellect evidently does not move anything without
desire,[34] since wish is desire, and any motion in accordance with reasoning
is in accordance with wish; desire, on the other hand, also moves us against
reasoning, since appetite is a kind of desire. Now, intellect is always correct, but desire and appearance may be either correct or incorrect. Hence in
every case the mover is the object of desire, but the object of desire is
either the good or the apparent good[35]—not every sort of good, but the
good that is achievable in action. What is achievable in action admits of
being otherwise.

Evidently, then, the potentiality of the soul that moves us is the one
called desire. People who divide the soul into parts, if they divide it
into separate parts corresponding to the different potentialities, will find
very many of them—the nutritive, perceptive, intellectual, and deliberative parts, and, moreover, the desiring part; for the difference between
these parts is wider than the one between the appetitive and emotional
parts.

Desires that are contrary to each other arise, however, when reason and
appetite are contrary, which happens in subjects that perceive time. For
intellect urges us to draw back because of what is to come, while appetite
<urges us on> because of what is present; for the pleasant thing that is
present appears both unqualifiedly pleasant and unqualifiedly good, because we do not see what is to come.

Hence the mover is one in species—the desiring part, insofar as it is
desiring. Indeed, the first mover of all is the object of desire, since it moves
us without being moved, by being present to understanding or appearance.
But the movers are numerically more than one.

We must distinguish three things—the mover, its instrument, and the
subject moved. There are two types of movers: the unmoved mover and the
moved mover. The unmoved mover is the good achievable in action, and
the moved mover is the desiring part; for the thing that is moved is moved

33. **starting point**: *arche*. See PRINCIPLE #2.

34. **moves nothing without desire**: On the roles of thought and desire see *EN*
1139a35.

35. **the good or the apparent good**: Cf. *EN* iii 4.

insofar as it desires, and desire, insofar as it is actual, is a sort of motion. The thing moved is the animal. When we reach the instrument by which desire moves, we reach something bodily, and so we should study it when we study the functions common to soul and body.

To summarize for the present: What moves something as an instrument is found where the same thing is both the starting point and the last stage. In the hinge-joint, for instance, the convex is last, and hence at rest, while the concave is the starting point, and hence is moved. These are different in account, though they are spatially inseparable. For since everything is moved by pushing and pulling, something must remain at rest, as in a circle, and the motion must originate from this.

In general, then, as we have said, an animal moves itself insofar as it has desire. For desire it needs appearance; and appearance is either rational appearance or the perceptual appearance that other animals share <with human beings>.

11

We should also consider what it is that moves incomplete animals, whose only form of perception is touch. Can they have appearance and appetite, or not? For they evidently have pleasure and pain; if they have these, they must have appetite. But how could they have appearance? Well, perhaps, just as they are moved indeterminately, so also they have appearance and appetite, but have them indeterminately.

Now, the other animals as well <as man> also have perceptual appearance, as we have said, but <only> reasoning animals have deliberative appearance. For when we come to the question whether one is to do this or that, we come to a task for reasoning. And <in this case> one must measure by one <standard>, since one pursues the greater <good>. And so one is able to make one object of appearance out of many. And this is why <non-rational animals> do not seem to have belief; it is because they lack the <appearance> resulting from reasoning.

That is why desire lacks the deliberative part. And sometimes one desire overcomes and moves another, while sometimes the second overcomes and moves the first, like one sphere moving another, whenever incontinence[36] occurs. By nature the <desire> that is superior is dominant in every case and moves <the agent>, and so it turns out that three motions are initiated <in the agent>. The part that has knowledge stays at rest and is not moved.

Now, one sort of supposition and statement is universal, while another is about what is particular; for the first says that this sort of agent ought to do this sort of thing, and the second says that this is this sort of thing and I am this sort of agent. Hence the second belief, not the universal belief, initiates motion; or <rather> both initiate motion, but the first does so by being more at rest, in contrast to the second.

36. **incontinence**: Cf. *EN* i 13, vii 3.

NICOMACHEAN ETHICS

There are three works of moral philosophy in the Aristotelian corpus: the Eudemian Ethics, *the* Magna Moralia *(considered by many scholars not to be a genuine work of Aristotle), and the* Nicomachean Ethics. *Of these it is the last—
one of the greatest works in all of moral philosophy—that represents the culmi-
nation of his mature thought.*

*In the extensive excerpts provided below, Aristotle discusses happiness and
human good (Book I); the nature of moral virtue (Book II); moral responsibility,
deliberation, and praise and blame (Book III); justice (Book V); the intellectual
virtues and practical wisdom (Book VI); weakness of the will (Book VII); and
happiness and contemplation (Book X).*

Book I

1

1094a Every craft and every investigation, and likewise every action and decision,
seems to aim at some good; hence the good has been well described as that
at which everything aims.

   However, there is an apparent difference among the ends aimed at. For
the end is sometimes an activity, sometimes a product beyond the activity;
5   and when there is an end beyond the action, the product is by nature better
than the activity.

   Since there are many actions, crafts and sciences, the ends turn out to be
many as well; for health is the end of medicine, a boat of boatbuilding,
10   victory of generalship, and wealth of household management.

   But whenever any of these sciences are subordinate to some one capacity—as e.g. bridlemaking and every other science producing equipment for
horses are subordinate to horsemanship, while this and every action in
warfare are in turn subordinate to generalship, and in the same way other
sciences are subordinate to further ones—in each of these the end of the
15   ruling science is more choiceworthy than all the ends subordinate to it,
since it is the end for which those ends are also pursued. And here it does
not matter whether the ends of the actions are the activities themselves, or
some product beyond them, as in the sciences we have mentioned.

Translated by T. Irwin

2

Suppose, then, that (a) there is some end of the things we pursue in our actions which we wish for because of itself, and because of which we wish for the other things; and (b) we do not choose everything because of something else, since (c) if we do, it will go on without limit, making desire empty and futile; then clearly (d) this end will be the good, i.e. the best good.

Then surely knowledge of this good is also of great importance for the conduct of our lives, and if, like archers, we have a target to aim at, we are more likely to hit the right mark.[1] If so, we should try to grasp, in outline at any rate, what the good is, and which science or capacity is concerned with it.

It seems to concern the most controlling science, the one that, more than any other, is the ruling science. And political science apparently has this character.

(1) For it is the one that prescribes which of the sciences ought to be studied in cities, and which ones each class in the city should learn, and how far.

(2) Again, we see that even the most honored capacities, e.g. generalship, household management and rhetoric, are subordinate to it.

(3) Further, it uses the other sciences concerned with action, and moreover legislates what must be done and what avoided.

Hence its end will include the ends of the other sciences, and so will be the human good.

<This is properly called political science;> for though admittedly the good is the same for a city as for an individual, still the good of the city is apparently a greater and more complete good to acquire and preserve. For while it is satisfactory to acquire and preserve the good even for an individual, it is finer and more divine to acquire and preserve it for a people and for cities. And so, since our investigation aims at these <goods, for an individual and for a city>, it is a sort of political science.

3

Our discussion will be adequate if its degree of clarity fits the subject-matter; for we should not seek the same degree of exactness in all sorts of arguments alike, any more than in the products of different crafts.

Moreover, what is fine and what is just, the topics of inquiry in political science, differ and vary so much that they seem to rest on convention only,

1. **and if . . . right mark:** Or: 'like archers who have a target to aim at, we are more likely to hit what is right <if we know what the target is>.' The version in the text implies that knowledge of the good gives us a target we would otherwise lack (cf. Plato, *Rep.* 519c2); the alternative version does not imply this.

not on nature. Goods, however, also vary in the same sort of way, since they cause harm to many people; for it has happened that some people have been destroyed because of their wealth, others because of their bravery.

Since these, then, are the sorts of things we argue from and about, it will
20   be satisfactory if we can indicate the truth roughly and in outline; since <that is to say> we argue from and about what holds good usually <but not universally>, it will be satisfactory if we can draw conclusions of the same sort.

Each of our claims, then, ought to be accepted in the same way <as claiming to hold good usually>, since the educated person seeks exactness
25   in each area to the extent that the nature of the subject allows; for apparently it is just as mistaken to demand demonstrations from a rhetorician as to accept <merely> persuasive arguments from a mathematician.

Further, each person judges well what he knows, and is a good judge
1095a about that; hence the good judge in a particular area is the person educated in that area, and the unconditionally good judge is the person educated in every area.

This is why a youth is not a suitable student of political science; for he lacks experience of the actions in life which political science argues from and about.

Moreover, since he tends to be guided by his feelings, his study will be
5   futile and useless; for its end is action, not knowledge. And here it does not matter whether he is young in years or immature in character, since the deficiency does not depend on age, but results from being guided in his life and in each of his pursuits by his feelings; for an immature person, like an incontinent person, gets no benefit from his knowledge.
10   If, however, we are guided by reason in forming our desires and in acting, then this knowledge will be of great benefit.

These are the preliminary points about the student, about the way our claims are to be accepted, and about what we intend to do.

4

Let us, then, begin again. Since every sort of knowledge and decision
15   pursues some good, what is that good which we say is the aim of political science? What <in other words> is the highest of all the goods pursued in action?

As far as its name goes, most people virtually agree <about what the good is>, since both the many and the cultivated call it happiness, and
20   suppose that living well and doing well are the same as being happy. But they disagree about what happiness is, and the many do not give the same answer as the wise.

For the many think it is something obvious and evident, e.g. pleasure, wealth or honor, some thinking one thing, others another; and indeed the

same person keeps changing his mind, since in sickness he thinks it is
health, in poverty wealth. And when they are conscious of their own   25
ignorance, they admire anyone who speaks of something grand and beyond
them.

<Among the wise,> however, some used to think that besides these
many goods there is some other good that is something in itself, and also
causes all these goods to be goods.

Presumably, then, it is rather futile to examine all these beliefs, and it is
enough to examine those that are most current or seem to have some   30
argument for them.

We must notice, however, the difference between arguments from origins
and arguments towards origins. For indeed Plato was right to be puzzled
about this, when he used to ask if <the argument> set out from the origins
or led towards them—just as on a race course the path may go from the 1095b
starting-line to the far end,[2] or back again.

For while we should certainly begin from origins that are known, things
are known in two ways; for some are known to us, some known unconditionally <but not necessarily known to us>. Presumably, then, the origin
we should begin from is what is known to *us*.

This is why we need to have been brought up in fine habits if we are to
be adequate students of what is fine and just, and of political questions   5
generally. For the origin we begin from is the belief that something is true,
and if this is apparent enough to us, we will not, at this stage, need the
reason why it is true in addition; and if we have this good upbringing, we
have the origins to begin from, or can easily acquire them.[3] Someone who
neither has them nor can acquire them should listen to Hesiod: 'He who   10
understands everything himself is best of all; he is noble also who listens
to one who has spoken well; but he who neither understands it himself nor
takes to heart what he hears from another is a useless man.'

5

But let us begin again from <the common beliefs> from which we di-
gressed. For, it would seem, people quite reasonably reach their conception   15
of the good, i.e. of happiness, from the lives <they lead>; for there are 17, 18

2. **far end:** Lit. 'limit'. Aristotle thinks of a Greek stadium, in which the midpoint
of the race is at the end farthest from the starting line.

3. **For the origin . . . acquire them:** Lit. 'For the origin is the that, and if this
appears adequately, he will not at all need in addition the because. Such a one has
origins or would get them easily.' The origins we are looking for are those known
without qualification, and we do not have them simply as a result of good upbringing; these tell us the 'because' or 'reason why'. The origins we have from good
upbringing are simply those that allow us to begin the inquiry. See 1095a2,
1179b25.

19   roughly three most favoured lives—the lives of gratification, of political
16   activity, and, third, of study.
17   The many, the most vulgar, would seem to conceive the good and happi-
19   ness as pleasure, and hence they also like the life of gratification. Here they
20   appear completely slavish, since the life they decide on is a life for grazing
     animals; and yet they have some argument in their defense, since many in
     positions of power feel the same way as Sardanapallus[4] <and also choose
     this life>.
          The cultivated people, those active <in politics>, conceive the good as
     honor, since this is more or less the end <normally pursued> in the politi-
     cal life. This, however, appears to be too superficial to be what we are
25   seeking, since it seems to depend more on those who honor than on the one
     honored, whereas we intuitively believe that the good is something of our
     own and hard to take from us.
          Further, it would seem, they pursue honor to convince themselves that
     they are good; at any rate, they seek to be honored by intelligent people,
     among people who know them, and for virtue. It is clear, then, that in the
30   view of active people at least, virtue is superior <to honor>.
          Perhaps, indeed, one might conceive virtue more than honor to be the
     end of the political life. However, this also is apparently too incomplete <to
     be the good>. For, it seems, someone might possess virtue but be asleep or
1096a inactive throughout his life; or, further, he might suffer the worst evils and
     misfortunes; and if this is the sort of life he leads, no one would count him
     happy, except to defend a philosopher's paradox. Enough about this, since it
     has been adequately discussed in the popular works[5] also.
5   The third life is the life of study, which we will examine in what follows.
          The money-maker's life is in a way forced on him <not chosen for itself>;
     and clearly wealth is not the good we are seeking, since it is <merely>
     useful, <choiceworthy only> for some other end. Hence one would be
     more inclined to suppose that <any of> the goods mentioned earlier is the
     end, since they are liked for themselves. But apparently they are not <the
10   end> either; and many arguments have been presented against them. Let
     us, then, dismiss them.

7

15   But let us return once again to the good we are looking for, and consider
     just what it could be, since it is apparently one thing in one action or craft,
     and another thing in another; for it is one thing in medicine, another in
     generalship, and so on for the rest.

4. **Sardanapallus:** An Assyrian king who lived in legendary luxury.

5. **the popular works:** (enkuklia) Probably these are by Aristotle himself, and are
the same as the 'popular' (or 'external', exōterika) works of 1102a26.

What, then, is the good in each of these cases? Surely it is that for the sake of which the other things are done; and in medicine this is health, in generalship victory, in house-building a house, in another case something   *20* else, but in every action and decision it is the end, since it is for the sake of the end that everyone does the other things.

And so, if there is some end of everything that is pursued in action, this will be the good pursued in action; and if there are more ends than one, these will be the goods pursued in action.

Our argument has progressed, then, to the same conclusion <as before, that the highest end is the good>; but we must try to clarify this still more.   *25*

Though apparently there are many ends, we choose some of them, e.g. wealth, flutes and, in general, instruments, because of something else; hence it is clear that not all ends are complete. But the best good is apparently something complete. Hence, if only one end is complete, this will be   *30* what we are looking for; and if more than one are complete, the most complete of these will be what we are looking for.

An end pursued in itself, we say, is more complete than an end pursued because of something else; and an end that is never choiceworthy because of something else is more complete than ends that are choiceworthy both in themselves and because of this end; and hence an end that is always <choiceworthy, and also> choiceworthy in itself, never because of something else, is unconditionally complete.

Now happiness more than anything else seems unconditionally complete, since we always <choose it, and also> choose it because of itself, never *1097b* because of something else.

Honor, pleasure, understanding and every virtue we certainly choose because of themselves, since we would choose each of them even if it had no further result, but we also choose them for the sake of happiness,   *5* supposing that through them we shall be happy. Happiness, by contrast, no one ever chooses for their sake, or for the sake of anything else at all.

The same conclusion <that happiness is complete> also appears to follow from self-sufficiency, since the complete good seems to be self-sufficient.

Now what we count as self-sufficient is not what suffices for a solitary person by himself, living an isolated life, but what suffices also for parents, children, wife and in general for friends and fellow-citizens, since a human   *10* being is a naturally political <animal>. Here, however, we must impose some limit; for if we extend the good to parents' parents and children's children and to friends of friends, we shall go on without limit; but we must examine this another time.

Anyhow, we regard something as self-sufficient when all by itself it makes a life choiceworthy and lacking nothing; and that is what we think   *15* happiness does.

Moreover, we think happiness is most choiceworthy of all goods, since it is not counted as one good among many. If it were counted as one among

many, then, clearly, we think that the addition of the smallest of goods would make it more choiceworthy; for <the smallest good> that is added becomes an extra quantity of goods <so creating a good larger than the original good>, and the larger of two goods is always more choiceworthy.
20   <But we do not think any addition can make happiness more choice-worthy; hence it is most choiceworthy.>

Happiness, then, is apparently something complete and self-sufficient, since it is the end of the things pursued in action.

But presumably the remark that the best good is happiness is apparently something <generally> agreed, and what we miss is a clearer statement of what the best good is.

Well, perhaps we shall find the best good if we first find the function of
25   a human being. For just as the good, i.e. <doing> well, for a flautist, a sculptor, and every craftsman, and, in general, for whatever has a function and <characteristic> action, seems to depend on its function, the same seems to be true for a human being, if a human being has some function.

Then do the carpenter and the leatherworker have their functions and
30   actions, while a human being has none, and is by nature idle, without any function? Or, just as eye, hand, foot and, in general, every <bodily> part apparently has its functions, may we likewise ascribe to a human being some function besides all of theirs?

What, then, could this be? For living is apparently shared with plants, but what we are looking for is the special function of a human being; hence
1098a we should set aside the life of nutrition and growth. The life next in order is some sort of life of sense-perception; but this too is apparently shared, with horse, ox and every animal. The remaining possibility, then, is some sort of life of action of the <part of the soul> that has reason.

Now this <part has two parts, which have reason in different ways>, one
5   as obeying the reason[6] <in the other part>, the other as itself having reason and thinking.[7] <We intend both.> Moreover, life is also spoken of in two ways <as capacity and as activity>, and we must take <a human being's special function to be> life as activity, since this seems to be called life to a fuller extent.

(a) We have found, then, that the human function is the soul's activity that expresses reason <as itself having reason> or requires reason <as obeying reason>. (b) Now the function of F, e.g. of a harpist, is the same in kind, so we say, as the function of an excellent F, e.g. an excellent harpist.

---

6. **obeying the reason:** Cf. 1102b26.

7. 'One as obeying the reason' (a4) = 'requires reason'—lit. 'not without reason—(a8) and refers to the role of non-rational desires. 'Itself having reason and think-ing' (a5) = 'expresses reason'—lit. 'according to reason'—(a7) and refers to the role of reason and rational desires. On these rational and non-rational parts of the soul see 1102b26.

(c) The same true unconditionally in every case, when we add to the   *10*
function the superior achievement that expresses the virtue; for a harpist's
function, e.g. is to play the harp, and a good harpist's is to do it well. (d)
Now we take the human function to be a certain kind of life, and take this
life to be the soul's activity and actions that express reason. (e) <Hence by
(c) and (d)> the excellent man's function is to do this finely and well. (f)
Each function is completed well when its completion expresses the proper   *15*
virtue. (g) Therefore <by (d), (e) and (f)> the human good turns out to be
the soul's activity that expresses virtue.

And if there are more virtues than one, the good will express the best
and most complete virtue. Moreover, it will be in a complete life. For one
swallow does not make a spring, nor does one day; nor, similarly, does one   *20*
day or a short time make us blessed and happy.

This, then, is a sketch of the good; for, presumably, the outline must
come first, to be filled in later. If the sketch is good, then anyone, it seems,
can advance and articulate it, and in such cases time is a good discoverer or
<at least> a good co-worker. That is also how the crafts have improved,   *25*
since anyone can add what is lacking <in the outline>.

However, we must also remember our previous remarks, so that we do
not look for the same degree of exactness in all areas, but the degree that
fits the subject-matter in each area and is proper to the investigation. For
the carpenter's and the geometer's inquiries about the right angle are dif-   *30*
ferent also; the carpenter's is confined to the right angle's usefulness for his
work, whereas the geometer's concerns what, or what sort of thing, the
right angle is, since he studies the truth. We must do the same, then, in
other areas too, <seeking the proper degree of exactness>, so that digres-
sions do not overwhelm our main task.

Nor should we make the same demand for an explanation in all cases. *1098b*
Rather, in some cases it is enough to prove that something is true without
explaining why it is true. This is so, e.g. with origins, where the fact that
something is true is the first principle, i.e. the origin.[8]

Some origins are studied by means of induction, some by means of
perception, some by means of some sort of habituation, and others by
other means. In each case we should try to find them out by means suited   *5*
to their nature, and work hard to define them well. For they have a great

---

8. **Rather, in . . . i.e. the origin:** Lit. 'But it is enough in some cases for the that to
be proved well, e.g. in the case of origins and the that is first and origin.' Here
Aristotle uses the phrase 'the that' for the ORIGINS known without qualification, i.e.
the first principles of his theory (in this case, the account of happiness), and not (as
in 1095b6) for the origins known to us, the starting-points in our inquiry. Starting-
points are beliefs that need some further 'because'. First principles provide the
necessary 'because', and a further 'because' cannot be given for the first principles,
since they are first, and themselves give the 'because'.

influence on what follows; for the origin seems to be more than half the whole,[9] and makes evident the answer to many of our questions.

8

However, we should examine the origin not only from the conclusion and
10   premises <of a deductive argument>, but also from what is said about it; for all the facts harmonize with a true account, whereas the truth soon clashes with a false one.

Goods are divided, then, into three types, some called external, some goods of the soul, others goods of the body; and the goods of the soul are
15   said[10] to be goods to the fullest extent and most of all, and the soul's actions and activities are ascribed to the soul. Hence the account <of the good> is sound, to judge by this belief anyhow—and it is an ancient belief agreed on by philosophers.

Our account is also correct in saying that some sort of actions and activities are the end; for then the end turns out to be a good of the soul,
20   not an external good.

The belief that the happy person lives well and does well in action also agrees with our account, since we have virtually said that the end is a sort of living well and doing well in action.

Further, all the features that people look for in happiness appear to be true of the end described in our account. For to some people it seems to be
25   virtue; to others intelligence; to others some sort of wisdom; to others again it seems to be these, or one of these, involving pleasure or requiring its addition; and others add in external prosperity as well.[11]

Some of these views are traditional, held by many, while others are held by a few reputable men; and it is reasonable for each group to be not entirely in error, but correct on one point at least, or even on most points.
30   First, our account agrees with those who say happiness is virtue <in general> or some <particular> virtue; for activity expressing virtue is proper to virtue. Presumably, though, it matters quite a bit whether we suppose that the best good consists in possessing or in using, i.e. in a state or in an activity <that actualizes the state>. For while someone may be in a

9. **the origin seems . . . :** A Greek proverb—i.e., 'well begun is more than half done'.

10. **are said:** Lit. 'we say'; but Aristotle must be reporting it as a widely held belief.

11. **involving . . . addition:** Lit. 'with pleasure or not without pleasure'. Aristotle seems to be distinguishing (a) life consisting of activities that are sources of pleasure in themselves, and (b) life consisting in activities that are not in themselves sources of pleasure, plus added sources of pleasure. The same distinction is assumed at 1099a15.

state that achieves no good, if, e.g., he is asleep or inactive in some other 1099a way, this cannot be true of the activity; for it will necessarily do actions and do well in them. And just as Olympic prizes are not for the finest and strongest, but for contestants, since it is only these who win; so also in life 5 <only> the fine and good people who act correctly win the prize.

Moreover, the life of these <active> people is also pleasant in itself. For being pleased is a condition of the soul, <hence included in the activity of the soul>. Further, each type of person finds pleasure in whatever he is called a lover of, so that a horse, e.g. pleases the horse-lover, a spectacle the lover of spectacles, and similarly what is just pleases the lover of justice, 10 and in general what expresses virtue pleases the lover of virtue. Hence the things that please most people conflict, because they are not pleasant by nature, whereas the things that please lovers of what is fine are things pleasant by nature; and actions expressing virtue are pleasant in this way; and so they both please lovers of what is fine and are pleasant in 15 themselves.

Hence their life does not need pleasure to be added <to virtuous activity> as some sort of ornament; rather, it has its pleasure within itself. For besides the reasons already given, someone who does not enjoy fine actions is not good; for no one would call him just, e.g., if he did not enjoy doing just actions, or generous if he did not enjoy generous actions, and 20 similarly for the other virtues. If this is so, then actions expressing the virtues are pleasant in themselves.

Moreover, these actions are good and fine as well as pleasant; indeed, they are good, fine and pleasant more than anything else, since on this question the excellent person has good judgement, and his judgement agrees with our conclusions.

Happiness, then, is best, finest and most pleasant, and these three features are not distinguished in the way suggested by the Delian inscription: 25 'What is most just is finest; being healthy is most beneficial; but it is most pleasant to win our heart's desire.' For all three features are found in the best activities, and happiness we say is these activities, or <rather> one of 30 them, the best one.

Nonetheless, happiness evidently also needs external goods to be added <to the activity>, as we said, since we cannot, or cannot easily, do fine actions if we lack the resources.

For, first of all, in many actions we use friends, wealth and political 1099b power just as we use instruments. Further, deprivation of certain <externals>—e.g. good birth, good children, beauty—mars our blessedness; for we do not altogether have the character of happiness if we look utterly repulsive or are ill-born, solitary or childless, and have it even less, presumably, if our children or friends are totally bad, or were good but have died. 5

And so, as we have said, happiness would seem to need this sort of

prosperity added also; that is why some people identify happiness with
good fortune, while others <reacting from one extreme to the other> identify it with virtue.

9

This <question about the role of fortune> raises a puzzle: Is happiness
acquired by learning, or habituation, or by some other form of cultivation?
10 Or is it the result of some divine fate, or even of fortune?

First, then, if the gods give any gift at all to human beings, it is reasonable for them to give happiness also; indeed, it is reasonable to give happiness more than any other human <good>, insofar as it is the best of
human <goods>. Presumably, however, this question is more suitable for a
different inquiry.

15 But even if it is not sent by the gods, but instead results from virtue and
some sort of learning or cultivation, happiness appears to be one of the
most divine things, since the prize and goal of virtue appears to be the best
good, something divine and blessed.

Moreover <if happiness comes in this way> it will be widely shared; for
anyone who is not deformed <in his capacity> for virtue will be able to
20 achieve happiness through some sort of learning and attention.

And since it is better to be happy in this way than because of fortune, it
is reasonable for this to be the way <we become> happy. For whatever is
natural is naturally in the finest state possible, and so are the products of
crafts and of every other cause, especially the best cause; and it would be
seriously inappropriate to entrust what is greatest and finest to fortune.

25 The answer to our question is also evident from our account <of happi-
ness>. For we have said it is a certain sort of activity of the soul expressing
virtue, <and hence not a product of fortune>; and some of the other goods
are necessary conditions <of happiness>, others are naturally useful and
cooperative as instruments <but are not parts of it>.

Further, this conclusion agrees with our opening remarks. For we took
30 the goal of political science to be the best good; and most of its attention is
devoted to the character of the citizens, to make them good people who do
fine actions, <which is reasonable if happiness depends on virtue, not on
fortune>.

It is not surprising, then, that we regard neither ox nor horse nor any
other kind of animal as happy, since none of them can share in this sort of
1100a activity. And for the same reason a child is not happy either, since his age
prevents him from doing these sorts of actions; and if he is called happy,
he is being congratulated because of anticipated blessedness, since, as we
5 have said, happiness requires both complete virtue and a complete life.

<Happiness needs a complete life.> For life includes many reversals of

fortune, good and bad, and the most prosperous person may fall into a
terrible disaster in old age, as the Trojan stories tell us about Priam; but if
someone has suffered these sorts of misfortunes and comes to a miserable
end, no one counts him happy.

13

Since happiness is an activity of the soul expressing complete virtue, we   5
must examine virtue; for that will perhaps also be a way to study happiness
better.

Moreover, the true politician seems to have spent more effort on virtue
than on anything else, since he wants to make the citizens good and law-
abiding. We find an example of this in the Spartan and Cretan legislators   10
and in any others with their concerns. Since, then, the examination of
virtue is proper for political science, the inquiry clearly suits our original
decision[12] <to pursue political science>.

It is clear that the virtue we must examine is human virtue, since we are
also seeking the human good and human happiness. And by human virtue
we mean virtue of the soul, not of the body, since we also say that happi-   15
ness is an activity of the soul. If this is so, then it is clear that the politician
must acquire some knowledge about the soul, just as someone setting out to
heal the eyes must acquire knowledge about the whole body as well. This is   20
all the more true to the extent that political science is better and more
honorable than medicine—and even among doctors the cultivated ones
devote a lot of effort to acquiring knowledge about the body. Hence the
politician as well <as the student of nature> must study the soul.

But he must study it for the purpose <of inquiring into virtue>, as far as
suffices for what he seeks; for a more exact treatment would presumably   25
take more effort than his purpose requires. <We> have discussed the soul
sufficiently <for our purposes> in <our> popular works as well[13] <as our
less popular>, and we should use this discussion.

We have said, e.g., that one <part> of the soul is nonrational, while one
has reason. Are these distinguished as parts of a body and everything
divisible into parts are? Or are they two only in account, and inseparable   30
by nature, as the convex and the concave are in a surface? It does not
matter for present purposes.

Consider the nonrational <part>. One <part> of it, i.e. the cause of
nutrition and growth, is seemingly plant-like and shared <with other living
things>: for we can ascribe this capacity of the soul to everything that is *1102b*

12. **decision:** The decision made in I.2.

13. **in <our>** . . . **as well:** Or perhaps 'even in the popular works', on which see
note to 1096a3.

nourished, including embryos, and the same one to complete living things, since this is more reasonable than to ascribe another capacity to them.

Hence the virtue of this capacity is apparently shared, not <specifically> human. For this part and capacity more than others seem to be active in sleep, and here the good and the bad person are least distinct, which is why happy people are said to be no better off than miserable people for half their lives.

And this lack of distinction is not surprising, since sleep is inactivity of the soul insofar as it is called excellent or base, unless to some small extent some movements penetrate <to our awareness>, and in this way the decent person comes to have better images <in dreams> than just any random person has. Enough about this, however, and let us leave aside the nutritive part, since by nature it has no share in human virtue.

Another nature in the soul would also seem to be nonrational, though in a way it shares in reason.

<Clearly it is nonrational.> For in the continent and the incontinent person we praise their reason, i.e. the <part> of the soul that has reason, because it exhorts them correctly and towards what is best; but they evidently also have in them some other <part> that is by nature something besides reason, conflicting and struggling with reason.

For just as paralysed parts of a body, when we decide to move them to the right, do the contrary and move off to the left, the same is true of the soul; for incontinent people have impulses in contrary directions. In bodies, admittedly, we see the part go astray, whereas we do not see it in the soul; nonetheless, presumably, we should suppose that the soul also has a <part> besides reason, contrary to and countering reason. The <precise> way it is different does not matter.

However, this <part> as well <as the rational part> appears, as we said, to share in reason. At any rate, in the continent person it obeys reason; and in the temperate and the brave person it presumably listens still better to reason, since there it agrees with reason in everything.

The nonrational <part>, then, as well <as the whole soul> apparently has two parts. For while the plant-like <part> shares in reason not at all, the <part> with appetites and in general desires shares in reason in a way, insofar as it both listens to reason and obeys it.

It listens in the way in which we are said to 'listen to reason'[14] from father or friends, not in the way in which we <'give the reason'> in mathematics.

The nonrational part also <obeys and> is persuaded in some way by
1103a reason, as is shown by chastening, and by every sort of reproof and exhortation.

If we ought to say, then, that this <part> also has reason, then the

14. **listen to reason:** Alternatively, 'take account'—lit., have *logos* (reason, account)—'of father or friends, not in the way in which we [give an account]. . . .'

<part> that has reason, as well <as the nonrational part> will have two parts, one that has reason to the full extent by having it within itself, and another <that has it> by listening to reason as to a father.

The distinction between virtues also reflects this difference. For some virtues are called virtues of thought, others virtues of character; wisdom,   5 comprehension and intelligence are called virtues of thought, generosity and temperance virtues of character.

For when we speak of someone's character we do not say that he is wise or has good comprehension, but that he is gentle or temperate. <Hence these are the virtues of character.> And yet, we also praise the wise person for his state, and the states that are praiseworthy are the ones we call   10 virtues. <Hence wisdom is also a virtue.>

Book II

1

Virtue, then, is of two sorts, virtue of thought and virtue of character. Virtue of thought arises and grows mostly from teaching, and hence needs   15 experience and time. Virtue of character <i.e. of *ēthos*> results from habit <*ethos*>; hence its name 'ethical', slightly varied from '*ethos*'.

Hence it is also clear that none of the virtues of character arises in us naturally.

For if something is by nature <in one condition>, habituation cannot   20 bring it into another condition. A stone, e.g., by nature moves downwards, and habituation could not make it move upwards, not even if you threw it up ten thousand times to habituate it; nor could habituation make fire move downwards, or bring anything that is by nature in one condition into another condition.

Thus the virtues arise in us neither by nature nor against nature. Rather, we are by nature able to acquire them, and reach our complete perfection   25 through habit.

Further, if something arises in us by nature, we first have the capacity for it, and later display the activity. This is clear in the case of the senses; for we did not acquire them by frequent seeing or hearing, but already had   30 them when we exercised them, and did not get them by exercising them.

Virtues, by contrast, we acquire, just as we acquire crafts, by having previously activated them. For we learn a craft by producing the same product that we must produce when we have learned it, becoming builders, e.g., by building and harpists by playing the harp; so also, then, we become just by doing just actions, temperate by doing temperate actions, brave by *1103b* doing brave actions.

What goes on in cities is evidence for this also. For the legislator makes the citizens good by habituating them, and this is the wish of every legisla-

5   tor; if he fails to do it well he misses his goal. \<The right\> habituation is
what makes the difference between a good political system and a bad one.

Further, just as in the case of a craft, the sources and means that develop
each virtue also ruin it. For playing the harp makes both good and bad
10   harpists, and it is analogous in the case of builders and all the rest; for
building well makes good builders, building badly, bad ones. If it were not
so, no teacher would be needed, but everyone would be born a good or a
bad craftsman.

It is the same, then, with the virtues. For actions in dealings with
15   \<other\> human beings make some people just, some unjust; actions in
terrifying situations and the acquired habit of fear or confidence make
some brave and others cowardly. The same is true of situations involving
appetites and anger; for one or another sort of conduct in these situations
20   makes some people temperate and gentle, others intemperate and irascible.

To sum up, then, in a single account: A state \<of character\> arises from
\<the repetition of\> similar activities. Hence we must display the right
activities, since differences in these imply corresponding differences in the
states. It is not unimportant, then, to acquire one sort of habit or another,
25   right from our youth; rather, it is very important, indeed all-important.

2

Our present inquiry does not aim, as our others do, at study; for the
purpose of our examination is not to know what virtue is, but to become
30   good, since otherwise the inquiry would be of no benefit to us. Hence we
must examine the right way to act, since, as we have said, the actions also
control the character of the states we acquire.

First, then, actions should express correct reason. That is a common
\<belief\>, and let us assume it; later we will say what correct reason is and
how it is related to the other virtues.

1104a   But let us take it as agreed in advance that every account of the actions
we must do has to be stated in outline, not exactly. As we also said at the
start, the type of accounts we demand should reflect the subject-matter;
and questions about actions and expediency, like questions about health,
have no fixed \<and invariable answers\>.

5   And when our general account is so inexact, the account of particular
cases is all the more inexact. For these fall under no craft or profession, and
the agents themselves must consider in each case what the opportune action is, as doctors and navigators do.

10   The account we offer, then, in our present inquiry is of this inexact sort;
still, we must try to offer help.

First, then, we should observe that these sorts of states naturally tend to
be ruined by excess and deficiency. We see this happen with strength and

health, which we mention because we must use what is evident as a witness to what is not.[15] For both excessive and deficient exercises ruin strength;   *15* and likewise, too much or too little eating or drinking ruins health, while the proportionate amount produces, increases and preserves it.

The same is true, then, of temperance, bravery and the other virtues. For if, e.g., someone avoids and is afraid of everything, standing firm against   *20* nothing, he becomes cowardly, but if he is afraid of nothing at all and goes to face everything, he becomes rash. Similarly, if he gratifies himself with every pleasure and refrains from none, he becomes intemperate, but if he avoids them all, as boors do, he becomes some sort of insensible person. Temperance and bravery, then, are ruined by excess and deficiency but   *25* preserved by the mean.

The same actions, then, are the sources and causes both of the emergence and growth of virtues and of their ruin; but further, the activities of the virtues will be found in these same actions. For this is also true of more   *30* evident cases, e.g. strength, which arises from eating a lot and from withstanding much hard labor, and it is the strong person who is most able to do these very things. It is the same with the virtues. Refraining from pleasures makes us become temperate, and when we have become temperate   *35* we are most able to refrain from pleasures. And it is similar with bravery; *1104b* habituation in disdaining what is fearful and in standing firm against it makes us become brave, and when we have become brave we shall be most able to stand firm.

3

But <actions are not enough>; we must take as a sign of someone's state his pleasure or pain in consequence of his action. For if someone who abstains   *5* from bodily pleasures enjoys the abstinence itself, then he is temperate, but if he is grieved by it, he is intemperate. Again, if he stands firm against terrifying situations and enjoys it, or at least does not find it painful, then he is brave, and if he finds it painful, he is cowardly.

<Pleasures and pains are appropriately taken as signs> because virtue of character is concerned with pleasures and pains.

(1) For it is pleasure that causes us to do base actions, and pain that   *10* causes us to abstain from fine ones. Hence we need to have had the appropriate upbringing—right from early youth, as Plato says—to make us find enjoyment or pain in the right things; for this is the correct education.

(2) Further, virtues are concerned with actions and feelings; but every feeling and every action implies pleasure or pain; hence, for this reason too,   *15* virtue is concerned with pleasures and pains.

---

15. For the maxim 'we must use . . .' cf. Anaxagoras, DK 59B21a.

(3) Corrective treatment <for vicious actions> also indicates <the relevance of pleasure and pain>, since it uses pleasures and pains; it uses them because such correction is a form of medical treatment, and medical treatment naturally operates through contraries.

20 (4) Further, as we said earlier, every state of soul is naturally related to and concerned with whatever naturally makes it better or worse; and pleasures and pains make people worse, from pursuing and avoiding the wrong ones, at the wrong time, in the wrong ways, or whatever other distinctions of that sort are needed in an account.

These <bad effects of pleasure and pain> are the reason why people actually define the virtues as ways of being unaffected and undisturbed
25 <by pleasures and pains>. They are wrong, however, because they speak <of being unaffected> unconditionally, not of being unaffected in the right or wrong way, at the right or wrong time, and the added specifications.

We assume, then, that virtue is the sort of state <with the appropriate specifications> that does the best actions concerned with pleasures and pains, and that vice is the contrary. The following points will also make it
30 evident that virtue and vice are concerned with the same things.

(5) There are three objects of choice—fine, expedient and pleasant—and three objects of avoidance—their contraries, shameful, harmful and painful. About all these, then, the good person is correct and the bad person is
35 in error, and especially about pleasure. For pleasure is shared with animals,
1105a and implied by every object of choice, since what is fine and what is expedient appear pleasant as well.

(6) Further, since pleasure grows up with all of us from infancy on, it is hard to rub out this feeling that is dyed into our lives; and we estimate
5 actions as well <as feelings>, some of us more, some less, by pleasure and pain. Hence, our whole inquiry must be about these, since good or bad enjoyment or pain is very important for our actions.

(7) Moreover, it is harder to fight pleasure than to fight emotion, <though that is hard enough>, as Heraclitus says. Now both craft and
10 virtue are concerned in every case with what is harder, since a good result is even better when it is harder. Hence, for this reason also, the whole inquiry, for virtue and political science alike, most consider pleasures and pains; for if we use these well, we shall be good, and if badly, bad.

In short, virtue is concerned with pleasures and pains; the actions that
15 are its sources also increase it or, if they are done differently, ruin it; and its activity is concerned with the same actions that are its sources.

4

However, someone might raise this puzzle: 'What do you mean by saying that to become just we must first do just actions and to become temperate we must first do temperate actions? For if we do what is grammatical or musical, we must already be grammarians or musicians. In the same way, then, if we do what is just or temperate, we must already be just or temperate.'

But surely this is not so even with the crafts, for it is possible to produce something grammatical by chance or by following someone else's instructions. To be a grammarian, then, we must both produce something grammatical and produce it in the way in which the grammarian produces it, i.e. expressing grammatical knowledge that is in us.

Moreover, in any case what is true of crafts is not true of virtues. For the products of a craft determine by their own character whether they have been produced well; and so it suffices that they are in the right state when they have been produced. But for actions expressing virtue to be done temperately or justly <and hence well> it does not suffice that they are themselves in the right state. Rather, the agent must also be in the right state when he does them. First, he must know <that he is doing virtuous actions>; second, he must decide on them, and decide on them for themselves; and, third, he must also do them from a firm and unchanging state.

As conditions for having a craft these three do not count, except for the knowing itself. As a condition for having a virtue, however, the knowing counts for nothing, or <rather> for only a little, whereas the other two conditions are very important, indeed all-important. And these other two conditions are achieved by the frequent doing of just and temperate actions.

Hence actions are called just or temperate when they are the sort that a just or temperate person would do. But the just and temperate person is not the one who <merely> does these actions, but the one who also does them in the way in which just or temperate people do them.

It is right, then, to say that a person comes to be just from doing just actions and temperate from doing temperate actions; for no one has even a prospect of becoming good from failing to do them.

The many, however, do not do these actions but take refuge in arguments, thinking that they are doing philosophy, and that this is the way to become excellent people. In this they are like a sick person who listens attentively to the doctor, but acts on none of his instructions. Such a course of treatment will not improve the state of his body; any more than will the many's way of doing philosophy improve the state of their souls.

5

Next we must examine what virtue is. Since there are three conditions arising in the soul—feelings, capacities and states—virtue must be one of these.

By feelings I mean appetite, anger, fear, confidence, envy, joy, love, hate, longing, jealousy, pity, in general whatever implies pleasure or pain.

25   By capacities I mean what we have when we are said to be capable of
these feelings—capable of, e.g., being angry or afraid or feeling pity.

By states I mean what we have when we are well or badly off in relation
to feelings. If, e.g., our feeling is too intense or slack, we are badly off in
relation to anger, but if it is intermediate, we are well off;[16] and the same is
true in the other cases.

First, then, neither virtues nor vices are feelings. (a) For we are called
30   excellent or base insofar as we have virtues or vices, not insofar as we have
feelings. (b) We are neither praised nor blamed insofar as we have feelings;
for we do not praise the angry or the frightened person, and do not blame
1106a the person who is simply angry, but only the person who is angry in a
particular way. But we are praised or blamed insofar as we have virtues or
vices. (c) We are angry and afraid without decision; but the virtues are
decisions of some kind, or <rather> require decision. (d) Besides, insofar
5   as we have feelings, we are said to be moved; but insofar as we have virtues
or vices, we are said to be in some condition rather than moved.

For these reasons the virtues are not capacities either; for we are neither
called good nor called bad insofar as we are simply capable of feelings.
10   Further, while we have capacities by nature, we do not become good or bad
by nature; we have discussed this before.

If, then, the virtues are neither feelings nor capacities, the remaining
possibility is that they are states. And so we have said what the genus of
virtue is.

6

15   But we must say not only, as we already have, that it is a state, but also
what sort of state it is.

It should be said, then, that every virtue causes its possessors to be in a
good state and to perform their functions well; the virtue of eyes, e.g.,
makes the eyes and their functioning excellent, because it makes us see
20   well; and similarly, the virtue of a horse makes the horse excellent, and
thereby good at galloping, at carrying its rider and at standing steady in
the face of the enemy. If this is true in every case, then the virtue of a
human being will likewise be the state that makes a human being good and
makes him perform his function well.

16. **By states . . . well off**: 'STATE', *hexis*, lit. 'having', is formed from *echein*, 'to
have'. 'Well (badly) off' translates *echein* with the adverb, lit. 'have well (badly)'.
(Greek says 'How do you have?' for the English 'How do you do?' or 'How are
you?') Here Aristotle argues that a state is not *merely* a capacity. He does not deny,
but indeed believes, that a state is a *type* of capacity; see e.g. 'able to' in 1104a32–
b3, indicating the type of capacity that is included in the state of character.

We have already said how this will be true, and it will also be evident   *25*
from our next remarks, if we consider the sort of nature that virtue has.

In everything continuous and divisible we can take more, less and equal,
and each of them either in the object itself or relative to us; and the equal
is some intermediate between excess and deficiency.

By the intermediate in the object I mean what is equidistant from each   *30*
extremity; this is one and the same for everyone. But relative to us the
intermediate is what is neither superfluous nor deficient; this is not one,
and is not the same for everyone.

If, e.g., ten are many and two are few, we take six as intermediate in the
object, since it exceeds <two> and is exceeded <by ten> by an equal   *35*
amount, <four>; this is what is intermediate by numerical proportion. But
that is not how we must take the intermediate that is relative to us. For if, *1106b*
e.g., ten pounds <of food> are a lot for someone to eat, and two pounds a
little, it does not follow that the trainer will prescribe six, since this might
also be either a little or a lot for the person who is to take it—for Milo <the
athlete> a little, but for the beginner in gymnastics a lot; and the same is
true for running and wrestling. In this way every scientific expert avoids   *5*
excess and deficiency and seeks and chooses what is intermediate—but
intermediate relative to us, not in the object.

This, then, is how each science produces its product[17] well, by focusing
on what is intermediate and making the product conform to that. This,
indeed, is why people regularly comment on well-made products that noth   *10*
ing could be added or subtracted, since they assume that excess or deficiency ruins a good <result> while the mean preserves it. Good craftsmen
also, we say, focus on what is intermediate when they produce their product. And since virtue, like nature, is better and more exact than any craft, it   *15*
will also aim at what is intermediate.

By virtue I mean virtue of character; for this <pursues the mean be-
cause> it is concerned with feelings and actions, and these admit of excess,
deficiency and an intermediate condition. We can be afraid, e.g., or be
confident, or have appetites, or get angry, or feel pity, in general have
pleasure or pain, both too much and too little, and in both ways not well;   *20*
but <having these feelings> at the right times, about the right things,
towards the right people, for the right end, and in the right way, is the
intermediate and best condition, and this is proper to virtue. Similarly,
actions also admit of excess, deficiency and the intermediate condition.

Now virtue is concerned with feelings and actions, in which excess and   *25*
deficiency are in error and incur blame, while the intermediate condition is
correct and wins praise, which are both proper features of virtue. Virtue,
then, is a mean, insofar as it aims at what is intermediate.

17. **product:** *Ergon*, also translated 'FUNCTION' in a16–24.

Moreover, there are many ways to be in error, since badness is proper to
30   what is unlimited, as the Pythagoreans pictured it, and good to what is
limited; but there is only one way to be correct. That is why error is easy
and correctness hard, since it is easy to miss the target and hard to hit it.
And so for this reason also excess and deficiency are proper to vice, the
35   mean to virtue; 'for we are noble in only one way, but bad in all sorts of
ways.'

Virtue, then, is (a) a state that decides, (b) <consisting> in a mean, (c)
1107a the mean relative to us, (d) which is defined by reference to reason, (e) i.e.,
to the reason by reference to which the intelligent person would define it. It
is a mean between two vices, one of excess and one of deficiency.

It is a mean for this reason also: Some vices miss what is right because
5   they are deficient, others because they are excessive, in feelings or in actions, while virtue finds and chooses what is intermediate.

Hence, as far as its substance and the account stating its essence are
concerned, virtue is a mean; but as far as the best <condition> and the
good <result> are concerned, it is an extremity.

But not every action or feeling admits of the mean. For the names of
10   some automatically include baseness, e.g. spite, shamelessness, envy <among
feelings>, and adultery, theft, murder, among actions. All of these and
similar things are called by these names because they themselves, not their
excesses or deficiencies, are base.

Hence in doing these things we can never be correct, but must invariably
15   be in error. We cannot do them well or not well—e.g. by committing
adultery with the right woman at the right time in the right way; on the
contrary, it is true unconditionally that to do any of them is to be in error.

<To think these admit of a mean>, therefore, is like thinking that unjust
20   or cowardly or intemperate action also admits of a mean, an excess and a
deficiency. For then there would be a mean of excess, a mean of deficiency,
an excess of excess and a deficiency of deficiency.

Rather, just as there is no excess or deficiency of temperance or of
bravery, since the intermediate is a sort of extreme <in achieving the
good>, so also there is no mean, and no excess or deficiency, of these
25   <vicious actions> either, but whatever way anyone does them, he is in
error. For in general there is no mean of excess or of deficiency, and no
excess or deficiency of a mean.

Book III

1

1109b Virtue, then, is about feelings and actions. These receive praise or blame
when they are voluntary, but pardon, sometimes even pity, when they are
involuntary. Hence, presumably, in examining virtue we must define the

voluntary and the involuntary. This is also useful to legislators, both for honors and for corrective treatments.   35

What comes about by force or because of ignorance seems to be involun- *1110a* tary. What is forced has an external origin, the sort of origin in which the agent or victim[18] contributes nothing—if, e.g., a wind or human beings who control him were to carry him off.

But now consider actions done because of fear of greater evils, or because of something fine. Suppose, e.g., a tyrant tells you to do something   5 shameful, when he has control over your parents and children, and if you do it, they will live, but if not, they will die. These cases raise dispute about whether they are voluntary or involuntary.

However, the same sort of thing also happens with throwing cargo overboard in storms; for no one willingly throws cargo overboard, uncondition-   10 ally, but anyone with any sense throws it overboard <under some conditions> to save himself and the others.

These sorts of actions, then, are mixed. But they would seem to be more like voluntary actions. For at the time they are done they are choiceworthy, and the goal of an action reflects the occasion; hence also we should call the action voluntary or involuntary with reference to the time when he does it. Now in fact he does it willingly; for in these sorts of actions he has   15 within him the origin of the movement of the limbs that are the instruments <of the action>, and when the origin of the actions is in him, it is also up to him to do them or not to do them. Hence actions of this sort are voluntary, though presumably the actions without <the appropriate> condition are involuntary, since no one would choose any action of this sort in itself.

For such <mixed> actions people are sometimes actually praised, when-   20 ever they endure something shameful or painful as the price of great and fine results; and if they do the reverse, they are blamed, since it is a base person who endures what is most shameful for nothing fine or for only some moderately fine result.

In some cases there is no praise, but there is pardon, whenever someone does a wrong action because of conditions of a sort that overstrain human   25 nature, and that no one would endure. But presumably there are some things we cannot be compelled to do, and rather than do them we should suffer the most terrible consequences and accept death; for the things that <allegedly> compelled Euripides' Alcmaeon to kill his mother appear ridiculous.

It is sometimes hard, however, to judge what <goods> should be chosen   30

18. **victim:** Lit. 'the one affected'. Perhaps 'the one having the feeling' (cf. 'feelings and actions', 1109b30). But more probably Aristotle is remarking that if I break a window because the wind blows me into it, I am a passive victim rather than an agent.

at the price of what <evils>, and what <evils> should be endured as the
price of what <goods>. And it is even harder to abide by our judgment,
since the results we expect <when we endure> are usually painful, and the
actions we are compelled <to endure, when we choose> are usually shame-
1110b ful. That is why those who have been compelled or not compelled receive
praise and blame.

What sorts of things, then, should we say are forced? Perhaps we should
say that something is forced unconditionally whenever its cause is external
and the agent contributes nothing. Other things are involuntary in themselves, but choiceworthy on this occasion and as the price of these
5   <goods>, and their origin is in the agent. These are involuntary in themselves, but, on this occasion and as the price of these <goods>, voluntary.
Still, they would seem to be more like voluntary actions, since actions
involve particular <conditions>, and <in mixed actions> these <condi-
tions> are voluntary. But what sort of thing should be chosen as the price
of what <good> is not easy to answer, since there are many differences in
particular <conditions>.

But suppose someone says that pleasant things and fine things force us,
10   since they are outside us and compel us. It will follow that for him everything is forced, since everyone in every action aims at something fine or
pleasant.

Moreover, if we are forced and unwilling to act, we find it painful; but if
something pleasant or fine is its cause, we do it with pleasure.

It is ridiculous, then, for <our opponent> to ascribe responsibility to
external <causes> and not to himself, when he is easily snared by such
15   things; and ridiculous to take responsibility for fine actions himself, but to
hold pleasant things responsible for his shameful actions.

What is forced, then, would seem to be what has its origin outside the
person forced, who contributes nothing.

Everything caused by ignorance is non-voluntary, but what is involuntary also causes pain and regret. For if someone's action was caused by
20   ignorance, but he now has no objection to the action, he has done it neither
willingly, since he did not know what it was, nor unwillingly, since he now
feels no pain. Hence, among those who act because of ignorance, the agent
who now regrets his action seems to be unwilling, while the agent with no
regrets may be called non-willing, since he is another case—for since he is
different, it is better if he has his own special name.

25   Further, action caused by ignorance would seem to be different from
action done in ignorance. For if the agent is drunk or angry, his action
seems to be caused by drunkenness or anger, not by ignorance, though it is
done in ignorance, not in knowledge.

<This ignorance does not make an action involuntary.> Certainly every
vicious person is ignorant of the actions he must do or avoid, and this sort

of error makes people unjust, and in general bad. But talk of involuntary 30
action is not meant to apply to <this> ignorance of what is beneficial.

For the cause of involuntary action is not <this> ignorance in the decision, which causes vice; it is not <in other words> ignorance of the universal, since that is a cause for blame. Rather, the cause is ignorance of the 1111a
particulars which the action consists in and is concerned with; for these
allow both pity and pardon, since an agent acts involuntarily if he is
ignorant of one of these particulars.

Presumably, then, it is not a bad idea to define these particulars, and say
what they are, and how many. They are: (1) who is doing it; (2) what he is
doing; (3) about what or to what he is doing it; (4) sometimes also what he 5
is doing it with, e.g. the instrument; (5) for what result, e.g. safety; (6) in
what way, e.g. gently or hard.

Now certainly someone could not be ignorant of *all* of these unless he
were mad. Nor, clearly, (1) could he be ignorant of who is doing it, since he
could hardly be ignorant of himself. But (2) he might be ignorant of what
he is doing, as when someone says that <the secret> slipped out while he
was speaking, or, as Aeschylus said about the mysteries, that he did not
know it was forbidden to reveal it; or, like the person with the catapult,
that he let it go when he <only> wanted to demonstrate it. (3) Again, he 10
might think that his son is an enemy, as Merope did; or (4) that the barbed
spear has a button on it, or that the stone is pumice-stone. (5) By giving
someone a drink to save his life we might kill him; (6) and wanting to
touch someone, as they do in sparring, we might wound him. 15

There is ignorance about all of these <particulars> that the action consists in. Hence someone who was ignorant of one of these seems to have
done an action unwillingly, especially when he was ignorant of the most
important of them; these seem to be (2) what he is doing, and (5) the result
for which he does it.

Hence it is action called involuntary with reference to *this* sort of igno- 20
rance <that we meant when we said that> the agent must, in addition, feel
pain and regret for his action.

Since, then, what is involuntary is what is forced or is caused by ignorance, what is voluntary seems to be what has its origin in the agent
himself when he knows the particulars that the action consists in.

<Our definition is sound.> For, presumably, it is not correct to say that
action caused by emotion or appetite is involuntary. 25

For, first of all, on this view none of the other animals will ever act
voluntarily; nor will children. <But clearly they do.>

Next, among all the actions caused by appetite or emotion do we do none
of them voluntarily? Or do we do the fine actions voluntarily and the
shameful involuntarily? Surely <the second answer> is ridiculous when
one and the same thing <i.e. appetite or emotion> causes <both fine and

30   shameful actions>. And presumably it is also absurd to say <as the first
answer implies> that things we ought to desire are involuntary; and in fact
we ought both to be angry at some things and to have an appetite for some
things, e.g. for health and learning.

Again, what is involuntary seems to be painful, whereas what expresses
our appetite seems to be pleasant.

Moreover, how are errors that express emotion any less voluntary than
those that express rational calculation? For both sorts of errors are to
1111b be avoided; and since nonrational feelings seem to be no less human
<than rational calculation>, actions resulting from emotion or appetite are
also proper to a human being; it is absurd, then, to regard them as involuntary.

2

5   Now that we have defined what is voluntary and what involuntary, the
next task is to discuss decision; for decision seems to be most proper to
virtue, and to distinguish characters from one another better than actions do.

Decision, then, is apparently voluntary, but not the same as what is
voluntary, which extends more widely. For children and the other animals
share in what is voluntary, but not in decision; and the actions we do on
10   the spur of the moment are said to be voluntary, but not to express decision.

Those who say decision is appetite or emotion or wish or some sort of
belief would seem to be wrong.

For decision is not shared with nonrational <animals>, but appetite and
emotion are shared with them.

Further, the incontinent person acts on appetite, not on decision, but the
15   continent person does the reverse and acts on decision, not on appetite.

Again, appetite is contrary to decision, but not to appetite.

Further, appetite's concern is what is pleasant and what is painful, but
neither of these is the concern of decision.

Still less is emotion decision; for actions caused by emotion seem least of
all to express decision.

20   But further, it is not wish either, though it is apparently close to it.

For, first, we do not decide to do what is impossible, and anyone claiming to decide to do it would seem a fool; but we do wish for what is
impossible, e.g. never to die, as well <as for what is possible>.

Further, we wish <not only for results we can achieve>, but also for
results that are <possible, but> not achievable through our own agency,
25   e.g. victory for some actor or athlete. But what we decide to do is never
anything of that sort, but what we think would come about through our
own agency.

Again, we wish for the end more <than for what promotes it>, but we decide to do what promotes the end.[19] We wish, e.g. to be healthy, but decide to do what will make us healthy; and we wish to be happy, and say so, but could not appropriately say we decide to be happy, since in general   *30* what we decide to do would seem to be what is up to us.

Nor is it belief.

For, first, belief seems to be about everything, no less about what is eternal and what is impossible <for us> than about what is up to us.

Moreover, beliefs are divided into true and false, not into good and bad, but decisions are divided into good and bad more than into true and false.

Now presumably no one even claims that decision is the same as belief *1112a* in general. But it is not the same as any kind of belief either.

For it is our decisions to do what is good or bad, not our beliefs, that make the characters we have.

Again, we decide to take or avoid something good or bad. We believe what it is, whom it benefits or how; but we do not exactly believe to take or   *5* avoid.

Further, decision is praised more for deciding on what is right, whereas belief is praised for believing rightly.

Moreover, we decide on something <even> when we know most completely that it is good;[20] but <what> we believe <is> what we do not quite know.

Again, those who make the best decisions do not seem to be the same as those with the best beliefs; on the contrary, some seem to have better beliefs, but to make the wrong choice because of vice.   *10*

We can agree that decision follows or implies belief. But that is irrelevant, since it is not the question we are asking; our question is whether decision is the *same* as some sort of belief.

Then what, or what sort of thing, is decision, since it is none of the things mentioned? Well, apparently it is voluntary, but not everything voluntary is decided. Then perhaps what is decided is the result of prior   *15* deliberation. For decision involves reason and thought, and even the name itself would seem to indicate that <what is decided, *prohaireton*> is chosen <*haireton*> before <*pro*> other things.

19. **What promotes the end:** Lit. 'things towards the end', *ta pros to telos*. 'Means to the end', a frequent rendering, is liable to mislead, since Aristotle is not concerned only with instrumental means; I can also decide on something as a good in itself that promotes a further good in itself by being a part of the further good.

20. <even> when . . .: Alternatively, and less probably, Aristotle might mean that knowing is a necessary condition for deciding.

3

But do we deliberate about everything, and is everything open to deliberation, or is there no deliberation about some things? By 'open to delib-
20   eration', presumably, we should mean what someone with some sense, not some fool or madman, might deliberate about.

Now no one deliberates about eternal things, e.g. about the universe, or about the incommensurability of the sides and the diagonal; nor about
25   things that are in movement but always come about the same way, either from necessity or by nature or by some other cause, e.g. the solstices or the rising of the stars; nor about what happens different ways at different times, e.g. droughts and rains; nor about what results from fortune, e.g. the
30   finding of a treasure. For none of these results could be achieved through our agency.

We deliberate about what is up to us, i.e. about the actions we can do; and this is what is left <besides the previous cases>. For causes seem to
33   include nature, necessity and fortune, but besides them mind and everything <operating> through human agency.
28   However, we do not deliberate about all human affairs; no Spartan, e.g.,
29   deliberates about how the Scythians might have the best political system. Rather, each group of human beings deliberates about the actions *they*
33   can do.
1112b   Now there is no deliberation about the sciences that are exact and self-sufficient, e.g. about letters, since we are in no doubt about how to write them <in spelling a word>. Rather, we deliberate about what results through our agency, but in different ways on different occasions, e.g. about
5   questions of medicine and money-making; more about navigation than about gymnastics, to the extent that it is less exactly worked out, and similarly with other <crafts>; and more about beliefs than about sciences, since we are more in doubt about them.

Deliberation concerns what is usually <one way rather than another>, where the outcome is unclear and the right way to act is undefined. And
10   we enlist partners in deliberation on large issues when we distrust our own ability to discern <the right answer>.

We deliberate not about ends, but about what promotes ends; a doctor, e.g., does not deliberate about whether he will cure, or an orator about whether he will persuade, or a politician about whether he will produce good order, or any other <expert> about the end <that his science
15   aims at>.

Rather, we first lay down the end, and then examine the ways and means[21] to achieve it. If it appears that any of several <possible> means

21. **ways and means:** Lit. 'how and through what things it will be'. 'Means' is a
convenient translation here, but may mislead us in the way noted in note to 1111b27.

will reach it, we consider which of them will reach it most easily and most finely; and if only one <possible> means reaches it, we consider how that means will reach it, and how the means itself is reached, until we come to the first cause, the last thing to be discovered.

For a deliberator would seem to inquire and analyse in the way de-   20
scribed, as though analysing a diagram. <The comparison is apt, since>, apparently, all deliberation is inquiry, though not all inquiry, e.g. in mathematics, is deliberation. And the last thing <found> in the analysis is the first that comes to be.

If we encounter an impossible step—e.g. we need money but cannot raise   25
it—we desist; but if the action appears possible, we undertake it. What is possible is what we could achieve through our agency <including what our friends could achieve for us>; for what our friends achieve is, in a way, achieved through our agency, since the origin is in us. <In crafts> we sometimes look for instruments, sometimes <for the way> to use them; so   30
also in other cases we sometimes look for the means to the end, sometimes for the proper use of the means or for the means to that proper use.

As we have said, then, a human being would seem to originate action; deliberation is about the actions he can do; and actions are for the sake of other things; hence we deliberate about what promotes an end, not about the end.

Nor do we deliberate about particulars, e.g. about whether this is a loaf 1113a or is cooked the right amount; for these are questions for perception, and if we keep on deliberating at each stage we shall go on without end.

What we deliberate about is the same as what we decide to do, except that by the time we decide to do it, it is definite; for what we decide to do is what we have judged <to be right> as a result of deliberation. For each of   5
us stops inquiring how to act as soon as he traces the origin to himself, and within himself to the dominant part; for this is the part that decides. This is also clear from the ancient political systems described by Homer; there the kings would first decide and then announce their decision to the people.

We have found, then, that what we decide to do is whatever action   10
among those up to us we deliberate about and desire to do. Hence also decision will be deliberative desire to do an action that is up to us; for when we have judged <that it is right> as a result of deliberation, our desire to do it expresses our wish.[22]

So much, then, for an outline of the sort of thing decision is about; it is about what promotes the end.

22. **expresses our wish:** Reading *boulēsin* rather than *bouleusin*, 'deliberation'. This passage and 1113b3–5 make it fairly clear that DECISION requires wish, not just any sort of desire.

4

15   Wish, we have said, is for the end. But to some it seems that wish is for the
good, to others that it is for the apparent good.

For those who say the good is what is wished, it follows that what
someone wishes if he chooses incorrectly is not wished at all. For if it is
wished, then <on this view> it is good; but what he wishes is in fact bad, if
20   it turns out that way. <Hence what he wishes is not wished, which is self-
contradictory.>

For those, on the other hand, who say the apparent good is wished, it
follows that there is nothing wished by nature. To each person what is
wished is what seems <good to him>; but different things, and indeed
contrary things, if it turns out that way, appear good to different people.
<Hence contrary things will be wished and nothing will be wished by
nature.>

If, then, these views do not satisfy us, should we say that, unconditionally and in reality, what is wished is the good, but to each person what
is wished is the apparent good?

25   To the excellent person, then, what is wished will be what is wished in
reality, while to the base person what is wished is whatever it turns out to
be <that appears good to him>. Similarly in the case of bodies, really
healthy things are healthy to people in good condition, while other things
are healthy to sickly people, and the same is true of what is bitter, sweet,
hot, heavy and so on.

30   For the excellent person judges each sort of thing correctly, and in each
case what is true appears to him. For each state <of character> has its own
special <view of> what is fine and pleasant, and presumably the excellent
person is far superior because he sees what is true in each case, being a sort
of standard and measure of what is fine and pleasant.

In the many, however, pleasure would seem to cause deception, since it
1113b   appears good when it is not; at any rate, they choose what is pleasant
because they assume it is good, and avoid pain because they assume it
is evil.

5

We have found, then, that we wish for the end, and deliberate and decide
about what promotes it; hence the actions concerned with what promotes
5   the end will express a decision and will be voluntary. Now the activities of
the virtues are concerned with <what promotes the end>; hence virtue is
also up to us, and so is vice.

For when acting is up to us, so is not acting, and when No is up to us, so
10   is Yes. Hence if acting, when it is fine, is up to us, then not acting, when it
is shameful, is also up to us; and if not acting, when it is fine, is up to us,

then acting, when it is shameful, is also up to us. Hence if doing, and likewise not doing, fine or shameful actions is up to us; and if, as we saw, <doing or not doing them> is <what it is> to be a good or bad person; then it follows that being decent or base is up to us.

The claim that no one is willingly bad or unwillingly blessed would seem   15
to be partly true but partly false. For while certainly no one is unwillingly blessed, vice is voluntary. If it is not, we must dispute the conclusion just reached, that a human being originates and fathers his own actions as he fathers his children. But if our conclusion appears true, and we cannot refer <actions> back to other origins beyond those in ourselves, then it   20
follows that whatever has its origin in us is itself up to us and voluntary.   ·

There would seem to be testimony in favor of our views not only in what each of us does as a private citizen, but also in what legislators themselves do. For they impose corrective treatments and penalties on anyone who does vicious actions, unless his action is forced or is caused by ignorance   25
that he is not responsible for; and they honor anyone who does fine actions; they assume that they will encourage the one and restrain the other. But no one encourages us to do anything that is not up to us and voluntary; people assume it is pointless to persuade us not to get hot or distressed or hungry or anything else of that sort, since persuasion will not stop it happening to us.

Indeed, legislators also impose corrective treatments for the ignorance   30
itself, if the person seems to be responsible for the ignorance. A drunk, e.g., pays a double penalty; for the origin is in him, since he controls whether he gets drunk, and his getting drunk is responsible for his ignorance.

They also impose corrective treatment on someone who <does a vicious action> in ignorance of some provision of law that he is required to know and that is not hard <to know>. And they impose it in other cases likewise 1114a for any other ignorance that seems to be caused by the agent's inattention; they assume it is up to him not to be ignorant, since he controls whether he pays attention.

But presumably his character makes him inattentive. Still, he is himself responsible for having this character, by living carelessly, and similarly for being unjust by cheating, or being intemperate by passing his time in   5
drinking and the like; for each type of activity produces the corresponding character. This is clear from those who train for any contest or action, since they continually practice the appropriate activities. <Only> a totally insensible person would not know that each type of activity is the source of the   10
corresponding state; hence if someone does what he knows will make him   12
unjust, he is willingly unjust.   13

Moreover, it is unreasonable for someone doing injustice not to wish to   11
be unjust, or for someone doing intemperate action not to wish to be   12
intemperate. This does not mean, however, that if he is unjust and wishes   13
to stop, he will stop and will be just.

15   For neither does a sick person recover his health <simply by wishing>; nonetheless, he is sick willingly, by living incontinently and disobeying the doctors, if that was how it happened. At that time, then, he was free not to be sick, though no longer free once he has let himself go, just as it was up to us to throw a stone, since the origin was in us, though we can no longer take it back once we have thrown it.

20   Similarly, then, the person who is <now> unjust or intemperate was originally free not to acquire this character, so that he has it willingly, though once he has acquired the character, he is no longer free not to have it <now>.

It is not only vices of the soul that are voluntary; vices of the body are also voluntary for some people, and we actually censure them. For we never censure someone if nature causes his ugliness; but if his lack of

25   training or attention causes it, we do censure him. The same is true for weakness or maiming; for everyone would pity, not reproach someone if he were blind by nature or because of a disease or a wound, but would censure him if his heavy drinking or some other form of intemperance made him blind.

Hence bodily vices that are up to us are censured, while those not up to

30   us are not censured. If so, then in the other cases also the vices that are censured will be up to us.

But someone may say, 'Everyone aims at the apparent good, and does not

1114b control how it appears; on the contrary, his character controls how the end appears to him.'

First, then, if each person is in some way responsible for his own state <of character>, then he is also himself in some way responsible for how <the end> appears.

Suppose, on the other hand, that no one is responsible for acting badly, but one does so because one is ignorant of the end, and thinks this is the

5   way to gain what is best for oneself. One's aiming at the end will not be one's own choice, but one needs a sort of natural, inborn sense of sight, to judge finely and to choose what is really good. Whoever by nature has this sense in a fine condition has a good nature. For this sense is the greatest

10   and finest thing, and one cannot acquire it or learn it from another; rather, its natural character determines his later condition, and when it is naturally good and fine, that is true and complete good nature.

If all this is true, then, surely virtue will be no more voluntary than vice?

15   For how the end appears is laid down, by nature or in whatever way, for the good and the bad person alike, and they trace all the other things back to the end in doing whatever actions they do.

Suppose, then, that it is not nature that makes the end appear however it appears to each person, but something also depends on him; or, alternatively, suppose that <how> the end <appears> is natural, but virtue is voluntary because the virtuous person does the other things voluntarily. In either case vice will be no less voluntary than virtue; for the bad person, no 20 less than the good, is responsible for his own actions, even if not for <how> the end <appears>.[23]

Now the virtues, as we say, are voluntary, since in fact we are ourselves in a way jointly responsible for our states of character, and by having the sort of character we have we lay down the sort of end we do.[24] Hence the vices will also be voluntary, since the same is true of them. 25

We have now discussed the virtues in general. We have described their genus in outline; they are means, and they are states. Certain actions produce them, and they cause us to do these same actions, expressing the virtues themselves, in the way that correct reason prescribes. They are up to us and voluntary.

Actions and states, however, are not voluntary in the same way. For we 30 are in control of actions from the origin to the end, when we know the particulars. With states, however, we are in control of the origin, but do 1115a not know, any more than with sicknesses, what the cumulative effect of particular actions will be; none the less, since it was up to us to exercise a capacity either this way or another way, states are voluntary.

Let us now take up the virtues again, and discuss each singly. Let us say what they are, what sorts of thing they are concerned with, and how they 5 are concerned with them; it will also be clear at the same time how many virtues there are.

Book V

1

The questions we must examine about justice and injustice are these: What 1129a sorts of actions are they concerned with? What sort of mean is justice? What are the extremes between which justice is intermediate? Let us exam- 5 ine them by the same type of investigation that we used in the topics discussed before.

We see that the state everyone means in speaking of justice is the state that makes us doers of just actions, that makes us do justice and wish what is just. In the same way they mean by injustice the state that makes us do 10 injustice and wish what is unjust. Let us also, then, <follow the common beliefs and> begin by assuming this in outline.

23. **for the bad . . .:** Lit. 'for similarly to the bad person also belongs the because of (*dia*) himself in the actions, even if not in the end'.

24. **Now the virtues . . . end we do:** Lit. 'If, then, the virtues . . .' But Aristotle clearly endorses it; he is reasserting his first reply (in b1–3).

For what is true of sciences and capacities is not true of states. For while one and the same capacity or science seems to have contrary activities, a state
15   that is a contrary has no contrary activities. Health, e.g., only makes us do healthy actions, not their contraries; for we say we are walking in a healthy way if <and only if> we are walking in the way a healthy person would.

Often one of a pair of contrary states is recognized from the other contrary; and often the states are recognized from their subjects. For if, e.g.,
20   the good state is evident, the bad state becomes evident too; and moreover the good state becomes evident from the things that have it, and the things from the state. For if, e.g., the good state is thickness of flesh, then the bad state will necessarily be thinness of flesh, and the thing that produces the good state will be what produces thickness of flesh.

It follows, usually, that if one of a pair of contraries is spoken of in more
25   ways than one, so is the other; if, e.g., what is just is spoken of in more ways than one, so is what is unjust.

Now it would seem that justice and injustice are both spoken of in more ways than one, but since the different ways are closely related, their homonymy is unnoticed, and is less clear than it is with distant homonyms
30   where the distance in appearance is wide (e.g., the bone below an animal's neck and what we lock doors with are called keys homonymously).

Let us, then, find the number of ways an unjust person is spoken of. Both the lawless person and the greedy and unfair person seem to be unjust; and so, clearly, both the lawful and the fair person will be just. Hence what is
1129b just will be both what is lawful and what is fair, and what is unjust will be both what is lawless and what is unfair.

Since the unjust person is greedy, he will be concerned with goods—not with all goods, but only with those involved in good and bad fortune, goods which are, <considered> unconditionally, always good, but for this or that person not always good. Though human beings pray for these and pursue
5   them, they are wrong; the right thing is to pray that what is good unconditionally will also be good for us, but to choose <only> what is good for us.

Now the unjust person <who chooses these goods> does not choose more in every case; in the case of what is bad unconditionally he actually
10   chooses less. But since what is less bad also seems to be good in a way, and greed aims at more of what is good, he seems to be greedy. In fact he is unfair; for unfairness includes <all these actions>, and is a common feature <of his choice of the greater good and of the lesser evil>.

Since, as we saw, the lawless person is unjust and the lawful person is just, it clearly follows that whatever is lawful is in some way just; for the provisions of legislative science are lawful, and we say that each of them is
15   just. Now in every matter they deal with the laws aim either[25] at the

25. **now in every matter** . . . Or: 'Now the laws deal with every matter, aiming either. . . .'

common benefit of all, or at the benefit of those in control, whose control rests on virtue or on some other such basis. And so in one way what we call just is whatever produces and maintains happiness and its parts for a political community.

Now the law instructs us to do the actions of a brave person—not to   20
leave the battle-line, e.g., or to flee, or to throw away our weapons; of a temperate person—not to commit adultery or wanton aggression; of a mild person—not to strike or revile another; and similarly requires actions that express the other virtues, and prohibits those that express the vices. The correctly established law does this correctly, and less carefully framed one   25
does this worse.

This type of justice, then, is complete virtue, not complete virtue unconditionally, but complete virtue in relation to another. And this is why justice often seems to be supreme among the virtues, and 'neither the evening star nor the morning star is so marvellous', and the proverb says 'And in justice all virtue is summed up.'   30

Moreover, justice is complete virtue to the highest degree because it is the complete exercise of complete virtue. And it is the complete exercise because the person who has justice is able to exercise virtue in relation to another, not only in what concerns himself; for many are able to exercise virtue in their own concerns but unable in what relates to another.

And hence Bias seems to have been correct in saying that ruling will   1130a
reveal the man, since a ruler is automatically related to another, and in a community. And for the same reason justice is the only virtue that seems to be another person's good, because it is related to another; for it does what   5
benefits another, either the ruler or the fellow-member of the community.

The worst person, therefore, is the one who exercises his vice towards himself and his friends as well <as towards others>. And the best person is not the one who exercises virtue <only> toward himself, but the one who <also> exercises it in relation to another, since this is a difficult task.

This type of justice, then, is the whole, not a part, of virtue, and the injustice contrary to it is the whole, not a part, of vice.   10

At the same time our discussion makes clear the difference between virtue and this type of justice. For virtue is the same as justice, but what it is to be virtue is not the same as what it is to be justice. Rather, in so far as virtue is related to another, it is justice, and insofar as it is a certain sort of state unconditionally it is virtue.

2

But we are looking for the type of justice, since we say there is one, that   15
consists in a part of virtue, and correspondingly for the type of injustice that is a part <of vice>.

Here is evidence that there is this type of justice and injustice:

First, if someone's activities express the other vices—if, e.g., cowardice
made him throw away his shield, or irritability made him revile someone,
or ungenerosity made him fail to help someone with money—what he does
20   is unjust, but not greedy. But when one acts from greed, in many cases his
action expresses none of these vices—certainly not all of them; but it still
expresses some type of wickedness, since we blame him, and <in particu-
lar> it expresses injustice. Hence there is another type of injustice that is a
part of the whole, and a way for a thing to be unjust that is a part of the
whole that is contrary to law.

25   Moreover, if A commits adultery for profit and makes a profit, while B
commits adultery because of his appetite, and spends money on it to his
own loss, B seems intemperate rather than greedy, while A seems unjust,
not intemperate. Clearly, then, this is because A acts to make a profit.

Further, we can refer every other unjust action to some vice—to intem-
30   perance if he committed adultery, to cowardice if he deserted his comrade
in the battle-line, to anger if he struck someone. But if he made an <unjust>
profit, we can refer it to no other vice except injustice.

Hence evidently (a) there is another type of injustice, special injustice,
besides the whole of injustice; and (b) it is synonymous with the whole,
1130b since the definition is in the same genus. For (b) both have their area of
competence in relation to another. But (a) special injustice is concerned
with honor or wealth or safety, or whatever single name will include all
these, and aims at the pleasure that results from making a profit; but the
5   concern of injustice as a whole is whatever concerns the excellent person.

Clearly, then, there is more than one type of justice, and there is another
type besides <the type that is> the whole of virtue; but we must still grasp
what it is, and what sort of thing it is.

What is unjust is divided into what is lawless and what is unfair, and
what is just into what is lawful and what is fair. The <general> injustice
10   previously described, then, is concerned with what is lawless. But what is
unfair is not the same as what is lawless, but related to it as part to whole,
since whatever is unfair is lawless, but not everything lawless is unfair.
Hence also the type of injustice and the way for a thing to be unjust <that
expresses unfairness> are not the same as the type <that expresses lawless-
15   ness>, but differ as parts from wholes. For this injustice <as unfairness> is
a part of the whole of injustice, and similarly justice <as fairness> is a part
of the whole of justice.

Hence we must describe special <as well as general> justice and injustice, and equally this way for a thing to be just or unjust.

20   Let us, then, set to one side the type of justice and injustice that corresponds to the whole of virtue, justice being the exercise of the whole of
virtue, and injustice of the whole of vice, in relation to another.

And it is evident how we must distinguish the way for a thing to be just or unjust that expresses this type of justice and injustice; for the majority of lawful actions, we might say, are the actions resulting from virtue as a whole. For the law instructs us to express each virtue, and forbids us to express each vice, in how we live. Moreover, the actions producing the   25 whole of virtue are the lawful actions that the laws prescribe for education promoting the common good.

We must wait till later, however, to determine whether the education that makes an individual an unconditionally good man is a task for political science or for another science; for, presumably, being a good man is not the same as being every sort of good citizen.[26]

Special justice, however, and the corresponding way for something to be   30 just <must be divided>.

One species is found in the distribution of honors or wealth or anything else that can be divided among members of a community who share in a political system; for here it is possible for one member to have a share equal or unequal to another's.

Another species concerns rectification in transactions. This species has   *1131a* two parts, since one sort of transaction is voluntary, and one involuntary. Voluntary transactions include selling, buying, lending, pledging, renting, depositing, hiring out—these are called voluntary because the origin of   5 these transactions is voluntary. Some involuntary ones are secret, e.g. theft, adultery, poisoning, pimping, slave-deception, murder by treachery, false witness; others are forcible, e.g. assault, imprisonment, murder, plunder, mutilation, slander, insult.

Book VI

1

Since we have said previously that we must choose the intermediate condi-   *1138b* tion, not the excess or the deficiency, and that the intermediate condition is   20 as correct reason says, let us now determine this, <i.e. what it says>.

For in all the states of character we have mentioned, as well as in the others, there is a target which the person who has reason focuses on and so tightens or relaxes; and there is a definition of the means, which we say are between excess and deficiency because they express correct reason.   25

To say this is admittedly true, but it is not at all clear. For in other pursuits directed by a science it is equally true that we must labour and be idle neither too much nor too little, but the intermediate amount prescribed

26. **being a good man . . .:** On the distinction between the virtues of a man and of a citizen see *Pol.* III. 4. The question about education is considered again in X. 9 and in *Pol.* VII.

30 by correct reason. But knowing only this, we would be none the wiser, e.g.
about the medicines to be applied to the body, if we were told we must
apply the ones that medical science prescribes and in the way that the
medical scientist applies them.

Similarly, then, our account of the states of the soul must not only be
true up to this point; we must also determine what correct reason is, i.e.
what its definition is.

35 After we divided the virtues of the soul we said that some are virtues of
1139a character and some of thought. And so, having finished our discussion of
the virtues of character, let us now discuss the others as follows, after
speaking first about the soul.

Previously, then, we said there are two parts of the soul, one that has
5 reason, and one nonrational. Now we should divide in the same way the
part that has reason.

Let us assume there are two parts that have reason; one with which we
study beings whose origins do not admit of being otherwise than they are,
and one with which we study beings whose origins admit of being otherwise. For when the beings are of different kinds, the parts of the soul
10 naturally suited to each of them are also of different kinds, since the parts
possess knowledge by being somehow similar and appropriate <to their
objects>.

Let us call one of these the scientific part, and the other the rationally
calculating part, since deliberating is the same as rationally calculating,
and no one deliberates about what cannot be otherwise. Hence the ra-
15 tionally calculating part is one part of the part of the soul that has reason.

Hence we should find the best state of the scientific and the best state of
the rationally calculating part; for this state is the virtue of each of them.
And since something's virtue is relative to its own proper function <we
must consider the function of each part>.

2

There are three <capacities> in the soul—perception, understanding,
desire—that control action and truth. Of these three perception clearly
20 originates no action, since beasts have perception, but no share in action.

As assertion and denial are to thought, so pursuit and avoidance are to
desire. Now virtue of character is a state that decides; and decision is a
deliberative desire. If, then, the decision is excellent, the reason must be
25 true and the desire correct, so that what reason asserts is what desire
pursues.

This, then, is thought and truth concerned with action. By contrast, when
thought is concerned with study, not with action or production, its good or
bad state consists <simply> in being true or false. For truth is the function

of whatever thinks; but the function of what thinks about action is truth   30
agreeing with correct desire.

Now the origin of an action—the source of the movement, not the
action's goal[27]—is decision, and the origin of decision is desire together
with reason that aims at some goal. Hence decision requires understanding
and thought, and also a state of character, since doing well or badly in   35
action requires both thought and character.

Thought by itself, however, moves nothing; what moves us is thought
aiming at some goal and concerned with action. For this is the sort of
thought that also originates productive thinking; for every producer in his 1139b
production aims at some <further> goal, and the unconditional goal is not
the product, which is only the <conditional> goal of some <production>,
and aims at some <further> goal. <An unconditional goal is> what we
achieve in *action*, since doing well in action is the goal.

Now desire is for the goal.[28] Hence decision is either understanding
combined with desire or desire combined with thought; and what origi-   5
nates movement in this way is a human being.

We do not decide to do what is already past; no one decides, e.g. to have
sacked Troy. For neither do we deliberate about what is past, but only about
what will be and admits <of being or not being>; and what is past does
not admit of not having happened. Hence Agathon is correct to say 'Of
this alone even a god is deprived—to make what is all done to have never   10
happened.'

Hence the function of each of the understanding parts is truth; and so
the virtue of each part will be the state that makes that part grasp the truth
most of all.

5

To grasp what intelligence is we should first study the sort of people we call   25
intelligent.

It seems proper, then, to an intelligent person to be able to deliberate
finely about what is good and beneficial for himself, not about some restricted area—e.g. about what promotes health or strength—but about
what promotes living well in general.

A sign of this is the fact that we call people intelligent about some
<restricted area> whenever they calculate well to promote some excellent

27. **the source:** Lit. 'that from which the movement <is> but not that for the sake of
which (*hou heneka*) <the movement is>'. Aristotle refers to the efficient and final
CAUSES. 'Goal' translates both *telos* and *hou heneka*.

28. **the goal. Now desire . . . :** A different punctuation would yield 'the goal, and
desire is for the goal. Hence . . .'.

30 end, in an area where there is no craft. Hence where \<living well\> as a whole is concerned, the deliberative person will also be intelligent.

Now no one deliberates about what cannot be otherwise or about what cannot be achieved by his action. Hence, if science involves demonstration, but there is no demonstration of anything whose origins admit of being *35* otherwise, since every such thing itself admits of being otherwise; and if *1140b* we cannot deliberate about what is by necessity; it follows that intelligence is not science nor yet craft-knowledge. It is not science, because what is done in action admits of being otherwise; and it is not craft-knowledge, because action and production belong to different kinds.

The remaining possibility, then, is that intelligence is a state grasping the *5* truth, involving reason, concerned with action about what is good or bad for a human being.

For production has its end beyond it; but action does not, since its end is doing well itself, \<and doing well is the concern of intelligence\>.

Hence Pericles and such people are the ones whom we regard as intelligent, because they are able to study what is good for themselves and for *10* human beings; and we think that household managers and politicians are such people.

This is also how we come to give temperance (*sōphrosunē*) its name, because we think that it preserves intelligence, (*sōzousan tēn phronēsin*). This is the sort of supposition that it preserves. For the sort of supposition that is corrupted and perverted by what is pleasant or painful is not every *15* sort—not, e.g., the supposition that the triangle does or does not have two right angles—but suppositions about what is done in action.

For the origin of what is done in action is the goal it aims at; and if pleasure or pain has corrupted someone, it follows that the origin will not appear to him. Hence it will not be apparent that this must be the goal and *20* cause of all his choice and action; for vice corrupts the origin.

Hence \<since intelligence is what temperance preserves, and what temperance preserves is a true supposition about action\>, intelligence must be a state grasping the truth, involving reason, and concerned with action about human goods.

Moreover, there is virtue \<or vice in the use\> of craft, but not \<in the use\> of intelligence. Further, in a craft, someone who makes errors voluntarily is more choiceworthy; but with intelligence, as with the virtues, the reverse is true. Clearly, then, intelligence is a virtue, not craft-*25* knowledge.

There are two parts of the soul that have reason. Intelligence is a virtue of one of them, of the part that has belief; for belief is concerned, as intelligence is, with what admits of being otherwise.

Moreover, it is not only a state involving reason. A sign of this is the fact that such a state can be forgotten, but intelligence cannot.

7

We ascribe wisdom in crafts to the people who have the most exact expertise in the crafts, e.g. we call Pheidias a wise stone-worker and Polycleitus a   10
wise bronze-worker, signifying nothing else by wisdom than excellence in a
craft. But we also think some people are wise in general, not wise in some
<restricted> area, or in some other <specific> way, as Homer says in the
Margites: 'The gods did not make him a digger or a plowman or wise in   15
anything else.' Clearly, then, wisdom is the most exact <form> of scientific
knowledge.

Hence the wise person must not only know what is derived from the
origins of a science, but also grasp the truth about the origins. Therefore
wisdom is understanding plus scientific knowledge; it is scientific knowledge of the most honorable things that has received <understanding as> its
coping-stone.

For it would be absurd for someone to think that political science or   20
intelligence is the most excellent science, when the best thing in the universe is not a human being <and the most excellent science must be of the
best things>.

Moreover, what is good and healthy for human beings and for fish is not
the same, but what is white or straight is always the same. Hence everyone
would also say that the content of wisdom is always the same, but the   25
content of intelligence is not. For the agent they would call intelligent is the
one who studies well each question about his own <good>, and he is the
one to whom they would entrust such questions. Hence intelligence is also
ascribed to some of the beasts, the ones that are evidently capable of
forethought about their own life.

It is also evident that wisdom is not the same as political science. For if
people are to say that science about what is beneficial to themselves <as   30
human beings> counts as wisdom, there will be many types of wisdom
<corresponding to the different species of animals>. For if there is no one
medical science about all beings, there is no one science about the good of
all animals, but a different science about each specific good. <Hence there
will be many types of wisdom, contrary to our assumption that it has
always the same content>.

And it does not matter if human beings are the best among the animals.
For there are other beings of a far more divine nature than human beings;
e.g., most evidently, the beings composing the universe.   1141b

What we have said makes it clear that wisdom is both scientific knowledge and understanding about what is by nature most honorable. That is
why people say that Anaxagoras or Thales or that sort of person is wise,   5
but not intelligent, when they see that he is ignorant of what benefits
himself. And so they say that what he knows is extraordinary, amazing,

difficult and divine, but useless, because it is not human goods that he looks for.

Intelligence, by contrast, is about human concerns, about what is open to
10   deliberation. For we say that deliberating well is the function of the intelligent person more than anyone else; but no one deliberates about what cannot be otherwise, or about what lacks a goal that is a good achievable in action. The unconditionally good deliberator is the one whose aim expresses rational calculation in pursuit of the best good for a human being that is achievable in action.

15   Nor is intelligence about universals only. It must also come to know particulars, since it is concerned with action and action is about particulars. Hence in other areas also some people who lack knowledge but have experience are better in action than others who have knowledge. For someone who knows that light meats are digestible and healthy, but not which sorts
20   of meats are light, will not produce health; the one who knows that bird meats are healthy will be better at producing health. And since intelligence is concerned with action, it must possess both <the universal and the particular knowledge> or the <particular> more <than the universal>. Here too, however, <as in medicine> there is a ruling <science>.

12

Someone might, however, be puzzled about what use they are.
20   For wisdom is not concerned with any sort of coming into being, and hence will not study any source of human happiness.

25   Admittedly intelligence will study this; but what do we need it for?
26   For knowledge of what is healthy or fit—i.e. of what results from the state of health, not of what produces it—makes us no readier to act appro-
27   priately if we are already healthy; for having the science of medicine or
21   gymnastic makes us no readier to act appropriately. Similarly, intelligence is the science of what is just and what is fine, and what is good for a human being; but this is how the good man acts; and if we are already good,
25   knowledge of them makes us no readier to act appropriately, since virtues are states <activated in actions>.

28   If we concede that intelligence is not useful for this, should we say it is useful for becoming good? In that case it will be no use to those who are
30   already excellent. Nor, however, will it be any use to those who are not. For it will not matter to them whether they have it themselves or take the advice of others who have it. The advice of others will be quite adequate for us, just as it is with health: we wish to be healthy, but still do not learn medical science.

Besides, it would seem absurd for intelligence, inferior as it is to wisdom,
35   to control it <as a superior. But this will be the result>, since the science that produces also rules and prescribes about its product.

We must discuss these questions; for so far we have only gone through the puzzles about them.

First of all, let us state that both intelligence and wisdom must be *1144a* choiceworthy in themselves, even if neither produces anything at all; for each is the virtue of one of the two <rational> parts <of the soul>.

Second, they do produce something. Wisdom produces happiness, not in the way that medical science produces health, but in the way that health   *5* produces <health>.²⁹ For since wisdom is a part of virtue as a whole, it makes us happy because it is a state that we possess and activate.

Further, we fulfil our function in so far as we have intelligence and virtue of character; for virtue makes the goal correct, and intelligence makes what promotes the goal <correct>. The fourth part of the soul, the nutritive   *10* part, has no such virtue <related to our function>, since no action is up to it to do or not to do.

To answer the claim that intelligence will make us no readier to do fine and just actions, we must begin from a little further back <in our discussion>.

Here is where we begin. We say that some people who do just actions are not yet thereby just, if, e.g., they do the actions prescribed by the laws,   *15* either unwillingly or because of ignorance or because of some other end, not because of the actions themselves, even though they do the right actions, those that the excellent person ought to do. Equally, however, it would seem to be possible for someone to do each type of action in the state that makes him a good person, i.e. because of decision and for the sake of the actions themselves.   *20*

Now virtue makes the decision correct; but the actions that are naturally to be done to fulfil the decision are the concern not of virtue, but of another capacity. We must get to know them more clearly before continuing our discussion.

There is a capacity, called cleverness, which is such as to be able to do the actions that tend to promote whatever goal is assumed and to achieve it.   *25* If, then, the goal is fine, cleverness is praiseworthy, and if the goal is base, cleverness is unscrupulousness; hence both intelligent and unscrupulous people are called clever.

Intelligence is not the same as this capacity <of cleverness>, though it requires it. Intelligence, this eye of the soul, cannot reach its fully devel-   *30* oped state without virtue, as we have said and as is clear. For inferences about actions have an origin: 'Since the end and the best good is this sort of thing', whatever it actually is—let it be any old thing for the sake of argument. And this <best good> is apparent only to the good person; for vice perverts us and produces false views about the origins of actions.   *35*

Evidently, then, we cannot be intelligent without being good.   *1144b*

---

29. **health produces <health>**: Less probably: 'health produces <happiness>'.

13

We must, then, also examine virtue over again. For virtue is similar <in this way> to intelligence; as intelligence is related to cleverness, not the same but similar, so natural virtue is related to full virtue.

For each of us seems to possess his type of character to some extent by
5   nature, since we are just, brave, prone to temperance, or have another feature, immediately from birth. However, we still search for some other condition as full goodness, and expect to possess these features in another way.

For these natural states belong to children and to beasts as well <as to adults>, but without understanding they are evidently harmful. At any
10   rate, this much would seem to be clear: just as a heavy body moving around unable to see suffers a heavy fall because it has no sight, so it is with virtue. <A naturally well-endowed person without understanding will harm himself.> But if someone acquires understanding, he improves in his actions; and the state he now has, though still similar <to the natural one>, will be virtue to the full extent.

And so, just as there are two sorts of conditions, cleverness and intel-
15   ligence, in the part of the soul that has belief, so also there are two in the part that has character, natural virtue and full virtue. And of these full virtue cannot be acquired without intelligence.

This is why some say that all the virtues are <instances of> intelligence, and why Socrates' inquiries were in one way correct, and in another way in
20   error. For in that he thought all the virtues are <instances of> intelligence,[30] he was in error; but in that he thought they all require intelligence, he was right.

Here is a sign of this: Whenever people now define virtue, they all say what state it is and what it is related to, and then add that it is the state that expresses correct reason. Now correct reason is reason that expresses intel-
25   ligence; it would seem, then, that they all in a way intuitively believe that the state expressing intelligence is virtue.

But we must make a slight change. For it is not merely the state expressing correct reason, but the state involving correct reason, that is virtue. And it is intelligence that is correct reason in this area. Socrates, then, thought, that the virtues are <instances of> reason because he thought they
30   are all <instances of> knowledge, whereas we think they involve reason.

What we have said, then, makes it clear that we cannot be fully good without intelligence, or intelligent without virtue of character.

In this way we can also solve the dialectical argument that someone might use to show that the virtues are separated from each other. For, <it is
35   argued>, since the same person is not naturally best suited for all the virtues, someone will already have one virtue before he has got another.

30. <instances of> intelligence: Lit. 'intelligences'; perhaps '<forms of> intelligence'.

This is indeed possible with the natural virtues. It is not possible, however, with the <full> virtues that someone must have to be called unconditionally good; for as soon as he has intelligence, which is a single state, he *1145a* has all the virtues as well.

And clearly, even if intelligence were useless in action, we would need it because it is the virtue of this part of the soul, and because the decision[31] will not be correct without intelligence or without virtue. For virtue makes   5 us reach the end in our action, while intelligence makes us reach what promotes the end.

Moreover, intelligence does not control wisdom or the better part of the soul, just as medical science does not control health. For it does not use health, but only aims to bring health into being; hence it prescribes for the sake of health, but does not prescribe to health. Besides, <saying that   10 intelligence controls wisdom> would be like saying that political science rules the gods because it prescribes about everything in the city.

Book VII

1

Next we should make a new beginning, and say that there are three condi-   15 tions of character to be avoided—vice, incontinence and bestiality. The contraries of two of these are clear; we call one virtue and the other continence.

The contrary to bestiality is most suitably called virtue superior to us, a heroic, indeed divine, sort of virtue. Thus Homer made Priam say that   20 Hector was remarkably good; 'nor did he look as though he were the child of a mortal man, but of a god.' Moreover, so they say, human beings become gods because of exceedingly great virtue.

Clearly, then, this is the sort of state that would be opposite to the bestial state. For indeed, just as a beast has neither virtue nor vice, so neither does   25 a god, but the god's state is more honorable than virtue, and the beast's belongs to some kind different from vice.

Now it is rare that a divine man exists. (This is what the Spartans habitually call him; whenever they very much admire someone, they say he is a divine man.) Similarly, the bestial person is also rare among human   30 beings. He is most often found in foreigners; but some bestial features also result from diseases and deformities. We also use 'bestial' as a term of reproach for people whose vice exceeds the human level.

We must make some remarks about this condition later. We have discussed vice earlier. We must now discuss incontinence, softness and self-   35 indulgence, and also continence and resistance; for we must not suppose *1145b*

31. **and because** . . . : Or 'and also, clearly, the decision . . .'

that continence and incontinence are concerned with the same states as
virtue and vice, or that they belong to a different kind.

As in the other cases we must set out the appearances, and first of all go
through the puzzles. In this way we must prove the common beliefs about
these ways of being affected—ideally, all the common beliefs, but if not all,
then most of them, and the most important. For if the objections are
solved, and the common beliefs are left, it will be an adequate proof.

Continence and resistance seem to be good and praiseworthy conditions,
while incontinence and softness seem to be base and blameworthy conditions.

The continent person seems to be the same as one who abides by his
rational calculation; and the incontinent person seems to be the same as
one who abandons it.

The incontinent person knows that his actions are base, but does them
because of his feelings, while the continent person knows that his appetites
are base, but because of reason does not follow them.

People think the temperate person is continent and resistant. Some think
that every continent and resistant person is temperate, while others do not.
Some people say the incontinent person is intemperate and the intemperate
incontinent, with no distinction; others say they are different.

Sometimes it is said that an intelligent person cannot be incontinent; but
sometimes it is said that some people are intelligent and clever, but still
incontinent.

Further, people are called incontinent about emotion, honor and gain.

These, then, are the things that are said.

2

We might be puzzled about the sort of correct supposition someone has
when he acts incontinently.

First of all, some say he cannot have knowledge <at the time he acts>.
For it would be terrible, Socrates thought, for knowledge to be in someone,
but mastered by something else, and dragged around like a slave. For
Socrates fought against the account <of incontinence> in general, in the
belief that there is no incontinence; for no one, he thought, supposes while
he acts that his action conflicts with what is best; our action conflicts with
what is best only because we are ignorant <of the conflict>.

This argument, then, contradicts things that appear manifestly. If ignorance causes the incontinent person to be affected as he is, then we must
look for the type of ignorance that it turns out to be; for it is evident, at any
rate, that before he is affected the person who acts incontinently does not
think <he should do the action he eventually does>.

Some people concede some of <Socrates' points>, but reject some of them. For they agree that nothing is superior to knowledge, but deny that no one's action conflicts with what has seemed better to him. Hence they say that when the incontinent person is overcome by pleasure he has only belief, not knowledge.   35

In that case, however, if he has belief, not knowledge, and what resists is not a strong supposition, but only a mild one, such as people have when 1146a they are in doubt, we will pardon failure to abide by these beliefs against strong appetites. In fact, however, we do not pardon vice, or any other blameworthy condition <and incontinence is one of these>.

Then is it intelligence that resists, since it is the strongest? This is absurd.   5 For on this view the same person will be both intelligent and incontinent; and no one would say that the intelligent person is the sort to do the worst actions willingly.

Besides, we have shown earlier that the intelligent person acts <on his knowledge>, since he is concerned with the last things, <i.e. particulars>, and that he has the other virtues.

Further, if the continent person must have strong and base appetites, the   10 temperate person will not be continent nor the continent person temperate. For the temperate person is not the sort to have either excessive or base appetites; but <the continent person> must have both.

For if his appetites are good, the state that prevents him from following them must be base, so that not all continence is excellent. If, on the other hand, the appetites are weak and not base, continence is nothing impres-   15 sive; and if they are base and weak, it is nothing great.

Besides, if continence makes someone prone to abide by every belief, it is bad, if, e.g., it makes him abide by a false as well <as a true> belief.

And if incontinence makes someone prone to abandon every belief, there will be an excellent type of incontinence. Neoptolemus, e.g., in Sophocles' *Philoctetes* is praiseworthy when, after being persuaded by Odysseus, he   20 does not abide by his resolve, because he feels pain at lying.

Besides, the sophistical argument is a puzzle. For <the sophists> wish to refute an <opponent, by showing> that his views have paradoxical results, so that they will be clever in encounters. Hence the inference that results is a puzzle; for thought is tied up, since it does not want to stand still because   25 the conclusion is displeasing, but it cannot advance because it cannot solve the argument.

A certain argument, then, concludes that foolishness combined with in-continence is virtue. For incontinence makes someone act contrary to what he supposes <is right>; but since he supposes that good things are bad and   30 that it is wrong to do them, he will do the good actions, not the bad.

Further, someone who acts to pursue what is pleasant because this is what he is persuaded and decides to do, seems to be better than someone who acts not because of rational calculation, but because of incontinence.

For the first person is the easier to cure, because he might be persuaded
otherwise; but the incontinent person illustrates the proverb 'If water
35   chokes us, what must we drink to wash it down?' For if he had been
1146b persuaded to do the action he does, he would have stopped when he was
was persuaded to act otherwise; but in fact, though already persuaded to
act otherwise, he still acts <wrongly>.

Further, is there incontinence and continence about everything? If so,
who is the simply incontinent? For no one has all the types of incontinence,
5   but we say that some people are simply incontinent.

These, then, are the sorts of puzzles that arise. We must undermine some
of these claims, and leave others intact; for the solution of the puzzle is the
discovery <of what we are seeking>.

3

First, then, we must examine whether the incontinent has knowledge or
not, and in what way he has it. Second, what should we take to be the
10   incontinent and the continent person's area of concern—every pleasure and
pain, or some definite subclass? Are the continent and the resistant person
the same or different? Similarly we must deal with the other questions that
are relevant to this study.

15   We begin the examination with this question: Are the continent and the
incontinent person distinguished <from others> (i) by their concerns, or
(ii) by their attitudes to them? In other words, is the incontinent person
incontinent (i) only by having these concerns, or instead (ii) by having this
attitude; or instead (iii) by both?

<Surely (iii) is right.> For <(i) is insufficient> since the simple inconti-
20   nent is not concerned with everything, but with the same things as the
intemperate person. Moreover, <(ii) is insufficient> since he is not incontinent simply by being inclined towards these things—that would make
incontinence the same as intemperance. Rather <as (iii) implies>, he is
incontinent by being inclined towards them in this way. For the intemperate
person acts on decision when he is led on, since he thinks it is right in
every case to pursue the pleasant thing at hand; but the incontinent person
thinks it is wrong to pursue it, yet still pursues it.

25   It is claimed that the incontinent person's action conflicts with true belief,
not with knowledge. But whether it is knowledge or belief that he has does
not matter for this argument. For some people with belief are in no doubt,
but think they have exact knowledge.

If, then, it is the weakness of their conviction that makes people with
belief, not people with knowledge, act in conflict with their supposition, it
follows that knowledge will <for these purposes> be no different from
30   belief; for, as Heraclitus makes clear, some people's convictions about what

they believe are no weaker than other people's convictions about what they know.

But we speak of knowing in two ways, and ascribe it both to someone who has it without using it and to someone who is using it. Hence it will matter whether someone has the knowledge that his action is wrong, without attending to his knowledge, or both has and attends to it. For this second case seems extraordinary, but wrong action when he does not attend to his knowledge does not seem extraordinary.

Besides, since there are two types of premisses, someone's action may well conflict with his knowledge if he has both types of premisses, but uses only the universal premiss and not the particular premiss.[32] For <the particular premiss states the particulars and> it is particular actions that are done.

Moreover, <in both types of premisses> there are different types of universal,[33] (a) one type referring to the agent himself, and (b) the other referring to the object. Perhaps e.g., someone knows that (a1) dry things benefit every human being, and that (a2) he himself is a human being, or that (b1) this sort of thing is dry; but he either does not have or does not activate the knowledge that (b2) this particular thing is of this sort.

Hence these ways <of knowing and not knowing> make such a remarkable difference that it seems quite intelligible <for someone acting against his knowledge> to have the one sort of knowledge <i.e. without (b2)>, but astounding if he has the other sort <including (b2)>.

Besides, human beings may have knowledge in a way different from those we have described. For we see that having without using includes different types of having; hence some people, e.g. those asleep or mad or drunk, both have knowledge in a way and do not have it.

Moreover, this is the condition of those affected by strong feelings.[34] For emotions, sexual appetites and some conditions of this sort clearly <both disturb knowledge and> disturb the body as well, and even produce fits of madness in some people.

Clearly, then <since incontinents are also affected by strong feelings>, we should say that they have knowledge in a way similar to these people.

Saying the words that come from knowledge is no sign <of fully having it>. For people affected in these ways even recite demonstrations and verses of Empedocles. Further, those who have just learnt something do not yet know it, though they string the words together; for it must grow into them, and this needs time.

32. **particular premise:** Lit. 'partial' (*kata meros*), mentioning particulars (*kath'hekasta*).

33. **types of universal:** Not universal premises, but universal terms or concepts (e.g. 'healthy' or 'dry').

34. **those affected . . . feelings:** Lit. 'those in affections' (*pathē*); see ATTRIBUTE #3.

Hence we must suppose that incontinents say the words in the way that actors do.

Further, we may also look at the cause in the following way, referring to
25   <human> nature. One belief (a) is universal; the other (b) is about particulars, and because they are particulars perception controls them. And in the cases where these two beliefs result in (c) one belief, it is necessary in purely theoretical beliefs for the soul to affirm what has been concluded, and in beliefs about production (d) to act at once on what has been concluded.[35]

If, e.g., (a) everything sweet must be tasted, and (b) this, some one
30   particular thing, is sweet, it is necessary (d) for someone who is able and unhindered also to act on this at the same time.

Suppose, then, that someone has (a) the universal belief, and it hinders him from tasting; he has (b) the second belief, that everything sweet is pleasant and this is sweet,[36] and this belief (b) is active; and he also has
35   appetite. Hence the belief (c) tells him to avoid this, but appetite leads him on, since it is capable of moving each of the <bodily> parts.
1147b   The result, then, is that in a way reason and belief make him act incontinently. The belief (b) is contrary to correct reason (a), but only coincidentally, not in itself. For it is the appetite, not the belief, that is contrary <in itself to correct reason>.

Hence beasts are not incontinent, because they have no universal sup-
5   position, but <only> appearance and memory of particulars.

How is the ignorance resolved, so that the incontinent person recovers his knowledge? The same account that applies to someone drunk or asleep applies here too, and is not special to this way of being affected. We must hear it from the natural scientists.

And since the last premiss (b) is a belief about something perceptible,
10   and controls action, this must be what the incontinent person does not have when he is being affected. Or rather the way he has it is not knowledge of it, but, as we saw, <merely> saying the words, as the drunk says the words of Empedocles.

Further, since the last term does not seem to be universal, or expressive

35. **And in the cases . . . :** Lit. (following the Greek word-order) 'Whenever one comes to be from them, it is necessary that the thing concluded, in the one case the soul affirms, and in productive <beliefs> does at once.' 'The thing concluded' is the object both of 'affirms' and 'does.'

36. **he has . . . is sweet:** Alternatively (i) 'everything sweet is pleasant' and (ii) 'this is sweet' might be taken as two distinct beliefs in which case 'this <belief> is active' (i.e. not merely potential) will refer to (ii).

Grammatically, 'Hence this belief . . . ' might refer to (a) rather than (c); but (a) hardly tells him to avoid this particular thing.

of knowledge in the same way as the universal term, even the result Socrates was looking for would seem to come about. For the knowledge that is   *15*
present when someone is affected by incontinence, and that is dragged
about because he is affected, is not the sort that seems to be knowledge to
the full extent <in (c)>, but only perceptual knowledge <in (b)>.

So much, then, for knowing and not knowing, and for how it is possible
to know and still to act incontinently.

Book X

6

We have now finished our discussion of the types of virtue; of friendship; *1176a*
and of pleasure. It remains for us to discuss happiness in outline, since we
take this to be the end of human <aims>. Our discussion will be shorter if
we first take up again what we said before.

We said, then, that happiness is not a state. For if it were, someone might
have it and yet be asleep for his whole life, living the life of a plant, or   *35*
suffer the greatest misfortunes. If we do not approve of this, we count *1176b*
happiness as an activity rather than a state, as we said before.

Some activities are necessary, i.e. choiceworthy for some other end,
while others are choiceworthy in themselves. Clearly, then, we should
count happiness as one of those activities that are choiceworthy in them-   *5*
selves, not as one of those choiceworthy for some other end. For happiness
lacks nothing, but is self-sufficient; and an activity is choiceworthy in itself
when nothing further beyond it is sought from it.

This seems to be the character of actions expressing virtue; for doing
fine and excellent actions is choiceworthy for itself.

But pleasant amusements also <seem to be choiceworthy in themselves>.
For they are not chosen for other ends, since they actually cause more harm   *10*
than benefit, by causing neglect of our bodies and possessions.

Moreover, most of those people congratulated for their happiness resort
to these sorts of pastimes. Hence people who are witty participants in them
have a good reputation with tyrants, since they offer themselves as pleasant   *15*
<partners> in the tyrant's aims, and these are the sort of people the tyrant
requires. And so these amusements seem to have the character of happiness because people in supreme power spend their leisure in them.

However, these sorts of people are presumably no evidence. For virtue
and understanding, the sources of excellent activities, do not depend on
holding supreme power. Further, these powerful people have had no taste   *20*
of pure and civilized pleasure, and so they resort to bodily pleasures. But
that is no reason to think these pleasures are most choiceworthy, since boys
also think that what they honor is best. Hence, just as different things

appear honorable to boys and to men, it is reasonable that in the same way different things appear honorable to base and to decent people.

25 As we have often said, then, what is honorable and pleasant is what is so to the excellent person; and to each type of person the activity expressing his own proper state is most choiceworthy; hence the activity expressing virtue is most choiceworthy to the excellent person <and hence is most honorable and pleasant>.

Happiness, then, is not found in amusement; for it would be absurd if 30 the end were amusement, and our lifelong efforts and sufferings aimed at amusing ourselves. For we choose practically everything for some other end—except for happiness, since it is <the> end; but serious work and toil aimed <only> at amusement appears stupid and excessively childish. Rather, it seems correct to amuse ourselves so that we can do something serious, as Anacharsis says; for amusement would seem to be relaxation, 35 and it is because we cannot toil continuously that we require relaxation. Relaxation, then, is not <the> end, since we pursue it <to prepare> for 1177a activity.

Further, the happy life seems to be a life expressing virtue, which is a life involving serious actions, and not consisting in amusement.

Besides, we say that things to be taken seriously are better than funny things that provide amusement, and that in each case the activity of the 5 better part and the better person is more serious and excellent; and the activity of what is better is superior, and thereby has more the character of happiness.

Moreover, anyone at all, even a slave, no less than the best person, might enjoy bodily pleasures; but no one would allow that a slave shares in happiness, if one does not <also allow that the slave shares in the sort of> life <needed for happiness>. Happiness, then, is found not in these pas-
10 times, but in the activities expressing virtue, as we also said previously.

7

If happiness, then, is activity expressing virtue, it is reasonable for it to express the supreme virtue, which will be the virtue of the best thing.

The best is understanding, or whatever else seems to be the natural ruler 15 and leader, and to understand what is fine and divine, by being itself either divine or the most divine element in us.

Hence complete happiness will be its activity expressing its proper virtue; and we have said[37] that this activity is the activity of study. This seems to agree with what has been said before, and also with the truth.

37. **We have said:** Where? Not explicitly; but cf. 1139a6–17, 1141a18–22, 1143b33–1144a6, 1145a6–11. Aristotle does not say here that the activity of understanding that constitutes happiness is exclusively concerned with study.

For this activity is supreme, since understanding is the supreme ele-   20
ment in us, and the objects of understanding are the supreme objects of
knowledge.

Besides, it is the most continuous activity, since we are more capable of
continuous study than of any continuous action.

We think pleasure must be mixed into happiness; and it is agreed that
the activity expressing wisdom is the pleasantest of the activities expressing virtue. At any rate, philosophy seems to have remarkably pure and firm   25
pleasures; and it is reasonable for those who have knowledge to spend their
lives more pleasantly than those who seek it.

Moreover, the self-sufficiency we spoke of will be found in study above
all.

For admittedly the wise person, the just person and the other virtuous
people all need the good things necessary for life. Still, when these are
adequately supplied, the just person needs other people as partners and   30
recipients of his just actions; and the same is true of the temperate person
and the brave person and each of the others.

But the wise person is able, and more able the wiser he is, to study even
by himself; and though he presumably does it better with colleagues, even
so he is more self-sufficient than any other <virtuous person>.   1177b

Besides, study seems to be liked because of itself alone, since it has no
result beyond having studied. But from the virtues concerned with action we try to a greater or lesser extent to gain something beyond the
action itself.

Happiness seems to be found in leisure, since we accept trouble so that   5
we can be at leisure, and fight wars so that we can be at peace. Now the
virtues concerned with action have their activities in politics or war, and
actions here seem to require trouble.

This seems completely true for actions in war, since no one chooses to
fight a war, and no one continues it, for the sake of fighting a war; for
someone would have to be a complete murderer if he made his friends his   10
enemies so that there could be battles and killings.

But the actions of the politician require trouble also. Beyond political
activities themselves these actions seek positions of power and honors; or
at least they seek happiness for the politician himself and for his fellow-
citizens, which is something different from political science itself, and   15
clearly is sought on the assumption that it is different.

Hence among actions expressing the virtues those in politics and war are
pre-eminently fine and great; but they require trouble, aim at some
<further> end, and are choiceworthy for something other than themselves.

But the activity of understanding, it seems, is superior in excellence
because it is the activity of study, aims at no end beyond itself and has its   20
own proper pleasure, which increases the activity. Further, self-sufficiency,
leisure, unwearied activity (as far as is possible for a human being), and

any other features ascribed to the blessed person, are evidently features of this activity.

25   Hence a human being's complete happiness will be this activity, if it receives a complete span of life, since nothing incomplete is proper to happiness.

Such a life would be superior to the human level. For someone will live it not insofar as he is a human being, but insofar as he has some divine element in him. And the activity of this divine element is as much superior

30   to the activity expressing the rest of virtue as this element is superior to the compound. Hence if understanding is something divine in comparison with a human being, so also will the life that expresses understanding be divine in comparison with human life.

We ought not to follow the proverb-writers, and 'think human, since you are human', or 'think mortal, since you are mortal'. Rather, as far as we

1178a can, we ought to be pro-immortal,[38] and go to all lengths to live a life that expresses our supreme element; for however much this element may lack in bulk, by much more it surpasses everything in power and value.

Moreover, each person seems to be his understanding, if he is his controlling and better element; it would be absurd, then, if he were to choose not his own life, but something else's.

5   And what we have said previously will also apply now. For what is proper to each thing's nature is supremely best and pleasantest for it; and hence for a human being the life expressing understanding will be supremely best and pleasantest, if understanding above all is the human being. This life, then, will also be happiest.

8

The life expressing the other kind of virtue <i.e. the kind concerned with action> is <happiest> in a secondary way because the activities expressing

10   this virtue are human.

For we do just and brave actions, and the others expressing the virtues, in relation to other people, by abiding by what fits each person in contracts, services, all types of actions, and also in feelings; and all these appear to be human conditions.

15   Indeed, some feelings actually seem to arise from the body; and in many ways virtue of character seems to be proper to feelings.

Besides, intelligence is yoked together with virtue of character, and so is this virtue with intelligence. For the origins of intelligence express the

---

38. **pro-immortal:** (*athanatizein*) Perhaps it means 'make oneself immortal'. But probably it is modelled on *mēdizein, lakōnizein,* used for pro-Medes (Persians) and pro-Laconians (Spartans).

virtues of character; and correctness in virtues of character expresses intelligence. And since these virtues are also connected to feelings, they are   *20*
concerned with the compound. Since the virtues of the compound are
human virtues, the life and the happiness expressing these virtues is also
human.

The virtue of understanding, however, is separated <from the com-
pound>. Let us say no more about it, since an exact account would be too
large a task for our present project.

Moreover, it seems to need external supplies very little, or <at any rate>
less than virtue of character needs them. For grant that they both need   *25*
necessary goods, and to the same extent, since there will be only a very
small difference even though the politician labors more about the body and
such-like. Still, there will be a large difference in <what is needed> for the
<proper> activities <of each type of virtue>.

For the generous person will need money for generous actions; and the
just person will need it for paying debts, since wishes are not clear, and   *30*
people who are not just pretend to wish to do justice. Similarly, the brave
person will need enough power, and the temperate person will need freedom <to do intemperate actions>, if they are to achieve anything that the
virtue requires. For how else will they, or any other virtuous people, make
their virtue clear?

Moreover, it is disputed whether it is decision or actions that is more in   *35*
control of virtue, on the assumption that virtue depends on both. Well,
certainly it is clear that what is complete depends on both; but for actions *1178b*
many external goods are needed, and the greater and finer the actions the
more numerous are the external goods needed.

But someone who is studying needs none of these goods, for that activity
at least; indeed, for study at least, we might say they are even hindrances.

In so far as he is a human being, however, and <hence> lives together   *5*
with a number of other human beings, he chooses to do the actions expressing virtue. Hence he will need the sorts of external goods <that are needed
for the virtues>, for living a human life.

In another way also it appears that complete happiness is some activity
of study. For we traditionally suppose that the gods more than anyone are
blessed and happy; but what sorts of actions ought we to ascribe to them?   *10*
Just actions? Surely they will appear ridiculous making contracts, returning
deposits and so on. Brave actions? Do they endure what <they find>
frightening and endure dangers because it is fine? Generous actions?
Whom will they give to? And surely it would be absurd for them to have
currency or anything like that. What would their temperate actions be?   *15*
Surely it is vulgar praise to say that they do not have base appetites. When
we go through them all, anything that concerns actions appears trivial and
unworthy of the gods.

However, we all traditionally suppose that they are alive and active,
20   since surely they are not asleep like Endymion. Then if someone is alive,
and action is excluded, and production even more, what is left but study?
Hence the gods' activity that is superior in blessedness will be an activity of
study. And so the human activity that is most akin to the gods' will, more
than any others, have the character of happiness.

A sign of this is the fact that other animals have no share in happiness,
25   being completely deprived of this activity of study. For the whole life of
the gods is blessed, and human life is blessed to the extent that it has
something resembling this sort of activity; but none of the other animals is
happy, because none of them shares in study at all. Hence happiness extends just as far as study extends, and the more someone studies, the
30   happier he is, not coincidentally but insofar as he studies, since study is
valuable in itself. And so <on this argument> happiness will be some kind
of study.

However, the happy person is a human being, and so will need external
35   prosperity also; for his nature is not self-sufficient for study, but he needs a
healthy body, and needs to have food and the other services provided.

1179a   Still, even though no one can be blessedly happy without external goods,
we must not think that to be happy we will need many large goods. For
self-sufficiency and action do not depend on excess, and we can do fine
actions even if we do not rule earth and sea; for even from moderate
5   resources we can do the actions expressing virtue. This is evident to see,
since many private citizens seem to do decent actions no less than people in
power do—even more, in fact. It is enough if moderate resources are provided; for the life of someone whose activity expresses virtue will be
happy.

10   Solon surely described happy people well, when he said they had been
moderately supplied with external goods, had done what he regarded as the
finest actions, and had lived their lives temperately. For it is possible to
have moderate possessions and still to do the right actions.

And Anaxagoras would seem to have supposed that the happy person
15   was neither rich nor powerful, since he said he would not be surprised if
the happy person appeared an absurd sort of person to the many. For the
many judge by externals, since these are all they perceive.

Hence the beliefs of the wise would seem to accord with our arguments.

These considerations do indeed produce some confidence. The truth,
however, in questions about action is judged from what we do and how we
20   live, since these are what control <the answers to such questions>. Hence
we ought to examine what has been said by applying it to what we do and
how we live; and if it harmonizes with what we do, we should accept it, but
if it conflicts we should count it <mere> words.

The person whose activity expresses understanding and who takes care

of understanding would seem to be in the best condition, and most loved
by the gods. For if the gods pay some attention to human beings, as they   25
seem to, it would be reasonable for them to take pleasure in what is best
and most akin to them, namely understanding; and reasonable for them to
benefit in return those who most of all like and honor understanding, on
the assumption that these people attend to what is beloved by the gods, and
act correctly and finely.

Clearly, all this is true of the wise person more than anyone else; hence   30
he is most loved by the gods. And it is likely that this same person will be
happiest; hence the wise person will be happier than anyone else on this
argument too.

9

We have now said enough in outlines about happiness and the virtues, and
about friendship and pleasure also. Should we then think that our decision   35
<to study these> has achieved its end? On the contrary, the aim of studies 1179b
about action, as we say, is surely not to study and know about each thing,
but rather to act on our knowledge. Hence knowing about virtue is not
enough, but we must also try to possess and exercise virtue, or become
good in any other way.

Now if arguments were sufficient by themselves to make people decent,   5
the rewards they would command would justifiably have been many and
large, as Theognis says, and rightly bestowed. In fact, however, arguments
seem to have enough influence to stimulate and encourage the civilized
ones among the young people, and perhaps to make virtue take possession
of a well-born character that truly loves what is fine; but they seem unable
to stimulate the many towards being fine and good.   10

For the many naturally obey fear, not shame; they avoid what is base
because of the penalties, not because it is disgraceful. For since they live by
their feelings, they pursue their proper pleasures and the sources of them,
and avoid the opposed pains, and have not even a notion of what is fine   15
and <hence> truly pleasant, since they have had no taste of it.

What argument could reform people like these? For it is impossible, or
not easy, to alter by argument what has long been absorbed by habit; but,
presumably, we should be satisfied to achieve some share in virtue when we
already have what we seem to need to become decent.[39]

Some think it is nature that makes people good; some think it is habit;   20
some that it is teaching.

The <contribution> of nature clearly is not up to us, but results from
some divine cause in those who have it, who are the truly fortunate ones.

39. **What we seem** . . . : Lit. 'through which we seem to become decent'.

Arguments and teaching surely do not influence everyone, but the soul
25 of the student needs to have been prepared by habits for enjoying and
hating finely, like ground that is to nourish seed. For someone whose life
follows his feelings would not even listen to an argument turning him away,
or comprehend it <if he did listen>; and in that state how could he be
persuaded to change? And in general feelings seem to yield to force, not to
argument.

30 Hence we must already in some way have a character suitable for virtue,
fond of what is fine and objecting to what is shameful.

But it is hard for someone to be trained correctly for virtue from his
youth if he has not been brought up under correct laws, since the many,
especially the young, do not find it pleasant to live in a temperate and
35 resistant way. Hence laws must prescribe their upbringing and practices;
for they will not find these things painful when they get used to them.

1180a Presumably, however, it is not enough to get the correct upbringing and
attention when they are young; rather, they must continue the same practices and be habituated to them when they become men. Hence we need
laws concerned with these things also, and in general with all of life. For
5 the many yield to compulsion more than to argument, and to sanctions
more than to what is fine.

This, some think, is why legislators should urge people towards virtue
and exhort them to aim at what is fine, on the assumption that anyone
whose good habits have prepared him decently will listen to them, but
should impose corrective treatments and penalties on anyone who disobeys
10 or lacks the right nature, and completely expel an incurable. For the decent
person, it is assumed, will attend to reason because his life aims at what is
fine, while the base person, since he desires pleasure, has to receive corrective treatment by pain, like a beast of burden; that is why it is said that the
pains imposed must be those most contrary to the pleasures he likes.

15 As we have said, then, someone who is to be good must be finely brought
up and habituated, and then must live in decent practices, doing nothing
base either willingly or unwillingly. And this will be true if his life follows
some sort of understanding and correct order that has influence over him.

A father's instructions, however, lack this influence and compelling
20 power; and so in general do the instructions of an individual man, unless
he is a king or someone like that. Law, however, has the power that compels; and law is reason that proceeds from a sort of intelligence and understanding. Besides, people become hostile to an individual human being
who opposes their impulses even if he is correct in opposing them;
whereas a law's prescription of what is decent is not burdensome.

25 And yet, only in Sparta, or in a few other cities as well, does the
legislator seem to have attended to upbringing and practices. In most other
cities they are neglected, and each individual citizen lives as he wishes,
'laying down the rules for his children and wife', like a Cyclops.

It is best, then, if the community attends to upbringing, and attends correctly. If, however, the community neglects it, it seems fitting for each   *30* individual to promote the virtue of his children and his friends—to be able to do it, or at least to decide to do it.

From what we have said, however, it seems he will be better able to do it if he acquires legislative science.[40] For, clearly, attention by the community   *35* works through laws, and decent attention works through excellent laws; *1180b* and whether the laws are written or unwritten, for the education of one or of many, seems unimportant, as it is in music, gymnastics and other practices. For just as in cities the provisions of law and the <prevailing> types of character have influence, similarly a father's words and habits have influ-   *5* ence, and all the more because of kinship and because of the benefits he does; for his children are already fond of him and naturally ready to obey.

Moreover, education adapted to an individual is actually better than a common education for everyone, just as individualized medical treatment is better. For though generally a feverish patient benefits from rest and starvation, presumably some patient does not; nor does the boxing instructor im-   *10* pose the same way of fighting on everyone. Hence it seems that treatment in particular cases is more exactly right when each person gets special attention, since he then more often gets the suitable treatment.

Nonetheless a doctor, a gymnastics trainer and everyone else will give the best individual attention if they also know universally what is good for   *15* all, or for these sorts. For sciences are said to be, and are, of what is common <to many particular cases>.

Admittedly someone without scientific knowledge may well attend properly to a single person, if his experience has allowed him to take exact note of what happens in each case, just as some people seem to be their own best doctors, though unable to help anyone else at all. None the less, pre-   *20* sumably, it seems that someone who wants to be an expert in a craft and a branch of study should progress to the universal, and come to know that, as far as possible; for that, as we have said, is what the sciences are about.

Then perhaps also someone who wishes to make people better by his attention, many people or few, should try to acquire legislative science, if we will become good through laws. For not just anyone can improve the   *25* condition of just anyone, or the person presented to him; but if anyone can it is the person with knowledge, just as in medical science and the others that require attention and intelligence.

Next, then, should we examine whence and how someone might acquire legislative science? Just as in other cases <we go to the practitioner>,   *30* should we go to the politicians? For, as we saw, legislative science seems to be a part of political science.

But is the case of political science perhaps apparently different from

40. **legislative science:** 'Science' is supplied in this phrase from here on.

the other sciences and capacities? For evidently in others the same people, e.g. doctors or painters, who transmit the capacity to others actively prac-
35   tice it themselves. By contrast, it is the sophists who advertise that they
1181a teach politics but none of them practices it. Instead, those who practice it are the political activists, and they seem to act on some sort of capacity and experience rather than thought.

For evidently they neither write nor speak on such questions, though presumably it would be finer to do this than to compose speeches for the
5   law courts or the Assembly; nor have they made politicians out of their own sons or any other friends of theirs. And yet it would be reasonable for them to do this if they were able; for there is nothing better than the political capacity that they could leave to their cities, and nothing better that they could decide to produce in themselves, or, therefore, in their closest friends.

10   Certainly experience would seem to contribute quite a lot; otherwise people would not have become better politicians by familiarity with politics. Hence those who aim to know about political science would seem to need experience as well.

By contrast, those of the sophists who advertise <that they teach political science> appear to be a long way from teaching; for they are altogether ignorant about the sort of thing political science is, and the sorts of things
15   it is about. For if they had known what it is, they would not have taken it to be the same as rhetoric, or something inferior to it, or thought it an easy task to assemble the laws with good reputations and then legislate. For they think they can select the best laws, as though the selection itself did not require comprehension, and as though correct judgment were not the most important thing, as it is in music.

20   It is those with experience in each area who judge the products correctly and who comprehend the method or way of completing them, and what fits with what; for if we lack experience, we must be satisfied with noticing that the product is well or badly made, as with painting. Now laws would
1181b seem to be the products of political science; how, then, could someone acquire legislative science, or judge which laws are best, from laws alone? For neither do we appear to become experts in medicine by reading textbooks.

And yet doctors not only try to describe the <recognized> treatments, but also distinguish different <physical> states, and try to say how each
5   type of patient might be cured and must be treated. And what they say seems to be useful to the experienced, though useless to the ignorant.

Similarly, then, collections of laws and political systems might also, presumably, be most useful if we are capable of studying them and of judging what is done finely or in the contrary way, and what sorts of
10   <elements> fit with what. Those who lack the <proper> state <of experi-

ence> when they go through these collections will not manage to judge finely, unless they can do it all by themselves <without training>, though they might come to comprehend them better by going through them.

Since, then, our predecessors have left the area of legislation uncharted, it is presumably better to examine it ourselves instead, and indeed to examine political systems in general, and so to complete the philosophy of human affairs, as far as we are able.

First, then, let us try to review any sound remarks our predecessors have made on particular topics. Then let us study the collected political systems, to see from them what sorts of things preserve and destroy cities, and political systems of different types; and what causes some cities to conduct politics well, and some badly.

For when we have studied these questions, we will perhaps grasp better what sort of political system is best; how each political system should be organized so as to be best; and what habits and laws it should follow.

Let us discuss this, then, starting from the beginning.

POLITICS

Aristotle's Politics *and Plato's* Republic *are the two great works of ancient political philosophy. But unlike the* Republic, *the* Politics *was probably not written as a single work; it is, rather, a collection of essays unified by a common theme. In the excerpts included below, Aristotle discusses the definition and structure of the state (Book I); criticizes the ideal societies proposed by Plato and others (Book II); classifies constitutions and such forms of government as democracy, oligarchy, and monarchy (Book III); and presents his own account of the best state (Book VII).*

Book I

1

1252a We see that every city is some sort of community, and that every community is constituted for the sake of some good, since everyone does everything for the sake of what seems good. Clearly, then, while all communities
5   aim at some good, the community that aims most of all at the good—at the good that most of all controls all the other goods—is the one that most of all controls and includes the others; and this is the one called the city, the political community.

It is wrong, then, to suppose, as some do, that the character of the politician, the king, the household manager, and the slave-master is the
10   same. People suppose this because they think the difference is not a difference in kind, but only in the number who are ruled, so that the ruler of a few is a master, the ruler of more people is a household-manager, and the ruler of still more people is a politician or a king—on the assumption that a large household is no different from a small city. And all they can say to distinguish a king from a politician is that someone who directs things himself is a king, whereas someone who follows the principles[1] of politi-
15   cal science, ruling and being ruled in turn, is a politician. These views are not true.

What we mean will be clear if the investigation follows our recognized line of inquiry. Just as in other cases we must divide the composite into
20   incomposites, since these are the smallest parts of the whole, so also in this

1. **principles:** *logoi.* See REASON.

case we must investigate the components of the city; for then we will also
see better the difference between these rulers, and the prospect of finding
any sort of scientific treatment[2] of the questions we have mentioned.

2

The best way to study this as well as other matters is to trace things back to   25
their beginnings[3] and observe their growth. First, then, those who cannot
exist without each other have to form pairs, as female and male do for
reproduction. And they do this not because of any decision, but from the
natural impulse that they share with other animals and with plants to leave   30
behind another of the same kind as oneself.

Self-preservation <rather than reproduction> is the basis of the natural
division between ruler and subject. For the capacity for rational foresight
makes one a natural ruler and natural master, and the capacity to execute
this foresight by bodily labor[4] makes another a subject and a natural slave;
that is why the interests of master and slave coincide.

Now there is a natural distinction between the female and the slave. For 1252b
nature makes nothing stingily, like a smith making a Delphic knife,[5] but
makes one thing for one function, since the best instrument for a particular
function is made exclusively for it, not for many others. Among foreigners,   5
however, female and slave have the same rank; the reason is that no foreigners are natural rulers, and so their community consists of a female
slave and a male slave. Hence the poets say 'It is to be expected that Greeks
rule over foreigners', assuming that the foreigner and the slave are naturally the same.

And so from these two communities <between female and male and   10
between slave and master> the first community that results is the household. Hesiod[6] was right when he said 'Get first of all a house, a wife, and a
plow-ox'—for the poor use an ox in place of a slave. Hence the community
naturally formed for every day is a household of 'breadbin-mates' (as
Charondas calls them) or (as Epimenides the Cretan says) 'manger-mates'.   15

The first community formed from a number of households for long-term
advantage is a village, and the most natural type of village would seem to
be an extension of a household, including children and grandchildren,
sometimes called 'milkmates'. That is why cities were also originally ruled

2. **scientific treatment**: Lit. 'belonging to a craft', *technikon*.

3. **beginnings**: *archai*. See PRINCIPLE #1.

4. **to execute . . . labor**: Read *tauta tōi sōmati poiein*. (OCT: 'to labor with one's
body'.)

5. **a Delphic knife**: like a Swiss army knife, with several different functions.

6. **Hesiod**: *Works and Days* 406.

20   by kings and some nations are ruled by kings even at present; they were
formed from communities ruled by kings—for in every household the
oldest member rules as its king, and the same is true in its extensions,
because the villagers are related by kinship. Homer[7] describes this when he
says 'Each rules over his children and wives', because they were isolated, as
households were in ancient times. And for the same reason everyone says
25   the gods are ruled by a king; it is because we were all ruled by kings in
ancient times, and some still are, and human beings ascribe to the gods a
human way of life, as well as a human form.

The complete community, formed from a number of villages, is a city.
Unlike the others, it has the full degree of practically every sort of self-
30   sufficiency; it comes to be for the sake of living, but remains in being for
the sake of living well. That is why every city is natural, since the previous
communities are natural. For the city is their end, and nature is an end; for
we say that something's nature (for instance, of a human being, a horse, or
a household) is the character it has when its coming to be is complete.
1253a   Moreover, the final cause and end is the best <good>, and self-sufficiency
is both the end and the best <good>.

It is evident, then, that the city exists by nature, and that a human being
is by nature a political animal. Anyone without a city because of his nature
rather than his fortune is either worthless or superior to a human being.
5   Like the man reviled by Homer,[8] 'he has no kin, no law, no home'. For his
natural isolation from a city gives him an appetite for war, since, like <a
solitary piece> in a game of checkers, he has no partner.

It is evident why a human being is more of a political animal than is any
bee or any gregarious animal; for nature, we say, does nothing pointlessly,
10   and a human being is the only animal with rational discourse. A voice
signifies pleasure and pain, and so the other animals, as well as human
beings, have it, since their nature is far enough advanced for them to
perceive pleasure and pain and to signify them to one another. But rational
15   discourse is for making clear what is expedient or harmful, and hence what
is just or unjust. For this is distinctive of human beings in contrast to the
other animals, that they are the only ones with a perception of good and
evil, and of just and unjust, and so on; and it is community in these that
produces a household and a city.

Further, the city is naturally prior to the household and to the individual,
20   since the whole is necessarily prior to the part. For if the whole animal is
dead, neither foot nor hand will survive, except homonymously, as if we
were speaking of a stone hand—for that is what a dead hand will be like.
Now everything is defined by its function and potentiality; and so anything

7. **Homer**: *Odyssey* ix 114, referring to the Cyclopes.
8. **Homer**: *Iliad* ix 63.

that has lost them should not be called the same thing, but a homonymous   *25*
thing.

Clearly, then, the city is also natural and is prior to the individual. For if
the individual separated from the city is not self-sufficient, his relation to it
corresponds to that of parts to wholes in other cases; and anyone who is
incapable of membership in a community, or who has no need of it because
he is self-sufficient, is no part of a city, and so is either a beast or a god.

Everyone has a natural impulse, then, towards this sort of community,   *30*
and whoever first constituted it is the cause of the greatest goods. For just as
a human being is the best of the animals if he has been completed, he is
also the worst of them if he is separated from law and the rule of justice.
For injustice is most formidable when it is armed, and a human being
naturally grows up armed and equipped for intelligence and virtue, but can   *35*
most readily use this equipment for ends that are contrary to intelligence
and virtue; hence without virtue he is the most unscrupulous and savage of
animals, the most excessive in pursuit of sex and food. Justice, however, is
political; for the rule of justice is an order in the political community, and
justice is the judgment of what is just.

Book II[9]

1

Our decision is to study the best political community for those who are *1260b*
capable of living, as far as possible, in the conditions they would aspire to
live in; hence we must also investigate the political systems that are found   *30*
in cities said to be well governed, and also any systems other people have
proposed that seem well conceived. Our aim is to see what the correct
condition is for a city and what is useful, and also to show that, in searching for something different from these systems, we are not behaving like
people who want above all to play the sophist, but are undertaking this line
of inquiry in response to the inadequacies of current systems. . . .

2

The proposal that all <the rulers'> women should be shared[10] raises many *1261a*
objections. In particular Socrates' arguments do not make it apparent why
he thinks this legislation is needed. Moreover, the end he prescribes for the

9. Book II is concerned with the proposals of various theorists and with the actual
states (e.g. Sparta and Crete) that some people have presented as models. The
extracts translated come from the criticism of Plato's *Republic*.

10. **The proposal . . . shared**: Plato, *Rep.* 457d.

city is impossible, taken literally, and he has not explained how else we
15 should take it. I refer to Socrates' assumption that it is best if all the city is
as unified as possible. It is evident, on the contrary, that as the city goes
further and further in the direction of unity, it will finally not even be a
city. For a city is by nature a mass of people; as it becomes more and more
unified, first the city will turn into a household, and then the household
20 will turn into just one person—for we would say that a household is more
unified than a city, and one person more unified than a household. And so,
even if someone were capable of completely unifying a city, he should not
do it, since he would destroy the city.

Besides, a city is composed, not merely of a number of human beings,
but of those different in kind—for similar people do not constitute a city.
25 For a city is different from an alliance; for since an alliance naturally aims
at assistance, the added quantity, even of something the same in kind,
makes the ally useful (like a weight that pulls a balance down further). A
city differs in the same way from a nation that is not scattered in separate
villages but <is all together>, as the Arcadians[11] are. <In contrast to these
30 cases,> the parts from which a unity comes to be must differ in kind.

This is why reciprocal equality preserves a city, as we said before in the
Ethics. Even free and equal people need this, since they cannot all rule at
the same time, but must rule for a year, or some other fixed length of time.
35 Such an arrangement ensures that they all rule—just as if cobblers and
carpenters were to change occupations, and the same people were not
cobblers or carpenters all the time. Since <the normal practice in the
crafts> is also better in the political community, it is clearly better if the
same people are, if possible, always rulers. But in some circumstances this
1261b is not possible, because all are naturally equal, and moreover it is just for
all to take part in ruling—whether it is a benefit or a burden. This
arrangement—where equals yield office to each other in turn and are similar when they are not holding office—at least imitates <the practice of the
5 crafts>; some rule and others are ruled, taking turns, as though they had
become other people. In the same way, among the rulers themselves, different ones rule in different ruling offices.

It is evident, then, from what we have said, that a city is not naturally
unified in the way that some claim it is and that the unity alleged to be the
greatest good for cities in fact destroys them, whereas a thing's good preserves it.
10 It is evident in another way too that attempts at excessive unification do
not benefit a city. For a household is more self-sufficient than an individual
person is; and a community of a mass of people counts as a city only if it

---

11. **Arcadians**: Their villages formed a federation, without the structure that Aristotle takes to be necessary for a *polis*.

proves to be self-sufficient. Since, then, what is more self-sufficient is more choiceworthy, what is less unified is <in this case> more choiceworthy than   15
what is more unified.

3

But even if it is indeed best if the community is as unified as possible, <Socrates'> argument does not seem to demonstrate that this will be the effect of agreement in saying 'mine' and 'not mine'[12]—though Socrates regards this agreement as a sign of the city's being completely unified.   20
For 'all' is said in two ways. If all, taken each one at a time, <speak of what is 'mine'>, then perhaps the <unity> that Socrates wants to produce would be more likely to result; for each one will call the same person his own son, and the same person his own wife, and will speak in the same way of property, and whatever else he has. In fact, however, those who share wives and children will not speak in this way. They will, all together,   25
not each taken one at a time, regard <wives and children as theirs>; and similarly, all together, not each taken one at a time, will regard property <as theirs>. Evidently, then, speaking of 'all' is a fallacious inference; for 'all', 'both', 'odd', and 'even' also produce contentious deductions in discus-   30
sions, because they are spoken of in these two ways. Hence if all say the same thing, the result is in one case fine, but not possible, and in the other case contributes nothing to concord.
Besides this, the proposal mentioned involves a further harm. For what is common to the largest number of people gets least attention, since people think most about what is private to them and think less about what is common, or else think about what is common only to the extent that it   35
applies to each of them. They care less about it because, in addition to other reasons, they assume that someone else is thinking about it—as in household service many attendants sometimes serve worse than a few. <In Socrates' city> each citizen will have a thousand sons, but not as sons of each taken one at a time; any given son will be the son of this father no more than of any other, and so all the fathers alike will care little   40
about them. . . .

4

. . . And in general the results of this sort of law <eliminating private 1262b property> are bound to be contrary to the results to be expected from correctly established laws, and contrary to Socrates' aim in prescribing   5

12. **agreement** . . . **'not mine'**: Lit. 'saying "mine" and "not mine" at the same time'. See Plato, *Rep.* 462c.

these arrangements about children and women. For we think friendship is
the greatest good for cities, since it best prevents civil conflict in them;
indeed Socrates himself praises the unity of the city more than anything
10   else, and, like other people, he takes unity to be the result of friendship. In
the same way, as we know, in the discussions of erotic love,[13] Aristophanes
says that erotic lovers love so intensely that they long to grow together and
make one person out of two. But whereas this union requires the perishing
15   of one or both of the lovers, sharing of wives and children will merely
make friendship in the city watery, and it will be least true that a father
speaks of 'my son' or a son of 'my father'. For just as a little of something
sweet mixed into a lot of water makes the mixture imperceptible, the same
20   is true of the mutual closeness resulting from these names <'father' and
'son'>, since this sort of political system is the least likely to ensure that a
father is especially concerned for his son, or a son for his father, or one
brother for another. For the two most important sources of care and friendship among human beings are the fact that something is one's own and the
fact that one likes it; neither can be true of those living under such a
political system. . . .

5

1263a . . . These, then, and others like them, are the disagreeable results of common ownership. The present arrangement would be far better, if it were
improved by good habits and ordered by correct laws. For in that case it
25   would have the advantages of both arrangements, i.e., of common and of
private ownership. For ownership ought to be common in a way, but
basically private; if different people attend to different things, no mutual
accusations result, and they will together contribute more, since each person keeps his mind on his own proper concerns. On the other hand, virtue
30   will make friends' possessions common (as the proverb says) for their use.
Even now there are traces of this arrangement in outline in some cities,
suggesting that it is not impossible, and, especially in well-governed cities,
some aspects are already there, and others might arise. For while each has
his own possessions, he offers his own for his friends to use and uses <his
35   friends'> possessions as common possessions. In Sparta, for instance, they
use one other's slaves practically as their own and do the same with horses
and dogs and with the fields around the countryside, if they need food for a
journey.
Evidently, then, it is better if we own possessions privately, but make
40   them common by our use of them. And it is the legislator's proper task to
see that the right sort of people develop.
Further, it is unbelievably more pleasant to regard something as one's

13. erotic love: See Plato, *Symp.* 192de.

own. For each person's love of himself is not pointless, but a natural ten- *1263b*
dency. Certainly, selfishness is quite rightly blamed; but selfishness is not
love of oneself, but excessive self-love. The same distinction applies to love
of money, since practically everyone loves himself and loves money. More-   5
over, the pleasantest thing is to please or to help our friends or guests or
companions, and we can do this when ownership is private.

These, then, are the results for those who unify the city excessively.
Moreover, they evidently remove any function for two virtues—
temperance towards women (since it is a fine action to refrain because of   10
temperance from a woman who is someone else's wife) and generosity with
our possessions (since no one's generosity will be evident, and no one
will do any generous action—for generosity has its function in the use of
possessions). . . .

Book III[14]

1

In investigating a political system and asking what, and of what sort, each *1274b*
system is, our first question should be to ask what the city is. For as things
are, this is disputed; some assert that the city has done some action, while   35
others assert that it was not the city, but the oligarchy or the tyrant that did
it. Moreover, we see that the politician's and the legislator's whole concern is
with the city, and that the political system is a particular sort of ordering of
those who live in the city.

Since the city is a composite, and we must proceed as we do with other
wholes that are constituted of many parts, it is clear that we must first of all 40
inquire into the citizen, since a city is a particular sort of mass of citizens.
And so we should examine who ought to be called a citizen and who the *1275a*
citizen is. For in fact there is often dispute about the citizen as well <as
about the city>, since not everyone agrees that the same person is a citizen;
someone who is a citizen in a democracy is often not a citizen in an   5
oligarchy.

We should omit those who acquire the title of citizen in some other way
<than by birth>—those who are created citizens, for instance. Someone is
not a citizen if he simply lives in a particular place; for resident aliens and
slaves live in the same place <as the citizens, but are not citizens>. Nor is
someone a citizen if he simply shares in the judicial system[15] to the extent

14. In Book III Aristotle turns to his own constructive theory, beginning with
questions about who is appropriately a member of the political community. This is
the foundation both for his analysis of existing states (Books IV–VI) and for his
own account of the ideal state (Book VIII).

15. **judicial system**: Lit. 'just things'.

10   of claiming justice and submitting to it; for this is also true of those who share judicial arrangements by treaty. (In many cities, indeed, resident aliens do not share fully in the judicial system, but must find a representative <to take up their case>, so that their share in this sort of community is in a way incomplete.)

15   What we say about these cases is similar to what we say about boys who are not yet of an age to be enrolled and about old men who have been released <from active participation>. For we say that these are citizens in a way, but not without qualification; we add the qualification that boys are incomplete citizens and that the old men are citizens past the proper age, or something like that (it does not matter exactly what we say, since what we mean is clear). For we are inquiring about those who are citizens without

20   qualification, in such a way that their claim admits of no ground for objection needing to be rectified. Similar puzzles and solutions apply to the dishonored[16] and to exiles.

    A citizen without qualification is defined, above all, as one who shares in judging and ruling.[17] Some types of rule are limited in time, so that some

25   ruling offices can never be held by the same person twice or can be held again only after a specified interval. Another type of ruler, however, is indefinite <in time>—for instance, the juryman or the assemblyman. Now, perhaps someone might say that these people are not rulers at all and that these functions do not count as sharing in ruling. Surely, however, it is ridiculous to deny that those with the most complete control are rulers.

30   Still, we need not suppose that this matters; it is simply an argument about a name, since the common feature applying to the juryman and the assemblyman has no name. And so, to make clear the distinction, let us call it indefinite rule. We take it, then, that those who share in ruling on these terms are citizens.

    This, then, is more or less the definition of citizen that best fits all those

35   called citizens. We must notice, however, that in cases where the subjects <of a property F> differ in species, and one is the primary F, another secondary, and so on in order, their common feature, in so far as they are F, is nothing, or only slight. Now, we see that political systems differ in

1275b species and that some are prior and some posterior, since the erroneous and deviant systems must be posterior to the correct ones (the meaning of 'deviant systems' will be clarified later); and so a different type of citizen must also correspond to each political system.

5   That is why the citizen fitting our definition is a citizen in a democracy

16. **dishonored**: *atimos*. This is the technical term for those deprived of civil rights (as a penalty for certain crimes); hence the dishonored are mentioned together with exiles as being deprived of the normal functions of a citizen.

17. **Ruling**: *archē*. See PRINCIPLE #5.

more than in the other systems, and in the other systems the citizen may
<have these functions>, but need not have them. For some systems have no
popular body, or recognized assembly <of all the people>, but only con-
vocations <of selected members>, and different judicial cases are decided
by different select bodies. (In Sparta, for instance, different types of cases
arising from treaties are decided by a different Overseer, cases of homicide   10
by the Elders, and other cases presumably by some other ruling official.
The same is true in Carthage, where ruling officials judge all the cases.)

Our way of distinguishing a citizen can still be corrected. In the non-
democratic political systems the assemblyman or juryman exercises a definite, not an indefinite, rule; for either all or some of these are assigned the   15
task of deliberating and sitting on juries, either on all questions or on some.
From this, then, it is clear who the citizen is; if it is open to someone to
share in deliberative and judicial rule, we say he is thereby a citizen of this
sort of city; and a city (to speak without qualification) is the collection of   20
such people that is adequate for self-sufficient life. . . .

4

The next question to be examined among those we have just mentioned is 1276b
whether or not we must take the virtue of a good man and of an excellent
citizen to be the same or different. And if we must search for this, we must
first grasp in some rough outline the virtue of a citizen.

Well, then, we say that a citizen, like a sailor, is one of a number of   20
associates. Now, sailors are dissimilar in their capacities—for one is an
oarsman, one a pilot, one a lookout, and another has some other name—
and clearly the most exact account of each one's virtue will be special to   25
him, but similarly some common account will also fit them all, since the
function of them all is to secure a safe voyage, and that is what each sailor
aims at. Similarly, then, the function of citizens, despite their dissimilarity,
is to secure the safety of the community; the political system is the community; hence the virtue of the citizen must be relative to the political   30
system.

If, then, there are several species of political system, there clearly cannot
be one virtue—complete virtue—of the excellent citizen. The good man, by
contrast, is good precisely in so far as he has one virtue—complete virtue.
Evidently, then, someone can be an excellent citizen without having the   35
virtue that makes someone an excellent man.

Moreover, we can raise a further puzzle in approaching the same discussion about the best political system. If a city cannot be composed entirely
of excellent men, still each must perform his own function well, and this   40
requires virtue; and since the citizens cannot all be similar, the virtue of a 1277a
citizen cannot be the same as that of a good man. For all must have the

virtue of the excellent citizen, since that is needed if the city is to be best;
5   but they cannot all have the virtue of the good man, if the citizens in the
excellent city cannot all be good men.[18]

Further, a city is constituted of dissimilar people, just as an animal is
necessarily constituted of soul and body, a soul is constituted of reason and
desire, a household is constituted of husband and wife, and possession is
constituted of master and slave. A city is constituted of all of these, and
10   moreover of different kinds of people; and so the citizens cannot all have
the same virtue, any more than the chorus-leader and ordinary member of
the chorus can have the same virtue.

This makes it evident why <the virtue of an excellent man and of an
excellent citizen> are not the same without qualification. But will the virtue
of one type of excellent citizen be the same as the virtue of an excellent
15   man? We say that an excellent ruler is good and intelligent, but that a
citizen need not be intelligent, so that (in some people's view) a ruler should
have a different type of education (just as we see the sons of kings educated
in horsemanship and warfare, and Euripides[19] says, 'For me none of these
subtleties . . . but what the city needs', on the assumption that there is a
20   type of education proper to a ruler).

Now, if the virtue of a good ruler and of a good man are the same, and
both the ruler and the ruled are citizens, it follows that the virtue of a man
is not the same without qualification as the virtue of a citizen but is the
same as the virtue of a certain kind of citizen <—a ruler>; for the virtue of
a ruler is not the same as the virtue of a citizen, and presumably that is
25   why Jason said he was starving when he was not tyrant, suggesting that he
did not know how to be a private citizen.

And yet someone is praised for being able both to rule and to be ruled,
and the virtue of an estimable citizen seems to be the ability both to rule
and to be ruled finely. If, then, we take the good man's virtue to be a virtue
in ruling, and the citizen's virtue to be both <in ruling and being ruled>,
30   the two abilities cannot be praiseworthy in the same way. Since, then, they
seem to be different in some cases, and it seems that the ruler and the ruled
must learn different things, while the citizen must know and share in both
ruling and being ruled, we may see what follows from that.

One type of rule is a master's rule over slaves. We say that this is con-
35   cerned with necessities; the ruler needs the knowledge of how to use these,
not the knowledge of how to produce them, which would actually be
slavish—I mean the ability to perform the actions of a servant. We speak of

18. **if the citizens . . . men**: Or 'unless it is necessary for all the citizens . . .'. For
Aristotle's view on this question see VII. 13.

19. **Euripides**: in a lost tragedy. This passage is also quoted in Plato, *Gorg.*
485e–486a.

several types of slaves, since there are several types of work. One type of work belongs to manual workers; as the name itself indicates, these are the ones who live by the work of their hands, and they include the menial 1277b craftsmen. That is why some cities gave the manual workers no share in ruling offices, before the extreme type of democracy arose. Hence neither the good politician nor the good citizen must learn the functions of people who are ruled in this way, unless he needs them for himself (for then it no 5 longer involves a master and a slave).

However, there is a type of rule that is exercised over people who are free and similar in kind <to the ruler>; this is called political rule. A ruler must learn this type of rule by being ruled himself—for instance, he must be 10 ruled by a cavalry officer to learn to rule as a cavalry officer, and ruled by a general or troop-leader or squadron-leader to learn to rule in these positions. Hence this is also a sound maxim, that you cannot rule well until you have been ruled. These virtues of ruler and ruled are different, but the good citizen must have the knowledge and ability both to be ruled and to 15 rule; and the virtue of a citizen is this knowledge of rule over free people, from both points of view.

Hence the good man has both virtues, even if the ruler has a different kind of temperance and justice. For, clearly, if a good person is ruled, but is a free citizen, his virtue—justice, for instance—is not of only one kind, but includes one kind for ruling and another for being ruled. Similarly, a man 20 and a woman have different kinds of temperance and bravery—for a man would seem cowardly if he were <only> as brave as a brave woman, and a woman would seem talkative if she were <only> as restrained as the good man is; and similarly household management is different for a man and a woman, since it is the man's task to acquire the goods and the woman's task 25 to preserve them. Intelligence is the only virtue that is distinctive of the ruler; for all the others, it would seem, must be common to rulers and ruled, but true belief, not intelligence, is the virtue of the ruled, since they correspond to flute-makers, whereas the rulers correspond to flute-players 30 who use the flutes.

From this, then, it is evident whether the virtue of the good man and of the excellent citizen are the same or different, and in what ways they are the same, and in what ways different. . . .

6

Now that these points have been determined, the next question to investi- 1278b gate is whether we should suppose there is one type or several types of political system, and, if there are several, what and how many they are, and what features differentiate them.

A political system is the ordering in a city of the various ruling offices,

10   and especially of the one that controls everything. For in every city the controlling element is the political body,[20] and the political body is the political system. I mean, for instance, that in democracies the common people are in control, and, by contrast, in oligarchies the few are in control, and we take the political systems of these cities to be different—and we

15   will give the same account of the other political systems as well.

First, then, we should state our assumption about what end the city is constituted for, and how many types of rule are concerned with human beings and with community of life.

In our first discussions, when we determined the features of rule over households and over slaves, we also said that a human being is by nature a

20   political animal. That is why, even when they have no need of mutual help, they desire none the less to live together; at the same time common advantage draws them together, to the extent that it contributes something to living finely for each person. Living finely, then, most of all is the goal of a city, both for all the citizens in common and for each separately. Still, they

25   also combine and maintain the political community for the sake of life itself. For presumably even life itself includes something fine in it, as long as its adversities are not overwhelming; and, clearly, most human beings still cling to life even if they must endure much suffering, finding that

30   simply being alive is a source of some well-being and natural delight.

Further, it is easy to distinguish the types of rule we have mentioned— indeed we often distinguish them in popular discussions. First comes the rule of master over slave, where the advantage of the natural slave and of

35   the natural master are in fact the same, but none the less the master rules for his own advantage, and for the slave's advantage <only> coincidentally (since the master cannot maintain his rule if the slave is being ruined).

By contrast, rule over children and wife and the whole household— called household-rule—is for the benefit of the ruled, or <coincidentally>

40   for some benefit common to ruler and ruled, but in itself for the benefit of

1279a the ruled. In the same way we see that the crafts—medicine and gymnastics, for instance—may also be coincidentally for the benefit of the craftsman as well as the subject, since the gymnastics trainer may sometimes be one of the people in training, just as the pilot is always one of the sailors;

5   and so the trainer or pilot considers the good of those he rules, but whenever he turns out to be one of them, he shares coincidentally in the benefit, since the pilot is a sailor, and the trainer is at the same time in training.

10   Hence, when a city is constituted on the basis of equality and similarity among the citizens, they think it right to take turns at ruling. In the past each did this in the naturally suitable way, thinking it right to take his turn in public service, and then in return to have someone else consider his

20. **political body**: *politeuma*. 'Government' would also be a suitable rendering; cf. 1279a25.

advantage afterwards, just as he previously was a ruler and considered the other's advantage. These days, however, people want to be rulers continuously, to gain the benefits of ruling and holding public office, and so they   15
pursue it as eagerly as they would if they were all sick and would all invariably recover their health if they became rulers.

It is evident, then, that all the political systems that consider the common advantage are correct types, conforming to what is just without qualification, whereas all those that consider only the advantage of the rulers are   20
erroneous types, deviations from the correct political systems—for these are the types of rule that a master exercises over slaves, whereas a city is a community of free citizens.

7

Now that this has been determined, the next task is to investigate how many political systems there are and what they are. First we consider the correct systems; for when we have determined these, we will have made the   25
deviant systems evident.

A political system and a political body[21] signify the same thing; the political body controls a city, and either one person or a few or the many must be in control. If, then, the one person or the few or the many rule for the common advantage, these political systems must be correct; and the   30
systems that aim at the special advantage of the one or the few or the mass of people[22] must be deviations—for either those who do not participate <in the political system> should not be called citizens, or they must <at least> share in the advantage.

The type of monarchy that considers the common advantage is usually called kingship. The corresponding type of rule by a few people, but more   35
than one, is called aristocracy, either because the best people are the rulers or because it aims at what is best for the city and those associated in it. Whenever the masses conduct political life for the common advantage, that system is called a polity—the name that is common to all the political systems. And this <name> is reasonable; for while one person or a few   40
people may excel in virtue, it is not easy for a larger number to be accom- 1279b
plished in every virtue, but they are accomplished in the virtue of war, since that requires a mass of people. That is why the controlling element in the political system consists of those who fight in wars, and those who own their own weapons are those who participate in the political system.

The deviations from these systems are tyranny, a deviation from king-   5

21. **political body**: *politeuma*. Or 'government'. Cf. 1278b11.

22. **mass of people**: *plēthos*. Or 'the majority'. Cf. 1274b41. The term normally refers (as *dēmos* does, in one of its uses) to the lower classes, not necessarily with any unfavorable suggestion.

ship; oligarchy, a deviation from aristocracy; and democracy, a deviation from polity. For tyranny is rule by one person, aiming at the advantage of the ruler himself; oligarchy aims at the advantage of the prosperous; and
10   democracy aims at the advantage of the disadvantaged; and none of these aims at what benefits the community.

8

We must spend a little longer, however, in saying what each of these political systems is. For the question raises some puzzles: and if we approach a line of inquiry from a philosophical point of view, not simply focussing on what is useful for action, it is appropriate not to overlook or
15   omit any point, but to make clear the truth about each question.

A tyranny, as we have said, is rule by one person who rules the political community as a master rules slaves. There is an oligarchy whenever possessors of property control the political system, and a democracy, by contrast, whenever those in control are the disadvantaged, those possessing no large property.
20   The first puzzle arises about this distinction. For suppose that the majority are prosperous and that they control the city, and it is a democracy whenever the masses are in control; and again suppose that in some city the disadvantaged are fewer in number than the prosperous, but are
25   stronger and control the political system, and there is said to be an oligarchy whenever a small number are in control. In these cases we do not seem to have drawn the right distinction between these political systems.

We might, then, combine being prosperous with small numbers, and being disadvantaged with large numbers, and hence classify the political systems by saying that an oligarchy is the system in which the prosperous
30   are few in number and hold the ruling offices, and that a democracy is the system in which the disadvantaged are many and hold the ruling offices. But these definitions raise another puzzle; what are we to call the systems we have just mentioned—the one in which the prosperous are in control of the system and are more numerous, and the one in which the disadvantaged are in control but are fewer in number—if there is no other political system apart from the ones we listed?
35   This argument, then, would seem to show that control by the few is coincidental to oligarchies, and control by the many to democracies, because in every city the prosperous are few in number and the disadvantaged are many. Hence the reasons we mentioned do not turn out to be reasons for distinguishing the systems <by the number in the ruling
40   group>. What really differentiates democracy from oligarchy is poverty
1280a and wealth. If the rulers rule because they are wealthy, whether they are few or many, the system must be an oligarchy, and if the disadvantaged rule, it must be a democracy; it comes about coincidentally, as we said, that

the prosperous are few and the disadvantaged are many. For only a few are   5
well off, but all <wealthy and poor> alike share free citizenship; wealth
and freedom cause the struggle between the two <groups> for control of
the political system.

9

First we must understand the received formulae of oligarchy and democracy, and the oligarchic and democratic <views of> justice; for everyone
touches on some sort of justice, but they make only limited progress and do   10
not describe the whole of what is fully just. Justice seems to be equality, for
instance, and indeed it is—but for equals, not for everyone. Again, inequality seems to be just; and so it is—but for unequals, not for everyone.
But these <partisans of each view> omit this part—equality or inequality
for whom—and so make the wrong judgment. The reason is that they are   15
giving judgment in their own case, and most people are practically always
bad judges in their own cases.

Justice is justice *for* certain people, and the division in the things <to be
distributed> corresponds to the division in those to whom <they are dis-
tributed>, as we have said before in the *Ethics*. Hence all sides agree about
the equal amount of the thing <to be distributed> but dispute about who
should receive it. They do this mainly for the reason we have just given,   20
that people are bad judges in their own cases, but also because each side
makes some progress in describing a sort of justice and so thinks it describes unqualified justice. For <supporters of oligarchy> think that if they
are unequal in some aspects—wealth, for instance—they are altogether
unequal, whereas <supporters of democracy> think that if they are equal
in some aspect—free status, for instance—they are altogether equal.   25

But they fail to mention the most important aspect. For if people combined and formed a <political> community in order to acquire possessions,
then someone's share in the city would correspond to his possessions, and
the supporters of oligarchy would seem to have a strong argument; for,
they say, if A has contributed one out of 100 minas and B has contributed   30
the other 99, it is not just for A to get the same return as B, either of the
original sum or of any later profits.

In fact, however, the <political> community does not aim simply at
staying alive, but aims predominantly at a good life. For if it aimed simply
at staying alive, then slaves and non-human animals would be members of
a city, whereas in fact they are not, since they do not participate in happiness or in a life guided by decision.

Nor does the city aim at an alliance, to prevent anyone from doing   35
injustice to anyone; or at exchange and dealings between its members. For
if this were the aim, then the Etruscans and the Carthaginians—and any
other peoples related by treaty—would all count as citizens of a single city;

at any rate, these have made conventions about imports, treaties to prohibit
40   doing injustice, and written articles of alliance. These peoples, however,
1280b have no common government, but each has its own government.[23] Moreover, neither people is concerned about the right character to form in the
citizens of the other city, or about how to remove injustice or any other vice
from the other city that is bound by the agreements; each is concerned only
5   to prevent the other city from doing injustice to it. By contrast, those who
are concerned with good government consider the virtues and vices of
citizens.

Hence it is evident that whatever is correctly called a city, not just for the
sake of argument, must be concerned with virtue. For <otherwise> the
community turns out to be <merely> an alliance, differing only in the
10   proximity of its members from the other alliances with more distant members. In that case law turns out to be an agreement and, as Lycophron the
sophist said, a mutual guarantor of just treatment, but unable to make the
citizens good and just.

To make it evident that we are right, suppose that we actually joined the
territories <of two allied states>, so that the cities of the Megarians and the
15   Corinthians had their walls adjacent; even so, they would not be one single
city, even if their citizens intermarried—though that is one sort of community that is distinctive of a city. Similarly, suppose people lived apart,
though not too far to prevent community, but had laws prohibiting unjust
20   treatment in exchanges (if, for instance, one was a carpenter, another a
farmer, another a cobbler, and so on), and there were ten thousand of
them, but their community extended no further than such matters as com-
merce and alliance; that would still not be enough to make a city.

25   Why is this? Surely it is not because their community is scattered. For if
they even lived closer together but in the same sort of community, each
treating his own household as a city, and they formed a purely defensive
alliance against unjust actions—even so, an exact study would not count
this as a city, if their intercourse when they live closer together is no
different from what it was when they lived apart.

30   Evidently, then, a city is not a community for living in the same place,
for preventing the unjust treatment of one member by another, and for
exchange. All these are necessary conditions for a city, but their presence
does not make a city. Rather, the city is a community for living well for
35   both households and families, aiming at a complete and self-sufficient life
(but this requires them to live in the same place and to intermarry). That is
why kinship-groups, brotherhoods, religious societies, and pursuits that
involve living together have developed in cities; these are the product of
friendship, since the decision to live together is friendship.

40   The end of a city, then, is living well, and these <pursuits> are for the

23. **government:** Or 'ruling offices', *archai*. See PRINCIPLE.

sake of the end. A city is the community of families and villages in a *1281a*
complete and self-sufficient life. This sort of life, as we say, is a happy and
fine life; hence we should suppose that a city aims at fine actions, not
<merely> at living together.

That is why someone who contributes most to this sort of community   5
has a greater share in the city than that of someone who is equal or
superior in free status or in family, but unequal in a citizen's virtue, and a
greater share than that of someone who excels in wealth but is excelled in
virtue.

It is evident, then, from what we have said that each of the parties
disputing about political systems is describing a part of justice.   10

10

A puzzle arises about which element ought to control the political system;
for it must be either the masses, or the wealthy, or the decent people, or the
single best person, or a tyrant. Each of these answers appears to raise
difficulties.

For if the poor, since they are more numerous, divide up the possessions   15
of the rich, is that not unjust? 'Well, <they might say,> it seemed just to the
controlling body.' But what could be a clearer case of extreme injustice?
Again, if the majority take everything and divide up the possessions of the
minority, evidently they are ruining the city; but a virtue does not ruin its   20
possessor and justice does not ruin a city, and so this law clearly cannot be
just. Moreover, <if such distributions are just,> all the tyrant's actions must
have been just too; for he is the stronger, and forces compliance, just as the
masses force the rich.

Then is it just for the rulers to be the minority and the rich? If, then, they   25
do these things, and plunder and confiscate the possessions of the masses,
this will be just. And if this is just, the corresponding action by the masses
is just too. Evidently, then, all these actions are base and not just.

Then ought the decent people to be rulers and in control of everything?
If they are, then surely all the others will necessarily be dishonored, since   30
they are denied the honor of holding political ruling offices. For we say that
ruling offices are positions of honor, and if the same people are rulers all
the time, the others will necessarily be dishonored. Then should the single
most excellent person be ruler? But that is an even narrower oligarchy,
since those dishonored are still more numerous.

Now, presumably someone might say that it is a bad arrangement if   35
a human being rather than law is in control at all, since any human
being has the feelings that normally arise in a human soul. If, then, the
law is in control, but it is oligarchic or democratic, how will that help
to avoid the puzzles? For the previous objections will arise in just the
same way.

11

40   Most of these puzzles must be postponed to another discussion. But it seems that the claim that the masses rather than the few best people must be in control is generally accepted,[24] and it seems that, though it raises a puzzle, it perhaps contains some truth.

1281b For even though each one among the many is not an excellent man, still it is possible that when they combine they are collectively, though not individually, better than the few best people, just as a dinner provided by many people's contributions is better than one provided at an individual's expense; for (on this view) they are many, and each has some part of virtue

5   and intelligence, so that when they combine, the masses become like one human being, with many feet, many hands, and many senses, and similarly for characters and for intellect. That is why the many are also better judges of the products of music and of poets; different individuals are better

10   judges of different parts, and all of them together are better judges of the whole.

Indeed it is this <combination of qualities> that makes an excellent man better than an ordinary individual among the many, just as it (supposedly) makes handsome people more handsome than plain people and makes a statue more handsome than the real things; for <in the statue> the dispersed features are gathered together in one figure, even though, taken

15   separately, this person's eye and some other part of someone else might be more handsome than <the corresponding parts of> the statue.

Now, it is not clear whether this claim about the superiority of the many over the few excellent ones could be true of every sort of common people and every sort of mass of people. Indeed, presumably, there are some of which it cannot be true; for if it were true of them, it would also be true of

20   beasts; and indeed there are some who are practically no better than beasts. But the claim may still be true for masses of a certain sort.

Hence we can use this argument to solve the previous puzzle, and the next one—which things should be controlled by the free citizens and the

25   mass of the citizens, those who have neither wealth nor any other claim to reputation for virtue? For it is not safe for them to share in the highest ruling offices, since an unjust character is bound to cause unjust actions, and lack of intelligence is bound to cause errors. On the other hand, if they are given nothing and have no share, that is dangerous; for any city that

30   holds many poor people in dishonor is bound to be full of enemies.

The remaining option, then, is for them to share in deliberating and judging. That is why both Solon and some other legislators assign them the election of ruling officials and the scrutinizing of officials, but do not allow

35   them to hold office individually. For all combined have adequate sense, and

24. **generally accepted**: lit. just 'said'. Text uncertain.

when they are mixed with the better people, they benefit cities (just as impure food mixed with pure makes the whole more useful than the smaller amount <of pure food>), but each taken separately is incompletely equipped for judging.

The first puzzle raised by this organization of the political system is this: The task of judging who has applied medicine correctly seems to belong to   40
the person who also has the task of applying the medicine and curing the patient from his present illness; and this is the medical expert. And the same is true for the other empirical techniques and for the crafts. And so 1282a
just as a medical expert should submit his conduct to scrutiny by medical experts, other experts should also be scrutinized by their peers.

Medical experts, however, include not only the practitioners and the supervising experts, but also those who are educated about the craft—for in   5
practically every craft there are people educated about it. And we assign the task of judging to the educated people no less than to those who know the craft.

The same puzzle seems to arise about selection <as about judging>. For selection is also properly a task for those who know the craft; it is the task of geometers, for instance, to select a geometer, and of pilots to select a   10
pilot.[25] For even if laymen have some share in selection for some types of production and craft, their share is no greater than that of people who know the craft. Hence, on this argument, the masses should not be given control either of selecting rulers or of scrutinizing them.

Presumably, however, this argument is not completely correct. First, it is   15
refuted by our earlier argument, as long as the masses are not too slavish; for though each one individually is a worse judge than one who knows the craft, all combined are better, or no worse. Second, the argument is mistaken because in some cases the producer is neither the only judge nor the best judge; this is so whenever laymen also recognize the products of a craft. It is not only the builder of the house, for instance, who knows it; its   20
user—the householder—is an even better judge. Similarly, a pilot is a better judge of a rudder than a carpenter is, and the diner, not the cook, is the judge of a feast. This, then, might seem to be an adequate solution of the puzzle.

There is another puzzle, however, following this one. For it seems absurd   25
for base people to control issues that are more important than the ones controlled by decent people; but scrutinies and elections to ruling offices are the most important thing, and in some political systems, as we have said, these functions are assigned to the common people, since the assembly controls all of these. And yet participation in the assembly, deliberative   30
council, and jury-court requires only a small property-qualification and no

25. **it is the task . . . a pilot:** Cf. Plato, *Prot.* 318bc.

minimum age, whereas a large qualification is needed to be a financial officer or general or to hold the highest ruling offices.

Well, the same solution applies to this puzzle also. For presumably this <policy that raises the puzzle> is also correct. For the ruler is not the
35   individual juryman or councilman or assemblyman, but the jury-court, the council, and the assembly; each individual councilman, assemblyman, or juryman is a part of the <collectives> we have mentioned. Hence it is just for the masses to control the most important things, since the common people, the council, and the jury-court are all composed of many members.
40   Moreover, the property of all these <collectively> is greater than the property of those who, one at a time or a few at a time, hold the high ruling
1282b offices. This, then, is how we settle these questions.

The puzzle that was raised first makes it especially evident that the laws, when they are correctly framed, must be in control, and that the ruler,
5   either one or many, must be in control where the laws are incapable of giving the exactly correct guidance, since it is not easy to determine these cases in a universal rule. But what sorts of laws are the correctly framed ones? This is not yet clear, and the previous puzzle remains unsolved. For the baseness or excellence, and justice or injustice, of laws depends on, and
10   matches, the character of political systems. It is evident, however, that the laws must at any rate be framed to fit the political system. And if this is so, then, clearly, the laws corresponding to correct systems will necessarily be just, and those corresponding to deviant systems not just.

12

15   In all types of science and craft the end is a good, and the greatest and best good is the end of the science that most controls all the others, and this is the political capacity. The political good is justice, and justice is the common benefit.[26] Everyone thinks justice is some sort of equality, and hence to
20   some extent they all agree with the philosophical discussions in which we have determined ethical questions; for they say that what is just is relative to the people involved and that it must be equality for equals. But we must find the relevant respect of equality or inequality; for this question raises a puzzle that concerns political philosophy.

For presumably someone might say that ruling offices ought to be un-
25   equally distributed in accordance with superiority in any good at all, if people are alike and not at all different in all of the other goods; for, it will be argued, superior people justly deserve to get more than other people get. In that case, however, anyone who excels in complexion, size, or any other good at all, will have a politically just <claim> to get more <goods>.

26. **justice is the common benefit**: Or 'the political good is the common benefit'?

Surely the falsity in this view is easy to spot, and is evident in the other   *30*
sciences and capacities. If two flute-players are at the same level in their
craft, we ought not to assign more flutes to the better-born one, since his
birth does not make him a better flute-player; rather, the one who excels in
the relevant function must be assigned the extra instruments.

If our point is not yet clear, it will become still more evident if we de-   *35*
velop it further. Suppose that A is superior to B in the flute-playing craft,
but far inferior to B in birth or beauty. Suppose even that each of these
other goods—i.e., good birth and beauty—is a greater good than the flute-
playing craft, and that B's superiority <in these respects> over A's flute-
playing is proportionately greater than A's superiority over B in the flute-   *40*
playing craft. Even in this case A should be given the better flutes. For if *1283a*
superiority in birth and wealth is relevant <to a distribution>, it ought to contribute to the relevant function, but in this case it contributes nothing to it.

Moreover, the argument we are opposing implies that every good is
comparable with every other; for if some particular size competes <with
some other good>, then size in general will also compete with wealth and   *5*
free status. And so if A's superiority over B in size is greater than B's
superiority over A in virtue, even though virtue in general is a greater good
than size, then all goods will be comparable; for if some amount is greater
than some other, clearly some amount is equal to it.

But since this is impossible, clearly it is also reasonable that in politics   *10*
not every sort of inequality is a ground for dispute about ruling offices. For
if A is quick and B is slow, it does not follow that A should have more and
B less; this sort of superiority receives its honor in gymnastic contests. The   *15*
goods that are grounds for dispute must be those that constitute the city.

Hence it is reasonable that the well-born and the free citizens and the
rich lay claims to honor. For <citizens> must be freemen, with some
property-qualification, since a city could not be composed entirely of disadvantaged people, any more than it could be composed of slaves. And yet,
if the city needs these, clearly it also needs justice and political virtue, since   *20*
these are also necessary conditions of living in a city. The difference is that
birth, free status, and wealth are <simply> necessary for a city to exist,
whereas justice and political virtue are necessary for living finely in a
city. . . .

Book VII

1

Anyone who is inquiring along the appropriate lines into the best political *1323a*
system must first determine what the most choiceworthy life is. If it is left
unclear what this is, it must also be unclear what the best political system

is; for those who have the best political system in their circumstances will characteristically be best-off, if nothing unexpected happens. That is why
20 we must first agree on what sort of life is most choiceworthy for (we may say)[27] everyone, and then agree on whether such a life is or is not the same for an individual as for a community. We may take it then, that the best life is discussed at sufficient length even in <our> popular discussions; and so we should use those now.

25 For certainly no one would dispute one classification <of goods>, at least, into external goods, goods in the body, and goods in the soul, or would deny that blessedly happy people ought to possess them all. For no one would count a person blessedly happy if he had no part of bravery,
30 temperance, justice, or wisdom, but was afraid of every passing fly, sank to any depth to satisfy his appetite for food or drink, ruined his closest friends for some trivial gain, and had his mind as full of senseless illusion as a child's or a madman's.

35 Everyone would agree with these statements, but people disagree about how much <of each good is needed> and about large amounts of them. For whereas they think any slight degree of virtue is quite enough, they seek extreme abundance of wealth, valuables, power, reputation, and all such things, without limit. We will tell them, on the contrary, that it is easy
40 to reach a confident belief about these questions, by simply attending to the facts.

For we see that people possess and keep external goods by having the
1323b virtues, not the other way round. Further, as we see, a happy life—whether such a life for human beings consists in enjoyment or in virtue or in both— belongs to those who go to extremes in well-ordered character and intellect,
5 but possess a moderate level of external goods, rather than to those who have more external goods than they can use, but are deficient in character and intellect.

Moreover, the same point is easy to notice if we approach the question by argument. For externals, like instruments, and everything useful for some purpose, have a limit, and excess of them is bound to harm, not to benefit,
10 the possessor; but each good of the soul becomes more useful as it ex- ceeds (if we are to attribute usefulness as well as fineness even to these goods).

And in general, clearly we will say that the best condition of one thing surpasses the best condition of another in proportion to the superiority of
15 the first thing over the second. And so, if the soul is more honorable,[28] both without qualification and in relation to us, than possessions and the body, it

27. (**we may say**): i.e., it may not be best for absolutely everyone. Aristotle often uses this phrase to apologize for a possible exaggeration that does not affect his main point.

28. **honorable**: or 'valuable'. Cf. *DA* 402a1–4.

follows that its best condition must be proportionately better than theirs. Further, these other things are naturally choiceworthy for the sake of the soul, and every intelligent person must choose them for its sake, not the   *20* soul for their sake.

Let us, then, take it as agreed that each person achieves happiness to the extent that he achieves virtue and intelligence, and acts in accordance with them. We appeal to the god as evidence; for he is happy and blessed, because of himself and the character that is naturally his, not through any   *25* external good. Indeed this is also why good fortune cannot be the same as happiness; for chance and fortune produce goods external to the soul, whereas no one is just or temperate from fortune or because of fortune.   *30*

The next point, relying on the same arguments, is that the happy city is also the best one, the one that acts finely. But no one can act finely without doing fine actions,²⁹ and neither a man nor a city does any fine actions without virtue and intelligence. Moreover, the bravery, justice, intelligence, and temperance of a city have the same capacity and form that belongs to a   *35* human being who is called brave, just, intelligent, and temperate.

So much, then, for a preface to our argument; for we can neither leave these questions untouched nor go through all the appropriate arguments, since this is a task for another discipline. For now, let us simply assume that   *40* the best life for an individual by himself, and the best common life for cities, is the life involving virtue that has sufficient <external> resources to *1324a* share in actions expressing virtue. In our present line of inquiry we must leave aside objections, and consider them later, if someone turns out to be unpersuaded by what we have said.

2

It remains to be said, however, whether we should or should not take   *5* happiness to be the same for an individual human being and for a city. But the answer to this is also evident; for everyone would agree that it is the same. For those who think an individual lives well in being rich also count a whole city blessed if it is rich, whereas those who honor the tyrant's way   *10* of life above all others would say that the happiest city is the one that rules over the most people; and if anyone thinks that virtue makes an individual happy, he will also say that the more excellent city is happier.

But now there are two questions to be investigated. First, which of these   *15* two lives is more choiceworthy—the one that involves taking part in political activities and sharing in the city, or the life of an alien, released from the political community? Second, what political system and what condition of the city should we regard as best (no matter whether we decide that participation in the city is choiceworthy for everyone, or only for most

29. **act finely . . . doing fine actions**: *kalōs prattein . . . prattein ta kala.*

20   people, not for everyone)? This second question—not the question about
        what is choiceworthy for the individual—is the task of political thought
        and study; and since we have decided to undertake a political investigation
        now, that first question will be a side-issue, and the second will be the main
        issue for this line of inquiry.

            First, then, it is evident that the best political system must be the order
25   that guides the life of anyone at all who does best and lives blessedly. But
        even those who agree that the life involving virtue is the most choiceworthy
        disagree about whether the active life of the citizen is choiceworthy, or the
        life of someone released from all externals—some life of study, which some
        people think is the only life for a philosopher—is more choiceworthy. For
30   practically all those, both in the past and now, who have most eagerly
        pursued virtue have evidently decided on one or other of these two lives,
        the political and the philosophical; and it is quite important to decide
35   which view is correct, since the intelligent individual, and the intelligent
        political system no less, will necessarily order life to aim at the best goal.

            Some people, however, think that ruling over one's neighbors as a master
        over slaves involves one of the worst injustices, and that even rule as a
        citizen over citizens, though it has nothing unjust about it, still interferes
        with the ruler's well-being. Others take just about the contrary view, sup-
40   posing that the only life for a man is the life of political activity, since, in
1324b   their view, the actions resulting from each virtue are open to those who
        undertake political action for the community, no less than to a private
        individual.

            Some, then, hold this view. But still others say that only the form of
        political system that rules as a master and a tyrant is happy. And so in
5   some cities the very aim of the political system and laws is to rule over
        neighboring peoples as slaves.

            And so, while most laws in most cities are pretty haphazard, still any
        city that has laws aiming to any extent at some end has them all aiming at
        domination, as in Sparta and Crete both the education and most of the
10   laws are organized for war. Moreover, all the <non-Greek> nations that
        have the power to get more <at the expense of others> honor this sort of
        power. For in some places there are even laws that incite them to this sort
        of virtue. The Carthaginians, for example, so it is said, decorate soldiers
15   with bracelets for the number of campaigns they have served in. Once the
        Macedonians had a law that someone who had not killed an enemy should
        wear a rope around his waist instead of a belt. The Scythians used to pass
        around a cup at feasts and forbade it to anyone who had not killed an
20   enemy. And the warlike Iberian nation place around someone's grave a
        number of stakes to mark the number of enemies he has killed. Many
        peoples have many similar practices established by laws or customs.

            If we are willing to examine this question, however, we will find it
25   utterly absurd to suppose that the politician's task is the ability to study

ways of ruling over neighboring peoples as willing or unwilling slaves. For
how could this be a politician's or lawgiver's task, since it is not even
lawful? It is unlawful to rule without regard to justice or injustice, and
domination may quite possibly be unjust. Moreover, we never see this in   *30*
the other sciences; it is not the doctor's or pilot's task to force his patients or
passengers if he fails to persuade them.

Most people, however, would seem to think the science of mastery over
slaves is political science; and they are not ashamed to treat other peoples
in ways that they reject as unjust and harmful among individuals. For   *35*
among themselves they seek to rule justly, but in relations with other
peoples they are indifferent to justice.

It is absurd, however, to deny that some creatures are, and some are not,
naturally suited to be ruled by masters. And so, if this is true, we must try
to rule as masters only over those suited to be ruled, not over everyone, just
as we must not try to hunt human beings for a feast or sacrifice, but only   *40*
animals that are suitable to be hunted; these are the wild animals that are *1325a*
suitable to eat.

Besides, a single city even by itself—if it has a fine political system, of
course—can be happy, if it is possible for a city to live in isolation somewhere, governed by excellent laws. The organization of this political system
will not aim at war or at domination over enemy states, since it is assumed   *5*
to have no enemies or wars.

Clearly, then, all the ways of training for war should be regarded as
fine—not, however, as the ultimate end of everything, but as promoting
that end. The excellent legislator's task is to consider how a city, or people,
or any other community, is to participate in a good life and in the happi-   *10*
ness available to it. However, some prescriptions of law will vary; and it is
the task of legislative science, if a city has neighbors, to see what practices
should be cultivated in relations with different sorts of neighbors and how
to apply the suitable ones to dealings with each neighboring city.

This question, however, about the right aim for the best political system,   *15*
will receive the proper discussion later.

3

We must reply to the two sides who agree that the life involving virtue is
the most choiceworthy but differ about the right way to practice it. For
those on one side refuse to hold any rule over citizens, since they suppose
that the free person's way of life is both different from the life of political   *20*
activity and the most choiceworthy of all lives. Those on the other side, on
the contrary, hold that the politically active life is the best of all, since, in
their view, someone who is inactive cannot possibly be acting well, and
good action is the same as happiness. In reply we say that each side is
partly right and partly wrong.

The one side is right to say that the free person's way of life is better than
25   the life of a master ruling slaves. This is true; for employing a slave, in so
far as he is a slave, is quite unimpressive, since there is nothing fine about
giving orders for the provision of necessities. But to suppose that every sort
of rule is the rule of a master over slaves is wrong. For there is just as great
a difference between rule over free people and rule over slaves as there is
30   between being naturally free and being naturally a slave. We have determined this sufficiently in the first discussions. Moreover, it is incorrect to
praise inactivity over activity; for happiness is activity, and, further, the
actions of just and temperate people achieve many fine goals.[30]

35   And yet, someone might perhaps take this conclusion to imply that
control over everyone is the best thing, thinking that this is the way to be in
control of the largest number of the finest actions. And so, on this view,
anyone capable of ruling must not resign rule to his neighbor, but must
seize it from him; a father must have no consideration for his sons, nor sons
40   for their father, nor in general one friend for another, nor consider them at
all in comparison to this goal <of ruling>, since what is best is most choiceworthy, and good action is best.

1325b   Now, presumably this claim <about ruling> is true, if brigands who rob
and use force get the most choiceworthy thing there is. But presumably
they cannot, and this assumption is false. For <the actions of an absolute
ruler> cannot be fine if he is not as far superior to his subjects as a man is
5   to his wife, or a father is to his children, or a master to his slaves. And so
someone who deviates from virtue can never achieve a great enough success thereby to outweigh his previous deviation.

For what is fine and just for people who are similar is <holding office> in
turn. For this is equal and similar treatment, whereas unequal treatment for
equal people and dissimilar treatment for similar people are against nature,
10   and nothing that is against nature is fine. That is why, if another person is
superior in virtue and in the capacity for the best actions, it is fine to follow
him, and just to obey him; but he must have not only virtue but also the
capacity for the actions.

15   If this is right, and we should take happiness to be good action, then the life
of action is best both for a whole city in common and for the individual.

However, the life of action need not, as some think, involve relations to
others, and the thoughts concerned with action need not be only those
20   carried out for the sake of the results of the action. On the contrary, the
studies and thoughts that include their own end and are carried out for
their own sakes must be far more concerned with action; for <their> end is
good action,[31] and hence it is a kind of action. And in fact, even in the case

---

30. **achieve many fine goals**: lit. 'have the end of many and fine things'.

31. **good action**: or 'doing well', *eupraxia*. This is the sort of ACTION that does not
involve motion (*kinēsis*) at all.

of external actions, those whom we regard as acting most fully are the master craftsmen whose plans <direct production>.

Nor, moreover, are cities necessarily inactive if their position is isolated 25 and they have decided to live in isolation. For a city can still have activities involving parts of itself, since the parts of the city have many communities with each other. And the same is also true of any individual human being; otherwise the god and the whole universe would hardly be in a fine condition, since they have no actions directed outside them, but only their own 30 proper actions involving themselves.

It is evident, then, that the same sort of life must be the best one both for an individual human being and for cities and human beings in common. . . .

13

We should now discuss the political system itself and say which people, and 1331b of what character, must constitute a city if it is to be blessedly happy and to 25 have a fine political system.

Everyone's welfare depends on two conditions; the goal and end of actions must be correctly laid down, and the actions promoting the end must 30 be found. For these may either conflict or harmonize with each other. Sometimes the goal has been finely laid down, but we fail to obtain it in our actions; sometimes we attain everything that promotes our end, but have laid down a bad end; and sometimes we fail on both counts (as in 35 medicine, for instance, when sometimes they neither make a correct judgment about the character of a healthy body nor manage to find the right productive process relative to the standard that has been laid down). In crafts and sciences we must master both the end and the actions advancing towards it.

It is evident, then, that everyone aims at living well and at happiness. In 40 fact, however, these are open to some and not to others, because of some- 1332a thing in fortune or nature—for living finely also needs resources, fewer if our condition is better, and more if it is worse. Others again, though happiness is open to them, seek it in the wrong way from the start. Our task is to see the best political system, the one that will result in the best 5 political life in the city; this will be the one that most of all results in happiness for the city. Hence we must not be ignorant of what happiness is.

We say, then—as we define it in the *Ethics*,[32] if those discussions are of any benefit—that happiness is complete activity and exercise of virtue, 10 complete without qualification, not conditionally.[33] By 'conditionally' I mean what is necessary, and by 'without qualification' I mean what is done

32. **Ethics**: Cf. *EN* 1098a16.
33. **conditionally**: Lit. 'on an assumption'. See NECESSITY #4.

finely. For in the case of just actions, for instance, penalties and corrective treatments result from virtue, but are necessary, and are done finely only to the extent that is possible for necessary actions,[34] since it is more choice-
15 worthy if neither a man nor a city needs any such thing. By contrast, actions leading to honors and prosperity are the finest actions without qualification; for while the other type of action involves merely the removal of some evil, these, on the contrary, construct and generate goods.

20   Now, certainly the excellent man will act finely in response to poverty or disease or any other ill fortune. Still, blessedness consists in the contrary of these. For we have determined this also in our ethical discussions, that the excellent person is the sort whose virtue makes unqualified goods good for
25 him; and clearly the ways in which he uses them must also be excellent and fine without qualification. Indeed this is why human beings think external goods cause happiness; it is as though they took the lyre rather than the performer's craft to be the cause of a splendidly fine performance.

It follows, then, from what has been said, that some conditions must be
30 presupposed, but some must be provided by the legislator. That is why, in establishing the city, we assume that the goods we want that are controlled by fortune (since we take fortune to control <externals>) are provided at the level we aspire to, but when we come to making the city excellent, it is a task not for fortune, but for science and decision.

Moreover, a city is excellent because the citizens who participate in the
35 political system are excellent; and in our city all the citizens participate in the political system. Hence we must consider how an excellent man comes to be; for even if it is possible for the citizens to be excellent all together without being so individually, still it is more choiceworthy for each to be excellent individually, since being excellent individually also implies being excellent all together <but the converse is not true>.

40   Now, people come to be good and excellent through three means— nature, habit, and reason. For, first of all, we must be born with the nature of a human being, not of some other animal; and then we must have the
1332b appropriate sort of body and soul. But in some cases being born with a given quality is no help, since habits alter it; for nature makes some things able to go either way, and habits change them for the worse or the better.

Now, whereas the other animals live mostly by nature, while some live to
5 some slight extent by habit, a human being also lives by reason, since he is the only animal who has it. And so these three ought to be in accord; for people do many actions contrary to habituation and nature because of reason, if they are persuaded that another way is better.

We have previously defined, then, the sort of nature that is needed if
10 people are to be easily handled by the legislator. Thereafter the task falls

---

34. **only to the extent that is possible for necessary actions:** Lit. just 'necessarily'.

to education, since some things are learnt by habituation, others by instruction. . . .

15

The goal appears to be the same for a community of human beings as for 1334a
an individual, and the best political system must conform to the same
standard that the best man conforms to. Evidently, then, it must possess the
virtues applying to leisure; for, as we have often said, the goal of war is   15
peace, and the goal of labor is leisure.

The virtues that are useful for leisure and for spending one's leisure time
are those whose function applies to leisure and those whose function applies to labor; for many necessary <goods> must be presupposed if leisure
is to be open to us. Hence it is fitting for the city to be temperate, brave, and 20
resistant; for, as the proverb says, slaves have no leisure, and those who
cannot face dangers bravely are slaves of their attackers.

Now, bravery and resistance are needed for labor, philosophy for leisure,
and temperance and justice in both circumstances—indeed, even more in   25
peace and leisure. For war compels us to be just and temperate, but enjoyment of good fortune and of peacetime makes people insolently aggressive
instead. Much justice and temperance, then, are needed by those who seem
to do best and to enjoy the <external> goods that bring congratulation for   30
blessedness. This will be true, for instance, of the people in the Isles of the
Blessed, if there are any, as the poets say there are; for these will have most
need of philosophy, temperance, and justice, to the extent that they more
than anyone else are at leisure, with abundance of all those <external>
goods.

It is evident, then, why the city that is to be happy and excellent needs to   35
share in the virtues. For it is shameful to be incapable of using goods
<properly>; it is even more shameful to be incapable of using them in
leisure, so that we appear good when we are laboring and fighting wars,
but slavish when we are at leisure in time of peace.   40

That is why we must not cultivate virtue as Sparta does. For the Spartans 1334b
are superior to other people not by rejecting other people's view that the
<externals> are the greatest goods, but by believing that a particular virtue
is the best way to secure these goods. But since they esteem these goods and
the enjoyment of them more highly than the enjoyment of the vir-
tues[35] . . . and that <virtue is to be cultivated> for itself, is evident from   5
this. The next thing to attend to, then, is the means and method of acquiring virtue.

35. **virtues** . . . There seems to be a passage missing from the manuscripts at this
point.

We have previously determined, then, that the acquisition of virtue depends on nature, habit, and reason; and among these we have previously determined the sort of natural characteristics people should have. The remaining question to study is whether education by reason or by habit should come first.

For reason and habit must achieve the best sort of harmony, since it is possible both for reason to fall short of the best basic assumption and for upbringing by habits to fail similarly. This at least, then, is evident first of all, as in other cases, that coming to be has some starting point, and the end resulting from one starting point is itself the starting point of another end. Now, the goal of nature for us is reason and understanding; hence the coming to be and the practice of habits must be arranged to aim at these.

Further, just as soul and body are two, so also we see that the soul has two parts, the non-rational and the rational, and these have two <characteristic> states, desire and understanding <respectively>. And just as the body comes to be before the soul, so also the non-rational part of the soul comes to be before the rational. This also is evident from the fact that emotion, wish, and also appetite are present in children as soon as they are born, whereas reasoning and understanding naturally arise in the course of growth.

First of all, then, attention to the body must precede attention to the soul, and, next, attention to desire must precede attention to understanding. Nonetheless, attention to desire must be for the sake of understanding, just as attention to the body must be for the sake of the soul.

SUGGESTIONS FOR FURTHER READING

N.B.: Volumes marked with an asterisk (*) are collections of essays.

The Presocratics and the Sophists

Many of the volumes in the first section are general histories of Presocratic philosophy or anthologies of articles, and should also be consulted for further readings on individual figures and movements. All of these entries contain further bibliographies.

Background and General Treatments of the Presocratics:

Barnes, J., *The Presocratic Philosophers*, Revised edition (London: Routledge and Kegan Paul, 1982).

*Caston, V., and D. Graham, eds., *Presocratic Philosophy: Essays in Honor of A. P. D. Mourelatos* (Aldershot: Ashgate Publishing Co., 2002).

Curd, P., "Presocratic Philosophy," *The Stanford Encyclopedia of Philosophy* (Fall 2008 Edition), Edward N. Zalta (ed.), available at http://plato.stanford.edu/archives/fall2008/entries/presocratics/.

*Curd, P., and D. H. Graham, eds., *The Oxford Handbook of Presocratic Philosophy* (New York: Oxford University Press, 2008).

Graham, D. W., *Explaining the Cosmos: The Ionian Tradition of Scientific Philosophy* (Princeton: Princeton University Press, 2006).

Guthrie, W. K. C., *A History of Greek Philosophy*, Vols. I, II, and III (Cambridge: Cambridge University Press, 1962, 1965, 1969).

Hussey, E., *The Presocratics* (London: Duckworth, 1972; reprinted, Indianapolis: Hackett, 1995).

*Long, A. A., ed., *The Cambridge Companion to Early Greek Philosophy* (Cambridge: Cambridge University Press, 1999).

*McCoy, J., *Early Greek Philosophy: Reason at the Beginning of Philosophy* (Washington, D.C.: The Catholic University of America Press, forthcoming).

McKirahan, R., *Philosophy Before Socrates*, 2nd ed. (Indianapolis: Hackett, 2011).

*Zeyl, D., *Encyclopedia of Classical Philosophy* (Westport, CT: Greenwood Press, 1997).

The Milesians:

Boudouris, K. J., ed., *Ionian Philosophy* (Athens: International Association for Greek Philosophy: International Center for Greek Philosophy and Culture, 1989).

Kahn, C. H., *Anaximander and the Origins of Greek Cosmology* (New York: Columbia University Press, 1960; reprinted, Indianapolis: Hackett, 1994).

Pythagoras and Early Pythagoreanism:

Burkert, W., *Lore and Science in Ancient Pythagoreanism*, E. Minar (tr.) (Cambridge, Mass.: Harvard University Press, 1972; First German ed., Nürnberg: Verlag Hans Carl, 1962).
Huffman, C., "Pythagoras," *The Stanford Encyclopedia of Philosophy* (*Winter 2009 Edition*), Edward N. Zalta (ed.), available at http://plato.stanford.edu/archives/win2009/entries/pythagoras/.
———, "Pythagoreanism," *The Stanford Encyclopedia of Philosophy* (*Fall 2008 Edition*), Edward N. Zalta (ed.), available at http://plato.stanford.edu/archives/fall2008/entries/pythagoreanism/.
Kahn, C. H., *Pythagoras and the Pythagoreans* (Indianapolis: Hackett, 2001).
Riedweg, C., *Pythagoras: His Life, Teaching and Influence* (Ithaca and London: Cornell University Press, 2005).

Xenophanes:

Lesher, J. H., "Xenophanes," *The Stanford Encyclopedia of Philosophy* (*Fall 2008 Edition*), Edward N. Zalta (ed.), available at http://plato.stanford.edu/archives/fall2008/entries/xenophanes/.
———, *Xenophanes of Colophon: Fragments: A Text and Translation with Commentary* (Toronto: University of Toronto Press, 1992).

Heraclitus:

Dilcher, R., *Studies in Heraclitus* (Hildesheim: Georg Olms, 1995).
Graham, D., "Heraclitus," *The Stanford Encyclopedia of Philosophy* (*Fall 2008 Edition*), Edward N. Zalta (ed.), available at http://plato.stanford.edu/archives/fall2008/entries/heraclitus/.
Kahn, C. H., *The Art and Thought of Heraclitus* (Cambridge: Cambridge University Press, 1979).
Robinson, T. M., *Heraclitus* (Toronto: University of Toronto Press, 1987).

Parmenides and Melissus:

Coxon, A. H., *The Fragments of Parmenides*, 2nd ed. revised and expanded, R. McKirahan (ed.) (Las Vegas: Parmenides Publishing, 2009).
Curd, P., *The Legacy of Parmenides: Eleatic Monism and Later Presocratic Thought*, 2nd ed. (Las Vegas: Parmenides Publishing, 2004).
Gallop, D., *Parmenides of Elea: Fragments* (Toronto: University of Toronto Press, 1984).
Mourelatos, A. P. D., *The Route of Parmenides*, 2nd ed. (Las Vegas: Parmenides Publishing, 2008).

Palmer, J. A., "Parmenides," *The Stanford Encyclopedia of Philosophy* (*Fall 2008 Edition*), Edward N. Zalta (ed.), available at http://plato.stanford.edu/archives/fall2008/entries/parmenides/.

———, *Parmenides and Presocratic Philosophy* (Oxford: Oxford University Press, 2009).

Zeno:

Grünbaum, A., *Modern Science and Zeno's Paradoxes* (London: Allen and Unwin, 1968).

Huggett, N. (ed.), *Space from Zeno to Einstein: Classic Readings with a Contemporary Commentary* (Cambridge, MA: MIT Press, 1999).

———, "Zeno's Paradoxes," *The Stanford Encyclopedia of Philosophy* (*Fall 2008 Edition*), Edward N. Zalta (ed.), available at http://plato.stanford.edu/archives/fall2008/entries/paradox-zeno/.

Makin, S., "Zeno of Elea" in E. Craig (ed.), *Routledge Encyclopedia of Philosophy*, vol. 9 (London and New York: Routledge, 1998): 843–53.

Palmer, J., "Zeno of Elea," *The Stanford Encyclopedia of Philosophy* (*Fall 2008 Edition*), Edward N. Zalta (ed.), available at http://plato.stanford.edu/archives/fall2008/entries/zeno-elea/.

Salmon, W. C. (ed.), *Zeno's Paradoxes Today*, 2nd ed. (Indianapolis: Hackett, 2001).

Vlastos, G., "Zeno of Elea" in P. Edwards (ed.), *The Encyclopedia of Philosophy*, vol. 8 (New York and London: Macmillan, 1967): 369–79. Reprinted in Vlastos, G., *Studies in Greek Philosophy, vol. 1: The Presocratics*, D. W. Graham (ed.) (Princeton: Princeton University Press, 1993): 241–63.

Empedocles:

Inwood, B., *The Poem of Empedocles*, 2nd ed. (Toronto: University of Toronto Press, 2001).

Kingsley, P., *Ancient Philosophy, Mystery, and Magic* (Oxford: Clarendon Press, 1995).

Parry, R., "Empedocles," *The Stanford Encyclopedia of Philosophy* (*Fall 2008 Edition*), Edward N. Zalta (ed.), available at http://plato.stanford.edu/archives/fall2008/entries/empedocles/.

*Pierris, A. (ed.), *The Empedoclean Kosmos: Structure, Process and the Question of Cyclicity* (Patras: Institute for Philosophical Research, 2005).

Wright, M. R., *Empedocles: the Extant Fragments* (New Haven: Yale University Press, 1981; reprinted, Indianapolis: Hackett Publishing, 1995).

Anaxagoras:

Curd, P., *Anaxagoras of Clazomenae: Fragments* (Toronto: University of Toronto Press, 2007).

Schofield, M., *An Essay on Anaxagoras* (Cambridge: Cambridge University Press, 1980).

Sider, D., *The Fragments of Anaxagoras*, 2nd ed. (Sankt Augustin: Academia Verlag, 2005).

Presocratic Atomism:

Berryman, S., "Ancient Atomism," *The Stanford Encyclopedia of Philosophy* (*Fall 2008 Edition*), Edward N. Zalta (ed.), available at http://plato.stanford.edu/archives/fall2008/entries/atomism-ancient/.
———, "Democritus," *The Stanford Encyclopedia of Philosophy* (*Fall 2008 Edition*), Edward N. Zalta (ed.), available at http://plato.stanford.edu/archives/fall2008/entries/democritus/.
———, "Leucippus," *The Stanford Encyclopedia of Philosophy* (*Fall 2008 Edition*), Edward N. Zalta (ed.), available at http://plato.stanford.edu/archives/fall2008/entries/leucippus/.
Cartledge, P., *Democritus* (London: Routledge, 1999).
———, *The Greek Cosmologists vol. 1: The Formation of the Atomic Theory and its Earliest Critics* (Cambridge: Cambridge University Press, 1987).
Taylor, C. C. W., *The Atomists: Leucippus and Democritus. Fragments* (Toronto: University of Toronto Press, 1999).

Philolaus of Croton:
(See also the section on Pythagoras)

Huffman, C. A., *Archytas of Tarentum: Pythagorean, Philosopher and Mathematician King* (Cambridge: Cambridge University Press, 2005).
———, "Philolaus," *The Stanford Encyclopedia of Philosophy* (*Fall 2008 Edition*), Edward N. Zalta (ed.), available at http://plato.stanford.edu/archives/fall2008/entries/philolaus/.
———, *Philolaus of Croton: Pythagorean and Presocratic* (Cambridge: Cambridge University Press, 1993).
———, "The Pythagorean Conception of the Soul" in Frede, D. (ed.), *Body and Soul in Ancient Philosophy* (Berlin: De Gruyter, 2009): 21–44.

The Sophists:

De Romilly, J., *The Great Sophists in Periclean Athens*, J. Lloyd (tr.) (Oxford: Oxford University Press, 1992).
Gagarin, M., and P. Woodruff, *Early Greek Political Thought from Homer to the Sophists* (Cambridge: Cambridge University Press, 1995).
Kerferd, G. B., *The Sophistic Movement* (Cambridge: Cambridge University Press, 1981a).
*———(ed.), *The Sophists and their Legacy* (Wiesbaden: Steiner, 1981b).
Sprague, R. K. (ed.), *The Older Sophists* (Columbia, SC: University of South Carolina Press, 1972; reprinted, Indianapolis: Hackett, 2001).

The Derveni Papyrus:

Betegh, G., *The Derveni Papyrus: Cosmology, Theology and Interpretation* (Cambridge: Cambridge University Press, 2004).
Kouremenos, T., G. M. Parássoglou, and K. Tsantsanoglou, *The Derveni Papyrus* (Firenze: L.S. Olschki, 2006).

Plato

For a more complete bibliography, see Kraut.

Background:

Irwin, T. H., *Classical Thought* (Oxford: Oxford University Press, 1989).
The Joint Association of Classical Teachers, *The World of Athens* (Cambridge: Cambridge University Press, 1984).

Socrates and Plato:

Allen, R. E., *Plato's Parmenides* (Minneapolis: University of Minnesota Press, 1983).
Annas, J., *An Introduction to Plato's Republic* (Oxford: Clarendon Press, 1981).
*Benson, Hugh H., *Essays on the Philosophy of Socrates* (New York: Oxford University Press, 1992).
Bostock, David, *Plato's Phaedo* (Oxford: Clarendon Press, 1986).
Brickhouse, Thomas C., and Nicholas D. Smith, *Plato's Socrates* (Oxford: Calrendon Press, 1994).
Burnyeat, Myles, and M. J. Levett, *The Theatetus of Plato* (Indianapolis: Hackett, 1990).
*Everson, S., *Companions to Ancient Thought 1: Epistemology* (Cambridge: Cambridge University Press, 1990).
*———, *Companions to Ancient Thought 2: Psychology* (Cambridge: Cambridge University Press, 1991).
Gallop, David, *Plato: Phaedo* (Oxford: Clarendon Press, 1975).
Grube, G. M. A., *Plato's Thought* (Indianapolis: Hackett, 1980).
Irwin, T. H., *Plato's Moral Theory* (Oxford: Clarendon Press, 1977).
———, *Plato: Gorgias* (Oxford: Clarendon Press, 1979).
*Kraut, Richard, *The Cambridge Companion to Plato* (Cambridge: Cambridge University Press, 1992).
Reeve, C.D.C., *Philosopher-Kings: The Argument of Plato's Republic* (Indianapolis: Hackett, 2006).
———, *Socrates in the Apology* (Indianapolis: Hackett, 1989).
Taylor, C.C.W., *Plato: Protagoras*, rev. ed. (Oxford: Clarendon Press, 1991).
Vlastos, G., *Plato's Universe* (Seattle: University of Washington Press, 1975).
*———, *Platonic Studies* (Princeton: Princeton University Press, 1981).
———, *Socrates: Ironist and Moral Philosopher* (Ithaca: Cornell University Press, 1991).
———, *Socratic Studies* (Cambridge: Cambridge University Press, 1994).

Aristotle

For a more complete bibliography see Barnes (1995).

Ackrill, J. L., *Aristotle the Philosopher* (Oxford: Oxford University Press, 1981).
Allan, D. J., *The Philosopher of Aristotle*, 2nd ed. (Oxford: Oxford University Press, 1970).
Barnes, Jonathan, *Aristotle* (Oxford: Oxford University Press, 1982).

———, *The Cambridge Companion to Aristotle* (Cambridge: Cambridge University Press, 1995).

Barnes, J., M. Schofield, and R. Sorabji (eds.), *Articles on Aristotle*, vols. 1–4 (London: Duckworth, 1975–79).

Cooper, John, *Reason and Human Good in Aristotle* (Cambridge, Mass.: Harvard University Press, 1975).

Furth, Montgomery, *Substance, Form and Psyche: An Aristotelean Metaphysics* (Ithaca: Cornell University Press, 1988).

*Gotthelf, A., and J. Lennox (eds.), *Philosophical Issues in Aristotle's Biology* (Cambridge: Cambridge University Press, 1987).

Irwin, T. H., *Aristotle's First Principles* (Oxford: Oxford University Press, 1988).

*Keyt, D., and F. D. Miller (eds.), *A Companion to Aristotle's* Politics (Oxford: Blackwell, 1991).

Kraut, Richard, *Aristotle on the Human Good* (Princeton: Princeton University Press, 1989).

Lear, Jonathan, *Aristotle: The Desire to Understand* (Cambridge: Cambridge University Press, 1988).

Lloyd, G. E. R., *Aristotle: The Growth and Structure of His Thought* (Cambridge: Cambridge University Press, 1968).

Loux, Michael, *Primary* Ousia: *An Essay on Aristotle's* Metaphysics Z *and* H (Ithaca: Cornell University Press, 1991).

Nussbaum, Martha, *The Fragility of Goodness: Luck and Ethics in Greek Tragedy and Philosophy* (Cambridge: Cambridge University Press, 1986).

*Nussbaum, M. C., and A. O. Rorty (eds.), *Essays on Aristotle's* De Anima (Oxford: Oxford University Press, 1992).

*Owen, G. E. L., *Logic, Science, and Dialectic: Collected Papers in Greek Philosophy* (Ithaca: Cornell University Press, 1986).

Reeve, C. D. C., *Practices of Reason: Aristotle's* Nicomachean Ethics (Oxford: Clarendon Press, 1992).

*Rorty, A. O. (ed.), *Essays on Aristotle's Ethics* (Berkeley: University of California Press, 1980).

Ross, W. D., *Aristotle,* 5th ed. rev. (New York: Barnes and Noble, 1949).

Witt, Charlotte, *Substance and Essence in Aristotle's* Metaphysics (Ithaca: Cornell University Press, 1989).

CONCORDANCE FOR THE PRESOCRATICS AND THE SOPHISTS

DK number	APR number or page
Alcmaeon (DK24)	
B1	p. 5
Anaxagoras (DK59)	9. Anaxagoras
A43	25
A46	26
A52	24
A58	27
A102	23
A117	28
B1	1
B2	2
B3	3
B4	4
B5	5
B6	6
B7	7
B8	8
B9	9
B10	10
B11	11
B12	12
B13	13
B14	14
B15	15
B16	16
B17	17
B18	18
B19	19
B21	20
B21a	21
B22	22
Antiphon (DK87)	14. Sophists
A44a	21
Aristotle	
Metaphysics 1.3 983a26–b6	2. Milesians 4

DK number	APR number or page
Aristotle, *Physics* 7.5 250a16–19	7. Zeno 13a
Physics 8.8 263a15–18	7. Zeno 9
Anaximander (DK12)	2. Milesians
A9	9
A10	12, 19
A11	10, 15
A15	11
A18	14
A21	13
A23	16
A26	17
A30	18, 20
B1	9
Anaximenes (DK13)	2. Milesians
A5	21
A6	26
A7	24, 28
A10	23
A17	29
A20	27
A21	30
B1	25
B2	22
Anonymous Iamblichi (DK89)	14. Sophists
6	23
7	23
Atomism: *See* Democritus *and* Leucippus	
Critias (DK88)	14. Sophists
B25	22

Democritus (DK68)	10. Atomism
A1	55
A37	5
A38	6
A40	39
A47	10, 22, 23, 26
A48b	14
A57	32
A58	20, 25
A59	9
A60	27
A66	28, 29
A68	30
A93	41
A104	42
A112	50
A129	35
A135	36, 43
B6	47
B7	49
B8	48
B9	44, 46
B11	45
B33	59
B69	57
B74	56
B117	51
B125	52
B155	33
B156	16
B164	38
B166	53
B189	60
B191	54
B214	58
B235	61

Diogenes of Apollonia (DK64)	13. Diogenes of Apollonia
A1	9
A6	10
A19	11
B1	1
B2	2
B3	3
B4	4
B5	5
B6	6
B7	7
B8	8

Dissoi Logoi (DK90)	14. Sophists
4	13

Empedocles (DK31)	8. Empedocles
B1	30
B2	34
B3a	36
B3b	35
B4	33
B5	32
B6	37
B7	38
B8	39
B9	41
B11	40
B12	43
B13	44
B14	45
B15	42
B16	46
B17	47
B20	48
B21	49
B22	55
B23	51
B25	54
B26	52
B27	62
B27a	63
B28	64
B29	65
B30	67
B31	68
B33	57
B34	58
B35	101
B36	102
B38	70
B42	73
B43	75
B44	72
B45	76
B46	77
B47	74
B48	78
B53	71
B54	71
B55	80
B56	81
B57	103
B58	104
B59	107
B60	105
B61	106
B62	95

B64	96	B129	3; Pythagoras 5
B65	98	B130	5
B66	97	B131	29
B67	99	B132	7
B68	100	B133	28
B71	82	B134	66
B73	84	B135	21
B75	91	B136	17
B76	50	B137	19
B78	6	B138	18
B79	93	B139	53
B80	94	B140	23
B81	61	B141	24
B82	89	B142	9
B83	92	B144	22
B84	109	B145	20
B85	85	B146	26
B86	86	B147	27
B87	109	B151	83
B88	108	Strasbourg Papyrus:	
B90	69	*ensemble* a	47
B91	56	*ensemble* b	50
B92	59	*ensemble* c	48
B93	60	*ensemble* d	53
B94	79	Wright fragment 152	90
B96	87		
B98	88	Eurytus (DK45)	12. Philolaus
B99	110	3	14, 15
B100	111		
B101	112	Gorgias (DK82)	14. Sophists
B102	113	B3	15
B104	114	B11	14
B105	119		
B106	117	Heraclitus (DK22)	5. Heraclitus
B107	118	B1	1
B108	120	B2	2
B109	115	B3	88
B110	116	B4	73
B111	31	B5	110
B112	1	B6	89
B113	3	B7	64
B114	2	B8	59
B115	8	B9	72
B117	12	B10	60
B118	14	B11	75
B119	13	B12	39
B121	15	B13	71
B124	16	B14	112
B125	10	B15	111
B126	11	B16	98
B127	25	B17	26
B128	4	B18	24

B19	29	B82	70
B20	97	B83	76
B21	22	B84a	55
B22	25	B85	109
B23	83	B86	9
B24	93	B87	31
B25	94	B88	82
B26	21	B89	20
B27	95	B90	49
B28	30	B91	40
B30	45	B92	113
B31	87	B93	16
B32	47	B94	88
B34	15	B95	108
B35	36	B96	99
B36	52	B97	32
B37	74	B98	65
B39	6	B99	90
B40	3; Pythagoras 2	B101	37
B41	46	B101a	63
B42	5	B102	77
B43	105	B103	79
B44	104	B104	8
B45	43	B107	13
B46	14	B108	10
B47	34	B110	107
B48	66	B111	84
B49	102	B112	18
B49a	41	B113	17
B50	11	B114	23
B51	61	B115	44
B52	103	B116	35
B53	58	B117	54
B54	38	B118	53
B55	62	B119	106
B56	33	B120	91
B57	7	B121	100
B58	85	B123	12
B59	67	B124	78
B60	68	B125	56
B61	69	B125a	101
B62	86	B126	80
B63	96	B129	4; Pythagoras 3
B64	48	B136	92
B65	50		
B67	81	Hesiod	
B70	28	*Theogony* 114–38	p. 2
B72	27		
B73	19	Hippias (DK86)	14. Sophists
B76	51	B6	19
B78	42		
B80	57	Homer	
		Iliad 2.484–92	p. 4

Leucippus (DK67)	10. Atomism
A1	37, 40
A6	3, 24
A7	7, 15
A8	6
A9	4
A13	13
A14	12, 31, 34
A15	11
A16	18, 21
A18	19
A19	8, 17
B2	1

Melissus (DK30)	11. Melissus
A5	11
B1	1
B2	2
B3	3
B4	4
B5	5
B6	6
B7	7
B8	8
B9	9
B10	10

P.Oxy. 53.3710, col. 2, 37–40	2. Milesians 3

Parmenides (DK28)	6. Parmenides
B1	1
B2	2
B3	3
B4	4
B5	5
B6	6
B7	7
B8	8
B9	9
B10	10
B11	11
B12	12
B13	13
B14	14
B15	15
B16	16
B17	17
B18	18
B19	19

Pherecydes (DK36)	
B4	Pythagoras 4

Philolaus (DK44)	12. Philolaus
B1	1
B2	2
B3	3
B4	4
B5	5
B6	6
B6a	7
B7	8
B8	13
B13	12
B16	10
B17	9
B20	11

Prodicus (DK84)	14. Sophists
B5	17

Protagoras (DK80)	14. Sophists
A5	1
B1	8
B3	2
B4	5
B7	6
B10	3
B11	4
A1	9, 10
A21	11, 12

Pythagoras (DK14)	3. Pythagoras and Early Pythagoreanism
1	7, 15
2	11
8	10
8a	8
10	6

Pythagorean School (DK58)	3. Pythagoras and Early Pythagoreanism
B4	17; Philolaus 16
B5	18, 20
B28	19
B40	9
C3	13
C4	11, 12
C6	14

Sextus Empiricus	
Against the Mathematicians 7.94–95	Pythagoreans 16

Thales (DK11)	2. Milesians		
A9	1	B23	13
A10	2	B24	14
A12	p. 2; Milesian 5	B25	16
A14	6	B26	15
A22	7, 8	B27	17
		B28	18
		B29	19
Xenophanes (DK21)	4. Xenophanes	B30	20
		B31	21
A12	28	B32	22
A30	29	B33	23
A32	30	B34	24
A33	34	B35	25
A38	32	B36	26
A39	35	B38	27
A40	31		
A44	33	Zeno (DK29)	7. Zeno
B1	1	A11	1
B2	2	A12	1
B7	3; Pythagoreans 1	A16	2
B8	4	A24	12
B10	5	A25	6, 8
B11	6	A26	7
B12	7	A27	10
B14	8	A28	11
B15	9	A29	13
B16	10	B1	4
B17	11	B2	3
B18	p. 4; 12	B3	5

GLOSSARY

FOR ARISTOTLE

ACCOUNT: see REASON

ACHIEVEMENT: see FUNCTION

ACTION, *praxis*

Aristotle uses *praxis* and the verb *prattein* (1) in a broad sense parallel to 'do'; (2) to distinguish voluntary actions from things that happen to us or things over which we have no control; (3) for rational action on a DECISION, which is not open to non-rational animals or to children; (4) for rational action in which the action itself is the end. Since ethics and politics are concerned with action in sense (4), they are 'practical' disciplines, in contrast to productive CRAFTS such as shoemaking, building, rhetoric, and poetics.

ACTUALITY, ACTIVITY, REALIZATION, *energeia*

1. *Energeia* is contrasted with POTENTIALITY, as actually walking, e.g., is contrasted with merely having the potentiality to walk. It seems to be equivalent to *entelecheia*, which is therefore also translated 'actuality' (except that when the two terms occur together in contexts that require different translations, 'realization' translates *entelecheia*, and 'actuality' translates *energeia*).

2. Aristotle sometimes distinguishes (a) first actuality (sometimes equivalent to STATE, *hexis*) from (b) second actuality, as in (a) knowing French, but not thinking or speaking in French at the time, in contrast to (b) speaking or thinking in French at the time, and so having actualized the potentiality still present in (a).

3. Sometimes the verb *energein* is rendered by 'be act' ive and *energeia* by 'activity'.

4. On the contrast between complete and incomplete actuality see MOTION.

AFFECTION: see ATTRIBUTE

aisthēsis: see PERCEPTION

aition, aitia: see CAUSE

ALWAYS, *aiei,* **EVERLASTING,** *aidion*

1. *Aiei* serves as a universal quantifier, and hence is often rendered 'in every case'.

2. What is always the case is sometimes identified with what is NECESSARY. Aristotle need not mean, however, that necessity is reducible to purely temporal concepts; probably he intends 'always' and 'everlasting' to have a modal sense.

APART FROM, BESIDES, *para*

1. Sometimes '*x* is *para y*' (with accusative) just means that *x* exists in addition to *y*. Sometimes it suggests that *x* is independent of *y*.

2. A special problem arises about *para* in statements about UNIVERSALS and PARTICU-LARS. Sometimes Aristotle allows that the universal is a 'one apart from the many'; but sometimes he uses such phrases to indicate the Platonic doctrine of SEPARATION, which he rejects.

APPEARANCE, *phantasia*

1. In its most general sense *phantasia* is simply the abstract noun corresponding to *phainesthai*, 'appear'. Hence my *phantasia* of x (the tree, Pythagoras' Theorem) is simply how x appears to me (whether x is sensible or non-sensible).

2. In its more specific sense *phantasia* is more closely connected to the senses, as opposed to the intellect. Hence Aristotle describes it as the product of PERCEPTION and memory. Here 'imagination' would be, in some ways, a suitable rendering. Appearance is present in all or most animals; this sort of appearance is perceptual, as distinct from rational appearance.

APPEARANCES, *phainomena*

1. *Phainomena* are literally 'things appearing', cognate with *phainesthai*, 'appear'. Two senses of *phainesthai* are marked by different grammatical constructions: (a) 'x appears to be F' (with the infinitive), or (b) 'x is evidently F' (with the participle; lit. 'x, being F, appears so'). Sense (b) implies, but sense (a) does not imply, that what appears F is F. Hence 'F *phainetai* to me' is sometimes translated 'I have the appearance of F' (i.e., I have an impression of F).

2. Aristotle believes that both empirical inquiry and dialectic should begin from the appearances. In a dialectical inquiry these appearances are also COMMON BELIEFS, *endoxa*.

3. Aristotle does not assume that all appearances are true; but a theory must respect and account for the most reasonable ones.

archē: see PRINCIPLE

aretē: see VIRTUE

ARGUMENT: see REASON

atomon: INDIVIDUAL

ATTRIBUTE, AFFECTION, FEELING, *pathos*

1. *Pathos* is cognate with *paschein* ('undergo', 'be affected'), which is correlative to *poiein* ('act on', 'produce').

2. In a wide sense (rendered by 'attribute') a *pathos* of x is something that 'happens to' x quite generally, i.e. something that is true of x. In some cases (though not always) a mere *pathos* of x is contrasted with x's essence.

3. In a narrower sense (rendered by 'affection' or 'feeling') a *pathos* is an 'affection' or 'passion', a mental state involving pleasure or pain.

BE, EXIST, *einai*

1. Aristotle uses the same word to indicate predication ('x is F') and existence ('x is', i.e. x exists). It is sometimes difficult to know which rendering suits a given context

better (since Aristotle does not always supply the '*F*', even in places where he seems to intend it).

2. Aristotle claims that being (*to on*, present participle) and beings (or things that are; *ta onta*) are spoken of in many ways, corresponding to the CATEGORIES. This probably refers to predicative being, since the categories provide the most general answers to the 'What is it?' question. See HOMONYMOUS.

3. Being (the result of a process of becoming) is sometimes contrasted with (the process of) coming to be. See also SUBSTANCE.

CAPABLE, CAPACITY: see POTENTIALITY

CATEGORIES: see PREDICATIONS

CAUSE, REASON, EXPLANATION, *aition, aitia*

1. In *Phys.* II 3, *GC* 335a28–336a12, *PA* 639b12, *Met.* 983a24–b6, Aristotle distinguishes the four types of *aition*: MATTER, FORM, the PRINCIPLE of MOTION (often called the 'efficient' cause, though Aristotle himself does not use this term), and the FINAL CAUSE (lit. 'that for the sake of which', *hou heneka* or 'end', *telos*).

2. We cite an *aition* in answer to the question 'Why?'; hence 'reason' and 'explanation' sometimes render *aition*.

3. In stating the cause Aristotle mentions different kinds of things: a substance; an event; a state; a substance performing or failing to perform an action. In these cases the substance can be said to be 'responsible' (*aitios*) for the action.

CHANCE: see LUCK

CHANGE: see MOTION

chōriston: SEPARABLE

COGNITION, *gnōsis*, **COGNIZE,** *gignōskein*: see KNOW

COINCIDENT, *sumbebēkos*

1. *Sumbebēkos* is derived from *sumbainein*, 'come about together', which often just means 'happen' or 'turn out'; and hence it has a wide range of uses. This makes 'accident' a misleading translation, since *sumbebēkota* include many things that are not, in the ordinary sense, accidents. 'Coincidence' is also too narrow, but 'coincide' is fairly close to the Greek term.

2. Aristotle recognizes two sorts of coincidents: (1) *G* is a coincident of *F* if (a) *G* belongs to *F* IN ITS OWN RIGHT, but (b) *G* is not the ESSENCE of *F*; e.g., a triangle has two right angles in its own right, but this is not the essence of a triangle. (2) *G* is a coincident of *F* if (a) *G* belongs to *F*, but (b) *F* is not essentially *G*. In this case *F*'s being *G* does not follow from the essence of *F*.

3. Coincidents of type (1) are especially important in the theory of demonstration. For demonstration begins with a DEFINITION of *F*, stating the essence of *F*, and proceeds to demonstrate the coincidents of *F* in its own right.

4. When Aristotle mentions coincidents without further specification, he usually has (2) in mind.

COME TO BE, *gignesthai*, COMING TO BE, *genesis*

Aristotle distinguishes unqualified (see WITHOUT QUALIFICATION) from qualified coming to be, *Phys.* 190a31–33. (a) In unqualified coming to be a SUBSTANCE did not exist at time t_1, but exists at t_2; hence we can say 'the tree came to be (= came into being)'. (b) In qualified coming to be one and the same substance remains in existence and changes in one of its non-essential properties. Hence from 'The tree came to be taller (= became taller)' we cannot infer 'The tree came to be (= came into being)'. Analogous distinctions apply to perishing, *phthora*.

COMMON BELIEFS, *endoxa*

These are one type of APPEARANCES, and are the starting point of DIALECTIC. Aristotle often reports the *endoxa* by using 'seems' (*dokei*, cognate with *doxa*, 'belief'. In these contexts 'seems' does not necessarily indicate tentativeness or hesitation, but simply the fact that the claim is a starting point for the construction of a theory (or sometimes a belief against which a theory can be tested) rather than a conclusion of a theoretical argument.

COMMUNITY, *koinōnia*

Koinōnia is cognate with *koinon*, 'common'. Aristotle believes that a *koinōnia* is created by every type of friendship. Hence the term includes both loose alliances and relatively casual relationships, close-knit communities and societies. 'Association' is sometimes a more natural rendering than 'community', since a *koinōnia* may be looser and more temporary than 'community' would suggest. However, 'community' is generally preferable, since it retains the connection with 'common' suggested by the Greek terms. Sometimes Aristotle's argument is easier to understand if the great variety of types of *koinōnia* is kept in mind.

COMPLETE, *teleion*

The term is cognate with *telos*, 'end' (see FOR SOMETHING); 'final' and 'perfect' are other possible translations. MOTION is an incomplete rather than complete ACTUALITY.

CRAFT, *technē*

1. A craft is a rational discipline, distinct from a theoretical science insofar as (1) it aims at production, and (2) it does not provide demonstrations.

2. Craft imitates NATURE, especially in being directed towards a FINAL CAUSE. Aristotle often uses examples of crafts to explain points about matter and form in natural organisms; but he is careful to distinguish the two cases.

3. Aristotle usually speaks as though the products of crafts (statues, beds etc.) are SUBSTANCES; but sometimes he expresses doubts.

DECISION, *prohairesis*

A decision results from wish (i.e. rational desire) for some end, focused by deliberation about what promotes the end; the result is a rational choice about what to do here and now to achieve the end.

DEDUCTION, *sullogismos*

1. The English derivative 'syllogism' is too narrow to capture the meaning of '*sullogismos*', which applies to inference more generally, and specifically to deduc-

tive inference proceeding from more general principles rather than from particular cases (in contrast to induction).

2. A 'syllogism' in the technical sense is a deductive argument with one of the formal structures that Aristotle describes in the *Prior Analytics*.

DEFINITION, *horismos*

1. The definition of F can replace the name 'F' while preserving truth, by saying what F is, and thereby stating the ESSENCE of F.

2. A 'nominal definition' (not an Aristotelian term) says what we take a name to SIGNIFY (e.g. 'thunder is a noise in the clouds') when we begin an inquiry, but does not state the essence. A 'real definition' states the essence.

3. The correct statement of a definition should involve terms that are better KNOWN by nature, not terms that are merely better known to us.

4. PARTICULARS do not have definitions (or at least do not have definitions of the primary sort).

5. Aristotle also speaks of the *horismos* when he means (as we would be inclined to put it) what the definition is of, i.e. the essence. He speaks of the *logos* in the same way.

6. In artifacts and natural organisms definitions involve reference to FORM and FUNCTION.

DIALECTIC, *dialektikē*

Dialektikē (an adjective with *technē* or *methodos* understood) is cognate with *dialegesthai*, 'discuss', and *dialogos*, 'dialogue'. Dialectic is the method Aristotle ascribes to Socrates in Plato's dialogues. He practices it himself in his major philosophical works, though without the overt form of a dialogue.

DIFFERENTIA, *diaphora*

A differentia divides a GENUS into its SPECIES. Aristotle mainly refers to differentiae not with abstract nouns (e.g. 'footedness') but with adjectives.

DISTINCTIVE, PROPER, SPECIAL, PRIVATE, *idion*

1. *Idion* refers to what is private as opposed to what is public (e.g. private as opposed to public property, or a private citizen as opposed to a public official).

2. Aristotle uses it as a technical term (Latin 'proprium') for a non-ESSENTIAL but necessary property of F, belonging to all and only Fs. He also uses the term less strictly, so that it includes essential properties.

3. *Idion* is rendered by 'proper' where Aristotle uses it for the object that is peculiar to each sense (e.g. color for sight, sound for hearing and so on), and for the proper PRINCIPLES of each science in contrast to common principles.

dunamis, dunaton: see POTENTIALITY

eidos: see FORM

END, *telos*: see FOR SOMETHING

endoxa: COMMON BELIEFS

energeia: see ACTUALITY

entelecheia: see ACTUALITY

epistēmē, epistasthai: see KNOW

ergon: see FUNCTION

ESSENCE

1. To state the essence of *F* is to answer the question 'What is *F*?', and to state the (real) DEFINITION of *F*.

2. Aristotle uses different phrases to refer to the essence: (a) 'Being *F*' (*to einai F*, also referring more generally to the definition or concept of *F*). (b) 'What *F* is' (*ti esti F*) or in general 'the what-it-is' (*to ti esti*). (c) 'What it is to be *F*' (*to ti ēn F einai*). This phrase probably means 'What it is for *F* to be *F*', indicating that one wants to know what *F* is INSOFAR as it is *F* (e.g. one wants to know that the man is qua man, not qua musician). (d) '*F* is essentially *G*' renders '*F* is *hoper G*' (i.e. '*F* is precisely what is *G*', especially where *G* is the GENUS of *F*).

3. An essential property of *F* is part of what *F* is IN ITS OWN RIGHT, not COINCIDENTALLY.

eudaimonia: see HAPPINESS

EXCELLENCE: see VIRTUE

EXIST: see BE

EXPLANATION: see CAUSE

FINAL CAUSE: see FOR SOMETHING

FOR SOMETHING, FINAL CAUSE, *heneka tou*

1. Aristotle uses 'for something' (*heneka tou*) for a goal-directed process, and uses 'that for the sake of which' (*to hou heneka*) for the goal or end (*telos*) to which the process is directed. 'Final cause' (from Latin 'finis', corresponding to the Greek *telos*) is a convenient technical term. Aristotle believes that the final cause is found in natural processes as well as in the products of CRAFT.

2. Different kinds of ends are relevant to production by crafts (and non-productive intentional ACTION) and to natural processes. (a) In production the end that plays a causal role is the result aimed at by a designer or producer. (b) In natural processes there is (in Aristotle's view) no intention or design. None the less some processes in natural organisms happen for the sake of a beneficial result to the organisms. This is true in cases where the fact that the process benefits the organism contributes to the causal explanation of why the process happens. Certain kinds of animals, for instance, have sharp teeth for the sake of their survival; this is true because the fact that sharp teeth contribute to the survival of those animals explains why the animals have sharp teeth.

FORM, SPECIES, SORT, *eidos*

1. In the most general sense, something's *eidos* is its character, sort, or type. Aristotle sometimes uses the term more narrowly, so that the *eidos* is what the

MATTER acquires in COMING TO BE, (when, e.g., the bronze is made into a statue, or the wood composes a tree. Here the form is PREDICATED of the matter, and is the formal CAUSE.

2. Aristotle argues that the form, rather than the matter or the compound of form and matter, is the primary sort of SUBSTANCE. Form is a THIS, the ACTUALITY that realizes the POTENTIALITY of the matter.

3. The form of F is what is defined in the DEFINITION or account of F, stating the ESSENCE of F. Hence 'account', logos, is often used interchangeably with 'form'.

4. The relation between the form, the matter, and the definition of things that are compounds of matter and form is not always clear; it is discussed at length in Met. vii 10–11.

5. In some cases (e.g. when a block of wood is made into a statue) the form is closely connected with the shape acquired by the matter. And so Aristotle readily uses morphē (lit. 'shape') to refer to the form. But since morphē is also applied to cases where functional properties rather than mere physical shape are intended, 'shape' would often be a misleading rendering; in these cases 'form' is used.

6. Non-sensible substances are form without matter.

7. In reproduction of animals form is transmitted by the male parent. Production by CRAFTS begins from form without matter and results in form in matter.

8. Aristotle uses 'eidos' for the species (e.g. man, horse), in contrast to both the PARTICULARS (e.g. this man) and the GENUS (e.g. animal). In these contexts it is translated 'species'. When the contrast between eidos and matter is involved, 'form' is used.

9. These different uses of 'eidos' make it all the more difficult to decide some disputed questions about (i) what Aristotle means by identifying substance with form; (ii) whether he thinks a substantial form (i.e. the sort of form that is a substance) is also a PARTICULAR; (iii) what he means by claiming that a substantial form is a THIS. Two main options that have been explored are these: (a) Aristotle identifies primary substance with a particular form, one that is peculiar to each particular substance (hence in living organisms it will be an individual soul. The particular form is a this, in contrast to a species form (e.g. man, horse) which is a UNIVERSAL, and therefore not a primary substance. (b) He identifies primary substance with the species form, which (on one conception of universals) is a universal; hence his conception of a this does not exclude species forms from being thises.

10. Sense-PERCEPTION involves the reception of the perceptible form (not the form that is identified with the substance) without the matter it is embodied in.

11. For similar reasons, UNDERSTANDING is the reception of intelligible forms without matter.

FORM, IDEA (PLATONIC), eidos, idea

As well as using eidos for the substantial forms and species that he believes in, Aristotle uses the term (interchangeably with idea, following Plato's practice) for the Forms or Ideas recognized by Plato (in these cases an initial capital is used for convenience, when it seems clear that Aristotle is talking about Platonic Forms).

FUNCTION, TASK, ACTIVITY, *ergon*

Ergon has the range of uses of the English 'work'. It is applied to an activity ('this is hard work') as well as to the result ('a great work of art'). Often 'function' is suitable; sometimes 'task' and 'activity' are used.

genesis: COMING TO BE

GENUS, *genos*

The term is cognate with *gignesthai*, 'COME TO BE', and originally means 'family' or 'race'. Aristotle uses it in a broader sense for a sort or kind (not always sharply distinguished from *eidos*), and in a narrower, technical sense. In the technical sense a genus is a secondary SUBSTANCE (e.g. animal) and a UNIVERSAL, divided by DIF-FERENTIAE (e.g. biped, quadruped) into species (e.g. man, horse; see FORM #9).

gignesthai: COME TO BE

haplōs: WITHOUT QUALIFICATION

HAPPINESS, *eudaimonia*

1. The term is derived from *eu*, 'well' and *daimōn*, 'divine being', and so suggests a life favored by the gods. Following common beliefs, Aristotle identifies happiness with the highest good, also described as 'living well'. Happiness is the COMPLETE end fully satisfying a person's correct rational desire.

2. The English 'happiness' may be a misleading rendering, if it suggests that Aristotle thinks pleasure or contentment or 'feeling happy' is the highest good. In fact he denies that pleasure is the same as *eudaimonia*; he thinks *eudaimonia* consists in living and acting a particular way, not simply in having a certain kind of pleasure (though he certainly thinks that the best sort of life includes pleasure in the appropriate actions).

HOMONYMOUS, *homōnumon*; SPOKEN OF IN MANY WAYS, *pollachōs legomenon*

1. *F*s are homonymous (lit. 'have the same name, *onoma*') if and only if (a) they share the name '*F*', but (b) they do not share the DEFINITION or ACCOUNT corresponding to '*F*'. Hence 'homonymy' is often used equivalently to 'spoken of in many ways'. Clause (b) above might be taken to mean (1) homonyms have no common element at all in their definitions; or (2) homonyms cannot have the whole of their definitions in common. Probably (2) captures Aristotle's intention in clause (b) (since some of his examples of definitions of homonyms seem to contain common elements).

2. When the definitions have little or nothing in common, we may speak of extreme homonymy. Here the homonymy is very clear, and it may simply be 'chance homonymy' (e.g. 'horse' applied to racehorses and clothes horses). In some cases homonymous *F*s are all perfectly genuine *F*s; but in some cases homonymy indicates *F*s that have only the name '*F*' but are not genuine *F*s, and in these cases Aristotle sometimes says 'not *F*, except homonymously'. Hence a statue of a horse is called a horse merely homonymously, and (in Aristotle's view) a dead hand or arm is a hand or arm merely homonymously.

3. When Aristotle has cases of extreme homonymy in mind, he sometimes contrasts homonymy with being spoken of in many ways. When he has this contrast in mind, he mentions cases where *F*s are all called *F* 'with reference to one thing' (*pros hen*);

this relation may be called 'focal connection'. Healthy things, e.g., have different definitions of 'healthy', but they are all called healthy by reference to health (since healthy diets are healthy because they promote health, and healthy appetites are healthy because they indicate health). Aristotle sometimes says that these focally connected things are spoken of in many ways (since they have no single definition), but are non-homonymous.

4. Homonymy and being spoken of in many ways are primarily relations between the things that have the names, not between the names themselves. Hence Aristotle usually says that horses (e.g.) are homonymous, not that the word 'horse' is homonymous. Sometimes, though, he attributes homonymy to names.

horismos: DEFINITION

hupokeimenon: SUBJECT

idea: see FORM, IDEA

idion: DISTINCTIVE

IN ITS OWN RIGHT, INTRINSIC, *kath'hauto*

1. G may belong to F in its own right (per se; lit. 'in accordance with itself') in either of two ways: (a) G is part of, or derivable from, the ESSENCE and DEFINITION of F, and G belongs to F INSOFAR AS it is F (belongs to F qua F); or (b) G contains F in its definition (as odd belongs to number in its own right, though not every number is odd.

2. Because of its connection with the essence, what belongs to F in F's own right is often contrasted with what belongs to F coincidentally.

INSOFAR AS, *hē(i)*

This is the dative of the relative pronoun, and means literally 'by which' or 'in the respect in which', often Latinized as 'qua'. When Aristotle says that x is G insofar as x is F, he means that x is G because x is F; x's being F is the basis for correctly predicating G of x. Socrates, e.g., is both a man and a musician; but it is qua man that he is an animal, and qua musician that he is incompetent.

INDIVIDUAL, INDIVISIBLE, *atomon*

1. What is *atomon* is in some way indivisible (lit. 'uncuttable'). Aristotle applies the term to mathematical points, and to the 'atoms' recognized by Democritus; Aristotle himself rejects indivisible magnitudes.

2. Aristotle says that x is an *atomon* F when he means that x is not divisible into further Fs. Hence Socrates is *atomon* insofar as he is a man and is not divisible into further men. In these cases an *atomon* is a PARTICULAR.

3. A species (see FORM #9) (e.g. man) is also said to be *atomon*, since—in contrast to the GENUS (e.g. animal), which is divisible into species—the species is not divisible into further species, though it is divisible into particulars.

4. 'The individual man' etc. is also used to translate *ho tis anthrōpos*, lit. 'the some man'. The indefinite *tis* ('some') is the nearest thing in Greek to an indefinite article.

INTELLECT: see UNDERSTANDING

INTELLIGENCE, UNDERSTANDING, *phronēsis*

Aristotle uses '*phronēsis*' (1) in a wider sense, referring to intelligent consciousness or understanding in general; (2) in his own specialized sense, for the deliberative VIRTUE of practical intellect (contrasted with theoretical wisdom, *sophia*).

katēgorein: PREDICATE

kath'hauto: IN ITS OWN RIGHT

kath'hekaston: PARTICULAR

katholou: UNIVERSAL

kinein, kinēsis: see MOTION

KNOW, *epistasthai, gignōskein, eidenai,* KNOWLEDGE, SCIENCE, *epistēmē,* KNOWN, *gnōrimon*

1. The relations between Aristotle's different epistemic verbs are not always clear. But in general: (1) *epistasthai* (cognate noun *epistēmē* = 'knowledge' or 'science') is most frequently associated with demonstrative science, or at any rate with a systematic discipline that is the source of the knowledge. (2) *gignōskein* and its cognates (*gnōrizein*, 'know' or 'come to know', *gnōsis*, 'knowledge', *gnōrimon*, 'known', *gnōrimōteron*, 'better known') often seem rather weaker. Where it is important to distinguish them from (1), we translate as 'recognize', 'cognize', 'cognition', or 'recognition'. It is appropriate to apply *gignōskein* to knowing or recognizing people and ordinary perceptible objects, but it would be odd to use *epistasthai* in such a context. (3) *eidenai* seems less specialized than either of the other two terms. (4) In English 'S knows that *p*' implies that (i) *p* is true and (roughly) (ii) S is justified in believing that *p*. The first implication holds for all three Greek verbs (though not in the phrase 'known to us'; see below). Something like the second implication holds (as Aristotle makes clear in *APo* i 2) for *epistasthai* and probably for *eidenai*, but it is less clear that it holds for *gignōskein*.

2. Aristotle often contrasts what is better known (*gnōrimon*) 'to us' with what is better known 'by nature' or 'WITHOUT QUALIFICATION'. The contrast is connected to the difference between types of *archai* (see PRINCIPLE #4). What is 'known to us' (i.e. 'known as far as we are concerned', or 'known in our view', and hence need not be true) is our *archē* insofar as it is the starting point; this consists of the APPEARANCES. What is 'known by nature' (i.e. is the sort of thing that makes it an appropriate object of knowledge, and hence must be true) is the result of successful investigation; this is the *archē* insofar as it is the first principle.

koinōnia: COMMUNITY

logos: see REASON

LUCK, CHANCE, FORTUNE, *tuchē*; CHANCE, *to automaton*

1. In Aristotle's strictest use, *to automaton* refers an event that is of the right sort to have a FINAL CAUSE, but actually has none. The subset of these events that come about from a DECISION are matters of *tuchē*. In these cases *tuchē* is rendered by 'luck', and *to automaton* by 'chance'.

2. When Aristotle does not have this contrast between luck and chance in mind, he tends to use *tuchē* (and cognates) to refer more broadly to *to automaton*, and still more broadly to COINCIDENTAL results (where no special similarity to events with final causes is implied).

MATTER, *hulē*

1. In ordinary Greek *hulē* means 'wood', and Aristotle extends this use to raw material in general. Matter is the SUBJECT of COMING TO BE and perishing, and so it is the subject from which a substance comes to be; the bronze from which the statue is made, and the material elements of which an organism is composed, are the matter.

2. Different types of matter are relative to different levels of organization. Wood is the 'proximate' (or 'closest') matter of the box, but earth is the matter of the wood, and only indirectly the matter of the box.

3. Most (though not all) interpreters believe that at the lowest level of organization Aristotle recognizes 'prime' (i.e. first) matter. This is the subject of the most basic qualities, and it remains throughout changes of one element into another.

4. Since matter is a subject, it seems to count as a SUBSTANCE; indeed, Aristotle sometimes suggests that matter is needed to make something a PARTICULAR subject at all. On the other hand, he insists that it is neither the only nor the primary sort of substance.

5. In speaking of the matter of a living organism Aristotle distinguishes its proximate from its non-proximate matter: (1) The living body and its organic parts are the proximate matter of the organism, and do not exist—except HOMONYMOUSLY—after the death of the organism. (2) By contrast, the material constituents of the living body and of its parts still exist after the death of the organism.

6. Most of Aristotle's remarks on matter apply to perceptible matter, which belongs to things that undergo coming to be, perishing, and MOTION. (A different sort of perceptible matter belongs to the imperishable heavenly bodies.) Mathematical objects are sometimes said to have intelligible matter (i.e. the extension that is determined by a specific geometrical figure).

7. Aristotle claims that matter does not admit of scientific KNOWLEDGE or of DEFINITION. This claim may be intended to apply to only some of the types of matter distinguished above.

metabolē: see MOTION

MORE, RATHER, *mallon*

When Aristotle says that x is *mallon* F than y, it is not always clear whether he means (a) 'x rather than y is F' (i.e. x is F and y is not F), or (b) 'x is F more than y' (i.e. x is F to a higher degree than y is without implying that either x or y either is or is not F).

morphē: see FORM #5

MOTION, PROCESS, CHANGE, *kinēsis*, MOVE, *kinein*

1. In many ways 'change' would be the best rendering of *kinēsis*, which extends more widely than motion, as we normally conceive it. But 'change' seems most

suitable for *metabolē*, which is often hard to distinguish from *kinēsis*, but sometimes is distinguished from it; moreover, 'changer' and 'unchanged changer' seem awkward. 'Change' has been used to translate both *kinein* and *metaballein* (and cognates) in passages where this resulted in more natural English and it seemed unimportant to mark the different Greek terms; but where it seemed important to distinguish them, 'move' has been used for *kinein* and 'change' for *metaballein*. The active voice *kinein* means 'move' in the sense of 'initiate motion', and the passive *kineisthai* means 'move' in the sense of 'be moved' or 'undergo motion' or 'be in motion'; this distinction has been marked in the translation at places where it seems important. 'Mover' is used in the active sense (i.e. initiator of motion).

2. Motion is defined as incomplete ACTUALITY (*Phys*. iii 1) and is contrasted with complete actuality. This contrast is connected with the division between *kinēsis* (here rendered 'process') and *energeia*.

NATURE, *phusis*

1. Aristotle (relying, as often, on dubious etymology) takes *phusis* to be the abstract noun cognate with *phuesthai*, 'grow' or 'be born' (cf. English 'native' and 'nativity').

2. Something has a nature if and only if it has an internal origin (see PRINCIPLE) initiating the subject's own MOTION and rest. This definition includes (a) the four elements, which, in Aristotle's view, have their own natural local motion; (b) living organisms, i.e. those natural objects whose internally caused motions include self-nourishment and reproduction.

3. Aristotle also uses 'nature' to refer generally to the natural world of material SUBSTANCES that have natures. This is the object of study for natural philosophy to which the *Physics* is devoted.

4. Aristotle believes that the study of nature requires study of the FORM as well as the MATTER; and so it requires study of FINAL CAUSES, and of conditional as well as unqualified necessity (see NECESSITY #4), *Phys* II 8–9, *PA* I 1.

5. The usual as well as the necessary is characteristic of nature.

6. Nature does nothing 'pointlessly' (*matēn*), for something done *matēn* has no point or end, and it is characteristic of nature to act for an end. (*Matēn* might also mean 'in vain', i.e. 'unsuccessfully'; but this is not what Aristotle usually means in saying that something is done *matēn*.)

NECESSITY, *ananke*, NECESSARY, *anankaion*

1. This is sometimes rendered by 'must' (which also renders *dei*).

2. Aristotle often suggests that it is necessary that *p* if and only if it is not possible that not-*p*.

3. Sometimes, however, he seems to imply that the formula just given does not provide an adequate definition of necessity. Sometimes he suggests that it provides a necessary but not a sufficient condition. Occasionally he suggests that it does not even provide a necessary condition.

4. Aristotle contrasts unqualified with conditional necessity. He has different sorts of conditions in mind in different contexts, so that what he treats as unconditional necessity (i.e. not relative to one sort of condition) in one passage may be described

as a type of conditional necessity (i.e. relative to another sort of condition) in another passage.

5. The necessary is contrasted both with the usual and with matters of chance (see LUCK) and COINCIDENCE.

6. Human voluntary action is not necessary, because its external circumstances do not by themselves make it impossible for the agent to do otherwise; the agent's own choice and DECISION also play a crucial role.

7. In a DEDUCTION the conclusion follows necessarily from the premisses (necessitas consequentiae), but the conclusion itself need not be necessary (necessitas consequentis), unless the premisses are also necessary.

8. Some kinds of necessity belong to a subject's NATURE, and some do not.

9. Aristotle takes not only some propositions and states of affairs, but also some SUBSTANCES, to be necessary. Their existence is necessary, insofar as they are everlasting (see ALWAYS) and essential to the universe.

ORIGIN: see PRINCIPLE

ousia: SUBSTANCE

PARTICULAR, *kath'hekaston*

1. The preposition *kata* in *kath'hekaston* means roughly 'taking one at a time' or 'by' (as in 'counting the army by regiments'). Hence 'taking Fs *kath'hekaston*' means 'taking Fs each one at a time', or 'taking Fs in turn', and so Aristotle uses the phrase *kath'hekaston* as a noun for each of the particular Fs taken one at a time. A particular is defined, in contrast to a UNIVERSAL, as what is not predicated of many things. Hence particulars include substances (e.g. Callias) and non-substances (e.g. the individual white, *Catg.* 1a25). It is characteristic of a particular to be INDIVIDUAL and numerically one. See also THIS.

2. Aristotle sometimes uses 'particular' and 'universal' to mark a contrast between the more and less specific or determinate; hence the 'particulars' are sometimes, e.g., the species (and hence universals) of a genus, rather than particulars such as Callias (for in dividing a genus, the things we take 'each one at a time' are the species).

3. Particulars (in the sense in which no universal is a particular) as such are not the objects of DEFINITION or scientific KNOWLEDGE.

pathos: see ATTRIBUTE

PERCEPTION, SENSE, SENSE-PERCEPTION, *aisthēsis*

1. *Aisthēsis* includes the five senses and the cognitive activity we perform with them. Each sense has its own proper (see DISTINCTIVE #3) object (e.g. color for sight), and the senses taken together have common objects. When we see an ordinary physical object (e.g. a chair, the son of Cleon), that is COINCIDENTAL perception, resulting from perceiving the perceptible qualities of the object.

2. Aristotle values sense-perception highly as a means to KNOWLEDGE, though it is not a sufficient condition for knowledge. He relies on it as a source of APPEARANCES

and empirical inquiry; in some cases he thinks it should be preferred over more general arguments as a source of reliable conclusions.

3. Perception primarily makes us aware of PARTICULARS, as opposed to UNIVERSALS.

phainomena: APPEARANCES

phantasia: APPEARANCE

phusis, phusikos: see NATURE

POINTLESS, *matēn*: see NATURE #6

poion: see QUALITY

POLITICAL SYSTEM, POLITY, *politeia*

Oligarchy, democracy, aristocracy, and so on are different forms of *politeia*. 'Constitution' is sometimes appropriate, but suggests something more narrowly legal than Aristotle has in mind; the character of the *politeia* depends on who controls the institutions, not simply on the constitutional character of the institutions themselves. The connection between *politeia*, *polis* ('city'), and *politēs* ('citizen') is lost in translation.

Aristotle also uses *politeia* for the restricted democracy described at *Pol.* 1279a38. Here it is translated by 'polity'.

POTENTIALITY, *dunamis*, POSSIBILITY, POSSIBLE, CAPABLE, POTENTIALLY, *dunaton*

1. (a) 'Possible' translates *dunaton* applied to a state of affairs ('it is possible that it will rain tomorrow'). (b) 'Can' or 'capable' translates *dunaton* and the cognate verb *dunasthai* applied to substances. (c) 'Potentiality' (or 'potentially') or 'capacity' translates the cognate noun *dunamis* applied to substances (see #3). This broad application of *dunaton* and its cognates sometimes creates some ambiguity in Aristotle's claims. 'Admit of', *endechesthai*, normally applies only to states of affairs, and does not appear to differ significantly in meaning from the use of *dunaton* for possibility.

2. What is possible is defined as (i) what is not impossible or as (ii) what is neither NECESSARY nor impossible (i.e., what is contingent).

3. *x* has a potentiality for *F* (in the primary way) by having an internal PRINCIPLE of *F*; in that case *F* is the ACTUALITY of the potentiality. Every such potentiality is a potentiality for *F* not in all circumstances, but in the appropriate circumstances.

4. Different levels of potentiality correspond to different degrees of closeness of the potentiality to the actuality. (The right combination of flour, water, and yeast has a higher-level potentiality for becoming bread, since it is closer to being bread; the wheat from which the flour is milled has a lower-level potentiality for becoming bread, since it is further from being bread.)

PREDICATE, *katēgorein*, THING PREDICATED, PREDICATION

1. Roughly speaking, *F* is predicated of *x* if and only if *x* is *F*; in this case *x* (e.g. this man) is the SUBJECT and *F* (e.g. man) is the thing predicated. Hence predication is normally a relation between non-linguistic items, not between words. Aristotle uses '*F* belongs (*huparchei*) to *x*' equivalently with '*F* is predicated of *x*'.

2. The grammatical subject and predicate of a sentence need not always identify the actual subject and thing predicated in the non-linguistic relation that is signified by the sentence. For instance, 'the musician' is the grammatical subject of 'the musician is a man'; but in Aristotle's view the man is the genuine subject and the musician is predicated of him. The grammatical structure, therefore, does not always correspond to the ontological subject and thing predicated.

3. In most cases the thing predicated is a universal.

PREDICATIONS, *katēgoriai*

1. Aristotle usually refers to the ten 'categories' as 'the figures (i.e. types) of predication', or 'the genera of predications', *genē tōn kategoriōn*. Sometimes he speaks of 'the predications', *katēgoriai*; this is the basis for the traditional label 'categories'.

2. The categories exemplify the fact that BEING is spoken of in many ways (see HOMONYMOUS). Each category answers the question 'What is it?' at the most general level about items of a certain sort (e.g. this man, this white color). The items seem to be sorted (rather unsystematically) by the different sorts of questions that might be asked about a substance, e.g. 'What is he?' (a man); 'How big is he?' (six feet tall), etc.

3. The names for the non-substance categories are usually rendered by the abstract nouns 'quality', 'quantity', etc.; but the Greek terms are neuter adjectives ('of what sort', 'how much', etc.; Latin 'quale', 'quantum') corresponding to interrogative adjectives. The items placed into categories are particulars (e.g. the individual white or a particular length) or universals (e.g. white, six feet long).

PRINCIPLE, ORIGIN, BEGINNING, STARTING-POINT, RULE, RULING OFFICE, *archē*

1. *Archē* (Latin 'principium') is cognate with *archein* ('begin', 'rule'), and the *archē* of x is in some way or other first in relation to x. Hence it is the beginning or origin.

2. Each of the four CAUSES is an *archē*. In these cases the *archē* is something non-linguistic and non-propositional. The use of 'principle' in these cases is perhaps slightly archaic English.

3. In an argument, description, or theory, the *archē* is 'that from which primarily a thing is known'. Often the sense of 'beginning' is also prominent. In these cases the principle is a proposition. But it should not be assumed that Aristotle always intends a sharp distinction between this and the type of *archē* mentioned in #2.

4. The *archē* that we try to discover is prior 'by nature' or 'prior WITHOUT QUALIFICATION' to the truths that are derived from it. What we begin our inquiry from is also called an *archē*; this sort of *archē* is 'prior to us' but not 'prior by nature' (see KNOW #2). In the case of what is prior to us, 'starting-point' is sometimes the best translation.

5. In political contexts (cf. 'first secretary', 'prime minister') *archē* refers to rule in general (as in 'the rule of the few') or to specific ruling offices (judge, general, etc.).

PROCESS: see MOTION

PROPER: see DISTINCTIVE

QUA: see INSOFAR AS

QUALITY, SORT OF THING, *poion*

Aristotle normally uses the adjective *poion* rather than the abstract noun *poiotēs* for the name of the category of quality (see PREDICATIONS). The question '*poion estin x?*' may be translated 'What sort of thing is *x*?'. But Aristotle uses *poion* in two different cases, corresponding to two different ways of understanding this question: (a) It refers to the category of quality. (Cf. 'What sort of meal was it?' 'Terrible.') (b) But it need not refer to the category of quality; it sometimes refers to the species in any category, including the category of substance. (Cf., 'What sort of animal is it?' 'A tiger.') Here (a) characterizes the subject, by predicating a quality, whereas (b) classifies the subject by mentioning a secondary SUBSTANCE (or other SPECIES; see FORM #8). The cognate term *toionde* is translated by 'this sort of thing'.

RATHER: see MORE

REALIZATION: see ACTUALITY

REASON, ACCOUNT, ARGUMENT, RATIONAL DISCOURSE, SENTENCE, STATEMENT, RATIO, *logos*

1. *Logos* refers to reason. It is characteristic of human beings, in contrast to non-rational animals, who cannot grasp UNIVERSALS.

2. One characteristic expression of *logos* is significant rational discourse, formed by the combination of thoughts.

3. The combination of thoughts and sentences produces a *logos*, i.e. argument. *Logos* refers especially to DEDUCTIVE argument, in contrast to appeal to APPEARANCES.

4. The *logos* of *F* is a verbal formula replacing the name '*F*'. This is translated 'account', and is often equivalent to a DEFINITION.

5. *Logos* is sometimes used for the thing or property defined rather than for the defining formula itself, and in Aristotle's view the thing defined by a definition of *x* is the FORM of *x* rather than the MATTER of *x*. Hence 'the *logos* of *x*' is often equivalent to 'the form of *x*'.

6. In mathematical contexts a *logos* is a ratio or proportion.

7. See also CAUSE.

RECOGNITION, *gnōsis*, RECOGNIZE, *gignōskein*: see KNOW

SENTENCE: see REASON

SEPARABLE, *chōriston*

1. *Chōriston* is formed from *chōrizein*, 'to separate'; it is hard to know whether in a given context it means 'separate' (i.e. is actually separated from something) or 'separable' (i.e. can be separated from something). (The same difficulty arises with many '-ton' endings.)

2. When Aristotle speaks of separability, he is usually interpreted to mean that *x* is separable from *y* if and only if it is possible for *x* to exist without *y* (i.e. *x* does not depend on *y* for its existence).

3. Sometimes, however, he describes this sort of separability as separability WITH-OUT QUALIFICATION, and contrasts it with separability in account, *logos* (see REA-SON), i.e. definitional independence.

4. Aristotle criticizes Plato for separating the FORMS, and claiming that they are separated, *kechōrismena* (perfect passive participle of *chōrizein*).

SIGNIFY, *sēmainein*

1. *Sēmainein* is cognate with *sēmeion* ('sign', 'indication'), and so means 'indicate'.

2. Aristotle standardly uses *sēmainein* where we would be inclined to speak of the meaning of a word. Hence 'mean' would often be a good translation.

3. However, not only words (e.g. 'man'), but also the corresponding things (e.g. man) are said to signify (as we say that spots signify measles).

SIMPLE: see WITHOUT QUALIFICATION

SPECIAL: see DISTINCTIVE

SPECIES: see FORM

SPOKEN OF IN MANY WAYS: see HOMONYMOUS

STARTING-POINT: see PRINCIPLE

STATE, *hexis*

Hexis is the abstract noun from *echein* 'have', which together with an adverb means 'be disposed in some way' (*echein pōs*); and so a hexis is a relatively fixed and permanent way a subject is disposed (it is a first, as opposed to a second, ACTU-ALITY). A person's character is constituted by the states that have been formed by habituation; and Aristotle claims that it is up to us to form our states of character.

SUBJECT, *hupokeimenon*

1. A subject (lit. 'underlying thing') is what has things PREDICATED of it. Not every grammatical subject-term, however, refers to a genuine (non-linguistic) subject.

2. A subject also underlies every change (see MOTION), both in non-substance CATEGORIES and in the category of SUBSTANCE. In the second case the subject is MATTER.

3. Aristotle does not sharply distinguish the uses of 'subject' in #1 and #2. He seems to have both in mind when he considers the claim of the subject to be substance.

4. The term is also used (cf. the English 'subject' = 'subject-matter') for that which is studied.

SUBSTANCE, ESSENCE, *ousia*

1. *Ousia* is the abstract noun formed from the verb 'to BE', and sometimes 'being' is the right translation. But 'being' is normally reserved for *to on*, the participle (= something that is) or for *einai* (the infinitive 'to be').

2. *Ousia* is the first of the ten CATEGORIES. Aristotle seems to pick it out in two ways: (a) *Ousia* is the SUBJECT of the other categories. It is either a primary sub-stance, which is a THIS and a PARTICULAR, and so a basic subject, or a secondary

substance, which is a species (see FORM #8) or GENUS of primary substances. (b) *Ousia* is what something is; the answer to the question 'What is *F*?' tells us the *ousia* of *F*. In these cases it is rendered by 'essence' (which is required when the *ousia* of a non-substance is being considered). It is often difficult to be sure which aspect of *ousia* Aristotle has in mind in a particular context; and it is often important, since (b) applies to non-substances as well as to substances. It is likely, however, that Aristotle thinks there is some systematic connection between (a) and (b), and in particular that substances (according to (a)) are primary bearers of essences. Hence it is not always clear whether the distinction between (a) and (b) is meant to be (i) a distinction between two kinds of substance (or two senses of the word '*ousia*') or (ii) a distinction between two criteria that (in Aristotle's view) are satisfied by one and the same thing.

3. Aristotle's elaborate discussion of substance in *Met.* VII raises several questions (see FORM #9): (a) Does he maintain, as he does in the *Catg.*, that a primary substance must be a PARTICULAR (see also THIS)? (b) In what sense does he believe that a substance must be a SUBJECT? (c) What does he mean by identifying form with substance? Is a substantial form a universal or a particular? (d) How can he retain the connection between being a substance and being an object of scientific KNOWLEDGE and DEFINITION? One series of answers results in the view that he identifies substances with particular forms; another series of answers implies that he identifies substances with species forms.

***sullogismos*:** DEDUCTION

***sumbebēkos*:** COINCIDENT

***technē*:** CRAFT

THIS, *tode ti*

1. The Greek might be rendered: (1) 'this something' (e.g. this dog); (2) 'some this', i.e. either (2a) some particular thing or (2b) something of some kind (e.g. some dog).

2. Aristotle often uses 'this' to refer to the category of substance, and *being a this* is especially characteristic of substance (though perhaps not confined to substance).

3. A *this* is numerically one, in contrast to a 'such' (see QUALITY). Aristotle often seems to assume that if a *this* is numerically one, it is also a PARTICULAR. Since he requires a SUBSTANCE to be a *this*, he seems to imply that a substance must be a particular. But the claim that substance is a particular is sometimes thought to be inconsistent with Aristotle's view (in *Met.* VII) that substance is to be identified with form. See further FORM #9, SUBSTANCE #3.

THIS SORT OF THING, *toionde*: see QUALITY

THOUGHT: see UNDERSTANDING

***ti esti*:** see ESSENCE

***ti ēn einai*:** see ESSENCE

***tode ti*:** THIS

tuchē: see LUCK

UNDERSTANDING, THOUGHT, INTELLECT, *nous*

1. Aristotle applies *nous* to the faculty or capacity (see POTENTIALITY) of rational thought (see also REASON) and to its exercise in acts of rational thinking. Hence the term is applied to both the first and the second ACTUALITY. See *DA* III 4. In many contexts 'thought' would be a suitable rendering.

2. Often, however, *nous* is a cognitive state that includes more than mere thinking. I can think (= have the thought) of going to the moon, without thinking that I will go the moon; but when Aristotle says I have *nous* that *p*, he means that I believe (and indeed KNOW) that *p*. For these contexts 'understanding' is more suitable.

3. In its broadest use, *nous* that *p* is any intellectual, as opposed to perceptual, grasp of the truth of *p*. In its narrowest use, *nous* applies to the non-demonstrative grasp of the PRINCIPLES that are premises for a demonstration.

UNIVERSAL, *katholou*

1. Aristotle's term is derived from the prepositional phrase *kata holou*, meaning 'taken as a whole', as opposed to 'taking each in turn' (*kath'hekaston*; see PARTICULAR #1). Sometimes it is appropriately rendered by 'generally'.

2. A universal is defined as 'what is of a nature to be predicated in the case of many things', *DI* 17a39. This might be taken to mean that (a) a universal is the sort of thing that can be predicated of many things, or (b) any universal must actually be predicated of many things. If Aristotle means (b), he denies the possibility of uninstantiated universals, and insists that if (e.g.) the universal horse exists, there must be a plurality of horses that it is predicated of. If he means (a), this definition does not commit him to denying the possibility of uninstantiated universals.

3. It is not clear whether Aristotle thinks it is possible for a universal to exist at one time and not to exist at another.

4. Universals are the primary objects of DEFINITION and scientific KNOWLEDGE.

5. Though Aristotle believes in the real (extra-mental, extra-linguistic) existence of universals APART FROM particulars, he denies that they are SEPARABLE. Hence he thinks it important to distinguish them from Platonic FORMS.

UNQUALIFIED: see WITHOUT QUALIFICATION

VIRTUE, *aretē*

1. Something has an *aretē* insofar as it is good at or for something; hence *aretē* is closely related to FUNCTION, and the term may refer to all sorts of excellences.

2. More narrowly understood, the virtues are the praiseworthy STATES of character and intellect that are discussed in the *EN*; these order the different parts of the soul so that they are properly suited to fulfill the human function in achieving the human good.

WHAT-IT-IS: see ESSENCE

WITHOUT QUALIFICATION, UNQUALIFIED, SIMPLY, UNCONDITIONALLY, WITHOUT EXCEPTION, *haplōs*

1. The adjective *haplous* is translated 'simple' (in contrast to compound), and sometimes the adverb *haplōs* is rendered by 'simply'.

2. Being *F* without qualification ('simpliciter') is contrasted with being a sort of *F*, or being *F* only in a particular way, or in a particular respect, or on an assumption.

3. In different contexts '*x* is *F* without qualification' may imply (a) that '*x* is *F*' is true entirely without exception, so that no qualification is needed; or (b) that '*x* is *F*' is true in standard, or appropriately understood, conditions (so that the relevant qualification is taken for granted).

4. Sometimes 'doing *F* without qualification' refers to the action-type described by 'doing *F*', as opposed to its particular action-tokens, which are described by 'doing *F* in these particular circumstances'.